LAW AND PRACTICE
OF THE SHERIFF COURTS IN SCOTLAND

LAW AND PRACTICE

OF THE

SHERIFF COURTS IN SCOTLAND

by

WM. JARDINE DOBIE, S.S.C.,

Sheriff-Subsitute of Lanarkshire, at Glasgow

CALEDONIAN BOOKS

Collieston, Aberdeenshire, Scotland

1986

Originally published by William Hodge & Co Ltd, Glasgow, in 1948

This edition published by Caledonian Books,
Collieston, Aberdeenshire, Scotland
1986

Caledonian Books is the publishing division of Aberdeen Rare Books,
dealers in secondhand and antiquarian Scottish law books.

ISBN 0 9506607 3 6

Printed and bound by Clark Constable,
Edinburgh and London

PREFACE.

THE present volume on Sheriff Court Practice is the result of a request to provide a second edition of the late Sheriff Fyfe's book on the same subject. When the matter was put in hand it was soon apparent that no normal revisal would meet the case. The older practice with which Sheriff Fyfe dealt at some length has now little more than an academic interest; many decisions of the Courts have helped to elucidate the provisions of the Act of 1907-13 which was none too clearly expressed; and fresh legislation has introduced its own problems and alterations. The framework of the original book has been retained, but little more of it remains as the text has been almost entirely rewritten.

The size of the volume created a problem in itself but it was considered inadvisable to omit the lengthy chapter on bankruptcy, or to leave out those on services, commissary practice and the statutory powers and duties of the Sheriff. The matter contained in these chapters is not usually available in works on practice and it was thought that its inclusion enhanced the value of the book to the practitioner. A chapter was written on workmen's compensation but in the end this was dispensed with in view of the impending transfer of that jurisdiction to another quarter. The statutory duties of the Sheriff have vastly increased in the last thirty years and the handling of this chapter presented some difficulty. Certain of these statutory jurisdictions are invoked almost daily, others are less frequently appealed to, while some are scarcely exercised at all. It was manifestly impossible to deal with all in detail, or even to be sure that all had been noted. But, where detailed treatment is not afforded, reference is made to any Act of Sederunt or decisions bearing upon procedure. In some parts of this chapter, and elsewhere when proceedings of an uncommon character are dealt with, opportunity has been taken to note where the appropriate styles may be obtained.

PREFACE.

In the original book the author had inserted many useful suggestions in regard to both pleading and practice. The policy of including such practical hints has been followed in the present volume and has been to some extent amplified.

On the question of precedents it is hoped that the practitioner has been referred to all decisions of the Supreme Court relevant to the point under discussion and also to any in the Sheriff Court which are likely to be of material assistance. The bearing of these references on the text has been made precise by the use of index numbers. The index itself has been prepared in such detail as should allow easy reference to any subject dealt with and, in accordance with modern practice, references therein are to pages and not to paragraphs. In many cases cross-references to other relevant pages have been inserted in the text itself.

The law has been stated as at 31st December, 1946, but a few references to later decisions have been added where this was possible without disturbing the text, and in some places the effect of impending legislation has been indicated by footnote.

The writer has to record his appreciation of assistance rendered by many in the Sheriff-clerks' service who provided information on various points. He is particularly grateful to Mr. J. G. Johnston, now Sheriff-clerk at Kirkcudbright, who read over the entire manuscript and made many suggestions and corrections.

GLASGOW, *February*, 1948.   W. J. D.

CONTENTS.

CHAPTER I

THE COURT

CHAPTER II

JURISDICTION

CHAPTER III

GROUNDS OF JURISDICTION

CHAPTER IV

THE LITIGANTS

CONTENTS.

CHAPTER V
The Action

CHAPTER VI
Service

CHAPTER VII
Undefended Cause

CHAPTER VIII
Defended Cause

CHAPTER IX
Trial of the Cause

CHAPTER X

INCIDENTAL PROCEDURE

CHAPTER XI

JUDGMENT

CHAPTER XII

OPERATING JUDGMENT

CHAPTER XIII

APPEAL

CHAPTER XIV

EXPENSES

CHAPTER XV

CIVIL JURY TRIAL

CHAPTER XVI

BANKRUPTCY

CHAPTER XVII

REMOVING

CHAPTER XVIII

SEQUESTRATION FOR RENT

CHAPTER XIX

SERVICE OF HEIRS

CHAPTER XX

Commissary Practice

CHAPTER XXI

Public Inquiries

CHAPTER XXII

Small Debt Court

CHAPTER XXIII

CHAPTER XXIV

Special Actions

CHAPTER XXV

STATUTORY POWERS AND DUTIES

STATUTORY POWERS AND DUTIES—*Continued*

TABLE OF CASES.

Cameron v. Mortimer (1872), 16.
Cameron v. Woolfson (1918), 208.
Cameron & Waterston v. Muir & Sons (1861), 311.
Campbell v. Alexander & Sons (1934), 81.
Campbell v. Ayr County Council (1905), 149.
Campbell v. Caledonian Railway Co. (1899), 169.
Campbell v. Campbell (1855), 92.
Campbell v. Campbell (1866), 37.
Campbell v. Campbell (1934), 249, 311.
Campbell v. Christie (1934), 629.
Campbell v. Craig (1911), 640, 642.
Campbell v. Duncan (1901), 11, 118.
Campbell v. Haddow (1890), 466.
Campbell v. Lothians & Findlay (1858), 270.
Campbell v. M'Allister (1893), 110.
Campbell v. Macpherson (1905), 117.
Campbell v. Scottish Educational News (1906), 352.
Campbell v. Train (1910), 50, 160.
Campbell v. Watson's Trustee (1898), 264.
Campbell & Co. (1899), 395.
Campbell Fraser & Co. v. Shepperd (1823), 232.
Campbell & Henry v. Hunter (1911), 130.
Campbell's Trustees v. Campbell (1903), 212.
Campbell's Trustees v. Kinloch (1925), 49.
Campbell's Trustees v. O'Neill (1911), 413, 415, 419.
Campbeltown Building Co. v. Magistrates of Campbeltown (1893), 641.
Campbeltown Shipbuilding Co. v. Robertson (1896), 173.
Cant v. Bayne (1868), 386.
Cant v. Pirnie's Trustees (1906), 492.
Capaldi v. Greenock Magistrates (1941), 43.
Cape v. M'Lure (1934), 501.
Carmichael v. Macintyre (1904), 488.
Carmichael v. Scottish Co-operative Wholesale Society (1934), 196.
Carnbroe Chemical Co. v. Lanark Middle Ward (1923-6), 104, 327, 650.
Carnwath v. West Calder Parish Council (1928), 644.
Carr v. Carr (1941), 498.
Carr & Sons v. M'Lennan, Blair & Co. (1885), 288.
Carrigan v. Cleland (1907), 81.
Carrigan v. Phillips (1905), 70.

Carron Co. v. Currie & Co. (1896), 271.
Carruthers' Trustee v. Finlay & Wilson (1897), 332.
Carson v. M'Dowall (1908), 293, 331.
Carswell & Son v. Finlay (1887), 226.
Carter v. Drysdale (1883), 586.
Casey v. Casey (1925), 20.
Cassells v. Filshie (1926), 329.
Cassidy v. Bilsland (1907), 246.
Cassilis, Countess of, v. Earl of Roxburgh (1679), 125.
Cassils & Co. v. Absalon (1907), 197, 199.
Cathcart v. Board of Agriculture (1915), 537, 553.
Cathcart v. Cathcart (1899), 525.
Cathcart v. Scott (1908), 59, 75.
Catto, Thomson & Co. v. Thomson & Son (1867), 195.
Caughie v. Robertson (1897), 70.
Caven v. Provost, &c., of Dalbeattie (1908), 236.
Central Motor Engineering Co. v. Galbraith (1918), 147, 157, 360, 396.
Central Private Clinic (1931), 576.
Cesari v. Anderson (1922), 412.
Cessford v. Commissioners of Millport (1899), 654.
Chamberlain v. Farr (1942), 659.
Chaney & Bull (1930), 574.
Chapman v. Balfour (1875), 93.
Cheyne v. M'Gungle (1860), 11, 118.
Christie v. Birrell (1910), 153.
Christie v. Christie (1917), 136, 525.
Christie v. Christie (1919), 498, 500, 524.
Christie v. Glasgow Corporation (1899), 320.
Christie v. Hoseason (1898), 490.
Christie v. Leven Magistrates (1912), 641, 642.
Christie v. Lowden (1890), 282.
Christie v. Macfarlane (1929), 335.
Christie v. Munro (1885), 156, 184.
Christie v. Orr (1927), 477.
Christie v. Ruxton (1862), 14.
Christie Bros. v. Remington Typewriter Co. (1912), 490.
Chrystal v. Chrystal (1900), 148.
Church of Scotland General Trustees v. Heritors of Rathven (1931), 128.
City of Glasgow Union Railway Co. v. Hunter (1870), 609.
Clan Lamont Society v. Lamont (1939), 90.
Clark v. Adams (1885), 586.
Clark v. Beattie (1909), 490.
Clark v. Campbell (1873), 515.

CHAPTER I.

THE COURT.

1. THE SHERIFF.

Originally the Sheriff was not necessarily a lawyer, and when, after 1748, he was required to be a lawyer, his qualification was three years' standing as an advocate.[1] This has since been altered on more than one occasion, and the qualification for a Sheriff is now five years' experience as an advocate or as a Sheriff-Substitute.[2]

[1] 20 Geo. II c. 43, sec. 29.
[2] 7 Edw. VII c. 51, sec. 12.

The Sheriff holds his office *ad vitam aut culpam*. He is removeable only for unfitness for office occasioned by " inability, neglect of duty, or misbehaviour.'' The right to remove a Sheriff from office is vested in the Secretary of State for Scotland, to be exercised upon a report by the Lord President and the Lord Justice-Clerk, and subject to a right of veto by Parliament.[1] The times and places for holding Courts, and the duties of the Sheriff generally, are now regulated by the Secretary of State for Scotland.[2]

[1] 7 Edw. VII c. 51, sec. 13.
[2] 7 Edw. VII c. 51, sec. 18.

The Sheriffs of the Counties of Midlothian and Lanark differ from the others, who are not resident judges, but mostly reside in Edinburgh, and continue in practice at the Bar, visiting their Sheriffdoms as occasion may require. The size and importance of these two Sheriffdoms has long necessitated the undivided attention of their Sheriffs being given to the work of the office, and in 1822 these two Sheriffs were made the subject of special Statute, under which they are required to reside within, or within six miles of, the Cities of Edinburgh and Glasgow respectively, during nine months of the year.[1]

[1] 3 Geo. IV c. 49, sec. 1.

Originally a separate Sheriff was appointed for each county, but amalgamation in 1870[1] reduced their number to fifteen. As vacancies in the office of Sheriff occur the Secretary of State for Scotland, with the approval of Parliament, may now promote

further unions and, pending any such, he may appoint an interim
Sheriff.[2] The present number of Sheriffs is twelve.

[1] 33 & 34 Vict. c. 86.
[2] 23 & 24 Geo. V c. 41, sec. 31.

In addition to the appellate judges of the Sheriff Court, the
office of Sheriff of Chancery, which was an independent office, was
created by Statute in 1847,[1] and is regulated by that Statute,
subject to alterations made by the Conveyancing Acts of 1868[2]
and 1874.[3] The duties of the Sheriff of Chancery mainly relate
to service of heirs. The office of Sheriff of Chancery has now been
united with that of the Sheriff of the Lothians and Peebles at
Edinburgh.[4]

[1] 10 & 11 Vict. c. 47.
[2] 31 & 32 Vict. c. 101, secs. 27-42.
[3] 37 & 38 Vict. c. 94, secs. 10 and 57.
[4] 23 & 24 Geo. V c. 41, sec. 31 (1).

The Sheriff in early days had many duties personally to perform,
but most of these duties have long ceased to exist, though the Sheriff
may apparently still require military aid in case of riot, and he
accounts to Exchequer for the fines collected in his Courts, and
executes Exchequer decrees.[1] There is little at the present time,
apart from his work as appellate judge, which the Sheriff may not
delegate, and which in practice does not devolve upon his
Substitute.[2]

[1] 19 & 20 Vict. c. 56, secs. 29-36.
[2] As to general duties of Sheriff and Sheriff-Substitute, see Glasgow
    Corporation v. Glasgow Churches' Council, 1944 S.C. 97.

The most important matters for which the Sheriff has still the
sole responsibility, although in the execution of his office he may
take the assistance of his Substitutes or others, are his duties
under the electoral laws. He is the returning officer at all Parliamentary elections (other than University elections) for constituencies
situated wholly within his Sheriffdom, special statutory provision
being made where the constituency is situated in more than one
Sheriffdom.[1] The writ for the election of a member of Parliament
is addressed to the Sheriff as returning officer,[2] and he is responsible
for the due observance of all the statutory rules relating to the
conduct of elections. He receives nominations of candidates: in
the case of a contest, makes the arrangements for taking a poll;
presides at the counting of the votes; decides all questions as to
the validity of the votes recorded; declares the election, and reports
the result to the Clerk of the Crown in Chancery, from whom he

received the writ.[3] When there is one election only within his jurisdiction, the Sheriff usually discharges his duties as returning officer personally, but where he is returning officer for more than one constituency, or is incapacitated, by sickness or unavoidable absence, from performing the duties, he may appoint a deputy—usually a Sheriff-Substitute—to act.[4] If no such appointment is made, or if the office of Sheriff is vacant at the time, a Sheriff-Substitute, as specified in the Act, acts as returning officer.[5]

[1] 7 & 8 Geo. V c. 64, sec. 43 (13) and Schedule 7; 9 & 10 Geo. VI c. 21, sec. 13.
[2] 35 & 36 Vict. c. 33, Schedule 2.
[3] 35 & 36 Vict. c. 33, secs. 2, 8, Schedule 1.
[4] 35 & 36 Vict. c. 33, sec. 8; 7 & 8 Geo. V c. 64, sec. 43 (13) ; 6 & 7 Geo. VI c. 48, sec. 33, Schedule VI.
[5] 7 & 8 Geo. V c. 64, sec. 43 (13) ; 6 & 7 Geo. VI c. 48, sec. 33, Schedule VI.

Amongst the matters with which, as a general rule, the Sheriff does not concern himself, and for which the Sheriff-Substitute has sole responsibility as judge of first instance, the most important are the administration of the Small Debt Acts and Bankruptcy Acts, as also a vast variety of summary applications both at common law and under Statutes, in many of which the judgment of the judge of first instance is final. It is competent in many cases for the Sheriff himself to act as judge of first instance if he chooses to do so, and, as regards the non-resident Sheriffs, it is a statutory requirement that they shall preside in the Small Debt Circuit Courts in use to be held within their Sheriffdoms, at least once a year, and in addition shall despatch such ordinary business as may then be available and as time may permit.[1]

[1] 7 Edw. VII c. 51, sec. 18.

2. The Sheriff-Substitute.

The evolution of the office of Sheriff-Substitute has resulted in his becoming the territorial judge of first instance, besides being, when the Sheriff is not actually functioning, the acting Sheriff in all matters not falling within the appellate jurisdiction of the Sheriff.[1] Originally, whether prepared by the Sheriff himself, or by the Sheriff-Substitute, there was only one judgment in the Sheriff Court in a judicial process, and that was the judgment of the Sheriff. If the Substitute heard the case, and if it were of importance, the Sheriff was probably consulted, but in the general case the judgment nominally of the Sheriff was really that of his Substitute. But, as the duties of both the Sheriff and his

Substitute grew in volume and in importance, what had at first been consultation gradually assumed the form of review. At first the judgment of the Sheriff-Substitute was appealable only by leave,[2] but in 1853 an interlocutor of the Sheriff-Substitute was officially recognized as an independent judgment, and appeal from the Sheriff-Substitute to the Sheriff as a right was given legislative sanction.[3] That Statute merely expressed what had become a recognized practice, although it had the apparent effect of introducing a right of appeal not hitherto officially recognized as part of the system of Scottish judicial procedure.

[1] Fleming v. Dickson, 1862, 1 M. 188.
[2] Act of Sederunt, 12th November, 1825, ch. xiv; Act of Sederunt, 10th July, 1839, sec. 98. See also 1 & 2 Vict. c. 119, secs. 4, 20.
[3] 16 & 17 Vict. c. 80, sec. 16.

When the Sheriff-Substitute was first required to have a legal training, the list of qualified persons comprised an advocate, a clerk to the Signet, a solicitor before the Supreme Courts, or a procurator—all of three years' standing.[1] The period of qualification was later raised from three to five years.[2] The Act of 1877, which made this alteration, mentions only " an advocate or a law agent," but by that time the Law Agents Act of 1873[3] had defined a law agent as including *inter alia* " every person entitled to practise as an agent in a Court of law in Scotland." The alteration of 1877, however, created this anomaly, that, for the office of Substitute, five years' experience was deemed requisite, whilst three years was sufficient for the presumably more responsible office of Sheriff.[4] The Sheriff Courts Act, 1907, removed this anomaly by making the period for both five years.[5]

[1] 6 Geo. IV c, 23, sec. 9.
[2] 40 & 41 Vict. c. 50, sec. 4.
[3] 36 & 37 Vict. c. 63, sec. 1.
[4] 20 Geo. II c. 43, sec. 29.
[5] 7 Edw. VII c. 51, sec. 12.

3. The Honorary Sheriff-Substitute.

The Honorary Sheriff-Substitute is an unpaid judge, nominated by the Sheriff, to hold office during the pleasure of the Sheriff, and for whom the Sheriff is answerable. An Honorary Sheriff-Substitute may exercise the whole powers and duties appertaining to the office of Sheriff-Substitute,[1] and he holds his office notwithstanding the death or removal of the Sheriff.[1]

[1] 7 Edw. VII c. 51, sec. 17. See also Mann v. Tait, 1892, 20 R. 13.

No legal qualification is required for an Honorary Sheriff-

Substitute, and he is not, if he happens to be a lawyer, precluded from practice,[1] as the salaried Sheriff-Substitute is. Prior to 1907 it was doubted whether an Honorary Sheriff-Substitute could, whilst holding office, be elected a member of Parliament, or even exercise the franchise.[2] All doubt has been dispelled by the Sheriff Courts Act, 1907, for the disability clause is expressly restricted to a salaried Sheriff-Substitute.[3] The Sheriff-clerk was at one time considered eligible for appointment as Honorary Sheriff-Substitute but he could not now be appointed.[4]

[1] See Henderson v. Warden, 1845, 17 Scot. Jur. 271.
[2] Wright v. Kellie, 1898, 1 F. 209.
[3] 7 Edw. VII c. 51, sec. 21.
[4] Binning v. Arnot, 1711, M. 7662; Stewart v. Lord Advocate, 1857, 29 Scot. Jur. 344; 2 Irv. 614.

4. JUDGES' POWERS AND DUTIES.

Most of the statutory enactments applicable to Sheriff Court judges apply both to the Sheriff and the Sheriff-Substitute. They are now alike Crown nominees, and they have similar tenure of office. They are now alike under the direction of the Secretary of State for Scotland, who may prescribe their duties. Subject to what is stated below they are alike entitled to a retiring allowance if disabled, after a specified period of service, from the exercise of their office by age or permanent infirmity. Neither whilst in office is eligible for election, as a member of Parliament, and both are debarred from voting in Parliamentary elections held within the Sheriffdom.[1]

[1] 7 Edw. VII c. 51, secs. 11, 13, 14, 18, 19, 20, 21.

Some of the enactments, however, apply to one judge only, and in some respects the Sheriff and Sheriff-Substitute differ. For instance (a) the Sheriff (except in Midlothian and Lanarkshire) is not necessarily resident, and is not debarred from practice, although he may not act as an advocate in any cause arising in his own Sheriffdom; whilst the Sheriff-Substitute is resident in his jurisdiction, and is debarred from practice;[1] (b) all interim Sheriffs-Substitute are paid by the Treasury, but interim Sheriffs are only so paid if the Sheriff is absent through illness, and if he is debarred from private practice; in other cases the interim Sheriff is remunerated at the Sheriff's expense;[2] (c) a Sheriff-Substitute cannot obtain a retiring allowance unless he has served at least ten years, whilst the Treasury have a discretion to make a modified allowance to a Sheriff, notwithstanding he may not have served

for ten years.[3] In the case of Sheriffs appointed after 28th July,
1933, retiring allowances will only be paid in the case of those
debarred from practice.[4]

[1] 7 Edw. VII c. 51, secs. 19, 21.
[2] Ibid., secs. 15 and 16; 23 & 24 Geo. V c. 41, sec. 32.
[3] 7 Edw. VII c. 51, sec. 20; 23 & 24 Geo. V c. 41, sec. 33.
[4] 23 & 24 Geo. V c. 41, sec. 33.

The Sheriff and the Sheriffs-Substitute—salaried and honorary—
are the only officials connected with the Sheriff Court of Scotland
who exercise strictly judicial functions. In the absence of special
direction from the Secretary of State for Scotland, and subject
to the Statutes, each Sheriff has authority to regulate the business
of his Sheriffdom, and to make all necessary orders for the instruction or direction of Court officials. Subject to this general control,
the judicial actings of the Sheriff and his Substitute are not, as
they once were, a common responsibility, but each has an independent judicial responsibility, the Sheriff-Substitute (now erroneously
so-called) having become an independent judge of first instance,
and the Sheriff's judicial function being in practice mainly
restricted to that of review. Some matters at common law, and
in accordance with long-established usage, as well as under various
Statutes, are relegated to the Sheriff alone; others are relegated
to the Sheriff-Substitute alone. In other cases certain classes of
business are in certain Sheriffdoms dealt with by the Sheriff and
in others disposed of by the Sheriff-Substitute. In some Statutes
the word " Sheriff " is defined as including " Sheriff-Substitute,"
but such a provision is not necessary, as the Interpretation Act
of 1889 provides, as regards Statutes passed after that date, that,
unless the contrary intention appears, " Sheriff " includes
" Sheriff-Substitute."[1] But this only expressed the recognized law,
for a quarter of a century earlier the Court of Session had ruled
" that all jurisdiction conferred on the Sheriff, to be exercised
in the Sheriff Court according to the ordinary rules and practice
in the Sheriff Court, is within the jurisdiction of the Sheriff-
Substitute also."[2]

[1] 52 & 53 Vict. c. 63, sec. 28.
[2] Fleming v. Dickson, 1862, 1 M. 188, Lord Cowan, p. 194.

5. THE SHERIFF-CLERK.

The office of Sheriff-clerk has existed from the earliest times,
though none of the Statutes strictly relating to Sheriff Court
procedure made special mention of the Sheriff-clerk till the Sheriff

Courts Act of 1825 directed that he was to discharge his duties personally.[1]

[1] 6 Geo. IV c. 23, sec. 6.

The Sheriff-clerk has from the earliest times been entitled to execute his office by deputy, and he was not precluded from doing so by the Act of 1825.[1] The older Statutes referring to the Sheriff-clerk's duties expressly recognize this, and specifically include the depute in the statutory enactments.[2] Formerly the deputes were appointed and dismissed by the Sheriff-clerk, and, having no independent authority, their commission fell on his death. But by the Sheriff Courts and Legal Officers (Scotland) Act, 1927, the right of appointing and—with certain qualifications—of dismissing Sheriff-clerks is vested in the Secretary of State for Scotland, who has also the power to appoint the necessary deputes, clerks, and assistants. The Secretary of State determines the appointees who are to be whole-time officers, and such officers are civil servants. With certain exceptions, and subject to the provisions of the Act regarding superannuation, existing officials are declared to hold office as if appointed by the Secretary of State. The Secretary of State is also empowered to make interim arrangements on vacancies occurring in the office of Sheriff-clerk or depute, or in the case of incapacity of any of these officers.[3] There is no statutory qualification for the office of Sheriff-clerk. He is at the present day an official with varied and often most important duties, and in some statutory matters he has to act upon his own initiative.

[1] Heddle v. Garioch, 1827, 5 S. 503.
[2] A. P. S. 1540, c. 12; 1555, c. 7.
[3] 17 & 18 Geo. V c. 35, secs. 1-7.

Sheriff-clerks and deputes who are appointed as whole-time officers are debarred from practising as solicitors or from carrying on any other employment to interfere with the discharge of their official duties.[1] Though not holding whole-time appointments they are precluded from acting as procurators in their own Courts,[2] unless they are personally parties to the cause, in which case the appropriate course is for the Sheriff to appoint a clerk *pro hac vice*.[3] This prohibition has been held not to prevent an unpaid depute, who had been appointed for service in an emergency, practising in the ordinary way when he was not officially acting as clerk.[4] Subject to the above, depute clerks in the Small Debt

Circuit Courts are not debarred from acting as procurators except in the Small Debt Courts in which they are officially acting.[5]

[1] 17 & 18 Geo. V c. 35, sec. 3.
[2] Acts of Sederunt, 6th March, 1783, and 10th July 1839, sec. 160; Smith, &c. v. Robertson, 1827, 5 S. 848; cf. Dickie v. Thomson, 1932, 48 Sh.Ct.Rep. 290.
[3] Manson v. Smith, 1871, 9 M. 492; Macbeth v. Innes, 1873, 11 M. 404.
[4] Edie v. Rigg, 1879, 17 S.L.R. 36.
[5] 7 Will. IV & 1 Vict. c. 41, sec. 25.

6. Auditor of Court.

The nomination of this official rests with the Sheriff, and the auditor holds office during the pleasure of the Sheriff. The Sheriff-clerk, or his depute, may also be the auditor, and one of these officials or a solicitor is normally appointed to the office, for which there is no statutory qualification. The Sheriff Courts Act, 1907, provides that "Expenses allowed in any action, whether in absence or *in foro*, shall, unless modified at a fixed amount, be taxed before decree is granted for them,"[1] but in undefended cases pursuer's solicitor has the option of charging an inclusive fee which obviates the need for taxation.[2] Fees payable by the litigants for the taxation of accounts now pass to the Exchequer. A neutral person may be appointed to tax any account in which the auditor is personally interested.

[1] 7 Edw. VII c. 51, Schedule I, Rule 99.
[2] C.A.S. M. II; Act of Sederunt, 7th May, 1935, Table of Fees I, 1 (b).

7. Procurator-Fiscal.

This official is appointed by the Lord Advocate, in whom the nomination is vested by the Sheriff Courts and Legal Officers Act, 1927.[1] His duties lie mainly in the Criminal Court, but he has some duties in the Civil Court also. The most important is the conduct of inquiries under the Fatal Accidents Inquiry Acts of 1895[2] and 1906.[3] In some quasi-criminal proceedings, such as breach of interdict and the like, the concurrence of the procurator-fiscal is requisite, although the proceedings are taken in the Civil Court.[4]

[1] 17 & 18 Geo. V c. 35, sec. 1 (2) (3).
[2] 58 & 59 Vict. c. 36.
[3] 6 Edw. VII c. 35.
[4] Northumberland v. Harris, 1832, 10 S. 366; Usher v. Magistrates of Edinburgh, 1839, 1 D. 639.

8. OFFICERS OF COURT.

The appointment of Sheriff-officers should be made by the Sheriff and not by a Sheriff-Substitute.[1] The officers are selected by the Sheriff after examination by him or others on his behalf as to their fitness for office, and they are required to find caution for the due discharge of their duties. Disapproval has been expressed in the Court of Session of a proposal to appoint an officer for the express purpose of acting for one employer alone, but an appointment by the Sheriff would appear to be a discretionary act of administration and not subject to appeal.[1]

[1] Stewart v. Reid, 1934 S.C. 69.

The officer and his cautioner will be liable to the employer for loss arising from negligence or delay in executing diligence in terms of the instructions given,[1] and to the debtor or defender for damages resulting from any improper use of the warrant.[2] In the general case the employer of the officer will also be responsible for his actings in executing diligence so far as these were authorized by him.[3] An officer has no authority beyond his warrant, but for the terms or legality of the warrant, if *ex facie* regular, he has no responsibility, and so will not incur any liability so long as he acts in conformity with it.[4] Any discretion as to the extent to which the officer is to give effect to his warrant must depend on the instructions given him.[5]

[1] Glen v. Black, 1841, 4 D. 36; Clason v. Black, 1842, 4 D. 743; Struthers v. Dykes, 1845, 7 D. 436, 1847, 9 D. 1437, 1850, 7 Bell's App. 390.
[2] Kennedy v. M'Kinnon, 1821, 1 S. 210; Inch v. Thomson, 1836, 14 S. 1129; Beattie v. M'Lellan, 1846, 8 D. 930; Gray v. Smart, 1892, 19 R. 692; Broomberg v. Reinhold & Co., 1942, 60 Sh.Ct.Rep. 45.
[3] Beattie v. M'Lellan, supra; Petersen v. M'Lean, 1868, 6 M. 218; Gray v. Smart, supra; Broomberg v. Reinhold & Co., &c., supra; Cf. Stewart v. Macdonald, 1784, M. 13989; Le Conte v. Douglas, &c., 1880, 8 R. 175.
[4] Scot v. Banks, 1628, M. 6016.
[5] Cullen v. Smith, 1847, 9 D. 606; Couper v. Bain, 1868, 7 M. 102.

An officer as such has not authority to receive payment of a debt and to grant a discharge for it, but the creditor may authorize him to do so. It is, in practice, very convenient that he should do so, but the debtor takes the risk of dealing with the officer. A debtor cannot plead against his creditor that he tendered payment, if the tender were made to the officer, and not to the creditor direct.[1] The officer's cautioner is not liable in respect of the embezzlement by the officer of money collected by him for his employer.[2]

[1] Inglis v. M'Intyre, 1862, 24 D. 541, Lord Cowan, p. 544.
[2] Ayr County Council v. Wyllie, 1935 S.C. 836.

The fees payable to officers are regulated by Act of Sederunt by the Court of Session.[1]

[1] 7 Edw. VII c. 51, sec. 40; C.A.S. M. III, as increased by later Acts of Sederunt.

Officers may be suspended or removed from office by the Sheriff who appointed them, or by his successor in office. As an officer must always have a cautioner subject to the Court's jurisdiction, he must find caution anew should his original cautioner die, or become bankrupt, or leave Scotland. The Sheriff may relieve a cautioner upon application.

A Sheriff-officer's commission authorizes his acting within the Sheriffdom of the Sheriff who grants it. The Small Debt Act of 1837 extended this authority to the other Sheriffdoms as regards citation and diligence under the Small Debt Acts, if the warrant had been endorsed by the Sheriff-clerk of the Sheriffdom where the warrant was to be executed.[1] In the following year, any Sheriff's warrant, which till then had been effective only in his own Sheriffdom, was made operative also in other jurisdictions upon endorsation,[2] but it had to be executed by an officer of the Sheriffdom of endorsement. In 1876 endorsation was dispensed with as regards warrants for service upon a defender subject to the jurisdiction of one Sheriff Court, but residing within another Sheriffdom.[3] Under the Sheriff Courts Act of 1907 endorsation is dispensed with as regards warrants of citation, or warrants or precepts of arrestment, proceeding upon depending actions or liquid documents of debt, and these may now be executed by an officer either of the Sheriffdom where the warrant was granted, or of that where it is to be executed.[4] But, in the case of ordinary Court decrees, endorsation is still necessary for operating diligence in execution,[5] and such warrants still require to be executed by an officer of the endorsing Court. In the case of small debt decrees endorsation is not necessary.[6]

[1] 7 Will. IV & 1 Vict. c. 41, secs. 12, 19, 34.
[2] 1 & 2 Vict. c. 119, sec. 24.
[3] 39 & 40 Vict. c. 70, sec. 12 (1).
[4] 7 Edw. VII c. 51, Schedule I, Rule 10.
[5] See 1 & 2 Vict. c. 114, sec. 13.
[6] 52 & 53 Vict. c. 26, sec. 11.

The extent to which a messenger-at-arms may act in Sheriff Court procedure is by no means clear. By the Sheriff Courts (Extracts) Act it is provided that execution on extracts issued under that Act—which does not apply to small debt procedure—shall be carried out by messengers-at-arms, officers of Court or others entitled to execute diligence thereon.[1] Under the Bankruptcy Act the Sheriff's warrant to apprehend the bankrupt and bring him for examination may be executed by messengers-at-arms and Sheriff-officers.[2] Similar provision for execution by messengers was contained in various Statutes now repealed.[3] The present Sheriff Courts Act seems to imply, but does not provide, that execution is to be by Sheriff-officer.[4]

[1] 55 & 56 Vict. c. 17, sec. 8.
[2] 3 & 4 Geo. V c. 20, sec. 84.
[3] 6 & 7 Will. IV c. 56, secs. 1, 4; 16 & 17 Vict. c. 80, sec. 30; 43 & 44 Vict. c. 34, sec. 9 (1).
[4] 7 Edw. VII c. 51, Schedule I, Rules 9, 10; Forms D, E, F, G.

It has been held in the Sheriff Court that, apart from statutory authority, a messenger-at-arms cannot act in Sheriff Court procedure and that he is not an officer of the Sheriff Court,[1] but an opposite view has been expressed in the Court of Session.[2] If sec. 3 of the Execution of Diligence Act can be read as applying to a warrant of service—which seems very doubtful—that section would imply that execution of such a warrant by a messenger is competent.[3] It is thought that the point must be regarded as an open one, but that a messenger has probably authority to act in Sheriff Court practice. In the Small Debt Court his status is more doubtful in view of the express indication in the Acts that Sheriff-officers are to function thereunder.[4]

[1] Hamilton v. Bain, 1857, I Guthrie's Select Cases 405. See also M'Culloch v. M'Laughlin, 1930 J.C. 8; Dove Wilson, Sheriff Court Practice, 4th edn. 45.
[2] Sutherland v. Standard Life Assurance Co., 1902, 4 F. 957, Lord Kincairney, p. 961. See also Finlayson v. Innes, 1803, 4 Pat. App. 443; Cheyne v. M'Gungle, 1860, 22 D. 1490; Campbell v. Duncan, 1901, 17 Sh.Ct.Rep. 155.
[3] 16 & 17 Geo. V c. 16, sec. 3. The Act, despite its title, is not confined to diligence.
[4] See 7 Will. IV & 1 Vict. c. 41, sec. 3; 52 & 53 Vict. c. 26, sec. 11. See also Dove Wilson, cit. supra.

9. SOLICITORS.

In the Sheriff Court, as in other Courts of law, a litigant may conduct his own case, but in the ordinary Sheriff Court it is not of frequent occurrence that a party conducts his case personally.

If he does, he must observe the rules of procedure, in the same manner as a solicitor.

Under the Small Debt Statutes, a party may appear personally, or be represented by a member of his family, or such other person as the Court may allow.[1] The original policy of the Small Debt Acts was to discourage professional pleaders,[1] and it was not till 1889 that remuneration to solicitors was recognized as falling within party and party costs.[2] Even then the duty was laid upon the Sheriff of selecting the cases in which a party might have the privilege of being assisted by his solicitor. But under the Sheriff Courts Act, 1907, appearance by a solicitor is now matter of right, not of privilege.[3] The practice in some Sheriff Courts of permitting non-professional pleaders in summary causes appears to be without statutory sanction.

[1] 7 Will. IV & 1 Vict. c. 41, secs. 14, 15 ; A and B, 1924, 40 Sh.Ct.Rep. 25.
[2] 52 & 53 Vict. c. 26, sec. 8.
[3] 7 Edw. VII c. 51, sec. 44.

In any Sheriff Court process, parties may be represented by counsel. While the Act and relative rules of procedure speak only of an agent, which expression is defined[1] as meaning " a law agent enrolled in terms of the Law Agents (Scotland) Act, 1873 "[2] —now a solicitor enrolled under the Solicitors (Scotland) Act, 1933[3]—it has long been recognized in practice that an advocate has right of audience before any tribunal in Scotland, unless expressly debarred by Statute, and the statutory provisions referred to do not deprive him of that right. Whether counsel's fees should in a particular case be included in party and party costs is a matter that rests with the Sheriff before whom counsel appears.[4]

[1] 7 Edw. VII c. 51, sec. 3 (g).
[2] 36 & 37 Vict. c. 63.
[3] 23 & 24 Geo. V c. 21, secs. 49, 50.
[4] See p. 335, infra.

Judicial proceedings before the Sheriff Courts are generally conducted by solicitors. Although local societies and faculties of procurators still exist, and retain certain functions under the Solicitors Act of 1933 any person enrolled or deemed to have been enrolled as a solicitor in pursuance of the Act of 1933, wherever his domicile or place of business may be, is entitled, upon payment of a small fee, to be put upon the roll of any Sheriff Court in Scotland, and there to practise.[1] A solicitor thus entitled to practise in any Sheriff Court may borrow a process although he has not a place of business within the jurisdiction of the Court.[2]

[1] 23 & 24 Geo. V c. 21, secs. 20, 46.
[2] 7 Edw. VII c. 51, Schedule I, Rule 16; 23 & 24 Geo. V c. 21, sec. 46.

When a solicitor has been admitted his name is enrolled on the Roll of Solicitors. The Court of Session may, in respect of a solicitor's professional misconduct, cause his name to be struck off the roll, or may suspend him from practice, or fine or censure him. By Part V of the 1933 Act provision is made for a Discipline Committee who are entitled to fine or censure a solicitor, subject to appeal to the Court. A solicitor's name may also be removed from the roll on his own application. A solicitor whose name has been struck off the roll may be restored by the Court.[1]

[1] 23 & 24 Geo. V c. 21, secs. 14, 19, 24-34. See Solicitors' Discipline (Scotland) Committee v. B, 1942 S.C. 293.

A woman could not formerly be enrolled as a solicitor,[1] but that disqualification has now been removed by the Sex Disqualification (Removal) Act, 1919.[2]

[1] Hall v. Incorporated Society of Law Agents, 1901, 3 F. 1059.
[2] 9 & 10 Geo. V c. 71, sec. 1.

An enrolled solicitor is entitled to subscribe the list of solicitors kept for any Sheriffdom, and thereafter to practise in the Courts of that Sheriffdom.[1] A solicitor is not entitled to plead before the Court of Session except in causes which, under the older practice of that Court, came before the Bill Chamber,[2] and in the case—unknown in modern practice—of a civil jury trial taken at a circuit town.[3]

[1] 23 & 24 Geo. V c. 21, secs. 20-22, 46. See Gray & Co. v. Paul, 1924, 41 Sh.Ct.Rep. 206.
[2] 23 & 24 Geo. V c. 41, sec. 3.
[3] 31 & 32 Vict. c. 100, sec. 50.

An unqualified person may not discharge the functions of a solicitor, unless permitted by Statute (as, for instance, under the Small Debt Acts[1]) under penalty of fine or imprisonment.[2] No person other than a qualified solicitor can recover fees for legal advice given, or for assistance rendered in the conduct of any legal process.[3]

[1] 7 Will. IV & 1 Vict. c. 41, sec. 15.
[2] 23 & 24 Geo. V c. 21, secs. 36, 40.
[3] Ibid., sec. 42.

Solicitors have a lien or right of retention over documents of their clients which have come into their hands in the course of their employment,[1] but not over those obtained merely as

productions from a process.[2]   The lien covers fees and ordinary
disbursements,[3] but not cash advances, nor the outstanding accounts
of other solicitors employed in England.[4]   A solicitor may also
obtain a charge and right to payment of his taxed expenses, out
of any property recovered or preserved for the client by Court
proceedings.[5]

[1] National Bank of Scotland v. White & Park, 1909 S.C. 1308.
[2] Callinan v. Bell, 1793, M. 6255.
[3] Skinner v. Paterson, 1826, 2 S. 354; Liquidator of Grand Empire
      Theatres v. Snodgrass, 1932 S.C. (H.L.) 73.
[4] Christie v. Ruxton, 1862, 24 D. 1182; Skinner v. Paterson, supra;
      Liquidator of Grand Empire Theatres v. Snodgrass, supra.
[5] 23 & 24 Geo. V c. 21, sec. 43.   See further, p. 331, infra.

The fees exigible by solicitors for the conduct of a Court
process are regulated by Act of Sederunt.[1]   In party and party
accounts only one solicitor for each party is normally recognized
as entitled to fees.   If he shares his fees with another solicitor
that is a private arrangement.   It is, with certain exceptions,
illegal for a solicitor to share fees with any unqualified person,[2]
and the sharing of fees between solicitors acting for the same
client is permitted only on certain conditions.[3]   A solicitor acting
for a disclosed client normally incurs no liability to another
solicitor employed by him.[4]   The liability of the client to the
other solicitor depends on circumstances.[5]

[1] 7 Edw. VII c. 51, sec. 40; Act of Sederunt, 7th May, 1935.
[2] 23 & 24 Geo. V c. 21, sec. 38.
[3] 23 & 24 Geo. V c. 41, sec. 37.
[4] 23 & 24 Geo. V c. 21, sec. 41.
[5] See M'Laren v. M'Dougall, 1881, 8 R. 626; Clark & Macdonald v.
      Schulze, 1902, 4 F. 448; Liquidator of Grand Empire Theatres v.
      Snodgrass, 1932 S.C. (H.L.) 73.

A solicitor who has conducted a Court process, in which his
client is found entitled to expenses, may obtain decree for these
expenses in his own name,[1] but he does not thereby discharge his
client of liability if he fail to recover under the decree.

[1] 7 Edw. VII c. 51, Schedule I, Rule 99.   See further, p. 329, infra.

The initial writ, by which an action is commenced, may be
signed by the pursuer or his solicitor, but in practice is almost
invariably signed by the solicitor.[1]   A solicitor acting without
authority, and thereby occasioning expense to another party may
render himself liable personally in damages or expenses.[2]

[1] 7 Edw. VII c. 51, Schedule I, Rule 3.
[2] Miller v. Rae, 1834, 13 S. 699; M'Call v. Sharp, 1862, 24 D. 393;
      Robertson v. Ross, 1873, 11 M. 910.

A solicitor, like any other skilled person, is liable for the consequences of gross negligence and want of skill in the exercise of his profession,[1] but negligence or want of skill is not necessarily to be inferred merely because he may have given professional advice which the event proved to be unsound.[2] He is not personally liable for all the statements made in Court pleadings, although he may have signed them, if he has been duly authorized to make them,[3] nor is he liable for error on the part of an officer[4] or of a correspondent-solicitor whom he may employ;[5] but for his own personal negligence or wrongful acts in the conduct of a Court process a solicitor may become liable, either to his own client[1] or to other parties.[6] A solicitor might possibly—although the grounds would require to be very clear—also be liable for defamatory statements made in the course of the conduct of Court proceedings if he acted maliciously,[7] and malice might possibly be inferred if such statements were obviously not pertinent to the issue in the cause. If, therefore, a client insist in having dangerous statements inserted in pleadings, it is a wise precaution to have the papers signed by the client.

[1] Hamilton v. Emslie, 1868, 7 M. 173; Simpson v. Kidstons & Co., (O.H.) 1913, 1 S.L.T. 74; Shane v. Girvan, (O.H.) 1927 S.N. 71, 1927 S.L.T. 460.
[2] Stewart v. M'Lean, Baird & Neilson, 1915 S.C. 13.
[3] Johnston v. Scott, 1829, 7 S. 234.
[4] Russell v. Hedderwick, 1859, 21 D. 1325.
[5] The correspondent would be liable to the client. See Hunter v. Farquharson, 1928, 45 Sh.Ct.Rep. 3.
[6] MacRobbie v. M'Lellan's Trustee, 1891, 18 R. 470.
[7] Bayne v. Macgregor, 1862, 24 D. 1126; 1863, 1 M. 615.

In every case the solicitor should obtain a mandate from his client. If he does not do so, he runs the risk of being held personally liable for expenses allowed against his client.[1] If his authority to act is challenged, he is bound to produce his mandate, and the opposing party is entitled to have the process sisted till he does so.[2] Possession by a defender's solicitor of the service copy of the writ is generally accepted as sufficiently vouching his authority to enter appearance and state a defence,[3] but, in special circumstances, a defender's solicitor, as well as a pursuer's solicitor, may be ordered to produce a mandate, especially in a case where there are several defenders called, and the solicitor has possession of only one service copy. A general mandate to act covers all ordinary procedure in a process. But it is very doubtful whether a solicitor's mandate invests him with any discretionary authority to bind his client, such as counsel possesses, in matters beyond the scope of routine procedure.[4] If it is proposed, for instance, to abandon an action,[5] or to compromise it,[4] or to appeal to, or contest an appeal taken by an opponent to, a higher Court,[6] or to submit the subject-matter of dispute to arbitration,[7] or refer it to a judicial referee,[8] or to delay executing diligence,[9] or to take any extraordinary step, the solicitor should see that he has his client's express authority to take the step.

[1] Cowan v. Farnie, 1836, 14 S. 634; Philip v. Gordon, 1848, 11 D. 175; M'Call v. Sharp, 1862, 24 D. 393; Robertson v. Ross, 1873, 11 M. 910.
[2] Philip v. Gordon, supra; Fischer & Co. v. Andersen, 1896, 23 R. 395.
[3] Muir v. Stevenson, 1850. 12 D. 512.
[4] See Weir v. Stevenson, &c., 1885, 1 Sh.Ct.Rep. 161; Torbat v. Torbat's Trustees, (O.H.) 1907, 14 S.L.T. 830; Hendry's Trustees v. Hendry, 1916, 53 S.L.R. 757; 1916, 2 S.L.T. 135; Smith v. Smith, (O.H.) 1927 S.N. 82; 1927 S.L.T. 462; Milne v. Spark, 1935, 51 Sh.Ct.Rep. 311.
[5] Urquhart v. Grigor, 1857, 19 D. 853.
[6] Macqueen & Macintosh v. Colvin, 1826, 4 S. 786; Stephen v. Skinner, 1863, 2 M. 287.
[7] Livingston v. Johnson, 1830, 8 S. 594.
[8] Black v. Laidlaw, 1844, 6 D. 1254.
[9] Cameron v. Mortimer, 1872, 10 M. 817.

CHAPTER II.

JURISDICTION.

1. GENERAL.

The various Statutes of the last hundred years, and in particular the Sheriff Courts Acts, 1907,[1] and 1913,[2] have greatly altered the complexion of the Sheriff Court jurisdiction. As reconstituted in 1907, the Sheriff Court has largely recovered its original character as a Court of practically universal jurisdiction. It also now exercises extensive and varied special jurisdiction conferred by Statute, though some matters are still beyond its scope. In some respects the Sheriff Court jurisdiction is privative, in others it is limited in extent; in some it does not exist at all. Where it does exist, and is not privative or appellate, it is concurrent with that of the Court of Session, unless the contrary is expressly provided by Statute.

[1] 7 Edw. VII c. 51, sec. 5.
[2] 2 & 3 Geo. V c. 28.

2. NOBILE OFFICIUM.

The Sheriff Court—like other inferior Courts in Scotland—has never possessed jurisdiction arising *ex nobile officio*.[1] This preeminent or extraordinary equity jurisdiction belongs alone to the Inner House of the Court of Session, which, as the Supreme Court of civil jurisdiction in Scotland, has an inherent and exclusive power of finding a remedy in circumstances in which no express process or established usage is available.[2] Much of what has long been recognized as exclusive Court of Session jurisdiction has been built up upon *nobile officium*, or equity power. But the distinction between common law and equity jurisdiction has never, in Scotland, been very marked, and in practice ordinary equity is administered in the Sheriff Court or in the Court of Session.

[1] Forbes, &c. v. Underwood, 1886, 13 R. 465.
[2] Erskine I 3, 22.

Various actions have been held incompetent in the Sheriff Court in respect that they involve an appeal to the *nobile officium*. These include an action to compel an arbiter to proceed :[1] an

action of proving the tenor :[2] and an action for a decree conform
to an English[3] or colonial[4] judgment.   It has also been indicated
that the Sheriff has no jurisdiction to control a local education
authority in their administration[5] or to entertain an action
against a judicial factor appointed by the Court of Session which
related to the discharge of his official duties.[6]

[1] Forbes, &c. v. Underwood, 1886, 13 R. 465.
[2] Dunbar & Co. v. Scottish County Investment Co., 1920 S.C. 210; cf.
    Elliott v. Galpern, 1927 S.C. 29.
[3] O'Connor v. Erskine, 1905, 22 Sh.Ct.Rep. 58.
[4] Stoddart, &c. v. Hotchkiss, 1916, 33 Sh.Ct.Rep, 60.
[5] Hunter v. School Board of Lochgilphead, 1886, 14 R. 135.
[6] Hallpenny v. Howden, 1894, 21 R. 945.

3. Consistorial.

The most important class of case which is to some extent still
incompetent in the Sheriff Court is that known as " consistorial."
Such cases were originally disposed of by the Bishop's Court and
later by the commissary.   Apart from Statute, neither the Sheriff
nor the Court of Session ever had jurisdiction as a Court of first
instance in consistorial causes, but the Act of 1830 conferred upon
the Court of Session privative jurisdiction in " actions of declarator
of marriage and of nullity of marriage, and all actions of
declarator of legitimacy and of bastardy, and all actions of divorce,
and all actions of separation *a mensa et thoro*,"[1] to which were
added in 1850 actions of adherence and all other consistorial
actions though not specially mentioned.[2]

[1] 11 Geo. IV and 1 Will. IV c. 69, sec. 33.
[2] 13 & 14 Vict. c. 36, sec. 16.

Since 1907 the Sheriff Court has had jurisdiction in actions
of aliment provided that as between husband and wife they are
actions of separation and aliment, adherence and aliment or
interim aliment and also in actions for regulating the custody of
children.[1]   At the same time jurisdiction in actions of declarator
was conferred on the Sheriff Court but there were excepted declarators of marriage or nullity of marriage and actions the direct or
main object of which is to determine the personal status of
individuals.[2]

[1] 7 Edw. VII c. 51, sec. 5 (2).
[2] Ibid., sec. 5 (1).

In this way the jurisdiction of the Court of Session has ceased
to be privative in actions of separation and aliment, and adherence

and aliment, and is now concurrent with that of the Sheriff Court, with power to the Sheriff, either on cause shown or *ex proprio motu*, to remit such a cause to the Court of Session.[1] The Court of Session, however, does not countenance the Sheriff exercising his power to remit, unless there is some special delicacy or difficulty in the case which makes a remit desirable.[2] The jurisdiction of the Court of Session is still privative as regards the other consistorial actions above referred to. The grounds of jurisdiction in any particular Sheriff Court in the case of actions of separation and aliment and adherence and aliment are dealt with later.[3] In actions of adherence and aliment, separation and aliment, interim aliment and actions regulating the custody of children decree in absence is not competent and proof must be led.[4]

[1] 7 Edw. VII c. 51, sec. 5 (1) (2); 2 & 3 Geo. V c. 28, Schedule I.
[2] Dunbar v. Dunbar, 1912 S.C. 19; Lamont v. Lamont, 1939 S.C. 484.
[3] See p. 525, infra.
[4] 7 Edw. VII c. 51, Schedule I, Rule 23; 2 & 3 Geo. V c. 28, Schedule II.

The " consistorial actions " which are still incompetent in the Sheriff Court are (a) declarator of marriage; (b) declarator of nullity of marriage; (c) declarator of legitimacy; (d) declarator of bastardy; (e) divorce;[1] and (f) action of putting to silence—the last named, which is not of frequent occurrence, being normally directed to negativing a claim to personal status.[2] These actions seem practically exhaustive of the cases involving questions of personal status which are met with in practice, and it is doubtful whether there are any others which would fall under the general exclusion from the Sheriff's jurisdiction of actions of declarator " the direct or main object of which is to determine the personal status of individuals."[2] It is to be observed that the exclusion applies only to questions of personal status, so that an action to determine the official status of an individual would apparently be competent. It has also to be noted that the words of exclusion above quoted are referable only to actions of declarator and therefore do not qualify the Sheriff's jurisdiction in the case of other actions between spouses falling under the next sub-head,[3] viz., actions of separation and aliment, adherence and aliment, and interim aliment, or those regulating the custody of children. So it has been held that the Sheriff could deal with an action of adherence and aliment in which aliment was claimed for a child whose paternity was denied by the defending husband.[4] This decision seems to infer a rather wider view of the Sheriff's jurisdiction than has sometimes been assumed, and, if followed out, may result in various questions affecting status being disposed of in the actions between spouses which are competent in the Sheriff Court.

[1] 11 Geo. IV & 1 Will. IV c. 69, sec. 33.
[2] 7 Edw. VII c. 51, sec. 5 (1); cf. Mackie v. Lyon, 1943, 59 Sh.Ct.Rep. 130.
[3] Ibid., sec. 5 (2); 2 & 3 Geo. V c. 28, Schedule I.
[4] Lamont v. Lamont, 1939 S.C. 484; cf. Casey v. Casey, 1925, 41 Sh.Ct.Rep. 300.

Apart from the point noted in the preceding paragraph that the exclusion relating to questions of status is referable only to actions of declarator it has long been recognized that if a question of status is merely ancillary to some other question which is the direct or main object of an action, the Sheriff Court may, for the purposes of that action, entertain and decide the question of status. This rule has been applied in an ordinary action when the existence of an irregular marriage had to be decided in. connexion with a pauper's settlement.[1] And in workmen's compensation procedure—where the position is rather special—the paternity of an illegitimate child[2] and the fact of an irregular marriage[3] have been held competent for the Sheriff to decide. But where a question of status is thus incidentally determined for the purpose of a particular case it is *res judicata* only as between the parties to that case.[4]

[1] M'Donald v. Mackenzie, 1891, 18 R. 502.
[2] Johnstone v. Spencer & Co., 1908 S.C. 1015.
[3] Turnbull v. Wilsons & Clyde Coal Co., 1935 S.C. 580; cf. Wallace v. Fife Coal Co., 1909 S.C. 682.
[4] Turnbull v. Wilsons & Clyde Coal Co., supra.

An action was not necessarily excluded from the jurisdiction of the Sheriff Court, merely because it related to the domestic relations. Aliment claims, for instance, between parents and children, where the parentage was not in dispute and claims against the fathers of illegitimate children, even where the paternity was disputed, have always been regarded as claims for debt and as competent in the Sheriff Court. Even between spouses, the Sheriff Court was accustomed to a limited effect to exercise jurisdiction in a claim by a wife for temporary aliment, pending a permanent settlement by the Court of Session.[1] This branch of the Sheriff's jurisdiction has now been extended by the express inclusion amongst the competent actions in the Sheriff Court of actions of aliment, provided that as between spouses they are actions of separation and aliment, adherence and aliment, or interim aliment.[2]

[1] Smith v. Smith, 1874, 1 R. 1010; M'Donald v. M'Donald, 1875, 2 R. 705.
[2] 7 Edw. VII c. 51, sec. 5 (2); 2 & 3 Geo. V c. 28, Schedule I. See further as to this matter, p. 523, infra.

Certain actions regarding the custody of children were always competent in the Sheriff Court, when no question of status was involved, and the crave was for the interim custody of the child. If a more permanent order was asked the Sheriff's jurisdiction prior to 1907 was somewhat doubtful.[1] The Sheriff has now jurisdiction in " actions for regulating the custody of children,"[2] and it has been held that this empowers him to deal with cases of permanent as contrasted with interim custody.[3] If such a case raises questions of difficulty or delicacy the Sheriff will probably remit it to the Court of Session for disposal, and he will be bound to do so if the issues raised fall under the Custody of Children Act, 1891, when the Supreme Court alone has jurisdiction.[3] By the Illegitimate Children (Scotland) Act, 1930,[4] the Sheriff is specially authorized to deal with the custody of, and access to, an illegitimate child, on application by one of the parents or in an action for aliment for the child. But if such an application raises questions under the Act of 1891 a remit to the Court of Session will apparently have to be made.[5] In actions relating to custody a crave may be made for warrant to search for and recover the person of the child. Decree in absence cannot be taken in actions for regulating the custody of children, and proof must be led.[6]

[1] Hood v. Hood, 1871, 9 M. 449, Lord President Inglis, p. 455.
[2] 7 Edw. VII c. 51, sec. 5 (2); 2 & 3 Geo. V c. 28, Schedule I.
[3] Murray v. Forsyth, 1917 S.C. 721; Dawkins v. Muir, 1922, 39 Sh.Ct.Rep. 45; Smith v. Corporation of Glasgow, 1933, 50 Sh.Ct.Rep. 103; Raeburn v. Dunleavy, 1934, 50 Sh.Ct.Rep. 107.
[4] 20 & 21 Geo. V c. 33, sec. 2.
[5] Raeburn v. Dunleavy, supra.
[6] 7 Edw. VII c. 51, Schedule I, Rule 23; 2 & 3 Geo. V c. 28, Schedule II.

In addition to the jurisdiction of the Sheriff, as above defined, he has power to deal with *inter alia* questions of custody under the Guardianship of Infants Acts, 1886 and 1925;[1] and he has also jurisdiction in applications under the Adoption of Children (Scotland) Act, 1930,[2] and the Registration of Births, Deaths and Marriages Acts, 1854 to 1934.[3] The Sheriff also deals with marriage licences under the Marriage (Scotland) Act, 1939,[4] and applications under the Intestate Husband's Estate Acts.[5] These matters are dealt with later.

[1] See p. 582, infra.
[2] See p. 543, infra.
[3] See p. 555, infra.
[4] See p. 560, infra.
[5] See p. 448, infra.

4. Recissory.

An action of reduction is not, strictly speaking, a declarator, nor a petitory action, nor a possessory action. It forms a class by itself, and is termed a recissory action. Actions of reduction, other than those relating to heritable title, are not expressly excepted in the jurisdiction clauses of the Sheriff Courts Act, 1907,[1] but this does not imply that such actions have been made competent in the Sheriff Court. Reductions were not previously competent in the Sheriff Court, and a new and important jurisdiction of this sort is not presumed to have been conferred by implication. By long established practice this class of action has been confined to the Court of Session.[2]

[1] 7 Edw. VII c. 51, sec. 5 (4).
[2] See Donald v. Donald, 1913 S.C. 274.

Although a reduction is not competent in the Sheriff Court as a direct action, deeds and writings which are founded on by either party in a Sheriff Court process may, in practical effect, be reduced in the Sheriff Court, for the Sheriff Courts Act enacts that " when a deed or writing is founded on by any party in a cause, all objections thereto may be stated and maintained by way of exception without the necessity of bringing a reduction thereof."[1] And there is no difference in result between such a challenge *ope exceptionis* and a formal reduction by separate action. But, where such an exception is stated and reduction would have been competent, the Sheriff has power to require caution, or order consignation.[1]

[1] 7 Edw. VII c. 51, Schedule I, Rules 50, 51.

What is covered by the wide expression, a deed or writing founded on, and how far a plea by exception should be admitted are matters to be determined in each particular case. Where the judgment of the Sheriff cannot be *res judicata* as to the validity of the document, or where the interests of parties not in the cause might be affected by the judgment, the rule does not apply.[1] Pleading by way of exception has been allowed in respect of the following documents : Sheriff-officer's execution,[2] resolution of a trading corporation,[3] discharge of a claim of damages,[4] minutes of meeting,[5] and an arbiter's award.[6] It has been held to be incompetent to plead *ope exceptionis* against a Sheriff Court decree *in foro*,[7] and, while in a Court of Session multiplepoinding, a decree in absence granted in the Supreme Court was set aside incidentally, it seems at least doubtful whether the same rule

would apply in the Sheriff Court.[8] A tenant sued under a lease
was held not entitled to take exception to it on the ground that
he was himself proprietor,[9] and pleading by exception was also
refused in an attack on a will as having been impetrated by
fraud and circumvention,[1] and in an objection to a limited
company's share register.[10] A plea *ope exceptionis* should only
be allowed when proper notice has been given to the other side,[11]
but it is available although the document attacked is the whole
foundation of the action or of the defence.[12]

[1] Donald v. Donald, 1913 S.C. 274.
[2] Scott v. Cook, 1886, 24 S.L.R. 34.
[3] Sadler v. Webster, 1893, 21 R. 107.
[4] Mackie v. Strachan, Kinmond & Co., 1896, 23 R. 1030.
[5] M'Gowan v. City of Glasgow Friendly Society, 1913 S.C. 991.
[6] Nivison v. Howat, 1883, 11 R. 182; Kilmaurs Dairy Association v.
    Brisbane, &c., Dairies, 1927, 43 Sh.Ct.Rep. 210; Blyth Building Co.
    v. Mason's Executor, 1937, 53 Sh.Ct.Rep. 180.
[7] Leggat Bros. v. Gray, 1912 S.C. 230.
[8] Jarvie's Trustees v. Bannatyne, 1927 S.C. 34. See also Neil v. M'Nair,
    1901, 3 F. (J.) 85, and Smith v. Hutchison, 1926, 42 Sh.Ct.Rep. 183.
[9] Duke of Argyll v. Muir, 1910 S.C. 96.
[10] National Bank, &c., Nominees v. Adamson, (O.H.) 1932 S.L.T. 492.
    See also Scottish Amalgamated Silks v. Macalister, (O.H.) 1930
    S.L.T. 593.
[11] Oswald v. Fairs, 1911 S.C. 257.
[12] Hopkinson v. Sanders, 1940, 57 Sh.Ct.Rep. 11.

An action with mixed conclusions brought in the Sheriff Court
need not necessarily be dismissed because these include a reductive
conclusion. If the separate conclusions are distinct, the action
may be entertained *quoad* the conclusions competent in the Sheriff
Court, and relevantly stated, although it may be dismissed *quoad*
other conclusions, which are not competent in the Sheriff Court.[1]

[1] Moroney & Co. v. Muir, 1867, 6 M. 7; Wilson v. Co-operative Store
    Co., &c., 1885, 13 R. 21.

To the general rule that reduction is competent only in the
Court of Session there are some statutory exceptions. A workman's contract of service, for instance, can be set aside, and a
contract of apprenticeship can be rescinded, under the summary
jurisdiction to that effect conferred upon the Sheriff by the
Employers and Workmen Act of 1875.[1] Under the Bankruptcy
(Scotland) Act, 1913,[2] also, certain deeds are voidable without
the necessity of an action of reduction. Resort may still be
required to the Court of Session, for the provisions of the Bankruptcy Act do not go the length of transferring jurisdiction in
actions of reduction to the Sheriff Court, but only empower the
Sheriff to set aside void or voidable deeds or alienations by way

of exception.[3] In the same way, under the Sheep Stocks Valuation
Act, 1937, an arbiter's award may be set aside by the Sheriff.[4]

[1] 38 & 39 Vict. c. 90, secs. 3, 6, 14.
[2] 3 & 4 Geo. V c. 20, sec. 8. See Dickson v. Murray, 1866, 4 M. 797;
M'Laren's Trustees v. National Bank, 1897, 24 R. 920.
[3] Dickson v. Murray, supra.
[4] 1 Edw. VIII & 1 Geo. VI c. 34, sec. 1 (2) ; Paynter v. Rutherford, &c.,
1939, 55 Sh.Ct.Rep. 305; Dunlop v. Mundell, &c., (O.H.) 1943
S.L.T. 286.

5. EXCHEQUER.

Exchequer causes proper are not competent in the Sheriff Court,
although the Sheriff, as the executive officer of the Exchequer,
is still charged with the duty of enforcing Exchequer decrees
within his Sheriffdom.[1] Formerly there was a separate Court
of Exchequer in Scotland, which had administrative as well as
judicial functions.[2] The former have long been transferred to
Treasury State Departments,[3] and in 1856 the judicial functions
were transferred to the Court of Session.[4] Indirectly, however,
Exchequer questions may be decided in the Sheriff Court, the
most common case being that where the Crown is a creditor in
competition with other creditors in a bankruptcy or other process.
When such a case arises in the course of a process not directly
initiated as an Exchequer claim, it is the prerogative of the Crown
to require the question to be determined by the Lord Ordinary
in Exchequer,[5] but, if this is not insisted in, a question so arising
in the Sheriff Court may competently be there determined. A
limited jurisdiction in Exchequer was conferred upon the Sheriff
Court under the Finance Act, 1894, which makes it competent to
appeal to the Sheriff against a charge for estate duty when the
value of the estate does not exceed £10,000.[6]

[1] 19 & 20 Vict. c. 56, secs. 29-36.
[2] 6 Anne c. 26.
[3] 3 & 4 Will. IV c. 13.
[4] 19 & 20 Vict. c. 56, sec. 1.
[5] Sharpe v. Miller, 1861, 23 D. 1015.
[6] 57 & 58 Vict. c. 30, secs. 10, 23 (2); 59 & 60 Vict. c. 28, sec. 22; Rules
of Court V, 20. See p. 589, infra.

6. ECCLESIASTICAL.

The Sheriff has no jurisdiction, even incidentally, in teind
questions proper, with the single exception of proceedings for
commutation and sale of fish teinds, which, under a Statute of
1864, are competent in the Sheriff Court.[1] Such matters as
augmentation of ministers' stipends, the erection or disjunction
of parishes, and the like, are dealt with in the Court of Session,

upon whom the functions of the Commissioners of Teinds were devolved. The jurisdiction vested in the Sheriff under the Church of Scotland (Property and Endowments) Act, 1925, will be considered later.[2]

[1] 27 & 28 Vict. c. 33. See p. 538, infra.
[2] See p. 567 et seq., infra.

7. HERITABLE.

The Sheriff Courts Act materially altered the law in regard to civil process relating to heritage. Formerly resort to the Court of Session was necessary to obtain a judicial declaration of the existence or non-existence of a heritable right, however unimportant.[1] The Sheriff Court was not deemed competent to declare a heritable right of any kind, but possessory questions relating to heritage, which were often of greater practical importance—as, for instance, a right to fish or an obligation to remove buildings—could competently be entertained in the Sheriff Court.[2] The Sheriff has always had jurisdiction in actions relating to heritage which involve merely questions of personal contract or delict where competition of right or title in the subjects is not in dispute.[3]

[1] Maxwell v. G. & S.W. Railway Co., 1866, 4 M. 447.
[2] Sutherland v. Thomson, 1876, 3 R. 485.
[3] See Anderson v. M'Gown, 1911 S.C. 441; Brady v. Miller's Properties, 1935, 51 Sh.Ct.Rep. 183; Duff v. West Craig, 1935, 51 Sh.Ct.Rep. 315.

Sheriff Court jurisdiction now covers actions relating to questions of heritable right or title (except actions of adjudication save in so far as formerly competent and actions of reduction), and it expressly includes all actions of declarator of irritancy and removing whether at the instance of a superior against a vassal or of a landlord against a tenant.[1]

[1] 7 Edw. VII c. 51, sec. 5 (4).

Broadly speaking, the Sheriff's jurisdiction in regard to heritage is now as extensive as in relation to moveables. It covers questions of absolute right, as contrasted with possessory questions—which have always been competent—and by Statute it expressly includes actions of declarator, as well as of division of commonty, and division or division and sale of common property.[1] It embraces interdicts,[2] actions of maills and duties,[3] and poinding of the ground,[4] as well as proceedings for erection of march fences, straightening of march fences, and division of runrig lands,[5] questions of nuisance,[6] or those arising from use

or abuse of property, and actions relating to the constitution
and exercise of servitudes.[7] Various questions between landlord
and tenant may be dealt with by the Sheriff. In addition to
removings and ejections,[8] and sequestration for rent,[9] the Sheriff
can deal with such diverse matters as ordaining the stocking or
plenishing of the subjects let,[10] appointing a judicial manager
on a deserted farm,[11] compelling the tenant to implement the
lease by taking possession,[12] deciding upon a tenant's counter
claim for damages against rent which he had retained,[13] and
ordering the inspection and repair of the premises let.[14] But in
the case of other proceedings relating to heritage an action for
a remit to a man of skill in order to obtain a report, though
competent in the general sense, may not always be granted.[15]
Actions of foreclosure and other applications under the Heritable
Securities Act are referred to later.[16]

[1] 7 Edw. VII c. 51, sec. 5 (1) (3).
[2] Ibid., sec. 6 (e).
[3] See p. 511, infra.
[4] See p. 521, infra.
[5] See p. 513, infra.
[6] See p. 73, infra.
[7] Questions relating to nuisance and servitudes were included in the
   Sheriff's jurisdiction in 1838 (1 & 2 Vict. c. 119, sec. 15), and, though
   not expressly repeated, are covered by the wider jurisdiction now
   conferred.
[8] See p. 404, infra.
[9] See p. 422, infra.
[10] M'Dougall v. Buchanan, 1867, 6 M. 120; Whitelaw v. Fulton, 1871,
   10 M. 27; Wright v. Wightman, 1875, 3 R. 68; Macdonald v.
   Mackessack, 1888, 16 R. 168.
[11] Gibson v. Clark, 1895, 23 R. 294.
[12] Robertson v. Cockburn, 1875, 3 R. 21.
[13] Fingland & Mitchell v. Howie, 1926 S.C. 319.
[14] Gordon's Trustees v. Melrose, 1870, 8 M. 906; Dickson, &c. v. Graham,
   1877, 4 R. 717; Lees v. Marr Typefounding Co., 1877, 4 R. 1088;
   but cf. Jenkins v. Gascoigne, 1907 S.C. 1189; Maclagan v. March-
   bank, 1911, 27 Sh.Ct.Rep. 282; M'Farlane v. Crawford, &c., 1919,
   35 Sh.Ct.Rep. 78.
[15] Magistrates of Kilmarnock v. Reid, 1897, 24 R. 388; Sutherland v.
   Squair, 1898, 25 R. 656; Jenkins v. Gascoigne, supra; M'Farlane v.
   Crawford, &c., supra.
[16] See p. 595, infra.

Adjudication remains incompetent in the Sheriff Court save
in so far as it was competent prior to 1907.[1] It is a diligence
in the form of an action, rather than, strictly speaking, an
action. It is of two kinds (a) adjudication in implement, still
competent only in the Court of Session, and which has usually
for its object the effectual vesting of heritable property in a party
who cannot otherwise obtain a valid title; and (b) adjudication
for debt, which has for its object the transference of a debtor's

heritable property to a creditor, subject to redemption. Originally all adjudications were competent in the Sheriff Court, but in 1672[2] the jurisdiction of the Sheriff was excluded, except as regards adjudication *contra hæreditatem jacentem*, by which a creditor might attach heritage vested in a deceased debtor, to which the heir in heritage had renounced succession. The process was seldom resorted to at any time, and, though it is probably still competent in the Sheriff Court, it has practically become obsolete there. The statutory process of adjudication on non-payment of a ground annual is dealt with later.[3]

[1] 7 Edw. VII c. 51, sec. 5 (4).
[2] Act 1672, c. 19.
[3] See p. 579, infra.

Actions of reduction relating to heritable property are expressly excepted from the Sheriff's jurisdiction,[1] but, as we have seen, actions of reduction of any sort are still incompetent in the Sheriff Court.[2] The express exclusion of actions of reduction in relation to questions of heritable right or title does not affect the Sheriff's right to deal *ope exceptionis* with a deed or writing in a question of heritable right when it would otherwise be appropriate to do so.

[1] 7 Edw. VII c. 51, sec. 5 (4).
[2] See p. 22, supra.

The present position, therefore, is that, except as regards adjudication (other than adjudication *contra hæreditatem jacentem*) and reduction, the jurisdiction of the Sheriff Court is now concurrent with that of the Court of Session in all questions relating to heritable right and title, whether these questions are declaratory or possessory. This broadened jurisdiction is, however, subject, within value limits, to a power of remitting the case to the Court of Session. Any action relating to heritage, whatever its value, may now be competently raised in the Sheriff Court; but if the value of the subjects in dispute exceeds £50 by the year or £1000 of capital[1] either party has the right at the closing of the record, or within six days thereafter, to require the cause to be remitted to the Court of Session.[2] This right applies to all actions relating to questions of heritable right or title, and to those relating to division of commonty, or division or division and sale of common property.[2] Removal to the Court of Session is, however, competent only if the cause really raises a heritable question. If it only raises a money question, although it concerns heritage, removal is not competent.[3]

1 See Bowie v. Marquis of Ailsa, 1887, 14 R. 649; Muirhead v. Gilmour, 1909, 1 S.L.T. 235.
2 7 Edw. VII c. 51, sec. 5.
3 Anderson v. M'Gown, 1911 S.C. 441; Duff v. West Craig, 1935, 51 Sh.Ct.Rep. 315.

This extension of jurisdiction of the Sheriff Court does not affect the powers exercised in burghs by the Dean of Guild Court. The function of the dean of guild is to see that in connexion with the erection or alteration of buildings in burghs, private property is not encroached upon, and the public interest is protected, and where special regulations exist, as they do in many burghs, that these regulations are complied with. The dean of guild, speaking broadly, has alone jurisdiction in questions relating to the legal title to build or to the mode of erection, but he does not exclude the civil Courts in questions relating to the use made of the property.[1] Questions of heritable right and title are not competent in the Dean of Guild Court,[2] but are now competent in the Sheriff Court. Some royal burghs, by their ancient charters, had conferred upon them right to exercise judicial or quasi-judicial authority. The jurisdiction of the Sheriff, as now extended, may cover matters in which a burgh Court also exercises jurisdiction, but that does not infer that the jurisdiction has been withdrawn from the burgh Court. It merely gives the litigant an option to choose his Court.

1 Manson v. Forrest, 1887, 14 R. 802; Robertson v. Thomas, 1887, 14 R. 822; cf. Botanic Gardens Picture House v. Adamson, 1924 S.C. 549.
2 Pitman v. Burnett's Trustees, 1881, 8 R. 914; Nicholson v. Glasgow Asylum, 1911 S.C. 391.

The Sheriff Court has always been in practice regarded as the appropriate Court in actions of sequestration for rent—which are not competent in the Court of Session[1]—and in removings. This is in no way affected by legislative changes. The Act of 1907 expressly declares that nothing therein contained shall derogate from any jurisdiction, powers, or authority then possessed or in use to be exercised by the Sheriffs of Scotland.[2]

1 Duncan v. Lodijensky, 1904, 6 F. 408.
2 7 Edw. VII c. 51, sec. 5.

8. SUSPENSION.

Suspension was a process originally competent only in the Court of Session. Its object is to prevent the execution of diligence or threatened diligence, and to preserve the *status quo* until an alleged illegality has been inquired into, or the rights of parties have been finally determined. It is akin to the process of interdict, which aims at the prevention of a threatened wrong, whilst matters are still intact, and an interdict conclusion is often conjoined with a craving for suspension. Suspension is not appropriate where appeal is competent, but if appeal is precluded, or is foreclosed by extract having been obtained, suspension may be competent.[1]

[1] Lamb v. Thomson, 1901, 4 F. 88; cf. Simpson v. Young, 1852, 14 D. 990; Watt Bros. & Co. v. Foyn, &c., 1879, 7 R. 126.

The Sheriff Courts Act, 1907, confers jurisdiction in suspensions of charges or threatened charges upon the decrees of Court granted by the Sheriff, or upon decrees of registration proceeding upon bonds, bills, contracts, or other obligations registered in the books of the Sheriff Court, the books of Council and Session or any others competent, where the debt exclusive of interest and expenses does not exceed £50.[1] The jurisdiction of the Sheriff Court is privative in suspensions as in other proceedings competent in the Sheriff Court where the cause does not exceed £50 in value, exclusive of interest and expenses.[2] But the value of a suspension will include any expenses decerned for in the decree sought to be suspended, so that suspension of a Sheriff Court decree for £48 of principal and £4 4s. of expenses would apparently be competent either in the Sheriff Court or the Court of Session.[3] And the Supreme Court will have jurisdiction whatever the value of the cause if suspension is sought of a charge which is not warranted by the decree on which it professes to proceed.[3] A decree upon which no charge can follow, as, for instance, a decree of absolvitor, cannot be the subject of a suspension.[4]

[1] 7 Edw. VII c. 51, sec. 5 (5).
[2] Ibid., sec. 7; Brown & Critchley v. Decorative Art Journals Co., 1922 S.C. 192.
[3] Aitchison v. M'Donald, 1911 S.C. 174.
[4] Danish Asiatic Co. v. Earl of Morton, 24th February, 1741, Elchie's Decisions " Suspension," No. 5; Findlay v. Duncan, 1854, 16 D. 938.

The statutory provisions regarding suspensions have left certain points in considerable doubt. The Act itself does not suggest any specialty as to the Court in which the suspension is to be brought, but Rule 123 provides that the person charged " may apply in the Sheriff Court of his domicile for suspension on caution of such charge and diligence." Apart from this rule the suspension would have been brought, not in the Court of the

suspender's domicile, but in the Court which had jurisdiction
over the holder of the decree.[1] It is thought that Rule 123 does
not exclude the other ground of jurisdiction, and that suspensions
may be competently brought in the Court which has jurisdiction
under sec. 6 of the Act over the defenders or holders of the decree,
as well as in the Court of the domicile of the person charged.
It is recognized that this plurality of jurisdiction apparently
results in a Sheriff having power to review by suspension a decree
of his own Court—which seems to follow in any case from Rule
123—and having the same power, on the more general grounds
of jurisdiction over a decree of another Sheriff in a different
Sheriffdom.[2] Until an authoritative decision is obtained the question as to the appropriate Court cannot be regarded as free
from doubt. The general practice appears to be to bring the
suspension in the Court which has, apart from Rule 123, jurisdiction over the holder of the decree. While the Sheriff is given
jurisdiction to suspend " charges or threatened charges," Rule 123
applies in terms only " where a charge has been given," and the
rule also refers to a charge on "letters of horning" following
on a decree. Letters of horning—which are seldom now seen in
practice—are not referred to in the corresponding section of the
Act, but the restriction of Rule 123 to charges actually given
seems to result in suspensions of threatened charges being competent only in a Court having jurisdiction against the holder
of the decree, and not in the Court of the suspender's domicile.
The Court of the suspender's domicile in the sense of the rule
is thought to mean the Court within whose territory he resides—or
possibly, in the case of a firm, company or corporation, where
it has its only, or principal, place of business—and that a Court
in which jurisdiction against the person charged has been got
by arrestment, prorogation or other adventitious means would
not be the Court of the domicile.

[1] 7 Edw. VII c. 51, sec. 6.
[2] See Brown & Critchley v. Decorative Art Journals Co., 1922 S.C. 192,
p. 202.

In the Sheriff Court a suspension is competent only if the
charge or threatened charge follows on a decree for payment
of money. A charge upon an *ad factum præstandum* decree, or
a warrant for imprisonment, can still be competently suspended
only in the Court of Session. The Supreme Court will not entertain
a suspension of one of its own decrees *in foro*,[1] but no such limitation appears in the jurisdiction conferred on the Sheriff, and
unless this is to be inferred—which seems very doubtful—then
a suspension within the statutory limits may competently be raised

in the Sheriff Court, whether the decree complained of has been granted *in foro* or in absence. So soon as a decree has been extracted, a charge on it is possible, but a charge may sometimes be prospectively threatened. Suspension appears to be competent so soon as a threat to charge has been made, or at least so soon as decree has been extracted.

1 Young v. List, &c., 1862, 24 D. 587, Lord Justice-Clerk Inglis, p. 588.

Suspension may be useful where a statutory power is being oppressively used, as, for instance, where the Sheriff has issued a summary warrant for recovery of rates. A ratepayer included in the certificate has no opportunity of being heard, although he may have a possible answer. The warrant is granted *de plano*, and it becomes a decree of Court upon which diligence may follow. A charge, or threatened charge, upon decree so obtained may now be conveniently suspended in the Sheriff Court.

9. ADMIRALTY.

In Scotland, up till 1830, Admiralty jurisdiction was independent. But in that year the High Court of Admiralty as a separate tribunal was abolished, and its jurisdiction was merged in that of the Court of Session and the Sheriff Court.[1] The form of, and procedure in, an Admiralty cause are now the same as in any other cause, but the law to be administered is Admiralty law which may not be the same as Scottish municipal law.[2]

1 11 Geo. IV & 1 Will. IV c. 69. sec. 21.
2 Currie v. M'Knight, 1896, 24 R. (H.L.) 1; Constant v. Christensen, 1912 S.C. 1371; Quinn, &c. v. Peacock & Co., 1917, 33 Sh.Ct.Rep. 205; Sheaf Steamship Co. v. Compania Transmediterranea, 1930 S.C. 660.

The Sheriff Courts Act, 1907, which repealed the provisions of the older Acts, provided that the powers and jurisdiction formerly competent to the High Court of Admiralty in Scotland in all maritime causes and proceedings civil and criminal, including such as apply to persons furth of Scotland, should be competent to the Sheriffs, provided the defender should, upon any legal ground of jurisdiction, be amenable to the jurisdiction of the Sheriff before whom such cause or proceeding might be raised, and provided also that it should not be competent to the Sheriff to try any crime committed on the seas which it would not be competent for him to try if the crime had been committed on land.[1] The Act further provided that, where Sheriffdoms are separated by a river, firth or estuary, the Sheriffs on either side

have concurrent jurisdictions over the intervening space occupied
by water.[1] Letters of arrestment may thus be issued from the
Court of the Sheriffdom on either side of the estuary, and actions
may be brought in whichever district the defender, under the
broadened regulations of present-day practice, is amenable, or
has been made amenable, to Sheriff Court jurisdiction.

[1] 7 Edw. VII c. 51, sec. 4.   See also Sheaf Steamship Co. v. Compania
Transmediterranea, 1930 S.C. 660.

The Sheriff's jurisdiction extends to and includes all navigable
rivers, ports, harbours, creeks, shores, and anchoring grounds
in or adjoining the Sheriffdom.[1] The jurisdiction in seaboard
territories extends to three miles from the shore. A party, therefore, guilty of delict at sea, within the three-mile limit, is in
the same position as if he had been on the shore of the adjacent
Sheriffdom, and, even if a foreigner, may, if found within the
Sheriffdom, and personally cited there, be rendered amenable
to its jurisdiction in an action arising out of the delict.[2] As
regards " all persons engaged in catching, curing, and dealing
in fish," the Herring Fishery Act of 1808 extended the jurisdiction
of the Sheriff Court to ten miles seaward.[3] Certain specialties
in relation to jurisdiction in maritime cases are dealt with in
detail later.[4]

[1] 7 Edw. VII c. 51, sec. 4.
[2] Macleod v. Dobson, 1900, 16 Sh.Ct.Rep. 33, 104.
[3] 48 Geo. III c. 110, sec. 60.   See Macpherson, &c. v. Ellen, 1914, 30
Sh.Ct.Rep. 206.
[4] See p. 617 et seq., infra.

Offences under the Sea Fisheries Acts may be dealt with under
the Summary Jurisdiction Acts by the Sheriff Court nearest to
the place where the offence was committed.[1] This provision in
relation to Sheriff Court jurisdiction does not apply to civil
actions, but it is competent to anyone injured by such offence to
ask that the question of damages be disposed of at the conclusion
of the trial.[2]

[1] 48 & 49 Vict. c. 70, sec. 7.
[2] Ibid., sec. 8.   See p. 665, infra.

10. Aircraft.

In terms of powers conferred under the Air Navigation Act,
1920,[1] jurisdiction has been conferred on all Courts having
Admiralty jurisdiction—which includes the Sheriff Court—to deal
with claims relating to wreck and salvage in connexion with

aircraft, and certain sections of the Merchant Shipping Act of 1894 are applied to such proceedings.[2] In such actions the ordinary powers, rules of practice and procedure for the time being in force in regard to the Admiralty jurisdiction of the Court are to apply.[3]

[1] 10 & 11 Geo. V c. 80, secs. 11, 14 (2); 26 Geo. V & 1 Edw. VIII c. 44, sec. 28, Schedule V.
[2] S.R. & O., 1938, No. 136.
[3] Ibid., sec. 4.

11. DECLARATORY.

Actions of declarator were formerly competent only in the Court of Session, but the jurisdiction of the Sheriff Court is now extended to include every kind of action of declarator, except declarators of marriage or nullity of marriage and actions to determine the personal status of individuals.[1] An action of proving the tenor, though of the nature of a declarator, is not competent in the Sheriff Court,[2] but proof of the terms of a missing document may be allowed incidentally in an action where it is founded on by one of the parties and the other who has or had it in his possession does not produce it.[3] An action which is in form a declarator but in substance a reduction cannot be dealt with in the Sheriff Court.[4] An action at common law for declarator that a person is dead has been held to be incompetent in the Sheriff Court as being one relating to status.[5]

[1] 7 Edw. VII c. 51, sec. 5 (1).
[2] Dunbar & Co. v. Scottish County Investment Co., 1920 S.C. 210.
[3] Elliott v. Galpern, 1927 S.C. 29.
[4] Cornhill Insurance Co. v. Fraser, Owen & Co., 1937, 53 Sh.Ct.Rep 168.
[5] Mackie v. Lyon, &c., 1943, 59 Sh.Ct.Rep. 130.

But although actions of declarator are now generally competent in the Sheriff Court, statutory actions of declarator may not be so.[1] In the case of all declarators brought under Statutes the Statutes should be consulted as to the competent forum. Generally speaking, any action of declarator is now competent in the Sheriff Court, unless it is barred by Statute. The competency of a declarator before the Sheriff was sustained though it related to a resolution of a limited company for voluntary liquidation, the jurisdiction in liquidations and in determining questions arising out of them being at that time in the Court of Session alone.[2]

[1] Clark v. Law, 1887, 3 Sh.Ct.Rep. 360; Motherwell v. Manwell, 1903, 5 F. 619.
[2] Grieve v. Kilmarnock Motor Co., 1923 S.C. 491.

The jurisdiction now conferred upon the Sheriff Court must be exercised within the recognized limits applicable to declaratory actions in general. Thus it is not competent now in the Sheriff Court, any more than in the Court of Session, merely to seek a judicial opinion upon an abstract question of law. The pursuer must have an actual interest to have some particular right declared to be his, and that must be a right which some other person is challenging. But it may suffice that a certain right is not clear, although it is not yet formally challenged, and the pursuer's interest may be to have his legal right declared before he proceeds to exercise it. The question of interest is liberally construed, and, if there is an actual or possible challenger, a litigant may bring an action of declarator to obtain a judicial finding upon a legal question, in the answer to which the pursuer has some real interest.[1] A declarator of a negative may be competent.[2]

[1] On the general question of competency see Harvey v. Harvey's Trustees, 1860, 22 D. 1310; Magistrates of Edinburgh v. Warrender, 1863, 1 M. 887; Fleming v. M'Lagan, 1879, 6 R. 588; Callender's Cable Co. v. Glasgow Corporation, 1900, 2 F. 397; Rothfield v. North British Railway Co., 1920 S.C. 805; Turner's Trustees v. Turner, 1943 S.C. 389.

[2] North British Railway Co. v. Birrell's Trustees, 1918 S.C. (H.L.) 33, Lord Dunedin, p. 47.

12. MINISTERIAL.

As judge ordinary of the bounds, the Sheriff has, both at common law and under Statute, very important jurisdiction, of an administrative or semi-judicial character, in regard to a great variety of matters. *Inter alia*, he is *ex officio* a justice of the peace, and also a commissioner of income tax; and he has administrative, as well as judicial, duties in connexion with the laws relating to bankruptcy, lunacy, registration of births, &c., the care of children, habitual drunkards, the poor law, the law relating to public health, and a great many other matters.

A ministerial duty of the Sheriff which does not properly fall within either his summary duties, or his ordinary Court duties, is presiding annually in February at the striking of fiars prices.[1] This duty may be discharged by the Sheriff or the Sheriff-Substitute. If by the latter, there is no appeal to the Sheriff. The fiars are the average prices of various kinds of grain crop. Separate fiars prices are struck in each county. These prices formerly regulated for the year the value of parish ministers' stipends, Crown compositions, and various payments under old leases and feus and other contracts. But, as a result of statutory schemes of standardization, fiars prices have been abolished in the case of grain feu duties[2] and they are being gradully superseded in the case of stipends.[3] Where there are more districts than one in a county, the fiars prices are struck at the Court of the district within which the county town is situated. Formerly the Sheriff summoned a jury of fifteen, of whom eight were heritors, and under his direction they received and tabulated the evidence tendered and ascertained the average, or, as it is termed, struck the fiars prices. To the result thus arrived at, the Sheriff interponed authority, and the prices so fixed became the criterion for ascertaining values for the year. Since 1918 the jury may be, and usually is, dispensed with and the Sheriff is directed to fix the fiars prices on such evidence as seems to him proper and sufficient. The result arrived at by the Fiars Court is not subject to review, although the Court of Session would probably interfere to remedy any gross irregularity of procedure, or obvious error.[4]

[1] See Codifying Act of Sederunt, L, XVI.
[2] 14 & 15 Geo. V c. 27, sec. 12.
[3] 15 & 16 Geo. V c. 33, secs. 1, 2.
[4] See Howden, &c. v. Earl of Haddington, 1851, 13 D. 522.

Another ministerial duty performed by the Sheriff is the supervision of the jury list.[1] He returns and summons jurors for the Supreme Court, as well as for the Sheriff Court.[2]

[1] See 6 Geo. IV c. 22.
[2] 31 & 32 Vict. c. 100, secs. 45-48.

One form of ministerial jurisdiction exercised by the Sheriff and now almost obsolete, is his power to detain upon a *fugæ* warrant a person proposing to evade diligence by fleeing the country. Formerly a creditor holding a debt in respect of which imprisonment was competent could have his debtor arrested in any Sheriffdom where he was found. To obtain the warrant the creditor deponed that the debtor was intending to flee the country, and set forth a *prima facie* case for his being detained till he found caution *de judicio sisti*. The warrant was an ancillary diligence, not one which of itself could operate payment of the debt. When the Debtors Act, 1880, abolished imprisonment for debt[1] the ancillary diligence fell with it, and as imprisonment became incompetent it became also incompetent to grant warrant against a person *in meditatione fugæ*. The only decrees which, after 1880, could warrant imprisonment were those : (a) *ad factum præstandum*; (b) for Crown taxes or penalties† ; (c) for statutory assessments ; and (d) for aliment. The Civil Imprisonment Act, 1882,[2] abolished imprisonment for an alimentary debt and substituted a new process under which six weeks' imprisonment might

† Alterations proposed by Crown Proceedings Bill.

be imposed for wilful failure to pay sums decerned for as aliment. The ancillary diligence of arrest *in meditatione fugœ* for alimentary debts fell in 1882, along with the imprisonment diligence itself, and it seems to be no longer competent to arrest, upon a *fugœ* warrant, a debtor in an alimentary debt.[3]

[1] 43 & 44 Vict. c. 34, sec. 4.
[2] 45 & 56 Vict. c. 42, secs. 3, 4.
[3] Glenday v. Johnston, 1905, 8 F. 24.

Imprisonment upon a decree *ad factum prœstandum* is now qualified by the Hire Purchase and Small Debt (Scotland) Act, 1932,[1] and the Law Reform (Miscellaneous Provisions) (Scotland) Act, 1940.[2] The other cases in which civil imprisonment is competent still remain, but in general arrestment upon a *fugœ* warrant may now be regarded as obsolete. An application for a *fugœ* warrant is a summary application, which requires no service, but a warrant is not granted till the creditor has made a deposition as to the verity of his claim, and as to the debtor's intention to abscond. If granted, the warrant may be brought under review by suspension in the Court of Session.[3]

[1] 22 & 23 Geo. V c. 38, sec. 7.
[2] 3 & 4 Geo. VI c. 42, sec. 1.
[3] Goudie v. East Lothian Bank, 1822, 2 S. 56.

The Sheriff, as judge ordinary, on the application of any of the recognized Courts of the Church of Scotland, is entitled and will generally be bound to issue letters of diligence against witnesses who neglect or refuse to attend on citation by the Church Court.[1]

[1] Presbytery of Lews v. Fraser, 1874, 1 R. 888.

13. CRIMINAL.

The common law criminal jurisdiction of the Sheriff extends to every description of crime committed within his Sheriffdom, except such as are, by Statute, excluded, and what are called the pleas of the Crown, which, by long-established practice, are relegated to the Court of Justiciary. It is not, however, within the scope of this work to enter in detail upon the powers and duties of the Sheriff in criminal matters proper.

14. DECLINATURE OF JURISDICTION.

Jurisdiction may, in certain special circumstances, be declined, either by the judge or by the parties. If an action is, from its nature, obviously not competent in the Sheriff Court, the Sheriff may decline to entertain it, even if no party object, but, on the other hand, if the Court has jurisdiction it must be exercised unless there is some recognized ground for refusing to do so.[1] Formerly certain persons were entitled to claim exemption from Sheriff Court jurisdiction. Peers and members of Parliament might not be sued during the sitting of Parliament, but this privilege no longer exists.[2] The Sheriff Court jurisdiction might also be declined by members of the College of Justice, including the Court of Session judges and their clerks, advocates and their clerks, officials of the Court of Session, Writers to the Signet, and probably (but doubtfully) solicitors before the Supreme Courts. The Sheriff Court Act of 1853 abolished this privilege,[3] and the provision of that Act is repeated in the Sheriff Courts Act, 1907.[4]

[1] Clements v. Macaulay, 1866, 4 M. 583, Lord Justice-Clerk Inglis. p. 593; Forbes, &c. v. Underwood, 1886, 13 R. 465, Lord President Inglis, p. 468; Société du Gaz de Paris v. Armateurs français, 1925 S.C. 332, 1926 S.C. (H.L.) 13.
[2] 10 Geo. III c. 50.
[3] 16 & 17 Vict. c. 80, sec. 48.
[4] 7 Edw. VII c. 51, sec. 10.

Relationship is a legal ground of declinature of a judge's jurisdiction, and, as it is statutory, it cannot be waived of consent. If a father, brother, or son of the judge, either by consanguinity or by affinity, or an uncle or nephew by consanguinity, is a party in a cause,[1] the judge should decline to exercise jurisdiction, and should he, by inadvertance, pronounce decree, it is not enforceable.[2] This ground of declinature does not apply where a party is uncle or nephew to the judge by affinity,[3] or where a party's wife is sister to the judge's wife;[4] but a plea of declinature has been sustained where a judge's daughter was the wife of a son of one of the parties.[5] Declinature was repelled where the judge's niece was married to the pursuer.[6] In an early case it was held that the declinature of the Sheriff did not preclude the Sheriff-Substitute from acting.[7]

[1] A.P.S. 1594, c. 212; 1681, c. 13; Erskine I, 2, 26.
[2] Ommanney v. Smith, 1851, 13 D. 678.
[3] Erskine v. Drummond. 1787, M. 2418.
[4] Goldie v. Hamilton, 16th February, 1816, F.C.
[5] Porterfield v. Stewart, 1821, 1 S. 10.
[6] Gordon v. Gordon's Trustees, 1866, 4 M. 501. See also Campbell v. Campbell, 1866, 4 M. 867; Moubray's Trustees v. Moubray, 1883, 10 R. 460; Moncrieff v. Moncrieff, 1904, 6 F. 1021.
[7] Wallace v. Colquhoun, 1823, 2 S. 139.

Interest on the part of a judge is also a ground for declining his jurisdiction. If the interest is direct and pecuniary it need

not be of a large amount,[1] but if it is not pecuniary it must be
substantial, and such as might bias the mind of the judge.[2] Mere
public interest, as being a member of a public corporation or
board, will not ground the plea.[3] A plea of declinature is valid,
although it may be—and normally will be—waived, where a
judge is personally a shareholder in an incorporated company.[1]
Partnership in an insurance company and ownership as a trustee
of stock or shares in an incorporated company have been by
Statute expressly abolished as grounds of declinature.[4] It appears
to be not a ground for declinature that a judge is a shareholder
in a chartered bank in Scotland.[5] A judge who has already
acted as counsel for one of the parties in connexion with the
matters at issue may not be disqualified but in practice he normally
declines.[6]

[1] Sellar v. Highland Railway Co., 1919 S.C. (H.L.) 19.
[2] Belfrage v. Davidson's Trustees, 1862, 24 D. 1132; Wildbridge v.
    Anderson, 1897, 25 R. (J.) 27; Goodall v. Bilsland, &c., 1909 S.C.
    1152; Gorman v. Wright, 1916 S.C. (J.) 44.
[3] Lord Advocate v. Edinburgh Commissioners of Supply, 1861, 23 D.
    933; Downie v. Fisherrow Harbour Trustees, 1903, 5 F. (J.) 101;
    Rae v. Hamilton, 1904, 6 F. (J.) 42.
[4] 31 & 32 Vict. c. 100, sec. 103.
[5] Act of Sederunt, 1st February, 1820; but not re-enacted in the Codify-
    ing Act of Sederunt or the Rules of Court.
[6] Hall v. Hall, 1891, 18 R. 690; Free Church of Scotland v. Macrae,
    1905, 7 F. 686; M'Cardle v. M'Cardle's Judicial Factor, 1906, 8 F.
    419.

Interest is not, like relationship, a radical disqualification
which renders proceedings null. It is merely a ground of
declinature which may be pleaded, but seldom is. If pleaded, it
is a plea in bar, and must be taken at an early stage of the
process. If in knowledge of the ground of declinature, the plea
of declinature is not timeously taken, it is held to be waived.[1]

[1] Duke of Atholl v. Robertson, 1869, 8 M. 299.

15. Exclusion of Jurisdiction.

In some matters the jurisdiction of the Sheriff is excluded by
Statute, as under the Public Health Act, 1897, where the jurisdiction of the resident Sheriff-Substitute is excluded in proceedings
for the formation of special drainage districts, which must be
taken before the Sheriff.[1] Amongst various other statutory exclu-
sions are those under the Friendly Societies Acts[2] and the Agricultural Holdings Act,[3] where special arrangements are made for the
settlement of disputes, and the jurisdiction of the Sheriff is also
excluded in those cases which fall to the Land Court to decide.[4]

Apart from Statute, some matters are privative to particular Courts by usage. If so, the jurisdiction of the Sheriff is excluded unless the Sheriff Court is that to which usage allocates the action. In general the Crown and those representing it are not, save by consent, subject to the jurisdiction of the Sheriff Court or any other inferior Court.[5]†

1 60 & 61 Vict. c. 38, sec. 122. See p. 651, infra.
2 59 & 60 Vict. c. 25, sec. 68; 8 Edw. VII c. 32, sec. 6. See p. 591, infra.
3 21 & 22 Geo. V c. 44, sec. 32.
4 See Maclaine v. MacFadyen, 1913, 30 Sh.Ct.Rep. 176; and cf. Rutherford v. M'Corquodale, 1934, 22 L.C. 53; Urquhart v. Department of Agriculture for Scotland, 1937, 26 L.C. 8.
5 Somerville v. Lord Advocate, 1893, 20 R. 1050; Magistrates of Helensburgh v. Brock, 1905, 13 S.L.T. 98.

Save to the very limited extent after explained[1] the Sheriff has at common law no power to appoint judicial factors. Under the Judicial Factors (Scotland) Act, 1880, the Sheriff may appoint factors *loco tutoris* and *curators bonis* in cases of estates, the yearly value of which (heritable and moveable together) does not exceed £100.[2] The Sheriff Court cannot appoint a judicial factor upon a testamentary trust estate, however small, but under the Bankruptcy (Scotland) Act, 1913, judicial factors on the estate of persons deceased, within certain limits, and judicial factors for the interim preservation of estates pending sequestration can be appointed by the Sheriff.[3] The Sheriff may also appoint a commissary factor.[4]

1 See next paragraph.
2 43 & 44 Vict. c. 4, secs. 3, 4.
3 3 & 4 Geo. V c. 20, secs. 14, 163.
4 See p. 441, infra.

It is a practice recognized in most Sheriff Courts that an *interim* factor, for an immediate special purpose, may be nominated by the Sheriff, although it is not clear upon what ground the practice rests. Such an appointment is usually temporary, pending the appointment of a person with a formal title. There is probably an inherent power in the Sheriff to make such an appointment for *interim* preservation as an incident to a litigation already before him.[1] And the Sheriff's right to appoint a judicial manager for a farm has been recognized by the Court of Session.[2] Again, where a trader has disappeared, but is not regarded as insolvent, there may be no call for bankruptcy proceedings, but a pressing temporary necessity for some one to take charge of stock and premises till inquiry is made for the missing person. Although the formal appointment of

† Alterations proposed by Crown Proceedings Bill.

a factor *loco absentis* is competent only in the Court of Session, the Sheriff is probably entitled, on the application, *ex parte*, of a creditor or other party interested, to appoint a factor for interim custody and preservation till more formal action is taken. Such proceedings, when not incidental to a pending litigation, are probably to be treated as " applications of a summary nature brought under the common law jurisdiction of the Sheriff."[3]

1 Drysdale v. Lawson, 1842, 4 D. 1061; cf. Rowe v. Rowe, 1872, 9 S.L.R. 493.
2 Affleck v. Affleck, 1862, 24 D. 291; Muir v. More Nisbett, &c., 1881, 19 S.L.R. 59; Gibson v. Clark, 1895, 23 R. 294. See also Stewart v. Mair, &c., 1911, 27 Sh.Ct.Rep. 337.
3 7 Edw. VII c. 51, sec. 3 (p).

Under the Trusts Act, 1921, the Sheriff has a limited jurisdiction which is explained later.[1]

1 See p. 667, infra.

The jurisdiction of Courts of law is excluded in the case of certain actions relating to trade unions. By the Act of 1871 the purposes of a union were not to be illegal merely because they were in restraint of trade,[1] but the Courts are not enabled by the Act to entertain legal proceedings for enforcing, or recovering damages for the breach of, certain agreements.[2] These agreements are those : (a) between members of a union concerning conditions of trade or work ;[3] (b) for payment of a subscription or penalty ;[4] (c) for the application of union funds in certain ways ;[5] (d) between one union and another ; and (e) to secure the performance of any of the above. An action for declarator that certain alterations on rules were *ultra vires* and for interdict against misapplication of funds has been held competent,[6] and provisions for benefit to a member's dependants are not within the scope of agreements which cannot be enforced in Court.[7] A declarator of membership of a union is competent,[8] as is also an action to enforce an arbiter's award although the claim dealt with in the arbitration could not have been entertained.[9] By the Act of 1906 an act done by a person in contemplation or furtherance of a trade dispute is not actionable merely because it induces another to break a contract of employment or interferes with another's trade, business or employment, or with his right to dispose of his capital or labour,[10] and an action against a union of workmen or masters, or against any members or officials on behalf of the union members, in respect of a wrong committed by or on behalf of the union cannot be entertained by the Courts.[11]

The position in regard to concerted action not falling under any of the Trade Union Acts has been recently considered in the House of Lords.[12]

[1] 34 & 35 Vict. c. 31, sec. 3.
[2] Ibid., sec. 4.
[3] Smith v. Scottish Typographical Association, 1919 S.C. 43; Aberdeen, &c., Slaters' Association v. Dickie & Son, 1924, 41 Sh.Ct.Rep. 95.
[4] Glasgow, &c., Potted Meat Manufacturers' Society v. Geddes, (O.H.) 1903, 10 S.L.T. 481; Rae v. Plate Glass Merchants' Association, 1919 S.C. 426.
[5] M'Kernan v. United Operative Masons' Association, 1874, 1 R. 453; Shanks v. United Operative Masons' Association, 1874, 1 R. 823; Aitken v. Associated Carpenters, &c., of Scotland, 1885, 12 R. 1206; M'Laren v. National Union of Dock Labourers, 1918 S.C. 834; Cameron v. Associated Society of Locomotive Engineers, &c., 1930, 46 Sh.Ct.Rep. 84; cf.. Amalgamated Society of Railway Servants v. Motherwell Branch, 1880, 7 R. 867; Wilkie v. King, 1911 S.C. 1310; M'Dowall v. M'Ghee, (O.H.) 1913, 2 S.L.T. 238.
[6] Wilson v. Scottish Typographical Association, 1912 S.C. 534.
[7] Love v. Amalgamated Society of Lithographic Printers, &c., 1912 S.C. 1078.
[8] Johnston v. Aberdeen Master Plumbers' Association, 1921 S.C. 62. See also Berry v. Transport, &c., Union, (O.H.) 1933 S.N. 110.
[9] Edinburgh Master Plumbers' Association v. Munro, 1928 S.C. 565.
[10] 6 Edw. VII c. 47, sec. 3. See Milligan & Co. v. Ayr Harbour Trustees, 1915 S.C. 937.
[11] Ibid., sec. 4; Caldwell v. Glasgow, &c., Aerated Water Manufacturers' Defence Association, 1909, 26 Sh.Ct.Rep. 94; Winter v. United Society of Boilermakers, &c., 1909, 26 Sh.Ct.Rep. 350; Shinwell v. National Sailors' Union, (O.H.) 1913, 2 S.L.T. 83; Wright & Sons v. M'Kay, &c., 1927, 44 Sh.Ct.Rep. 109.
[12] Crofter Hand Woven Harris Tweed Co. v. Veitch, 1942 S.C. (H.L.) 1.

Certain classes of action may be time-barred by Statute. The principal Act in this connexion is the Public Authorities Protection Act which provides that an action against any person for any act done in pursuance, or execution, or intended execution, of any Act of Parliament, or of any public duty or authority, or in respect of any alleged neglect or default in the execution of any such Act, duty, or authority, is competent only when it is commenced within six months after the act, neglect or default complained of, or, in case of a continuance of injury or damage, within six months after the ceasing thereof.[1] This limitation does not apply to proceedings by a Government Department against any local authority or officer of such authority,[1] nor to actions for any act done in pursuance or execution or intended execution of any Act of Parliament, or in respect of any alleged neglect or default in the execution of any Act of Parliament, or on account of any act done in any case instituted under an Act of Parliament, when that Act of Parliament applies to Scotland only and contains

a limitation of the time and other conditions for the action in
question.[2]

[1] 56 & 57 Vict. c. 61, sec. 1.
[2] Ibid., sec. 3; Montgomerie & Co. v. Haddington Corporation, 1908
    S.C. 127, 1908 S.C. (H.L.) 6; Kemp v. Glasgow Corporation, 1919
    S.C. 71, 1920 S.C. (H.L.) 73.

The Act applies though the crave is not for any pecuniary
conclusion, e.g., reduction,[1] but it cannot exclude an interdict as
ex hypothesi the wrong will still be continuing.[2] The mere fact
that the defenders are a public body acting under Statute will
not entitle them to the protection of the Act if the main cause
of action does not fairly fall within the words of the Statute,[3]
and the Act will not protect a public servant who has acted out
of private malice.[4] A body incorporated by royal charter does
not merely on that account have the protection of the Act in
carrying out its functions,[5] but the Act will protect a public
authority in carrying out profit-earning undertakings under
statutory powers.[6] A natural person may be a public authority
within the meaning of the Act.[7]

[1] Latham v. Glasgow Corporation, 1921 S.C. 694; cf. Stirling v.
    Stirling County Council, (O.H.) 1900, 7 S.L.T. 353.
[2] Farquhar & Gill v. Magistrates of Aberdeen, 1912 S.C. 1294, Lord
    President Dunedin, p. 1302.
[3] Magistrates of Edinburgh v. Heriot's Trust, (O.H.) 1900, 7 S.L.T.
    371; M'Phie v. Magistrates of Greenock, 1904, 7 F. 246; Lanark-
    shire Upper Ward District Committee v. Airdrie, Coatbridge and
    District Water Trustees, 1906, 8 F. 777; Grant & Sons v. Magis-
    trates of Dufftown, 1924 S.C. 952; Crawford Brothers v. Com-
    missioners of Northern Lighthouses, 1923 S.L.T. 689, 1924 S.L.T.
    105, 1925 S.C. (H.L.) 22; Blackley v. Ayr County Council, (O.H.)
    1934 S.L.T. 398; Robert Baird v. Corporation of Glasgow, 1934
    S.C. 359.
[4] M'Ternan v. Bennett, 1898, 1 F. 333.
[5] Ayr v. St. Andrew's Ambulance Association, 1918 S.C. 158.
[6] Spittal v. Corporation of Glasgow, 1904, 6 F. 828. See also Conolly
    v. Managers of Stranraer Reformatory, (O.H.) 1904, 11 S.L.T.
    638; Clyde Salvage Co. v. Anstruther Union Harbour Commis-
    sioners, (O.H.) 1908, 15 S.L.T. 888.
[7] Wilson v. 1st Edinburgh City Royal Garrison Artillery Volunteers,
    1904, 7 F. 168; Lanart v. Clark, 1945 S.C. 1.

If the protection of the Act is sought it must be founded on in
the defences,[1] but this is not necessary if the Statute is merely
to be used in relation to an award of expenses to the defender.[2]
The date from which the time limit begins to run is the date of
the act complained of even though the effect of the injuries then
sustained continues thereafter.[3] If a continuing act inflicts continuing injury the date from which the time limit runs is the
date when the act and the injury first cease to concur.[4] Where

the last day of the period expired on a Sunday it was held that
an action served on a Monday, on a warrant of service got that
day, was not timeously brought.[5] Proceedings taken to obtain
the benefit of the poor's roll in order to raise an action are not
the commencement of an action within the meaning of the Act.[6]
An amendment increasing the sum sued for has been allowed
although craved after the six months had expired.[7]

[1] Hunter v. Dundee Water Commissioners, 1920 S.C. 628, Lord President
Clyde, p. 630.
[2] Hunter v. Dundee Water Commissioners, supra.
[3] Spittal v. Corporation of Glasgow, 1904, 6 F. 828.
[4] Brownlie & Son v. Magistrates of Barrhead, 1923 S.C. 915, 1925 S.C.
(H.L.) 41.
[5] M'Niven v. Glasgow Corporation, 1920 S.C. 584.
[6] M'Ternan v. Bennett, 1898, 1 F. 333.
[7] Mackie v. Glasgow Corporation, (O.H.) 1924 S.L.T. 510. See also
Pompa's Trustees v. Edinburgh Magistrates, 1942 S.C. 119.

Other Acts which impose time limits on the raising of actions
include the following :—

(1) Riot Act, 1715; Seditious Meetings Act, 1817; Riotous
Assemblies Act, 1822.[1]

(2) Poor Law (Scotland) Act, 1845.[2]

(3) Public Health (Scotland) Act, 1897.[3]

(4) Maritime Conventions Act, 1911.[4]

(5) Moneylenders Act, 1927.[5]

[1] 1 Geo. I, Stat. 2, c. 5, sec. 9; 57 Geo. III c. 19. sec. 38; 3 Geo. IV
c. 33, secs. 10, 11, 15; Capaldi v. Greenock Magistrates, 1941 S.C.
310; Pompa's Trustees v. Edinburgh Magistrates, 1942 S.C. 119.
[2] 8 & 9 Vict. c. 83, sec. 86; Oakely v. Campbell, 1867, 6 M. 12; M'Coll
v. Babtie, 1882, 9 R. 470.
[3] 60 & 61 Vict. c. 38, sec. 166; Edwards v. Parochial Board of Kinloss,
1891, 18 R. 867; Mitchell v. Magistrates of Aberdeen, 1893, 20 R.
253; Sutherland v. Magistrates of Aberdeen, 1894, 22 R. 95; Duncan
v. Magistrates of Hamilton, 1902, 5 F. 160; Paterson v. Glasgow
Corporation, (O.H.) 1908, 16 S.L.T. 224; Corporation of Glasgow
v. Smithfield, &c., Meat Co., 1912 S.C. 364; Brash v. Magistrates
of Peebles, 1926 S.C. 995.
[4] 1 & 2 Geo. V c. 57, sec. 8; Dorie Steamship Co., 1923 S.C. 593;
" Reresby " v. " Cobetas," (O.H.) 1923 S.L.T. 719; Essien v.
Clan Line Steamers, (O.H.) 1925 S.N. 75.
[5] 17 & 18 Geo. V c. 21, sec. 13 (1) ; Harry Smith v. Craig, 1938 S.C.
620.

The jurisdiction of the Sheriff Court, as of other Courts of
law, may be, and frequently is, excluded by contract. In insurance
policies, in friendly society rules, in partnership agreements, and
in many executorial contracts of all sorts, it is a common stipulation that disputes arising shall be settled by arbitration and not
by Courts of law. But to exclude the jurisdiction of a Court of

law, and restrict a party's remedy to arbitration, the language
of the contract must be clear and distinct.[1]

[1] M'Connell & Reid v. Smith, 1911 S.C. 635; on general effect of such
clauses see Lord Dunedin in Sanderson & Son v. Armour & Co.,
1922 S.C. (H.L.) 117.

The jurisdiction of the civil Courts is excluded in questions
arising between individuals engaged in military service and their
regiment or officers, as regards military affairs.[1] Apart from
this a soldier remains subject, in his personal capacity, to the
jurisdiction of the civil Courts. Military disputes of the nature
above indicted are in effect settled by internal procedure under
military law.[2] Thus an action in the civil Courts by a member
of a regiment, against his regiment, for payment of services
rendered to the regiment would be incompetent and the soldier
would require to proceed under military law.

[1] Dawkins v. Paulet, 1869 L.R. 5 Q.B. 94, Lush, J., p. 121. See also
Marks v. Frogley, 1898 L.R. 1 Q.B. 899.
[2] 44 & 45 Vict. c. 58, secs. 42, 43.

16. TRANSFER.

The Sheriff Court Rules provide for a cause being transferred
to another Sheriffdom in three different situations: (1) where
there are two or more defenders and the action has been brought
in the Court of the domicile of one and is transferred to another
Court having jurisdiction over any of the defenders;[1] (2) where,
upon sufficient cause shown, a cause is remitted to another
Sheriffdom irrespective of jurisdiction;[2] and (3) where a plea of
no jurisdiction is sustained and the cause is remitted to the Court
before which it should apparently have been brought.[3]

[1] 7 Edw. VII c. 51, Schedule I, Rule 19.
[2] Ibid., Rule 20.
[3] Ibid., Rule 21.

The power of transfer is an exception to the general rule that
a Court must exercise the jurisdiction it possesses. In that sense
it is akin to the position where a plea is taken of *forum non
conveniens*. That plea implies that there is another Court of
competent jurisdiction, in which the party taking the plea submits
that the case could be tried more suitably for the interests of all
the parties, and for the ends of justice.[1] Normally the plea is
taken when the question arises between a Court in this country
and a Court in some other country, and a selection of cases in
which the plea has been considered is noted below.[2] The elements
to be taken into account by the Sheriff in considering the question

of transfer of a cause will be to some extent similar, though certain of the grounds which would support the transfer of a case to the Courts of another country cannot apply where the transfer is merely to another Sheriffdom. The convenience of, and the probable expense to, the parties to the cause[3] will generally be the usual considerations to be urged in support of a transfer or remit under Rules 19 and 20.

[1] Société du Gaz de Paris v. Société Armateurs français, 1926 S.C. (H.L.) 13, Lord Dunedin, p. 18.
[2] Martin v. Stopford-Blair's Executors, 1879, 7 R. 329; Williamson v. North Eastern Railway Co., 1884, 11 R. 596; Sim v. Robinow, 1892, 19 R. 665; Hay v. Jackson & Co., 1911 S.C. 876; Montgomery v. Zarifi, 1917 S.C. 627; Foster v. Foster's Trustees, 1923 S.C. 212; Société du Gaz de Paris v. Société Armateurs français, supra; Lawford v Lawford's Trustees, 1927 S.C. 360; Robinson v. Robinson's Trustees, 1930 S.C. (H.L.) 20; Sheaf Steamship Co. v. Compania Transmediterrania, 1930 S.C. 660; Woodbury v. Sutherland's Trustees, 1938 S.C. 689.
[3] Lamb & Co. v. Pearson, &c., 1912, 28 Sh.Ct.Rep. 80.

Under Rule 19 an action against several defenders brought in the Sheriff Court of the domicile of one of them may be transferred to any other Court—which presumably means any other Sheriff Court—which has jurisdiction over any of the defenders.[1] The rule does not cover a case brought in a Court having jurisdiction over one defender though not on the ground of domicile, for the right of transfer is a special statutory power which is conferred only in cases where the original ground of jurisdiction is domicile.[2] The transfer need not be to a Court having jurisdiction over another defender—though this will be the usual case—but it could be to another Court having jurisdiction over the same defender as where he resided in one jurisdiction and carried on business in another. The Sheriff has no power to transfer a cause to the Court of Session nor would that Court adopt on appeal an action which was only competent in the Supreme Court.[3] The Sheriff's power of transfer under this rule is to be exercised by him when he considers it expedient to do so, and he will no doubt have regard to the considerations indicated in the cases referred to above. The rule makes no provision for review of the interlocutor transferring the cause, but it has been held that, with leave, it can be appealed to the Sheriff.[4] On the transfer being made the action is to proceed in all respects as if it had been originally brought in the Court to which it has been transferred.[1] It might be thought that the receiving Court has no discretion in the matter and has no option but to accept the process, but a remit back is probably as competent here as under Rule 20.[5] This rule differs from the two which follow in that no provision for finality is attached to the transferring interlocutor. In many cases the transfer will be made at the instance, or with the concurrence, of the defender who is subject to the Court to whose jurisdiction the cause is transmitted. If this is not so the rule does not appear to preclude a plea of no jurisdiction if that is not barred by anything that has transpired in the original Court.

[1] 7 Edw. VII c. 51, Schedule I, Rule 19.
[2] See Graham v. Young, &c., 1926, 43 Sh.Ct.Rep. 3, p. 4.
[3] Gillan v. Barony Parish Council, 1898, 1 F. 183.
[4] Lamb & Co. v. Pearson, &c., 1911, 28 Sh.Ct.Rep. 80.
[5] See next paragraph, infra.

Rule 20 authorizes a Sheriff, upon sufficient cause shown, to remit a cause to another Sheriffdom by interlocutor stating his reasons for doing so, and such interlocutor if issued by the Sheriff-Substitute is, with his leave, and within seven days, subject to review by the Sheriff, but is not further subject to review.[1] Rules 19 and 21 deal with transfers to another Court having jurisdiction, but this rule appears to authorize a transfer on grounds of expediency to another Court irrespective of the question whether or not it has jurisdiction over the defenders or any of them, and it is understood to be so acted on in practice.[2] It is also acted upon in transfers, not to another Sheriffdom, but to another Court in the same Sheriffdom. In view of the stringent provision as to review it might be thought that the receiving Court had no option but to accept and deal with the case. There appears to be no reported authority on the point, but a remit back by the receiving Court is not unknown in practice when the reasons for the transfer are not considered adequate. A remit on the ground of contingency[3] might be made under this rule, but the usual ground will be convenience in respect of the residence of the witnesses.[2]

[1] 7 Edw. VII c. 51, Schedule I, Rule 20.
[2] Walden v. Campbell, 1940 S.L.T. (Sh.Ct.) 39.
[3] Cuthbertson v. Young, 1851, 13 D. 1308; Robertson v. Duke of Athole, 1869, 8 M. 304.

Under Rule 21 when a plea of no jurisdiction is sustained the Sheriff, in place of dismissing the action, may, if he thinks proper and on such conditions as to expenses as he may think fit, remit the cause to the Sheriff before whom it appears to him it ought to have been brought.[1] On this being done the cause thereafter proceeds in all respects as if it has been originally brought in the Court to which it has been transferred. The interlocutor making the remit, if issued by the Sheriff-Substitute, is subject to review by the Sheriff, only with leave of the Sheriff-

Substitute and within seven days of its date, and is not further subject to review.[1] This provision as to finality would not, it is thought, preclude the defender from maintaining a plea of no jurisdiction in the Court to which the case had been transmitted, unless he was debarred from doing so by something which had transpired in the original Court.

[1] 7 Edw. VII c. 51, Schedule I, Rule 21.

The power of transfer may be exercised whether the action is being treated as an ordinary or a summary cause. There appears to be no reason why an undefended cause should not be transferred under Rules 19 and 20 if there were any grounds for such a transfer, but it would be advisable in such an event to order intimation to the defender.[1] Transfers under these rules will generally be made during the early stages of an action, but it seems competent to transfer at any stage and Rules 20 and 21 contemplate a transfer by the Sheriff on appeal.[2] Where a transfer is ordered the process is transmitted by the Sheriff-clerk of the original Court to the Sheriff-clerk of the receiving Court.

[1] 7 Edw. VII c. 51, Schedule I, Rules 19, 20.
[2] Ibid., Rules 20, 21.

17. PRIVATIVE JURISDICTION.

The Sheriff Court has (subject to the exception noted below) privative jurisdiction in all actions which are competent in that Court, where the value of the cause, exclusive of interest and expenses, does not exceed £50.[1] Such cases must not only be brought in the Sheriff Court but they are not subject to review in the Court of Session save where the Sheriff, after final judgment on an appeal to him, on the motion of either party made within seven days of the final interlocutor, certifies the cause as suitable for appeal to the Court of Session.[2] This privative jurisdiction has been encroached upon by the Administration of Justice Act, 1933,[3] sec. 10 of which permits the summary trial in the Court of Session of certain cases, including cases which would have been competent in the Court of Session but for sec. 7 of the Sheriff Courts Act of 1907.[1] Apart from this provision causes of a value of £50 and less may be brought in the Court of Session if they are not competent in the Sheriff Court. Possession of heritage within the jurisdiction is a ground of jurisdiction in the Sheriff Court, only if the action relates to the property,[4] but there is no such limitation in the jurisdiction of the Supreme Court, so that an action for not over £50 against an owner of Scottish heritage, but not relating to the subjects, is competent only in the Court of Session,[5] and it seems that in such a case arrestment to found jurisdiction in a Sheriff Court would be ineffective as the defender is not a person " not otherwise subject to the jurisdiction of the Courts of Scotland."[6] If in such a case the action relates to the property the Sheriff Court alone has jurisdiction.[7] Similarly if arrestments are used to found jurisdiction in Scotland and the defender is not otherwise subject to the jurisdiction of the Scottish Courts the action, if not over £50 in value, must be brought in the Sheriff Court.[8]

[1] 7 Edw. VII c. 51, sec. 7.
[2] Ibid., sec. 28 (1) (d).
[3] 23 & 24 Geo. V c. 41, sec. 10.
[4] 7 Edw. VII c. 51, sec. 6 (d).
[5] Strachan v. Pharmaceutical Society of Great Britain, 1901, 8 S.L.T. 373; Pagan & Osborne v. Haig, 1910 S.C. 341.
[6] 7 Edw. VII c. 51, sec. 6 (c).
[7] Allan v. Alexander's Trustees, 1908, 16 S.L.T. 491.
[8] Dickson & Walker v. John Mitchell & Co., 1910 S.C. 139.

In an action *ad factum præstandum* if there is an alternative petitory conclusion the amount of this conclusion determines the value.[1] But the alternative petitory conclusion has been held not to be decisive if it is indefinite as where, failing delivery of the items claimed, the crave was for £10 or such other sum as should be ascertained as the value.[2] If the action is without petitory conclusions as for delivery (even of articles of apparently small value), or interdict, or relating to the possession of property, the value will generally be taken to be over £50,[3] and the same rule applies in declarators, as where a tramway passenger was sued in the Court of Session for declarator that a 2d. fare was valid and enforceable.[4] But in a more recent case without petitory conclusions, where the record disclosed that the value at stake was admittedly under the limit, the Court accepted the value so disclosed.[5]

[1] Singer Manufacturing Co. v. Jessiman, 1881, 8 R. 695; Dickson v. Bryan, 1889, 16 R. 673; Lamonby v. Foulds, 1928 S.C. 89.
[2] Shotts Iron Co. v. Kerr, 1871, 10 M. 195; Aberdeen v. Wilson, 1872, 10 M. 971.
[3] Purves v. Brock, 1867, 5 M. 1003; Galloway v. M'Ghie, 1869, 41 Scot. Jur. 400; Henry v. Morrison, 1881, 8 R. 692; Thomson v. Barclay, 1883. 10 R. 694; Broatch v. Pattison, 1898, 1 F. 303.
[4] Edinburgh, &c., Tramways Co. v. Torbain, 1876, 3 R. 655; 4 R. (H.L.) 87.
[5] General Guarantee Corporation v. Alexander, 1918 S.C. 662.

In an ordinary petitory action the sum for which payment is craved, exclusive of interest and expenses, is the criterion of value, and the interest thus excluded is not merely the interest due after the date of citation.[1] Despite the decision last noted it seems arguable that what were truly arrears of interest might be aggregated with principal to arrive at value, and this point appears to be still left open. Where action is taken to recover the balance due on an account the sum sued for is the criterion, though the account contain items of much larger amount,[2] but the sum sued for was ignored in a case where it had been brought below the limit by the pursuer having credited or set off a sum due by him to the defender on an entirely separate transaction.[3] An action for rent was dismissed in the Court of Session because the defender was entitled to deduct the amount of certain rates which left a net sum below £50.[4] When a claim for £42 was refused a preferable ranking on a fund of £18 the value of the case was, on appeal, held to be over the then limit of £25,[5] but where there were disputed claims of £53 and £12 to be ranked on a fund of £17 the value was held to be under that limit.[6]

[1] Bowie v. Donaldson, 1922 S.C. 9.
[2] Stevens, Sons & Co. v. Grant, 1877, 5 R. 19.
[3] Inglis v. Smith, 1859, 21 D. 822.
[4] Campbell's Trustees v. Kinloch, (O.H.) 1925 S.L.T. 189.
[5] Henderson v. Grant, 1896, 23 R. 659.
[6] Dobbie v. Thomson, 1880, 7 R. 983.

Although there is only a petitory crave for a sum within the limit of the Sheriff's privative jurisdiction that will not be conclusive should the nature of the action be such .that something of greater value—taking the case outside the limit—is at stake and is dependent on the result of the case. A common example is where the sum sued for is rent[1] or other periodic payment,[2] and the decision will rule a question of continuing liability which takes the case beyond the limit of value. But apart from questions of continuing liability, a case containing a small pecuniary crave may involve questions of greater value which take it beyond the limit.[3] Thus an action for rent may involve a decision as to the validity of the lease.[4] In an action of filiation and aliment an appeal to the Court of Session was—with some difficulty—allowed, although the child had died and the total and final pecuniary value was under £6.[5] But the element of value which is claimed to raise the case above the limit must be inherent in the case, and not some mere extrinsic and incidental result of it.[6] An action of interdict to stop the sale of furniture valued at £13 under a poinding was held to be appealable to the Court of Session.[7]

[1] Drummond v. Hunter, 1869, 7 M. 347; Cunningham v. Black, 1883, 10 R. 441; Duke of Argyll v. Muir, 1910 S.C. 96; cf. North British Railway Co. v. M'Arthur, 1889, 17 R. 30; Welsh v. Duncan, 1893, 20 R. 1014.

2 Hamilton v. Hamilton, 1877, 4 R. 688; Den v. Lumsden, 1891, 19 R.
77; Paisley Parish Council v. Glasgow Parish Council, &c., 1907
S.C. 674; Stevenson v. Sharp, 1910 S.C. 580; Abrahams v. Campbell,
1911 S.C. 353; cf. Macfarlane v. Friendly Society of Stornoway,
1870, 8 M. 438; Standard Shipowners' Association v. Taylor, 1896,
23 R. 870; Stirling Parish Council v. Perth Parish Council, 1898,
25 R. 964; Melrose Parish Council v. Hawick Parish Council, 1912
S.C. 1029.
3 Raimes Clark & Co. v. Swan's Trustee, (O.H.) 1902, 10 S.L.T. 316;
Aitchison v. M'Donald, 1911 S.C. 174.
4 Drummond v. Hunter, supra; Cunningham v. Black, supra; Duke of
Argyll v. Muir, supra.
5 M'Donald v. Ross, 1929 S.C. 240. See also Tait v. Lees, 1903, 5 F.
304, and cf. Melrose Parish Council v. Hawick Parish Council,
supra.
6 Brown & Critchley v. Decorative Art Journals Co., 1922 S.C. 192;
cf. Aitchison v. M'Donald, supra.
7 Brady v. Napier & Son, 1944 S.C. 18.

Where there are several parties on one side or the other the
separate sums due to or by each may be aggregated to ascertain
the value of the cause,[1] but only if the parties have community
of interest.[2] Where actions have been conjoined the combined
sums are the criterion of value[3]—at any rate where the claims
are all on the one side. The effect of a counter-claim as affecting
value can arise only on the question of appeal as *ex hypothesi*
the principal action is for not more than £50. In *Bowie* v.
Donaldson[4] the sum claimed was £50 but there was a counter-
claim, which was not being pressed, for £75, and appeal to the
Court of Session was held incompetent as the value of the cause
was not over £50. Lord Salvesen alone dealt with the situation
created by the counter-claim and stated that however large a
counter-claim might be it could not increase the value of the
original cause. It is thought, with deference, that this may have
to be reconsidered, and if the result of claim and counter-claim
is that the defender is assoilzied in the principal action but gets
decree for over £50 on the counter-claim it is difficult to see that
appeal could be refused. Apart from *Bowie*[4] it might have been
argued that, as a counter-claim is to be dealt with " as if it had
been stated in a substantive action,"[5] the value of the case was
the aggregate of claim and counter-claim. But it is doubtful
if this is a sound view.[6]

[1] Dykes v. Merry & Cunninghame, 1869, 7 M. 603; Nelson, Donkin
& Co. v. Browne, 1876, 3 R. 810; Birrell v. Taylor, 1884, 12 R. 151.
[2] Bruce v. Henderson, 1889, 17 R. 276; Brotherston v. Livingston, 1892,
20 R. 1; Sneddon v. Addie & Sons Collieries, (O.H.) 1927 S.N. 164.
[3] Campbell, &c. v. Train, 1910 S.C. 147.
[4] 1922 S.C. 9.
[5] 7 Edw. VII c. 51, Schedule I, Rule 55.
[6] See Gottlieb v. Fons Patent Inkwell, 1916, 33 Sh.Ct.Rep. 70; Murphy

v. Muir, 1927 S.L.T. (Sh.Ct.) 55; Cleave & Son v. Letters & Co., 1929, 45 Sh.Ct.Rep. 223; Kinnaird & Son v. Millar, 1931, 47 Sh.Ct.Rep. 320; Macfarlane v. Macdougall, 1931, 47 Sh.Ct.Rep. 325.

The result of a change in value during the course of the proceedings is another question which is, on the authorities, left in some confusion. The older practice favoured the matter being tested by the sum originally claimed irrespective of subsequent events which had reduced the amount.[1] More recent practice has tended to substitute as the criterion the amount at issue when the case comes on appeal to the Court of Session.[2] The older decisions are not expressly over-ruled, but it is doubtful if in similar circumstances they would be repeated.[3]

[1] Wilson v. Wallace, 1858, 20 D. 764; Buie v. Stiven, 1863, 2 M. 208; Armour v. Munro, &c., 1899, 7 S.L.T. 21; Tait v. Lees, 1903, 5 F. 304.
[2] Cairns v. Murray, 1884, 12 R. 167; Muirhead v. Gilmour, 1909, 1 S.L.T. 235; David Allen, &c. v. Dundee, &c., Billposting Co., 1912 S.C. 970; cf. Lamonby v. Foulds, 1928 S.C. 89.
[3] Cf. reasons in Tait v. Lees, supra, and M'Donald v. Ross, 1929 S.C. 240.

In actions of accounting it is usual to crave payment of a stated sum, or such other sum as may be found due. It is competent to grant a decree for a larger sum than that stated,[1] but it has been held that on such a crave an appeal is incompetent against a decree for a sum that is in fact below the limit.[2] On the analogy of the cases where a pecuniary alternative to a crave for delivery is left indefinite[3] it is thought that the value of an accounting should be regarded as over £50, unless it clearly appears from the record that the value is in fact under the limit. In an action of damages brought in the Court of Session, where the sum sued for was apparently much overstated, the Court would not accept the argument that the pursuer could never recover as much as the then limit of £25.[4] The criterion of value in suspensions has already been dealt with.[5]

[1] Spottiswoode v. Hopkirk, 1853, 16 D. 59.
[2] Stott v. Gray, 1834, 12 S. 828.
[3] Shotts Iron Co. v. Kerr, 1871, 10 M. 195; Aberdeen v. Wilson, 1872, 10 M. 971.
[4] Soutar v. Mulhern, 1907 S.C. 723.
[5] See p. 29, supra.

In addition to the general privative jurisdiction of the Sheriff various statutory provisions have relegated to the Sheriff Court a privative jurisdiction in relation to the matters to which they refer. Certain of these statutory powers and duties of the Sheriff which involve privative jurisdiction are considered in detail later.[1]

[1] See p. 532 et seq., infra.

CHAPTER III.

GROUNDS OF JURISDICTION.

1. GENERAL.

The Sheriff Courts Act defines various grounds upon which jurisdiction against defenders may be based in the Sheriff Court.[1] It seems clear that the statutory grounds there specified are not exhaustive of the Sheriff's jurisdiction,[2] and it is expressly provided by the Act that its terms are not to derogate from any jurisdiction already possessed or exercised by the Sheriff.[3] Thus at common law the situation of moveables within the Sheriffdom creates jurisdiction to deal with them,[4] as does the citation within the jurisdiction of a person without a fixed residence[5] and the situation of a company's registered office.[6]

[1] 7 Edw. VII c. 51, sec. 6.
[2] See Martin v. Szyszka, 1943 S.C. 203. See also Muir v. Matassa, 1935 S.L.T. (Sh.Ct.) 55.
[3] 7 Edw. VII c. 51, sec. 5.
[4] See p. 75, infra.
[5] M'Niven v. M'Kinnon, 1834, 12 S. 453; Linn v. Casadinos, 1881, 8 R. 849; Martin v. Szyszka, supra.
[6] See p. 60, infra.

2. RATIONE DOMICILII.

Every person resident within a Sheriffdom is liable to be sued in its Courts. Where a Sheriffdom is divided into districts, with district Courts, a resident within any district is amenable to the district Court. It appears to be competent to take action against a defender in any of the Courts, or at any rate in the principal Court, of a Sheriffdom although the defender resides in another district of the Sheriffdom and in what may have been originally a separate Sheriffdom.[1] But the Sheriff has a discretion whether to cite a defender who is resident in another district,[2] and the latitude above indicated seems to be inapplicable in small debt cases.[3] Actions relating to questions of heritable right or title must be brought in the Court of the jurisdiction and district where the property forming the subject of the dispute is situated.[4] Joint defenders, all subject to the jurisdiction of a Sheriff Court, may be sued in the Court within whose jurisdiction any one of them resides.[5] But whilst a pursuer has thus apparently the choice of *forum*, his choice is not absolute, for the action may be transferred by the Sheriff to another Court.[6]

[1] Tait v. Johnston, 1891, 18 R. 606; Kelso District Committee v. Fairbairn, 1891, 3 White 94; M'Cormick v. Campbell, 1926, 42 Sh.Ct.Rep. 124. A practical difficulty may arise in such a case if there are separate Sheriff-clerks for each county. The Sheriff-clerk of one county would have no authority to sign a warrant to cite a defender to the principal Court if in another county. In such circumstances the signature of the Sheriff would be necessary. (See Mactavish & Co. v. Cameron, infra.)
[2] Davidson v. Davidson, 1891, 18 R. 884; M'Cormick v. Campbell, supra.
[3] Mactavish & Co. v. Cameron, 1899, 15 Sh.Ct.Rep. 292. See also Clelland v. Young, 1896, 13 Sh.Ct.Rep. 33.
[4] 7 Edw. VII c. 51, sec. 5.
[5] Ibid., sec. 6 (a).
[6] See p. 44 et seq., supra.

Under the Sheriff Courts Act the Sheriff has jurisdiction where the defender (or where there are several defenders over each of whom a Sheriff Court has jurisdiction in terms of the Act, where one of them) resides within the jurisdiction, or having resided there for at least forty days has ceased to reside there for less than forty days and has no known residence in Scotland.[1] This sub-section is generally regarded as being declaratory of the common law in relation to jurisdiction *ratione domicilii*, so that decisions on that topic will usually be applicable.[2]

[1] 7 Edw. VII c. 51, sec. 6 (a)
[2] Duncan & Dykes, Principles of Civil Jurisdiction, 340; Martin v. Szyszka, 1943 S.C. 203, Lord Wark, p. 213.

At common law jurisdiction *ratione domicilii* rests upon the fact of residence alone,[1] and domicile of origin and domicile of succession are generally of no moment.[2] If it is clearly established that a particular place is that which a person has selected as his dwelling-place, that of itself is sufficient to subject him to the jurisdiction, no matter whether at the moment the defender is actually at that residence or not.[3]

[1] Erskine I, 2, 16; Joel v. Gill, 1859, 21 D. 929; Johnston v. Strachan, 1861, 23 D. 758, Lord Kinloch, p. 763.
[2] Tasker v. Grieve, 1905, 8 F. 45; Kerr v. R. & W. Ferguson, 1931 S.C. 736.
[3] Steel v. Lindsay, 1881, 9 R. 160, but cf. M'Cord v. M'Cord, 1946 S.C. 198.

The qualifying period of residence sufficient to found jurisdiction has been long fixed at forty days.[1] This does not rest upon Statute, but is matter of practice. Even shorter residence than forty days might suffice if it were clear that the defender had taken up residence in a Sheriffdom *animo remanendi*,[2] but the general rule is, "that a residence of forty days is sufficient—not mere presence within the territory, travelling about, and never fixed in any one place—but continuous residence in one locality for forty days. According to the principles of Scottish law, therefore, one who has resided constantly at one place within Scotland for forty days is subject to the jurisdiction of the Scottish Courts *ratione domicilii.*"[3]

[1] Erskine I, 2, 16.
[2] Home v. Eccles, 1725, M. 3704.
[3] Joel v. Gill, 1859, 21 D. 929, Lord Justice-Clerk Inglis, p. 939.

The continuity of personal residence does not require to be absolute, so long as absence does not negative the aspect of residence. It is a question of circumstances always.[1] But the fact that a man had settled his wife and family in a dwelling-house within a territory, would not in itself be sufficient to constitute jurisdiction if he was not in fact resident there.[2] Similarly, if a man were judicially separated from his wife, and living apart from his family, the family residence would not necessarily be his domicile.

[1] Irvine v. ,euchar, 1707, M. 3703; Ritchie & M'Cormick v. Fraser, 1852, ₅ D. 205.
[2] Arnott v. Peden, 1915, 31 Sh.Ct.Rep. 288; Croft v. Croft, 1923, 39 Sh.Ct.Rep. 80; M'Cord v. M'Cord, 1946 S.C. 198.

A residence, to constitute a domicile for purposes of jurisdiction, must be reasonably the defender's own residence. The fact, however, that he has sojourned for forty days in a friend's house,[1] or even in a hotel or lodgings,[2] although it does not necessarily make that place his own home, may make it his domicile in the above sense. For founding jurisdiction this is more likely to be inferred if the person have no dwelling-house of his own. A foreign soldier stationed on war service in a Scottish county may be resident there for the purpose of jurisdiction.[3]

[1] Ritchie & M'Cormick v. Fraser, 1852, 15 D. 205.
[2] Joel v. Gill, 1859, 21 D. 929.
[3] Martin v. Szyszka, 1943 S.C. 203. See also Robertson v. M'Millan, 1942, 59 Sh.Ct.Rep. 12 (Scottish soldier).

Seafaring men when on shore, military men on furlough, travellers, and other itinerants having no fixed abode, may acquire a domicile of citation in less than forty days if personal service is effected on them within the jurisdiction. That is held to be the case not only in the Court of Session[1] but also in the Sheriff Court.[2] Soldiers and sailors who have a fixed abode do not necessarily lose their domicile by going abroad on service, and it has been held that such a person may be cited at his domicile, although at the moment he may be non-resident there.[3] If the citation is objected to, a pursuer may in special circumstances be barred by his actings from pleading that the citation was valid.[4] But an action of filiation and aliment brought against a conscript soldier in the Sheriffdom of his residence before joining the army was dismissed on the ground that residence for the purpose of jurisdiction in the Sheriff Court means actual and not merely constructive residence.[5] See the case undernoted as to questions arising under the Army Act.[6]

[1] Linn v. Casadinos, 1881, 8 R. 849; cf. M'Neill v. M'Neill, (O.H.) 1919, 2 S.L.T. 127.
[2] M'Niven v. M'Kinnon, 1834, 12 S. 453; Mackenzie & Co. v. Detchon, 1891, 7 Sh.Ct.Rep. 255; Lloyds Variety Agency v. Dainton, 1914, 31 Sh.Ct.Rep. 41; Martin v. Szyszka, 1943 S.C. 203; cf. Emordy v. Wheatley, 1924, 41 Sh.Ct.Rep. 76.
[3] Brown v. M'Callum, 1845, 7 D. 423; in the Sheriff Court the matter of jurisdiction would seem to turn on the Act, sec. 6 (a).
[4] Morrison v. Vallance's Executors, 1907 S.C. 999.
[5] Findlay v. Donachie, 1944 S.C. 306. See also M'Cord v. M'Cord, 1946 S.C. 198.
[6] M'Kinnon v. M'Quillian, 1912, 28 Sh.Ct.Rep. 268.

The rule as to domicile of citation applies to parties whose domicile is not personal, but derivative. Thus the domicile of a wife or a child is normally that of the husband or father,[1] but a wife may have a domicile of citation of her own, as, for instance, when she is judicially separated or when she is personally resident in the Sheriffdom, her husband being abroad or elsewhere outwith its jurisdiction.[2] A minor may be forisfamiliated, although still a minor, and he may have a domicile of citation elsewhere than at his father's house. In the case of a lunatic the last residence before incapacity supervened is usually taken for the purpose of jurisdiction.[3]

[1] Steel v. Lindsay, 1881, 9 R. 160; Henry, 1896, 12 Sh.Ct.Rep. 121.
[2] As in Arnott v. Peden, 1915, 31 Sh.Ct.Rep. 288.
[3] Henry, supra; M'Cormick, &c., 1896, 13 Sh.Ct.Rep. 184; Dougall, &c., 1906, 22 Sh.Ct.Rep. 292.

Sec. 6 (a) of the Sheriff Courts Act, 1907, if literally construed, might appear to alter the general law as above explained by dispensing with the necessity for forty days' residence to constitute jurisdiction, for it requires merely that the defender " resides within the jurisdiction or having resided there for at least forty days has ceased to reside there for less than forty days and has no known residence in Scotland."[1] But the established law prior to this Statute required the residence to be clearly *animo remanendi*, or to extend to forty days, before it constituted a jurisdiction domicile, and as in projecting that jurisdiction for a further period of forty days, the latter portion of the section recognized that established law, it is thought that the Act does not affect the residential qualification as previously recognized by the law, and that when it speaks of a defender who " resides within the jurisdiction " it refers to a defender who had, in accordance with the established law of Scotland, acquired a domicile of citation there by forty days' residence there, or by settlement there *animo remanendi*.[2]

[1] 7 Edw. VII c. 51, sec. 6 (a) ; 2 & 3 Geo. V c. 28, Schedule I.
[2] Duncan & Dykes, Principles of Civil Jurisdiction 340 ; Martin v. Szyszka, 1943 S.C. 203, Lord Wark, p. 213. See also Lloyd's Variety Agency v. Dainton, 1914, 31 Sh.Ct.Rep, 41 ; M'Cormick v. Campbell, 1926, 42 Sh.Ct.Rep. 124.

Once a defender has acquired a domicile of citation in any Sheriffdom in Scotland, if he changes his residence into another Sheriffdom, forty days' further residence is not required in the new jurisdiction. If his new address is disclosed, his creditor can follow him there at once.[1] If his new address has not been disclosed, then the effect of the Statute is that the old domicile determines where the defender may be competently sued during a further period of forty days.[2] For instance, if a defender has resided within Sheriffdom A for forty days prior to 28th May, and has departed without disclosing his new address, he may be sued in Sheriffdom A up till 6th July. If, however, he have left Sheriffdom A, and openly settled himself in Sheriffdom B, with a known address, then his creditor must follow him there, and may sue him in Sheriffdom B only, and that at any time after 28th May.

[1] Ferguson, Shaw & Son v. M'Coll, 1897, 14 Sh.Ct.Rep. 107.
[2] 7 Edw. VII c. 51, sec. 6 (a) ; M'Lardy & Co. v. Irvine, 1911, 27 Sh.Ct.Rep. 94.

The Statute gives no direction as to the mode of citation of the defender who has left within forty days, but has not disclosed his new address. It might happen that the defender could still be served personally, but that is unlikely. Keyhole service would apparently be effectual if the house were closed,[1] and the effect of the sub-section[2] might be thought to make the old address the " legal domicile or proper place of citation "[3] in the sense of the Citation Amendment Act and thus render valid postal citation at that address.[4] But such a postal citation, if undelivered, is simply returned to the Court, which is unsatisfactory, and in practice service by officer is usually insisted on in such cases. It is thought that service by officer at the old address would constitute service at the dwelling-place despite the defender's removal.[5] In a doubtful case, as where the defender might have gone abroad, citation both at the dwelling-house and edictally might be prudent. The above does not apply to foreigners.[6]

[1] M'Lardy & Co. v. Irvine, 1911, 27 Sh.Ct.Rep. 94.
[2] 7 Edw. VII c. 57, sec. 6 (a).
[3] 45 & 46 Vict. c. 77, sec. 3.
[4] Hart, jun., &c. v. Grant & Wylie, &c., 1907, 23 Sh.Ct.Rep. 186. See also Morrison v. Vallance's Executors, 1907 S.C. 999; Fraser v. Macfadyen, 1939, 56 Sh.Ct.Rep. 66; Hutchison v. Goodale, 1940 S.L.T. (Sh.Ct.) 24.
[5] Act of Sederunt, 14th December, 1805, sec. 1; Morrison v. Vallance's Executors, supra.
[6] See next paragraph.

The projected jurisdiction of forty days at the original domicile of citation is expressly applied to the case of a person who has no known residence in Scotland.[1] The words used might suggest that the case contemplated was that of a person who had left his original domicile, but who had still a residence somewhere in Scotland, although he had not disclosed it to his creditor. Probably the better reading is that jurisdiction subsists wherever the defender is so long as he has no known residence in Scotland.[2] Normally in the case of a foreigner jurisdiction in this country ceases as soon as he leaves.[3] But it could be argued that the terms of the enactment apply comprehensively to every defender who has acquired a domicile of citation whether he was originally a foreigner or not, and that a foreigner who has come to Scotland, acquired a domicile of citation, and gone back to his native land could be sued in the Sheriff Court where he had acquired a domicile, provided the creditor brought his action within forty days of the foreigner's departure. It is thought that the terms of the Act have not this effect[4]—which would give a wider jurisdiction to the Sheriff than to the Court of Session—and that the provision should be read as subject to the general rule that in the case of a foreigner jurisdiction ceases as soon as he leaves his residence.[5] On the other hand, when the defender is not a foreigner but has left to go abroad, the jurisdiction appears to continue for the period stated.[5]

[1] 7 Edw. VII c. 51, sec. 6 (a); 2 & 3 Geo. V c. 28, Schedule I.
[2] See Fraser v. Macfadyen, 1939, 56 Sh.Ct.Rep. 66.
[3] Corstorphine v. Kasten, 1898, 1 F. 287; Buchan v. Grimaldi, 1905, 7 F. 917.
[4] Duncan & Dykes, Principles of Civil Jurisdiction 342; Roche v. Graham, 1939 S.L.T. (Sh.Ct.) 18.
[5] Fraser v. Macfadyen, supra; Hutchison v. Goodale, 1940 S.L.T. (Sh.Ct.) 24.

3. Joint Defenders.

Prior to 1907 joint defenders dwelling within the same
Sheriffdom could be jointly sued there, but if the defenders were
domiciled in different jurisdictions an action against them collectively could be brought only in the Court of Session, however trifling
the value of the case might be.   It is now competent to bring an
action in any Sheriff Court in whose jurisdiction any one of the
several joint defenders is resident provided each of the joint
defenders is subject to the jurisdiction of some Sheriff Court.[1]
This assimilates the practice of the ordinary Sheriff Court to that
of the Small Debt Court.[2]   Possible abuse of this privilege is
guarded against by the Sheriff having discretionary power to remit
the case to another Sheriffdom with jurisdiction over any of the
defenders, if he thinks this expedient.[3]

[1] 7 Edw. VII c. 51, sec. 6 (a) ; 2 & 3 Geo. V c. 28, Schedule I.
[2] 52 & 53 Vict. c. 26, sec. 3.
[3] 7 Edw. VII c. 51, Schedule I, Rule 19; Lamb & Co. v. Pearson, &c.,
1911, 28 Sh.Ct.Rep. 80.

As above indicated, it is a statutory requisite of convening
defenders in the one Sheriffdom that all should be subject to the
jurisdiction of some Sheriff Court.   Thus two defenders resident
in a Sheriffdom and a foreigner cannot be convened together in
terms of the section.   Any doubt on this subject[1] was removed
by the alterations on this clause effected by the Sheriff Courts Act,
1913.[2]   The sub-section depends upon residence and its terms cannot be applied where action is taken in a Court whose jurisdiction
one of the defenders has prorogated, nor can such an action
apparently be transferred to another Sheriffdom.[3]

[1] See Neilson-Sproul v. MacIntyre, &c., 1910, 26 Sh.Ct.Rep. 259.
[2] 7 Edw. VII c. 51, sec. 6 (a) ; 2 & 3 Geo. V c. 28, Schedule I.
[3] Graham v. Young, &c., 1926, 43 Sh.Ct.Rep. 3.

The question has been raised whether the above statutory rule
that all the joint defenders must be subject to the jurisdiction
of a Sheriff Court suffers an exception in the case of a body of
trustees, one of whom resides within a Sheriffdom and against
none of whom there is a personal conclusion, but who are sued
only in their official capacity as trustees.   The idea that executors
in their official capacity were subject to the jurisdiction of the
Sheriff Court from which their confirmation issued was negatived
in the case of *Halliday*.[1]   But ten years later, in *Thompson's*

case,[2] the Court sustained jurisdiction against two trustees, one of whom was furth of Scotland, the trust estate and the other trustee being within the Sheriffdom. Before the sub-section under consideration took its present shape it had been held in the Sheriff Court that where one trustee resided within a Sheriffdom, and the other was furth of Scotland, both might be sued in the Sheriff Court of the Scottish resident.[3] The matter is not free from difficulty, but, as jurisdiction is not conferred by implication, and as joint defenders do not fall within the sub-section unless they are all subject to the jurisdiction of some Sheriff Court, there seems no reason why the same principle should not apply to a body of trustees.[4]

[1] Halliday's Executors v. Halliday's Executors, 1886, 14 R. 251.
[2] Thompson v. Wilson's Trustees, 1895, 22 R. 866.
[3] Cathcart v. Scott, 1908, 25 Sh.Ct.Rep. 16; Aston v. Barclay, 1912, 29 Sh.Ct.Rep. 10.
[4] See Dalziel v. Coulthurst's Executors, 1934 S.C. 564.

4. CARRYING ON BUSINESS.

A person (which includes a company, corporation, association or firm or a board corporate or unincorporate) who carries on business and has a place of business within the jurisdiction, and is cited either personally or at such place of business is subject to the jurisdiction of the Sheriffdom.[1] To conform to the sub-section all these three requisites must concur. As to a place of business intersected by the boundary of the Sheriffdom see the case undernoted.[2] This ground of jurisdiction is not in substitution for, but in addition to, that *ratione domicilii*, and a defender may be sued and cited at his place of business, although he have no dwelling-place within Scotland. The mode of effecting service at a place of business is similar to that at a dwelling-place.

[1] 7 Edw. VII c. 51, sec. 6 (b).
[2] Connell & Co. v. Dempsie, 1873, 10 S.L.R. 393.

The business domicile in its present aspect was a statutory creation first introduced by the Sheriff Courts Act, 1876.[1] Even prior to that, however, the common law recognized this jurisdiction to a limited extent, and as a company or business concern cannot have a dwelling-place, in practice the place of business was regarded as its domicile of citation. The principle was that a place of business in a Sheriffdom gave jurisdiction in actions relating to matters arising out of the business conducted there.[2] That common law jurisdiction still remains,[3] and, apart from the present Act, a limited company can always be sued in the Sheriffdom where its registered office is situated.[4]

1 39 & 40 Vict. c. 70, sec. 46.
2 Harris v. Gillespie, 1875, 2 R. 1003; Hughes v. J. & W. Stewart, 1907 S.C. 791.
3 Grigor v. Jamieson & Son, 1915, 32 Sh.Ct.Rep. 93.
4 Brown & Critchley v. Decorative Art Journals Co., 1922 S.C. 192.

In invoking the statutory ground of jurisdiction it is immaterial whether the place of business is a principal or a subordinate one,[1] or whether the action relates to matters arising within the Sheriffdom.[2] It is also immaterial that the defender is a foreign company which has registered in this country the names of persons to accept service of process.[3] It has usually been held to be essential that the business operations are still being continued.[4] If in the above sense the defender has a place of business situated within the Sheriffdom jurisdiction will be established provided that the defender actually carries on business, and that he is cited personally, or at the place of business within the Sheriffdom.

1 Hay's Trustees v. London & North-Western Railway Company, 1909 S.C. 707; M'Aulay v. Glasgow Corporation, 1930 S.L.T. (Sh.Ct.) 47 (tramway lines and depot); cf. Wilson v. Pattison, 1891, 7 Sh.Ct.Rep. 305 (carriers' quarters); M'Laughlin v. Dumbarton Steamboat Co., 1899, 19 Sh.Ct.Rep. 270.
2 Henderson's Trustees v. Paton, 1887, 4 Sh.Ct.Rep. 17 (maills and duties).
3 Paterson v. Establissements Hutchinson, 1915, 32 Sh.Ct.Rep. 105.
4 Dallas's v. Hodge & Co., 1909, 26 Sh.Ct.Rep. 214; Bruce v. British Motor Trading Corporation, 1924 S.C. 908; cf. Mouat v. Lee, 1891, 18 R. 876; Mackay v. Penman, 1922, 38 Sh.Ct.Rep. 189.

The expression used in the 1876 Act was " trade or business " —an expression which lent countenance to the narrow view that the jurisdiction thereby conferred was limited to traders. The 1907 Act requires the defender simply to carry on business, a definition which is undoubtedly wider. It is thought that this would still not cover one who was merely the joint tenant of a farm[1] and not concerned in the farm business, or a judicial factor selling off farm stock.[2] But it has been held to include a farmer (though not living on the farm),[3] an actor[4] and a showman.[5] In the last two cases jurisdiction failed because there was no place of business.

1 M'Bey v. Knight, 1879, 7 R. 255; Mackay v. Toms, 1944, 60 Sh.Ct.Rep. 169.
2 Ferguson v. Dyer, 1882, 9 R. 671.
3 M'Diarmid v. Urquhart, 1891, 7 Sh.Ct.Rep. 328.
4 Robb v. Lely, 1922, 38 Sh.Ct.Rep. 81.
5 Emordy v. Wheatley, 1924, 41 Sh.Ct.Rep. 76.

It may now be taken as established that the place of business which the Statute requires is not satisfied by a mere agency or the appointment of representatives.[1]

[1] Laidlaw v. Provident, &c., Insurance Company, 1890, 17 R. 544; Roberts v. Provincial Homes Investment Co., 1907 S.C. (J) 7.

5. Arrestment ad Fundandam Jurisdictionem.

Jurisdiction founded upon arrestment is, as regards the Sheriff Court, statutory, although the principle underlying it has long been recognized in the law of Scotland and of other commercial countries. It is a principle of expediency which applies generally where a defender has no domicile of citation in Scotland, and is a foreigner who has moveable property of any description which can be arrested within Scotland.

In the older practice letters authorizing arrestment *ad fundandam jurisdictionem* were issued by the Sheriff as judge ordinary of the locality where the property proposed to be arrested was situated, but the action founded upon that arrestment had generally to be brought in the Court of Session.

In 1877 a limited jurisdiction by arrestment was conferred on the Sheriff Court and by the Sheriff Courts Act, 1907, jurisdiction is now conferred when the defender is a person not otherwise subject to the jurisdiction of the Courts of Scotland, and a ship or vessel of which he is owner or part owner or master, or goods, debts, money, or other moveable property belonging to him have been arrested within the jurisdiction.[1] To found jurisdiction by arrestment in the Sheriff Court it is essential that the defender be not otherwise subject to the jurisdiction of the Courts of Scotland. Thus if a foreigner owns heritage in Scotland an action for however small an amount but not relating to the heritage must be brought in the Court of Session, as jurisdiction by arrestment cannot be founded in that case in the Sheriff Court.[2]

[1] 7 Edw. VII c. 51, sec. 6 (c).
[2] Pagan & Osborne v. Haig, 1910 S.C. 341.

No recent cases are reported in regard to jurisdiction by arrestment against foreign executors, but from a series of old decisions it would appear that special considerations apply. In general the Court have declined to admit jurisdiction by arrestment as sufficient for an action of accounting or payment against the foreign executors of a deceased foreigner,[1] though such jurisdiction appears to suffice for an action to constitute the debt.[2] And if the foreign executor has come to this country for confirmation arrestment here seems to found jurisdiction in the normal manner.[3]

[1] Houston v. Stirling, 1825, 1 W. & S., 199; Brown's Trustees v. Palmer, 1830, 9 S. 224; Macmaster v. Macmaster, 1833, 11 S. 685.
[2] Ashton, Hodgson & Co. v. Mackrill, 1773, M. 4835; Houston v. Stirling, supra; Forrest v. Forrest, 1863, 1 M. 806.
[3] M'Morine v. Cowie, 1845, 7 D. 270.   See also Innerarity & Co. v. Gilmore, 1840, 2 D. 813.

An arrestment to found jurisdiction is used for the special purpose only of making the defender subject to the jurisdiction of the Court.   The modern view is that such an arrestment does not place a *nexus* on the property so that the arrestee is not precluded from parting with the subjects arrested, and a ship which has been arrested in this way is not prevented from sailing away.[1] If it is desired to retain the arrested property within the jurisdiction of the Sheriff Court where it has been found, a warrant to arrest on the dependence should be craved in the initial writ, and the property attached under that warrant.

[1] Craig v. Brunsgaard, Kjosterud & Co., 1896, 23 R. 500; Leggat Brothers v. Gray, 1908 S.C. 67; Fraser-Johnston Engineering Co. v. Jeffs, 1920 S.C. 222.   See also North v. Stewart, 1890, 17 R. (H.L.) 60, Lord Watson, p. 63.

Any moveable property which might competently be arrested in execution of a decree is arrestable to found jurisdiction,[1] but it must be property which is not elusory in value, and which belongs to the defender personally, or which must be accounted for to him.   Mere smallness in amount is immaterial and a debt of 9s. 3d.[2] and a door plate[3] have been held to be sufficient.   But the subjects arrested must have some mercantile value, and plans and documents[4] or a pattern book[5] have been held to be not enough.   A contingent,[6] and as yet unascertained,[7] debt as well as a defeasible right[8] are now recognized as arrestable.   And the date as at which the matter has to be judged is the date when the arrestments are laid on.[9]   An arrestment used in the hands of a Scottish limited company will found jurisdiction in Scotland against foreigners who are registered shareholders in the company, notwithstanding that at the moment the arrestment is used there is no money due to shareholders, in the shape of declared dividend or otherwise.   But uncalled capital is not normally arrestable in the hands of shareholders, no call having been made upon them.[10]

[1] Leggat Brothers v. Gray, 1908 S.C. 67.
[2] Ross v. Ross, 1878, 5 R. 1013.
[3] Dalrymple v. Lancashire Trust and Mortgage Insurance Corporation, (O.H.) 1894, 2 S.L.T. 79.
[4] Trowsdale's Trustee v. Forcett Railway Co., 1870, 9 M. 88.

[5] Millar & Lang v. Poole, (O.H.) 1907, 15 S.L.T. 76.
[6] MacLaren & Co. v. Preston, (O.H.) 1893, 1 S.L.T. 75.
[7] Baines & Tait v. Compagnie Generale des Mines d'Asphalte, 1879, 6 R.
   846; Agnew v. Norwest Construction Co., 1935 S.C. 771.
[8] North v. Stewart, 1890, 17 R. (H.L.) 60.
[9] North v. Stewart, supra; Shankland & Co. v. M'Gildowny, 1912 S.C.
   857.
[10] Lindsay v. Martona Rubber Estates, 1912, 28 Sh.Ct.Rep. 76.

Where a claim of damages was arrested it was held that jurisdiction depended on pursuer proving that something had in fact
been attached.[1] The same rule was applied where the question
depended on the state of accounts between the arrestee and the
defender.[2] But the practice in such cases has varied[3] and the
test is said to be that at the date of arrestment there must be
a present duty of accountability.[4] An arrestment in the hands of
the Clerk of Court of money consigned by the defender and which
was returnable to him in terms of settlement was held to be bad,[4]
but such an arrestment was sustained where the consigned money
was by order of Court payable to defenders by the time the arrestment was used.[5] Where a claim of damages arising out of a motor
car accident had been intimated, but liability was not admitted,
arrestments in the hands of an insurance company bound to
indemnify the motorist were held to be ineffective.[6]

[1] Smith v. Rosenbloom, (O.H.) 1915, 53 S.L.R. 5.
[2] Napier, Shanks & Bell v. Halvorsen, 1892, 19 R. 412; Mitchell &
   Muil v. Feniscliffe Products Co., 1920, 57 S.L.R. 277.
[3] Baines & Tait v. Compagnie Generale des Mines d'Asphalte, 1879, 6 R.
   846.
[4] Shankland & Co. v. M'Gildowny, 1912 S.C. 857.
[5] Scottish Iron & Steel Co. v. Gilleaux & Collinet, 1913, 30 Sh.Ct.Rep. 42.
[6] Kerr v. R. & W. Ferguson, 1931 S.C. 736.

Arrestment of a ship may found jurisdiction against a defender
in a representative capacity. Thus, a foreign ship, the owner
of which may be unknown, may be attached, and an action raised
in the Sheriff Court, directed against the shipmaster as representing the owner, but not against any other, as, for instance,
a mortgagee in possession.[1] But as regards property other than
maritime, the Statute is more narrowly expressed, and is therefore
to be more strictly construed, when the subjects arrested are goods,
debts, money, or other moveable property. Such assets must
" belong " to the defender and not be merely in his custody as
the ship is in the custody of the master. Where a deposit receipt
stood in name of trustees, but was payable on the order of the
solicitor and a beneficiary, an arrestment of sums due by the
bank to the beneficiary attached no part of the sum on deposit.[2]
It is immaterial that the pursuers have only recently parted with

possession of the subjects arrested,[3] but it is essential that the
holder of the fund or subject is legally bound to make payment
or delivery to the defender,[4] or be accountable to him. In a
shipping case arising out of a collision jurisdiction is effectually
founded against a defender by arresting a ship of his, other than
that alleged to be at fault in the collision.[5] A vessel owned by
a foreign government is generally immune from arrestment.[6]

[1] Jones v. Samuel, 1862, 24 D. 319.
[2] Clark v. National Bank, 1890, 27 S.L.R. 628.
[3] Pollock, Whyte & Waddell v. Old Park Forge, (O.H.) 1907, 15 S.L.T.
    3; Braby & Co. v. Danks & Co., (O.H.) 1907, 15 S.L.T. 161. But
    see Millar & Lang v. Poole, (O.H.) 1907, 15 S.L.T. 76 (effect of
    mala fides)
[4] Mitchell, &c. v. Burn, 1874, 1 R. 900; Young v. Aktiebolaget Ofverums
    Bruk, 1890, 18 R. 163; Whittall v. Christie, 1894, 22 R. 91; Heron v.
    Winfields, 1894, 22 R. 182; J. & C. Murray v. Wallace Marrs & Co.,
    1914 S.C. 114; Moore & Weinberg v. Ernsthausen, 1917 S.C. (H.L.)
    25; Young & Saunders v. Gordon, 1924, 40 Sh.Ct.Rep. 272.
[5] Sheaf Steamship Co. v. Compania Transmediterranea, 1930 S.C. 660.
[6] The "Victoria" v. The "Quillwark," (O.H.) 1922 S.L.T. 68.

Goods are not arrestable to found jurisdiction if they are in
the arrestee's own hands or in the hands of a person who is a
mere custodier for the owner, and has himself no title to retain
the goods.[1] Arrestment would also seem to be incompetent in
the hands of a pledgee, who has made advances upon deposit of
the goods under a special contract, stipulating that, failing
redemption within a specified time, the pledgee becomes the owner,
and the redemption period has expired, although the pledgee may
not yet have had his forfeiture title judicially declared. Arrestment of a visitor's luggage in the hands of a hotel has been found
ineffective as the hotel had not truly possession of the subjects.[2]
Arrestment of money taken from a prisoner was also held to be
incompetent in the hands of the police.[3]

[1] Bell Com. II, 70; Denholm Young & Co. v. MacElwee, 1918, 34
    Sh.Ct.Rep. 193; Grant, Melrose & Tennant v. du Cros, 1927, 43
    Sh.Ct.Rep. 347.
[2] Hutchison v. Hutchison, (O.H.) 1912, 1 S.L.T. 219.
[3] Guthrie v. Morren, 1939, 55 Sh.Ct.Rep. 172.

An arrestment to found jurisdiction is personal to the defender
against whom it is used and it falls by his death.[1] Moreover it
founds jurisdiction only for the particular action in respect of
which it was used. So if new pursuers are added by amendment
or otherwise the jurisdiction will have to be founded of new, and
a subsequent action even between the same parties requires a fresh
arrestment.[2] But it has been held that the jurisdiction founded
by arrestment holds in respect of an action as competently

amended.[3] As express power is now given to add new parties by amendment[4] it could be argued that the rule in *Andersen*[2] no longer applies, but it is thought that the reason for that decision still holds good.

[1] Cameron v. Chapman, 1838, 16 S. 907; Mackenzie v. Drummond's Executors, 1868, 6 M. 932.
[2] Goodwin & Hogarth v. Purfield, 1871, 10 M. 214; Andersen v. Harboe, 1871, 10 M. 217.
[3] Hope v. Derwent Rolling Mills, 1905, 7 F. 837; cf. Morley v. Jackson, 1888, 16 R. 78.
[4] 7 Edw. VII c. 51, Schedule I, Rule 79.

The initial writ should narrate any arrestment relied upon as creating jurisdiction, and the defender may plead invalidity of the arrestment process. Such a plea, however, must be stated as a plea in bar. A defender who has entered upon litiscontestation on the merits will not afterwards be allowed to plead that the arrestment *ad fundandam jurisdictionem* was inept. Such a plea though not in the defences may be added at adjustment but would probably not be available by amendment after the record was closed.[1] Irregularities in the arrestment, or in the execution, if not in essentials may be disregarded.[2] Where jurisdiction is founded by arrestment the defender, though he has appeared in the process, is not debarred from objecting to the regularity of the service on him.[3]

[1] Fraser-Johnston Engineering Co. v. Jeffs, 1920 S.C. 222.
[2] Fraser-Johnston Engineering Co. v. Jeffs, supra; Stirling Bonding Co. v. Great West Wine Co., (O.H.) 1927 S.L.T. 579.
[3] 7 Edw. VII c. 51, Schedule I, Rule 13.

The original object contemplated by the principle of jurisdiction by arrestment was probably the recovery of debts, and it has in practice been regarded as a commercial rather than a universal form of founding jurisdiction. In the Supreme Court where the matter is not regulated by Statute, jurisdiction by arrestment does not extend to actions relating to status[1] or declarators,[2] but it probably covers actions *ad factum praestandum*.[3] The terms of the Sheriff Courts Act, 1907, which are quite unqualified, lay down in express terms that upon arrestment may follow, not only a claim for money, but an action of any kind which is now competent in the Sheriff Court.[4] The specialties regarding jurisdiction in actions of status probably take such actions, so far as they are competent in the Sheriff Court, outwith the scope of jurisdiction founded by arrestment,[5] and jurisdiction founded in this way seems inappropriate, and is probably ineffective, in the case of various summary applications, notwithstanding the express

terms of the section.[4] These terms were not directly considered in
the *Union Electric Co.'s* case.[3] A foreign pursuer may use arrestment to found jurisdiction against another foreigner.[6]

[1] Morley v. Jackson, 1888, 16 R. 78.
[2] Williams v. Royal College of Veterinary Surgeons, (O.H.) 1897, 5
S.L.T. 208.
[3] Powell v. Mackenzie & Co., (O.H.) 1900, 8 S.L.T. 182; Union Electric
Co. v. Holman & Co., 1913 S.C. 954.
[4] 7 Edw. VII c. 51, sec. 6, cf. p. 30, supra, and pp. 103, 515, infra.
[5] Holt v. Holt, 1908, 25 Sh.Ct.Rep. 112. See M'Cord v. M'Cord. 1946
S.C. 198, Lord Justice-Clerk Cooper, p. 201.
[6] Tyne Improvement Commissioners v. Aktieselkabet Aalborg Damps-
kibsselskab, (O.H.) 1905, 12 S.L.T. 693.

This preliminary arrestment is necessary only in the case of
a person who is not subject to the jurisdiction of the Scottish Courts
at the time of the initiation of an action against him. It is
not required where a person was subject to the jurisdiction of
the Courts when the action was raised, but has since ceased to be
so, and a defender who had a Scottish domicile when he was sued,
although he subsequently left Scotland, was held liable to be called
as defender in an action of furthcoming to make good arrestments,
without the necessity of fresh arrestment to found jurisdiction.[1]
The furthcoming, although in form a separate process, was there
regarded as really a continuation of the same judicial proceedings.

[1] Burns v. Monro, 1844, 6 D. 1352.

There is no provision in the Sheriff Courts Acts as to the
time within which an action may be brought in the jurisdiction
to which a defender has been made subject by arrestment *ad
fundandam jurisdictionem*. An arrestment on the dependence falls
if the action is not served within twenty days,[1] but that does
not apply to an arrestment to found jurisdiction. There seems
no specific obligation upon the user of the arrestment to bring
his action within any particular time, but he will act wisely if
he follows the usual practice of bringing it immediately after
the arrestment. Jurisdiction has been sustained for an action
not served for over two months after the arrestment,[2] and probably
an action would be regarded as timeously brought if served within
a year and day. It has been said, however, that there must be
no unreasonable delay in bringing the action.[3] The arrestment
should be executed prior to or at the same time as the serving of
the writ.[4]

[1] 7 Edw. VII c. 51, Schedule I, Rule 127.
[2] Jacobo v. Scott, (O.H.) 1895, 2 S.L.T. 455; Craig v. Brunsgaärd
Kjosterud & Co., 1896, 23 R. 500.

[3] Craig v. Brunsgaard Kjosterud & Co., supra.
[4] Walls' Trustees v. Drynan, 1888, 15 R. 359; North v. Stewart, 1890, 17 R. (H.L.) 60.

An application for letters of arrestment is made at common law to the Sheriff as judge ordinary of the bounds within which is situated the property proposed to be arrested. The application is an *ex parte* summary application which requires no service and which is normally granted *de plano*. It contains a condescendence and pleas in law, should disclose the nature of the action to be raised, and aver that the defender is not subject to the jurisdiction of the Courts of Scotland. The warrant is executed in the same manner as a warrant to arrest on the dependence, or in execution, but the officer's execution should bear that it was made *ad fundandam jurisdictionem*. The cost of arrestment *ad fundandam jurisdictionem* falls within party and party expenses in the action which follows upon it.[1]

[1] Smith v. Owners of " Crystal Spring," 1890, 7 Sh.Ct.Rep. 67; Wallace v. Toye, 1912, 28 Sh.Ct.Rep. 50.   See also Brodersen Vaughan & Co. v. Falcks Rederiaktieselskabet, (O.H.) 1921, 2 S.L.T. 231.

The fact that arrestment is a means of founding jurisdiction in the Sheriff Court does not infer that the letters of arrestment must necessarily issue from the Sheriff Court. Letters of arrestment may also be applied for in the Court of Session, and while these are no longer required in Court of Session procedure[1] they appear to be still available, and they will warrant arrestment to found jurisdiction for an action to be brought in the Sheriff Court.[2] The warrant in that case can be executed only by a messenger-at-arms.[3]

[1] Rules of Court of Session, 1936, II, 6.
[2] Dickson & Walker v. Mitchell, &c., 1910 S.C. 139.
[3] Buchanan v. British National Premium Provident Association, (O.H.) 1903, 11 S.L.T. 465.

6. RECONVENTION.

Although he may not be otherwise subject to the jurisdiction of the Scottish Courts, a foreigner will render himself liable to be sued in the Sheriff Court if he himself brings an action in that Court, and thus becomes liable to the jurisdiction *ex reconventione*. The principle at common law is that a foreigner cannot avail himself of the Scottish Court, by suing an action there, without also subjecting himself to its jurisdiction if the defender in his action have a claim against him arising out of the same matter. The foreigner need not necessarily have raised a substantive action. It is enough that he is a party in a process pending before the Court, as, for instance, lodging a claim in a bankruptcy process[1] or liquidation,[2] or in a multiplepoinding.[3]

[1] Barr v. Smith & Chamberlain, 1879, 7 R. 247.
[2] California Redwood Co. v. Merchant Banking Co., 1886, 13 R. 1202.
[3] Colville v. Colville, 1891, 7 Sh.Ct.Rep. 266.

It was doubted at one time whether the principle of reconvention was not restricted in its operation to the Supreme Court, but it has long been recognized in the Sheriff Court that a foreigner suing in the Sheriff Court for any claim may, at common law, be made to answer there also for any counter-claim arising out of the contract sued on, or in *eodem negotio*, or *ejusdem generis*.[1] A counter-action could not be entertained in the Sheriff Court if the cause of it arose out of a different contract, or a different set of circumstances than those of the leading action, and the same rule holds in the Court of Session.[2] But in the Sheriff Court the element of contingency has now been eliminated, for the Sheriff Courts Act, 1907,[3] expressly sanctions any cross action, without restriction as to how it arose so long as it is one which is competent in the Sheriff Court. All that the Act requires is that in the second action the party sued is the pursuer in an action pending within the jurisdiction against the party suing,[3] but it is now doubtful whether this provision can receive literal effect.[4] It does not, it is thought, prejudice the common law extension to claims in bankruptcy, liquidation and multiplepoindings above referred to.[5] It has been held that an action by a foreigner in the Sheriff Court justifies an action against the foreigner in the Court of Session.[6]

[1] Skirving v. Barr, 1874, I Guthrie's Select Cases 248; Oakbank Oil Co. v. Lecky, 1878, I Guthrie's Select Cases 251.
[2] Thompson v. Whitehead, 1862, 24 D. 331.
[3] 7 Edw. VII c. 51, sec. 6 (h); Ponton's Executors v. Ponton, 1913 S.C. 598; Finklestein v. Commercial Enlargers, &c., 1924, 40 Sh.Ct.Rep. 196.
[4] Kitson v. Kitson, 1945 S.C. 434.
[5] See definition of pursuer in 7 Edw. VII c. 51, sec. 3 (n).
[6] Burrell v. Gerbruder van Uden, (O.H.) 1914, 2 S.L.T. 394.

Originally, reconvention was conceived as applying between a Scotsman and a foreigner, but in the Sheriff Court it has long been accepted as applicable between Scotsmen in different Sheriffdoms,[1] and the wide terms of the Act confirm this application. Apart from reconvention a defender sued in any Sheriffdom may there set up any counter-claim against the party who is suing him, and that without serving a formal action, for it is no longer necessary to state such counter-claim in a substantive action. It is sufficient to set it forth (in a separate statement) in the defences in the leading action, and when it is so stated the Sheriff is directed to " deal with it as if it had been stated in a substantive action."[2] But the defender's claim, whether stated in a substantive action, or by way of counter-claim, must be of a nature which is competent in the Sheriff Court.

[1] Skirving v. Barr, 1874, I Guthrie's Select Cases 248.
[2] 7 Edw. VII c. 51, Schedule I, Rules 43, 55.

The view prevailed at one time that jurisdiction *ex reconventione* existed at common law so long as any step remained to be taken in the original action, and a cross action was regarded as timeously brought if the leading action had not yet been extracted, or expenses decerned for.[1] But the modern view is that jurisdiction by reconvention is not available when the original action has been finally disposed of on the merits.[2] In the Sheriff Court the question arising on the terms of the Act is whether the first action is " pending " but it is thought that the later decision in the Supreme Court, though not in the circumstances binding, would probably be followed.[3] An action by a foreigner suing in a representative capacity does not render him liable to a counter-claim directed against him as an individual.[4]

[1] Allan v. Wormser, Harris & Co., 1894, 21 R. 866.
[2] Hurst, Nelson & Co. v. Spencer Whatley, 1912 S.C. 1041.
[3] But on a plea of lis alibi pendens the older view apparently holds; Kennedy v. Macdonald, 1876, 3 R. 813.
[4] Ponton's Executors v. Ponton, 1913 S.C. 598.

7. DELICT.

Another mode in which a person may become subject to the jurisdiction of a Sheriff Court in Scotland is through his personal delict. Where the action arises out of the delict of the defender within the jurisdiction, and he is personally cited there, he is liable to be sued there.[1] Delict is a relative term, which has a general and a legal meaning, but it is thought to have been used in the Sheriff Courts Act, 1907, in its broadest sense, and to mean that a man is not to be permitted to evade the consequences of his negligence or fault or wrong-doing within a Sheriffdom on the plea that he is not subject to the jurisdiction. In such a case, and without any preliminary arrestment to found jurisdiction being required, he may be cited personally to answer in the civil Court for delict committed within a Sheriffdom. If, for instance, a foreigner attacks a person in Scotland, he may be dealt with under the criminal law. But he is also liable under the civil law to a claim of damages for assault, and for that he must answer in the local civil Court, if he is personally cited within its jurisdiction. The same principle applies in actions arising out of other forms of delict or quasi delict, such as slander actions,[2] and actions founded upon personal fault or negligence.[3] It was at one time held that actions of affiliation and aliment are founded on delict,[4] but that appears to be erroneous.[5] Such an action against an English defender may be competent under the Summary Jurisdiction (Process) Act, 1881,[6] though in the case decided on this point[7] it may be thought that a somewhat generous view was taken of the defender being " within the jurisdiction of the Court."

[1] 7 Edw. VII c. 51, sec. 6 (i).
[2] Kermick v. Watson, 1871, 9 M. 984; Parnell v. Walter, 1889, 16 R. 917.
[3] Macleod v. Dobson, 1900, 16 Sh.Ct.Rep. 33, 104.
[4] Drennan v. Smith, 1887, 3 Sh.Ct.Rep. 326; Carrigan v. Phillips, 1905, 21 Sh.Ct.Rep. 335.
[5] M'Intosh v. Nilsson, 1935, 51 Sh.Ct.Rep. 137.
[6] 44 & 45 Vict. c. 24, sec. 6.
[7] Sheridan v. Ball, 1921, 39 Sh.Ct.Rep. 163.

This ground of jurisdiction is conditional upon personal service, as distinguished from postal service.[1] To make a person, not otherwise subject to it, amenable to the jurisdiction of a Sheriff Court, not only must the action arise out of the delict of the defender within the jurisdiction, but the defender must be personally cited there.[2]

[1] Davidson v. Gourlay, 1906, 22 Sh.Ct.Rep. 242; Kerr v. R. & W. Ferguson, 1931 S.C. 736.
[2] 7 Edw. VII c. 51, sec. 6 (i).

Joint delinquents may be sued jointly and severally if the action as laid against all of them arises out of the same delict.[1] But each defender must be served personally. When an action was brought against the executors of the deceased wrongdoers it was held that personal service on one executor was not sufficient.[2] An action against one delinquent may not debar a later action against another if satisfaction has not been obtained as a result of the first.[3]

[1] Caughie v. Robertson, 1897, 25 R. 1; Sim v. Muir's Trustees, 1906, 8 F. 1091; Fleming v. Gemmill, 1908 S.C. 340; Ellerman Lines v. Clyde Trustees, &c., 1909 S.C. 690.
[2] Dalziel v. Coulthurst's Executors, 1934 S.C. 564.
[3] Steven v. Broady Norman & Co., 1928 S.C. 351.

It is thought that the words of sec. 6 (i) include cases laid upon quasi delict and—though this has been doubted—that they would cover a case laid upon the negligence of a servant.[1] But in any event the common law has always recognized that in cases of quasi delict redress can be found at the place where the wrong has been committed, provided the defender is personally cited there.[2] It is thought that a pursuer could still appeal to the common law and there no distinction is drawn between delict and quasi delict.[3] The fact that the wrong has not been committed by the defender but by one for whom he is responsible does not alter the rule that personal service must be made on the defender himself.[1]

[1] Henderson v. Muir, 1910, 26 Sh.Ct.Rep. 158.
[2] Kermick v. Watson, 1871, 9 M. 984.
[3] See Kerr v. R. & W. Ferguson, 1931 S.C. 736; Dalziel v. Coulthurst's Executors, 1934 S.C. 564.

An action for interdict against an alleged wrong being committed, or threatened to be committed, within the jurisdiction is always competent whether the defender is otherwise subject to the jurisdiction or not.[1] In this case personal service is not essential.

[1] 7 Edw. VII c. 51, sec. 6 (e).

8. RATIONE REI SITÆ.

A person who is owner, part owner, or tenant or joint tenant of heritable property situated within any Sheriffdom is subject to the jurisdiction of the Courts of that Sheriffdom, although he may not reside there, or have a place of business there, provided that the action which is brought relates to such property or to his interest therein.[1] Tenant in the above sense includes sub-tenant.[2] Even if the owner or tenant of such property be a foreigner, no antecedent arrestment process is necessary to render him subject to the jurisdiction. The fact of ownership or tenancy of heritable property is of itself sufficient to create jurisdiction for all actions relating to that heritable property, and it is immaterial whether the defender's interest is as an individual or as a trustee.[1] As in the case of other grounds of jurisdiction the action must be of a kind which is competent in the Sheriff Court. Neither under the Act nor at common law does the ownership of heritage in the Sheriffdom give the Sheriff any general jurisdiction over the owner.[3] It has been held that an action for a share of the cost of repairs related to the property within the meaning of the section, though the defender had already agreed in writing to pay the amount,[4] and a tenant's action for reimbursement of the cost of repairs

paid for by him has also been held to fall under the section.[5]
But when bills of exchange sued upon were said to be secured on
a property,[6] and where an action arose out of the defenders'
alleged negligence in connexion with a hoist in their property,[7]
it was held that the section did not apply.

[1] 7 Edw. VII c. 51, sec. 6 (d).
[2] Ibid., sec. 3 (b).
[3] Maxwell v. Horwood's Trustees, 1902, 4 F. 489.
[4] Fletcher v. Kinloch, 1915, 31 Sh.Ct.Rep. 159.
[5] Allan v. Alexander's Trustees, (O.H.) 1908, 16 S.L.T. 491.
[6] Gordon v. Nicoll, 1913, 29 Sh.Ct.Rep. 213.
[7] Brady v. Miller's Properties, 1935, 51 Sh.Ct.Rep. 183.

Even where the defender had his residence within another
Sheriffdom, actions relating to heritable property could nevertheless be brought in the Sheriff Court of the district within which
the property lay.   This was always the practice as regards such
actions as sequestration for rent, poinding of the ground, removing,
and the like, and actions relating to the possession of the property
or of pertinents within it.[1]   This jurisdiction is now defined by
Statute as extending to all actions relating to the property, or
to the defender's interest in it.[2]   Generally such an action could
also be brought in any other Sheriffdom, to the jurisdiction of
which the defender might be subject by residence or otherwise,
but if the action relates to questions of heritable right or title,
including irritancy and removing, or to division of commonties,
or division, or division and sale, of common property the action
must be raised in the Court of the jurisdiction and district where
the property forming the subject in dispute is situated, and all
parties against whom the action may be brought are to be subject
to that jurisdiction for the purposes of the action.[3]   It is thought
that the statutory extension as above has brought within the
jurisdiction of the Sheriff various cases which were formerly outside it.[4]

[1] Mouat v. Lee, 1891, 18 R. 876; Culross Special Water District Com-
     mittee v. Smith-Sligo's Trustees, 1891, 19 R. 58; Duncan v. Lodi-
     jensky, 1904, 6 F. 408.
[2] 7 Edw. VII c. 51, sec. 6 (d).
[3] Ibid., sec. 5; Thom v. Young, 1931, 47 Sh.Ct.Rep. 69; Duff v. West
     Craig, 1935, 51 Sh.Ct.Rep. 315.   See also Stark's Trustees v.
     Cooper's Trustees, 1900, 2 F. 1257.
[4] E.g., Pollokshaws Commissioners v. M'Lean, 1899, 2 F. 96; Maxwell v.
     Horwood's Trustees, 1902, 4 F. 489.

It is thought that ownership of property will be regarded in
the same way as in the Supreme Court where right rather than
feudal title is the test.   Thus a binding contract to purchase has

been held to be enough,[1] the radical right to the subjects may
be sufficient,[2] but a mere claim on a trust estate comprising
heritage will not suffice.[3] Title itself without actual ownership
will not do,[4] and feudal divestiture,[5] or even delivery of an
absolute conveyance,[6] will generally terminate ownership, but an
agreement to sell on improbative missives has been held not to
divest the seller.[7] A bondholder is, it is thought, an owner of
heritable property within the meaning of the section.[8] From
the wording used it is thought that the intention is that ownership as a trustee should be sufficient to give jurisdiction against
the owner as an individual,[9] but such a question is unlikely to
arise as the action must relate to the property owned by the trust.

[1] Thorburn v. Dempster, 1900, 2 F. 583.
[2] Smith v. Stuart, 1894, 22 R, 130.
[3] Gemmell v. Emery, (O.H.) 1905, 13 S.L.T. 490; cf. Smith v. Stuart,
    supra.
[4] Hastie v. Steel, 1886, 13 R. 843.
[5] Buchan v. Grimaldi, 1905, 7 F. 917.
[6] Bowman v. Wright, 1877, 4 R. 322.
[7] Dowie & Co. v. Tennant, 1891, 18 R. 986.
[8] Ashburton v. Escombe, 1892, 20 R. 187; Love v. Love, 1907 S.C. 728.
[9] Cf. Mackenzie v. Drummond's Executors, 1868, 6 M. 932; Smith v.
    Stuart, supra.

In connexion with the division of commonties it is provided
that the Act of 1695 concerning that matter is to be read and
construed as if it conferred jurisdiction upon the Sheriff Court
in the same manner as upon the Court of Session.[1] Actions
regarding servitudes, nuisance and the like will normally fall
under sec. 6 (d) or (e), but it is thought that the Sheriff still
has jurisdiction in such cases irrespective of the Act where the
property in question is within the jurisdiction.[2]

[1] 7 Edw. VII c. 51, sec. 5 (3).
[2] Culross Special Water District Committee v. Smith-Sligo's Trustees,
    1891, 19 R. 58.

Certain provisions of the Sheriff Courts Act, 1907, and relative
Rules of Procedure are, so far as appropriate, made applicable
to the Small Debt Court.[1] There, as in the Ordinary Court,
for instance, tenant includes sub-tenant, and there also an action,
if it is in its nature competent, lies against a defender who is
owner, or part owner, or tenant, or joint tenant, whether individually or as a trustee of heritable property within the jurisdiction,
provided the action relates to such property or to his interest
therein.[2] But the express enactment, which includes questions
relating to heritable right or title within the jurisdiction of the
Sheriff Court, and the direction that such actions must be raised

in the district Court where the property lies, are not amongst those which are made applicable, and they are not appropriate to the Small Debt Court.[3] The Small Debt Court jurisdiction, therefore, as regards the kind of action there competent, is not affected by the Sheriff Courts Act, 1907, but in the case of actions which relate to heritable property, the jurisdiction over defenders is somewhat widened. The Small Debt Statutes contain within themselves a process code for sequestration for rent, for an amount within the Small Debt limit.[4]

[1] 7 Edw. VII c. 51, sec. 45.
[2] Ibid., sec. 6 (d).
[3] Ibid., sec. 5.
[4] 7 Will. IV & 1 Vict. c. 41, secs. 1-5, 20. See p. 482, infra.

In the Small Debt Court a claim relating to heritable property —apart from sequestrations for rent and ejections—is only competent if it can be stated as a debt or demand,[1] and it must follow the procedure of the Small Debt Acts. An action of damages may be brought against a person having an interest in heritable property, individually or as a trustee, or as part owner, or joint or sub-tenant; but that is not normally an action relating to heritable right or title which, under the Sheriff Courts Act, 1907, requires to be raised in the Sheriffdom or district where the property lies,[2] nor will it usually be one relating to the property in the sense we are now considering.[3] Under the Small Debt Act of 1837[4] an action is directed to be brought in the Court within the jurisdiction of which the defender shall reside, or to the jurisdiction of which he shall be amenable. The defender in such an action, therefore, may be sued in the Court of his residence, although the property lies elsewhere. If, however, he has no residence within the jurisdiction, then in the Small Debt Court, as in the ordinary Court, he may be amenable to the jurisdiction *ratione rei sitæ*, provided the action is one which relates to the property.[3]

[1] 7 Will. IV & 1 Vict. c. 41, sec. 2.
[2] 7 Edw. VII c. 51, sec. 5.
[3] Brady v. Miller's Properties. 1935. 51 Sh.Ct.Rep. 183.
[4] 7 Will. IV & 1 Vict. c. 41. sec. 26.

Jurisdiction *ratione rei sitæ* is not limited to actions relating to heritable property, and by Statute actions of furthcoming or multiplepoinding may be brought either in the Court within the jurisdiction of which the fund or subject *in medio* is situated, or in the Court to the jurisdiction of which the arrestee or holder of the fund is subject.[1] But the situation of moveable property at common law has always ruled the jurisdiction in any action in which it was necessary to deal with the actual property itself. That jurisdiction is over the property, not over the defender, the cases in which it is most commonly exercised being maritime subjects which it is desired to safeguard, perishable goods within the Sheriffdom, and which it is in the interest of all concerned to have converted into cash,[2] or goods or livestock, the ownership of which is in dispute,[3] or goods unclaimed held by a custodier for behoof of whom it may concern and lying within the Sheriffdom. On the same ground the Sheriff Court deals with claims arising directly out of the administration of a trust within its jurisdiction[4] and can decide the right to a lair in a cemetery within its territory.[5] And the same principle has been applied to interdicts of the sale of poinded goods[6] which would not fall under sec. 6 (e).

[1] 7 Edw. VII c. 51, sec. 6 (g).
[2] Bannatyne v. Newendorff, 1841, 3 D. 429.
[3] Scottish Central Railway Co. v. Ferguson, 1863, 1 M. 750; Pender v. Lamont, 1917, 33 Sh.Ct.Rep. 310; Muir v. Matassa, 1935, 51 Sh.Ct.Rep. 251. See also White v. Magistrates of Dundee, 1915 S.C. 395.
[4] Thomson v. Wilson's Trustees, 1895, 22 R. 866; cf. Cathcart, &c. v. Scott, &c., 1908, 25 Sh.Ct.Rep. 16.
[5] Service v. Blues, 1891, 7 Sh.Ct.Rep. 303.
[6] Taylors v. Hepper & Co., 1905, 21 Sh.Ct.Rep. 93; Urquhart & Son v. Wood, 1906, 22 Sh.Ct.Rep. 255.

9. RATIONE CONTRACTUS.

A person not otherwise subject to the jurisdiction of a Sheriff Court may become so *ratione contractus*. The original theory of this jurisdiction, as developed at common law in the Supreme Court, was that a foreigner who had made a contract, soluble within Scotland, presumably agreed with the other contracting party that legal questions relating to that contract should be determined within Scotland according to Scots law. An action for this purpose lay in the Court of Session, if the foreigner was personally cited within Scotland.[1]

[1] Erskine I, 2, 20; Sinclair v. Smith, 1860, 22 D. 1475.

The Sheriff Court also exercised this jurisdiction in order to enforce a contract to be performed within the Sheriffdom, if the defender had been personally cited within that Sheriffdom, although the contract itself had been made elsewhere.[1] But in an action of damages for non-fulfilment of a contract (not for its enforcement) it was doubtful whether the Sheriff of the county where the contract was made, but within which the defender had no residence, had jurisdiction.[2]

[1] Pirie v. Warden, 1867, 5 M. 497.
[2] Logan v. Thomson, 1859, 31 Scot. Jur. 174.

The definition of jurisdiction *ratione contractus* in the Sheriff Courts Act, 1907, takes no account of where the contract was made and the Sheriff can entertain any action (of a class competent in the Sheriff Courts) which relates to a contract, the place of execution or performance of which is within the jurisdiction if the defender is personally cited there.[1] Personal citation within the Sheriffdom is essential; postal citation is not enough.[2] Jurisdiction is conferred in respect of any action which relates to the contract, which seems to include an action to declare its meaning, or for its enforcement, or for damages for its non-fulfilment.[3] In effect this assimilates the Sheriff Court jurisdiction *ratione contractus* to that of the Court of Session, except that, for the Court of Session, citation of the defender within Scotland is sufficient, but for the Sheriff Court the defender must be personally cited within the Sheriffdom.

[1] 7 Edw. VII c. 51, sec. 6 (f).
[2] Bird v. Brown, 1887, 25 S.L.R. 1; Davidson v. Gourlay, 1906, 22 Sh.Ct.Rep. 242; Kerr v. R. & W. Ferguson, 1931 S.C. 736.
[3] Sinclair v. Smith, 1860, 22 D. 1475; Robertson v. Neely, 1895, 12 Sh.Ct.Rep. 182; Goodall v. Robb, 1901, 17 Sh.Ct.Rep. 162; cf. Johnston v. Strachan, 1861, 23 D. 758.

The wide inclusion of all actions relating to the contract might be construed as covering actions by parties other than the contracting parties as, for instance, actions of damages or interdicts by a third party in respect of operations arising out of the contract. These might fall under one of the other grounds of jurisdiction, but it is thought that this statutory provision was intended to read, and can only reasonably be read, as applying to questions between the contracting parties themselves, arising out of their contract.

10. PROROGATION.

A person not subject to the jurisdiction of the Sheriff Court may elect to make himself subject to it, by prorogating jurisdiction.[1] But he cannot thereby make competent in the Sheriff Court any action which is otherwise incompetent, for prorogating jurisdiction only means waiving a litigant's personal right to object to being sued in that Court. It does not remedy or remove a radical incompetency.[2] If the action is not competent in the Sheriff Court, then the Sheriff cannot entertain it, however willing both parties may be to waive all objections and prorogate jurisdiction.

1 7 Edw. VII c. 51, sec. 6 (j); but cf. M'Cord v. M'Cord, 1946 S.C. 198, at p. 201.
2 Ringer v. Churchill, 1840, 2 D. 307.

There is no prescribed form for a defender prorogating jurisdiction. It may be done antecedently by agreement contained in a contract or document dealing also with other matters,[1] but it must be clearly expressed.[2] It seems doubtful whether the submission to the jurisdiction contained in bonds of caution for executors dative is sufficient to prorogate jurisdiction.[3] Agreements to prorogate jurisdiction in a Sheriff Court are void if contained in or relating to certain contracts of sale or hire.[4] In the process prorogation may be evidenced by a formal minute, or by an endorsement on the initial writ signed by defender or his solicitor, and if service is accepted it may be combined with the acceptance of service.

1 Elderslie Steamship Co. v. Burrell & Son, 1895, 22 R. 389; Lawrence v. Taylor, (O.H.) 1934 S.L.T. 76.
2 Styring v. Mayor of Oporovec, (O.H.) 1931 S.L.T. 493.
3 Kyd v. Readdie, 1902, 19 Sh.Ct.Rep. 88; cf. Kirkwood, &c. v. Kirkwood, &c., 1889, 6 Sh.Ct.Rep. 43.
4 Law Reform (Miscellaneous Provisions) (Scotland) Act, 1940 (3 & 4 Geo. VI c. 42), sec. 4. See p. 479, infra.

A defender who might challenge the jurisdiction and does not do so, but defends an action on the merits, will normally be held to have prorogated the jurisdiction,[1] but it is not too late to add a plea of no jurisdiction at adjustment.[2] A party outside the action originally may also prorogate the jurisdiction by having himself sisted as a party to the cause.[3] Prorogation of the jurisdiction by one of several defenders is not sufficient to subject the other defenders to the jurisdiction also under sec. 6 (a) of the Act.[4] The effect of prorogating jurisdiction is to put the defender in every respect in the same position as if he had been in fact subject to the jurisdiction upon one of the other qualifying grounds. Statutory provision is made in regard to prorogation resulting from a convention with a foreign state.[5]

1 White v. Spottiswood, 1846, 8 D. 952; Longmuir v. Longmuir, 1850, 12 D. 926; Dundee, &c. Investment Co. v. Macdonald, 1884, 11 R. 537; Assets Co. v. Falla's Trustees, 1894, 22 R. 178; cf. Mitchell v. Stewart, (O.H.) 1907, 14 S.L.T. 685.
2 Fraser-Johnston Engineering Co. v. Jeffs, 1920 S.C. 222; cf. Kirkwood, &c. v. Kirkwood, &c., 1889, 6 Sh.Ct.Rep. 43.
3 Gill v. Cutler, 1895, 23 R. 371.
4 Graham v. Young, &c., 1926, 43 Sh.Ct.Rep. 3; 7 Edw. VII c. 51, sec. 6 (a).
5 3 & 4 Geo. VI c. 42, sec. 7.

CHAPTER IV.

THE LITIGANTS.

1. GENERAL.

The Sheriff Court may in general entertain an action at the instance of any person, a Scotsman or a foreigner, against a defender who is, upon one or other of the grounds just discussed, liable to the jurisdiction of that Sheriffdom. There are, however, some personal disabilities which may, either absolutely or conditionally, prevent persons suing, or prevent their being sued, even where the Court has normally jurisdiction.

2. OUTLAW.

No person who has been placed beyond the pale of the law can either sue or defend an action in any civil Court. A person under sentence of death, and who is thus civilly dead, can neither be a pursuer nor a defender. Neither can a person who has been outlawed,[1] unless and until he be reponed.

[1] Erskine II, 5, 60. See also Macrae v. Hyndman, 1836, 15 S. 54; 1839, 1 Macl. & R. 645.

3. CONVICT.

A person who has been sentenced to penal servitude and removed to a convict prison, even for a lengthened period, has, nevertheless, a title to sue, and may be sued; but whether he should be sued in the jurisdiction of his ordinary residence, or that of the prison, depends upon the circumstances. The provision of the Sheriff Courts Act,[1] continuing the jurisdiction arising from residence for a period of forty days after a person has left it, will not usually apply to the case of a convict, because his residence in Scotland is known. But a convict does not necessarily lose his domicile of citation merely because he is temporarily removed from his place of residence to a prison, if the place of residence still remains his home, to which he probably will return.[2] In such a case it is thought that he may still be sued in the Sheriff Court of his residence, and cited at his residence in the ordinary way, although, if the fact that the defender is in prison is brought to the knowledge of the Court, the pursuer would probably be ordered,

78

in addition to such citation, to serve on or notify the defender at the prison. If a defender might be prejudiced in conducting a defence by his being in prison, the Court might sist the action till his release, unless the matter were urgent. Where the convict had no home when arrested, or his family home had been broken up after his conviction, it is thought that a convict should be sued in the Sheriffdom where his prison is situated as that is *de facto* his residence.

1 7 Edw. VII c. 51, sec. 6 (a).
2 Martin v. Szyszka, 1943 S.C. 203, Lord Justice-Clerk Cooper, pp. 207-8.

4. BANKRUPT.

A person may, by operation of law, be deprived of his legal status, and so disentitled to sue or defend an action. Thus, after sequestration in bankruptcy, claims by the estate are enforced at the instance of the trustee, not of the bankrupt; and claims by creditors are established in the manner prescribed by the bankruptcy Statutes, not by action against the bankrupt. But an action pending at the date of the bankruptcy may be continued in name of the bankrupt if, after being afforded an opportunity of sisting himself, the trustee declines to do so,[1] or an action may be raised by a bankrupt in special circumstances, though in either case the Court may require the bankrupt to find caution for expenses. Generally the bankrupt will be allowed to sue a claim abandoned by the trustee,[2] but he cannot sue for a debt falling under the sequestration.[3] He may be permitted to take action to impugn a settlement made by the trustee,[4] and generally he has been allowed to sue for behoof of the estate, although not reinvested, if the trustee has been discharged.[5] In addition to such cases, which depend on the bankrupt's radical right in the estate, he can sue actions of a personal nature, such as declarator of marriage or breach of promise of marriage, though the result may affect the estate.[6] He may also sue for injury to his own character.[7]

1 See Fleming v. Walker's Trustees, 1876, 4 R. 112, and cases there cited.
2 Fleming v. Walker's Trustees, supra; cf. Douglas v. Maclachlan, 1881, 8 R. 470; Macdonald v. Mackintosh, 1905, 7 F. 771.
3 Graham v. Mackenzie, 1871, 9 M. 798.
4 Clarke v. Cumming, 1891, 28 S.L.R. 343.
5 Whyte v. Murray, 1888, 16 R. 95; Geddes v. Quistorp, 1889, 17 R. 278; cf. Whyte v. Forbes, 1890, 17 R. 895.
6 See Goudy, Bankruptcy, 4th edn., 365-6; Greenhill v. Ford, 1822, 1 S. 296; Beckham v. Drake, 1849, 2 H. of L. Ca. 579; Borthwick v. Borthwick, 1896, 24 R. 211.
7 See Thom v. Bridges, 1857, 19 D. 721, Lord Justice-Clerk Hope, p. 723; Jackson v. M'Kechnie, 1875, 3 R. 130.

A trustee in bankruptcy, who sists himself in an action initiated by the bankrupt, must accept liability if unsuccessful for the expenses of the litigation from its initiation.[1] If a counter-claim larger than that sued for has been stated by way of defence, the trustee accepts the risk of its being established, in which case, if the defender gets decree for the difference, he will rank as a creditor therefor. A trustee may be found liable in expenses personally, or as an individual, but it is thought that this is not necessary and that he is, in any event, liable as an individual to the successful party.[2]

[1] Torbet v. Borthwick, 1849, 11 D. 694.
[2] Kilmarnock Theatre Co. v. Buchanan, 1911 S.C. 607; Mulholland v. Macfarlane's Trustees, 1928 S.L.T. 251; cf. Craig v. Hogg, 1896, 24 R. 6; Barrie v. Barrie's Trustees, 1933 S.C. 132.

The rules governing the finding of caution for expenses in the case of bankrupt and impecunious litigants are considered in detail later.[1]

[1] See p. 311, infra.

5. MARRIED WOMAN.

By the Married Women's Property (Scotland) Act, 1920, the husband's right of administration is wholly abolished, and a married woman is now capable of suing and being sued as if she were not married.[1] Her husband, if major and *capax*, is her curator only if she is a minor and till she comes of age.[1] If, in such a case, the husband is also a minor or *incapax* the wife's father or other curator continues to act till she comes of age, or till her husband's curatory begins.[1] As a result of the Act a husband can no longer appear in Court for his wife as a party litigant.[2] A wife may now sue her husband on contract[3] but not on delict.[4]

[1] 10 & 11 Geo. V c. 64, secs. 1, 2, 3.
[2] Gordon v. Nakeski-Cumming, 1924 S.C. 939.
[3] Raitt v. Raitt, 1922, 39 Sh.Ct.Rep. 133; Millar v. Millar, 1940 S.C. 56 (ejection from house).
[4] Harper v. Harper, 1929 S.C. 220; cf. Bruce v. Murray, (O.H.) 1926 S.L.T. 236; Cameron v. Glasgow Corporation, 1936 S.C. (H.L.) 26.

6. PUPIL AND MINOR.

Pupils cannot in general sue alone. An action in the interest of a pupil is sued in name of his father as tutor and administrator-in-law if alive, or his mother if the father is dead, or his tutors if he have any. Failing tutors, the action is brought in the pupil's name, and the Court will appoint a tutor *ad litem*.[1] If the father is alive and *capax* and has no adverse interest an action at the instance of the pupil alone is incompetent,[2] and the Court will not normally appoint a tutor *ad litem* in such a case.[3] If the father is insane the action would probably be brought in name of the pupil alone.[4] Similarly, a pupil cannot be sued without calling his father or other tutors, and, if there are none, the Court will appoint a tutor *ad litem*. Such an appointment is competent though no appearance has been made for the pupil.[5]

[1] Ward v. Walker, 1920 S.C. 80.
[2] Carrigan v. Cleland, (O.H.) 1907, 15 S.L.T. 543.
[3] Lowther v. Chien, 1935, 52 Sh.Ct.Rep. 197.
[4] See M'Rae v. Glasgow Corporation, (O.H.) 1915, 2 S.L.T. 94. See also M'Donald v. Glasgow Corporation, (O.H.) 1915, 2 S.L.T. 249.
[5] Drummond's Trustees v. Peel's Trustees, 1929 S.C. 484.

An action by a minor above the age of puberty is sued in name of the minor, with concurrence of his curator at law. If there be none, the Court will, if necessary, appoint a curator *ad litem*. In like manner a minor may be sued in his own name, but his curators should be called. If he have none, the Court will appoint a curator *ad litem*.[1]

[1] Cunningham v. Smith, 1880, 7 R. 424; M'Dowall, &c. v. Carson, 1907, 24 Sh.Ct.Rep. 72.

When the appointment of a tutor or curator *ad litem* is necessary, the Court may appoint one, although neither party move for it. He is appointed only for a particular process, not to act generally. He is not required to find caution, and, unless in special circumstances, he is not personally liable for expenses.[1] A tutor *ad litem* appointed to a pupil has power to compromise,[2] but a curator *ad litem* to a minor has not.[3] A tutor or curator *ad litem* cannot validly continue to act if his ward becomes insane.[4] The remuneration and expenses of a curator *ad litem* are part of the ordinary expenses of process and are recoverable from a defender following the acceptance of a tender.[5]

[1] Fraser v. Pattie, 1847, 9 D. 903.
[2] Dewar v. Dewar's Trustees, (O.H.) 1906, 14 S.L.T. 238.
[3] Stephenson v. Lorimer, 1844, 6 D. 377.
[4] Moodie v. Dempster, 1931 S.C. 553.
[5] Campbell v. Alexander & Sons, (O.H.) 1934 S.L.T. 52.

A minor is not to be forced into litigation merely by the other parties procuring the appointment of a curator *ad litem*, and it does not appear to be competent to appoint a curator *ad litem*

to a minor who has not appeared in an action, or who does not
desire to litigate.[1]

[1] Mackenzie's Trustees v. Mackenzie, 1908 S.C. 995; cf. Drummond's
    Trustees v. Peel's Trustees, 1929 S.C. 484, in the case of a pupil.

Service in ordinary form on a minor and on his father as
curator at law, or upon a minor and his tutors and curators if
known to pursuer, or if unknown, on the minor himself in ordinary
form and upon his tutors and curators edictally, is declared to
be good and sufficient service on the minor for every purpose of
law.[1]

[1] 7 Edw. VII c. 51, Schedule I, Rule 14.

If a defender pleads that he is a minor, the action is not dismissed, but is intimated to the defender's father or curator. If
he decline to sist himself, the Court may appoint a curator *ad
litem*.[1] Formerly, it was necessary to bring a supplementary
action against the curator, but, as the addition of parties is
amongst the amendments sanctioned by the Sheriff Courts Act,
a curator desiring to sist himself may by order of Court be included
in the instance.[2]

[1] M'Conochie v. Binnie, 1847, 9 D. 791; Cunningham v. Smith, 1880, 7 R.
    424.
[2] 7 Edw. VII c. 51, Schedule I, Rule 79.

Where in an action of damages by or for behoof of a person
under legal disability, arising either out of injury sustained by
such person, or out of the death of some other person in respect
of whose death the person under legal disability is entitled to
damages, a sum of money becomes payable to such person, such
sum, unless otherwise ordered, is to be paid into Court, and to
be invested, applied or otherwise dealt with and administered
by the Court in such manner as the Court in its discretion thinks
fit for the benefit of the person entitled thereo, and the receipt
of the Sheriff-clerk is to be a sufficient discharge in respect of
the amount paid in.[1] The Sheriff-clerk of any Sheriff Court is
also authorized, at the request of any competent Court within the
British Dominions, to accept custody of any sum of money paid
into such Court in any action of damages by or for behoof of
a person under legal disability, provided always that such person
is then resident within the jurisdiction of such Sheriff Court, and
such sum is to be invested or otherwise dealt with as in the above
provisions.[1] Where any money is paid into Court as above it
is thereafter to be paid out by the Sheriff-clerk, or otherwise
applied for the benefit of the person entitled thereto, after such

intimation and service and such inquiry as the Sheriff may direct.[1]
All applications under these provisions are to be by minute by
or on behalf of the person entitled to the payment.[1] Provision
is also made for the manner of investing such payments, and for
the Sheriff-clerk issuing receipts, and advising the King's and Lord
Treasurer's Remembrancer.[2] The provisions, it will be noted,
apply only in cases of damages arising out of injury or death.
Probably this would cover damages for slander.

[1] Act of Sederunt, 16th July, 1936 (adding, inter alia, Rule 172 to the
  Act).
[2] Act of Sederunt of 10th February, 1939 (amending Rule 172).

7. INSANE PERSON.

An insane person cannot sue an action in his own name, or
even with a curator *ad litem*. If it is necessary to raise an action
for him, a *curator bonis* sues in his official capacity. Such a
curator is appointed by the Court of Session, or, if the yearly
value of the insane person's estate does not exceed £100, he may
be appointed by the Sheriff.[1] Damages recovered for an insane
person would fall under the provisions detailed above, but the
Court would in that case presumably order them to be paid to
the *curator bonis* as pursuer.

[1] 43 & 44 Vict. c. 4. See p. 604, infra.

If, in the course of a process, a defender becomes insane, the
proper course is that the process be sisted till a *curator bonis* has
been appointed.[1] There is authority for the appointment of a
curator *ad litem* to an insane defender who has not appeared.[2]
But the propriety of this has been doubted and the matter may
require to be reconsidered.[3] Where in a pending process the
defender alleged that the pursuer was insane, a preliminary proof
on this point was, in somewhat special circumstances, allowed.[4]

[1] Anderson's Trustees v. Skinner, 1871, 8 S.L.R. 325; Moodie v. Dempster,
  1931 S.C. 553; cf. Davidson v. Scott's Shipbuilding, &c., Co., 1926
  S.C. 970.
[2] Rossie v. Rossie, (O.H.) 1899, 6 S.L.T. 357; Scott v. Scott, 1908 S.C.
  1124.
[3] Macdonald's Trustee v. Medhurst, 1915 S.C. 879; Drummond's Trustees
  v. Peel's Trustees, 1929 S.C. 484; Moodie v. Dempster, supra.
[4] A B v. C D, 1937 S.C. 408, 3696.

8. DEAF AND DUMB PERSONS.

The incapacity of those who are deaf and dumb does not affect
their legal rights and privileges, and they are entitled to sue and
may be sued in normal fashion. Appointment of a curator *ad*

litem is not necessary. Proceedings in which they take part personally are conducted through an interpreter.

9. ASSIGNEE.

The holder of a special assignation may sue for the assigned claim in his own name as assignee, setting forth his title in the initial writ. If the claim is competently assigned the defender cannot object to answer the assignee, but he is entitled to be satisfied as to his title to sue. If the assignee's title expressly authorizes the claim to be sued for in the cedent's name, the action may be so brought, but the assignee as the true *dominus litis* may be required to sist himself, as the defender is entitled to have him made a party to the action.[1] When the pursuer has no title to sue at the date of raising of the action a later assignation will not cure the defect.[2]

[1] Fraser v. Dunbar, 1839, 1 D. 882; cf. Waddel v. Hope, 1843, 6 D. 160.
[2] Symington v. Campbell, 1894, 21 R. 434; cf. Middle Ward District Committee of Lanarkshire County Council v. Marshall, 1896, 24 R. 139; Doughty Shipping Co. v. North British Railway Co., (O.H.) 1909, 1 S.L.T. 267; Westville Shipping Co. v. Abram Steamship Co., 1923 S.C. (H.L.) 68.

When, in the course of a litigation, the interest is transferred, either by direct assignment or by operation of law—as, for instance, to executors in the case of a litigant's death, or to a trustee in the case of his bankruptcy, the party to whom the interest has passed may claim to be sisted,[1] or the other parties may require him to sist himself. This may be done even after judgment has been pronounced.[2] But a representative who has no interest in the merits of a case will not be allowed to proceed with it merely to recover expenses.[3] An executor has no title to institute an action of damages for personal injuries sustained by the deceased though he may take up and insist in an action raised by the deceased before his death.[4]

[1] Mavor v. Aberdeen Educational Trust, (O.H.) 1902, 10 S.L.T. 156; Martin's Executor v. M'Ghee, 1914 S.C. 628.
[2] Scott v. Mill's Trustees, 1923 S.C. 726; Cumming v. Stewart, 1928 S.C. 709.
[3] Martin's Executor v. M'Ghee, supra.
[4] Stewart v. London, Midland & Scottish Railway Co., 1943 S.C. (H.L.) 19.

10. CAUTIONER.

Formerly a cautioner could not be sued till the principal debtor had first been discussed. But the Mercantile Law Amendment Act of 1856 made it competent to sue both or either of the

principal debtor and the cautioner.[1] The more common practice
is to sue both jointly and severally, unless the cautioner has made
it an express contract condition that creditors shall first discuss
the principal debtor.

[1] 19 & 20 Vict. c. 60, sec. 8; Morrison v. Harkness, 1870, 9 M. 35.

As a cautioner has relief against the principal debtor and his
co-cautioners, any one cautioner may sue for relief against the
principal debtor, if he is being sued for payment by the creditor,
and may proceed against his co-cautioners if he has paid more
than his own share of the cautionary obligation.[1] A cautioner
who pays the creditor is entitled to an assignation of the debt
and diligence, so that he may come in place of the creditor. But
the cautioner's title to sue is not based upon his being an assignee,
and he has a cause of action against the debtor or his co-cautioners
on account of the fact that he has been called upon to pay the
full debt, or has paid it, whether he has taken a formal assignation or not.[2]

[1] Erskine III, 3, 65; Bell's Principles, 255.
[2] Low v. Farquharson, 1831, 9 S. 411; M'Kechnie v. M'Farlane, 1831,
    10 S. 126.

11. FIRM-NOMINATE.

A co-partnery, consisting of two or more disclosed persons
associated for business purposes, has always been regarded as a
separate *persona* in the eye of the law, and as such entitled to
sue, and liable to be sued, in any civil process in the firm-name.[1]

[1] Erskine III, 3, 18, 20; Bell's Principles, 357.

A decree against a firm warrants diligence against the partners,[1]
so that in an action for a firm's debt, brought while the firm
subsists, it is not necessary, although it is competent, to call
the individual partners. They are liable if the debt is constituted
against the firm, and in the general case they are liable as individuals, only when the debt has been constituted against the firm.
But there may be special circumstances which entitle a creditor
to ask decree against the individual partners, failing decree against
the firm, and in an action based on fraud the partners charged
with the fraud should be specified.[2] A firm may always sue
in the name of the whole partners.[3] When two of three partners
disclaimed a defence the remaining partner was held to have no
title to defend.[4]

[1] 53 & 54 Vict. c. 39, sec. 4 (2); 7 Edw. VII c. 51, Schedule I, Rule 11.
[2] Thomson & Co. v. Pattison Elder & Co., 1895, 22 R. 432.

³ Plotzker v. Lucas, 1907 S.C. 315.
⁴ Marquis of Breadalbane v. Toberonochy Slate Quarry Co., &c., 1916,
    33 Sh.Ct.Rep. 154.

After the dissolution of a firm, an action for a firm's debt
is directed against all or any of the individuals who were the
partners. They are designed as the partners of the now dissolved
firm. The fact and date of the dissolution of the firm should
be set forth in the initial writ. It is not in such a case necessary
to call the firm itself, but all the known partners who are within
the jurisdiction of the Courts of Scotland should be included in
the instance.¹ It may be competent for a dissolved firm to sue
in the firm-name,² but the usual practice is to sue in name of
the partners or surviving partners,³ and this is a good instance
though a partner has died after the dissolution.⁴

¹ Muir v. Collett, 1862, 24 D. 1119; M'Naught v. Milligan, 1885, 13 R.
    366.
² Brims & Mackay v. Pattullo, 1907 S.C. 1106.
³ Menzies, &c. v. M'Laren & Co., 1898, 15 Sh.Ct.Rep. 297.   See also
    John & Francis Anderson v. Balnagown Estates Co., 1939 S.C. 168.
⁴ Nicoll v. Reid, 1877, 5 R. 137.

Where default is made by a firm or person in registering
particulars under the Registration of Business Names Act the
rights of such defaulter, under contracts relating to the business
in connexion with which the default was made, are not enforceable by action.¹ On cause shown the Court of Session may grant
relief against the above disability,² and in any proceedings in
the Sheriff Court commenced by a defaulter to enforce a contract,
relief may be granted in that Court in respect of that particular
contract.³

¹ 6 & 7 Geo. V c. 58, secs. 1, 8.   See also Anderson v. Livingstone, 1932
    S.N. 82; John & Francis Anderson v. Balnagown Estates Co., 1939
    S.C. 168.
² Clydesdale Motor Transport Co., 1922 S.C. 18; J. J. & P. M'Lachlan,
    1929 S.C. 357; Wilson & Co. v. Whyte, 1929, 45 Sh.Ct.Rep. 97.
³ 6 & 7 Geo. V c. 58, secs. 8 (2), 23; Clydesdale Motor Transport Co.
    v. M'Cosh & Devine, 1921, 38 Sh.Ct.Rep. 109.

12. FIRM-DESCRIPTIVE.

Prior to 1907 a descriptive firm could not sue or be sued under
its firm-name. But the Sheriff Courts Act, 1907, made it competent to sue a descriptive firm; and the amending Act of 1913
made it competent for such a firm to sue.¹ Creditors are therefore
no longer hampered in pursuing such debtors, for a debtor's
business designation is now also his process designation, and a

firm may be sued and diligence done against it in its descriptive name alone without mentioning partners.

[1] 7 Edw. VII c. 51, sec. 3 (e), and Schedule I, Rules 11 and 151; 2 & 3 Geo. V c. 28, Schedule II.

The effect of this, however, is not to restrict the creditor's diligence to firm's assets, and a decree against a descriptive firm is a warrant for diligence, not only against that firm, but also against any persons who may be discovered to be partners in the concern using the descriptive name.[1] The effect of the Statute is simply to put a firm-nominate and a firm-descriptive on the same footing as regards actions and diligence. The provisions of the Registration of Business Names Act, 1916, are referred to above.[2]

[1] 53 & 54 Vict. c. 39, sec. 4 (2) ; 7 Edw. VII c. 51, Schedule I, Rule 11 ; 2 & 3 Geo. V c. 28, Schedule II ; Ewing & Co. v. M'Clelland, 1860, 22 D. 1347.
[2] See p. 86, supra.

13. CORPORATIONS, ASSOCIATIONS AND OTHER BODIES.

The Rules to the Sheriff Courts Act authorize any individual or individuals, or any corporation or association carrying on business under a firm, or trading, or descriptive name to sue or be sued in such name, without the addition of the name or names of the individual or individuals, or of any member or official of the corporation or association ; and an extract decree in such an action, or a decree of registration, is to be a warrant for diligence against the corporation, association or firm, and the individual or individuals.[1]

[1] 7 Edw. VII c. 51, Schedule I, Rule 11 ; 2 & 3 Geo. V c. 28, Schedule II.

Banking corporations could, under Statute, sue and be sued in name of one of their principal officials.[1] But this is now superseded by the above Rules of Court.

[1] 7 Geo. IV c. 67, sec. 1.

Formerly a voluntary society, consisting of a certain number of persons associated together for any purpose, was not, in its associated capacity, a *persona* in law capable of suing or being sued. The whole of the members required to be set forth in the instance.

This rule was attended with great inconvenience, and was relaxed in cases where the membership was very large, and the business of the association was entrusted to a properly constituted committee of management. The office-bearers of an association were also recognized by the Courts as being entitled, in their official character, to enforce contracts which had been expressly made with them in that character, and in like manner they were liable to be sued for implement of obligations officially undertaken by them as such office-bearers.[1]

[1] Somerville v. Rowbotham, 1862, 24 D. 1187; Renton Football Club v. M'Dowall, 1891, 18 R. 670; Pagan & Osborne v. Haig, 1910 S.C. 341.

The necessity for including either the whole members of a society, or the members of a committee, in the instance has now been abrogated in the case of an association carrying on business under a firm, or trading, or descriptive name.[1] When the association does not carry on business the broadening of the definition of " person " to include an association of any description and the definitions of " pursuer " and " defender " may be sufficient to justify the association suing, or being sued, in its own name alone.[2] If the constitution or rules of the association prescribe the manner in which the association may sue and be sued, the instance may be expressed as directed by the constitution.[3] If there is no specific direction, the association should sue, or may be sued, under the description by which it is commonly known. But a decree obtained against such an association is not a warrant for diligence against an official or member not called in the action.[4] For this reason it may be advisable, and it appears quite competent, to include as defenders any known officials, particularly if they have been contracting parties.[5]

[1] Cockburn Ex-Service Men's Club v. Thomson, 1924, 40 Sh.Ct.Rep. 176; Lanark United Football Club v. Bathgate Football Club, 1927, 43 Sh.Ct.Rep. 12.
[2] 7 Edw. VII c. 51, sec. 3 (e) (n) and (o). See also Greengairs Rovers Football Club, &c. v. Blades, &c., 1910, 26 Sh.Ct.Rep. 280; cf. Mid-Atholl Public Hall Committee, &c. v. Macdonald, &c., 1929, 45 Sh.Ct.Rep. 274.
[3] Whitecraigs Golf Club v. Ker, 1923 S.L.T. (Sh.Ct.) 23.
[4] Aitchison v. M'Donald, 1911 S.C. 174.
[5] Bryson & Co. v. Glasgow Civil Service, &c., Guild, 1915, 32 Sh.Ct.Rep. 23.

The Sheriff Courts Acts do not affect the statutory provision that certain actions against public bodies must be brought within six months of the cause of action arising,[1] nor do they abrogate other provisions regulating methods of suing particular bodies. Thus actions against the Crown or a public department are usually not laid against a minister or the department, but against the

Lord Advocate.[2] But certain departments sue and are sued in their own name: The Minister of Transport[3]; the Minister of Pensions[4]; and the General Board of Control for Scotland.[5] Certain Scottish departments have had their functions transferred to the Secretary of State for Scotland. These departments are the Scottish Education Department, the Department of Health for Scotland, the Department of Agriculture for Scotland, the Prisons Department for Scotland, and the Fishery Board for Scotland.[6] In the case of these departments the proper instance is the Secretary of State for Scotland.[6] A town council sues and is sued in its corporate name, "the Provost (or Lord Provost), Magistrates and Councillors" of the burgh, and if the burgh is the defender the action must be served upon the town-clerk.[7] Special statutory provision is made in connexion with actions by or against a friendly society.[8] A registered trade union may sue and be sued in name of its trustees or of any other officer authorized by its rules,[9] or in its own registered name.[10] In calling an official to account the action should be brought by the trustees.[11] An unregistered union would fall under the rule above stated as to associations.[12]

[1] 56 & 57 Vict. c. 61, secs. 1, 3.
[2] 20 & 21 Vict. c. 44.
[3] 9 & 10 Geo. V c. 50, sec. 26.
[4] 6 & 7 Geo. V c. 65, sec. 6.
[5] 3 & 4 Geo. V c. 38, sec. 19 (1).
[6] 2 & 3 Geo VI c. 20, sec. 1 (1) (8).
[7] 63 & 64 Vict. c. 49, sec. 9.
[8] 59 & 60 Vict. c. 25, secs. 68, 94; 8 Edw. VII c. 32, secs. 6, 11.
[9] 34 & 35 Vict. c. 31, sec. 9.
[10] Cameron v. Associated Society of Locomotive Engineers and Firemen, 1930, 46 Sh.Ct.Rep. 84; Berry v. Transport and General Workers' Union, (O.H.) 1933 S.N. 110.
[11] 34 & 35 Vict. c. 31, sec. 11.
[12] See p. 87, supra. See also Aberdeen, &c., Master Slaters' Association v. Dickie & Son, 1924, 41 Sh.Ct.Rep. 95.

Whilst it may not be essential, it may be thought desirable, to associate one or more individuals in the instance, especially in the case of an association which has no local habitation of its own.[1] The scheme of the Statute, however, appears to be that all kinds of associated bodies, including nominate firms with disclosed partners, shall be put upon the same footing as regards instance and jurisdiction. Citation in all such cases is to be made at the principal place of business (including the place of business or office of the clerk or secretary of any corporation or association) if it is within the jurisdiction of the Court where the action is brought; or, if not, at any place of business or office where such business is carried on within its jurisdiction.[2]

[1] Mid-Atholl Public Hall Committee, &c. v. Macdonald, &c., 1929, 45 Sh.Ct.Rep. 274.   See also Alyth Light Symphony Band, &c. v. Ross, 1929, 46 Sh.Ct.Rep. 62; Clan Lamont Society, &c. v. Lamont, 1939, 55 Sh.Ct.Rep. 155.
[2] 7 Edw. VII c. 51, Schedule I, Rule 11; 2 & 3 Geo. V c. 28, Schedule II.

There is no statutory definition of the term "place of business." In the common commercial case, it requires no definition, but when the clerk or secretary of an association is referred to as having a place of business within the jurisdiction there may be some dubiety as to the meaning. The secretary of an amateur dramatic club might not himself be a householder, and might be an employee in the warehouse of one having no connexion with the club. What the Rule contemplates, it is thought, is that, where there is no separate place set apart for conducting the business of the club, the place where the secretary in fact, does conduct that business becomes the club's place of business for citation purposes, whether that place be business premises or the secretary's dwelling-house, or apartments, and that the club, as an associated body, would be competently cited by service upon the secretary at that place.

Local authorities and other similar public bodies sue, and are sued, under their official descriptive name without the addition of the names of members or officials as, the County Council of the County of Lanark. Although it is not now necessary, it is thought to be still competent to call the members of such an authority or corporation, and if called only in their official capacity, a minority are bound by the majority as to defending, and cannot dissociate themselves by minute of disclaimer.[1]

[1] Eadie v. Glasgow Corporation, 1908 S.C. 207.

14. VEXATIOUS LITIGANT.

A person who may ostensibly have a title to sue, and a case to state, may be precluded from suing, if he has been declared a vexatious litigant. The victim of excessive litigiosity may complain to the Lord Advocate, who may obtain from the Court of Session an order that no legal proceedings shall be instituted by the person complained of in the Court of Session or any other Court, unless leave has been obtained from the Court of Session on their being satisfied that the proposed proceeding is not vexatious. Such an order is granted if the Court of Session is satisfied "that any person has habitually and persistently instituted vexatious legal proceedings, without any reasonable ground for instituting such proceedings, whether in the Court of Session or in any inferior Court, and whether against the same person or against different persons."[1] There does not appear to be any reported case in which such an order has been granted.

[1] 61 & 62 Vict. c. 35.

15. MANDATORY.

The general rule is that no one is bound to litigate in Scotland with a person who is not subject to the jurisdiction of the Scottish Courts, for every litigant is entitled to have some one responsible to the Court for the conduct of the case, and responsible to him for expenses, should he ultimately succeed.[1] Accordingly, either a pursuer or a defender may be asked to sist a mandatory but the granting of such a motion is within the discretion of the Court.[2] A motion to order a party to sist a mandatory may be made at any stage of a cause, but it should be made so soon as the circumstances emerge which render a mandatory necessary, because the objection to a party litigating without a mandatory may be waived by implication, as well as expressly, and the Court may be disinclined to grant a motion which has been too long delayed.[3]

[1] See Lawson's Trustees v. British Linen Co., 1874, 1 R. 1065.
[2] Gordon's Trustees v. Forbes, 1904, 6 F. 455.
[3] See M'Crae v. Bryson, 1922 S.L.T. 664 (caution for expenses).

In the normal case a pursuer resident outwith Scotland will require to sist a mandatory, even though he is of Scottish domicile.[1] In view of the Judgments Extension Acts,[2] this rule does not apply to residents in England or Northern Ireland,[3] unless in special circumstances.[4] But residents in the Irish Free State fall under the general rule.[5] The rule may be relaxed in special cases, as where only one out of several pursuers is abroad,[6] where pursuer is abroad on foreign service,[7] or where he holds a judgment and is respondent in an appeal for the defender,[8] and where the pursuer has a *prima facie* case.[9] The rule is less strictly applied in consistorial causes,[10] and where the pursuer has heritage in Scotland which is not affected by the action.[11] A foreigner coming to reside in Scotland will not in general have to sist a mandatory.[12]

[1] Railton v. Mathews, 1844, 6 D. 1348; Bruce v. Smith, (O.H.) 1865, 1 S.L.R. 53.
[2] 31 & 32 Vict. c. 54; 45 & 46 Vict. c. 31.
[3] Lawson's Trustees v. British Linen Co., 1874, 1 R 1065; Dessau v. Daish, 1897, 24 R. 976; Hudson v. Innes & Grieve, 1907, 24 Sh.Ct.Rep. 190; M'Gildowney v. Hart, 1911, 27 Sh.Ct.Rep. 37.
[4] Lawson v. Young, 1891, 7 Sh.Ct.Rep. 319.
[5] Calton v. Calder & Co., 1928, 44 Sh.Ct.Rep. 206. See also Cooney v. Dunne, (O.H.) 1925 S.L.T. 22.

6 Gale v. Bennett, 1857, 19 D. 665 (consenting husband); Antermony Coal Co. v. Wingate & Co., 1866, 4 M. 544; Robb's Trustees v. Hutton, 1866, 4 M. 546; Armour v. Glasgow Royal Infirmary, (O.H.) 1908, 16 S.L.T. 435.

7 Graham v. Graham's Trustees, 1901, 4 F. 1.

8 Aitkenhead v. Bunten & Co., 1892, 19 R. 803. See also Seaman v. Butters, (O.H.) 1911, 2 S.L.T. 198 (complainer in suspension).

9 M'Lean v. M'Garvey, (O.H.) 1908, 16 S.L.T. 174.

10 Campbell v. Campbell, 1855, 17 D. 514; Low v. Low, (O.H.) 1905, 12 S.L.T. 817; Scott v. Scott, 1924 S.C. 843.

11 Caledonian, &c., Railway Co. v. Turner, 1849, 12 D. 406; Lawson's Trustees v. British Linen Co., supra.

12 Faulks v. Whitehead, 1854, 16 D. 718; Withers v. Lattimore, 1921, 37 Sh.Ct.Rep. 147; cf. Nero v. Gunn & Cameron, 1886, 2 Sh.Ct.Rep. 342; Dickey v. British Mexican Railway Co., (O.H.) 1893, 1 S.L.T. 273.

As a general rule a claimant in a multiplepoinding, who is resident abroad, will not be required to sist a mandatory.[1] But a mandatory has been required from a claimant in a Scottish sequestration,[2] from an objector to the accounts of a judicial factor who had reclaimed against an interlocutor repelling his objections,[3] and from claimants in a liquidation who were contesting the liquidator's deliverance.[4]

1 Buik v. Patullo, 1855, 17 D. 568; North British Railway Co. v. White, &c., 1881, 9 R. 97; Stow's Trustees v. Silvester, (O.H.) 1900, 8 S.L.T. 253; Town and County Bank v. Lilienfield, (O.H.) 1900, 8 S.L.T. 227; Gordon's Trustees v. Forbes, 1904, 6 F. 455; Elmslie v. Pauline, 1905, 7 F. 541.

2 Ford v. King, 1844, 6 D. 1163.

3 Lowson v. Lowson, 1902, 4 F. 692.

4 Liquidators of Bruce Peebles & Co. v. Stern & Watt, (O.H.) 1909, 47 S.L.R. 77.

In the case of a defender the rule in regard to sisting a mandatory is rather less strictly applied,[1] and the grounds on which the rule may be relaxed, as stated above, are equally applicable. But in several cases a defender who has gone abroad after the action was raised has been ordered to sist a mandatory,[2] and it is thought that any suspicion that the defender had left the country with a view to evading a decree against him would have that result. Where a defender had heritage in Scotland, but the property was the subject of the litigation, a mandatory was ordered.[3] A defending husband in an action of divorce has been required to sist a mandatory,[4] but where the jurisdiction of the Courts here was doubtful the motion for a mandatory was refused.[5]

1 Simla Bank v. Home, 1870, 8 M. 781; M'Donald's Trustees v. Stewart, 1891, 18 R. 491; Morton v. Smith, (O.H.) 1902, 9 S.L.T. 396; Florence v. Smith, 1913 S.C. 393.

[2] Young v. Carter, (O.H.) 1907, 14 S.L.T. 829; Dampskibsselskabet Neptune v. Blasquez, (O.H.) 1908, 15 S.L.T. 1046; Bank of Scotland v. Rorie, (O.H.) 1908, 16 S.L.T. 130; Holmes v. M'Murrich, 1920 S.C. 631; Irvine v. Reid, 1921, 37 Sh.Ct.Rep. 108.
[3] Sandilands v. Sandilands, 1848, 10 D. 1091; Morton v. Smith, supra.
[4] Tingman v. Tingman, 1854, 17 D. 122.
[5] D'Ernesti v. D'Ernesti, 1882, 9 R. 655; Taylor v. Taylor, (O.H.) 1919, 1 S.L.T. 169.

The mandatory must be an independent party—not a co-litigant with the absent person[1]—and he must be solvent and in the same rank of life as the principal.[2] He must be resident in Scotland or in England or Northern Ireland.[3] The mandatory must accept the position unconditionally and he becomes liable for all expenses, past as well as future,[4] his liability being joint and several with the principal. But a mandatory for a litigant on the poor's roll is not apparently liable for expenses.[5] If an absent litigant who has sisted a mandatory comes to reside in this country the mandatory may be allowed to withdraw,[6] but he remains liable to the date of withdrawal, notwithstanding the principal's residence here.[7] If a mandatory dies or becomes insolvent the opponent is entitled to have a new mandatory sisted.[8] A mandatory is responsible for the proper conduct of the case, but he is not entitled without special authority to settle the action.[9] He is not liable for interim aliment to a spouse in a consistorial case.[10]

[1] Barstow v. Smith, 1851, 13 D. 854.
[2] Railton v. Matthews, 1844, 7 D. 105; M'Kinlay v. M'Kinlay, 1849, 11 D. 1022.
[3] Blow v. Ecuadorian Association, 1903, 5 F. 444.
[4] Pease, Wrays & Trigg v. Smith & Jameson, 4th June, 1822, F.C.; 1 S. 452; Robertson & Co. v. Exley & Co., 1833, 11 S. 320; Renfrew v. Magistrates of Glasgow, 1861, 23 D. 1003.
[5] Middlemas v. Brown, 1828, 6 S. 511.
[6] Shedden v. Patrick, 1853, 15 D. 379; Bracken v. Blasquez, 1891, 18 R. 819.
[7] Erskine v. Walker's Trustees, 1883, 10 R. 717. See also Chapman v. Balfour, 1875, 2 R. 291.
[8] Pease, Wrays & Trigg v. Smith & Jameson, supra; Harker v. Dickson, 1856, 18 D. 793.
[9] Thom v. Bain, 1888, 15 R. 613.
[10] Webster v. Webster, (O.H.) 1896, 33 S.L.R. 369.

If a pursuer sue with a mandatory this appears in the instance. If a mandatory is ordered to be sisted a minute is lodged with the mandatory's name and designation, and a formal mandate may be demanded.[1] A refusal of a motion for a mandatory is *in hoc statu*, and the motion may be renewed later.[2] Failure to sist on the part of a pursuer entails a decree of absolvitor,[3] and in the

case of a defender decree as craved will be granted.[4] The office
of mandatory falls by the death of the principal.[5]

[1] Gunn & Co. v. Couper, 1871, 10 M. 116.
[2] Aitkenhead v. Bunten & Co., 1892, 19 R. 803.
[3] Train v. Little, 1911 S.C. 736.
[4] 7 Edw. VII c. 51, Schedule I, Rule 56.
[5] See Marshall v. Connon, 1848, 21 Scot. Jur. 63.

A party who is not a foreigner, and may not require to sist
a mandatory, may nevertheless be sometimes ordered to produce
a mandate to satisfy the Court and the opposing party of his
instructions to sue or defend. This may happen where a party
is suing as factor or commissioner, or as a trustee, or an official
of a corporation, or generally where any person is suing or defending an action for another.[1] It may also arise where it is alleged
that the pursuer or defender has not authorized the proceedings
or the defence taken in his name.[2]

[1] Hepburn v. Tait, 1874, 1 R. 875 ; Fischer & Co. v. Andersen, 1896, 23 R.
    395.
[2] Hepburn v. Tait, supra.

CHAPTER V.

THE ACTION.

1. GENERAL.

The Sheriff Courts Act declares that " action or cause includes every civil proceeding competent in the ordinary Sheriff Court."[1] This repeats the definition of the Act of 1876.[2] Every civil proceeding, except a Small Debt action, now proceeds in the ordinary Sheriff Court. In this definition the word " ordinary " is not applied to the action, but to the Court. Under the present Act a civil proceeding may be what is known as an ordinary action (although that is not a statutory expression); or it may be a summary cause[3]; or it may be a summary application[4]; or it may be a statutory arbitration under the Workmen's Compensation Act[5]; or it may be an appeal allowed to the Sheriff under Statute; but these terms refer only to the procedure to be followed. They are all alike civil proceedings in the ordinary Sheriff Court, as distinguished from civil proceedings in the Small Debt Court. Accordingly, although the subsequent procedure in each of these is different, the initial procedure is the same. They all commence with an initial writ in the form provided by the Act.[6] At the date of the Act there were three exceptions to this (a) proceedings in services of heirs regulated by the Conveyancing Acts of 1868 and 1874[7]; (b) Small Debt proceedings regulated by the Small Debt Acts of 1837 and 1889[8] as amended by the Sheriff Courts Act and by certain later Acts; and (c) summary removings, which are regulated by special directions in the Sheriff Courts Act.[9] Since the date of the Act special forms differing from the normal initial writ have been provided in the case of applications under the Adoption of Children Act, 1930.[10] A special statutory form is also provided for applications under the Intestate Husband's Estate Acts.[11]

---

[1] 7 Edw. VII c. 51, sec. 3 (d) ; 2 & 3 Geo. V c. 28, Schedule I.
[2] 39 & 40 Vict. c. 70, sec. 3.
[3] 7 Edw. VII c. 51, sec. 3 (i).
[4] Ibid., sec. 3 (p).
[5] 15 & 16 Geo. V c. 84.
[6] 7 Edw. VII c. 51, Schedule I, Rule 1.
[7] 31 & 32 Vict. c. 101, sec. 27 et seq. ; 37 & 38 Vict. c. 94, sec. 10.
[8] 7 Will. IV & 1 Vict. c. 41; 52 & 53 Vict. c. 26.
[9] 7 Edw. VII c. 51, sec. 38, Schedule I, Rules 115-122; 2 & 3 Geo. V c. 28, Schedule II.
[10] 20 & 21 Geo. V c. 37. See p. 546, infra.
[11] See 9 & 10 Geo. V c. 9, Schedule.

2. ORDINARY ACTION.

The term " ordinary action," although not a statutory term, is a convenient and well-understood term, and it is in this work used as referring to the civil business brought before the Sheriff Court, other than that appropriated to special Courts, or that which, within the ordinary Court itself, is regulated by special enactments.

3. SUMMARY CAUSE.

This, in name, was a new creation of the Sheriff Courts Act, 1907, but it was not new in principle.[1] It preserved, in substance, the machinery for the recovery of debts not exceeding £50, which was introduced by the Debts Recovery Act of 1867,[2] which was repealed by the Sheriff Courts Act. In some Sheriff Courts non-professional representatives are allowed to appear in summary causes—a practice for which there appears to be no statutory authority.

[1] 7 Edw. VII c. 51, secs. 3 (i), 8, Schedule I, Rule 41; 2 & 3 Geo. V c. 28, Schedule II.
[2] 30 & 31 Vict. c. 96.

The " summary cause " procedure is applicable to all actions (except those under the Small Debt Acts and the Workmen's Compensation Act) for payment of money not exceeding £50, exclusive of interest and expenses, and all actions in which either the parties admit that the value of the action, exclusive of interest and expenses, does not exceed £50, or which they consent at any stage shall be tried summarily.[1] This definition of a summary cause contains the amendments made by the Act of 1913 which removed certain difficulties that had arisen on the original Act. Under the original definition summary causes were thought to be limited to actions for payment of money and nothing else.[2]

[1] 7 Edw. VII c. 51, sec. 3 (i); 2 & 3 Geo. V c. 28, Schedule I.
[2] Abrahams v. Campbell, 1911 S.C. 353.

Actions not exceeding £50 in value, exclusive of interest and expenses, are within the privative jurisdiction of the Sheriff Court,[1] and consideration has already been given to the rules by which such value is judged.[2] The first branch of the definition of a summary cause is an action for payment of money not exceeding £50 in amount exclusive of interest and expenses, and in conformity with the view expressed in the first edition of this work it has now been decided that the interest thus excluded is not merely the interest due after the date of citation.[3] But it is thought to be still an open question whether what are truly arrears of interest might not be aggregated with principal to arrive at the sum sued for. Where the only crave in the writ is for payment of money it seems from the terms of the definition that the sum sued for is the decisive factor to the exclusion of any other elements of value. But there has been a tendency to read the definition less strictly, and to exclude from summary causes actions for payments within the limits of value but in which wider interests appear to be involved, as shown by the terms of the crave[4] or by the real point in dispute when issue is joined between the parties.[5] Thus when the crave itself discloses a case of continuing liability it seems that the sum sued for is not necessarily conclusive.[4]

[1] 7 Edw. VII c. 51, sec. 7; 2 & 3 Geo. V c. 28, Schedule I.
[2] See p. 48 et seq., supra.
[3] Bowie v. Donaldson, 1922 S.C. 9.
[4] Stevenson v. Sharp, 1910 S.C. 580.
[5] Duke of Argyll v. Muir, 1910 S.C. 96. See further, p. 49, supra.

Summary causes also include all actions in which the parties admit that the value of the action, exclusive of interest and expenses, does not exceed £50. There are many actions where it is obvious that the value of the action does not exceed £50. If it is not obvious, it is open to a party desiring to have an action regarded as a summary cause to make a specific averment that the value does not exceed £50; and if this is a fact within the other party's knowledge, and he does not deny it, he will be held as admitting it.[1] An action which is not for payment of money, and in which the value is not expressly or by implication admitted to be not over £50, exclusive of interest and expenses, will not be a summary cause.[2]

[1] 7 Edw. VII c. 51, Schedule I, Rule 44; 2 & 3 Geo. V c. 28, Schedule II.
[2] M'Leod v. Munro, 1930, 47 Sh.Ct.Rep. 21.

The determination of whether an action is a summary cause will in practice rest in the first instance with the Sheriff-clerk, for it is he who issues the warrant for service, and the warrant is not the same in an ordinary action as in a summary cause. In a summary cause it requires the defender to appear and answer in Court upon a date set forth in the warrant. In an ordinary action it requires the defender to lodge a notice of appearance if he intends to defend.[1] The Sheriff-clerk can only judge of the *ex facie* value, and the ultimate determination of whether an action is a summary cause will rest with the Sheriff. It is thought that at any stage of the case the Sheriff can have a case hitherto treated as an ordinary action treated as a summary cause and *vice versa*.[2]

The use of the wrong form of warrant of service does not affect the competency of the proceedings.[3]

[1] 7 Edw. VII c. 51, Schedule I, Rule 4.
[2] United Creameries Co. v. Boyd & Co., 1912 S.C. 617; Purves v. Graham, 1924 S.C. 477.
[3] Muir & Weir v. Petrie, 1910, 27 Sh.Ct.Rep. 151; Thirtle, &c. v. Copin, 1912, 29 Sh.Ct.Rep. 13; MacGregor v. M'Kinnon, 1915, 32 Sh.Ct.Rep. 3.

Summary cause also includes any action which the parties themselves at any stage of the case consent shall be tried summarily.[1] If an action has in fact been dealt with as a summary cause it will be treated as such for purposes of appeal,[2] and if an action has been dealt with throughout as an ordinary action it will generally have the right of appeal of an ordinary action.[3]

[1] 7 Edw. VII c. 51, sec. 3 (i); 2 & 3 Geo. V c. 28, Schedule I.
[2] Summerlee Iron Co. v. Duff, 1920 S.C. 291.
[3] Ross v. Ross, 1920 S.C. 530.

The question has been raised whether in a money claim the character of a summary cause is changed, as regards procedure, when a defence by way of a money counter-claim exceeding £50 is stated. Under the Act a counter-claim stated in defence is to be dealt with as if stated in a substantive action,[1] and the defender may get decree for the excess of his claim over the pursuer's. It has been stated[2]—though it may with deference be doubted[3]—that the amount of a counter-claim is not to be taken into account in computing the value of the cause for purposes of appeal. On the question raised above two conflicting judgments have been given by Sheriffs-Principal of Lanarkshire, but in the later of these it was held that a counter-claim for over £50 could be lodged in a summary cause and dealt with and that the character of the summary cause was not thereby changed.[4]

[1] 7 Edw. VII c. 51, Schedule I, Rule 55.
[2] Bowie v. Donaldson, 1922 S.C. 9, Lord Salvesen, p. 13.
[3] See p. 50, supra.
[4] Gottlieb v. Fons Patent Inkwell, 1916, 33 Sh.Ct.Rep. 70; Cleave & Son v. Letters & Co., 1929, 45 Sh.Ct.Rep. 223.

There is nothing in the Statute, or in the procedure rules, to prevent an ordinary action and a summary cause being conjoined. But such a course may often be inconvenient, and the actions may have to be disjoined before final judgment is pronounced. It is in all cases a question of circumstances. If the ordinary action is raised subsequent to, and in answer to, a summary cause, and if its object appears to be merely to hamper the summary cause procedure, an order for conjunction will not, it is thought, be readily granted. If the circumstances warrant conjunction, then the proper course would seem to be to remit the summary cause process to the other.[1]

[1] See on this topic generally, M'Donald v. M'Donald, 1912, 29 Sh.Ct.Rep. 157.

A summary cause is, in its nature, not different from an ordinary action. They are alike actions; they alike commence by initial writ; and they are served upon the same induciæ. It is in regard to procedure only that there is any difference. The differences in procedure, briefly stated, are: (1) In the warrant of citation in an ordinary action the defender is called upon, if he means to defend, to lodge a formal notice of appearance; whilst in a summary cause he is called upon to attend and answer at a time and place set forth in the warrant of citation.[1] (2) In an ordinary action decree in absence may be granted so soon as the induciæ has expired, and appearance has not been entered, without waiting for a formal sitting of the ordinary Court, whilst the summary cause must be called at the appointed place and time, and decree in absence cannot be granted till then, because until it is so called it cannot be seen whether the defender means to answer. (3) In an ordinary action which is defended, there must be formal defences, and a record is made up and the evidence is recorded; whilst in a summary cause the Sheriff has an entirely free hand to order such procedure as he thinks requisite. It is not necessary, although it is usual, to have formal defences. It is neither necessary nor usual to have the record closed,[2] and the evidence is not necessarily recorded. The only statutory process direction is that the Sheriff may order defences if he thinks fit, or he may note on the writ or separately the defender's pleas, and may appoint a diet for the trial of the cause, or he " may order such other procedure as the circumstances seem to him to require."[3] As the record is not closed it is a common practice to add adjustments after a further stage of procedure has been reached, but it is clear that these may be objected to if they prejudice an opponent as where it is attempted to add a preliminary plea after an order for proof is made or to include substantial new averments of fact on the eve of the proof itself. A summary cause is to be disposed of without a record of the evidence, unless on the motion of either party, made before the examination of witnesses is begun, the Sheriff shall order that the evidence be recorded.[4] Although it might be assumed that the Sheriff has a discretion to refuse a motion to have the evidence recorded, it has been decided that such a motion if made must be granted.[5] The interlocutor disposing of the case must contain findings in

fact and law.[4]   (4) In an ordinary action exceeding £50 in value
there is, subject to the provisions of the Act, full right of appeal;
whilst in a summary cause there is an appeal to the Sheriff on fact
and law if the evidence is recorded, but on law only if the evidence
is not recorded,[4] and appeal beyond the Sheriff is only competent
if the Sheriff, after final judgment, certifies the case as suitable
for appeal to the Court of Session.[6]

[1] 7 Edw. VII c. 51, Schedule I, Rule 4.
[2] Cf. National Cash Register Co. v. Hunter, 1915, 32 Sh.Ct.Rep. 121.
[3] 7 Edw. VII c. 51, Schedule I, Rule 41; 2 & 3 Geo. V c. 28, Schedule II.
   See also M'Lelland v. Mackay, 1908, 24 Sh.Ct.Rep. 157; Park v.
   Coltness Iron Co., 1913 S.C. 1163.
[4] Ibid., sec. 8; 2 & 3 Geo. V c. 28, Schedule I.
[5] Stewart v. Gourlay, 1939, 56 Sh.Ct.Rep. 3; Weiner v. Tod Cunningham
   & Petrie, 1941, 57 Sh.Ct.Rep. 58.
[6] 7 Edw. VII c. 51, secs. 27-28; 2 & 3 Geo. V c. 28, Schedule I.   See
   further in regard to appeals, p. 302, infra.

The procedure in a summary cause is to be carried through
" without delay."[1]   In vacation there may be greater promptitude
in obtaining decree in an ordinary undefended action, because
a decree in absence may be granted immediately upon the expiry
of the induciæ, when a notice of appearance has not been lodged,
without waiting for a formal sitting of the Court.   In a summary
cause the warrant of citation requires a defender to " answer
within the Sheriff Court-house," but the form indicates that such
appearance may be in chambers[2] and thus not at a formal sitting
of the Court.   It appears, therefore, as if it were competent for
a defender to be cited to attend in chambers, although in practice
this does not seem to be done.[3]   During session, the summary
cause in matter of expedition should have the advantage of the
ordinary action.   No time need be occupied in waiting for pleadings or for adjustment, for in many actions for debt not exceeding
£50 formal pleadings are of little assistance.   The pursuer's case
is set forth in the initial writ.   The Sheriff can note the defender's
case in answer, and the case may go to trial at once and be decided
within a very short time.   It is thought that in too many cases
full advantage is not taken of the expeditious procedure which is
possible in summary causes, but in many Courts these are treated
in much the same way as ordinary actions, save that the record
is not formally closed.

[1] 7 Edw. VII c. 51, sec. 8; 2 & 3 Geo. V c. 28, Schedule I.
[2] Ibid., Schedule I, Rule 4, Form B.
[3] The objection may arise from a doubt whether an attendance of this
   kind can be validly made other than in open Court.

4. SUMMARY APPLICATION.

The summary application is neither a new process nor a new name, although it was first officially defined in the Sheriff Courts Act, 1907.[1] The Sheriff has always had jurisdiction to deal in a summary manner with many common law applications. Such applications, for instance, as for a precept of arrestment *jurisdictionis fundandæ causa;* for warrants to disinter bodies, to make post-mortem examinations, to cite witnesses in an arbitration, or before a presbytery, to realize perishable goods, to sell undelivered or rejected goods, to seal repositories, to sell stray cattle, to bring a prisoner from prison to give evidence in a civil cause, to carry back sequestrated effects, and many others, are dealt with by the Sheriff under his common law powers as judge ordinary of the bounds. In many of these common law applications a warrant may be granted *de plano.* The great majority of summary applications, however, are brought in the Sheriff Court under Statutes.

[1] 7 Edw. VII c. 51, sec. 3 (p).

A summary application should not be confounded with a " summary cause," the one having no connexion with the other. The provisions of the Act with regard to summary causes do not apply to summary applications, with the exception of Rule 4 and Form B, which prescribe the same mode of citation.[1]

[1] 7 Edw. VII c. 51, Schedule I, Rule 4, Form B.

Summary application as now defined means and includes all applications of a summary nature, brought under the common law jurisdiction of the Sheriff, and all applications, whether by appeal or otherwise, brought under any Act of Parliament which provides, or according to any practice in the Sheriff Court which allows, that the same shall be disposed of in a summary manner, but which does not more particularly define in what form the same shall be heard, tried and determined.[1]

[1] 7 Edw. VII c. 51, sec. 3 (p).

The Act provides[1] that in summary applications (where a hearing is necessary) the Sheriff shall appoint the application to be heard at a diet to be fixed by him, and at that, or any subsequent diet (without record of the evidence unless the Sheriff shall order a record), shall summarily dispose of the matter and give his judgment in writing. This procedure is to apply where by Statute any application is to be heard, tried and determined summarily, or in the manner provided by sec. 52 of the Sheriff Courts (Scotland)

Act, 1876,[2] and it should be followed in all cases, except those brought under Statutes conferring summary jurisdiction on the Sheriff, where other procedure is particularly prescribed.

[1] 7 Edw. VII c. 51, sec. 50.
[2] 39 & 40 Vict. c. 70, sec. 52 (now repealed).

The Act of 1907 did not introduce a uniform method of appeal in summary applications, when appeal is competent, but it expressly reserved existing appeal rights by providing that " nothing contained in this Act shall affect any right of appeal provided by any Act of Parliament under which a summary application is brought."[1]	Apart from such statutory rights of appeal it is thought that the general rule holds that a right of appeal exists unless it is excluded expressly or by implication.[2]

[1] 7 Edw. VII c. 51, sec. 50.
[2] See further in regard to appeals, p. 305, infra.

A summary application of any sort is a civil proceeding in the ordinary Sheriff Court. It is therefore an " action," and must be commenced by initial writ.[1]	It is served (when service is necessary, which it sometimes is not) in the same manner as a summary cause, by requiring the defender to attend and answer to the citation, at a place, and at an hour, on a day named.[2]	The use of the warrant of citation in the form appropriate for an ordinary action does not preclude the process being dealt with as a summary application if the Sheriff considers it to be such,[3] and if the process continues as an ordinary cause an objection to the competency of that procedure will not be entertained.[4]	The only other instruction about procedure is the brief, but comprehensive direction that the Sheriff " shall summarily dispose of the matter and give his judgment in writing."[5]	The evidence need not be recorded, unless so ordered, and the form of judgment is not prescribed.[6]	Rule 82 of Schedule I of the Act, which requires a judgment to set forth findings in fact and in law separately, with a note setting forth the grounds of judgment,[7] is inappropriate in the case of many summary applications, and it has been pointed out in the Court of Session that the procedure rules appended to the Act do not necessarily apply to summary applications.[8]	There may be cases, however, in which the usual form of judgment would be convenient, as, for instance, in an application under Statute, where there is a right of appeal.	In the majority of summary applications at common law the usual form of judgment is simply, " Grants warrant as craved."	On

the question of recovery of penalties by a summary application,
see the case noted.[9]

[1] 7 Edw. VII c. 51, sec. 3 (d), Schedule I, Rule 1; 2 & 3 Geo. V c. 28,
    Schedule I.
[2] Ibid., Rule 4, Form B.
[3] Thirtle, &c. v. Copin, 1912, 29 Sh.Ct.Rep. 13.   See also United
    Creameries Co. v. Boyd & Co., 1912 S.C. 617; Purves v. Graham,
    1924 S.C. 477.
[4] Comrie v. Gow & Sons, 1931, 47 Sh.Ct.Rep. 159.   See also Muir &
    Weir v. Petrie, 1910, 27 Sh.Ct.Rep. 151; Thirtle, &c. v. Copin,
    supra; MacGregor v. M'Kinnon, 1915, 32 Sh.Ct.Rep. 3.
[5] 7 Edw. VII c. 51, sec. 50.   See also Park v. Coltness Iron Co., 1913
    S.C. 1163; Stanners v. Thom, 1920, 36 Sh.Ct.Rep. 87.
[6] Ibid., sec. 50.
[7] Ibid., Schedule I, Rule 82.
[8] See O'Donnell v. Wilson, 1910 S.C. 799; Park v. Coltness Iron Co.,
    supra.
[9] Glasgow Goldsmiths' Co. v. Mackenzie & Co., 1911, 28 Sh.Ct.Rep. 27.

In the case of summary applications prescribed by Statute the
Act itself in many cases specifies the Court in which it is to be
brought.   But as a summary application is an action, and the
jurisdiction clauses of the Act[1] are appropriate to " any action,"
a summary application may, in other cases, be brought wherever
an ordinary action is competent, although it is doubtful whether
jurisdiction may be founded by arrestment for bringing a summary
application, and such a course seems inappropriate.   A defender
in a summary application may, it is thought, prorogate jurisdiction, unless barred by the Statute authorizing the application,
which may itself prescribe the Court in which the application must
be brought.

[1] 7 Edw. VII c. 51, sec. 6.

The proceedings in a summary application are entirely in
the Sheriff's discretion.   His only compulsory duty is to give his
judgment in writing.   In many cases no pleadings are necessary,
but there are cases in which the exact attitude of the contending
parties can be best seen by their putting in papers.   If the case
seems to the Sheriff to make this course desirable, there is nothing
in the Act to forbid it, and in practice written papers are frequently
ordered.   A small debt action has of consent been held to be a
summary application with consequent right of appeal.[1]

[1] Craig v. Lorn District Committee, 1911, 28 Sh.Ct.Rep. 14.

5. THE INITIAL WRIT.

Except as regards proceedings for service of heirs, summary
removings, small debt proceedings, and proceedings for which

special statutory forms have been provided, every action (*i.e.*, every civil proceeding) commences in the same form, whether it is, as regards subsequent procedure, treated as an ordinary action, a summary cause, a summary application, or an appeal. It is imperative that " all actions shall be commenced by writ as nearly as may be in the Form A."[1] An appeal against the resolution of a local authority is an " action " which is commenced by initial writ in the usual form.[2]

[1] 7 Edw. VII c. 51, Schedule I, Rule 1.
[2] Carnbroe Chemical Co., &c. v. District Committee of Middle Ward of Lanark County Council, 1923-1926, 43 Sh.Ct.Rep. 163.

The initial writ by which all actions are commenced is defined as meaning " the statement of claim, petition, note of appeal, or other document by which the action is initiated."[1] The form of the writ consists of five parts : (a) the Sheriffdom and place of the Court ; (b) the instance ; (c) the crave ; (d) the condescendence ; and (e) the note of pleas in law. There is no further direction as to form, except that the crave is to " set forth the specific decree, warrant, or order asked,"[2] that is to say, all that pursuer expects to find in his extract decree if he is successful in the litigation. This implies that the crave must be unambiguous and definite, and such as it is competent for the Sheriff Court to grant.

[1] 7 Edw. VII c. 51, sec. 3 (k).
[2] Ibid., Schedule I, Form A ; 2 & 3 Geo. V c. 28, Schedule II.

The one essential requisite of the initial writ is that, within the four corners of it shall be found the whole case which pursuer lays. If there is no appearance made for the defender the writ will be the only process, and the judgment of the Court may simply be " decerns as craved." That will justify inserting in the extract decree only what is craved in the writ. Interest upon a money claim, especially if claimed from a date prior to the raising of the action, and expenses of process, if sought, should be included in the crave of the writ, notwithstanding that Form A of the 1913 Act does not,[1] as the 1876 Act did,[2] specially direct that they must be asked for. It is thought that a crave for a principal sum does not entitle the Court to decern also for interest. And while a Court of law has an inherent right to award, or withhold, expenses in a judicial process,[3] it is doubtful whether expenses not craved could be awarded if the action were undefended.

[1] 7 Edw. VII c. 51, Schedule I, Rule 1, Form A ; 2 & 3 Geo. V c. 28, Schedule II.
[2] 39 & 40 Vict. c. 70, Schedule A, Note.
[3] Ledgerwood v. M'Kenna, 1868, 7 M. 261. See further, p. 310. infra.

If a warrant to arrest on the dependence is wanted, it should be asked for in the crave of the initial writ, although it has been held competent to insert such a warrant in the first deliverance when it was not so craved[1]; where it is craved the warrant is not necessarily, although it is usually, granted as matter of course. It is competent only in an action with a crave for payment of money, other than expenses[2]; and even in money claims a warrant for arrestment on the dependence may be refused, if the debt is future or contingent and it is not specially averred that the defender is *vergens ad inopiam;* or *in meditatione fugæ;* or is secreting his funds.[3] Arrestment on the dependence is competent in an action of separation and aliment, but its use should be limited to a case where the defender is in one of the categories above specified.[4] Arrestment on the dependence is available not only where there is a pecuniary crave along with another crave, as in separation and aliment, but where the pecuniary crave is merely alternative as in an action for delivery, or, alternatively, for damages.[5] Arrestment on the dependence is more fully dealt with later.[6]

[1] A. L. Muir & Son v. Robert Muir & Co., (O.H.) 1910, 1 S.L.T. 414.
[2] Stafford v. M'Laurin, 1875, 3 R. 148.
[3] Symington v. Symington, 1875, 3 R. 205; Burns v. Burns, 1879, 7 R. 355; Crear v. Morrison, 1882, 9 R. 890; Ellison v. Ellison, 1901, 4 F. 257.
[4] Burns v. Burns, supra; Johnson v. Johnson, 1910, 26 Sh.Ct.Rep. 134; Noble v. Noble, (O.H.) 1921, 1 S.L.T. 57.
[5] More v. Stirling & Sons, 1822, 1 S. 547.
[6] See p. 260 et seq., infra.

The writ which commences a civil proceeding of any kind must be authenticated by the signature of the pursuer or his solicitor.[1] The statutory form appears to require such signature only at the end of the crave,[1] and it is thought that this is sufficient, but it is usual to sign also at the end of the pleas. If pursuer has, at that stage, a solicitor representing him, the solicitor's name and address are also to be endorsed upon the back of the service copy of the writ.[1] The solicitor whose name is to be put upon the service copy (for the obvious purpose of informing the defender's solicitor with whom he may communicate) is not necessarily the solicitor who actually signs the writ (for any enrolled solicitor may sign a writ on behalf of another solicitor),[2] but the solicitor who is responsible for the issue of the writ. He must be a solicitor who is enrolled in the Court which grants the first warrant upon the initial writ, because applying for a warrant is " practising " in that Court, and a solicitor may not practise in any Court unless he has subscribed the list of that Court.[3] As the warrant for service is endorsed upon the initial writ itself the solicitor must borrow the writ in order to effect service, and a solicitor can borrow a process only if he is entitled to practise within the jurisdiction of the Court.[4] After a process has been tabled the initial writ cannot be borrowed unless by special order of the Sheriff.[5]

[1] 7 Edw. VII c. 51, Schedule I, Rule 3, Form A; cf. Sharp v. M'Cowan, 1879, 6 R. 1208.
[2] On this topic see Muir's Sequestration, 1911, 27 Sh.Ct.Rep. 327.
[3] 23 & 24 Geo. V c. 21, sec. 22.
[4] Ibid., sec. 46; 7 Edw. VII c. 51, Schedule I, Rule 16; 2 & 3 Geo. V c. 28, Schedule II.
[5] 7 Edw. VII c. 51, Schedule I, Rule 16; 2 & 3 Geo. V c. 28, Schedule II.

An initial writ must be presented, and a warrant on it may be competently granted, only in the Sheriffdom where there is jurisdiction against the defender, and it should be lodged in the Court of the appropriate district of that Sheriffdom, where there are more district Courts than one. Actions relating to questions of heritable right or title, including irritancy and removing, or to division of commonties or division, or division and sale, of common property, if raised in the Sheriff Court, must be raised in the Sheriff Court of the jurisdiction and district where the property forming the subject of dispute is situated.[1] Apart from this specialty it is thought that a defender can be sued in any of the Courts, or at all events in the principal Court of a Sheriffdom though he resides in another district, and in what may have been at one time a separate Sheriffdom.[2] This latitude is apparently not applicable in small debt cases,[3] and in other cases the Sheriff has a discretion as to citing a defender resident in another district,[4] and is always entitled to transfer a cause from one district of his Sheriffdom to another.[5] In practice a writ will not usually be accepted in other than the appropriate district, and if transmitted by post it will usually be sent on to the proper Court for attention.

[1] 7 Edw. VII c. 51, sec. 5.
[2] Tait v. Johnston, 1891, 18 R. 606; Kelso District Committee v. Fairbairn, 1891, 3 White 94; M'Cormick v. Campbell, 1926, 42 Sh.Ct.Rep. 124.
[3] Mactavish & Co. v. Cameron, 1899, 15 Sh.Ct.Rep. 292.
[4] Davidson v. Davidson, 1891, 18 R. 884; M'Cormick v. Campbell, supra.
[5] Tait v. Johnston, supra; Davidson v. Davidson, supra; M'Cormick v. Campbell, supra.

6. The Instance.

" Pursuer " and " defender " were not defined in any of the previous Sheriff Court Acts. In the present Act " pursuer " means and includes any person making a claim or demand, or seeking any warrant or order competent in the Sheriff Court; and "defender" means and includes any person who is required to be called in any action.[1] In addition "person" is defined to include company, corporation or association, and firm of any description, nominate or descriptive, or any board, corporate or unincorporate.[1] The manner in which any individual or individuals, or any corporation or association, carrying on business under a firm or trading or descriptive name may sue or be sued has already been considered.[2] Several persons can join as pursuers if they have a common ground of action such as preventing the pollution of a river in which they are jointly interested, seeking to establish a right of way, or contesting illegal assessments.[3] But it is not enough that each may have a separate and independent claim, personal to himself, against the same defender.[4] An action by several unconnected pursuers may be made competent by the withdrawal of all but one of the pursuers.[5] It is thought that there is a sufficient community of interest to justify joint action in all cases where several creditors have right under one debt or obligation, but each pursuer should crave in respect of the share of the debt to which he personally is entitled.[6] Joint owners are in the same position.

[1] 7 Edw. VII c. 51, sec. 3 (e) (n) (o).
[2] See p. 86 et seq., supra.
[3] Torrie v. Duke of Athol, 1849, 12 D. 328; 1852, 1 Macq. 65; Hay v. Earl of Morton, 1861, 24 D. 116; Cowan & Sons v. Duke of Buccleuch, 1876, 4 R. (H.L.) 14; Stirling County Council v. Magistrates of Falkirk, 1912 S.C. 1281; cf. Arthur v. Aird, 1907 S.C. 1170.
[4] Douglas v. Tait, 1884, 12 R. 10; Fischer & Co. v. Andersen, 1896, 23 R. 395; Ballantyne v. Ballantyne's Trustees, (O.H.) 1897, 4 S.L.T. 337; Brims & Mackay v. Pattullo, 1907 S.C. 1106; Paxton v. Brown, 1908 S.C. 406; Sime v. J. & A. D. Grimond, 1920, 1 S.L.T. 270; Smith-Shand's Trustees v. Forbes, 1921 S.C. 820; London and North Eastern Railway Co., &c. v. Reid's Trustee, 1945, 61 Sh.Ct.Rep. 135.
[5] Fischer & Co. v. Andersen, supra; Paxton v. Brown, supra.
[6] M'Lachlan's Executors v. Scott, 1850, 12 D. 467.

Where a wrong is done which entitles several persons to reparation they have generally the option of suing separately or together, a separate sum being, in the latter case, craved for each pursuer.[1] The familiar example is a road accident in which several persons are injured and claim damages in respect of the negligence of one or both of the drivers. Where relatives claim damages and/or *solatium* in respect of the death of one person they should all sue together. Separate actions in such a case, if not incompetent, are discouraged on the score of expense,[2] and an isolated action by one of several children for *solatium* for an unauthorized post-

mortem examination of the father's body was dismissed as no
averment was made as to the attitude of the other possible
claimants.[3] Where a father had known of an action for *solatium*
and damages by the widow and children of his son and had
taken no action he was not allowed to bring a subsequent action
on his own account.[4] Where certain of the claimants with a joint
cause of action will not concur the action should be intimated to
them.[5] In claims arising from breach of trust the general rule
applies, and each beneficiary may bring a separate action.[6] One
pursuer suing as administrator for several pupil children must
claim a separate sum for each,[7] and in such a case a lump tender
is ineffective.[8] If the grounds of action are wrongful acts of the
defender, which are similar but separate, joint action by the
parties affected is not allowed.[9]

[1] Cowan & Sons v. Duke of Buccleuch, 1876, 4 R. (H.L.) 14; Mitchell v.
Grierson, 1894, 21 R. 367; Benevolent Yearly Society v. Young &
Gall, 1894, 10 Sh.Ct.Rep. 288; Brown's Trustees v. Hay, 1897, 24 R.
1108; Baptist Union of Scotland v. Anderson, 1927, 43 Sh.Ct.Rep.
209; Armstrong v. Paterson Brothers, 1935 S.C. 464; Golden v.
Jeffers, (O.H.) 1936 S.L.T. 388.
[2] Slorach v. Kerr & Co., 1921 S.C. 285. See also Kinnaird v. M'Lean,
1942 S.C. 448.
[3] Pollok v. Workman, 1900, 2 F. 354.
[4] Kinnaird v. M'Lean, supra.
[5] Smith v. Wilsons & Clyde Coal Co., 1893, 21 R. 162; cf. Grant v. Wood
Brothers, (O.H.) 1902, 10 S.L.T. 296 (where other claimants renounced their rights).
[6] Allen v. M'Combie's Trustees, 1909 S.C. 710; cf. Benevolent Yearly
Society v. Young & Gall, supra.
[7] Gray v. Caledonian Railway Co., 1912 S.C. 339.
[8] Murphy v. Smith, 1920 S.C. 104.
[9] Gibson v. Macqueen, 1866, 5 M. 113; Killin v. Weir, 1905, 7 F. 526;
Cruickshank, &c. v. Great Northern Railway Co., 1919, 37 Sh.Ct.Rep.
62; Roberton, &c. v. Lauchope Coal Co., 1937, 53 Sh.Ct.Rep. 13;
cf. Golden v. Jeffers, supra.

The claims of a pursuer against separate and unconnected
defenders should not be combined in one action.[1] In laying an
action against joint defenders, regard should be had to the nature
of their joint liability. If that liability is joint and several and
is constituted by writ,[2] or if it arises *ex delicto*,[3] any one may
be sued for the full amount due. If the obligation is not by writ
or by delict all who are liable must be called together as defenders,[4]
and, where the liability is not joint and several but merely joint,
all the joint obligants must be called in order that the full sum
can be craved, each defender being in that case only liable for
his share.[5] Although the fault or negligence of two or more persons
may have been different in kind, they may be sued together, if their

collective acts have resulted in one wrong which has caused loss
and damage to pursuer. In that case they may be sued jointly
and severally,[6] but if the separate acts have produced separate
wrongs the defenders, though they may be sued together, must be
concluded against for separate amounts.[7] Regard should also be
had to whether any persons other than the direct defenders have
an interest, and, if so, such other persons should be called.[8]

[1] Exchange Loan Co. v. Levenson, 1905, 21 Sh.Ct.Rep. 33; cf. Miller, &c.
v. Forrester, &c., (O.H.) 1897, 5 S.L.T. 71.
[2] Neilson v. Wilson, 1890, 17 R. 608; Rankine v. Logie Den Land Co.,
1902, 4 F. 1074.
[3] Croskery v. Gilmour's Trustees, 1890, 17 R. 697; Sim v. Muir's Trustees,
1906, 8 F. 1091; Ellerman Lines v. Clyde Navigation Trustees, 1909
S.C. 690; Reid v. Clark, (O.H.) 1913, 2 S.L.T. 330; 1914, 1 S.L.T. 86.
[4] Neilson v. Wilson, supra. See also Thomson v. Aitken, 1934, 50
Sh.Ct.Rep. 233. (Negligence and breach of contract.)
[5] Bell's Principles, 52, 53.
[6] Belmont Laundry Co. v. Aberdeen Steam Laundry Co., 1898, 1 F. 45;
Fleming v. Gemmill, 1908 S.C. 340; Goodall v. Forbes, 1909 S.C.
1300; Rose Street Foundry, &c., Co. v. Lewis & Sons, 1917 S.C. 341.
[7] Barr v. Neilson, 1868, 6 M. 651; Taylor v. M'Dougall, 1885, 12 R. 1304;
Smyth v. Muir, 1891, 19 R. 81; Sinclair v. Caithness Flagstone Co.,
1898, 25 R. 703; Hannay v. Muir, 1898, 1 F. 306; Conway v. Dalziel,
1901, 3 F. 918; Hook v. M'Callum, 1905, 7 F. 528; Mellis & Son
v. California Company of Porters, &c., 1917, 34 Sh.Ct.Rep. 3;
Fleming v. M'Gillivray, 1946 S.C. 1.
[8] Mackinnon v. Macdonald, 1905, 7 F. 589.

When an action has been laid against defenders who are called
jointly and severally it may competently proceed against one or
more of them, although it may have been found irrelevant against
others,[1] or although one of the defenders may have been settled
with.[2] When defenders are sued jointly and severally any of
them may be found liable for the whole sum, and if some are
assoilzied others can be decerned against jointly and severally.[3]
It is also competent on such a crave to pronounce a " joint "
decree only.[4] If one of several defenders gets out, and the case
is to be remitted to the Court of Session, the remit should be
delayed until any expenses found due to the defender who has
got out are taxed and an extract has been obtained by him. After
the remit he cannot get his extract in the Sheriff Court, and
may have to be at the trouble and expense of seeking a decree
of new in the Court of Session.[5] A decree obtained against one
of several joint delinquents, but which is unsatisfied, does not
debar a further action against others who may be also liable[6];
and where one defender in an action against two parties at fault
was assoilzied the other defender was held to have no right to
appeal.[7] A joint and several crave has been held competent in

an action for delivery.[8] Where two or more defenders are held jointly and severally liable in damages or expenses, the Court may decide as to the proportions in which they shall be liable to contribute *inter se*.[9]

[1] Robinson v. Reid's Trustees, 1900, 2 F. 928; Gibson v. Irvine, (O.H.) 1900, 7 S.L.T. 391; Baird's Trustees v. Leechman, &c., (O.H.) 1903, 10 S.L.T. 515; Fleming v. Gemmill, 1908 S.C. 340; Mackenzie v. Macallister, 1909 S.C. 367. See also Thomson v. Aitken, 1934, 50 Sh.Ct.Rep. 233.

[2] Douglas v. Hogarth, 1901, 4 F. 148.

[3] Fleming v. Gemmill, supra.

[4] Gillespie v. Paisley Road Trustees, (O.H.) 1900, 7 S.L.T. 350.

[5] Gavin v. Henderson & Co., 1910 S.C. 357.

[6] Steven v. Broady Norman & Co., 1928 S.C. 351.

[7] M'Dermott v. Western S.M.T. Co., 1937 S.C. 239.

[8] Sinclair v. Fleming, 1909, 25 Sh.Ct.Rep. 268.

[9] 3 & 4 Geo. VI c. 42, sec. 3 (1). See Bromberg v. Reinhold & Co., 1942, 60 Sh.Ct.Rep. 45; Anderson v. St. Andrew's Ambulance Association, 1943 S.C. 248. See also 8 & 9 Geo. VI c. 28, secs. 1, 5.

Every person whose name appears in the instance is not necessarily a party to the cause, in the sense of being liable in expenses to the other parties. The pursuer may require to sue with consent of some person who has himself no beneficial interest in the result of the litigation, or it may be necessary to call, along with a defender, some person who has an *ex facie* legal, or a probable personal, interest; but such persons are not litigants in the strict sense, and, in general, a consenter does not merely by his consent incur liability for expenses.[1] No operative decree can be pronounced against a defender who is called merely for any interest he may have,[2] and a person who has merely concurred with one of the parties cannot exercise the right of appeal.[3]

[1] Whitehead v. Blaik, 1893, 20 R. 1045; Armstrong v. Thompson, (O.H.) 1895, 2 S.L.T. 537; Currie v. Cowan & Co., (O.H.) 1911, 2 S.L.T. 467; Gordon v. Henderson, 1922, 38 Sh.Ct.Rep. 293.

[2] Campbell v. M'Allister, (O.H.) 1893, 1 S.L.T. 14.

[3] Martin v. Lindsay, 1894, 21 R. 759.

Facts and circumstances may warrant a consenting party being held liable in expenses, and a consenter will generally be made responsible for expenses if he has actively participated in the conduct of the case.[1] A father who brings an action for pupil children, and is thus more than a consenter, is liable for expenses,[2] and in many cases husbands concurring with wives—when such concurrence was necessary—have been held liable,[3] as have also fathers consenting for minor children.[4] The extent of the rule is not too well defined but it is thought that there may be less

likelihood of such liability when the consent is for a defender.[5]
This topic is further discussed in the chapter on expenses.[6]

[1] M'Ilwaine v. Stewart's Trustees, 1914 S.C. 934.
[2] White v. Steel, 1894, 21 R. 649; Wilkinson v. Kinneil, &c., Coal Co., 1897, 24 R. 1001.
[3] Lindsay v. Kerr, 1891, 28 S.L.R. 267; Macgown v. Cramb, 1898, 25 R. 634; Maxwell v. Young, 1901, 3 F. 638; Picken v. Caledonian Railway Co., 1901, 4 F. 39; Schmidt v. Caledonian Railway Co., 1903, 5 F. 648; Kerr v. Malcolm, (O.H.) 1906, 14 S.L.T. 358; Herriot v. Jacobsen, 1909 S.C. 1228; M'Ilwaine v. Stewart's Trustees, supra. See also M'Millan v. Mackinlay, 1926 S.C. 673; Todd, &c. v. Wilson, 1930, 46 Sh.Ct.Rep. 17.
[4] Fraser v. Cameron, 1892, 19 R. 564; Wilkinson v. Kinneil, &c., Coal Co., supra; Rodger v. Weir, 1917 S.C. 300.
[5] Rodger v. Weir, supra.
[6] See p. 316, infra.

Both pursuer and defender should be clearly identified in the instance. The general rule may be taken now to be that parties are sufficiently designed in a Court process if such particulars are given as are sufficient to identify the person who is intended, and errors in names and addresses which are, in this sense, immaterial will be disregarded.[1] A party may in the course of the process be ordained to disclose his true address.[2] If any error occurs, the powers of correction by amendment under the Act are more extensive than they previously were. In defended cases amendment of the instance is specially provided for,[3] and in undefended cases any error or defect in the writ may be corrected.[4]

[1] Joel v. Gill, 1859, 22 D. 6; Spalding v. Valentine & Co., 1883, 10 R. 1092; Cruickshank v. Gow & Sons, 1888, 15 R. 326; Improved Edinburgh Property Investment Building Society v. White, 1906, 8 F. 903; Anderson v. Stoddart, 1923 S.C. 755; cf. Brown v. Rodger, 1884, 12 R. 340.
[2] Murdoch v. Young, (O.H.) 1909, 2 S.L.T. 450; Stein v. Stein, 1936 S.C. 268.
[3] 7 Edw. VII c. 51, Schedule I, Rule 79. See Riach v. Wallace, 1899, 1 F. 718; Watt v. Smith's Trustees, 1901, 9 S.L.T. 215.
[4] Ibid., Rule 26.

The statutory power to amend in defended cases sanctions adding a party,[1] but does not countenance an amendment which is really the substitution of a new defender for the defender originally called.[2] If the wrong defender has been called the instance is radically bad, and cannot be cured by amendment. But if the instance is good so far as it goes, but is incomplete because others are interested besides the defender who has been called, the instance may be amended by adding such other parties, instead of bringing

a supplementary action as was formerly necessary. The general
rules in regard to amendment are discussed later.[3]

[1] 7 Edw. VII c. 51, Schedule I, Rule 79. See Cooney v. Murdoch, 1918,
    34 Sh.Ct.Rep. 318.
[2] Clugston v. Scottish Women's Friendly Society, 1913, 30 Sh.Ct.Rep.
    150; Scotland v. British Order of Ancient Free Gardeners' Friendly
    Society, &c., 1916, 33 Sh.Ct.Rep. 93; M'Kenzie v. Jones, 1926, 42
    Sh.Ct.Rep. 289; cf. Bethune, &c. v. Turnbull, 1918, 34 Sh.Ct.Rep.
    309.
[3] See p. 234, infra.

A nominal party, who is not the true litigant, may be called
upon to disclose the real *dominus litis*, and if necessary a preliminary proof on this point may be allowed.[1] When ascertained
the Court may require the true *dominus* to be sisted as a party
to the cause, or that caution be found for expenses.[2] Such a
course is adopted only in special circumstances.[3] The general
definition of *dominus litis* is " a party with a direct interest in
the subject matter of the litigation . . . having the control and
direction of the suit, with power to retard it, or push it on, or
put an end to it altogether."[4] The mere circumstance that a party
is giving a pursuer financial aid to carry on a litigation does
not of itself infer that the financier is the *dominus litis*.[5] It is
thought to be competent for a defender to move for a *dominus litis*
being sisted at any time before expenses have been decerned for.

[1] Jenkins v. Robertson, 1869, 7 M. 739; Robertson v. Duke of Atholl,
    1905, 8 F. 150; Rutherford v. Licences and General Insurance Co.,
    (O.H.) 1934 S.L.T. 47.
[2] Jenkins v. Robertson, supra; Robertson v. Duke of Atholl, supra.
[3] Fraser v. Dunbar, 1839, 1 D. 882; Waddel v. Hope, 1843, 6 D. 160;
    Potter v. Hamilton, 1870, 8 M. 1064; Hepburn v. Tait, 1874, 1 R.
    875; M'Cuaig v. M'Cuaig, 1909 S.C. 355; Drysdale v. Reid, &c.,
    1919, 36 Sh.Ct.Rep. 124, and other cases, supra.
[4] Mathieson v. Thomson, 1853, 16 D. 19, Lord Rutherfurd, p. 23. See
    also Fraser v. Malloch, 1896, 23 R. 619; Cairns v. M'Gregor, 1931
    S.C. 84.
[5] Cairns v. M'Gregor, supra.

If a party is ordered to be sisted as a *dominus litis*, or if
caution for expenses has to be found, and that is not done, the
party against whom such an order is made would, it is thought,
be barred from proceeding further with the action and the other
party could then move for absolvitor, or that the action be dismissed, or for decree as craved, upon the ground that an order
made by the Sheriff had not been implemented.[1] Subject to proper
intimation it is competent to grant decree against the *dominus litis*
in the original action though the *dominus* has not become a party
to the process.[2] But the usual procedure is to raise a separate
action against the party who is alleged to have been the *dominus*

if he has not been a party to the original process. In addition to the authorities already cited reference may be made to the undernoted cases for the circumstances in which liability will attach to a party as *dominus litis*.[3] The liability of the *dominus* is for expenses only, and he is not responsible for the principal sum sued for.[4] The position in regard to a *dominus litis* is further discussed in the chapter on expenses.[5]

[1] 7 Edw. VII c. 51, Schedule I, Rule 56.
[2] M'Millan v. Mackinlay, 1926 S.C. 673; Davidson v. Whatmough, (O.H.) 1930 S.L.T. 536; Main v. Rankin & Sons, 1929 S.C. 40.
[3] Kerr v. Employers' Liability Assurance Corporation, 1899, 2 F. 17; Stevenson v. Sneddon, 1900, 3 F. 182; Harvey v. Corporation of Glasgow, 1915 S.C. 600.
[4] Nairn v. South-East Lancashire Insurance Co., 1930 S.C. 606.
[5] See p. 317, infra.

When a party sues or is sued in other than his personal character the capacity in which he appears must be set forth in the instance.[1] An executor may sue although not yet confirmed, but must produce his confirmation before he can get extract or obtain payment.[2] A body of trustees may sue by the quorum authorized by the deed of trust or by a majority,[3] but an impersonal description such as " the trustees of A " without any individual names of the trustees is not a name under which trustees can either sue or defend.[4] The title of a firm as trustees under a trust deed for creditors has been sustained.[5] When the pursuer's character is descriptive, as, for instance, a trustee in bankruptcy or a *curator bonis*, this appears in the instance, but where the pursuer's title requires explanation, as in the case of an assignee, it will be more convenient to set forth fuller particulars in the condescendence. Thus, a pursuer who sues for an assigned debt would design himself as A B, assignee of C D, in the instance, and in the condescendence would narrate that the debt sued for had been incurred to C D and assigned to A B conform to title set forth. An executor has no title to institute an action of damages for personal injury sustained by the deceased though he may insist in such an action if raised by the deceased himself.[6]

[1] 7 Edw. VII c. 51, Schedule I, Form A; 2 & 3 Geo. V c. 28, Schedule II.
[2] Maitland v. Cockerell, 1827, 6 S. 109; Bone v. Morrison, 1866, 5 M. 240; Mackay v. Mackay, 1914 S.C. 200.
[3] Blisset's Trustees v. Hope's Trustees, 1854, 16 D. 482. See 11 & 12 Geo. V c. 58, sec. 3 (c).
[4] Bell v. Trotter's Trustees, 1841, 3 D. 380.
[5] Pollard & Bird v. National Finance Co., &c., 1915, 32 Sh.Ct.Rep. 101.
[6] Stewart v. London, Midland & Scottish Railway Co., 1943 S.C. (H.L.) 19.

Where a defender is sued in a representative or special character the crave will be for decree against him in that capacity and not in his personal character. In the case of trustees such a crave does not preclude decree for expenses being granted against them as individuals.[1] In special circumstances, as where trustees carry on a business, they may be sued as individuals.[2]

[1] Mulholland v. Macfarlane's Trustees. (O.H.) 1928 S.L.T. 251.
[2] Johnston v. Waddell, (O.H.) 1928 S.N. 81.

CHAPTER VI.

SERVICE.

1. WARRANT OF CITATION.

In the great majority of cases, before the Court can entertain any action (other than a summary application which is to be disposed of *de plano*) it must be served upon the defender. An error in the service, if not timeously noticed and corrected, may be fatal to the action. The first step in effecting service is to obtain a warrant. This is in practice written upon the initial writ, although there is no statutory enactment on the subject. A warrant of citation is in general signed by the Sheriff-clerk, but any warrant may be signed by the Sheriff himself, and the Sheriff must sign all warrants which (a) alter the normal induciæ; (b) grant interim interdict; (c) grant warrant to sequestrate; or (d) are other than the usual one for citation and arrestment.[1] Thus the Sheriff-clerk may sign a warrant to arrest a ship, but if a warrant to dismantle is also sought that must be signed by the Sheriff. In some Sheriff Courts it is the practice to have warrants of citation in all applications brought under special Statutes signed by the Sheriff, although this does not appear to be necessary.

[1] 7 Edw. VII c. 51, Schedule I, Rule 7.

The Act of 1907 introduced a distinction in the forms of warrant which requires attention at this stage of the case. In an ordinary action the defender is required, if he intend to defend, to lodge a notice of appearance.[1] In every other kind of application, where citation is necessary, he is required to attend and answer at a fixed time and place.[1] This latter form of warrant is required in summary causes and summary removings, in summary applications where citation is necessary, and in cases under the Workmen's Compensation Act.[1] The use of the wrong form of warrant will not affect the competency of the proceedings.[2] There is no statutory time limit for service; but a warrant of service is thought to ·be inept after the lapse of a year and day. Where arrestment on the dependence has been used prior to service, it falls if the action

115

is not served within twenty days thereafter.[3]　As to an error in the warrant see the case noted.[4]

[1] 7 Edw. VII c. 51, Schedule I, Rule 4, Forms B and C.
[2] Muir & Weir v. Petrie, 1910, 27 Sh.Ct.Rep. 151; Thirtle, &c. v. Copin, 1912, 29 Sh.Ct.Rep. 13; MacGregor v. M'Kinnon, 1915, 32 Sh.Ct.Rep. 3.
[3] 7 Edw. VII c. 51, Schedule I, Rule 127; 2 & 3 Geo. V c. 28, Schedule II.
[4] Stevenson v. Wilson, 1941, 58 Sh.Ct.Rep. 74.

2. Induciæ.

The normal induciæ of citation is seven days.[1]　But when the defender is in Orkney or Shetland, or any of the other islands of Scotland, the normal induciæ is fourteen days.[1]　It is so also if the defender is furth of Scotland.[1]　The Sheriff may shorten or extend the normal induciæ, but not so as in any case to be less than forty-eight hours.[1]

[1] 7 Edw. VII c. 51, Schedule I, Rules 5, 6.

The induciæ is the same in an ordinary action and in a summary cause.　But summary applications, where service is necessary, are sometimes served upon a short induciæ or from two to four days.　In sequestrations for rent it is also usual to shorten the induciæ.　The power to shorten the induciæ formerly existed.[1] The power to extend it was introduced in 1907, but is not likely to be exercised unless in exceptional circumstances.

[1] 39 & 40 Vict. c. 70, sec. 8.　See Muir v. More Nisbett, 1881, 19 S.L.R. 59.

3. Execution of Citation.

Formal citation is not always necessary.　The defender or his agent may accept service.　He may also dispense with the induciæ. When service is accepted a docquet to that effect, holograph of the defender or of his solicitor, is endorsed upon the initial writ, and such a docquet is equivalent to an execution of citation.　A defender who receives a writ with warrant of citation for the purpose of accepting service is not entitled to retain the writ but must return it on demand.[1]　Where a defender obstructs formal service, but is in knowledge of the process raised against him, the want of formal execution of citation may not prevent decree being granted.[2]　The date of commencement of an action is the date of the acceptance of, or execution of, service,[3] for no action can be regarded as initiated until it has been served.　Exceptions to this rule are a sequestration process, in which the date of commencement is the date of the first deliverance,[4] and a petition for winding up a company when the winding up is deemed to commence on the presentation of the petition or as from the date of any earlier resolution to wind up voluntarily.[5]

[1] Campbell v. Macpherson, 1905. 22 Sh.Ct.Rep. 88.
[2] Busby v. Clark, 1904, 7 F. 162.
[3] Alston v. Macdougall, 1887, 15 R. 78; Gibson v. Clark, 1895, 23 R. 294.
[4] 3 & 4 Geo. V c. 20, sec. 41.
[5] 19 & 20 Geo. V c. 23, sec. 175.

Execution of the warrant of citation is effected by delivery or transmission to the defender of a copy of the writ and warrant, along with a schedule of citation signed by the officer or solicitor who serves it. The name and address of the pursuer's solicitor must be upon the back of every service copy.[1] The copy writ served should be a full copy including condescendence and pleas. The effect of a discrepancy between the principal writ and the service copy will depend on the nature of the error.[2] In a broad sense citation falls into two categories (a) by registered letter, which is the method normally adopted and which can be effected either by a solicitor or an officer, and (b) citation which is competent to an officer only and which is either personal service or service at the dwelling-house.

[1] 7 Edw. VII c. 51, Schedule I, Rule 3. See National Cash Register Co. v. Hunter, 1915, 32 Sh.Ct.Rep. 121; Muir v. National Bank, 1943, 59 Sh.Ct.Rep. 51.
[2] Lochrie v. M'Gregor, 1911 S.C. 21. See National Cash Register Co. v. Hunter, supra; Muir v. National Bank, supra.

The Citation Amendment Act of 1882 introduced postal service, which is the form now most commonly in use. That Statute, however, expressly reserved the existing law and practice as regards citation, so that postal citation, or citation by officer is optional.[1] Personal citation can be effected only by an officer. This normally means a Sheriff-officer. It seems possible that citation by a messenger-at-arms would be accepted but this has never been definitely decided.[2] The Sheriff's authority to any suitable person to execute a warrant under the Execution of Diligence (Scotland) Act, 1926,[3] is clearly not intended to apply to executing a warrant of citation, and it is thought that it could not be read as having that effect. Where personal citation is not essential, postal citation may be made either by an officer or by a solicitor, even although the solicitor is a party in the cause.[4] In all cases where service is made by an officer the officer must be one who has no personal interest in the action.[5]

[1] 45 & 46 Vict. c. 77, sec. 6.

[2] Finlayson v. Innes, 1803, 4 Pat. App. 443; Hamilton v. Bain, 1857, 1 Guthrie's Select Cases, 405; Cheyne v. M'Gungle, 1860, 22 D. 1490; Campbell v. Duncan, 1901, 17 Sh.Ct.Rep. 155; Sutherland v. Standard Life Assurance Co., 1902, 4 F. 957; M'Culloch v. M'Laughlin, 1930 J.C. 8. See p. 11, supra.
[3] 16 & 17 Geo. V c. 16, sec. 3.
[4] Addison v. Brown, 1906, 8 F. 443.
[5] Dalgleish v. Scott, 1822, 1 S. 506.

Under the Sheriff Courts Act, 1907, execution of citation by an officer may be made either by an officer of the Sheriffdom whence the warrant issues, or by an officer of the Sheriffdom where service is to be made.[1] In the case of citation by a solicitor the matter seems to be left by the statutory provisions in some confusion. The general authority of the Citation Amendment Act sanctioning citation by " an enrolled law-agent "[2] was thought to be qualified by the Law Agents Act, 1873,[3] and to be limited to an agent practising in the Court whence the warrant of citation issued. By the Execution of Diligence Act, 1926, enrolled law-agent in the relevant section of the Citation Amendment Act is defined in the case of a warrant issued from the Sheriff Court as meaning an agent on the roll of agents practising in any Sheriff Court of the Sheriffdom in which the warrant is to be executed[4]—not the Sheriffdom from which the warrant was issued. The roll of agents under the Law Agents Act is now superseded by the list of solicitors under the Solicitors (Scotland) Act, 1933,[5] but otherwise the matter is left as amended by the Act of 1926. No difficulty arises if the writ has to be served on persons within the Sheriffdom in which the solicitor is entitled to practise, but the definition introduced in 1926 might be thought to raise the doubt whether a solicitor practising in the Sheriffdom from which the warrant has issued can competently cite by registered letter in the case of a defender resident outwith that Sheriffdom, unless the solicitor happens also to be entitled to practise in the Sheriffdom in which that defender resides. In practice warrants of service are executed by the solicitor practising in the Court from which the warrant issued irrespective of the defender's place of abode, and it is thought that the Act of 1926 would be read as not affecting this practice.[6]

[1] 7 Edw. VII c. 51, Schedule I, Rule 10.
[2] 45 & 46 Vict. c. 77, sec. 3.
[3] 36 & 37 Vict. c. 63, sec. 16.
[4] 16 & 17 Geo. V c. 16, sec. 4; cf. earlier decisions in Mouat v. Lee, 1891, 18 R. 876, and Kerr, (O.H.) 1906, 14 S.L.T. 412.
[5] 23 & 24 Geo. V c. 21, secs. 20, 22.
[6] Cf. M'Gregor v. Brown, Davies & Tait, 1886, 2 Sh.Ct.Rep. 172. It would be difficult for the Sheriff-clerk to say whether a solicitor serving a writ was enrolled in a Sheriffdom or district other than his own.

Certain statutory requisites must be observed in postal citation, whether made by a solicitor or an officer : (a) the citation must specify the date of posting[1] ; (b) on the envelope containing the writ there must be a written or printed notice stating that it contains a Court citation, and giving the name and address of the Sheriff-clerk to whom it is to be returned if delivery cannot be made[1] ; (c) the citation, when it does not require the defender to appear and answer at a fixed date, must set forth that the induciæ is reckoned from twenty-four hours after the date of posting mentioned in it[2] ; (d) a copy of the initial writ, and a copy of the warrant of citation must accompany the citation which is to be subjoined to the writ[3] ; and (e) the letter containing the citation must be registered, and the post office receipt for the registered letter must accompany the execution of citation[1] and should be affixed to it. Postal citation is by Statute only permissible when the warrant is being executed in Scotland.[4] The postal service of an edictal citation is discussed later.[5]

[1] 45 & 46 Vict. c. 77, sec. 4.
[2] Ibid., and 7 Edw. VII c. 51, Schedule I, Rule 8, Form D. See also Addison v. Brown, 1906, 8 F. 443.
[3] 45 & 46 Vict. c. 77, sec. 3.
[4] Ibid. See Williams v. Williams, 1931 S.C. 196.
[5] See p. 121, infra.

The Citation Amendment Act of 1882 did not provide a form of citation, but only the form of execution of citation.[1] The Sheriff Courts Act, 1907, provided a form of citation, as well as a form of execution, the latter of which is directed to be " appended to or indorsed upon the initial writ,"[2] and in practice is generally a printed form which is gummed to the writ.[3] These forms should be followed. The general direction in the form of execution to " set forth the mode of service "[2] seems to invite the use of the relevant portion of the form of execution provided by the Citation Amendment Act,[1] when the citation is made by post.

[1] 45 & 46 Vict. c. 77, Schedule I.
[2] 7 Edw. VII c. 51, Schedule I, Rule 8, Forms D and E.
[3] Hunter. (O.H.) 1908, 15 S.L.T. 716.

All warrants upon actions directed against a defender furth of Scotland should contain authority to cite edictally,[1] for edictal citation may not be competent unless the warrant expressly authorizes it.[2]

[1] 7 Edw. VII c. 51, Schedule I, Rules 7, 15.
[2] Miller, 1853, 16 D. 109.

Although edictal citation is in general appropriate only when a defender is furth of Scotland it may also be required when his whereabouts are unknown. Under the Rules it is used for citing the unknown tutors and curators of a minor.[1] And in some cases, too, the defender's address may be unknown to the pursuer. In such circumstances the Rules do not expressly provide for the method of citation so the matter is regulated by the general practice in regard to edictal citation. It seems clear that edictal citation is not limited to cases in which it is averred that the defender is abroad, and if a defender has left his usual residence for forty days and his present address is unknown edictal citation is appropriate and warrant to cite in this way should be granted in such a case as the only method of convening the defender.[2] In a doubtful case, as where a defender had left his residence within forty days of citation and it was thought that he might be abroad, citation both at the last dwelling place and edictally might be prudent. Where the defender is a foreigner, then, if he is still subject to the jurisdiction of the Sheriff Court after he has left the country—as by arrestment—citation should be edictal whether he has left within forty days or not.[3] Edictal citation might be sustained even though it afterwards transpired that the defender was at the time in Scotland if he induced the belief in the pursuer that he had gone abroad. Whether the citation is good in such a case is a question of circumstances.[4] Where the defender is merely on a temporary absence abroad edictal citation may not be necessary.[5]

[1] 7 Edw. VII c. 51, Schedule I, Rule 14.
[2] Act of Sederunt, 14th December, 1805. See Corstorphine v. Kasten, 1898, 1 F. 287; Morrison v. Vallance's Executors, 1907 S.C. 999. See also Morrison, Dick & M'Culloch v. Turner, 1897, 14 Sh.Ct.Rep. 109.
[3] Corstorphine v. Kasten, supra.
[4] Sandbach v. Caldwell, 1825, 4 S. 171; Robertson v. M'Culloch, 1836, 14 S. 950; Clark-Kennedy v. Clark-Kennedy, (O.H.) 1908, 15 S.L.T. 844.
[5] Gibson v. Clark, 1895, 23 R. 294.

Edictal citation is competent in a small debt as well as an ordinary Court process.[1] Leaving a summons with a servant is also good service of a small debt summons[2]; but, although a defender may not be furth of Scotland, there may at the moment be nobody in his premises to receive a summons, in which event it is, in certain circumstances, competent for the officer, under the Citation Act of 1871, to affix the small debt summons to the gate or door of defender's premises, and also send a duplicate by post to defender's last known address, or to any address which the officer, after diligent inquiry, may deem most likely to find the defender. The requisites for this method of procedure are that the officer is satisfied that the defender is refusing access or concealing himself to avoid citation or that defender has within forty days removed from his house or premises and that his present dwelling place is unknown.[3]

[1] 7 Edw. VII v. 51, sec. 45, Schedule I, Rule 15.
[2] 7 Will. IV & 1 Vict. c. 41, sec. 3; 34 & 35 Vict. c. 42, sec. 3.
[3] 34 & 35 Vict. c. 42, sec. 3. See also Bell, &c. v. Bowman & Co., 1918, 35 Sh.Ct.Rep. 90.

Edictal citation is made at the office of the Extractor of the Court of Session, New Register House, Edinburgh, either by delivery there of the citation, or by transmitting it by post.[1] If the citation is postal a certified copy of the warrant has to be sent by registered letter addressed to the Extractor of the Court of Session, New Register House, Edinburgh, of which copy the Extractor has to acknowledge receipt.[1] In practice both writ and warrant are sent and are certified by the solicitor who effects the service. Where the defender has no known address in the United Kingdom, service upon the Extractor of the Court of Session is sufficient; but, if the defender has a known residence or place of business in England or Ireland, a copy of the writ and citation is sent to that address by registered letter and the execution of citation must bear that this has been done.[1]

[1] 7 Edw. VII c. 51, Schedule I, Rule 15; 18 & 19 Geo. V c. 34. sec. 8; S.R. & O., 1929, No. 588; Act of Sederunt, 19th July, 1929; 1 Edw. VIII & 1 Geo. VI c. 43, sec. 13; Act of Sederunt, 9th July, 1937.

The signature of a solicitor alone to the execution of postal citation is sufficient, but it must be the personal signature of the solicitor who made the citation.[1] One solicitor may sign an initial writ on behalf of another, but one solicitor should not sign an execution of citation for another.[2] Nor can the execution be signed by a clerk for a solicitor, even if the letter has been actually registered ·and posted by that clerk.[3] An execution of citation by an officer must in general be attested by one witness, but this is dispensed with when the officer's citation is made by post.[4] The officer's execution must specify whether the citation was personal or, if not, the mode of citation.[3]

[1] 45 & 46 Vict. c. 77, secs. 3, 4. Schedule I.
[2] Tait v. Johnston, 1891, 18 R. 606.
[3] Wilson, 1885, 13 R. 342.
[4] 7 Edw. VII c. 51, Schedule I, Rule 9, Form E. See also 45 & 46 Vict. c. 77, secs. 3, 4, Schedule I.

The Citation Amendment Act of 1882 requires the registered post letter to be sent to the defender's known residence or place of business or to his last known address if it continues to be his legal domicile or proper place of citation.[1] It might be thought that the Act merely altered the method of citation and not the place where it might be made, and that the place to which the letter is to be directed is the place where an officer in person might legally effect service upon a defender. But apparently the Act is to be read as going further than this, and in the case of an individual defender it is optional to send a postal citation either to his residence or place of business.[2] This is apart from the section extending the Sheriff's jurisdiction to a defender who carries on business and has a place of business within the jurisdiction and who is cited either personally or at such place of business.[3] In that case citation even by officer is competent at the place of business though the defender also resides within the Sheriffdom.[4] The question has been already discussed as to the proper method of citation of a defender who is not a foreigner and who has resided within the jurisdiction for at least forty days and has ceased to reside there for less than forty days but has no known residence in Scotland.[5] In the case of a foreigner, jurisdiction from residence normally ceases as soon as he leaves, and if he is still subject to the jurisdiction—say, by arrestment—citation should be made edictally.[6] Where a defender had gone abroad temporarily citation at his dwelling-house was sustained.[7]

[1] 45 & 46 Vict. c. 77, sec. 3.
[2] Rachkind v. Donald & Sons, 1916 S.C. 751, Lord Salvesen, p. 755; Bruce v. British Motor Trading Corporation, 1924 S.C. 908.
[3] 7 Edw. VII c. 51, sec. 6 (b).
[4] Rachkind v. Donald & Sons, supra.
[5] See p. 56, supra.
[6] Corstorphine v. Kasten, 1898, 1 F. 287; Buchan v. Grimaldi, 1905, 7 F. 917.
[7] Gibson v. Clark, 1895, 23 R. 294.

If the postal letter cannot be delivered, the Citation Amendment Act directs the post office officials to return it immediately to the Clerk of Court[1]; but it is possible that a letter may not be delivered, and yet not be returned to the Sheriff-clerk within the induciae. In that case pursuer, at the first calling, may move for decree in absence, because ex facie the service has been validly effected. If the letter has not been delivered, then—save where it has been tendered and refused as explained below—the action has not been served, and the Sheriff-clerk is directed to notify the return of the letter to the pursuer.[1] The Court may then, the matter being still open, order re-service, and substitute a new diet of appearance.[1] But if decree in absence has been taken this does not appear to be competent, as the Sheriff cannot recall his own decree, and the pursuer's only remedy may be to raise a new action. In practice an ordinary action is usually re-served by an officer, so soon as it is so returned through the post office. In a summary cause and in a small debt action, if there is not time to re-serve before the appointed diet of compearance, a warrant for re-service for a fresh diet is asked. Such re-service is usually ordered to be made otherwise than by postal citation, but this is in the discretion of the Sheriff.[2]

[1] 45 & 46 Vict. c. 77, sec. 4 (5).
[2] Ibid., sec. 4 (5) ; 7 Edw. VII c. 51, Schedule I, Rule 12.

Where the letter is returned because the defender, or others for him, refused to accept delivery of it, that is to say, in post office phraseology, when it is returned marked " Refused," an order for re-service does not follow as matter of course. If the Sheriff is satisfied that the letter has been tendered at the proper address and refused, he may hold the tender as equivalent to a valid citation and decree in absence may follow upon it.[1] It is for the Sheriff to decide on the information put before him whether the tender of the letter is to be accepted as service.[2] If he decides that it is, this does not foreclose the matter finally, and a reduction of the decree will be competent if refusal of the letter was not in fact made by the defender or by someone on his authority.[3] If the defender in fact received the letter it is immaterial that it was not actually delivered at his premises.[4]

[1] 45 & 46 Vict. c. 77, sec. 4 (5).
[2] Roberts v. Crawford, 1884, 22 S.L.R. 135 ; Spaulding v. Marjoribanks, (O.H.) 1903, 11 S.L.T. 71 ; Busby v. Clark, 1904, 7 F. 162 ; Matheson v. Fraser, (O.H.) 1911, 2 S.L.T. 493.
[3] Bruce v British Motor Trading Corporation, 1924 S.C. 908.
[4] Steuart v. Ree, 1885, 12 R. 563.

In certain cases citation by an officer is still necessary. The personal service, which is necessary in certain cases to found jurisdiction, can only be made in this way.[1] Leaving a writ in the hands of a servant or affixing it to the door or putting it in the keyhole is not in such cases compliance with the statutory requirement of personal service. Even when it is not used to found jurisdiction, personal service is always the safest mode of citation, but the additional expense of such service beyond the cost of postal citation will not be allowed on taxation unless it is shown that postal service was not expedient in the circumstances.[2] Keyhole citation also can only be made by an officer. This never satisfactory mode still subsists as a competent mode of citation[3] in any process other than one under the Small Debt Acts. As regards small debt procedure, it was abolished in 1871 and another method was substituted as before explained.[4]

[1] 7 Edw. VII c. 51. sec. 6 (b) (f) (i).
[2] 45 & 46 Vict. c. 77, sec. 6; Macleod v. Davidson, 1887, 14 R. 298.
[3] See next two paragraphs.
[4] See p. 120, supra.

When service is made by an officer it may (apart from postal service which, as above explained, may be made either by an officer or a solicitor) be made in various ways: (a) the copy of the writ and schedule of citation may be delivered into the hands of the defender personally wherever he can be found; (b) if the defender is not found personally after inquiry the writ and schedule may be left with a servant in the house to be given to the defender[1]; (c) if the officer cannot obtain access after giving six audible knocks he may affix a copy of the writ and schedule to the door of the premises, or put it in the keyhole.[1] In all cases of citation by an officer (other than postal service or a citation upon a small debt summons, or a summary removal complaint[2]), at least one witness must be present, and must sign the execution along with the officer, and the execution must state whether the citation was personal or otherwise, and the mode of it, if not personal.[3]

[1] Act 1540, c. 75.
[2] 7 Will. IV & 1 Vict. c. 41, sec. 3; 7 Edw. VII c. 51, Schedule I, Rule 119.
[3] 7 Edw. VII c. 51, Schedule I, Rule 9, Form E.

In the case of personal service it is sufficient if the writ and schedule are tendered to the defender and he refuses to accept them.[1] It has been suggested that personal service might be good though the defender's presence had been obtained by illegal means,[2] but this seems doubtful.[3] In the case of citation at the dwelling place, the *locus* of citation is the defender's actual and usual residence,[4] and, if he has more than one, citation at any may be good.[5] The case of a defender normally resident in Scotland who has been absent for not more than forty days has been already discussed.[6] If the defender cannot be found at such dwelling place the writ and schedule are to be offered to a servant, who is thought to be any person legitimately found on the premises.[7] If such person will not accept the citation the officer proceeds as when he cannot get access and affixes the writ and schedule to the principal door of the house or puts them in the keyhole.[8] Apart from special circumstances in which it may be ordered, service on a defender's solicitor is not service on the defender. Where a defender carries on business within the jurisdiction he may be cited by officer at his place of business, though his residence is also within the Sheriffdom.[9]

[1] Stair IV, 38, 15; Busby v. Clark, 1904, 7 F. 162; cf. Macgregor, 1848, 11 D. 285 (inability to serve on a lunatic).
[2] International Exhibition v. Bapty, 1891, 18 R. 843.
[3] Borjesson v. Carlberg, 1878, 5 R. (H.L.) 217.
[4] See Corstorphine v. Kasten, 1898, 1 F. 287, but for this form of service a place of business is not necessarily equivalent to the dwelling-place; Sharp, Fairlie & Co. v. Garden, 1822, 1 S. 337; cf. note 9, infra.
[5] Douglas & Heron v. Armstrong, 1779, M. 3700; Macdonald v. Sinclair, 1843, 5 D. 1253.
[6] See p. 56, supra.
[7] A v. B, 1834, 12 S. 347. See also Countess of Cassilis v. Earl of Roxburgh, 1679, M. 3695.
[8] Act 1540, c. 75.
[9] Rachkind v. Donald & Sons, 1916 S.C. 751.

Actions of separation and aliment and adherence and aliment directed against a foreigner will not be usually met with in the Sheriff Court, but if the defender in such an action is in fact abroad when service is made there may be some doubt as to the appropriate mode of citation. The Conjugal Rights Amendment Act of 1861 directed that, in every consistorial cause (which is defined to include actions of adherence and separation) service upon a defender not resident in Scotland must be personal, unless the Court is satisfied that he cannot be found, when edictal citation is sufficient, but there must also in that case be service on the children of the marriage, if any, and on one or more of the defender's next-of-kin (other than the children) if such parties are known and are resident within the United Kingdom.[1] The Court of Session Act of 1868 provided that the personal service thus required might be executed by delivery of the service copy of the writ (and relative schedule of citation) to the defender by any person duly authorized by the pursuer.[2] These provisions have been recently modified by Rules of Court which, in the case of Court of Session procedure, sanction postal, as an alternative to personal, citation where the defender is resident at a known address furth of Scotland.[3] Despite the apparent universality of the terms of sec. 10 of the 1861 Act it is thought that the procedure there laid down is applicable only in the Court of Session, and that when actions of adherence and separation were made competent in the Sheriff Court this did not import into that Court the procedure referred to.[4] It follows that such actions will be subject to the ordinary rules in regard to citation, though personal service on a defender in a consistorial cause may be recommended as a matter of expediency, and is probably advisable if the defender is abroad and if this form of service is possible. In a recent judgment the Court of Session have held that citation by registered letter on a defender in a consistorial cause resident abroad may be sufficient in that Court if the defender is shown to have received the citation.[5]

[1] 24 & 25 Vict. c. 86, secs. 10, 19. See Laughland v. Laughland, (O.H.) 1882, 19 S.L.R. 645 ; as to proof of defender's address being unknown, see Clark-Kennedy v. Clark-Kennedy, (O.H.) 1908, 15 S.L.T. 844.
[2] 31 & 32 Vict. c. 100, sec. 100. See Colvin v. Colvin, (O.H.) 1923 S.L.T. 728.
[3] Rules of Court, 1936, III, 24.
[4] Cf. 37 & 38 Vict. c. 31.
[5] Williams v. Williams, 1931 S.C. 196.

Citation by officer has been greatly simplified by the legislation of the last century. Any warrant of citation or warrant or precept of arrestment whether on a depending action or a document of debt may be competently executed in any Sheriffdom without endorsation by the Sheriff-clerk of that Sheriffdom, and any such warrant or precept may be executed either by an officer of the Court which granted the warrant or precept or by an officer of the jurisdiction where it is to be executed.[1] The officer must not have any personal interest in the action.[2] One witness is sufficient for the execution of citation, but a witness is dispensed with in a small debt or summary removing process, and when the officer's citation is by post.[3] Any person not under fourteen years of age is a competent witness.[4]

[1] 7 Edw. VII c. 51, Schedule I, Rule 10.
[2] Dalgliesh v. Scott, 1822, 1 S. 506.
[3] 7 Edw. VII c. 51, Schedule I, Rules 9, 119, Form E ; 7 Will. IV & 1 Vict. c. 41, sec. 3.
[4] Davidson v. Charteris, 1758, M. 16899.

Citation should, unless in exceptional circumstances, be made within reasonable hours and it is probably incompetent on a Sunday.[1] The attesting witness must be actually present at the citation, and he is required to sign the execution along with the officer.[2] When an action is served, but nothing more is done for a year and a day from the last day for appearance, the instance falls.[3]

[1] Oliphant v. Douglas, 1633, M. 15002; Stair III, 1, 37; III, 3. 11; IV, 47, 27. This point was expressly reserved in M'Niven v. Glasgow Corporation, 1920 S.C. 584.
[2] 7 Edw. VII c. 51, Schedule I, Rule 9.
[3] M'Kidd v. Manson, 1882, 9 R. 790.

If an irregularity occurs in citation, the remedy is to repeat the citation. Where the authority of the Sheriff is required for re-service, it may be granted on such conditions as to the Sheriff shall seem just.[1] Normally it will be granted as a matter of course when an attempt at citation has been made and has failed. But where the failure to serve is owing to carelessness, conditions may be attached to granting it. In a summary cause where a pursuer obtains warrant to cite for a particular diet, if he lets it lie till it is too late to execute it, re-service upon the same warrant is not competent, and the proper course is for the Court to grant a fresh warrant of citation. A party who appears may not plead irregularity of service, and his appearance is deemed to remedy any defect in the service unless where jurisdiction has been constituted by citation or by arrestment *ad fundandam jurisdictionem*.[2] But defenders sisted in a case could apparently plead irregularity of service on the original defender who had not appeared.[3] If objection to the citation is taken in subsequent proceedings the execution of citation may have to be reduced.[4]

[1] 7 Edw. VII c. 51, Schedule I, Rule 12.
[2] Ibid., Rule 13.
[3] Morrison v. Vallance's Executors, 1907 S.C. 999.
[4] Tait v. Johnston, 1891, 18 R. 606; Reid v. Clark, (O.H.) 1914, 2 S.L.T. 68.

In the case of any individual or individuals, or any corporation or association, carrying on business under a firm or trading or descriptive name citation may be made at the principal place where such business is carried on (including the place of business or office of the clerk or secretary of any corporation or association) when such place is within the jurisdiction of the Sheriff Court in which the action is brought, or otherwise at any place of business or office at which such business is carried on within the jurisdiction of such Sheriff Court.[1] It is thought that in the case of a club or voluntary association this would justify citation at the place from which the secretary in fact conducted its business, whether that place was the secretary's place of business, dwelling-house or apartments.[2] Apart from the above provision the common law rule is that in the case of a trading company or firm the place of business corresponds to the residence of an individual.[3] A company incorporated under the Companies Act can be cited at its registered office,[4] but if the registered office is not, and another place of business is, within the jurisdiction, citation should be at that place of business. If neither the registered office nor any place of business is within the jurisdiction—as

might happen if jurisdiction was founded by arrestment—it is
thought that the registered office is the proper place for citation.

1 7 Edw. VII c. 51, Schedule I, Rule 11; 2 & 3 Geo. V c. 28, Schedule II.
   It is essential for such citation that the business is still being
   carried on. See Bruce v. British Motor Trading Corporation, 1924
   S.C. 908.
2 See p. 90, supra.
3 See Rachkind v. Donald & Sons, 1916 S.C. 751, Lord Salvesen, p. 754.
4 19 & 20 Geo. V c. 23, sec. 370. See Brown & Critchley v. Decorative
   Art Journals Co., 1922 S.C. 192.

In the case of public corporations the method of citation may
be prescribed by their charter or constitution, or by Statute, but
if such place of citation is outwith the jurisdiction, and there is
a place of business within it, it is suggested that citation be
made at the latter.   Town councils are cited by service on the
town-clerk,[1] but other local authorities are cited in their corporate
name at their official address.   Special statutory provision is made
in the case of friendly societies.[2]   An action against the General
Assembly of the Church of Scotland should be served on the
moderator, the principal clerks, and the procurator,[3] but where
the matter refers to property, the Church of Scotland general
trustees are usually the proper defenders.[4]   Presbyteries and synods
are validly cited through their office-bearers.[5]   Where the Lord
Advocate is sued on behalf of a Government department service
should be made on him at the Crown Office.[6]   In the case of writs
to be served under the Merchant Shipping Act reference should
be made to the Statute.[7]

1 63 & 64 Vict. c. 49, sec. 9.
2 59 & 60 Vict. c. 25, secs. 68, 94; 8 Edw. VII c. 32, secs. 6, 11.
3 Cruickshank v. Gordon, 1843, 5 D. 909.
4 See Church of Scotland General Trustees v. Heritors of Rathven, 1931
   S.C. 215.
5 Skerret v. Oliver, 1896, 23 R. 468.
6 See p. 89, supra.
7 57 & 58 Vict. c. 60, sec. 696. See p. 624, infra.

In the case of a minor defender service in ordinary form on
him and on his father, as curator at law, or upon a minor and
his tutors and curators, if known to pursuer, or, if they are not
known, upon the minor himself, in ordinary form, and his tutors
and curators edictally, is declared to be good and sufficient service
on the minor for every purpose of law.[1]   A corresponding practice
should be followed in the case of a pupil defender, and where
no appearance is made a curator *ad litem* can be appointed.[2]

1 7 Edw. VII c. 51, Schedule I, Rule 14.
2 Drummond's Trustees v. Peel's Trustees, 1929 S.C. 484.

CHAPTER VII.

UNDEFENDED CAUSE.

1. DECREE.

If the defender in an ordinary cause does not lodge a notice of appearance within the induciæ, or if he fails to appear at the diet to which he has been cited in a summary cause or summary application, the pursuer may obtain decree in absence.[1] To do so the pursuer or his solicitor endorses on the initial writ a minute craving decree.[1] An ordinary action becomes an undefended cause immediately upon the expiry of the induciæ, if the defender has not meantime lodged a notice of appearance. The case does not require to be called in Court, and the pursuer need not wait for a sitting of the Court. Decree must be taken or at least the case must be enrolled within a year and a day after the induciæ has expired,[2] but if arrestment on the dependence has been used prior to service, the arrestment falls unless the action is served within twenty days from the execution of the arrestment and unless the decree in absence is taken within twenty days of the expiry of the induciæ.[3] In a summary cause, the fixed date of compearance must arrive before it is known whether or not the action is undefended. The action must accordingly be called on the appointed day. If the defender do not then appear, decree in absence may be granted on a minute being endorsed on the writ in the same way as in an ordinary cause. It is thought that the diet for appearance in a summary cause need not be an ordinary sitting of the Court and the form of warrant indicates that a defender can be cited to appear in chambers,[4] although this is not in practice usually done.[5]

[1] 7 Edw. VII c. 51, Schedule I, Rule 23; 2 & 3 Geo. V c. 28, Schedule II.
[2] 7 Edw. VII c. 51, Schedule I, Rule 101; M'Kidd v. Manson, 1882, 9 R. 790; Belfrage v. Blyth, 1910, 26 Sh.Ct.Rep. 295; Hillhead Garage v. Bunten & Miller, 1924, 40 Sh.Ct.Rep. 208; Hughes v. Scott, 1940, 56 Sh.Ct.Rep. 176.
[3] 7 Edw. VII c. 51, Schedule I, Rule 127; 2 & 3 Geo. V c. 28, Schedule II.
[4] See Ibid., Schedule I, Form B.
[5] The reason may be a doubt whether an attendance of this kind may be other than in open Court.

In an undefended action, where a notice of appearance has not been lodged, the case is not tabled,[1] and in a summary cause where the defender does not appear at the diet to which he has been cited it has been held that the pursuer, by continuing the case to a later date, is not prevented from asking decree in absence on an earlier day.[2] Where the writ has alternative craves the minute asking decree must state which crave is desired. Where a solicitor's account is sued for the account must be remitted for taxation before decree is taken. In certain actions such as those craving payment failing delivery, or a warrant of ejection failing plenishing or caution, there is a first interlocutory order which is intimated to the defender and failing implement of its terms the final decree is pronounced.

[1] Raimes, Clark & Co. v. Glass, 1909, 25 Sh.Ct.Rep. 309.
[2] Campbell & Henry v. Hunter, 1911, 27 Sh.Ct.Rep. 26.

The above provisions for taking decree in absence are declared not to apply in the case of actions of separation and aliment, adherence and aliment, interim aliment, or for regulating custody of children.[1] There is no express direction in the Act that in such actions the pursuer must substantiate her case, but the Court of Session practice is followed in the Sheriff Court and the pursuer has to lead evidence to support her averments.[2] Decree granted after this inquiry is still a decree in absence. If the defender appears at this diet, the pursuer's evidence will not usually be heard unless the defender is prepared to proceed with the proof at that time. He may be allowed to lodge a notice of appearance, and the case may then be sent to the roll as a defended cause. It is not appropriate to repone the defender, for as yet no decree in absence has been pronounced.

[1] 7 Edw. VII c. 51, Schedule I, Rule 23; 2 & 3 Geo. V c. 28, Schedule II.
[2] Grant v. Grant, 1908, 24 Sh.Ct.Rep. 114.

In addition to the above consistorial actions there are other classes of statutory proceedings in which decree is not granted without inquiry by proof or otherwise. These include declarators that a deed is validly subscribed,[1] applications under the Intestate Husband's Estate Acts,[2] declarators of the amount of a widow's terce,[3] applications for adoption orders,[4] actions by moneylenders where the interest exceeds 48 per cent.,[5] and declarators that a will is holograph.[6]

[1] 37 & 38 Vict. c. 94, sec. 39.
[2] 1 & 2 Geo. V c. 10; 9 & 10 Geo. V c. 9, secs. 1, 2.
[3] 14 & 15 Geo. V c. 27, sec. 21.
[4] 20 & 21 Geo. V c. 37, secs. 1, 3.
[5] Act of Sederunt, 24th February, 1933, sec. 5.
[6] Act of Sederunt, 19th July, 1935.

A decree in absence, which has not been recalled or brought under review by suspension or by reduction, becomes final, and entitled to all the privileges of a decree *in foro*, in six months from its date or from the date of charge upon it, where the service of the writ, or of the charge, has been personal; in any other case, in twenty years from the date of decree.[1] The privilege which attaches to a decree *in foro* is that the defender cannot be reponed. The decree can then be challenged only by suspension, if competent, or by reduction. A decree *in foro* cannot be pleaded against *ope exceptionis* in the Sheriff Court,[2] but a decree in absence may be, at any rate in a process of multiplepoinding in the Supreme Court.[3] The position in regard to errors in a decree is discussed later.[4]

[1] 7 Edw. VII c. 51, Schedule I, Rule 25.
[2] Leggat Bros. v. Gray, 1912 S.C. 230. See also Neil v. M'Nair, 1901, 3 F. (J.) 85; Smith v. Hutchison, 1926, 42 Sh.Ct.Rep. 183.
[3] Jarvie's Trustees v. Bannatyne, 1927 S.C. 34.
[4] See p. 253, infra.

If pursuer purposes to restrict the crave of his initial writ, he can do so in his minute craving decree in absence,[1] or in a separate minute. The restriction of the crave does not usually necessitate any notice being given to the defender, and the restricted writ does not require to be re-served. But a restriction which affected the nature of the action as, for instance, reducing an ordinary action to one appropriate in the Small Debt Court, might have a bearing upon the expenses to be awarded, unless the restriction was necessitated by a payment having been made after service of the action. Apart from any such restriction decree must be granted as craved and the Sheriff has no power to vary the crave *ex proprio motu*.[2]

[1] 7 Edw. VII c. 51, Schedule I, Rule 23; 2 & 3 Geo. V c. 28, Schedule II.
[2] Terry v. Murray, 1947 S.C. 10.

When a decree in absence is being obtained decree may be taken at the same time or later for expenses as the same may be certified by a note endorsed upon the initial writ by the Auditor of Court.[1] As an alternative to the expenses being adjusted by the auditor, pursuer's solicitor may elect to charge an inclusive fee fixed by the table of fees, and this election is signified by minute endorsed on the writ before extract is ordered.[2] Normally this will be done in the minute in which decree is craved. When expenses are fixed by the auditor no formal remit to him is required, and he acts on a note by the Sheriff-clerk endorsed on the writ showing that no appearance has been made for the defender.

[1] 7 Edw. VII c. 51, Schedule I, Rule 23; 2 & 3 Geo. V c. 28, Schedule II.
[2] Act of Sederunt, 7th May, 1935; Table of Fees, I, 1 (b).

The endorsement of the minute upon the writ craving decree in absence enables the decree to be signed at any time after the action has become an undefended cause. The writ with the minute endorsed is left with the Sheriff-clerk, who procures the decree in absence signed by the Sheriff in ordinary course. There is no form prescribed for the minute craving decree, and, as it is to be endorsed upon the writ, all that is required is a brief request which, in respect the defender has not lodged a notice of appearance (or has not answered), craves decree in terms of the crave of the writ with expenses as certified by the auditor amounting to a certain sum, or with expenses in respect of which the pursuer's solicitor elects to take the scale fee, plus certain specified outlays amounting in all to a certain sum.

A decree in absence should not be confounded with a decree by default. A decree in absence is granted when a defender fails to lodge a notice of appearance within the induciæ or fails to answer in a summary cause or application at the diet to which he has been cited. If the defender appear at the diet of compearance, or if notice of appearance is lodged, the case cannot be an undefended cause, and a decree pronounced after the defender has once appeared is not a decree in absence, but a decree by default. A decree by default is a decree *in foro*. It has been held that a notice of appearance, save of consent, cannot be withdrawn and the pursuer thus becomes entitled, once appearance has been entered, to obtain a decree *in foro*.[1]

[1] Cuthbert v. Stuart-Gray, 1904, 21 Sh.Ct.Rep. 31.

2. EXTRACT.

An extract of a decree in absence may be obtained after the expiry of seven days from the date of the Sheriff's judgment.[1] Formerly the judgment had to be signed within the Sheriffdom, but this is not now the case.[1] The date of such judgment, like the date of every other interlocutor, is deemed to be the date upon which it is entered in the books of Court.[1] A decree in absence, therefore, is not extractable till after the lapse of seven clear days from the entry of the decree in the Act Book of the Court, and the Sheriff does not appear to have power to shorten this period.[2] This applies to a decree in absence in either an ordinary action or a summary cause. The lodging of a reponing note is not declared to have the effect of preventing extract of the decree and the decree could apparently be extracted, though no diligence upon it is competent.[3]

1 7 Edw. VII c. 51, Schedule I, Rules 24, 83.
2 Ibid., Schedule I, Rule 85; 17 & 18 Geo. V c. 35, sec. 21.
3 Ibid., Schedule I, Rule 32.

An extract is the warrant for making a decree or order of Court operative. When *ex facie* regular it proves itself, and it is presumed in law to be conform to the interlocutor on which it bears to proceed.[1] Formerly it was a cumbrous document, but the Sheriff Courts (Scotland) Extracts Act of 1892 simplified and cheapened the procedure by introducing brief forms of extract, which are declared to be as valid and sufficient as the extended forms previously in use.[2] The Statute also provides that any party interested may demand from the Sheriff-clerk a full or more extended extract.[3]

1 Stair IV, 42, 10; Erskine IV, 2, 6.
2 55 & 56 Vict. c. 17, sec. 4.
3 Ibid., sec. 6.

The essential contents of the extract now are (a) the Court; (b) the parties; (c) the date of decree; (d) the decerniture; and (e) a warrant for the appropriate execution. Where imprisonment may follow, the special character of the debt should also be mentioned, as, for instance, for aliment.[1] The extract is dated from the seat of the Court which granted the decree, and is signed by the Sheriff-clerk.[1] It was at one time considered that no decree could be extracted unless it contained the word " decerns," but the Act of 1892 declared the use of this word to be unnecessary.[2] It also defined " interest " to mean interest at 5 per cent. per annum unless otherwise stated.[3] The import of the short forms of warrants of execution is contained in the Act.[4]

1 55 & 56 Vict. c. 17, Schedule.
2 Ibid., sec. 4.
3 Ibid., sec. 9.
4 Ibid., sec. 7.

The direction of the Extracts Act is that the extract is to be in the scheduled form, or as near thereto as the circumstances permit.[1] If a particular case is not scheduled, the extract is to be modelled on the forms of the schedule, with such variations as the nature of the case or form of the action or proceeding may necessarily require, or as an alternative the older form may be used.[2] No extract is to be held invalid on account of form if it be sound in substance.[3] The position in regard to errors in a judgment or extract is discussed later.[4] The statutory forms of extract may have the effect of supplying an omission in the judgment. Thus where a defender was ordained to consign, but no time was stated, the extract, following the statutory form, granted warrant for execution after a charge of seven days. It was held that this was justified and that the form had supplied what was lacking in the interlocutor.[5]

[1] 55 & 56 Vict. c. 17, sec. 4.
[2] Ibid., sec. 5.
[3] Ibid., sec. 11.
[4] See pp. 248, 253. infra.
[5] M'Lintock v. Prinzen & van Glabbeek, &c., 1902, 4 F. 948. See also
　Hardie v. Brown, Barker & Bell, (O.H.) 1907, 15 S.L.T. 539.

An extract is not essential to make every interlocutor of the Sheriff operative. In many summary applications the interlocutor is its own warrant for execution, and in formal intermediate steps of process an extract is not in general required. An extract is necessary when an interim or final judgment, in whole or in part, deals with the merits of the cause, and makes a decerniture against, or an order upon, one or other of the parties, which, if not voluntarily implemented, requires to be enforced by diligence. The Extract Act of 1892 does not apply to small debt cases, summary ejections, commissary proceedings, or services of heirs, or proceedings for completing titles, nor to proceedings under the Summary Jurisdiction Act.[1] These are dealt with under other Statutes.

[1] 55 & 56 Vict. c. 17, sec. 2.

3. Reponing.

Reponing is the placing of a defender, who has been decerned against in absence, in the same position as if that decree had not been granted. A defender who, by inadvertence, had allowed decree to pass against him in absence had formerly only the remedy of suspension in the Court of Session. The Court of Session Act of 1825[1] first introduced the system of reponing defenders against decrees in absence. The Sheriff Court Act of 1853[2] introduced the modern reponing note. The Act of 1876[3] allowed a defender to be reponed on simple motion, if made within seven days, or at a later date but before implement, if the defender could give a sufficient explanation of his failure to appear. The Sheriff Courts Act, 1907,[4] makes no distinction between reponing before and after seven days. It adopts the principle of the written note, introduced in 1853, but makes some important alterations on the practice.

1 6 Geo. IV c. 120, sec. 43.
2 16 & 17 Vict. c. 80, sec. 2, Schedule B.
3 39 & 40 Vict. c. 70, sec. 14.
4 7 Edw. VII c. 51, Schedule I, Rules 27, 33.

The Sheriff-Substitute can repone a defender only against a decree in absence. If the judgment complained of is a decree by default, then it is a decree *in foro*, and reponing in the Sheriff Court is incompetent.[1] But, if it is an appealable judgment, an appeal may be noted, and the Appellate Court may indirectly repone the defender, if the circumstances warrant this course, by recalling the decree and remitting the case back.[2]

1 West v. Hair, 1926, 43 Sh.Ct.Rep. 118.
2 See p. 250, infra.

Under the present procedure a defender may, at any time before implement of a decree in absence, apply to be reponed by lodging with the Sheriff-clerk and serving upon the pursuer a note setting forth his proposed defence, and his explanation of his failure to appear. Along with the reponing note the defender has also to consign the sum of £2 in the hands of the Sheriff-clerk.[1] A party other than the defender himself may apply to be reponed if he would be entitled to be sisted as a party to the action.[2] Thus an executrix of a deceased defender[2] and a trustee for a defender's creditors[3] have been reponed. In a furthcoming an arrestee can be reponed.[4]

1 7 Edw. VII c. 51, Schedule I, Rules 27, 28.
2 Pearson & Jackson v. Allison, 1871, 9 M. 473.
3 Barrie v. Hosie, 1933, 49 Sh.Ct.Rep. 114; cf. Primrose, Thomson & Co. v. Crawford, 1913, 29 Sh.Ct.Rep. 243; London and North-Eastern Railway Co., &c. v. Reid Bros., 1944, 61 Sh.Ct.Rep. 22.
4 Fraser v. Savings Investment Trust, 1912, 28 Sh.Ct.Rep. 224.

Reponing is a matter which is now entirely in the discretion of the Sheriff. Upon consignation being made the Sheriff, if satisfied with the defender's explanation, may recall the decree so far as not implemented, whereupon the action proceeds in all respects as if the defender had appeared. On the other hand, if the Sheriff is not satisfied with the defender's explanations he may refuse the reponing note.[1] The usual practice is that the Sheriff should also be satisfied that the defender has a stateable defence.[2] Reponing notes may be lodged in many different circumstances, but it has been pointed out that in the reported cases

they have been granted only where the defender has been misled
by someone connected with the pursuer, where the defender was
under some excusable mistake in fact, or where he was not within
reasonable reach of legal advice.[3]   A defender has not in general
been reponed in respect of his own neglect or delay,[4] but the
requirement that the Sheriff should be satisfied with the defender's
explanation leaves him with a wide discretion, and in some Courts
reponing is granted as a matter of course if a defender has a
stateable case and can give any reasonable excuse for his failure
to appear.[5]   In a consistorial case reponing may be granted after
proof has been taken.[6]

[1] 7 Edw. VII c. 51, Schedule I, Rules 29, 30.
[2] Nisbet, &c. v. Macleod, 1923, 39 Sh.Ct.Rep. 248.
[3] Robert M'Coll v. M'Donald, 1933 S.L.T. (Sh.Ct.) 4.
[4] Reponing was granted in these cases: Christie v. Christie, 1917, 34
    Sh.Ct.Rep. 123; Nisbet, &c. v. Macleod, supra; Mess v. Mutch,
    1928, 45 Sh.Ct.Rep. 54; Wards v. Wards, 1929, 45 Sh.Ct.Rep. 305;
    Young v. Snaddon, 1931, 48 Sh.Ct.Rep. 19; Macmillan v. Ellis, 1941,
    58 Sh.Ct.Rep. 48; London and North-Eastern Railway Co., &c. v.
    Reid Bros., &c., 1944, 61 Sh.Ct.Rep. 22; and was refused in these
    cases: Rodger v. Mackay, 1904, 21 Sh.Ct.Rep. 29; Thow v. Thow,
    1908, 24 Sh.Ct.Rep. 329; Logan, &c. v. Miller, 1910, 27 Sh.Ct.Rep.
    25; Fraser v. Savings Investment Trust, 1912, 28 Sh.Ct.Rep. 224;
    Macphail v. West-End Hiring Co., 1915, 32 Sh.Ct.Rep. 225; Robert
    M'Coll v. M'Donald, supra; Graham v. Finlay, 1937, 53 Sh.Ct.Rep.
    218; Ramsay v. Russell, 1939, 56 Sh.Ct.Rep. 63; Deuchar v.
    MacAllan, 1943, 59 Sh.Ct.Rep. 202; Macdonald v. Kennedy, 1943,
    60 Sh.Ct.Rep. 108.
[5] This is in accord with the view taken in the Court of Session on an
    appeal against a Sheriff Court decree by default, M'Kelvie v. Scottish
    Steel Scaffolding Co., 1938 S.C. 278.
[6] Christie v. Christie, supra.

The Act gives no form for a reponing note, but defender is
required to set forth in it his proposed defence and his explanation of his failure to appear.[1]   The defence here meant is the
general answer to pursuer's case, as set forth in the initial writ.
If the defence indicated in the reponing note is obviously of
an irrelevant or frivolous nature, the Sheriff may refuse it.[2]   What
is contemplated is that the matter of reponing shall be decided
upon the note itself, without inquiry by proof.   It is thought that
in all cases pursuer is entitled to be heard, if he wants to be
heard; and in practice a diet is usually appointed.

[1] 7 Edw. VII c. 51, Schedule I, Rule 27.
[2] Fraser v. Savings Investment Trust, 1912, 28 Sh.Ct.Rep. 224; Nisbet,
    &c. v. Macleod, 1923, 39 Sh.Ct.Rep. 248.

A reponing note, when duly lodged and intimated to the
pursuer or to his solicitor, operates as a sist of diligence,[1] but it
does not recall it.   Thus an arrestment on the dependence stands,

notwithstanding that defender may be reponed. The defender may fail in his defence, and the pursuer is not to be deprived of the benefit of any diligence he may meantime have used. The terms of the rule[1] justify service of the reponing note, and this is usually done without any order of Court. Alternatively, an interlocutor ordering service and appointing a diet for hearing parties may be pronounced.

[1] 7 Edw. VII c. 51, Schedule I, Rule 32.

Reponing is open to a defender at any time before implement of the decree.[1] Matters, however, may not be intact, and it may not be possible to place the defender just where he was before the decree in absence was pronounced, for the decree may have been partially implemented. The fact that the Sheriff is to recall the decree so far as not implemented[2] seems to make it clear that reponing is competent even though the decree has been implemented to some extent.

[1] 7 Edw. VII c. 51, Schedule I, Rule 27.
[2] Ibid., Rule 29.

What is " implement " of a decree in absence is a question of circumstances. If the decree has been fully implemented as by payment by defender or recovery by pursuer of the sum decerned for there can be no reponing. So also if by voluntary payment by the defender, or by the use of diligence by pursuer, half the sum decerned for in absence is already in pursuer's pocket, the reponing has no effect upon that half, and the defence can be entertained only to the effect of showing why the other half should not be paid. And under a decree ordaining delivery of fifty articles, if the pursuer has already obtained possession of thirty, the defender can be reponed only against the order to deliver the other twenty.

The general principle is that, to whatever extent the pursuer has actually obtained what he sought, the defender is barred from being reponed, but if pursuer, however near he may have come to it, has not actually got what the decree entitled him to have, the defender is still in time to seek to be reponed, as, for instance, where an arrestment has attached funds, but the arrestment has not yet been made operative by decree of furthcoming.[1] But where a poinding has been executed, even although it has not been reported or followed by a sale, the decree has been implemented in the reponing sense to the extent of the poinding.[2] It has been indicated that imprisonment following on a decree should be regarded as implement,[3] but imprisonment is now in certain cases restricted by Statute.[4]

[1] Paul v. Macrae, 1887, 3 Sh.Ct.Rep. 338.
[2] Stephenson v. Dobbins, 1852, 14 D. 510; Anderson v. Anderson, 1855, 17 D. 804; Rowan v. Mercer, 1863, 4 Irvine 377; M'Niven v. Orr, 1905, 22 Sh.Ct.Rep. 9.
[3] M'Lachlan v. Rutherford & Co., 1854, 16 D. 937.
[4] 3 & 4 Geo. VI c. 42, sec. 1 (1). See also 22 & 23 Geo. V c. 38, sec. 7 (1) (vi).

Under the earlier Acts the sum to be consigned with a reponing note was treated as expenses, and the Sheriff had a discretion as to its disposal.[1] The present provision is that, whether the reponing note is granted or refused, the pursuer is entitled to uplift the consigned money.[2] The Sheriff has no discretion in the matter. Different views have been expressed as to whether the £2 is a payment to account of expenses or not.[3] It seems to be clear that the pursuer has right to the sum by virtue of the Act itself, and that even if the defender succeeds he cannot recover the amount, and his expenses presumably start as from the date when he was reponed. It may not seem reasonable that the pursuer, if successful, should retain the £2 and charge his opponent in full with the expenses of taking the original decree and of the procedure in connexion with reponing, but it is difficult to see that the defender can in such a case insist on the £2 being credited towards expenses. A decision that the £2 could not be returned to defender even where the reponing note was lodged in error may be thought open to doubt.[1]

[1] See 16 & 17 Vict. c. 80, sec. 2; 39 & 40 Vict. c. 70, sec. 14.
[2] 7 Edw. VII c. 51, Schedule I, Rule 31.
[3] A & Co. v. B, 1911, 27 Sh.Ct.Rep. 214; Hart v. Barras, 1920, 38 Sh.Ct.Rep. 27.
[4] Hart v. Barras, supra.

An interlocutor or order recalling, or incidental to the recall of a decree in absence is final and not subject to review,[1] but an interlocutor refusing a reponing note may be appealed to the Sheriff Principal or to the Court of Session.[2] The Sheriff-Substitute cannot effectively grant leave to appeal against an interlocutor sustaining a reponing note and recalling a decree in absence.[3]

[1] 7 Edw. VII c. 51, Schedule I, Rule 33; 2 & 3 Geo. V c. 28, Schedule II.
[2] Ibid., secs. 27, 28; 2 & 3 Geo. V c. 28, Schedule I.
[3] Mess v. Mutch, 1928, 45 Sh.Ct.Rep. 54.

CHAPTER VIII.

DEFENDED CAUSE.

1. APPEARANCE.

An action is " defended " when appearance is made by or for the defender. Formerly it was thought that a defender might withdraw his notice of appearance before, or at, the first calling, but that is not now competent,[1] and the Sheriff Courts Act, 1907, directs the Sheriff-clerk, so soon as appearance has been entered, to enrol the case for tabling.[2] In an ordinary action, appearance is made by defender exhibiting to the Sheriff-clerk the service copy of the writ and lodging a notice of appearance before the expiry of the induciæ.[3] The notice of appearance is in the terms shown in the rule.[3] In a summary cause, appearance is made by defender or his solicitor answering when the case is called at the diet appointed in the warrant of citation. But the effect is in each case the same. A decree in absence cannot then be granted, even if defender do nothing more than appear, for, whether he go on to defend the action or not, the mere fact of his making appearance makes the action a defended cause ; and, if defender do not go on to defend, judgment is given against him in the form of a decree by default, not a decree in absence. It is thought that the time for entering appearance cannot be prorogated by the Sheriff under Rule 56,[4] but a late notice of appearance is in practice accepted of consent. A defender who lodges defences cannot disclaim appearance which has been made in his name.[5]

1 Cuthbert v. Stuart-Gray, 1904, 21 Sh.Ct.Rep. 31.
2 7 Edw. VII c. 51, Schedule I, Rule 34.
3 Ibid., Rule 22 ; 2 & 3 Geo. V c. 28, Schedule II.
4 Ibid., Rule 56.
5 A B v. C D, 1905, 21 Sh.Ct.Rep. 303.

The practice in this matter in the Sheriff Court differs from that of the Court of Session, where a decree in respect of no defences is a decree in absence.[1] The practice in the Sheriff Court is now regulated by the terms of the Sheriff Courts Act, 1907,[2] but that only expresses what had always been the practice in the Sheriff Court.

1 Rules of Court II, 17.
2 7 Edw. VII c. 51, Schedule I, Rules 23, 56 ; 2 & 3 Geo. V c. 28, Schedule II.

2. Tabling.

Under the Sheriff Courts Act, 1907, " tabling " became an official step in every ordinary cause and was a new process name. The Act directs that, where appearance has been entered, the Sheriff-clerk shall enrol the cause for tabling on the first Court day occurring after the expiry of the induciæ.[1] If the case is not then tabled and if protestation has not been craved, it drops from the roll; but by leave of the Sheriff it may be enrolled for tabling within three months on such conditions as to notice, re-service or expenses or otherwise as the Sheriff may impose.[2] If arrestment on the dependence has been used prior to service, it falls in the case of defended actions unless the action is tabled within twenty days of the first ordinary Court day occurring after the expiry of the induciæ.[3] It is the pursuer's duty to table the case, and it is the defender's privilege, if the case is not tabled, to ask protestation. But where there are several defenders the case will not be enrolled for tabling till the induciæ has expired against the defender last served. From the wording of the rules it would appear that the process of tabling is restricted to ordinary causes and that a summary cause is not tabled at the diet of appearance appointed in the warrant of citation. But for purposes of protestation and arrestment on the dependence it is thought that the diet of appearance in a summary cause must necessarily be regarded as tabling.

[1] 7 Edw. VII c. 51, Schedule I, Rule 34.
[2] Ibid., Rule 35.
[3] Ibid., Rule 127; 2 & 3 Geo. V c. 28, Schedule II.

The pursuer's solicitor who is to table the case should be in Court when the case calls, and it is not sufficient that the writ has been handed in at the Court before the Sheriff has taken his seat on the Bench.[1] Where a case has not been tabled, and where the defender has not craved protestation and the case has not been re-enrolled for tabling under Rule 35, there appears to be no method by which it can be revived, and the action simply falls. It cannot, after the expiry of year and day, be treated as an action which is asleep and which can be wakened.[2] Irregularities at the stage of tabling resulting from a wrong date on the service copy writ may be a ground for suspension of the proceedings.[3]

[1] Higgins v. Atkinson, 1908, 24 Sh.Ct.Rep. 385.
[2] Robb & Crosbie v. Forbes, 1911, 27 Sh.Ct.Rep. 162. See also M'Kidd v. Manson, 1882, 9 R. 790; Belfrage v. Blyth, 1910, 24 Sh.Ct.Rep. 295.
[3] Wilson v. Gorman, (O.H.) 1924 S.L.T. 112.

3. Process.

In an ordinary action, when a notice of appearance has been lodged, it becomes the duty of the pursuer to make up a process, and there should be lodged at tabling with the Sheriff-clerk, principal and duplicate interlocutor sheets, and a principal and borrowing inventory of process.[1] After defences have been lodged, and before the diet for adjustment, the pursuer must also lodge a certified copy of the initial writ and warrant thereon.[2] The process begins its course when the action is tabled, or called, and thereafter may be borrowed. The principal interlocutor sheets and borrowing inventory of process remain always with the Sheriff-clerk[1]; so does the principal initial writ unless the Sheriff grants a special warrant to give it out.[3] The items of a process are numbered in their order as put in, but the Sheriff-clerk must endorse upon all pleadings the date on which they are lodged.[1] In a summary cause a process is not usually made up, but in certain circumstances it may be convenient to have this done. Formerly the terms of a lost interlocutor could only be set up in an action of proving the tenor but now a copy—authenticated in such a manner as the Sheriff may require—may be substituted for any number of process which has been lost or destroyed.[4]

[1] 7 Edw. VII c. 51, Schedule I, Rule 18.
[2] Ibid., Rule 46; 2 & 3 Geo. V c. 28, Schedule II.
[3] Ibid., Rule 16; 2 & 3 Geo. V c. 28, Schedule II.
[4] Ibid., Rule 17.

A process may be borrowed only by a solicitor entitled to practise in the jurisdiction or by his duly authorized clerk, for whom he is responsible.[1] It is not necessary that the solicitor have a place of business in the Sheriffdom.[2]

[1] 7 Edw. VII c. 51, Schedule I, Rule 16; 2 & 3 Geo. V c. 28, Schedule II.
[2] 23 & 24 Geo. V c. 21, sec. 46 (which repeals 36 & 37 Vict. c. 63, sec. 15).

The solicitor who borrows a process is responsible for its return, and if he fails to return it for any diet at which it is required he may be fined in a sum not exceeding £1.[1] This is a penalty personal to the solicitor for which his client has no liability. It is optional to, not imperative upon, the Sheriff to impose the penalty. If he does so, there is no appeal, but the Sheriff himself may, on cause shown, recall his order.[1] For the purpose of these provisions every solicitor practising before his Court is subject to the jurisdiction of the Sheriff.[1]

¹ 7 Edw. VII c. 51, Schedule I, Rule 57.

Formerly, when a solicitor failed to return a process, the only remedy was for the other solicitor to institute against him a process caption in which, after intimation, a warrant of imprisonment might be granted against the solicitor (or his clerk) who had borrowed and failed to return the process. A caption process of this sort is still competent, and is the appropriate remedy where, as sometimes happens, after a case is finished, a process is held up to prevent extract being issued. This would probably be regarded as a form of contempt of Court.[1] All remedies (including caption) competent to enforce the return of a borrowed process may proceed on the warrant of the Court from whose custody the process was obtained, and that whether the borrower is or is not resident within its jurisdiction.[2] If documents in a process are held up in the course of the litigation, the other side, if defending, might obtain absolvitor if the documents were essential to the case and were not forthcoming. In any case if an order for their return was not implemented decree as craved, or of absolvitor, might be granted under Rule 56.[3]

¹ Levison v. Jewish Chronicle, (O.H.) 1924 S.L.T. 755. See also Watt v. Thomson, 1868, 6 M. 1112; 8 M. (H.L.) 77; 11 M. 960; 1 R. (H.L.) 21; Gregson v. Grant, (O.H.) 1910, 2 S.L.T. 16.
² 7 Edw. VII c. 51, Schedule I, Rule 16; 2 & 3 Geo. V c. 28, Schedule II.
³ Ibid., Rule 56.

4. PROTESTATION.

Protestation is the defender's remedy against a pursuer who does not proceed with a process which he has instituted. By this means the defender can force the pursuer either to proceed with his process or let it fall. The defender must exercise this privilege in an ordinary action at the diet at which the pursuer should table his case, which is (a) the first Court day occurring after the expiry of the induciæ upon which the Sheriff-clerk has enrolled the case for tabling, or (b) any Court day, not later than three months thereafter, upon which the Sheriff has directed the case to be again enrolled for tabling.[1] If the pursuer do not at such diet table the cause the defender may produce the service copy of the writ and crave protestation, which the Sheriff may grant and may modify the amount of protestation money payable to the defender.[2] Two or three guineas is a usual award. Where a case has not been tabled and protestation has not been craved there seems no reason why the defender should not, within three months of the first diet, ask the Sheriff to direct the case to be again enrolled for tabling so that he can then crave protestation if the case is not tabled. Where there are two or more defenders, protestation taken by one may be available to others who have in fact concurred in applying for protestation but the process will not fall *quoad* any remaining defenders.[3] Extract is granted after a lapse of seven days in normal circumstances, or forty-eight hours where arrestments have been used, and upon protestation being extracted the instance falls, any arrestment on the dependence, of course, falling also.[4] While tabling appears under the rules to be restricted to an ordinary cause it is thought that this would not be held to deprive a defender of his right to protestation and that in a summary cause the diet for appearance must be taken as equivalent to tabling. It has been pointed out that a motion for absolvitor in respect of the pursuer's failure to table is not appropriate.[5]

[1] 7 Edw. VII c. 51, Schedule I, Rules 34, 35.
[2] Ibid., Rule 36.
[3] Sceales v. Commercial Bank, 1839, 1 D. 465.
[4] 7 Edw. VII c. 51, Schedule I, Rules 37, 38.
[5] Higgins v. Atkinson, 1908, 24 Sh.Ct.Rep. 385.

There is no appeal against an interlocutor granting protestation, but, before extract, the Sheriff himself may recall the protestation, and the pursuer may be allowed to proceed with his action upon payment to defender of the protestation money, and upon such other conditions as the Sheriff may think fit.[1] If, however, the protestation is extracted, the process comes to an end and pursuer would then require, if he wanted to revive it, to serve a fresh initial writ and table a new action.[2]

[1] 7 Edw. VII c. 51, Schedule I, Rule 39.
[2] Ibid., Rule 38.

5. LOST PROCESS.

Formerly much inconvenience resulted from a part or the whole of the process going amissing, and to set up the terms of documents which had been produced in Court, but had been lost, an action of proving the tenor was sometimes necessary. But this matter is now dealt with by Rule 17 which provides that when any number of process is lost or destroyed, a copy thereof, authenticated in such manner as the Sheriff may require, may be substituted, and shall, for the purposes of the action, be equivalent to the original.[1] The rule covers every document in a process, including the initial writ and interlocutor sheets. To bring a document within its provision, it is sufficient that it has been marked a number of process.

1 7 Edw. VII c. 51, Schedule I, Rule 17.

What is a copy, and what is " authentication," are questions of circumstances in each case. Excerpts from books, correspondence, and the like should present no difficulty, but there may be documents upon the appearance of which much may depend—as, for instance, bills of exchange or bills of lading—and it may often be impossible to get an exact duplicate. In the case of formal deeds there may be no duplicate. If a lease were lost a tenant's copy, made at the time the lease was entered into, certified by the landlord's solicitor or factor as a correct copy, would probably be accepted by the Court as a sufficiently authenticated copy. But if the copy had to be made up from a draft, it might come near to setting up the lost deed instead of substituting a copy of it. No hard and fast interpretation can be put upon this rule. But it is thought that it does not sanction a document being set up, as distinguished from an admitted copy of a document being substituted for a lost original, and cases may still occur where a document of importance may have to be set up in a separate action of proving the tenor.

It is only competent to substitute a copy of a document which has been produced and marked a number of process. It is not enough that a document is founded on in the pleadings, if it has not come into the process. Thus, if a document is produced along with the initial writ, or with defences, and that document gets lost, a copy may be substituted; but if the document has not been produced with the pleading, but is merely referred to in it, it has never become a number of process, and so, if it goes amissing, the Sheriff has no power to substitute a copy, unless of consent of all parties.

6. PROCEDURE AFTER TABLING.

(1) *General*.

Until 1853 actions in the Sheriff Court were almost entirely conducted by written pleadings, except in the Small Debt Court, where oral pleading has always been recognized. The only relic of written pleading which was saved by the Act of 1853,[1] and which still survives, is the optional power in the Sheriff in appeal proceedings to order written arguments, in the shape of a reclaiming petition and answers, in place of hearing parties orally. The rules further provide that the Sheriff may, on the motion of both parties, dispose of the appeal without even an oral hearing.[2] The Sheriff has a like latitude as regards appeals upon the ground of confidentiality taken in the course of a proof. He is broadly directed, with or without a hearing, and with the least possible delay, to dispose of such appeal.[3]

[1] 16 & 17 Vict. c. 80, sec. 16.
[2] 7 Edw. VII c. 51, Schedule I, Rules 89, 90; 2 & 3 Geo. V c. 28, Schedule II.
[3] Ibid., Rule 76.

(2) *Summary Cause.*

As has already been pointed out,[1] there are no statutory requirements as to procedure in a summary cause, except that in defended causes, (a) if defences are not ordered a note of the defence is taken by the Sheriff[2]; (b) a diet must be fixed for the trial of the cause, or such other procedure ordered as the circumstances seem to the Sheriff to require[2]; and (c) as in other cases the final judgment on the merits must be in writing and contain findings in fact and findings in law.[3] Whilst formal pleadings are not compulsory, they are quite competent, and it is in the Sheriff's discretion to adopt as procedure in a summary cause such of the rules as he considers appropriate. The usual practice is to have written defences, but not to have the record closed. The evidence in a summary cause need not be recorded unless on the motion of either party the Sheriff orders that the evidence be recorded.[4] If such a motion is made it is held that the Sheriff must accede to it.[5]

[1] See p. 99, supra.
[2] 7 Edw. VII c. 51, sec. 8, Schedule I, Rule 41.
[3] Ibid., Rule 82.
[4] Ibid., sec. 8. See p. 99, supra.
[5] Stewart v. Gourlay, 1939, 56 Sh.Ct.Rep. 3; Weiner v. Tod, Cunningham & Petrie, 1941, 57 Sh.Ct.Rep. 58.

In some Courts the Sheriffs grant decrees by instalments in summary causes in the same way as in small debt causes. This may be a continuation of the practice in the Debts Recovery Court which dealt with cases roughly equivalent to what are now summary causes. But in the Debts Recovery Court the right to grant an instalment decree was statutory, by the express adoption of the relevant section in the Small Debt Act.[1] There is no similar authority in regard to summary causes. The matter seems to rest entirely on practice and it may be open to challenge as having no statutory sanction.

[1] 30 & 31 Vict. c. 96, sec. 5 ; 7 Will. IV & 1 Vict. c. 41, sec. 19.

Of consent of parties, any defended action (other than a claim under the Workmen's Compensation Act) may at any stage become a summary cause.[1] If an action not falling within the summary cause definition is of consent desired to be tried as such, the parties should put it in a joint minute craving the Court to direct that it be tried as a summary cause. Such a minute may be put in at any stage of a cause, but the obviously convenient stage is at the tabling. The Sheriff's decision on this motion is final.[1]

[1] 7 Edw. VII c. 51, Schedule I, Rule 40.

(3) Ordinary Action.

(a) *The Condescendence.*—The condescendence, as a statutory necessity, was introduced by the Sheriff Court Act of 1876.[1] The present rule (as amended by the Act of 1913) is that there shall be annexed to the initial writ a statement (in the form of an articulate condescendence) of the facts which form the ground of action, and a note of the pursuer's pleas in law, which condescendence and note of pleas in law shall be held to constitute part of the initial writ.[2]

[1] 39 & 40 Vict. c. 70, sec. 6.
[2] 7 Edw. VII c. 51, Schedule I, Rule 2 ; 2 & 3 Geo. V c. 28, Schedule II.

The object of a condescendence is to set forth in detail the grounds of action, and it should disclose the pursuer's whole case, including his title and interest to sue. The condescendence is a pursuer's explanatory paper, and it should set forth succinctly, and in articulate articles, the grounds of action and the whole pleas in law upon which he is to ask the Court to give decree. A plea ought to contain a proposition in law to which the Court is asked to give effect.[1]

[1] Mitchell v. Aberdeen Insurance Committee, 1918 S.C. 415, Lord Justice-Clerk Scott Dickson, p. 430, Lord Dundas, p. 433.

(b) *The Defences.*—In an ordinary action defences are due to be lodged either at the tabling of the case or within six days thereafter.[1] That is a statutory provision, but an order for defences is usually made. In a summary cause the Sheriff may or may not order defences.[2] If ordered the interlocutor will state when they are due. It is essential that defences be lodged on the due date, irrespective of the Court being then in vacation.[3] But in all cases the Sheriff may prorogate the time for lodging defences even after the original period has expired.[4]

[1] 7 Edw. VII c. 51, Schedule I, Rule 42; 2 & 3 Geo. V c. 28, Schedule II.
[2] Ibid., Schedule I, Rule 41; 2 & 3 Geo. V c. 28, Schedule II.
[3] Lord Brooke v. Marchioness of Huntly, 1911, 2 S.L.T. 382.
[4] Macnab v. Nelson, 1909 S.C. 1102.

The statutory direction is that defences shall be in the form of articulate answers to the condescendence, with a note of defender's pleas in law, and, where necessary, a statement of facts.[1] This separate statement of facts is essential when the defender states a counter-claim.[1] It is also appropriate where defender's case rests on facts not disclosed in the pursuer's condescendence; where it is advisable for defender to state the facts in his own way; where his case raises an entirely new issue; or where he wishes to have explicit answers by pursuer to facts on which he is to rely. When defender has put in a statement of facts the pursuer will normally be appointed to answer it while the case is at adjustment.[2] Although the defender has a preliminary plea—as one to jurisdiction—which might dispose of the action, he cannot reserve his answers and defence on the merits. Defences on these lines should be refused as incompetent, as the whole defence must be stated at the one time.[3]

[1] 7 Edw. VII c. 51, Schedule I, Rule 43; 2 & 3 Geo. V c. 28, Schedule II.
[2] 7 Edw. VII c. 51, Schedule I, Rule 49.
[3] Thorburn v. Dempster, 1900, 2 F. 583.

A party is, by Rule 44, bound to answer every statement of fact made by the other party, and, if a statement made by one party of a fact within the knowledge of the other party is not denied by that other party, the latter is held as admitting the fact so stated.[1] A mere non-admission will not in such circumstances be accepted.[2] This applies even if the other party intends to plead that the statements in question are irrelevant. If a party makes evasive answers, he runs a risk of being held as admitting his opponent's statements, because he does not distinctly deny them. Qualified admissions must be taken with their qualifications,[3] but if the other party at a proof succeeds in removing the qualification, he may then be able to found upon the admissions.[4]

[1] 7 Edw. VII c. 51, Schedule I, Rule 44; 2 & 3 Geo. V c. 28, Schedule II. See also Central Motor Engineering Co. v. Galbraith, 1918 S.C. 755; Gilmour v. Scottish Clan Motorways, (O.H.) 1928 S.N. 19.
[2] Pegler v. Northern Agricultural Implement Co., 1877, 4 R. 435, Lord President Inglis, p. 438.

3 Picken v. Arundale & Co., 1872, 10 M. 987; Gelston v. Christie, 1875, 2 R. 982; Chrystal v. Chrystal, 1900, 2 F. 373; Walker v. Garlick, (O.H.) 1940 S.L.T. 208.
4 Scottish North Eastern Railway Co. v. Napier, 1859, 21 D. 700; Robertson & Co. v. Bird & Co., 1897, 24 R. 1076.

Defences should explicitly bear in the heading for whom they are lodged.[1] Where there are more defenders than one, each is entitled, but not bound, to lodge separate defences. Where the ground of defence is the same, a question may arise as to whether, if the defence is successful, each defender is entitled to expenses at any rate after the closing of the record.[2] If the grounds of defence are different each defender should lodge separate defences.

1 Fernie v. Bell, (O.H.) 1894, 2 S.L.T. 311.
2 Anderson v. M'Cracken Brothers, 1900, 2 F. 780.

The defence may involve a challenge of a deed or writing founded on, objections to which may be stated and maintained by way of exception, without the necessity of bringing a reduction thereof.[1] But this rule does not make it competent to deal by way of exception with a document when the Sheriff's judgment cannot finally dispose of the question, as, for instance, an exception to the validity of a will taken in the course of a petition to complete title.[2] Nor does it entitle a defender in all circumstances to challenge a deed or writing. His right to do so depends upon such elements as the nature of the deed or writing, and whether he has a title and interest to challenge it. A deed or writing, for instance, might be challenged as not constituting an obligation enforceable at law against the defender, although in itself a valid deed. Where the validity of the deed itself is challenged, the challenger must himself have a title to sue an action of reduction. Thus a tenant, who can himself show no title to the property, cannot challenge the validity of his landlord's title, *ope exceptionis*, because he could not bring an action of reduction of the title.[3]

1 7 Edw. VII c. 51, Schedule I, Rule 50.
2 Donald v. Donald, 1913 S.C. 274. See further, p. 22, supra.
3 Duke of Argyll v. Muir, 1910 S.C. 96.

A party who has not been called as defender in a case may be allowed to appear and lodge defences. This may happen where public rights are at stake as in the case of rights of way,[1] but it may also occur in other cases where a party, though not a defender, will usually be permitted to appear and defend if he can show a title and interest to intervene.[2]

1 Macfie v. Scottish Rights of Way Society, 1884, 11 R. 1094; Houldsworth v. School Board of Cambusnethan, 1904, 7 F. 291; cf. Hope v. Landward Committee of Parish Council of Inveresk, 1906, 8 F. 896.

² Scottish Heritages Co. v. North British Property Investment Co., 1885, 12 R. 550; Glasgow Shipowners' Association, &c. v. Clyde Navigation Trustees, 1885, 12 R. 695; Bruce v. Calder, 1903, 20 Sh.Ct.Rep. 288; Ross v. Ross, &c., (O.H.) 1909, 2 S.L.T. 117; Gas Power, &c., Co. v. Power Gas Corporation, 1911 S.C. 27; Zurich, &c., Insurance Co. v. Livingston, 1938 S.C. 582; cf. Laing's Sewing Machine Co. v. Norrie & Sons, 1877, 5 R. 29; Heron v. Martin, 1893, 20 R. 1001; Muir v. Glasgow Corporation, 1917, 2 S.L.T. 106.

Only in exceptional circumstances will a defender be allowed to appear in the process by minute.[1] In the normal case a defender must lodge defences if he desires to be a party to the litigation, and a minute will either be refused or disregarded.[2] Defences which have been lodged may be withdrawn by minute, and decree granted to the pursuer.[3] Where it is alleged that defences have been lodged without authority the proper course is to allow time for the production of a mandate.[4]

[1] Macpherson v. Macdonald Fraser & Co., 1905, 12 S.L.T. 824.
[2] Ramsay v. M'Laren, (O.H.) 1936 S.L.T. 35. See also Campbell v. Ayr County Council, (O.H.) 1905, 13 S.L.T. 193.
[3] Ower v. Crichton, (O.H.) 1902, 10 S.L.T. 279.
[4] Fischer & Co. v. Andersen, 1896, 23 R. 395.

(c) *Judicial Tender.*—If a defender propose to make a tender to the pursuer, he may do so in the defences (although this practice has recently been deprecated[1]) or he may lodge a minute of tender with his defences or at any other stage of the case. Whether it is in the defences, or by separate minute, a judicial tender must meet the crave of the pursuer. A tender in respect of one of several craves with expenses applicable to that crave is a good tender.[2] But if there are several pursuers with separate claims the tender, to be effective, must allocate a separate sum to each.[3] In an action of count and reckoning the pursuer's right to demand an accounting should be recognized, and in an action of damages for slander the words complained of should be retracted, as well as money damages offered.[4] It is not necessary that the defender admit the use of the words complained of and an apology for the words, if used, is sufficient.[5] The tender must be unqualified and unconditional,[6] and must include an offer of expenses up to the date of tender,[7] and such expenses must be on the scale appropriate to the action as brought.[8] But where no claim had been intimated before an action was raised a tender without expenses made on service of the writ was effective.[9] A tender has an important effect upon the question of expenses which will be discussed later.[10] One of several defenders may make a tender on his own account, and the pursuer may accept it, without discontinuing the action against the others, to recover any balance

still due. A tender should not be brought to the notice of the
Sheriff,[1] and it is now in practice usually placed in a sealed
envelope by the Sheriff-clerk. In view of the effect of a tender it
is essential that it be brought to the notice of the other side and
the proper practice is to intimate it when it is lodged. The lodging
of a tender does not imply that the defender has waived a plea
of no jurisdiction.[11]

[1] Avery v. Cantilever Shoe Co., 1942 S.C. 469.
[2] John Hamilton & Co. v. Fleming & Co., (O.H.) 1918, 1 S.L.T. 229.
[3] Boyle v. Olsen, 1912 S.C. 1235; Flanagan v. Dempster, Moore & Co.,
      1928 S.C. 308. See also M'Crae v. Bryson, (O.H.) 1923 S.L.T. 164;
      1923 S.C. 896; Peggie v. Keddie, 1932 S.C. 721.
[4] Faulks v. Park, 1854, 17 D. 247; Malcolm v. Moore, 1901, 4 F. 23;
      Mitchell v. Nicoll, 1890, 17 R. 795; Sturrock v. Deas & Co.,
      (O.H.) 1913, 1 S.L.T. 60. See also Hunter v. Russell, 1901, 3 F.
      596; Davidson v. Panti, 1915, 1 S.L.T. 273 (tender of apology
      without damages).
[5] Malcolm v. Moore, supra.
[6] Gunn v. Marquis of Breadalbane, 1849, 11 D. 1046; Low v. Spences,
      (O.H.) 1895, 3 S.L.T. 170. See also Thomson & Co. v. Dailly, 1897,
      24 R. 1173.
[7] Little v. Burns, 1881, 9 R. 118; Mavor & Coulson v. Grierson, 1892,
      19 R. 868; Wick v. Wick, 1898, 1 F. 199; Addison v. Kellock,
      (O.H.) 1906, 14 S.L.T. 410.
[8] Gordon v. O'Hara, 1931 S.C. 172. See also Watson v. Speedie Bros.,
      1932, 49 Sh.Ct.Rep. 83; Bruce v. Notman, 1936 S.L.T. (Sh.Ct.) 24.
[9] Lees v. Gordon, (O.H.) 1929 S.L.T. 400; cf. Burke v. Magistrates of
      Dunfermline, 1932 S.N. 68; Gordon v. Edinburgh Corporation,
      (O.H.) 1946 S.N. 40.
[10] See p. 335, infra.
[11] Grangemouth and Forth Towing Co. v. Netherlands East Indies
      Government, (O.H.) 1942 S.L.T. 228.

A tender may be withdrawn at any time prior to its acceptance,
but, apart from formal withdrawal, any important change of
circumstances will render the tender inoperative.[1] Thus where
judgment had been given after the tender had been lodged the
pursuer was not allowed to accept when the case was on appeal.[2]
An offer to settle made before an action is raised and repeated
on record though without any offer of expenses will generally
protect the defender in the same way as a tender.[3] Offers not
repeated on record, or made only after the action is in Court,
have not the same effect, but they may be taken into account by
the Court in disposing of the question of expenses.[4] A tender is
usually accepted by minute, but it is thought that a letter of
acceptance is binding.[5] In either case the pursuer's solicitor
should have express authority to accept.[6]

[1] Macrae v. Edinburgh Street Tramways Co., 1885, 13 R. 265. See also
      M'Millan v. Meikleham, (O.H.) 1934 S.L.T. 357.
[2] Bright v. Low, 1940 S.C. 280.

3 Gunn v. Hunter, 1886, 13 R. 573; Nash v. Warren Smith, (O.H.) 1894, 2 S.L.T. 319; Black v. Fife Coal Co., 1909 S.C. 152; 1912 S.C. (H.L.) 33; cf. Bryden v. Devlin, (O.H.) 1899, 6 S.L.T. 297.
4 Little v. Burns, 1881, 9 R. 118; Critchley v. Campbell, 1884, 11 R. 475; Miller v. M'Phun, 1895, 22 R. 600; Wick v. Wick, 1898, 1 F. 199; Gore v. Leith Salvage & Towage Co., 1925 S.N. 12; Pearce & Co. v. " Hans Maersk," 1935 S.C. 703.
5 Penman & Sons v. Crawford, 1903, 20 Sh.Ct.Rep. 123.
6 Weir v. Stevenson, &c., 1885, 1 Sh.Ct.Rep. 161.

(d) *Counter-claim.*—The defence may be, or may include, a counter-claim. Formerly a counter-claim could only be pleaded to the effect of set off. The present rule provides that, where a defender pleads a counter-claim, it is sufficient that he states same in the defences, and the Sheriff may thereafter deal with it as if it had been stated in a substantive action, and may grant decree for it in whole or in part, or for the difference between it and the claim sued on.[1] The counter-claim must be stated in a separate statement of facts.[2] The stating of a counter-claim by way of defence is optional to the defender, and, if the counter-claim is in any way complex, it may be desirable to bring a substantive counter-action. The defender should plead that he is entitled to decree for his counter-claim, or to set it off against pursuer's claim, and should state the amount (if any) for which he claims decree.

[1] 7 Edw. VII c. 51, Schedule I, Rule 55.
[2] Ibid., Rule 43; 2 & 3 Geo. V c. 28, Schedule II; M'Lellan v. Finnie & Co., 1916, 33 Sh.Ct.Rep. 235.

While the position may be different in small debt procedure[1] it seems clear that in the Ordinary Court the counter-claim must be one that can be set off pecuniarily against the sum sued for, and it has been settled that a money counter-claim cannot be pleaded in defence in an action of declarator,[2] or in an action *ad factum præstandum* without any pecuniary conclusion.[3] A counter-claim, which is subject to these restrictions, must be distinguished from what is really a defence to the principal claim. Thus in an action for delivery, or removing, or declarator, it might be a sufficient answer that the defender had a right of lien, or that the pursuer was in breach of some obligation to the defender. While these may be valid defences to the action they are not counter-claims and cannot be pleaded as such.[4]

[1] See Bernstein v. Holloway, 1909, 26 Sh.Ct.Rep. 32. See p. 473, infra.
[2] Macnab v. Nelson, 1909 S.C. 1102.
[3] Airdrie Market, &c., Ltd. v. M'Laughlin, 1924, 41 Sh.Ct.Rep. 67.
[4] Macnab v. Nelson, supra, Lord President Dunedin, pp. 1109, 1110; Mackay v. Macdonald, 1917, 34 Sh.Ct.Rep. 156.

The rule in regard to counter-claims affects procedure only, and its main object was to allow a defender to get a decree for payment in his favour without having to raise a counter-action. The rule does not alter the general law in regard to compensation or set off, and it does not justify one claim being set off against another when this would not have been competent formerly. Thus in actions for rent the tenant's counter-claim has been allowed where it arose from a breach of the landlord's obligation under the lease,[1] but refused as a set off where it was a general claim of damages.[2] Damages for late delivery may be set against an action for the price of the goods even without a counter-claim.[3] But in an action for an instalment of a purchase price the defender's counter-claim of damages for misrepresentations inducing the contract was repelled as a defence, as it did not arise from the contract but from antecedent delict.[4] So also a defender was not allowed to meet a claim for payment by setting off damages arising out of another matter.[5] The above cases in which counter-claims were repelled must now be considered in relation to the more recent case of *Armour & Melvin* v. *Mitchell*,[6] where the defender had no answer to an action for payment for goods supplied, but counter-claimed for other goods and services supplied to the pursuer, all of which were disputed. The pursuer's claim being thus liquid and the defender's illiquid, the Court granted decree to the pursuer, and allowed the defender a proof in respect of his counter-claim. This result appears inconsistent with some of the views expressed as to the rule in prior cases when the same course could apparently have been followed. It is thought that the correct view of the rule is that indicated by *Armour & Melvin*[6]—even though the proof on the counter-claim was conceded in that case by pursuer—and that while a counter-claim which cannot be set off against the principal claim is no obstacle to pursuer getting decree *de plano* for a sum admittedly due, it does not follow that the counter-claim must be repelled. If the principal claim has to be established by proof an allowance of proof on both claim and counter-claim seems the proper course if there is no reason why such a course is inappropriate or inconvenient in the circumstances.[7] The above appears to have been the view which was originally taken in the Sheriff Court.[8] Where a defender has been brought into Court by a public authority it has been indicated that he may not be precluded by the Public Authorities Protection Act from pleading in a counter-claim some act or default which arose more than six months prior to the action against him.[9]

[1] Fingland & Mitchell v. Howie, 1926 S.C. 319.

[2] Christie v. Birrell, 1910 S.C. 986.

[3] British Motor Body Co. v. Thomas Shaw (Dundee), Ltd., 1914 S.C. 922. See also Associated Producing, &c., Co. v. Leishman, 1936, 53 Sh.Ct.Rep. 244.

[4] Smart v. Wilkinson, 1928 S.C. 383; Clingan's Trustees v. M'Kinnon, 1911, 28 Sh.Ct.Rep. 35. See also Lohmann v. Lohmann Manufacturing Co., 1912, 28 Sh.Ct.Rep. 191.

[5] Aarons & Co. v. Macdonald, 1913, 29 Sh.Ct.Rep. 315; Lindsay v. Scottish Motor Traction Co., 1915, 31 Sh.Ct.Rep. 175.

[6] 1934 S.C. 94.

[7] Herbert v. Scottish Bricks, 1945, 62 Sh.Ct.Rep. 23.

[8] Clyde Salvage Co. v. Good & MacKinnon, 1908, 25 Sh.Ct.Rep. 61; Hinchcliffe & Co. v. Binning, 1910, 26 Sh.Ct.Rep. 181.

[9] Scottish Milk Marketing Board v. Stewart, 1938, 55 Sh.Ct.Rep. 21.

The opinion has been expressed that, if the pursuer abandons his action,[1] any counter-claim which has been stated cannot be further insisted on in that action, the view being that the defender is not entitled to demand that the process should be treated as a living process for the purpose of trying his counter-claim.[2] The position is not however materially different from that in *Armour & Melvin* v. *Mitchell*,[3] where the pursuer obtained decree and proof was allowed to defender in respect of his counter-claim, and it is thought that on the wording of the rule such a course is competent. The Court presumably has a discretion in the matter, and the state of the pleadings may be a relevant factor for consideration.[4]

[1] See 7 Edw. VII c. 51, Schedule I, Rule 81.

[2] Airdrie Market Buildings, &c. v. M'Laughlin, 1924, 41 Sh.Ct.Rep. 67, p. 68. See also Craw v. Malcolm, 1908, 24 Sh.Ct.Rep. 268.

[3] 1934 S.C. 94.

[4] See Craw v. Malcolm, supra.

It is competent to counter-claim for a larger sum than £50 in a summary cause. Conflicting views have been expressed as to the result of such a course on the character of the action, but the later opinion is that the action remains a summary cause notwithstanding the amount of the counter-claim.[1] Where a counter-claim has been stated and dismissed it has been held that the defender cannot raise a separate action until the first action has been finally disposed of. This was decided on the ground that the original action might ultimately be appealed and the counter-claim thus be revived so that the plea of *lis alibi pendens* was still open to the original pursuer.[2] It is thought, however, that the original defender could in such circumstances make certain of his right to proceed with the second action in all cases by giving up his right to proceed with the counter-claim and so stating in the later action.[3]

1 Gottlieb v. Fons Patent Inkwell, 1916, 33 Sh.Ct.Rep. 70; Cleave & Son v. Letters & Co., 1929, 45 Sh.Ct.Rep. 223.
2 Stevenson v. Fraser & Carmichael, 1914, 30 Sh.Ct.Rep. 277.
3 Laidlaw v. Smith, 1834, 12 S. 538; Gracie v. Kerr, 1846, 19 Scot. Jur. 60; M'Aulay v. Cowe, 1873, 1 R. 307.

(e) *Revisal.*—Revisal of pleadings has always rested with the Sheriff. The Sheriff Court Act of 1876 expressly declared that " neither party shall be entitled as matter of right to ask for a revisal of his pleadings; but it shall be competent for the Sheriff to allow or order a revisal of the pleadings upon just cause shown."[1] The Act of 1907 leaves the matter also with the Sheriff, who may, upon cause shown or *ex proprio motu*, order a revisal of the pleadings.[2] The time for revisal is fixed by the Sheriff. In modern practice revisal of pleadings is seldom required.

1 39 & 40 Vict. c. 70, sec. 17.
2 7 Edw. VII c. 51, Schedule I, Rule 49. See Logan v. Henderson & Co., 1877, 1 Guthrie's Select Cases 416.

(f) *Productions.*—Much time and trouble are often saved if documents upon which either party relies are produced with the initial writ. In a summary cause, if a document of debt is founded on, it is often a convenience to lodge it with the Sheriff-clerk, along with the initial writ, at the first calling. By the rules each party must, along with his pleadings, or at latest before the closing of the record, if required by any other party in the action, or by the Sheriff, lodge any documents founded on in the pleadings, so far as the same are within his custody or power.[1] Where such documents are not produced by either party, or where they are in the hands of third parties, the Sheriff may, on the motion of either party, grant commission and diligence for their recovery, and may on that account delay closing the record.[2] It is also provided that the Sheriff may order production of documents at any stage of the case, and may allow a party, at any time before judgment, to produce any document which he has failed to produce timeously, upon such conditions as to expenses and further proof as to the Sheriff shall seem just.[3] As will be indicated later this last rule does not, it is thought, add to the right of recovery before the record is closed. Non-implement by a party to the cause of an order to produce documents within his control would be default in the sense of Rule 56, entitling the other party to ask for decree.[4]

1 7 Edw. VII c. 51, Schedule I, Rule 47.
2 Ibid., Rule 48.
3 Ibid., Rule 68 (a). See Act of Sederunt of 16th July, 1936.
4 Ibid., Rule 56.

It is thought to be clear that the documents which a party is entitled to call upon his opponent to produce before the record is closed are those founded on by the opponent. It is not enough that a party in his own pleadings makes reference to a document, or that he himself founds on it. A party cannot, for instance, by merely saying in his own pleadings that certain transactions have been treated in a particular way in his opponent's books, get a diligence to recover these books before the record has been closed.[1]

[1] Wright v. Valentine, 1910, 26 Sh.Ct.Rep. 26, 151. See also Cameron, &c. v. Ferrier, 1913, 29 Sh.Ct.Rep. 125.

Production of documents founded on before the closing of the record can, it is thought, be insisted on as a matter of right. The mere fact that production may disclose more than other parties in the case are at that stage entitled to know, is not apparently pleadable as an excuse for non-production. The statutory rule gives an unqualified right to each party in a cause to see the documents founded on in the pleadings of all the other parties, and to see them before the record is closed. This right arises wherever the productions are founded on by an opponent and are within his control. The Court has apparently no discretion in the matter but must, it is thought, if required by the other party, order production.[1]

[1] See views expressed in Wright v. Valentine. 1910, 26 Sh.Ct.Rep. 26, 151; cf. Reavis v. Clan Line Steamers, 1926 S.C. 215.

Where the documents are in the hands of third parties it is thought that the Sheriff has a discretion as to granting diligence to recover them. In such a case the practice in the Court of Session would probably be adopted and the Sheriff would probably grant diligence before the closing of the record only where it appeared to be reasonably necessary that a party, for the purpose of preparing or adjusting his pleadings, should see the documents called for.[1] But when the object of seeking production is merely to support facts which can be stated without reference to the actual documents, the granting of diligence for recovery will probably be deferred until after the record has been closed and a proof allowed. While Rule 68 (a) authorizes the Sheriff to order production of documents at any stage of the case it is thought that this does not apply to the period before the record is closed, or that in any case it does not extend the right to have documents produced at that stage.[2] Apart from the Rules of Procedure it is thought to be clear that the Court has an inherent power to order documents to be produced prior to the record being closed, and that this power should be exercised where a document is not founded on in the pleadings but its production is necessary for the preparation or adjustment of the pleadings.[3]

1 Marshall & Sons v. Spiers & Son, (O.H.) 1882, 19 S.L.R. 696; Christie v. Munro, (O.H.) 1885, 23 S.L.R. 267; Dalgleish's Trustees v. Matheson's Trustees, (O.H.) 1902, 10 S.L.T. 56; Caledonian Railway Co. v. Crocket & Co., 1902, 10 S.L.T. 89; Bradley v. Maguire, (O.H.) 1920, 2 S.L.T. 417; Jamieson v. Jamieson, (O.H.) 1928 S.L.T. 427. See also Braby & Co. v. Story, (O.H.) 1896, 3 S.L.T. 325; Graeme-Hunter v. Glasgow Iron & Steel Co., (O.H.) 1908, 16 S.L.T. 15.
2 Thornycroft & Co. v. Ricketts, 1935, 51 Sh.Ct.Rep. 194.
3 Orr v. Orr, 1936, 53 Sh.Ct.Rep. 89.

(g) *Adjustment.*—Under the older Statutes the meeting for adjustment of pleadings was a ceremonial affair, but the diet for adjustment is now a formal step in the process. The rules provide that upon defences being lodged the Sheriff-clerk shall enrol the action for adjustment on an ordinary Court day occurring not less than four days after defences have been lodged,[1] but in practice the diet for adjustment is frequently fixed in the interlocutor ordering defences. After defences have been lodged and before the diet for adjustment the pursuer must lodge in process a certified copy of the initial writ and warrant, which is borrowable, and is a sufficient warrant for arrestment on the dependence where that is competent.[2] There is no direction for transmission of the process to the Sheriff, and it is in the adjustment roll that he first sees and applies his mind to the pleadings. If defender has lodged a separate statement of facts pursuer will at this stage be ordered to answer it within a specified time.[3] The adjustment diet, according to the rules, may not be adjourned more than once, except upon special cause shown.[1] When the pleadings have been adjusted the Sheriff is directed to close the record.[4] These rules, read together, mean that, when the parties have had reasonable opportunity afforded them (at the adjustment diet and as a result of one but usually more adjournments) of adjusting their pleadings, the Sheriff may hold the pleadings as adjusted, and close the record. Not later than six days thereafter the pursuer must lodge in process a certified copy of the closed record.[4]

1 7 Edw. VII c. 51, Schedule I, Rule 45; 2 & 3 Geo. V c. 28, Schedule II.
2 Ibid., Rule 46; 2 & 3 Geo. V c. 28, Schedule II.
3 Ibid., Rule 49.
4 Ibid., Rule 52.

As soon as defences are lodged the pursuer should adjust his condescendence so as to answer the defender's averments. In doing

so he should add such further averments of fact and such additional
pleas as may be required. On such adjustments being intimated
the defender should make the corresponding adjustments on the
defences. In adjusting the pleadings the rule must be kept in
view that every statement of fact made by one party must be
answered by the other party; and if a statement made by one
party of a fact within the knowledge of the other party is not
denied by that party the latter is held as admitting the fact so
stated.[1] In such circumstances a mere non-admission will be
ineffective.[2] The position in regard to qualified admissions has
been already mentioned.[3]

[1] 7 Edw. VII c. 51, Schedule I, Rule 44; 2 & 3 Geo. V c. 28, Schedule II.
   See also Central Motor Engineering Co. v. Galbraith, 1918 S.C. 755;
   Gilmour v. Scottish Clan Motorways, (O.H.) 1928 S.N. 19.
[2] Pegler v. Northern Agricultural Implement Co., 1877, 4 R. 434, Lord
   President Inglis, p. 438.
[3] See p. 147, supra.

There is no provision in the Statute to enable one party to
compel another party to adjust. But the power of the Court to fix
peremptory diets, and make peremptory orders is enough to afford
a remedy against purely dilatory tactics. The Sheriff is the sole
judge of the point of time at which the pleadings are to be held
as adjusted, and the record closed, and he is also the sole judge
of what is sufficient cause to warrant an adjournment of the
adjustment diet.

The extent of the alterations permitted at adjustment is practically unlimited save that they must be relevant to the crave of
the writ. The writ itself, apart from the condescendence and pleas,
cannot be altered except by amendment. In connexion with the
pleadings in general it is desirable that separate branches of the
averments should be kept to separate articles of the condescendence,
and it is essential when a case is rested on different grounds in
law that the averments and pleas in support of these should be
kept distinct.[1] The averments on each side must give fair notice
of all the evidence which it is proposed to lead.[2] They should
consist of statements of fact and should not be argumentative.

[1] M'Grath v. Glasgow Coal Co., 1909 S.C. 1250; Keenan v. Glasgow
   Corporation, 1923 S.C. 611.
[2] See Ward v. Coltness Iron Co., 1944 S.C. 318, Lord President Normand,
   p. 322.

While there is now no statutory enactment on the point it is
thought that the Sheriff has an inherent power to delete from
a record any matters that are improper or plainly irrelevant.[1]
And, as in the Supreme Court, there seems no reason why this

power should not be exercised after a record has been closed, though
it will be more convenient and appropriate that it should be raised
at adjustment.[1] In some cases the averments complained of have
been excluded from probation,[2] but in general they have been
ordered to be deleted from the record.[3]

[1] Robertson v. Smith, 1904, 21 Sh:Ct.Rep. 100; Kennan v. Stranraer
Creamery Co., 1908, 24 Sh.Ct.Rep. 326; cf. M'Isaac v. Leonard,
1915, 31 Sh.Ct.Rep. 303.
[2] Inglis v. National Bank of Scotland, 1909 S.C. 1038; M'Isaac v.
Leonard, supra; A v. C, (O.H.) 1922 S.L.T. 34; Galloway v.
Cruickshank, (O.H.) 1928 S.N. 159; Scott v. Cormack Heating
Engineers, 1942 S.C. 159.
[3] Wardrope v. Duke of Hamilton, 1876, 3 R. 876; A v. B, 1895, 22 R.
402; Thomson v. Landale, (O.H.) 1897, 5 S.L.T. 204; Robertson
v. Smith, supra; H v. P, 1905, 8 F. 232; Heriot-Hill v. Heriot-Hill,
(O.H.) 1906, 14 S.L.T. 182; Kennan v. Stranraer Creamery Co.,
supra; M v. S, (O.H.) 1909, 1 S.L.T. 192; Oliver v. Borland, (O.H.)
1911, 2 S.L.T. 46; C v. M, 1923 S.C. 1; cf. Press v. Press, (O.H.)
1925 S.L.T. 425; MacTaggart v. MacKillop, 1938 S.C. 847.

A party may lay his case upon alternative averments of fact
which are contradictory and mutually exclusive, provided that
either of them, if proved, would entitle him to succeed.[1] But
where alternative averments of fact are made the weaker of the
alternatives is the one by which the relevancy of the averments
will be judged,[2] and where one branch of a case which is alternatively averred is relevant and the other is not the action will be
dismissed.[3]

[1] Clarke v. Edinburgh and District Tramways Co., 1914 S.C. 775.
[2] Hope v. Hope's Trustees, 1898, 1 F. (H.L.) 1, Lord Watson, p. 3.
[3] Murray v. Wyllie, 1916 S.C. 356.

All alterations or additions made on the record must be authenticated on the writ and defences by the Sheriff's initials.[1] This is
merely done for identification, and the fact that the Sheriff has
initialled an alteration does not mean that he has approved of it
as relevant. It is not necessary for the parties' solicitors to initial
alterations made at adjustment, and such initialling by a solicitor
will not be accepted as equivalent to authentication by the Sheriff.[2]
An alteration made, even of consent, upon the pleadings, after the
record has been closed, is not adjustment, but amendment, which
can be made only by leave.

[1] 7 Edw. VII c. 51, Schedule I, Rule 53.
[2] Kilcoyne v. Wilson, 1907 S.C. 86.

(h) *Conjunction and Contingency.*—Either before the closing
of the record or afterwards, a motion may be made for conjunction
of contingent actions. There is no statutory direction as to this,

but it has long been the practice that, where two or more processes are before the Court, relating to the same subject-matter, expense should be minimized by conjoining them, and conducting them thereafter as one process. The chief considerations are economy and convenience.[1] Conjunction may be made at any stage, but, where the actions are both pending, a convenient stage is at adjustment. To warrant actions being conjoined they must have contingency. What will amount to that is a question of circumstances, but it must be something more than merely that inquiry into the facts set forth in the one action might throw some light upon the other action.[2] When separate pursuers in conjoined actions are contesting each other's case each pursuer should be expressly given the right to cross-examine the witnesses for the other.[3] After conjunction the actions become in effect one process and all subsequent steps in procedure apply to each action.

[1] Wilson v. Rapp, (O.H.) 1911 S.C. 1360.
[2] Western Bank v. Douglas, 1860, 22 D. 447.
[3] Boyle v. Olsen, 1912 S.C. 1235.

As a general rule, actions will not be conjoined if the one is at a much more advanced stage than the other, or if the one is for recovery of a liquid, and the other of an illiquid claim,[1] or where the actions are different in their nature,[2] or the defence in the one action is upon different grounds from that in the other[3]; nor will actions be conjoined if the motion for conjunction is made for some ulterior motive[4] or the effect of conjunction would be to give one party any advantage over another.[5] Actions proceeding on different grounds though between the same parties will not as a rule be conjoined.[6]

[1] M'Leay v. Rose, 1826, 4 S. 481.
[2] Mackay v. Greenhill, 1858, 20 D. 1251.
[3] National Exchange Company v. Drew, 1861, 23 D. 1278.
[4] Hay, &c. v. M'Millan, 1916, 33 Sh.Ct.Rep. 241.
[5] Lawson v. Fyffe, 1891, 8 Sh.Ct.Rep. 218.
[6] Phillips v. Miller, (O.H.) 1894, 1 S.L.T. 498; M'Fadyen v. United Alkali Co., (O.H.) 1897, 4 S.L.T. 321.

Conjunction is competent, even although the parties to the actions may be different, if the subject-matter is the same,[1] as where two or more pursuers are making the same demand upon the same defender,[2] or where two or more defenders are resisting the same claim of a pursuer upon the same pleas.[3] The actions formerly required to be before the same Court, but the wide scope of the transfer powers of the Sheriff under the Sheriff Courts Act, 1907, indicates the possibility of effecting conjunction of actions raised in different Sheriff Courts. The Sheriff may remit a cause

to another district or another Sheriffdom upon sufficient cause,
and the avoiding of several litigations to settle the same dispute,
by remitting actions in which there is contingency to one Court
for conjunction, would probably be regarded as sufficient cause.[4]
There is no power in the Sheriff to require a cause to be remitted
to his Court from another Court. The conjunction of a summary
and an ordinary cause has been already discussed.[5] There is a
statutory power in the Sheriff to conjoin actions under the
Employers' Liability Act arising out of the same occurrence, or
cause of action, though at the instance of different parties and in
respect of different injuries.[6]

[1] M'Dowall v. Campbell, 1838, 16 S. 629.
[2] Gatt v. Angus Shipping Co., (O.H.) 1907, 14 S.L.T. 749; Boyle v.
Olsen, 1912 S.C. 1235.
[3] Cowan & Sons, &c. v. Duke of Buccleuch, &c., 1876, 4 R. (H.L.) 14.
[4] 7 Edw. VII c. 51, Schedule I, Rule 20.
[5] See p. 98, supra.
[6] 43 & 44 Vict. c. 42, sec. 6.

A Sheriff Court process may be transmitted to the Court of
Session under sec. 74 of the Court of Session Act, 1868, which
authorizes a Sheriff Court process to be transmitted to the Court
of Session, upon the ground that there is a contingency between it
and a pending Court of Session process.[1] It is then within the
power of the Court of Session to conjoin the actions,[2] but such
conjunction does not take effect automatically as a result of the
remit.[3] This is not a Sheriff Court step of process and the Sheriff
does not consider, or decide, the question of contingency. The
motion for transmission of the process is made in the Court of
Session, where the party moving for transmission presents a copy
of the Sheriff Court pleadings and interlocutors certified by the
Sheriff-clerk.[1] The Sheriff makes no order at all, and transmission
of the process is made by the Sheriff-clerk upon the direct order
of the Court of Session.

[1] 31 & 32 Vict. c. 100, secs. 74, 75; Wilson v. Junor, (O.H.) 1907, 15
S.L.T. 182.
[2] See M'Fadyen v. United Alkali Co., (O.H.) 1897, 4 S.L.T. 321.
[3] See Campbell, &c. v. Train, 1910 S.C. 147, p. 149.

It is necessary for transmission *ob contingentiam* that both
processes should still be in dependence.[1] As in the case of conjunction, the main consideration is not the identity of the parties
but of the subject-matter of the actions.[2] In regard to the
circumstances which constitute contingency, reference can be made
to the cases in which contingency was established[3] and to those
in which the remit or transmission was refused.[4] A jury trial

in the Court of Session may be allowed in a case transmitted *ob contingentiam*.[5]

[1] See Gordon v. Ross, 1827, 6 S. 257; Bryce v. Chalmers, 1859, 22 D. 213; Forster v. Grigor, 1871, 9 M. 397.
[2] Cuthbertson v. Young, 1851, 13 D. 1308; Duke of Atholl v. Robertson, 1869, 8 M. 304.
[3] Gordon v. Ross, supra; Jaffray v. Gordon, 1830, 8 S. 803; Cochrane v. Hamilton, 1847, 9 D. 794; Cleland v. Clason & Clark, 1850, 7 Bell's App. 153; Cuthbertson v. Young, supra; Powrie v. Powrie, 1868, 6 M. 1111; Reid v. Reid's Trustees, 1873, 45 Scot. Jur. 191; M'Fadyen v. United Alkali Co., (O.H.) 1897, 4 S.L.T. 321; Wilson v. Junor, (O.H.) 1907, 15 S.L.T. 182.
[4] Earl of Mansfield v. Aitchison, 1829, 8 S. 243; Buchanan v. Douglas, 1851, 13 D. 547; Blaikie v. Aberdeen Railway, 1854, 16 D. 496; Liquidators Western Bank v. Douglas, &c., 1860, 22 D. 447; Duke of Atholl v. Robertson, supra; Higgins v. Macfie, 1931 S.N. 18.
[5] Forte v. Rutherford, 1933 S.L.T. 109.

Actions which have been conjoined may, in the discretion of the Court, be disjoined upon cause shown.[1] This may be necessary or advisable in some cases before judgment is given, as, for instance, where an ordinary action and a summary cause have been conjoined to avoid the expense of separate proofs.[2]

[1] Turner v. Tunnock's Trustees, 1864, 2 M. 509.
[2] M'Donald v. M'Donald, 1912, 29 Sh.Ct.Rep. 157. See also Yellowlees v. Alexander, 1882, 9 R. 765.

Apart from any question of conjunction or contingency an order may be obtained in the Court of Session for transmission of any Sheriff Court process to the Supreme Court for production in process in an action in the latter Court.[1] Special provision is made in this connexion in petitions for suspension of a Sheriff Court decree.[2]

[1] Rules of Court, 1936, II, 30.
[2] Ibid., IV, 52.

(i) *Closing Record.*—The closing of the record is an important process step, and, as it forecloses either party from making further alterations without leave, it is the interest of both to see that the pleadings of each are complete before the record is closed. Formerly it was considered that pleas in law might be added at any stage, without special leave of the Court; but in modern practice the addition or deletion of a plea in law after closing can now only be done by amendment. All pleas, whether preliminary or on the merits, should be stated before the record is closed.[1]

[1] Thorburn v. Dempster, 1900, 2 F. 583.

In a summary cause the record is not usually closed and in some cases there may be no written defences.[1] If there are pleadings they should be adjusted, and if this is thought advisable the record may be closed, in the same manner as in an ordinary action, but this is not a statutory requirement, and will be regulated by the Sheriff.[2]

[1] 7 Edw. VII c. 51, sec. 8, Schedule I, Rule 41; 2 & 3 Geo. V c. 28. Schedules I, II.
[2] National Cash Register Co. v. Hunter, 1915, 32 Sh.Ct.Rep. 121.

When the record has been closed, it is the duty of the pursuer within six days to lodge in process a certified copy of the closed record for the use of the Sheriff.[1]

[1] 7 Edw. VII c. 51, Schedule I, Rule 52; 2 & 3 Geo. V c. 28, Schedule II.

At the closing of the record various courses are open for the final disposal of the action. Where it relates to questions of heritable right or title, or to division of commonty or division or division and sale of common property, and the value of the subjects in dispute exceeds £50 by the year or £1000 in all, or where it relates to a right of moveable succession of over £1000 in value either party may at the closing of the record or within six days thereafter require the cause to be remitted to the Court of Session.[1] If proof is allowed at closing certain actions may be remitted to the Court of Session for jury trial[2] while others may be tried by jury in the Sheriff Court.[3] If the issue in the case, or the immediate issue to be decided, is one of law and not fact the case may be sent to the debate roll.[4] Other possibilities are that the case may be sisted for a given period or to await some happening[5]; a remit may be made to a man of skill to report[6] or parties may agree to a judicial reference[7]; one party may refer the case to the oath of his adversary[8]; or the case may by agreement be disposed of as a summary cause,[9] or remitted to the Small Debt roll.[10]

[1] See p. 169, infra.
[2] See p. 305, infra.
[3] See p. 339, infra.
[4] See p. 180, infra.
[5] See p. 176, infra.
[6] See p. 173, infra.
[7] See p. 171, infra.
[8] See p. 229, infra.
[9] See p. 98, supra.
[10] See p. 178, infra.

(j) *Interim Decree.*—An interim decree is a judgment of the Court disposing of some part of the cause, but not dealing with the whole crave of the writ. In some circumstances, chiefly in cases of separation or adherence and aliment, an interim decree for aliment may be granted before the record is closed, but such a decree is not generally granted till the Sheriff has applied his mind to the case, and this he does not normally do till the case is adjusted. At that stage the whole case should be disclosed, and the propriety of granting an interim decree can then appropriately be considered.

An interim decree may be craved whenever it appears from the pleas or pleadings that there is a partial admission by defender of the claim or demand made by the pursuer. It is within the discretion of the Court to grant or refuse an interim decree,[1] and it is a relevant consideration that the defender has a contingent claim on the pursuer for the expenses of the action, if the defence succeeds in respect of the matters still in dispute. In certain circumstances an interim decree can be obtained even before the record is closed.[2]

[1] See Dalziel v. Scott, 1831, 3 Scot. Jur. 591; Banks v. Lang, 1845, 17 Scot. Jur. 536; Elliot v. Aiken, 1869, 7 M. 894; Nivison v. Howat, 1883, 11 R. 182.

[2] M'Kinlay v. M'Kinlay, 1849, 11 D. 1022; Conacher v. Conacher, 1857, 20 D. 252.

An interim decree is appealable to the Sheriff if it is an interlocutor (a) granting or refusing interdict; (b) granting interim decree for payment of money other than expenses; or (c) making an order *ad factum præstandum*.[1] An interim decree is appealable either to the Sheriff or to the Court of Session, if it is for payment of money (other than expenses).[1] An order to consign is not an interim decree for payment of money in the appeal sense, but it is an order *ad factum præstandum*,[2] and as such is appealable. An interim decree authorising an officer or official of Court to pay out money in his hands to a party,[3] or granting warrant to uplift consigned money,[4] is an appealable interim decree for payment of money.

[1] 7 Edw. VII c. 51, secs. 27, 28; 2 & 3 Geo. V c. 28, Schedule I.

[2] Mackenzie v. Balerno Paper Mill Co., 1883, 10 R. 1147. See also Menzies v. Templeton, 1896, 12 Sh.Ct.Rep. 323.

[3] Baird v. Glendinning, 1874, 2 R. 25.

[4] Sinclair v. Baikie, 1884, 11 R. 413.

An interim decree, like any other decree, is extractable in a summary cause in seven days, and in an ordinary action in fourteen days, but the Sheriff may in ordinary causes and it is thought also in summary causes exercise his power of allowing earlier extract.[1]

[1] 7 Edw. VII c. 51, Schedule I, Rule 85. See p. 255, infra.

(k) *Consignation.*—The defender, whilst partially admitting the pursuer's claim, may so qualify his admissions as not to warrant an interim decree being granted, as, for instance, he may admit holding a fund or a subject, but claim a lien or right of retention over it or he may make general admissions which show that a balance will ultimately be due, but is not yet due; or he may admit a debt, but may claim deductions which are in dispute[1] or may admit the debt but dispute the pursuer's title to sue for it[2]; or he may admit an *ex facie* regular document of debt, but propose to attack it *ope exceptionis*. In such circumstances the pursuer may, at the closing of the record or otherwise ask the Sheriff to order the defender to consign the fund admittedly held by him, or to consign a general sum, or to place a subject in neutral custody. An order for consignation does not decide, or affect, any question raised in the case, and is merely a preservation order.[3] A sum of money is ordered to be consigned in the hands of the Sheriff-clerk. A subject is usually placed in a public store. In a summary cause an order for consignation may be moved for when pleas are noted.

[1] Cumming v. Williamson, 1842, 4 D. 1304.
[2] Rolfe v. Drummond, 1862, 1 M. 39.
[3] See generally as to consignation Littlejohn v. Reynolds, &c., 1890, 6 Sh.Ct.Rep. 321.

The consignation is recorded in the consignation register kept by the Sheriff-clerk, and which is to be made patent to interested parties or their solicitors.[1] An interlocutor requiring consignation could apparently be appealed against as an order *ad factum præstandum*.[2]

[1] Sheriff Courts Consignations (Scotland) Act, 1893 (56 & 57 Vict. c. 44, sec. 3).
[2] See p. 163, supra.

In any process for the distribution of an estate of a deceased person, a consigned fund is not to be paid out till the Sheriff-clerk has seen a certificate by the proper revenue officer, that all income tax, estate, legacy, or succession duties and any other duty payable to the Commissioners of Inland Revenue have been duly settled.[1]

[1] Codifying Act of Sederunt L. III, 1. Act of Sederunt, 16th July, 1936, sec. 3.

A defender may voluntarily make consignation, if it is in his interest to do so[1] (as, for instance, in order to found a claim for expenses if pursuer ultimately gets judgment for less than the consigned sum), or the Court in its discretion may order, or refuse to order, consignation.[2] When the defence to a claim based upon a bill of exchange is an attack upon the validity of the bill, sec. 100 of the Bills of Exchange Act, 1882, expressly reserves the right of the Court to order caution or consignation as a condition of a sist or suspension of diligence.[3] In the same way where objection to a deed or writing founded on by any party to a cause is made

by way of exception the Sheriff may, where an action of reduction would be competent, order caution or consignation.[4] The
Court has also a discretion under the Sale of Goods Act, 1893, to
order consignation of, or caution for, the price, or part thereof,
where a seller sues for the price of goods which a buyer might
have rejected, but which he has elected to retain and claim
damages.[5]

[1] As in Brodie & Hall v. Di Placido, 1938, 55 Sh.Ct.Rep. 82; but there
   is no authority for consignation in anticipation of a threatened
   action, A B & Co., v. C D, 1908, 25 Sh.Ct.Rep. 106.
[2] Donaldson v. Finlay, Bannatyne & Co., 1846, 5 Bell's App. 105; Cowan
   v. Western Bank, 1860, 22 D. 1260.
[3] 45 & 46 Vict. c. 61, sec. 100.
[4] 7 Edw. VII c. 51, Schedule I, Rule 51. See also Brodie & Hall v.
   Di Placido, supra; Winter v. Kerr, 1895, 12 Sh.Ct.Rep. 77.
[5] 56 & 57 Vict. c. 71, sec. 59. See Lee & Brown v. Menzies, 1896, 12
   Sh.Ct.Rep. 273; Motor Plants v. D. Stewart & Co., (O.H.) 1909,
   1 S.L.T. 478; Gorrie & Son v. Northern Laundry Co., 1910, 27
   Sh.Ct.Rep. 66; Gunn, Collie & Topping v. Purdie, 1946 S.L.T.
   (Sh.Ct.) 11.

(l) *Realization.*—If the action relate to goods of a perishable
nature, or to live stock, the cost of keeping which during a litigation may be considerable, either party may move for the realization
of the goods or stock, and consignation of the proceeds. If this
is to be moved for, previous notice should be given, and it may be
convenient to have a crave for warrant of sale in the initial writ.
If it is not considered necessary, or advisable, to realize the subject
of action, the Sheriff may, upon the motion of either party, make
an order for its present safe custody.

(m) *Preliminary Pleas.*—The Act provides that, if preliminary
pleas have been stated, the Sheriff shall first dispose of them, unless
he thinks that, from their being connected with the merits, or on
any other ground, they should be reserved till a future stage of
the cause.[1] This is merely a statutory expression of recognized
Court practice, and it emphasizes the desirability, wherever possible, of disposing of, and not reserving, preliminary pleas.[2]

[1] 7 Edw. VII c. 51, Schedule I, Rule 54.
[2] See Docherty v. M'Alpine & Sons, 1899, 2 F. 128; Hunter v. Darngavil
   Coal Co., 1900, 3 F. 10; Sinclair v. Lochgelly Iron Co., 1905. 13
   S.L.T. 103; cf. Oates v. Redpath Brown & Co., (O.H.) 1926 S.L.T.
   211; Gardner v. Hastie, (O.H.) 1928 S.L.T. 497.

Formerly pleas in defence were classed under (a) dilatory
defences, which included every kind of plea which, if sustained,
terminated the case in the defender's favour, but did not cut off
the pursuer's right to bring a fresh action. These include incompetency, irrelevancy, and no title to sue; and (b) peremptory

defences, which entered into the merits of the case, generally necessitating some inquiry into, or admission of, facts, and if successful, extinguished the pursuer's right of action. Such pleas include those of payment, prescription, *res judicata*, and *lis alibi pendens*. In modern practice these distinctions are not maintained, and pleas in law are regarded as preliminary pleas if they are such as, when sustained, render inquiry into the merits of the cause unnecessary, and themselves afford a ground for final judgment and as pleas on the merits, if they are such as cannot be either sustained or repelled without some inquiry into the merits of the cause. Some pleas may be either preliminary pleas or pleas on the merits, and how such a plea is to be treated may depend upon the manner in which the pleadings are framed. If there are agreed facts, it may be disposed of without proof. If the facts are not agreed, it may be necessary to have a proof *primo loco* upon these particular facts.[1]

[1] See generally the cases cited in the preceding paragraph.

A preliminary plea, like a plea on the merits, must be founded upon averments in the pleadings. The averment, and the plea founded upon it, ought together to present a legal proposition complete in itself, without reference to other pleas. Thus if a plea that the action is incompetent is based upon a statutory bar of action, the Statute must be averred; or, if the plea is, " all parties not called," the defences should set forth the other parties who should have been called.[1] It is convenient, where possible, to confine to a separate article in the pleading the narration of the particular fact upon which a specific plea in law is based. Some preliminary pleas, however, such as incompetency and irrelevancy, are based, not upon specific averments, but upon the nature of the case as laid, or the pleadings as a whole. General statements are not pleas in law, and a plea that " in the circumstances set forth decree should be granted," is not sufficient.[2]

[1] See North British Railway Co. v. Brown, Gordon & Co., 1857, 19 D. 840.

[2] Young & Co. v. Graham, 1860, 23 D. 36. See also 7 Edw. VII c. 51, Schedule I, Rules 2, 43; 2 & 3 Geo. V c. 28, Schedule II.

A preliminary plea of incompetency should not be reserved. An action may be incompetent (a) because its object is not attainable in a civil process at all; (b) because the law has provided some other remedy than a Court process for the cause of action, as, for instance, arbitration[1]; (c) because some other form of action is alone appropriate to the circumstances; (d) because some condition-precedent has not been complied with, as, in an action against a company in liquidation brought without the sanction of the Court as required by the Companies Act; or (e) because of the manner in which the particular action is laid, as, for instance, when it is laid under Statute instead of at common law, or *vice versa*. It is *pars judicis* to take notice of some forms of incompetency, and the Court may dismiss an obviously incompetent action even without a plea.[2] A party pleading incompetency should not act inconsistently with his plea, as he might be held to have waived it.[3]

[1] Where the action is barred by an arbitration clause in a contract the usual plea is for a sist pending the arbitration; Wilson & M'Farlane v. Stewart & Co., 1898, 25 R. 655.

[2] Hamilton v. Murray, 1830, 9 S. 143; Macgregor, &c. v. Macfarlane, &c., 1914, 31 Sh.Ct.Rep. 104.

[3] North British Railway Co. v. Carter, 1870, 8 M. 998.

An action, though competent, may not be relevantly stated, and a preliminary plea may be taken on the ground that the averments made do not support the crave. Formerly, if a plea of irrelevancy were sustained, the action was dismissed, but the powers of amendment are now so wide that the party whose pleading is thus attacked is often allowed to amend upon payment of certain expenses. This course is appropriate where the averments are defective or wanting in specification, not where they are altogether inept to support the craving or pleas.[1] But if a party contemplates amendment as a reply to a plea to the relevancy he should make his position clear before avizandum is made in the debate roll otherwise his action may be dismissed and he may require to appeal in order to be allowed to amend.

[1] See Paterson v. Wallace, 1909 S.C. 20.

Averments are irrelevant wherever the facts set forth, if proved, do not warrant the plea in law based upon these facts. Pleadings may be irrelevant also, if the facts themselves are not set forth with sufficient specification. Competency and relevancy pleas are sometimes confused. Broadly speaking, an action is incompetent when the crave of the initial writ cannot be granted by the Court in which the action is brought; and pleadings are irrelevant when the facts averred are insufficient to justify or support the crave or the defences. Where there are alternative averments relevancy depends on the weaker alternative.[1]

[1] Hope v. Hope's Trustees, 1898, 1 F. (H.L.) 1, Lord Watson, p. 3. See also Murray v. Wyllie, 1916 S.C. 356.

The question of relevancy must be raised in a plea. The Court will not *ex proprio motu* dismiss an action which is merely irrelevant, and the question of relevancy arises, therefore, only in defended actions. If such a plea is not stated or insisted in at the proper time, and the case is allowed to go to proof upon a closed record, without the relevancy having been challenged, neither party will be lightly permitted to add a relevancy plea. Formerly a party was in such circumstances held to have waived his right to do so, but the powers of amendment are now so broad[1] that this rule cannot now be regarded as absolute. But if the question of relevancy is raised after the case has been sent for proof, payment of part of the other party's expenses will usually be required. In a summary cause, where no formal record is made up, an interlocutor appointing a diet of proof will foreclose the question of relevancy, to the same effect as an interlocutor in an ordinary action closing the record.

[1] 7 Edw. VII c. 51, Schedule I, Rule 79.

If a plea to the relevancy is sustained, the action will be dismissed. This is a final appealable judgment, but a dismissal on the ground of incompetency or irrelevancy does not found a plea of *res judicata* and does not prevent an action in competent form and relevantly stated being brought on the same grounds either in the Sheriff Court or in the Court of Session.[1] It is not essential that a relevancy plea be disposed of upon the closed record without inquiry into the merits. If such inquiry is necessary the question of relevancy is reserved by allowing a proof before answer.

[1] Duke of Sutherland v. Reed, 1890, 18 R. 252; Menzies v. Menzies, 1893, 20 R. (H.L.) 108, Lord Watson, p. 110; Govan Old Victualling Society v. Wagstaff, 1907, 44 S.L.R. 295.

A proof before answer is frequently allowed where the pursuer's averments are of doubtful relevancy, but the Court does not see its way to dismiss the action without inquiry.[1] It may also be allowed in other circumstances as where partial proof is necessary to establish the existence or identity of a document on the terms of which the case may turn. In modern practice an allowance of proof before answer is usually confined to cases where a decision on the relevancy is to be reserved, and such an allowance of proof does not sanction the admission of incompetent evidence.[2] Occasionally the expression has been used where it was intended to reserve a question as to the competency of evidence but this is not usual.[3]

When a relevancy plea is sustained after a proof the form of judgment will normally be dismissal and not absolvitor.

¹ Govan v. J. & W. M'Killop, 1907, 15 S.L.T. 658; Inglis v. National Bank of Scotland, 1909 S.C. 1038; Stewart v. Astor & Faith, 1925 S.L.T. 7.
² Robertson v. Murphy, 1867, 6 M. 114.
³ See Stuart v. Stuart, 1869, 7 M. 366; Macvean v. Maclean, 1873, 11 M. 506; cf. Thomson v. Fraser, 1868, 7 M. 39; Haldane (Speirs' Factor) v. Speirs, 1872, 10 M. 537. See also Moncrieff v. Sievwright, 1896, 33 S.L.R. 456.

Other preliminary pleas may be taken, the disposal of which may exclude any further inquiry into the case. Typical examples of these are cases where the pursuer's claims are alleged to have been settled or discharged,¹ or where they are said to be barred by the omission of some preliminary as the want of statutory notice.² Proof will usually be required to establish such defences and it will often be convenient to have a preliminary proof for that purpose.³ On the other hand, if the point taken is merely a separate branch of the merits a proof on the whole case will usually be allowed.⁴ A plea of no jurisdiction should in general be disposed of *ante omnia*, and if necessary a limited proof of the facts on which it is based should be allowed *primo loco*.⁵

¹ Docherty v. M'Alpine & Sons, 1899, 2 F. 128; Hunter v. Darngavil Coal Co., 1900, 3 F. 10; Sinclair v. Lochgelly Iron & Coal Co., (O.H.) 1905, 13 S.L.T. 103; Gray v. Rivet Bolt and Nut Co., (O.H.) 1912, 2 S.L.T. 341; Davies v. Hunter, (O.H.) 1933 S.L.T. 158; cf. Campbell v. Caledonian Railway Co., 1899, 1 F. 887.
² Duncan v. Fife Coal Co., 1905, 7 F. 958.
³ Cases cited, supra. See also Gilillan v. Middle Ward District Committee of Lanarkshire County Council, (O.H.) 1902, 9 S.L.T. 432; 10 S.L.T. 274; M'Lean v. Hassard, (O.H.) 1903, 10 S.L.T. 593; Robertson v. Duke of Atholl, 1905, 8 F. 150; Rutherford v. Licenses, &c., Insurance Co., (O.H.) 1934 S.L.T. 47; A B v. C D, 1937 S.C. 408; cf. M'Kinnon v. Keith, (O.H.) 1912, 2 S.L.T. 501.
⁴ Oates v. Redpath Brown & Co., (O.H.) 1926 S.L.T. 211; Gardner v. Hastie, (O.H.) 1928 S.L.T. 497.
⁵ M'Leod v. Tancred, Arrol & Co., 1890, 17 R. 514; Donald v. Baird, &c., (O.H.) 1907, 15 S.L.T. 427; Methven Simpson v. Gray & Goskirk, 1905, 22 Sh.Ct.Rep. 342.

(n) *Removal to Court of Session.*—The preliminary pleas having been disposed of, or reserved, the next normal step in process is to allow a proof. But in certain cases the Sheriff Court procedure may be interrupted by the action being removed to the Court of Session.

At the closing of the record, or within six days thereafter, either party may require the remission to the Court of Session of (a) actions relating to questions of heritable right and title where the value of the subject in dispute exceeds £1000, or £50 yearly;

(b) actions relating to moveable succession where the value of the subject in dispute exceeds £1000; and (c) actions relating to division of commonty, or division, or division and sale, of common property, where the value of the subject in dispute exceeds £1000, or £50 yearly.[1] To obtain the remit a note in specified terms is written on the interlocutor sheet and signed by the party desiring it, or his solicitor.[2] Within four days thereafter the Sheriff-clerk sends written notice to the other side, and transmits the process to the Court of Session.[2] Failure by the Sheriff-clerk to notify the other side does not invalidate the procedure, but the Court of Session may remedy any disadvantage thereby occasioned.[2] For purposes of remit the value is not that of the whole subject but of the portion about which the parties are at issue.[3] Cases which relate only incidentally to heritable property cannot be remitted as raising questions of heritable right and title.[4]

[1] 7 Edw. VII c. 51, sec. 5.
[2] Rules of Court, 1936, V, 14.
[3] Muirhead v. Gilmour, 1909, 46 S.L.R. 425. See also Bowie v. Marquis of Ailsa, 1887, 14 R. 649.
[4] Anderson v. M'Gown, 1911 S.C. 441. See also Macandrew v. Dods, 1908 S.C. 51; Nicholson v. Glasgow Blind Asylum, 1911 S.C. 391; Duff v. West Craig, 1935, 51 Sh.Ct.Rep. 315.

In the case of actions of aliment (which as between spouses are actions of separation and aliment, adherence and aliment, or interim aliment) and actions for regulating the custody of children the Sheriff may, on cause shown or *ex proprio motu*, remit the cause to the Court of Session.[1] This may be done at any stage of the case, but the most convenient stage will be at the closing of the record. Generally a case so remitted to the Court of Session remains there for disposal, but it is within the Court's discretion to send it back to the Sheriff Court, and this will be done in remits *ex proprio motu* where there are no questions of special difficulty or delicacy to justify the cause being remitted.[2] Certain rights of removal to the Court of Session previously existed and are thought to be still operative. These include applications brought under the Guardianship of Infants Acts[3] and under the Rivers Pollution Prevention Act, 1876.[4]

[1] 7 Edw. VII c. 51, sec. 5.
[2] Dunbar v. Dunbar, 1912 S.C. 19; Lamont v. Lamont, 1939 S.C. 484.
[3] 49 & 50 Vict. c. 27, sec. 10; 15 & 16 Geo. V c. 45.
[4] 39 & 40 Vict. c. 75, secs. 11, 21. See Midlothian County Council v. Pumpherston Oil Co., 1902, 4 F. 996; Lanark County Council v. Magistrates of Airdrie, &c., 1906, 8 F. 802.

An action may be removed to the Court of Session for jury trial. This practice was introduced by the Judicature Act of 1825[1] when jury trial was not competent in civil causes in the Sheriff Court. The removal was effected upon the initiative of a party, and the Sheriff himself had no power to remit for this purpose. The present procedure for removal for jury trial is dealt with in detail later.[2]

[1] 6 Geo. IV c. 120, sec. 40.
[2] See p. 305, infra.

(4) *Judicial Reference.*

Most actions which are not dealt with by jury trial or disposed of on preliminary pleas go to proof before the Sheriff. But in certain cases the decision of the cause may be devolved upon a judicial referee, in which event the function of the Sheriff is largely restricted to granting a decree to make the judicial referee's report operative. A judicial reference is competent at any stage, but the convenient stage is at the closing of the record. If made at a later stage, there are referred to the judicial referee only such questions raised on record as have not already been disposed of by the Court.[1] After a judicial reference the Court will not allow an amendment of record which enlarges the scope of the reference.[2]

[1] Brown's Trustees v. Horne, 1907 S.C. 1027, Lord Kinnear, p. 1033.
[2] Brown's Trustees v. Horne, supra.

A reference may be either of the whole or of part of the cause. It is only competent to refer of consent of both parties, and the consent is expressed in a minute, which may be signed by the party or his solicitor. If signed by the solicitor, he should procure a special mandate.[1] Until the authority of the Court has been interponed to the reference either party may resile[2] unless barred,[3] but thereafter it can be recalled only of consent.[4] The interlocutor following on the minute refers the case to the referee selected by the parties. In practice one referee is selected. The procedure is in effect the substitution of an arbiter for a judge, and the proceedings before the referee follow the practice in arbitrations.

[1] Livingston v. Johnson, 1830, 8 S. 594; Black v. Laidlaw, 1844, 6 D. 1254.
[2] Reid v. Henderson, 1841, 3 D. 1102.
[3] As in Fairley v. M'Gown, 1836, 14 S. 470.
[4] Walker & Co. v. Stewart, 1855, 2 Macq. 424.

Although a judicial referee is selected, the character of a Court process is not altogether lost, and the aid of the Court may be invoked for such purposes as to compel the attendance of witnesses before the referee, to recover documents, &c. The process may, it is thought, fall asleep if there are no proceedings in it for year and day.[1] The Court may not review the referee's award on the merits, but may control its form, and may remit it back for correction if it is informal, or incomplete, or if the referee has not exhausted the reference,[2] or has not taken proof on disputed matters of fact. Objections which warrant the Court interfering must, however, be substantial, and of such a nature as might ground an action for reduction of an arbiter's award.[3] The Court can entertain such objections on being moved for decree in terms of the referee s report and a separate action of reduction is unnecessary,[4] but the Court will not interfere upon trivial points of form, or complaints as to procedure.[3] The question of expenses in the reference may be disposed of by the referee with special or express authority,[5] or it may be left to be dealt with by the Court. The referee is entitled to a fee,[6] and the Court fixes his and his clerk's remuneration if it has not been agreed upon. If one party has paid the referee's or clerk's fee, the Court may decern the other party to reimburse his share.[7]

[1] See Watson v. Stewart, 1872, 10 M. 494.
[2] Lord Advocate v. Heddle, 1856, 18 D. 1211; Cormack & Son v. Magourty, 1928, 45 Sh.Ct.Rep. 103.
[3] Robertson v. Davidson, 1833, 11 S. 659; Rogerson v. Rogerson, 1885, 12 R. 583.
[4] Mackenzie v. Girvan, 1840, 3 D. 318, per Lord Moncreiff, p. 327; Hook v. Lodge Colinton & Currie, 1931, 47 Sh.Ct.Rep. 144.
[5] Henderson v. Paul, 1867, 5 M. 613, 628; Hilton v. Walkers. 1867, 5 M. 969.
[6] Macintyre Brothers v. Smith, 1913 S.C. 129.
[7] Edinburgh Oil Gas Co. v. Clyne's Trustees, &c., 1835, 13 S. 413; Drummond v. Leslie, 1835, 13 S. 684.

A judicial reference is competent in a summary cause as well as in an ordinary action and the appropriate time will be when pleadings are being adjusted or, where there are not formal pleadings, at the diet when pleas are noted. When the reference is completed, the process—whether ordinary or summary—comes back to the Court, so that judicial authority may be interponed to the referee's report. Subject to what is stated above the decision of the referee is final both as regards fact and law, upon the matters referred.[1] When the Sheriff interpones authority to the referee's report his interlocutor is in form a Court judgment, but it is not subject to review on the merits of the award.[1] The parties may competently exclude any review at all of the interlocutor applying the referee's award,[2] and if in place of making a reference they constitute the Sheriff an arbiter his decision will not be subject to appeal,[3] but such exclusion of the rights of appeal will not be readily assumed. If the judicial referee dies before making an award, the process reverts to its position as at the date of the remit.[4] The reference unlike an ordinary submission does not fall by the death of a party[5] but it falls if the principal process falls.[6]

[1] Mackenzie v. Girvan, 1840, 3 D. 318.
[2] Shiels, &c. v. Shiels' Trustees, 1874, 1 R. 502.
[3] Dykes v. Merry & Cunninghame, 1869, 7 M. 603; cf. Lindsay v. Walker's Trustees, 1877, 4 R. 870; Gordon v. Bruce & Co., 1897, 24 R. 844.
[4] Mackenzie v. Girvan, supra, Lord Moncreiff, p. 329.
[5] Watmore v. Burns, 1839, 1 D. 743.
[6] Gillon v. Simpson, 1859, 21 D. 243.

(5) *Remit to Man of Skill.*

It is a competent, and convenient, mode of ascertaining matters of fact, whether in an ordinary action or in a summary cause, to remit to a man of skill to make a report. This differs from a judicial reference in that it is only a mode of ascertaining facts, upon which the Court will pronounce judgment, not a devolution of the cause upon a referee for his decision. A judicial referee may decide both upon fact and law. A judicial reporter normally reports upon matters of fact, except in special cases, as in a remit to a solicitor who may express an opinion upon title deeds or legal questions. The general object of a remit is to provide a basis of fact for the Sheriff's judgment in law.[1] As a report from a man of skill often renders proof unnecessary, if not incompetent, a remit will not in general be granted till the record has been closed. But it is competent and may in special circumstances be convenient, for the information of the Court, to make a remit before that stage is reached.[2] The Sheriff Courts Act leaves the time of making a remit an open question.[3]

[1] Nisbet v. Mitchell-Innes, 1880, 7 R. 575; Scott v. Somerville, (O.H.) 1895, 3 S.L.T. 218; Campbeltown Shipbuilding Co. v. Robertson, 1896, 14 Sh.Ct.Rep. 244.
[2] See Mushet v. Duke of Buccleuch, 1851, 13 D. 715.
[3] 7 Edw. VII c. 51, Schedule I, Rule 60.

It is now provided by Statute that the Sheriff may remit to any person of skill, or other person, to report on any matter of fact; and that when such remit is made of consent of both parties, the report of such person shall be final and conclusive with respect to the matter of the remit.[1] While a remit may probably be made by the Sheriff at his own hand the expediency of making it may be questioned.[2] When a remit is made on the motion of one party without objection by the other it is thought that this is a remit of consent and that the report of the man of skill is conclusive upon the matter of fact with which it deals.[3] It is in general the right of each party in a cause to prove his case by leading evidence before the Court, and it is very doubtful whether the statutory provision empowers the Court to force one of the parties against his will to accept a remit in place of proof, save in special circumstances in which a remit is particularly appropriate.[2] A remit which involves questions of law as well as of fact is not encouraged.[4]

[1] 7 Edw. VII c. 51, Schedule I, Rule 60.
[2] Quin v. Gardner & Sons, 1888, 15 R. 776; Magistrates of Kilmarnock v. Reid, 1897, 24 R. 388; Sutherland v. Squair, 1898, 25 R. 656; cf. Broxburn Oil Co. v. Morrison, 1903, 5 F. 694.
[3] Pearce Brothers v. Irons, 1869, 7 M. 571; Barclay v. Bruce's Trustees, (O.H.) 1904, 12 S.L.T. 100.
[4] Quin v. Gardner & Sons, supra.

A remit has been considered a suitable method of ascertaining such facts as the nature and condition of fences in a farm, or machinery in a factory[1]; the amount to be allowed for the average annual cost of repairs in connexion with assessments for parish rates,[2] and the nature of items claimed to be fixtures.[3] Remits are also commonly made in cases of nuisance and pollution in order to ascertain the position, or to investigate remedial measures.[4] In actions of count reckoning and payment, and in other cases where the investigation of accounts is necessary, it is usual to remit to an accountant to report. Normally such a remit does not necessarily exclude proof, and proof may be allowed later, on objections to the accountant's report.[5] The provisions regulating such remits in the Court of Session[6] do not apply to the Sheriff Court, but procedure on similar lines might be followed. It has been held incompetent to bring an action in the Sheriff Court merely for the purpose of getting a remit to a man of skill to report on contract work with the view of matters being followed up after his report has been made.[7] A remit is frequently made when it is necessary to ascertain the facts in non-contentious business, but in declarators regarding terce under the Conveyancing Act inquiry must apparently be by proof.[8]

[1] Magistrates of Kilmarnock v. Reid, 1897, 24 R. 388, Lord President Robertson, p. 392. See also M'Donald, 1882, 10 R. 172.
[2] Broxburn Oil Co. v. Morrison, 1903, 5 F. 694.
[3] Nisbet v. Mitchell-Innes, 1880, 7 R. 575. See also Quin v. Gardner & Sons, 1888, 15 R. 776, Lord Shand, p. 780.
[4] Dodd v. Hilson, 1874, 1 R. 527; Dykes v. Allanshaw Coal Co., (O.H.) 1894, 1 S.L.T. 530; Earl of Kintore v. Pirie & Sons, 1905, 8 F. 1058; 1906, 8 F. (H.L.) 16; M'Ewen v. Steedman & M'Alister, 1913 S.C. 761.
[5] Binnie v. Binnie's Trustees, 1889, 16 R. (H.L.) 23.

6 31 & 32 Vict. c. 100, sec. 81, et seq.
7 Magistrates of Kilmarnock v. Reid, supra; Sutherland v. Squair, 1898, 25 R. 656.
8 Dickson v. Dickson, (O.H.) 1931 S.L.T. 75.

Notwithstanding that the report of a skilled reporter has been obtained of consent, and is therefore conclusive as to the facts reported upon, the parties are entitled to be heard upon the report before it is adopted by the Sheriff. Objection may be made to the report on such grounds as that the reporter has not exhausted the terms of the remit, or that he has dealt with matters not remitted to him, or has made errors in calculation, or the like, and the Court may direct the reporter to take back his report for revisal in the light of such objections.[1] The Sheriff may re-remit as often as may be necessary to obtain a complete report, exhaustive of the original remit, or to get additional information from the reporter.[2] A remit for a report after a proof when a change of circumstances has occurred is not incompetent,[3] and a report at this stage may be appropriate in cases of pollution and nuisance.[4] When the report does not cover the whole questions at issue an allowance of proof to clear up outstanding points is not incompetent, though a second remit will usually be the more appropriate course.[5] Where the report is based partly upon facts and partly upon opinion, the reporter's grounds of opinion may be attacked. In an accountant's report the manner in which the figures should be arranged, so as to present a true account, the question whether they should appear under capital or income, or how they should be treated in a balance sheet, or the like, are matters of opinion. Where English counsel in a remit to ascertain a point in English law differed in their opinions the Court remitted to other counsel.[6]

[1] Cameron v. Anderson, 1844, 7 D. 92.
[2] Lyle & Wallace v. M'Kechnie, 1922, 38 Sh.Ct.Rep. 167.
[3] Leonard, &c. v. Lindsay & Benzie, 1886, 13 R. 958.
[4] Earl of Kintore v. Pirie & Sons, 1905, 8 F. 1058; 1906, 8 F. (H.L.) 16; M'Ewen v. Steedman & M'Alister, 1913 S.C. 761.
[5] Steel v. Steel, 1898, 25 R. 715.
[6] Fyffe v. Fyffe, 1840, 2 D. 1001.

A remit to a man of skill is sometimes made to relieve the Court of investigation work. The most familiar instances are remits to the Auditor of Court to tax expenses allowed, or to tax a professional account sued for; remits to adjust a draft deed; remits to a solicitor in company applications; and remits to the accountant of Court in factory and similar applications. Reports under such remits are not conclusive, and an operative judgment must be pronounced by the Court, either giving effect to or modifying the reporter's recommendations.

The functions of the reporter will differ according to the nature and terms of the remit. In contentious cases he must act with fairness to both sides. It will not be necessary for him in all cases to hear parties,[1] but if the remit instructs him to do so he must hear them in presence of each other.[2] A formal hearing may not be necessary if the reporter has met the parties and afforded them an opportunity in each other's presence of offering their respective explanations and representations.[3]

[1] See Marshall v. Callander, &c., Hydropathic Co., 1897, 24 R. 712; North British Railway Co. v. Wilson, 1911 S.C. 730. See also Darling v. Butters Bros., 1901, 17 Sh.Ct.Rep. 272.
[2] M'Farlane & Gibb v. Strachan, 1884, 12 R. 114.
[3] Lyle & Wallace v. M'Kechnie, 1922, 38 Sh.Ct.Rep. 167.

The direction of the Act, as regards the expense attending remits, is (a) that, if made upon the motion of one party, the party moving for a remit is liable in the first instance; and (b) that, if made upon joint motion, or by the Sheriff *ex proprio motu*, the expenses are in the first instance to be paid by the parties equally, unless the Sheriff shall otherwise order.[1] The liability is laid upon the parties, not upon the solicitors. Decree for a reporter's fee may be given in his favour in the process[2] after the report has been lodged. Normally the parties will at this stage be found liable jointly and severally for the fee, but they may be found liable jointly when each is responsible *in hoc statu* for only one-half of the fee.[3] The reporter may withhold his report, and retain the vouchers and documents which have come into his hands in the course of executing the remit, till he obtain payment of his fees. Where one party has taken up a report, and paid the whole fee, the other party cannot compel him to disclose it unless by paying his half of the fee.[4] When the amount of the reporter's fee is challenged the Sheriff may remit to the auditor who will fix the amount of the fee subject to revision by the Sheriff.[5]

[1] 7 Edw. VII.c. 51, Schedule I, Rule 60.
[2] Ballantine v. Reddie, 1884, 22 S.L.R. 136.
[3] See Davidson v. Watson, 1925 S.C. 883.
[4] Sutherland v. Goalen, 1855, 17 D. 509.
[5] Allen v. Tudhope, 1890, 6 Sh.Ct.Rep. 276.

(6) *Sisting an Action.*

If any reason exists why a case should not, at the closing of the record, be sent to proof or debate, or if, at any stage, circumstances arise which make it inexpedient to continue a litigation, but the pursuer does not desire to abandon it, the Court may in its discretion sist the action till the further orders of Court. An action should not, generally speaking, be sisted if the effect of doing so would be to give one party an unfair advantage, as, for instance, to enable an illiquid debt to be constituted,[1] or if the circumstances are such that the action should be dismissed.[2] Thus an action which has been served prematurely, as for a debt not yet due, should be dismissed and not sisted because there was no relevant cause of action at the date the action was raised.[3]

[1] Mackie v. Mackie, (O.H.) 1897, 5 S.L.T. 42; cf. Munro v. Macdonald's Executors, 1866, 4 M. 687; Ross v. Ross, 1895, 22 R. 461.
[2] North British Railway Co. v. North British Grain Storage, &c., Co., 1897, 24 R. 687.
[3] Cf. Macvean v. Maclean, &c., 1873, 11 M. 764.

If there was, at the date of raising an action, a relevant cause of action, but it is inexpedient at the moment to proceed with the case, it may be conveniently sisted. Perhaps the most common case is where the point at issue in the action falls to be decided by arbitration and the process is sisted to await the arbiter's award.[1] So also a process may be sisted to await the issue of a pending litigation, or of another action to be raised to decide some point that cannot be disposed of in the first action.[2] If a sist is asked in respect of other pending proceedings it will generally be refused if the record has not yet been closed.[3] A sist is also appropriate where circumstances have arisen since the action was raised which, according as they may eventuate, may render the action unnecessary[4]; where a party has become bankrupt and his trustee requires time to investigate the circumstances before deciding whether to sist himself as a party; or where a document founded on requires to be stamped,[5] or one of the parties requires to complete title.[6] The granting of a motion to sist is in the discretion of the Court,[7] and it may be refused if prejudice is likely to be suffered by the other party to the action.[8]

[1] See Wilson & M'Farlane v. Stewart & Co., 1898, 25 R. 655; Barr v. Queensferry Commissioners, 1899, 1 F. 630; Crawford Bros. v. Commissioners of Northern Lighthouses, 1925 S.C. (H.L.) 22; Palmer v. South East Lancashire Insurance Co., (O.H.) 1932 S.L.T. 68.
[2] Loudon & Co. v. Young, &c., 1856, 18 D. 856; Smellie v. Thomson, 1868, 6 M. 1024; Earl of Lauderdale v. Wedderburn, (O.H.) 1903, 11 S.L.T. 194; Duke of Argyll v. Muir, 1910 S.C. 96; Foster v. Foster's Trustees, 1923 S.C. 212; cf. Thomson v. North British & Mercantile Insurance Co., 1868, 6 M. 310.
[3] Clydesdale Bank v. Cohen, 1943 S.C. 244.
[4] Paterson v. Paterson, 1899, 2 F. 81.
[5] Neil v. Leslie, 1867, 5 M. 634.
[6] Stiven v. Brown, 1871, 8 S.L.R. 626.
[7] Phosphate Sewage Co. v. Molleson, 1876, 3 R. (H.L.) 77.
[8] M'Crae v. Bryson, 1922 S.L.T. 664.

An action may be sisted on the motion of either party, or by the Sheriff *ex proprio motu*. An interlocutor sisting an action can be appealed without leave from the Sheriff-Substitute to the Sheriff or to the Court of Session and from the Sheriff to the Court of Session.[1] An interlocutor refusing to sist an action is not appealable without leave.[1] A sist does not apparently prevent an action from falling asleep.[2] A sist may be recalled upon the motion of either party, but the recall, like the sisting, is in the discretion of the Court. While it stands, an order sisting an action precludes any step of process, however formal, being taken. No interlocutor can be pronounced till the sist has been recalled, when the action resumes the character of a pending process.

[1] 7 Edw. VII c. 51, secs. 27, 28; 2 & 3 Geo. V c. 28, Schedule I.
[2] American Mortgage Co. of Scotland v. Sidway, (O.H.) 1906, 44 S.L.R. 170. See 7 Edw. VII c. 51, Schedule I, Rule 101.

(7) *Remit to and from Small Debt Roll.*

Any action, whether a summary cause or an ordinary action, irrespective of its value, may of consent be disposed of as a small debt action. This, it is thought, applies only to actions of a nature competent in the Small Debt Court, such as actions for payment, or for delivery, or of multiplepoinding. An action of declarator, or for count and reckoning, or for separation, or the like, not being competent in the Small Debt Court, cannot be remitted to the Small Debt Roll. Where such a remit is desired a minute is lodged, signed by both parties or their solicitors, agreeing to the case being disposed of under the Small Debt Acts. On such a minute being lodged the Sheriff must remit the action to the Small Debt Roll and the whole process and provisions of the Small Debt Acts then become applicable to the cause.[1] The Sheriff may, either upon cause shown, or *ex proprio motu*, remit a cause from his Small Debt Roll to be tried as an ordinary action[2]; but it is only of consent of parties that he may bring a case from the Ordinary to the Small Debt Roll.[1]

[1] 7 Edw. VII c. 51, Schedule I, Rule 61.
[2] Ibid., sec. 48.

Actions for delivery are competent in the Small Debt Court, and actions for the custody of children are now competent in the Ordinary Court,[1] but it seems clear that an action for delivery of the person of a child is not one of the actions which may be remitted from the roll of ordinary actions to the Small Debt Roll. Such an action cannot be initiated in the Small Debt Court, because the Small Debt Amendment Act of 1889, which made an

action of delivery competent in that Court, applies only to
" corporeal moveables."[2] It is not therefore competent, even of
consent, to raise an action seeking delivery of a child in the
Small Debt Court, nor is it competent to remit it to that Court
from the Ordinary Roll.

[1] 7 Edw. VII c. 51, sec. 5 (2).
[2] 52 & 53 Vict. c. 26, sec. 2.

An action so remitted from the Ordinary to the Small Debt
Roll becomes in every respect a small debt process, and it is disposed of in the Small Debt Court. When the necessary minute
is lodged the case is at once put upon the Small Debt Roll. The
table of fees contains a special provision to meet cases remitted
in this way to the Small Debt Roll. The expenses up to the lodging
of the joint minute will be fixed in accordance with the scale
applicable to the action in its original character, but thereafter
the solicitor's fee is restricted to £1 6s. 8d.[1] The expenses, which
will be decerned for in the Small Debt Court, may thus include :
(a) expenses on the ordinary scale, from the raising of the action
till the date of remit to the Small Debt Roll ; (b) thereafter expenses
on the Small Debt Court scale which may include legal charges
not exceeding in all £1 6s. 8d.

[1] Codifying Act of Sederunt, Book M, chap. II, as amended by Act
of Sederunt of 7th May, 1935; Table of Fees IX, 4.

Provision is also made for remitting a small debt case to the
Ordinary Roll.[1] If the Sheriff is of opinion that the importance
of the questions raised in the case warrant that course he may at
any stage either on cause shown or *ex proprio motu* remit the case
to his Ordinary Court Roll.[1] The small debt action, when so
transferred, is to proceed in all respects (including appeal) as if it
had been originally raised in the Ordinary Court.[1] Such a remitted
case (being under £50 in value) appears to fall within the present
definition of a summary cause,[2] and it will thus have the right of
appeal competent in a summary cause including a right of appeal
to the Court of Session if the Sheriff after final judgment on appeal
certifies the case as suitable for appeal.[3] On being remitted, the
action ceases to be a small debt action, unless of consent it is
remitted back to the Small Debt Roll. If this is not done, the
judgment in the action is not appealable to the Justiciary Court,
for that is appropriate only to a small debt action, and the remitted
cause has lost that character. The making or refusing of the

remit is in the discretion of the Sheriff and reference may be made
to the undernoted cases.[4]

1 7 Edw. VII c. 51, sec. 48.
2 Ibid., sec. 3 (i) ; 2 & 3 Geo. V c. 28, Schedule I; cf. Price v. Canadian
　　Pacific Railway Co., 1911 S.C. 631.
3 Ibid., secs. 8, 27, 28; 2 & 3 Geo. V c. 28, Schedule I.
4 Munro v. North British Railway Co., 1904, 21 Sh.Ct.Rep. 19; Brown
　　v. Corporation of Glasgow, 1909, 25 Sh.Ct.Rep. 185.

There is no prescribed stage at which, nor time within
which, a case may be remitted either from the Ordinary to the
Small Debt Roll, or from the Small Debt to the Ordinary Roll. It
appears to be competent at any stage.[1] In an ordinary action, the
circumstances which make it appropriate for small debt procedure
may not have emerged at the initial stages of the case, but by the
time the record is closed they should have done so, and the appropriate time for a remit to the Small Debt Roll would appear to be
at the closing of the record. In the converse case of remit from the
Small Debt Court the issue will be clear from the first, and, if the
case is appropriate for treatment as an ordinary action, it should
be remitted at the first calling, before any procedure is entered
upon. In both cases, however, the power of remitting is unrestricted
as to time, and it is probably not incompetent to remit a Small
Debt Court cause to the Ordinary Court Roll, at any time before
judgment in it has been recorded in the Small Debt Court book.[1]
In the case noted the remit was made from the Small Debt Court
when the case was at avizandum after proof.[1]

1 See Wigtownshire Creamery Co. v. Portpatrick & Wigtownshire Joint
　　Committee, 1903, 6 F. (J.) 3.

(8) *Debate Roll.*

Where a case is not disposed of in one of the ways indicated
above, and is not appropriate for jury trial in the Sheriff Court,
the Sheriff will at the closing of the record in the normal case
either allow a proof or appoint the case to be debated. It is
specially provided that if, at the closing of the record, the parties
renounce probation, they shall sign a minute to that effect on the
interlocutor sheet, and the Sheriff may order the case to be debated
then or at a subsequent diet.[1] The course here indicated may be
advisable in special cases,[2] but it is not the usual custom in normal
circumstances to require probation to be renounced before a case
is sent for debate.[3] And where an action does not raise issues of
fact but only questions of law it will be sent to the Debate Roll for
disposal as a matter of course.[4] Apart from such a case a debate
will be ordered where it is necessary to deal with preliminary pleas

which ought to be discussed before a proof is taken, and the statutory instruction is that the Sheriff shall first dispose of such pleas unless he thinks that, from their being connected with the merits, or on any other ground, they should be reserved till a future stage of the cause.[5] The nature of such preliminary pleas and the manner of their disposal have been already discussed.[6]

[1] 7 Edw. VII c. 51, Schedule I, Rule 58.
[2] Watson v. Watson's Trustees, 1926 S.C. (H.L.) 27.
[3] William Beardmore & Co. v. Park's Executrix, 1927 S.C. 533.
[1] See Congested Districts (Scotland) Commissioners v. MacInnes, 1910, 26 Sh.Ct.Rep. 343.
[5] 7 Edw. VII c. 51, Schedule I, Rule 54.
[6] See p. 165 et seq., supra.

(9) *Order for Proof.*

An action which is not sent to the Debate Roll, will in normal circumstances proceed to trial before the Sheriff, and at the closing of the record, the Sheriff may allow a proof.[1] As already mentioned, that may be a proof before answer, or a proof on the merits, according as the preliminary pleas have, or have not, been disposed of.[2] The interlocutor should formally allow a proof and such an interlocutor is amongst those which are subject to appeal.[3] In a summary cause the Sheriff may appoint a diet for the trial of the cause or may order such other procedure as he thinks proper.[4] If inquiry is needed a proof will normally be allowed in the usual way and such an interlocutor has been held to be open to appeal in a summary as in the ordinary cause.[5]

[1] 7 Edw. VII c. 51, Schedule I, Rule 59.
[2] See p. 168, supra.
[3] 7 Edw. VII c. 51, sec. 27.
[4] Ibid., Rule 41.
[5] Salmond v. Ross, 1919, 36 Sh.Ct.Rep. 146.

Certain distinctions are sometimes recognized in regard to the form of an order for proof. Thus, if the case comprises only averments for the pursuer, denied by the defender, the order may allow the pursuer a proof of his averments and the defender a conjunct probation.[1] Where both parties make substantive averments, the proper order is to allow parties a proof of their respective averments, and pursuer a conjunct probation.[1] If defender admits the pursuer's case, and sets up in answer a separate case, the order may allow the defender a proof, and the pursuer a conjunct probation. In modern practice where both parties make averments the order may simply allow a proof, or allow parties a proof of their averments. It is thought that this is sufficient and that each party is then required to lead evidence in support of his own case, and in anticipation of his opponent's case. Sometimes an order is made for proof *habili modo* the effect of which is that, while the order for proof is otherwise in general terms, parole proof may not be competent in respect of certain averments, and it is left to the Sheriff at the proof to decide whether any particular fact can be proved by parole or only by writ.[2]

[1] See Scott & Co. v. Forrest & Turnbull, 1897, 24 R. 877.
[2] See Gill v. Gill, 1907 S.C. 532, Lord Justice-Clerk Macdonald, p. 535; Smith's Trustees v. Smith, 1911 S.C. 653; Macneil v. MacMillan, 1930, 46 Sh.Ct.Rep. 282; Kennedy v. Macrae, 1946 S.L.T. 198.

In the absence of express direction to the contrary, the pursuer leads at the proof. Sometimes the onus of proof is on the defender, or he may be the party who requires to establish the issue which has gone to proof. In such circumstances the defender should be appointed to lead. This is largely a matter of convenience, and does not necessarily infer that in all cases where the defender is appointed to lead the *onus* of proof rests upon him.[1] If the defender is to lead this should be ordered in the interlocutor allowing the proof, thus avoiding a discussion on the point when the proof is about to begin. Where an allowance of proof has been affirmed on appeal it may be too late thereafter to ask that the defender be appointed to lead.[2]

[1] Gibson v. Adams, 1875, 3 R. 144.
[2] Marquis of Breadalbane v. M'Nab, 1903, 20 Sh.Ct.Rep. 51.

If an open proof is not allowed the particular restriction of the inquiry should be set forth in the interlocutor, whether the restriction is as regards the subject-matter or the form of the proof. Thus, where a pursuer makes averments which it is not competent to prove by parole, the order should specifically allow a proof by writ or oath of the defender and a similar restriction should be made where definite parts of the case can only be proved in this manner.[1] Proof may also be refused of any separable part of the case which is irrelevant so as to prevent such averments going to proof.[2] If a separation as above cannot be made a proof *habili modo* may be allowed[3] or a proof before answer may be ordered.[4] If an averment is made of some fact which if proved would not be competent evidence in the case that averment should be excluded from probation.[5]

[1] Gibson v. Adams, 1875, 3 R. 144. See also Hallet v. Ryrie and Others, (O.H.) 1907, 15 S.L.T. 367. See p. 233, infra.
[2] Barr v. Bain, 1896, 23 R. 1090; Soeder v. Soeder, 1897, 24 R. 278; P. & W. MacLellan v. Peattie's Trustees, 1903, 5 F. 1031.
[3] Gill v. Gill, 1907 S.C. 532, and other cases cited at top of this page.

[4] Moncrieff v. Sievwright, 1896, 33 S.L.R. 456, and other cases cited on p. 169, supra.
[5] Scott v. Cormack Heating Engineers, 1942 S.C. 159.

The date and place for taking the proof are commonly set forth in the interlocutor allowing proof, but these may be the subject of a subsequent interlocutor. An interlocutor allowing proof is appealable, although no time and place for taking it have been fixed[1]; but an interlocutor merely fixing a time and place at which a proof already allowed shall proceed is not appealable.

[1] 7 Edw. VII c. 51, sec. 27 (d).

If, at the diet of proof, one party only appears, he does not in the normal case require to lead any evidence. The party not appearing is held as confessed, and the party appearing may crave decree by default.[1] If neither party appear, the action is dismissed.[1] These provisions do not apply where the party does not appear at a diet of proof but is represented by a solicitor even though the latter is not prepared to proceed. In such a case, if the Sheriff is not disposed to adjourn the diet, the other party may be allowed to proceed with the proof.[2] Decree by default cannot be taken in the case of consistorial actions where the pursuer must in all circumstances establish his case before decree will be granted.[3]

[1] 7 Edw. VII c. 51, Schedule I, Rule 56.
[2] Finlay v. Bush, 1925, 41 Sh.Ct.Rep. 171; Jack v. Wardrop, 1927, 44 Sh.Ct.Rep. 61.
[3] 7 Edw. VII c. 51, Schedule I, Rule 23; 2 & 3 Geo. V c. 28, Schedule II. See p. 130, supra

CHAPTER IX.

TRIAL OF THE CAUSE.

1. INSPECTION BY COURT.

In some actions, specially those concerning heritable property,
and the execution of works, it may be convenient for the judge,
before hearing evidence, to see the *locus*. If this is considered
desirable, the order fixing a time and place for the proof should
also appoint parties or their solicitors to meet with the Sheriff
on the ground. The proper time is -before the commencement
of the proof, for the object of an inspection is to enable the
Sheriff to follow the evidence led, not for the purpose of criticising
evidence after it has been led.[1] Such a visit should be made in
presence of parties' solicitors.[1]

[1] Hattie v. Leitch, 1889, 16 R. 1128; 5 Sh.Ct.Rep. 333.

2. INSPECTION BY PARTIES.

In like manner, not for the purpose of superseding proof,
but for its better understanding, each party is entitled to reasonable facility from the other for the inspection, personally, or by
others on his behalf, of buildings, works, vehicles, material, &c.,
which are the subject of an action.[1] If reasonable access is not
voluntarily afforded, the Court may order a party to afford it,[1]
but the identity of the parties who are to be sent to inspect
must be disclosed.[2] Normally an order for inspection will only
be made after proof has been allowed, but it may be granted before
the closing of the record if it is necessary for the adjustment of
the pleadings.[3] A preliminary application for an inspection before
an action is raised if not incompetent will only be considered in
exceptional circumstances.[4] If the article to be inspected is portable
its production in Court may be ordered.[5]

[1] Bell v. Hamilton's Trustees, 1889, 16 R. 1001; Stevenson v. Gray &
Sons, (O.H.) 1902, 9 S.L.T. 489; Murray v. Waterproofing Co.,
(O.H.) 1914, 1 S.L.T. 46.
[2] Clippens Oil Co. v. Edinburgh Water Trustees, (O.H.) 1904, 12 S.L.T.
40.
[3] Christie v. Munro, (O.H.) 1885, 23 S.L.R. 267; Murray v. Waterproofing Co., supra; cf. Gallacher v. Linlithgow Oil Co., 1891,
8 Sh.Ct.Rep. 13.
[4] Irvine v. William Dixon, 1890, 6 Sh.Ct.Rep. 192.
[5] MacTaggart, &c. v. MacKillop, (O.H.) 1938 S.L.T. 559.

A party who alleges personal injury and sues for damages in respect thereof, is bound to submit himself to medical examination on behalf of the defender, and, if necessary, the Sheriff will make an order for this purpose,[1] even before the record is closed,[2] if such medical examination is reasonably necessary to enable a defender to state his defence. Similarly, in consistorial cases a pursuer, but not a defender, will normally be required to submit to medical examination on behalf of the other party.[3] But a defender who alleges the pursuer is insane must make out a *prima facie* case before he can get an order for medical examination.[4] A person who can be medically examined at or near his home will not usually be required to travel to another district at the request of the party desiring the examination.[5]

[1] Junner v. North British Railway Co., 1877, 4 R. 686.
[2] Smyth v. Gow, (O.H.) 1895, 2 S.L.T. 473.
[3] X v. Y, (O.H.) 1922 S.L.T. 158; cf. A B v. C D, (O.H.) 1908, 15 S.L.T. 911.
[4] A B v. C D, 1937 S.C. 408, 696.
[5] M'Donald v. Western S.M.T. Co., 1945 S.C. 47.

3. ASSESSORS.

In maritime causes, as defined below, the Court, or either party, may require a skilled assessor to sit with the Sheriff to hear evidence. This is regulated by the Nautical Assessors (Scotland) Act, 1894,[1] and relative Act of Sederunt.[2] Intimation of the assessor proposed to be summoned has to be given by the Sheriff-clerk to the parties eight days before the proof, and any party proposing to object to the appointment must lodge a minute containing his grounds of objection within two days of receipt of the intimation.[2] Any such objection has to be disposed of by the Court at least three days before the proof, and, if sustained, the same procedure is to be followed to secure another assessor, the proof, if necessary, being adjourned.[3] In practice objection is seldom made to the proposed nominee of the Sheriff. The assessor is selected from a list approved by the Sheriff, which is in force for three years, but assessors already on the list may be approved in a subsequent list.[4] If all the assessors on the list are successfully objected to the motion for an assessor would seem to fall, for there is no provision for a nomination *pro hac vice*, either by the Sheriff-Substitute or the Sheriff. The party moving for an assessor is required to consign the costs involved.[5] If an assessor is summoned *ex proprio motu* by the Court, the pursuer of the action makes the consignation unless the Court otherwise orders.[5] It is the duty of the Sheriff-clerk to arrange for the assessor's attendance.[3]

[1] 57 & 58 Vict. c. 40 (superseded as to Court of Session by Rules of Court, 1936).
[2] C.A.S. Book L, chap. I.
[3] Ibid., sec. 1.
[4] 57 & 58 Vict. c. 40, sec. 4.
[5] C.A.S. Book L, chap. I, sec. 3.

The official qualification for a nautical assessor is that he must be a person " of nautical skill and experience."[1] Objection taken to an assessor by any of the parties may be either personal or in respect of his qualification.[1] The latter ground of objection will presumably be related to the particular subject of the action —as in a case involving questions of navigation only, where it might reasonably be objected that the proposed assessor, although an eminent marine engineer, had no experience in navigation. Assessors may be summoned either for a proof or at any subsequent hearing whether on appeal or otherwise.[1] One assessor is summoned for a proof and one or more, in the discretion of the Court, for an appeal.[2]

[1] 57 & 58 Vict. c. 40, sec. 2.
[2] C.A.S. Book L, chap. I, sec. 1.

The scope of the Nautical Assessors Act is very wide. It applies not only to actions arising out of, or relating to, collisions at sea, but also to actions relating to salvage and towage, or any other maritime matter.[1] This broad definition might be thought to cover many actions, arising upon contract, relating to the building, employment, or insurance of ships. In practice, however, in most Sheriff Courts, a nautical assessor is asked for only in collision and salvage cases, and applications for assessors are few in proportion to the number of maritime actions entertained in the Sheriff Courts.

[1] 57 & 58 Vict. c. 40, sec. 2.

Where an assessor is present the Sheriff must note any questions submitted by him to the assessor and the assessor's answers thereto.[1] The assessor is not a judge in the case and it is for the Sheriff to pronounce upon the trustworthiness of the evidence led before him.[2] Nor can the opinion of the assessor be taken as evidence upon a point upon which no evidence was led at the proof.[3] The opinion has been expressed that, when a nautical assessor is present, expert evidence on matters of nautical skill or experience is incompetent,[4] but this has not, as in the Court of Session,[5] been made a matter of express provision. A nautical assessor cannot function at a jury trial.[6] As to the death of an assessor before the close of the proof see the case undernoted.[7]

[1] 57 & 58 Vict. c. 40, sec. 3; s.s. "Rowan" v. s.s. "West Camak," 1923 S.C. 316.
[2] Cambo Shipping Co. v. Dampskibsselskabet Carl, 1920 S.C. 26.
[3] "Nerano" v. "Dromedary," 1895, 22 R. 237.
[4] "Bogota" v. "Alconda," 1923 S.C. 526.
[5] See Rules of Court, 1936, I, 52; III, 10 (g).
[6] M'Lean v. Johnstone, 1906, 8 F. 836; Leadbetter v. Dublin, &c., Steam Packet Co., 1907 S.C. 538; Kerr, &c. v. Screw Colliery Co., (O.H.) 1907, 15 S.L.T. 444; Rodger v. Glen-Coats, 1913, 1 S.L.T. 434.
[7] Ravelston Steamship Co. v. Sieberg Brothers, 1946 S.C. 349.

The Employers' Liability Act of 1880 also sanctions the Court calling in an assessor in cases laid upon that Statute, which are being tried without a jury, but the qualification for an assessor is not defined, and the Sheriff is not restricted to an official list of assessors.[1] The function of the assessors is to ascertain the amount of the compensation,[1] but their appointment seems to be unknown in modern practice.

[1] 43 & 44 Vict. c. 42, sec. 6 (2).

Under the Patents and Designs Act of 1907, in any action for infringement or revocation of a patent the Court may *ex proprio motu*, and must, on the request of either of the parties to the proceedings, call in an assessor and try the case wholly or partially with his assistance.[1] The qualification for an assessor is not defined beyond that he is to be a person "specially qualified,"[1] and the selection rests with the Sheriff. An assessor can also be called in by the Court on appeal.[2]

[1] 7 Edw. VII c. 29, secs. 31 (1); 94 (1).
[2] Ibid., sec. 31 (2).

When it is competent to have an assessor in an ordinary action, or in a summary cause, the appropriate time for moving for an assessor is at the date of ordering proof, but the motion may be made later. It should in all cases be made a reasonable time before the diet of proof, and in maritime cases it should be at such time as will enable the Sheriff-clerk to intimate the name of the proposed assessor eight days before the proof.[1] It is not usual for an assessor to be called in after proof has been led, but the Nautical Assessors Act provides that, in a maritime cause, an assessor may be called in at the trial or at any subsequent

hearing whether on appeal or otherwise.[2] A Court of Appeal
may have an assessor, although the judge of first instance had not.

1 See p. 185, supra.
2 57 & 58 Vict. c. 40, sec. 2.

4. Witnesses.

Every citizen is bound to assist constituted judicial authority
in the administration of justice, and so every person who has
knowledge of the facts and circumstances upon which Court proceedings depend is a competent witness, including the parties
in the cause, and their solicitors or servants. If a party adduces
his own solicitor as a witness, he cannot object to pertinent cross-
examination on the ground of confidentiality.[1] It is not necessary
that a witness should be cited to attend. He may attend voluntarily, and citation is only a means of enforcing his attendance.
Any person who is in the presence of the Court may be called
to give evidence, whether he has been formally cited, or is there
as a party in the cause, or as an outsider. How he comes to be
present is of no consequence. What alone is of consequence is
that he has knowledge of facts which, in the interests of justice,
the Court desires to be informed upon. If he has such knowledge
he is a competent witness.[2]

1 15 Vict. c. 27, sec. 1.
2 Watson v. Livingstone, 1902, 5 F. 171.   See also 15 Vict. c. 27, sec. 1;
        Dickson on Evidence, sec. 1260.

Formerly there were some personal disabilities which precluded
a witness from giving evidence. Consanguinity, interest, agency,
and other disabilities restricted the scope of available testimony,
but the Evidence Act of 1840[1] commenced the relaxation of the
older rules by declaring that it should neither be a ground for
a witness declining to give evidence, nor an objection to the
evidence itself, that a witness was a parent, or child, or collateral
relation, of any party; nor should it be imperative to reject the
testimony of a witness who had been present in Court during the
proceedings. The Evidence Acts of 1852[2] and 1853[3] removed the
disability which formerly attached to those who had been convicted
of crime, and to solicitors, husbands and wives, and interested
parties generally, so that in present-day practice practically no
sane person (other than an outlaw) is disqualified for giving
testimony in a Court of Law. The modern view is that no competent evidence should be excluded, but all evidence is weighed

and all witnesses may be examined on any points tending to affect their credibility.

[1] 3 & 4 Vict. c. 59, secs. 1, 3.
[2] 15 Vict. c. 27, sec. 1.
[3] 16 Vict. c. 20, secs. 2, 3.

Children, however young, are competent witnesses if they are able to answer intelligently. Children under twelve are not sworn, but are admonished to speak the truth.[1] Persons over fourteen are sworn,[1] and between the ages of twelve and fourteen the matter is in the discretion of the judge.[2] Relationship to a party in the cause does not now disqualify a witness. Nor is the character of a witness a disqualification for giving evidence. These are elements for consideration in weighing the evidence given, but they do not warrant the exclusion of a witness. An insane person is not a competent witness, but it is not a good objection to a witness that he has at some time been an inmate of a lunatic asylum.[3] Insanity supervening between the date of the matters spoken to and the proof will in general be enough to exclude a witness.[4] A deaf and dumb person may competently give testimony, through a sworn interpreter or by written question and answer.[5]

[1] Dickson on Evidence, sec. 1549.
[2] Anderson v. M'Farlane, 1899, 1 F. (J.) 36.
[3] Sheriff & Mitchell, 1866, 5 Irv. 226; Lord Advocate v. M'Kenzie, 1869, 1 Coup. 244; Lord Advocate v. Stott, 1894, 1 Adam 386.
[4] Sheriff & Mitchell, supra; Lord Advocate v. M'Kenzie, supra.
[5] Montgomery, 1855. 2 Irv. 222; Lord Advocate v. Howison, 1871, 2 Coup. 153; cf. O'Neil & Gollan, 1858, 3 Irv. 93.

5. PRECOGNITION.

In criminal practice attendance by prospective witnesses for precognition is compulsory, and may be enforced at the instance of the procurator-fiscal, but there is no machinery in civil practice to compel a prospective witness to attend for precognition.[1] If a witness has unreasonably refused to attend for precognition, the Court might be asked to refuse him a witness fee, but that is all that can be done. The Court will not make any order either against a party in the cause or an outsider to submit to precognition, or to grant facilities for precognition of witnesses who may be in his employment.[1] The names of witnesses may, in certain circumstances, be recovered from an opponent.[2]

[1] Henderson v. Patrick Thomson, 1911 S.C. 246.
[2] Henderson v. Patrick Thomson, supra; Clarke v. Edinburgh and District Tramways Co., 1914 S.C. 775; Macphee v. Corporation of Glasgow, 1915 S.C. 990.

In Scotland precognitions in civil causes are not taken on oath, and a witness is not usually asked, and cannot be forced, to sign his precognition. A precognition is not documentary evidence, and, even where a witness has died, his precognition, whether taken in connexion with the same proceedings or not, will not be admitted as evidence.[1] Considerable divergence of judicial opinion has arisen on the question whether statements made by a witness in precognition may be put to him for the purpose of discrediting his testimony in the box. It appears to be now settled that this will not be allowed if the statements were truly made on precognition,[2] but that previous statements made by the witness may be so used if they were not precognitions.[3] This point may arise in connexion with the use in civil proceedings of statements made to the police, and the distinction between what is and what is not a precognition may be a fine one. It is thought that, in the above connexions, it would make no difference that the witness had signed his precognition.

1 Graham v. Western Bank, 1865, 3 M. 617; Stevenson v. Stevenson, 1893, 31 S.L.R. 129; Robertson v. Robertson, (O.H.) 1894, 2 S.L.T. 354.
2 M'Neilie v. H.M. Advocate, 1929 J.C. 50.
3 Gilmour v. Hansen, 1920 S.C. 598; Binnie v. Black, (O.H.) 1923 S.L.T. 98; M'Neilie v. H.M. Advocate, supra.

6. Attestation.

Subject to what has already been stated in regard to children, a witness cannot competently give evidence unless he has made oath or affirmation that he will speak the truth. The usual form of oath administered to a witness in Scotland is, " I swear by Almighty God, and as I shall answer to God at the great day of judgment, that I will tell the truth, the whole truth, and nothing but the truth." When a witness objects to being sworn on the ground that he has no religious belief or that the taking of an oath is contrary to his religious belief he is permitted to make a solemn affirmation instead.[1] The form of affirmation is, " I do solemnly, sincerely, and truly declare and affirm that I will tell the truth, the whole truth, and nothing but the truth."[1] A witness who refuses to swear or affirm in the prescribed form can be punished for contempt of Court.[2] The Court of its own initiative takes no cognisance of the nationality or special faith of any witness; but if it is brought to its notice that some further formality is necessary to make an oath or affirmation binding upon the conscience of the witness, or if the witness himself desires to add some additional ceremony peculiar to his faith or country, the Court may order or permit its observance. Thus, a witness may desire to swear on the Bible; a Jew may be sworn on the Pentateuch with his hat on his head ; a Mohammedan on the Koran ; or a Chinaman by the ceremony of breaking a saucer. An oath is binding if administered in a form and with ceremonies which the witness has accepted without objection, or has declared to be binding on him.[3]

[1] 51 & 52 Vict. c. 46, secs. 1, 2.
[2] Bonnar v. Simpson, &c., 1836, 1 Swin. 39; M'Laughlin v. Douglas, 1863, 4 Irv. 273.
[3] 1 & 2 Vict. c. 105; 23 & 24 Geo. V c. 20, secs, 1, 7, 8.

7. CITATION OF WITNESSES.

Whilst the evidence of any person who is present before the Court may be required and accepted, no person is bound to attend as a witness unless he has been formally cited. A certified copy of the interlocutor allowing proof, or fixing a trial diet, or a diet for examination of witnesses or havers, is sufficient warrant for citing witnesses and havers.[1] The interlocutor should expressly bear that the diet is for proof or trial.[2] Citation must be made upon an induciæ of not less than forty-eight hours[1]; but longer notice should be, and generally is, given. In the case of postal citation the induciæ runs from twenty-four hours after the date of posting.[3] A witness or haver duly cited as above and who, after tender of his travelling expenses if these have been demanded, fails to attend before the Sheriff or a commissioner may be ordained by the Sheriff to forfeit a penalty not exceeding forty shillings unless a reasonable excuse is offered and sustained.[1] The party who cited the witness or haver may get decree for the penalty.[1] The above rule seems to imply that a witness or haver who has demanded his travelling expenses and has not been paid is not bound to answer the citation, and is not liable in the penalty for non-attendance. The rule does not expressly direct that a witness is to be tendered his travelling expenses along with the citation, and the non-payment of such expenses seems only to be relevant if they have been demanded. But it will be wise in most cases if it is desired to ensure attendance, to tender the travelling expenses, or a ticket, or to make other arrangements for the witnesses being brought to the Court. The above provisions apply to witnesses within Scotland and there is no means of compelling the attendance in Scotland of a witness who is outwith the country.[4]

[1] 7 Edw. VII c. 51, Schedule I, Rule 71.
[2] Grant v. Grant, 1908, 24 Sh.Ct.Rep. 114.
[3] 45 & 46 Vict. c. 77, sec. 4 (2).
[4] See p. 209, infra.

The form of citation of witnesses and havers requires that the witness be notified of the names of the pursuer and defender in the action and of the place and date where his attendance is required.[1] The citation also specifies the penalty for non-attendance, and is dated and signed either by an officer, or by the solicitor of the party citing the witness.[1] In neither case is a witness to the citation now necessary.[1] The citation of a witness or haver may be made by solicitor or officer by post, or may be served personally by an officer in the same manner as a citation of a party, but unless the Sheriff is of opinion that citation by an officer was justified, only postal citation fees will be allowed as party and party expenses.[2] Despite the unfortunate wording of the heading of Rule 10 it is thought that it would apply to a warrant to cite witnesses and that such a warrant does not require endorsement when executing the citation of witnesses in another Sheriffdom.[3] The same rule provides that an officer either of the Sheriffdom which granted the warrant, or of the Sheriffdom where it is to be executed, may execute the warrant.[3] The general position in regard to a solicitor serving a citation on a person resident outside the jurisdiction of the Court before which the solicitor is entitled to practise has already been discussed.[4]

[1] 7 Edw. VII c. 51, Schedule I, Rule 72; Forms F., G.
[2] 45 & 46 Vict. c. 77, sec. 6.
[3] 7 Edw. VII c. 51, Schedule I, Rule 10.
[4] See p. 118, supra.

A witness or haver who has been duly cited and fails to attend in a civil cause is not only liable in a monetary penalty, but also to arrest under letters of second diligence.[1] Such letters authorize officers of Court to apprehend the witness and commit him to prison till he find caution to appear when called upon. The letters are effectual in any Sheriffdom in Scotland without endorsation.[1] The expense of this procedure falls upon the witness or haver, and may be decerned for in favour of the party who requires his attendance.[1] If the citation is returned marked " refused " it is not necessary to await the diet, and letters of second diligence may be issued forthwith.[2] As a general rule the Court will compel the attendance of witnesses to facts only, not of witnesses to opinion.[3]

[1] 7 Edw. VII c. 51, Schedule I, Rule 73.
[2] 45 & 46 Vict. c. 77, sec. 4 (5); Steedman v. Steedman, (O.H.) 1886, 23 S.L.R. 856.
[3] Gilmour v. North British Railway Co., (O.H.) 1893, 1 S.L.T. 370.

8. Payment of Witnesses and Havers.

A witness, although entitled to have his travelling expenses prepaid, is not entitled to refuse to attend, or to refuse to give his evidence, unless his fee also is prepaid. His fee is a debt for which the party who cites the witness is liable, but it is not incurred till the witness has attended for examination. When a solicitor cites a witness he, as well as his client, is personally liable for the witness's fee,[1] save where the client is on the poor's roll in which case the solicitor is not liable unless the fee is recovered by him personally.[2] When the citation is by officer, the party alone is liable. Fees payable to witnesses vary according to the standing of the witness.[3] They are fixed by the Auditor of Court, subject to revision by the Sheriff upon objections to the auditor's report. A solicitor who cites a haver is in the same way liable for the haver's fee and expenses.[4]

[1] 7 Edw. VII c. 51, Schedule I, Rule 72.
[2] Ibid., Rule 167.
[3] C.A.S., M. II; Act of Sederunt, 7th May, 1935, Table of Fees IV.
[4] Bayley v. Middleton, 1909, 1 S.L.T. 493.

9. Documentary Evidence.

It is provided by the rules that each party shall, along with his pleadings, or at latest before the closing of the record, if required by any other party in the action or by the Sheriff, lodge any documents founded on in the pleadings, so far as the same are within his custody or power.[1] Where such documents are not produced by either party, or where they are in the hands of third parties, the Sheriff may, on the motion of either party, grant commission and diligence for their recovery, and may on that account delay closing the record.[2] These rules relate to documents founded on in the pleadings, but it is also provided that at any time after a proof has been allowed, or an order made for jury trial, the Sheriff may, upon the motion of either party, grant commission and diligence for the recovery of such documents as the Sheriff shall deem relevant to the case.[3] Further the Sheriff may order production of documents at any stage of the cause, and may allow a party at any time before judgment to produce any document he has failed to produce timeously upon such conditions, as to expenses and allowing further proof, as to the Sheriff shall seem just.[4] An interlocutor of the Sheriff-Substitute granting diligence for recovery of documents, is not appealable without leave,[5] but an interlocutor refusing a diligence may be appealable as importing a refusal of proof.[6] For purposes of appeal the refusal of part of a specification should appear in the interlocutor.[7]

[1] 7 Edw. VII c. 51, Schedule I, Rule 47.
[2] Ibid., Rule 48.
[3] Ibid., Rule 62.
[4] Ibid., Rule 68 (a) ; Act of Sederunt, 16th July, 1936.
[5] Stewart v. Kennedy, 1890, 17 R. 755; Baikie v. Doull, 1908, 24 Sh.Ct.Rep. 211.
[6] Thomson & Co. v. Bowater & Sons, 1918 S.C. 316; cf. Dick v Blairgowrie Town Council, 1910, 27 Sh.Ct.Rep. 243.
[7] Thomson & Co. v. Bowater & Sons, supra.

Except to the limited extent of enforcing production of documents founded on in the pleadings, diligence to recover documents is not in general asked or granted till the record has been closed, and proof allowed. The principles which govern the recovery of documents before the record is closed have been already discussed.[1] Rule 68 (a) above quoted[2] which authorizes the Sheriff to order production at any stage of the case does not, it is thought, apply to the period before the record is closed nor extend the right to have documents produced at that stage.[3] An application for bank book entries under the Bankers' Books Evidence Act, 1879,[4] may be granted before the closing of the record.[5] While the Sheriff has power to order the production of documents at any stage of the cause, the parties should move for recovery of documents a reasonable length of time before the proof. If a party fails to take steps to recover a document by diligence he will not be allowed to prove its contents by parole even though it is probable that the document would not in fact have been recovered.[6]

[1] See p. 154, supra.
[2] 7 Edw. VII c. 51, Schedule I, Rule 68 (a) ; Act of Sederunt, 16th July, 1936.
[3] Thornycroft & Co. v. Ricketts, 1935, 51 Sh.Ct.Rep. 194.
[4] 42 Vict. c. 11.
[5] Burrows, 1905, 21 Sh.Ct.Rep. 215.
[6] Dowgray v. Gilmour, 1907 S.C. 715.

A specification will not be allowed unless there are averments on record to warrant it, but the approval of a specification does not infer that every document covered by it is relevant evidence.[1] Rule 62[2] which authorizes diligence for the recovery of such documents as the Sheriff shall deem relevant to the case is not thought to have intended or effected any change in the established practice in this connexion. And it is clear that the Sheriff cannot determine the relevancy of the various productions called for in a specification when the diligence is asked. Some of the letters in a correspondence, for instance, may be relevant evidence and some not, and some may be confidential. The rule, as interpreted in practice, means that diligence is refused only if the documents are beyond the scope of the case laid on record, and so clearly cannot be relevant evidence. There is no rule that documents called for must clearly be admissible in evidence: the rule is that diligence is refused only if it is shown that they cannot be evidence.[3] Where proof of the averments on record has been allowed a diligence for recovery of documents cannot be refused on the ground that these averments are irrelevant.[4]

[1] Duke of Hamilton's Trustees v. Woodside Coal Co., 1897, 24 R. 294, Lord M'Laren, p. 296; Wheatley v. Anderson, &c., 1927 S.C. 133, Lord Justice-Clerk Alness, p. 142.
[2] 7 Edw. VII c. 51, Schedule I, Rule 62.
[3] Mackirdy v. Glasgow and Transvaal Options, 1903, 40 S.L.R. 313, Lord Kinnear, p. 314. See also Livingstone v. Dinwoodie, 1860, 22 D. 1333.
[4] Duke of Hamilton's Trustees v. Woodside Coal Co., supra; cf. Macqueen v. Mackie & Co., 1920 S.C. 544.

The documents to be recovered under diligence must not only be related to averments on record, but these averments must have been remitted to probation.[1] Further if the proof is limited in its scope, as to writ or oath, the documents called for must be such as fall within the limited scope of the proof which has been allowed.[2] Writings cannot be recovered where the best evidence of their contents is that of the parties who wrote them and such parties are available as witnesses.[3] In the same way documents cannot be recovered where their sole use would be for purposes of cross-examination.[4] Recovery under diligence in this way relates only to documents and not to an article such as a typewriter in relation to which an order for production is the appropriate step.[5] Photographs taken of the *locus* of a road accident and of the vehicles involved have been held not recoverable by diligence.[6]

[1] Scott Simpson & Wallis v. Forrest & Turnbull, 1897, 24 R. 877.
[2] Catto, Thomson & Co. v. Thomson & Son, &c., 1867, 6 M. 54.
[3] Livingstone v. Dinwoodie, 1860, 22 D. 1333; M'Neill v. Campbell, &c., 1880, 7 R. 574; County Council of Fife v. Thoms, 1898, 25 R. 1097; French v. Purnell, (O.H.) 1931 S.L.T. 85.
[4] French v. Purnell, supra.
[5] MacTaggart, &c. v. MacKillop, (O.H.) 1938 S.L.T. 559.
[6] Anderson v. St. Andrew's Ambulance Association, &c., 1942 S.C. 555.

Where documents called for are in the hands of the police, or of a government department, the question whether they should be produced is a matter to be decided by the Court and is not left to the commissioner to deal with.[1] The practice in the Court of Session in such cases is to order intimation to be made to the Lord Advocate, who may consent to the documents being produced, or refuse to produce on the ground of public interest.

Notwithstanding such refusal the Supreme Court at one time pro-
fessed to have an inherent power to order production[2] but this
does not appear to be the case.[3] The right to withhold production
is not affected by the department in question being a party to the
case.[4] It is suggested that in the Sheriff Court the same course
should be followed of intimating in such cases to the Lord Advocate,
and if he refused production the matter would then be at an end.[5]

[1] Sheridan v. Peel, 1907 S.C. 577, Lord President Dunedin, p. 580.
[2] Sheridan v. Peel, supra; Admiralty v. Aberdeen Steam Trawling, &c.,
Co., 1909 S.C. 335; Henderson v. M'Gown, 1916 S.C. 821; Wilson's
Executors v. Bank of England, (O.H.) 1925 S.L.T. 81; Caffrey v.
Lord Inverclyde, 1930 S.C. 762; Rogers v. Orr, 1939 S.C. 492.
See also Dowgray v. Gilmour, 1907 S.C. 715; Carmichael v. Scottish
Co-operative Wholesale Society, (O.H.) 1934 S.L.T. 158.
[3] See Duncan v. Cammel Laird & Co., [1942] A.C. 624.
[4] Admiralty v. Aberdeen Steam Trawling, &c., Co., supra.
[5] Cf. Paterson v. Rolls Royce, 1944, 61 Sh.Ct.Rep. 63; M'Rae v. M'Rae,
1946 S.N. 104.

Communications which have passed between parties on the same
side of a litigation *post litem motam* are generally regarded as
confidential and not recoverable.[1] This principle was applied in
the case of communications between master and servant[2] but modern
practice requires the production of reports and the like made at the
time, or immediately after the event, and *ante litem motam*.[3] In
this way lists of witnesses may be recovered if these are on the same
paper as the report.[4] Communications between solicitor and client
are in general confidential,[5] but may be recovered so far as they
disclose only records of facts and not advice.[6] And in various
special circumstances recovery has been allowed.[7] Where an illegal
search of a house was alleged the occupier was held entitled to be
furnished with the names of the officers concerned and an order
for such to be furnished was made in an action brought by him for
this purpose against the chief constable.[8]

[1] Rose v. Medical Insurance Co., 1847, 10 D. 156; Tannett, Walker
& Co. v. Hannay & Sons, 1873, 11 M. 931; cf. Logan v. Miller,
(O.H.) 1920, 1 S.L.T. 211.
[2] Muir v. Edinburgh Tramways Co., 1909 S.C. 244.
[3] Finlay v. Glasgow Corporation, 1915 S.C. 615; Whitehill v. Glasgow
Corporation, 1915 S.C. 1015; Sneddon v. Glasgow Corporation,
(O.H.) 1935 S.L.T. 74; cf. French v. Purnell, (O.H.) 1931 S.L.T. 85.
[4] Macphee v. Glasgow Corporation, 1915 S.C. 990; M'Culloch v. Glasgow
Corporation, 1918 S.C. 155; cf. M'Bride v. Lewis, (O.H.) 1922
S.L.T. 380.
[5] Lumsdaine v. Balfour, 1828, 7 S. 7.
[6] Caledonian Railway Co. v. Symington, 1913 S.C. 885.
[7] Fowler v. Mackenzie, 1872, 44 Scot. Jur. 332; 1874, 11 S.L.R. 485;
Fraser v. Malloch, (O.H.) 1895, 3 S.L.T. 211; Mackenzie v.
Mackenzie's Trustees, 1916, 53 S.L.R. 219; Earl of Morton v.
Fleming, (O.H.) 1921, 1 S.L.T. 205.
[8] De Duca v. Sillitoe, 1935, 52 Sh.Ct.Rep. 18.

In special circumstances the Sheriff himself may preside at a diet for the examination of havers; but in ordinary practice a commissioner is appointed by the Court to take the oaths of the havers and receive the productions. The documents called for are set forth in a specification lodged in process and intimated to the other side, and diligence for recovery is granted for these in whole or in part. The rules and practice relating to the citation and attendance of witnesses before the Court itself, are applicable also to proceedings before a commissioner. The citation of a haver should specify what he is called upon to produce, and the specification may be quoted or a copy be attached to the citation. Both parties to the action should receive intimation of the diet.[1] If documents are tendered which the specification clearly does not cover, the commissioner may reject them, but if there is room for dubiety as to whether they are covered by the specification, the safer course is to receive them, subject to objection, and let the Court decide later as to their admission in evidence. In certain circumstances the Court has given the commissioner the help of an accountant in examining business books.[2]

[1] Craig v. Craig, (O.H.) 1905, 13 S.L.T. 556.
[2] William Whiteley v. Dobson Molle & Co., (O.H.) 1902, 10 S.L.T. 71; Municipal Council of Johannesburg v. Stewart & Co., (O.H.) 1911, 1 S.L.T. 359; cf. Cassils & Co. v. Absalon, (O.H.) 1907, 15 S.L.T. 48.

The Act and rules give no direction as to procedure before a commissioner when a haver objects to produce documents in his possession on the ground of confidentiality or otherwise. The commissioner has no power to enforce production of documents from an unwilling haver. If a haver's objection to produce is repelled by the commissioner the document, if produced, may be sealed up by the commissioner to await the decision of the Sheriff —the haver being entitled to be heard on the point.[1] If, in such circumstances, the haver refuses to produce, the fact is noted in the commissioner's report, and, if his ruling is upheld, a further diet may be fixed, and the haver again called on to produce.[2] If there is still refusal to produce, the matter may be dealt with as contempt of Court. As an alternative to a second diet before the commissioner the haver may be cited to produce at the diet of proof. If the objection is repelled, the haver must then make the production called for, unless an appeal is taken forthwith. The rules provide that where objection is taken in Court to the production of documents on the ground of confidentiality, hypothec, or otherwise, the decision on the point is to be minuted in the notes of evidence, and the objector, or any party to the cause, may, with leave of the Court, take an appeal in open Court to

the Sheriff, who is to dispose of it, with or without a hearing,
with the least possible delay.[3] Such an appeal does not remove
the case from the Sheriff-Substitute, who may proceed with it
as regards points not necessarily dependent on the ruling appealed
against.[4]

1 County Council of Fife v. Thoms, 1898, 25 R. 1097; Train & M'Intyre
    v. William Forbes, (O.H.) 1925 S.L.T. 286.
2 M'Donald v. M'Donald, 1881, 8 R. 357.
3 7 Edw. VII c. 51, Schedule I, Rule 76.
4 Ibid., Rule 77.

Objections to documents themselves, as, for instance, want
of requisite stamp, non-attestation, or the like, are not disposed
of by the commissioner, but he may refer to such objections in
his report. The productions are not put in evidence merely by
being produced before the commissioner, and they should be
lodged in process with an inventory of productions. When the
party who has recovered them offers to put them in as evidence
the question of their admissibility may be raised, and if raised
must be then decided by the Court.

Business books, not only of the opposing party, but of third
parties, may be recovered if they contain entries relevant to the
issue.[1] Books are often recovered to show damage to a business
resulting from personal injury[2] or slander.[3] But a call for books
may be sustained in connexion with damages for breach of promise
or seduction,[4] or to show the authorship of a slanderous statement.[5] As a rule letter books, or the corresponding files of
duplicate letters, cannot be called for to recover copies until the
party seeking to recover has used all due diligence to recover the
originals.[6] Books are not usually themselves put in evidence,
for they generally contain entries relating to matters other than
those referred to in the action. An excerpt taken from the books
at the sight of the commissioner, and certified by him, is the
proper form of production of book entries in a process. The
selection of the excerpts is a matter for the commissioner. Books
when produced remain in the commissioner's hands, and the party
producing the books should have the opportunity of being present
at any inspection of them by the commissioner.[7] Diligence to
recover records of a hospital has been granted.[8]

1 Graham v. Sprot, 1847, 9 D. 545; Robertson v. Earl of Dudley, 1875,
    2 R. 935; Craig v. North British Railway Co., 1888, 15 R. 808;
    Fraser v. Fraser's Trustees, (O.H.) 1897, 4 S.L.T. 228; Mackenzie
    v. Mackenzie's Trustees, 1916, 53 S.L.R. 219; Craig v. Chassels,
    (O.H.) 1917, 2 S.L.T. 242.
2 Johnston v. Caledonian Railway Co., 1892, 20 R. 222.
3 Gray v. Wyllie, 1904, 6 F. 448.

[4] Somerville v. Thomson, 1896, 23 R. 576; Stroyan v. M'Whirter, (O.H.) 1901, 9 S.L.T. 242; Robertson v. Hamilton, (O.H.) 1915, 2 S.L.T. 195.

[5] Cunningham v. Duncan & Jamieson, 1889, 16 R. 383. See also Ogston & Tennant v. " Daily Record," 1909 S.C. 1000; Reid v. Johnston & Co., 1912 S.C. 187.

[6] Caledonian Railway Co. v. Symington, 1912 S.C. 1033.

[7] Cassils & Co. v. Absalon, (O.H.) 1907, 15 S.L.T. 48.

[8] Travers v. Brown, Fraser & Co., 1943, 59 Sh.Ct.Rep. 200; Kelly v. Kelly, (O.H.) 1946 S.L.T. 208. See also Black v. Bairds & Dalmellington, 1939 S.C. 472; M'Rae v. M'Rae, 1946 S.N. 104; MacArthur v. MacArthur, 1946, 62 Sh.Ct.Rep. 137.

Although excerpts are put in evidence, exhibition of the books themselves may in certain cases be required at the proof, for much may depend upon the appearance of a book, or upon the position and surroundings of a particular entry, and exhibition of the book itself may be necessary to show the facts which are of importance. If the entries are in any way peculiar the commissioner should endeavour to make his excerpt as nearly as possible a facsimile copy of the book. The excerpt may require to embrace more than the particular entry relating to the action, as where an entry has been interlined in a cash book, or apparently entered under a wrong date, when it may be necessary that a complete page of the book be excerpted. When they present peculiarities the commissioner should report specially upon the appearance of the books.

A call in a specification for certain specified books and also documents and papers was held to cover letters and copies of letters.[1] Loose documents, called for in slump, like correspondence between certain parties, within specified dates, may be put in without examination of each document, unless the production of any is objected to; but books are exhibited that the commissioner may take relevant excerpts as before explained. The solicitor of the party calling for production is not, as is sometimes assumed, entitled to get the book into his own hands, and to search for such information as he hopes to find in it.[2] If the book requires to leave the hands of the haver, the only other person entitled to handle it is the judge or the commissioner.

[1] National Exchange Co. v. Drew & Dick, 1857, 19 D. 689.

[2] Cassils & Co. v. Absalon, (O.H.) 1907, 15 S.L.T. 48.

A haver is examined on oath and he may be required to answer some questions in regard to the documents called for. He may be interrogated to ascertain whether what is handed in is all that exists of the class of document called for, or, if the haver depone that the documents called for are not in his custody, he may be

interrogated as to whether he ever held them, and as to his knowledge of where they now are.[1] If the haver depone that he had
a document but destroyed it he may be asked when, where and
why he destroyed it, and any further questions that may help to
establish what became of a document he once had.[2] He cannot be
asked any questions about a document which is produced or any
questions about the contents of any document.[3] A haver who
produces documents at the call of one party may be asked by
another party if he has any other documents bearing on the
issues raised in the action, and if he has any he is bound to produce
them.[4] A diet for recovery of documents is not, however, to be
used as an occasion for precognition, and the deposition of a haver
cannot be used as evidence of facts.[5]

[1] Act of Sederunt, 22nd February, 1688; Cullen v. Thomson & Kerr,
1863, 1 M. 284.
[2] Home v. Hardy, 1842, 4 D. 1184; Cullen v. Thomson & Kerr, supra;
Gordon v. Davidson, 1865, 3 M. 938.
[3] Somervell v. Somervell, (O.H.) 1900, 8 S.L.T. 84.
[4] Dunlop's Trustees v. Belhaven, 1852, 14 D. 825.
[5] Gibson v. Ewan, 1852, 25 Scot. Jur. 163.

A solicitor who has the custody of documents may competently
be called by a third party as a haver, although his client is not
called, and as a general rule, subject to any plea of confidentiality,
a solicitor must produce whatever documents his principal could
have been compelled to produce.[1] In such circumstances the
solicitor cannot plead his right of lien against the third party,[2]
but the solicitor's own client may not be able to make use of the
productions without paying the solicitor's account.[3] Where, however, the solicitor is called upon by his own client to produce
documents over which he has a lien, he is entitled to decline to
produce on the client's call if that might defeat, or prejudice, his
right.[4] A haver, before making production, is entitled to be
paid his fees for searching and attendance,[5] as well as the amount
of an account due him by the party by whom he has been cited.[4]
He is only entitled to insist on payment of copying fees of extracts
if he has been asked to make the copies.[5]

[1] Scott v. Napier, 1749, 1 Pat. App. 441; Noble v. Scott, 1843, 5 D.
723; M'Cowan v. Wright, 1852, 15 D. 229.
[2] Montgomerie v. A B, 1845, 7 D. 553; M'Intosh v. Chalmers, 1883,
11 R. 8.
[3] Montgomerie v. A B, supra.
[4] Mackinnon v. Guildford, (O.H.) 1894, 2 S.L.T. 309.
[5] Forsyth v. Pringle Taylor & Lamond Lowson, (O.H.) 1906, 14 S.L.T.
658.

Documents recovered under diligence pass into the custody of the
Court for the particular purpose of being used as evidence in the

action in which they are produced. When that purpose has been served the solicitor of the party who called for them should see that they are borrowed up and returned to the person who produced them. They cannot be used as productions in another process, or for any other purpose.

It is now provided that, where a proof is allowed, all documents, plans, maps, models, and other productions intended to be used or put in evidence at the proof must be lodged with the Sheriff-clerk on or before the fourth day prior to the proof, and intimation of the lodging sent to the solicitor for the opposite party at the same time.[1] No other production can be used or put in evidence at the proof, unless of consent of parties, or by permission of the Sheriff, on cause shown to his satisfaction and on such terms as he shall direct.[1] These provisions, it is thought, do not apply to documents which are used solely for purposes of cross-examination.[2] Productions and other steps of process which have been borrowed must be returned to process before noon on the day preceding the proof.[1] The above rule must be kept in view in lodging documents recovered under diligence, but if productions are numerous it is convenient that they should be lodged in good time before the proof. A similar rule applies in regard to lodging productions before a jury trial.[3]

[1] 7 Edw. VII c. 51, Schedule I, Rule 68; Act of Sederunt, 16th July, 1936.
[2] See Livingstone v. Dinwoodie, 1860, 22 D. 1333; Paterson & Sons v. Kit Coffee Co., (O.H.) 1908, 16 S.L.T. 180.
[3] 7 Edw. VII c. 51, Schedule I, Rule 142.

When a specification of documents has been approved by the Court, the expense thereof and of the execution of the commission will normally be allowed as party and party expenses, even although no documents have been recovered[1]; but if a party does recover documents, and does not put them in evidence, he will not, as a rule, be allowed the expense of the commission, even if upon the merits he is successful and is found entitled to expenses.[2]

[1] M'Leod v. Leslie, 1868, 5 S.L.R. 687.
[2] Mackie & Stark v. Cruickshank, 1896, 4 S.L.T. 84.

Extracts from public records are generally received as evidence, but in certain circumstances it may be necessary to produce the records themselves. It is now provided that, where any party to a cause desires to obtain from the Keeper of the Registers and Records of Scotland production of the originals of any register or deed under his custody, he must apply by motion to the Sheriff, after seven days' written notice of such application given to the keeper in charge of the originals.[1] On such application the Sheriff may, by interlocutor, certify that it is necessary for the ends of justice that the application should be granted, and a certified copy of the interlocutor is then sent by letter by the applicant to the principal clerk of session.[1] The letter asks for an order from the Lords of Council and Session authorizing the keeper to exhibit the original register or deed in the hands of an official to the Sheriff.[1] The above application is submitted by the principal clerk of session to a Lord Ordinary in chambers who, if satisfied, grants the necessary warrant, a certified copy of which is then served upon the Keeper of the Registers and Records of Scotland.[1] The expense attending the transmission and exhibition of such original register or deed is defrayed in the first instance by the party applying for it.[1] Where Sheriff Court records have been transmitted to the Keeper of the Registers and Records of Scotland, and any such record is required for the purposes of any proceedings in the High Court of Justiciary, the Court of Session, or any Sheriff Court, the keeper will retransmit such record to the clerk of such Court on any order of a judge of the High Court or Court of Session or of the Sheriff, and any record so retransmitted is to be returned by the clerk of Court to the keeper as soon as it has served the purpose for which it was transmitted.[2] A certified copy of the interlocutor should, it is thought, be sent to the keeper in this case also. The Court of Session has sanctioned a chemical test of a document which was in a public register,[3] but it is doubtful if the Sheriff has power to authorize a test of this nature.

[1] 7 Edw. VII c. 51, Schedule I, Rule 68 (b) ; Act of Sederunt, 16th July, 1936.
[2] 1 Edw. VIII & 1 Geo. VI c. 43, sec. 2.
[3] Irvine v. Powrie's Trustees, 1915 S.C. 1006.

Documents which are already productions in a Court process may be required as evidence in another process. If the same solicitor requires them they can be borrowed ; but if this cannot be done, the Sheriff-clerk, as custodier of the process, may be cited as a haver. The Supreme Court may order the production of a Sheriff Court process,[1] but the Sheriff has no such authority, even over a process in another Sheriff Court. Documents which are in the custody of a Court or other official may be recovered by diligence but, as already stated, this will in general only be possible if the department or the Lord Advocate does not object.[2] Thus declarations of an accused person, or precognitions of witnesses taken for the purpose of possible criminal prosecution, or documents recovered in the course of criminal investigation will not in general be recoverable,[2] but criminal records of public facts may be used as evidence in a civil cause, as in the case of an extract conviction of a crime or statutory contravention. A document illegally obtained may be accepted as a production in a case.[3]

[1] Rules of Court, 1936, II, 30. See Brown v. Glenboig, &c., Fireclay Co., (O.H.) 1911, 1 S.L.T. 27; Docherty v. Niddrie & Benhar Coal Co., (O.H.) 1911, 1 S.L.T. 396.
[2] Arthur v. Lindsay, 1895, 22 R. 417; cf. Mills v. Kelvin & James White, 1912 S.C. 995. See further, p. 195, supra.
[3] MacColl v. MacColl, (O.H.) 1946 S.L.T. 312.

Special statutory provision is made in the case of bankers' books. Where the bank is not a party to the cause a bank official cannot in general be compelled to produce the bank's books, or to give evidence in regard to their contents, unless under a special order of the Court.[1] With or without summoning the bank, a party to a cause may obtain an order of Court to enable him to inspect and take copies from bankers' books, and such order if obtained has to be served on the bank three clear days before the inspection, unless the Court otherwise directs.[2] A copy of an entry in a banker's book spoken to by someone who has examined it with the original entry and found it correct is *prima facie* evidence of the entry, provided it is proved that the book was one of the ordinary books of the bank, that the entry was made in the ordinary course of business, and that the book is in the bank's custody or control.[3] The post office and other savings banks fall under the provisions of the Act.[4] An order for inspection under the Act may be granted before the closing of the record.[5] In practice the statutory procedure is not often required. Calls for entries in bankers' books may be included in a specification, but if the call is allowed copies of the entries are often obtained and of consent are accepted as sufficient. Where the bank is itself a party to the cause its records are not protected by the Act and can be recovered in the ordinary way.

[1] 42 Vict. c. 11, sec. 6.
[2] Ibid., sec. 7.
[3] Ibid., secs. 3, 4, 5.
[4] 42 Vict. c. 11, sec. 9; Forrest v. MacGregor, (O.H.) 1913, 1 S.L.T. 372.
[5] Burrows, 1905, 21 Sh.Ct.Rep. 215.

If a document founded on is not sufficiently stamped it must be properly stamped before it can be looked at by the Court,[1] and if necessary the action can be sisted for a reasonable time to enable this to be done.[2] Alternatively, if the document is capable of being stamped after execution, the amount of stamp duty and penalty may be consigned with the Sheriff-clerk, and the document may then be received in evidence[1] or the document may be borrowed by the party founding on it and stamped.[3] The question of ultimate liability for the expense of procuring the deed stamped is not determined at that stage, but is dealt with as part of the question of expenses,[4] but the consignation falls to be made by the party founding on the document.[2] Where a document has been uplifted by one of the parties and stamped it is immaterial that no penalty has been exacted and that the stamp duty has not been adjudicated.[2] Stamping may be done after a proof has been closed and before judgment,[4] or after judgment when the case is on appeal.[5]

[1] 54 & 55 Vict. c. 39, sec. 14.
[2] Rice v. Hall, 1916, 34 Sh.Ct.Rep. 296.
[3] See Lord Provost, &c., of Dundee v. Vance, 1946, 62 Sh.Ct.Rep. 116.
[4] Neil v. Leslie, 1867, 5 M. 634; M'Douall v. Caird, 1870, 8 M. 1012; Weinschell, (O.H.) 1916, 2 S.L.T. 346.
[5] See Hislop v. Thomson, 1878, 5 R. 794.

In the case of a bilateral deed or of a document upon which both parties are entitled to found the general rule is that the cost of after-stamping should be shared between them. It follows, therefore, that the party who founds on such a document and so has meantime to provide the expense of stamping it, does not, although he may be successful in the litigation, recover from the other party this expense in full, but only half of it.[1] If the stamping of the document has been fruitless the party who has had it stamped will usually be left to bear the cost himself. The obligation to stamp is not avoided by a copy of the document being of consent held as equivalent to the principal.[2]

[1] See Hislop v. Thomson, 1878, 5 R. 794, Lord President Inglis, p. 795.
[2] Cowan v. Stewart, 1872, 10 M. 735.

Under the Stamp Act of 1891[1] it is *pars judicis* to take notice of any omission or insufficiency of stamp, whether the document is objected to or not, but the Court will not require a document to be stamped if the necessity for a stamp, or the amount of it, is dubious. " This is not a provision compelling judges to raise test cases or try doubtful questions regarding the stamping of instruments. I think that they are only bound to intervene to protect the Revenue, where there is an undoubted case of insufficient stamping, or an attempted evasion of the Stamp Act."[2]

[1] 54 & 55 Vict. c. 39, sec. 14. See also Livingston v. Aitken, 1890, 7 Sh.Ct.Rep. 45.
[2] Francesco v. De Meo, 1908 S.C. 7, Lord Ardwall, p. 11; O'Brien v. O'Brien, 1910, 26 Sh.Ct.Rep. 268.

Documents which are not themselves probative must in general be proved by the party founding upon them; but certain documents may be put in evidence without being produced or spoken to by a witness. British Acts of Parliament and Statutory Rules and Orders require neither proof nor production and are cited by reference merely. Under the Documentary Evidence Act of 1868, Government orders, proclamations, or regulations are proved by the production of the *Gazette* containing them, or of a copy order, proclamation or regulation printed by the Government printer, or a copy certified as provided in the Act. Such production is declared to be *prima facie* evidence and it is therefore open to challenge.[1] Official extracts from civil or criminal Courts such as extract decrees or convictions are probative and are competent evidence of the records they contain.

[1] 31 & 32 Vict. c. 37, sec. 2.

10. Evidence to Lie in Retentis.

It is provided in the rules that evidence in danger of being lost may be taken to lie *in retentis*, and that, if satisfied that it is desirable so to do, the Sheriff may, upon the motion of either party at any time, either take such evidence himself, or grant authority to a commissioner to do so.[1] Old age, serious illness, and the fact that the witness has necessarily to leave the country, are the usual grounds on which evidence is so taken, but there appears to be complete discretion in the Sheriff to follow this course in any case where evidence is in danger of being lost. Normally such a motion is made after the record has been closed, and proof has been allowed, but the rule indicates that authority to take evidence in this way can be asked at any time after the action has been served.[2] The practice of preserving evidence even before an action is raised, which is competent in the Court of Session,[3] is thought to be not available in the Sheriff Court.[4] The witness whose evidence is to be taken in this way may be one of the parties in the case.[5]

[1] 7 Edw. VII c. 51, Schedule I, Rule 63.
[2] See Hansen v. Donaldson, 1873, 1 R. 237.
[3] See Galloway Water Power Co. v. Carmichael, 1937 S.C. 135.
[4] Dove Wilson, Sheriff Court Practice (4th edn.), 276.
[5] Hansen v. Donaldson, supra; Samson & Co. v. Hough, &c., 1886, 13 R. 1154; Anderson v. Morrison, 1905, 7 F. 561; Anderson, 1912 S.C. 1144; cf. Craig v. Walker, (O.H.) 1930 S.N. 144.

The general rule is that a witness over seventy years of age cannot be compelled to attend Court, and that, unless he is agreeable to come to Court, his evidence must be taken on commission.[1]

Where the commission to take evidence to lie *in retentis* is asked on the ground of ill-health it should be supported by a medical certificate on soul and conscience. If the certificate is challenged a neutral medical man may be appointed to examine the witness and report.[2] Where a witness is about to leave the country a commission will normally be granted as a matter of course if the witness's departure is occasioned by duty or business,[3] but if it is a mere case of pleasure or personal convenience leave to take the evidence to lie *in retentis* will not generally be granted.[4]

[1] See Wilson v. Young, (O.H.) 1896, 4 S.L.T. 73.
[2] Lunn v. Watt, (O.H.) 1911, 2 S.L.T. 479.
[3] Hansen v Donaldson, 1873, 1 R. 237; Anderson, 1912 S.C. 1144.
[4] Grant v. Countess of Seafield, 1926 S.C. 274; see also 1926 S.N. 22.

The application for the commission will normally be by written motion, but a more formal application by initial writ may be necessary if the commission is applied for before appearance has been entered or defences lodged. The interlocutor granting commission to take evidence to lie *in retentis* should embody the reason for granting it, and should name the witness or witnesses to be examined. If individual names cannot be ascertained it seems competent to grant a general order, as, for instance, to take the evidence of " the officers and crew " of a named vessel, but this practice should only be adopted in special circumstances and the interests of the other party to the case must be considered and safeguarded.[1] In one case where a pursuer sought a commission to examine an aged defender the pursuer formally waived his right thereafter to refer the cause to the defender's oath.[2] A certified copy of the interlocutor is sufficient authority for the commissioner to act.

[1] See Gardner v. Magistrates of Kilrenny, 1825, 3 S. 613; Ramsay v. Cochrane, 1825, 3 S. 643; Morrison v. Cowan, 1828, 6 S. 1082; cf. Western Ranches v. Nelson's Trustees, 1898, 25 R. 527; Crawford & Law v. Allan Steamship Co., (O.H.) 1908, 16 S.L.T. 434. See also Lord Advocate, 1925 S.C. 568.
[2] Laing v. Nixon, 1866, 4 M. 327.

The formal citation of a witness to give evidence to lie *in retentis* is not always necessary, and if the witness is ill or aged the commissioner may require to attend on the witness. If citation is necessary it is made in the same way as citation of a witness to attend a proof or trial.[1] A certified copy of the interlocutor granting the commission is generally regarded as sufficient warrant for citation although Rule 70 refers to an interlocutor fixing the diet of examination before the commissioner—an arrangement which is unknown in practice. As in the case of witnesses cited to attend

Court, it is thought that a warrant of citation to attend before a commissioner does not require endorsation, and that if executed by an officer, it may be executed within Scotland either by an officer of the Court granting the warrant, or of the Court within whose jurisdiction it is executed.[2] The general practice in regard to a solicitor serving a citation upon a person resident outwith the jurisdiction of the Court before which he is entitled to practice has been already considered.[3]

[1] 7 Edw. VII c. 51, Schedule I, Rules 71-73. See p. 191, supra.
[2] Ibid., Rule 10.
[3] See p. 118, supra.

Under the former practice the commissioner had to be the clerk of Court, his acting depute, a solicitor of at least three years standing, a justice of the peace, or other magistrate.[1] As this restriction is not now in force any suitable person may be appointed, but the practice still is to appoint the clerk of Court or one of the other parties mentioned if this is suitable in the circumstances. There must be a special appointment in each case of a named commissioner.

[1] Act of Sederunt, 10th July, 1839, sec. 69.

The procedure before a commissioner is the same as that before the Court. Interrogatories[1] are usually required only in cases when there is no skilled legal assistance to conduct an examination. The commissioner may record the evidence by his own hand, or may have it taken down by a clerk or a shorthand writer nominated by him and to whom he administers the oath *de fideli administratione*.[2] The notes taken by the clerk and certified by him, or the extended shorthand notes certified by the shorthand writer, are the record of the evidence.[2] The commissioner may, if he thinks fit, dictate to the clerk or shorthand writer what he is to record.[2] The commissioner has power to deal with objections to the competency of evidence led before him, but if the matter is of importance he may prefer to have evidence, which is objected to, separately recorded so as to leave the decision as to its competency to the Sheriff.[3] The party moving for the commission, and his solicitor, are both personally liable for the shorthand writer's fee. The party moving for the commission is also liable for the fees of the commissioner and his clerk, the amount of which, failing agreement, will be fixed by the Sheriff. The commissioner might, it is thought, insist upon his fee being provided for, before he enters upon his duties, or at any rate withhold delivery of the report of the commission till the fee was paid.

¹ See p. 211, infra.
² 7 Edw. VII c. 51, Schedule I, Rule 65.
³ Ibid., Rule 74.

The commissioner makes a report to the Court of the proceedings under the commission. This may be a separate paper, the record of the evidence being made a production, along with any other productions, but in practice the record of the evidence is embodied in the report signed by the commissioner and the clerk. If the evidence is not recorded in shorthand it is thought that the witness should sign and also the commissioner and clerk. These suggestions are made notwithstanding the general terms of Rule 65.[1] The commissioner should also initial and number all productions made, and any such should be included in an inventory. The expense of a commission will generally be allowed against an opponent, if the incurring of that expense was reasonable in the circumstances at the time, even if the witness appear at the trial and the report of the commission is thus not used.[2] The use of the report as evidence is only dealt with in the rules in the case of jury trials, where it is provided that, if the Sheriff is satisfied that the deponing witness is dead, or cannot attend the trial owing to absence, infirmity or other sufficient cause, he may, on the motion of any party to the cause—and irrespective of which party moved for the commission—direct that the report be read to the jury, and when so read it is to form part of the evidence in the cause.[3] But if the witness attends Court and goes in the box then, neither at trials nor proofs can the report be used as evidence or even for the purpose of contradicting what the witness has stated in Court.[4] If the witness does not attend Court then in proofs, as in trials, the reason for his absence should be stated and the report should be formally incorporated in the evidence for the party who obtained the commission, though in all cases the Court has probably the power to admit the report as evidence where this has not been done.[5] But it is at least doubtful whether in proofs the party who has not obtained the commission can insist on the report being put in and used as evidence against the wishes of his opponent.[6]

¹ 7 Edw. VII c. 51, Schedule I, Rule 65.
² Couper v. Cullen, 1874, 1 R. 1101; Graham v. Borthwick, 1875, 2 R. 812; Spite & Co. v. Bow M'Lachlan & Co., 1907, 24 Sh.Ct.Rep. 58; North of Scotland Bank v. Mackenzie, (O.H.) 1925 S.L.T. 352; Gilchrist v. National Cash Register Co., 1929 S.C. 272; cf. Speirs v. Caledonian Railway Co., 1921 S.C. 889.
³ 7 Edw. VII c. 51, Schedule I, Rule 138.
⁴ Ibid. See Forrest v. Low's Trustees, 1907 S.C. 1240.
⁵ Cameron v. Woolfson, 1918 S.C. 190.
⁶ See Pickford v. Johnstone, 1890, 6 Sh.Ct.Rep. 252.

11. Proof on Commisssion.

The evidence of a witness may be taken by commission in the same way as evidence to lie *in retentis* if the witness is resident beyond the jurisdiction of the Court, or if, though resident within the jurisdiction, he resides at some place remote from the seat of the Court, or if he is, by reason of illness, age or infirmity, unable to attend the proof or trial.[1] As already indicated a witness over seventy cannot in general be required to attend Court, and if the disability is illness or infirmity this should be supported by a medical certificate on soul and conscience.[2] The evidence of a party may be taken on commission, but the Court will require stronger reasons for granting such a commission than in the case of one who is only a witness.[3] A commission to take the evidence of a pursuer who was resident abroad was, with some difficulty, granted in the course of a proof.[4] Normally the commission should be applied for in time to have the report of the commission available before the proof begins. Notwithstanding the wide terms in which the first part of the rule is expressed it is thought that a commission to examine any witness who resides in Scotland will not readily be granted except on the ground of old age or ill-health. If the witness's mental capacity is doubtful the position will generally be left to the commissioner to judge of and a preliminary medical examination for this purpose has been refused.[5]

[1] 7 Edw. VII c. 51, Schedule I, Rule 70.
[2] See p. 205, supra.
[3] See p. 205, supra, and cases there cited.
[4] Lyell, &c. v. Harthill Thistle Pipe Band, &c., 1905, 21 Sh.Ct.Rep. 294.
[5] M'Intyre v. M'Intyre, (O.H.) 1920, 1 S.L.T. 207.

There is no power in the Sheriff Court to compel the attendance in Scotland of a witness who is resident furth of Scotland. Where the witness is in England or Northern Ireland[1] a commissioner may be appointed to take the evidence of the witness there, and attendance can be compelled before the commissioner under the Evidence by Commission Act, 1843.[2] The case of a witness who is resident elsewhere abroad is considered below.[3]

[1] As to Ireland, see 10 & 11 Geo. V c. 67, sec. 69 (a) ; S.R. & O., 1921, No. 1804, sec. 5 ; 13 Geo. V (Session 2) c. 2, sec. 6 (1) (a) ; S.R. & O., 1923, No. 405, sec. 3.
[2] 6 & 7 Vict. c. 82, secs. 5-7. See also 22 Vict. c. 20.
[3] See p. 210 et seq., infra.

The qualification of the person to be appointed commissioner, the citation of witnesses resident in Scotland and the conduct of the examination are the same as in the case of evidence taken to lie *in retentis*.[1] Witnesses in England or Northern Ireland are cited as laid down in the Evidence by Commission Act, 1843.[2] On the evidence being concluded, the commissioner closes the commission and reports it to the Court. He may retain it till he has received his fee, which, if not agreed upon, is fixed by the Sheriff. Evidence taken to lie *in retentis* may or may not be used in a case, but proof on commission is part of the proof allowed in the cause, and the report therefore is put in process upon the conclusion of the commission proceedings. The solicitor instructing a commissioner appears to be personally liable for his fee.[3]

[1] See p. 205 et seq., supra.
[2] 6 & 7 Vict. c. 82, secs. 5-7.
[3] Watson v. Cowan, 1913, 1 S.L.T. 435.

12. Witnesses Abroad.

Where the witness to be examined is in a British Dominion or Colony, or is in India, or the Irish Free State,[1] the matter may proceed under the Evidence by Commission Act, 1859,[2] in terms of which the Sheriff will appoint a commissioner to take the evidence of the witness, and the aid of the Court in the Dominion is invoked to compel the attendance of the witness for examination before the commissioner. Alternatively, the procedure under the Evidence by Commission Act, 1885,[3] may be adopted. In that case the commission from the Sheriff Court is addressed to the Court in the Dominion and that Court then nominates the commissioner who takes the evidence. Interrogatories are not prescribed by either of the Acts and their use will depend on what is expedient in each case.[4] They will be needed in all cases where the witness cannot be examined in the usual way. If incriminating questions may be put to the witness the commissioner should be specially instructed to advise him of his rights.[5]

[1] See 13 Geo. V (Session 2) c. 2, sec. 6 (1) (a); S.R. & O., 1923, No. 405, secs. 2, 3.
[2] 22 Vict. c. 20.
[3] 48 & 49 Vict. c. 74.
[4] See Dexter & Carpenter v. Waugh & Robertson, 1925 S.C. 28.
[5] Muir v. Muir, 1873, 11 M. 529.

Where the witness whose evidence is required is resident outwith the British Empire application is made in the Sheriff Court by a minute asking the issue of a letter of request addressed to the foreign tribunal within whose jurisdiction the witness resides.[1] After consideration of the minute, and any objections, the Sheriff may authorize the issue of a letter of request in prescribed form which asks the foreign Court to arrange for the examination of the witness.[2] The letter of request is prepared by the party seeking the evidence, and is lodged with the minute. If it is granted the party has to lodge a translation of it for use abroad.[3] The evidence in such cases must be taken on interrogatories, and the party who has obtained the commission must lodge a translation of the interrogatories also.[3] The letter of request, interrogatories and translations are sent by the Sheriff-clerk to the Foreign Office. The completed interrogatories, with any productions, are sent back through the Foreign Office to the Sheriff-clerk.[4] It is a condition precedent to the issue of the letter of request that the solicitor of the party applying for it should become personally bound for the whole expenses of executing the commission, and should consign such sum as the Sheriff shall fix.[5] The evidence of a party to the cause may be taken on commission,[6] but the Court has a discretion in the matter,[6] and even in the case of an ordinary witness a commission has been refused where his evidence was of special importance.[7]

[1] Codifying Act of Sederunt, L. II, 1.
[2] Ibid., 2, Schedule B.
[3] Ibid., 4, 5, Schedule B.
[4] Ibid., 5.
[5] Ibid., 3.
[6] Samson & Co. v. Hough, 1886, 13 R. 1154; Robertson v. Robertson, (O.H.) 1897, 4 S.L.T. 358; Lyell, &c. v. Harthill Thistle Pipe Band, &c., 1905, 21 Sh.Ct.Rep. 294.
[7] Western Ranches v. Nelson's Trustees, 1898, 25 R. 527.

As an alternative to the procedure laid down by the Act of Sederunt a commission may be obtained in ordinary form to have the evidence of the witness in the foreign country taken before a commissioner appointed by the Sheriff. If a British Consul is available at the place of examination a suitable appointment is of the Consul, whom failing, the Vice-Consul.[1] But the weakness of this arrangement is that there is no means of compelling the attendance of the witness for examination and the result of the commission is dependent on whether the witness will voluntarily attend to be examined.

[1] See Lawson v. Donaldson, 1893, 10 Sh.Ct.Rep. 110.

Where interrogatories are necessary the party seeking the evidence will be appointed to lodge his interrogatories or questions to be put to the witness, and the other party will be allowed thereafter to lodge his cross-interrogatories. These are adjusted, if necessary, after a hearing before the Sheriff, and the adjusted interrogatories are appointed to be put to the witness. This is done by the queries being read *seriatim* to the witness by the commissioner, who records the answers as given. It is always competent to the commissioner to put any further questions either *ex proprio motu*, or at the request of parties' representatives, if present, in order to elucidate the position. It is customary for the final interrogatory to embody a general authority to the commissioner to put such further questions.

13. PROOF OF LAW OF OTHER COUNTRIES.

It is sometimes necessary, in a cause raised in the Scottish Courts, to ascertain the law of other countries. Foreign law—which in this connexion includes the law of England and Ireland, and of the British Dominions—is, as regards our Courts, a matter of fact.[1] A relevant averment of what the foreign law is must appear in the pleadings,[2] and upon such an averment proof may be led. Opinion evidence may be given as to the foreign law, and barristers or others qualified to speak on the subject are the usual witnesses. It seems doubtful if evidence by solicitors would be accepted as sufficient.[3] Foreign Statutes, text-books and decisions may be referred to by the witnesses. It is also competent to make a remit to a suitable person in order to ascertain the foreign law as a matter of fact.[4]

[1] Girvin, Roper & Co. v. Monteith, 1895, 23 R. 129; Campbell's Trustees v. Campbell, 1903, 5 F. 366; Brown's Trustees v. Gregson, 1919 S.C. 438; 1920 S.C. (H.L.) 87; Higgins v. Ewing's Trustees, 1925 S.C. 440.
[2] Campbell's Trustees v. Campbell, supra; Stuart v. Potter, Choate & Prentice, 1911, 48 S.L.R. 657; Higgins v. Ewing's Trustees, supra.
[3] Dinwoodie's Executrix v. Carruther's Executor, 1895, 23 R. 234, Lord Young, p. 238.
[4] Welsh v. Milne, 1844, 7 D. 213. See 7 Edw. VII c. 51, Schedule I, Rule 60. See also p. 175, supra.

If the law to be ascertained is that of a foreign country outwith the British Dominions the Sheriff Court cannot obtain an opinion from the foreign Court under the Foreign Law Ascertainment Act, as that Act applies only to the Court of Session or the Justiciary Court in Scotland.[1] In such a case the foreign law must be ascertained as a matter of fact in one of the methods above indicated. On the other hand, the law of a British Dominion— which includes England and Ireland—may be ascertained in the Sheriff Court, as in the Court of Session, under the provisions of the British Law Ascertainment Act of 1859.[2] That Statute applies to any action depending in any Court within His Majesty's Dominions, and an action is defined as including "every judicial proceeding instituted in any Court." Although the remit is made to a Superior Court it is thought to be clear that the remitting Court need not be a Superior Court.[3]

[1] 24 Vict. c. 11, secs. 1, 4.
[2] 22 & 23 Vict. c. 63, secs. 1, 5.
[3] See Macomish's Executors v. Jones, 1932 S.C. 108.

When it is necessary or expedient for the proper disposal of the action to ascertain the law applicable to the facts of the case, the Sheriff is empowered to state a case for the opinion of a Superior Court of the country, the law of which it is desired to ascertain.[1] The parties may agree upon the facts to be submitted, or, if necessary, they may be heard upon the terms of the stated case which fall to be adjusted or approved by the Sheriff. The whole facts, as set forth on record, to which the law is to be applied should be stated and to these are added the questions of law on which an opinion is required. The Sheriff-clerk will transmit the stated case to the tribunal selected, and there the parties in the cause may apply to be heard before the opinion is given upon the stated case.[1] The opinion is certified by the clerk of the Court which delivers it, and is given to each of the parties who may require it.[2] Any party may then move the Sheriff to apply the law so ascertained to the facts as stated on record.[3] The opinion is not binding on the House of Lords if given by a Court whose judgments are subject to review by the House.[4]

[1] 22 & 23 Vict. c. 63, sec. 1.
[2] Ibid., sec. 2.
[3] Ibid., sec. 3.
[4] Ibid., sec. 4.

14. CONDUCT OF PROOF.

(a) *Examination of Witnesses.*—Each party's solicitor must decide the number of witnesses he shall call, and the order in which they shall be called, but his client although successful may be refused the expenses of an unnecessary number of witnesses. If one day is not sufficient to overtake the evidence, the diet should be fixed so as to admit of the proof being taken on successive days, and the witnesses should be cited accordingly. If the proof is adjourned for an interval, witnesses not taken should be again cited for the adjourned diet. Witnesses who have been cited must attend personally and give their evidence upon oath in the box. Under the Administration of Justice (Scotland) Act, 1933,[1] it is made competent by Act of Sederunt to provide for the admission of affidavits in lieu of parole evidence, but so far this has not been generally done.[2]

[1] 23 & 24 Geo. V c. 41, sec. 34 (1) (c).
[2] cf. Act of Sederunt, 19th July, 1935, 1 (2) (Holograph Wills).

Witnesses are examined separately, and not in the hearing of other intended witnesses, but this rule may be waived by the other party to the case. If a witness has been present in Court, without consent of the other side during an earlier part of the proceedings, his evidence need not be rejected, but may be admitted at the discretion of the Court if it appears that the witness's presence was not the consequence of culpable negligence or criminal intent, and that the witness has not been unduly instructed or influenced by what took place during his presence in Court, or that injustice will not be done by examining the witness.[1] In modern practice witnesses are not commonly excluded on this ground, but if a witness has inadvertently been present in Court, it may be thought well to note that fact upon the notes of evidence. In many cases the witness, when he leaves the witness-box, remains in Court unless objection is taken by a party in the cause. But if there is a prospect of a witness being recalled[2] he should not be allowed to remain in Court. In any case, a witness who has been examined should not, until the proof has been concluded, be allowed to hold any communication with witnesses still to be taken relative to the proceedings. If he does so, he may seriously affect the weight to be attached to the evidence of unexamined witnesses, with whom he has spoken after being himself examined.

[1] 3 & 4 Vict. c. 59, sec. 3.
[2] See 15 Vict. c. 27, sec. 4. See also Robertson v. Steuart, 1874. 1 R. 532; Hoey v. Hoey, 1884, 11 R. 578; cf. Begg v. Begg, 1887, 14 R. 497.

An exception to the exclusion from Court of unexamined witnesses is commonly made in the case of skilled witnesses who are to speak to matters of opinion, but this is a matter of arrangement and the leave of the Court or the consent of the other party should be obtained. As a rule such witnesses should not hear each other's evidence. As matter of right the parties to the action and their solicitors are the only persons entitled to be present while witnesses are being examined, though they intend to give evidence themselves later.[1] A skilled witness called to give an opinion is entitled to hear stated, or to read, a statement of the facts in regard to which he is asked to express an opinion; but in the general case the business of a witness is to state facts, not opinions, and the examination of a witness should be directed only to eliciting the facts.

[1] Perman v. Binny's Trustees, (O.H.) 1925 S.L.T. 123.

The examination is conducted in English. If a witness is unable to speak English he may be examined through a sworn

interpreter. If a witness speaks English but is unable to articulate
distinctly enough to be generally understood some one who understands his mode of speech may act as interpreter, but the witness
must be capable of being put on oath and of understanding its
nature.[1] A dumb person is a competent witness whose sign or
lip language may be interpreted.[2] It is competent, and may be
more satisfactory in some cases, for the witness to write down
the answers to questions put to him. But in the general case, even
where the witness is both deaf and dumb, the examination is
commonly conducted through an interpreter.

[1] White, 1842, 1 Broun 228; cf. Lord Advocate v. Howison, 1871, 2
   Coup. 153.
[2] Montgomery, 1855, 2 Irv. 222; Lord Advocate v. Howison, supra;
   cf. O'Neil & Gollan, 1858, 3 Irv. 93.

In the examination-in-chief of a witness, leading questions,
which suggest the answer desired by the examiner, should be
avoided. It is often necessary to put on record narrative or intro-
ductory matter or facts not really in dispute, and over this a
witness may generally be led without objection, but, when material
facts are the subject of inquiry, the evidence of a witness is lessened
in value if his statement is an answer to a leading question.[1] Where
the witness is hostile[2] to the examiner leading questions are permissible. If exception is taken to leading questions the question as put
may be objected to, or the objector may ask that the evidence be
recorded as question and answer instead of as narrative. As to the
recording of objections to questions and their disposal see the case
noted.[3]

[1] See Bishop v. Bryce, 1910 S.C. 426, Lord President Dunedin, p. 431;
   M'Kenzie v. M'Kenzie, 1943 S.C. 108.
[2] See further as to the examination of hostile witnesses, p. 218, infra.
[3] Hewat v. Edinburgh Corporation, 1944 S.C. 30.

When a witness is speaking to facts, it is presumed that he is
speaking from his own knowledge. If it turns out that his knowledge is second-hand, his evidence will be discarded as hearsay.
But if the witness do know the facts, his evidence is not necessarily
restricted to stating them baldly. Thus a witness may be asked not
only to repeat the exact expression which he heard used, but may
be asked also his impression at the time as to whether the speaker
meant his remark to be taken seriously or jocularly, or whether
the remark was part of a general discussion or altercation. While
elucidation of this kind is permissible, and often necessary, evidence
of mere impressions alone is not competent testimony.[1]

[1] See A B v. C D, 1848, 11 D. 289.

In general, where a witness accepts a fact which he does not himself know, but has only heard, his belief is of no consequence; but it is different when the witness is expressing a belief formed in his mind because of his own knowledge of certain facts. Thus, a person may competently express his opinion that a document is in the handwriting of a particular person although he did not see the document written. Opinion evidence is also admissible where, from the nature of the case, opinion or belief alone is possible, as in the case of professional or expert witnesses. Skilled witnesses, however, ought not to be asked their general opinion upon the merits of the case, but only their opinion upon specific facts put to them.

The rule as to rejection of hearsay evidence does not apply where the object is to establish what had been said by a deceased person. Evidence of statements made by a deceased person is admissible, the degree of weight to be attached to such evidence being a question of circumstances. Depositions made in prior proceedings may be used in a later action when the witnesses are dead,[1] but a precognition or similar statement of an intended witness, who has died between the date of precognition and the date of trial, will not be received as evidence.[2] Statements made by a party to a cause are admissible as evidence against him, and so a party may be asked what he said on a particular occasion. Hearsay evidence of what was said by a person who has since become insane must, it is thought, be admitted in the same way as if the person had died.[3] Hearsay evidence as to statements made by the defender's employee against whom fault is alleged, has been refused.[4]

[1] Geils v. Geils, 1855, 17 D. 397; Robertson v. Robertson, (O.H.) 1894, 2 S.L.T. 353; Coutts v. Wear, (O.H.) 1914, 2 S.L.T. 86.
[2] Graham v. Western Bank, 1865, 3 M. 617; Stevenson v. Stevenson, 1893, 31 S.L.R. 129; Robertson v. Robertson, supra.
[3] Dickson on Evidence, sec. 268.
[4] Livingstone v. Strachan, Crerar & Jones, 1923 S.C. 794; Scott v. Cormack Heating Engineers, 1942 S.C. 159.

If written evidence is necessary to establish a right or to prove an essential fact its place cannot be taken by oral testimony,[1] and the terms of the document must be established in a proving of the tenor.[2] But this rule may be relaxed if the writing has been either destroyed or withheld by the party founding on its non-production.[3] If written evidence is not the only method of proving the right founded on, parole evidence of the terms of the writing may be competent if it is established that the document does not exist or that it cannot be recovered by diligence.[4] In the case of ordinary commercial documents, or correspondence, of which a draft or copy has not been preserved, it may be competent, after the absence of the documents has been reasonably explained, to ask a witness to give his recollection of their general import. When a document is in existence, and has been recovered, the witness should have it before him when being questioned upon it. In general a party may not by parole testimony contradict or traverse a written document to which he is a party,[5] but he may supplement or explain it.[6] It is always competent to ask a party in a cause what his version is of the meaning of his own document. In special cases, even a third party witness might be asked to supplement the statements in a writing, as, for instance, a solicitor who has drawn a deed, bearing to be granted for good and onerous causes, might be asked (subject to his right to plead confidentiality) what were the causes referred to.[7]

[1] Mackinnon's Trustee v. Bank of Scotland, 1915 S.C. 411; Walker v. Nisbet, 1915 S.C. 639.
[2] Shaw v. Shaw's Trustees, 1876, 3 R. 813.
[3] Young v. Thomson, 1909 S.C. 529; Drummond v. China Tiles, &c., 1909 S.C. 1049; Enever v. Craig, 1913, 2 S.L.T. 30.
[4] Gibson v. Anderson, 1846, 9 D. 1; Longworth v. Yelverton, 1862, 24 D. 696; Steele v. Law, (O.H.) 1895, 3 S.L.T. 190; Dowgray v. Gilmour, 1907 S.C. 715.
[5] Kirkpatrick v. Allanshaw Coal Co., 1880, 8 R. 327; M'Allister v. M'Gallagley, 1911 S.C. 112.
[6] Renison v. Bryce, 1898, 25 R. 521; Macdonald v. Newall, 1898, 1 F. 68; Welwood's Trustees v. Mungall, 1921 S.C. 911.
[7] Ivison v. Edinburgh Silk Co., 1846, 9 D. 1039.

A medical, scientific or skilled witness sometimes gives his evidence-in-chief in the form of a report in writing which is lodged in process. If such a report contains hearsay statements these are not evidence, and, if disclosed in a jury trial, they may result in the verdict being set aside.[1] An ordinary witness gives his evidence in answer to questions, but he is entitled to refresh his memory by referring to book entries, made by himself or on his behalf, or to his notes made at or about the time to which the facts relate, and when they were fresh in his recollection. In the same way a witness by referring to his signature may be able to state that he was a party to a document, though he has forgotten the fact of signing it, and a witness by reference to his signature or handwriting may be able to identify a production as having been previously seen or examined by him. In general, book entries and notes made contemporaneously by the witness may be available as evidence, but other writings though not properly evidence may be used to refresh the witness's memory. Writings of the latter class need not necessarily be produced in process, but must be shown to the opposite party if called for.[2]

[1] See Grant v. H.M. Advocate, 1938 J.C. 7.
[2] See Niven v. Hart, 1898, 25 R. (J.) 89.

A witness is not entitled to refuse to give his testimony, merely because the subject-matter is disagreeable to him, or because the part he took in events under review may make him appear foolish, or may affect his civil rights or his credit.[1] He may, however, refuse to answer any questions if the answer might tend to incriminate him or render him, individually, or as art and part with others, subject to a criminal prosecution.[2] But if no prosecution can follow the witness is obliged to answer.[3] In proceedings instituted in consequence of adultery it is provided by Statute that no witness is liable to be asked, or bound to answer, any question tending to show guilt of adultery unless the witness has already given evidence in the same case in disproof of adultery.[4] The privilege is personal to the witness[5] and may be waived by him.[6] If he takes advantage of it neither the question nor the declinature to answer is noted.[7]

[1] See Pender, 1836, 1 Swin. 25; A B v. Binny, 1858, 20 D. 1058.   See
    also 46 Geo. III c. 37.
[2] Dickson on Evidence, sec. 1786.
[3] Macmillan v. Murray, 1920 J.C. 13.
[4] 37 & 38 Vict. c. 64, sec. 2.
[5] Kirkwood v. Kirkwood, 1875, 3 R. 235.
[6] Bannatyne v. Bannatyne, 1886, 13 R. 619.
[7] Cook v. Cook, 1876, 4 R. 78.

In affiliation cases it has long been a common practice for the pursuer to call the defender as the first witness. The Supreme Court has on various occasions expressed disapproval of the practice, but has not pronounced it incompetent,[1] and it is thought that, in spite of this disapproval, solicitors acting for pursuers in such cases will generally continue the practice if it appears in the circumstances to offer them any advantage.[2] If he is not called by pursuer, the defender may not go into the witness-box at all, and in such a case the fact that he has not tendered himself as a witness will not generally be held to corroborate the pursuer's evidence.[3]

[1] M'Arthur v. M'Queen, 1901, 3 F. 1010; M'Whirter v. Lynch, 1909 S.C.
    112; Fraser v. Smith, 1937 S.N. 67; cf. Darroch v. Kerr, 1901, 4 F.
    396.
[2] Mackay v. Munn, 1909, 25 Sh.Ct.Rep. 369.
[3] Faddes v. M'Neish, 1923 S.C. 443.

As a general rule, a party is not entitled to discredit a witness called by himself, but he may be allowed to do so when the calling of such a witness was unavoidable in respect of the scarcity of available evidence, or in other cases if the witness turns out to be unreliable.[1] Where the evidence of a witness turned out to be unfavourable to the side for which he was called, and to be contrary to the other evidence for that side, a practice had grown up of the examining solicitor asking leave of the Court to treat the witness as hostile so as to conduct his examination with a view to discrediting the witness. This practice has now been denounced in the Court of Session and any submission as to a witness's evidence falls to be made at the hearing of evidence and not during the examination.[2] If a witness who gives evidence contradictory of the rest of the party's case is not disclaimed in this way his testimony may tend to destroy that of witnesses who are favourable.[3] The Evidence Act of 1852[4] made it competent to ask a witness if he had, upon some other occasion, made a statement different from that he was giving in evidence and to prove such different statement. If it is intended to discredit a witness, a foundation must be laid for the contradictory proof by examining the witness himself, in detail, as to the different statement intended to be proved against him.[5] If necessary the witness can be recalled for this purpose,[6] but it has been held incompetent to discredit in anticipation a witness not yet called.[7] It would seem that statements made on precognition cannot be used to discredit a witness.[8]

[1] Gall v. Gall, 1870, 9 M. 177; Darroch v. Kerr, 1901, 4 F. 396. See also M'Ghee v. Glasgow Coal Co., 1923 S.C. 293.
[2] Avery v. Cantilever Shoe Co., 1942 S.C. 469.
[3] M'Ghee v. Glasgow Coal Co., supra.
[4] 15 Vict. c. 27, sec. 3.
[5] Gall v. Gall, supra; M'Taggart v. H.M. Advocate, 1934 J.C. 33. See also M'Kenzie v. M'Kenzie, 1943 S.C. 108.
[6] Robertson v. Steuart, 1874, 1 R. 532; Hoey v. Hoey, 1884, 11 R. 578.
[7] Livingstone v. Strachan, Crerar & Jones, 1923 S.C. 794.
[8] Binnie v. Black, (O.H.) 1923 S.L.T. 98; M'Neilie v. H.M. Advocate, 1929 J.C. 50; cf. Gilmour v. Hansen, 1920 S.C. 598.

A witness may refuse to disclose matters which are confidential. In general, communications between spouses are so protected, unless the protection is waived.[1] But there is no protection if the conduct of the spouses is in issue as in an action of separation.[1] Communications between solicitor and client are generally protected as confidential.[2] But the privilege of pleading confidentiality belongs to the client, who may waive it, and the solicitor is then bound to give his evidence.[3] If a client calls his solicitor as a witness, he waives the privilege.[3] In general, communications between a doctor and his patient are not protected.[4] There is no authority in Scotland deciding that confessions to a clergyman or priest are confidential, and the matter would have to be decided according to the circumstances of the case.[5] Communications between parties on the same side of a case are generally regarded as confidential.[6]

[1] Dickson on Evidence, secs. 1660, 1661; 16 Vict. c. 20, sec. 3.
[2] Dickson on Evidence, sec. 1663, et seq.
[3] Ibid., secs. 1682, 1683; 15 Vict. c. 27, sec. 1.

[4] Ibid., sec. 1688. See also A B v. C D, 1851, 14 D. 177; Watson v. M'Ewan, 1905, 7 F. (H.L.) 109.

[5] Dickson on Evidence, sec. 1684, et seq.

[6] Rose v. Medical, &c., Insurance Society, 1847, 10 D. 156; Logan v. Miller, (O.H.) 1920, 1 S.L.T. 211. See further, p. 196, supra.

Besides examining in chief the witnesses called to support his own case as laid, a pursuer should also exhaust each witness in respect of any evidence he can give about the defence stated, or upon any separate case laid for the defender.[1] In other words in present-day practice the pursuer leads his conjunct probation along with his proof-in-chief.[1] At one time a party led in the first instance evidence to support his own averments (his proof-in-chief), but the evidence which he led to contradict his opponent's proof (his conjunct proof) was not brought forward till his opponent had led his proof-in-chief, and when it was brought forward it was restricted to controverting his opponent's proof-in-chief.

[1] Gairdner v. Young, 1874, 2 R. 173; Dick & Stevenson v. Mackay, 1880, 7 R. 778, Lord Shand, p. 791.

Failure to examine a witness upon some fact which is in dispute and of which the witness has knowledge may be held equivalent to the abandonment of that part of the case by the party who has adduced the witness in question.[1] But failure of a defender to give evidence at all will not generally be regarded as an admission of averments made against him by pursuer and which he might have been expected to deny.[2]

[1] See A B v. C D, 1844, 6 D. 1148; Watson v. Board of Trade, 1892, 19 R. 1078; Turner v. Board of Trade, 1894, 22 R. 18; The "Nerano" v. The "Dromedary," 1895, 22 R. 237; Crawford v. Granite City Steamship Co., 1906, 8 F. 1013.

[2] Faddes v. M'Neish, 1923 S.C. 443. See also Nelson v. Easdale Slate Quarries Co., (O.H.) 1910, 1 S.L.T. 21.

(b) *Cross-examination.*—Much greater latitude is permitted in cross-examination than in examination-in-chief, and a witness may fairly be questioned, not only in regard to the facts themselves, but also in regard to the sources of his knowledge of the facts, his inaccuracy of memory, his attitude towards the parties to the cause, his interests, or his prejudices, all of which may cast a light upon his testimony, or influence the weight which should be attached to it.[1] Leading questions are generally permissible in cross-examination, and as one object of cross-examination is to test the reliability of the testimony given, whatever may reasonably affect the credibility of the witness or may tend to show that his views are distorted or exaggerated, or the like, is relevant cross-examination.[1] Cross-examination, like examination-in-chief, must be kept within the cause, and it is not competent to cross-examine a witness in regard to facts wholly irrelevant to the cause with the object of afterwards leading evidence to contradict him, and so impairing his testimony.[2] In addition to testing evidence already given in chief, the cross-examiner can elicit from the witness evidence of any facts favourable to the cross-examiner's case.[3] Such questions are not cross to anything stated by the witness in examination-in-chief.

[1] See generally Dickson on Evidence, sec. 1763, et seq.
[2] Ibid., sec. 1794.
[3] 3 & 4 Vict. c. 59, sec. 4.

Notice has already been taken of the fact that where it is intended to discredit a witness by proving a previous statement of his of different import the witness himself must be cross-examined in detail as to the statement intended to be proved against him.[1] The same precaution must be taken if it is intended to prove facts known to the witness though not actually spoken to by him in the box. Failure to cross-examine a witness upon any point spoken to by him in his examination-in-chief will generally be taken to mean that such point is no longer disputed by the cross-examiner, and that the other side need not elaborate their evidence on this point.[2]

[1] See p. 219, supra.
[2] Keenan v. Scottish Wholesale Co-operative Society, 1914 S.C. 959. See also M'Kenzie v. M'Kenzie, 1943 S.C. 108.

(c) *Re-examination.*—Upon the conclusion of the cross-examination, the examiner-in-chief is entitled to re-examine the witness and to interrogate him on any matters first raised in the cross-examination. He may also clear up any doubts which have arisen in regard to facts spoken to by the witness, or dispel any complexion which the cross-examination has tended to put upon the facts themselves, or upon the explanation of them given by the witness. The re-examiner is not entitled to open up any new matter with the witness, nor is he entitled to go back upon his examination-in-chief in regard to points which the cross-examination has not touched. The object of re-examination is not to supply omissions in the examination-in-chief, but to clear up the evidence of the witness upon points already dealt with by both sides. If any point has inadvertently been omitted the proper course is to ask a question to be put by the Court. The re-examination ends the testimony of the witness, unless the Court desires to put any questions to him, but a witness may be recalled before the proof has been closed, if the Court permit.[1]

[1] 15 Vict. c. 27, sec. 4. See also Robertson v. Steuart, 1874, 1 R. 532; Hoey v. Hoey, 1884, 11 R. 578; Begg v. Begg, 1887, 14 R. 497; Saunders v. Paterson, 1905, 7 F. (J.) 58; M'Neilie v. H.M. Advocate, 1929 J.C. 50; Davidson v. M'Fadyean, 1942 J.C. 95.

(d) *Proof in Replication.*—In present-day practice an order for proof in replication is not frequent, as each party not only supports his own case in evidence, but leads proof in anticipation to meet his opponent's case. But after a pursuer has closed his proof some point may come out in the defender's proof which the pursuer could not reasonably have anticipated, and in that event it is still competent to allow a proof in replication, the nature and extent of which should be specified in the interlocutor allowing the additional proof.[1] In some cases it may be sufficient to obtain the leave of the Court to recall one or more witnesses to clear up the point which pursuer has not sufficiently anticipated in his proof and thus avoid the necessity of a formal proof in replication. The general question of additional evidence being led after the proof is closed is considered later.[2]

[1] See Rankine v. Roberts, 1873, 1 R. 225; Gairdner v. Young, 1874, 2 R. 173; Kessack v. Kessack, 1899, 1 F. 398.
[2] See p. 225, infra.

(e) *Appeal during Proof.*—Objections to the competency of evidence do not necessarily interrupt the course of a proof, but may delay the issue of judgment, and may reopen the proof. If an objection to evidence is taken, the objection, and answer made to it, and the ruling of the Sheriff or commissioner, are noted upon the notes of evidence, but the examination of the witness nevertheless proceeds.[1] The rule[1] requires that the noting should be made, if desired by the objector, but it is thought that, when an objection is sustained, the matter should be also noted, if desired by the other side. If the Sheriff or commissioner considers the objection of sufficient importance he may direct that the evidence objected to should be taken on a separate paper.[1] It is not competent, during the course of a proof, to submit to review any judgment pronounced upon the competency of evidence,[1] but at the close of the proof or within seven days thereafter, the Sheriff-Substitute (if he has not in the interval given judgment in the case) may grant leave to appeal the objections taken during the course of the proof to the Sheriff.[2] The precise form in which the appeal is to be taken is not prescribed, but a note of appeal in the usual form should be written on the interlocutor sheet,[3] and should state that the appeal is upon the objections to the admissibility of evidence taken in the course of the proof. The Sheriff is directed, with or without a hearing, to dispose of such appeal with the least possible delay, and if he decides that evidence accepted should not have been allowed, he may delete the same from the notes of evidence.[2] If, on the other hand, he thinks that the evidence sought to be led should have been allowed, he may direct it to be taken before the case is disposed of on the merits.[2]

[1] 7 Edw. VII c. 51, Schedule I, Rule 74. See also Hewat v. Edinburgh Corporation, 1944 S.C. 30.
[2] Ibid., Rule 75.
[3] See ibid., Rule 87.

It has been held that the procedure by incidental appeal above referred to is the appropriate remedy where a party is dissatisfied with the admission or rejection of evidence in the course of a proof.[1] And, where questions which were apparently competent were disallowed at a proof, and no such appeal was taken, the Court of Session, on an appeal on the merits, declined to allow the questions to be put as additional proof on the ground that it was then too late to review the Sheriff-Substitute's ruling.[1] While that case was concerned with a motion to be allowed to lead additional proof the opinions indicate that in all cases of admission or rejection of evidence, where no appeal is taken at the time, the matter will probably not be open to review at a later appeal on the merits. If an appeal is taken at the time the matter does not go beyond the Sheriff, but as a later appeal to the Supreme Court has the effect of submitting to review the whole of the interlocutors in the case[2] the Sheriff's decision on the admission of evidence will be in that case open to attack.

[1] Jackson v. M'Kay, 1923 S.C. 286.
[2] 7 Edw. VII c. 51, sec. 29.

A similar summary appeal to the Sheriff is allowed upon an objection to produce documents or to give oral evidence upon the plea of confidentiality. The provision is that if any person, whether a party to the cause or not, pleads before the Sheriff-Substitute confidentiality with reference to documentary or oral evidence, or objects to produce documents on pleas of alleged hypothec or otherwise, the Sheriff-Substitute is to minute his decision on such pleas on the notes of evidence, and any party to the cause, or the party pleading confidentiality may, by leave of the Sheriff-Substitute in open Court, take an appeal to the Sheriff, who is directed to dispose of it with the least possible delay, with or without a hearing.[1] Although not specifically stated, it is assumed that such an appeal is open to a party pleading a right of hypothec as indicated in the earlier part of the rule.

1 7 Edw. VII c. 51, Schedule I, Rule 76.

The succeeding rule provides that such incidental appeal shall not remove the cause from the Sheriff-Substitute, who may proceed with the cause as regards points not necessarily dependent upon the ruling so appealed against.[1] This provision appears to refer only to an appeal on the ground of confidentiality and the like under Rule 76, but it might be held to apply also to an appeal on questions of admissibility of evidence, although the prospect of the Sheriff-Substitute proceeding with the cause in such circumstances seems a little remote.

1 7 Edw. VII c. 51, Schedule I, Rule 77.

The provisions of the above-mentioned rules[1] relating to incidental appeal upon the competency of evidence are not appropriate to a summary cause, unless there is a record of the evidence. But if notes of evidence are taken an appeal seems competent in a summary as in an ordinary cause on any questions of admission of evidence raised at the proof. While the rules regarding appeals upon the admission of evidence clearly contemplate only cases where the evidence is recorded[1] the rule dealing with appeals on grounds of confidentiality or hypothec is dependent on a record of the evidence only to the extent that the Sheriff-Substitute's decision is to be minuted thereon.[2] It is thought, although with some hesitation, that an incidental appeal under Rule 76 might be competent in a summary cause even when the evidence had not been recorded.

1 7 Edw. VII c. 51, Schedule I, Rules 74, 75.
2 Ibid., Rule 76.

(f) *Close of Proof.*—The proof is directed to be taken as far as possible continuously, but the Sheriff may adjourn the diet from time to time.[1] The pursuer leads in the proof, unless the defender has been ordained to lead. The latter may be the position where the pursuer's case is admitted on record, and defender sets up a counter-claim, or where a pursuer sues upon a document of debt which the defender admits to be genuine, but pleads has been discharged.[2] The party who leads is generally required to close his proof, before the other party leads any evidence; but of consent a party's proof is sometimes closed subject to future examination of a named witness, who, for sufficient reason, cannot attend, the other party meantime proceeding with his proof. When a party has led all his evidence, the shorthand notes record that his proof is closed.

At the conclusion of the proof an interlocutor may be pronounced, declaring the proof to be closed, and appointing a hearing thereon, or, if parties have been heard, making avizandum.

[1] 7 Edw. VII c. 51, Schedule I, Rule 69.
[2] And see further. p. 182, supra.

Where the Sheriff-Substitute died in the course of a proof it was held that as one of the parties did not agree to the notes of evidence already taken being utilized the whole evidence must be taken of new.[1] Of consent of both parties these notes might have been used. In a case in the Court of Session where the whole evidence had been taken but judgment had not been issued the Court of consent of parties approved of the notes of evidence being used,[2] but it is thought that such a course could not be followed against the wish of either party.[1]

[1] Lumsden v. Lang's Trustees, 1939, 55 Sh.Ct.Rep. 223; Ravelston Steamship Co. v. Sieberg Brothers, 1946 S.C. 349.
[2] Ferguson v. Ferguson, 1936 S.C. 808.

(g) *Reopening the Proof.*—After the proof has been closed, neither party can insist upon leading further evidence upon the case as it stood when the order for proof was made; but, as the Court is empowered to allow amendment at any stage,[1] a record may be opened up even after a proof has been closed, and further proof may in that case be allowed. As a general rule an amendment which involves additional proof will not be allowed unless for some sufficiently good reason and subject to a condition in regard to the payment of expenses.[2]

[1] 7 Edw. VII c. 51, Schedule I, Rule 79. See further. p. 239, infra.
[2] See M'Kenzie v. Jones, 1926, 42 Sh.Ct.Rep. 289; Union Bank of Scotland v. Fulton, &c., 1928, 45 Sh.Ct.Rep. 62.

The Sheriff-Substitute had, under an Act of Sederunt of 1839,[1] power to allow additional proof, if weighty reasons were shown to him for doing so. But that provision fell with the repeal of the Act of 1838 to which it related.[2] Under the present Statute authority is given to the Sheriff to allow further proof when a case is before him on appeal,[3] and this provision has been held to withdraw by implication any general or inherent power in the Sheriff-Substitute to allow additional proof, apart from that following on an amendment.[4] There is, however, another provision that the Sheriff—which includes the Sheriff-Substitute—may allow a party, at any time before judgment, to produce any document which he has failed to produce timeously upon such conditions as to payment of expenses and allowing further proof as to the Sheriff shall

seem just.[5] The result appears to be that, apart from proof following upon an amendment of record, additional proof cannot be
allowed by the Sheriff-Substitute unless it is allowed as relative to
a document which one of the parties has failed to produce timeously,
and has been allowed to lodge at a later stage. When an appeal has
been taken to the Supreme Court special statutory provision is
made for additional proof being taken in the Court of Session.[6]

1 Act of Sederunt, 10th July, 1839, sec. 83.
2 1 & 2 Vict. c. 119 (rep. 7 Edw. VII c. 51, Schedule II).
3 7 Edw. VII c. 51, sec. 27; as to effect of this provision, see p. 297, infra.
4 Hogan v. Cunningham, 1915, 32 Sh.Ct.Rep. 67; M'Ghee v. Ellingham,
    1932, 49 Sh.Ct.Rep. 282; Grierson v. M'Garva, 1934, 50 Sh.Ct.Rep.
    88.   See also Cook v. Crane, 1922 S.C. 631.
5 7 Edw. VII c. 51, Schedule I, Rule 68a.   See Crawford & Elliot v.
    Wainstein, 1924 S.L.T. (Sh.Ct.) 18.
6 31 & 32 Vict. c. 100, sec. 72.   See Gairdner v. Macarthur, 1915 S.C.
    589.

In cases where additional proof can competently be allowed such
a motion will only be granted if a sufficient reason is shown for
doing so.   Reference may be made to the undernoted cases dealing
with further evidence relative to a document which has been produced.[1]   In other cases it is not in general a sufficient reason for
reopening the proof that a branch of the case has been omitted to
be proved,[2] or that a witness who might have been called at the
proof was not called,[3] and where parties had renounced probation
in the Sheriff Court a motion on appeal to amend the record with
a view to proof being allowed was refused.[4]   As a general rule
before additional proof will be allowed, it will require to be shown
to the Court that a party has been prejudiced through no fault of
himself or his solicitor, but solely owing to circumstances beyond
his control.[5]   The power in the Sheriff on appeal to allow further
evidence is not limited to a case of res noviter, but would apply to
a case of new evidence even about matters already dealt with in
the proof.[6]   The Sheriff's discretion on a motion for such additional
proof is one with which the Court of Session will not as a rule interfere if the discretion has not been unreasonably exercised,[6] but the
Sheriff has no power to order further proof ex proprio motu.[7]

1 Coul v. Ayr County Council, 1909 S.C. 422; Crawford & Elliot v.
    Wainstein, 1924 S.L.T. (Sh.Ct.) 18.   See also Reid v. Haldane's
    Trustees, 1891, 18 R. 744; Liquidator of Universal Stock Exchange
    Co. v. Howat, 1891, 19 R. 128.
2 Cruickshank, Fraser & Co. v. Caledonian Railway Co., 1876, 3 R. 484;
    Glengarnock Iron, &c., Co. v. Cooper & Co., 1895, 22 R. 672.
3 Mabon v. Cairns, 1875, 3 R. 47; Allan v. Stott, 1893, 20 R. 804; Barnes
    v. Hannay, 1922, 38 Sh.Ct.Rep. 202.   See also Miller v. North
    British Locomotive Co., 1909 S.C. 698.
4 Carswell & Son v. Finlay, 1887, 24 S.L.R. 643.

⁵ Brown v. Gordon, 1870, 8 M. 432; Mitchell v. Sellar, 1915 S.C. 360; Gairdner v. Macarthur, 1915 S.C. 589; Balfour-Kinnear v. Balfour-Kinnear, 1919 S.C. 391; M'Ghee v. Ellingham, 1932, 49 Sh.Ct.Rep. 282; Grierson v. M'Garva, 1934, 50 Sh.Ct.Rep. 88.
⁶ Cook v. Crane, 1922 S.C. 631.
⁷ Hutchison v. Davidson, 1945 S.C. 395.

Where additional proof is taken on appeal to the Court of Session it is provided that such proof is to be taken in the same way as other proofs in cases depending before the Inner House.[1] No provision is made for the manner in which further proof allowed by the Sheriff on appeal to him is to be taken,[2] but probably the most convenient course is a remit to the Sheriff-Substitute to take the proof and report same to the Sheriff.[3] In a recent case where additional proof was allowed in an appeal to the Court of Session on a minute of *res noviter* a remit was made to the Sheriff-Substitute to take the additional proof.[4]

[1] 31 & 32 Vict. c. 100, sec. 72.
[2] 7 Edw. VII c. 51, sec. 27.
[3] See Cook v. Crane, 1922 S.C. 631.
[4] Macfarlane v. Raeburn, 1946 S.L.T. 164.

15. RECORD OF EVIDENCE.

Evidence before the Sheriff or a commissioner may be taken down by the Sheriff or commissioner, or by a clerk or shorthand writer nominated by the Sheriff or commissioner, to whom the oath *de fideli administratione* is administered.[1] The evidence may be recorded in narrative form, or by question and answer as the Sheriff or commissioner shall direct, and the extended notes of evidence, certified by the clerk or shorthand writer, are the notes of the oral evidence in the cause.[1] The Sheriff or commissioner may, if he think fit, dictate to the clerk or shorthand writer what he is to record,[1] but in practice evidence is taken direct by the shorthand writer without dictation by the Sheriff. The Act directs that a summary cause is to be disposed of without a record of the evidence, unless on the motion of either party the Sheriff shall order that the evidence be recorded.[2] It has been held that if a motion is made to have the evidence recorded the Sheriff has no discretion in the matter and that the motion must be granted.[3]

[1] 7 Edw. VII c. 51, Schedule I, Rule 65.
[2] Ibid., sec. 8.
[3] Stewart v. Gourlay, 1939, 56 Sh.Ct.Rep. 3. See further, p. 99, supra.

In the case of evidence taken on commission the shorthand writer's fees are paid in the first instance by the party who moved for the commission, and in a proof or jury trial by the parties equally.[1] The latter rule applies in summary causes where the evidence has been recorded at the request of one of the parties.[2] It is also provided that parties' solicitors are personally liable for the shorthand writer's fees,[1] but this does not apply to a solicitor for the poor.[3] The cost of the shorthand notes taken at the proof is a good charge, as party and party costs, against an unsuccessful party, even if no use has been made of the notes.[4] The Sheriff is empowered to make an order directing payment of the shorthand writer's account to be made.[1] Such an order, if not implemented before judgment, would entitle the Sheriff to dismiss an action, or to grant decree of absolvitor under Rule 56.[5]

[1] 7 Edw. VII c. 51, Schedule I, Rule 67.
[2] Weiner v. Tod, Cunningham & Petrie, 1941, 57 Sh.Ct.Rep. 58.
[3] 7 Edw. VII c. 51, Schedule I, Rule 167.
[4] Marshall v. Shearer Brothers, (O.H.) 1903, 11 S.L.T. 71.
[5] 7 Edw. VII c. 51, Schedule I, Rule 56.

If the correctness of the notes of evidence or of a deposition be questioned, the Sheriff may satisfy himself in regard thereto by the examination of witnesses or otherwise, and may amend the record of evidence or the deposition.[1] This may be a useful power, but in practice the revision of notes of evidence is usually confined to the correction of obvious errors, and the re-examination of witnesses will seldom be resorted to for this purpose. In a case where the notes of evidence were manifestly inaccurate and incomplete the Sheriff on appeal remitted to the Sheriff-Substitute to take the whole evidence of new.[2] The same order was made in an earlier case where an application was made to the *nobile officium* of the Court of Session when part of the shorthand notes had been accidentally destroyed.[3] It is thought that in such a case the Sheriff-Substitute would himself adopt this course.[3] If the notes of evidence themselves were lost after they were in process another copy might be substituted under Rule 17.[4]

[1] 7 Edw. VII c. 51, Schedule I, Rule 66.
[2] Wilson v. MacQueen, 1925, 41 Sh.Ct.Rep. 278.
[3] Yates v. Robertson, 1891, 18 R. 1206.
[4] 7 Edw. VII c. 51, Schedule I, Rule 17.

16. Hearing.

At the close of the proof, or at an adjourned diet, if the Sheriff sees fit to postpone the hearing, the Sheriff is directed to hear the parties or their solicitors.[1] It is not essential that the extended notes of evidence be before the Court, or before the parties, at the debate, but in complicated cases it may be convenient. After the hearing the Sheriff is directed to pronounce judgment with the least possible delay.[1]

[1] 7 Edw. VII c. 51, Schedule I, Rule 78.

17. REFERENCE TO OATH.

All other proof may be superseded by a party electing to refer to the oath of the opposing party. This is a privilege which subsists so long as the action itself is pending. Even where decree on the merits has been granted, if extract has not been obtained, the cause is still pending, and reference to oath is still competent.[1] The reference may be retracted in the discretion of the Court, and on such conditions as may be imposed at any time up to the actual moment of making oath.[2] If a party has been called as a witness by the other party and examined, reference to his oath is not thereafter competent.[3] And if a party has given evidence on his own behalf and has been cross-examined on the merits of the case by the other side, a motion to refer to that party's oath will not generally be granted.[4] The adducing of a party as a witness by the adverse party has not the effect of a reference to the oath of the party adduced.[3]

[1] Longworth v. Yelverton, 1865, 5 M. (H.L.) 144; Aikman v. Aikman's Trustees, 1868, 6 M. 277.
[2] Bennie v. Mack, 1832, 10 S. 255; Dick v. Hutton, 1876, 3 R. 448.
[3] 16 Vict. c. 20, sec. 5.
[4] Macleay v. Campbell, 1876, 3 R. 999; Pollok v. Whiteford, 1936 S.C. 402. See also Dewar v. Pearson, 1866, 4 M. 493; Swanson v. Gallie, 1870, 9 M. 208.

Reference to oath can only take the place of competent proof. It is not competent, for instance, by referring a case to the oath of party, to evade an objection that parole proof is incompetent. Thus, a contract to which writing is essential cannot be set up by averment and reference to oath.[1] The reference is competent only in regard to matters of fact, which are specifically averred[2] in a competent and relevantly stated action, and a party cannot, by deposition on oath, contradict his own averments on record, nor can a party refer to his opponent's oath with a view to establishing facts plainly inconsistent with his own averments.[3] A motion to refer the whole cause to the defender's oath was refused where certain of pursuer's averments were not covered by the conclusions of the summons.[4] Where there are alternative craves and one is referred to oath the other is held as departed from.[5]

[1] Dickson, Evidence, sec. 1416.
[2] M'Farlane v. Watt, 1828, 6 S. 1095.
[3] Dickson, Evidence, sec. 1421.
[4] Thomson v. Simpson, 1844, 7 D. 106.
[5] Thomson v. Philp, 1867, 5 M. 679.

The mode of referring to oath is by minute signed either by the party desiring the reference or his solicitor,[1] who should have special authority to make the reference.[2] The reference must be unconditional. It is effective in the process in which it is made and in any subsequent proceedings involving the same matter and depending on the facts deponed to.[3] But the deposition cannot be used in any other process depending upon different facts.[3] If made prior to decree the reference to oath may be confined to individual points of fact, but after decree any reference must be of the whole case or of such part as will be conclusive.[4]

[1] 7 Edw. VII c. 51, Schedule I, Rule 64.
[2] Dickson, Evidence, sec. 1444.
[3] Ibid., sec. 1496.
[4] Ibid., sec. 1439, et seq.

The minute does not become operative till the Court has interponed authority to it, and an interlocutor should be pronounced formally sustaining the reference.[1] The Court has a discretion to refuse the reference, if obvious injustice would result, or it may attach conditions in allowing the reference.[2] Thus consignation may be required where the competency of the reference is doubtful, or the procedure is obviously taken merely to get delay.[3] In practice, however, a reference to oath is generally regarded as the privilege of a litigant, of which he is not to be deprived unless in special circumstances.[2]

[1] See Pollok v. Whiteford, 1936 S.C. 402.
[2] Dickson, Evidence, sec. 1418.
[3] Conacher v. Conacher, 1859, 21 D. 597.

Reference to oath is not competent unless there is an unqualified issue before the Court. The record should be complete, and all preliminary pleas disposed of before a minute of reference is lodged.[1] Although the oath of party is not, strictly speaking, proof, it takes the place of proof, so that if another mode of disposing of the case has already been adopted, as, for instance, by reference to a judicial referee, the reference to oath is incompetent.[2] But a reference to oath is open although the parties have renounced probation.[3] Objection to a reference to oath should be taken at the time the reference is proposed, as otherwise the reference may be held as acquiesced in.[4]

[1] Dickson, Evidence, secs. 1422-3.
[2] M'Laren v. Shore, 1883, 10 R. 1067.
[3] Anstruther v. Wilkie, 1856, 18 D. 405.
[4] See Broom & Co. v. Edgley & Co., 1843, 5 D. 1087.

The deposition of the witness may be taken in shorthand, in the same manner as evidence,[1] and the power to correct the shorthand notes covers a deposition[2]; but, unless to correct an obvious clerical error, the Court is not likely to interfere with the recorded deposition. An examination under a reference to oath is conducted by the solicitor of the party who has made the reference. The solicitor of the deponent is entitled to be present,[3] but cannot cross-examine, although he may take objection to incompetent questions[4] and may suggest questions to be put by the Court.[5] All that the deponent says, although not said in answer to questions put to him, is part of the oath.[6] If documents are referred to they may be put in process, and incorporated in the deposition by reference,[7] but documents will not in general be recoverable by diligence for use at the reference.[8] When a deposition has been made it must stand. The interrogator is not of right entitled to enter upon a re-examination to clear up points. If there is ambiguity, the Court may put, or allow, questions with the view of clearing it up.

[1] 7 Edw. VII c. 51, Schedule I, Rule 65.
[2] Ibid., Rule 66.
[3] Blair v. M'Phun, 1856, 18 D. 1202.
[4] Dickson, Evidence, sec. 1486.
[5] Heslop v. Runcie, 1894, 22 R. 83.
[6] Paterson v. Cowie's Executor, 1905, 7 F. (J.) 68.
[7] See Jackson v. Cochrane, 1873, 11 M. 475; Broatch v. Dodds, 1892, 19 R. 855.
[8] Miller's Trustees v. M'Donald, (O.H.) 1931 S.L.T. 101.

The reference must be of matters of fact only, not of questions of law.[1] Particular facts may be referred. If so, these must be specifically set forth in the minute of reference.[2] If the deponent refuse to answer competent and relevant questions, he is held as confessed,[3] but he is not bound to answer an incriminating question.[4] If a party fail to appear at the diet for making oath the Sheriff may hold him as confessed, and decern accordingly.[5] It is generally stated that the oath may be taken either before the Sheriff or before a commissioner. Under the Act of Sederunt of 1839[6] a commissioner could be appointed to take the oath if the Sheriff could not attend or in any case of special emergency. That Act of Sederunt has now fallen with the repeal of the Act of 1838 to which it related,[7] and the present Act contains no direct provision for the oath being taken before a commissioner. It may be thought that the combined effect of Rules 64 and 65[8] is to recognize that the oath is competent before a commissioner, but in the absence of any direct authority it seems at least doubtful whether the Sheriff, who cannot delegate the taking of evidence save in the cases for which special provision is made, can in the general case delegate the taking of an oath on reference. There is stronger ground for thinking that if the deponent can be brought within the terms of Rules 63 or 70[9] the appointment of a commissioner is competent, although neither rule is happily expressed to cover the taking of an oath on reference.

[1] Taylor & Sons v. Hall, 1829, 7 S. 565; Conacher v. Robertson, 1829, 8 S. 141.
[2] See Finlay v. Outram, 1851, 14 D. 48; Stewart v. Clark, 1871, 8 S.L.R. 524.
[3] Murray v. Murray, 1839, 1 D. 484.
[4] Dickson, Evidence, secs. 1428-9.
[5] 7 Edw. VII c. 51, Schedule I, Rule 64. See also Rule 56.
[6] Act of Sederunt, 10th July, 1839, sec. 79.
[7] 1 & 2 Vict. c. 119 (rep. 7 Edw. VII c. 51, Schedule II).
[8] 7 Edw. VII c. 51, Schedule I, Rules 64 and 65.
[9] Ibid., Rules 63 and 70.

In determining the import of the reference, the matter is purely one of construing what the deponent has sworn to, and questions of credibility cannot be raised. The sole question is *quid juratum est*, not *quid verum est*.[1] The oath may be qualified by the deponent and the question then is whether any admissions made by him must be taken as subject to the qualification, or, in other words, whether the qualifications are intrinsic or extrinsic of the admission. Authority on this topic must be sought elsewhere. The construction of the deposition is not in general affected by averments on record.[2] The deposition is normally conclusive against the deponent only. Thus the oath of a bankrupt binds himself, but does not affect his creditors,[3] or, in an action of multiplepoinding, the oath of an arrestee binds the arrestee, but does not affect the common debtor,[4] or, in an action laid upon a debt which has been assigned, the oath of the cedent cannot, after intimation of the assignation, affect the debt.[5]

[1] Erskine iv, 2, 8; Fenning v. Meldrum, 1876, 4 R. 148.
[2] Penney v. Aitken, 1927 S.C. 673.
[3] Campbell Fraser & Co. v. Shepperd, 1823, 2 S. 517; Mein v. Towers, 1829, 7 S. 902; Ferrier v. Graham, 1831, 9 S. 419; Dyce v. Paterson, 1846, 9 D. 310; Thomson v. Duncan, 1855, 17 D. 1081.
[4] Erskine iii, 6, 16.
[5] Erskine iii, 5, 9.

The reference is in the general case to the oath of the opposing party, but in the case of household supplies the constitution of the debt may be referred to the oath of the wife and the resting owing to that of the husband.[1] Reference to the oath of an executor appears to be incompetent, and in the case of trustees is available only in certain circumstances.[2] Reference to the oath of a party's solicitor is not competent.[3] The question whether the oath of one partner will bind the firm appears to be still in some doubt.[4] In the usual case the minute simply refers the cause, or part of it, to the oath of the other party, but if the reference is to the oath of a person or persons not parties to the cause these persons should be specified in the minute, and their relationship to the other party should be stated. If a person is named in the minute the oath of that person alone can be taken, and if there is a reference to the oaths of several persons the reference is not exhausted by the oath of one of them.[5]

[1] Mitchell v. Moultry, 1882, 10 R. 378.
[2] Dickson, Evidence, secs. 1463-4.
[3] Sawers v. Clark, 1892, 19 R. 1090.
[4] Dickson, Evidence, secs. 1450-3.
[5] Cleland v. M'Lellan, 1851, 13 D. 504.   See also Bertram & Co. v. Stewart's Trustees, 1874, 2 R. 255.

In a case where it is found that the averments are provable only by writ or oath the party on whom the *onus* of proof lies may be allowed *primo loco* a proof by writ and the other party a conjunct probation also by writ. A specified time may be stated within which the writings have to be lodged. If proof by writ is not forthcoming the party bearing the *onus* may be appointed to lodge a minute referring the case to the oath of his opponent. Alternatively there may be a finding that the averments can only be proved by writ or oath, and a proof may be allowed to pursuer *habili modo*, and to defenders a conjunct probation.[1]

[1] Hallet v. Ryrie, &c., (O.H.) 1907, 15 S.L.T. 367; cf. Muir v. Steven, 1896, 12 Sh.Ct.Rep. 368; M'Cracken v. M'Cracken, 1927, 44 Sh.Ct.Rep. 297, p. 299.

Reference to oath is competent in a summary cause in the same manner as in an ordinary action. In the latter case it may be made so soon as the record has been closed and preliminary pleas disposed of. In a summary cause pleas should have been noted or defences lodged and any preliminary pleas dealt with.

CHAPTER X.

INCIDENTAL PROCEDURE.

1. GENERAL.

The rules make no provision for the procedure in relation to incidental motions, but in practice these are made by written motion, lodged in process and intimated to the other side. Such written motions are required in connexion with various steps of procedure where the step is not one which necessarily results from the case being already in the roll. Thus applications for an award of interim aliment, for a case to be restored to the roll for further procedure, for the examination of a witness on commission, and to fix a diet of proof (when this is not done at closing the record or following a debate) are all usually made by written motion.

2. AMENDMENT.

The Sheriff Courts Act, 1907, very greatly extended the power of amendment of pleadings. The present rule is that, upon the motion of either party, the Sheriff may, at any stage of the cause, and upon such conditions as to expenses, re-service or otherwise as he shall deem proper, allow a record to be altered or amended to the effect of determining the real question in controversy (including amendment of the instance and the initial writ and the adding of parties) notwithstanding that the conclusions of the action may thereby be enlarged or altered.[1] Amendment is necessary when at any stage of the cause alterations are desired in regard to the parties to the action, or the crave of the writ, or when any alteration whether on the instance, the crave or the pleadings is desired after the record has been closed.

[1] 7 Edw. VII c. 51, Schedule I, Rule 79.

Amendment is not the appropriate procedure for every alteration required on the writ or defences especially where the Statute provides a different remedy. Thus amendment is not to be confused with abandonment. It is competent, by way of amendment, to convene additional defenders in an action, but it is not competent to drop the action against one of several defenders by simply deleting his name by way of amendment. In such circumstances the proper course is to abandon the action against that defender,[1] who then obtains decree of dismissal with payment of his expenses, or alternatively gets decree of absolvitor with expenses as matter of right.[2] In the case of amendment, the awarding of expenses is in the discretion of the Sheriff.[3] Where an action has been incompetently laid against two defenders and has been dismissed as against one, it can proceed against the other without amendment.[4]

[1] See Scotland v. British Order of Ancient Free Gardeners' Friendly Society, &c., 1916, 33 Sh.Ct.Rep. 93; Malcolmson v. Sampson, &c., 1927, 44 Sh.Ct.Rep. 88; cf. Lamont & Co. v. Reid, &c., 1925, 42 Sh.Ct.Rep. 262.
[2] 7 Edw. VII c. 51, Schedule I, Rule 81.
[3] Ibid., Rule 79.
[4] Thomson v. Aitken, 1934, 50 Sh.Ct.Rep. 233. See also Fleming v. M'Gillivray, 1946 S.C. 1.

If one of several pursuers desires to retire from the case, that pursuer may put in a minute of abandonment.[1] In other cases where an action was incompetent as a result of the combination of various pursuers in one process, amendment was allowed to strike out the pursuers whose removal was necessary to render the action competent.[2]

[1] See Todd & Higginbotham v. Magistrates of Glasgow, (O.H.) 1879, 16 S.L.R. 718.
[2] Fischer & Co. v. Andersen, 1896, 23 R. 395; Paxton v. Brown, 1908 S.C. 406; Smith-Shand's Trustees v. Forbes, 1921 S.C. 820.

It is in the discretion of the Sheriff to allow amendment, and the primary consideration is whether the amendment is directed to determining the real question in controversy. In many cases proposed amendments of the instance have been refused. Thus a pursuer has not been permitted to add or substitute new defenders when this created what was substantially a new case,[1] or when such a step was necessary to render the action competent.[2] And a pursuer was not allowed to substitute a new defender for one against whom the action had been abandoned.[3] On the other hand where the liability of a third party was indicated by the original defender the former was allowed to be added as a defender.[4] Additional defenders may be added by amendment even when the case is on appeal to the Court of Session.[5] An amendment to add a new pursuer was allowed where the original pursuer had the substantial right, but was without a registered title.[6] But the addition of a new pursuer was refused where this was necessary to make the action relevant.[7] It has been suggested that the wide powers of amendment now competent in the Court of Session are implicit in the more general terms of the Sheriff Court Rule,[8] but it is thought

that there is room for distinction. In the Court of Session express
authority is now conferred to effect a cure by amendment where an
action has been begun in name of the wrong pursuer or directed
against the wrong defender.[9] It is thought that such a radical
defect could not be cured by amendment apart from express
authority, and that Rule 79 as construed by the above decisions
does not justify such a course being adopted.

   [1] M'Kenzie v. Jones, 1926, 42 Sh.Ct.Rep. 289; Kirkwood v. Campbell,
      1926, 43 Sh.Ct.Rep. 17.
   [2] Clugston v. Scottish Women's Friendly Society, 1913, 30 Sh.Ct.Rep.
      150.
   [3] Scotland v. British Order of Ancient Free Gardeners' Friendly Society,
      1916, 33 Sh.Ct.Rep. 93.
   [4] Cooney v. Murdoch, 1918, 34 Sh.Ct.Rep. 318; cf. Caven v. Provost,
      &c., of Dalbeattie, 1908, 25 Sh.Ct.Rep. 109.
   [5] Henderson v. Campbell Bros., 1937 S.C. 91.
   [6] Handy Washer Syndicate v. Vanderaa, 1921, 38 Sh.Ct.Rep. 95.
   [7] Invergordon Auction Co. v. Macmillan, 1908, 24 Sh.Ct.Rep. 187.
   [8] Lewis, Sheriff Court Practice (8th edn.), 170. See also Bethune, &c.
      v. Turnbull, 1918, 34 Sh.Ct.Rep. 309.
   [9] Rules of Court, 1936, II, 20 (a) (i) (v). See Rackstraw v. Douglas,
      1919 S.C. 354.

    Where another defender is to be added by amendment he must
be subject to the jurisdiction of the Court. An interlocutor is
pronounced directing service of the writ on the new defender, with
a copy of the interlocutor, and he is appointed to enter appearance
in the usual way.[1]

   [1] See Cooney v. Murdoch, 1918, 34 Sh.Ct.Rep. 318.

    Where parties are added in a case the application may be made
by way of amendment at the instance of the opposite party to the
action. But parties may also be added, or substituted, at their
request, and this generally happens where a change of circumstances
has occurred in the course of the action. Thus where a party
whether pursuer or defender has died, become bankrupt, or assigned
his interest in the course of the process the deceased's executor or
other representative,[1] the bankrupt's trustee[2] or the assignee[3] can
be sisted in place of the original party. This is done by minute
of sist and it would seem competent to grant a sist of this kind
even after final judgment if this has been pronounced in ignorance
of the party's death.[4] If the representative does not move to be
sisted, intimation can be made to him with a view to his doing so,
but he cannot be compelled to be a party to the process.[5] In
addition to those cases where the new parties are truly representatives of the original litigant a person wholly outside the case may
be sisted at his own request if he shows that he has a legitimate
interest to be made a party to the cause.[6] A party who is sisted

may be found liable in expenses incurred before as well as after he was sisted.[7]

[1] Martin's Executor v. M'Ghee, 1914 S.C. 628; Cumming v. Stewart, 1928 S.C. 709; X v Y, 1945 S.L.T. (Sh.Ct.) 2.
[2] Ellis v. Ellis, 1870, 8 M. 805; Gowans v. Adams, (O.H.) 1906, 14 S.L.T. 328.
[3] Parker v. Welsh, (O.H.) 1894, 2 S.L.T. 122; Fearn v. Cowpar, (O.H.) 1899, 7 S.L.T. 68; cf. Harvey v. Clark, &c., 1911, 28 Sh.Ct.Rep. 75.
[4] Scott v. Mills' Trustees, 1923 S.C. 726; Cumming v. Stewart, supra.
[5] Finklestone, &c. v. Smellie, 1916, 32 Sh.Ct.Rep. 244.
[6] See Macfie v. Scottish Rights of Way Society, 1884, 11 R. 1094 (society acting in public interest); Orr Ewing's Trustees, 1884, 12 R. 343 (beneficiary); Bruce v. Calder, 1903, 20 Sh.Ct.Rep. 288 (creditors); Addison v. Brown, (O.H.) 1910, 1 S.L.T. 185 (attestor of cautioner); Alexander v. Picken, 1946 S.L.T. 91 (local authority craving sist in right of way case on appeal to Court of Session). See also Lord Blantyre v. Lord Advocate, 1876, 13 S.L.R. 213; Glasgow Shipowners' Association v. Clyde Navigation Trustees, 1885, 12 R. 695; and cf. Laing's Sewing Machine Co. v. Norrie & Sons, 1877, 5 R. 29; Gas Power, &c., Co. v. Power Gas Corporation, 1911 S.C. 27; Muir v. Corporation of Glasgow, (O.H.) 1917, 2 S.L.T. 106.
[7] Ellis v. Ellis, supra.

Where the amendment which is proposed is an alteration on the crave of the writ the motion has generally been refused when the effect of the amendment would be a radical change in the remedy sought or an entire alteration in the nature of the crave.[1] But an amendment has been allowed which added a crave that was really ancillary to one originally in the writ.[2] In the same way the addition of an alternative crave will be permitted,[3] and the deletion of part of the crave has been allowed.[4] Where the alteration is on the defences, and not on the crave of the writ, greater latitude seems to be allowed, and an amendment raising an entirely new defence at a late stage in the case was permitted subject to payment of expenses.[5] It seems to be a sufficient reason to refuse an amendment that it is irrelevant.[6]

[1] Ford v. Ford, 1911, 28 Sh.Ct.Rep. 226; Watt Bros. v. Cormack, 1912, 29 Sh.Ct.Rep. 242; Patten v. Morison, 1919, 35 Sh.Ct.Rep. 252; Mound Motors v. Murphy, 1936, 53 Sh.Ct.Rep. 93; Richards v. Cameron, 1946, 62 Sh.Ct.Rep. 106. Cf. Amalgamated Welding Co. v. Vincent, 1946, 63 Sh.Ct.Rep. 7.
[2] Marwick v. Budge, 1933, 50 Sh.Ct.Rep. 54.
[3] Summerlee Iron Co. v. Caledonian Railway Co., 1911 S.C. 458; Mound Motors v. Murphy, supra; Delsen v. Tippett & Clyde Rubber Works Co., 1942, 59 Sh.Ct.Rep. 10.
[4] Gillespie v. Duncan, 1933, 50 Sh.Ct.Rep. 60.
[5] Mitchell v. Shanks, 1922, 40 Sh.Ct.Rep. 139. See also M'Lelland v. Mackay, 1908, 24 Sh.Ct.Rep. 157.
[6] Dick & Stevenson v. Woodside Steel & Iron Co., 1888, 16 R. 242.

When an amendment is allowed the Sheriff may impose such conditions as to expenses as he thinks proper.[1] The general principle is that expenses caused by the amendment should be placed on the party who has made the amendment. So where substantial amendments are made during the latter stages of a case it usually means that most of the prior procedure is rendered useless, and in such cases the normal condition is to find the party desiring the amendment liable in the whole of the expenses since the closing of the record.[2] This rule may be applied to amendments made after proof,[3] after the case is at avizandum,[4] or when it is on appeal.[5] Where an amendment for the pursuer made his case relevant the defender was allowed expenses from the inception of the action up to the date of amendment.[6] An amendment may be substantial and yet may not nullify earlier procedure, and thus not result in the other side having been put to unnecessary expense. In such a case a modified award of expenses will be appropriate.[7] In the same way amendments made on appeal may justify an award to the other side of merely the appeal expenses to date.[8] Minor amendments may be made at the cost of a nominal award,[9] and on an open record, or where the alteration is slight, there may be no occasion for any expenses being awarded.[10] If it is difficult at the time to reach any equitable result the expenses may be reserved.[11] Where expenses are awarded the amendment may be allowed only on these being paid,[2] or it may be provided that there should be no further procedure till the expenses awarded have been paid.[12] Where a pursuer in the Court of Session did not pay expenses of an amendment awarded against him the defender was assoilzied.[13] In the Sheriff Court, Rule 56 could be applied.[14]

1 7 Edw. VII c. 51, Schedule I, Rule 79.
2 Mitchell v. Shanks, 1922, 40 Sh.Ct.Rep. 139.
3 Stevens v. Motherwell Entertainments, 1914 S.C. 957.
4 Gray v. Scottish Society for Prevention of Cruelty to Animals, 1890, 17 R. 789.
5 Morgan, Gellibrand & Co. v. Dundee Gem Line Steam Shipping Co., 1890, 18 R. 205.
6 Haughton v. North British Railway Co., 1892, 20 R. 113.
7 Woodbury v. Sutherland's Trustees, (O.H.) 1939 S.L.T. 93.
8 Murdison v. Scottish Football Union, 1896, 23 R. 449.
9 Macdonald v. Forsyth, 1898, 25 R. 870.
10 Gillespie v. Duncan, 1933, 50 Sh.Ct.Rep. 60.
11 Clippens Oil Co. v. Edinburgh and District Water Trustees, 1905, 7 F. 914; William Beardmore & Co. v. Park's Executrix, (O.H.) 1932 S.L.T. 218.
12 Morgan, Gellibrand & Co. v. Dundee Gem Line Steam Shipping Co., supra; Haughton v. North British Railway Co., supra.
13 Dougall v. Caledonian Railway Co., 1913 S.C. 349.
14 7 Edw. VII c. 51, Schedule I, Rule 56.

Rule 80 provides that no amendment shall have the effect of validating diligence used prior thereto on the dependence of the action so as to prejudice the rights of creditors of the defender interested in defeating such diligence, but such amendment shall be operative to the effect of obviating objections to such diligence when stated by the defender himself, or by any person representing him by a title, or in right of a debt contracted by him, subsequent to the execution of such diligence.[1] This provision is common to both the Sheriff Court and the Court of Session.[2] Though the rule is not very happily expressed in this connexion it is thought that under the latter portion the representative of the defender is precluded from objecting only if his title is subsequent in date to the execution of the diligence. It must be kept in view that amendment, though allowed, may not in fact cure the defect which it is intended to remedy, and the opposing party may still insist in objections to the form of the action.[3] There is apparently nothing incompetent in amending an amendment.[4]

[1] 7 Edw. VII c. 51, Schedule I, Rule 80.
[2] See 39 & 40 Vict. c. 70, sec. 24; 31 & 32 Vict. c. 100, sec. 29; Rules of Court, 1936, II, 20 (c). See also Fischer & Co. v. Andersen, 1896, 23 R. 395.
[3] See Bank of Scotland v. Fergusson, 1898, 1 F. 96; Hope v. Derwent Rolling Mills Co., 1905, 7 F. 837.
[4] Lynch v. Stewart, 1871, 9 M. 860.

There are no statutory provisions in regard to the method of making amendments. If comparatively unimportant, a motion to amend as proposed at the Bar may be sufficient. But usually the proposed amendment should be embodied in a minute. If the amendment is to be allowed the other party should be given an opportunity of lodging answers. If amendments are made after the record has been closed it is usual to open up the record, and, the amendments having been made, of new to close it. The amendment and answers, whether contained in a minute or not, should be written on the original pleadings and on the record, if any, and these alterations should be authenticated by the Sheriff's initials.[1]

[1] 7 Edw. VII c. 51, Schedule I, Rule 53.

Under the rule the Sheriff may allow amendment at any stage of the cause.[1] Thus amendments may be allowed after proof has been taken, though stronger reasons may be needed for amending at that stage than might suffice earlier in the action.[2] Amendment may also be made when the case is at avizandum[3] or when it is on appeal,[4] but not after a judicial reference has been made.[5] Where proceedings are subject to a time limit an amendment has been allowed enlarging the sum sued for after the time limit had expired.[6] An amendment may be incompetent if it is inconsistent with interlocutors already pronounced which have not been brought under review,[7] and a proposed amendment was refused where the new averments were of facts similar to others already averred, and the purpose of the amendment was merely to obtain additional proof of these similar facts.[8] Where an amendment was allowed at the close of a proof, and judgment was given without the other party having a proper opportunity to meet the altered situation, it was held on appeal that the amendment should not have been received.[9] Where at a proof facts are established which disclose an additional ground of action or defence these facts cannot be founded on without the record being amended so as to incorporate them in the case.[10] An amendment increasing the sum sued for has been allowed though the defenders had lodged a minute consenting to decree against them as originally craved.[11]

[1] 7 Edw. VII c. 51, Schedule I, Rule 79.
[2] See M'Kenzie v. Jones, 1926, 42 Sh.Ct.Rep. 289; Union Bank of Scotland v. Fulton, 1928, 45 Sh.Ct.Rep. 62; and cf. Coul v. Ayr County Council, 1909 S.C. 422; Stevens v. Motherwell Entertainments, 1914 S.C. 957.
[3] Gray v. Scottish Society for Prevention of Cruelty to Animals, 1890, 17 R. 789; Govan Rope, &c., Co. v. Weir & Co.. 1897, 24 R. 368.
[4] Rose v. Johnston, 1878, 5 R. 600; Guinness, Mahon & Co. v. Coats Iron Co., 1891, 18 R. 441; Stevens v. Motherwell Entertainments, supra; Henderson v. Campbell Bros., 1937 S.C. 91. See also Gairdner v. Macarthur, 1914, 30 Sh.Ct.Rep. 179; 1915 S.C. 589.
[5] Brown's Trustees v. Horne, 1907 S.C. 1027.
[6] Mackie v. Glasgow Corporation, &c., (O.H.) 1924 S.L.T. 510.
[7] Arthur v. Lindsay, 1895, 22 R. 417; Terrell v. Ker, 1900, 2 F. 1055. See also MacGown v. Cramb, 1897, 24 R. 481.
[8] Brown v. Hastie & Co., 1904, 6 F. 1001.
[9] Oswald v. Fairs, 1911 S.C. 257.
[10] Black v. John Williams & Co., 1924 S.C. (H.L.) 23; Vitruvia S.S. Co. v. Ropner Shipping Co., 1924 S.C. (H.L.) 31.
[11] Cowie v. Carron Co., 1945 S.C. 280.

Amendment is competent in a summary cause as well as in an ordinary action, subject to such conditions as to expenses, re-service or otherwise as the Sheriff shall deem proper.[1] In view of the wide discretion given to the Sheriff in regard to procedure in summary causes,[2] greater latitude would appear to be permissible in connexion with amendment in such cases.[3] Thus in a defended summary cause it may be competent, by way of amendment, practically to substitute a new case or a new defence for that originally set up. But when a party desires to amend in such a way as practically to subvert his original pleading, and to set up a new case, the Court will probably attach stringent conditions in regard to expenses. As the record is not usually closed in a summary cause there is generally not the same need for amendment of the condescendence, answers, and pleas.

[1] 7 Edw. VII c. 51, Schedule I, Rule 79.
[2] Ibid., sec. 8; Schedule I, Rule 41; 2 & 3 Geo. V c. 28, Schedule II.
[3] See M'Lelland v. Mackay, 1908, 24 Sh.Ct.Rep. 157.

In an undefended action the Sheriff may allow the pursuer to amend any error or defect in the initial writ, and may, if he see fit, order the amended writ to be served on the defender, and may allow him to appear within such time as he may think proper.[1] The reference to error or defect in the writ suggests a restriction in the scope of amendment in undefended, as compared with defended, cases. If the defect is radical, as, for instance, the wrong ground of action has been libelled, it is doubtful whether amendment is competent or appropriate and it is better to serve a fresh action.

[1] 7 Edw. VII c. 51, Schedule I, Rule 26.

As in defended cases[1] the rule provides that amendment of an undefended action shall not have the effect of validating diligence used on the dependence of the action so as to prejudice creditors of the defender, but that such amendment shall be operative to the effect of obviating objections to such diligence when stated by the defender himself, or by any persons representing him by a title, or in right of a debt contracted by him, subsequent to the using of such diligence.[2]

[1] See p. 238, supra.
[2] 7 Edw. VII c. 51, Schedule I, Rule 26.

It is also provided in the case of undefended actions that the expense occasioned by any such amendment shall not be chargeable against the defender, and that any diligence which was competent upon the original writ shall be competent upon the amended writ.[1] It is not clear what meaning is to be attached to the latter provision. As the power to amend is not as broad in an undefended as in a defended cause, it is difficult to visualize such a change in the form of action as would give this provision any practical effect. It can hardly be intended that, if the pecuniary crave in an undefended action was dropped by amendment, arrestment on the dependence would remain competent merely because of the original form of the writ.

[1] 7 Edw. VII c. 51, Schedule I, Rule 26.

It is specially provided that the Sheriff, when a case is before him on appeal, may open up the record *ex proprio motu* if it

shall appear to him not to have been properly made up.[1] It is
not clear that this provides anything more than would be covered
by the normal powers of amendment[2] which in any Court are
available on appeal.[3]

[1] 7 Edw. VII c. 51, sec. 27; 2 & 3 Geo. V c. 28, Schedule I.
[2] Hutchison v. Davidson, 1945 S.C. 395.
[3] See p. 239, supra.

3. Deletion of Irrelevant or Scandalous Averments.

Conflicting decisions have been given on the question whether
the Sheriff is empowered to order the deletion of averments as
irrelevant or scandalous,[1] but it appears to be the better view
that such a power is inherent in the Court. In certain cases the
averments complained of have been allowed to remain on record
but have been excluded from probation.[2] An objection of this kind
should be raised before the record is closed though a discussion
upon it may be postponed until the record has been closed.[3]

[1] Robertson v. Smith, 1904, 21 Sh.Ct.Rep. 100; Kennan v. Stranraer
Creamery Co., 1908, 24 Sh.Ct.Rep. 326; M'Isaac v. Leonard, 1915,
31 Sh.Ct.Rep. 303.
[2] Inglis v. National Bank of Scotland, 1909 S.C. 1038; A v. C, (O.H.)
1922 S.L.T. 34; M'Isaac v. Leonard, supra; Galloway v. Cruickshank, (O.H.) 1928 S.N. 159; Scott v. Cormack Heating Engineers,
1942 S.C. 159; cf. A v. B, 1895, 22 R. 402; H v. P, 1905, 8 F. 232;
Oliver v. Borland, (O.H.) 1911, 2 S.L.T. 46; C v. M, 1923 S.C. 1.
[3] Kennan v. Stranraer Creamery Co., supra; M'Isaac v. Leonard, supra.

4. Wakening.

If no interlocutor has been pronounced in a cause for a year
and a day, the action is held to have fallen asleep,[1] and it is
necessary to have the cause wakened before any further procedure
can take place. If all parties want it wakened, a minute to that
effect is endorsed on the interlocutor sheet and subscribed by the
parties or their solicitors.[2] If the parties do not all concur, a
party desiring to have the action wakened may lodge a minute
which is intimated and published as the Sheriff shall direct.[3] The
solicitor of the party applying to have the cause wakened has to
lodge a certificate of intimation and publication, and, if satisfied,
the Sheriff may then waken the cause and proceed with it.[3] The
action resumes at the stage at which it fell asleep, and the interlocutor wakening the cause may conveniently send it to the appropriate roll for procedure, or otherwise provide for the next step
in the process.

[1] 7 Edw. VII c. 51, Schedule I, Rule 101.
[2] Ibid., Rule 102.
[3] Ibid., Rule 103.

The period of a year and day runs consecutively during session and vacation alike. A sist of process does not apparently prevent an action from falling asleep,[1] but the cause will be kept awake by the pronouncement of any interlocutor, however formal. An action which has been served, but in which no other step has been taken within a year and day of the expiry of the induciæ, cannot be wakened; nor can it be revived by applying for a new warrant of service.[2] In such circumstances a new action must be brought.[3] Wakening is competent although the cause has been asleep for longer than the period of the negative prescription,[4] or although the cause is undefended.[5]

[1] American Mortgage Co. of Scotland v. Sidway, (O.H.) 1906, 44 S.L.R. 170.
[2] M'Kidd v. Manson, 1882, 9 R. 790; Belfrage v. Blyth, 1910, 26 Sh.Ct.Rep. 295; Hillhead Garage v. Bunten & Miller, 1924, 40 Sh.Ct.Rep. 208; Hughes v. Scott, 1940, 56 Sh.Ct.Rep. 176.
[3] Robb & Crosbie v. Forbes, 1911, 27 Sh.Ct.Rep. 162.
[4] Barr v. Wallace, 1912, 29 Sh.Ct.Rep. 171.
[5] Hunter v. Duke of Leinster, (O.H.) 1933 S.L.T. 518.

5. ABANDONMENT.

A pursuer may, at any stage of an action, before an interlocutor granting absolvitor or dismissing the action has been pronounced, offer to abandon the action.[1] A minute to that effect is lodged, signed by the pursuer or his solicitor, and, upon payment to defender of his expenses, the Sheriff may dismiss the action and pursuer may bring a new action if otherwise competent.[1] If the pursuer fails, within fourteen days of the date of taxation, to pay the defender's expenses, the defender is entitled to decree of absolvitor with expenses.[1]

[1] 7 Edw. VII c. 51, Schedule I, Rule 81.

It might have been thought that Rule 81 prescribed the only manner in which an action could now be abandoned in the Sheriff Court, but it has been held that abandonment at common law is still competent. Common law abandonment has been recognized as a means of releasing one of several defenders from a case,[1] and as the appropriate method where a pursuer desired to abandon absolutely and without reserving right to bring a fresh action.[2] In the case of common law abandonment expenses are in the discretion of the Court but the defender is entitled to absolvitor.[1] It was formerly held that abandonment immediately after service of the writ might be made by letter and by judicial admission in a new action.[3] In view of the recognition of abandonment other that under Rule 81 it may be that this procedure is still competent,

but the position is doubtful and it is thought that even at this
stage abandonment should be made under Rule 81.

1 Malcolmson v. Sampson, &c., 1927, 44 Sh.Ct.Rep. 88; cf. Scotland
    v. British Order of Ancient Free Gardeners' Friendly Society, &c.,
    1916, 33 Sh.Ct.Rep. 93.
2 Goldie v. Chrysler Motors, 1938, 55 Sh.Ct.Rep. 99.
3 Laidlaw v. Smith, 1834, 12 S. 538; M'Aulay v. Cowe, 1873, 1 R.
    307.   See also Roxburgh v. Commercial Bank of Scotland, 1903,
    19 Sh.Ct.Rep. 248.

When abandonment is made under Rule 81 the minute should
simply state that the pursuer offers to abandon the action in terms
of the Act.   If a solicitor signs the minute he should get a special
mandate, as a general agency mandate does not cover abandoning
an action.[1]   The defender, upon the minute being lodged, obtains
his expenses taxed, and upon payment of these expenses the action
is dismissed, leaving the pursuer free to bring a new action if
competent.   If defender will not accept payment of the taxed
expenses, the pursuer may get the action dismissed by consigning
the amount of the expenses.[2]   Payment of defender's expenses is an
essential condition of abandonment which can only be departed
from of consent of parties.[3]   Till the abandoned action is actually
out of Court, a new action is not competent.[4]

1 See Urquhart v. Grigor, 1857, 19 D. 853.
2 See Lawson v. Low, 1845, 7 D. 960.
3 Scott v. Thurso River Harbour Trustees, 1895, 23 R. 268.
4 Aitken v. Dick, 1863, 1 M. 1038; Kennedy v. Macdonald, 1876, 3 R.
    813.   See also Lee v. Pollock's Trustees, 1906, 8 F. 857, Lord
    President Dunedin, p. 860.

A minute of abandonment may be withdrawn at any time previous to the entry in the Court books[1] of an interlocutor sustaining
the minute and dismissing the action.[2]   The Court may impose
conditions as to expenses in granting leave to withdraw the minute,
but if the minute stands, and the pursuer timeously pays or consigns the defender's expenses, the Court has no option, and is bound
to dismiss the action.   In this connexion it is thought to be clear
that the use in the rule of the phrase " offer to abandon " in no
way qualifies the pursuer's right to abandon on the terms laid down
in the rule.   If a minute of abandonment is withdrawn the pursuer
may be required to show that his proceedings have been *in bona fide*
before he is allowed to go on with the case.[3]

1 See 7 Edw. VII c. 51, Schedule I, Rule 83.
2 Todd & Higginbotham v. Glasgow Corporation, 1879, 16 S.L.R. 718;
    Dalgleish v. Mitchell, 1886, 23 S.L.R. 552; Lee v. Pollock's Trustees,
    1906, 8 F. 857.
3 Lee v. Pollock's Trustees, supra.

As stated above,[1] abandonment is the appropriate method for releasing one of several defenders, and it is not necessary that the other defenders consent.[2] It is also the proper course when one of several pursuers desires to withdraw from an action.[3] Where pursuers had obtained decree in absence against one of two defenders it was held that they could not thereafter abandon the action against that defender in order to insist in their claim against the other.[4] It seems doubtful whether partial abandonment withdrawing part of what was originally craved is competent and in such circumstances the correct procedure is by minute of restriction.[5] Where an action in which there was a counter-claim was abandoned it was held that the defender could not thereafter proceed with his counter-claim.[6] But this decision turned partly on the manner in which the counter-claim was stated, and it is thought that, on the terms of Rule 55,[7] a counter-claim can proceed although the original claim of the pursuer has been abandoned.[8]

[1] See p. 235, supra.
[2] Malcolmson v. Sampson, &c., 1927, 44 Sh.Ct.Rep. 88.
[3] Todd & Higginbotham v. Glasgow Corporation, 1879, 16 S.L.R. 718.
[4] Lamont & Co. v. Reid, &c., 1925, 42 Sh.Ct.Rep. 262.
[5] M'Sorley v. Archibald, 1922 S.C. 26.
[6] Craw v. Malcolm, 1908, 24 Sh.Ct.Rep. 268.
[7] 7 Edw. VII c. 51, Schedule I, Rule 55.
[8] Armour & Melvin v. Mitchell, 1934 S.C. 94.

The expenses to which a defender is entitled on abandonment will normally be those which he could have recovered from the pursuer on a decree of absolvitor with expenses, and prior findings as to expenses will not usually be affected or disturbed.[1] The Court will not grant decree for expenses against the pursuer, as upon the minute of abandonment, as it is optional to the pursuer to pay these and the defender's *compulsiter* if payment is not made is to obtain absolvitor with expenses, when a decree can be granted, but it is thought that this does not prevent the Sheriff from dealing with objections to the auditor's report arising on taxation of the defender's account of expenses.[2]

[1] Nobel's Explosives Co. v. British Dominions General Insurance Co., 1919 S.C. 455; Lord Hamilton v. Glasgow Dairy Co., 1933 S.C. 18; cf. P v. P, 1940 S.C. 389.
[2] See Lee v. Pollock's Trustees, 1906, 8 F. 857; Buchanan & French v. Watson, 1910, 26 Sh.Ct.Rep. 246. See also Todd & Higginbotham v. Glasgow Corporation, 1879, 16 S.L.R. 718.

A defender does not proceed by abandonment, but if he is not to insist in his defences he should lodge a minute withdrawing them and consenting to decree.[1] Apart from such formal withdrawal, if the defender ceases to attend the cause the pursuer may ask decree by default.[2]

[1] See Paterson v. St. Andrew's Magistrates, 1880, 7 R. 712; Ower v. Crichton, 1902, (O.H.) 10 S.L.T. 279.
[2] 7 Edw. VII c. 51, Schedule I, Rule 56.

6. DISCLAIMER.

A minute of disclaimer is somewhat akin to a minute of abandonment. It is the mode by which a party, who has been made a litigant either as pursuer or defender without his consent, gets out of the process. Parties will be heard on the minute of disclaimer and, if necessary, answers to it may be lodged.[1] If the minute is sustained the disclaimer may be awarded expenses against the parties who have convened him in the process without his consent,[2] or against the solicitor who used his name without authority.[3]

[1] See Cambuslang West Church Committee v. Bryce, 1897, 25 R. 322; Muir & Rutherford v. Ford & Torrie, 1932, 49 Sh.Ct.Rep. 214.
[2] Cambuslang West Church Committee v. Bryce, supra.
[3] Fairlie v. Fairlie's Trustees, (O.H.) 1903, 11 S.L.T. 51; cf. Cassidy v. Bilsland, 1907, 15 S.L.T. 615. See also Ferguson, Davidson & Co. v. Paterson & Dobbie, 1898, 1 F. 227.

Where a sole pursuer, or all the pursuers, disclaim, it is not generally competent to sist another party as pursuer as no valid action has been brought into Court.[1] Where a corporation is a party to a cause dissenting members cannot disclaim the proceedings as the corporation is bound to act as resolved by a majority.[2] The opposite view has been taken in relation to a body of trustees.[3]

[1] Ferguson, Davidson & Co. v. Paterson & Dobbie, 1898, 1 F. 227; Gordon v. Purves, 1903, 11 S.L.T. 38. See also p. 235, supra.
[2] Eadie v. Glasgow Corporation, 1908 S.C. 207.
[3] Fairlie v. Fairlie's Trustees, (O.H.) 1903, 11 S.L.T. 51.

CHAPTER XI.

JUDGMENT.

1. FORM.

Rule 82 provides that in his final judgment on the merits the Sheriff shall set forth his findings in fact and in law separately; and that to all interlocutors, except those of a formal nature, he shall append a note setting forth the grounds upon which he has proceeded.[1] These provisions apply both in summary[2] and in ordinary causes. In the case of summary applications the Sheriff is directed to dispose of the matter summarily and to give his judgment in writing.[3] In view of this direction Rule 82 is probably inapplicable to summary applications, but it is thought that, where such an application is contested a note of the grounds of judgment should be appended to the interlocutor disposing of it, and that, where evidence has been taken, there should be findings in fact and in law. The note and findings should be given in all such applications where there is a right of appeal.[4] The findings in fact, as well as the findings in law, must be in the interlocutor itself, and not in the note,[5] and it has been indicated that the findings in fact should include not only the bare facts upon which the judgment is based, but all the relevant facts material to the contentions of either of the parties.[6] Besides the obvious convenience to any appellate Court, the separation of findings in fact and findings in law is of importance if the case goes to the House of Lords, for, if a cause has originated in the Sheriff Court, the findings in law only are subject to review in the supreme tribunal.[7] The findings should be numbered.[8] Where two or more defenders are found jointly and severally liable in damages or expenses the Court may decide as to the proportion in which they shall be liable to contribute *inter se*.[9] In cases to which the Law Reform (Contributory Negligence) Act applies the total damages as well as the sum recoverable must be stated.[10]

[1] 7 Edw. VII c. 51, Schedule I, Rule 82.
[2] See also ibid., sec. 8.
[3] Ibid., sec. 50.
[4] See Kerr v. Annandale Steamship Co., 1926, 43 Sh.Ct.Rep. 44.
[5] Glasgow Gas Co. v. Working Men's Abstinence Society, 1866, 4 M. 1041; Melrose v. Spalding, 1868, 6 M. 952; Mackay v. Mackenzie, 1894, 21 R. 894; M'Caffer v. Allan, 1896, 33 S.L.R. 601.

6 Little v. Stevenson & Co., 1896, 23 R. (H.L.) 12, Lord Herschell, p. 15.
7 6 Geo. IV, c. 120, sec. 40. See Mackay v. Dick & Stevenson, 1881,
　　8 R. (H.L.) 37; Caird v. Sime, 1887, 14 R. (H.L.) 37.
8 Calderwood v. Magistrates of Dundee, 1944 S.C. 24.
9 3 & 4 Geo. VI c. 42, sec. 3 (1). See Broomberg v. Reinhold & Co.,
　　1942, 60 Sh.Ct.Rep. 45; Anderson v. St. Andrews' Ambulance
　　Association, 1943 S.C. 248.
10 8 & 9 Geo. VI c. 28, sec. 1.

2. DATE.

The Sheriff may pronounce or sign any judgment or interlocutor
when furth of his Sheriffdom, but the date of every interlocutor
is deemed to be the date of its entry in the books of Court.[1]
Omission to sign a merely formal interlocutor may not invalidate
a process, but if an interlocutor of consequence, as, for instance,
allowing proof, is unsigned, all the subsequent proceedings may
be held to be inept.[2]

1 7 Edw. VII c. 57, Schedule I, Rule 83.
2 Smith v. M'Aulay & Co., 1846, 9 D. 190.

3. REVISION.

A clerical or incidental error may be corrected before extract,
or before transmission of the process in an appeal,[1] but if any party
desires an alteration in an interlocutor, he should call attention to
it immediately the interlocutor is issued.[2] Corrections should be
initialled by the Sheriff.[3] What is a " clerical or incidental "
error is a question of circumstances, but it is thought that it would
include any reasonable correction which did not alter the substance
of the judgment.[4] When a party had failed to move for expenses
a later motion for these was held not to be a competent correction
of the interlocutor.[5] If an interlocutor has been pronounced in
error, it may be recalled or corrected of consent,[6] but it is doubtful
whether the Sheriff has the same powers as the Court of Session[7] to
deal with an interlocutor otherwise than of consent where the
alteration goes beyond the correction of a clerical or incidental
error. Where an interlocutor bears to be granted of consent and
the giving of consent is denied the matter can probably be
reopened.[8] It is not competent to issue a second interlocutor
modifying or explaining an earlier one.[9]

1 7 Edw. VII c. 51, Schedule I, Rule 84.
2 Kennedy v. Clyde Shipping Co., 1908 S.C. 895; Bruce v. Bruce, 1945
　　S.C. 353. See also Burke v. Harvey, (O.H.) 1916, 2 S.L.T. 315;
　　Lauder v. National Bank of Scotland, (O.H.) 1918, 1 S.L.T. 43;
　　Torry v. Torry, (O.H.) 1919, 1 S.L.T. 161.
3 Clark & Macdonald v. Bain, 1895, 23 R. 102.
4 See Cuthill v. Burns, 1862, 24 D. 849; Moncreiffe v. Perth Police
　　Commissioners, 1886, 13 R. 921; and other cases, supra.

[5] Campbell v. Campbell, (O.H.) 1934 S.L.T. 45.
[6] Rottenburg v. Duncan, 1896, 24 R. 35; Gillon's Trustees v. Gillon, 1903, 40 S.L.R. 461.
[7] See Ritchie v. Ferguson, 1848, 12 D. 119; Harvey v. Lindsay, 1875, 2 R. 980.
[8] See Whyte v. Whyte, 1895, 23 R. 320.
[9] Edington v. Astley, 1829, 8 S. 192.

Where an interlocutor had been pronounced in ignorance of the fact that one of the parties to a case had died, the Court of Session on the deceased's representatives being sisted, repeated the interlocutor to suit the altered circumstances.[1] It is thought that in a similar situation the Sheriff would be entitled to follow the same course.

[1] Scott v. Mills' Trustees, 1923 S.C. 726; Cumming v. Stewart, 1928 S.C. 709.

A decree granted after both parties have been heard, and where both have been represented in the course of the process, is, in the strictest sense, a judgment *in foro;* but, in practice the expression decree *in foro* receives a wider interpretation, and every decree which is pronounced by the Sheriff-Substitute or the Sheriff, in a case in which the defender has appeared, is a decree *in foro*, as distinguished from a decree in absence, which is granted as a matter of course where the defender does not answer at all.

4. Decree by Default.

Where a process is not followed out to a conclusion on the merits, but, in the course of it, one party fails to prosecute his side of the litigation, the other party may become entitled to decree, and this is in practice termed a decree by default. Such a decree can be granted only in a defended cause, but it may be granted either in a summary cause process, or an ordinary action process, the relevant provisions of the Act[1] being applicable to both. The rule provides that in a defended action (including a jury cause) when any production or pleading has not been lodged, or order implemented, within the time required by Statute or ordered by the Sheriff, or where in a defended action either party fails to appear, by himself or his agent, at any diet, or fails to make payment of any Court dues or deposit, the Sheriff may grant decree as craved, or of absolvitor, or may dismiss the action, with expenses, but the Sheriff may upon cause shown prorogate the time for lodging any production or pleading, or implementing any order.[1] If all parties fail to appear the Sheriff is directed, unless sufficient reason appear to the contrary, to dismiss the action.[1] Similar provision is made in the case of non-payment of Court fees collected by the Sheriff-clerk.[2] Failure to pay shorthand writer's fees after an order for payment had been made by the Court[3] would apparently fall under Rule 56.

[1] 7 Edw. VII c. 51, Schedule I, Rule 56.
[2] See Act of Sederunt, 16th July, 1929, sec. 2.
[3] 7 Edw. VII c. 51, Schedule I, Rule 67.

A judgment by default may be pronounced at any time after appearance has been made by or for the defender, that is to say, at any time after the action has become a defended cause, and where the granting of decree in absence has thus become incompetent. Reponing is not a competent remedy for any failure on the part of a defender who has once appeared, because reponing applies only to a decree in absence,[1] and a decree by default is not a decree in absence. Although it may be pronounced in the absence of the other party from an appointed diet, it is a decree *in foro*. Failure to lodge defences entitles the pursuer to decree by default and not to a decree in absence.[2]

[1] See 7 Edw. VII c. 51, Schedule I, Rules 27-33. See also West v. Hair, 1926, 43 Sh.Ct.Rep. 118.
[2] See West v. Hair, supra.

A decree by default is a final judgment which the Sheriff at his own hand cannot alter, although on appeal the Sheriff Principal or the Court of Session might in effect repone the defender, by recalling the decree and remitting the cause back, if the circumstances appeared to warrant that being done, and upon conditions as to expenses. No general principle can be inferred from the decisions as to the circumstances in which a defender will be reponed on appeal.[1] In many of the cases the default had arisen from neglect, or from an over-sight, on the part of the defender's solicitor. In such cases reponing has sometimes been granted on payment of expenses,[2] and sometimes it has been refused.[3] Where the default occurred in the course of settlement negotiations the defender was reponed on payment of modified expenses,[4] and reponing was also granted in another case where the default was a failure to lodge accounts.[5] In a recent case[6] the Court indicated a general willingness to repone in cases of default occasioned by carelessness, if there was a real defence on the merits, but they refused to repone in that case as the defence appeared to have no substantial foundation. Where decree of absolvitor is granted by default a new action

on the same grounds is incompetent while the original decree
stands.[7]

[1] Hyslop v. Flaherty, 1933 S.C. 588.
[2] Morrison v. Smith, 1876, 4 R. 9; Vickers & Son v. Nibloe, 1877, 4 R.
729; Robb v. Eglin, 1877, 14 S.L.R. 473; King v. Gavan, 1880,
17 S.L.R. 583; M'Carthy v. Emery, 1897, 24 R. 610.
[3] M'Gibbon v. Thomson, 1877, 4 R. 1085; Stevenson v. Hutcheson &
Anderson, 1885, 12 R. 923; Bain v. Lawson & Son, 1899, 1 F. 576;
Lanark County Council v. Motherwell Commissioners, 1901, 4 F.
151; Lord Brooke v. Marchioness of Huntly, 1911, 49 S.L.R. 71;
Galpern v. Thomson, 1917 S.C. 24.
[4] Bainbridge v. Bainbridge, 1879, 6 R. 541.
[5] Brown's Trustees v. Milne, 1897, 24 R. 1139.
[6] M'Kelvie v. Scottish Steel Scaffolding Co., 1938 S.C. 278.
[7] Forest v. Dunlop, 1875, 3 R. 15.

One of the situations in which decree by default is competent
is where a party fails to appear by himself or his agent at any
diet.[1] In a summary cause the defender is required to answer at
the first diet, when the case is called. If he fails to appear at this
diet the decree given is a decree in absence not a decree by default.
Rule 56 does not apply in such circumstances as it relates only to
defended actions. On the other hand, in a summary cause, if the
defender answers at the first diet, and the pursuer fails to appear,
the defender's remedy it is thought is to crave protestation under
Rule 36,[2] not to crave decree by default under Rule 56. This is on
the view that for the purpose of the former rule the first diet in a
summary cause must be regarded as the equivalent of tabling in an
ordinary action. The distinction between a decree in absence and
a decree by default is not of much moment in a summary cause, for
either decree is extractable in seven days.[3] It is, however, of some
consequence in an ordinary action, for the decree in absence is
extractable after the lapse of seven days,[4] and the decree by default
not till after the lapse of fourteen days, unless the Sheriff shortens
the period.[3]

[1] 7 Edw. VII c. 51, Schedule I, Rule 56. Where a party appears by an
agent who is not prepared to proceed with the case at that stage
a decree by default is not appropriate; Finlay v. Bush, 1925 S.L.T.
(Sh.Ct.) 140; Jack v. Wardrop, 1927, 44 Sh.Ct.Rep. 61.
[2] Ibid., Schedule I, Rule 36; Higgins v. Atkinson, 1908, 24 Sh.Ct.Rep.
385.
[3] Ibid., Schedule I, Rule 85; 17 & 18 Geo. V c. 35, sec. 21.
[4] Ibid., Schedule I, Rule 24.

Although a party has made himself liable to decree by default,
such decree need not necessarily be pronounced, and the matter is
left to the discretion of the Sheriff.[1] The statutory alternatives
are: (a) To grant decree as craved, or of absolvitor; (b) to dismiss
the action with expenses; or (c) upon cause shown to prorogate the

time for lodging any production or pleading or implementing **any** order.[1] In a case of failure to appear it is thought that the Sheriff **has a** discretion to afford the defaulting party another opportunity of appearing at a later diet. It is competent for the Sheriff to prorogate the time for lodging a paper or implementing an order, either during the currency of the period originally allowed or after its expiry.[2]

[1] 7 Edw. VII c. 51, Schedule I, Rule 56.
[2] Macnab v. Nelson, 1909 S.C. 1102.

5. GOVERNMENT AND OTHER DUTIES.

It is provided by Act of Sederunt that no decree, warrant or order for payment of any consigned money, and no decree, warrant or order for transfer or conveyance to any person of any stocks, shares or other property, heritable or moveable, in any process for the distribution of the estate of any deceased, pending in the Sheriff Court, shall issue until there is lodged with the Sheriff-clerk a certificate by the proper officer in the department of Inland Revenue that all income tax, estate duty, legacy duty, succession duty and any other duty payable to the commissioners of Inland Revenue have been paid and satisfied to the department in respect of any such money, stocks, shares or other property or any part thereof so to be paid, transferred or conveyed as aforesaid.[1] The first part of the above provision as to consigned money is in general terms and does not seem to be limited to a process for distribution of a deceased's estate. But in practice the provision is not applied in cases where no question of duty or tax can arise, as in consignation not in relation to a deceased's estate where no interest has accrued up to the order for payment.

[1] Codifying Act of Sederunt, L, III, 1; Act of Sederunt, 16th July, 1936, sec. 3.

CHAPTER XII.

OPERATING JUDGMENT.

1. Extract.

The foundation for diligence in execution of a decree of Court is an extract of the judgment, containing the warrant for execution, and as regards the form of extract, there is no difference between a summary cause and an ordinary action, although there is a difference in the time within which extract may be obtained.

The form of extract is regulated by the Sheriff Courts (Scotland) Extracts Act, 1892,[1] but the Act does not apply to extracts in the Small Debt Court, in summary ejections under sec. 38, and Rules 115 to 122, of the Sheriff Courts Act, 1907, in commissary or executry proceedings, in proceedings for service of heirs or completing titles, or in proceedings under the Summary Jurisdiction (Scotland) Act, 1908.[2] An abbreviated form of extract is provided in the Act,[1] and the import of the warrant of execution is defined by the Statute.[3] In cases not specially provided for the form of extract is to be modelled on the forms contained in the schedule to the Act.[4] It is not necessary for the purpose of extracting that the decree should contain the word " decerns."[1]

[1] 55 & 56 Vict. c. 17, sec. 4.
[2] Ibid., sec. 2.
[3] Ibid., sec. 7.
[4] Ibid., sec. 5.

The extract of a decree for payment expressly authorizes immediate arrestment and also grants warrant for poinding after a charge has been given, the induciæ of the charge being stated in the extract.[1] Where imprisonment of the debtor is a competent remedy warrant for this is included.[2]

[1] 55 & 56 Vict. c. 17, Schedule I.
[2] Ibid., sec. 7 (1).

Extracting a final judgment is the official closing of the process. After extract, no further step can be taken, and reference to oath is not competent. Neither can the decree be corrected or altered, for the process is no longer depending.[1] Accordingly, if it is desired to supersede extract for a certain time, that should be

253

expressed in the decree itself, for the Sheriff has no power to stay execution upon a final decree which has been extracted.

1 See Edington v. Astley, 1829, 8 S. 192, and cf. Clark & Macdonald v. Bain, 1895, 23 R. 102; Mitchell's Trustees, 1930 S.C. 180.

The time within which an extract may be demanded is (a) on a decree in absence, whether in a summary cause or an ordinary action, seven days[1]; (b) on any decree in a summary cause, seven days[2]; (c) on any decree in an ordinary action—not being in absence or for expenses—fourteen days[2]; (d) on a decree for expenses, whether in a summary cause or an ordinary action, seven days.[3] Extract of a decree disposing of the merits does not preclude the subsequent issue of extract of a later interlocutor decerning for expenses.[4]

1 7 Edw. VII c. 51, Schedule I, Rule 24.
2 Ibid., Rule 85.
3 Ibid., Rule 98.
4 Tennents v. Romanes, 1881, 8 R. 824; Mackintosh v. Young, (O.H.) 1886, 23 S.L.R. 634; 2 Sh.Ct.Rep. 196. See also Crichton Bros. v. Crichton, 1901, 4 F. 271.

The time for extract in all cases counts from the date of the interlocutor, that is, from the date upon which it is entered in the Court books,[1] and the days which must elapse are clear days. In an ordinary action the Sheriff is given express power to shorten the normal time for extract,[2] and extract of a decree for expenses is to be issued after the lapse of seven days unless otherwise directed by the Sheriff,[3] which implies that in this case the time for extract may be either shortened or extended. Apart from these provisions the Sheriff may indirectly extend the time by superseding extract,[4] or, in certain interlocutors, by making the issue of extract conditional upon caution being found[5]; but conditions of this sort are not alterations of the statutory extract time, but rather part of the decree. In the case of decrees other than those in absence and for expenses it is provided that extract may be issued within the times already stated unless an appeal has been taken or leave to appeal has been applied for, but application for leave to appeal does not preclude the issue of extract unless leave is granted and an appeal is taken within seven days after leave is granted.[6]

1 7 Edw. VII c. 51, Schedule I, Rule 83.
2 Ibid., Rule 85.
3 Ibid., Rule 98.
4 See Bruce v. M'Lellan, 1925 S.C. 103; MacLean v. Clan Line Steamers, 1925 S.C. 256.
5 See Simpson v. Jack, 1888, 16 R. 131.
6 7 Edw. VII c. 51, Schedule I, Rule 85; 17 & 18 Geo. V c. 35, sec. 21.

The terms of Rule 85[1] raise a doubt as to whether the Sheriff has the power of shortening the period of extract in a summary cause. As the rule is punctuated it suggests that, as regards shortening the period, a distinction is intended to be created between a " summary cause " in the first part of the rule, and " any other cause " in the second part. But as punctuation is not used in the interpretation of Statutes, and as the Sheriff formerly had the power of shortening the extract period it is thought that the Rule should not be construed so as to take away this power. While the matter is not free from doubt the view that the last clause in the rule is intended to qualify the period of extract in both summary and ordinary causes is to some extent supported by the manner in which the recent amendment of this rule has been effected.[2] It is thought that the Sheriff has no power to shorten the period of seven days for extracting a decree in absence.[3]

[1] 7 Edw. VII c. 51, Schedule I, Rule 85.
[2] See 17 & 18 Geo. V c. 35, sec. 21.
[3] 7 Edw. VII c. 51, Schedule I, Rule 24. See Dove Wilson, Sheriff Court Practice, 4th edn., pp. 131, 326.

Where interest is included in a decree or extract it is deemed to be at the rate of 5 per cent. per annum, unless otherwise stated.[1] If interest has been craved in the initial writ it is generally asked and decerned for as from the date of citation. If it is not decerned for at all, interest will run only from the date of the decree, and, where the decree has been affirmed on appeal, from the date of the judgment on appeal.[2] A decree for expenses is deemed to include the expenses of extract.[3] A person tendering payment of taxed expenses before their formal approval is entitled to deduction of the unincurred items,[4] but the party in whose favour a decree on the merits has been granted will be entitled to the expenses of extracting that decree if he has an interest to obtain an extract.[5]

[1] 55 & 56 Vict. c. 17, sec. 9.
[2] See Wallace v. Henderson, 1876, 4 R. 264; Roger v. J. & P. Cochrane & Co., 1910 S.C. 1.
[3] 7 Edw. VII c. 51, Schedule I, Rule 98.
[4] Leith Magistrates v. Gibb, 1882, 19 S.L.R. 399; Bannatyne v. M'Lean, 1884, 11 R. 681.
[5] Orr v. Smith, (O.H.) 1891, 28 S.L.R. 539; Rutherglen Parish Council v. Glenbucket Parish Council, (O.H.) 1896, 33 S.L.R. 368; Glasgow District Subway Co. v. M'Callum, 1896, 12 Sh.Ct.Rep. 148.

2. REGISTRATION DECREE.

The warrant for executing diligence is not necessarily an extract of a decree in a Court process. Any writ containing a clause of consent to registration for execution may be recorded in the books of Court, and an extract is, for purposes of diligence, equivalent to an extract following upon a decree of Court.[1] So also sums due under bills of exchange or promissory notes need not necessarily be sued for in an action unless the bill has not been timeously presented and noted for non-payment. If it has been, the more expeditious mode is to record the notarial protest; and an extract registered protest warrants diligence to the same effect as an extract proceeding upon a decree pronounced in an action.[1]

[1] 40 & 41 Vict. c. 40, secs. 2, 3.

3. CHARGE.

As a preliminary to poinding or imprisonment upon an extract decree a party decerned against must be formally charged to implement the decree of Court. There is an exception to this in small debt causes, where the defender was present when decree was pronounced.[1] The person in whose name a charge may be given is not necessarily the person who is the pursuer or creditor named in the decree. A charge may be given by any person in right of the decree, as an assignee, or trustee in bankruptcy, or executor. If the charge is to be given at the instance of a person other than the person named in the decree, the party in right of the decree endorses a minute upon the extract, setting forth his title, and, upon the Sheriff-clerk writing a fiat upon the extract, it becomes operative at the instance of such third person.[2] Such a creditor may charge, although he is a foreigner, without a mandatory, but if the charge is suspended, he will generally have to sist a mandatory in the suspension process.[3]

[1] 7 Will. IV & 1 Vict. c. 41, sec. 13. See p. 485, infra.
[2] 1 & 2 Vict. c. 114, sec. 12.
[3] Ross v. Shaw, 1849, 11 D. 984.

A charge must in the general case be executed by a Sheriff-officer or a messenger-at-arms.[1] But to this general rule there are two exceptions. (1) A charge on a small debt decree for payment of money may be executed by registered letter if the place of execution is in one of the islands of Scotland, or in a county where there is no resident Sheriff-officer, or is more than twelve miles distant from the seat of the Court which granted the decree.[2] The procedure is detailed in the Act, and the registered letter may be sent by Sheriff-officer or messenger-at-arms, but if none such is resident in the Sheriffdom where the place of execution is situated a solicitor enrolled in such Sheriffdom may send the registered letter.[2] The pursuer's solicitor may apparently act in the matter. (2) Where an extract decree of any Scottish Court is presented to the Sheriff within whose jurisdiction it is to be executed and he is satisfied that no messenger or officer is reasonably available to execute it he may authorize some other person—but not the solicitor of the person presenting the decree—to execute the decree.[3] The appropriate procedure would appear to be by minute endorsed on the decree. Apart from the special provisions referred to above in relation to small debt decrees postal service of a charge is not competent.[4]

[1] 55 & 56 Vict. c. 17, sec. 8.
[2] 16 & 17 Geo. V c. 16, sec. 2. See this more fully discussed, p. 486, infra.
[3] Ibid., sec. 3.
[4] Gow & Sons v. Thomson, 1895, 1 Adam 534; Whyte, Ridsdale & Co., 1912 S.C. 1095.

The provisions of Rule 10 of the Sheriff Courts Act, 1907,[1] do not extend to a charge, and where a charge has to be executed in another Sheriffdom from that in which the decree was obtained it is still necessary to have the extract endorsed by the Sheriff-clerk of that Sheriffdom,[2] and it is still requisite that the charge be given by an officer of that Sheriffdom. The extract is presented to the Sheriff-clerk with a minute endorsed craving concurrence, and when the Sheriff-clerk has written a fiat on the extract it becomes operative for diligence to the like effect, as if it had been issued in the Sheriffdom where it is to be executed.

[1] 7 Edw. VII c. 51, Schedule I, Rule 10.
[2] 1 & 2 Vict. c. 114, sec. 13.

The officer executing a charge must be accompanied by one witness who subscribes the execution of charge along with the officer.[1] Subject to the special provisions stated above[2] a charge upon an individual must be served personally, or at his dwelling-place by being left with some person therein, or, if admittance cannot be obtained, by affixing the charge to the door or putting it in the keyhole.[3] If the debtor is furth of Scotland service of the charge is made edictally.[4] If a charge is invalid, the whole subsequent diligence may be inoperative. A trifling error in a charge or execution will not invalidate it[5]; but if a material error occurs[6] the charge should be withdrawn, by letter addressed to the debtor, and a fresh charge should be given.[7] A charge for more than is truly due is good for the sum due and only bad quoad the excess.[8]

[1] 1 & 2 Vict. c. 114, sec. 32.
[2] See p. 256, supra.
[3] Act 1540, c. 75.

4 7 Edw. VII c. 51, Schedule I, Rule 15.
5 Henderson v. Rollo, &c., 1871, 10 M. 104; M'Kellar v. Dallas, 1928
    S.C. 503.
6 See Graham v. Bell, 1875, 2 R. 972; Hardie v. Brown, Barker & Bell,
    (O.H.) 1907, 15 S.L.T. 539; Anderton v. Law, 1911, 27 Sh.Ct.Rep.
    87; Paterson v. Scottish Insurance Commissioners, (O.H.) 1915, 2
    S.L.T. 178; Dunbar & Co. v. Mitchell, (O.H.) 1928 S.L.T. 225.
7 Clark v. Hamilton & Lee, 1875, 3 R. 166.
8 Haughhead Coal Co v. Gallocher, (O.H.) 1903, 11 S.L.T. 156. See
    also Graham Stewart, Diligence, 304.

It is competent to charge any corporation or association, or
any individual or individuals carrying on business under a firm
or trading or descriptive name, under such name at the principal
place where such business is carried on (including in the case of
a corporation or association the place of business or office of their
clerk or secretary) or where such principal place of business is
furth of Scotland, at any place of business in Scotland at which
such business is carried on.[1] This provision does not apply to
an individual who trades or carries on business under his own
name.[2]

1 7 Edw. VII c. 51, Schedule I, Rule 151; 2 & 3 Geo. V c. 28, Schedule
    II. See also Rule 11; 2 & 3 Geo. V c. 28, Schedule II.
2 Imperial Tobacco Co. v. Mackay, 1928 S.L.T. (Sh.Ct.) 8.

A decree against a firm is a warrant to charge each partner,[1]
but not a person who is not a partner but who has held himself
out as a partner.[2] A decree obtained against an unincorporated
body such as a club is not a warrant for a charge against an
individual alleged to be a member or official of the club but who
is not named in the decree.[3] If there is any statutory enactment
requiring any corporation or board or society to be cited in a
particular manner, the same direction should be followed in
executing a charge; but, in the absence of such special direction,
the usual methods will be adopted, whether the body to be charged
is a public or private corporation.

1 53 & 54 Vict. c. 39, sec. 4 (2).
2 Brember v. Rutherford, 1901, 4 F. 62.
3 Aitchison v. M'Donald, 1911 S.C. 174.

The provision which bars a person who has appeared from
challenging the validity of citation[1] does not apply to execution
of diligence. An execution, however, if *ex facie* regular, is presumptive evidence of the fact and manner of execution, and of
the fact that the defender has been charged, and this presumption
normally applies till the execution is reduced.[2] If the execution
is *ex facie* regular and the objection is not patent, a process of

reduction may be necessary to set aside the execution[2] but the objection may also be competently taken *ope exceptionis*.[3]

[1] 7 Edw. VI c. 51, Schedule I, Rule 13.
[2] Dickson, Evidence, sec. 1279.
[3] Scott v. Cook, 1886, 24 S.L.R. 34.

The charge must be dated,[1] and the days of charge must conform to the warrant. Where several persons are charged, the execution should state the date upon which each was charged. The charge given upon an extract decree for payment of money certiorates the debtor that, if he fail to obey the charge, recovery may be made by poinding, and it is given also under the pain of imprisonment where imprisonment is competent.[2] The charge upon a decree *ad factum præstandum* is given under the pain of imprisonment,[3] and in a removing process under pain of ejectment.[4] In regard to a charge upon a decree for both payment and delivery see the case undernoted.[5]

[1] See Beattie v. M'Lellan, 1844, 6 D. 1088.
[2] 55 & 56 Vict. c. 17, sec. 7 (1).
[3] Ibid., sec. 7 (2). See p. 284, infra, as to modification of law in regard to imprisonment in certain cases.
[4] Ibid., sec. 7 (4).
[5] Hardie v. Brown, Barker & Bell, (O.H.) 1907, 15 S.L.T. 539.

The charge, which must be signed by the messenger or officer, must specify the parties to the action, the date of the decree on which it proceeds,[1] the induciæ on which the charge is given, the amount charged for and the date of service. If payments to account of the sum in the decree have been made these should be specified,[2] and a charge for more than is truly due is bad *quoad* the excess.[3] It is essential that the name of the officer be given[4] and that the creditor under the decree be clearly specified.[5] In the execution of the charge the method by which service was effected should be stated.[6]

[1] Beattie v. M'Lellan, 1844, 6 D. 1088; Graham v. Bell, 1875, 2 R. 972; cf. Henderson v. Rollo, 1871, 10 M. 104.
[2] See M'Martin v. Forbes, 1824, 3 S. 275.
[3] Haughhead Coal Co. v. Gallocher, (O.H.) 1903, 11 S.L.T. 156. See also Graham Stewart, Diligence, 304.
[4] Paterson v. Scottish Insurance Commissioners, (O.H.) 1915, 2 S.L.T. 178.
[5] Dunbar & Co. v. Mitchell, (O.H.) 1928 S.L.T. 225.
[6] See Stewart v. Macdonald, 1860, 22 D. 1514.

The Sheriff Courts Act, 1907, does not, as the 1876 Act did,[1] prescribe the days of charge. But this is regulated by the Sheriff Courts Extracts Act of 1892, which provides for a charge of seven days.[2] Edictal execution is competent when the debtor is furth of Scotland, and the charge is given upon fourteen days' induciæ.[3] In the case of edictal execution where the party charged has a known residence or place of business in England or Northern Ireland a copy of the decree and charge must be posted in a registered letter to the party at such address and the execution must bear that this has been done.[4] The Sheriff has no power to shorten the induciæ of charge.

[1] 39 & 40 Vict. c. 70, sec. 8.
[2] See 55 & 56 Vict. c. 17, Schedule, No. 1.
[3] Ibid., sec. 7 (6); 7 Edw. VII c. 51, Schedule I, Rule 15.
[4] 7 Edw. VII c. 51, Schedule I, Rule 15.

Registration of the extract decree and execution of expired charge in the Sheriff Court Register of Hornings has the effect of accumulating the debt and interest into one capital sum, upon which interest runs from the date of registration.[1]

[1] 1 & 2 Vict. c. 114, sec. 10.

4. ARRESTMENT.

Arrestment is the appropriate diligence for the attachment of a debtor's moveable property which is in the custody of a third party. If it is in defender's own custody, poinding is the proper diligence, but under the Sale of Goods Act, an unpaid seller of goods still in his custody may arrest them in his own hands.[1] By arrestment a debtor's property may be secured, for the benefit of his creditor, before, as well as after, judgment, arrestment before judgment being termed arrestment on the dependence, and that after judgment arrestment in execution. An extract of a Sheriff Court decree is itself a statutory warrant for arrestment in execution.[2] For arrestment on the dependence a special warrant is required, but once it has been executed and the arrestment has become effective it remains in force for the prescriptive period. It is not affected by decree being granted in the action and it is thought that arrestment in execution on the decree is not necessary in order to attach the arrested fund.[3] A warrant to arrest on the dependence is commonly included in the first warrant of citation, but the writ does not necessarily require to be served before arrestment can be used. In many cases it may be advisable to use arrestments before the service of the writ, but in that case the writ must be served within twenty days from the date of the execution of the arrestment, and, in the case of defended actions, must be tabled within twenty days of the first ordinary Court day occurring after the expiry of the induciæ, and in the case of undefended actions decree in absence must be taken within twenty days of the expiry of the induciæ, otherwise the arrestment falls.[4] In the above connexion it is thought that the first diet in a summary cause must be held to be the " tabling." The manner of execution is the same, whether the arrestment is on the dependence or after judgment. The validity of arrestments on the dependence was sustained where warrant to arrest had been granted although the initial writ had contained no crave for such a warrant.[5] The specialities in arrestments on small debt summonses are dealt with later.[6]

[1] 56 & 57 Vict. c. 71, sec. 40.
[2] 55 & 56 Vict. c. 17, sec. 7.
[3] See p. 265, infra.
[4] 7 Edw. VII c. 51, Schedule I, Rule 127; 2 & 3 Geo. V c. 28, Schedule II.
[5] Muir & Son v. Muir & Co., (O.H.) 1910, 1 S.L.T. 414.
[6] See pp. 469, 470, infra.

An arrestment upon a Sheriff Court warrant is competent only within Scotland. The provision of the Debtors (Scotland) Act, 1838, authorizing arrestment edictally upon an arrestee furth of Scotland, applies only to a Court of Session warrant.[1] Formerly a warrant to arrest on the dependence, or a precept of arrestment, if executed in another Sheriffdom, required first to be endorsed by the Sheriff-clerk of that Sheriffdom, and was executed by an officer of that Sheriffdom, but a warrant or precept of arrestment proceeding upon a depending action or liquid document of debt may now be executed in any Sheriffdom without endorsation, and may be executed by an officer either of the Sheriffdom where the warrant or precept was granted, or of that where it is to be executed.[2] These provisions do not apply to arrestments used in execution upon a decree, and in that case a warrant of concurrence must still be obtained from the Sheriff-clerk of the county where the arrestments are to be executed, and the officer executing the arrestments must be an officer of that Sheriffdom.[3]

[1] 1 & 2 Vict. c. 114, secs. 16-18.
[2] 7 Edw. VII c. 51, Schedule I, Rule 10.
[3] 1 & 2 Vict. c. 114, sec. 13.

An arrestment may proceed upon a precept issued in the Sheriff Court, and the rules provide that separate precepts of arrestment may be issued by the Sheriff-clerk upon production to him of a writ containing pecuniary conclusions upon which a warrant of citation has been granted, or of a liquid document of debt.[1] It is not necessary to present an initial writ formally craving a precept of arrestment and production to the Sheriff-clerk of the requisite grounds is sufficient. The production of a writ with pecuniary conclusions is necessary only in the exceptional case where, in the crave of the writ, a warrant to arrest on the dependence has been omitted. If a warrant to arrest is craved it will be included in the warrant of citation, and a separate precept is in practice applied for only where a ground of debt exists, but a writ has not been taken out.

1 7 Edw. VII c. 51, Schedule I, Rule 46; 2 & 3 Geo. V c. 28, Schedule II.

Neither under a warrant to arrest on the dependence, nor upon a separate precept, is arrestment on the dependence competent unless in respect of a pecuniary claim (other than expenses),[1] but it is enough that such a claim exists, although it may be only alternative or subsidiary to some other claim or demand. It is not competent, for instance, to crave warrant to arrest on the dependence where the claim is for declarator or delivery alone, but if an alternative pecuniary crave is included arrestment is competent. So also arrestment may be competent upon the dependence of an action of count and reckoning, if there is also a conclusion for a money payment, but in general a warrant to arrest on the dependence is not granted upon future or contingent claims, unless it is averred that the defender is *vergens ad inopiam* or *in meditatione fugæ*.[2] Arrestment on the dependence is competent in actions of separation and aliment,[3] but not in an action of affiliation and aliment raised before the birth of the child where the defender is not alleged to be *vergens ad inopiam* or *in meditatione fugæ*.[4] A precept of arrestment will be issued only in respect of a specific existing debt against a specified debtor, and the precept should disclose the grounds of debt.

1 Ketchen v. Grant, 1871, 9 M. 966; Stafford v. M'Laurin, 1875, 3 R. 148.
2 See Ellison v. Ellison, 1901, 4 F. 257.
3 Symington v. Symington, 1875, 3 R. 205; Burns v. Burns, 1879, 7 R. 355; Speirs v. Speirs, 1938, 54 Sh.Ct.Rep. 208; cf. Johnson v. Johnson, 1910, 26 Sh.Ct.Rep. 134.
4 Speedie v. Steel, 1941 S.L.T. (Sh.Ct.) 2.

It is thought that a precept of arrestment cannot be competently issued to a defender, upon defences being lodged stating a counter-claim. Rule 55 empowers the Sheriff to deal with such a claim as if it had been stated in a substantive action.[1] But Rule 46 only authorizes a precept to be issued upon production of a writ containing pecuniary conclusions upon which a warrant of citation has been granted, or of a liquid document of debt.[2] It seems clear that a statement of counter-claim by way of defence does not fall within the terms of Rule 46.[3] If a defender desires to arrest upon a counter-claim he should raise a substantive action and get in that action a warrant to arrest.

[1] 7 Edw. VII c. 51, Schedule I, Rule 55.
[2] Ibid., Rule 46; 2 & 3 Geo. V c. 28, Schedule II.
[3] Cf. express provision for arrestment in Court of Session in Rules of Court, 1936, II, 13 (c).

Save in the case of small debt procedure as after mentioned,[1] arrestments must be executed by a messenger or officer and postal execution is incompetent. Either a messenger-at-arms or a Sheriff-officer may arrest in execution on a decree,[2] but the statutory provision which authorizes this does not apply to arrestments on the dependence. It is thought that a messenger could probably act in that case also, but the matter is not clearly decided.[3] In the case of individuals the execution may be either personal or at the dwelling-place. Arrestments used in the hands of companies should be executed at their registered office,[4] and in the case of firms at the place of business. If the schedule of arrestment has not been personally served upon an arrestee it is necessary, to make the arrestment effectual, that a copy of the schedule be also sent by postal registered letter to the last known place of abode of the arrestee, or if such place of abode is unknown, or if the arrestee is a firm or corporation, to the arrestee's principal place of business if known, or if not known to any known place of business of the arrestee, and the officer in his execution must certify that this has been done, and specify the address to which the postal intimation was sent.[5] It has been held to be immaterial that the postal intimation was not sent till eight days after service at the place of business,[6] but execution of the arrestment will not be completed until the postal intimation has been effected. The execution is sufficient if the subjects to be attached are described in general terms, but if any specific fund or subject is known to be in the arrestee's hands, and it is desired to attach that, there may be added to the general description " and particularly," with a specification of such special fund or subject.[7]

[1] See p. 470, infra.
[2] 55 & 56 Vict. c. 17, sec. 8.
[3] See p. 11, supra.
[4] See Corson v. Macmillan, 1927 S.L.T. (Sh.Ct.) 13.
[5] 7 Edw. VII c. 51, Schedule I, Rule 126.
[6] Hart, jun. v. Grant & Wylie, &c., 1907, 23 Sh.Ct.Rep. 186.
[7] See Metzenburg v. Highland Railway Co., 1869, 7 M. 919; Macintyre v. Caledonian Railway Co., 1909, 25 Sh.Ct.Rep. 329.

Rule 11,[1] which sanctions actions by or against firms under a descriptive name alone, further provides that an extract decree in such an action is a valid warrant for diligence against such firm.

It seems clear that this provision does not apply to arrestment on the dependence and that in the case of diligence in execution of a decree it relates only to such diligence as is used directly against the defender. There is thus no provision for the case where an arrestee is a firm with a descriptive name, and in such a case, whether arrestment is used on the dependence or in execution, it is thought that the common law rule of practice still holds, and that service is necessary not only on the firm at its place of business, but personally or at the dwelling-place of three partners if there are as many.[2]

[1] 7 Edw. VII c. 51, Schedule I, Rule 11; 2 & 3 Geo. V c. 28, Schedule II.
[2] See Dove Wilson, Sheriff Court Practice, 4th edn., pp. 98, 211; Graham Stewart, Diligence, 32.

In the case of a corporation, if the Act or Charter by which it is constituted contains no other provision, an arrestment is properly served if left with a servant at the corporation's place of business, and under the provisions of the Act of 1876 this has been held to be so far equivalent to personal service that postal service of a copy schedule in addition is not necessary.[1] As the present Rule 126[2] is not in precisely the same terms as the provisions of the 1876 Act[3] it may be considered advisable also to post a copy addressed to the corporation at its principal place of business, but as the authorities stand it is thought that this is not essential, either in the case of a corporation or a limited company, where there has been valid service otherwise at the place of business or registered office.[4] Arrestments used in the hands of a firm would fall into the same category, but here again the additional postal intimation may be considered advisable.

[1] Campbell v. Watson's Trustee, 1898, 25 R. 690.
[2] 7 Edw. VII c. 51, Schedule I, Rule 126.
[3] 39 & 40 Vict. c. 70, sec. 12 (5).
[4] Campbell v. Watson's Trustee, supra; Macintyre v. Caledonian Railway Co., 1909, 25 Sh.Ct.Rep. 329; cf. Corson v. Macmillan, 1927 S.L.T. (Sh.Ct.) 13; Graham Stewart, Diligence, 29.

The authority to arrest on the dependence is the warrant included in the order for service, or the precept of arrestment issued by the Sheriff-clerk, or the certified copy writ and warrant lodged by the pursuer in a defended action.[1] The extract decree is the warrant to arrest in execution. It is essential that the warrant be in the hands of the officer or messenger when he executes the arrestment, otherwise the arrestment is made without authority and is bad.[2]

[1] 7 Edw. VII c. 51, Schedule I, Rule 46; 2 & 3 Geo. V c. 28, Schedule II.
[2] MacKillop v. Mactaggart, (O.H.) 1939 S.L.T. 65.

Under Rule 127 of the Act the execution of an arrestment on the dependence which has been used prior to service must be reported to the Sheriff-clerk forthwith.[1] Under this rule a delay of twenty days in reporting the arrestment was held to render it ineffective.[2] The rule does not apply to an arrestment on the dependence used after the writ has been served.[3]

[1] 7 Edw. VII c. 51, Schedule I, Rule 127; 2 & 3 Geo. V c. 28, Schedule II.
[2] Johnson v. Johnson, 1910, 26 Sh.Ct.Rep. 134. See also Macintyre v. Caledonian Railway Co., &c., 1909, 25 Sh.Ct.Rep. 329; A B, &c. v. E F, 1910, 26 Sh.Ct.Rep. 172.
[3] Henley's Tyre & Rubber Co. v. Swan, 1929 S.L.T. (Sh.Ct.) 47.

An arrestment prescribes in three years.[1] In the case of arrestment in execution of decrees, whether of registration or constitution, the three years run from the date of execution of arrestment; in the case of arrestment on the dependence, from the date of the final decree in the cause[2]; and, when the arrestment is used upon a future or contingent debt, from the date the debt becomes due, or the contingency is purified.[1] Arrestments used under the Small Debt Acts prescribe in three months from the date of execution.[3]

[1] 1 & 2 Vict. c. 114, sec. 22.
[2] Graham Stewart, Diligence, 223.
[3] 7 Will. IV & 1 Vict. c. 41, sec. 6.

As we have seen, arrestment on the dependence may be used before service of the writ,[1] and it may be used at any time after service while the action is still pending. It is generally available to the pursuer until he can obtain an extract decree and thus is able to use arrestments in execution.[2] Despite a certain diversity of judicial opinion on the point it is thought to be clear that when arrestment on the dependence has been used it is not necessary to use arrestments again to attach the same subjects when decree has been obtained. If a furthcoming is necessary it is brought on the arrestments used on the dependence.[3] Where there have been arrestments on the dependence and a plea of no jurisdiction is sustained, but the cause is transferred to another Sheriffdom which has jurisdiction, it would seem from the wording of the rule under which such a transfer is made[4] that the arrestments remain effective notwithstanding the sustaining of the plea to the jurisdiction.

[1] See p. 260, supra.
[2] Graham Stewart, Diligence, 22.
[3] Ibid., 231. See also Abercrombie v. Edgar & Crerar, (O.H.) 1923 S.L.T. 271.
[4] 7 Edw. VII c. 51, Schedule I, Rule 21.

An arrestment may be recalled or restricted by the Sheriff who granted the warrant, with or without caution or consignation. As a general rule, the expense of laying on or recalling arrestments falls upon the party using the arrestments, or the party applying for recall.[1] The Personal Diligence Act provides that the Sheriff from whose books a warrant of arrestment has been issued may recall or restrict the arrestment with or without caution.[2] The procedure is by petition of the debtor or defender intimated to the creditor or pursuer to which answers are to be lodged, and the matter is to be disposed of as in summary causes, the Sheriff's judgment being subject to review in the Court of Session.[2] After an action is in progress, an arrestment used on the dependence is sometimes of consent recalled on consignation, upon motion of a party, although this is not strictly correct procedure as laid down in the Act.[3] Recall of arrestment may be desired before a writ has been served, and in that case there is no process in which to make a motion. Applications for recall or restriction usually relate to arrestments used on the dependence, but it has been held that the statutory procedure is available in the case of arrestments used in execution.[4] Where a warrant of concurrence has been obtained it has been held that the Sheriff granting the concurrence is the Sheriff who is entitled to recall the arrestment.[5] There is some doubt as to whether in addition to the statutory right of appeal to the Court of Session there is also an appeal to the Sheriff.[6]

[1] Roy v. Turner, 1891, 18 R. 717. See also Muir & Co. v. United Collieries, 1908 S.C. 768.
[2] 1 & 2 Vict. c. 114, sec. 21.
[3] See Buchanan v. Black, 1882, 9 R. 926; Gordon v. Bruce & Co., 1897, 24 R. 844; Stuart v. Stuart, (O.H.) 1926 S.L.T. 31.
[4] Gillies v. Bow, 1877, Guthrie's Select Cases I, 196.
[5] Comrie v. Gow & Sons, 1931, 47 Sh.Ct.Rep. 159; cf. Irvine v. Gow & Sons, 1910, 26 Sh.Ct.Rep. 174.
[6] Johnson v. Johnson, 1910, 26 Sh.Ct.Rep. 134; A B v. E F, 1910, 26 Sh.Ct.Rep. 172; Irvine v. Gow & Sons, supra; Kennedy v. Kennedy, 1910, 27 Sh.Ct.Rep. 71; Swan v. Kirk, 1931, 47 Sh.Ct.Rep. 217; cf. M'Garva v. M'Brierley, 1917, 33 Sh.Ct.Rep. 283.

An application for recall of arrestments is not competent at the instance of a third party, who alleges that the arrested fund or subject belongs to him. The proper course in such circumstances is to have the dispute dealt with in the furthcoming or in a multiplepoinding process.[1] An application for recall is competent at the instance of any party in the cause against whom arrestment has been used. It is not competent for the arrestee to seek recall where the subject arrested is a debt or sum of money, but he may in certain circumstances petition for recall where a corporeal moveable is arrested.[2] The validity of an arrestment itself is a matter for determination in a furthcoming process, but when no furthcoming had been brought the Court in a petition for recall disposed of a question as to the liability of the arrested fund to the diligence of creditors.[3] In the normal case the questions dealt with in a petition for recall are (1) whether there was justification for using arrestments at all; and (2) if so, whether caution should be made a condition of recall.[4] The validity of an arrestment is determined by the *lex loci rei sitæ*.[5]

[1] Vincent v. Chalmers & Co.'s Trustee, 1877, 5 R. 43: Brand v. Kent, 1892, 20 R. 29; " Nordsoen " v. Mackie, Koth & Co., 1911 S.C. 172.   See also M'Morran v. Glover, jun., &c., 1937, 53 Sh.Ct.Rep. 87.
[2] Barclay, Curle & Co. v. Laing & Sons, 1908 S.C. 82.
[3] Lord Ruthven v. Drummond, 1908 S.C. 1154.
[4] Vincent v. Chalmers & Co.'s Trustee, supra, Lord President Inglis at p. 44.
[5] Inglis v. Robertson & Baxter, 1898, 25 R. (H.L.) 70.   See also Royal Bank v. Securities Insurance Co., (O.H.) 1897, 4 S.L.T. 232.

A warrant or precept of arrestment authorizes arrestment in the hands of the arrestee only of money which is due to, or goods which belong to, the debtor at the time the arrestment is laid on, and the schedule and execution must bear that the subject arrested belongs to defender.[1] What is carried by an arrestment is only what is in the arrestee's hands at the moment the schedule is served upon him, and arrestments are preferable in the order of service.   An arrestment, the execution of which sets forth that it was used within certain hours upon a date, may take precedence of one used on the same date, but without mention of hours.[2] On the question of preference it is immaterial which of several arresters gets the first decree of furthcoming,[3] or in the case of arrestments on the dependence who obtains the first decree in his action.[3]

[1] Marshall & Sons v. Robertson, 1904, 21 Sh.Ct.Rep. 243.
[2] Hertz v. Itzig, 1865, 3 M. 813.   See further in regard to similar points, Graham Stewart, Diligence, 138.
[3] Graham Stewart, Diligence, 137, and cases cited.

Alimentary provisions are arrestable by the attachment of termly payments as they fall due, but are only available for ordinary creditors after an allowance to the alimentary beneficiary for current expenses has been made, and after the satisfaction of current alimentary debts and any arrears of alimentary debts.[1] It is a question of circumstances whether emoluments by way of salary, pension, or annuity, are arrestable.   Salaries paid by the Crown, including the wages of workmen in Government service, are not subject to arrestment, and the same is probably true of Crown pensions.[2]* In the case of ministers' stipends, professors'

* Alterations proposed by Crown Proceedings Bill.

salaries, and the like, the general rule is that any surplus beyond what is reasonably necessary for maintenance is arrestable.[3] Police pensions, which are by Statute not assignable, have been held to be not subject to arrestment,[4] but the salary of a constable can be attached.[5] The earnings of " labourers, farm servants, manufacturers, artificers, and workpeople " are protected from arrestment save for the excess over 35s. per week, but such earnings may be arrested in execution of a decree for an alimentary debt, or for rates and taxes.[6] Wages of seamen or apprenticed seamen cannot be arrested,[7] and arrestment of any wages on the dependence of a small debt summons is not competent.[8] A workman's tools and all normal wearing apparel are in general exempted from diligence.[9] Workmen's compensation, sums paid for redemption of compensation, and capital compensation due to dependants are not subject to arrestment.[10]

[1] Lord Ruthven v. Pulford & Sons, 1909 S.C. 951, Lord M'Laren, p. 954.
[2] Mulvenna v. The Admiralty, 1926 S.C. 842.
[3] See Simpson v. Jack, 1888, 16 R. 131; Graham Stewart, Diligence, 100.
[4] Macfarlane v. Glasgow Corporation, 1934, 50 Sh.Ct.Rep. 247.
[5] Young v. Turnbull, (O.H.) 1928 S.N. 46.
[6] 33 & 34 Vict. c. 63, secs. 1, 2; 14 & 15 Geo. V c. 16, sec. 2.
[7] 57 & 58 Vict. c. 60, sec. 163.
[8] 8 & 9 Vict. c. 39.
[9] See Graham Stewart, Diligence, 345; cf. Steele v. Eagles, 1922, 39 Sh.Ct.Rep. 68.
[10] 15 & 16 Geo. V c. 84, sec. 40; William Baird & Co. v. Campbell, 1928 S.C. 314.

Various cases have been decided in regard to the earnings which are protected by the Act of 1870. The statutory limit of 35s. is to be calculated as the amount due for the week in which the arrestment was used, and not the proportion of the week's wages actually earned at the date of arrestment.[1] Protection has been afforded to the full extent of net earnings which were under the limit, though a sum over the limit was paid to the workman who had to pay others who worked with him.[2] A gamekeeper's wages have been held to be protected at common law,[3] and a golf greenkeeper's wages were held to fall under the Act though he carried on a supplementary trade on his own account.[4] In the case of a farm servant it has been held that the limit is calculated by aggregating wages both in money and in kind,[5] but where a van salesman received both wages and commission he was regarded as having a dual employment, and the commission was treated as a separate item which was not protected but was only attached so far as earned at the date of arrestment.[6] The position of special payments to fishermen and seamen is dealt with in the cases undernoted.[7] Where wages are paid in advance they cannot be arrested.[8] Wages are not protected against arrestment when diligence is used on a decree for an alimentary debt, and this is held to include a decree for expenses in such an action,[9] but arrestment on the dependence of an action for an alimentary debt has no such privilege.[10] The wages of a clerk do not appear to fall under the protection of the Act, but there is authority for the proposition that at common law wages in general are only arrestable beyond what is necessary for proper maintenance.[11] A music hall artiste's salary has been held to be "wages" and thus protected against arrestment on a small debt decree.[12]

[1] Shiel & Co. v. Skinner & Co., &c., 1933, 50 Sh.Ct.Rep. 101.
[2] M'Murchy v. Emslie & Guthrie, 1888, 15 R. 375; Thomson v. Barrett, &c., 1888, 4 Sh.Ct.Rep. 242.
[3] Marjoribanks v. Watson, &c., 1903, 19 Sh.Ct.Rep. 279; cf. Munro v. M'Callum, 1893, 9 Sh.Ct.Rep. 171.
[4] Auchterlonie v. M'Kelvie, &c., 1907, 24 Sh.Ct.Rep. 130.
[5] Skinner & Co. v. Anderson, &c., 1915, 31 Sh.Ct.Rep. 256.
[6] M'Aulay v. Smith, &c., 1913, 30 Sh.Ct.Rep. 162.
[7] Caledonian Banking Co. v. Johnston & Sons, 1886, 2 Sh.Ct.Rep. 131; M'Ritchie v. Milne, &c., 1886, 3 Sh.Ct.Rep. 176; Gouick v. Bruce & Co., 1895, 11 Sh.Ct.Rep. 142.
[8] Eddie v. M'Avoy, 1893, 9 Sh.Ct.Rep. 366; Morrison v. Eastern Brass-founding Co., &c., 1918, 34 Sh.Ct.Rep. 216.
[9] Hunter v. Wilson, &c., 1916, 33 Sh.Ct.Rep. 209.
[10] Mathew v. M'Leish, 1875, Guthrie's Select Cases I, 371; Harkness v. Williamson, 1904, 21 Sh.Ct.Rep. 85.
[11] See Graham Stewart, Diligence, 101; Thomson v. Cohen, 1915, 32 Sh.Ct.Rep. 15.
[12] Locke v. Chard, 1908, 24 Sh.Ct.Rep. 305.

A fund which has been earmarked and appropriated to a special purpose may not in the general case be arrested so as to defeat that purpose.[1] But this protection from arrestment is limited to cases where the appropriation in the hands of the holder of the fund is such that some third party has acquired a right in the fund. Thus money consigned in the hands of the Clerk of Court may be arrested so long as the object of the consignation is not thereby defeated,[2] and if the party to meet whose alleged claim the consignation was made be found not entitled to it, or if a surplus remain after satisfying his claim, the fund, or the surplus, is available to other creditors of the party whose money was consigned. But the consignor himself, after the other party has become entitled to the money, is not permitted to prevent the consigned fund reaching him, by arresting it upon an alleged separate claim against the other party.[3] The arrestment of stolen money, or the funds of an arrested person, in the hands of the police or the procurator-fiscal is apparently incompetent.[4] It has been held that where sequestration of a bankrupt's estate has been awarded but no trustee has been elected arrestment of the bankrupt's funds is incompetent.[5]

[1] See Brown v. Port Seton Harbour Commissioners, 1898, 1 F. 373, and cases there cited, also British Linen Co. v. Kansas Investment Co., (O.H.) 1895, 3 S.L.T. 138.
[2] Pollock v. Scott, 1844, 6 D. 1297; Campbell v. Lothians & Findlay, 1858, 21 D. 63.
[3] Cuthill v. Hamilton, 1830, 8 S. 487.
[4] Guthrie v. Morren, 1939, 55 Sh.Ct.Rep. 172, and cases there cited; cf. Suter Hartmann, &c., Co. v. Gillespie, 1908, 24 Sh.Ct.Rep. 207.
[5] Hodgson & Son v. United Thread Mills, &c., 1935 S.L.T. (Sh.Ct.) 26; cf. M'Lardy & Co. v. Mutter, Howey & Co., &c., 1933, 50 Sh.Ct.Rep. 100.

Rent is arrestable, but only as regards arrears, and the current term's rent. Future payments not yet due are not arrestable. An arrestment used during the currency of a term attaches the rent of that term,[1] even if, by agreement between the landlord and tenant, payment is postponed till after the legal term.[2] Arrestment on the term day does not attach the rent for the period then commencing.[3]

[1] Livingston v. Kinloch, 1795, M. 769.
[2] Handyside v. Corbyn & Lee, 15 Jan., 1813, F.C.
[3] Wright v. Cunningham, 1802, M. 15919.

Funds may be arrestable, although not presently payable, if the debtor has a vested interest. Thus, a *jus crediti* under a trust deed may be attached in the hands of a trustee, although the estate consists of heritage which has not yet been realized.[1] If the estate is held by a body of trustees, a schedule of arrestment should be served upon each of them,[2] or at least upon so many of them as constitute a quorum.[3]

[1] Kyle's Trustees v. White, 1827, 6 S. 40; Learmont v. Shearer, 1866, 4 M. 540.
[2] M'Laren, Wills and Succession, 3rd edn., 851.
[3] Black v. Scott, 1830, 8 S. 367; as to terms of schedule served on trustees see Gracie v. Gracie, 1910 S.C. 899.

An arrestment can competently be used only in the hands of a direct debtor to the common debtor. Service of an arrestment for a debt due by a firm should be executed against the firm, and, if necessary, the partners, as already indicated,[1] and not against one partner only.[2] If the arrestee has no liability to the common debtor the arrestment in his hands is inept. But it is sufficient that, in principle, the arrestee is liable to account and pay—or is under an obligation to pay arising from contract or delict—to the common debtor, although the exact amount in which he is liable has not at the moment been ascertained.[3] While arrestment is normally valid only if used in the hands of the actual debtor to the common debtor, in exceptional cases an arrestment may be validly used in the hands of a representative of the arrestee proper, as, for instance, a commissioner entrusted with full management of the arrestee's affairs,[4] or a tutor or curator,[5] or, in some circumstances, a solicitor.[6] But an arrestment in the hands of a bank agent will not attach money due by the bank to a customer.[7] Such an arrestment should be executed against the bank itself. The usual practice is to use arrestments at the head office of the bank and to send separate intimation to the branch where the funds are.[8] As to arrestments in the hands of a company in liquidation, see the case undernoted.[9]

[1] See p. 264, supra.
[2] Hay v. Dufourcet, 1880, 7 R. 972; cf. Ewing & Co. v. M'Clelland, 1860, 22 D. 1347.
[3] See Riley v. Ellis, 1910 S.C. 934; Boland v. White Cross Insurance Association, 1926 S.C. 1066; Park, Dobson & Co. v. Taylor & Son, 1929 S.C. 571.
[4] Carron Co. v. Currie & Co., (O.H.) 1896, 33 S.L.R. 578.
[5] Erskine III, 6, 4.
[6] Ritchie v. M'Lachlan, 1870, 8 M. 815.
[7] Graham v. Macfarlane & Co., 1869, 7 M. 640. See Allan's Executor v. Union Bank, 1909 S.C. 206.
[8] See Graham Stewart, Diligence, 33.
[9] Burns v. Gillies, 1906, 8 F. 460.

An arrestment on the dependence covers interest and expenses in the process in which the debt is sued for.[1] Formerly it did not cover the expenses of a process of furthcoming to make good the arrested fund, but the arrested fund, if sufficient, may now be made available for this expense also.[2]

[1] Graham Stewart, Diligence, 133.
[2] 7 Edw. VII c. 51, Schedule I, Rule 129.

The finding of caution, or making consignation, may be made a condition of recalling an arrestment.[1] When an arrestment is loosed on caution, the obligation of the cautioner properly is that the arrested fund or subject will be made forthcoming to the arrester, if he obtain judgment, but the more common and convenient form is an obligation to pay the arrester such sum as he may obtain judgment for against the principal debtor to the extent of the arrested fund, and in many cases the cautioner's liability is limited to a sum fixed by the Court.[2] Only an arrestment on the dependence is, in the general case, loosed on caution, but an arrestment in execution, following a decree, may also be recalled on caution or consignation in special circumstances.[3] Apart from recall on caution or consignation arrestments which are excessive may be restricted[4] and oppressive arrestments may be recalled *de plano*.[5]

1 See generally Erskine III, 6, 12.
2 Burns v. Burns, 1879, 7 R. 355; M'Phedron & Currie v. M'Callum, 1888, 16 R. 45.
3 James v. James, 1886, 13 R. 1153; Cormack & Sons v. Semple, 1890, 7 Sh.Ct.Rep. 100.
4 Dunn v. Davidson, 1892, 8 Sh.Ct.Rep. 121; Noble v. Noble, (O.H.) 1921, 1 S.L.T. 57; Conzemius v. Findlay, 1924, 41 Sh.Ct.Rep. 337; Swan v. Kirk, 1931, 47 Sh.Ct.Rep. 217.
5 Dick & Parker v. Langloan Iron, &c., Co., 1904, 21 Sh.Ct.Rep. 139; Lapsley v. Lapsley, 1915, 31 Sh.Ct.Rep. 330; Pett v. Kopke, 1917, 34 Sh.Ct.Rep. 261.

An arrestment in itself has no effect in transferring the ownership of funds or property, except upon an Exchequer decree.[1] Its use on the dependence of an action is merely to preserve the property, to be available to the creditor if he obtain judgment against the common debtor. After decree is obtained a separate process is necessary to make the property available and this takes the form of an action of furthcoming, or, where there are competing arrestments, an action of multiplepoinding.

1 19 & 20 Vict. c. 56, sec. 30.

A ship, as a moveable subject, is attached by arrestment, but the process is somewhat different from that used for goods or money. The schedule of arrestment is affixed to the ship's mast, or upon the stern post, and, if there is any fear that the ship may be removed, a warrant to dismantle should be asked. An ordinary warrant authorizing arrestment on the dependence is sufficient for the arrestment,[1] but not for the dismantling of a ship. The former practice in most Sheriff Courts was to require a separate application for warrant to dismantle, setting forth the circumstances which were relied upon as justifying the dismantling. In modern practice, a separate application is not always insisted in, but in the initial writ the crave for warrant to arrest on the dependence should include warrant to dismantle maritime subjects. It is thought that the warrant when granted should be signed by the Sheriff-Substitute. A ship can be arrested only if she is within the jurisdiction of the Court and is either in harbour or is at anchor in a roadstead.[2] If she has begun a voyage that cannot be interrupted by arrestment.[3] If the ship sails, despite an arrestment used on the dependence the defender may be required to find caution before being allowed to prosecute his defence.

[1] Clark v. Loos, 1853, 15 D. 750.
[2] See Kennedy v. M'Kinnon, 1821, 1 S. 210; Petersen v. M'Lean, &c., 1868, 6 M. 218; Borjesson, &c. v. Carlberg, &c., 1878, 5 R. (H.L.) 215.
[3] Borjesson, &c. v. Carlberg, &c., supra.
[4] Meron v. Umland, (O.H.) 1896, 3 S.L.T. 286.

An arrestee who, in the knowledge of an arrestment, parts with the fund or subject arrested, to the prejudice of the arrester, is liable to him for the value of the fund or subject arrested up to the limit of the amount secured by arrestment,[1] or, if the value of the fund or subject cannot be ascertained, for payment of the amount of the arrestor's debt.[2] He is also theoretically in contempt of Court,[3] but the proceedings at the instance of the arrester do not in modern practice take the form of a summary complaint, as in the case of breach of interdict. The arrester proceeds by initial writ, and craves payment of damages on the lines already indicated.

[1] See Graham Stewart, Diligence, 221.
[2] Macarthur v. Bruce, 1760, M. 803.
[3] See Inglis & Bow v. Smith, &c., 1867, 5 M. 320.

Errors in the schedule of arrestment or in the execution may be fatal to the diligence. In some cases the Court have ignored mistakes where no prejudice has resulted,[1] but an error in the date of the decree on which the arrestment proceeds,[2] or the misdescription of one of the parties,[3] will generally render the diligence invalid.

[1] Pollock, Whyte & Waddell v. Old Park Forge, (O.H.) 1907, 15 S.L.T. 3; Baird v. Baird, (O.H.) 1910, 1 S.L.T. 95; cf. Gracie v. Gracie, 1910 S.C. 899; MacTaggart v. MacKillop, (O.H.) 1938 S.L.T. 100.
[2] Graham v. Bell, 1875, 2 R. 972; Grant v. Rattray, &c., 1906, 23 Sh.Ct.Rep. 115.
[3] Burns v. Gillies, 1906, 8 F. 460; Gibb v. Lee, 1908, 45 S.L.R. 833; Lattimore v. Singleton, Dunn & Co., (O.H.) 1911, 2 S.L.T. 360; cf. Pollock, Whyte & Waddell v. Old Park Forge, supra.

5. Furthcoming.

The purpose of the action of furthcoming is to make good to the creditor the arrested fund or subjects. The action is commenced by initial writ at the instance of the party who used the arrestment, and is directed against the arrestee and also the arrestee's original creditor who is, in this process, called the common debtor. It is competent to bring an action of furthcoming in the Sheriff Court (a) within whose jurisdiction the arrested fund or subject is situated, or (b) to whose jurisdiction the arrestee or holder of the fund is subject.[1] It is immaterial that the common debtor is not subject to either of these jurisdictions[1] but he should receive fair notice of the proceedings so as to allow him to appear if he so desires.[2]

[1] 7 Edw. VII c. 51, sec. 6 (g), and Schedule I, Rule 128.
[2] See Leggat Bros. v. Gray, 1912 S.C. 230.

It is competent to bring a furthcoming if an arrested fund is vested in the common debtor, although it may not yet be payable to him; but it should be kept in mind that arrestments prescribe in three years.[1] The action, therefore, should be brought within the three years in order to interrupt the prescription, although actual payment may not be craved until some later date.[2]

[1] 1669, c. 9; 1 & 2 Vict. c. 114, sec. 22.
[2] Jameson v. Sharp, &c., 1887, 14 R. 643.

It is thought to be clear that when arrestment has been used on the dependence, it is not essential to arrest again in execution, after decree has been obtained.[1] The arrestee is not entitled to challenge the arrester's claim against the common debtor.[2] The arrestee may dispute the validity of the arrestment, but beyond that he can plead against the arrester only such defences as he could have pleaded against the common debtor, as, for instance, a lien or retention right over a subject arrested, or that he is not indebted to the common debtor, or that other creditors of the common debtor have also used arrestments.[2] He may apparently refer a defence against payment to the debtor's oath.[3] So far as it is still open to him to do so the common debtor can challenge the arrester's claim upon which the arrestment was used, which is the basis of the action of furthcoming, and he may also challenge the validity of the arrestment itself.

[1] See p. 265, supra.
[2] Houston v. Aberdeen Town and County Bank, 1849, 11 D. 1490.
[3] See Graham Stewart, Diligence, 236, and cases cited; cf. M'Aulay v. Smith, &c., 1913, 30 Sh.Ct.Rep. 162.

When either the arrestee, or the common debtor, defends the action of furthcoming, the procedure, as nearly as may be, follows that of an ordinary action,[1] but any person who has an interest in the fund or subject arrested, although not called, may appear in a furthcoming process.[2] As a decree of furthcoming divests both the arrestee and the common debtor, and conveys the arrested fund to the arrester, and an extract of the decree in the furthcoming will preclude all questions of compensation or retention on the part of the arrestee, he has an interest to see that any such pleas are considered in the furthcoming process. The common debtor has a double interest—he has to see that decree of furthcoming does not go out against the arrestee for more than his debt to the arrester, and he has to see that the arrestee fully disclose the arrested fund or subject. Where either or both, therefore, defend, a record will be made up, and proof allowed if necessary, to determine the situation, not only as between the arrester, on the one hand, and the arrestee and the common debtor, on the other hand; but also as between the common debtor and the arrestee.

[1] 7 Edw. VII c. 51, Schedule I, Rule 132.
[2] Walker v. United Creameries, 1928 S.L.T. (Sh.Ct.) 21.

When the arrested subject is not money, the crave of the initial writ should include such conclusions as are necessary to make a decree in the furthcoming operative to afford the arrester the benefit of the arrested subject,[1] as, for instance, warrant should be asked for the sale of property, or for the sale or transfer of shares,[2] or the surrender or sale of an insurance policy,[3] or otherwise as the case may be.

[1] Lucas' Trustees v. Campbell & Scott, 1894, 21 R. 1096.
[2] Valentine v. Grangemouth Coal Co., (O.H.) 1897, 5 S.L.T. 47.
[3] Clark v. Scottish Amicable Life Assurance Society, 1922 S.L.T. (Sh.Ct.) 88.

When an arrestment has been loosed on caution, the cautioner is called as defender along with the common debtor in the action of furthcoming, but it is proper also to call the arrestee for his interest, for the cautioner's liability to the arrester is no greater than the arrestee's liability to the common debtor, and the arrestee has therefore an interest to appear if he so desire.[1]

[1] Stair III, 1, 36; Bell's Commentaries II, 67; cf. Graham Stewart, Diligence, 241.

When the arrested subject is a ship, the form of making good the arrestment is an action for warrant to sell in which all the owners, so far as known, should be called as defenders. The crave is for authority to sell, and to apply the proceeds to the arrester's debt.

Where warrant to sell arrested subjects is necessary the pursuer is entitled to recover the expenses of sale out of the proceeds, and in all cases he can recover the principal sum in the decree on which the diligence has proceeded with interest to the date of payment, and the expenses decerned for. It is also now provided in the Sheriff Courts Act that the expenses of bringing the furth-

coming may be made good out of the arrested subjects,[1] but where
the principal debt is already secured by arrestment this does not
entitle the pursuer to use a further arrestment merely to secure
the expenses of the furthcoming.[2] It would appear that the expenses
of the arrestment itself are not recoverable out of the arrested
subjects.[3]

[1] 7 Edw. VII c. 51, Schedule I, Rule 129.
[2] Lawsons v. Campbell, 1925, 41 Sh.Ct.Rep. 229.
[3] Graham Stewart, Diligence, 133.

Where more than one arrestment has been served upon the same
arrestee the more suitable form of action to make good the arrested
fund, and determine who has best right to it, is an action of
multiplepoinding. This may be brought in the Sheriff Court
within whose jurisdiction the fund or subject which has been
arrested lies, or to whose jurisdiction the arrestee is subject.[1]
Procedure in actions of multiplepoinding is dealt with in detail
later.[2] When competition between two claimants to the arrested
fund arises after a furthcoming has been brought, the question
may be dealt with in the furthcoming process,[3] or that process
may be sisted and a multiplepoinding brought to supersede it.[4]

[1] 7 Edw. VII c. 51, Schedule I, Rule 128.
[2] See p. 514 et seq., infra.
[3] As in Walker v. United Creameries, &c., 1928 S.L.T. (Sh.Ct.) 21.
[4] As in Pollard v. Galloway & Nivison, 1881, 9 R. 21; cf. Ross, &c.
      v. Brunton, &c., 1913, 30 Sh.Ct.Rep. 141.

6. POINDING AND SALE.

The moveable effects of a debtor, who has failed to implement
a decree for payment, after being duly charged, are made available to the creditor by poinding and sale, the proceedings in
regard to which are regulated by the Debtors (Scotland) Act, 1838.[1]
Poinding is appropriate when such moveable property is in the
custody or control of the debtor himself. If it is in the hands of
a third party, the appropriate diligence is arrestment. If the
effects are in the creditor's own possession poinding is competent,
and arrestment is not.[2] The extract of a Sheriff Court decree
for payment contains a warrant to poind, after the expiry of the
days of charge.[3]

[1] 1 & 2 Vict. c. 114, secs. 23, 30.
[2] Lochhead v. Graham, 1883, 11 R. 201.
[3] 55 & 56 Vict. c. 17, sec. 7 (1), Schedule I.

Such moveables only as are corporeal may be poinded, except
for Crown debts, for recovery of which this diligence is, by the
Exchequer Act, 1856, extended to include bank notes, money,

bonds, bills, stocking, and implements of husbandry of all kinds.[1] In practice bank notes are not usually attached under an ordinary poinding, but if the question were raised for decision they might be held to be poindable.[2] Some moveables are generally exempt from poinding, as, for instance, agricultural implements, and horses used in tillage during the tillage season, if there are any other effects available.[3] It is also held that wearing apparel to a reasonable amount, and working tools so far as necessary for the debtor's livelihood, are not poindable.[4] By established practice ships are not poinded, but arrested, although an order made under the Merchant Shipping Act, 1894, for payment of seamen's wages can apparently be operated by poinding.[5] Goods already sequestrated for rent may be poinded to attach any reversion.[6]

[1] 19 & 20 Vict. c. 56, sec. 32.
[2] Graham Stewart, Diligence, 340.
[3] 1503 c. 98.
[4] Graham Stewart, Diligence, 345, and cases cited.
[5] 57 & 58 Vict. c. 60, sec. 693.
[6] Wyllie v. Fisher, 1907 S.C. 686.

The poinding may proceed at any time after the expiry of the days of charge, and there is no time limit within which it must be executed. It is carried out by a messenger-at-arms or an officer of Court,[1] without any further warrant than the extract decree. That extract carries authority to open shut and lockfast places, if that be necessary to enable the officer to execute the poinding.[2] The goods poinded are appraised by two valuators, and set forth in a schedule,[3] each article being separately valued and entered,[4] and a copy of the schedule of poinding is delivered by the officer to the debtor, or to the custodian of the poinded effects, the execution, signed by the officer and the valuators, being reported to the Sheriff within eight days, unless the Sheriff on cause shown extends the time.[3] When the goods are appraised they are offered to the debtor at the appraised value, and may be acquired by him or those acting for him—but not by third parties[5]—at that value. The poinding must be commenced before sunset and completed during daylight.[6] Poinding by the Crown under the Taxes Management Act follows its own procedure and witnesses at the poinding are not necessary.[7]

[1] 55 & 56 Vict. c. 17, sec. 8.
[2] Ibid., sec. 7 (1).
[3] 1 & 2 Vict. c. 114, secs. 23-25.
[4] See Le Conte v. Douglas, 1880, 8 R. 175.
[5] Hogg v. Taylor, 1934 S.L.T. (Sh.Ct.) 36.
[6] Graham Stewart, Diligence, 338; Urquhart & Son v. Wood, 1906, 22 Sh.Ct.Rep. 255.
[7] 43 & 44 Vict. c. 19, sec. 97; Norman v. Dymock, 1932 S.C. 131.

A poinding may be interrupted by payment being made of the debt. Receiving the debt is not within the normal scope of duty of the officer executing the poinding, and if he had not authority to collect the debt, the person paying runs the risk of having again to pay to the creditor, if payment does not reach him through the officer.[1] The proceedings must be stopped if the debtor tenders the amount in the decree, principal, interest, and expenses, or the appraised value of the poinded effects.[2] The officer cannot demand the dues of charge, or expenses incurred in the poinding, although these are charges for which the debtor may be made liable otherwise.[2] The person making payment is entitled to have a marking made upon the extract decree, but he is not entitled to delivery of it.[3] If the officer has no mandate to receive payment the debtor should consign in the creditor's name and deliver the deposit receipt to the officer who should then stop the poinding.[1]

[1] Graham Stewart, Diligence, 351.
[2] Ibid., 350.
[3] Inglis v. M'Intyre, 1862, 24 D. 541.

The poinding may also be interrupted by some person appearing and claiming the poinded effects as his. When this happens the officer should examine the claimant on oath and consider any documents of title produced.[1] On the evidence adduced he may desist from poinding, or he may proceed and narrate the evidence in his execution, leaving the objector to appear by minute in the poinding process,[2] but he should in any case preserve an inventory of the effects on the premises. If the claim turns out to be groundless and collusive, the interrupter may be liable to the creditor in damages.[3] The debtor's wife may competently appear as a third party claiming the effects.[1]

[1] Maxwell v. Controller of Clearing House, 1923 S.L.T. (Sh.Ct.) 137; Cameron v. Cuthbertson, 1924 S.L.T. (Sh.Ct.) 67; Farrell v. Gordon & Co., 1928, 44 Sh.Ct.Rep. 208.
[2] Lamb v. Wood, 1904, 6 F. 1091.
[3] Erskine III, 6, 27; cf. M'Connell v. Brew, 1907, 23 Sh.Ct.Rep. 261.

Bankruptcy interrupts a poinding. If the officer is certiorated that an award of sequestration of the debtor's estates has been granted, he must desist, even although the poinding creditor may possibly be a preferable creditor. The officer should complete an inventory but the creditor must allow the trustee in bankruptcy to realize the effects, and his remedy is to claim a preference in the sequestration process.[1]

[1] Sinclair v. Edinburgh Parish Council, 1909 S.C. 1353.

At any time before completion of poinding, any other creditor who holds a warrant to poind, that is to say, who holds an extracted decree for payment on which a charge has been given and has expired, may claim to be conjoined.[1] The officer is, at the moment, the sole judge of whether a creditor should be conjoined; but if the warrant produced is *ex facie* regular, the officer should endeavour to poind sufficient to cover the judgment debts of both the poinding creditor, and the intervening creditor.

[1] 1 & 2 Vict. c. 114, sec. 23; Graham Stewart, Diligence, 355.

The report of poinding should set forth the designations of the creditor, the debtor, and the valuators, the debt and the diligence, as well as a list of the poinded articles and their value.[1] It narrates the delivery of the schedule to the holder of the goods,[1] and also any evidence from objectors, and is signed by the officer and the valuators. Upon the report of the poinding, the Sheriff may grant a warrant for the sale to proceed at a time and place fixed, the time not to be less than eight, or more than twenty, days after publication of notice of sale.[1] The Sheriff may direct the manner in which notice is to be given, and a copy of the warrant of sale must be served at least six days before the date of sale, upon the debtor, and also upon the person in whose custody the poinded effects may be.[1] Such service may be made by an officer or by registered post letter.[2] Undue delay in applying for a warrant for sale may be a ground for refusing the warrant,[3] but when an arrestment is used after poinding and before a sale, by a creditor of the poinder the sale will still proceed and the debtor to protect himself should suspend the charge and interdict the poinding.[4]

[1] 1 & 2 Vict. c. 114, secs. 25, 26.
[2] Lochhead v. Graham, 1883, 11 R. 201.
[3] Graham Stewart, Diligence, 360.
[4] Ferguson v. Bothwell, 1882, 9 R. 687.

If at the sale no offerer appear to offer the upset price, which is not to be less than the appraised value, the articles are delivered by the judge of the roup to the poinding, and any conjoined, creditor, or their solicitors, to be applied as at their appraised value in satisfaction *pro tanto* of the debt, interest, and expenses.[1] The poinding creditor, or any other creditor, may purchase at the sale.[2] If a sale is effected, or the articles are delivered in satisfaction of the debt, a report of sale or delivery is lodged, and on a sale the roup rolls or certified copies and an account of the proceeds and the expenses of sale are also lodged, all within eight days of the sale.[3] The Sheriff may order the free proceeds to be consigned, although, where there is no competition, this is in practice not always done. If there be no competing claims, the proceeds of sale may be paid to the poinding creditor and any conjoined creditor; but if there are competing claims, the right to the consigned fund is determined in the same manner as in a multiplepoinding.[3]

[1] 1 & 2 Vict. c. 114, sec. 27.
[2] Ibid., sec. 29.
[3] Ibid., sec. 28.

The procedure at a sale under a poinding is by Statute under the direction of the Sheriff. He has thus general authority to do whatever is necessary to afford creditors the benefit of the poinding process. If the goods poinded are perishable he may order their immediate disposal, or if they are in an insecure place he may order their removal into safe custody.[1]

[1] 1 & 2 Vict. c. 113, sec. 26.

The convenient, and not uncommon, practice of the officer handing over the proceeds to the poinding creditor without an order of Court does not seem to be sanctioned by the statutory directions, and cases may be conceived where this practice if recognized might prejudice creditors other than the poinding creditor, who might be entitled to participate. It has been held that such a payment without an order of Court does not prejudice the participation in the proceeds of another creditor who had intimated a claim to the Sheriff-clerk and that in such circumstances an order for consignation could still be made.[1]

[1] Gillon & Co. v. Christison, 1909, 25 Sh.Ct.Rep. 283.

If the goods of a third party have been erroneously included in a poinding schedule, the proper course for a party claiming their ownership is to intervene in the poinding process, by minute, and object to such goods being included in the warrant of sale.[1] If the warrant of sale has been already granted, the remedy is to interdict the sale.[2] As to a third party's rights after sale, see the cases undernoted.[3]

[1] Lamb v. Wood, 1904, 6 F. 1091; cf. Ross v. Sinclair, 1904, 20 Sh.Ct.Rep. 317.
[2] Jack v. Waddell's Trustees, 1918 S.C. 73; cf. Ross v. Sinclair, supra.
[3] Boyle v. James Miller & Partners, 1942 S.L.T. (Sh.Ct.) 33; Grant & Co. v. Napier & Son, 1943, 59 Sh.Ct.Rep. 109.

A person who unlawfully intromits with, or carries off, poinded effects is liable to be imprisoned till he restore the effects, or pay to the poinding creditor double their appraised value.[1] A

warrant for his imprisonment may be obtained upon an application at the instance of the poinding creditor without the concurrence of the procurator-fiscal, for, although imprisonment may
follow, this is a civil process.[2] Such application may be presented,
and warrant granted, either in the Sheriff Court within whose
jurisdiction the poinding was executed, or in the Court where
the party so interfering with the poinded effects has his domicile.[1]
Apart from an application under the Act the poinding creditor
may bring an action of damages in ordinary form at common
law.[3]

[1] 1 & 2 Vict. c. 114, sec. 30.
[2] Wilson v. M'Kellar, 1896, 24 R. 254. See also Dickson v. Bryan,
1889, 16 R. 673; A and B v. Allan, 1910, 27 Sh.Ct.Rep. 139; and
Encyclopædia of Scottish Legal Styles VII, 269.
[3] Graham Stewart, Diligence, 358. See Angus Brothers v. Crocket,
1909, 25 Sh.Ct.Rep. 322, p. 326.

7. IMPRISONMENT.

A Sheriff Court extract decree is a warrant for imprisonment,
when imprisonment is competent, and in such cases the nature of
the debt must be stated in the extract.[1] It is now competent to
imprison only for non-payment of (a) Crown taxes,* fines, or
penalties, the term not to exceed twelve months[2]; (b) rates and
assessments, the term not to exceed six weeks in respect of rates
of any one year[3]; (c) alimentary debts, when failure to pay is
wilful, the term not to exceed six weeks[4]; and (d) for wilful refusal
to implement a decree *ad factum præstandum*. Imprisonment
under a *meditatione fugæ* warrant is no longer competent.[5]

[1] 55 & 56 Vict. c. 17, sec. 7 (1) and Schedule, General Directions.
[2] 43 & 44 Vict. c. 34, sec. 4. See Walker v. Bryce, 1881, 9 R. 249.
[3] Ibid.; 45 & 46 Vict. c. 42, sec. 5.
[4] 43 & 44 Vict. c. 34, sec. 4; 45 & 46 Vict. c. 42, secs. 3, 4.
[5] Glenday v. Johnston, 1905, 8 F. 24. See p. 35, supra.

In the case of debts, other than alimentary, when imprisonment is competent, the procedure is regulated by the Debtors
(Scotland) Act, 1838. The extract decree and execution of charge
are produced to the Sheriff-clerk within year and day of the
expiry of the charge and are registered by him.[1] The party
desiring to imprison a defender presents the extract with certificate
of registration thereon, and having endorsed a minute subscribed
by himself or his solicitor craving warrant for imprisonment,
the Sheriff-clerk writes thereon " Fiat ut petitur." This deliverance is authority to officers of Court to apprehend, and, if necessary for that purpose, to open shut and lockfast places, and is
authority also to prison authorities to receive and detain the

* Alterations proposed by Crown Proceedings Bill.

prisoner till liberated in due course of law.[2] The warrant is
executed by a Sheriff officer or a messenger-at-arms.[3] Certain
provisions in favour of defenders under decrees *ad factum
præstandum* are considered later.[4]

[1] 1 & 2 Vict. c. 114, sec. 10.
[2] Ibid., sec. 11, Schedule, No. 8.
[3] 55 & 56 Vict. c. 17, sec. 8.
[4] See pp. 284, 479, infra.

As regards alimentary debts, the procedure is under the Civil
Imprisonment Act, 1882. There must be failure to pay within the
days of charge sums of aliment and any expenses decerned for.[1]
The charge should not be made under pain of imprisonment.[2]
The creditor's application is to be disposed of summarily without
any written pleadings,[3] and the usual procedure is by minute
craving warrant to imprison, which is contained in an official
printed form. Upon this being lodged the debtor is cited to
attend to show cause why warrant should not be granted.[3] The
onus is on the debtor to show that his failure to pay has not been
wilful.[1] If he fail to do so, or fails to appear, warrant may be
granted for his imprisonment for a time not exceeding six weeks.
Postal citation of the debtor, though competent, is not recommended, and in some Courts warrant of imprisonment is not
granted without personal citation. The Sheriff's judgment is not
appealable in so far as it grants or refuses imprisonment in
respect of failure to pay,[4]—the debtor's remedy being by way of
suspension—but in other cases, as in questions whether the decree
is one for aliment, appeal is competent.[5] If it is proved to the
satisfaction of the Sheriff that, since the commencement of the
action in which the decree was pronounced, the debtor has not
possessed or been able to earn the means of paying what is due,
or such instalments as the Sheriff considers reasonable, the application will be refused.[1] Expenses are not awarded in such applications.[6] The practice of granting lengthy adjournments in these
cases has been adversely criticized in the Court of Session, and such
a course seems incompetent without affording the debtor an opportunity of showing his inability to pay at the first diet.[7]

[1] 45 & 46 Vict. c. 42, sec. 4.
[2] Whiteford v. Gibson, (O.H.) 1899, 7 S.L.T. 233; Torbet v. Morrison,
1902, 18 Sh.Ct.Rep. 183; Shanks v. Shanks, 1910, 27 Sh.Ct.Rep. 57.
[3] See Cook v. Wallace & Wilson, 1889, 16 R. 565.
[4] Strain v. Strain, 1886, 13 R. 1029; Christie v. Lowden, 1890, 6
Sh.Ct.Rep. 140.
[5] Tevendale v. Duncan, 1883, 10 R. 852; Purdon v. Purdon, 1884,
Guthrie's Select Cases II, 160; Crosbie v. Crosbie, 1902, 4 F. 945.
[6] Strain v. Strain, 1888, 4 Sh.Ct.Rep. 125; Wilson v. Wilson, 1936, 52
Sh.Ct.Rep. 200.
[7] Cain v. M'Colm, 1892, 19 R. 813.

To justify the debtor being imprisoned the case must be within the precise terms of the Statute. Thus it has been held that imprisonment is not competent on a decree of registration following on a bond for aliment,[1] nor upon a decree for arrears of aliment for an illegitimate child fixed by agreement, the decree in the latter case being regarded as a claim of relief.[2] In the case of arrears of aliment imprisonment is competent if aliment is still due,[3] but not after the duty of providing aliment has ceased.[4] It would seem that an offer by the father of an illegitimate child to assume custody would not now affect his liability to imprisonment for failure to pay aliment.[5] A public authority which has maintained some person out of public funds cannot enforce by imprisonment a decree obtained against the party liable to them in reimbursement of their outlay[6]; nor can an agent-disburser so enforce a decree for expenses obtained in his own name.[7] It is thought to be clear that an assignee who obtains right to an alimentary decree cannot enforce the decree by imprisonment.[8] But an order to pay to an inspector of poor or other person may now be granted by the Court, and such order may be enforced by imprisonment.[9] Imprisonment in respect of expenses of an action which is not wholly or mainly for aliment appears to be incompetent.[10]

[1] M'Geekie v. Cameron, 1897, 13 Sh.Ct.Rep. 357.
[2] Stewart v. Scott, 1934 S.L.T. (Sh.Ct.) 24.
[3] Cain v. M'Colm, 1892, 19 R. 813; Park v. Roberts, 1906, 22 Sh.Ct.Rep. 322.
[4] Glenday v. Johnston, 1905, 8 F. 24.
[5] 20 & 21 Geo. V c. 33, sec. 2 (2); cf. Wilson v. Lindsey, (O.H.) 1893, 1 S.L.T. 272.
[6] Tevendale v. Duncan, 1883, 10 R. 852; Mackay v. Resolis Parish Council, 1899, 1 F. 521. See 20 & 21 Geo. V c. 33, sec. 4.
[7] Bulloch, &c. v. Pollock, 1887, 3 Sh.Ct.Rep. 249.
[8] Cain v. M'Colm, supra, Lord M'Laren, p. 817. See 20 & 21 Geo. V c. 33, sec. 4.
[9] 20 & 21 Geo. V c. 33, sec. 4.
[10] Renwick v. Blair, 1910, 27 Sh.Ct.Rep. 210; Mitchell v. Mitchell, 1912, 28 Sh.Ct.Rep. 183; Smith v. Smith, 1914, 30 Sh.Ct.Rep. 178.

Imprisonment of the debtor does not to any extent operate as a satisfaction or extinction of the debt, or interfere with the creditor's other remedies for recovery,[1] and imprisonment may be granted of new at intervals of not less than six months against the same person in respect of failure to pay the same sums of aliment and expenses so far as outstanding, or any sums afterwards accruing due under the decree.[2] The creditor has no responsibility for alimenting the debtor while he is in prison.[3]

[1] 45 & 46 Vict. c. 42, sec. 4 (5).
[2] Ibid., sec. 4 (4); cf. Walker v. Bryce, 1881, 9 R. 249 (Act of 1880).
[3] Ibid., sec. 4 (6).

In decrees *ad factum præstandum* the time within which implement is to be carried out should be stated,[1] but if this is not done the charge will be on an induciæ of seven days.[2] It is now provided, however, that no person may be apprehended or imprisoned for failure to comply with a decree *ad factum præstandum* save after certain procedure in Court.[3] The person in right of such a decree—which would seem to include an assignee —may apply to the Court by which the decree was granted, and, if the Court is satisfied that the person against whom the decree was granted is wilfully refusing to comply with it, warrant to imprison for any period up to six months may be granted.[4] The onus in this case is on the creditor to show wilful refusal, and it is presumably necessary that a charge should have expired without implement of the decree. Imprisonment does not operate to extinguish the obligation under the decree, and the creditor is not liable to aliment the debtor while in prison.[5] Where the Court is satisfied that a debtor who is in prison has complied, or is no longer wilfully refusing to comply, with the decree immediate liberation may be ordered.[6] In lieu of granting warrant to imprison, the Court may recall the original decree and grant an order for payment or such other order as seems just, and where delivery of corporeal moveables is sought may grant warrant to officers of Court to search for, take possession of, and deliver such moveables to the creditor.[7] The last-mentioned warrant is deemed to include authority to open shut and lockfast places.[8] The above provisions do not apply to decrees obtained in the Small Debt Court.[9] The procedure to be followed to obtain a warrant to imprison is not laid down but application may be made by minute in the original action. Warrant is usually granted to cite the defender to a stated diet at which pursuer is appointed to lead proof of wilful refusal and defender is appointed if he so desires to lead conjunct probation.

[1] Macdonald v. Mackessack, 1888, 16 R. 168.
[2] M'Lintock v. Prinzen & Van Glabbeek, 1902, 4 F. 948.
[3] 3 & 4 Geo. VI c. 42, sec. 1 (1).
[4] Ibid., sec. 1 (1) (i).
[5] Ibid., sec. 1 (1) (iii) (iv).
[6] Ibid., sec. 1 (1) (ii).
[7] Ibid., sec. 1 (2).
[8] Ibid., sec. 1 (3).
[9] Ibid., sec. 1 (4). See further, p. 479, infra.

8. Inhibition.

The object of inhibition is to prevent a debtor dealing with his heritable property to the prejudice of creditors. It may be used either before or after judgment, but it is not competent on the dependence where the only pecuniary crave in the writ is the crave for expenses.[1] Thus, inhibition may be used on the dependence in an action with mixed craves, as, for instance, separation and aliment,[2] and also in an action with alternative craves such as delivery, with an alternative crave for damages.[3] It is directed against the alienation of lands and heritages, but its effect is merely prohibitory, and of itself it gives the inhibitor no title to, and effects no transfer of, the lands. It is made operative by an action of adjudication in the Court of Session. Inhibition is not competent upon a small debt decree.[4]

[1] Weir v. Otto, 1870. 8 M. 1070; Stafford v. M'Laurin, 1875, 3 R. 148.
[2] Burns v. Burns, 1879, 7 R. 355.
[3] More v. Stirling & Sons, 1822, 1 S. 547.
[4] Lamont, 1867. 6 M. 84.

Inhibition is not, properly speaking, a Sheriff Court process, for it proceeds upon letters issued under the Signet. Production of a Sheriff Court decree, other than a small debt decree, in the Petition Department of the Court of Session[1] is sufficient warrant for issuing letters of inhibition, and a notice thereof, setting forth the names and designations of the persons by and against whom the same are raised and the date of signeting, is registered in the Register of Inhibitions and Adjudications.[2] If this is done, and the execution is registered within twenty-one days of the date of registration of the notice, the inhibition takes effect from the date of the registration of the notice, otherwise it takes effect only from the date of the registration of the execution.[2] A charge on the decree is not a necessary preliminary to the issue of letters of inhibition. When inhibition is desired on the dependence an initial writ, with a pecuniary crave as above described, or a certified copy of the writ is produced. Inhibition may be recalled in the Court of Session, and where there is no depending process before that Court the procedure is by petition to the Inner House. Inhibitions prescribe in five years.[3]

[1] Rules of Court, 1936, IV, 1 (b).
[2] 31 & 32 Vict. c. 101, sec. 155; 14 & 15 Geo. V c. 27, sec. 44.
[3] 14 & 15 Geo. V c. 27, sec. 44 (3) (a).

9. ADJUDICATION.

Inhibition may be followed by an action of adjudication. Inhibition is not a necessary preliminary to an adjudication, but its use may affect the ranking of creditors where there is a competition. Adjudication is a Court of Session process, and is not competent in the Sheriff Court except to the limited extent

of adjudication *contra hæreditatem jacentem*, and in the case of
the statutory process of adjudication available to the holder of
a ground annual.[1] Decree in the action of adjudication adjudges
to the creditor the debtor's heritable estate, to the value of the
amount of the creditor's constituted debt, principal, interest and
expenses, and also further interest up to the date of redemption
of the heritage. The decree of adjudication, or an abbreviate,
is recorded and operates as a title to the adjudger, but the
right is redeemable within ten years. Meantime, the decree of
adjudication may be made the foundation for an action of maills
and duties, under which the creditor will take the rents.[2]

1 See p. 579, infra.
2 See generally Graham Stewart, Diligence, 576, et seq.

10. JUDGMENTS EXTENSION ACT.

Formerly, a judgment of a Scottish Court was not operative
in England or Ireland, and to enforce it there a separate action
in the sister kingdom was necessary. Under the Judgments
Extension Act of 1868,[1] a system of registration of decrees of
the Courts of the three kingdoms was introduced, but in Scotland
this applied only to Court of Session judgments. In 1882 the
registration principle was applied also to the inferior Courts,
which as regards Scotland means the Sheriff Court, including
the Small Debt Court.[2] Neither of these Acts now applies as
between this country and the Irish Free State.[3] The Administration of Justice Act, 1920, which makes corresponding provisions
between Great Britain and the Dominions relates only to decrees
of superior Courts.[4]

1 31 & 32 Vict. c. 54.
2 45 & 46 Vict. c. 31, sec. 2.
3 Calton v. Calder & Co., 1928, 44 Sh.Ct.Rep. 206.
4 10 & 11 Geo. V c. 81.

When a certificate of judgment obtained in an inferior Court
of one kingdom has been registered in another, it becomes, for
diligence purposes, equivalent to a judgment of the Court where
it is so registered, and may be executed according to the practice
of the Court of registration.[1] But such execution is only available under the Act against " any goods or chattels " of the
defender which are within the jurisdiction of the Court of registration[1]—debts and sums of money being thus excluded from
attachment.[2] The certificate of judgment will be presented where
it is intended to execute diligence against the defender. Thus, a
certificate of the judgment of a County Court in England or

Northern Ireland may be presented to the Sheriff-clerk of any Sheriff Court in Scotland for registration, whereupon it becomes a warrant for diligence to the extent above indicated, as if it had been pronounced in that Sheriff Court. The induciæ of the charge upon a certificate is fifteen days.[3]

[1] 45 & 46 Vict. c. 31, secs. 4, 5; Codifying Act of Sederunt L, IX.
[2] See Dove Wilson, Sheriff Court Practice, 4th edn., 354, 360; Graham Stewart, Diligence, 438.
[3] Codifying Act of Sederunt L, IX, 2.

This registration privilege applies only to judgments for " debt, damages, or costs."[1] Such judgments include not only decrees for payment, interim or final, but also decrees of absolvitor or dismissal with expenses, and decrees in absence as well as decrees in *foro*. A judgment cannot be registered under the Act after the lapse of twelve months from its date.[2] After that time, the privilege of registration is lost, and resort must be made to the former practice of using the judgment as a basis for a decree-conform in the Court of the sister kingdom. An action brought to obtain a decree-conform would not appear to be competent in the Sheriff Court.[3]

[1] 45 & 46 Vict. c. 31, sec. 3.
[2] Ibid., sec. 4.
[3] O'Connor v. Erskine, 1905, 22 Sh.Ct.Rep. 58.

It is not competent to register a certificate of judgment for an amount greater than could have been recovered in an action in the Court of registration.[1] This does not affect the registration of English or Northern Irish judgments in a Sheriffdom in Scotland, for there is no restriction in Scotland as to the amount which may be sued for in the Sheriff Court. But, in the converse case, registration of a Scottish judgment in an English or Northern Irish County Court may be precluded by the amount for which judgment has been given being in excess of the limit of County Court jurisdiction. In that event, the certificate of judgment may be registered in England or Northern Ireland in the Register of Scotch Judgments created by the Judgments Extension Act of 1868[2] for Court of Session judgments, in like manner as if the certificate had been that of a Court of Session judgment.[1]

[1] 45 & 46 Vict. c. 31, sec. 9.
[2] 31 & 32 Vict. c. 54, sec. 3.

The privileges of the Inferior Courts Judgments Extension Act do not apply to a judgment of a Sheriff Court in Scotland against a person who, at the time of raising the action upon which the judgment proceeds, was domiciled in England or Ireland, " unless the whole cause of action shall have arisen, or the obligation to which the judgment relates ought to have been fulfilled,'' within the jurisdiction of such Sheriff Court, and the action was personally served on defender within that district.[1] It has been held that the above limitation is intended to apply only in the case of defenders and that a decree for expenses is enforceable against an English or Irish pursuer although the action had not been personally served on the defender.[2]

[1] 45 & 46 Vict. c. 31, sec. 10.
[3] Carr & Sons v. M'Lennan Blair & Co., 1885, 1 Sh.Ct.Rep. 262; Hudson v. Innes & Grieve, 1907, 24 Sh.Ct.Rep. 190.

So far as diligence is concerned, the Court has the same control and jurisdiction in the case of a registered certificate of a judgment as it has in regard to diligence upon one of its own judgments.[1] It is further provided that the Court which registers a certificate of judgment may order the registration to be cancelled on proof of the setting aside or satisfaction of the judgment.[2] This is most likely to be necessary where some error has occurred, for the Act directs that a certificate of judgment is not to be granted until the appeal days have elapsed, and upon proof that the judgment has not been satisfied.[3]

[1] 45 & 46 Vict. c. 31, sec. 6.
[2] Ibid., sec. 7.
[3] Ibid., sec. 3.

If a judgment to which the Act does not apply is sought to be enforced by registration, a prohibition or injunction against the enforcement of the judgment may be obtained in England or Northern Ireland by the person against whom the judgment is proposed to be enforced. In like manner, if an English or Northern Irish judgment is proposed to be enforced by registration in the Sheriff Court in Scotland, suspension and interdict may be applied for in the Court of Session.[1] Under this section the Court has to consider only whether the judgment proposed to be registered is one which falls within the Act.

[1] 45 & 46 Vict. c. 31, sec. 10.

The special provisions for the registration of an English bastardy or maintenance order under the Summary Jurisdiction (Process) Act, 1881, are considered later.[1]

[1] See p. 666, infra.

CHAPTER XIII.

APPEAL.

1. Value.

The Sheriff Courts Act, 1907, provides that, subject to the provisions of that Act and of the Small Debt Acts, all causes not exceeding £50 in value, exclusive of interest and expenses, competent in the Sheriff Court, shall be brought and followed forth in the Sheriff Court only, and shall not be subject to review by the Court of Session.[1] It is further provided that no appeal to the Court of Session is competent where the cause does not exceed £50 in value, exclusive of interest and expenses, or is being tried as a summary cause, unless the case has first been taken to the Sheriff on appeal, and, after final judgment by him, he certifies it as a case suitable for appeal to the Court of Session.[2] The motion for the Sheriff's certificate must be made within seven days of the date of the final interlocutor.[2]

[1] 7 Edw. VII c. 51, sec. 7; 2 & 3 Geo. V c. 28, Schedule I.
[2] Ibid., sec. 28; 2 & 3 Geo. V c. 28, sec. 2.

The principles for determining the value of a cause have already been considered in connexion with the privative jurisdiction of the Sheriff Court, and reference should be made to what is there written.[1]

[1] See p. 47, et seq., supra.

2. Appeals in Ordinary Causes.

(1) Appeal to the Sheriff.

(a) General.—This mode of review, by appeal from a single judge to another single judge, is, in Scotland, peculiar to the Sheriff Court. Originally there was no such intermediate appeal, but the practice grew of taking the opinion of the Sheriff as a method of appeal and after its formal recognition in the Act of Sederunt of 1839[1] the matter was regulated by successive Sheriff Courts Acts.

[1] Act of Sederunt, 10th July, 1839, secs. 98-100.

(b) *Appealable Interlocutors.*—Appeal from the Sheriff-Substitute to the Sheriff is competent without leave in the case of the following interlocutors :—

(1) A final judgment[1] as defined below.[2]

(2) An interlocutor granting or refusing interdict, interim or final.[3] But interim interdict, though appealed against will be binding until recalled.[4]

(3) An interlocutor granting an interim decree for payment of money other than a decree for expenses.[5] This is held to include warrant to uplift consigned money[6]—if this is in substance a decree for payment[7]—and warrant on a judicial manager to pay from a fund in his hands,[8] but not an order to consign,[9] which, however, falls under the next head. A decree for expenses may be appealed against if it is contained in an interlocutor allowing proof, granting an interim decree for payment or making another order which is itself appealable. In such a case the appellant may restrict his argument to a challenge of the decree for expenses, and thus in effect bring it alone under review.[10]

(4) An interlocutor making an order *ad factum præstandum*.[5] This includes an order to carry back hypothecated furniture,[11] and an order to consign,[12] but not an order for caution[13] or to sist a mandatory.[14] An order for caution may fall under the next head.

(5) An interlocutor sisting an action.[15] This has been held to include an incidental sist of process till caution has been found,[16] and an interlocutor which, though not in form a sist, is equivalent to an interlocutor sisting process.[17]

(6) An interlocutor allowing, or refusing, or limiting, the mode of proof, not being an interlocutor fixing a diet for jury trial.[18] This will cover an interlocutor of new allowing proof,[19] and one refusing recovery of writings,[20] but not one granting a diligence,[21] or ordering accounts.[22]

(7) An interlocutor refusing a reponing note.[23] An interlocutor which recalls or is incidental to the recall of a decree in absence is not appealable.[24]

Apart from these cases specified in the Act there would appear to be a general right of appeal to the Sheriff against an interlocutor of his Substitute which is incompetent.[25]

[1] 7 Edw. VII c. 51, sec. 27.
[2] See p. 291, infra.
[3] 7 Edw. VII c. 51, sec. 27 (a). See Gauldie v. Magistrates of Arbroath, 1936 S.C. 861 (question of interim interdict reserved).
[4] Ibid., sec. 29.
[5] Ibid., sec. 27 (b).

[6] Sinclair v. Baikie, 1884, 11 R. 413.
[7] Hughes' Trustee v. Hughes, 1925 S.C. 25.
[8] Baird v. Glendinning, 1874, 2 R. 25.
[9] Maxton v. Bone, 1886, 13 R. 912.
[10] See Nelson v. Wilson & Sons, 1913, 29 Sh.Ct.Rep. 90.
[11] Menzies, &c. v. Templeton, 1896, 12 Sh.Ct.Rep. 323.
[12] Mackenzie v. Balerno Paper Mill Co., 1883, 10 R. 1147.
[13] Jack v. Carmichael, 1894, 10 Sh.Ct.Rep. 242.
[14] Lawson v. Young, 1891, 7 Sh.Ct.Rep. 319.
[15] 7 Edw. VII c. 51, sec. 27 (c).
[16] Horn & Co. v. Tangyes, 1906, 8 F. 475.
[17] Watson v. Stewart, 1872, 10 M. 494.
[18] 7 Edw. VII c. 51, sec. 27 (d).
[19] Kinnes v. Fleming, 1881, 8 R. 386; Sinclair v. M'Coll, 1894, 10 Sh.Ct.Rep. 144.
[20] Thomson & Co. v. Bowater & Sons, 1918 S.C. 316.
[21] Stewart v. Kennedy, 1890, 17 R. 755; Baikie v. Doull, 1908, 24 Sh.Ct.Rep. 211; Dick v. Blairgowrie Town Council, 1910, 27 Sh.Ct.Rep. 243.
[22] Lamont & Co. v. Dublin, &c., Steam Packet Co., 1908 S.C. 1017.
[23] 7 Edw. VII c. 51, sec. 27 (e); 2 & 3 Geo. V c. 28, Schedule I.
[24] 7 Edw. VII c. 51, Schedule I, Rule 33.
[25] See Archer's Trustees v. Alexander & Sons, 1910, 27 Sh.Ct.Rep. 11; Maxwells v. Adam, 1911, 2 S.L.T. 149. See also Bone v. School Board of Sorn, 1886, 13 R. 768; County Council of Roxburgh v. Dalrymple's Trustees, 1894, 21 R. 1063.

In addition to the foregoing interlocutors in which appeals are competent without leave, appeals may be taken in the case of any other interlocutors against which the Sheriff-Substitute, either *ex proprio motu*, or on the motion of any party, grants leave to appeal.[1] Without prejudice to the above general right of appeal with leave, the Act specifies various particular cases where an appeal is competent with leave. These are interlocutors remitting the cause to another Sheriffdom,[2] where the Sheriff's judgment on appeal is not further subject to review, and appeals on questions of admissibility of evidence[3] and on questions of confidentiality and hypothec in connexion with documentary or oral evidence, which the Sheriff, with or without a hearing, is directed to dispose of with the least possible delay.[4]

[1] 7 Edw. VII c. 51, sec. 27 (f); 2 & 3 Geo. V c. 28, Schedule I.
[2] Ibid., Schedule I, Rules 20, 21. See also Lamb & Co. v. Pearson, 1911, 28 Sh.Ct.Rep. 80 (Rule 19).
[3] Ibid., Rule 75. See p. 222, supra.
[4] Ibid., Rule 76. See p. 223, supra.

A final judgment is defined in the Act as an interlocutor which, by itself, or taken along with previous interlocutors, disposes of the subject-matter of the cause, notwithstanding that judgment may not have been pronounced on every question raised, and that expenses found due may not have been modified, taxed or decerned for.[1] It is immaterial that the interlocutor is a decree by default,[2] and it is probably also immaterial that certain questions in the case affecting parties other than the appellant have not been disposed of.[3] In the light of provisions regulating appeal to the Court of Session, it has been held that an interlocutor disposing of a claim in a competition is a final interlocutor for purposes of appeal to that Court.[4] In an appeal to the Sheriff the matter would have to be decided on the terms of the Sheriff Courts Act itself, but it is thought that the same result would be reached.

[1] 7 Edw. VII c. 51, sec. 3 (h).
[2] As in Laurence v. Gray, 1908, 25 Sh.Ct.Rep. 19.
[3] See Duke of Roxburghe, 1875, 2 R. 715. See also Glasgow Corporation v. General Accident, &c., Corporation, 1914 S.C. 835.
[4] Glasgow Corporation v. General Accident, &c., Corporation, supra; cf. Strichen Endowments v. Diverall, 1891, 19 R. 79.

In the normal case it is essential for a final judgment that the liability for expenses should have been disposed of. So, where the merits of the case have been dealt with, and a later interlocutor decides the liability for the expenses, appeal against the later interlocutor is competent.[1] The earlier interlocutor dealing with the merits only is not a final judgment.[2] Where the merits and the liability for expenses have been disposed of, either together or in separate interlocutors, and no appeal has been taken, a subsequent interlocutor decerning for expenses already found due is not a final judgment and cannot be appealed against as such,[3] though it is open to appeal with leave.[4] Where the merits and expenses are both disposed of, a reservation as to modification of the expenses will not prevent the interlocutor being a final judgment, but the subsequent interlocutor dealing with the modification will also be regarded as a final judgment.[5] While there seems to have been some doubt upon the point it is thought to be now clear that where there are objections to the auditor's report the interlocutor disposing of these is not a final judgment but is to be treated as a mere decerniture for expenses already found due.[6] An interlocutor fixing the scale of taxation for expenses already awarded is not a final judgment.[7] Where the Sheriff had partially disposed of the merits but refused to deal with expenses at that stage the party against whom the judgment was given was held entitled to bring the matter before the Court of Session by suspension and interdict.[8]

[1] Fleming v. North of Scotland Banking Co., 1881, 9 R. 11; Bowman's Trustees v. Scott's Trustees, 1901, 3 F. 450; Barrie v. Caledonian Railway Co., 1902, 5 F. 30; Caldwell v. Dykes, 1906, 8 F. 839; Wyllie v. Fisher, 1907 S.C. 686; Garrioch v. Glass, 1911 S.C. 453.

[2] Greenock Parochial Board v. Miller & Brown, 1877, 4 R. 737; Russell v. Allan, 1877, 5 R. 22; Burns v. Waddell, 1897, 24 R. 325; Caledonian Railway Co. v. Glasgow Corporation, 1900, 2 F. 871; Houstoun v. Gault, 1925 S.C. 429.

[3] Tennents v. Romanes, 1881, 8 R. 824; Thompson & Co. v. King, 1883, 10 R. 469; Stirling Maxwell's Trustees v. Kirkintilloch Police Commissioners, 1883, 11 R. 1; M'Kinstrey v. Plean Colliery Co., 1910, 27 Sh.Ct.Rep. 62. See also Carson v. M'Dowall, 1908, 24 Sh.Ct.Rep. 324 (refusal of decree in name of agent disburser).

[4] Laurenson v. Gordon, 1901, 18 Sh.Ct.Rep. 319; Dalton & Co. v. Boyle & Co., 1909, 26 Sh.Ct.Rep. 53.

[5] Taylor's Trustees v. M'Gairgan, 1896, 23 R. 738; Inglis v. National Bank of Scotland, 1911 S.C. 6.

[6] M'Alley v. Marshall's Trustees, 1913 S.C. 890; M'Kinstrey v. Plean Colliery Co., supra; cf. Stirling Maxwell's Trustees v. Kirkintilloch Police Commissioners, supra.

[7] Shaw v. Browne, 1886, 2 Sh.Ct.Rep. 203.

[8] Caledonian Railway Co. v. Cochran's Trustees, 1897, 24 R. 855.

Where the merits of the case have in fact been disposed of and expenses have been dealt with, the interlocutor is a final judgment though the case is continued for purposes which are merely executorial.[1]

[1] Malcolm v. M'Intyre, 1877, 5 R. 22; M'Ewan v. Sharp, 1899, 1 F. 393; Turner's Trustees v. Steel, 1900, 2 F. 363; cf. Jardine v. Magistrates of Moffat, 1907 S.C. 1065.

In a multiplepoinding an interlocutor sustaining the competency and ordering claims is not a final judgment,[1] nor is an interlocutor finding a claimant entitled to be ranked but not granting an operative decree.[2] But an interlocutor disposing of a claim in a competition has been held to be a final judgment.[3] It has also been held that the following interlocutors are not final judgments: allowing proof by writ or oath,[4] refusing an order for caption,[5] and granting protestation.[6] An interlocutor dismissing one crave in an action and allowing proof *quoad* the other craves is not a final judgment.[7]

[1] Gordon v. Graham, 1874, 1 R. 1081; Macduff v. Macduff, 1893, 9 Sh.Ct.Rep. 243.

[2] Strichen Endowments v. Diverall, 1891, 19 R. 79.

[3] Glasgow Corporation v. General Accident Fire and Life Assurance Corporation, 1914 S.C. 835.

[4] Shirra v. Robertson, 1873, 11 M. 660; Wilson v. Brakenridge, 1888, 15 R. 587.

[5] Broatch v. Pattison, 1898, 1 F. 303.

[6] Robertson v. Black & Watson, 1901, 18 Sh.Ct.Rep. 98.

[7] Ludlow v. Strang, 1938 S.C. 551.

Appeal from the Sheriff-Substitute to the Sheriff or to the Court of Session may be excluded by the actings of parties or by special circumstances. Thus, appeal is incompetent if the Sheriff-Substitute was not acting in his judicial capacity[1]; if parties had agreed to accept his decision as final[2]—which must, however, be evidenced by more than mere deviations from normal procedure[3]—or if the judgment appealed against has been pronounced of consent.[4] An appeal is also incompetent if the appellant has no title to insist in it. On the latter ground a defender on whose averments a second defender had been added was not allowed to appeal against an interlocutor dismissing the action as against the second defender.[5]

[1] Magistrates of Glasgow v. Glasgow District Subway Co., 1893, 21 R. 52; cf. Ross v. Ross, 1920 S.C. 530.
[2] Shiels v. Shiels' Trustees, 1874, 1 R. 502; cf. Lindsay v. Walker's Trustees, 1877, 4 R. 870; Steel v. Steel, 1898, 25 R. 715.
[3] Gordon v. Bruce & Co., 1897, 24 R. 844; Stark's Trustees v. Duncan, 1906, 8 F. 429.
[4] Whyte v. Whyte, 1895, 23 R. 320; Paterson v. Kidd's Trustees, 1896, 23 R. 737; cf. Pirrie v. M'Neil, 1922 S.L.T. 160.
[5] M'Dermott v. Western S.M.T. Co., &c., 1937 S.C. 239.

(c) *Time for Appealing.*—The time within which appeal is competent varies in the case of different interlocutors, and is as follows :—

(1) Final judgments : three months from date of judgment, if not sooner extracted or implemented.[1] Extract of such judgments is competent in causes, other than summary causes, after a lapse of fourteen days from the date of the decree, or at such earlier date as the Sheriff may allow extract.[2]

(2) Interlocutory judgments in which appeal is competent without leave : fourteen days from date of interlocutor, if not sooner extracted,[1] extract being competent within the time above set forth.[2]

(3) Interlocutors under which leave to appeal is required : fourteen days unless sooner extracted.[1] But in this case the time runs not from the date of the interlocutor appealed against, but from the date of the interlocutor granting leave to appeal, because only then is there an appealable interlocutor.[3] Extract is competent within the time above set forth, unless either an appeal has been taken or leave to appeal has been applied for. In the latter case the issue of extract is not precluded unless leave is granted and an appeal is taken within seven days after leave is granted.[2] The effect of the above provisions— which were amended in 1927—is to extend the time for appealing, so that, if the application for leave is made within fourteen days, appeal is competent until the expiry of seven days from the date when leave is granted, when the interlocutor may be extracted and the right of appeal is lost. Apart from the right being cut off by extract, appeal would apparently be

competent up to fourteen days from the date of the interlocutor granting leave to appeal.

(4) Interlocutor granting interim interdict: fourteen days from the date of intimation thereof.[4]

After extract an interlocutor is not open to appeal even with consent of the other party to the cause,[5] and an appeal which is otherwise incompetent cannot be heard even of consent of parties.[6]

[1] 7 Edw. VII c. 51, Schedule I, Rule 86.
[2] Ibid., Rule 85; 17 & 18 Geo. V c. 35, sec. 21.
[3] M'Cabe v. Mount Vernon Colliery Co., 1925 S.C. 574.
[4] 7 Edw. VII c. 51, Schedule I, Rule 86; 2 & 3 Geo. V c. 28, Schedule II.
[5] Walker v. Wotherspoon, 1916, 35 Sh.Ct.Rep. 74; cf. Weir v. Tudhope, 1892, 19 R. 858 (extract of earlier interlocutors than that appealed against).
[6] Burns v. Waddell & Son, 1897, 24 R. 325; Millom and Askam Hematite Co. v. Simpson, 1897, 14 Sh.Ct.Rep. 206.

In addition to these general time-limits the following special cases are dealt with in other rules:—

(5) Appeal from ruling on question of confidentiality in regard to documentary or oral evidence, or on objection to produce on ground of hypothec or otherwise: in open Court at the proof.[1]

(6) Appeal from interlocutor transferring a cause under Rules 20 and 21: seven days.[2] An interlocutor transferring a cause under Rule 19 would be appealable with leave as in (3) above.[3]

(7) Appeal on question of admissibility of evidence at close of proof or within seven days thereafter if judgment not pronounced in the meantime.[4]

[1] 7 Edw. VII c. 51, Schedule I, Rule 76.
[2] Ibid., Rules 20, 21.
[3] See Lamb & Co. v. Pearson, 1911, 28 Sh.Ct.Rep. 80.
[4] 7 Edw. VII c. 51, Schedule I, Rule 75.

The date of every interlocutor is deemed to be the date upon which it is entered in the books of the Court.[1] If the date of such entry differs from the date of the interlocutor the date of entry should be noted on the interlocutor, as otherwise there is nothing in the process to show if an appeal has been taken timeously. Where an appeal taken to the Court of Session has been abandoned the appellant cannot thereafter appeal to the Sheriff,[2] nor can an appeal to the Sheriff be superseded by one to the Court of Session.[3] It has been indicated that this rule may not apply where the appeal has been marked to the wrong appellate tribunal by mistake, or where an appeal is withdrawn of consent of both parties.[3] When an appellant did not insist on his appeal before the Sheriff, and it was dismissed on this ground, he was not allowed to appeal against that interlocutor to the Court of Session.[4] Where an interlocutor assoilzieing two defenders was extracted by one and the extract bore that that one only had been assoilzied it was held that the extract, though incomplete, was, while it stood unreduced, a bar to the pursuer taking an appeal.[5] Extract of a decree for expenses will not bar appeal against a previous final judgment which has not been extracted.[6]

[1] 7 Edw. VII c. 51, Schedule I, Rule 83.
[2] Clark v. Comrie, 1910, 1 S.L.T. 404.
[3] J. & J. Fraser v. Smith, 1937 S.C. 667.
[4] Manchester and County Bank v. Moore, 1909 S.C. 246.
[5] Hutchison v. Robson, &c., 1930, 47 Sh.Ct.Rep. 109; cf. Menzies v. Templeton, 1896, 12 Sh.Ct.Rep. 323.
[6] Macfarlane v. Thomson, 1884, 12 R. 232.

(d) *Procedure in Appeals.*—The appeal is taken by a note of appeal dated and signed by the appellant or his solicitor in these terms: " The pursuer (or defender or other party) appeals to the Sheriff."[1] This is written on the interlocutor sheet, but if that is not in the hands of the Sheriff-clerk it may be written on a separate paper, which is lodged with a certificate by the Sheriff-clerk that the interlocutor sheet is not in his hands.[1] If an appellant intends to ask for review of only a portion of the interlocutor appealed against he should intimate this limitation of his appeal to the opposite party. An appeal is competent only to review an interlocutor and not to modify an opinion or observation in the relative note.[2]

[1] 7 Edw. VII c. 51, Schedule I, Rule 87.
[2] Kennedy v. Macrae, 1946 S.L.T. 198.

Within two days of the appeal being taken the Sheriff-clerk transmits the process to the Sheriff, and sends written notice of the appeal to the other parties or their solicitors, but failure to give such notice does not invalidate the appeal.[1] It is optional to the Sheriff either to order a reclaiming petition and answers, or to hear parties orally[2]—the latter being the usual practice. The reclaiming petition and answers should contain written arguments for both sides, and in conformity with earlier practice should avoid quotation from other parts of the process, except where this is indispensable.[3] On the motion of both parties the Sheriff may, if he see fit, dispose of the appeal without either written arguments or an oral hearing.[4] In the Court of Session, when a respondent does not appear to support a judgment appealed against, the appellant is not entitled to have the judgment reversed by default but must satisfy the Court that such judgment is in fact wrong.[5]   It is thought that the same principle should apply in the case of an appeal to the Sheriff.

[1] 7 Edw. VII c. 51, Schedule I, Rule 88.
[2] Ibid., Rule 89; 2 & 3 Geo. V c. 28, Schedule II.
[3] See 39 & 40 Vict. c. 70, sec. 30.
[4] 7 Edw. VII c. 51, Schedule I, Rule 90; 2 & 3 Geo. V c. 28, Schedule II.
[5] Alder v. Clark, 1880, 7 R. 1093; Dunbar v. Macadam, 1884, 11 R. 652.

When the action is before the Sheriff on appeal it is provided that he may open the record *ex proprio motu* if it appears to him not to have been properly made up, or may allow further proof.[1] It is not clear how the Sheriff can act at his own hand in such a matter, and the enactment seems to provide nothing more than could be obtained under the ordinary powers of amendment[2] It has been held that the Sheriff cannot under this provision, *ex proprio motu*, allow or order further proof.[2]   The Act provides that an appeal is effectual to submit to review the whole of the interlocutors pronounced in the cause, and the appeal is available to, and may be insisted in, by all other parties to the case though they have not noted separate appeals.[3]   But a party's acquiescence in an interlocutor which might have been appealed against at the time may preclude him asking review of the interlocutor when an appeal is taken at a later stage.[4]   It would appear that the extracting of any of the prior interlocutors does not prevent these being reviewed on appeal.[5]   Appeals may be taken notwithstanding the death, resignation or removal of a Sheriff, and these are heard by the succeeding Sheriff when he takes office.[6]

[1] 7 Edw. VII c. 51, sec. 27; 2 & 3 Geo. V c. 28, Schedule I.
[2] Hutchison v. Davidson, 1945 S.C. 395.
[3] 7 Edw. VII c. 51, sec. 29.
[4] Ferguson's Trustee v. Reid, 1931 S.C. 714.   See also Cunningham & Co. v. Benn Bros., 1920, 37 Sh.Ct.Rep. 76; Macaskill v. Nicol, 1943 S.C. 17.
[5] Weir v. Tudhope, 1892, 19 R. 858.
[6] 7 Edw. VII c. 51, sec. 27.

Notwithstanding that an appeal has been taken the Sheriff-Substitute may (a) regulate all matters relating to interim possession; (b) make any order for the preservation or sale of property to which the action relates; (c) make any order for the preservation of evidence; or (d) make in his discretion any interim order which a due regard to the interests of the parties may require.[1] Any such orders are not ordinary interlocutors in the cause, and as the process is no longer with the Sheriff-Substitute they

will be written on a separate sheet.[2]   Such orders are not subject
to review except by the Sheriff at the hearing of the appeal.[1]   An
appeal does not prevent immediate execution of a warrant of
sequestration for rent, or of warrants to take inventories, or place
effects in custody *ad interim*, or warrants for interim preservation.[3]
An interim interdict, though appealed against, is binding until
recalled.[4]   After an appeal has been noted the appellant is not
entitled to abandon it unless of consent of all parties, or by leave
of the Sheriff.[5]   It has been held that when a consistorial cause
is on appeal a motion by the wife for interim aliment is properly
made to the Sheriff-Substitute.[6]

[1] 7 Edw. VII c. 51, Schedule I, Rule 91.   See also Trainer v. Renfrewshire Upper Ward District Committee, 1907 S.C. 1117.
[2] See Trainer v. Renfrewshire Upper District Committee, supra, Lord
   President Dunedin, p. 1119.
[3] 7 Edw. VII c. 51, sec. 29.
[4] Ibid.   See also Rule 91, and Trainer v. Renfrewshire Upper District
   Committee, supra.
[5] Ibid., Schedule I, Rule 96.
[6] A B v C B, 1939 S.L.T. (Sh.Ct.) 11.

Where an interlocutor is affirmed on appeal the expenses of
the appeal are not carried unless this is expressly stated.[1]   If the
interlocutor affirming the judgment is silent as to expenses these
may be lost to the respondent.[1]

[1] Macdonald v. M'Eachan, 1880, 7 R. 574.

(2) *Appeal to the Court of Session.*

(a) *General.*—It has long been recognized in principle that
the Court of Session, as the Supreme Court of Scotland, has
power to review the judgments of the inferior Courts, including
the Sheriff Court.[1]   The general rule is that, unless review by
the Court of Session is, by express statutory enactment, or by
clear implication, excluded, every judgment of the Sheriff Court
or other inferior Court, is subject to review by the Court of
Session.[1]   There is an exception to this general rule in cases where
the inferior Court judgment is the decision of a Court to which
a discretion in some particular matter has been relegated by
Statute.   In such cases the appellate Court will not, as a rule,
entertain an appeal.[2]

[1] Harper v. Inspector of Rutherglen, 1903, 6 F. 23, Lord Trayner, p. 25;
   Jeffray v. Angus, 1909 S.C. 400, Lord Justice-Clerk Macdonald,
   p. 402.
[2] Strain v. Strain, 1886, 13 R. 1029; Crosbie v. Crosbie, 1902, 4 F. 945.
   See also New Mining, &c., Syndicate v. Chalmers & Hunter, 1909
   S.C. 1390.

The Sheriff Court Statutes did not create this right of review, but only regulated it. Originally the judgment of the Supreme Court was obtained by a separate process of advocation. In 1868 the process of advocation was abolished and the short note of appeal was adopted as the mode of appeal from the Sheriff Court to the Court of Session.[1]

[1] 31 & 32 Vict. c. 100, secs. 64, 65.

(b) *Appealable Interlocutors.*—Subject to the limit of value already specified,[1] appeal from the Sheriff or the Sheriff-Substitute to the Court of Session is competent in the case of the following interlocutors :—

(1) A final judgment[2] as already defined.[3]

(2) An interlocutor granting interim decree for payment of money other than a decree for expenses.[2] This is held to include warrant to uplift consigned money[4]—if this is in substance a decree for payment[5]—and warrant on a judicial manager to pay from a fund in his hands,[6] but not an order to consign.[7]

(3) An interlocutor sisting an action.[2] This has been held to include an incidental sist of process till caution has been found,[8] and an interlocutor which, though not in form a sist, is equivalent to an interlocutor sisting process.[9]

(4) An interlocutor refusing a reponing note[2]—an interlocutor which recalls or is incidental to the recall of a decree in absence not being appealable.[10]

(5) An interlocutor against which the Sheriff or Sheriff-Substitute, either *ex proprio motu* or on the motion of any party, grants leave to appeal.[2]

Apart from the statutory instances of appeal specified above, there is a general right in the Court of Session to intervene in respect of any incompetent or irregular proceedings in the Sheriff Court or in case of failure to exercise jurisdiction or exceeding the jurisdiction of that Court.[11] Reference has already been made to cases in which appeal is incompetent in respect that the Sheriff-Substitute has not acted in his judicial capacity, or that the parties, by their conduct of the case, have excluded any right of appeal.[12]

[1] See p. 301, supra.
[2] 7 Edw. VII c. 51, sec. 28; 2 & 3 Geo. V c. 28, sec. 2.
[3] See p. 291, supra.

4 Sinclair v. Baikie, 1884, 11 R. 413.
5 Hughes' Trustee v. Hughes, 1925 S.C. 25.
6 Baird v. Glendinning, 1874, 2 R. 25.
7 Maxton v. Bone, 1886, 13 R. 912.
8 Horn & Co. v. Tangyes, 1906, 8 F. 475.
9 Watson v. Stewart, 1872, 10 M. 494.
10 7 Edw. VII c. 51, Schedule I, Rule 33.
11 Dalgleish v. Leitch, 1889, 2 White, 302; Penny v. Scott, 1894, 22 R.
    5; Heddle v. Magistrates of Leith, 1898, 25 R. 801; Allen & Sons v.
    Corporation of Edinburgh, 1909 S.C. 70; Moss' Empires v. Assessor
    for Glasgow, 1917 S.C. (H.L.) 1, Lord Kinnear, p. 6.
12 See p. 293, supra.

(c) *Time for Appealing.*—The time within which appeals may
be taken from interlocutors of either the Sheriff or the Sheriff-
Substitute to the Court of Session is as follows:—

(1) Final judgments: three months from date of judgment
if not sooner extracted or implemented.[1] Extract may be issued
in causes other than summary causes after a lapse of fourteen
days, or at such earlier date as the Sheriff may allow extract.[2]

(2) Other judgments in which appeal is competent without
leave, being those falling under (2) (3) and (4) of the foregoing
paragraph: fourteen days from date of interlocutor appealed
against if not sooner extracted.[1] (Where the appeal is from
a judgment of the Sheriff Principal the words in the rule are
" if not sooner extracted or implemented.") Extract is competent within the time above stated.[2]

(3) Interlocutors under which leave to appeal is required:
fourteen days from date of interlocutor granting leave to appeal
unless sooner extracted.[3] (Where the interlocutor is by the
Sheriff Principal the words are " if not sooner extracted or
implemented.") Extract is competent within the time above
stated, unless an appeal has been taken or leave to appeal has
been applied for.[2] In the latter case extract is not precluded
unless leave to appeal is granted and an appeal is taken within
seven days after leave is granted.[2] This provision has the
effect of extending the time for appealing so that, if the application for leave is made within fourteen days, appeal is competent
until the expiry of seven days from the date of the interlocutor
granting leave, when extract may be issued. Apart from the
issue of extract appeal would be competent up to fourteen days
from the date of the interlocutor granting leave.[4]

1 7 Edw. VII c. 51, Schedule I, Rules 86, 92.
2 Ibid., Rule 85; 17 & 18 Geo. V c. 35, sec. 21.
3 Ibid., Rules 86, 92; M'Cabe v. Mount Vernon Colliery Co., 1925 S.C.
    574. See p. 294, supra.
4 See M'Cabe v. Mount Vernon Colliery Co., supra.

The date of every interlocutor is deemed to be the date upon which it is entered in the books of the Court.[1] Where an appeal taken to the Court of Session has been abandoned the appellant cannot thereafter appeal to the Sheriff,[2] nor can an appeal to the Sheriff be superseded by one to the Court of Session.[3] But this rule may not apply where the appeal has been marked to the wrong appellate tribunal by mistake, nor where an appeal is withdrawn of consent of both parties.[3] When an appellant did not insist in his appeal before the Sheriff, and it was dismissed on that ground, he was not allowed to appeal against that interlocutor to the Court of Session.[4] Extract of a decree for expenses will not bar appeal against a previous final judgment which has not been extracted.[5]

[1] 7 Edw. VII c. 51, Schedule I, Rule 83.
[2] Clark v. Comrie, 1910, 1 S.L.T. 404.
[3] J. & J. Fraser v. Smith, 1937 S.C. 667.
[4] Manchester and County Bank v. Moore, 1909 S.C. 246.
[5] Macfarlane v. Thompson, 1884, 12 R. 232.

(d) *Procedure in Appeals.*—The appeal is taken by note of appeal written by the appellant or his solicitor on the interlocutor sheet, or other written record containing the interlocutor appealed against, or on a separate sheet lodged with the Sheriff-clerk.[1] The note is signed by the appellant or his solicitor, and dated, and is to be as nearly as may be in the following terms: " The (pursuer, applicant, claimant, defender, respondent or other party) appeals to the Court of Session."[1] Within four days after an appeal has been taken the Sheriff-clerk transmits the process to the Deputy Principal Clerk of the General Department of the Court of Session.[1] Within the same period the Sheriff-clerk sends a written notice of the appeal to the other party or parties, or to his or their solicitor or solicitors.[1] Failure to give such notice does not invalidate the appeal, but the Appeal Court may give such remedy as they think proper for any disadvantage or inconvenience thereby occasioned.[1] The subsequent procedure in the Court of Session is prescribed by the Rules of Court.[2]

[1] Rules of Court, 1936, V 8.
[2] Ibid., V 8-13.

Notwithstanding that an appeal has been taken, the Sheriff is entitled to regulate interim possession and make other interim orders as already detailed.[1] An appeal does not prevent immediate execution of a warrant of sequestration for rent, or of warrants to take inventories, or place effects in custody *ad interim*, or warrants for interim preservation.[2] An interim interdict, though appealed against, is binding until recalled.[3] After an appeal has been noted the appellant cannot abandon it unless of consent of all parties or by leave of the Court of Session.[4] The appeal is effectual to submit to review all interlocutors pronounced in the cause, and is available to other parties who have not noted appeals,[2] all as more fully explained above.[5]

[1] 7 Edw. VII c. 51, Schedule I, Rule 91. See p. 297, supra.
[2] Ibid., sec. 29.
[3] Ibid. See also Rule 91 and Trainer v. Renfrewshire Upper District Committee, 1907 S.C. 1117.
[4] Ibid., Schedule I, Rule 96.
[5] See p. 297, supra.

3. APPEALS IN SUMMARY CAUSES.

Where a judgment disposing of the case has been given in a summary cause in which the evidence has been recorded the Act provides that the judgment of the Sheriff-Substitute on fact and law may be brought under review of the Sheriff in ordinary form, but where the evidence has not been recorded the findings in law only are subject to review.[1] It is thought to be clear that this provision does not limit the right of appeal in final judgments on summary causes to those pronounced after proof, and that final judgments in cases where no proof has been taken are subject to appeal to the Sheriff in the usual way.[2] The reference to a judgment which disposes of the case is thought to mean the same as a final judgment as already defined.[3]

[1] 7 Edw. VII c. 51, sec. 8; 2 & 3 Geo. V c. 28, Schedule I.
[2] See generally on this section Duke of Argyll v. Muir, 1910 S.C. 96.
[3] See p. 291, supra. See also Duke of Argyll v. Muir, supra.

Interlocutory judgments in summary causes are appealable to the Sheriff in the same way as in ordinary causes.[1] The interlocutors which can be appealed in this way, with or without leave, have been already detailed.[2]

[1] 7 Edw. VII c. 51, sec. 27; 2 & 3 Geo. V c. 28, Schedule I; Salmond v. Ross, 1919, 36 Sh.Ct.Rep. 146. See generally Duke of Argyll v. Muir, 1910 S.C. 96.
[2] See p. 290, et seq., supra.

It is enacted by the Sheriff Courts Act that, subject to the provisions of the Act, causes not exceeding £50 in value, exclusive of interest and expenses,[1] are not subject to review by the Court of Session.[2] In no case can an interlocutor of the Sheriff-Substitute in such a cause be appealed direct to the Court of Session, but there is a limited right of appeal to the Court of Session from a final judgment of the Sheriff on appeal. The provision is that no appeal is competent to the Court of Session where the cause does not exceed £50 in value, or is being tried as a summary cause, unless the Sheriff after final judgment by him on an appeal, on the motion of either party made within seven days of the date of the final interlocutor, certifies the cause as suitable for appeal to the Court of Session.[3] It will be noticed that this limited right of appeal applies not only to actions which are summary causes because they are under the statutory limit of value, but also to any action which is in fact being tried as a summary cause,[4] though the value may be beyond the statutory limit.[5]

[1] For principles in fixing value see p. 48, et seq., supra.
[2] 7 Edw. VII c. 51, sec. 7.
[3] Ibid., sec. 28 (1) (d) ; 2 & 3 Geo. V c. 28, sec. 2.
[4] See ibid., sec. 3 (i).
[5] See Summerlee Iron Co. v. Duff, 1920 S.C. 291. (In this case it appears to have been overlooked that appeal is not competent from a judgment of the Sheriff-Substitute.)

In the case of appeals in summary causes to the Sheriff the time limit for noting appeals is as follows :—

(1) Final judgments : three months from date of judgment if not sooner extracted or implemented.[1] Extract can be issued after a lapse of seven days from the date of the decree,[2] but it is thought that in summary as in ordinary cases the Sheriff may allow earlier extract.[3]

(2) Interlocutory judgments in which appeal is competent without leave : fourteen days from date of interlocutor if not sooner extracted,[1] extract being competent as above.[2]

(3) Interlocutors where leave to appeal is required : fourteen days from the date of interlocutor granting leave unless sooner extracted.[4] Extract is competent as above, unless either an appeal is taken or leave to appeal is applied for. In the latter case extract is not prevented unless leave is granted and an appeal is taken within seven days thereafter.[2] Leave should be applied for within the seven days to prevent the issue of extract, but if extract is not issued leave can be applied for after the seven days have expired. When leave to appeal is asked appeal is competent up to seven days after leave is granted when extract may be issued and the right of appeal is lost. Apart from the right being lost by extract appeal would apparently be competent within fourteen days of leave to appeal being granted.[5]

(4) Interlocutors granting interim interdict : fourteen days from the date of intimation thereof.[6]

[1] 7 Edw. VII c. 51, Schedule I, Rule 86.
[2] Ibid., Rule 85; 17 & 18 Geo. V c. 35, sec. 21.
[3] See p. 255. supra.
[4] 7 Edw. VII c. 51, Schedule I, Rule 86; M'Cabe v. Mount Vernon Colliery Co., 1925 S.C. 574.
[5] See M'Cabe v. Mount Vernon Colliery Co., supra.
[6] 7 Edw. VII c. 51, Schedule I, Rule 86; 2 & 3 Geo. V c. 28, Schedule II.

As already stated, appeal to the Court of Session in a summary cause is competent only after final judgment by the Sheriff on appeal and when the Sheriff, on the motion of either party made within seven days of the date of the final interlocutor, certifies the cause as suitable for appeal to the Court of Session.[1] Appeal is competent within three months of the final judgment unless it is sooner extracted or implemented.[2] Extract can be issued within seven days of the judgment.[3] It is not clear whether the motion for a certificate of suitability for appeal is to be regarded as an application for leave to appeal which has now the effect of preventing extract until it is disposed of and (if granted) until seven days after it is granted.[3] Strictly read, Rule 85 does not apply to such certificates, and in that view extract may be issued at once on the lapse of seven days from the judgment, irrespective of any motion for a certificate. It is thought, however, that the motion for a certificate and the application for leave to appeal should be regarded as synonymous,[4] so that, if the motion for a certificate is made—as it must be—within seven days of the judgment, extract could not be issued until either the motion was refused, or, if granted, till the expiry of seven days from the interlocutor granting the certificate. On the other view of the matter, appeal might be cut off by extract if it is within three months of the judgment.

[1] 7 Edw. VII c. 51, sec. 28 (1) (d) ; 2 & 3 Geo. V c. 28, sec. 2.
[2] Ibid., Schedule I, Rule 86.
[3] Ibid., Rule 85; 17 & 18 Geo. V c. 35, sec. 21.
[4] Cf. Dumfriesshire County Council v. Langholm Magistrates, 1913 S.C. 307.

The procedure in summary causes in appeals to the Sheriff, or to the Court of Session—where this is competent—is the same as in ordinary causes, and reference can be made to what has already been written on this matter.[1]

[1] See pp. 296, 301, supra.

4. APPEALS IN SUMMARY APPLICATIONS.

In the case of summary applications[1] appeal from the Sheriff-Substitute to the Sheriff and—subject to the normal limit of value—to the Court of Session, will, it is thought, be competent in all cases where such appeal is not excluded by express provision of any Statute under which the application may be brought or by clear implication from such provisions.[2] Where appeal is competent the normal forms and procedure will apply.[2] If the evidence has not been recorded any judgment on the facts cannot be reviewed.[3] To a large extent summary applications arise under Statute, and detailed consideration of various applications under different Statutes is given later.[4]

[1] See 7 Edw. VII c. 51, secs. 3 (p), 50.
[2] See Magistrates of Portobello v. Magistrates of Edinburgh, 1882, 10 R. 130; M'Callum, 1924, 41 Sh.Ct.Rep. 51; Kerr v. Annandale Steamship Co., 1926, 43 Sh.Ct.Rep. 44.
[3] Sinclair, &c. v. Spence, 1883, 10 R. 1077.
[4] See p. 533, et seq., infra.

5. REMOVAL TO COURT OF SESSION FOR JURY TRIAL.

This is not an appeal for review of a Sheriff Court judgment, but the permanent removal of a cause from the Sheriff Court to the Court of Session for jury trial.

The Act provides that in cases originating in the Sheriff Court—other than claims by employees against employers to be noticed presently—where the claim is in amount or value above £50, either party, who may conceive that the cause should be tried by jury, may require it to be remitted to the Court of Session for that purpose.[1] The excepted causes are claims by employees against employers in respect of injury caused by accident arising out of and in the course of their employment and concluding for damages under the Employers' Liability Act, 1880, or at common law, or alternatively at common law or under the Employers' Liability Act.[1] Employee is defined to include the legal personal representatives of an employee, and any person who, by the law of Scotland, may be entitled to solatium in respect of the death of an employee.[2] In stating the limit of value the section does not say " exclusive of interest and expenses,"[3] but interest is not likely to arise as part of the sum sued for in an action appropriate for jury trial, and expenses would not in any case be taken into account in fixing the value of the cause.

[1] 7 Edw. VII c. 51, sec. 30; 2 & 3 Geo. V c. 28, Schedule I.
[2] 7 Edw. VII c. 51, sec. 3 (q); 2 & 3 Geo. V c. 28, Schedule I; cf. Lawrie v. Banknock Coal Co., 1912 S.C. (H.L.) 20, and cases there cited.
[3] Cf. 7 Edw. VII c. 51, sec. 7.

The application for remission of the cause is competent only when an order has been pronounced allowing proof—other than an order for proof to lie *in retentis*, or for recovery of documents —and it must be made within six days of the interlocutor allowing proof.[1] Where there is an interlocutor allowing a proof and a later interlocutor fixing the date of the proof the application for remission must be made within six days of the first interlocutor.[2] Where the Sheriff-Substitute has allowed a proof and his interlocutor is appealed to the Sheriff who affirms it the six days run from the Sheriff's interlocutor,[3] but where an appeal against an allowance of proof is taken to the Court of Session it is too late thereafter to ask for a remit for jury trial even though the Court of Session has affirmed the allowance of proof.[4] An appeal to the Sheriff against his Substitute's allowance of proof cannot be taken if there has meantime been an application for a remit for jury trial,[5] nor can application for a remit be made while the Substitute's allowance of proof is under appeal to the Sheriff.[6]

[1] 7 Edw. VII c. 51, sec. 30; 2 & 3 Geo. V c. 28, Schedule I.
[2] Kinnes v. Fleming, 1881, 8 R. 386; Williams v. Watt & Wilson, 1889, 16 R. 687.
[3] See Davidson v. Davidson's Executor, 1891, 18 R. 1069; Ellerman Lines v. Clyde Navigation Trustees, 1909 S.C. 694, Lord President Dunedin, p. 697.
[4] Ellerman Lines v. Clyde Navigation Trustees, supra.
[5] Rae v. Burgh of Falkirk, 1937 S.C. 673.
[6] M'Arthur v. Boucher, 1887, 15 R. 117; Ritchie v. Lanarkshire County Council, 1931 S.N. 33.

Remission for jury trial is competent on an allowance of proof in respect of part of the case only,[1] and also in respect of an allowance of proof on the merits where proof on a preliminary point has already been held in the Sheriff Court.[2] Where the proof allowed is on a purely preliminary point remission for jury trial is incompetent.[3] Remission for jury trial will also be excluded where the proof allowed is by writ or oath only,[4] but not where the proof by writ or oath is in respect of part of the averments only and a general proof is allowed *quoad* the remainder.[5] Remission for jury trial will not be allowed where the allowance of proof has been made of consent of parties,[6] or where it is made on the direction of the Court of Session to allow a proof.[7]

[1] Conroy v. Inglis, 1895, 22 R. 620; M'Cafferty v. M'Cabe, 1898, 25 R. 872.
[2] M'Coll v. Gardner & Co., 1898, 25 R. 395.
[3] Curran v. M'Alpine & Son, 1898, 1 F. 326.
[4] Shirra v. Robertson, 1873, 11 M. 660; Wilson v. Brackenridge, 1888, 15 R. 587; Glasgow Central Stores v. Goodson, 1901, 3 F. 1075.
[5] Robertson v. Earl of Dudley, 1875, 2 R. 935.

When a remit is made for jury trial the Court of Session can deal with objections not only to the competency but to the relevancy,[1] and the remit may be asked solely for the purpose of having the action dismissed as irrelevant.[2] If the Court of Session consider the case unsuitable for jury trial they may remit it back to the Sheriff, or remit it to a Lord Ordinary, or send it for proof before one of the judges of the Division before whom the cause depends.[3] If an issue is approved the usual course is to remit the case to a Lord Ordinary for trial. It has been stated that in deciding between a remit back to the Sheriff for proof, and sending for proof before a Lord Ordinary, the Court will have regard to the fact that in the one case there is a possible ultimate appeal to the House of Lords on the facts and in the other there is not.[4] The Court of Session will also consider whether the case is of the class appropriated by Statute to jury trial, and will take into account the probable value of the cause in relation to the limit of value in the Act.[4] In many cases jury trial has been refused where it was clear that a reasonable award of damages would not amount to £50,[5] or where the averments did not make it clear that an award of that amount was to be expected.[6] The same result has followed where legal questions were involved in the point at issue,[7] where only part of the crave of the writ was suitable for jury trial,[8] and where the sist of a widow in place of a deceased pursuer introduced complications which might have misled a jury in assessing damages.[9] In actions of damages for slander the seriousness of the case may not be measured by the amount of damages alone.[10] Where jury trial is refused, and the case is remitted back to the Sheriff, payment of any expenses awarded by the Court of Session is not by implication a condition precedent to the party proceeding with the case in the Sheriff Court.[11]

[1] Rules of Court, 1936, V 15 (a).
[2] See Keith Bros. v. Maxwell's Judicial Factor, 1890, 17 R. 799; Ellerman Lines v. Clyde Navigation Trustees, 1909 S.C. 694.
[3] 7 Edw. VII c. 51, sec. 30.
[4] Sharples v. Yuill & Co., 1905, 7 F. 657, Lord President Dunedin, p. 664. See also Granger v. Glasgow Corporation, 1945 S.C. 57.
[5] Dawson v. Stewart & Shaw, 1905, 7 F. 769; M'Laughlan v. Clyde Valley, &c., Co., 1905, 8 F. 131; Kennedy v. Bruce, 1907 S.C. 845; Smellie v. Whitelaw, 1907, 14 S.L.T. 865; Houston v. M'Indoe, 1934 S.C. 362; Armstrong v. Paterson Bros., 1935 S.C. 464; cf. Sharples v. Yuill & Co., supra; Mackie v. Davidson, 1913 S.C. 675; Fraser v. Tod & Sons, 1922 S.C. 6; Stevenson v. Glasgow Corporation, 1922 S.L.T. 185.

6 Barclay v. Smith & Co., 1913 S.C. 473; Ogg v. Scott, 1915 S.C. 168;
    Greer v. Glasgow Corporation, 1915 S.C. 171; Monaghan v. United
    Co-operative Baking Society, 1917 S.C. 12; Brown v. Campbell,
    1924 S.C. 1048.
7 Grant v. Fleming & Co., 1914 S.C. 228; Woods v. A.C.S. Motors,
    1930 S.C. 1035; cf. Jones v. Magistrates of Hamilton, 1929 S.C. 89.
8 M'Sorley v. Archibald, 1922 S.C. 26.
9 Reid v. Lanarkshire Traction Co., 1933 S.C. 416.
10 Alberti v. Bernardi, 1921 S.C. 468.
11 Crawford v. North British Railway Co., 1914, 31 Sh.Ct.Rep. 128.

The party desiring the cause to be remitted for jury trial
has to write on the interlocutor sheet in the Sheriff Court a note
in the following terms : " The pursuer (or defender or other
party) requires the cause to be remitted to the Court of Session."
The note is signed by the party making the application, or his
solicitor, and bears the date on which it is signed.[1] Within four
days of the application being made the Sheriff-clerk sends written
notice thereof to the opposite party or his solicitor. Failure
to give such notice does not invalidate the remission, but the Court
of Session may give such remedy for any disadvantage or inconvenience thereby occasioned as may be thought proper.[2] Within
four days of the application the Sheriff-clerk transmits the process
to the Deputy Principal Clerk of the General Department of the
Court of Session who causes to be written on the interlocutor sheet
a note of the day on which it is received.[3] Subsequent procedure
is as laid down in the Rules of Court.[4]

1 Rules of Court, V 14 (a).
2 Ibid., V 14 (b).
3 Ibid., V 14 (c).
4 Ibid., V 15.

6. Statutory Appeals.

Specialties in relation to appeals which are regulated by various
Statutes are considered later.[1]

1 See p. 533, et seq., infra.

CHAPTER XIV.

EXPENSES.

1. General.

The expenses of the successful party in a contested litigation were originally regarded as damages due by the unsuccessful party, in reparation of the loss incurred by the successful party, in consequence of his opponent's bad faith in litigating. But this view has long ceased to apply, and a litigant who contests a cause, even if not personally interested, as, for instance, a trustee sisted in room of a bankrupt party, and however much in good faith he acts, may be held liable in expenses if he is unsuccessful.[1]

[1] Torbet v. Borthwick, 1849, 11 D. 694. See also White v. Steel, 1894, 21 R. 649.

Where expenses have been reserved in a judgment dealing with preliminary pleas, and afterwards decree is given for expenses in general terms, that decree carries the reserved expenses.[1] And where certain expenses have been declared to be expenses in the cause these go as a matter of right to the party getting a general finding for expenses, and he cannot be deprived of them on the ground that he has been unsuccessful in that branch of the litigation.[2]

[1] Caledonian Railway Co. v. Chisholm, 1889, 16 R. 622; Alston & Orr v. Allan, 1910 S.C. 304.
[2] Glasgow & South Western Railway Co. v. Magistrates of Ayr, 1911 S.C. 298.

It frequently happens that much expense is incurred in the discussion of a claim before it reaches the Court, but costs incurred prior to the service of a writ are not judicial expenses. A defender can avoid liability for expenses if he satisfy the claim or demand before the initial writ has been served.[1] A creditor is not entitled to refuse to accept payment of a claim unless the expense in taking legal advice is also paid. If he insist upon serving his action in such circumstances, proof that payment of the full sum claimed was tendered, before the service of a writ, will generally preclude the creditor getting expenses. A defender must also be afforded the opportunity of meeting the pursuer's claim or demand before

he can be held liable in any expenses. If no previous demand
has been made, and a defender pays immediately after service,
the pursuer will not in general be allowed expenses.[2]

[1] Mintons v. Hawley & Co., 1882, 20 S.L.R. 126.
[2] Leith Magistrates v. Lennon, 1881, 18 S.L.R. 313.

It is not competent to consign in the hands of the Sheriff-clerk
a sum representing the pursuer's crave in a threatened action
not yet raised,[1] and such consignation, if made, will not defeat
the claim of a successful pursuer to expenses when the action is
raised.[1]

[1] Alexander v. Campbell's Trustees, 1903, 5 F. 634; A B & Co. v. C D,
1908, 25 Sh.Ct.Rep. 106.

2. CRAVE FOR EXPENSES.

Expenses should be craved in the initial writ. The Act does
not expressly direct that expenses must be craved, and, even
when not craved, it is probably within the discretion of the
Court, unless debarred by statutory provision, to award or refuse
expenses in a contested cause.[1] But it is at least doubtful whether
expenses can be awarded in an undefended cause if they are not
craved.

[1] Heggie & Co. v. Selkrig, 1826, 4 S. 510; Rooney v. Cormack, 1895,
23 R. 11; Thomson v. Edinburgh and District Tramways Co., 1901,
3 F. 355; Mitchell v. Baird, 1902, 4 F. 809; Warrand v. Watson,
1907 S.C. 432; Pollich v. Heatley, 1910 S.C. 469; Society of
Accountants in Edinburgh v. Lord Advocate, (O.H.) 1924 S.L.T.
194; Society of Accountants in Edinburgh v. Scottish Board of
Health, (O.H.) 1924 S.L.T. 199.

It is usually stated that the inherent power to award expenses
is limited to proceedings that are judicial, and that, apart from
special statutory direction on the point, there is no power to
deal with expenses in processes that are purely administrative.[1]
The more correct view may be that the power to award expenses
is present even in administrative processes but that an award
of expenses in such processes does not necessarily follow the result as
in ordinary causes.[2] Even in administrative proceedings expenses
are usually awarded if the proceedings, or the objections taken,
are regarded as vexatious.[3]

[1] Cuninghame v. M'Gregor, 1904, 6 F. 955; Liddall v. Ballingry Parish
Council, 1908 S.C. 1082; Burgh of Tobermory v. Capaldi, 1938
S.L.T. (Sh.Ct.) 38; cf. Steele v. Lanark Middle Ward, 1928 S.L.T.
(Sh.Ct.) 20.
[2] See Liddall v. Ballingry Parish Council, supra.
[3] Dunbartonshire County Council v. Clydebank Commissioners, 1901, 4 F.
111; cf. White v. Magistrates of Rutherglen, 1897, 24 R. 446.

Expenses should be asked at the time the merits of the case are disposed of. If they are not then asked it may be too late to move for them subsequently.[1]

[1] Fraser v. Fraser, (O.H.) 1903, 11 S.L.T. 70; Jack v. King, 1932, 48 Sh.Ct.Rep. 242; Campbell v. Campbell, 1934 S.L.T. 45.

3. Interim Expenses.

In general, the matter of expenses is dealt with only when final judgment is pronounced, but an award of expenses may be made during the course of a process, as, for instance, where amendment is allowed.[1] Interim decree may be granted for such expenses, and may be extracted and enforced without waiting for the conclusion of the process.[2] An interim award of expenses is frequently made in a separation and aliment case.[3] In an action of multiple-poinding a decree for expenses in favour of the real raiser may be granted during the progress of the process.[4]

[1] 7 Edw. VII c. 51, Schedule I, Rule 79.
[2] See further as to expenses of amendment, p. 237, supra.
[3] See p. 527, infra.
[4] See 7 Edw. VII c. 51, Schedule I, Rule 129.

Apart from statutory provision, the wide discretion of the Court on the matter of expenses may warrant the Sheriff granting a decree for expenses before the close of a litigation. Thus when a special point has been raised, which is distinct from the merits of the cause, and which the ultimate decision will not affect, the expenses of proof or discussion requisite to settle that point may be dealt with when the point has been settled, although the main litigation is still pending.[1] Where an interim award is modified to a fixed sum it disposes finally of the expenses so dealt with, and no further expenses for that part of the case can be recovered, but if the award is in general terms it is treated as a payment to account.[2] The question whether an interim decree for expenses involves payment as a condition precedent to proceeding with the case is discussed later.[3]

[1] Waddel v. Hope, 1843, 6 D. 160; Vaughan v. Davidson, 1854, 16 D. 922.
[2] Strangford v. Hurlet, &c., Alum Co., 1861, 23 D. 534; Cameron & Waterston v. Muir & Sons, 1861, 23 D. 535.
[3] See p. 337, infra.

4. Caution for Expenses.

Whether a bankrupt will be ordered to find caution for expenses is a question of circumstances. Generally a bankrupt pursuer will be required to do so, whether he is under sequestration or a trust deed, as in neither case has he any real interest in the result of the suit. Caution has been ordered where action was taken to reduce a decree of cessio[1]; where a bankrupt firm assumed a partner stated to be solvent[2]; in a bankrupt's appeal against the rejection of a claim in another sequestration[3]; and where the bankrupt was merely a consenter.[4] Where pursuer was made bankrupt by defenders the practice has varied.[5] In actions of damages for slander, caution has 'sometimes been dispensed with,[6] but has more frequently been required.[7] Caution was not required in a number of cases where the pursuer had, notwithstanding the bankruptcy, a substantial interest in the result of the action,[8] and where he had been permitted to carry on a business in respect of which the litigation arose.[9] A bankrupt executor with no executry funds has been required to find caution.[10] In petitions for the bankrupt's discharge caution is not required,[11] and in various exceptional circumstances it has also been dispensed with.[12]

1 Gilmour v. Donnelly, (O.H.) 1899, 7 S.L.T. 267.
2 Fraser v. Mackenzie, 1874, 12 S.L.R. 74.
3 Dunsmore's Trustee v. Stewart, 1891, 19 R. 4.
4 Douglas v. M'Kinlay, 1902, 5 F. 260; cf. Willox v. Farrell, 1849, 11 D. 1206; Horn v. Sanderson & Muirhead, 1872, 10 M. 295.
5 Fraser v. M'Murrich, 1924 S.C. 93; Rennie v. Campbell Bros., (O.H.) 1929 S.L.T. 27; Neil v. South East Lancashire Insurance Co., 1930 S.C. 629.
6 Scott v. Johnston, 1885, 12 R. 1022; Macrae v. Sutherland, 1889, 16 R. 476.
7 Clarke v. Muller, 1884, 11 R. 418; Collier v. Ritchie & Co., 1884, 12 R. 47; Scott v. Roy, 1886, 13 R. 1173; Watson v. Williamson, (O.H.) 1895, 3 S.L.T. 21; Brown v. Oliver & Co., (O.H.) 1895, 3 S.L.T. 43; Powell v. Long, 1896, 23 R. 955; Munro v. Mudie, (O.H.) 1901, 9 S.L.T. 53; Cook v. Kinghorn, (O.H.) 1904, 12 S.L.T. 186; Miller v. J. M. Smith, (O.H.) 1908, 16 S.L.T. 268; Johnston v. Laird & Son, (O.H.) 1915, 2 S.L.T. 24; Will v. Sneddon, Campbell & Munro, 1931 S.C. 164.
8 M'Alister v. Swinburne, 1873, 1 R. 166; Cooper v. Frame & Co., 1893, 20 R. 920; Derrick v. Derrick, (O.H.) 1901, 8 S.L.T. 321; Paton v. Paton's Trustee, (O.H.) 1901, 8 S.L.T. 455; Paterson v. Wright, 1937, 53 Sh.Ct.Rep. 108; cf. Buchanan v. Peyton, (O.H.) 1897, 4 S.L.T. 324.
9 Burnett v. Murray, 1877, 14 S.L.R. 616; Kennedy v. Crawford, (O.H.) 1899, 7 S.L.T. 26; M'Call v. Gattens, (O.H.) 1905, 13 S.L.T. 149.
10 Birnie v. M'Bain, &c., 1914, 30 Sh.Ct.Rep. 174.
11 Melrose-Drover v. Heddle, 1905, 7 F. 852; Scott v. Scott's Trustees, 1914 S.C. 704.
12 Ferguson v. Leslie, 1873, 11 S.L.R. 16; Ritchie v. M'Intosh, 1881, 8 R. 747; Rogerson v. Rogerson's Trustee, (O.H.) 1885, 22 S.L.R. 673; Thom v. Andrew, 1888, 15 R. 780; Thom v. Caledonian Railway Co., (O.H.) 1902, 9 S.L.T. 440; M'Quator v. Wellwood, (O.H.) 1908, 16 S.L.T. 110; Gallagher v. Edinburgh Corporation, (O.H.) 1929 S.L.T. 356; Dingley v. Black, &c., 1934, 51 Sh.Ct.Rep. 171.

Mere impecuniosity on the part of a pursuer is not of itself sufficient to justify a demand for caution for expenses.[1]   In several cases a pursuer in receipt of poor relief has been required to sue *in forma pauperis* or to find caution,[2] but this is not always done.[3] And a pursuer refused admission to the poor's roll as having no probable cause, has sometimes been allowed to sue without finding caution and on other occasions has had to find caution.[4] But an impecunious pursuer put forward as a cloak for others will generally have to find caution.[5]

[1] Porteous v. Pearl Life Assurance Co., (O.H.) 1901, 8 S.L.T. 430; Cunningham v. Skinner, 1902, 4 F. 1124; Nakeski-Cumming v. Gordon's Judicial Factor, 1923 S.C. 770. See also Hepburn v. Tait, 1874, 1 R. 875.

[2] Hunter v. Clark, 1874, 1 R. 1154; Robertson v. Suburban District Committee of Midlothian County Council, 1898, 25 R. 569; Fraser v. Mackintosh, (O.H.) 1901, 9 S.L.T. 117; Maclean v. Maclaren, (O.H.) 1910, 1 S.L.T. 29.

[3] Macdonald v. Simpsons, 1882, 9 R. 696; Johnstone v. Dryden, 1890, 18 R. 191.

[4] Thompson v. North British Railway Co., 1882, 9 R. 1101; Robertson v. Meikle, (O.H.) 1890, 28 S.L.R. 18; Buchanan v. Ballantine, (O.H.) 1911 S.C. 1368; Gore v. Westfield Autocar Co., 1923 S.C. 100.

[5] Jenkins v. Robertson, 1869, 7 M. 739; Robertson v. Duke of Atholl, 1905, 8 F. 150.

A defender who is bankrupt will not, in general, be ordered to find caution for expenses,[1] but this may be done if the defender is in reality the pursuer in the issue at stake,[2] if he has apparently no interest to maintain the defence,[3] or if other circumstances are present which justify such a course.[4] There appears to be no authority for a defender who is merely impecunious being required to find caution.

[1] Buchanan v. Stevenson, 1880, 8 R. 220; Stiven v. Fleming, 1885, 22 S.L.R. 673; Lawrie v. Pearson, 1888, 16 R. 62: Crichton Bros. v. Crichton, 1902, 5 F. 178; Drew v. Robertson, (O.H.) 1903, 11 S.L.T. 67; Johnstone v. Henderson, 1906, 8 F. 689; Mackay v. Boswall-Preston, 1916 S.C. 96.

[2] Ferguson, Lamont & Co.'s Trustee v. Lamont, 1889, 17 R. 282; Robb v. Dickson, (O.H.) 1901, 9 S.L.T. 224: Professional and Civil Service Supply Association v. Lawson, (O.H.) 1913, 2 S.L.T. 55.

[3] Smith's Trustee v. M'Cheyne, 1879, 16 S.L.R. 592: Stevenson v. Lee, 1886, 13 R. 913; Finklestone, &c. v. Smellie, 1916, 32 Sh.Ct.Rep. 244; Macrae's Trustees v. Macrae, 1945, 62 Sh.Ct.Rep. 48.

[4] Macnaughtan, &c. v. Thurman & Co., 1908, 24 Sh.Ct.Rep. 80; Robertson v. M'Caw, 1911 S.C. 650; Govers & Co. v. Findlay & Wallace, 1922, 39 Sh.Ct.Rep. 201; Swan & Sons v. Speirs, 1925, 41 Sh.Ct.Rep. 218.

Under the Companies Act[1] a limited company, which is pursuer in an action, may be required to find caution " if it appears by credible testimony that there is reason to believe that the company will be unable to pay " the defender's expenses, and proceedings may be stayed until such security is given.[2] The section has been held not to apply to a pursuing company which was defending a judgment on appeal,[3] nor to a company which has brought an action to reduce a decree by registration,[4] and a motion for caution has been refused where the action was brought by a company in liquidation and the liquidator,[5] and where a defending company had reclaimed against an adverse judgment.[6]

[1] 19 & 20 Geo. V c. 23, sec. 371. .
[2] Southern Bowling Club v. Edinburgh Evening News, (O.H.) 1901, 9 S.L.T. 35; New Mining, &c., Syndicate v. Chalmers & Hunter, 1909 S.C. 1390; Brownrigg Coal Co. v. Sneddon, 1911 S.C. 1064; Edinburgh Entertainments v. Stevenson, 1925 S.C. 848.
[3] Star Fire, &c., Insurance Co. v. Davidson & Sons, 1902, 4 F. 997.
[4] English's Coasting, &c., Co. v. British Finance Co., 1886, 13 R. 430.
[5] Motor Plants v. D. Stewart & Co., (O.H.) 1909, 1 S.L.T. 478.
[6] Sinclair v. Glasgow and London Contract Corporation, 1904, 6 F. 818.

A party who is to move for caution for expenses should do so timeously, and if he delay until a proof or trial is approaching the motion may be refused as being too late.[1] A written motion seems appropriate. If the bankruptcy occur during the dependence of an action, a motion for caution, or that the trustee in bankruptcy be sisted, should be made at once. In special circumstances it may be necessary to state the grounds for the motion on record, or in the motion or minute.[2] If caution is ordered it may extend to expenses already incurred, as well as expenses to be incurred.[3] If a pursuer fails to find caution as ordered the defender is entitled to absolvitor[4]; if it is the defender who fails to find caution the pursuer will get decree as craved.[5] An order for caution can competently be modified or superseded on a change of circumstances.[6]

[1] Simpson v. Allan, 1894, 31 S.L.R. 572; M'Crae v. Bryson, (O.H.) 1922 S.L.T. 574.
[2] Nakeski-Cumming v. Gordon's Factor, 1923 S.C. 770.
[3] Douglas v. M'Kinlay, 1902, 5 F. 260; Govers & Co. v. Findlay & Wallace, 1922, 39 Sh.Ct.Rep. 201; Swan & Sons v. Speirs, 1925, 41 Sh.Ct.Rep. 218.
[4] Gray v. Ireland, 1884, 11 R. 1104; Teulon v. Seaton, 1885, 12 R. 1179.
[5] 7 Edw. VII c. 51, Schedule I, Rule 56. See Govers & Co. v. Findlay & Wallace, supra; Swan & Sons v. Speirs, supra.
[6] Whyte v. City of Perth Co-operative Society, 1932 S.C. 482.

5. AWARDING OF EXPENSES.

It is not possible here to discuss in detail the circumstances in which the Court will award or withhold expenses, but the general rule is that expenses follow the fortunes of the case and fall to the party who is successful.[1] The effect of failure in a particular part or branch of a case is noticed later.[2] But a successful party may be refused expenses for various reasons, the most usual of which is to mark the dissatisfaction of the Court at the party's conduct which led to the litigation, or at the conduct of the case.[3] In more exceptional cases in the same class the successful party may be found liable in expenses to his opponent.[4] This result may also follow where a party, though unsuccessful, is held to be entitled to get a decree of Court for his protection as in objections to a title on a sale of heritage.[5] Divided success may result in a modification of expenses, or a party being awarded a stated proportion of his total costs,[6] or in neither party being found entitled to expenses.[7] In general, expenses must be dealt with in the action itself, a separate action for expenses being usually incompetent,[8] and the Court must exercise its discretion in regard to expenses in a judicial manner.[9]

[1] See Shepherd v. Elliot, 1896, 23 R. 695, Lord President Robertson, p. 696; Wood & Co. v. Mackay, 1906, 8 F. 625; Feeney v. Fife Coal Co., 1918 S.C. 197.

[2] See p. 324, infra.

[3] Shepherd v. Elliot, supra, p. 696. See Robb v. Logiealmond School Board, 1875, 2 R. 698; Ewart v. Brown, 1882, 10 R. 163; Armour v. Duff & Co., 1912 S.C. 120; Robinson v. National Bank of Scotland, 1916 S.C. (H.L.) 154; cf. Wood & Co. v. Mackay, supra.

[4] Barrie v. Caledonian Railway Co., 1902, 5 F. 30; Hamilton v. M'Lauchlan, 1908, 16 S.L.T. 341; Wilson v. Kerrigan, 1912, 28 Sh.Ct.Rep. 313; Baker v. Glasgow Corporation, 1916 S.C. 199; Goldie v. Chrysler Motors, 1938, 55 Sh.Ct.Rep. 99.

[5] Howard & Wyndham v. Richmond's Trustees, 1890, 17 R. 990; Harland Engineering Co. v. Stark's Trustees, 1914, 2 S.L.T. 292; cf. Roscoe v. Mackersy, 1905, 7 F. 761. See also Crawford v. Magistrates of Paisley, 1870, 8 M. 693; Dunbarton Magistrates v. Edinburgh University, (O.H.) 1909, 1 S.L.T. 51.

[6] E.g., Strang v. Brown & Son, 1882, 19 S.L.R. 890.

[7] E.g., Dalkeith Police Commissioners v. Duke of Buccleuch, 1889, 16 R. 575.

[8] Young, &c. v. Nith Commissioners, &c., 1880, 7 R. 891; Wood v. Wood's Trustees, 1904, 6 F. 640; Cullen's Executors v. Kilmarnock Theatre Co., (O.H.) 1913, 1 S.L.T. 290; cf. Clark v. Henderson, 1875, 2 R. 428.

[9] Breslin v. Barr & Thornton, 1923 S.C. 90.

In cases which arise out of the construction of settlements or testamentary writings the usual practice is that parties, whether successful in their contentions or not, should have their expenses out of the estate.[1] But this principle is not extended to questions as to the construction of a Statute[2] or as to a testator's domicile.[3]

Special rules in regard to expenses apply in consistorial causes and these are considered later.[4]

[1] Gibson's Trustees v. Wilson, 1899, 1 F. 1016; Wordie's Trustees v. Wordie, 1916 S.C. (H.L.) 126; Lethem v. Evans, (O.H.) 1918, 1 S.L.T. 27; cf. Bannerman's Trustees v. Bannerman, 1915 S.C. 398; Macculloch v. M'Culloch's Trustees, 1903, 6 F. (H.L.) 3.
[2] Dundas's Trustees v. Dundas's Trustees, 1912 S.C. 375.
[3] Brooks v. Brooks' Trustees, 1902, 4 F. 1014.
[4] See p. 527, infra.

It is the usual, but not the invariable, rule that a creditor must constitute his debt at his own expense against a deceased's estate.[1] A pursuer in an action of affiliation and aliment is entitled to constitute her claim by obtaining decree although the defender does not deny paternity, and has paid all sums due to date, but the pursuer in such an action is not entitled to her expenses.[2] Where several pursuers have claims it is a question how far full expenses in each action can be allowed against the defender.[3] As to expenses in relation to a counter-claim see the cases noted.[4]

[1] Earl of Rosslyn v. Lawson, 1872, 9 S.L.R. 291; Harper v. Connor's Trustees, 1927, 43 Sh.Ct.Rep. 138; Barclay's Bank v. Lawton's Trustees, (O.H.) 1928 S.L.T. 298; Ferrier v. Crockart, &c., (O.H.) 1937 S.L.T. 205.
[2] Robbie v. Dawes, 1924 S.C. 749.
[3] See Adam v. Rio Grande Rubber Estates, 1915 S.C. 484; Barrie v. Scottish Motor Traction Co., 1920 S.C. 704.
[4] Brooks & Bohm v. Kitchencraft Co., 1944 S.C. 25; Macfarlane v. Macdougall, 1931, 47 Sh.Ct.Rep. 325.

A trustee or person suing in some other representative capacity may be found personally liable to his opponents in expenses, but it is thought that a finding in these terms is not necessary, and that the usual finding against a party in a representative capacity infers personal liability to the opponent, without prejudice to any right of relief against trust or other funds which may be open to the party found liable.[1]

[1] Kilmarnock Theatre Co. v. Buchanan, 1911 S.C. 607; Mulholland v. Macfarlane's Trustees, (O.H.) 1928 S.L.T. 251; cf. Craig v. Hogg, 1896, 24 R. 6; Fulwood v. Dumfries Harbour Commissioners, 1907 S.C. 735; Barrie v. Barrie's Trustees, 1933 S.C. 132.

A party who merely consents to an action is not liable in expenses on that account alone.[1] This immunity applies to a husband who has consented to an action by his wife[2]—which consent is not now necessary—and to a parent consenting to an action by a minor.[3] On the other hand, where a parent sues as tutor and administrator for a pupil the parent incurs liability for expenses.[4] And a consenter who takes an active part in the litigation will be held liable in expenses.[5] Participation by a husband in a suit by his wife, to which he is not a consenter, may involve him in expenses, though his intervention is not to the extent which would justify him being regarded as *dominus litis.*[6]

[1] See M'Millan v. Mackinlay, 1926 S.C. 673.
[2] See Kerr v. Malcolm, (O.H.) 1906, 14 S.L.T. 358.
[3] Armstrong v. Thompson, (O.H.) 1895, 2 S.L.T. 537; Currie v. Cowan & Co., (O.H.) 1911, 2 S.L.T. 467.
[4] White v. Steel, 1894, 21 R. 649.
[5] Lindsay v. Kerr, 1891, 28 S.L.R. 267; Macgown v. Cramb, 1898, 25 R. 634: M'Ilwaine v. Stewart's Trustees, 1914 S.C. 934; Rodger v. Weir, 1917 S.C. 300.
[6] M'Millan v. Mackinlay, supra.

Apart from any question of consent or relationship, a person may be liable for the expenses of a litigation on the ground that he was *dominus litis.* Various definitions of what is necessary to constitute this liability have been suggested, but it is probably essential that there should have been an interest in the outcome of the case, and also the control of it to such a degree that the party who is alleged to be the true *dominus* had the right to say whether the action should proceed or be compromised or abandoned.[1] The *dominus litis* is liable in expenses only and is not responsible for the principal sum[2]; if he withdraws during the course of the action he will be liable in expenses only up to that date.[3] Liability as *dominus litis* may be determined in the principal action[4] or in a subsequent process.[5]

[1] See Cairns v. M'Gregor, 1931 S.C. 84, and cases cited there.
[2] Nairn v. South-East Lancashire Insurance Co., 1930 S.C. 606.
[3] Main v. Rankin & Sons, 1929 S.C. 40.
[4] As in Main v. Rankin & Sons, supra; Davidson v. Whatmough, (O.H.) 1930 S.N. 102.
[5] As in Cairns v. M'Gregor, supra. See also Swirles v. Isles, 1930 S.C. 696; Rutherford v. Licences, &c., Insurance Co., (O.H.) 1934 S.L.T. 47.

Where several parties on the same side of a case are jointly represented, and only certain of them are found entitled to expenses in general terms, the expenses so awarded are not the full judicial costs of that side of the case, but the successful parties' proportional share of such judicial expenses.[1] Thus, if two parties out of three receive an award of expenses the expenses awarded will generally be treated as two-thirds of the costs of the joint representation of their side.[1] But an award of expenses

against one of several parties on the same side generally infers
liability for the normal judicial expenses of the other side.[2]

[1] Robertson v. Steuart, 1875, 2 R. 970; Arthur v. Lindsay, 1895, 22 R.
904; Crawford v. Adams, 1900, 3 F. 296.
[2] See Macleod v. Heritors of Morvern, 1870, 8 M. 528.

Where there are several pursuers who may sue together in
connexion with claims arising out of the same subject-matter they
will not in general receive the expenses of separate actions if
they sue separately.[1] Where several related pursuers sue together
in a family suit, and one is unsuccessful, the Court have in some
cases disregarded the unsuccessful pursuer in the matter of expenses,
and have awarded the successful pursuers the full expenses of
the action.[2] The taxation of expenses in such cases of joint
litigants is dealt with above.[3] Where one of several pursuers
abandons an action the defender is entitled to expenses against
that pursuer without waiting the issue of the case in relation
to the others.[4] Where one or more of several pursuers dies in
the course of an action the surviving pursuers, if successful, are
entitled to their expenses in the usual way.[5]

[1] See Slorach v. Kerr & Co., 1921 S.C. 285.
[2] M'Phail v. Caledonian Railway Co., 1903, 5 F. 306; Peggie v. Keddie,
1932 S.C. 721, Lord Hunter, p. 724; but cf. Lythgoe v. Banks,
(O.H.) 1933 S.N. 39.
[3] See previous page.
[4] Maxtone v. Muir, 1846, 18 Scot. Jur. 452.
[5] Hay v. Earl of Morton, 1862, 24 D. 1054.

Where there are several unrelated pursuers, and some are
successful and others are not, the position in regard to expenses
is somewhat complicated, and reference may be made to the undernoted cases in which this question has arisen.[1]

[1] Karrman v. Crosbie, 1898, 25 R. 931; Grangemouth, &c., Towing
Co. v. "River Clyde" Co., (O.H.) 1908, 16 S.L.T. 638; Wilson
v. Rapp, (O.H.) 1911 S.C. 1360.

When several defenders have similar interests they should
combine as from the closing of the record and be represented
by one solicitor.[1] Normally they will be entitled to separate
expenses to the closing, and thereafter to one set of expenses and
a watching fee.[1] In some cases there should be a combined
defence from the start,[2] and separate representation is not

encouraged at all on appeal.[3] Questions of this kind should be raised on the motion for expenses and not after taxation.[4]

[1] Anderson v. M'Cracken Bros., 1900, 2 F. 780. See also Liquidator of Consolidated Copper Co. of Canada v. Peddie, 1877, 5 R. 393; Stott v. Fender, 1878, 16 S.L.R. 5; Bell v. Goodall, 1883, 10 R. 905; Barrie v. Scottish Motor Traction Co., 1920 S.C. 704; and cf. Stewart's Trustees v. Robertson, 1874, 1 R. 334; Welsh v. Eastern Cemetery Co., 1894, 31 S.L.R. 687.
[2] J. & G. Cockburn v. City Club, (O.H.) 1905, 12 S.L.T. 678.
[3] Duncan v. Salmond, 1874, 1 R. 839.

Where two or more defenders conduct separate defences, and the pursuer succeeds against both or all of them, they may be found liable in expenses jointly and severally, but a motion to this effect must be made when expenses are awarded.[1] If one or more of the defenders is successful, and the other or others unsuccessful, the result in regard to expenses will largely depend on the circumstances of the case.[2] If the defender who succeeds has been brought into the case at the instigation of the defender who has failed,[3] or if the latter's averments have blamed the successful defender, or necessarily imply such blame, the unsuccessful defender will generally be held liable in expenses to the successful defender, as well as to the pursuer.[4] But a successful defender is probably entitled, if he wishes, to get a decree for expenses against the pursuer, and a pursuer so held liable will get a right of relief against the unsuccessful defender.[5] Where two or more persons are found liable jointly and severally in expenses, the Court may decide as to the proportions in which they are to be liable to contribute *inter se.*[6] Where two defenders are assoilzied both will normally get expenses against the pursuer.[7]

[1] Warrand v. Watson, 1907 S.C. 432.
[2] See M'Crae v. Bryson, 1923 S.C. 896; Keating v. Anderson, 1925 S.C. 19.
[3] Morrison v. Waters & Co., 1906, 8 F. 867; Kennedy v. Shotts Iron Co., 1913 S.C. 1143.
[4] Craig v. Aberdeen Harbour Commissioners, 1909 S.C. 736; M'Crae v. Bryson, supra; Stuart v. Hannah, (O.H.) 1927 S.L.T. 117; cf. M'Intyre v. Ellams & Curry, (O.H.) 1938 S.L.T. 413.
[5] Keating v. Anderson, supra. See also Walker v. Frame, (O.H.) 1939 S.N. 102.
[6] 3 & 4 Geo. VI c. 42, sec. 3.
[7] See Johnstone v. Clyde Navigation Trustees, (O.H.) 1946 S.N. 102.

6. SOLICITOR AND CLIENT EXPENSES.

A decree for expenses expressed in general terms ordinarily means expenses as between party and party.[1] Under the Public Authorities Protection Act of 1893, the defender, if successful, is entitled to expenses as between solicitor and client, if the action has been directed against him in respect of any act done in pursuance or execution or intended execution of any Act of Parliament, or of any public duty or authority, or in respect of any alleged neglect or default in the execution of any such Act, duty, or authority.[2] The judgment awarding expenses in such a case must bear that expenses are allowed as between solicitor and client, otherwise the ordinary rule will apply, and the Court will not in general alter this at a later stage.[3] The Act applies to expenses in an appeal,[4] but it does not affect the right of the Court to refuse expenses to a successful defender for good cause or to modify expenses which are awarded.[5]

[1] Fletcher's Trustees v. Fletcher, 1888, 15 R. 862.
[2] 56 & 57 Vict. c. 61, sec. 1.
[3] Aberchirder Magistrates v. Banff District Committee, 1906, 8 F. 571.
[4] Aird v. Tarbert School Board, 1907 S.C. 305; Smith v. Glasgow Education Authority, 1933 S.C. (H.L.) 51.
[5] Aird v. Tarbert School Board, supra.

The Act does not apply if action is time-barred by another Statute.[1] An award of expenses under the Act may be made though the Act has not been founded on till after the closing of the record,[2] or even though the Act is not pleaded on record at all,[3] but there must be averments, and if necessary proof, that the grounds of action bring the case within the terms of the section.[4] The motion for expenses under the Act must be made when the expenses are awarded, and it will not be entertained at a later stage.[5] A public authority sisting itself as defender in an existing action has not the benefit of the Act.[6] Other decisions as to whether the grounds of action bring it within the terms of the Act are dealt with elsewhere.[7]

[1] 56 & 57 Vict. c. 61, sec. 3. See Davidson v. Anderson, (O.H.) 1905, 13 S.L.T. 298; Kemp v. Glasgow Corporation, 1919 S.C. 71.
[2] Christie v. Glasgow Corporation, 1899, 36 S.L.R. 694.
[3] Hunter v. Dundee Water Commissioners, 1920 S.C. 628.
[4] Hunter v. Dundee Water Commissioners, supra; Livingstonia Steamship Co. v. Clyde Navigation Trustees, 1928 S.C. 270.
[5] Walsh v. Magistrates of Pollokshaws, (O.H.) 1907, 14 S.L.T. 845; Edinburgh and District Water Trustees v. Sommerville & Sons, 1907 S.C. 355. See Mitchell v. Orkney Harbour Commissioners, 1922 S.L.T. (Sh.Ct.) 110, as to motion made first on appeal.
[6] M'Robert v. Reid, 1914 S.C. 633.
[7] See p. 41, supra.

Apart from express statutory authority, the Sheriff has power to award expenses as between solicitor and client in other actions, and in certain cases expenses are normally taxed as between solicitor and client. In consistorial cases the wife who is awarded expenses is generally entitled to have these taxed on the matrimonial scale, that is as between solicitor and client, payable by a third party,[1] and this rule now applies to expenses awarded to an impecunious husband if the wife has separate estate.[2] The rule does not apply to an action regarding custody of children.[3] In petitions for winding up companies expenses awarded are usually taxed as between solicitor and client.[4] Where expenses are awarded to trustees out of the trust estate such an award normally infers taxation as between solicitor and client.[5] This is generally expressed in the interlocutor, and, where the expenses come out of a separate fund and not the general trust estate, an award in normal terms will result in party and party taxation.[6] In the matter of expenses a judicial factor or a curator is entitled to the same treatment as a trustee.[7]

[1] Grant v. Grant, 1905, 43 S.L.R. 109; Wright v. Wright, 1910, 26 Sh.Ct.Rep. 111; Thomson v. Thomson, 1929, 45 Sh.Ct.Rep. 240; P v. P, 1940 S.C. 389; cf. A B v. C B, 1918 S.C. 19.
[2] Adair v. Adair, (O.H.) 1925 S.L.T. 286.
[3] A B v. C B, 1906, 8 F. 973.
[4] M'Gregor v. Ballachulish Slate Quarries, 1908 S.C. 1.
[5] Davidson's Trustees v. Simmons, 1896, 23 R. 1117; Merrilees v. Leckie's Trustees, 1908 S.C. 576.
[6] M'Gregor's Trustees v. Kimbell, 1912 S.C. 261.
[7] Fowler, (O.H.) 1917, 1 S.L.T. 266; Miln's Judicial Factor v. Spence's Trustees, (O.H.) 1929 S.L.T. 279.

Where a trustee, factor, or the like is awarded expenses as between solicitor and client this involves that the party receives all his reasonable expenses out of the estate, and the scale of taxation applied is that known as solicitor and client, client paying.[1] In other cases, such as awards to spouses or to public authorities under the Public Authorities Protection Act, the expenses are taxed on an intermediate scale known as solicitor and client, third party paying.[1]

[1] See this matter discussed in Miln's Judicial Factor v. Spence's Trustees, (O.H.) 1929 S.L.T. 279. See also Thomson v. Thomson, 1929, 45 Sh.Ct.Rep. 240.

7. TAXATION.

Expenses may be taxed upon either of two scales. The lower scale applies where the amount of principal craved does not exceed £50; the higher is applicable to causes exceeding that amount.[1] Where the pecuniary amount or value of the question in dispute cannot be ascertained from the process, the Sheriff determines according to which scale the account shall be taxed.[2] In actions of damages the scale of taxation of the pursuer's expenses is regulated, not by the sum concluded for, but by the sum decerned for, unless the Sheriff otherwise directs.[3] If the demand made does not exceed the value which may be competently concluded for in the Small Debt Court, small debt expenses only are to be allowed, unless the Sheriff appoint otherwise, and if the principal sum decerned for does not exceed £20 the Sheriff may allow small debt expenses only.[4] In all cases the Sheriff may appoint that expenses shall be subject to modification, or he may direct that expenses be taxed according to the scale applicable to the amount decerned for.[5] He may also direct an account falling under the lower scale to be taxed according to the higher scale, if he is of opinion that the sum concluded for does not truly represent the nature and importance of the case.[6] The Sheriff has probably no power to give an instalment decree for expenses.[7] In an action of interdict proceeding as an ordinary cause, and without any crave for damages, it has been held that, in the absence of any direction as to the scale and despite the small value of the proceedings interdicted, taxation should be on the higher scale.[8]

[1] Act of Sederunt, 7th May, 1935, General Regulation I. See as to several pursuers suing for separate sums Japp v. Adams, 1939 S.C. 439.
[2] Ibid., General Regulation V.
[3] Ibid., General Regulation II (3). See also Japp v. Adams, supra.
[4] Ibid., General Regulation II (4) (5). See Forestry Commissioners v. MacDougall, 1935, 52 Sh.Ct.Rep. 255.
[5] Ibid., General Regulation I, II (1).
[6] Ibid., General Regulation II (2).
[7] Archer's Trustees v. Alexander & Sons, 1910, 27 Sh.Ct.Rep. 11.
[8] M'Leod v. Munro, 1930, 47 Sh.Ct.Rep. 21.

In certain procedure connected with jury trials, and in connexion with bankruptcy and executry business only one scale of charges is given.[1] In the case of the specified fees in jury trials it is provided that, if the verdict is of less than £50, only half of these specified fees is to be allowed as judicial expenses[2]—a rule that is presumably intended to apply only if the pursuer is successful. In ordinary removings and ejections the ordinary table applies, and the scale is determined by the annual amount of the rent.[3] When the rent is not set forth as exceeding £50 the lower scale applies.[3] An action does not cease to be an ordinary removing because the defender pleads the terms of the Rent Restriction Acts,[4] but ordinary removings and ejections do not include removings during the currency of the lease, nor ejections for the removal of a squatter.[5] In such cases the Court ought to fix the scale of taxation.

[1] Act of Sederunt, 7th May, 1935, General Regulation III. See Cross v. Ferrie, 1940, 58 Sh.Ct.Rep. 40, as to scale in sequestrations.
[2] Ibid., Table of Fees, ch. I, 16.
[3] Ibid., General Regulation IV.
[4] Tod & Sons v. Sinclair, 1921, 38 Sh.Ct.Rep. 114.
[5] Stark. &c. v. Harland Engineering Co., 1915, 31 Sh.Ct.Rep. 277.

In actions where there is a counter-claim there is no general rule which justifies the aggregation of claim and counter-claim for the purpose of determining the scale on which expenses are to be taxed. But in practice this course has been followed in two cases which are reported.[1] In view of the doubt which exists as to the value of the cause where a counter-claim is involved[2] the scale for taxation ought to be determined by the Court before the account is taxed. Where a crave for payment of £82 was reduced by minute of restriction, after the record was closed, to £33 10s., it was held that the expenses were not thereby affected and fell to be taxed on the higher scale.[3]

[1] Murphy v. Muir, 1927, 43 Sh.Ct.Rep. 235; Kinnaird & Son v. Millar, 1931, 47 Sh.Ct.Rep. 320; cf. Sinclair v. Wood, 1912, 28 Sh.Ct.Rep. 359.
[2] See p. 50, supra.
[3] M'Innes v. Finlay, 1916, 33 Sh.Ct.Rep. 3.

In a summary cause, expenses are, as a rule, taxed upon the lower scale,[1] but if the sum decerned for does not exceed £20, the Sheriff may allow small debt expenses only.[2] When a small debt action has been remitted to the Ordinary Court Roll, the cause is to proceed in all respects, including appeal, as if it had been originally raised in the Ordinary Court.[3] The matter of expenses is in the Sheriff's discretion, and the ordinary fees will normally apply from the time the case appears on the Ordinary Court Roll. Failing any special directions the account will be taxed on the lower scale if, as will usually be the case, the action concludes for a payment of not over £50.[1]

[1] Act of Sederunt, 7th May, 1935, General Regulation I.
[2] Ibid., General Regulation II (5).
[3] 7 Edw. VII c. 51, sec. 48.

Besides his general discretion to award expenses subject to modification, the Sheriff may disallow particular charges relative to procedure which he regards as unnecessary, or irregular, the general direction being that only such expenses are to be allowed, in taxing accounts between party and party, as are necessary for conducting the case in a proper manner, and with due regard to economy.[1] Further, though a party has obtained a general award of expenses, if he has been unsuccessful in any particular part of the case, or through his fault has occasioned any part of the expense, he is not to be allowed on taxation the expense of such parts of the proceedings.[2] The last-mentioned regulation has been held not to apply to any part of the expenses which have been declared expenses in the cause,[3] nor to the expenses of discussing preliminary pleas,[4] and these particular expenses were allowed under a general finding despite lack of success in regard to them. But such a provision has been applied in spite of a special modification of expenses in respect of non-success,[5] and its application by the auditor was upheld in a case where the Lord Ordinary had given a general finding and had intended all expenses to be covered.[6] A defender awarded expenses on abandonment was held not entitled to the costs of earlier unsuccessful appeals on his part.[7] In view of the above ruling in regard to the expenses of discussing preliminary pleas, the party who succeeds in such debates should raise the question of these expenses at the time or, if necessary, have them specially dealt with at the close of the case.[8]

[1] Act of Sederunt, 7th May, 1935, General Regulation X.
[2] Ibid., General Regulation XI.
[3] Glasgow & South-Western Railway Co. v. Magistrates of Ayr, 1911 S.C. 298.
[4] Earl of Lauderdale v. Wedderburn, 1911 S.C. 4.
[5] Arthur v. Lindsay, 1895, 22 R. 904; Aitken v. Classen, 1928 S.C. 628; cf. Ralston v. Caledonian Railway Co., 1878, 5 R. 671; Dick & Stevenson v. Mackay, 1880, 7 R. 778.
[6] Craig v. Craig, 1906, 14 S.L.T. 469.
[7] Lord Hamilton v. Glasgow Dairy Co., 1933 S.C. 18.
[8] See Thomson v. Simons & Co., 1943, 60 Sh.Ct.Rep. 106.

Where a party—other than a solicitor—conducts his own case he is not entitled to any expenses in respect of loss of time, or travelling or subsistence allowances, in respect of his attendance at debates or hearings,[1] but a party who appears as a witness is entitled to the usual witness fee and expenses of travelling and maintenance.[2] A solicitor who conducts his own case is entitled to the usual professional charges.[3]

[1] Forbes v. Whyte, 1891, 18 R. 688.
[2] Dairon v. Dairon, 1900, 3 F. 230; Woodward v. Woodward, 1910, 2 S.L.T. 248; Dalton & Co. v. Boyle & Co., 1909, 26 Sh.Ct.Rep. 53; Cochran v. Paton & Co., 1920, 36 Sh.Ct.Rep. 118.
[3] A B v. C D, 1912, 29 Sh.Ct.Rep. 166.

In the normal case taxation of expenses by the Auditor of Court is an essential preliminary to obtaining decree for them unless the expenses have been modified at a fixed sum, so that taxation is not necessary. But under the present Table of Fees the pursuer's solicitor has the option, in undefended cases, of charging an inclusive fee to cover all work down to the obtaining of the extract decree, outlays being chargeable in addition.[1] In that case also taxation is unnecessary. The option is exercised by pursuer's solicitor endorsing a minute to the above effect on the initial writ before ordering extract of the decree.[1] In practice the option to take the inclusive fee is incorporated in the minute craving decree. Apart from the above two cases, expenses allowed in any action, whether in absence or *in foro*, must be taxed before decree is granted for them.[2] In order to have the expenses taxed an account thereof is lodged in process and thereafter transmitted to the Auditor of Court for taxation in presence of parties' solicitors. Intimation of the diet of taxation is made by sending the opposite party a copy of the account. In a report annexed to the account the auditor states the amount at which the account has been taxed by him.

[1] Act of Sederunt, 7th May, 1935, Table of Fees, ch. I, 1 (b).
[2] 7 Edw. VII c. 51, Schedule I, Rule 99.

If exception is to be taken to any of the auditor's rulings on taxation, a note of objections to his report must be lodged within two days of the lodging in process of the report, and such objections are to be disposed of by the Sheriff in a summary manner, with or without answers.[1] No provision is made for the party whose account is taxed intimating to his opponent when the account with the auditor's report has been lodged, and while the Sheriff-clerk may, as a matter of courtesy, inform a prospective objector when the account is lodged, the onus is on the party to ascertain this for himself by inquiring. The rule contemplates that there may be formal answers to the objections, and, where the objections are serious, it may sometimes be convenient that answers be ordered. In the ordinary case, however, there is not likely to be any advantage in this, and in practice answers are seldom put in. Objections may be stated for both parties.

[1] 7 Edw. VII c. 51, Schedule I, Rule 100.

The note of objection should be specific, and should deal with each item separately, setting forth the objection to the auditor's method of dealing with that item, and what the objector proposes should be substituted for the auditor's finding.[1] There is no rule expressly requiring an objector to notify the other party that he is lodging a note of objections to the auditor's report, or to intimate the diet fixed for disposing of the objections, but in

practice a copy of the note of objections is sent to the other side
with a note of the diet.

¹ Crossan v. Caledonian Railway Co., 1902, 5 F. 187.

It has been laid down by a series of decisions of the Court of
Session that, where expenses are to be dealt with in some special
manner, a motion to that effect must be made at the time when
the expenses are being awarded, and that where a general award
has been made it is too late to seek to have this modified on
objections to the auditor's report. All that can be dealt with
at that stage are questions of taxation, and not those that affect
the basis of the award itself. This rule has been applied in the
case of the following attempted modifications of a general award :
to exclude reserved expenses carried by a general finding[1] ; to
have a party and party award treated as one between solicitor
and client[2] ; to have a general award of expenses to parties who
had been separately represented treated as only a joint award[3] ;
to have parties who had been found liable generally decerned
against jointly and severally[4] ; and to exclude certain expenses
carried by a general award.[5] The Court of Session has also
applied the rule in two Sheriff Court appeals[6] where it refused
to alter the scale upon which the auditor had taxed an account
of expenses. In both cases the Court considered that the correct
scale had been applied, but indicated that the motion in any
case came too late.[6] There has been considerable controversy as
to whether the Court of Session rule should be applied in the
Sheriff Court itself where the question is as to the appropriate
scale of taxation, and it has been pointed out that there is a
sharp divergence of practice between the two Courts, for, in
the Court of Session, expenses are awarded after judgment given
in open Court and upon a motion for expenses made at the Bar,
whereas in the Sheriff Court expenses are normally awarded by
the Sheriff without parties being heard upon the subject.[7] There
is also the further distinction that in the Court of Session party
and party expenses can, in the usual case, be taxed on only one
scale, and the import of the award appears on the face of the
interlocutor, whereas in the Sheriff Court there are at least two
possible scales of taxation, and a general award may itself be
ambiguous as the circumstances may be such that the Sheriff
should have fixed the scale of taxation, or this may depend on
the sum sued, or decerned, for.

¹ Macfie v. Blair, 1884, 22 S.L.R. 224.
² Fletcher's Trustees v. Fletcher, 1888, 15 R. 862; Mackellar v.
    Mackellar, 1898, 25 R. 883; Magistrates of Aberchirder v. Banff
    District Committee, 1906, 8 F. 571.

3 Murray v. Macfarlane's Trustees, 1895, 23 R. 80.
4 Warrand v. Watson, 1907 S.C. 432; Young, &c. v. Burgh of Darvel, 1923 S.C. 745.   See also s.s. "Fullwood" v. Dumfries Harbour Commissioners, 1907 S.C. 735; Alyth Light Symphony Band v. Ross, 1929, 46 Sh.Ct.Rep. 62.
5 Anderson's Trustees v. Donaldson & Co., 1908 S.C. 385.
6 Murray v. Rennie & Angus, 1897, 24 R. 1026; Mickel v. M'Coard, 1913 S.C. 1036.
7 See Carnbroe Chemical Co. v. Lanark Middle Ward, 1924, 43 Sh.Ct.Rep. 163.

While the decisions in the Sheriff Court show certain differences of opinion, the following conclusions seem to be justified. Where the pecuniary value of the question in dispute cannot be ascertained from the process, and under Regulation V of the Table of Fees, the scale falls to be fixed by the Sheriff, and this is not done in the interlocutor awarding expenses, the right of the Court to fix the scale remains, and while this ought to be done before the taxation,[1] it is competent to do so even after the account has been taxed.[2] The same latitude has been indicated to be applicable in two cases where the position was complicated by a counter-claim though these decisions may be doubtful,[3] and if an account has been taxed on the scale which is admittedly appropriate according to the circumstances of the case, it is probably too late, after taxation, to ask that the Court should make a special direction under one of the sub-heads of Regulation II and appoint taxation on the other scale.[4] It is not clear that such a motion can be entertained after an award has been made and before the account is submitted for taxation, but the Sheriff may possibly be entitled, under the General Regulations, to make such a direction at that stage if the question is raised without delay.[5] In order to eliminate the difficulties that occur in this connexion, it is suggested that where any doubt in regard to the appropriate scale may arise, parties should be heard upon the point before the award is made, and that the matter should be raised, but not necessarily fully discussed, at the close of the proof or hearing on the merits. The limitation above suggested on the Sheriff's power to give a special direction as to taxation under Regulation II does not apply where the question is whether on the award as made the auditor has taxed on the proper scale. A reversal of the auditor on this point can only be made after taxation, and it involves, not any special direction, but the interpretation of the award as made. The allowance of a special debate fee, and the sanctioning of the employment of counsel, have been treated as matters that may be dealt with on objections to the auditor's report.[6]

1 Johnstone Corporation v. Smith & M'Laurin, 1937, 53 Sh.Ct.Rep. 317.
2 Carnbroe Chemical Co. v. Lanark Middle Ward, 1924, 43 Sh.Ct.Rep. 163. See also M'Leod v. Munro, 1930, 47 Sh.Ct.Rep. 21; and cf. Stark v. Harland Engineering Co., 1915, 31 Sh.Ct.Rep. 277.
3 Murphy v. Muir, 1927, 43 Sh.Ct.Rep. 235; Kinnaird & Sons v. Millar, 1931, 47 Sh.Ct.Rep. 320.
4 Murray v. Rennie & Angus, 1897, 24 R. 1026; Mickel v. M'Coard, 1913 S.C. 1036; Tod & Sons v. Sinclair, 1921, 38 Sh.Ct.Rep. 114; M'Stay v. Murdostoun Colliery Co., 1924, 40 Sh.Ct.Rep. 334.
5 Act of Sederunt, 7th May, 1935, Regulation II. See Kennedy v. Clyde Shipping Co., 1908 S.C. 895.
6 Harris v. Lamont, 1925, 41 Sh.Ct.Rep. 243. But see p. 335, infra.

If there are no objections lodged, or after they have been disposed of, the Sheriff, by interlocutor, approves of the auditor's report and decerns for the taxed expenses. Such decree may be extracted after the lapse of seven days, unless otherwise directed by the Sheriff.[1] The rule which postpones the time for issuing extract on an application being made for leave to appeal does not apply to a decree for expenses.[2] The rule relating to decrees for expenses[1] appears to give the Sheriff a wider discretion than that of the general extract rule,[2] and to make it competent for him to shorten or to extend the extract period of a decree for expenses.

1 7 Edw. VII c. 51, Schedule I, Rule 98.
2 Ibid., Rule 85; 17 & 18 Geo. V c. 35, sec. 21. See p. 254, supra.

An interlocutor approving of the auditor's report, and granting decree for the taxed amount of the expenses, is not appealable as a final judgment.[1] When objections have been stated to the auditor's report, there have been doubts whether the judgment disposing of these objections is appealable as a final judgment, but it is thought that it is not.[1] Interlocutors granting decree for expenses, whether after objections or without objections, can be appealed with leave.[2]

1 See further on this point at p. 292, supra.
2 See p. 291, supra.

Every decree for expenses includes decree for the expense of extract,[1] and the account of expenses is taxed upon the footing that the decree will be extracted. A party who pays immediately upon taxation, and so renders extract unnecessary, is generally entitled to deduction of the items under this head included in the taxed account, but not actually incurred[2]; but extract may be regarded as necessary in the interests of the holder of the decree and he may be held entitled to extract it irrespective of payment if the decree is not merely for payment of money, but is a decree of declarator or the like.[3] Interest runs on a decree for expenses from its date, that is, from the date of its entry in the Court books.[4] A pursuer paying the expenses included in an extract decree of absolvitor is not entitled to delivery of the extract.[5]

[1] 7 Edw. VII c. 51, Schedule I, Rule 98; 55 & 56 Vict. c. 17, Schedule, "General Directions."
[2] Leith Magistrates v. Gibb, 1882, 19 S.L.R. 399; Bannatyne v. M'Lean, 1884, 11 R. 681.
[3] Orr v. Smith, 1891, 28 S.L.R. 589; Rutherglen Parish Council v. Glenbucket Parish Council, (O.H.) 1896, 33 S.L.R. 368; Glasgow District Subway Co. v. M'Callum, 1896, 12 Sh.Ct.Rep. 148.
[4] Wallace v. Henderson, 1876, 4 R. 264.
[5] Williams v. Carmichael, (O.H.) 1874, 11 S.L.R. 530.

8. DECREE IN SOLICITOR'S NAME.

When expenses are found due to the successful party in a litigation his solicitor may interpose to obtain the decree for expenses in his name.[1] When this is done the solicitor has a claim for expenses which is not affected by any set-off at the instance of the debtor against the client. The granting of decree in the solicitor's name is a matter which is in the discretion of the Court.[1] The proper time to move for decree in name of the solicitor is when an interlocutor is asked for approving of the auditor's report, and decerning for the taxed expenses, or, if expenses are to be modified, when the fixed sum is decerned for. Although practice seems to sanction decree being asked in the name of the solicitor without prior intimation,[2] it is thought that notification of decree being asked should always be given, and that a written motion should be lodged. When a case has been appealed to the Court of Session expenses in both Courts may be decerned for in name of the Sheriff Court solicitor, if the Edinburgh solicitor consents and the other party to the case does not object.[3]

[1] 7 Edw. VII c. 51, Schedule I, Rule 99.
[2] See Rorie v. Macpherson, 1910, 26 Sh.Ct.Rep. 232.
[3] Smith v. Gordon, 1908, 45 S.L.R. 513; Cassels v. Filshie, 1926 S.L.T. 497; West v. Cow, 1929 S.C. 783.

The right of a solicitor to obtain decree in his own name for expenses does not go so far as to entitle him—save in certain circumstances—to carry on a process on his own account so as to secure a decree in his own name for expenses.[1] In general the Court will allow the solicitor to be sisted as a party if an

award of expenses has been made and the case is compromised by
the client on appeal,[2] or where the case has reached a stage at
which a finding for expenses will naturally follow, although, as
yet, no formal interlocutor dealing with expenses has been pronounced,[3] or where the parties to a cause have collusively come
to an agreement with the view of defeating recovery of expenses
by a party's solicitor.[4] In the general case the solicitor's motion
will not be granted if there has been no investigation into the
facts.[5] In practice decree in the solicitor's name may be granted
if asked at any time before extract, even though decree for expenses
has already been given in name of the client.[6]

[1] Elliot v. Elliot, 1893, 1 S.L.T. 261; Wales v. Wales, (O.H.) 1902,
    9 S.L.T. 371; Riddle v. Riddle, (O.H.) 1904, 12 S.L.T. 361.
[2] Ammon v. Tod, 1912 S.C. 306.
[3] Cornwall v. Walker, 1871, 8 S.L.R. 442.
[4] Crawford v. Smith, (O.H.) 1900, 8 S.L.T. 249.
[5] Clark v. Henderson, 1875, 2 R. 428.
[6] Brown v. Brown, 1929 S.L.T. (Sh.Ct.) 44.

A solicitor may be found personally liable in expenses to an
opponent if he conducts a litigation without his client's authority,[1]
and in one case, when the fault of a solicitor had necessitated
his client asking to be reponed, this was allowed subject to the
solicitor personally paying the expenses of the other party.[2]

[1] Cowan v. Farnie, 1836, 14 S. 634; Philip v. Gordon, 1848, 11 D.
    175; Robertson v. Ross, 1873, 11 M. 910; cf. Mitchell & Baxter v.
    Cheyne, 1891, 19 R. 324.
[2] M'Kechnie v. Halliday, 1856, 18 D. 659.

In general, a solicitor's right to have decree for expenses in
his own name will be defeated if there are cross awards of expenses
which ought to be set against each other. This situation arises
where pursuer and defender each receive awards of expenses in
the same case,[1] even though these are made at different times.[2]
The same principle applies in the case of separate actions if they
arise out of the same subject-matter,[3] but not if they are merely
between the same parties.[4] On the other hand, decree in name
of the solicitor as agent-disburser will be allowed in the case of
the second of two cross awards if the first has already gone out
in name of the other solicitor,[5] or, in the case of two actions, if
the decree in the earlier has already been extracted and become
a judgment debt.[6] A possibility of a counter award of expenses
at a later stage will not prevent a solicitor getting decree in his
name in respect of expenses already awarded.[7] A right of relief
between parties in respect of expenses is not treated as a cross
award to the effect of defeating the solicitor's right to decree.[8]

A solicitor may ask for decree even after he has retired from
the case,[9] and the right to decree exists in statutory arbitrations
under the Workmen's Compensation Act as in ordinary actions.[10]
Where an arrestment had been used against the client the solicitor's
motion has been granted under reservation of the effect of the
arrestment,[11] but in such a case it would seem that the arrestment
has the preference unless the solicitor has by notice interpelled
the party liable in the expenses from making payment before
the arrestment was used.[12] Decree has been granted in the
solicitor's name despite the intervening sequestration of the client,[13]
and decree may be given in the country solicitor's name in appeals
to the Court of Session.[14] An appeal against an interlocutor
allowing decree in the solicitor's name is competent only with
leave.[15]

[1] Stothart v. Johnston's Trustees, 1823, 2 Mur. 549; Warburton v.
    Hamilton, 1826, 4 S. 631; M'Owan v. Wilson, 1888, 4 Sh.Ct.Rep.
    346; Masco Cabinet Co. v. Martin, 1912 S.C. 896.
[2] Graham v. M'Arthur, 1826, 5 S. 49; Gordon v. Davidson, 1865. 3 M.
    938; Macgillivray v. Mackintosh, 1891. 19 R. 103; Dixon v. Murray,
    1894, (O.H.) 1 S.L.T. 600; Grieve's Trustees v. Grieve, 1907 S.C.
    963.
[3] Portobello Pier Co. v. Clift, 1877, 4 R. 685; Oliver v. Wilkie, 1901,
    4 F. 362; Lochgelly Iron & Coal Co. v. Sinclair, 1907 S.C. 442.
[4] Paterson v. Wilson, 1883, 11 R. 358; Stuart v. Moss, 1886, 13 R. 572;
    Strain v. Strain, 1890, 17 R. 566; Bruce v. Adamson, 1900, (O.H.)
    8 S.L.T. 17; Fine v. Edinburgh Life Assurance Co., 1909 S.C.
    636; Holt v. National Bank of Scotland, (O.H.) 1927 S.L.T. 664.
[5] Blasquez v. Scott, 1893, 1 S.L.T. 357.
[6] Paolo v. Parias, 1897, 24 R. 1030; Fine v. Edinburgh Life Assurance
    Co., supra; Wm. Baird & Co. v. Campbell, 1928 S.C. 487; Wm.
    Baird & Co. v. M'Bride, 1928 S.N. 31.
[7] Hugh Nelson & Co. v. Glasgow Corporation, 1908 S.C. 879.
[8] Jackson & Co. v. Laing, 1929 S.C. 426.
[9] Holt v. National Bank of Scotland, supra.
[10] Coakley v. Summerlee Iron Co., 1929 S.C. 182.
[11] Connolly v. Magistrates of Clydebank, 1929 S.N. 14; Donoghue v.
    Stevenson, (O.H.) 1932 S.L.T. 520.
[12] Buchanan v. Royal Insurance Co., &c., 1937, 53 Sh.Ct.Rep. 314; cf.
    Agnew v. Norwest Construction Co., 1935 S.C. 771.
[13] Union Bank of Scotland v. Macmillan, 1930, 47 Sh.Ct.Rep. 15.
[14] West v. Cow, 1929 S.C. 783.
[15] 7 Edw. VII c. 51, secs. 27, 28; Carson v. M'Dowall, 1908, 24
    Sh.Ct.Rep. 324.

Where a solicitor is employed to pursue or defend any action
the Court may declare the solicitor entitled to a charge for the
taxed expenses of, or in reference to, the action upon and against,
and a right to payment out of, the property, of whatsoever nature,
kind or tenure the same may be, which has been recovered or
preserved by the solicitor on behalf of his client, and the Court
may make such orders for taxation of, and for raising and pay-

ment of, such expenses out of the property as may seem proper to the Court.[1] And all acts done or deeds granted by the client after the date of the declaration, except acts or deeds in favour of a *bona fide* purchaser or lender, are declared to be void and of no effect against such charge or right.[1] The granting of a charging order is in the discretion of the Court.[2]

[1] 23 & 24 Geo. V c. 21, sec. 43. See also Stenhouse v. Stenhouse's Trustees, (O.H.) 1903, 10 S.L.T. 684; Paton v. Paton's Trustees, (O.H.) 1905, 13 S.L.T. 96.
[2] Carruthers' Trustee v. Finlay & Wilson, 1897, 24 R. 363.

The charging order covers extrajudicial expenses and the right to the order is not defeated by arrestment having been used against the fund recovered or preserved,[1] nor by the client having gone into voluntary liquidation and the fund being in England,[2] and the right has been held to extend to the Glasgow solicitor who got up a case as well as to the Edinburgh solicitor who actually attended the case.[3] But it is essential for the application of the section that the fund sought to be charged should have been actually recovered or preserved on behalf of the client,[4] and a charging order was not allowed to prejudice the right of the other party to the case to set off certain expenses against the principal sum.[5] A charging order has been refused where the client entitled to the fund had been already sequestrated.[6]

[1] Automobile Gas Producer Syndicate v. Caledonian Railway Co., (O.H.) 1909, 1 S.L.T. 499.
[2] Philip v. Willson, 1911 S.C. 1203; cf. Tait & Co. v. Wallace, (O.H.) 1894, 2 S.L.T. 261.
[3] Bannatyne, Kirkwood France & Co., 1907 S.C. 705.
[4] See Carruthers' Trustee v. Finlay & Wilson, 1897, 24 R. 363; Hutchison v. Hutchison's Trustees, 1902, 40 S.L.R. 200, 10 S.L.T. 562; Smart & Co. v. Stewart, (O.H.) 1911, 49 S.L.R. 66. 2 S.L.T. 340.
[5] O'Keefe v. Grieve's Trustees, (O.H.) 1917, 1 S.L.T. 305.
[6] Tait & Co. v. Wallace, (O.H.) 1894, 2 S.L.T. 261; Pollock & Son v. Crawford, 1900, 16 Sh.Ct.Rep. 124.

Whether any property has been recovered or preserved in the sense of the Act is, in each case, a question of circumstances, and reference may be made to the undernoted cases.[1] A charging order may be obtained by a solicitor for the poor.[2]

[1] Carruthers' Trustee v. Finlay & Wilson, 1897, 24 R. 363; Hutchison v. Hutchison's Trustees, (O.H.) 1902, 40 S.L.R. 200, 10 S.L.T. 562; Smart & Co. v. Stewart, (O.H.) 1911, 49 S.L.R. 66, 1911, 2 S.L.T. 340.
[2] Cameron v. M'Donald, (O.H.) 1935 S.N. 25.

9. Witnesses.

In general, witness fees and charges for precognitions are allowed only for witnesses who are actually examined, or are held as concurring with a witness who has been examined.[1] It may happen, however, that a party who has brought necessary witnesses does not require to examine them, because of some change of circumstances at the proof, as, for instance, his opponents not insisting in the particular matter to which these witnesses were intended to speak, or by judgment being given in the absence of the other party without evidence being led. Under the Sheriff Court Table of Fees charges for precognitions and for attendances of the witnesses not examined will only be allowed if a motion for such allowance is made at the time or within eight days thereafter, and if the allowance is sanctioned by the Court, the witnesses' names and addresses being noted.[2] If the motion is not made at the time, but within the eight days, the charge for the motion itself will not be allowed.[2] Witnesses who do not reside in the town of the place of trial or proof are entitled to witness fees for the time necessarily occupied in going to, remaining at, and returning from the proof, besides reasonable travelling and maintenance charges, according to their station in life.[3] A party to the case who gives evidence is entitled to the usual expenses.[4]

[1] See Barrie v. Scottish Motor Traction Co., (O.H.) 1936 S.L.T. 143.
[2] Act of Sederunt, 7th May, 1935, Table of Fees, ch. I, 12 (c).
[3] Ibid., ch. IV, 3 (b).
[4] See p. 324, supra.

Skilled witnesses are entitled to special charges for making investigations prior to a proof or trial to qualify them for giving evidence.[1] Such charges are allowed in addition to their ordinary witness fees at a rate in the discretion of the auditor.[1] But it is a condition of such special charges that the Court, on a motion made at the trial or proof or within eight days thereafter, if the Court is in session, or in vacation, within the first eight days of the ensuing session, certifies such skilled persons for additional remuneration.[1] The present Act of Sederunt does not define a skilled witness, but " skilled persons " may probably be read as including not only professional or scientific witnesses, but any other skilled person who, in the Sheriff's opinion, was reasonably entitled to visit a locus, or examine work, or make calculations, or otherwise occupy time before the date of the proof or trial in order to qualify himself for giving evidence.

[1] Act of Sederunt, 7th May, 1935, Table of Fees, ch. IV, 3 (a).

It has been held in the Court of Session on a similar provision that the eight days count from the date of judgment in proofs, and from the date of the verdict in jury trials.[1] A similar ruling has been applied in the Sheriff Court,[2] but the opposite view has also been taken,[3] and the practice does not appear to be settled. It is not necessary that the motion be disposed of within the eight days, and if a motion craving the certificate is lodged within the time that is sufficient.[4] The appropriate time for making the motion is at the close of the proof or trial, and in the Court of Session, if this is not done, the charges for a subsequent enrolment are not recoverable from an opponent.[5] Certification by the Court is unnecessary if the case it settled before the proof or trial,[6] but where certification is necessary omission to apply for it is not a matter that can be rectified on appeal.[7] The additional allowance under the table is for preliminary investigations only.[8]

[1] Scott v. Lanarkshire, &c., Railway Co., 1897, 5 S.L.T. 165; Davidson v. Scott, 1915 S.C. 1120; M'Ghee v. William Beardmore & Co., (O.H.) 1946 S.N. 59.
[2] Duncan v. Ballantyne, 1938, 55 Sh.Ct.Rep. 122; Henderson v. Burgh of Airdrie, 1943, 59 Sh.Ct.Rep. 100. See MacDonald v. Robertson, 1910, 27 Sh.Ct.Rep. 103, p. 107.
[3] O'Neil v. Hopkinson, 1944 S.L.T. (Sh.Ct.) 27.
[4] John Haig & Co. v. Boswall-Preston, 1915 S.C. 339; cf. MacDonald v. Robertson, supra; Black v. Crawford, 1912, 28 Sh.Ct.Rep. 308.
[5] Davidson v. Scott, supra.
[6] Clements v. Edinburgh Corporation, 1905, 7 F. 651; Storrie v. Mitchell, (O.H.) 1937 S.L.T. 624; cf. Sneddon v. Baton Collieries, 1922 S.C. 83. See also Mill v. Dundas, 1920 S.C. 208 (settlement in course of trial); White v. Avery, 1915, 31 Sh.Ct.Rep. 344 (witness not giving evidence.
[7] Gibson v. West Lothian Oil Co., 1887, 14 R. 578; Reid v. Orkney County Council, 1912 S.C. 627.
[8] See Ferguson v. Johnston, 1886, 13 R. 635; Ebbw Vale Co. v. Murray, 1898, 25 R. 925; Govan v. M'Killop, 1909 S.C. 562; Caledonian Railway Co. v. Greenock Corporation, 1922 S.C. 299.

10. Counsel's Fees.

While a party is always entitled to be represented in Court by counsel, fees to counsel will only be allowed as judicial expenses when the employment is sanctioned by the Court.[1] When sanctioned the allowance is limited to party and party expenses, and no fees to counsel are allowed till after the closing of the record.[1] Fees are in general limited to attendances in Court, and fees for one consultation only in course of the case are allowed, unless counsel is employed both before the Sheriff-Substitute and on appeal to the Sheriff, when an additional fee may be allowed for a consultation prior to the debate on appeal.[1]

[1] Act of Sederunt, 7th May, 1935, Table of Fees, ch. I, 19 (a) (b).

Whether counsel's fees should be sanctioned as judicial costs in the Sheriff Court is a matter in the discretion of the Sheriff in each particular case. His sanction may be given at any time before the taxation of the expenses,[1] and an appellate Court will not, in general, interfere with the discretion of the judge of first instance in this matter. It is probably competent for an appellate tribunal to sanction the employment of counsel, but the motion should be made before the judge who tried the case, and the Appeal Court will not readily intervene if sanction has not been asked in the Court below.[2] The sanction may cover the employment of senior counsel,[3] and the recall on appeal of an interlocutor containing the sanction will not nullify the sanction itself.[4] Sanction may be granted though counsel have been employed by one side only.[5] The fees to be allowed are not necessarily limited to those actually sent to counsel before sanction was obtained.[6]

[1] Purvis v. Dowie, 1869, 7 M. 764; M'Kercher v. M'Quarrie, 1887, 14 R. 1038; Swanson v. Gardner & Co., 1916, 33 Sh.Ct.Rep. 117. The sanction of counsel after taxation of the account—see Harris v. Lamont, 1925, 41 Sh.Ct.Rep. 243—is thought to be not justifiable.
[2] Mackenzie v. Blakeney, 1879, 7 R. 51; Wood's Trustees v. Wood, 1900, 2 F. 870; Reid v. Orkney County Council, 1912 S.C. 627.
[3] Alpine v. Dumbarton Heritors, (O.H.) 1908, 16 S.L.T. 388; Garden, Haig-Scott & Wallace v. Prudential Approved Society, (O.H.) 1927 S.L.T. 393.
[4] Taylor v. Steel-Maitland, 1913 S.C. 978.
[5] Cochran v. Paton & Co., 1920, 36 Sh.Ct.Rep. 3; Elliott v. North British Railway Co., 1922, 38 Sh.Ct.Rep. 17; Scottish Milk Agency v. Leiper, 1930, 47 Sh.Ct.Rep. 106.
[6] Christie, &c. v. Macfarlane, 1929, 45 Sh.Ct.Rep. 243.

11. EFFECT OF TENDER.

A tender does not affect the awarding of expenses if the pursuer obtains decree for a sum greater than that tendered.[1] But if he obtains decree for the sum tendered, or less, he will be entitled to expenses up to the date of tender, and after that date he will be liable in expenses to the defender.[2] While these are the rules generally applied the Court retains its discretion as to expenses, and in marginal cases, or in special circumstances, these general rules may be disregarded.[3] The essentials of an effective tender, and the effect of extra-judicial offers, have been already considered.[4] Where a tender is declined, and the defender is ultimately found entitled to expenses since its date, the Court may supersede extract of the pursuer's decree for the principal sum till defender's expenses have been taxed and decerned for.[5]

[1] See Heriot v. Thomson, 1833, 12 S. 145.

2 Mitchells v. Nicoll, 1890, 17 R. 795; Brodie v. MacGregor, 1901, 4 F. 93; John Hamilton & Co. v. Fleming & Co., (O.H.) 1918, 1 S.L.T. 229; M'Lean v. Galbraith Stores, 1935 S.C. 165.

3 Smith v. Baird, 1843, 16 Scot. Jur. 133; Wilkie v. Bethune, 1848, 11 D. 132; Muckarsie v. Dickson, 1848, 11 D. 164; Webster v. Alexander, 1859, 21 D. 1214; Aitchison v. Steven, 1864, 3 M. 81; Cutlar v. M'Leod's Trustees, 1876, 13 S.L.R. 308; M'Lellan v. Finnie & Co., 1916, 33 Sh.Ct.Rep. 235.

4 See pp. 149, 150, supra.

5 Bruce v. M'Lellan, 1925 S.C. 103.

Where a case is settled by tender and acceptance the expenses awarded to the pursuer include the costs of considering and accepting the tender,[1] and where a tender is refused and pursuer subsequently gets an award of expenses the costs of considering the declined tender are included.[1] Expenses awarded to the date of a tender are normally held to cover expenses necessarily incurred, in the natural course of the case, till the date when the tender should have been accepted on a reasonable view of the circumstances of the case.[2] If a tender is not in this sense timeously accepted, but is ultimately accepted, the defender will usually be awarded expenses subsequent to the date when timeous acceptance should have been made.[3] But where expenses are awarded against a pursuer in respect of a declined tender these will be held to run from the actual date of the tender unless this is qualified in the interlocutor awarding them.[4] The question of withdrawing a tender has been already noticed.[5]

1 Philip v. Dixon, 1852, 15 D. 228; M'Dougall v. Caledonian Railway Co., 1878, 5 R. 1011; Irvin v. Fairfield Shipbuilding Co., 1899, 1 F. 595; M'Millan v. Central S.M.T. Co., (O.H.) 1947 S.N. 20.

2 M'Laughlin v. Glasgow Tramway & Omnibus Co., 1897, 24 R. 992; Allan v. Bell Bros., (O.H.) 1927 S.L.T. 213.

3 Jack v. Black, 1911 S.C. 691.

4 M'Lean v. Galbraith Stores, 1935 S.C. 165.

5 See p. 150, supra.

Where several pursuers sue in one action, or where actions are conjoined, a tender cannot be competently made by offering a lump sum to cover all the claims, and the defender must tender a separate sum to each pursuer.[1] In the result various parties may require to be differently dealt with in relation to expenses according to the general principles already considered.[2]

1 Boyle v. Olsen, 1912 S.C. 1235; Flanagan v. Dempster, Moore & Co., 1928 S.C. 308; cf. John Hamilton & Co. v. Fleming & Co., (O.H.) 1918, 1 S.L.T. 229.

2 See Flanagan v. Dempster, Moore & Co., supra; Clegg v. M'Kirdy & M'Millan, 1932 S.C. 442; Peggie v. Keddie, 1932 S.C. 721.

12. Payment of Expenses as Condition of Proceeding.

Where a partial award of expenses is made in the course of a case, it may, or may not, be made a condition of the action being allowed to proceed that these expenses should be paid.[1] A party is generally found liable in such expenses because he has been responsible for causing the expenses, and where radical amendment of a record has been allowed,[2] or a postponement of a case is granted,[3] or a party is reponed against a decree by default,[4] the Court may make payment of the expenses awarded a condition precedent of the case proceeding further. The mere fact that an award of expenses has been made does not imply that payment is a condition precedent to the action proceeding.[5]

[1] Wight v. Ewing, 1834, 12 S. 535; Wallace v. Henderson, 1876, 4 R. 264; Byres' Trustees v. Gemmell, (O.H.) 1896, 4 S.L.T. 21; Nixon v. Houston, 1898, 1 F. 78.
[2] Morgan, Gellibrand & Co. v. Dundee Gem Line Steam Shipping Co., 1890, 18 R. 205; Stevens v. Motherwell Entertainments, 1914 S.C. 957.
[3] Nixon v. Houston, supra.
[4] M'Carthy v. Emery, 1897, 24 R. 610.
[5] Crawford v. North British Railway Co., 1914, 31 Sh.Ct.Rep. 128.

Where a second action is raised between the same parties, and there is an outstanding award of expenses in the earlier action, it is within the discretion of the Court to insist on the earlier expenses being paid before the later action is allowed to proceed. If the two actions, though between the same parties, are entirely separate, as where an unsuccessful action of damages for breach of contract was followed by one for slander, no condition as to payment of the earlier expenses will generally be made.[1] But where the two actions relate to the same subject-matter payment of the expenses in the first will usually be made a condition of proceeding with the second.[2]

[1] Stuart v. Moss, 1886, 13 R. 572.
[2] Irvine v. Kinloch, 1885, 13 R. 172; M'Murchy v. Maclullich, 1889, 16 R. 678; Wilson v. Crichton, (O.H.) 1898, 5 S.L.T. 350; Somervell v. Tait, &c., 1908, 15 S.L.T. 1015, 16 S.L.T. 139; Swanson v. Gardner & Co., 1916, 33 Sh.Ct.Rep. 123.

13. Appeals on Question of Expenses.

Appeals for review of an interlocutor dealing with expenses only, without challenging the judgment on the merits are competent,[1] but are not encouraged.[2] It has been stated that such appeals, whether to the Sheriff Principal or to the Court of Session, should not be entertained unless there has been an obvious miscarriage of justice in the interlocutor under appeal, or the expenses have become substantially more valuable than the merits of the case.[3] Appeals of this kind have also been given effect to where a question of principle was involved,[4] but even in such cases, where an appeal would normally be considered, it will not be entertained if the point to be argued has not been raised in the Court below.[5] It is competent to take advantage of an opponent's appeal in order to raise a question of expenses only.[6]

[1] Fleming v. North of Scotland Banking Co., 1881, 9 R. 11.
[2] Bowman's Trustees v. Scott's Trustees, 1901, 3 F. 450; Crawford v. Glen, 1902, 18 Sh.Ct.Rep. 351.
[3] Caldwell v. Dykes, 1906, 8 F. 839, Lord President Dunedin, p. 840. See also Wyllie v. Fisher, 1907 S.C. 686; Garrioch v. Glass, 1911 S.C. 453.
[4] Barrie v. Caledonian Railway Co., 1902, 5 F. 30; Caldwell v. Dykes, supra; Jack v. Black, 1911 S.C. 691; Brooks & Bohm v. Kitchencraft Co., 1944 S.L.T. 191.
[5] Aird v. Tarbert School Board, 1907 S.C. 22.
[6] Bonner's Trustees v. Bonner, 1902, 4 F. 429. See 7 Edw. VII c. 51, sec. 29.

14. Action by Solicitor for Account.

An action by a solicitor against his client for payment of his business account proceeds in ordinary form, but decree will not be granted for payment, save of consent, without the account being taxed. Even where the action is undefended the first order is a remit to the auditor to tax the account and to report.[1]

[1] A special summary form of procedure in such a case—which does not seem to have had any particular advantages—has apparently fallen with the Act of Sederunt of 1839; see secs. 110-112.

CHAPTER XV.

CIVIL JURY TRIAL.

1. WHEN COMPETENT.

It is competent for either of the parties in a certain class of actions to require the cause to be tried in the Sheriff Court before a jury.[1] The Court has not power *ex proprio motu* to send a cause for jury trial, nor has the Sheriff power to refuse a motion for jury trial. If it is moved for in the appropriate class of case he must grant the motion. But this right of trial by jury in the Sheriff Court is restricted to actions by employees against employers concluding for damages either at common law or under the Employers' Liability Act, 1880, or, alternatively, under the Act or at common law in respect of injury caused by accident arising out of and in the course of the employment and in which the claim exceeds £50.[1] For the purpose of these provisions " employee " includes the legal personal representative of an employee and any person who by the law of Scotland may be entitled to solatium in respect of the death of an employee.[2]

[1] 7 Edw. VII c. 51, sec. 31; 2 & 3 Geo. V c. 28, Schedule I.
[2] Ibid., sec. 3 (q); 2 & 3 Geo. V c. 28, Schedule I.

A motion for trial by jury in the Sheriff Court may be made as soon as proof has been allowed, and must be made within six days of the date of entry in the Court books of the interlocutor allowing proof.[1] The motion, it is thought, is timeously made if lodged within the six days, although not heard until later.[2] The possibility of trial by jury emphasizes the desirability in this class of action of first disposing of preliminary pleas, as directed by Rule 54,[3] for the inconvenience is obvious of sending a case to a jury while pleas as to relevancy or competency are still open.

[1] 7 Edw. VII c. 51, sec. 31, Schedule I, Rule 83.
[2] See Black v. Crawford, 1912, 28 Sh.Ct.Rep. 308; John Haig & Co. v. Boswall-Preston, 1915 S.C. 339; cf. MacDonald v. Robertson, 1910, 27 Sh.Ct.Rep. 103.
[3] 7 Edw. VII c. 51, Schedule I, Rule 54.

Upon a strict reading of the Act it might be argued that even an allowance of interim proof, as, for instance, upon a jurisdiction plea, might warrant a motion for jury trial.[1] The intention, however, appears to be that a motion for jury trial should not be entertained unless, and until, proof upon the merits of the cause has been allowed. It is thought that the decisions in regard to removal of cases to the Court of Session for jury trial are generally in point, and that, while jury trial in the Sheriff Court would not be allowed in lieu of proof on a purely preliminary point, it might be permitted on an allowance of proof in respect of part of the case only, and would be competent in respect of the merits, where proof on a preliminary point had already been held.[2]

[1] 7 Edw. VII c. 51, sec. 31.
[2] See p. 306, supra.

An interlocutor allowing proof is appealable to the Sheriff without leave and to the Court of Session with leave,[1] but an interlocutor appointing the case to be tried by jury is not appealable save with leave.[1] Motions to close the record, to allow proof, and for jury trial, are sometimes made all at the one diet; but, although this may be done, and all these motions may be dealt with in one interlocutor, it is more convenient to allow proof by separate interlocutor. A motion for jury trial does not debar appeal upon the interlocutor allowing proof, and the allowance or refusal of jury trial might be brought under review in this way.

[1] 7 Edw. VII c. 51, secs. 27, 28; 2 & 3 Geo. V c. 28, sec. 2.

2. THE JURY.

The jury consists of seven persons, of whom two are special and five are common jurors, chosen from a panel of five special and ten common jurors[1] to be cited from the Sheriff Court jury book in the manner prescribed by law, or in use to be followed for the citation of jurors in Scotland.[2] The rules further provide that all statutory or other regulations and customs relative to the citation, non-attendance, selection, and swearing of jurors shall apply,[2] with the qualification that the right of challenge which each party may exercise is limited to one special and one common juror; and in this matter, where there are more pursuers or defenders than one, they must act collectively, and not individually.[3] The practical effects of these provisions seem to be (a) that for each civil jury cause in the Sheriff Court a panel of fifteen is to be cited, from which seven are selected[1]; (b) that of these fifteen, four only may be challenged, two for pursuers and two for defenders[3]; and (c) that if there are joint pursuers or joint defenders they must agree upon the jurors to be challenged, otherwise the right of challenge falls.[3] No provision is made for the list of jurors who have been cited being made available for inspection by the parties, but it ought to be lodged a reasonable time before the trial for this purpose.

[1] 7 Edw. VII c. 51, sec. 31, Schedule I, Rule 133.
[2] Ibid., Rule 134.
[3] Ibid., Rule 135.

In Scotland the qualification of a common juror is the ownership in his or her own right, whether in fee or in liferent, of heritable property within the Sheriffdom of the yearly value of £5, or the ownership of personal property of the value of £200.[1] The qualification of a special juror is the payment of land tax upon £100 valued rent[2]; payment of Crown taxes upon a house rental of £30 a year[2]; residence in the Sheriffdom and ownership of heritable property of the value of £100 a year[3]; or residence in the Sheriffdom and possession of personal property worth £1000.[3]

[1] 6 Geo. IV c. 22, sec. 1; 10 & 11 Geo. V c. 53, sec. 3.
[2] 55 Geo. III c. 42, sec. 24.
[3] 7 Geo. IV c. 8, sec. 1.

No person is eligible as a juror till he has reached the age of twenty-one, and he ceases to be eligible at the age of sixty.[1] Certain persons also are exempted in respect of their occupations, although otherwise qualified. These include (a) peers[2] (b) judges, including Sheriffs and magistrates of royal burghs[2]; (c) clergymen of all religious denominations whether acting or retired[2]; (d) the clerks and officials of all law Courts, all officers of the law, and all practising advocates and solicitors[2]; (e) professors in universities[2]; (f) physicians, surgeons,[2] and registered dentists[3]; (g) customs, excise, and inland revenue officials[2]; (h) army and navy officers[2] and soldiers[4]; (i) officers and men of the Territorial Army[5]; (j) officers of the post-office[6]; (k) income tax commissioners[7]; (l) lighthouse-keepers and their assistants[8]; (m) police officers[9]; and (n) factory inspectors.[10]

[1] 6 Geo. IV c. 22, sec. 1.
[2] Ibid., sec. 2.
[3] 41 & 42 Vict. c. 33, sec. 30.
[4] 44 & 45 Vict. c. 58, sec. 147.
[5] 7 Edw. VII c. 9, sec. 23 (4).
[6] 8 Edw. VII c. 48, sec. 43.
[7] 43 & 44 Vict. c. 19, sec. 40.
[8] 32 & 33 Vict. c. 36.
[9] 20 & 21 Vict. c. 72, sec. 18.
[10] 1 Edw. VIII & 1 Geo. VI c. 67, sec. 122 (6).

Jurors may also be exempted in certain counties on the ground of their residence at an inconvenient distance from the seat of the Court.[1] The Sheriff, with the approval of the Secretary of State for Scotland, may fix a distance limit for each Court House, residence beyond which limit exempts an otherwise qualified person from being called to serve as a juror.[1] This applies only to the Sheriff Court, and does not affect the liability of such persons to be called to serve as jurors at the Circuit Justiciary Courts.[1] In making up the jury list for the Sheriff Court, however, the Sheriff-clerk is entitled to omit the names of persons resident beyond the prescribed limit.[1]

[1] 1 & 2 Vict. c. 119, sec. 27.

Women are now eligible to serve on a jury, the Sex Disqualification (Removal) Act having provided that no person shall be exempted by sex or marriage from the liability to serve as a juror.[1] Special provisions have been made in regard to the service of women on juries, and those are briefly as follows. The Sheriff may in his discretion, on an application made by the parties or any of them, or at his own instance, order that the jury shall be composed of men only or of women only, as the case may require.[1] In the Sheriff Court such a motion must be made at the time when a date is appointed for the trial.[2] If the motion is granted the Sheriff-clerk makes up a jury list of men only or of women only as the case may be.[3] If no such order is made the jury list is composed as nearly as possible of equal numbers of men and women; and the proportions of men and women included as special jurors are also to be as nearly as possible equal.[4]

[1] 9 & 10 Geo. V c. 71, sec. 1; 10 & 11 Geo. V c. 53, sec. 1.
[2] Act of Sederunt, 5th February, 1921, sec. 1 (a).
[3] Ibid., sec. 2 (b).
[4] Ibid., sec. 3.

The names of those appearing on the jury list are placed in the box or glass, according as they are special or common jurors, but irrespective of whether they are men or women; and the ballot is carried through in the manner formerly in use.[1] The Sheriff is entitled, however, on an application made by a woman to be exempted from service to grant such exemption in respect of the nature of the evidence to be given or of the issues to be tried.[2] Apart from this special exemption any woman summoned to serve on a jury may apply to be exempted from service on account of pregnancy or other feminine condition or ailment.[3] Her application must be made to the Sheriff-clerk as soon as may be after receipt of her citation, and, unless on special cause shown, not later than the third day before the trial, and must be supported by evidence, by medical certificate or otherwise, vouching her unfitness to serve.[3] The Sheriff-clerk disposes of such applications, with or without consulting the Sheriff, but the Sheriff may, at any time before the jury is empanelled, grant exemption in his discretion to any woman in respect of any of the foregoing reasons.[3]

[1] Act of Sederunt, 5th February, 1921, sec. 4. See next page.
[2] 9 & 10 Geo. V c. 71, sec. 1.
[3] Act of Sederunt, 5th February, 1921, sec. 5.

3. PROCEDURE.

When a jury trial has been ordered the Sheriff is directed to order a time and place for the trial which is not to be sooner than fourteen days from the date of his interlocutor.[1] Documents or productions intended to be put in evidence, or referred to at the trial, must be lodged with the clerk of Court four days before the date fixed for the trial, but the Sheriff may allow productions to be exhibited and produced at the trial if he is satisfied that they could not reasonably have been lodged earlier, and that reasonable notice has been given to the other parties of intention to produce at the trial.[2] It is thought that the above provision as to lodging productions does not apply to such as are used merely for the cross-examination of witnesses.[3]

[1] 7 Edw. VII c. 51, sec. 32; 2 & 3 Geo. V c. '28, sec. 6.
[2] 7 Edw. VII c. 51, Schedule I, Rule 142.
[3] See Livingstone v. Dinwoodie, 1860, 22 D. 1333; Paterson & Sons v. Kit Coffee Co., (O.H.) 1908, 16 S.L.T. 180.

The rule in regard to failure to appear or to implement any order of the Court is expressly applied to jury causes, so that failure to lodge any production or pleading within the time required or ordered, or failure to appear, or to pay Court dues or to deposit, may entail decree as craved, or decree of absolvitor or dismissal being granted.[1] Where either party fails to appear by himself or his solicitor at the trial the Sheriff would be entitled to grant decree to the other party under this rule without the jury being empanelled.[1] In the special case of failure to deposit the jury fees the Sheriff is expressly authorized to dismiss the cause.[2]

[1] 7 Edw. VII c. 51, Schedule I, Rule 56. See further p. 346, supra.
[2] See p. 249, infra.

For a civil trial in the Sheriff Court a jury is to be cited, selected, and sworn according to the usual practice in use in

Scotland.[1] A juror is cited by registered post letter, directed
to him by the Sheriff-clerk at his residence, as stated in the jurors'
roll made up by the Sheriff-clerk, and a certificate of posting
under the hand of the Sheriff-clerk or his depute, is equivalent
to an execution of citation.[2] When a jury is to be empanelled
the jurors are selected by writing on separate slips the names
of each of the panel of fifteen, placing the names of the five
special jurors, irrespective of sex, in one glass, and those of
the ten common jurors in another, and drawing from each
alternately in order, commencing with one from the special jurors
and then in succession two from the common jurors[3]; but in the
case of a Sheriff Court jury the second draw from the common
jurors' glass will be three instead of two, in order to make up
the number to seven. The jury when empanelled is sworn by
the Sheriff-clerk, who administers to them the following oath:
"You swear by God, as you shall answer to God at the great day
of judgment, that you shall well and truly try this issue and a
true verdict give according to the evidence."[4]

[1] 7 Edw. VII c. 51, Schedule I, Rule 134.
[2] 31 & 32 Vict. c. 100, sec. 47.
[3] Ibid., sec. 44.
[4] 55 Geo. III c. 42, sec. 31.

The law and practice relating to the taking of evidence in
proofs before the Sheriff is declared to apply to jury trials,[1]
but there are also certain special provisions. Unless all the parties
appearing in the case put in a minute (which may be signed by
their solicitors) dispensing with a record of the proceedings, such
a record is to be taken by an official shorthand writer of the Court,
but his notes need not be extended unless an appeal is taken and
the Appellate Court orders their production. In that event it
is the duty of the appellant to procure the extended notes, certified
by the shorthand writer, and to lodge same in the Court of
Session.[1] Where no shorthand notes have been taken the Sheriff's
interlocutor applying the verdict is not subject to review.[2] It is
competent in a jury trial to take evidence to lie *in retentis*, and
if the Sheriff is satisfied that the deponing witness is dead or
cannot attend the trial owing to absence or infirmity or other
sufficient cause, he may direct the report of the commission to be
read to the jury.[3] Such direction may be given by the Sheriff
on the motion of any party to the cause and irrespective of which
party moved for the commission.[3] When read to the jury the
report of the commission forms part of the evidence in the cause.[3]
But depositions cannot be read or referred to, even for purposes
of cross-examination, if the witness attends at the trial.[3] It is

competent to recover documents under specification for a jury trial, for that also is part of the practice in proofs. As in proofs the shorthand writer is to be paid by the parties equally in the first instance, and the Sheriff may make an order directing payment to be made.[4] The incidental appeal to the Sheriff in the course of a proof upon a question of competency of evidence or confidentiality of documents is not available in a jury trial, but exceptions taken in the course of the trial to rulings of the Sheriff in regard to admission or rejection of evidence or in regard to points of law laid down in the course of the trial or in the Sheriff's charge to the jury must, if required by the party taking the exception, be recorded to the Sheriff's dictation upon the official shorthand notes before the jury proceed to consider their verdict.[5]

[1] 7 Edw. VII c. 51, Schedule I, Rule 137; Rules of Court, 1936, V 13 (a).
[2] Ibid., Rule 147. See Adair v. Colville & Sons, 1922 S.C. 672.
[3] Ibid., Rule 138.
[4] Ibid., Rules 67, 137.
[5] Ibid., Rule 139.

Amendment of record is competent at any stage of the cause, and a cause which is being tried before a jury is not excepted.[1] But an amendment of the record, proposed at the inception of or during the progress of a jury trial, is a different matter from an amendment proposed in the course of a proof, and in most cases such an amendment would not be entertained.[2]

[1] 7 Edw. VII c. 51, sec. 32, Schedule I, Rule 79.
[2] See Kenny v. Ninian & Son, 1926, 42 Sh.Ct.Rep. 272.

Each juror who is empanelled is entitled to a fee of 10s. per day. To meet this expense, the party who moves for jury trial is required to deposit with the Sheriff-clerk the sum of £3 10s. on each day the trial proceeds, before the proceedings commence.[1] The proceedings commence with the calling of the diet. The party liable for this disbursement must therefore be prepared to deposit this sum with the Sheriff-clerk, at the latest when the case is called upon to proceed. After he has been put into the jury box, the juror would appear to be entitled to his 10s., even although the case should come to an end immediately thereafter; but the depositor is entitled to get back his deposit if the jury trial is not proceeded with.[1] This, it is thought means, if it becomes unnecessary to empanel a jury, as, for instance, if a settlement is arranged before the opening of the trial. A juror is not entitled to any consideration for attending the Court. He is remunerated only if he is empanelled. The sum deposited

forms part of the expenses of the cause.[1] It is specially provided
that, failing the deposit being made, the Sheriff may dismiss
the cause.[1] This provision is not appropriate in the possible,
though unlikely, event of the defender having moved for a jury
trial, and it is thought that in that case the Sheriff would be
entitled to proceed if necessary under the more ample powers
under Rule 56.[2]

[1] 7 Edw. VII c. 51, sec. 33.
[2] Ibid., Schedule I, Rule 56. See p. 249, et seq., supra.

There is no provision in the rules for opening speeches by the
solicitors for the parties, but it is convenient that there should be
opening statements of this kind in order to acquaint the jury
with the general nature of the case, and of the questions at issue.
Concluding speeches are contemplated by the rules because it is
provided that, immediately after or as soon as practicable after the
conclusion of the speeches, or if none be made, after the conclusion of the evidence, the Sheriff shall charge the jury if he deem
it necessary to do so.[1]

[1] 7 Edw. VII c. 51, Schedule I, Rule 141.

It was originally provided by the Act that the questions of
fact to be put to the jury should be set forth in an interlocutor
pronounced after parties had been heard, and at the same time
as the date and place of trial were fixed.[1] But this was altered
by the amending Act of 1913, and it is now provided that at the
trial the Sheriff may, or if required by either party shall, after
the conclusion of the evidence, propone to the jury question or
questions of fact to be answered by them, and the jury in their
verdict shall give specific answers to such question or questions.[2]

[1] 7 Edw. VII c. 51, sec. 32.
[2] 2 & 3 Geo. V c. 28, sec. 6.

The statutory provisions for jury trial in the Sheriff Court
have been adversely criticized in several cases which went on
appeal to the Court of Session, and they have been found difficult
to work out in practice. Part of the difficulty which has been
experienced relates to the questions to be put to the jury. Differing
from the practice in the Court of Session the Sheriff Court system
for jury trial contemplates that the jury will in the usual case
give, not a verdict in general terms for one or other of the parties,
but answers to specific questions. It has been pointed out that,
as the provision now stands, a general verdict is competent, but
if either or both of the parties so require the Sheriff must propone
to the jury questions of fact to be answered by them.[1] Apparently

the Sheriff has no option but to put the questions proposed by the parties, if these are proper questions of fact, but it has been said that he may discard questions of law, or of mixed fact and law, or questions that are indeterminate and non-specific.[1] In connexion with questions of mixed fact and law, however, it was stressed in the later case of *Adair*[2] that an appropriate question was one which raised the issue of fault in relation to which the Sheriff would have to give the necessary directions on law to the jury. Difficulties may arise if the jury's answers are not sufficient as findings in fact for the determination of the case,[3] but it has been indicated that if special questions have been put it is incompetent to take also a general verdict.[1] It has been pointed out that objections to the questions to be put to the jury and to any relative direction by the Sheriff might be made matter of exception and thus be available to be brought under review in a subsequent appeal.[4]

[1] See Ferguson v. North British Railway Co., 1915 S.C. 566, Lord Anderson, pp. 584-585; Adair v. Colville & Sons, 1926 S.C. (H.L.) 51, Lord Dunedin, p. 57.
[2] Adair v. Colville & Sons, 1924 S.C. 981; 1926 S.C. (H.L.) 51.
[3] See Taylor v. Sutherland, 1910 S.C. 644.
[4] See Adair v. Colville & Sons, 1924 S.C. 981, Lord Skerrington, p. 993; 1926 S.C. (H.L.) 51, Lord Dunedin, p. 56.

It seems clear that much of the difficulty experienced in connexion with jury trials in the Sheriff Court would be removed if the Sheriff were left to put to the jury a general question in the form of the issue adopted in the Court of Session.[1] In this way the jury would merely be asked to find in general terms, such as whether on or about a specified place and date the pursuer was injured in his person (or otherwise) through the fault of the defender to the loss, injury and damage of the pursuer. On such an issue it is thought that the Sheriff would, as the presiding judge does in the Court of Session, direct the jury in his charge on any point of law they would require to have in view in considering their verdict. In the Supreme Court a general question on contributory negligence—when that was a competent defence—could be put in a separate counter issue.[2] Any misdirection in law would be open to review on appeal.[3] On a general issue such as has been indicated the jury would simply find for the pursuer or the defender.

[1] See Ferguson v. North British Railway Co., 1915 S.C. 566, Lord Anderson, p. 585; Adair v. Colville & Sons, 1926 S.C. (H.L.) 51, Lord Dunedin, p. 57.
[2] See Smith v. Petterson, 1940 S.C. 18.
[3] 7 Edw. VII c. 51, sec. 31.

As already indicated it is for the parties to decide whether special questions are to be put to the jury, but it is not definitely stated whether, in addition to the questions proposed by the parties, the Sheriff may also put questions of his own. It seems clear, however, that the Sheriff has authority to put questions in such circumstances,[1] as he undoubtedly has where the parties do not themselves propose any questions,[2] and it is thought that he ought to intervene in this way if it is clear to him that the questions proposed may not elicit answers sufficient for the disposal of the case.

[1] See Adair v. Colville & Sons, 1924 S.C. 981; 1926 S.C. (H.L.) 51.
[2] 7 Edw. VII c. 51, sec. 32.

In the rules as originally framed it was provided that, in addition to their answers to the questions put to them, the jury should state in their verdict the amount at which they assessed the damages, in the event of damages being awarded.[1] This rule was wholly repealed in 1913,[2] and the position in regard to damages has been left in a state of uncertainty. It is still one of the statutory grounds of appeal that the award of damages is inadequate or is excessive,[3] and in the form of note of appeal one of the grounds indicated is that the damages awarded by the jury were excessive.[4] These indications support the view—which it is thought is correct—that the amount of damages is essentially a matter for the jury to deal with. If a general issue, as in the Court of Session, is being put to the jury they may be asked in general terms to assess the damages if they find for the pursuer. If special questions are put the jury do not specifically find for either party and they ought in that case to assess damages contingently in the event of such being awarded. If a special question is put to them in regard to damages it should be framed to make this clear, otherwise an award of damages may be claimed to infer a verdict for the pursuer.

[1] 7 Edw. VII c. 51, Schedule I, Rule 144.
[2] 2 & 3 Geo. V c. 28, Schedule II.
[3] 7 Edw. VII c. 51, sec. 31.
[4] Ibid., Schedule I; Form M.

4. VERDICT.

The verdict of the jury in a Sheriff Court trial comprises answers to the questions put by the Sheriff. After the lapse of one hour from the time the jury is enclosed a verdict by a majority may be returned.[1] When specific questions of fact are put to the jury they do not decide the legal question whether the pursuer is entitled to damages. When they have answered the questions their verdict is recorded upon the interlocutor sheets and signed by the Sheriff-clerk.[2] When this is done the duty of the jury is over and they are discharged.[2] Whether, upon the facts as found by the jury, the pursuer is entitled in law to damages is a question decided, not by the jury, but by the judge, after hearing parties on a motion to apply the verdict. Such a motion may be made by either party as soon as the verdict has been recorded, or within fourteen days thereafter.[3] If no motion is made within the period stated it could be argued that the proceedings must fall, as the prorogation power under Rule 56 does not in terms apply to an extension of this fourteen days' period.[4] It is thought, however, that the Court would avoid such a result, more especially as Rule 146 is not expressed in peremptory terms.[3]

[1] 7 Edw. VII c. 51, Schedule I, Rule 143.
[2] Ibid., Rule 145.
[3] Ibid., Rule 146.
[4] Ibid., Rule 56.

In the form of general issue as used in the Court of Session the jury decide the question whether the pursuer is entitled to an award of damages, as well as fix the amount of it. In the Sheriff Court when special questions of fact are put to the jury they do not decide the question of liability for damages, although they fix the amount of these.[1] That is argued before the Sheriff upon the answers returned by the jury, and the Sheriff may make avizandum.[2] As soon as practicable thereafter the Sheriff is directed to issue an interlocutor applying the verdict.[2] If the Sheriff decides that the facts found by the jury do not infer legal liability for damages he will grant absolvitor or dismiss the action; but if he holds that the facts found by the jury do infer legal liability for damages he will decern for the sum assessed by the jury in name of damages, with the amount of which he cannot interfere. It has been held that the Sheriff's interlocutor applying the verdict should not incorporate the findings in fact made by the jury.[3] In the interlocutor applying the verdict the Sheriff is to dispose of the question of expenses.[4]

[1] See as to this, preceding page.
[2] 7 Edw. VII c. 51, Schedule I, Rule 146. See M'Govern v. James Nimmo & Co., 1938 S.C. (H.L.) 18.
[3] M'Vicar v. Robertson & Son, 1910 S.C. 396; cf. Kenny v. Ninian & Son, 1926, 42 Sh.Ct.Rep. 272.
[4] 7 Edw. VII c. 51, Schedule I, Rule 146.

The above is the position where special questions of fact are put to the jury, and such questions must be put if the parties or either of them so require.[1] But, as already pointed out, a general issue, involving a general verdict by the jury for one party or the other, is also competent.[1] If a general issue is put to the jury the practice will be assimilated to that of the Court of Session.[1]

[1] See p. 346, et seq., supra.

In a Court of Session jury trial further procedure for review is not by way of appeal, as in the Sheriff Court, but by way of bill of exception or motion for a new trial. But, in the Sheriff Court jury trial system, the interlocutor of the Sheriff applying the jury's verdict is declared to be the final judgment in the cause and is subject to review only in the statutory manner, and on the statutory grounds.[1] If no shorthand notes of the proceedings have been taken the interlocutor applying the verdict is not subject to review.[2]

[1] 7 Edw. VII c. 51, sec. 31, Schedule I, Rule 148; 2 & 3 Geo. V c. 28, Schedules I, II.
[2] 7 Edw. VII c. 51, Schedule I, Rule 147. See Adair v. Colville & Sons, 1922 S.C. 672; 1926 S.C. (H.L.) 51.

If shorthand notes have been taken in the Sheriff Court any party in the cause may, within fourteen days of the final interlocutor applying the verdict, but not later, appeal to the Court of Session by lodging with the Sheriff-clerk a note of appeal in the Form M in the Schedule annexed to the Act.[1] This form states the grounds of the appeal and it is thought that its use is not superseded by the later Rules of Court of 1936.[2] Where the notes of evidence were voluminous it was held, in an appeal on the ground that the verdict was contrary to evidence, that it was sufficient to state that the jury's answers to certain numbered questions were contrary to the evidence.[3] Within three days of receiving the note of appeal the Sheriff-clerk is directed to notify the other parties in the cause and transmit the process to the Depute Principal Clerk of the General Department of the Court of Session at Edinburgh.[4] Further procedure in the Court of Session is regulated by the Rules of Court.[2]

[1] 7 Edw. VII c. 51, Schedule I, Rule 148.
[2] Rules of Court, 1936, V 7-13.
[3] Forsyth v. Plean Colliery Co., 1925 S.C. 76.
[4] 7 Edw. VII c. 51, Schedule I, Rule 149.

Appeals in jury trials are competent only upon one or more of the following grounds : (1) that the verdict has been erroneously applied by the Sheriff; (2) that the verdict is contrary to the evidence; (3) that the Sheriff had, in the course of the trial, unduly refused or admitted evidence or misdirected the jury; and (4) that the award of damages is inadequate or excessive.[1]

[1] 7 Edw. VII c. 51, sec. 31.

If the question raised in the appeal is whether the Sheriff has erroneously applied the verdict, the Appeal Court need not send back the case for new trial, nor need they send it back to the Sheriff Court at all. If they find that the verdict was erroneously applied they may give judgment accordingly,[1] which it is thought means that the Appeal Court may give judgment in accordance with what they consider to be the correct application of the jury's verdict.

[1] 7 Edw. VII c. 51, sec. 31; 2 & 3 Geo. V c. 28, Schedule I.

No incidental appeal is competent in the course of a jury trial, and in no circumstances is there any appeal from the Sheriff-Substitute to the Sheriff. All questions arising must await the final interlocutor, for then only is any part of the proceedings subject to review. Exceptions to the Sheriff's rulings in the course of the trial are directed to be noted, to his dictation, in the shorthand notes,[1] and any exception so noted comes up for review if and when an appeal is taken against the final interlocutor. The form of note of appeal includes misdirection of the jury upon a point of law, and the appellant is directed to state the point of law.[2] The usual exceptions to the Sheriff's rulings will relate to the admission or rejection of evidence, but exceptions are competent to any points of law laid down in the course of the trial or in the Sheriff's charge to the jury.[1] Where special questions of fact are put to the jury there will normally be no necessity for directions in law to be given at that stage, but it has been pointed out that there may be directions relative to the questions to which exception may be taken,[3] and where a general issue is put to the jury directions in law and exceptions thereto may be appropriate.

[1] 7 Edw. VII c. 51, Schedule I, Rule 139.
[2] Ibid., sec. 31, Schedule I, Form M; 2 & 3 Geo. V c. 28, Schedule I.
[3] See Adair v. Colville & Sons, 1924 S.C. 981, Lord Skerrington, p. 993; 1926 S.C. (H.L.) 51, Lord Dunedin, p. 56.

An appeal upon the ground that the verdict of a jury is contrary to the evidence is not likely to prevail, unless it can be shown (1) that, upon no possible view of the evidence led, could the jury reasonably arrive at the result embodied in their verdict[1]; (2) that no legal evidence had been led at the trial sufficient to support that result[2]; or (3) that the result is directly contrary to the weight of the evidence which was led.[3] That a view of the evidence different from that taken by the jury might be taken by some other person, or even by the Court of Appeal, is not enough. As the verdict in a Sheriff Court jury trial is in many cases represented by the answers to specific questions upon matters of fact the probability of the answers not being warranted by the evidence led is minimized, and appeals on this ground are not numerous.

[1] Kinnell v. Peebles, 1890, 17 R. 416; Campbell v. Scottish Educational News, 1906, 8 F. 691; M'Ghee v. Glasgow Coal Co., 1923 S.C. 293; Lowe v. Bristol Motor Omnibus Co., 1934 S.C. 1.
[2] Littlejohn v. Brown & Co., 1909 S.C. 169; cf. Spindlow v. Glasgow Corporation, 1933 S.C. 580.
[3] Fraser v. Edinburgh Tramway Co., 1882, 10 R. 264; Ross v. M'Kittrick, 1886, 14 R. 255; Kinnell v. Peebles, supra; Campbell v. Scottish Educational News, supra.

If, after hearing parties upon an appeal in respect that the verdict is contrary to evidence, the Appeal Court are unanimously of opinion that the verdict under review is contrary to evidence, and, further, that they have before them all the evidence that could be reasonably expected to be obtained relevant to the case, they are entitled to set aside the verdict, and, in place of granting a new trial, to enter judgment for the party unsuccessful at the trial.[1]

[1] 10 Edw. VII and 1 Geo. V c. 31, sec. 2. See Madden v. Glasgow Corporation, 1923 S.C. 102.

As regards the admission, or rejection, of evidence the elements which enter into the question of competency are the same in a jury trial as in a proof before the Sheriff.[1] If exception is taken to the rejection of evidence, it must be shown, before the appeal can succeed, that the evidence was available and that it was relevant and material.[2] If the exception taken is to some direction to the jury this may relate to any point of law laid down in the course of the trial or in the Sheriff's charge to the jury.[3] It is thought that an appeal on the grounds dealt with in this paragraph is competent only if the exception has been formally noted in terms of Rule 139.[4]

[1] See p. 213, et seq., supra.
[2] Scott v. Wilson, 1826, 3 Murray 529.
[3] 7 Edw. VII c. 51, Schedule I, Rule 139. See M'Coll v. Alloa Coal Co., 1909, 46 S.L.R. 465.
[4] See Adamson v. Fife Coal Co., 1909 S.C. 580, Lord Justice-Clerk Macdonald, p. 586.

An appeal upon the ground that an award of damages is excessive is not likely to be sustained unless there has been a gross mistake in the assessment,[1] and the usual practice is not to interfere with the award unless it is more than twice as large as is reasonable.[2] In the Court of Session the inadequacy of the award is now, but was not formerly, a ground for granting a new trial,[3] but verdicts were in practice set aside on this account when they were regarded as perverse.[4] In the Sheriff Court, where this has all along been one of the statutory grounds of attack on the verdict, it is thought that the same standards should apply as in attacks on the ground of excess of damages.[5] If an appeal as to the amount of damages is allowed the Appeal Court may itself assess the damages only if both parties consent to this being done.[6]

[1] Landell v. Landell, 1841, 3 D. 819, p. 825; Thoms v. Caledonian Railway Co., 1913 S.C. 804; M'Kiernan v. Glasgow Corporation, 1919 S.C. 407.
[2] Young v. Glasgow Tramway Co., 1882, 10 R. 242, Lord President Inglis, p. 245; Elliot v. Glasgow Corporation, 1922 S.C. 146.
[3] Cf. Madden v. Glasgow Corporation, 1923 S.C. 102; Aitken v. Laidlay, 1938 S.C. 303.
[4] Gibson v. Kyle, 1933 S.C. 30, and cases there cited.
[5] See Aitken v. Laidlay, supra.
[6] Boal v. Scottish Catholic Printing Co., 1908 S.C. 667; cf. Madden v. Glasgow Corporation, supra.

In the Court of Session the verdict of a jury may be set aside, not only on various particular grounds, but on any other ground that is essential to the justice of the cause.[1] In the Sheriff Court no appeal is competent except on the grounds specified in the Act.[2] If circumstances arose which showed that there had been a clear miscarriage of justice, and no other remedy was open, an action of reduction might be brought in order to annul the verdict.[3]

[1] 55 Geo. III c. 42, sec. 6; Rules of Court, 1936, II, 47 (a).
[2] See Adamson v. Fife Coal Co., 1909 S.C. 580.
[3] See Adair v. Colville & Sons, 1926 S.C. (H.L.) 51.

If, on appeal, the judges are equally divided in opinion the verdict is to stand.[1] As already pointed out, where the Appeal Court find that the verdict was erroneously applied they may themselves grant judgment without sending the case back to the Sheriff,[2] and where they are unanimously of opinion that the verdict is contrary to evidence and that all relevant evidence is before them they may also give judgment themselves.[3] In the former case they may act by a majority; in the latter they must be unanimous.

[1] 7 Edw. VII c. 51, sec. 31.
[2] See p. 351, supra.
[3] See preceding page.

If the result of the appeal is an order for a new trial, the party wishing to proceed with the cause must furnish the Sheriff-clerk with a certified copy of the interlocutor making such order and must borrow the Sheriff Court process and transmit it to the Sheriff-clerk. The Sheriff is directed by the Act as soon as possible to fix the date of the new trial.[1] From the point at which it is resumed in the Sheriff Court, the proceedings follow the directions as for an original trial.[1] A new jury will be cited and the evidence led of new, without reference to the former trial.

[1] 7 Edw. VII c. 51, Schedule I, Rule 150.

CHAPTER XVI.

BANKRUPTCY.

1. JURISDICTION.

In Scotland the bankruptcy Statutes are in the main administered by the Sheriff. The jurisdiction of the Court of Session
is concurrent with that of the Sheriff Court, as regards awarding
sequestration,[1] in the matter of a deed of arrangement,[2] as regards
appeal against creditors' resolutions or a trustee's deliverance,[3]
and as regards the discharge of the trustee and bankrupt,[4] but the
practical conduct of a sequestration process is always relegated
to the Sheriff Court. The debtor must be subject to the jurisdiction
of the Supreme Courts of Scotland at the date of an application
for sequestration of his estates, or, if dead, he must have been
so subject at the date of his death.[5] But if sequestration is awarded
in the Supreme Court, it is remitted to the appropriate Sheriff
Court to be worked out.[6]

[1] 3 & 4 Geo. V c. 20, sec. 16.
[2] Ibid., sec. 34.
[3] Ibid., sec. 165.
[4] Ibid., secs. 135, 143, 152.
[5] Ibid., sec. 11.   See Joel v. Gill, 1859, 21 D. 929, 22 D. 6; Strickland,
    (O.H.) 1911, 1 S.L.T. 212; Weinschel, 1916, 2 S.L.T. 91, 205;
    Gairdner v. Macarthur, (O.H.) 1918, 56 S.L.R. 20; Wylie, (O.H.)
    1928 S.L.T. 665.
[6] Ibid., sec. 17.

An application in the Sheriff Court for sequestration of a
debtor's estates, whether made by the debtor himself or by a
creditor, is commenced by initial writ in the usual form. Other
applications to the Court at the instance of creditors, or of the
trustee in bankruptcy, or of the bankrupt, which are made in
virtue of powers under the bankruptcy Statutes, are in the same
form. The procedure in summary sequestrations, which differs
to some extent from that in ordinary sequestrations, will be dealt
with later.[1]

[1] See p. 396, infra.

The Sheriff Court, in which an application for sequestration
may be brought, is that for the county in which the debtor for a
year—which presumably means during the whole year—prior to

the application, or for a year prior to his death, as the case may be, has resided or carried on business.[1] When proof on the question of jurisdiction is required it is taken at or after the diet of appearance to which the debtor is cited.[2]

[1] 3 & 4 Geo. V c. 20, sec. 16. See Strickland, (O.H.) 1911, 1 S.L.T. 212; Weinschel, 1916, 2 S.L.T. 91, 205; Gairdner v. Macarthur, (O.H.) 1918, 56 S.L.R. 20; Wylie, (O.H.) 1928 S.L.T. 665.
[2] Hope v. Macdougall, 1893, 21 R. 49. See also Train v. Steven, 1904, 7 F. 47.

No sequestration may be awarded by any Court after production of evidence that sequestration has already been awarded in another Court and is still undischarged.[1] If, in ignorance that sequestration had already been awarded, a second award is made, the later is remitted to the Sheriff of the county which has made the earlier award, on production of a certificate from the clerk of the Sheriff Court where sequestration was first awarded.[2] When the awards in different Courts bear the same date, either may be appealed to the Supreme Court which remits the sequestration to such Sheriff Court as is deemed expedient.[2] Such a remit is also made where one award has been made by the Court of Session and one by a Sheriff Court, or where the award is by the Court of Session only.[2] Thus when there is one application only to the Sheriff Court it is necessarily in the Sheriff Court of the bankrupt's residential or business domicile; but when there is one application to the Court of Session alone, or conflicting Sheriff Court applications of the same date, or a Court of Session application and one or more in the Sheriff Courts, the Court of Session may select any Sheriff Court in Scotland as the convenient *forum*. Apart from the above, there may be a competition where a petition by the debtor is presented during the currency of the induciæ on a creditor's petition. In such a case the matter is in the discretion of the Court and sequestration may be awarded on the debtor's petition if there is no apparent prejudice to creditors by so doing.[3] Notice of remit to a Sheriff Court is given in the *Edinburgh Gazette*.[2] There is no objection to a second sequestration being granted in the same Court while the former one granted in it is still undischarged.[4]

[1] 3 & 4 Geo. V c. 20, sec. 16.
[2] Ibid., secs. 16, 17.
[3] Duncan, &c., (O.H.) 1936 S.L.T. 162. See also Reid, (O.H.) 1895, 3 S.L.T. 37; Mackie, (O.H.) 1898, 5 S.L.T. 316; cf. Blair & Co. v. Mackenzie, (O.H.) 1899, 1 F. 854; Govan, (O.H.) 1901, 8 S.L.T. 415; Calder & Co., (O.H.) 1904, 12 S.L.T. 398. See also Kellock v. Anderson, 1875, 3 R. 239; Tennent v. Martin & Dunlop, 1879, 6 R. 786; Fletcher v. Anderson, 1883, 10 R. 835.
[4] Mellor v. Drummond, (O.H.) 1919, 2 S.L.T. 68; Cook v. M'Dougall, 1923 S.C. 86.

2. Application by Debtor.

An application by, or with the concurrence of, a debtor, or with the concurrence of a deceased debtor's successor, requires no service or intimation.[1] It needs only the concurrence of one or more creditors whose debts amount together to at least £50.[2] The debts may be liquid or illiquid but must not be contingent.[2] An application by a debtor without the concurrence of creditors is competent only in a summary sequestration.[3] It is not necessary that the debtor be bankrupt or insolvent. An affidavit and claim, and account with relative vouchers, by the concurring creditor or creditors are produced with the application, and if the application and productions are *ex facie* regular, sequestration is forthwith awarded.[4] If the application is not signed by the debtor, the solicitor signing it must produce a special mandate authorizing the application to be made.[4] If the necessary productions are not presented with the petition the application must be dismissed.[4] An interlocutor awarding sequestration is not appealable, the remedy in the case of an award not made with the consent of the debtor or of his successors being an application for recall.[5] If the Sheriff should refuse to award sequestration (which is unlikely on a debtor's petition) it appears to be competent to appeal that judgment,[6] although the more expeditious course would be to make a fresh application in the Court of Session. Appeal may be competent against deliverances prior to the award of sequestration such as an interlocutor allowing a proof as to the validity of a petitioning creditor's claim.[7] The award of sequestration is intimated in the *Edinburgh Gazette* and the *London Gazette*.[8]

[1] 3 & 4 Geo. V c. 20, sec. 28.
[2] Ibid., sec. 12.
[3] Ibid., sec. 175 (1). See p. 397, infra.
[4] Ibid., secs. 20, 28.
[5] Ibid., sec. 30. See p. 361, infra.
[6] Marr & Sons v. Lindsay, 1881, 8 R. 784.
[7] Purves v. Groat, 1900, 2 F. 1174.
[8] 3 & 4 Geo. V c. 20, sec. 44.

3. Application by Creditor.

The application may be made by a creditor or creditors qualified as indicated in the preceding paragraph,[1] and it must be accompanied by an affidavit and claim and vouchers, and be presented within four months of the debtor's notour bankruptcy unless he is a concurring party.[2] An award of sequestration is not granted *de plano* if the application is made by a creditor without concurrence of the debtor or his successors. Service is ordered upon

the debtor or his successor who is required to show cause why
sequestration of the estates should not be awarded.[3] If the service
is made personally or at a dwelling-house or place of business, the
induciæ is not less than six or more than fourteen days.[4] If
made edictally the induciæ is fourteen days.[4] At the same time
the Sheriff directs intimation of the warrant and of the diet of
appearance in the *Edinburgh Gazette*. If desired, the Sheriff,
in the first deliverance, also grants diligence to recover evidence
of the debtor's notour bankruptcy, or other facts necessary to be
established.[3] Where a debtor is apprehensive of sequestration
being applied for he may lodge a caveat asking that he may be
heard before any order is pronounced and the same course may
be taken by a creditor who has applied for sequestration to enable
him to be heard in the first instance should the debtor himself
apply on his own petition. The statutory direction to cite the
debtor is peremptory, and even where, in virtue of a caveat, the
debtor objects to the jurisdiction, or to the vouchers produced,
warrant to cite must be granted and these matters disposed of
thereafter.[5] The necessary productions must be presented with
the petition itself and where a defective oath was challenged the
petitioner was not allowed to rectify the defect by lodging an
amended affidavit.[6] If the debtor intends to oppose the granting
of sequestration the usual practice is to lodge a notice of appearance
upon which a diet for hearing parties is appointed.

[1] 3 & 4 Geo. V c. 20, sec. 11.
[2] Ibid., secs. 11, 13; as to time for lodging productions, see Muir's
    Sequestration, 1911, 27 Sh.Ct.Rep. 327.
[3] Ibid., sec. 25.
[4] Ibid., sec. 27.
[5] Hope v. Macdougall, 1893, 21 R. 49; Train v. Steven, 1904, 7 F. 47.
[6] Younger & Son, (O.H.) 1926 S.L.T. 238; cf. Muir's Sequestration,
    1911, 27 Sh.Ct.Rep. 327.

In addition to proving citation of the debtor the creditor must
at the first diet produce evidence to show (a) that the debtor is
notour bankrupt,[1] which is normally proved by showing that he
has been charged to make payment of a debt and that the charge
has expired without payment,[2] and (b) that for the year immediately preceding the presentation of the application—or, in the
case of a deceased debtor, for the year preceding his death—he
has resided or had a dwelling-place or place of business in the
Sheriffdom, or, if the debtor is a company, that the company
has for that time carried on business in the Sheriffdom, and a
partner has resided or had a dwelling-house in the Sheriffdom,
or the company has had a place of business within the Sheriffdom.[3]
On these facts being established at the diet of compearance,

sequestration is awarded, unless the debtor or his successor appear
and (a) show cause why sequestration cannot be competently
awarded, or (b) pay instantly the debts in respect of which he
was made bankrupt or produce written evidence of such payment,
and also pay, or produce written evidence of payment of, the
debt of the petitioner and any other creditors appearing and
concurring.[4] In special circumstances consignation of the amount
due may be allowed,[5] but in general, if all the requisites for
sequestration are present, the Court has no discretion but must
make the award.[6] The award of sequestration is intimated in
the *Edinburgh Gazette* and in the *London Gazette*.[7]

[1] 3 & 4 Geo. V c. 20, sec. 11.
[2] M'Nab v. Clarke, 1889, 16 R. 610; Scottish Milk Marketing Board
v. Wood, 1936 S.C. 604.
[3] 3 & 4 Geo. V c. 20, secs. 11, 16.
[4] Ibid., sec. 29.
[5] Laird v. Scott, (O.H.) 1914, 1 S.L.T. 368; M'Cumiskey Bros. v.
MacLaine, (O.H.) 1922 S.L.T. 104.
[6] Stuart & Stuart v. Macleod, 1891, 19 R. 223.
[7] 3 & 4 Geo. V c. 20, sec. 44.

When service upon the debtor or his successor is necessary it
may competently be made within Scotland (a) personally, or (b) by
posting in a registered letter a copy of the writ and warrant to
him at his dwelling-place or place of business, or the dwelling-
house or place of business last occupied by him.[1] If he is furth
of Scotland it is made at the office of the Extractor of the Court
of Session, and at the dwelling-house or place of business last
occupied by him.[2] When citation is made edictally and the
address of the debtor in England or Ireland is known, a copy
of the petition must be sent to him at that address by registered
letter posted on the day on which the induciæ of the petition
begins to run.[3] A witness is not required to an execution of
citation by an officer.[4] Citation in terms of the Citation Amendment Act of 1882[5] is now expressly authorized by Statute in
reference to sequestration.[4] A mere clerical error in the service
copy petition will not prevent an award of sequestration being
made,[6] and the debtor by appearing in the process may be barred
from objecting to the citation.[7]

[1] 3 & 4 Geo. V c. 20, sec. 25.
[2] Ibid.; 18 & 19 Geo. V c. 34, sec. 8; S.R. & O., 1929, No. 588; Act of
Sederunt, 19th July, 1929; 1 Edw. VIII & 1 Geo. VI c. 43, sec. 13;
Act of Sederunt, 9th July, 1937.
[3] 3 & 4 Geo. V c. 20, sec. 27.
[4] Ibid.. sec. 171.
[5] 45 & 46 Vict. c. 77, sec. 3.
[6] Lochrie v. M'Gregor, 1911 S.C. 21
[7] Gairdner v. Macarthur, (O.H.) 1918, 2 S.L.T. 123.

When the debtor is a company—which includes a body corporate, politic or collegiate, and a partnership[1]—citation is made by leaving a copy of the petition and warrant at the place where the business of the company is, or was last, carried on, provided a partner, clerk or servant of the company is there.[2] Failing that the copy is left at the dwelling-house of any of the acting partners, and if the house of such partner cannot be found, at the office of the Extractor of the Court of Session.[3] Sequestration may be awarded of the estates of the company and partners jointly or of their respective estates separately,[2] but if the sequestration of partners' estates is desired they should be separately cited.[4]

[1] 3 & 4 Geo. V c. 20, sec. 2.
[2] Ibid., sec. 26.
[3] Ibid.; Act of Sederunt, 19th July, 1929; Act of Sederunt, 9th July, 1937.
[4] See Central Motor Engineering Co. v. Galbraith, 1918 S.C. 755.

If a petitioning or concurring creditor dies or withdraws any other creditor may sist himself and pursue the process.[1] Thus a petitioning creditor desiring to withdraw cannot stop the proceedings; he can only withdraw himself as a party. This he does by lodging a minute craving the Court to permit him to withdraw, or consenting to the application for sequestration being dismissed. If another creditor lodges a minute craving to be sisted, and produces an affidavit and claim and vouchers, and these are *ex facie* regular, it is thought that the Court is bound to sist him. Such an intervening creditor need not be qualified as to the amount of his debt in the same way as an original petitioner, and it seems to be sufficient that if required to do so he satisfies the Court before sequestration is awarded that he is a creditor.[2] The Statute provides no time limit for a creditor being sisted in place of one who has withdrawn, and this appears to be competent even after an interval from the time of the withdrawal,[3] if the original application has not in the meantime been dismissed for lack of prosecution. Where an application for sequestration is withdrawn or dismissed, warrant should be asked to clear the personal registers and the interlocutor may appoint a certified copy of the deliverance to be transmitted to the Keeper of the Register of Inhibitions and Adjudications for that purpose. The petitioning or concurring creditor is entitled to payment by the trustee, out of the first funds coming into his hands, of the expenses of obtaining the sequestration and other procedure prior to the trustee's election.[4]

[1] 3 & 4 Geo. V c. 20, sec. 33.
[2] Stewart v. Wetherdair, 1928 S.C. 577. See also Allan v. Thomson, 1840, 3 D. 152.
[3] See Forsyth, 1883, 10 R. 1061.
[4] 3 & 4 Geo. V c. 20, sec. 40.

4. REGISTRATION OF SEQUESTRATION.

The party applying for sequestration must present, or transmit by post, before the expiration of the second lawful day after the first deliverance of the Sheriff an abbreviate of the petition and deliverance in the form prescribed by the Act signed by him or his solicitor, to the Keeper of the Registers of Inhibitions and Adjudications at Edinburgh who records and returns the abbreviate with a certificate thereon.[1] The same party must also, within four days after a copy of the deliverance awarding sequestration could be received in course of post in Edinburgh, insert a notice in statutory form in the *Edinburgh Gazette*, and within six days of the same date must insert a similar notice in the *London Gazette*.[2] Omission to insert the notice or errors in the notice inserted may be rectified on application to the Court of Session.[3]

[1] 3 & 4 Geo. V c. 20, sec. 44, Schedule A, Nos. 1 and 2.
[2] Ibid., sec. 44, Schedule B.
[3] Robertson, 1909 S.C. 444; Morgan, 1922 S.C. 589.

5. RECALL.

The deliverance awarding sequestration is not subject to review and the Sheriff has no jurisdiction to recall the sequestration, which is competent only in the Court of Session.[1] Within forty days after the deliverance awarding sequestration, a petition for recall may be presented in the Court of Session at the instance of the debtor if he has not consented to the sequestration (or, in certain circumstances, the representatives of a deceased debtor), or of any creditor[2]; but, after the lapse of the forty days, recall is, in general, competent only at the instance of nine-tenths in number and value of the creditors ranked on the estate.[3] Pending any petition for recall, and until recall is granted, the sequestration proceedings go on as if no such petition had been presented.[4] The usual grounds upon which recall is asked are irregularities in the proceedings leading to sequestration or the existence of a prior sequestration.[5] Appeal is competent against the deliverance of a Sheriff refusing a petition for sequestration.[6] The Court of Session may also recall a sequestration for the purpose of transferring the administration of the estate to England or Ireland,[7] and they may declare the sequestration at an end when recall cannot be made under the Act.[8]

[1] 3 & 4 Geo. V c. 20, sec. 30.
[2] Ibid. See 23 & 24 Geo. V c. 41, sec. 3; Rules of Court, 1936, IV 1 (a) (vii).
[3] 3 & 4 Geo. V c. 20, sec. 31. See Livingstone's Creditors v. Livingstone's Trustee, (O.H.) 1937 S.L.T. 391.
[4] Ibid., sec. 32.
[5] As to recall in case of a competing sequestration, see Kellock v. Anderson, 1875, 3 R. 239; Tennent v. Martin & Dunlop, 1879, 6 R. 786; Fletcher v. Anderson, 1883, 10 R. 835.
[6] Marr & Sons v. Lindsay, 1881, 8 R. 784.
[7] 3 & 4 Geo. V c. 20, sec. 43.
[8] Craig & Co., 1946 S.C. 19.

6. CREDITORS' MEETING.

In the deliverance awarding sequestration, the date and place are fixed for the first meeting of creditors to elect a trustee and commissioners which is held not earlier than six nor later than twelve days from the *Gazette* notice of the award.[1] A possible first duty of the Sheriff is to preside at this meeting, in which event the Sheriff-clerk or his depute also attends and writes the minutes.[2] Neither the Sheriff nor the Sheriff-clerk, however, requires to attend the meeting, unless required by two or more creditors to do so,[2] and in practice the Sheriff is seldom requisitioned. In his absence the creditors elect a preses,[2] who reports the proceedings to the Sheriff.[3] The process then remains with the Sheriff-clerk till a trustee is finally appointed, after which the process is delivered to the trustee, who is thereafter responsible for it.[3]

[1] 3 & 4 Geo. V c. 20, sec. 63.
[2] Ibid., sec. 64. See A. & G. V. Mann v. Tait, 1892, 20 R. 13. It has been held that the preses need not be a creditor, Aitken's Sequestration, 1910, 26 Sh.Ct.Rep. 165.
[3] Ibid., sec. 66.

7. ELECTION OF TRUSTEE.

If the Sheriff is present at the meeting of creditors he declares the person chosen by the creditors to be trustee, or, if there are objections or competition, he decides the issue either then or at a later hearing within four days of the meeting.[1] When the Sheriff is not present at the meeting then upon the proceedings being reported by production of the minutes, and if there are no objections or competition for the office, he declares the election of the trustee.[2] The trustee may not be the bankrupt or any one conjunct or confident with the bankrupt or having an interest opposed to the general body of creditors or resident outwith the jurisdiction of the Court of Session.[3] Upon the trustee finding caution to the extent fixed by the minute of the creditors' meeting, his election is confirmed by the Sheriff.[4] Caution must be found within seven days of the deliverance declaring the election.[4] In such incidental steps of procedure no formal written application or motion is necessary. The trustee's official title is an act and warrant, which is issued by the Sheriff-clerk and operates to transfer to him the whole estates of the bankrupt.[5] A copy of the act and warrant is sent by the Sheriff-clerk to the accountant within three days of its issue, and a copy, certified by the Sheriff-clerk and authenticated by a judge of the Court of Session, is received as *prima facie* evidence of the trustee's title in any Court of law in England or Ireland, or elsewhere in His Majesty's dominions.[5] Within ten days after the trustee's election is confirmed he must present an abbreviate in statutory form signed by him or his solicitor to the Keeper of the Register of Inhibitions and Adjudications to be recorded.[6]

[1] 3 & 4 Geo. V c. 20, sec. 65.
[2] Ibid., sec. 66.
[3] Ibid., sec. 64.
[4] Ibid., secs. 67, 69, 70.
[5] Ibid., sec. 70.
[6] Ibid., sec. 75.

If there is a competition for the office of trustee, or objections to the candidate or candidates, the parties concerned may, within four days of the election meeting, lodge objections to the votes recorded, to the eligibility of the trustee, or to the conduct of the proceedings.[1] These objections must be specific, and such as can be disposed of upon the affidavits and vouchers, with such instruction of each objection as is immediately available, for proof at large is not allowed in a competition process, though diligence may be granted to recover documents which instantly verify the objections.[2] There are no written pleadings beyond the notes of objections. After hearing parties the Sheriff gives his decision in writing, and the grounds of it in a note, and these are put in process.[1] The Sheriff's judgment declaring the election of a trustee is not subject to review by appeal, suspension or otherwise,[3] but, if he find that no election of trustee has been made, that judgment is appealable.[4] Appeals were at one time thought competent in the case of interlocutory deliverances prior to the judgment declaring the election, but it is thought that such appeals would not now be allowed.[5]

[1] 3 & 4 Geo. V c. 20, sec. 66. See generally as to objections, Shaw v. Sinclair, 1927, 44 Sh.Ct.Rep. 218.
[2] Rhind v. Mitchell, 1846, 9 D. 231; Wylie v. Kyd, 1884, 11 R. 968; Reid v. Strathie, 1887, 14 R. 847. See Moncur v. Macdonald, 1887, 14 R. 305.
[3] 3 & 4 Geo. V c. 20, sec. 67; Bannatyne v. Thomson, 1902, 5 F. 221; Yeaman v. Little, 1906, 8 F. 702; Grierson v. Ogilvy's Trustee, 1908 S.C. 959; cf. Farquharson v. Sutherland, 1883, 15 R. 759.
[4] See Miller v. Duncan, 1858, 20 D. 803; Wiseman v. Skene, 1870, 8 M. 661.
[5] Galt v. Macrae, 1880, 7 R. 888. See Yeaman v. Little, supra; Grierson v. Ogilvy's Trustee, supra.

8. REMOVAL OF TRUSTEE.

A majority in number and value of the creditors present at a meeting called for the purpose may—without reasons assigned[1]—remove the trustee or accept of his resignation.[2] Appeal to the Sheriff is competent against a resolution of the creditors removing a trustee, his decision being in turn subject to review by the Court of Session.[3] The trustee may also be removed by the Court of Session or the Sheriff, upon the application of one-fourth of the creditors in value. Such application is served on the trustee and intimated in the *Edinburgh Gazette*,[2] and if sufficient reason is shown[4] the trustee is removed and a meeting of creditors is appointed to be held to devolve the estate on the trustee next in succession or to elect a new trustee.[2]

[1] Wallace v. Gibson, 1824, 3 S. 73; Walker v. Walker, 1835, 13 S. 428.
[2] 3 & 4 Geo. V c. 20, sec. 71.
[3] Ibid., secs. 165, 166.
[4] See Aytoun v. Macculloch, 1824, 3 S. 80; Brown v. Burt, 1848, 11 D. 338; Richmond v. M'Phun, 1854, 16 D. 546.

If the accountant of Court is dissatisfied with the trustee's conduct in the sequestration, or if complaint is made to him by a creditor, he inquires into the matter and, if not satisfied with the explanation given, he reports to the Court of Session or the Sheriff, who, after hearing the trustee and investigating the whole matter, may censure or remove the trustee or deal otherwise with him as justice may require.[1] The accountant is also directed to report to the Court of Session, or to the Sheriff, any disobedience by the trustee of any requisition or order by the accountant, and generally any matters which he may deem necessary to report and the Court is empowered to deal summarily with the matter as accords of law.[2] When such a report from the accountant is received the usual practice is to appoint a copy to be served on the trustee and to ordain the latter to appear personally before the Sheriff and at that or a subsequent hearing the matter is generally disposed of.

[1] 3 & 4 Geo. V c. 20, sec. 158. See Accountant in Bankruptcy v. Peacock's Trustee, 1867, 6 M. 158; Lang v. Hally, 1870, 8 M. 753; Accountant in Bankruptcy v. Davie, 1884, 11 R. 1013.
[2] Ibid., sec. 160.

The Sheriff has also a concurrent jurisdiction with the Court of Session to dismiss a trustee who has kept in his hands for more than ten days funds exceeding £50 belonging to the estate.[1] Any qualified creditor may complain of this to the Court of Session or the Sheriff,[1] and, in the Sheriff Court, the complaint will take the form of an initial writ, narrating the circumstances and craving the Court to dismiss the trustee. The onus of proving that the money was kept up from innocent causes rests upon the trustee.[1] If he fail to prove this he is liable to be dismissed, to forfeit his claim for remuneration, and to be mulct in expenses.[1] The trustee and commissioners, as well as any judicial factor, are amenable to the Sheriff though resident beyond his territory, at the instance of any party interested, to account for their intromissions and management. The procedure is by initial writ served on the party complained about. If the application fails the respondent is entitled to expenses, either out of the estate or from the party who has complained, as the Sheriff shall direct.[2]

[1] 3 & 4 Geo. V c. 20, sec. 79.
[2] Ibid., sec. 82. See M'Adam v. Martin's Trustee, 1884, 12 R. 358; Tough's Trustee v. Edinburgh Parish Council, 1918 S.C. 107.

In the event of the trustee being discharged, or dying, or resigning, or being removed, or remaining furth of Scotland for three months continuously, whilst the sequestration process is pending, any commissioner or any creditor may apply to the Court of Session or the Sheriff for an order to hold a meeting for devolving the estate on the trustee next in succession, or for electing a new trustee.[1] In the absence of special directions as to how such application is to be made, the appropriate mode would seem to be a summary application, by initial writ, narrating the facts complained of, and craving the Sheriff to appoint a meeting of creditors to be held. If the crave is granted, the new meeting is advertised in the *Edinburgh Gazette* and held, and a new trustee elected and confirmed, in the same manner as in the case of the original trustee.[1] The above section does not apply to a case where both the bankrupt and the trustee have been discharged.[2]

[1] 3 & 4 Geo. V c. 20, sec. 71.
[2] Cockburn's Trustees, 1941 S.C. 187. See next paragraph.

The Sheriff cannot order a meeting to be held to elect a new trustee in any circumstances in which the Statute does not empower him to do so.[1] In circumstances not falling within sec. 71, the Court of Session may *ex nobile officio* order a meeting to be held to elect a new trustee[2]; but the Sheriff at his own hand cannot do this.[1] In such cases a remit may be made by the Court of Session to the Sheriff Court,[3] and the Sheriff may direct the holding of a meeting of creditors, if so authorized, when the subsequent procedure is as in the original process; or the Court may authorize the Accountant of Court to convene a meeting of creditors to elect a new trustee.[4]

1 Cockburn's Trustees, 1941 S.C. 187.
2 Gentles, 1870, 9 M. 176; Cockburn's Trustees, supra.
3 See Young, 1888, 16 R. 92.
4 Accountant in Bankruptcy v. Davie, 1884, 11 R. 1013.

The bankrupt has no direct voice in the appointment of a trustee or commissioners, nor has he any statutory power to apply for their removal. In one case a bankrupt presented a petition to the Court of Session for the removal of the trustee, and *ex nobile officio* the Court, without deciding as to the competence of the application, directed a meeting of creditors to be held to consider the position.[1] But the *nobile officium* of the Court of Session will not generally be exercised in matters in regard to which there is statutory direction, and the removal of a trustee can generally be effected only in the way provided by the Act as above set forth.

1 Robertson v. Mitchell, 1871, 9 M. 741.

9. COMMISSIONERS.

The Sheriff has the duty of confirming the election of the commissioners who are appointed at the same meeting as the trustee.[1] Their title is a minute, entered in the sederunt book, and signed by the Sheriff, without any more formal confirmation.[1] The decision of the Sheriff as to the persons elected is final.[1] The commissioners do not require to find caution. No person is eligible as a commissioner who is disqualified to be a trustee,[1] and it is within the scope of the Sheriff's authority to refuse to confirm the appointment as commissioner of any person obviously disqualified, or whose disqualification can be instantly verified by an objector. A commissioner who is a mandatory loses his office if written intimation of recall of the mandate is sent to the trustee,[1] and a majority of creditors in value—not number and value[2]—at any meeting called for the purpose may remove a commissioner and elect a successor.[3] If the accountant of Court, at his own hand

by the Court of Session unless made by the Sheriff before whom the sequestration comes to depend.[5]

[1] 3 & 4 Geo. V c. 20, sec. 15.   See Coupland's Sequestration, 1885, 2 Sh.Ct.Rep. 56.
[2] Bannatyne v. Thomson, 1902, 5 F. 221.
[3] 3 & 4 Geo. V c. 20, sec. 168.
[4] See ibid., sec. 17.
[5] Ibid., sec. 18.

11. BANKRUPTCY EXAMINATION.

The Sheriff presides at the public examination of the bankrupt and of third parties who can give information relative to the estate.[1]   Within eight days of the date of his act and warrant the trustee applies to the Sheriff to name a day for the public examination of the bankrupt.[2]   This takes the form of an initial writ, lodged in the sequestration process, narrating his appointment as trustee, and craving an examination diet.   This application is granted *de plano*, and then served upon the bankrupt, who is ordained to attend for examination on a date not sooner than seven, nor later than fourteen, days from the date of the interlocutor.[2]   The date fixed must be intimated by *Gazette* notice and circular to the creditors.[2]   In practice the intimation is made in the first issue of the *Gazette* after the order is granted.

[1] 3 & 4 Geo. V c. 20, secs. 83, 86, 88.
[2] Ibid., sec. 83.

The examination of the bankrupt is generally conducted in public, and its object is to elicit, for the information of the trustee, facts tending to show where there is any estate which the trustee may take and realize for the benefit of the creditors.   The Statute invests the trustee with a discretion to take the examination either in public or in private.[1]   Thus if the trustee moves that the examination be conducted in public, the Sheriff has no discretion, but must so order.[1]

[1] 3 & 4 Geo. V c. 20, sec. 88; Wright v. Guild, 1878, 6 R. 289.

When the bankrupt is abroad, or is prevented from attending by a lawful cause, that is to say, by some cause which, in the opinion of the Sheriff, reasonably excuses him,[1] the Sheriff may grant commission[2] to take the examination of the bankrupt.[3] But when there is no good reason for absenting himself, the bankrupt must attend personally, and, if necessary, the Sheriff may grant a warrant for his apprehension, which may be executed by a messenger or Sheriff-officer anywhere within Scotland.[3]   If he is furth of Scotland, but within the United Kingdom, a warrant may be obtained from the Court of Session to apprehend him and bring him to the place fixed for his examination.[4] When the bankrupt is in prison the Sheriff may grant warrant to authorize his attendance.

[1] See Sinclair & Bremner's Trustee, 1897, 5 S.L.T. 136.
[2] There seems to be no definition of the persons who may be appointed commissioners. The terms of sec. 69 of the Act of Sederunt of 10th July, 1839, do not appear to be applicable, and in any case are now ineffective (Inglis' Trustees v. Macpherson, 1910 S.C. 46).
[3] 3 & 4 Geo. V c. 20, sec. 84.
[4] Ibid., sec. 85. See 4 & 5 Geo. V c. 59, secs. 121-123.

The Sheriff may, at any time, on the application of the trustee —made by initial writ—order an examination of the bankrupt's wife and family, clerks, servants, factors, solicitors, and others who can give information relative to his estate.[1] These parties may be examined in public or in private in the trustees' discretion,[2] or if necessary the examination may be on commission.[1] If such parties are desired to produce documents, the crave should ask that they be ordered to exhibit or produce certain specified documents. The keeping of the examination within due bounds is often difficult, and sometimes delicate. Creditors may not be examined upon their own claims and the trustee is not entitled to use his power of examining third parties in order to investigate collateral matters or the merits of claims upon the estate.[3] The object of the examination, both as regards the bankrupt and third parties, is to ascertain what the bankrupt's estate consists of, where it is, and what he has done with it, or to affect it.[4] If he can aid this inquiry, no person is entitled to withhold his information, merely because he is an actual or possible creditor or litigant,[5] but it is not the purpose of the examination to settle the validity of creditors' claims, or the soundness of litigants' pleas.[3] A bankruptcy examination is an inquiry rather than a proof, and the rules of evidence are not so strictly regarded as in a proof.[6] The Sheriff is the judge of what is relevant and reasonable inquiry, but his ruling is open to review by appeal within eight days to the Court of Session.[7] The Act provides that the bankrupt and third parties under examination must answer all lawful questions relating to the affairs of the bankrupt,[8] and objections to questions may be taken by any creditor or by the bankrupt or third party under examination, or, in the case of questions by a creditor, by the trustee.

[1] 3 & 4 Geo. V c. 20, sec. 86.
[2] Ibid., sec. 88; Wright v. Guild, 1878, 6 R. 289.

[3] Sawers v. Balgarnie, 1858, 21 D. 153; Delvoitte & Co. v. Baillie's Trustee, 1877, 5 R. 143; Brash v. Arnott's Trustee, 1888, 15 R. 583; Jacks' Trustee v. Jacks' Trustees, 1910 S.C. 34.
[4] Delvoitte v. Baillie's Trustee, supra, Lord President Inglis, p. 144.
[5] See Brash v. Arnott's Trustee, supra.
[6] Sawers v. Balgarnie, supra; M'Kay v. M'Lachlan, 1863, 1 M. 440; Park v. Robson, 1871, 10 M. 10.
[7] 3 & 4 Geo. V c. 20, sec. 166. See cases in note 3, supra; as to manner of appeal see Rules of Court, 1936, V 7 and 8, and pp. 375, 391, infra.
[8] Ibid., sec. 87.

Failing the attendance of third parties at the diet fixed for their examination, a warrant for their apprehension may be issued, and may be executed within Scotland in like manner as a warrant for the apprehension of the bankrupt[1]; but when the third party is not the wife, nor member of the family, nor clerk or servant of the bankrupt, a warrant for apprehension will not be granted unless eight days have elapsed from the service of the warrant, or the trustee makes oath of his reasonable belief that the witness intends to leave the country to avoid being examined.[1] If the party to be examined cannot attend, the Sheriff may grant a commission to take his evidence,[1] but the provision for bringing the bankrupt from England or Ireland does not extend to third party witnesses, and apart from a commission there is no provision for procuring their evidence if they are furth of Scotland. The English Bankruptcy Act of 1914 provides that Courts having bankruptcy jurisdiction in the three kingdoms are to enforce each other's orders, in the same manner as if the order had been made in their own Courts.[2] Accordingly, the Sheriff, in making an order for the examination of either the bankrupt or third parties furth of Scotland, may embody in it a request to the County Court of the domicile of the witness to give effect to the order, and that Court will compel the witness to attend before the County Court for examination there.[3]

[1] 3 & 4 Geo. V c. 20, sec. 86.
[2] 4 & 5 Geo. V c. 59, secs. 121-123.
[3] See Park v. Robson, 1871, 10 M. 10.

The ordinary rules of procedure in recording evidence, which are in operation in the Sheriff Court, apply to examinations in bankruptcy of the bankrupt and third parties.[1] The deponent must be sworn, or make an affirmation, in the same manner as a witness in a litigation.[1] The record of the evidence may be taken down by the Sheriff or commissioner or by a shorthand writer, under the supervision of the Sheriff or commissioner, but not necessarily to his dictation, and the shorthand writer's notes of evidence, certified by him, form the official record of the examination.[2] The record of the evidence of third parties does not necessarily require to be signed by the witnesses or by the Sheriff, unless in the opinion of the Sheriff such authentication is necessary.[1] The deposition of the bankrupt is in practice written into the sederunt book, and is signed by the bankrupt and the Sheriff. The Act provides that the examination of the bankrupt is to be authenticated in the ordinary way as a regular deposition[1]; and that the statutory oath, which closes the examination, must be engrossed and signed in the sederunt book,[3] so it is convenient to have the entire examination there recorded. The depositions of third parties are in practice recorded like evidence in proofs in civil cases,[2] and are not now usually signed, either by the witness or by the Sheriff. The Sheriff may order the bankrupt or other persons under examination to produce any books, papers, deeds or other documents in their custody relative to the bankrupt's affairs, and cause the same or copies to be delivered to the trustee.[4] The state of affairs with any additions or alterations made by the bankrupt is signed by him and the Sheriff.[3]

[1] 3 & 4 Geo. V c. 20, sec. 88.
[2] Ibid.; 7 Edw. VII c. 51, Schedule I, Rule 65.
[3] 3 & 4 Geo. V c. 20, sec. 91.
[4] Ibid., sec. 87.

If the bankrupt refuses to sign his examination or if he, or a third party under examination, refuses to be sworn or to answer, to the satisfaction of the Sheriff, any lawful question put to him by the Sheriff or trustee or creditor, or refuses to produce books, deeds or other documents in his custody or power relating to the estate the Sheriff may grant warrant to commit such person to prison till the order is complied with.[1] The warrant must specify the question and answer, or the book, deed or document or the refusal to swear or sign in respect of which it is granted.[1] Imprisonment in such a case is not a punishment, but a compulsitor, and it must cease as soon as the person complies or the information is otherwise obtained.[2] In the case of refusal to be sworn or to sign, the Sheriff would be entitled to commit to prison forthwith, but in the case of refusal to answer or produce it is thought that the Sheriff should first pronounce a formal deliverance ordering the party to answer or produce and if that order is not implemented or appealed against[3] a warrant to imprison may be granted. The appropriate person to apply for the warrant is the trustee, but it is thought that a creditor could apply if the refusal to answer related to a question put by him. The warrant to imprison is not subject to review, but the party imprisoned may apply by petition to the Court of Session for recall of the warrant.[4]

1 3 & 4 Geo. V c. 20, sec. 89.
2 Bell's Commentaries ii, 327; Nicol v. Edmond, 1851, 13 D. 614.
3 See p. 370, supra.
4 3 & 4 Geo. V c. 20, sec. 89. See Auld, (O.H.) 1888, 25 S.L.R. 434.

The examination may be adjourned by the Sheriff or commissioner to an early specified date,[1] but creditors are not entitled to postponement in order to test statements made by the bankrupt.[2] Primarily the examination of the bankrupt is conducted by the trustee or the solicitor in the sequestration, and questions may also be put by the Sheriff.[3] But creditors or mandatories for creditors may also put questions with the sanction of the Sheriff.[4] In practice the rule is that, after the trustee has closed his examination, any creditor, or his mandatory, or his solicitor may put supplementary questions, which, if relevant and competent, will be allowed even in the face of an objection by the trustee that the answer may be injurious to the general body of creditors.[5] A solicitor representing the bankrupt has no authority under the Act to examine or cross-examine his client or other parties who may give evidence. At times his assistance may be useful in clearing up matters relevant to the inquiry in hand but his intervention can only take the form of suggesting questions to be put by the trustee or by the Court. Third parties who are not creditors but whose names may be mentioned in the depositions have no standing to put questions or to intervene in the examination.

1 3 & 4 Geo. V c. 20, secs. 84, 86. See Wright v. Guild, 1878, 6 R. 289.
2 Unger v. Blogg, 1867, 5 M. 1049.
3 3 & 4 Geo. V c. 20, sec. 89.
4 Ibid.; Smyth v. M'Clelland, 1843, 6 D. 331.
5 Barstow v. Hutcheson, 1849, 11 D. 687; Wright v. Wink, 1852, 24 Scot. Jur. 230; cf. Delvoitte & Co. v. Baillie's Trustee, 1877, 5 R. 143.

If the trustee obtains full information privately from the bankrupt or others, there is no object to be served by a formal examination, and the fact that the trustee is satisfied is recorded in the sederunt book and the statutory oath is administered. Thus it frequently occurs that, at the examination diet, the trustee states that he is satisfied with the explanations obtained, and that he has no questions to ask. In that event no examination takes place. But if the bankrupt is sworn, and is asked by the trustee any question, however formal, an examination by the trustee has been made, and a creditor may then, with the leave of the Court, proceed tò put questions.[1] On the other hand if, at the diet, the trustee does not proceed at all with the examination, the Court has no discretion to allow creditors to intervene. If creditors are dissatisfied, they can report to the accountant of Court,[2] and the accountant has authority to direct a meeting of creditors to be held if requisite for the preservation or due management of the estate, or more speedy realizing and division of the funds or winding up of the estate[2]; or the accountant might report the trustee's conduct to the Court of Session or the Sheriff for direction.[3] But neither the accountant nor the Court is likely, unless in exceptional circumstances, to interfere with the trustee's discretion in a matter of this sort. As regards examining the bankrupt (but not third parties), dissatisfied creditors (if they constitute a sufficient majority) may treat the first examination as closed, and proceed to procure a new diet. The Sheriff may, upon the application of the trustee, order the bankrupt to be examined as often as he shall see fit.[4] The trustee is bound to call a meeting of creditors upon the requisition of one-fourth in value of the creditors entitled to vote,[5] and the meeting of creditors is entitled to give directions to the trustee. In this indirect way the requisite majority of creditors might compel the examination of the bankrupt.[6]

[1] 3 & 4 Geo. V c. 20, sec. 89.
[2] Ibid., sec. 159.
[3] Ibid., sec. 160.
[4] Ibid., sec. 84.
[5] Ibid., sec. 93.
[6] Cf. Somerville v. Darlington, 1859, 21 D. 467.

12. Appeal from Creditors' Resolution.

The Sheriff may occasionally be appealed to when a difference of opinion arises as to the management and disposal of the estate. At the statutory meeting held after the bankrupt's examination, when the trustee submits a report upon the estate, the creditors may give directions to the trustee for the recovery, management or disposal of the estate,[1] and there may be room for difference of opinion upon policy, such as carrying on a business for a time, the adoption of current contracts, or the like. A resolution of the creditors, whether at this or at any other meeting, is appealable to the Sheriff or the Court of Session within fourteen days.[2] The parties entitled to appeal appear to be (a) the minority creditors; (b) any other creditor, whether he was present at the meeting or not; (c) the bankrupt, upon whose possible reversionary interest the policy of the resolution may have an important bearing; and (d) the trustee, if the interests of the estate justify him in appealing,[3] or in other special circumstances as where the resolution has given directions contrary to the bankruptcy Statutes. A note of appeal, which should narrate the date and terms of the resolution, and the remedy suggested must be lodged with and marked by the Sheriff-clerk within fourteen days of the meeting.[2] In practice the note of appeal is in the form of an initial writ.[4] The Act provides that the Sheriff shall appoint a copy of the note of appeal and of his deliverance thereon to be served on the respondent, or his mandatory or known solicitor, and shall appoint the respondent to appear at a specified diet when parties are heard, and the Sheriff may decide the matter without a record, provided he specifies the facts and the grounds of his judgment.[2] Alternatively, he may order the parties to lodge minutes containing their averments in fact and pleas in law without argument, and may proceed in a summary way, holding these documents as a closed record, and in pronouncing judgment he must assign his reasons.[2] In the case of an appeal against a resolution of creditors it is thought that the note of appeal should be served on the creditors who voted in favour of the resolution and also upon the bankrupt and trustee if their interests are involved, but that no one need be named as a respondent.[5] In place of deciding the question raised the Sheriff may, in the first place, order a new meeting of creditors to be held to reconsider the resolution complained against.[2] The Sheriff's judgment may be appealed to the Court of Session by note of appeal, written on the interlocutor sheet within eight days of the judgment, signed by the appellant or his solicitor, and bearing the date on which it is signed.[6]

[1] 3 & 4 Geo. V c. 20, sec. 92.
[2] Ibid., sec. 165.
[3] See Witham v. Teenan's Trustee, 1884, 11 R. 776.
[4] See p. 391, infra.
[5] See Purdom, &c. v. Spence, 1853, 16 D. 164; Aberdeen, &c., Bank v. Scottish Equitable Insurance Co., 1859, 22 D. 162.
[6] Rules of Court, 1936, V 7, 8; 3 & 4 Geo. V c. 20, sec. 166.

13. Deed of Arrangement.

Another duty of the Sheriff under the bankruptcy Statutes is to decide upon the reasonableness of a deed of arrangement, and, if satisfied with it, to end the sequestration. At the meeting for the election of the trustee or at a subsequent meeting called for the purpose, a majority in number and three-fourths in value of the creditors present or represented may resolve that the estate be wound up by deed of arrangement and that an application be made to the Sheriff or the Court of Session to sist procedure for not more than two months.[1] If it is so resolved at the first meeting, a trustee need not be elected,[1] but it may be desirable, although it is not essential, to appoint a judicial factor.[2] If the resolution is adopted after a trustee has been elected his duties as trustee are suspended, and his functions become rather those of a judicial factor to preserve the estate, and, if there is a going business, to carry it on, or to supervise the bankrupt in carrying it on. Where a trustee is in office at the date of the sist, it is not competent to appoint a judicial factor, but the Sheriff may give such directions to the trustee as he may think necessary.[3] The creditors voting at the meeting must have their claims duly vouched.[4]

[1] 3 & 4 Geo. V c. 20, sec. 34.
[2] Ibid., sec. 36.
[3] Brown v. Bayley's Trustees, 1910 S.C. 76.
[4] North of Scotland Banking Co. v. Ireland, 1880, 8 R. 117.

Within four days of the meeting at which such a resolution is passed, the bankrupt, or a person appointed for the purpose by the meeting, reports the resolution to the Sheriff and craves that the sequestration process be sisted for a period not exceeding two months.[1] This is done by initial writ in the ordinary form which is intimated to any dissentient creditors. The Sheriff may hear any party having an interest,[2] which at that stage would appear to include (a) the bankrupt; (b) creditors; (c) persons holding or managing any part of the estate; or (d) any person who can qualify an interest which might be prejudiced by the sequestration process being sisted. But as the resolution has at this stage gone no further than that a deed of arrangement be the mode of working out the sequestration, and its terms are not yet before the Sheriff, his duty is in practice restricted to satisfying himself of the regularity of the proceedings at the meeting, that the resolution was carried by the requisite majority, and that it has been reported to him within four days. If he is satisfied of these technical details, and that the application is reasonable, the process is sisted.[2] Failing the matter being reported within four days the sequestration must proceed.[3]

[1] 3 & 4 Geo. V c. 20, sec. 35.
[2] Ibid. See Hunter's Sequestration, 1930, 46 Sh.Ct.Rep. 290.
[3] Ibid., sec. 38.

When the completed deed of arrangement is ready it is presented to the Sheriff for approval.[1] The creditors themselves adjust the deed, and get it signed by, or by authority of, the requisite majority in number and three-fourths in value of the creditors, and by the bankrupt.[1] It must be presented within the period of the sist and if the last day of the sist is a *dies non* it cannot be received on the following day.[2] As the power to sist is statutory it is thought that the Sheriff cannot extend the period under Rule 56 of the Sheriff Courts Act.[3] If the deed of arrangement is not timeously presented the sequestration proceeds. If it is timeously presented, the Sheriff must satisfy himself that the deed of arrangement was duly entered into and executed, and that it is reasonable.[1] It is not the practice to lodge any further application to the Court when the deed of arrangement is produced, but the Sheriff is empowered by the Act to make such intimation thereof as he may think proper, and to hear parties having an interest, and make any inquiry he may think necessary.[1] There is no prescribed mode of inquiry, but the general practice is to order intimation by circular to the creditors who have not signed the deed and by advertisement in the *Edinburgh Gazette* and a local newspaper requesting all who wish to oppose the approval of the deed to lodge a notice of appearance. A declaration is taken from the bankrupt confirming the list of creditors and that there are no non-concurring creditors to whom circulars have not been sent. If necessary a diet is fixed for hearing any persons who appear. As the Sheriff's power to inquire is unrestricted, it is competent to take proof, but in practice this is not always done. If the deed is regularly executed, and in conformity with the Statute, it has usually been approved, unless an objector can instantly verify some substantial objection,[4] but the Court of Session have recently pointed out that the Sheriff's duty is to decide whether the reasonableness of the arrangement has been established and that he cannot rely merely on failure by creditors to aver and prove that it is unreasonable.[5] Whether the Sheriff is to be satisfied by explanations given him, or should have evidence on oath from the bankrupt and others, must depend on the circumstances present in each case.[5]

[1] 3 & 4 Geo. V c. 20, sec. 37.
[2] Hunter's Sequestration, 1929, 46 Sh.Ct.Rep. 52.
[3] 7 Edw. VII c. 51, Schedule I, Rule 56.
[4] See Hendrie's Sequestration, 1894, 10 Sh.Ct.Rep. 107; Kinloch Campbell & Co.'s Sequestration, 1894, 10 Sh.Ct.Rep. 180; Tait's Sequestration, 1912, 29 Sh.Ct.Rep. 94; Williamson's Sequestration, 1923 S.L.T. 123; Hunter's Squestration, 1930, 46 Sh.Ct.Rep. 290; 47 Sh.Ct.Rep. 51; Fraser's Sequestration, 1935, 51 Sh.Ct.Rep. 225.
[5] Stone v. Woodhouse, Hambly & Co., 1937 S.C. 824.

The Sheriff's interlocutor approving of the deed of arrangement also declares the sequestration at an end, and, when this interlocutor has been entered in the register of sequestrations, and an abbreviate recorded in the Register of Inhibitions and Adjudi-

cations,[1] the effect is (a) that the sequestration is in the same
position as if it had been recalled; and (b) that all the creditors,
whether they concurred or not, are bound by the deed of arrangement.[2] But an appeal to the Court of Session is competent against
an interlocutor approving or refusing to approve of a deed of
arrangement,[3] and if objection is taken to the claims of certain
creditors the Court of Session may remit to the Sheriff to allow
these claims to be properly vouched.[4] The statutory time limit
of two months applies to the production of the deed to the Sheriff
and not to its judicial approval.[4]

[1] 3 & 4 Geo. V c. 20, secs. 30, 39.
[2] Ibid., sec. 37.
[3] Coutts & Co. v. Jones, 1900, 2 F. 1066.
[4] Williamson's Sequestration, 1923 S.L.T. 123; cf. Hunter's Sequestration,
    1930, 46 Sh.Ct.Rep. 290.

Although the sequestration thus comes to an end as a judicial
process, the Act provides that the sequestration shall receive full
effect in so far as may be necessary for the purpose of preventing,
challenging, or setting aside preferences over the estate.[1] While
the trustee or creditors may thus challenge preferences in realizing
and distributing the estate, the bankrupt, if reinvested under
the deed of arrangement, cannot do so unless specially empowered,[2]
nor can a purchaser from the creditors unless the right has been
specially assigned.[3] There is no statutory provision for the discharge of the bankrupt where the estate is wound up under a
deed of arrangement and this is a matter to be dealt with in the
deed itself. The provisions of the Act relative to deeds of arrangement extend to and include settlements and arrangements by way
of composition,[4] and where it was provided that certain payments
should be made by the bankrupt by instalments and he failed
to make one payment, a creditor was held entitled to sue him
for his whole debt less the sums actually received.[5] Where a
sequestration has been brought to an end on approval of a deed
of arrangement a subsequent creditor would apparently be entitled
to apply for sequestration although the debtor's estate was still
being administered under the deed of arrangement.[6]

[1] 3 & 4 Geo. V c. 20, sec. 37.
[2] Bell's Commentaries ii, 351-2.
[3] Smith & Co. v. Smyth, 1889, 16 R. 392.
[4] 3 & 4 Geo. V c. 20, sec. 34.
[5] Alexander & Austin v. Yuille, 1873, 1 R. 185.
[6] A v. B, (O.H.) 1912, 2 S.L.T. 498.

The provisions for working out a deed of arrangement, in
cases where a trustee has been appointed, leave the trustee in

a somewhat indefinite position. Approval of the deed of arrangement brings the sequestration to an end. But the machinery for procuring the. trustee's discharge, after a final division of the funds, is not applicable, and there is no other statutory machinery available. In the ordinary case of a deed of arrangement, the trustee has not intromitted with the estate, but merely preserved it, and no one has any interest except the bankrupt if he is reinvested under the deed. An application by the trustee, and his cautioner if there is one, with consent of the bankrupt, or intimated to the bankrupt, for authority to the Sheriff-clerk to deliver up the bond of caution, seems a competent proceeding in the Sheriff Court and no other procedure appears to be available. The trustee must deliver up the sederunt book to the accountant of Court. If the resolution is not timeously reported, or if the Sheriff refuses to sist the sequestration, or if the deed of arrangement is not timeously produced to the Sheriff or is not approved by him, the sequestration proceeds, and the period of time subsequent to the resolution of the creditors is not reckoned in calculating periods of time prescribed in the Act.[1] The Act authorizes the Sheriff to make all necessary orders by appointing meetings of creditors and otherwise for resuming the necessary procedure in the sequestration.[2] Once a deed of arrangement has been signed and although it has not been formally approved by the Court it is thought that neither the bankrupt nor the creditors would be entitled to resile save on cause shown.[3]

[1] 3 & 4 Geo. V c. 20, sec. 38.
[2] Ibid. See form of petition in Eucyclopœdia of Scottish Legal Styles, VIII, p. 243.
[3] See Lee v. Stevenson's Trustee, 1883, 11 R. 26.

14. COMPOSITION SETTLEMENT.

The Act provides for an offer of composition being made by or on behalf of the bankrupt at the meeting for the election of a trustee,[1] and if a majority in number and three-fourths in value of the creditors then present agree to entertain the offer for consideration[1] it may be accepted by a similar majority in number and value at the meeting after the bankrupt's examination.[2] The offer may also be made at the meeting held after the bankrupt's examination or at a later meeting called for the purpose, a subsequent meeting being called by the trustee if necessary for the purpose of accepting the offer.[3] Security for payment of the composition must be offered[1] and accepted,[2] and a formal bond of caution is executed.[2]

[1] 3 & 4 Geo. V c. 20, sec. 134.
[2] Ibid., sec. 135.
[3] Ibid., sec. 136.

The Sheriff's duties in regard to a composition offer are somewhat similar to those in respect of a deed of arrangement. The trustee makes a formal report, with the information to enable the Court to judge of the arrangement.[1] The report may be made to the Court of Session or the Sheriff Court as the trustee may select, and in the latter case the report and bond of caution are lodged with the Sheriff-clerk,[1] along with the *Edinburgh Gazette* containing the notice of the meeting to accept the offer, certificate of posting of circulars calling the meeting, and the minutes of both meetings. Before the Sheriff approves of the composition settlement, the trustee's accounts must have been audited by the commissioners, his commission fixed by them, such commission and the sequestration expenses paid or provided for, and the balance due by or to the trustee ascertained.[2] The commissioners' findings on these matters are subject to review by the Sheriff on complaint by the trustee, the bankrupt or any of the creditors, but such review cannot be granted if the deliverance bringing the sequestration to an end has meantime been pronounced.[3] An offer of composition once made cannot be withdrawn without cause assigned.[4]

[1] 3 & 4 Geo. V c. 20, sec. 135.
[2] Ibid., sec. 138.
[3] Franklin v. Landale, 1840, 3 D. 188; Clark v. Whyte, 1843, 5 D. 772.
[4] Lee v. Stevenson's Trustee, 1883, 11 R. 26.

It is usual to order service of the trustee's report on any creditors who have voted against the acceptance of the composition, and, if they appear to oppose the approval of the offer, they may be appointed to lodge objections, and the bankrupt or the trustee to answer them. Apart from creditors it would seem that the trustee and the bankrupt's cautioner are entitled to object.[1] The normal grounds of objection relate to irregularities in the procedure,[2] fraud or collusion,[3] insufficient caution,[4] unreasonableness of the composition,[5] and failure to pay or provide for the sequestration expenses or the trustee's remuneration.[6] In addition to hearing parties the Sheriff may order inquiry, but if, after hearing any objections, he finds that the offer, with the security, has been duly made, and is reasonable, and has been assented to by the requisite majority he pronounces a deliverance approving thereof.[7]

If the Sheriff refuses to sustain the offer or if he rejects the vote
of any creditor he must specify the grounds of refusal or rejection.[7]
It has been held that in place of objecting as above, creditors may
appeal in the usual way against the resolution of the meeting
accepting the composition.[8]

[1] See Ironside v. Gray, 1841, 4 D. 629; Miller v. Keith, 1872, 11 M. 164;
Lee v. Stevenson's Trustee, 1883, 11 R. 26.
[2] Lee v. Stevenson's Trustee, supra.
[3] Urquhart, 1855, 17 D. 773.
[4] Bell's Commentaries ii, 355.
[5] Bradshaw v. Kirkwood & Sons, 1904, 7 F. 249.
[6] M'Carter v. Aikman, 1893, 20 R. 1090.
[7] 3 & 4 Geo. V c. 20, sec. 135.
[8] M'George v. M'George's Creditors, 1887, 14 R. 841.

A deliverance sustaining or refusing a composition offer is
appealable.[1] If the interlocutor is one of approval, and there is
no appeal taken, or if an appeal is refused, the bankrupt or his
successor or other party offering the composition makes a declaration (or, if required by the trustee or any creditor, an oath)
before the Sheriff that a full surrender has been made and that
there has been no collusive preference, security, payment or agreement in order to obtain concurrence to the offer of composition.[2]
Where necessary a commission may be granted to take the declaration.[2] If the Sheriff is satisfied with the declaration he pronounces
a further interlocutor discharging the bankrupt, declaring the
sequestration at an end, and reinvesting the bankrupt in his
estates.[2] This also is an appealable deliverance,[1] but the prior
question of the approval of the composition settlement cannot be
raised under this appeal.[3] That must be separately and timeously
submitted to review, upon the interlocutor in which the composition offer is approved of.[3] If the composition offered is less than
5s. in the £ a proof has to be allowed to enable the bankrupt
to show that he cannot be held responsible for his failure to pay
that amount. The trustee obtains his discharge by application
to the Sheriff in which warrant is also asked for delivery of the
bond of caution.[4] Prior to discharge the sederunt book has to
be transmitted to the accountant. The petition for discharge, if
not concurred in by the bankrupt and his cautioner, should be
intimated to these parties. If an offer of composition is made
and rejected, or if it has become ineffective, no other offer of
composition can be entertained unless nine-tenths in number and
value of all the creditors assent thereto in writing.[5]

[1] 3 & 4 Geo. V c. 20, sec. 166. As to manner of appeal, see pp. 375, 391.
[2] Ibid., sec. 137.

3 Scottish Provincial Assurance Co. v. Christie, 1859, 21 D. 333.
4 Encyclopædia of Scottish Legal Styles, VIII, p. 340.
5 3 & 4 Geo. V c. 20, sec. 142.

15. APPEAL AGAINST TRUSTEE'S DELIVERANCE.

An appeal to the Sheriff or the Court of Session may be taken against deliverances of the trustee (a) by a creditor in respect of the rejection of his claim; (b) by a creditor in respect of the admission or rejection of another creditor's claim[1]; (c) by the bankrupt (if he can show an interest) against the admission of a creditor's claim.[2]   The appeal to the Sheriff is a summary application,[3] and is presented in the form of an initial writ, narrating the deliverance of the trustee and craving its recall.[4]   The initial writ containing the appeal must be lodged with and marked by the Sheriff-clerk before the expiry of fourteen days from the date of the *Gazette* notice of payment of the dividend,[5] or in the case of an appeal by the bankrupt within fourteen days from the date of the deliverance.[6]   Where the appeal is by a creditor against the trustee's deliverance on his own claim, the trustee alone need be called as defender, but when the appeal concerns the claims of other creditors these creditors, as well as the trustee, should be called.[7]   The directions of the Bankruptcy Act as to procedure are similar to those of the Sheriff Court Act in regard to summary applications.[8]   It is in the Sheriff's discretion whether formal pleadings are required, whether a formal record be made up and closed, and whether evidence be led and/or recorded.[8]   The general intention is that the procedure is to be summary, but the decision must be in writing and must contain the reasons for the judgment.[9] If there is no record the Sheriff is directed to specify the facts and assign the grounds of his judgment.[9]   The Sheriff's judgment is an appealable deliverance, which may be submitted to review of the Court of Session by note of appeal written on the interlocutor sheet within eight days of the date of the deliverance, signed by the appellant or his solicitor, and bearing the date of signature.[10]   Where a claim has been rejected on adjudication for a first dividend, and no appeal has been taken, a subsequent appeal following on adjudication for the second dividend appears to be incompetent.[11]

1 3 & 4 Geo. V c. 20, sec. 124.
2 Ibid., sec. 165; Robertson v. Robertson's Trustee, 1885, 13 R. 424.
3 7 Edw. VII c. 51, sec. 50.
4 See Encyclopædia of Scottish Legal Styles, VIII, pp. 303-4.
5 3 & 4 Geo. V c. 20, secs. 124, 127, 129.
6 Ibid., sec. 165.
7 Skinner's Trustee v. Keith, 1887, 14 R. 563.
8 3 & 4 Geo. V c. 20, secs. 124, 165; 7 Edw. VII c. 51, sec. 50.

[9] 3 & 4 Geo. V c. 20, sec. 165.
[10] Ibid., sec. 166; Rules of Court, 1936, V 7, 8.
[11] Mactavish v. Stewart, 1930, 46 Sh.Ct.Rep. 268.

16. DISCHARGE OF TRUSTEE.

After final division of the funds he has ingathered, the trustee may apply to the Sheriff or to the Court of Session for his discharge, but before an application is made to the Court, a creditors' meeting must have been held to consider the conduct of the trustee.[1] The Sheriff, after considering the minutes of the creditors' meeting, and hearing any creditor, may pronounce or refuse decree of exoneration and discharge.[1] It does not appear to be essential to the granting of the trustee's discharge that the creditors have expressly approved of his conduct, but the application for discharge should be intimated to any objecting creditors, unless in special circumstances as where there is to be a reversion.[2] The bankrupt has no *locus standi* to object to the trustee's discharge,[3] and while the competency of objection by the accountant has been doubted[4] the usual practice is to apply for a report from him before discharge is granted. The application for discharge may be served on the accountant,[2] but a common practice now is for the trustee to transmit the sederunt book and obtain an acknowledgment before making his application. As the accountant's acknowledgment states that the trustee is entitled to discharge this obviates service on or a remit to the accountant. Any creditor is entitled to be heard on the question of discharge[5] and it is a good objection that the trustee has not yet fully executed his office,[6] or that available funds have not been ingathered.[5] A creditor will not be heard to oppose the trustee's discharge upon trifling irregularities in the conduct of the sequestration process,[7] but if there is failure to observe the statutory requirements to a material degree discharge may be refused or postponed.[8] The trustee's application for discharge is by initial writ in the usual form and it is held that an application of this kind is available to the representatives of a trustee who has died.[9] The process should be returned to the Court by the trustee at this stage. When discharge has been granted the Sheriff-clerk transmits to the accountant a signed extract of the decree which is entered in the register of sequestrations and the trustee's bond of caution is delivered up.

[1] 3 & 4 Geo. V c. 20, sec. 152.
[2] Milne v. M'Callum, 1878, 5 R. 546; Lindsay v. Hendrie, 1879, 6 R. 1246.
[3] Couper's Sequestration, 1892, 8 Sh.Ct.Rep. 207; M'Culloch, 1896, 12 Sh.Ct.Rep. 361; cf. Duke v. Somervell, (O.H.) 1903, 41 S.L.R. 20.

4 M'Cracken's Sequestration, 1896, 13 Sh.Ct.Rep. 60.
5 Hamilton's Trustee v. Caldwell, 1918 S.C. 190.
6 Bannatyne, 10th February, 1810, F.C.
7 Bruce, 1825, 4 S. 151; Craig v. Mitchell, 1895, 2 S.L.T. 488; 3 S.L.T. 20.
8 Dundas v. Lawrie, 1822, 1 S. 238; Stewart & Muir, 1828, 6 S. 749;
　　Wyllie, 1835, 14 S. 179.
9 Elder's Trustees, 1903, 5 F. 431.

17. DISCHARGE OF BANKRUPT.

The bankrupt may apply to the Sheriff or to the Court of Session for discharge. In the Sheriff Court the procedure is by summary application in the form of an initial writ narrating shortly the situation of the sequestration process. The application may be made at any time after the meeting held after the examination and at that stage requires the concurrence of all the creditors; after six months from the award of sequestration the concurrence of a majority in number and four-fifths in value is needed; after twelve months from the award a majority in number and two-thirds in value must concur; and after eighteen months from the award a majority in number and value is sufficient.[1] On the expiry of two years from the award of sequestration the bankrupt requires no concurrence of creditors.[1] The creditors' concurrence must refer in terms to the trustee's report mentioned below.[1] and if this is omitted the concurrence is held to be invalid.[2] No special form for instructing such concurrence is provided, but it should be in writing and may consist of minutes of the meeting at which the consents were given.[3] The usual practice is for the creditors or their mandatories to sign a short minute of concurrence and for the trustee to certify that the necessary consents have been obtained. The application for discharge is intimated to each creditor, whether he has lodged a claim or not, and is published in the *Edinburgh Gazette*, and if, at a diet not less than twenty-one days after the posting of the circulars to creditors and publication in the *Gazette*, no objector appears, the bankrupt will be found entitled to his discharge,[1] unless the case falls under one of the statutory provisions referred to in the next paragraph. Before the bankrupt can present his application the trustee must prepare a report on his conduct and compliance with the statutory requirements, the disclosure and surrender of the estate, and the cause of the bankruptcy.[1] The trustee's report is *prima facie* evidence of the facts set forth in it, but its terms may be challenged before the Court[4] and proof may be allowed.[5] If the trustee is dead or not available a remit may be made to the accountant of Court for

a report.[6] The trustee's report is demandable by the bankrupt
on the expiry of five months from the award of sequestration,[7]
and the trustee may not charge the bankrupt for its preparation.[8]

[1] 3 & 4 Geo. V c. 20, sec. 143.
[2] Scott & Campbell v. Couper, 1872, 10 M. 626.
[3] Bell's Commentaries, ii, 371.
[4] Findlay v. Donaldson's Trustees, 1832, 10 S. 813; Dixon's Trustees
    v. Campbell, 1867, 5 M. 767; Cooper v. Fraser, 1872, 11 M. 38;
    Cruickshank v. Gowans, 1899, 1 F. 692.
[5] Cooper v. Fraser, supra.
[6] White, 1893, 20 R. 600; Meldrum, 1895, 2 S.L.T. 405; Mackay, 1896,
    24 R. 210.   (These cases seem to imply an appeal to the nobile
    officium of the Court of Session, but in practice the same course
    is followed in the Sheriff Court.)
[7] 3 & 4 Geo. V c. 20, sec. 143; Mather v. M'Kittrick, 1881, 8 R. 952.
[8] White v. Robertson, 1879, 6 R. 854.

Apart from express statutory provisions the Sheriff has complete
discretion as to granting or refusing the bankrupt's discharge,
and discharge may be granted in spite of an unfavourable report
by the trustee.[1]   Where the dividend paid is less than 5s. in the
£ the Act prohibits discharge being granted unless the bankrupt
satisfies the Court that the failure to pay 5s. in the £ is due
to circumstances for which he cannot justly be held responsible.[2]
Whether or not the bankrupt is responsible in the sense of the
Act is held to be largely a matter for the judge of first instance,
and, while his judgment is subject to review,[2] it will not be readily
interfered with on appeal.[1]   Proof is usually necessary in cases
which fall under the section in question, and, where discharge is
refused under its provisions, the bankrupt may pay an additional
dividend to make up 5s. in the £ and then apply as if such a
dividend had been originally paid.[2]   In cases falling under the
section the first deliverance usually appoints intimation to the
accountant that he may report, and the second deliverance—proceeding on the reports by the trustee and the accountant, the
Gazette notice, certificate of posting intimation to the creditors,
and the absence of opposition by creditors—allows a proof as to
the bankrupt's responsibility for failure to pay 5s. in the £.
The Act also provides that discharge may be refused although two
years have elapsed from the date of sequestration and although
there is no opposition by creditors if it appears from the report
of the accountant of Court or other sufficient evidence that the
bankrupt has fraudulently concealed any part of his estate or
effects or has wilfully failed to comply with any of the provisions
of the Act.[3]   In this case also the Court of Session will hesitate

to interfere with the exercise of the Sheriff's discretion in granting or refusing discharge.[4]

[1] Buchanan v. Wallace, 1882, 9 R. 621; Shand, (O.H.) 1882, 19 S.L.R. 562; Bell v. Bell's Trustee, 1908 S.C. 853. See also Bremner, 1900, 2 F. 1114; Inglis, (O.H.) 1937 S.L.T. 619. (The view as to responsibility expressed in Cohen, 1944, 60 Sh.Ct.Rep. 59, appears to be unusually stringent.)
[2] 3 & 4 Geo. V c. 20, sec. 146.
[3] Ibid., sec. 149.
[4] See Millar, 1877, 5 R. 144.

A creditor is entitled to oppose the application for discharge although he has not proved his debt in the sequestration,[1] and he is not precluded from opposing because he has previously consented to the application.[2] The trustee may also oppose. While the Sheriff is expressly empowered to hear evidence both from the bankrupt and objectors on the question whether the failure to pay 5s. in the £ is due to circumstances for which the bankrupt is responsible,[3] it has been held that he is not bound to do so, and he may proceed on any information that is before him and which satisfies him on this point.[4] But he may require further evidence at any later stage before discharge is actually granted if he considers any points require to be cleared up before the bankrupt is discharged.[4] He may also obtain a report from the accountant of Court and this is usually got in all cases where the application is made after two years from the award of sequestration and there is no concurrence of creditors. Where there is opposition to the discharge it is usually based on (a) some defect in procedure in the application for discharge[5]; (b) failure by the bankrupt to comply with the statutory requirements, such as failure to disclose or to surrender estate; (c) fraudulent or collusive dealings by the bankrupt[6]; and (d) gross extravagance or reckless trading.[7] If there are no assets to meet the expenses of the sequestration the bankrupt will generally not get his discharge till these are settled.[8] If the trustee's report is, from the bankrupt's point of view, defective or incorrect the Court will not ordain him to furnish a fresh report and the bankrupt must make his submissions on this head when he applies for discharge.[9]

[1] Cant v. Bayne, 1868, 6 M. 368.
[2] See Reid v. Buchanan, 1838, 16 S. 549.
[3] 3 & 4 Geo. V c. 20, sec. 146 (2).
[4] Alison v. Robertson's Trustees, 1890, 18 R. 212.
[5] Scott & Campbell v. Couper, 1872, 10 M. 626.
[6] Millar, 1877, 5 R. 144
[7] Learmonth v. Paterson, 1858, 20 D. 418; Dixon's Trustees v. Campbell, 1867, 5 M. 767; Inglis v. Lyle, (O.H.) 1928 S.N. 58; Reid & Son's Sequestration, 1939, 55 Sh.Ct.Rep. 287.

8 M'Carter v. Aikman, 1893, 20 R. 1090; Bathgate's Sequestration, 1914, 30 Sh.Ct.Rep. 158.
9 Cruickshank v. Gowans, 1899, 1 F. 692; Hamilton v. Yule, 1903, 19 Sh.Ct.Rep. 35.

The Act provides that if there is opposition to the discharge, either on the part of the trustee or creditors, the Sheriff may either find the bankrupt entitled to his discharge or refuse the discharge, or he may defer consideration of the matter for such period as he may think proper and may annex such conditions to the discharge as the justice of the case may require.[1] Thus the Court may, as a condition of discharge, require the bankrupt to make available for his creditors a stated proportion of his salary or emoluments,[2] or it may find the bankrupt entitled to discharge but postpone granting it[3]—or postpone extract[4]—till a later date. If there is opposition and the objectors are successful the bankrupt may be found liable to them in expenses[5]; if the objectors are not successful it is not uncommon to find no expenses due, especially if the objections taken were reasonable.[6] It is not the practice to make the bankrupt find caution for expenses on an application for discharge even if he takes an appeal.[7] In one case where no creditors appeared at the meeting to elect a trustee,[8] and in another where a trustee was elected but the creditors failed to take the necessary steps to have his election confirmed,[9] the Court of Session granted a discharge to the bankrupt in virtue of the *nobile officium*—a course that would not, it is thought, be available in the Sheriff Court.

1 3 & 4 Geo. V c. 20, sec. 143.
2 Leslie v. Cumming & Spence, 1900, 2 F. 643; Hamilton v. Caldwell, 1916 S.C. 809; cf. Liddell's Motor Services, 1937, 53 Sh.Ct.Rep. 196.
3 Bell v. Bell's Trustee, 1908 S.C. 853.
4 Buchanan v. Wallace, 1882, 9 R. 621; Shand, (O.H.) 1882, 19 S.L.R. 562.
5 Mackenzie v. Keith, &c., 1925, 41 Sh.Ct.Rep. 340; Marwick, 1925, 42 Sh.Ct.Rep. 53; Levin, 1927, 43 Sh.Ct.Rep. 139; cf. Clarke v. Crockatt & Co., 1883, 11 R. 246.
6 Bain v. Milne, 1870, 8 M. 784; Sieber's Sequestration, 1894, 10 Sh.Ct.Rep. 237; Wilson's Sequestration, 1915, 32 Sh.Ct.Rep. 148; Alexander's Sequestration, 1917, 34 Sh.Ct.Rep. 277.
7 Melrose-Drover v. Heddle, 1905, 7 F. 852; Scott v. Scott's Trustee, 1914 S.C. 704.
8 Sinclair, 1932 S.N. 53.
9 Aitken v. Robson, 1914 S.C. 224.

The interlocutor finding the bankrupt entitled to his discharge also appoints him to appear and make a declaration in terms indicated by the Act that a full surrender has been made and that there has been no collusive preference, security, payment or agreement in order to obtain any creditor's concurrence to his discharge.[1] If required by the trustee or any creditor the declaration must be given by oath.[1] If the bankrupt is at the time beyond the jurisdiction, or is by some lawful cause prevented from attending to make the declaration, commission may be granted to any fit person to take the declaration or oath.[1] Where the bankrupt has died there is authority for a declaration being made by his representatives to the best of their knowledge or belief,[2] and where a bankrupt had become insane the Court of Session, in exercise of the *nobile officium*, dispensed with any declaration being granted.[3] If satisfied with the declaration or oath the Sheriff discharges the bankrupt of all debts or obligations for which he was liable at the date of sequestration, and the Sheriff-clerk thereupon transmits a signed extract of the deliverance to the accountant of Court, who enters it in the register of sequestrations.[1] An abbreviate of the deliverance is also issued by the Sheriff-clerk and is recorded in the register of inhibitions and adjudications.[4]

1 3 & 4 Geo. V c. 20, sec. 144.
2 Robertson's Trustee, 1842, 4 D. 627; Walker, 1842, 4 D. 742; cf. Gray's Executrices, (O.H.) 1928 S.L.T. 558.
3 Roberts, 1901, 3 F. 779.
4 3 & 4 Geo. V c. 20, sec. 145.

The deliverance awarding discharge can be appealed to the Court of Session by note of appeal, written on the interlocutor sheet in the way described below, within eight days of the deliverance.[1] Such an appeal does not, however, submit to review the previous interlocutor finding the bankrupt entitled to discharge which becomes final if not appealed against within eight days of its date.[2] A deliverance refusing, postponing or qualifying the right to discharge is subject to review in the same way.[1] As already indicated, the Court of Session are slow to interfere with the Sheriff's discretion as to discharge, particularly in cases where he has found the bankrupt entitled to discharge.[3]

1 3 & 4 Geo. V c. 20, secs. 146 (3), 166; Rules of Court, 1936, V 7, 8. See p. 391, infra.
2 Alison v. Robertson's Trustees, 1890, 18 R. 212.
3 See p. 385, supra.

18. MISCELLANEOUS PROCEDURE.

In the course of a sequestration process many other occasions may arise in which the aid of the Sheriff may be invoked. In such cases the procedure is by summary application, in the form of an initial writ, narrating the circumstances and stating the judicial aid desired. These applications are lodged in, and form part of, the sequestration process. The principal classes of applica-

tion specified in the Act are these : (a) application by a creditor
before a trustee is appointed to have an annuity or a contingent
claim valued, the bankrupt and the petitioning or concurring
creditor and any interim judicial factor being called as defenders[1] ;
(b) application by the trustee with the concurrence of creditors
for authority to make a special allowance to the bankrupt[2]—in
this case the minute of the creditors' meeting and the accountant's
report approving of the allowance should be produced ; (c) application by the trustee calling the bankrupt as defender and requiring
him to give information or assistance, to submit to medical examination for life assurance in connexion with the realization of a
contingent right or to sign deeds, all which the Sheriff may ordain
him to do under pain of imprisonment[3] ; (d) application by the
trustee, intimated in the *Gazette* and served on the bankrupt for
declarator that certain assets acquired by the bankrupt after
sequestration are vested in the trustee[4] ; (e) application by the
trustee to have determined any excess of an alimentary provision
of which the bankrupt may be in right, and to order payment of
such excess to the trustee, the bankrupt and any trustees charged
with payment of the provision being called as defenders[4] ; (f) application by a person claiming estate improperly included in the
sequestration, the application being served on the trustee who is
ordained to answer within a stated period[5] ; (g) application by
the trustee for a vesting order in respect of heritable estate
belonging to a deceased bankrupt whose successor has made up title
thereto, the application being served on the successor who is
required to answer within fourteen days[6] ; (h) application by
the trustee or a posterior creditor requiring a selling creditor
and the purchaser of heritable estate—who will be called as
defenders—to account for any reversion of the price[7] ; (i) application by the trustee for approval of a scheme of ranking and
division of price of heritage sold, the application being served
on the bankrupt, the accountant of Court, and the parties interested
in the application of the price[8] ; (j) application to the Sheriff on
a report by the accountant to determine the amount of the trustee's
commission on a difference having arisen between the commissioners and the accountant[9] ; (k) application by the trustee and
commissioners to authorize an alteration of the period for payment
of dividends[10] ; (l) application by the trustee calling the bankrupt
as defender and craving an order for payment to the trustee of
such portion of pay, half-pay or pension as any Government
Department concerned may consent to[11] ; (m) application by the
trustee or a creditor calling another creditor as defender and
craving that the latter should be found to have forfeited his claim

on the estate in respect of collusion[12]; (n) application by the trustee calling the bankrupt as defender and craving delivery of letters posted to the bankrupt to be opened in presence of the Court.[13]

[1] 3 & 4 Geo. V c. 20, secs. 49, 50.
[2] Ibid., sec. 74.
[3] Ibid., secs. 77, 78.
[4] Ibid., sec. 98. See also 14 & 15 Geo. V c. 27, sec. 44 (4) (b).
[5] Ibid., sec. 99.
[6] Ibid., sec. 101.
[7] Ibid., sec. 108.
[8] Ibid., secs, 112, 113.
[9] Ibid., sec. 122.
[10] Ibid., sec. 132.
[11] Ibid., sec. 148.
[12] Ibid., sec. 150.
[13] Ibid., sec. 187; Bird v. Lamont, (O.H.) 1912, 2 S.L.T. 356.

19. PROCEDURE RULES.

In a bankruptcy process conducted in the Sheriff Court the Sheriff Court rules of procedure apply where they are appropriate, and are not excluded by the Bankruptcy Act.[1] In some matters a bankruptcy process differs from an ordinary process. It does not fall asleep in a year and a day[2]; citation may be made by a competent officer without a witness[3]; certain deeds and writings, which might otherwise require stamping, are, when used for bankruptcy purposes, exempt from stamp duty[4]; and the rights of appeal are regulated by the Bankruptcy Statute and the Rules of Court and not by the Sheriff Court Act.[5] But in the broad sense a bankruptcy process is a Sheriff Court process not different from any other, and unless these are excluded it is subject to the rules which regulate the conduct of process generally.[1]

[1] See Scott & Allan v. Anstruther, 1848, 10 D. 732; Lindsay v. Hendrie, 1879, 6 R. 1246.
[2] 3 & 4 Geo. V c. 20, sec. 42.
[3] Ibid., sec. 171.
[4] Ibid., sec. 189.
[5] See next page.

While applications brought for the purpose of carrying out the provisions of the Bankruptcy Act are in general summary applications within the meaning of the Sheriff Courts Acts, it does not follow that every action by a bankruptcy trustee is necessarily a summary application. Actions by a bankruptcy trustee to cut down gratuitous alienations, or preferences, granted by an insolvent, proceed by way of ordinary action and not as summary applications. In the same way a trustee seeking to recover debts and enforce obligations to which the bankrupt had right, sues, in the manner of any other pursuer, an action for payment or implement.

In the Bankruptcy Act, the paper to be used for bringing a deliverance of the trustee or a resolution of creditors under review of the Sheriff is described as a " note of appeal."[1] But in practice an appeal to the Sheriff in a bankruptcy process is commenced by an initial writ in ordinary form, though it may be titled as a note of appeal. A judgment of the Sheriff, if further appeal is competent, is brought under review of the Court of Session by note of appeal in the same way as in an ordinary action.[2] The provisions of the Bankruptcy Act which contemplated a note of appeal written on a separate paper[2] are superseded by the Rules of Court which require the note of appeal to be written in the usual way on the interlocutor sheet or the paper which contains the deliverance appealed against.[3] This has to be done within eight days after the date of the deliverance appealed against and the note of appeal has to be signed by the appellant or his solicitor and to bear the date on which it is signed.[3] Within four days of the appeal being taken the Sheriff-clerk is directed to transmit the process to the Court of Session and to notify the other parties interested.[3] There is in bankruptcy proceedings no appeal from the Sheriff-Substitute to the Sheriff, but every deliverance pronounced in the Sheriff Court is appealable to the Court of Session, unless appeal is excluded by the Statute as, for instance, the deliverance awarding sequestration,[4] and the interlocutor declaring the election of the trustee[5]; and an ultimate appeal to the House of Lords is competent, unless barred by the Act, as upon the question of the bankrupt's right to a discharge, notwithstanding a dividend of less than 5s. per £, regarding which the judgment of the Inner House is final.[6] As appeals in sequestrations are purely the creation of the Bankruptcy Act the ordinary rule that appeals submit to review prior interlocutors in the cause[7] does not apply, so that an appeal taken against the deliverance discharging the bankrupt does not open up to review the earlier interlocutor finding him entitled to discharge.[8] An action calling the trustee to account under the Act is subject to appeal only under the Act and there is thus no right of appeal to the Sheriff.[9] Expenses in sequestrations are the subject of special provisions in the Table of Fees.[10]

[1] 3 & 4 Geo. V c. 20, sec. 165.
[2] Ibid., sec. 166.
[3] Rules of Court, 1936, V 7, 8.
[4] 3 & 4 Geo. V c. 20, sec. 30.
[5] Ibid., sec. 67.
[6] Ibid., sec. 146 (3).

⁷ See 7 Edw. VII c. 51, sec. 29.
⁸ Alison v. Robertson's Trustees, 1890, 18 R. 212.
⁹ Edinburgh Parish Council v. Craig, 1916, 34 Sh.Ct.Rep. 36; Tough's
    Trustee v. Edinburgh Parish Council, 1918 S.C. 107.
¹⁰ Act of Sederunt, 7th May, 1935, chap. VI.   See Cross v. Ferrie, 1940,
    58 Sh.Ct.Rep. 40; 1942 S.L.T. (News), p. 43.

20. Deceased Debtor.

An application for sequestration of the estates of a deceased debtor is only competent in the Sheriff Court if the deceased had resided or carried on business within the Sheriffdom for the year —that is during the whole year—preceding his death.[1] If he had not so resided or carried on business, but had resided within Scotland, and was at the time of his death subject to the jurisdiction of the Supreme Courts of Scotland, application is competent only in the Court of Session.[2] The petition may be presented by a mandatory of the deceased without the concurrence of creditors or by a creditor or creditors qualified as in the case of a living debtor.[3] The petitioning creditor does not, in the case of a deceased debtor, necessarily require to instruct notour bankruptcy, as is essential in the case of a living debtor, but while a creditor's petition may be presented at any time after the debtor's death sequestration cannot be awarded till the expiry of six months from the date of death, unless the debtor was notour bankrupt at the time of his death, or the application is made with the concurrence of the successors, or they renounce the succession.[4] On a mandatory's petition it is thought that the award can be made at once, and where the petition is made by or with the concurrence of the debtor's successors, or if they renounce the succession, the award is made forthwith on presentation.[5] " Successors " is defined to include all persons who have succeeded to any property which was vested in a party deceased at the time of his death, whether as heirs, heirs-apparent, trustees under voluntary conveyances, representatives by deed or otherwise, executors, administrators, or nearest of kin, or as assignees or legatees, and the term also includes singular successors where they have acquired the right.[6] Under a definition so wide, the persons whose concurrence should be asked is left somewhat vague, but they include all who have a direct interest in the succession. Where the petition is by a creditor without concurrence all such successors should be called as defenders in addition to the general intimation by *Gazette* notice. A successor, as well as a creditor, may oppose the granting of an award of sequestration.[7] If notour bankruptcy is proved, or if the successors concur in the petition or renounce the succession and sequestration can thus be awarded at once, a meeting to elect a trustee will be held, as in the case of a living debtor[4]; but if notour bankruptcy is not established, and the successors neither concur nor renounce, the awarding of sequestration is deferred for six months,[4] and a judicial factor may be appointed.[8] In his affidavit produced with the petition or in a separate oath the petitioning creditor must specify the place where the deceased resided, or had a dwelling-house, or carried on business in Scotland at the time of his death, and whether he was then owner of estates in Scotland.[9]

[1] 3 & 4 Geo. V. c. 20, sec. 16.
[2] Ibid., secs. 11, 16.
[3] Ibid., sec. 11. See p. 357, supra.
[4] Ibid., sec. 13.
[5] Ibid., secs. 13, 28.
[6] Ibid., sec. 2.
[7] Ibid., sec. 29.
[8] Ibid., sec. 14; J. & G. Stewart v. Waldie, (O.H.) 1926 S.L.T. 526.
[9] Ibid., sec. 23.

The proceedings subsequent to the meeting for the election of a trustee are the same in the case of a deceased debtor as in the case of a living debtor, except that there is no bankruptcy examination. But there may be examination of third parties, and, in other respects, the statutory provisions apply, except so far as they are personal to the bankrupt. In a case where there was admittedly a surplus on the estate the heir at law was held entitled, pending the sequestration, to a conveyance of heritage not required for the payment of debts.[1] In the case of a deceased debtor there appears to be no provision for a discharge of his estate and for investment of his successors, but reference may be made to the cases noted.[2]

[1] Bell's Trustees v. Bell's Trustee, 1882, 10 R. 370.
[2] See Robertson's Trustee, 1842, 4 D. 627; Walker, 1842, 4 D. 742; Gray's Executrices, (O.H.) 1928 S.L.T. 558.

In place of sequestration of the estates of a deceased person the Bankruptcy Act provides another process which is applicable where a deceased person has left no settlement appointing trustees or other parties with power to manage his estate or part thereof, or where such parties do not accept or act.[1] In such a case one or more creditors, or any person having an interest in the succession, may apply for the appointment of a judicial factor who winds up the estate under the supervision of the accountant of Court.[1] Where the assets of the deceased are estimated not to exceed £500 the application for a factor may be made to the Sheriff of the Sheriffdom within which the deceased resided, or carried on business, during the year immediately preceding the date of the application, or within which heritage belonging to the deceased at the time of his death is situated.[1] If there is no heritage the application is apparently competent only within a year of the death. The application is a summary application made by initial writ in the usual form and such intimation as may be considered necessary is to be made to the creditors of the deceased and other parties interested.[1] In the Court of Session the procedure is regulated by Rules of Court,[2] but in the Sheriff Court the procedure laid down for the appointment of judicial factors under the Judicial Factors (Scotland) Act, 1880, is to apply.[3]

[1] 3 & 4 Geo. V c. 20, sec. 163.
[2] Rules of Court, 1936, IV, 13.
[3] Act of Sederunt 16th July, 1936, 1 B; 7 Edw. VII c. 51, Schedule I, Rule 170. See p. 604, et seq., infra.

There are conflicting decisions in the Court of Session as to whether a judicial factor should be appointed on a deceased's estate under the Bankruptcy Act where an application for sequestration has already been presented and an interim factor has been appointed in view of the fact that sequestration cannot be granted till the expiry of six months from the death.[1] The question is probably one of circumstances in each case. It is in the discretion of the Court whether a factor should be appointed on an intestate estate where there is an executor or other person *in titulo* to deal with it or someone who is entitled and willing to take up the administration.[2]

[1] See 22 S.L.Rev., p. 99; Youngson, &c., (O.H.) 1911, 2 S.L.T. 448.
[2] Macfarlane, 1857, 19 D. 656; Masterton v. Erskine's Trustees, 1887, 14 R. 712; Begg & Co., (O.H.) 1893, 1 S.L.T. 274; Curle's Trustees, (O.H.) 1893, 1 S.L.T. 340; London and Brazilian Bank v. Lumsden's Trustees, (O.H.) 1913, 1 S.L.T. 262.

21. COMPANY DEBTOR.

Wherever sequestration proceedings at the instance of creditors are competent in the Sheriff Court against an individual bankrupt, they are, with the exceptions undernoted, competent against any company or corporation. In the Bankruptcy Act the expressions " debtor " and " bankrupt " apply to companies as well as individuals, and " company " is defined to include bodies corporate, politic or collegiate and partnerships and " partner of a company " includes the members of such bodies.[1] Besides the company itself being made notour bankrupt in the ordinary way, notour bankruptcy of a company may be constituted by an partner being rendered notour bankrupt for a company debt.[2]

But diligence against a partner for a private debt, or even an application by a partner for sequestration of his own estates, has no effect in constituting notour bankruptcy against the company. Notour bankruptcy may be thus constituted only when the partner is in law liable personally for company debts, and notwithstanding the definition above referred to, members of corporate bodies, who are not personally liable for the debts of the corporation, cannot be made the medium for rendering the corporation notour bankrupt. A company registered under the Companies Act is not a company in the sense of the Bankruptcy Act, and its estates are not liable to sequestration,[3] nor are bodies such as railway companies, which are by Statute exempted from ordinary diligence or which can be wound up only by statutory authority.[4] It has been held recently that a club is not liable to sequestration,[5] but a body of trustees or executors[6] and a royal burgh[7] may be sequestrated. A dissolved company is not a deceased debtor, so that its estates cannot be sequestrated at the instance of a creditor unless it is notour bankrupt.[8]

[1] 3 & 4 Geo. V c. 20, sec. 2.
[2] Ibid., sec. 6.   See Mullen v. Campbell, (O.H.) 1923 S.L.T. 497.
[3] Standard Property Investment Co. v. Dunblane Hydropathic, 1884, 12 R. 328.
[4] 30 & 31 Vict. c. 126, sec. 4; Haldane v. Girvan, &c., Railway Co., 1881, 8 R. 669; Haldane v. Rushton, 1881, 9 R. 253.
[5] Pitreavie Golf Club v. Penman, (O.H.) 1934 S.L.T. 247.
[6] Campbell & Co., (O.H.) 1899, 6 S.L.T. 406; Bain, (O.H.) 1901, 9 S.L.T. 14.
[7] Wotherspoon v. Magistrates of Linlithgow, 1863, 2 M. 348.
[8] Stewart & M'Donald v. Brown, 1898, 25 R. 1042.

Sequestration of a company is competent if it have within— which apparently means at any time within—a year before the presentation of the petition carried on business in Scotland and any partner have resided or had a dwelling-house in Scotland, or if the company had a place of business in Scotland.[1] Sequestration is competent in the Sheriff Court of any county in which the debtor, which includes a company debtor,[2] resided or carried on business for the year—which presumably means during the whole year—preceding the date of the petition.[3] The combined effect of these provisions appears to be that sequestration is competent in a Sheriff Court if the company has, during the year —that is during the whole year—before the petition is presented, had a place of business, and has therefore carried on business, within the Sheriffdom, or if the company during the same period has carried on business—without necessarily having a place of business—within the Sheriffdom and a partner has resided or had a dwelling-place within the Sheriffdom during the same period.

In the latter case it may be sufficient that the partner's residence
or dwelling-place was within Scotland though not within the
Sheriffdom, and that it was at any time within, though not necessarily during the whole of, the year.

¹ 3 & 4 Geo. V c. 20, sec. 1i.
² Ibid., sec. 2.
³ Ibid., sec. 16.

A company, being a separate *persona* in law, may apply for
sequestration of its estates under the Bankruptcy Act, or may be
sequestrated at the instance of creditors, independently of its
partners,¹ and a descriptive firm, which may be sued and charged
under its descriptive name,² may be sequestrated under that name
also. The sequestration of a company proceeds in the same manner
as that of an individual; but if a company and its partners are
all sequestrated, as is common where there are known partners
liable for company debts, the estates of the company and those
of the partners are separate estates, which must be separately
administered, and upon which it is competent, although not
essential nor usual, to elect separate trustees. In the case of a
creditor's application, citation may be made (a) by leaving a copy
of the petition and warrant at the place where the company is
carrying on, or last carried on, business, if a partner or servant
is there; (b) failing that, by leaving same at the dwelling-house
of any acting partner; or (c) if the house of such partner cannot
be found by serving such copies edictally.¹ Citation may be made
by officer or postally.³ It is doubtful whether, if the company
only has been cited as above, the estates of the individual partners
who have not been cited may be sequestrated as well.⁴

¹ 3 & 4 Geo. V c. 20, sec. 26.
² 7 Edw. VII c. 51, Schedule I, Rules 11, 151; 2 & 3 Geo. V c. 28,
    Schedule II.
³ 3 & 4 Geo. V c. 20, sec. 171.
⁴ Central Motor Engineering Co. v. Galbraith, 1918 S.C. 755. See also
    Mullen v. Campbell, (O.H.) 1923 S.L.T. 497.

22. SUMMARY SEQUESTRATION.

The process of *cessio bonorum* was abolished in 1913 and in
its place was introduced a form of summary sequestration designed
for the winding up of small insolvent estates. Summary sequestration is available wherever a debtor's assets of every description
do not in the aggregate exceed £300 in value, but it is not
applicable to the estate of a deceased debtor.¹ So far as not
expressly modified by the statutory provisions to be noted below
the normal procedure in a sequestration applies.² The petition

for summary sequestration is presented in any Sheriffdom within which the debtor resided or carried on business during—which it is thought means at any time during—the year immediately preceding the date of the petition.[3] The petition may be at the instance of the debtor without the concurrence of any creditor, or if the debtor be notour bankrupt it may be presented within four months of the constitution of notour bankruptcy by any creditor for £10 or more, or by several creditors with claims aggregating that amount.[3] In a creditors' application if they do not know within which Sheriffdom the debtor resided or carried on business within the requisite period, or if the debtor is furth of Scotland, the petition may be presented in the Court of Session.[3] It is understood that in some Sheriff Courts where heritage burdened by a bond is included in the debtor's estate, only the value of the reversion is taken into account in arriving at the total assets.[4]

[1] 3 & 4 Geo. V c. 20, sec. 174.
[2] Ibid., secs. 174, 176.
[3] Ibid., sec. 175 (1) (2).
[4] Cf. Calley v. Cargill, 1927, 44 Sh.Ct.Rep. 177, p. 179. See Goudy Bankruptcy (4th edn.), 713.

The application for summary sequestration is made by initial writ in the usual form which should aver that the debtor's total assets are within the required limit, should crave that the sequestration should proceed as a summary sequestration, and should contain a plea to the same effect. With a petition presented by the debtor himself—who need not be bankrupt or insolvent—he must lodge a state of affairs signed by him and containing the particulars required to be provided by him in an ordinary sequestration.[1] In a debtor's petition a mandate is required when the writ is not signed by the debtor himself. In a creditors' application the first deliverance is a warrant to cite and an order on the debtor to lodge a similar state of affairs with the Sheriff-clerk within six days after service.[1] The deliverance will also order intimation in the *Gazette* and (if necessary) grant diligence to recover evidence.[2] A creditor produces with his writ an affidavit and vouchers necessary to prove the debt, and evidence of notour bankruptcy if this is in his hands. In a debtor's application the petition and state of affairs are not borrowable, but a certified copy petition and state of affairs are lodged with the petition and these may be borrowed.[3]

[1] 3 & 4 Geo. V c. 20, sec. 175 (3) (4).
[2] Ibid., secs. 25, 27.
[3] Act of Sederunt, 25th May, 1937, sec. 1.

The Act provides that the Sheriff may refuse the application, with or without expenses, or may award sequestration,[1] and that the sequestration if awarded may be recalled[1] as in the case of an ordinary sequestration.[2] Differing from an ordinary sequestration the Sheriff has thus a discretion to grant or refuse an application for summary sequestration though all the statutory requisites have been complied with. A debtor's application was refused where it was held to be an attempt to abuse the process,[3] and a creditor's petition was dismissed where practically all the creditors had acceded to a trust deed.[4] But the discretion must be exercised judicially and there must be adequate grounds for refusing an application which is in order.[5] The *Gazette* notice of an award of summary sequestration is inserted in the *Edinburgh Gazette* alone, and it differs from that in an ordinary sequestration.[6] Expenses are now regulated by a special chapter in the Table of Fees.[7]

[1] 3 & 4 Geo. V c. 175 (5).
[2] See p. 361, supra.
[3] Mackay's Sequestration, 1917, 34 Sh.Ct.Rep. 152; cf. Marburg v. Drysdale, 1933, 49 Sh.Ct.Rep. 316.
[4] Reading Trust v. Adamson, 1935, 52 Sh.Ct.Rep. 225.
[5] Montgomery v. MacCallum, 1935, 52 Sh.Ct.Rep. 227.
[6] See Encyclopædia of Scottish Legal Styles, VIII, p. 345; Act of Sederunt, 25th May, 1937, sec. 2.
[7] Act of Sederunt, 7th May, 1935, chap. VII. See 1942 S.L.T. (News), p. 43.

Where the Sheriff to whom an application for summary sequestration is presented awards sequestration he may either order that the sequestration shall proceed as a summary sequestration or, if he is of opinion that it is not expedient that the sequestration should so proceed, either in respect that the state of affairs shows that the assets exceed £300 or for some other reason, he may make no such order.[1] In the latter case the Act provides that the sections relating to summary sequestrations shall no longer apply.[1] The terms of the sub-section are somewhat unfortunately worded. On a strict reading it would appear that as sequestration has *ex hypothesi* been awarded, then, if it is not to proceed as a summary sequestration, it must continue as an ordinary sequestration. But the circumstances may be such that an ordinary sequestration could not be competently awarded by the Sheriff, for example, the claims of petitioning or concurring creditors may not amount to £50, or the debtor may not have resided or carried on business in the Sheriffdom for the whole of the preceding year. If in such a case an award is made but there is no order that the sequestration proceed as a summary sequestration and it pro-

ceeds as an ordinary sequestration an application for recall would
seem to be competent in respect that the statutory requisites for
an ordinary award were not present. In a case where the creditor's
claim was under £50 and the assets were over £300 the Sheriff,
in exercise of his discretion under sub-section (5), refused to
award sequestration.[2] While the terms of the sub-section under
consideration do not seem to make refusal of the application
essential in such circumstances the same course will no doubt be
followed in other cases where the alternative is to sanction proceedings which are at least of doubtful competency. While the
wording of the sub-section may be read as inferring that the
Sheriff has discretion to sanction a summary sequestration even
if the assets exceed £300 it is thought that such is not the case
and that in these circumstances a summary sequestration is incompetent.[3] The Sheriff's decision is final on the question whether
the sequestration is or is not to proceed as a summary sequestration.[1] As in the case of an ordinary sequestration appeal is
available against an interlocutor refusing an award, but is not
competent against a deliverance awarding sequestration where
an application for recall is the only remedy.[4]

[1] 3 & 4 Geo. V c. 20, sec. 175 (6). (In practice the debtor seldom lodges
a state of affairs before the actual award of sequestration.)
[2] Calley v. Cargill, 1927, 44 Sh.Ct.Rep. 177.
[3] See 3 & 4 Geo. V c. 20, sec. 174.
[4] See p. 357, supra.

The election of the trustee and commissioners is as in an
ordinary sequestration,[1] and, within seven days of the deliverance
declaring his election, the trustee applies orally to the Sheriff who
ordains the bankrupt to appear before him for public examination at a specified day and hour.[2] It is understood that the
trustee's application is in practice accepted if made within seven
days of the deliverance confirming the election. The diet for
examination in an ordinary sequestration must be not less than
seven nor more than fourteen days from the Sheriff's interlocutor,[3]
but it is doubtful if this applies—or in certain circumstances can
apply—in a summary sequestration. Not less than seven days
before the diet of examination the trustee notifies the bankrupt—
which should be done by formal citation—to attend the diet,[4] and
he also inserts a notice in prescribed form in the *Edinburgh
Gazette*,[5] and posts to all known creditors, including those who
have claimed or are mentioned in the state of affairs, a circular
containing certain particulars including the date for lodging
claims and the time and place of the second meeting of creditors.[4]

If the examination of third parties is necessary a written application is apparently required.[6]

1 See pp. 362, 366, supra.
2 3 & 4 Geo. V c. 20, sec. 176 (1).
3 Ibid., sec. 83.
4 Ibid., sec. 176 (3).
5 Act of Sederunt, 25th May, 1937, sec. 3.
6 See Encyclopædia of Scottish Legal Styles, VIII, 347.

Where no trustee or no commissioners have been elected in a
summary sequestration at the first statutory meeting of creditors,
or at any lawful adjournment thereof, or where, for any reason,
the first statutory meeting has not been duly called or held, a
creditor of any amount who produces an oath as required for a
petitioning creditor may apply by note in the original process
to the Sheriff who awarded sequestration, or to whom the proceedings have been remitted, to appoint a special meeting to be
held in order to get the position rectified.[1] The Sheriff may grant
or refuse the application or do otherwise as he may deem proper.[1]
If he grants it the creditor who has applied must, within four
days after a copy of the Sheriff's deliverance could be received
in due course of post in Edinburgh, insert a notice in the *Edinburgh
Gazette* of the meeting appointed to be held, and of such particulars
in the original notice of sequestration[2] as have not already appeared
in the *Gazette*.[1] The meeting in question is to be held not earlier
than six nor later than twelve days from the issue of the *Gazette*
containing the notice, and at such place within the county as the
Sheriff may fix, and the purpose of the meeting is to make the
necessary elections and do such other acts as should have been
done at the first statutory meeting and were not done.[1] The
Sheriff may order such intimation or service of the application
as he may deem proper.[1]

1 Act of Sederunt, 25th May, 1937, sec. 1.
2 See 3 & 4 Geo. V c. 20, Schedule B.

Provision is made for the trustee taking possession of the
bankrupt's property and papers, adjudicating upon claims before
the second meeting of creditors, and notifying creditors whose
claims are rejected.[1] Creditors who are to object to the rejection
of their claim, or the admission or ranking of other claims, and
the bankrupt, if he is to object to the admission of any claim,
must give to the trustee and also to the other creditor—if the
admission or ranking of another claim is to be objected to—notice
by registered letter specifying particulars of the objection and
posted three days before the second meeting, and a copy of the

letter and the post office receipt must be produced to the meeting.[2]
If such notice is given the trustee applies orally to the Sheriff
to fix a diet for the summary disposal of the objections, and, if
a diet is fixed, the Sheriff-clerk issues to the bankrupt, the trustee,
or any creditor desiring to lead evidence, a diligence to cite
witnesses and havers for that or any adjourned diet.[2] When
necessary the Sheriff may grant second diligence.[2] At the diet
the Sheriff hears parties *viva voce*, and, after such proof, if any,
as he may allow, disposes of the objections summarily and settles
the ranking objected to. If any of the parties so desire the
proof must be recorded and the Sheriff is empowered to adjourn
consideration of any of the matters mentioned in the sub-section
to another diet or diets.[2] In disposing of the objections the
Sheriff makes findings in fact and in law.[2] Where the proof has
not been recorded the findings in fact are final but appeal is
competent against the findings in law; where the proof has been
recorded both sets of findings are open to appeal.[2] Apparently
by mistake the sub-section limits the right of appeal in the latter
case to "any creditor," but it is thought that any party would
be held entitled to appeal. Further procedure is as in appeals
in ordinary sequestrations.[3]

[1] 3 & 4 Geo. V c. 20, sec. 176 (2) (5).
[2] Ibid., sec. 176 (6) (a) (b) (c) (d).
[3] See p. 391, supra.

At the second meeting of creditors a date for payment of a
dividend may be fixed or the matter may be postponed.[1] If
at this meeting it appears to the trustee and commissioners that
there will be no funds for division amongst the creditors the
latter are required to direct the trustee to report orally to the
Sheriff.[1] Failing any such direction the trustee may report at
his own hand either then or at any subsequent period.[1] On such
a report being made the Sheriff may dispense with any further
procedure in the sequestration.[1] At least ten days before the
date fixed for payment of any dividend the trustee's accounts are
audited by, and his remuneration is fixed by, the commissioners
whose decision is subject to appeal to the accountant of Court.[2]
The business account of the trustee's solicitor is taxed by the Sheriff
Court auditor and is produced to the commissioners' meeting.[2]
If a second or subsequent dividend is available notice is given
of the dividend and of the date for lodging claims in order to
participate therein.[3] The trustee's adjudication upon any new
claims is subject to appeal as stated in the preceding paragraph,
but notice of objection to his deliverance must be posted at least

three days before the date for payment of the dividend.[3] Provision is made for the postponement of payment of the dividend
until any appeal is determined, for the remodelling of the state
of ranking and for the taxation and adjustment of any additional
accounts of the trustee or his solicitor.[3]

[1] 3 & 4 Geo. V c. 20, sec.176 (7) (8).
[2] Ibid., sec. 176 (9).
[3] Ibid., sec. 176 (10).

If the trustee has not been already discharged he must within
ten days after the expiry of six months from the date of his
Act and Warrant make a report to the accountant of Court containing certain prescribed particulars.[1] The accountant is required
to express his approval or disapproval of the trustee's reasons
for failing to realize the estate, and a similar report is to be
sent in within ten days after the expiry of three months from
the date of the previous one.[1] After the final division of the
funds, or if the Sheriff has dispensed with further procedure, the
trustee may take steps to obtain his discharge.[2] He delivers to
the accountant the sederunt book and accounts and a list of
unclaimed dividends and the accountant may grant a certificate
that the trustee is entitled to his discharge if he is satisfied that
the trustee has complied with all the statutory provisions, and
is otherwise entitled to be discharged, and on deposit by him in
bank of any unclaimed dividends and unapplied balances.[2] The
trustee reports orally to the Sheriff the issue of the certificate,
and the Sheriff fixes a diet for hearing any objections.[2] At least
seven days before the hearing the trustee must publish in the
Gazette a notice intimating the diet.[2] If the bankrupt or any
creditor appears, parties are heard *viva voce* or the Sheriff may
note any objections and answers, and, after any proof he may
allow, he may dispose of the matter summarily by granting or
refusing discharge.[2] The Sheriff may adjourn consideration of
any of the matters in question till a later diet or diets, and he
may grant warrant to cite witnesses or havers.[2] If discharge
is granted the Sheriff's judgment is final and his interlocutor
orders the bond of caution to be delivered up.[2] A signed extract
of the discharge is transmitted by the Sheriff-clerk to the accountant.[2] If discharge is refused the trustee may appeal to the Court
of Session.[3]

[1] 3 & 4 Geo. V c. 20, sec. 176 (13).
[2] Ibid., sec. 176 (14) (15).
[3] Ibid., sec. 176 (16). See p. 391, supra.

The Act provides that, where the Sheriff has dispensed with further procedure in a summary sequestration the bankrupt may at any time petition the Sheriff for his discharge, and the provisions of the Act relating to a bankrupt's discharge apply except those as to the periods at which the bankrupt may so petition and as to the consent of creditors.[1] The effect of this provision appears to be that where the Sheriff, for the reason already indicated,[2] dispenses with further procedure the bankrupt may forthwith, or at any later date, apply for his discharge, without the consent of creditors, in the manner and subject to the conditions relating to discharge in an ordinary sequestration.[3] In the case of a deed of arrangement or payment of composition the position as to discharge is the same as in an ordinary sequestration,[4] and where the winding up is by dividend the procedure is also the same.[3] In the last case it seems that the periods for application and the consent of creditors apply as in an ordinary sequestration.

[1] 3 & 4 Geo. V c. 20, sec. 176 (17).
[2] See p. 401, supra.
[3] See p. 384, supra.
[4] See pp. 378, 381, supra.

CHAPTER XVII.

REMOVING.

1. PURPOSE.

The process of removing is the procedure by which a landlord formally rids himself of a tenant who has ceased to have a title to occupy subjects in respect (a) that the period of his lease has expired or (b) that, although the period has not yet elapsed, circumstances have occurred which entitle the landlord to determine the lease. A formal action of removing is, as hereafter explained,[1] not always necessary, but when it is required it follows the usual course of an ordinary action.[2] In special circumstances a declarator may be necessary along with the removing to show pursuer's title to sue.[3]

[1] See p. 410, et seq., supra.
[2] MacGregor v. M'Kinnon, 1915, 32 Sh.Ct.Rep. 3.
[3] See Forsyth v. Stronach, 1945, 62 Sh.Ct.Rep. 127.

2. JURISDICTION.

The Act of 1907 provides that the Sheriff's jurisdiction includes " Actions relating to questions of heritable right or title . . . including all actions of declarator of irritancy and removing whether at the instance of a superior against a vassal or of a landlord against a tenant."[1] It is not clear why actions of removing have been included in actions relating to questions of heritable right or title which will seldom be the case in practice, but it would seem that if an action of removing can be shown to raise a question of heritable right and title either party may at the closing of the record or within six days thereafter require the cause to be remitted to the Court of Session if the value of the subjects in dispute exceeds £50 by the year or £1000 in value.[2] Actions of irritancy and removing are to be brought in the Court of the jurisdiction and district where the property forming the subject in dispute—which in this instance must mean those from which it is sought to remove or eject the defender—is situated and all parties against whom the action is brought are in such action subject to that jurisdiction.[3]

[1] 7 Edw. VII c. 51, sec. 5 (4).
[2] Ibid., sec. 5 (a).
[3] Ibid., sec. 5.

3. Subjects Let for Less than a Year.

Where houses or other heritable subjects are let for a shorter period than a year—irrespective of the amount of the rent or the nature of the subjects let—the proprietor or his factor, or any other person by law authorized to pursue a process of removing, may present to the Sheriff a summary application for removing.[1] The application is made on an official printed form of " Summary Removing Petition or Complaint," and, save where written answers are given in as explained below,[2] the proceedings are conducted as in a small debt case. Decree in such an application is declared to have the full force and effect of a decree of removing and warrant of ejection.[1] Applications of this kind are competent only against a tenant, not a squatter, but would apparently be available in the case of a house let during employment but terminable on notice.[3]

[1] 7 Edw. VII c. 51, sec. 38; Schedule I, Rule 115.
[2] See p. 407, infra.
[3] Magistrates of Buckhaven and Methil v. Wemyss Coal Co., 1928 S.C. 66; Earl of Eglinton v. M'Luckie, 1944 S.L.T. (Sh.Ct.) 21.

The Sheriff Courts Act provides that, in the absence of express stipulation, notice of removal must be given (a) where the let is for a period not exceeding four months, as many days before the ish as is equal to at least one-third of the full period of let, and (b) where the let exceeds four months, but is less than one year, at least forty days before the ish.[1] These provisions are modified in the case of houses falling under the House Letting and Rating (Scotland) Act, 1911, generally described as " small dwelling-houses," and which fall to be treated as subjects let for less than a year.[2] The latter Act provides that, if such houses are let for a period of more than three months, at least forty days' notice is required, and, if let for a period of three months or less, the notice given must be equal to at least one-third of the period of the let unless the let is for a shorter period than a month when five days' notice is sufficient.[3] Lets of small dwelling-houses, if for less than one month, must terminate on a Monday, and, if for a longer period, on the 28th day of a month or (if that is a Sunday) on the Monday following,[4] and such lets are, by notice as above, terminable on the day on which the next payment of rent falls due, if that is a lawful date for termination as above specified, or, if it is not, then on the lawful date for termination next following.[3] If the occupier of a small dwelling-house is in arrear with his rent for a period of not less than seven days he may be given forty-eight hours' notice to terminate

the let, and a certificate by or on behalf of the owner is *prima
facie* evidence of such arrears.[5]

[1] 7 Edw. VII c. 51, sec. 38.
[2] See Falkirk, &c., Co-operative Society v. Potter, 1921, 38 Sh.Ct.Rep.
       276
[3] 1 & 2 Geo. V c. 53, sec. 4.
[4] Ibid., sec. 3.
[5] Ibid., sec. 5.

Notice to terminate the let of a small dwelling-house is directed
to be given in accordance with the provisions of the Sheriff Courts
Act,[1] but that Act does not provide any special form of notice
in respect of lets for less than a year. In practice Form J is used,[2]
and the notice may be given by a messenger-at-arms or Sheriff
officer—by delivery and not by posting—or by registered letter
signed by the person entitled to give such notice, or by his solicitor
or factor, posted in time to admit of its being delivered at the
address thereon, on or prior to the last date upon which the
notice must be given, addressed to the person entitled to receive
the notice, and bearing his then known address, or, if that
is unknown, his last known address.[3] A certificate of notice
should be endorsed on a copy of the notice and signed by the
person sending it.[4] It seems clear that the notice must be in
writing.[5]

[1] 1 & 2 Geo. V c. 53, sec. 4.
[2] Cf. Barr & Sons v. Muncie, 1920, 39 Sh.Ct.Rep. 50.
[3] 7 Edw. VII c. 51, Schedule I, Rule 113.
[4] Ibid.   See Schedule I, Rule 114 (though this rule does not in terms
       apply).
[5] Aitken v. Morris, 1921, 38 Sh.Ct.Rep. 70.

The warrant to cite upon an application for summary removing
proceeds on an induciæ of two days and appoints the defender
to answer at a specified time and place.[1] When citation is made
by an officer it seems the better view that a witness is not required.[2]
The warrant of citation is signed by the Sheriff-clerk,[1] and it
and the defender's service copy are declared to be sufficient
warrant to cite witnesses.[3] Save as explained below the case is
conducted and disposed of in the summary manner in which
proceedings are dealt with in the Small Debt Court and is not
subject to review.[4] It is thought to be clear that this latter
provision excludes even the limited right of review competent in
small debt cases, but it may not exclude review by suspension on
an averment that the let is for a year or more.[5] Appearance in
Court need not be by a solicitor but may be by any person whom
the Court allows to appear.[6] If the defender has found caution

for violent profits, or if such caution has been dispensed with, he is entitled to give in written answers and, if such answers are lodged, the case proceeds as an ordinary action of removing and is subject to review in common form.[7]

1 7 Edw. VII c. 51, Schedule I, Rule 116.
2 Ibid., Schedule I, Rule 119; 2 & 3 Geo. V c. 28, Schedule II; 34 & 35 Vict. c. 42, sec. 4; cf. Lewis Sheriff Court Practice, 8th edn., 276; Wallace Sheriff Court Practice, 504.
3 7 Edw. VII c. 51, Schedule I, Rule 118.
4 Ibid., Schedule I, Rule 119; 2 & 3 Geo. V c. 28, Schedule II.
5 Robertson v. Thorburn, 1927 S.L.T. 562.
6 A v. B, 1924, 40 Sh.Ct.Rep. 25.
7 7 Edw. VII c. 51, Schedule I, Rules 121, 122; 2 & 3 Geo. V c. 28, Schedule II.

If the defender fails to appear the Sheriff may dispose of the case in his absence,[1] and it is thought that, in the normal case, he must grant decree. Where decree in absence is granted the Sheriff may give directions for the preservation of defender's goods and effects.[1] If defender, within three days of the granting of decree in absence, satisfies the Sheriff that there was reasonable excuse for his non-appearance the Sheriff may rehear the case and, if the decree has not been implemented, he may recall it on such conditions as to expenses or otherwise as he shall deem reasonable.[1] The lodging of a minute within the period would keep the matter open, but a verbal explanation at the bar by or on behalf of the defender would probably be sufficient.[2]

1 7 Edw. VII c. 51, Schedule I, Rule 117.
2 Reference may be made to the procedure for rehearing in cases under the Rent Restrictions Acts. See Acts of Sederunt, 14th December, 1923, and 17th November, 1925.

Special forms of extract decrees of ejection, absolvitor and dismissal are provided by Act of Sederunt.[1] Where ejection is granted it is to be not sooner than a specified day at 12 o'clock noon.[1] In the case of decrees in absence it seems advisable that three days at least should elapse before the date of ejection in view of the defender's right to apply for a rehearing. In the case of subjects to which the House Letting and Rating Act applies no delay beyond forty-eight hours is to be granted unless on cause shown and stated in the interlocutor, or on caution for, or consignation of, any rent due.[2] Reference is made later to the effect of the Rent Restrictions Acts.[3]

1 Act of Sederunt, 3rd February, 1933, sec. 7, Schedule F.
2 1 & 2 Geo. V c. 53, sec. 6 (2).
3 See p. 419, infra.

4. Subjects under the Agricultural Holdings Acts.

The subjects falling under the Acts are any piece of land—irrespective of size or extent—held by a tenant, which is either wholly agricultural or wholly pastoral, or in part agricultural and as to the rest pastoral, or in whole or in part cultivated as a market garden, and which is not let to the tenant during his continuance in any office, appointment or employment held under the landlord.[1] Special provision is made for notice of termination of tenancy unless (1) where the tenant has been sequestrated or has incurred an irritancy[2]; (2) where land is resumed by the landlord under the terms of the lease for building, planting, feuing or other purposes[3]; or (3) where the holding is let for any period less than a year.[4] In the latter case the above provisions in regard to notice relative to summary removings will apply.

[1] 13 & 14 Geo. V c. 10, sec. 49.
[2] Ibid., sec. 26 (4).
[3] Ibid., sec. 26 (5). No notice is usually necessary in such a case. See Kininmonth v. British Aluminium Co., 1915 S.C. 271; also Earl of Morton v. Gray, 1919, 36 Sh.Ct.Rep. 67.
[4] Ibid., sec. 26 (5).

Apart from the exceptions last mentioned the tenancy in such a holding is not terminated save on written notice by either party to the other, the period of notice being : (1) Not less than one year nor more than two years before the termination of the lease in leases for three years and upwards entered into before 24th December, 1920, or in leases of two years and upwards entered into on or after that date[1]; (2) not less than six months before the termination of the lease in leases from year to year or for any other period less than three years entered into before 24th December, 1920, and in leases from year to year or for any other period less than two years entered into on or after that date[1]; (3) not less than one year nor more than two years where a lease is renewed from year to year by tacit relocation.[2] It seems to follow from the last provision that, in the case of a yearly let renewed by tacit relocation, six months' notice would suffice in the first or original year of the let, but that at least a year's notice is required thereafter. It is not competent to contract out of the above provisions as to notice, and, failing such notice, the lease is renewed by tacit relocation.[3]

[1] 13 & 14 Geo. V c. 5, sec. 26 (1).
[2] Ibid., sec. 26 (2).
[3] Duguid v. Muirhead, (O.H.) 1926 S.C. 1078.

Notice by the landlord to the tenant under the section in question must be given either in the same manner as notice of removal under sec. 6 of the Removal Terms (Scotland) Act, 1886, or in the form and manner prescribed by the Sheriff Courts Act of 1907, and such notice, in the case of an agricultural holding, is to come in place of the notice required by the last-mentioned Act.[1] The result of this provision is that, where the land in the holding exceeds two acres in extent, notice should be in terms of Form H of Schedule I to the Sheriff Courts Act,[2] and, where the land does not exceed two acres in extent, it should be in terms of Form J to said Schedule,[3] and in either case should be given by a messenger-at-arms or Sheriff-officer or by registered letter in terms of Rule 113 to the Sheriff Courts Act,[4] the details of which have already been narrated.[5] This notice must be given in one of the three ways mentioned : notice by unregistered letter is not enough.[6] Evidence of notice to remove having been given in the Forms H or J is obtained by certificate under Rule 114 in the same way as in other removings under the Sheriff Courts Act.[7]

[1] 13 & 14 Geo. V c. 10, sec. 26 (3) (b).
[2] 7 Edw. VII c. 51, Schedule I, Rule 111. See Watters v. Hunter, 1927 S.C. 310.
[3] Ibid., Rule 112.
[4] Ibid., Rule 113; 49 & 50 Vict. c. 50, sec. 6.
[5] See p. 406, supra.
[6] Department of Agriculture v. Goodfellow, 1931 S.C. 556.
[7] 7 Edw. VII c. 51, Schedule I, Rule 114. See p. 411, infra.

The procedure relating to removings in the Sheriff Court applies to removings from agricultural holdings subject to the period of notice being as above indicated and not as specified in the Sheriff Courts Act.[1] As a result the methods of procedure under secs. 34 and 35 of the last-mentioned Act are available in the case of agricultural holdings subject to the above modification in the period of notice, but the last proviso to sec. 35, dispensing with any notice to remove in certain circumstances, will not apply to such holdings.

[1] 13 & 14 Geo. V c. 10, sec. 26 (3) (a).

5. Lands Exceeding Two Acres in Extent.

Where lands exceeding two acres in extent—which do not form an agricultural holding[1] —are let for any period not less than a year under a probative lease specifying a term of endurance, with or without an obligation on the tenant to remove without

warning, an action of removing may be unnecessary provided
notice to remove has been given.[2] In such circumstances, if previous
written notice to remove has been given, where the lease is for
three years or more, not less than one year nor more than two
years before the termination of the lease, and where the lease is
from year to year or by tacit relocation or for any other period
less than three years, not less than six months before the termination of the lease, then the lease or an extract thereof from the
books of any Court of record has the same force and effect as an
extract decree of removing obtained in an ordinary action at the
instance of the lessor, or any one in his right, against the lessee
or any party in possession, and the lease or extract, with authority
in writing signed by the lessor, or any one in his right or by
his factor or solicitor, is sufficient warrant to any Sheriff-officer
or messenger-at-arms of the Sheriffdom[3] within which the lands
are situated to eject the party in possession at the expiry of the
term or terms of endurance of the lease.[2]

[1] See p. 408, supra.
[2] 7 Edw. VII c. 51, sec. 34.
[3] This presumably means any messenger having a place of business
within the Sheriffdom.

It seems clear that the above provisions apply whether the
lands alone are let, or whether the lease is of lands over two
acres in extent along with houses, and it is expressly provided
that, where there is a separate ish as regards lands and houses
or otherwise, the notice above specified must be given before that
ish which is first in date.[1] The last provision as contained in
the Act appears to apply only to leases of less than three years,
but it is thought that this rule is common to all leases.[2] If
written notice as above is not given the lease is held to be renewed
by tacit relocation for another year and thereafter from year
to year.[1] It would seem that the statutory provisions as to notice
supersede any contractual stipulations in the lease itself.[3] The
statutory provisions are declared not to affect the landlord's right
to remove a tenant who has been sequestrated, or who has incurred
an irritancy or other liability to removal by non-payment of rent,
and the provisions as to notice do not apply to stipulations in a
lease entitling the landlord to resume land for building, planting,
feuing or other purposes.[1] It is also provided that removal or
ejectment in virtue of sec. 34 is not competent after six weeks
from the date of the ish last in date, and also that the terms of

the section do not prevent proceedings under any lease in common form.[1]

[1] 7 Edw. VII c. 51, sec. 34.
[2] Rankine, Leases, 3rd edn., 567.   See Montgomerie v. Wilson, 1924, 40 Sh.Ct.Rep. 113.
[3] See Duguid v. Muirhead, (O.H.) 1926 S.C. 1078, pp. 1082-3.

The notice required to be given is to be as nearly as may be in the Form H annexed to the Sheriff Courts Act,[1] and may be given by a messenger-at-arms or Sheriff-officer—by delivery and not by posting—or by registered letter signed by the person entitled to give such notice or by his solicitor or factor, posted in time to admit of its being delivered at the address thereon, on or prior to the last date upon which the notice must be given, addressed to the person entitled to receive the notice and bearing his then known address, or, if that is unknown, his last known address.[2] The notice must be given in one of the three ways mentioned : notice by unregistered letter is not enough.[3]   A certificate of notice dated and endorsed upon the lease or extract and signed by the Sheriff-officer, messenger-at-arms or by the person giving the notice, or his solicitor or factor, or an acknowledgment of notice endorsed on the lease or extract by the party in possession, or his solicitor, is sufficient evidence that notice has been given.[4]

[1] 7 Edw. VII c. 51, Schedule I, Rule 111.   See Watters v. Hunter, 1927 S.C. 310.
[2] Ibid., Rule 113.
[3] Department of Agriculture v. Goodfellow, 1931 S.C. 556.
[4] 7 Edw. VII c. 51, Schedule I, Rule 114.

Where a tenant in possession of lands exceeding two acres in extent, whether with or without a written lease, grants a letter of removal, either at the date of entering upon the lease or at any other time,[1] in terms of Form I annexed to the Act,[2] which is either holograph or attested by one witness, such letter has the same effect as an extract decree of removing and is a sufficient warrant for ejection[1] in the same way as the Act provides in the case of a lease or extract thereof,[3] and is operative against the granter of the letter of removal or any party in his right within the same time—that is not later than six weeks from the ish last in date—and in the same manner, after notice to remove has been given as above indicated.[4]   The certificate or acknowledgment of notice is endorsed on the letter of removal.[5]   But where the letter of removal is dated and signed within twelve

months before the date of removal or before the first ish, if there
is more than one ish, no notice by either party is necessary.[1]

[1] 7 Edw. VII c. 51, sec. 35.
[2] Ibid., Schedule I, Rule 111, Form I.
[3] See p. 410, supra.
[4] See p. 410, supra.
[5] 7 Edw. VII c. 51, Schedule I, Rule 114.

In the above two cases falling under secs. 34 and 35 of the
Act, no process of removing or ejection is necessary and the tenant
may be ejected without any decree given in Court. But the landlord need not use the shorthand methods provided by these sections
and in cases where there is a *bona fide* dispute it may be more
convenient to have the matter brought into Court by an ordinary
action of removing[1] under which, if decree is granted, the defender
will be ordained to flit and remove under pain of ejection.[2] An
action of removing may be raised at any time provided the tenant
has bound himself to remove by writing dated and signed within
twelve months of the term of removal or of the ish first in date
if there is more than one.[3] It is thought that the " writing "
referred to need not be either holograph or tested, and it has been
held that it is something different from the lease itself.[4] If no
such writing has been granted an action of removing may be raised
at any time, in the case of leases of three years and upwards, if
not less than one year nor more than two years elapse between
the notice of removal and the removal term first in date, and,
in the case of leases, written or verbal, from year to year, or
for any period less than three years or under tacit relocation if
not less than six months elapse between the notice of removal and
the removal term first in date.[3]

[1] See MacGregor v. M'Kinnon, 1915, 32 Sh.Ct.Rep. 3.
[2] As to competency of separate crave for ejection failing defender
removing, see Patten v. Morison, 1919, 35 Sh.Ct.Rep. 252; Graham
v. Lister, &c., 1919, 35 Sh.Ct.Rep. 281.
[3] 7 Edw. VII c. 51, Schedule I, Rule 110.
[4] Cesari, &c. v. Anderson, 1922, 38 Sh.Ct.Rep. 137.

Where lands exceeding two acres in extent are occupied by a
tenant without any written lease and the tenant has not granted
a letter of removal the lease may be terminated on written notice
by or on behalf of one party to the other not less than six months
before the determination of the tenancy.[1] The notice is in Form H
annexed to the Act[2] and is given and evidenced as already
explained.[3] As in this case there is no lease the certificate of
notice is endorsed on a copy of the notice certified as correct
by the person, Sheriff-officer, messenger-at-arms, solicitor or

factor sending the same, the certificate itself being signed by such party and being sufficient evidence that notice has been given.[4] If the tenant fails to remove after notice has been given the proprietor may apply for and obtain a summary warrant of ejection against the tenant and every one deriving right from him.[1] It is thought that the summary warrant of ejection referred to in this section is identical with the warrant for summary ejection provided for under sec. 37 of the Act. The application is made by initial writ craving warrant summarily to eject the defender and is treated as an ordinary cause.[5] Technically the action is one of removing and the tenant is entitled to state such defences as would have been open to him in a removing.[6]

[1] 7 Edw. VII c. 51, sec. 36.
[2] Ibid., Schedule I, Rule 111, Form H.
[3] See p. 411, supra.
[4] 7 Edw. VII c. 51, Schedule I, Rule 114.
[5] Cf. Campbell's Trustees v. O'Neill, 1911 S.C. 188.
[6] See Campbell's Trustees v. O'Neill, supra.

6. Subjects other than Lands Exceeding Two Acres in Extent.

In the case of all heritable subjects (other than lands exceeding two acres in extent) let for a year or more other provisions apply.[1] In addition to the above general class of subjects the section is expressly applied to houses with or without land attached not exceeding two acres in extent, lands not exceeding two acres in extent let without houses, mills, fishings and shootings,[1] but all these appear to be covered by the more general description. In such cases notice is to be given in writing to the one party by or on behalf of the other as nearly as may be in the Form J annexed to the Act.[2] It is provided that notice is to be given at least forty days before 15th May or 11th November, according as the ish is Whitsunday or Martinmas.[1] No provision as to length of notice is made where the ish is other than at Whitsunday or Martinmas, but probably forty days' notice before the actual ish is sufficient.[3] Notice for Whitsunday given on 5th April has been held to be insufficient.[4] The notice is given by messenger-at-arms, or Sheriff-officer or by registered letter as already explained,[5] and a certificate of notice dated and endorsed upon a certified copy of the notice signed by the party sending the notice is sufficient evidence that the notice has been given.[6]

[1] 7 Edw. VII c. 51, sec. 37.
[2] Ibid., Schedule I, Rule 112, Form J.
[3] See Rankine, Leases, 3rd edn., 573.
[4] M'Leod v. George, 1933, 49 Sh.Ct.Rep. 302.
[5] 7 Edw. VII c. 51, Schedule I, Rule 113. See p. 406, supra.
[6] Ibid., Rule 114.

Notice as above, whether given to the landlord or to the tenant, entitles the proprietor to apply to the Sheriff for what the Act describes as " a warrant for summary ejection in common form " against the tenant and every one deriving right from him.[1] The application is made by initial writ craving warrant summarily to eject the defender and is technically an action of removing all as already explained.[2] While written notice as above is an essential preliminary to an application for a warrant for summary ejection[3] an action of removing in ordinary form can competently be brought in the case of urban properties following an informal notice to quit which is sufficient at common law.[4] There are Sheriff Court decisions to the effect that, if an action of removing from an urban property is brought forty days before Whitsunday, in terms of an Act of Sederunt of 1756,[5] no notice of removing is required.[6] These decisions seem to ignore the fact that the Act of Sederunt does not apply to urban subjects[7] though it may well be that an action brought at such a time would be held as giving the tenant adequate notice to quit. Although notice to remove has been given in statutory form there seems to be nothing incompetent in the action following upon it being in ordinary form and not a statutory application for summary ejection.[8]

[1] 7 Edw. VII c. 51, sec. 37.
[2] See previous page.
[3] Taylor v. Brown, 1913, 30 Sh.Ct.Rep. 215; Plumb v. Maynall, 1920, 37 Sh.Ct.Rep. 23.
[4] Craighall Cast-Stone Co. v. Wood Bros., 1931 S.C. 66, and see Gillies v. Fairlie, 1919, 36 Sh.Ct.Rep. 6; Grant v. Bannerman, 1919, 36 Sh.Ct.Rep. 59; Lord Advocate v. Dykes, 1921, 37 Sh.Ct.Rep. 133; Kirk v. Aitchman, 1928, 45 Sh.Ct.Rep. 317; cf. Ritchie v. Lyon, 1939, 56 Sh.Ct.Rep. 39.
[5] Now C.A.S. L, XV, 2.
[6] Green v. Young, 1919, 35 Sh.Ct.Rep. 201; Kerr v. Young, 1920, 36 Sh.Ct.Rep. 184.
[7] Wright v. Wightman, 1875, 3 R. 68; Rankine, Leases, 3rd edn. 562.
[8] Reid v. Anderson, 1919, 36 Sh.Ct.Rep. 11.

7. Form of Notices.

The rules provide that notices of removal given in terms of the Act are to be as nearly as may be in the forms prescribed in the Schedule,[1] and there have been a number of decisions as to the extent to which the statutory forms may be departed from. Slight discrepancies may, generally speaking, be ignored, but any material deviation from the prescribed form may render the notice inept.[2] A misdescription of the subjects is usually fatal,[3] and a notice relating to part only of the subjects let is altogether ineffectual.[4] Where the removal term is 28th May it would probably be held immaterial that a notice in Form J after requiring removal at Whitsunday did not add, as it should, " being the 28th day of May,"[5] but if the notice in such a case required removal on 15th May it would probably be held to be bad.[6] The notice must definitely require the tenant's removal, and one couched in conditional terms will be ineffectual.[7] There are conflicting decisions as to whether a notice given by an officer must state on whose behalf it is given.[8] Notice in proper form but by unregistered letter does not fulfil the requirements of Rule 113.[9]

[1] 7 Edw. VII c. 51, Schedule I, Rules 111, 112.
[2] Patten v. Morison, 1919, 35 Sh.Ct.Rep. 252; Grant v. Bannerman, 1919, 36 Sh.Ct.Rep. 59; Core v. Gray, 1919, 36 Sh.Ct.Rep. 113; Oban Town Council v. Erwin, 1945 S.L.T. (Sh.Ct.) 27; Richards v. Cameron, 1946, 62 Sh.Ct.Rep. 106; cf. Naysmith v. Maxwell, 1924, 41 Sh.Ct.Rep. 318; Rutherford v. Oswald, 1945 S.L.T. (Sh.Ct.) 9.
[3] Scott v. Livingstone, 1919 S.C. 1. See also Cameron v. Ferrier, 1912, 28 Sh.Ct.Rep. 220; cf. Naysmith v. Maxwell, supra.
[4] Gates v. Blair, 1923 S.C. 430.
[5] Campbell's Trustees v. O'Neill, 1911 S.C. 188.
[6] Macdonald v. Cameron, 1916, 32 Sh.Ct.Rep. 261; Anderson v. Scott, 1938, 55 Sh.Ct.Rep. 143.
[7] Murray, &c. v. Grieve, 1920, 36 Sh.Ct.Rep. 126; Ritchie v. Lyon, 1939, 56 Sh.Ct.Rep. 39; cf. Watt, &c. v. Findlay, 1920, 37 Sh.Ct.Rep. 34.
[8] M'Lauchlin v. Mowat, 1920, 36 Sh.Ct.Rep. 116; Seggie v. Haggart, 1925, 42 Sh.Ct.Rep. 284.
[9] 7 Edw. VII c. 51, Schedule I, Rule 113; Department of Agriculture for Scotland v. Goodfellow, 1931 S.C. 556.

8. EXTRAORDINARY REMOVINGS.

The foregoing paragraphs deal generally with the cases of removing or ejection of a tenant at the expiry or natural termination of a lease. Where removal is desired before the natural termination the process is one of extraordinary removing to which the special provisions of the Act of 1907 have no application. For an extraordinary removing in this sense an ordinary action of removing requires to be raised and the cases in which this is necessary include the following : (1) where an agricultural tenant is two years in arrear with his rent[1] ; (2) in cases where the landlord's hypothec has been abolished and the tenant of an agricultural holding[2] is six months in arrear with his rent the landlord may bring an action of removing at the next ensuing term of Whitsunday or Martinmas and decree will be granted unless the tenant pays or finds caution for the outstanding arrears as well as security for a further year's rent[3] ; (3) in agricultural subjects where the tenant is one year in arrear, or deserts possession or leaves the subjects unlaboured, and the remedy under (2) above is not available,[4] the landlord may take action to ordain the tenant to find caution for the arrears and for the next five years' rents failing which he will be removed[5]; (4) where the tenant has incurred a conventional irritancy under a lease the appropriate remedy is an action of declarator of the irritancy and removing.[6] In the last case the declarator of the irritancy is usually combined with a removing, but in certain circumstances it may be enough to bring a removing alone.[7]

[1] Codifying Act of Sederunt, L, XV, 4.
[2] For definition, see p. 408, supra.
[3] 13 & 14 Geo. V c. 10, sec. 25.   See Fletcher v. Fletcher, 1930, 47 Sh.Ct.Rep. 336.
[4] Ibid., sec. 25 (3).
[5] Codifying Act of Sederunt, L, XV, 5.
[6] See 7 Edw. VII c. 51, sec. 34.
[7] Duke of Argyll v. Campbeltown Coal Co., 1924 S.C. 844.

9. Caution for Violent Profits.

Under the older practice the defender in an action or a process of ejection—other than an ejection against a party without a title—was required to find caution for violent profits if his defence was not instantly verifiable as contrasted with having to be established by proof in the ordinary way.[1] To give the landlord this right it was essential that his own title to sue did not itself require proof.[2] If it did both parties stood in the ·same position and caution could not be demanded.[2] The right to caution applied generally in ordinary removings, and whether it could be demanded in extraordinary removings depended on circumstances.[2] In the case of ordinary removings at any rate the landlord's demand for caution as a matter of right has now been abrogated and the Sheriff is given a discretion to order or dispense with caution.[3] By Rule 110 of the Act of 1907 it is provided that the Sheriff may in any defended action of removing order the defender to find caution for violent profits.[3] The rule applies to ordinary removings in respect of subjects let for a year or more.[3] In the case of lets for less than a year Rule 121 appears to infer a similar option by recognizing that caution may be dispensed with.[4]

[1] See Rankine, Leases, 3rd edn., 580.
[2] Ibid., 582.
[3] 7 Edw. VII c. 51, Schedule I, Rule 110.   See Milne v. Darroch, 1934, 53 Sh.Ct.Rep. 3.
[4] Ibid., Rule 121 ; 2 & 3 Geo. V c. 28, Schedule II.   See also p. 407, infra.

The measure of violent profits may generally be taken as the aggregate of (1) any damage done to the subjects by the defender, and (2) the profit which the pursuer could have made out of the property.[1] The motion for caution can be made as soon as appearance has been entered, and, if an order for caution is made and not implemented, decree of removal or ejection may be granted at once. The interlocutor ordering caution is only appealable with leave.[2]

[1] See Rankine, Leases, 3rd edn., 585; also Gardner v. Beresford's Trustees, 1877, 4 R. 1091.
[2] Jack v. Carmichael, 1892, 10 Sh.Ct.Rep. 242; Buchanan v. Dickson, 1934, 51 Sh.Ct.Rep. 41.

10. EJECTION OF PERSON WITHOUT TITLE.

In the case of one holding subjects *vi, clam, aut precario* the appropriate remedy for the owner of the property is an action of ejection[1] which proceeds as an ordinary cause but craves the summary ejection of defender. Such an action falls under the jurisdiction of the Sheriff at common law, and is not specially dealt with in the Act of 1907. To justify this form of process the defender must either never have had a title to occupy or any such title must have been legally terminated.[2] If the defender has a title to occupy an action of ejection is not competent and an action of removing must be brought, but it is not a valid objection to an action of removing that the defender has no title to occupy, and therefore an action of ejection would have been competent and appropriate.[3] A proprietor in personal occupation of security subjects who has made default in payment of principal or interest is by Statute deemed to occupy without a title and can be removed by an action of ejection,[4] but this remedy is not available to the holder of an *ex facie* absolute disposition with back letter.[5] Caution for violent profits cannot be demanded in an action of ejection.[4] The right of appeal in such actions is considered later.[6] Proceedings by way of ejection are not rendered incompetent by the fact that a question of law is involved.[7]

[1] See Rankine, Leases, 3rd edn., 593.
[2] Ibid. See Scottish Property Investment Society v. Horne, 1881, 8 R. 737; Gibson & Son v. Gibson, 1899, 36 S.L.R. 522; Dunbar's Trustees v. Bruce, 1900, 3 F. 137; Walker v. Kerr, 1917 S.C. 102; Lowe v. Gardiner, 1921 S.C. 211; Scottish Supply Association v. Mackie, 1921 S.C. 882; Cooney v. Taylor, 1922 S.L.T. (Sh.Ct.) 6; Steven v. Mackay, 1931, 54 Sh.Ct.Rep. 234; Stonehaven Town Council v. Masson, 1938, 54 Sh.Ct.Rep. 142; cf. Breadalbane v. Cameron, 1923 S.L.T. (Sh.Ct.) 6; Eastman v. Barclay, 1930, 48 Sh.Ct.Rep. 90.
[3] Breadalbane v. Cameron, supra; Earl of Eglinton v. M'Luckie, 1944 S.L.T. (Sh.Ct.) 21.
[4] Inglis' Trustees v. Macpherson, 1910 S.C. 46.
[5] Scottish Property Investment Society v. Horne, supra.
[6] See next page.
[7] Cairns v. Innes, 1942 S.C. 164.

11. Extract Decrees.

Under sec. 113 of the Act of Sederunt of 1839 a decree of removing could be extracted forty-eight hours after the inter-locutor was signed,[1] but that Act of Sederunt has fallen with the repeal of the Sheriff Courts Act of 1838,[2] and, as in the case of other interlocutors, extract may be issued after the expiry of seven days in the case of a decree in absence (or if the action is being tried as a summary cause), or after a lapse of fourteen days in the case of a decree *in foro*, or at such earlier date as the Sheriff may allow.[3] A decree of removing will normally be put into execution at once but it has been held that a delay of three weeks in giving a charge after the term of removing does not amount to waiver on the part of the landlord.[4] Under a decree of removing the defender is charged to remove on forty-eight hours' warning under pain of ejection.[5] If the charge is not obeyed the Sheriff-officer can carry out the ejection without further recourse to the Court.[5] It is not necessary in a summary ejection to give the defender a charge before ejecting him.[6]

[1] Act of Sederunt, 10th July, 1839, sec. 113.
[2] Inglis' Trustees v. Macpherson, 1910 S.C. 46.
[3] 7 Edw. VII c. 51, Schedule I, Rule 85. See p. 254, supra.
[4] Taylor v. Earl of Moray, 1892, 19 R. 399.
[5] 55 & 56 Vict. c. 17, sec. 7 (4).
[6] See 55 & 56 Vict. c. 17, Schedule Form 9.

12. Review.

Under the Court of Session Act of 1825 it was provided that where a judgment of an inferior Court ordained a tenant to remove from lands or houses the tenant could only have the judgment reviewed by suspension.[1] The above provision was held inappli-cable to cases where the defender was in possession without a title[2] or was not a tenant[3] and thus the restriction of review to suspension did not apply to ejection of squatters and the like.[4] Nor did the section apply where decree of removing was not granted but refused. But it was held to apply where a warrant for summary ejection was asked under sec. 37 of the Sheriff Courts Act on the ground that such an action was in substance a removing[5] —a view which it is thought would equally apply to a summary warrant of ejection asked under sec. 36. The restriction in the mode of review applied only when the matter was taken to the

Court of Session and appeal from the Sheriff-Substitute to the Sheriff was available in the usual way.

1 6 Geo. IV c. 120, sec. 44.
2 Barbour v. Chalmers & Co., 1891, 18 R. 610.
3 Clark v. Clarke, 1890, 17 R. 1064.
4 Robb v. Brearton, 1895, 22 R. 885.
5 Campbell's Trustees v. O'Neill, 1911 S.C. 188; Mackay v. Menzies, 1937 S.C. 691.

By the Rules of Court of 1936[1] as amended in 1938[2] it is provided that the rules contained in sec. 3 of chap. V shall, notwithstanding any provision in any Act of Parliament to the contrary, apply with regard to all appeals from any interlocutor, judgment or determination (including decrees of removing) pronounced by any inferior Court (other than the Land Court) which may competently be submitted to review to the Court of Session or to a judge thereof.[1] By the amendment of 1938 the words " which may competently be submitted to review " were substituted for " against which it is competent to appeal "[2]; and it is thought that this amendment and the express reference to decrees of removing result in the virtual repeal of sec. 44 of the 1825 Act and provide a right of appeal in lieu of suspension in the cases referred to in the preceding paragraph where suspension alone was formerly competent. The method of appeal is thus the same as has been already described in the case of other actions.[3]

1 Rules of Court, 18th March, 1936, V 7.
2 Act of Sederunt, 12th July, 1938.
3 See p. 289, et seq., supra.

13. Rent Restrictions Acts.

The progress and result of processes of removing and ejection are materially affected by the Rent Restrictions Acts which, in one form or another, have been continually in force since 1915. The main provision of the Acts as affecting such a process is that no order for recovery of possession of any dwelling-house to which the Acts apply, or for the ejectment of a tenant therefrom, shall be made unless (1) the Court considers it reasonable to make such an order, and (2) one or more of certain specified circumstances are present, one of which is that any rent lawfully due from the tenant has not been paid.[1] It is further provided that at the time of the application for, or the making of, any such order or one for ejectment, or, if such order has been made and not executed, then at any subsequent time, the Court may adjourn the application, or stay or suspend execution of the order, or postpone the date of possession, for such period and subject to such conditions (if any) in regard to payment of rent, arrears or profits and otherwise as the Court thinks fit, and if such conditions are complied with the Court may discharge or rescind the order for possession.[2] As a result of these provisions decree is usually given against a tenant who is protected by the Acts and is in arrear with his rent, only after several continuations granted on condition that he makes some payment in addition to current rent in order to reduce the arrears. By Act of Sederunt applications under the Acts are to be made by initial writ or by minute in any pending process[3], and in the case of a summary removing the process is deemed to be pending though decree for ejection has been given, and the decree and warrant have been given up to the party in right of it, provided it has not been executed.[4] Applications made by initial writ are to be dealt with as summary applications.[3] Applications to stay or suspend execution on the decree, or to discharge, rescind or vary the decree, are made by minute in prescribed form on which a warrant is granted to cite the pursuer in the original application on two days' induciæ and an interim sist of execution is granted if asked.[4] Thereafter parties are heard and the matter is disposed of in such a way as may be appropriate.

[1] 23 & 24 Geo. V c. 32, sec. 3 (1), Schedule I.
[2] 10 & 11 Geo. V c. 17, sec. 5 (2); 13 & 14 Geo. V c. 32, sec. 4.
[3] Act of Sederunt, 14th December, 1923, sec. 2.
[4] Act of Sederunt, 17th November, 1925.

14. SUPERIOR AND VASSAL.

Included among the actions relating to questions of heritable right or title which are expressly declared to be competent in the Sheriff Court are all actions of declarator of irritancy and removing whether at the instance of a superior against a vassal or of a landlord against a tenant.[1] In such actions against a vassal the normal crave is for declarator of the irritancy, of the avoidance thereby of the feu right, and of the superior's right to enter into possession and dispose of the subjects; and for an order on the vassal to flit and remove from the subjects within a stated time failing which for warrant for his summary ejection. The action proceeds as an ordinary cause and the only specialty is contained in a loosely phrased provision in Rule 110 of the 1907 Act.[2] This requires the pursuer to call as parties to the action the last entered vassal and such heritable creditors and holders of postponed ground burdens as are disclosed by a search for twenty years prior to the raising of the action, the expenses of the search being declared to form part of pursuer's expenses of process.[2] The last entered vassal is presumably intended to mean whoever is infeft as owner of the feu, and the reference to holders of postponed ground burdens appears to infer that all parties with rights heritably secured on the subjects and disclosed by the search ought to be convened as defenders. The action falls to be raised in the Sheriff Court of the jurisdiction and district where the subjects are situated, and there would appear to be a right in either party to have the cause remitted to the Court of Session at the closing of record or within six days thereafter, if the action raises a question of heritable right or title and the value of the property exceeds £50 by the year or £1000 in value.[3]

[1] 7 **Edw. VII** c. 51, sec. 5 (4).
[2] Ibid., Schedule I, Rule 110.
[3] Ibid., sec. 5.

CHAPTER XVIII.

SEQUESTRATION FOR RENT.

1. Purpose.

Proceedings in a process of sequestration for rent are competent only in the Sheriff Court,[1] and should be raised in the Sheriff Court of the district where the subject of let is situated. The purpose of this process is to make available to a landlord in security, or in satisfaction of rent, moveables over which the landlord has a right of hypothec. By the Hypothec Abolition (Scotland) Act, 1880, the right was abolished as regards rent of lands exceeding two acres in extent (including rent of any buildings thereon) let for agriculture or pasture.[2] In the case of agricultural holdings other remedies for non-payment of rent are now available to a landlord,[3] and certain modifications in the right of hypothec have also been made in the case of urban properties.[4] Where sequestration for rent is available in non-urban subjects it must be exercised within three months after the last term of payment, for the crop of any one year is hypothecated only for the rent of that year, and neither stock nor crop can be sequestrated after the lapse of three months.[5]

[1] Duncan v. Lodijensky, 1904, 6 F. 408.
[2] 43 Vict. c. 12, sec. 1.
[3] 13 & 14 Geo. V c. 10, sec. 25.
[4] 1 & 2 Geo. V c. 53, sec. 10; 10 & 11 Geo. V c. 17, secs. 16 (1), 18 (1) (a).
[5] See Rankine, Leases, 3rd edn., 384.

The process of sequestration is largely used for the recovery of rents of urban subjects, but, as the hypothec falls three months after the last term of payment of rent, sequestration is inept unless brought within that period.[1] In " small dwelling-houses "[2] there is an exemption from hypothec in the case of furniture to be selected by the occupier to the value of £10 and of all bedding and tools used as a means of livelihood by the occupier or any member of his family.[3] It is competent for a landlord to sequestrate either in security or for payment, and in the most common form of process there is a craving for both. Sequestration in security is usually asked on averments that the tenant is *vergens ad inopiam*, or is removing effects, or otherwise endangering the hypothec,[4]

and if the rent is duly paid no expenses will usually be awarded
to either party.[5] But the landlord may be found entitled to his
expenses in such circumstances if he shows that his action was
justified.[6] In neither sequestration for payment nor in security
is there any notice given to the tenant. Upon presentation of
an application for sequestration the Sheriff, unless a caveat has
been lodged, usually sequestrates the tenant's effects and grants
warrant to inventory and secure.[7] Such a warrant includes
authority to open shut and lockfast places, and it will be signed
by the Sheriff.[8]

[1] See Rankine, Leases, 3rd edn., 384.
[2] 1 & 2 Geo. V c. 53, sec. 1; 10 & 11 Geo. V c. 17, secs. 16 (1), 18 (1) (a).
[3] 1 & 2 Geo. V c. 53, sec. 10.
[4] See Donald v. Leitch, 1886, 13 R. 790, where the need for such aver-
    ments is not definitely decided; also Macguire v. Hayes & Co.,
    1897, 13 Sh.Ct.Rep. 197.
[5] Nicol v. Mercer, 1902, 18 Sh.Ct.Rep, 253; Kilburn v. Wilson, 1903,
    19 Sh.Ct.Rep. 249; cf. Sinclair v. Morrison, 1902, 18 Sh.Ct.Rep.
    254.
[6] Scott v. Mansergh, 1905, 21 Sh.Ct.Rep. 283; Primrose's Trustees v.
    Cocker, 1905, 22 Sh.Ct.Rep. 111; M'Gregor v. Scott, 1906, 22
    Sh.Ct.Rep. 270.
[7] 7 Edw. VII c. 51, Schedule I, Rule 105.
[8] Ibid., Rule 7.

2. PROCEDURE.

Where there is power to sub-let, whether express or implied,
a principal tenant may pursue an action of sequestration against
his sub-tenant; and this process is also available to a heritable
creditor if he is in possession of the subjects under a decree of
maills and duties.[1] Joint proprietors may sue jointly, or each
may sue a sequestration process for his own share of the rent[2];
and the process is open to a liferenter[3] or one who has obtained
an assignation to a landlord's right.[4] Under the Small Debt
Act " landlord " is defined to include any person having a right
to exact rent, whether as owner, liferenter, heritable creditor in
possession, principal tenant or otherwise.[5]

[1] See Forsyth v. Aird, 1853, 16 D. 197; MacRosty v. Phillips, 1897, 13
    Sh.Ct.Rep. 274; 1898, 14 Sh.Ct.Rep. 69.
[2] Stewart v. Wand, 1842, 4 D. 622.
[3] Rankine, Leases, 3rd edn., 369; cf. Zuill v. Buchanan, 1833, 11 S. 682.
[4] See Guthrie & M'Connachy v. Smith, 1880, 8 R. 107; Duncan & Son
    v. Smith, 1904, 20 Sh.Ct.Rep. 161.
[5] 7 Will. IV & 1 Vict. c. 41, sec. 37.

The writ usually craves (a) sequestration in security and/or
for payment of rent past due and to become due; (b) warrant to sell
and for payment to pursuer from the proceeds; (c) decree against

defender for any balance due; (d) order to replenish if insufficient
effects are left on the premises after sale; and (e) failing replenishment warrant to eject defender and authority to pursuer to relet
the premises. The proceedings are not affected by the tenant's
sequestration in bankruptcy.[1]

[1] Hardie v. Adamson, 1922, 39 Sh.Ct.Rep. 229.

The first deliverance sequestrating the tenant's effects—which
must be signed by the Sheriff—has no effect in passing the property
in the articles inventoried. It merely identifies the articles as
under sequestration. The inventory may be appended to the writ
with the officer's execution of service, or there may be a separate
execution of the inventory specifying the articles secured and it
is conclusive of what is sequestrated.[1] The inventory includes
all items subject to the hypothec irrespective of their value in
relation to the rent due.[2] The Sheriff may order the sequestrated
effects to be sold, and the proceeds consigned.[3] A tenant who
interferes with articles so sequestrated may become liable to fine
or imprisonment for breach of sequestration,[4] and third parties
who defeat a sequestration may also be liable in damages to the
landlord.[5]

[1] Horsburgh v. Morton, 1825, 3 S. 596. It is not necessary to appraise
the items in the inventory—Town Council of Lochgilphead v.
M'Intyre, 1940, 59 Sh.Ct.Rep. 178.
[2] Breadalbane v. Toberonochy Slate Quarry Co., 1916, 33 Sh.Ct.Rep. 154.
[3] 7 Edw. VII c. 51, Schedule I, Rule 106.
[4] See Bell's Principles, 1244; Goldie v. Oswald, 1839, 1 D. 426.
[5] Jack v .M'Caig, 1880, 7 R. 465.

3. BREACH.

Breach of sequestration, like breach of interdict, is contempt
of Court, for the sequestrated articles, when they have been inventoried by an officer of Court, are theoretically in the custody of
the Court.[1] The complaint takes the form of a summary application at the instance of the landlord, the initial writ in which
narrates the sequestration, and the alleged breach of it, and craves
the Court to ordain the defender to appear personally and to
restore the articles or find caution for the rent. The landlord must
obtain the concurrence of the procurator-fiscal to the application
which also craves the imposition of a fine on the defender and
imprisonment failing payment of the fine. If the defender do
not appear, wilful breach of sequestration is presumed, and decree
and warrant of imprisonment may follow, but the defender may

appear and show that, in the circumstances, his action was not wilful, in which case no penalty is usually enforced.[2]

[1] Bell's Principles, 1244.
[2] Kippen v. Oppenheim, 1846, 8 D. 957.

4. WARRANT TO CARRY BACK.

When articles subject to hypothec have been removed before sequestration has been granted the landlord may obtain a warrant to bring them back to his premises to be sequestrated, for articles subject to hypothec cannot validly be sequestrated and inventoried elsewhere than upon the premises let. To obtain a warrant the landlord includes such a crave in his writ or lodges a separate minute or endorses such a minute upon the writ. The minute enumerates the articles removed, states how they were removed and where they are, and craves warrant to bring them back. Whilst warrant to carry back may be granted *de plano* if averments are made which seem to justify this course the usual practice is to intimate to the tenant and to any third party in whose custody the articles are before the warrant is granted.[1] A pursuer who acts upon a warrant obtained without notice to the defender does so at his own risk and may be liable in damages if it was taken without due cause.[2]

[1] Johnston v. Young, 1890, 18 R. (J.) 6; M'Laughlan v. Reilly, 1892, 20 R. 41; cf. Shearer v. Nicoll, (O.H.) 1935 S.L.T. 313.
[2] Gray v. Weir, 1891, 19 R. 25; Jack v. Black, 1911 S.C. 691.

To justify a warrant to carry back being granted, the articles must be still subject to the landlord's hypothec. Thus, in the case which not infrequently occurs, where a tenant has occupied a dwelling-house for a year ending at Whitsunday, and has at that term duly paid his rent and before 28th May removed his furniture, the landlord is not entitled to warrant to carry back the furniture to sequestrate it in security of further rent, for the furniture, not having been in the house on or after 28th May, never was subject to hypothec for rent accruing after Whitsunday.[1] But sequestration has been held competent when applied for between 15th and 28th May in respect of rent due in advance on 15th May and unpaid.[2]

45; M'Queen v. Armstrong, 1908, 24 Sh.Ct.Rep. 377.
[1] Thomson v. Barclay, 1883, 10 R. 694; Sawers v. Kinnair, 1897. 25 R.
[2] Henderson v. Huzzard, 1934, 50 Sh.Ct.Rep. 300.

5. Decree.

Warrant of sale in a sequestration process is not granted till the term of payment of the rent has passed. In an action of sequestration in security only, after sequestration is granted in the first deliverance, the case is generally continued till the term of payment. If the rent is not then paid, and the action is defended, the case will proceed in the same manner as any other defended action. In an action of sequestration for past due rent only, or in the most common form of action, which combines sequestration for payment of past due rent with sequestration in security of current rent, when appearance is entered the action (after sequestration is granted) follows the usual procedure applicable to a defended action. In order to ensure that the sequestrated effects will be available when wanted, the Sheriff may, at the first calling or at any subsequent stage, appoint a person to take charge of the effects, or may require the tenant to find caution that they shall be made furthcoming.[1]

[1] 7 Edw. VII c. 51, Schedule I, Rule 109.

If the action is undefended, or if the defence is repelled and rent is past due, the Sheriff grants warrant to sell so much of the sequestrated effects as will satisfy the rent, interest and expenses. The usual form of minute craving decree is appended to the writ for this purpose. The sale is carried out at the sight of an officer of Court, or of such other person as the Court may appoint,[1] who is usually a licensed auctioneer, and after such intimation as the Court orders, which is usually by newspaper advertisement and by handbills. The sale must be reported by the pursuer to the Sheriff-clerk within fourteen days, and he must lodge the roup rolls or certified copies thereof and a state of debt.[2] The report of the sale specifies any surplus and with it are lodged as productions, in addition to the roup roll, any vouchers for outlays and the newspaper containing the advertisement. If there is a surplus that should be consigned with the Sheriff-clerk, and the defender may move to uplift it. If there is a deficit the Sheriff may, in the interlocutor approving the report of the sale or by separate interlocutor, give decree against the defender for any balance remaining due.[3] If, after sale, rent is still due or may become due, and the subjects are displenished, the landlord may ask for replenishment or caution, and, failing that, for ejection and warrant to relet. Such craves are usually included in the original writ, but if not they may be contained in a minute lodged at this stage.

¹ 7 Edw. VII c. 51, Schedule I, Rule 106.
² Ibid., Rule 107.
³ Ibid., Rule 108.

Sequestration for rent is competent in the Small Debt Court, if the whole rent in respect of which sequestration is asked does not exceed £20.¹ Originally the small debt process covered only rent past due, but it now extends to all sequestrations applied for *currente termino* or in security.² Every sequestration for rent, whether in the ordinary or in the Small Debt Court, must be recorded in the special register kept by the Sheriff-clerk under the Hypothec Amendment Act of 1867,³ or in the Act Book of Court or other suitable register.⁴ Procedure in sequestration for rent in the Small Debt Court is dealt with in more detail below.⁵

¹ 7 Will. IV & 1 Vict. c. 51. sec. 5; 7 Edw. VII c. 51, sec. 42.
² 7 Edw. VII c. 51, sec. 43.
³ 30 & 31 Vict. c. 42, sec. 7.
⁴ Act of Sederunt, 3rd February, 1933, sec. 2.
⁵ See p. 482, infra.

A party sued in a process of sequestration may enter appearance in the usual way, but, as an alternative, he may at any time after service of the writ apply to have the sequestration recalled upon caution or consignation. Before the first diet of compearance this application is by a separate writ, narrating the sequestration process and craving recall, in the same manner as an application for recall of arrestments. In the general case the defender's more convenient course is to await the first calling, and then to tender caution or make consignation,¹ and to move for recall of the sequestration. If sequestration is recalled on general caution, and decree is ultimately granted, the cautioner as well as the tenant is liable both for the rent and the expenses of the process.²

¹ See Alexander v. Campbell's Trustees, 1903, 5 F. 634.
² Clark v. Duncan, 1833, 12 S. 158.

6. Third Party.

A party not called as a defender may have an interest in a sequestration process, as owner of effects ostensibly falling within the landlord's hypothec, but which are not really the property of the tenant. An officer making an inventory under a sequestration warrant is entitled to include all the effects which he finds upon the premises, and mere intimation by a third party to the officer of a claim to the ownership of effects within the premises has no effect in the sequestration process. If a third party desires to vindicate his alleged proprietary interest, he may intervene in the process and ask the Court to exclude from the warrant of sale the articles in question, and at that stage interdict is not an appropriate remedy,[1] but if warrant of sale has been granted the proper course is to raise an action of interdict in the Sheriff Court, narrating in the initial writ the inclusion of such effects in the sequestration inventory and the claimant's title to the ownership thereof, and craving interdict against their being sold.[2]

[1] Lindsay v. Earl of Wemyss, 1872, 10 M. 708; Hoare v. Mackay, (O.H.) 1905, 13 S.L.T. 588; M'Intosh v. Potts, 1905, 7 F. 765.
[2] Jack v. Waddell's Trustees, 1918 S.C. 73.

The third party claimant who wishes to intervene before a warrant of sale is granted lodges a minute in the sequestration craving leave to compear, specifying the articles he claims and asking that *quoad* them the sequestration be recalled.[1] The minute should specify the grounds on which the articles fall to be excluded —other than merely ownership in the claimant—and should include a note of pleas in law.[1] The minute is served on the pursuer. Answers are ordered and a record is made up. The minute and answers will usually be treated as initiating a separate cause.[1]

[1] See Ryan v. Little, 1910 S.C. 219; Boni v. M'Iver, 1933, 49 Sh.Ct.Rep. 191.

Superiors have a right of hypothec similar, but preferable, to that of a landlord, and this can be made good in an action of sequestration for feu duty.[1] In practice a superior usually resorts to a poinding of the ground.

[1] Yuille v. Lawrie, 1823, 2 S. 155; Anderson's Trustees v. Donaldson & Co., 1908 S.C. 38.

CHAPTER XIX.

SERVICE OF HEIRS.

1. JURISDICTION.

Judicial procedure for obtaining a formal title upon succession to heritable property is one of the matters in which the Court of Session has not concurrent jurisdiction with the Sheriff Court. The local Sheriff's jurisdiction in this matter is, however, concurrent with that of the Sheriff of Chancery, and in some cases the jurisdiction of the Sheriff of Chancery is privative. The office of Sheriff of Chancery is now united with that of Sheriff of the Lothians and Peebles at Edinburgh.[1] The process is regulated by the Conveyancing Acts of 1868 and 1874, and an extract decree of service granted by the Sheriff, recorded and extracted in the manner prescribed by Statute, is equivalent to the retour of a service under the older law and practice.[2]

[1] 23 & 24 Geo. V c. 41, sec. 31 (1).
[2] 31 & 32 Vict. c. 101, sec. 37.

2. FORM OF APPLICATION.

An application relating to service of heirs is a civil proceeding in the Ordinary Sheriff Court, and is therefore an " action," but it is not commenced by an intial writ in the usual form[1] but by petition in the form prescribed by the conveyancing Statutes,[2] addressed to the appropriate local Sheriff or to the Sheriff of Chancery, as the case may be, setting forth the facts and circumstances in narrative form, and concluding with a prayer to serve the petitioner heir. The petition is to be signed by the petitioner or his mandatory,[3] so that a solicitor who signs for a petitioner has to obtain a special mandate, which must be holograph or tested and may be contained in some more general deed.

[1] 7 Edw. VII c. 51, sec. 3 (d), Schedule I, Rule 1.
[2] 31 & 32 Vict. c. 101, sec. 29, Schedules P, Q; 37 & 38 Vict. c. 94, secs. 10, 43, Schedule E.
[3] 31 & 32 Vict. c. 101, sec. 29.

3. FORUM.

A petition for general service may be presented in the Sheriff Court of the county, or district of a county, within which the deceased proprietor of the heritable subjects had at the time of his death his ordinary or principal domicile; or, in the option of the petitioner, it may be presented to the Sheriff of Chancery at Edinburgh.[1] If the deceased had no domicile in Scotland (or if his domicile is unknown or doubtful) it is presented to the Sheriff of Chancery.[1]

[1] 31 & 32 Vict. c. 101, sec. 28. See also A B, 1895, 12 Sh.Ct.Rep. 253.

A petition for special service may be presented either to the Sheriff of Chancery, or in the Sheriff Court of the county or district where the lands (or the burgh containing the lands) lie.[1] If the lands are in different counties, or in several burghs in different counties, the petition must be presented to the Sheriff of Chancery.[1] County in relation to services means geographical county and not the registration district,[2] and if a Sheriffdom comprises two or more counties these remain separate so far as services are concerned.

[1] 31 & 32 Vict. c. 101, sec. 28.
[2] E.g., subjects in Glasgow lie in Lanarkshire.

If a petitioner craves general service and special service, in the same character,[1] he may combine the applications in one petition and such combined petition is in practice accepted in the county where the lands lie though that is not the county of the domicile of the deceased proprietor. The combined petition may also be presented to the Sheriff of Chancery.

[1] 31 & 32 Vict. c. 101, sec. 48.

4. Procedure.

No procedure can take place upon the petition till it has been published.[1] The publication is arranged for by the Sheriff-clerk and is made edictally at Edinburgh in all cases, and also in the local jurisdiction where the lands lie or where the deceased's domicile was (if known and in Scotland) upon the walls of the district Court-house.[1] Notice by registered postal letter is also given by the Sheriff-clerk to any person who has lodged a caveat.[2] After the lapse of fifteen days from the last date of publication, or twenty days in the case of publication in Orkney and Shetland, or thirty days where a deceased proprietor has died abroad, evidence may be taken by the Sheriff or his commissioner.[3] Notice of the expiry of the induciæ is given by the Sheriff-clerk. Any justice of the peace,[3] any notary public admitted to practise in Scotland,[4] or the provost or a bailie of any city or royal or parliamentary burgh may act as commissioner without special appointment, or a commissioner may be appointed by the Sheriff.[3] The petitioner's solicitor, though qualified as above, should not act as commissioner.[5] The ordinary Sheriff Court rules as to taking evidence on commission apply, and when the commissioner has reported the evidence the Sheriff may serve the petitioner, or refuse the service, or dismiss the petition. The petitioner's solicitor appears to be a competent witness,[6] although it is understood that the Chancery Office does not accept this view, and for that reason it is well to avoid having the solicitor as one of the witnesses. If the Sheriff think it necessary or desirable he may, before pronouncing decree, require additional evidence,[7] or may hear interested parties, but where there is no competition decree is usually granted immediately upon the evidence being reported to the Sheriff.

[1] 31 & 32 Vict. c. 101, sec. 30.
[2] Ibid., sec. 31.
[3] Ibid., sec. 33.
[4] Ibid., sec. 3.
[5] A B, 1869, 12 Sh.Ct.Rep. 254.
[6] Boyle, 1853, 15 D. 432; 16 Vict. c. 20, sec. 2.
[7] Wilson, 1917, 34 Sh.Ct.Rep. 101.

Where documentary evidence falls to be produced, as will be the case in all petitions for special service or for service as heir of provision, an inventory of productions must be made out and this is certified either by the Sheriff or by the commissioner who takes the proof.[1] The inventory and productions are lodged with the Sheriff-clerk along with the proof. It has been held that the Sheriff may competently grant diligence for recovery of documents.[2]

[1] 31 & 32 Vict. c. 101, sec. 33.
[2] Irving's Trustees v. Irving, (O.H.) 1894, 1 S.L.T. 665.

Petitions for service may be amended or restricted. Incidental errors can usually be corrected without a minute, but for more serious alterations a minute of amendment or restriction is desirable. Amendment is not competent after the decree has been extracted. It is for the Sheriff to decide whether republication is necessary following an amendment being allowed.

5. COMPETITION.

If there are competing petitions, they may be conjoined and proof heard in regard to the one claim as against the other, in the same manner as in any other competitive process.[1] The Sheriff is also directed to dispose of the question of expenses at the same time as he pronounces decree upon the petitions, and a diet for hearing the competitors is usually fixed, after the evidence has been received, and before decree is pronounced.[1]

[1] 31 & 32 Vict. c. 101, sec. 35.

6. APPEAL.

There is no appeal from the Sheriff-Substitute to the Sheriff. But when either the local Sheriff or the Sheriff of Chancery has refused to serve a petitioner, or has dismissed a petition, or has repelled the objection of an opposing party, his judgment is subject to review by the Court of Session, upon a note of appeal, which may be signed within fifteen days of the date of the judgment, or where the proceedings have taken place in Orkney and Shetland within twenty days.[1] The procedure in such appeals is now regulated by the Rules of Court.[2] If the Court of Session decide that service should be granted, they do not themselves pronounce decree, but remit the process back to the Sheriff that he may do so.[1]

[1] 31 & 32 Vict. c. 101, sec. 42.
[2] Rules of Court, 1936, V 7-13.

In opposed and competitive petitions, any of the parties may remove the proceedings to the Court of Session for jury trial at any time before proof is begun.[1] To do so a note is written on the interlocutor sheet requiring the cause to be remitted to the Court of Session and the procedure is regulated by the Rules of Court.[2] If the result of the Court of Session proceedings is that service is to be granted, a remit is made to the Sheriff to grant decree.[1]

[1] 31 & 32 Vict. c. J01, sec. 41.
[2] Rules of Court, 1936, V 14-15.

7. OBJECTION.

Any interested person may appear in a service process, but the usual ground of opposition is that the objector has a competent claim to be served heir.[1] He need not necessarily present a competing petition, although it is convenient that he should do so, nor does he require to lodge a notice of appearance.[1] He must, however, state his objections in writing, which may be done by minute, and the Sheriff is directed to dispose of the objections in a summary manner, but he may hear parties and if necessary may make up a record, upon the petition and minute of objections, and take proof.[1] As an interlocutor repelling objections is subject

to appeal[2] a note should be appended setting forth the grounds
of judgment.[3]

¹ 31 & 32 Vict. c. 101, sec. 40.   See Moncrieff v. Moncrieff, 1904, 6 F.
   1021 ; Sim v. Duncan, 1900, 2 F. 434.
² Ibid., sec. 42.
³ 7 Edw. VII c. 51, Schedule I, Rule 82.

8. Extract.

When final decree of service has been pronounced by the Sheriff
of a county the Sheriff-clerk transmits the process to the Keeper
of the Registers and Records of Scotland, the decree is recorded,
and an extract thereof is sent to the Sheriff-clerk for issue to the
party.[1] If decree of service applicable to separate parcels of land
has been prayed for, and the lands are identified in the petition,
separate extracts may be given out if this has been craved in the
petition.[1]

¹ 31 & 32 Vict. c. 101, sec. 36.   See S.R. & O., 1922, No. 670; Act of
   Sederunt, 15th July, 1932.

9. Reduction.

Decree of service may be challenged in an action of reduction
by a party alleging a competing title within twenty years of the
heir's infeftment and entering into possession.[1] Decree will not
be reduced on account of a mistaken description of the character
of the heir, if it appear that he was, in fact, the proper successor
to the deceased proprietor.[2] The Court of Session may in an
action of reduction allow further evidence to be taken or may
direct the case to be tried by jury.[1] If reduction is granted the
extract decree must be recorded in the sasine register.[3]

¹ 31 & 32 Vict. c. 101, sec. 43; 37 & 38 Vict. c. 94, sec. 13.
² 37 & 38 Vict. c. 94, sec. 11.
³ 14 & 15 Geo. V c. 27, sec. 46; Mulhearn v. Dunlop, (O.H.) 1929 S.L.T.
   59.

10. Completion of Title.

The procedure for obtaining special service is, by the Conveyancing Act, 1874, made applicable to the case of a person
desiring to procure himself infeft in lands to which his author
had only a personal right as heir by survivance of his ancestor.[1]
The Sheriff's decree sets forth the links in the chain of title between
the proprietor last infeft and the petitioner, and, when recorded
in the appropriate register, this decree has the same effect as an
extract decree of special service.[1]

¹ 37 & 38 Vict. c. 94, sec. 10, Schedule E.

11. Heir of Last Surviving Trustee.

The heir of the last surviving trustee may be an heir of provision under the will or other deed constituting the trust if
such heir is called in the description. In that case he may serve
as heir of provision in trust.[1] If this is not the position the heir
of the last surviving trustee may under Statute complete title
to the estate held in trust in the same way as any other heir,
but in that case he does not (except in certain circumstances)
administer the trust but conveys the estate to a new trustee, a
judicial factor or the beneficiaries.[2]

[1] See White v. Anderson, (O.H.) 1904, 12 S.L.T. 493; Brown v. Hastie,
    1912 S.C. 304; Glasgow Western Infirmary v. Cairns, (O.H.) 1944
    S.C. 488.
[2] 37 & 38 Vict. c. 94, sec. 43.

CHAPTER XX.

COMMISSARY PRACTICE.

1. INTRODUCTORY.

As in the case of succession to heritage, so also in the case of a moveable succession, the Sheriff is the official who declares the title of the successor. The original jurisdiction in such matters was in the Commissary Courts, but these were finally abolished as separate tribunals in 1876, and their powers and duties transferred to the Sheriff Court.[1] The Sheriff Courts Act of 1907 did not affect the special regulations applicable to commissary practice, but in some respects altered the forms of process. Thus regard must still be had to the older Statutes, and to the relative Acts of Sederunt, as well as to the schedule of modern procedure rules.

[1] 39 & 40 Vict. c. 70, sec. 35.

2. EXECUTOR-NOMINATE.

An executor-nominate does not require to apply to the Court by formal action to obtain appointment, for the will itself contains his appointment; but to enable him to uplift and discharge debts, and generally to administer the estate, the executor must be confirmed by the Sheriff. The duty of the Court is rather administrative than judicial, and is largely discharged by the Sheriff-clerk. In the ordinary case the executor produces the instrument nominating him, along with an inventory of the estate of the deceased, duly sworn to, both of which are recorded in the books of Court, whereupon the Sheriff-clerk issues a writ of confirmation, called a "testament-testamentar," ratifying the appointment of the executor, and authorizing him to administer the estate.[1] An executor-nominate, unlike an executor-dative, does not require to find caution for his intromissions.[2] Failing an executor-nominate or, if none has been appointed, testamentary trustees, and, failing them, a general disponee or universal legatory, or residuary legatee, is held to be an executor-nominate and is entitled to confirmation as such.[3]

[1] 21 & 22 Vict. c. 56, secs. 8, 10; Act of Sederunt, 3rd February, 1933, sec. 5, Schedules B, C.
[2] 4 Geo. IV c. 98, sec. 2.
[3] 63 & 64 Vict. c. 55, sec. 3.

In the normal case the inventory and the writ containing the appointment are forwarded to the Sheriff-clerk conducting commissary business for the county or district of the deceased's domicile and no local solicitor is needed.[1] But if the authentication of the testamentary writing is irregular or its terms *quoad* the appointment are ambiguous or there are other peculiarities, the Sheriff-clerk may intimate that he cannot issue confirmation without the authority of the Sheriff, and in that case an initial writ for warrant to issue confirmation must be presented by a solicitor entitled to practice in the Court. The position in regard to caveats is dealt with below.[2]

[1] C.A.S., V 5.
[2] See next page.

In the case of a competition for the office of executor turning on the validity of different testamentary writings the duty of the Sheriff as commissary judge is to determine the question on the face of the deeds put before him, and he is not entitled to go into such matters as the power of the testator to grant one of the testamentary writings.[1] Questions of the latter kind fall to be determined by a tribunal other than the Commissary Court.[1]

[1] See Martin v. Ferguson's Trustees, 1892, 19 R. 474; MacHardy v. Steele, 1902, 4 F. 765. See also Young v. Bell, 1921, 40 Sh.Ct.Rep. 221.

3. EXECUTOR-DATIVE.

Where there are no executors-nominate executors-dative may be appointed by the Sheriff. An application to the Court for such appointment is commenced by initial writ in terms of the Sheriff Courts Act.[1] The initial writ, besides giving the name and designation of the deceased, and the date and place of his death, should state where he had his ordinary or principal domicile, and also the character in which the pursuer craves to be appointed executor —as, for instance, relict, next-of-kin, creditor, or legatee.

[1] 7 Edw. VII c. 51, sec. 3 (d), Schedule I, Rule 1.

4. PROCEDURE.

No defenders are called in the application for appointment and no service is necessary, but the application is intimated by the Sheriff-clerk on the walls of the Court-house, or in a conspicuous place in the Court and in his office, and at the office of the Extractor of the Court of Session in Edinburgh.[1] Any person interested is entitled to appear to oppose the appointment craved, but, in general, opposition is made on the ground that the objector has himself a title to the office, and in that case he should present a competing application; if he is not competing for appointment he lodges answers. When a competing application is presented the Sheriff will order intimation to prior applicants, and to any executor already decerned upon any part of the deceased's estate.[2] After confirmation in one application has been issued, a competing application is incompetent, without reduction of the grant of confirmation. But a competing application can be presented without a reduction if the original grant has been extracted but confirmation has not been issued.[3]

[1] 21 & 22 Vict. c. 56, sec. 4. See S.R. & O., 1929, No. 588; Act of Sederunt, 19th July, 1929; Act of Sederunt, 9th July, 1937.
[2] 39 & 40 Vict. c. 70, sec. 44.
[3] Webster v. Shiress, 1878, 6 R. 102.

A caveat may be lodged[1] either against confirmation being issued or against an application for appointment as executor. The party who has lodged the caveat receives intimation when the application is made, and, if the caveat is against the issue of confirmation, he must lodge a note of objections. The applicant is then required to lodge a writ answering the objections and craving confirmation. The matter at issue is disposed of on these pleadings or the objector may be ordained to answer the application for confirmation. If the caveat is against an application for appointment the objector, on receiving intimation of the application being presented, should lodge answers or a competing application. Caveats fall on the expiry of one month but may be renewed.[2]

[1] See C.A.S., L, V 4.
[2] Act of Sederunt, 16th July, 1929, Part II, 26.

An opposed application for the appointment of an executor, or a conjoined process of competing applications, in effect becomes an ordinary Court process in which a record may be made up, and, if necessary, proof taken, as in any other contested cause, and the judgment of the Sheriff is subject to review in common form. In an unopposed application, if the pursuer is a relative of the deceased, the relationship is in practice assumed to be as stated, but if the applicant claims on other grounds he must produce with his initial writ *prima facie* evidence of his title to the office, as, for instance, the will appointing him a legatee, or the documents vouching the debt of a creditor.

An application for appointment of an executor may be called in Court on the first Ordinary Court day occurring after the lapse of nine days from the date of the certificate of intimation which is endorsed by the Sheriff-clerk upon the initial writ.[1] If there is no opposition decree will be granted decerning the pursuer executor as craved. If the application is in order the Sheriff has apparently no discretion in the matter.[2] If the application is opposed the Sheriff may order objections or answers, as the circumstances may require, or may continue the case that a competing application may be conjoined. In some Sheriffdoms formal calling in Court of unopposed applications is dispensed with. In such cases a minute craving decree is usually required though in certain Courts this is not asked.

[1] 21 & 22 Vict. c. 56, secs. 5, 6; 39 & 40 Vict. c. 70, sec. 44.
[2] Henderson, 1906, 22 Sh.Ct.Rep. 186.

5. CONFIRMATION.

When decree has been pronounced decerning a person executor on an unopposed application, extract may be given out after the lapse of three days.[1] In a contested case extract is not issued until after the lapse of fourteen days unless the Sheriff shortens the time.[2] Such an appointment may give the executor a title to sue a debtor to the deceased, but it does not invest him with full power to uplift and discharge or administer the estate. To obtain a complete title he must first make payment of any Government duties, lodge an inventory of the estate, and obtain confirmation in the same manner as an executor-nominate. The title issued to the executor who has been appointed by the Court is termed a " testament-dative."

[1] 21 & 22 Vict. c. 56, sec. 6.
[2] 7 Edw. VII c. 51, Schedule I, Rule 85

Confirmation will not be issued to an executor-dative until he has found caution for the amount of the estate confirmed to, or for such less amount as the Sheriff may accept.[1] If restriction is asked the executor must apply by initial writ setting forth any facts and circumstances which are relied upon as warranting the caution being restricted, and craving an order restricting the amount. The application for restriction should not be included in the petition for appointment.[2] The usual procedure is to order public intimation by newspaper notice and to allow objections to be lodged within ten days or other short time. The cautioner must not be beneficially interested in the estate, and must be subject to the jurisdiction of the Scottish Courts. In modern practice caution is usually found through an insurance or guarantee company. The bond of caution is never delivered up.

[1] 4 Geo. IV c. 98, sec. 2.
[2] Girdwood, &c., 1930, 46 Sh.Ct.Rep. 115.

Provision is now made for the issue of certificates each confined to one item of estate—the total holding in British Government stocks and in any one company or concern being reckoned as one item—which *quoad* such item are to be valid and effectual to anyone acting on the faith of them as if the confirmation itself had been exhibited.[1] Such certificates—which are now confined to estate situated in Scotland[2]—may, if desired, be obtained by parties other than the executor.[3]

[1] Act of Sederunt, 3rd February, 1933, sec. 5; Act of Sederunt, 11th December, 1936.
[2] Act of Sederunt, 11th December, 1936, Schedule.
[3] Watt, 1942 S.C. 214.

6. Forum.

The application for the appointment of an executor must be presented to the Sheriff Court of the county or district within which the deceased person was domiciled.[1] If the deceased was domiciled furth of Scotland or had no fixed or known domicile, but left property within Scotland, the application must be presented in the Sheriff Court at Edinburgh.[1]

[1] 21 & 22 Vict. c. 56, sec. 3.

7. Testament Implying Nomination.

If a testamentary writing is so expressed as to create doubt whether or not a party named in it has been nominated as executor, the party claiming that office may apply to the Court, not for appointment as executor-dative, but for confirmation as executor-nominate.[1] In modern practice the application would crave warrant to issue confirmation. In the general case such applications will involve merely a construction of the testamentary writing, and the Sheriff may decide the question *de plano*, but in some cases it may be desirable first to order public advertisement. If the crave is granted the applicant is confirmed executor-nominate, and does not require to find caution.

[1] See Tod, 1890, 18 R. 152; Martin v. Ferguson's Trustees, 1892, 19 R. 474.

8. Recall of Appointment of Executor.

The appointment of an executor-dative may be recalled in the

Sheriff Court where decree was granted if confirmation has not yet been issued.[1] The crave for recall is usually made in an application by one having a prior title to the office of executor, and who also craves for his own appointment in room of the party already appointed. He should ask intimation to the party who has already obtained the decree. If not, the Court will order intimation to him. Incidental applications for recall of decrees appointing executors may be necessary where a will appointing executors has been found, or in order to correct an error in naming or designing an executor, or in respect of the death of one of those appointed. Such applications may be made by minute endorsed on the initial writ craving recall and, if appropriate, a new appointment in the terms desired.

[1] See Webster v. Shiress, 1878, 6 R. 102; Johnstone, &c. v. Johnstone, 1903, 20 Sh.Ct.Rep. 50.

9. CONJUNCTION OF APPLICANTS.

A person who cannot challenge the title of another to the office, but who has himself the same relationship and qualification, may, before confirmation is issued, apply to be conjoined in the office of executor-dative. The initial writ should narrate the appointment already made and the pursuer's relationship to the deceased, and to the executor already appointed, and crave that he be conjoined in the office of executor. Intimation should be asked to be made to the executor already appointed.

10. EXECUTOR-CREDITOR.

Where no executors confirm to an estate, a creditor of the deceased, with a liquid or duly constituted debt, may apply for his appointment as executor-dative *qua* creditor. In his initial writ the pursuer will set forth the nature of his debt, and he must produce his documents of debt. Notice of the application must be inserted at least once in the *Edinburgh Gazette* and a copy of the *Gazette* is produced in process.[1] As explained below,[2] the creditor may if desired take up the office of executor only so far as necessary to satisfy his debt.

[1] 4 Geo. IV c. 98, sec. 4.
[2] See next page.

Not only a creditor of the deceased, but a creditor of the deceased's next-of-kin, having first constituted his debt against the next-of-kin, is entitled to apply for the office of executor for the purpose of making good his debt out of the portion of the deceased's estate falling to the next-of-kin. The initial writ should narrate the fact of the decease, the interest of the next-of-kin in the deceased person's estate, and the particulars of the pursuer's claim against him. The document of debt should be produced. The death of the next-of-kin does not prevent the creditor's confirming.[1]

[1] Smith's Trustees v. Grant, 1862, 24 D. 1142.

To entitle him to administer the estate of the deceased, even to the extent of operating payment of his own debt, an executor-creditor must obtain confirmation in the same manner as any other executor, and must give up a complete inventory of the estate and find caution, but he may confirm only to part of the estate, in which event he finds caution only to the extent to which he confirms.[1] Applications by creditors are not very common, for, if the deceased person has left estate, it can be sequestrated under the bankruptcy Statutes, or creditors may find other means of attaching it and making it available for payment of debts. An application by an executor-creditor is not an appropriate process in which to try questions as to the ownership of articles included in the executor-creditor's inventory of the estate.[2]

[1] 4 Geo. IV c. 98, sec. 4.
[2] Tait's Executry, 1918, 34 Sh.Ct.Rep. 306.

11. MINOR.

A minor may be nominated as an executor, or may apply to the Court for his appointment to the office. In the latter case the application will usually be by the minor with consent of his legal guardians, or of a factor appointed for the purpose. The appointment of a factor in such circumstances was always within the scope of the commissary[1] and this power has now devolved upon the Sheriff. The minor may be decerned as executor, and then a factor appointed to act for him in the discharge of his office; but the more convenient practice is for the Court first to appoint a factor for the minor, and then for the factor to apply for the office of executor *qua* factor. The factor in such a case is subject to the supervision of the Accountant of Court,[2] and the appointment is usually made without any service or intimation. The factor has to find caution as such and also as executor if appointed.[3]

He has been found entitled to judicial discharge *qua* factor and to have his bond of caution in that capacity delivered up.[4]

[1] See Johnstone v. Lowden, &c., 1838, 16 S. 541.
[2] Accountant of Court, 1907 S.C. 909.
[3] See further Currie, Confirmation, 5th edn., 89, 90.
[4] Haston, 1930, 46 Sh.Ct.Rep. 141.

It appears to be competent—though it is obviously very inconvenient—for a pupil to be confirmed as executor-nominate or appointed executor-dative. The appointment of a commissary factor, as explained in the preceding paragraph, is the appropriate course. If an application for appointment is made at the instance of a pupil it should proceed in name of his legal guardian.[1] As an alternative to the appointment of a commissary factor in such cases, a factor *loco tutoris* may be appointed and it is understood that this course is recommended by the Accountant of Court.

[1] See generally Currie, Confirmation, 5th edn., 89, 90.

12. MARRIED WOMAN.

A married woman may be appointed executrix-dative to a deceased person in any character for which she possesses the necessary qualifications.

13. STATUTORY SUCCESSORS.

In virtue of their statutory rights of succession various parties are entitled to be appointed executors-dative either alone or in conjunction with the next-of-kin.[1] These statutory successors comprise the surviving husband,[2] the widow,[3] the father,[4] the mother,[5] the brothers and sisters uterine,[6] and an illegitimate child.[7]

[1] See Muir, 1876, 4 R. 74; Webster v. Shiress, 1878, 6 R. 102; Stewart v. Kerr, 1890, 17 R. 707.
[2] 3 & 4 Geo. VI c. 42, sec. 5.
[3] 1 & 2 Geo. V c. 10; 9 & 10 Geo. V c. 9; 3 & 4 Geo. VI c. 42, sec. 5.
[4] 18 & 19 Vict. c. 23, sec. 3.
[5] 9 & 10 Geo. V c. 61, sec. 1.
[6] 18 & 19 Vict. c. 23, sec. 5.
[7] 16 & 17 Geo. V c. 60, sec. 9.

14. LEGATEE.

A legatee of a deceased person is entitled to the office of executor if the deceased have no known next-of-kin. As has been already pointed out,[1] failing appointment of executors or testamentary trustees, a general disponee, universal legatory, or residuary legatee is held to be an executor-nominate and entitled to confirmation as such.[2] In other cases the legatee may be appointed executor-dative and must find caution in the usual way.

[1] See p. 435, supra.
[2] 63 & 64 Vict. c. 55, sec. 3.

15. FUNERATOR.

Appointment of an executor-dative as funerator is competent when the next-of-kin are unknown or unable to act or will not come forward to do so. The undertaker may apply, or anyone who has paid his account and produces the receipt. The applicant must aver all that is known about the next-of-kin. There is an official instruction that the King's and Lord Treasurer's Remembrancer should have notice of all applications for appointment *qua* funerator, and in some Courts the application is not received or proceeded with until such intimation has been given by the petitioner's solicitor and a reply received. Intimation is also usually ordered in the *Edinburgh Gazette*.

16. FOREIGNER.

An executor to administer the estates of a deceased foreigner, who had acquired a domicile in Scotland and died there, leaving estate situated in Scotland, may be appointed in the usual way. It does not disqualify an applicant for the office of executor that he is himself a foreigner, but his cautioner must be subject to the jurisdiction of the Scottish Courts. Nor is an enemy alien necessarily debarred from appointment.[1] Subject to the existence of a convention in reciprocal terms in the foreign State, it is provided that where the subject of a foreign State dies here, and there is no person with a title to administer his estate in Scotland, the local consul, vice-consul or consular agent of the foreign State may apply for appointment as executor.[2] The application will be published and the procedure observed as in the case of a next-of-kin, and the executor will in like manner require to find caution before confirmation.

[1] Schulze, 1917, 1 S.L.T. 176; Crolla, 1942 S.L.T. 66.
[2] 24 & 25 Vict. c. 121, sec. 4.

17. APPEAL.

In commissary procedure appeal is competent in the usual way to the Sheriff or to the Court of Session—either directly or after appeal to the Sheriff—and from the Court of Session to the House of Lords. If the Court of Session desires to recall an appointment made in the Sheriff Court and make another appointment, or to make an appointment not made in the Sheriff Court, they remit to the Sheriff with directions and do not themselves appoint.[1]

[1] Denman v. Torry, 1899, 1 F. 881; Crolla, 1942 S.L.T. 66.

18. SEALING REPOSITORIES.

It occasionally happens that a person dies leaving effects of which no one can at the moment take charge; or that a person in charge of the deceased's house desires to avoid the responsibility of the custody of his effects. In such a case any interested person, such as a relative or a housekeeper, may apply to the Court to have the repositories of the deceased sealed up, and the effects preserved in safe custody till some one obtains an official title to administer the estate. Such an application is usually presented immediately after the death and craves the Court to authorize the Sheriff-clerk or his depute to seal up the repositories meantime, and after the interment of the deceased to open them and inventory the effects. Alternatively, the crave may be to authorize the Sheriff-clerk to examine the repositories and take possession of the effects. Such applications are not intended for the settlement of competing claims to the custody of the effects,[1] but represent the ministerial intervention of the Sheriff to preserve the estate. They are common law summary applications which in the normal case require no service or intimation, and the warrant sought is usually granted *de plano* if the pursuer avers any ostensible interest to make the application. In the unlikely event of such an application being presented after a petition for appointment of an executor-dative had been lodged service of the application would be ordered on that petitioner. The person appointed under the application usually takes immediately into his own custody testamentary writings found in the house, or money, or documents of debt, or valuables. A report of the proceedings is made and lodged in process and if a will is found the executors under it may apply by minute for delivery of it and of the effects.

[1] See Milligan v. Milligan, 1827, 5 S. 206.

19. CONFIRMATION OF SMALL ESTATES.

In the case of small estates not over £500 in value, inclusive of heritable and moveable estate, a simplified procedure is available.[1] No initial writ is required, nor is there any publication. The applicant, if he is an executor-nominate, produces the will at the Sheriff Court of the deceased's domicile, or the Sheriff Court at Edinburgh, as the case may be, and provides the necessary information and particulars. The Sheriff-clerk has to be satisfied that the estate is within the value limit, and that the applicant is entitled to confirmation. If these conditions are fulfilled, the inventory and relative affidavit are filled up by the Sheriff-clerk, and the confirmation is issued, the applicant, if not an executor-nominate, first finding caution. In the case of an executor-dative the Sheriff-clerk may require such proof as he thinks sufficient to establish identity and relationship, and in practice two witnesses are usually required.

    1 38 & 39 Vict. c. 41; 39 & 40 Vict. c. 24; 44 & 45 Vict. c. 12, secs. 33-37; 57 & 58 Vict. c. 30, sec. 16; 63 & 64 Vict. c. 55, sec. 9; 9 & 10 Geo. VI c. 64, Schedule 10, Part III.

20. PRESUMPTION OF LIFE ACT.

Where a person has disappeared and has not been heard of for at least seven years proceedings may be taken to find the date of death, or the presumed date of death, so that the estate may be appropriated by those who would have taken it in the event of the missing person having actually died at the date found by the Court.[1] If the value of the missing person's estate in Scotland, the right to which depends on his death, does not exceed £500 proceedings are competent in the Sheriff Court.[2] It has been held competent to combine the statutory declarator with conclusions for accounting and payment.[3] An action at common law for declarator that a person is dead has been held to be incompetent in the Sheriff Court as one raising a question of status.[4]

    1 54 & 55 Vict. c. 29, sec. 3.
    2 Ibid., sec. 12 (1) (b).
    3 M'Gregor v. Mackechnie, 1917, 34 Sh.Ct.Rep. 174.
    4 Mackie v. Lyon, 1943, 59 Sh.Ct.Rep. 130.

The value which is to be regarded is that of all property in Scotland, heritable and moveable, real and personal, and any right or interest therein of any description.[1] The Act does not apply to a sum due under a life insurance policy upon the life of the missing person, and the claimants under such a policy must establish their claim as if the Act had not been passed.[2]

    1 54 & 55 Vict. c. 29, sec. 12 (2).
    2 Ibid., sec. 11.

The Court of Session has a general concurrent jurisdiction with the Sheriff Court in applications under this Statute, and, if the value of the estate as above defined exceeds £500, the Court of Session is the only competent Court.[1] In the Sheriff Court the application must be made in the Court of the county in which the estate, or the greater part thereof, is situate.[1]

[1] 54 & 55 Vict. c. 29, sec. 12.

The application is made by initial writ, narrating the fact of the disappearance of the missing person, including any material facts and circumstances tending to fix the probable date of death, and craving the Court to find and declare the date at which the missing person was last known to be alive; and that he died at some specific date within seven years of the date at which he was last known to be alive; or, if there is not evidence to fix a specific date, to declare that the date upon which he is presumed to have died is a date exactly seven years after the date on which he was last known to be alive.[1] The general process direction in the Act is that the Sheriff shall direct such intimation and service and such investigation or inquiry as he may think fit.[2] The usual practice is to order intimation by newspaper advertisement and service on any interested parties. Proof is taken whether the application is opposed or not. It is not usually necessary to order answers, but when appearance has been entered and the application is to be opposed this will be done, and it may be convenient to make up a formal record. The judgment of the Sheriff-Substitute is appealable to the Sheriff, and the judgment of either the Sheriff-Substitute or the Sheriff is appealable to the Court of Session in the same manner as in an ordinary action,[2] the right of appeal to the Court of Session being barred where the value of the cause does not exceed £50, unless the Sheriff certifies the cause as suitable for appeal [3]

[1] 54 & 55 Vict. c. 29, sec. 3.
[2] Ibid., sec. 12 (1) (b).
[3] 7 Edw. VII c. 51, secs. 7, 28 (1); 2 & 3 Geo. V c. 28, sec. 2.

The persons entitled to make application to the Court under the Act are: (a) any person entitled to succeed to any estate on the death of the missing person, as, for instance, a disponee or legatee under a settlement, or an heir in heritage, or one of the next-of-kin; (b) any person entitled to estate the transmission of which to the petitioner depends upon the death of the missing person; or (c) the fiar of any estate burdened with a liferent to the missing person.[1] The Statute is not in express terms available to creditors, either of the missing person or of a person entitled to make an application. But a creditor holding an assignation or conveyance of estate which passes on the missing person's death is probably within the definition of the second class of applicant above specified. The statutory procedure is not available to fix a date of death for the purpose of proving that an admittedly deceased person had survived until a certain date,[2] but it is available to increase the share of beneficiaries under a will by cutting out the right of a possible competing beneficiary by fixing his death at a date before the succession opened.[3]

[1] 54 & 55 Vict. c. 29, sec. 3.
[2] Murray v. Chalmers, (O.H) 1913, 1 S.L.T. 223.
[3] Barr v. Campbell, 1925 S.C. 317.

Another type of application under the Act may be made by *pro indiviso* proprietors of heritable estate in Scotland where one of the proprietors has disappeared and has not been heard of for seven years or more.[1] The application in that case is to authorize a sale, the missing person's share of the proceeds being paid into bank for his behoof and treated as heritable estate of his which is subject to the provisions of the Act.[1]

[1] 54 & 55 Vict. c. 29, sec. 4.

A decree under the Act has of itself no effect in transferring the estate of the missing person. It merely fixes the date of his death. The person interested will require thereafter, in a separate process, to take the appropriate steps to procure himself confirmed executor or otherwise to obtain a title to the estate. If the estate is intestate moveable succession, the Statute only applies if the missing person was a domiciled Scotsman at the date at which he is proved or presumed to have died.[1] In practice this is held to mean that the absentee's last known domicile was in Scotland. A finding as to domicile is often inserted in the interlocutor. In the case of succession to heritable property the absentee's domicile is immaterial.[2]

[1] 54 & 55 Vict. c. 29, sec. 3.
[2] Jones, (O.H.) 1923 S.L.T. 31.

On decree under the Act being granted the party entitled to the absentee's estate may proceed to make up titles, and enter upon possession of the estate, and sell or burden it, all as if the missing person had actually died at the date specified in the decree.[1] But within thirteen years the party taking the estate may be called upon to account, and to denude, by the missing person himself, if he returns, or by any person deriving right from him, which is preferable to that of the holder of the decree.[2]

[1] 54 & 55 Vict. c. 29, sec. 3.
[2] Ibid., sec. 6.

21. Intestate Husband's Estate Acts.

Under the Intestate Husband's Estate Acts the widow of a domiciled Scotsman dying after 18th August, 1911, leaving no lawful issue—which is held to mean children or remoter issue[1]—is entitled to the whole of his heritable and moveable estate if the net value of that does not exceed £500, or, if it does, she is a creditor on the estate to that extent with interest at 4 per cent. from the date of death till payment.[2] In the latter case the widow's rights in the estate are apportioned rateably between the heritable and moveable estate,[3] and she retains her rights of terce and *jus relictæ* in the balance of the estate after her statutory rights have been satisfied.[4] Originally the above provisions applied only in the case of total intestacy,[5] but in the case of deaths after 17th July, 1940, they apply, with certain modifications, to cases of partial intestacy as well.[6] As from the same date a surviving husband is given the same rights in his deceased wife's estate as a widow was given in her deceased husband's estate by the earlier Acts.[7] Although this provision is somewhat loosely expressed, it is thought that where a deceased wife's estate is over £500 the surviving husband's rights in the balance are his own proper rights of courtesy and *jus relicti*.

[1] Grant v. Munro, 1916, 1 S.L.T. 338.
[2] 1 & 2 Geo. V c. 10, secs. 1, 2.
[3] Ibid., sec. 3.
[4] Ibid., sec. 4.
[5] Taylor's Executors v. Taylor, 1918 S.C. 207; Gill v. Gill, 1938 S.C. 65.
[6] 3 & 4 Geo. VI c. 42, sec. 5 (2).
[7] Ibid., sec. 5 (1).

For the purposes of the Acts the net value of the moveable estate is ascertained after deduction of debts, funeral and testamentary—which is presumably intended to mean administrative or executry—expenses of the intestate, and all other lawful liabilities and charges to which the estate is subject.[1] Death duties apparently fall to be included among the deductions.[2] No special provision is made in regard to the valuation of the heritable estate except that this is to be determined by the Sheriff.[3] It would appear that the value of the estate is to be taken at the date of death and that any later fluctuations in value are to be ignored.[4]

[1] 1 & 2 Geo. V c. 10, sec. 6.
[2] See 9 & 10 Geo. V c. 9, Schedule (Deductions).
[3] Ibid., sec. 3.
[4] In re Heath, [1907] 2 Ch. 270.

In order to work out the rights provided by the Acts the
surviving spouse presents, in the Sheriff Court of the county in
which the deceased spouse was domiciled at the time of death, or
if that county is uncertain, in the Sheriff Court of the Lothians
and Peebles at Edinburgh, a summary application in the form
of the schedule to the Act of 1919.[1] Appended to the application
is an inventory of the estate and deductions in statutory form.[1]
For the purpose of jurisdiction the Sheriff to whom the application is presented decides as to domicile and his decision is, for
this purpose, final and not subject to review.[2] If the surviving
spouse has died without having made the necessary application it
is competent for his or her executors, or any other person deriving
right immediately or otherwise from such spouse, to make a similar
application.[3]

[1] 9 & 10 Geo. V c. 9, sec. 1.
[2] Ibid., sec. 3 (3).
[3] 1 & 2 Geo. VI c. 24, sec. 10.   See also 3 & 4 Geo. VI c. 42, sec. 5 (3),
   and Encyclopædia of Scottish Legal Styles VI, 239.

On such an application being presented the Sheriff is directed to
order intimation of the application and relative inventory to be
given to the intestate's heir-at-law, if the estate consists of or
includes heritage, and to the heir *in mobilibus* if it consists of or
includes moveables.[1] If such parties are unknown, and cannot
be ascertained after such inquiry as the Sheriff thinks fit, intimation to them may be dispensed with.[1] Although there is no
opposition decree is not granted *de plano*, and the Sheriff has to
be satisfied, after such inquiry as he deems proper, that the
applicant is entitled under the Acts to the whole or part of the
estate. For the purpose of this inquiry proof may be allowed
in the usual way, or some less formal method of inquiry may be
adopted by the Sheriff. In the inventory appended to the initial
writ[2] it is suggested that—although the statutory form does not
seem to require this—burdens and conditions of title should be
referred to at the end of the description of any heritable property,
but not in the case of heritable securities.[3] A deduction of title
is required in the case of heritable estate where the deceased was
not infeft and this will be in the form provided by the Conveyancing
Act of 1924.[4] In the case of heritable securities it seems to be
unnecessary to connect the deceased with the original creditor or
with the person who had the last recorded title, but it may be
considered desirable to do this by adding a reference in the terms
provided by the 1924 Act.[5] Debts heritably secured are deducted
from the value of the property itself but moveable debts are included
in the deduction at the end; death duties on both heritage and

moveables have apparently to be lumped together and deducted at the end.[2]

[1] 9 & 10 Geo. V c. 9, sec. 2.
[2] Ibid., Schedule.
[3] 14 & 15 Geo. V c. 27, sec. 9.
[4] Ibid., sec. 3, Schedule A, Form 1.
[5] Ibid., Schedule K, Note 2.

If the Sheriff determines that the total net value of the estate does not exceed £500 he is directed to pronounce decree declaring that the estate belongs wholly and exclusively to the applicant.[1] On a stamped inventory of the estate being lodged such decree is a sufficient warrant for issuing confirmation of the moveable estate in favour of the applicant as executrix (executor) dative *qua* relict.[1] Caution will require to be found in the usual way. An extract decree recorded in the appropriate register of sasines, which contains a description of the heritage and the heritable securities and security subjects, or which has a schedule annexed containing the statutory particulars of these as in the inventory appended to the initial writ, has the effect of infefting the applicant in the heritable estate and in the heritable securities.[1]

[1] 9 & 10 Geo. V c. 9, sec. 3 (1).

If the Sheriff determines that the net value of the estate exceeds £500 he is directed to grant decree for £500 and interest in favour of the applicant against the defender or against the several defenders jointly and severally, and the applicant is entitled to recover that sum and interest from the deceased's executor-dative on the expiry of six months from the death, so far as the executor has any free moveable estate in his hands after payment of debts and other proper charges and deductions.[1] But the decree is only to operate against the defender or defenders so far as they benefit from the succession.[1] An extract of the decree, recorded in the appropriate Register of Sasines, and which contains a description of the heritage, or has a schedule appended containing the particulars required in the inventory annexed to the writ, has the effect of a duly recorded bond and disposition in security over the heritable estate for £500, and interest at 4 per cent. from the date of death until payment, granted by the deceased in favour of the applicant containing all usual and necessary clauses including power of sale, and as if the deceased had been subject to no legal incapacity and had been infeft in the heritage at the date of his death, and as if the sum in the bond were due at the date of recording the decree, but the real security in the applicant's favour is postponed to all debts and obligations of the deceased.[1]

Further the applicant is entitled to recover in all no more than £500 and interest as above out of the whole estate, heritable and moveable, and this is to be borne as between the heir-at-law and the representatives of the moveable estate in proportions as already stated.[1] In this case, differing from that of an estate under £500, the surviving spouse has no preferential right to the office of executor and an executor must be appointed in the usual way.

[1] 9 & 10 Geo. V c. 9, sec. 3 (2).

The procedure under the Acts is subject to the usual rights of appeal to the Sheriff and the Court of Session.[1]

[1] See Gill v. Gill, 1938 S.C. 65

22. DECLARATOR THAT WILL IS HOLOGRAPH.

Special provision has been made by Act of Sederunt for actions of declarator that a testamentary writing of a deceased person is holograph. The process is begun by initial writ in the usual form, and save in so far as special procedure is laid down it proceeds as an ordinary action.[1] The writ is served on the deceased's heir-at-law and on such other persons interested as the Sheriff may direct.[1] Decree is not granted *de plano*, though there is no opposition, but the Sheriff may accept evidence by affidavit.[1] These may be endorsed on the will or extract or be separate, and may be taken before a magistrate, commissioner for oaths, justice of the peace or notary public (provided such party is not the pursuer's solicitor or a partner or servant of such solicitor) or before a commissioner appointed by the Sheriff.[1] The affidavits are to be two or more in number, and affidavits by persons patrimonially interested in the estate are competent and are directed to be " duly considered by the Sheriff."[1] The Sheriff may in any case call for further affidavits, or allow further proof to be taken in the usual way.[1] The procedure under the Act of Sederunt does not affect the commissary practice of accepting affidavits to prove a holograph will for purposes of confirmation,[2] and where confirmation has been issued to executors-nominate prior to 1st July, 1938, the testamentary writing on which confirmation was issued is deemed to be probative.[3] A holograph writing may be set up incidentally without a declarator in another action in which it is founded on.[4]

[1] Act of Sederunt, 19th July, 1935, sec. 1.
[2] Ibid., sec. 2.
[3] 1 & 2 Geo. VI c. 24, sec. 11.
[4] M'Pherson v. Cameron's Executor, 1942 S.L.T. (Sh.Ct.) 26.

CHAPTER XXI.

PUBLIC INQUIRIES.

1. Fatal Accidents, &c.

It is the duty of the Sheriff to preside at certain public inquiries of which the most numerous are those held under the Fatal Accidents Inquiry Act. The original Statute of 1895 covered all cases of death of any person or persons, whether employers or employed, engaged in any industrial employment or occupation in Scotland due, or reasonably believed to be due, to accident occurring in the course of such employment or occupation.[1] The Fatal Accidents and Sudden Deaths Inquiry Act of 1906 extended the scope of this process to include all cases of sudden or suspicious death in Scotland in connexion with which the Lord Advocate directs a public inquiry to be held.[2] The Sheriff may preside at such inquiries, but in practice they are conducted before the Sheriff-Substitute, whose decision is final upon any question, as to the competency of evidence or otherwise, arising in the course of the inquiry. If the Sheriff or Sheriff-Substitute, for any reason satisfactory to the Secretary of State for Scotland, is unable to hold the inquiry, a person holding the qualification for a Sheriff-Substitute may be appointed by the Secretary of State to hold it.[3]

[1] 58 & 59 Vict. c. 36, sec. 2.
[2] 6 Edw. VII c. 35.
[3] 58 & 59 Vict. c. 36, sec. 4 (3).

Upon the occurrence of a death falling within the Statute, or in regard to which the Lord Advocate has directed a public inquiry to be held, it becomes the duty of the procurator-fiscal of the district within which the accident or death occurred (a) to collect evidence in regard to the death; (b) to present a petition to the Sheriff craving him to hold a public inquiry; and (c) to furnish the Sheriff-clerk with information as to the relatives and the employer of the deceased person.[1] If several deaths have resulted from the one accident one inquiry is held in regard to all of them.[2] Upon presentation of the petition the Sheriff orders an inquiry and fixes a time and place for holding it.[3] The inquiry is to be held as soon as reasonably possible in the Court-house nearest to the place where the accident occurred, unless there are special circumstances which seem to the Sheriff to make it expedient to hold it in some other Court-house or other building which is available and convenient.[3] In the interlocutor ordering an inquiry, warrant is included to cite witnesses and havers for all interested parties.[3] It is the duty of the Sheriff-clerk to intimate the time and place of the inquiry by letter to the wife or husband or nearest known relative, and to the employer of the deceased.[4] The Sheriff-clerk also intimates the time and place for the inquiry in the local press, and notifies any government official or department having a statutory right to inquire into the circumstances of the accident.[4] Provision is made for inspection and for recovery of productions.[5]

[1] 58 & 59 Vict. c. 36, sec. 3 (1).
[2] Ibid., sec. 3 (2).
[3] Ibid., sec. 4 (1).
[4] Ibid., sec. 4 (2).
[5] Ibid., sec. 5 (2).

The inquiry is held before a jury of seven, two special and five common jurors being selected from a panel of fifteen.[1] Challenge of jurors is not competent as in a criminal trial, but the employer of the deceased and all persons engaged under the employer are disqualified.[1] This or any other objection to a juror may be taken by any person interested in the inquiry, and the Sheriff decides whether a challenged juror shall serve.[1] The persons interested who may appear and take part in, and lead evidence at, the inquiry (personally or by counsel or solicitor, or by any other person by leave of the Sheriff) include (a) the deceased's relatives; (b) the employer; (c) any person engaged under the same employer as the deceased[2]; (d) any person authorized by any trades union or friendly society of which the deceased was a member[3]; (e) an inspector of mines; (f) a factory inspector; and (g) any other persons whom the Sheriff may consider to have a just interest in the inquiry.[2] The inquiry is open to the public and the fiscal or his depute leads evidence as to the cause of death and the circumstances of the accident.[4]

[1] 58 & 59 Vict. c. 36, sec. 4 (4) (5) (6).
[2] Ibid., sec. 5 (3).
[3] 6 Edw. VII c. 35, sec. 2.
[4] 58 & 59 Vict. c. 36, sec. 5 (1); 1 & 2 Geo. VI c. 48, sec. 9.

The evidence is led, and the inquiry conducted, as nearly as possible in the manner observed at a criminal jury trial, and the ordinary rules of evidence apply.[1] Examination as a witness or haver does not bar subsequent criminal proceedings against the party examined, but no witness is compelled to answer any question tending to show him guilty of any crime or offence.[1] The evidence is recorded under the supervision of the Sheriff, and may be taken in shorthand,[1] but it is not written out unless the Sheriff so directs, either *ex proprio motu* or on application by anyone appearing or entitled to appear at the inquiry made not later than one month thereafter.[2] At the close of the evidence the Sheriff usually indicates to the jury the form of verdict which he proposes, but parties have a right to be heard if they desire to address the jury.[3] The jury may return a verdict by a majority after the lapse of an hour,[4] and the verdict is recorded in the books of Court[5]; but it is not competent to use it in evidence, or to found upon it, in any subsequent judicial proceedings, civil or criminal, arising out of the same accident.[6] At the conclusion of the inquiry the Sheriff-clerk (a) furnishes to the procurator-fiscal, to be by him transmitted to the Crown Agent, the record of evidence (if this has been written out)[2] and the productions, a copy of the application to hold an inquiry, and a copy of the verdict; (b) in a mining or factory accident, transmits copies of the proceedings to the Inspector of Mines or the Inspector of Factories, as the case may be.[5] Copies are also obtainable on payment by any person interested in the inquiry.[5]

[1] 58 & 59 Vict. c. 36, sec. 5 (4).
[2] 23 & 24 Geo. V c. 41, sec. 38.
[3] 6 Edw. VII c. 35, sec. 2.
[4] 58 & 59 Vict. c. 36, sec. 4 (8).
[5] Ibid., sec. 5 (5).
[6] Ibid., sec. 6.

The verdict of the jury is required to set forth, so far as such particulars have been proved, (a) the place and date of the accident and death; (b) the cause or causes of the accident or death; (c) the person or persons, if any, to whose fault or negligence the accident was attributable; (d) precautions, if any, by which the accident might have been avoided; (e) any defects in the system or mode of working which contributed to the accident; and (f) any other facts the jury think relevant to the inquiry.[1] In practice verdicts are usually given in purely formal terms as to the circumstances of the accident and death, and findings of fault are not often included. In addition to the statutory requirements, the verdict of the jury may contain, as a rider, opinions or recommendations as to the conduct of work.

[1] 6 Edw. VII c. 35, sec. 2.

2. BOARD OF TRADE.

(a) *Shipping Casualties.*—The Sheriff or the Sheriff-Substitute is a " judge " within the meaning of the Shipping Casualties Rules, 1923,[1] made under the authority of Part VI of the Merchant Shipping Act, 1894,[2] and the Sheriff may thus be required to hold a public inquiry into the circumstances attending a shipping casualty. Upon receiving a request to this effect from the Board of Trade the Sheriff fixes a time and place for the inquiry which is held in the Court-house or other suitable place.[2] By the same interlocutor warrant is usually granted for citing witnesses and havers. Notice is given by the Board of Trade by registered letter[3] to the owner, master, and officers of the ship, and to any other person whom the Board considers entitled to notice.[4] Any person so notified becomes a party in the inquiry,[5] and is entitled to take part, personally or by counsel or solicitor, in the proceedings. The notice embodies the questions which the Board of Trade propose to raise at the inquiry,[4] but these may be amended by a subsequent notice before the hearing of the inquiry,[4] and may also be modified by the Board of Trade after the evidence of the Board's witnesses has been concluded.[6] Any person may appear at the inquiry by leave of the Sheriff and thereby becomes a party to the inquiry.[7] Every party to the inquiry has a possible liability for costs.[8] In conducting the inquiry the Sheriff has the powers which he exercises as a Court of summary jurisdiction.[9]

[1] S.R. & O., 1923, No. 752, sec. 2.
[2] 57 & 58 Vict. c. 60, secs. 466 (12), 479.
[3] S.R. & O., 1923. No. 752, sec. 28.
[4] Ibid., sec. 3.
[5] Ibid., sec. 4.
[6] Ibid., sec. 11.
[7] Ibid., sec. 5.
[8] Ibid., sec. 16.
[9] 57 & 58 Vict. c. 60, sec. 466 (10).

The Court consists of the Sheriff and one or more assessors.[1] The assessors are appointed by the Secretary of State on the requisition of the Board of Trade, and are notified of the place and date of the inquiry by the Secretary of State.[2] When the investigation involves possible suspension of the certificates of a master or officers, at least two assessors are appointed.[3] If the conduct of an engineer is involved, one of the assessors is selected from the engineer class.[4] The assessors are selected from a list comprising (1) certificated shipmasters of five years' experience in the merchant service; (2) certificated engineers of five years' experience in the merchant service; (3) certain naval officers; and (4) other persons of special skill or knowledge selected by the Secretary of State.[5]

[1] 57 & 58 Vict. c. 60, sec. 466 (3).
[2] S.R. & O., 1923, No. 752, secs. 22-26.
[3] Ibid., sec. 23.
[4] Ibid., sec. 24.
[5] Ibid., App. Part II.

Diligence for recovery of documents is not competent, but any party may, by registered letter, give notice to any other party, requiring him to produce documents at the inquiry diet; and, if this notice is not complied with, the party who gave the notice is entitled to lead secondary evidence of the contents of the documents called for.[1] A party may also by a like notice call upon any other party to admit any documents, and if such admission is not made then, unless the Sheriff considers the refusal was reasonable, the party who refused to make the admission may be found liable for the costs of proving the documents whatever the result of the inquiry may be.[2] If such a notice is not given the expenses of proving a document are not to be allowed unless the auditor considers that expense has been saved by omitting the notice.[2] It is not competent to take evidence on commission to lie *in retentis*, but an affidavit or statutory declaration may, by leave of the Sheriff, be used as evidence at the inquiry.[3]

[1] S.R. & O., 1923, No. 752, secs. 6, 28.
[2] Ibid., sec. 7.
[3] Ibid., sec. 8.

At the time and place appointed, the Court may proceed with the inquiry, whether all or any of the parties served with a notice are present or not.[1] The inquiry may be adjourned from time to time, and place to place, but the Sheriff may impose terms, as to payment of costs or otherwise, as a condition of granting an adjournment, and that whether the adjournment is asked by the Board of Trade or by any other party to the inquiry.[2] In practice adjournments are, as far as possible, avoided, and the proceedings are taken *de die in diem* till concluded.

[1] S.R. & O., 1923, No. 752, sec. 9.
[2] Ibid., sec. 14.

The Board of Trade witnesses are first examined and each party in the inquiry may then cross-examine them in the order allowed by the Sheriff, after which they may be re-examined by the Board of Trade.[1] At the conclusion of the Board of Trade evidence, the party representing the Board is required to state, in open Court, the questions in regard to the casualty, and the conduct of the ship's officers or others, upon which the opinion of the Court is desired.[2] At this stage modifications on the questions already notified may be made by the Board of Trade.[2] Each party is entitled to be heard upon these questions and to lead evidence, each witness called by him being subject to cross-examination and re-examination in such order as the Court shall allow.[3] The Board of Trade may also produce and examine further witnesses.[3]

It may happen that a question as to possible blame arises between two or more of the parties, in which event the party alleging blame will usually lead evidence and the other parties cross-examine if they so desire, the party blamed being allowed to cross-examine last. The rules of evidence which apply in proofs are not strictly enforced and witnesses already examined for the Board of Trade may be recalled by any party.[3] The Sheriff may in general allow such examination, cross-examination, or re-examination as he thinks necessary to expiscate the facts and, as the presiding judge, he has the right to question witnesses. The rules make no provision as to the assessors doing so, but in practice, and with the permission of the judge, the assessors do question the witness after all the parties have finished, and before the judge puts any questions. At the conclusion of the evidence each party is entitled to be heard, and the Board of Trade may address the Court in reply on the whole case.[4] The judgment of the Court is given in the form of answers to the questions proposed by the Board of Trade. If an officer's certificate is cancelled or suspended, the judgment must be given in open Court.[5] If not, it may be delivered either *viva voce* or in writing, and if in writing will be sent to the parties by the Sheriff-clerk[5]; but in practice judgment is usually delivered in open Court whether certificates are involved or not.

[1] S.R. & O., 1923, No. 752, sec. 10.
[2] Ibid., sec. 11.
[3] Ibid., sec. 12.
[4] Ibid., sec. 13.
[5] Ibid., sec. 15.

The Sheriff may order the costs of the inquiry, or any part thereof, to be paid by any party to the inquiry.[1] If a party is found liable to the Board of Trade in costs the order for payment is in favour of the solicitor to the Board of Trade.[2] If the Board is found liable to a party the order is in favour of that party.[2] It is usually only in exceptional cases, and where fault is proved, that a party in such an inquiry is found liable in costs. An imposition of costs, when made, is rather by way of penalty for blame in connexion with the casualty, than a finding for expenses in the ordinary acceptation of the term. The ship's officers can be penalized by suspension or cancellation of their certificates, but shipbuilders, shipowners, charterers, or stevedores may sometimes be parties to an inquiry, and an order for payment of costs is the only mode in which such parties can be reached, if blame for the casualty is attributable to them.

[1] S.R. & O., 1923, No. 752, sec. 16
[2] Ibid., App. Part I, No. 2.

At the conclusion of the inquiry it is the duty of the Sheriff to make a report in a prescribed form to the Board of Trade.[1] This is signed by the Sheriff, and also by the nautical assessors if they concur in it.[1] But if any assessor does not concur in the report, as stated by the Sheriff, he need not sign it, and he must then make an independent report to the Board of Trade explaining his dissent.[2] The report itself contains only the finding of the Court, as delivered in open Court or communicated in writing to the parties, but it is accompanied by an annex (which is not part of the judgment, and is not communicated to the parties before being sent to the Board of Trade), setting forth in detail the circumstances of the case, the Court's opinion as to the cause of the casualty and the conduct of any persons implicated and whether and for what reason any certificate is suspended or cancelled.[1] On application by any party the Board of Trade must furnish him with a copy of the report.[3]

[1] S.R. & O., 1923, No. 752, sec. 17, App. Part I, No. 3.
[2] 57 & 58 Vict. c. 60, sec. 466 (6).
[3] S.R. & O., 1923, No. 752, sec. 18.

The decision of the Court in a Board of Trade inquiry is the judgment of the Sheriff, although it may have been pronounced under the advice of the assessors. When a decision is given with respect to the cancelling or suspension of a certificate,[1] or when a finding of fault is made against any person[2] the judgment is subject to review by a Division of the Court of Session unless there is to be a rehearing of the case as explained below.[3] Within twenty-eight days of the decision being pronounced, or twenty-one days of the issue in London of the print of the Sheriff's report to the Board of Trade, or if not printed within twenty-one days from the date of the *London Gazette* containing notice of receipt by the Board of Trade of the Court's report, any party in the inquiry may notify the other parties of his intention to appeal.[4] The notice should probably be given by registered letter.[5] Such an appeal is apparently now subject to the Rules of Court so that the appellant must within the time stated write the usual note of appeal on the minute of procedure or other written record containing the decision.[6] Within two days of the appeal being set down for hearing, the appellant must notify the other parties of the general grounds of the appeal.[4] It may be well to send this by registered letter.[5] Before the hearing, the appellant, if a party other than the Board of Trade, must find caution for the

costs of the appeal, to an amount fixed by the Sheriff, by deposit
or otherwise.[7]

1 57 & 58 Vict. c. 60, sec. 475 (3).
2 6 Edw. VII c. 48, sec. 66.
3 See paragraph below.
4 S.R. & O., 1923, No. 752, sec. 20 (a) (b).　See also sec. 27 as to
computation of time.
5 Ibid., sec. 28.
6 Rules of Court, 1936, V 7, 8.　See p. 298, et seq., supra, as to appeals
generally.
7 S.R. & O., 1923. No. 752, sec. 20 (c).　See Thain v. Board of Trade,
1923 S.C. 548.

The Appeal Court also has the assistance of assessors,[1] and the
proceedings are conducted as in an ordinary hearing upon an
appeal from the Sheriff Court.[2]　The process before the Appeal
Court consists of the minute of procedure before the Sheriff along
with the notes of evidence, the Sheriff's report to the Board of
Trade and relative annex, and the appellants' notice giving the
grounds of his appeal.[3]　The Appeal Court may hear further
evidence on questions of fact, or in regard to circumstances which
have occurred since the date of the Sheriff's judgment, and may
order other parties to be called.[4]　The Appeal Court may award
expenses to or against any party.[5]　On the conclusion of the proceedings the Appeal Court makes a report to the Board of Trade.[6]

1 S.R. & O., 1923, No. 752. sec. 20 (e).
2 Ibid., sec. 20 (j).
3 Ibid., sec. 20 (f) (g).
4 Ibid., sec. 20 (f) (h).
5 Ibid., sec. 20 (i).
6 Ibid., sec. 20 (k).

The Board of Trade may direct a rehearing in any investigation
and must do so in certain circumstances.[1]　They may order the
case to be reheard before the same Court as conducted the original
inquiry, or by a wreck commissioner or a judge of the Court of
Session.[1]　Certain of the provisions as to procedure in appeals
apply in the case of a rehearing.[2]　Although the position is by
no means clear it would seem that there is not intended to be
any right of appeal following a rehearing.[1]

1 57 & 58 Vict. c. 60, sec. 475.
2 S.R. & O., 1923, No. 752, sec. 21.

(b) *Survey.*—Analogous to the procedure of the Board of Trade
inquiry in the Sheriff Court, although it takes the form of an
appeal, is that of the inquiry held by the Sheriff under the Merchant
Shipping Act, 1894, in a dispute between a Board of Trade surveyor and a shipowner as to whether a passenger vessel is so con-

structed as to entitle her to a passenger certificate. Such an appeal to the Sheriff is not of frequent occurrence, but occasionally an owner may appeal to the Court of Survey for the port or district where the vessel is,[1] which, in Scotland may mean the Sheriff (or the Sheriff-Substitute) sitting with two assessors.[2] The proceedings may be begun by appeal in the form of an initial writ and the procedure is similar to that in a Board of Trade inquiry into a shipping casualty.[3] The judge and each surveyor may survey the ship, or the judge may appoint any person to survey and report.[4] The Court may either sustain or refuse the appeal, but in either case must make a report to the Board of Trade.[5] If the Court find that the vessel is entitled to a certificate it is granted by the Board of Trade, the judgment of the Court superseding the necessity for the local surveyor's declaration. Sitting as a Court of Survey the Sheriff has power to award costs to or against any party, and in general these should follow the event.[6] The decision of a Court of Survey is not subject to review.

[1] 57 & 58 Vict. c. 60, secs. 274, 275.
[2] Ibid., sec. 487.
[3] See Rules of Court of Survey, 1876 and 1877 (printed in M'Millan, Scottish Maritime Practice, pp. 359, 368).
[4] 57 & 58 Vict. c. 60, sec. 488 (2) (3).
[5] Ibid., secs. 275 (2), 488 (7).
[6] Ibid., sec. 275 (3).

In addition to the matter referred to in the preceding paragraph a Court of Survey may be appealed to on the refusal of a clearance certificate to an emigrant ship[1] and the refusal of a certificate as to lights and fog signals.[2] Such appeals are dealt with as in the preceding paragraph. Appeal may also be made to a Court of Survey where a vessel is detained as unsafe.[3] This is made to the Court for the port or district where the ship is detained.[3] The judge of the Court may order the ship to be released or finally detained, but unless one assessor concurs in the detention the ship is released.[4] The procedure is as already indicated, but in this case the expenses are not in the hands of the Court but are recoverable separately.[5]

[1] 57 & 58 Vict. c. 60, sec. 318.
[2] Ibid., sec. 420.
[3] Ibid., secs. 459, 462; 60 & 61 Vict. c. 59, sec. 1: 6 Edw. VII c. 48, secs. 2, 85.
[4] Ibid., sec. 488 (5).
[5] Ibid., sec. 460.

(c) *Conduct of Ship's Officers.*—The Sheriff Court may also become a Court of Inquiry into the conduct of ship's officers, under the provisions of the Merchant Shipping Act. If it is reported by the local Marine Board, or otherwise to the Board of Trade, that any certificated master, mate, or engineer is, from incompetency or misconduct, unfit to discharge his duties, or that he has failed, in a case of collision, to assist another vessel or to give information required by the Act, the Board may (a) appoint a person to hold an inquiry; (b) direct the local Marine Board to do so; or (c) direct an inquiry to be held before a Court of summary jurisdiction, which in Scotland means the Sheriff Court.[1] In holding such an inquiry the Sheriff has the same powers, and the procedure as to conduct of the case and report to the Board of Trade is the same, as in an inquiry into a shipping casualty.[2] Presumably the intention is that there is a similar right of appeal. The Board of Trade may direct the person who has made the charge against the officer to conduct the case.[2]

[1] 57 & 58 Vict. c. 60, sec. 471 (1) (2).
[2] Ibid., sec. 471 (4).

3. PROVISIONAL ORDERS.

Under the Burgh Police Act application may be made in certain circumstances to the Secretary of State for Scotland for a provisional order[1] and on receipt of such application the Secretary of State may direct the Sheriff—which appears to include Sheriff-Substitute[2]—or other commissioner or commissioners to hold a local inquiry in the district in respect to the matters mentioned in the application.[3] At least fourteen days' notice of the time, place and subject of the inquiry must be given in two consecutive weeks in a newspaper published or circulating in the district.[3] For the purposes of the inquiry the Sheriff is empowered to take the assistance of valuators, accountants, engineers or other persons of skill to such extent as he may deem necessary,[3] and, after the conclusion of the inquiry, the Sheriff is directed to make a written report to the Secretary of State.[3] If such an inquiry is directed in connexion with a provisional order which is *ultra vires* the proceedings may be stopped by interdict.[4]

[1] 55 & 56 Vict. c. 55, sec. 45.
[2] Ibid., sec. 4 (30).
[3] Ibid., sec. 46.
[4] Russell v. Magistrates of Hamilton, 1897, 25 R. 350.

4. POLICE INQUIRIES.

Under the Police Appeals Act a member of a police force who is punished by dismissal, or by being required to resign, or by reduction in rank or pay may appeal to the Secretary of State, who, unless he considers that the case can be determined without oral evidence, appoints the Sheriff—excluding the Sheriff-Substitute —to hold an inquiry and report.[1] Rules have been made in connexion with such inquiries, and reference should be made to them for the details of the prescribed procedure.[2]

[1] 17 & 18 Geo. V c. 19, secs. 1, 2, 6; 6 & 7 Geo. VI c. 8, sec. 1.
[2] S.R. & O., 1943, No. 481, sec. 13.

CHAPTER XXII.

SMALL DEBT COURT.

1. Jurisdiction.

By the Sheriff Courts Act, 1907, the value limit in the Small Debt Court was raised to £20,[1] and many provisions of that Statute were made applicable to small debt procedure.[2] The competency of an action in the Small Debt Court is determined by the sum sued for, and it is competent to sue for a debt exceeding £20 if the sum sued for is restricted to £20. In that case, if deductions are made by the disallowance of items, these come off the amount of the debt, not off the restricted sum.[3] Accordingly, the full amount of the debt should be specified and then restricted to £20. The Small Debt Court has not privative jurisdiction in the case of debts not exceeding £20 and such may be sued for in the ordinary Court as summary causes, but if that is done small debt expenses only may be awarded.[4]

[1] 7 Edw. VII c. 51, sec. 42.
[2] Ibid., sec. 45.
[3] Dalgleish & Kerr v. Anderson, 1883, 20 S.L.R. 412.
[4] Act of Sederunt, 7th May, 1935, Gen. Reg. II (4) (5).

If a pursuer in the Small Debt Court sues for less than his prestable claim or demand, he is held to have abandoned the remaining portion of it.[1] It is not competent to sue for part of a due debt, reserving right to sue again for another part; nor is it competent to split a claim of over £20, and bring two or more small debt actions.[2] But this bar exists only when the first action has been heard and determined.[3] A small debt action taken out, but abandoned before decree is pronounced, does not bar another action,[3] and a second action against the same debtor is not barred if it relates to a separate claim,[4] or is in respect of a claim that could not have competently been included in the first action.[5]

[1] 7 Will. IV & 1 Vict. c. 41, sec. 2; cf. St. George Co-operative Society v. Murray, 1918, 34 Sh.Ct.Rep. 229.
[2] Hewat v. MacFarlane, 1906, 23 Sh.Ct.Rep. 109; Caledonian Railway Co. v. Findlater, 1914, 31 Sh.Ct.Rep. 25.
[3] Nelson v. Lanark County Council, 1890, 7 Sh.Ct.Rep. 3; Baird & Stevenson v. O'Hare, 1911, 27 Sh.Ct.Rep. 365.
[4] Fraser v. Ferguson, 1870, 42 Scot. Jur. 396; John v. Chalmers & Son, 1909, 26 Sh.Ct.Rep. 34; Schultze Co. v. M'Lagan, 1915, 32 Sh.Ct.Rep. 71.
[5] Findlay's Trustees v. Shanks, 1930 S.L.T. (Sh.Ct.) 32.

Where heritable subjects are let for less than a year, irrespective of the amount of the rent, an action of summary removing against the tenant is to be conducted and disposed of—except where written answers are lodged—in the same way as proceedings under the Small Debt Acts.[1] Details of the procedure in such cases have been already dealt with.[2]

[1] 7 Edw. VII c. 51, sec. 38, Schedule I, Rules 115-122; 2 & 3 Geo. V c. 28, Schedule II.
[2] See p. 405, et seq., supra.

The Sheriff's jurisdiction over defenders in the Small Debt Court is, as regards actions competent in that Court, now practically co-extensive with his jurisdiction in the Ordinary Court. The jurisdiction clauses of the Sheriff Courts Act, 1907, are, so far as appropriate, applicable also to a Small Debt Court.[1] It is, accordingly, now competent to sue a small debt action against joint defenders in the Sheriff Court where any one of them has acquired a residential domicile (provided a Sheriff Court has jurisdiction over each of them), and this remains competent for forty days after such defender has left that domicile, if his present residence in Scotland is unknown.[2] As in the Ordinary Court, any person who carries on business within the jurisdiction and is cited personally or at such place of business, is liable to the jurisdiction of that Sheriffdom, irrespective of domicile.[3] The power to transfer an action to another Court where one of several defenders is domiciled is also applicable to the Small Debt Court.[4]

[1] 7 Edw. VII c. 51, secs. 6, 45.
[2] Ibid., secs. 6 (a), 45; 2 & 3 Geo. V c. 28, Schedule I. See p. 52, et seq., supra.
[3] Ibid., secs. 6 (b), 45; 2 & 3 Geo V c. 28, Schedule I. See p. 59, et seq., supra.
[4] Ibid., sec. 45, Schedule I, Rule 19.

The broadened definition of " person " in the Sheriff Courts Act, 1907,[1] with the relative citation rule, is also applicable to the Small Debt Court. Accordingly, any kind of corporation or association carrying on business under a firm or trading or descriptive name can now sue and be sued in the Small Debt Court, and that under its business designation alone, service being made at the principal place of business of the corporation or association, if that is within the jurisdiction, and, if not, at any place of business or office at which such business is carried on within the jurisdiction, and the term principal place of business includes the office or place of business of the clerk or secretary of any corporation or association.[2]

[1] 7 Edw. VII c. 51, secs. 3 (e), 45.
[2] Ibid., Schedule I, Rule 11; 2 & 3 Geo. V c. 28, Schedule II. See p. 127, supra.

The further grounds of jurisdiction over defenders in the Sheriff Court apply where these arise from (a) arrestment *ad fundandam jurisdictionem*[1]; (b) ownership or tenancy of heritable property within the jurisdiction where the action relates to the property[2]; (c) the place of performance of a contract within the jurisdiction where the defender is personally cited there[3]; (d) the situation within the jurisdiction of the fund *in medio* in a furthcoming or multiplepoinding, or the fact of the arrestee or holder of the fund being subject to the jurisdiction[4]; (e) reconvention[5]; (f) delict of the defender within the jurisdiction where he is personally cited there[6]; and (g) prorogation.[7] Further details as to these various grounds of jurisdiction can be sought where they have been already dealt with.[8]

[1] 7 Edw. VII c. 51, secs. 6 (c), 45. See p. 61, et seq., supra.
[2] Ibid., secs. 6 (d), 45. See p. 71, et seq., supra.
[3] Ibid., secs. 6 (f), 45. See p. 75, et seq., supra.
[4] Ibid., secs. 6 (g), 45. See p. 74, supra.
[5] Ibid., secs. 6 (h), 45. See p. 67, supra.
[6] Ibid., secs. 6 (i), 45. See p. 69, supra.
[7] Ibid., secs. 6 (j), 45. See p. 76, supra. See also p. 479, infra, as to exclusion of prorogation in cases arising out of hire purchase agreements.
[8] See pages noted above.

The territorial jurisdiction of the Sheriff in the Small Debt Court is the same as in other proceedings in the Sheriff Court.[1]

[1] 7 Edw. VII c. 51, secs. 4, 45.

2. COMPETENT ACTIONS.

Every kind of action competent in the Ordinary Court is not competent in the Small Debt Court, which was instituted, and is still intended, mainly for the recovery of debts. The Statute of 1837 speaks of a " debt, demand, or penalty,"[1] but statutory penalties are now generally recovered under the provisions of the Summary Jurisdiction Act.[2]

[1] 7 Will. IV & 1 Vict. c. 41, sec. 2.
[2] Glasgow District Railway Co. v. Hutchison's Trustees, 1884, 11 R. (J.) 43.

Procedure in the Small Debt Court in actions of delivery,[1] and multiplepoinding,[2], and in furthcomings,[3] sequestrations for rent,[4] and actions relating to hire purchase agreements[5] is dealt with later. Reference has already been made to summary removings which in certain circumstances are disposed of in the same way as small debt proceedings.[6] Jurisdiction to deal with disputes between employers and workmen under the Employers and Workmen Act, 1875, is also conferred on the Small Debt Court by that Act.[7]

[1] See p. 477, infra.
[2] See p. 481, infra.
[3] See p. 481, infra.
[4] See p. 482, infra.
[5] See p. 478, infra.
[6] See p. 405, supra.
[7] 38 & 39 Vict. c. 90, secs. 4, 14.　See p. 484, infra.

It is competent to sue in the Small Debt Court for such a debt as continuing aliment,[1] and to decern for future payments or instalments over a period of twelve months, so long as the whole sum sued for does not exceed £20.[2]　An action of affiliation and aliment where the child has died is commonly brought in the Small Debt Court if the amount due is within the limit of value.[3] The test of value in the Small Debt Court is the sum sued for and the fact that the decision may virtually settle a question of future liability does not affect the competency.[4]

[1] See Nixon v. Caldwell, 1876, 3 R. (J.) 31 ; cf. Strang v. Strang, 1882, 19 S.L.R. 724.
[2] 52 & 53 Vict. c. 26, sec. 9.
[3] But a pursuer has the option of taking action in the Ordinary Court; Campbell v. Haddow, 1890, 7 Sh.Ct.Rep. 13.
[4] Nixon v. Caldwell, supra ; Gerry v. High, 1877, Guthrie's Select Cases I, 417.

If parties in an ordinary action so desire they may lodge in process a minute, signed by them or their solicitors, agreeing to the cause being disposed of in the manner provided under the Small Debt Acts.[1]　On that being done the Sheriff must remit the case to the Small Debt Roll and the whole powers and provisions of the Small Debt Acts then become applicable to the case.[1]　This matter has already been discussed in detail.[2]

[1] 7 Edw. VII c. 51, Schedule I, Rule 61.
[2] See p. 178, supra.

A small debt case may at any stage[1] be remitted to the Ordinary Roll either by the Sheriff *ex proprio motu*, or on cause shown, if the Sheriff is of opinion that the importance of the question raised warrants that course.[2]　If the remit is made the case proceeds in all respects (including appeal) as if it had been originally raised in the Ordinary Court.[2]　A case so remitted comes within the present definition of a summary cause[3] and is subject to the rights of appeal competent in such causes.[4]　The existence of conflicting decisions in the Small Debt Court is a sufficient reason for making such a remit.[5]

[1] See Wigtownshire Creamery Co. v. Portpatrick, &c., Joint Committee, 1903, 6 F. (J.) 3.
[2] 7 Edw. VII c. 51, sec. 48.
[3] Ibid., sec. 3 (i); 2 & 3 Geo. V c. 28, Schedule I; cf. Price v. Canadian Pacific Railway Co., 1911 S.C. 631.
[4] See p. 302, supra.
[5] Munro v. North British Railway Co., 1904, 21 Sh.Ct.Rep. 19; cf. Brown v. Corporation of Glasgow, 1909, 25 Sh.Ct.Rep. 185.

A claim upon a debit and credit account bringing out a balance due to the pursuer may be sued for in the Small Debt Court. But the question whether a defender is bound to count and reckon with the pursuer is not one which can be competently decided in the Small Debt Court, and an action of count, reckoning, and payment with alternative conclusions in the usual form is appropriate only as an ordinary action.[1]

[1] See Pollock v. Fulton, 1906, 22 Sh.Ct.Rep. 161.

3. PROCEDURE.

Statutory provisions as to procedure in the Sheriff Court in general do not necessarily apply also in the Small Debt Court.[1] The scheme of the 1907 Act is to apply only certain of the Procedure Rules to the Small Debt Court and this supports the view—which is thought to be correct—that provisions not made expressly applicable to small debt procedure do not apply there. But there seems no reason for excluding from the Small Debt Court common law rules of practice or procedure.[2]

[1] Wilson v. Glasgow Tramways Co., 1878, 5 R. 981; Leven v. Provincial Homes Investment Co., 1904, 6 F. (J.) 62; M'Kenzie v. Geekie, 1930, 46 Sh.Ct.Rep. 221.
[2] Martin v. Caledonian Railway Co., 1911, 27 Sh.Ct.Rep. 152.

A small debt action is commenced by a summons, in the form of Schedule A of the Small Debt Act, 1837, as now amended.[1] It sets forth the names of the pursuer and defender, and any special character in which they appear, with a brief statement of the claim or demand, and the grounds of it, and it calls upon the defender to answer at a set diet.[1] The small debt summons contains also warrant to cite witnesses and havers, and warrant to arrest on the dependence.[1] It is signed by the Sheriff-clerk, and is a sufficient warrant for the citation of the defender.[1] The grounds of action may be stated in the summons but are usually set out in a separate statement or account. A copy of any such statement or account is served with the summons.[1] The last date in the account should be stated in the summons.[1]　An account consisting of a series of entries " To goods " under different dates has been held to be sufficient, but the action was for a balance only and invoices had apparently been furnished.[2]　It is thought that in the normal case such an account without further details would not be sufficient.　The special provisions in regard to claims by moneylenders are referred to elsewhere.[3]

[1] 7 Will. IV & 1 Vict. c. 41, sec. 3, Schedule A ; Act of Sederunt, 3rd February, 1933, sec. 6.
[2] Cox Bros. v. Jackson & Lamb, 1877, 4 R. 898.
[3] See p. 627, et seq., infra.

If the defender has already had a statement furnished to him by passbook or otherwise it may suffice to incorporate the account by reference, as, for instance, " Goods as per passbook in defender's possession."　Certain kinds of debts which are in use to be stated in a slump sum, as, for instance, a doctor's bill, may be sufficiently libelled as, say, professional services for a certain period.[1]　In such a case, if details are called for, the practice is to continue the case to a future diet, that details may be furnished.

[1] See Mowat v. Martine, 1856, 2 Irvine 435.

Citation on a defender may be made as follows :—

1. By Sheriff-officer's service on defender personally or at his dwelling place or if a company—which presumably includes a partnership—at its ordinary place of business.[1]　By virtue of the Sheriff Court Rules service at the principal place of business, if within the jurisdiction, and, if not, at any place of business within the jurisdiction is sufficient, and place of business in the case of a corporation or association includes the office or place of business of its clerk or secretary.[2]　A witness to the citation is not required.[3]　It seems at least doubtful whether a messenger-at-arms can serve a small debt summons.[4]　If the officer is satisfied that the defender is refusing access or is concealing himself to avoid service, or that he has removed within a period of forty days, his present address being unknown, the officer may affix the summons to the gate or door, or leave it with an inmate, and send by registered post a copy summons to the address which after diligent inquiry he deems most likely to find defender, or to his last known address, and, in that case, the affixing of the summons and the posting of the copy constitute valid citation.[5]　The execution of citation states the endeavours to effect service and the circumstances that prevented it, and is accompanied by the post-office

receipt.[5] It has been indicated that this method of service is only available in citation at a dwelling-house or residence.[6]

2. By an officer or solicitor serving by registered post under the Citation Amendment Act, 1882, and reference is made to what has been already written on this point.[7]

3. By edictal citation where that is necessary and competent.[8]

[1] 7 Will IV & 1 Vict. c. 41, sec. 3.
[2] 7 Edw. VII c. 51, Schedule I, Rule 11; 2 & 3 Geo. V c. 28, Schedule II. See p. 127, supra.
[3] 7 Will. IV & 1 Vict. c. 41, sec. 3; 34 & 35 Vict. c. 42, sec. 4.
[4] M'Culloch v. M'Laughlin, 1930 J.C. 8; and earlier cases cited, p. 118, supra.
[5] 34 & 35 Vict. c. 42, sec. 3.
[6] Bell v. Bowman & Co., 1918, 35 Sh.Ct.Rep. 90.
[7] See p. 117, et seq., supra.
[8] See p. 120, supra.

The minimum induciæ of citation upon a small debt summons is six days.[1] The provision of the Sheriff Courts Act, empowering the Sheriff to shorten or extend the induciæ in an ordinary action does not apply in the Small Debt Court,[2] and there is no power under the Small Debt Acts to shorten the induciæ. It is competent, however, to extend it, and in edictal citation the induciæ is always fourteen days. In actions of furthcoming and multiplepoinding there is a special induciæ of twelve days when the common debtor is not within the Sheriffdom.[3] As in the case of ordinary actions endorsement is not necessary for service beyond the county from which the warrant was issued[4]; service of new may be ordered[4]; and a party appearing may not state any objection to the regularity of the service.[4] Where a circuit Small Debt Court is held a defender may be cited either to the circuit Court or to the principal Small Debt Court.[5] Where several counties are combined into one Sheriffdom a small debt summons signed by the Sheriff-clerk of one county, citing to that Court a defender from another county, has been held to be invalid in respect that the Sheriff-clerk's powers did not extend over the combined Sheriffdom.[6]

[1] 7 Will. IV & 1 Vict. c. 41, sec. 3.
[2] 7 Edw. VII c. 51, sec. 45, Schedule I, Rule 6.
[3] 7 Will. IV & 1 Vict. c. 41, secs. 9, 10.
[4] 7 Edw. VII c. 51, sec. 45, Schedule I, Rules 10, 12, 13. See pp. 126, 127, supra.
[5] Stewart v. M'Gregor & Sons, 1868, 40 Scot. Jur. 654.
[6] Mactavish & Co. v. Cameron, 1899, 15 Sh.Ct.Rep. 292.

Arrestment on the dependence of a small debt action, if executed by an officer but not served personally, is not effectual against the arrestee, unless the officer sends a copy of the schedule of arrestment by registered post to the last known place of abode of the

arrestee.[1] If the place of abode is unknown, or if the arrestee
is a firm or corporation, the postal intimation is made at the
arrestee's principal place of business if known, or, if not known,
at any known place of business of the arrestee. In either case the
officer must certify in his execution that this has been done and
specify the address to which postal intimation was sent.[1] In this
matter, there is no difference between Small Debt and Ordinary
Court arrestment.

[1] 7 Edw. VII c. 51, sec. 45, Schedule I, Rule 126.

An arrestment upon any warrant or decree of the Small Debt
Court—which includes an arrestment on the dependence—may be
executed by registered letter containing the schedule of arrestment
posted to the residence or place of business of the arrestee, or
to his last known address if it continues to be his legal domicile
or proper place of citation.[1] Arrestments may be so executed by
a Sheriff-officer who would otherwise be entitled to execute the
arrestments, or by a messenger-at-arms resident in the Sheriffdom
where the place of execution is situated, or if no officer or messenger
is resident in the Sheriffdom by a solicitor enrolled in the Sheriffdom[1]—the pursuer's solicitor being apparently competent to act.[2]
While the messenger must be resident, and the solicitor must be
enrolled, in the Sheriffdom where the arrestments are to be executed
a Sheriff-officer of any county can execute them.[3] The arrestments
date from the actual time of delivery of the registered letter, and
provision is made in regard to proof of delivery and to refusal of
the registered letter.[1] Rule 126[4] does not apply to arrestments
executed as above,[5] and endorsement is not necessary in small debt
procedure where diligence has to be executed in another Sheriffdom.[6]

[1] 16 & 17 Geo. V c. 16, secs. 2, 5.
[2] Cf. 16 & 17 Geo. V c. 16, sec. 3.
[3] 52 & 53 Vict. c. 26, sec. 11; 16 & 17 Geo. V c. 16, sec. 2 (2) (b).
[4] 7 Edw. VII c. 51, Schedule I, Rule 126.
[5] 16 & 17 Geo. V c. 16, sec. 2 (2) (g).
[6] 52 & 53 Vict. c. 26, sec. 11.

An arrestment in the Small Debt Court falls on the expiry of
three months from its date, unless it is renewed by special warrant
or order intimated to the arrestee, which keeps it in force for
another three months when it can be again renewed, or unless an
action of furthcoming or multiplepoinding is brought in the Small
Debt Court within the three months when it remains in force till
the termination of such action.[1] The requirements of immediate
reporting of arrestments, and of service of an action on which

arrestments have been used on the dependence within twenty days of executing the arrestments, apply as in the case of ordinary actions.[2] Wages cannot be arrested on the dependence of a small debt summons,[3] and the salary of a music hall artiste has been held to be protected on this ground.[4]

[1] 7 Will. IV & 1 Vict. c. 41, sec. 6.
[2] 7 Edw. VII c. 51, sec. 45, Rule 127; 2 & 3 Geo. V c. 28, Schedule II. See pp. 260, 265, supra.
[3] 8 & 9 Vict. c. 39. See generally as to restriction of arrestments at pp. 266, 272, supra.
[4] Locke v. Chard, 1908, 24 Sh.Ct.Rep. 305.

In order to have such arrestments recalled the defender may consign the amount of the claim, and a fixed sum for expenses, in the hands of the Sheriff-clerk of the Sheriffdom where the arrestment has been used, or the Sheriffdom where the action is pending, or he may find caution to the satisfaction of the first-mentioned Sheriff-clerk that the arrested subjects will be forthcoming.[1] If consignation is made where the action is pending the defender obtains a certificate from that Sheriff-clerk and produces it to the Sheriff-clerk of the Sheriffdom where the arrestments have been used, or, if the case is disposed of, he produces to that Sheriff-clerk evidence of a decree of absolvitor or of payment or consignation of the sums decerned for.[1] A certificate in statutory form by the Sheriff-clerk of the Sheriffdom where the arrestments were used operates as a warrant for loosing the arrestments.[1]

[1] 7 Will. IV & 1 Vict. c. 41, sec. 8, Schedule C.

In the Small Debt Court a party may appear personally, or be represented by one of his family, or by such person—other than an officer of Court—as the Sheriff shall allow,[1] or he may appear by or along with a solicitor whose fee may be included as part of the expenses of the cause.[2] The Sheriff appears to have a complete discretion as to the person—not being an officer of Court—whom he may allow to represent a party.[3]

[1] 7 Will. IV & 1 Vict. c. 41, sec. 15.
[2] 7 Edw. VII c. 51, sec. 44.
[3] A v. B, 1923, 40 Sh.Ct.Rep. 25.

The whole proceedings in the Small Debt Court are summary in their nature. If the defender do not appear, decree in absence may be granted against him.[1] If the pursuer do not appear, the defender is entitled to decree of absolvitor.[1] But such decrees need not necessarily be granted, for the Sheriff has a discretion to adjourn the case to a subsequent Court day, if good reason for

delay is stated.[1] When decree is granted the Sheriff in his discretion may allow the sum decerned for to be paid by instalments.[2]
There is no distinction in the Small Debt Court, as in the Ordinary
Court, between a decree by default and a decree in absence. If
the defender is not present, or represented, at the diet at which
decree is pronounced, it is a decree in absence. The provisions as
to protestation and reponing in the Ordinary Court do not apply
to the Small Debt Court, but the ordinary powers of amendment
are available in either defended or undefended cases.[3] If judgment is given in the absence of either party the Act of 1837 provides a remedy by sist.[4] It has been held that an order on a
defender to find caution for the sum sued for is not competent
in the Small Debt Court.[5]

[1] 7 Will. IV & 1 Vict. c. 41, sec. 15.
[2] Ibid., sec. 18; 14 & 15 Geo. V c. 16, sec. 1.   See Friedlander & Co.
    v. Hutton, 1901, 18 Sh.Ct.Rep. 138.
[3] 7 Edw. VII c. 51, sec. 45, Schedule I, Rules 26, 79, 80.
[4] See p. 475, infra.
[5] Paterson v. Paterson's Trustees, 1872, 2 Coup. 234.

The only official record of proceedings in the Small Debt Court
is made in the statutory book of causes, which must contain certain
prescribed particulars of the cases.[1] A copy of the Roll of causes
to be tried on each Court day is directed to be exhibited at the
Court-house, at least an hour before the sitting of the Court, and
to remain there during the sitting,[1] but in some Courts this direction is not followed. The Sheriff-clerk, or other officer of Court, is
required to call the causes in the roll in their order.[1] Judgment
is pronounced orally in Court, but this may be delayed and the case
may be adjourned to a specified future date for judgment; or the
Sheriff may make avizandum and give judgment within seven days.[2]
These provisions as to judgment probably apply only to a final
judgment.[3]

[1] 7 Will. IV & 1 Vict. c. 41, sec. 17.
[2] 52 & 53 Vict. c. 26, sec. 10.
[3] Paterson & Sons v. Robinson, 1895, 22 R. (J.) 45.

The decree in a small debt action is usually endorsed upon the
summons, and in practice the whole proceedings are embodied in
one printed paper. If this goes amissing a second extract of the
decree may be issued which may be written upon a separate paper,
and has the same force and effect in all respects as the first extract.[1]
As in an ordinary action a lost number of process may be replaced
by a copy authenticated as the Sheriff may require.[2]

[1] 7 Edw. VII c. 51, sec. 47.
[2] Ibid., sec. 45, Schedule I, Rule 17.

In addition to the ordinary provisions as to amendment already referred to[1] the representative, or assignee, or trustee of a pursuer who has died, or assigned his rights, or become bankrupt may be sisted in his place upon a verbal application to the Sheriff, made in Court.[2] In the same way the representative or trustee of a defender who has died or become bankrupt may be sisted in his stead.[2] A party who acquires right to a small debt decree can enforce it after the Sheriff-clerk has endorsed a fiat upon it in the same way as in an ordinary action.[3]

[1] See previous page.
[2] 52 & 53 Vict. c. 26. sec. 4.
[3] Ibid., sec. 5; 1 & 2 Vict. c. 114, sec. 12. See p. 256, supra.

In the Small Debt Court, as in the Ordinary Court, objections to a deed or writing founded on may be stated and maintained by way of exception without the necessity of bringing a reduction,[1] and reference is made to what has been already written on this point.[2] The rule authorizing an order on the objector to find caution or consignation does not apply in the Small Debt Court.[3]

[1] 7 Edw. VII c. 51, sec. 45, Schedule I, Rule 50. See also Wilson v. Glasgow Tramways Co., 1878, 5 R. 981; Neil v. M'Nair, 1901, 3 F. (J.) 85.
[2] See p. 22, supra.
[3] 7 Edw. VII c. 51, sec. 45, Schedule I, Rule 51.

Defence by way of counter-claim is in a somewhat different position in the Small Debt Court from the same defence in the Ordinary Court. Under the Act of 1837 it was provided that a copy of any counter-claim had to be served on the pursuer at least one free day before the day of appearance, otherwise the claim could not be pleaded except of consent.[1] By the Sheriff Courts Act, 1907, the rule permitting a counter-claim to be stated in the defences is applied to small debt procedure,[2] but in view of the absence of written defences in the Small Debt Court and of the consequent lack of notice to the pursuer it has been held that the provisions of the Act of 1837 have not been superseded and that service of a counter-claim in terms thereof is still necessary.[3] Frequently this procedure is avoided by a counter-claim tabled at the diet of appearance being received of consent. When the counter-claim is not larger in amount than the pursuer's claim in the summons, service of a counter-claim is the method usually adopted and the counter-claim is pled only by way of set-off. But when the defender seeks to recover from pursuer a sum larger than the sum sued for it is probably better that the defender should state his counter-claim in the form of a substantive action.

¹ 7 Will. IV & 1 Vict. c. 41, sec. 11; for form of counter-claim see Lees, Small Debt Handbook, 204.
² 7 Edw. VII c. 51, sec. 45, Schedule I, Rule 55.
³ Johnstone v. M'George, 1908, 24 Sh.Ct.Rep. 83; Simons & Co. v. Miller, 1909, 25 Sh.Ct.Rep. 122. See also Taylor v. Ormond & Co., 1906, 8 F. (J.) 76.

A counter-claim may be pleaded in a small debt cause, notwithstanding that the defender is a foreigner, or a person resident or carrying on business in another Sheriffdom.¹ The original direction was that the counter-claim had to be served upon the pursuer by an officer,² but it may now be served by post.³

¹ 7 Edw. VII c. 51, secs. 6 (h), 45.
² 7 Will. IV & 1 Vict. c. 41, sec. 11.
³ 45 & 46 Vict. c. 77, sec. 3.

The authorities dealing with the nature of counter-claims which may be pleaded are unsatisfactory. Originally small debt summonses were for payment of money only and the counter-claims intended were claims of the same nature.¹ It appears to have been the practice, however, to admit illiquid counter-claims against liquid principal claims,² and it was held in the Small Debt Court that a counter-claim for payment could be dealt with in an action for delivery with which the payment was apparently not connected.³ This latter judgment proceeded on a Justiciary Court decision which does not appear to settle any general question.⁴ In this matter there seems no ground for distinction between the Ordinary Court and the Small Debt Court, and it is suggested that counterclaims in the latter should be admitted only when they conform to what is held to be competent in the Ordinary Court.⁵ As to the position where the principal claim is admitted see the case undernoted.⁶

¹ 7 Will. IV & 1 Vict. c. 41, secs. 2, 11.
² Lees, Small Debt Handbook, 38; but cf. Jack & Co. v. Hutchison, 1911, 27 Sh.Ct.Rep. 96.
³ Bernstein v. Holloway, 1909, 26 Sh.Ct.Rep. 32.
⁴ Rollands v. Rolland, 1907, 15 S.L.T. 141.
⁵ See p. 151, et seq., supra.
⁶ M'Bey v. Laird, 1946, 62 Sh.Ct.Rep. 140.

The small debt summons—or the service copy in the case of the defender—is the warrant for citing witnesses and havers.¹ Endorsement by the Sheriff-clerk of the jurisdiction where the witness is to be cited is not required,² and the warrant may be

executed by an officer of the Court which granted the warrant,
or by an officer of the Sheriffdom within which it is to be executed.[2]
No witness to the citation is required.[3] Postal citation is also
competent in the usual way.[4] The minimum induciæ of citation
is forty-eight hours, and letters of second diligence may be granted
to compel the attendance of a witness or haver who fails to answer
to the citation.[5] The privilege of claiming that travelling expenses
be tendered before the issue of second diligence does not seem to
extend to witnesses cited for the Small Debt Court.[6]

[1] 7 Will. IV & 1 Vict. c. 41, sec. 3.
[2] 7 Edw. VII c. 51, sec. 45, Schedule I, Rule 10.
[3] 34 & 35 Vict. c. 42, sec. 4.
[4] 45 & 46 Vict. c. 77, sec. 3. See further, p. 117, et seq., supra.
[5] 7 Will. IV & 1 Vict. c. 41, sec. 12.
[6] 7 Edw. VII c. 51, sec. 45, Schedule I, Rule 71.

Commission to take evidence may be granted in the Small Debt
Court, and also remits to men of skill.[1] Diligence for recovery
of documents appears to be competent[2] and the rules giving power
to transfer a cause to another Court having jurisdiction over
any of several defenders, and to transfer on sustaining a plea of
no jurisdiction are applied to small debt procedure.[3] But the
power to remit to another Sheriffdom on cause shown is not available.[4] A small debt cause does not fall asleep in year and day.[5]
A right of abandonment in the Small Debt Court has been recognized.[6] The special provisions as to actions by moneylenders are
dealt with later.[7]

[1] 7 Edw. VII c. 51, sec. 45, Schedule I, Rules 60, 63, 70.
[2] Taylor v. Marshall, 1919, 35 Sh.Ct.Rep. 176.
[3] 7 Edw. VII c. 51, sec. 45, Schedule I, Rules 19, 21.
[4] Ibid., Rule 20.
[5] Kean v. Lindsay, 1852, 25 Scot. Jur. 8.
[6] Martin v. Caledonian Railway Co., 1911, 27 Sh.Ct.Rep. 152. See
  also Goldie v. Chrysler Motors, 1938, 55 Sh.Ct.Rep. 99.
[7] See p. 627, infra.

In the Small Debt Court a decree granted in absence against
a defender may be opened up by consigning with the Sheriff-clerk
the expenses decerned for, and a further sum of ten shillings to
meet further expenses and obtaining a warrant sisting the case
for a future Court day, and authorizing the citation of the pursuer
for that day.[1] In the same way when decree of absolvitor has been
granted in absence of the pursuer he may obtain a sist by consigning within one calendar month thereafter the expenses decerned
for and a further sum of five shillings.[1] An appeal to the High

Court against the granting of a sist was held competent[2] but the decision has since been disapproved.[3]

[1] 7 Will. IV & 1 Vict. c. 41, sec. 16.
[2] Gow & Sons v. Thomson, 1895, 1 Adam 534; Welsh v. Semple, 1894, 2 S.L.T. 11.
[3] Murdoch v. Glasgow Corporation, 1932 J.C. 61.

By a series of cases decided on appeal[1] it was held that a sist was not competent if litiscontestation had taken place. The question arose in cases where both parties had been present at one diet and the case had been adjourned to a later date or continued for proof, when one party had failed to appear. The test suggested was whether parties had joined issue at the first diet, and, if they had, a sist was refused as the decree was held to be not granted in absence. This distinction—which seems inappropriate to the procedure in the Small Debt Court—appears to be now departed from and it is suggested that the only test of the competency of a sist is whether the decree has been in fact pronounced in the absence of the party in question.[2]

[1] Worrall, Hallam & Co. v. M'Dowall, 1885, 13 R. (J.) 4; M'Neil v. M'Neil, 1891, 18 R. (J.) 38; Oliver v. Simpson, 1898, 1 F. (J.) 12; Netherwood & Lee v. Scott, 1907, 24 Sh.Ct.Rep. 39.
[2] Ratcliffe v. Farquharson, 1908 S.C. (J.) 71. See also Montgomery v. Loughran, 1891, 18 R. (J.) 25; Aschengrau v. Hillson & Co., 1912, 28 Sh.Ct.Rep. 141.

A defender must apply for a sist before a charge is given, or, if given, before implement of the decree and within three months of the charge.[1] The execution of a poinding prevents a sist being granted,[2] but the use of arrestments does not.[3] It is thought that a defender is entitled to obtain a sist, so long as the decree has not been fully implemented, and when payments had been made by a third party a defender who was sought to be made liable for a small balance of expenses was held entitled to a sist.[4] If a decree is not enforced by poinding or imprisonment within a year from its date, or from the date of a charge upon it, it cannot be enforced without a new charge being given.[1] If a second charge is given a sist is competent within three months thereafter,[5] but a sist is not competent where only one charge has been given and application has not been made for a sist within three months thereafter, even though a year has elapsed since the charge was given.[6] Each party may sist the case once only.[7]

[1] 7 Will. IV & 1 Vict. c. 41, sec. 16.
[2] Wyllie v. Lawson, 1863, 4 Irvine 441; Sinclair v. Aird & Co., 1917, 33 Sh.Ct.Rep. 251.
[3] Paul v. Macrae, 1887, 3 Sh.Ct.Rep. 338; Murray & Sons v. Adams, 1909, 25 Sh.Ct.Rep. 152.

[4] See Kegan v. Crumblish, 1896, 12 Sh.Ct.Rep. 30; Christie v. Orr, 1927, 44 Sh.Ct.Rep. 33; Lees, Small Debt Handbook, 54.
[5] Lochie & Co. v. Brown, 1863, 4 Irvine 363.
[6] Aldin v. Kelvin Motors, 1937 J.C. 1.
[7] Grange v. M'Kenzie, 1866, 5 Irvine 324.

The fees payable to the Sheriff-clerk and the Sheriff-officer are prescribed by Statute,[1] and fees to a solicitor may be allowed in addition.[2] The solicitor may obtain decree for expenses in his own name,[3] and a solicitor conducting his own case has been held entitled to his fees.[4] When a small debt summons was served and returned to the Court for calling the defender who paid before the calling was held liable for pursuer's solicitor's fee for attending the calling.[5]

[1] 7 Will. IV & 1 Vict. c. 41, sec. 32; Act of Sederunt, 16th July, 1929; Codifying Act of Sederunt, M. iii; Act of Sederunt, 20th July, 1945; Act of Sederunt, 13th July, 1946.
[2] 7 Edw. VII c. 51, sec. 44. See Act of Sederunt, 7th May, 1935, chap. IX.
[3] 52 & 53 Vict. c. 26, sec. 12.
[4] Stewart v. Ollason, 1917, 34 Sh.Ct.Rep. 124.
[5] Glyco Metal Co. v. Allan & Son, 1907, 23 Sh.Ct.Rep. 145.

4. ACTION OF DELIVERY.

(a) *Small Debt Amendment Act.*—An action *ad factum præstandum* is not in general competent in the Small Debt Court, but an action for delivery of corporeal moveables was made competent by the Act of 1889.[1] The term corporeal moveables includes all articles which are capable of being taken tangible possession of.[2] It would include such items as a written agreement[3] or a season ticket,[4] but would not cover such moveable property as stocks and shares or a patent right, or any other property not capable of being handled and moved from one place to another.[5] The action is competent only if the value of the moveables of which delivery is sought is proved to the satisfaction of the Sheriff not to exceed £20,[1] and it is competent, although not imperative, to sue alternatively for the money value (not exceeding £20) of the articles claimed.[1] Specialties in regard to cases arising out of hire purchase agreements are dealt with later.[6]

[1] 52 & 53 Vict. c. 26, sec. 2.
[2] See Bell's Principles, 1285.
[3] Baird v. Refuge Assurance Co., 1890, 6 Sh.Ct.Rep. 187.
[4] See Stewart v. M'Dougall, 1907, 14 S.L.T. 921; 15 S.L.T. 662.
[5] Bell's Principles. 1338.
[6] See next page.

It is not possible to modify the value to make an action of delivery competent, as in the case of a debt, for the pursuer must

satisfy the Court that the value does not exceed £20.[1] In practice
competency in respect of value is assumed, if the action is
unopposed, and, if contested, the value[2] may be vouched by the
pursuer's oath, or, without oral evidence at all, by the production
of documents, or in suitable circumstances, by a remit.   The
summons may ask for delivery only or for delivery and alternatively payment.   Warrant to search and take possession if desired
should be asked for,[3] but if pursuers have right to enter and
take possession under their contract an action for delivery may
be unnecessary and incompetent.[4]   When decree is asked in Court
the pursuer must, if the summons has an alternative crave, elect
whether to take decree for delivery or decree for payment of the
money value.[5]   If the defender in an action for delivery claims
the right to retain the articles against payment of a debt this
should be stated as a counter-claim served on pursuer.[6]

[1] 52 & 53 Vict. c. 26, sec. 2.
[2] This has been said to mean the value to the pursuer; Jay & Co. v.
    Paton, 1907, 23 Sh.Ct.Rep. 329.
[3] See next page.
[4] Bruce Brothers v. M'Vittie, 1943, 62 Sh.Ct.Rep. 20; Bell Brothers v.
    Hamilton and Wilkie, 1945, 62 Sh.Ct.Rep. 31.
[5] Dalbooca v. Millar, &c., 1905, 21 Sh.Ct.Rep. 183.
[6] Rollands v. Rolland, 1907, 15 S.L.T. 141; Bernstein v. Holloway,
    1909, 26 Sh.Ct.Rep. 32.   See p. 473, supra.

Prior to the passing of the Hire Purchase and Small Debt Act
of 1932[1] decrees for delivery in the Small Debt Court were enforceable by imprisonment under the warrant in the decree itself.   But
no person may now be apprehened or imprisoned for failure to
comply with a small debt decree for delivery save in accordance
with the statutory provisions[2] as set out below.

[1] 22 & 23 Geo. V c. 38.
[2] Ibid., sec. 7.

(b) *Hire Purchase and Small Debt (Scotland) Act.*—By the
Hire Purchase and Small Debt (Scotland) Act, 1932, certain provisions are made in regard to contracts to which the Act applies.
These are contracts of hire purchase—as defined by the Act—
entered into after 12th July, 1932, and relating to articles not
exceeding £20 in value.[1]   That value is taken as being the sum
of the instalments stipulated for in the contract,[2] and where there
are several articles hired the Act only applies where the aggregate
value of the articles is not over £20.[3]   If decree of delivery is
granted in respect of default by a defender under a contract
to which the Act applies the defender may retain or recover the
article hired on making payment to the pursuer within fourteen

days of the decree of any unpaid instalments, the expenses awarded in the action and any expenses incurred by the pursuer in obtaining possession under the decree.[4] The last-mentioned expenses are, failing agreement, to be determined by the Court which has granted the decree on an application presented by the defender, and which is to be disposed of summarily without any written pleadings.[4] A motion in the small debt process is probably intended.

[1] 22 & 23 Geo. V c. 38, sec. 1.
[2] Ibid., sec. 10 (2).
[3] Bell Brothers v. Hamilton and Wilkie, 1945, 62 Sh.Ct.Rep. 31.
[4] 22 & 23 Geo. V c. 38, sec. 5.

The Act contains various provisions as to hire purchase agreements which deal with matters other than procedure—and are therefore not touched on here—and also certain provisions as to procedure not restricted to actions arising out of hire purchase contracts. By one of its sections, part of which has since been repealed and re-enacted in 1940, any agreement to prorogate the jurisdiction of any particular Court is declared void if it is contained in, or relates to, a contract of purchase or hire purchase as defined by the Act of 1940.[1] The Act of 1932 also authorized the inclusion in small debt decrees of delivery of a warrant to Sheriff-officers to search for and take possession of the moveables to which the decree relates and this warrant includes authority to open shut and lock-fast places.[2] If this warrant is desired it should be asked for in the small debt summons. The premises to be searched must be in the occupation of the defender as owner or tenant.[2]

[1] 3 & 4 Geo. VI c. 42, sec. 4.
[2] 22 & 23 Geo. V c. 38, sec. 6.

The right to enforce decrees of delivery from the Small Debt Court by imprisonment is abolished by the Act, which also provides that no person may be apprehended or imprisoned for failure to comply with a small debt decree for delivery of moveables except in accordance with certain provisions laid down in the Act.[1] These provisions relate to all small debt decrees for delivery and are not limited to those arising out of hire purchase contracts. If delivery is not made within ten days after such a decree has been granted the pursuer may then make application for warrant to imprison the defender,[2] apparently irrespective of whether he has been charged on the decree or not, but a charge may be thought desirable if defender was not personally present when the decree was pronounced. Such application is to be disposed of summarily without any written pleadings, and is to be served on the defender on seven days' induciæ.[2] Divergent views have been expressed as to the procedure in such applications but the intention in the Act is thought to be that they should be presented as summary applications in the Ordinary Sheriff Court and not in the Small Debt Court, nor as part of the existing small debt action for delivery.[3] If in such an application it is proved that the defender is wilfully refusing to comply with the decree the Court may order his imprisonment for any period not exceeding six weeks, or it may recall the decree and substitute one for payment, or make such other order as appears to the Court to be just and equitable.[4] In the case of a substituted decree it has been held that the expenses of a charge served on the defender, but not the expenses of the application to imprison, should be included in the sum decerned for.[5] A defender imprisoned under such a decree may obtain immediate liberation when the Court is satisfied that delivery has been made in accordance with the decree, or that the defender is no longer wilfully refusing to comply with the decree, and any person to whom delivery is made in terms of the decree is required to intimate such delivery forthwith to the Court.[6] Imprisonment under the Act is without prejudice to any other competent diligence or execution.[7] Where a defender is imprisoned the pursuer is not liable to aliment him or to contribute to his aliment.[8] A decree is held to be complied with if the defender delivers to (a) any person specified in a notice by pursuer to defender and residing or carrying on business within a radius of two miles from the place where any person who acted for pursuer in the formation or conclusion of the contract resided or carried on business when he so acted, or (b) failing any such notice to any person who so acted as agent for pursuer.[9] In making applications under the Act the time limit for enforcing small debt decrees must be kept in view.[10]

[1] 22 & 23 Geo. V c. 38, sec. 7 (1).
[2] Ibid., sec. 7 (1) (i) (ii) (iii).
[3] Bell Bros. (H.P.) v. Hunt, 1933, 49 Sh.Ct.Rep. 288; Aron Taximeter Co. v. Russell, 1934, 50 Sh.Ct.Rep. 75.
[4] 22 & 23 Geo. V c. 38, sec. 7 (1) (iv).
[5] Cuthbertson & Co. v. Darcy, 1933, 50 Sh.Ct.Rep. 80.
[6] 22 & 23 Geo. V c. 38, sec. 7 (1) (v).
[7] Ibid., sec. 7 (1) (vi).
[8] Ibid., sec. 7 (1) (vii).
[9] Ibid., sec. 7 (2).
[10] 7 Will. IV & 1 Vict. c. 41, sec. 13. See p. 486, infra.

No cause, action or proceeding on, or arising out of, any hire purchase contract to which the Act applies, which may competently be brought or instituted in the Small Debt Court, may be brought or instituted except in that Court.[1] But that is not to affect or prejudice the Sheriff's power to remit a cause to his ordinary roll.[1]

[1] 22 & 23 Geo. V c. 38, sec. 8.

5. MULTIPLEPOINDING.

An action of multiplepoinding may proceed in the Small Debt Court, where the fund, or the value of the subject, *in medio* does not exceed £20.[1] It may be brought in the Court to the jurisdiction of which the holder of the fund is amenable[1]; or in the Sheriffdom where the fund or subject is situated.[2] That a fund or subject is claimed by more than one person, under competing arrestments or otherwise, is the statutory ground upon which a small debt action of multiplepoinding may be competently based.[1] The action may be raised by the holder of the fund, or by a claimant in his name, and the claimant and common debtor and the holder—if he is not the real raiser—are cited as defenders.[1] The matter of intimation, by newspaper advertisements or otherwise, is left in the discretion of the Sheriff, the general direction being that all interested parties are to have an opportunity of claiming upon the fund *in medio*, and that judgment preferring a claimant is not to be given at the first calling, or until due intimation has been given.[1] In practice the competency of the action, and the existence of the fund *in medio*, are usually inquired into at the first calling, and the case is then continued to a future Court to hear claimants, parties meantime being ordered to lodge claims of which a statutory form is given.[1] The designation of the real raiser must be set forth in the summons, and he may be allowed his expenses preferably out of the fund.[3] A certificate that all government duties have been paid is required before any order for payment or transfer of property can be granted.[4]

[1] 7 Will. IV & 1 Vict. c. 41, sec. 10, Schedule E.
[2] 7 Edw. VII c. 51, secs. 6 (g), 45, Schedule I, Rule 128.
[3] Ibid., Rule 129.
[4] Codifying Act of Sederunt, L. III, 1; Act of Sederunt, 16th July, 1936, sec. 3.

6. FURTHCOMING.

An action of furthcoming may be brought in the Small Debt Court, where the sum sought to be recovered under the furthcoming does not exceed £20, exclusive of expenses and dues of extract.[1] This action, like a multiplepoinding, may be brought either in the Court to whose jurisdiction the arrestee or holder of the fund is amenable, or in that within whose jurisdiction the arrested fund is situated, irrespective of where the common debtor may reside.[2] The procedure is regulated by the Small Debt Act of 1837, and the summons is served on the arrestee and the common debtor.[1] If the common debtor is not within the county in which the action is brought the minimum induciæ is twelve days.[1] If goods or effects have been arrested the Sheriff may order these to be sold.[3] In the Small Debt Court, as in the Ordinary Court, the expenses of bringing the action of furthcoming may be made good out of the arrested fund if it is sufficient.[4] If not, the common debtor will be found liable for these expenses.

[1] 7 Will. IV and 1 Vict. c. 41, sec. 9, Schedule D.
[2] Ibid.; 7 Edw. VII c. 51, secs. 6 (g) 45, Schedule I, Rule 128.
[3] See 7 Will. IV & 1 Vict. c. 41, sec. 20.
[4] 7 Edw. VII c. 51, Schedule I, Rule 129.

7. SEQUESTRATION FOR RENT.

The Small Debt Court can deal with sequestrations for rent if the total rent in respect of which sequestration is asked does not exceed £20.[1] Sequestration is competent either *currente termino* or in security.[2] The summons contains warrant to inventory and secure the effects, and the officer, when he executes the warrant, has the effects appraised by two persons, who may also be witnesses to the sequestration and who need not be skilled appraisers.[1] The appraisers should be sworn, as the report of sale bears that the goods were appraised on oath.[3] An inventory and appraisement is given to or left for the tenant who is cited to appear in Court at a diet not sooner than the sixth day after service.[1] The execution of the citation and sequestration with the appraisement must be returned by the officer to the Sheriff-clerk within three days.[1] At the calling of the cause the Sheriff may (a) recall the sequestration in whole or in part; or (b) grant decree for the rent found due and warrant for sale of the sequestrated effects[1]; or (c), if the action is in security, continue the cause till a Court day after the term. The Sheriff may give directions as to the carrying out of the sale[1] but in the absence of such directions, the sequestrated goods are carried to the cross or most public place in the town or village, or the nearest town or village, and sold by public roup between the hours of eleven and three, after at least two hours' notice by the town crier.[4] In practice, the goods are usually directed to be sold on the premises, or at an auction sale room, and intimation is given by handbills or newspaper advertisement. The surplus, if any, arising upon the sale, after paying the sums decerned for, and any expenses awarded, and the cost of the sequestration and sale, are returned to the owner of the goods, or, if the owner cannot be found, consigned with the Sheriff-clerk.[4] Such a consigned fund is arrestable in the hands of the Sheriff-clerk.[5] The effects cannot be sold for less than the appraised value.[6] If they are not so sold they are delivered, at the appraised value, to the creditor in satisfaction *pro tanto* of the sum due as above and within eight days of sale or delivery the officer must report the proceedings to the Sheriff-clerk.[4] A warrant of sequestration covers authority to the officer to open shut and lockfast places if necessary.[7] Sales carried through under the small debt procedure do not require the formalities laid down in the Debtors Act of 1838.[8]

[1] 7 Will. IV & 1 Vict. c. 41, sec. 5, Schedule B.
[2] 7 Edw. VII c. 51, sec. 43.
[3] See Le Conte v. Douglas, 1880, 8 R. 175.
[4] 7 Will. IV & 1 Vict. c. 41, sec. 20.
[5] Gatherar v. Muirhead & Turnbull, 1909, 25 Sh.Ct.Rep. 357; cf. Shankland & Co. v. M'Gildowny, 1912 S.C. 857.
[6] Lees, Small Debt Handbook, 66.
[7] 52 & 53 Vict. c. 26, sec. 7.
[8] See Brady v. Napier & Son, 1944 S.C. 18.

If after sequestration the tenant pays to the pursuers the rent claimed with expenses, or consigns the rent and £2 to cover expenses in the hands of the Clerk of Court, the sequestration is *ipso facto* recalled on the clerk writing and signing on the back of the summons the words " payment made " (which he is bound to do on production of evidence of payment of the rent and expenses) or on the clerk similarly writing and signing the words " consignation made," and in that case on intimation of recall being made by officer to the pursuer.[1] Consignation before sequestration is inept and does not bar sequestration being granted.[2]

[1] 7 Will. IV & 1 Vict. c. 41, sec. 5; form of intimation in Lees, Small Debt Handbook, 209.
[2] Alexander v. Campbell's Trustees, 1903, 5 F. 634.

Where any sum consisting of arrears of rent is directed to be paid by instalments the Sheriff may annex conditions as to the punctual payment of rent to become due in future, and if such condition is not complied with the Sheriff may rescind or vary the direction as to payment by instalments.[1]

[1] 14 & 15 Geo. V c. 16, sec. 1.

If the sequestration is for past due rent and the statutory requirements have been complied with the Sheriff must grant expenses to the pursuer,[1] and if decree for rent is granted warrant to sell the sequestrated effects must also be granted.[2] As in the Ordinary Court the sequestration must be registered.[3] A summons of sequestration is held not to infer the abandonment of a claim to arrears of rent due for an earlier period.[4]

[1] Renfrew v. Hall, 1901, 4 F. (J.) 27.
[2] Clark v. Lowe, 1900, 2 F. (J.) 49.
[3] 30 & 31 Vict. c. 42, sec. 7; Act of Sederunt, 3rd February, 1933, sec. 2. See further, p. 427, supra.
[4] Findlay, &c. v. Shanks, 1929, 46 Sh.Ct.Rep. 70.

Where a warrant of sale has been granted for the rent, and the officer has reported that the premises are displenished, the Sheriff may grant warrant to the landlord to eject the tenant and re-let the premises.[1] Notice of at least forty-eight hours of the landlord's intention to ask an ejectment warrant is given to the tenant, by registered letter sent to his last known address.[1] If the tenant appears, he is heard, but the proceedings are summary. A tenant who has displenished premises seldom appears, and in practice the warrant to eject is granted upon the expiry of the induciæ of notice. Warrant to carry back effects removed in breach of hypothec, or of the sequestration, may be applied for by minute.[2]

[1] 52 & 53 Vict. c. 26, sec. 6.
[2] Form of minute in Lees, Small Debt Handbook, 208-209; as to circumstances in which this is granted, see p. 425, supra.

8. SUMMARY REMOVINGS.

Where heritable subjects—irrespective of their nature or of the amount of rent—are let for a shorter period than a year, an action of summary removing in respect of them is brought, and in general conducted, as in a small debt case. The procedure in such applications has already been dealt with.[1]

[1] See p. 405, supra.

9. EMPLOYERS AND WORKMEN DISPUTES.

Under the Employers and Workmen Act of 1875, the Small Debt Court is given a special jurisdiction as regards disputes arising between employers and workmen.[1] The Court is authorized by the Act to set off one claim against the other, although not liquidated; to rescind contracts; and to accept security and order performance of a contract which has been broken.[2] The Act applies to apprentices and the Court may order an apprentice to perform his duty under pain of imprisonment; or may rescind the contract, and order repayment of any premium; or decern for damages against any cautioner of the apprentice, or accept security for the apprentice's performance of his duties.[3] Domestic servants are excluded from the Act as are also apprentices for whom there has been paid a premium exceeding £25.[4]

[1] 38 & 39 Vict. c. 90, secs. 4, 14.
[2] Ibid., secs. 3, 4. See Wilson v. Glasgow Tramways Co., 1878, 5 R. 981; Cowdenbeath Coal Co. v. Drylie, 1886, 3 Sh.Ct.Rep. 3.
[3] Ibid., secs. 5, 6, 7.
[4] Ibid., secs. 10, 12, 13; 43 & 44 Vict. c. 16, sec 11.

A special form of summons is provided by Act of Sederunt and forms of various orders are also given.[1] So far as not specially provided for the usual small debt forms may be used.[2] It is specially provided that no notice of a set-off or counter-claim need be given by a defender.[3]

[1] Act of Sederunt, 29th January, 1876, sec. 1.
[2] Ibid., secs. 1, 2.
[3] Ibid., sec. 4.

10. DILIGENCE.

An extract decree in the Small Debt Court is written on the summons or separately and is signed by the Sheriff-clerk.[1] Any party to a cause may obtain an extract[2] and a second and further extract may be issued to have the same effect as the first extract.[3]

[1] 52 & 53 Vict. c. 26, sec. 13.
[2] Ibid., sec. 12.
[3] 7 Edw. VII c. 51, sec. 47.

The proceedings in execution of a decree are not materially different in Ordinary Court and Small Debt Court practice. The extract decree is a warrant for execution by arrestment, or by poinding and sale, or by imprisonment if competent.[1] It is not a foundation for inhibition.[2] A charge is requisite on a small debt decree only if the defender was not personally present when decree was pronounced.[1] If he was so present diligence can proceed after the lapse of ten free days and no charge is necessary. A defender is not personally present if he is merely represented by a solicitor or other person.[3]

[1] 7 Will. IV & 1 Vict. c. 41, sec. 13.
[2] Lamont, 1867, 6 M. 84.
[3] Shiell v. Mossman, 1871, 10 M. 58.

Normally a charge is given by a Sheriff-officer, but a witness is not required.[1] As in the case of other decrees the Sheriff having jurisdiction where a small debt decree falls to be executed if satisfied that no officer is reasonably available may authorize any suitable person (other than the solicitor for the holder of the decree) to

execute the decree.[2]   Where a charge has to be given upon a small
debt decree for payment of money at a place distant more than
twelve miles from the seat of the Court where the decree was
granted, or in any of the islands of Scotland, or in any county
where there is no resident Sheriff-officer, the charge may be given
by registered letter.[3]   The registered letter containing the charge
is posted to the known residence or place of business of the debtor,
or to his last known address if it continues to be his legal domicile
or proper place of citation.[4]   It may be sent by a Sheriff-officer
of the Sheriffdom where the charge is to be executed, or by a
messenger-at-arms resident in that Sheriffdom, or, if no officer or
messenger resides in the Sheriffdom, by a solicitor enrolled there.[4]
The pursuer's solicitor could apparently act.   The envelope is to
contain a notice requiring its return, if undelivered, to the officer
or other person who sent it and the execution is to be accompanied
by the post office receipt.[4]   If the validity of the charge is questioned, and a post office certificate of delivery is produced, the
letter is presumed to have been delivered as specified in the certificate unless the debtor proves that it was not, and if it is proved
that the letter was tendered and refused the Court may hold that
as equivalent to delivery.[4]   An association, company or firm may
be charged as on an ordinary decree.[5]   Where a postal charge is not
given endorsation of the decree is apparently necessary before a
charge can be given in another county than that in which the
decree was granted.[6]

[1] 52 & 53 Vict. c. 26, sec. 11.
[2] 16 & 17 Geo. V c. 16, sec. 3.   See p. 257, supra.
[3] Ibid.. sec. 2 (1).
[4] Ibid., sec. 2 (2).
[5] 7 Edw. VII c. 51. sec. 45, Schedule I, Rule 151.   See p. 258, supra.
[6] Neither 52 & 53 Vict. c. 26, sec. 11, nor 7 Edw. VII c. 51, Schedule I,
    Rule 10, affect this question.

If a decree is not enforced by poinding or imprisonment within
a year from its date, or from the date of a charge for payment
given thereon, the decree cannot be enforced without a new charge
being given.[1]

[1] 7 Will. IV & 1 Vict. c. 41, sec. 13.

Upon the expiry of the charge on the decree, or after the lapse
of ten free days from the date of the decree if defender was
personally present when it was pronounced, the debtor's effects may
be poinded and sold.[1]   The effects poinded are appraised, inventoried and sold in the manner already described in the case of
sequestration for rent and sale thereunder.[2]   A breach of poinding

is dealt with by prosecution under the Summary Jurisdiction
(Scotland) Act, 1908.[3]

[1] 7 Will. IV & 1 Vict. c. 41, sec. 13.
[2] See p. 482, supra.
[3] Thomson & Co. v. Wood, 1896, 12 Sh.Ct.Rep. 241; Perritt v. Bell,
1896, 12 Sh.Ct.Rep. 327. See also 8 Edw. VII c. 65, Schedule C.

Arrestments in execution on a small debt decree are served in
the same way as arrestments on the dependence and reference is
made to what has already been written on this topic in regard to
the expiry of such arrestments.[1]

[1] See p. 470, supra.

11. APPEAL.

The judgment of the Sheriff-Substitute in the Small Debt Court
is not appealable to the Sheriff, nor is the judgment subject to
reduction or suspension or to review at all,[1] except to the limited
extent allowed by the Small Debt Act of 1837, which sanctions a
small debt decree being submitted to review of the High Court of
Justiciary at the next ensuing circuit sitting, or, where there
are no Circuit Courts, at Edinburgh. The only grounds of appeal
are (a) corruption or malice and oppression on the part of the
Sheriff; or (b) such deviations in point of form from the statutory
enactments as the Court shall think took place wilfully, or have
prevented substantial justice being done; or (c) incompetency,
including defect of jurisdiction.[2] The provision in the Sheriff
Courts Act, conferring upon that Court jurisdiction in suspensions
of charges on decrees granted by the Sheriff,[3] is subject to the earlier
provision of the Small Debt Act which expressly bars suspension
or reduction of a small debt decree. But in the exceptional cases
in which suspension of a charge on such a decree is competent[4] it
would appear that such a suspension is now competent in the
Sheriff Court and in that Court alone.[5] A small debt action has
of consent been held to be a summary application with consequent
right of appeal.[6]

[1] 7 Will. IV & 1 Vict. c. 41, sec. 30.
[2] Ibid., secs. 30, 31.
[3] 7 Edw. VII c. 51, sec. 5 (5).
[4] See Samuel v. Mackenzie & Bell, 1876, 4 R. 187; cf. Wilson v. Scott,
1890, 18 R. 233. See p. 489, infra.
[5] Brown & Critchley v. Decorative Art Journals Co., 1922 S.C. 192;
cf. Aitchison v. M'Donald, 1911 S.C. 174.
[6] Craig v. Lorn District Committee, 1911, 28 Sh.Ct.Rep. 14.

It is difficult to reconcile the cases in regard to the competency
of appeals, or to group them consistently under the various grounds

of appeal. Corruption or malice and oppression indicate something done by the Sheriff from motives of his own or from caprice,[1] and an appeal allowed because the statement of claim disclosed no legal ground of liability may now be a doubtful precedent.[2] A refusal to hear parties is a sufficient ground for appeal,[3] as is also the hearing of one side and the refusal to hear the other.[4] Appeal is also competent if the Sheriff refuse, without reason, to hear competent evidence,[5] but not merely if he has made a mistake in regard to the evidence to be admitted or has allowed incompetent evidence to be adduced.[6] Appeals have also been allowed where the Sheriff considered a counter-claim which had not been intimated,[7] where he refused to grant a decree which the pursuer had a statutory right to require,[8] and where he granted warrant to carry back sequestrated goods without any notice given to defender.[9] Incompetency, in the sense of the Act, will cover cases in which the Sheriff had no right to entertain the action in respect that he had no power to grant the decree given,[10] or had no jurisdiction.[11] But appeal may be refused where the question of jurisdiction is a matter personal to the defender and is thus one for the Sheriff to decide.[12] Appeals have been entertained where decree has been granted for something different from what was sued for,[13] and where an incompetent form of multiplepoinding was entertained which led to substantial injustice.[14] Appeal is only competent against a final judgment in the Small Debt Court.[15]

[1] Robson v. Menzies, 1913 S.C. (J.) 90, Lord Justice-General Dunedin, p. 94; cf. Millar v. Strathmore Auction Co., 1906, 8 F. (J.) 71.

[2] Patrick Henderson & Sons v. National Telephone Co., 1909 S.C. (J.) 46; cf. Inverness County Council v. Morrison, 1910 S.C. (J.) 80.

[3] Gow & Sons v. M'Ewan, 1897, 34 S.L.R. 421; M'Culloch v. M'Laughlin, 1930 J.C. 8.

[4] Robson v. Menzies, supra, Lord Justice-General Dunedin, p. 95.

[5] Gordon v. Mulholland, 1891, 18 R. (J.) 18; Reid & Son v. Sinclair Bros., 1894, 22 R. (J.) 12; Renfrew v. Hall, 1901, 4 F. (J.) 27; Stalker v. Somerville, 1901, 4 F. (J.) 31; Carmichael v. Macintyre, 1904, 6 F. (J.) 48; Paterson v. Cowie's Executor, 1905, 7 F. (J.) 68; Cowe v. M'Dougall, 1908, 16 S.L.T. 478; Robson v. Menzies, supra, Lord Justice-General Dunedin, p. 96; cf. Brown v. Edinburgh House Proprietors Co., 1902, 10 S.L.T. 311. See also Spence v. Bryce, 1885, 12 R. (J.) 43.

[6] Hare v. Nicol's Trustees, 1871, 43 Scot. Jur. 389; Sprott v. Portpatrick, &c., Committee, 1898, 25 R. (J.) 71; Crieff Magistrates v. Young, 1906, 8 F. (J.) 48.

[7] Taylor v. Ormond & Co., 1906, 8 F. (J.) 76; Rollands v. Rolland, 1907, 15 S.L.T. 141; Mair's Trustees v. Miller, 1908 S.C. (J.) 74.

[8] Clark v. Lowe, 1900, 2 F. (J.) 49.

[9] Johnston v. Young, 1890, 18 R. (J.) 6.

[10] See Robson v. Menzies, supra, Lord Justice-General Dunedin, p. 93.

[11] Ibid.; also Russell & Co. v. Murray, 1892, 19 R. (J.) 61; Roberts v. Provincial Homes Co., 1907 S.C. (J.) 7.

12 Wilson v. Glasgow Tramways Co., 1878, 5 R. 981; Allison v. Balmain, 1882, 10 R. (J.) 12; Findlay v. Crabb, 1886, 13 R. (J.) 53; Leven v. Provincial Homes Co., 1904, 6 F. (J.) 62.
13 Glasgow & S.W. Railway v. Wilson, 1855, 2 Irvine, 162; Singer Manufacturing Co. v. Beale & Mactavish, 1905, 8 F. (J.) 29; Mair's Trustees v. Miller, supra.
14 Britannic Assurance Co. v. Henderson, 1912 S.C. (J.) 31.
15 Murdoch v. Glasgow Corporation, 1932 J.C. 61.

The appeal may be taken in open Court at the time of judgment, or it may be lodged with the Sheriff-clerk within ten days thereafter.[1] In either case the practice is to lodge a written minute or note of appeal, setting forth the facts of the case and the grounds of appeal, and craving the remedy sought from the Appeal Court. This must be served upon the opposite party, within ten days after judgment and at least fifteen days before the diet of the Justiciary Court.[1] At the time the appeal is lodged the appellant must find caution, to the satisfaction of the Sheriff-clerk, to abide by the judgment of the Appeal Court, and to pay the costs, if any, awarded against him.[1] Productions to be founded on must be initialled by the Sheriff, and witnesses whose evidence is to be referred to must be noted by him on the summons which markings are to be made only if required by one of the parties.[2] The Appeal Court may itself dispose of the case or it may remit to the Sheriff for inquiry or with directions.[3] The expenses are usually modified but full expenses may be allowed.[4]

1 20 Geo. II c. 43, secs. 34, 36; 7 Will. IV & 1 Vict. c. 41, sec. 31.
2 7 Will. IV & 1 Vict. c. 41, sec. 31.
3 Glass v. Laughlin, 1876, 4 R. 108; Spence v. Bryce, 1885, 12 R. (J.) 43; Russell & Co. v. Murray, 1892, 19 R. (J.) 61.
4 Allison v. Balmain, 1882, 10 R. (J.) 12.

In addition to the restrictions on rights of appeal the 1837 Act provides that no decree in the Small Debt Court is to be subject to reduction, advocation, suspension, or appeal or any other form of review or stay of execution, other than provided by the Act, either on account of any omission or irregularity or informality in the citation or proceedings, or on the merits, or on any ground or reason whatever.[1] But that provision does not bar suspension or reduction if there is some fundamental illegality as where the Sheriff-clerk who signed the summons was himself pursuer,[2] or solicitor for one of the parties,[3] or where the summons was served on the wrong person.[4] Suspension of diligence used on a small debt decree is generally excluded if that involves an attack on the decree itself,[5] but suspension is competent if it attacks irregular diligence used on a decree which is not itself challenged,[6] or if, by payment or otherwise, a decree is no longer a ground for

diligence.[7]   In the same way reduction of an extract which had
been wrongfully altered after decree was granted was not excluded,[8]
but reduction in respect of irregularities leading up to the decree
will not in general be entertained.[9]   The finality provisions of the
1837 Act have been held to exclude claims of damages arising from
irregularities leading up to a decree[10] but irregularities in diligence
following on a decree are not protected,[11] nor is warrant to carry
back in a sequestration for rent.[12]   The protection of the finality
provisions was refused where a claim of damages was made in
respect of diligence on a decree in absence which was subject to an
irregularity and had since been recalled on a sist obtained by the
defender.[13]   The above provisions of the Small Debt Act do not
affect statutory rights of appeal—as under the Friendly Societies
Acts—which may apply to proceedings brought in the Small Debt
Court.[14]

[1] 7 Will. IV & 1 Vict. c. 41, sec. 30.
[2] Manson v. Smith, 1871, 9 M. 492.
[3] Gray v. Hardie, 1888, 1 White 561.
[4] Brown v. Rodger, 1884, 12 R. 340; but cf. Spalding v. Valentine &
Co., 1883, 10 R. 1092; Cruickshank v. Gow & Sons, 1888, 15 R.
326; Quinn v. Walker, 1940 S.L.T. 172.
[5] Wilson v. Scott, 1890, 18 R. 233; Christie v. Hoseason, 1898, 6 S.L.T.
123; Crawford v. Copland & Lye, 1901, 9 S.L.T. 76; Curdie v.
Hay, (O.H.) 1902, 10 S.L.T. 435; Beveridge v. Macfarlane & Co.,
(O.H.) 1906, 14 S.L.T. 169; Christie Bros. v. Remington Type-
writing Co., (O.H.) 1912, 1 S.L.T. 123.
[6] Shiell v. Mosman, 1871, 10 M. 58; cf. Beveridge v. Macfarlane & Co.,
supra.
[7] Samuel v. Mackenzie & Bell, 1876, 4 R. 187.
[8] Murchie v. Fairbairn, 1863, 1 M. 800.
[9] Lenon v. Tully, 1879, 6 R. 1253; Robertson v. Pringle, 1887, 14 R. 474;
Riach v. Wallace, 1899, 2 F. 149.
[10] Gray v. Smart, 1892, 19 R. 692; MacLean v. Mackenzie, (O.H.) 1895,
3 S.L.T. 142; Scott v. Young, (O.H.) 1895, 4 S.L.T. 324; Jackson
v. Lillie & Russell, (O.H.) 1902, 10 S.L.T. 448; Gray v. Macintosh
& Co., (O.H.) 1906, 14 S.L.T. 403.
[11] Gray v. Smart, supra; Reid v. Gow & Sons. (O.H.) 1903, 10 S.L.T.
606.
[12] M'Donald v. Grant, (O.H.) 1904, 11 S.L.T. 575; Jack v. Black, 1911
S.C. 691; Shearer v. Nicoll, (O.H.) 1935 S.L.T. 313.
[13] Clark v. Beattie, 1909 S.C. 299.
[14] Linton v. City of Glasgow Friendly Society, 1895, 23 R. 51; Smith v.
Scottish Legal Life Assurance Society, 1912 S.C. 611.

CHAPTER XXIII.

THE POOR'S ROLL.

It is a recognized principle of judicial procedure in the Courts of Scotland that free legal assistance should be afforded to those who are unable to pay for this in the usual way. In civil causes the applicant for the benefit of the poor's roll must obtain a certificate of poverty, and have his case inquired into and reported upon by the procurators for the poor.[1] The certificate of poverty is granted by the inspector or assistant inspector of poor of the burgh or district of the county where the applicant resides and bears that the applicant is unable, through poverty, to pay for the conduct of legal proceedings.[1] The application for the benefit of the poor's roll is lodged along with the certificate, and the Sheriff then remits the application to the solicitors for the poor, who notify the parties of the time and place of their inquiry.[1]

[1] 7 Edw. VII c. 51, Schedule I, Rules 162, 163.

The solicitors for the poor are directed to inquire and report whether the applicant is entitled to the benefit of the poor's roll, as well as whether he has a probable cause of action.[1] The applicant's solicitor may not act as a reporter,[2] and in practice the remit is made to reporters other than the solicitor for the applicant. If the report is favourable the Sheriff appoints one of the solicitors for the poor to take charge of the applicant's case.[1] But objection by the other side may be taken to the report on the finding as to poverty, but not as to probable cause.[3] The interlocutor granting or refusing the application for admission may be appealed to the Sheriff Principal,[4] or to the Court of Session. It is not necessary for the reporters to have precognitions submitted with applications for admission to the poor's roll, but if precognitions are lodged the contents of them are available to the other side.[5] A minor is not denied the benefit of the poor's roll because his father appears as curator and his income is above the recognized limit.[6]

[1] 7 Edw. VII c. 51, Schedule I, Rules 163, 164. See Hastie v. Hastie, 1924, 41 Sh.Ct.Rep. 111.
[2] M'Kean v. Herbison, 1913 S.C. 548.
[3] Hunter v. Hunter, 1929, 46 Sh.Ct.Rep. 104. See also M'Intosh v. Roy, 1898, 25 R. 899.
[4] Apparently without leave—see Hunter v. Hunter, supra—as a final judgment in the application.

5 Cant v. Pirnie's Trustees, 1906, 8 F. 1120; M'Gregor v. Kinloch, 1914, 30 Sh.Ct.Rep. 282; Coyle v. Star Motor Express Co., 1934, 51 Sh.Ct.Rep. 115.
6 M'Gregor v. Kinloch, supra; as to husband and wife see Cummings v. Houston, 1919, 36 Sh.Ct.Rep. 121.

It is in the power of the Sheriff at any time to deprive a litigant of the benefit of the poor's roll,[1] but in practice this will only be done, in the course of a litigation, if it is alleged that there has been a change of circumstances since the application was made.[2] The request for removal will be by motion in the pending action, and if the Sheriff-Substitute on such a motion deprives a litigant of the benefit of the poor's roll, there is an appeal, with leave, to the Sheriff.[2] A litigant may be deprived of the benefit of the poor's roll if he fails to instruct his solicitor,[3] and if he insists in an appeal against his solicitor's advice a further remit to the reporters may be made to see if there is still a probable cause.[4]

1 7 Edw. VII c. 51, Schedule I, Rule 169.
2 Mahon v. Boyd, 1930, 46 Sh.Ct.Rep. 258.
3 Biagi v. Biagi, 1936 S.C. 148.
4 Gore v. Westfield Autocar Co., 1923 S.C. 100; Smith v. Smith, 1925 S.C. 714. See also Watt v. Haddington Corporation, 1929 S.C. 481.

The solicitors for the poor hold office for one year, but are eligible for renomination.[1] They are appointed by vote of the solicitors enrolled in the Court books, or, where there are districts with separate Courts, in each district Court.[2] An annual meeting of solicitors for this purpose is convened by order of the Sheriff, by notice posted upon the walls of each Court-house, and in each Sheriff-clerk's office, within the county or district.[3] The names of the solicitors selected are reported to the Sheriff who may confirm the nominations or may decline to do so.[4] If the meeting fails to make nominations, or if the Sheriff refuses to confirm the nomination of any solicitor, he may either himself nominate, or may appoint another meeting to be held.[5] Nominations made by a local law society do not constitute proper nominations under the rules.[6]

1 7 Edw. VII c. 51, Schedule I, Rule 158; 2 & 3 Geo. V c. 28, Schedule II.
2 Ibid., Rule 152.
3 Ibid., Rules 152, 153.
4 Ibid., Rules 154, 155.
5 Ibid., Rule 157.
6 Smith, 1923, 41 Sh.Ct.Rep. 36.

Six days before the list of solicitors is submitted to the Sheriff for confirmation the Sheriff-clerk notifies each solicitor who has been selected by the meeting, and such solicitor may, before the nominations are confirmed, represent to the Sheriff any reason why his nomination should not be confirmed.[1] The fact that the solicitor has not an office in the district is not a ground of exemption from duty.[2] The decision of the Sheriff is final. In the matter of appointment of the solicitors for the poor, " Sheriff " does not include Sheriff-Substitute.[3]

[1] 7 Edw. VII c. 51, Schedule I, Rule 156.
[2] Frew, 1922 S.L.T. (Sh.Ct.) 140.
[3] 7 Edw. VII c. 51. Schedule I, Rule 161.

The solicitors for the poor act as directed by the Sheriff or—as is the usual case—as they themselves arrange.[1] They act for the poor in all cases, civil and criminal, including attendance at Circuit Courts.[1] The solicitors in their respective districts assist each other by taking precognitions or evidence on commission or otherwise as may be requisite and reasonable.[2] A solicitor who is assigned a poor's case conducts it to a final issue although he may meantime have ceased to serve on the poor's roll.[3]

[1] 7 Edw. VII c. 51, Schedule I, Rule 159.
[2] Ibid., Rule 160.
[3] Ibid., Rule 165.

Each solicitor for the poor is bound, within six months of the expiry of his year of office, to furnish the Sheriff-clerk with a signed list of the cases in which he has acted, showing the amounts he has recovered, and, if he has recovered Court dues, he is bound to account for them at the same time, and to remit the amount of any subsequently recovered.[1]

[1] Act of Sederunt, 16th July, 1929, sec. 7.

A party admitted to the benefit of the poor's roll is not in the first instance liable for dues of Court, nor for the fees of the solicitor appointed to conduct his case, nor for fees of officers of Court.[1] But such a party is liable for outlays made by his solicitor on his behalf and with his sanction.[1] He is also liable to pay the solicitor's fees, officer's fees, and the Court dues if he recovers these from the opposite party,[2] and if necessary the solicitor may obtain a charging order on any estate recovered.[3] A party citing witnesses is liable for their fees, notwithstanding that he is suing *in forma pauperis*, but the solicitor is not, unless he personally recovers these from the opposite party.[2] Nor is the solicitor for the poor liable for shorthand writer's fees, Court dues or officer's fees unless he recovers these personally.[2] A haver—and presumably also a witness—cited to appear at the instance of a litigant on the poor's roll is entitled to object to do so till some provision is made for his expenses.[4]

1 7 Edw. VII c. 51, Schedule I, Rules 166, 167, 168.
2 Ibid., Rule 167; Act of Sederunt, 16th July, 1929, sec. 7.
3 Cameron v. M'Donald, (O.H.) 1935 S.N. 25.
4 Dickson v. Taylor, 1914, 30 Sh.Ct.Rep. 338.

CHAPTER XXIV.

SPECIAL ACTIONS.

1. ACCOUNTING.

An action of accounting asks the defender to produce an account, and the money crave asks for payment of the sum found due and is in supplement of the crave for an accounting. Failing appearance of the defender, or failing production of the account, decree is asked for a stated sum. An accounting is regarded as a money claim, and arrestment on the dependence is competent. But the money crave does not necessarily limit the amount to which the pursuer is entitled, if an accounting is gone into, and he will obtain decree for whatever sum the accounting discloses to be due.[1] If the liability to account is not admitted a record will be made up, and if necessary a proof taken and judgment pronounced disposing of this question. When liability to account is admitted, or has been established, the defender is ordered to produce an account within a specified time. The pursuer is allowed to lodge objections to the account and the defender to lodge answers to the objections. A record may be made up on the objections and answers and proof may be allowed if necessary. Where investigation of books is necessary the most convenient course may be to remit to an accountant to make a report.

[1] Spottiswoode v. Hopkirk, 1853, 16 D. 59.

If accounting is craved for in general terms, that means that the period at which the account is to close is the date of citation.[1] If a continuing account is wanted the crave should ask that the defender be ordained to state an account down to the date of the decree to be pronounced in the action.[2] An accounting is not competent against a servant of the pursuer as the accounts in that case are the pursuer's own accounts.[3] Nor is it generally competent at the instance of an employee against his employer,[4] or a bankrupt against his trustee in bankruptcy who has been discharged.[5] To justify the action being raised there must be on the one side an obligation to account and on the other a right to demand accounts.

[1] See Wallace v. Henderson, 1875, 2 R. 999.
[2] See Wauchope v. North British Railway Co., 1860, 23 D. 191, p. 201.
[3] Govan Old Victualling Society v. Wagstaff, 1907, 44 S.L.R. 295.
[4] Swanson v. Gardner & Co., 1916, 33 Sh.Ct.Rep. 117.
[5] Hemming v. Galbraith, 1908 S.C. 897; cf. Ritchie v. M'Intosh, 1881, 8 R. 747.

If it is admitted or is apparent that upon an accounting a sum will be due, although the exact amount of it is not ascertained, the Court may order the defender to consign a stated sum. Such an order is a decree *ad factum præstandum*, which may be separately enforced, although the process will still go on.[1] If no time for making consignation is expressed in the interlocutor, the extract warrants a charge upon seven days' induciæ.[2]

[1] Mackenzie v. Balerno Paper Mill Co., 1883, 10 R. 1147; M'Lintock v. Prinzen & Van Glabbeek, 1902, 4 F. 948; as to enforcement of such decrees, see p. 284, supra.
[2] M'Lintock v. Prinzen & Van Glabbeek, supra.

2. Ad Factum Præstandum.

An action *ad factum præstandum* is brought to compel a defender to do something which, at common law, or under contract, he is bound to do, and which, in existing circumstances, it is possible for him to do. If performance has become impossible, the Court will not grant decree *ad factum præstandum* for no Court will grant a decree which cannot be made operative.[1] The remedy for non-implement of an obligation is an action of damages, and a conclusion for damages is an alternative crave in the great majority of actions *ad factum præstandum*. But if implement is not impossible the pursuer is not bound to restrict his claim to one of damages.[2] Agreements to prorogate jurisdiction in the Sheriff Court are void in the case of certain contracts of hire purchase.[3]

[1] Cocker v. Crombie, 1893, 20 R. 954; Gall v. Loyal Glenbogie Lodge, 1900, 2 F. 1187; cf. M'Kellar v. Dallas, 1928 S.C. 503.
[2] Stewart v. Kennedy, 1890. 17 R. (H.L.) 1, Lord Watson, p. 10.
[3] 3 & 4 Geo. VI c. 42, sec. 4. See p. 479. supra.

Subject to recent statutory modifications already referred to,[1] decree in this class of action warrants execution by imprisonment, but the Court has a discretion to refuse decree *ad factum præstandum*, even where implement is possible.[2] Where no alternative crave for damages has been made such a crave may be added by amendment.[3] It is probably better in such a case that the original crave for implement remain and that the crave for damages be added as an alternative. Although a contrary view seems to have been indicated,[4] it is thought that an amendment on the above lines is competent even though implement has become impossible so that the new crave becomes the only one which could be granted.[3] The procedure for obtaining warrant to imprison on a decree *ad factum præstandum*, which has been altered by recent legislation, has been already dealt with.[1]

[1] See p. 284, supra.
[2] Moore v. Paterson, 1881, 9 R. 337; Grahame v. Kirkcaldy Magistrates, 1882, 9 R. (H.L.) 91; Dampskibsaktieselskapet Aurdal v. Compania de Navegacion La Estrella, 1916 S.C. 882.
[3] Summerlee Iron Co. v. Caledonian Railway Co., 1911 S.C. 458.
[4] Mound Motors v. Murphy, 1936, 53 Sh.Ct.Rep. 93.

The initial writ for delivery may be framed in various ways. If it craves delivery alone it can be enforced by imprisonment, but this compulsitor is now modified by Statute.[1] Alternatively the writ itself may crave warrant to search and take possession, or the crave may be for delivery, and failing delivery, for payment of a sum of money. In the last form of writ it is optional to the Court as already explained to grant decree for specific implement or for the alternative sum sued for.[2] A crave for delivery has been held competent against two defenders.[3] If the specific thing which falls to be delivered has perished without fault there may be no claim either for delivery or for damages.[4] If a defender asks for and obtains decree for delivery only he cannot on failure to deliver move for warrant to search[5] although this may be obtained by means of the statutory procedure now available.[1] A crave for delivery has been held incompetent where pursuers, under a hire-purchase agreement, had power to enter and take possession of the article in question.[6]

[1] See p. 284, supra.
[2] See previous page.
[3] Sinclair v. Gardner, 1915, 32 Sh.Ct.Rep. 211.
[4] Leitch v. Edinburgh Ice and Cold Storage Co., 1900, 2 F. 904.
[5] Napier & Son v. Reid, 1943, 59 Sh.Ct.Rep. 117.
[6] Bruce Bros. v. M'Vittie, 1944, 62 Sh.Ct.Rep. 20; Bell Bros. v. Hamilton and Wilkie, 1945, 62 Sh.Ct.Rep. 31.

Where the action is one for implement other than delivery the crave of the writ may be for implement alone, and in that case the decree is enforceable by imprisonment—subject to the recent statutory modifications already referred to—or it may be for implement and alternatively for damages. As already mentioned, the Court may refuse to grant a decree for specific implement, but if decree for implement is granted it is—subject as above—enforceable by imprisonment even though the writ contains an alternative crave for damages.[1] In framing the crave of the writ the method of implement asked must be specifically stated.[2] A crave for implement has been held competent against the executor of the person originally bound under the contract where such executor was in a position to carry out performance of what was asked.[3] Where a person has refused to sign a document, as ordered by the Court, the Court of Session grant warrant to the Clerk of Court to sign in his place.[4] But this is done in exercise of the *nobile officium* and such a course is not apparently competent in the Sheriff Court.

[1] M'Kellar v. Dallas, 1928 S.C. 503.
[2] Robertson v. Cockburn, 1875, 3 R. 21; Middleton v. Leslie, 1892, 19 R. 801.
[3] Beardmore & Co. v. Barry, 1928 S.C. 101; 1928 S.C. (H.L.) 47; cf. Russell v. Menzies, &c., 1903, 20 Sh.Ct.Rep. 41.
[4] Wallace's Curator Bonis v. Wallace, 1924 S.C. 212; Pennell's Trustee, 1928 S.C. 605.

3. ALIMENTARY.

Some alimentary claims have always been enforceable in the Sheriff Court. These included actions in which no question of status was involved, as claims for aliment for an illegitimate child, or claims at the instance of parents against children, and *vice versa*. These cases remain competent as before, but by Statute the jurisdiction of the Sheriff is now extended to include actions of aliment provided that, as between husband and wife, these are actions of separation and aliment, adherence and aliment or interim aliment and also actions for regulating the custody of children.[1] In actions of aliment between spouses—not conjoined with separation or adherence—the Act has not extended the jurisdiction of the Sheriff beyond the provision of interim aliment, which is intended to regulate the position until it is determined in a consistorial action. This was always competent under the former practice[2] and a competent action is not excluded by the fact that it includes a crave for aliment to a child whose paternity is denied by the defending husband.[3] An action by a wife for arrears of aliment under a contract is really one for debt and is competent apart from the Act,[4] but where interim aliment—in the sense above indicated—is claimed decree in absence cannot be granted in view of the provisions of the Act[5] although a decree of consent in a defended case appears to be competent.[6]

[1] 7 Edw. VII c. 51, sec. 5 (2); 2 & 3 Geo. V c. 28, Schedule I.
[2] Smith v. Smith, 1874, 1 R. 1010; the circumstances in Christie v. Christie, 1919 S.C. 576, were special. See also Carr v. Carr, 1941, 57 Sh.Ct.Rep. 124.
[3] Lamont v. Lamont, 1939 S.C. 484.
[4] See Douglas v. Douglas, 1931, 47 Sh.Ct.Rep. 303.
[5] 7 Edw. VII c. 51, Schedule I, Rule 23; 2 & 3 Geo. V c. 28, Schedule II.
[6] See Christie v. Christie, supra.

Even in actions of adherence and aliment and separation and aliment, where the Sheriff can grant more than an interim award, the decree for aliment is open to review and alteration on any change in circumstances.[1] And such alteration in the rate of aliment is competent whether or not the original award contains any reservation to this effect. Aliment due under a contract may be reviewed as well as aliment due under a decree, and in the Sheriff Court this could be done in an action of separation and aliment or adherence and aliment.[2] Applications to review or recall any decree for aliment, whether in favour of a spouse, parent, child or any other person, are made by minute in the original process.[3] Service of the minute is ordered on the opposite party and answers are appointed within a specified time.[3] The application is disposed of without making up a record and after such proof or other procedure as the Court considers necessary.[3] An interim modification has been held competent[4] and where the husband was without income the aliment was reduced to a merely nominal rate.[5] The provision made for review of aliment cannot be used to avoid the effect of a decree of adherence and aliment on the plea that the pursuer had refused to accept adherence when offered.[6]

[1] Macdonald v. Macdonald, 1881, 8 R. 985; Hay v. Hay, 1882, 9 R. 667; Stewart v. Stewart, 1886, 13 R. 1052.
[2] See Scott v. Scott, 1894, 21 R. 853; M'Keddie v. M'Keddie, (O.H.) 1902, 9 S.L.T. 381. But it has to be kept in view that the Court will in general not enforce a contract of voluntary separation save for recovery of arrears of aliment.
[3] 7 Edw. VII c. 51, Schedule I, Rule 171; Act of Sederunt, 16th July, 1936. See earlier cases : Richardson v. Richardson, 1931, 48 Sh.Ct.Rep. 124; Gray v. Gray, 1933, 50 Sh.Ct.Rep. 186; Thomson v. Thomson, 1934, 50 Sh.Ct.Rep. 270. See also Dowswell v. Dowswell, 1943 S.C. 23.
[4] Auld v. Auld, 1933, 49 Sh.Ct.Rep. 179.
[5] Brotherston v. Brotherston, 1938 S.L.T. (Sh.Ct.) 39.
[6] Robertson v. Robertson, 1940 S.L.T. (Sh.Ct.) 43.

Under the rules decree in absence cannot be granted in the Sheriff Court in actions of adherence and aliment, separation and aliment and interim aliment and in undefended actions proof must be led before decree can be obtained.[1] A decree of consent would appear to be competent in a defended action for interim aliment.[2] Decree in absence is available in other actions of aliment such as between parents and children, in actions of affiliation and aliment[3] and in actions for arrears of aliment due under a contract. In the case of actions of aliment in general and in those between spouses which are actions of adherence and aliment, separation and aliment, or interim aliment and in actions for regulating the custody of children, the Sheriff may at any stage of the cause, and either on cause shown or *ex proprio motu*, remit the action to the Court of Session.[4] But the Sheriff should only make such a remit in cases of special difficulty and the Court of Session may send a case back if they consider there are no special grounds for the remit.[5] It is difficult to see why such a remit is made competent in actions of interim aliment or in those of aliment not between spouses and substantial justification would be needed for a remit in these cases. Actions of adherence and aliment and separation and aliment are dealt with in detail later.[6]

[1] 7 Edw. VII c. 51, Schedule I, Rule 23; 2 & 3 Geo. V c. 28, Schedule II.
[2] Christie v. Christie, 1919 S.C. 576.
[3] See Silver v. Walker, 1938 S.C. 595. In practice decrees are granted in absence in such cases without question and they must decern for the aliment as craved (Terry v. Murray, 1947 S.C. 10).
[4] 7 Edw. VII c. 51, sec. 6; 2 & 3 Geo. V c. 28, Schedule I.
[5] Dunbar v. Dunbar, 1912 S.C. 19; Lamont v. Lamont, 1939 S.C. 484.
[6] See p. 523, infra.

In actions of affiliation and aliment it is unnecessary to preface the crave for payment by a declarator that the defender is the father of the child, but, if that is not done, payment should be craved in respect of a child " of which the defender is the father."[1] In 1919 the customary rate of aliment awarded against a defender as his half of the aliment for the child was raised to 4s. 6d. per week, the inlying expenses allowed being £2 2s.,[2] but the Court in awarding aliment and inlying expenses is now by Statute directed to have regard to the means and position of the parties and the whole circumstances of the case.[3] As a result of this provision the customary rate of contribution is no longer binding, and it has been pointed out that, in exceptional circumstances, the defender might be ordered to pay more or less than half of the total amount of aliment.[4] But if other than the customary rate is to be asked it is necessary that proper averments of the circumstances on each side should be given, and, if paternity is not in issue, the matter should in most cases be adjusted without proof.[4] Any award of aliment in such cases may be recalled or varied at a later date,[5] the procedure being by minute as already explained.[6] Orders for aliment of a child may now be made up to the age of sixteen.[7] Where decree in absence is granted in an action of affiliation and aliment it must decern for aliment as craved, and the Sheriff cannot ex proprio motu award aliment at a lower rate.[8]

[1] Silver v. Walker, 1938 S.C. 595. See also the terms of sec. 1 (2) of 20 & 21 Geo. V c. 33.
[2] Forbes v. Matthew, 1919 S.C. 242.
[3] 20 & 21 Geo. V c. 33, sec. 1 (2).
[4] Mottram v. Butchart, 1939 S.C. 89.
[5] 20 & 21 Geo. V c. 33, sec. 1 (4).
[6] See previous page.
[7] 20 & 21 Geo. V c. 33, sec. 1 (1); 2 & 3 Geo. VI c. 4, sec. 1.
[8] Terry v. Murray, 1947 S.C. 10.

Other material alterations in regard to procedure in such cases were made by the Illegitimate Children (Scotland) Act of 1930. Apart from any common law obligation the parents' liability for aliment now endures until the child attains sixteen,[1] and the father cannot meet the mother's claim for aliment by an offer of custody, and any such offer does not affect his liability for aliment.[2] The Court may also, on application by either parent or in any action for aliment of an illegitimate child, make an order as to custody and access, having regard to the child's welfare, and the conduct and wishes of the parents, and may, on application by either parent, recall or vary such order.[3] The application in such cases is by minute as in the case of variation of aliment.[4]

[1] 20 & 21 Geo. V c. 33, sec. 1 (1). See also 2 & 3 Geo. VI c. 4, sec. 1.
[2] Ibid., sec. 2 (2).
[3] Ibid., sec. 2 (1). See Paterson v. M'Nicoll, 1933, 49 Sh.Ct.Rep. 271; Hepburn v. Williamson, 1933, 50 Sh.Ct.Rep. 37.
[4] See p. 499, supra.

Various decisions have been given as to whether the above statutory provisions are retrospective. It seems to be the better view that, where a decree for aliment has been given before the date of the Act, the pursuer cannot come back to have the period extended until the child attains sixteen.[1] The effect of an offer by the father to assume custody before the passing of the Act, but after the child had reached seven, has been considered in several cases.[2] The Act is not limited in its application to children born before it came into operation, and its provisions as to aliment and custody apply to those born after its date.[3]

[1] Cape v. M'Lure, 1934, 51 Sh.Ct.Rep. 52; cf. Shields v. Murray, 1935 S.L.T. (Sh.Ct.) 8.
[2] Ward v. Ainslie, 1930, 47 Sh.Ct.Rep. 138; Presly v. Duguid, 1932, 49 Sh.Ct.Rep. 14; Kerr v. Henderson, 1933, 49 Sh.Ct.Rep. 303.
[3] Paterson v. M'Nicoll, 1933, 49 Sh.Ct.Rep. 271. See also Hepburn v. Williamson, 1933, 50 Sh.Ct.Rep. 37.

An unmarried woman who is pregnant may now raise an action of affiliation and aliment before the birth of her child, but no proof can be taken, and no declaration of paternity nor decree for payment pronounced till after the birth, unless the action is undefended, or paternity is admitted, when the Court may grant decree before the birth for a sum to account of inlying expenses, and for aliment to begin as at the date of birth, and, after the birth, may decern for the balance of inlying expenses and may review and alter the sum awarded as aliment.[1] Such an action may not be raised before the birth of the child unless the pursuer produces a declaration, sworn before a justice of the peace or magistrate, that the defender is the father of the child, and a medical certificate that she is pregnant and specifying the expected date of birth.[2] The action cannot be raised more than three months before the date specified in the certificate.[2] In such an action, if the defender originally denies liability, he will usually be held liable in expenses although he admits paternity as soon as the child is born.[3] Arrestments used on the dependence of an action of this kind were recalled when it was not alleged that the defender was *vergens ad inopiam*, or *in meditatione fugæ* or depleting his funds.[4]

[1] 20 & 21 Geo. V c. 33, sec. 3 (1).
[2] Ibid., sec. 3 (2).
[3] Auld v. Wilson, 1932, 48 Sh.Ct.Rep. 257; Morton v. Duff, 1942, 58 Sh.Ct.Rep. 89.
[4] Speedie v. Steel, 1941 S.L.T. (Sh.Ct.) 2.

Where the Court grants, or has granted, decree for aliment to an illegitimate child it may, on granting decree or later, on application of the inspector of poor with consent of the person in whose favour the decree was granted, or on the application of any other person authorized by the person in whose favour the decree was granted, order that any sums due under the decree should be paid to the inspector of poor or other person authorized as above.[1] If such an order is made the inspector or other person may enforce the decree by diligence, including imprisonment, but must pay over any sums recovered to the person to whom the decree was granted, or expend the sums for behoof of the child.[2]

[1] 20 & 21 Geo. V c. 33, sec. 4.
[2] Ibid.; cf. as to imprisonment generally in such cases, p. 281, et seq., supra.

On the application of any person entitled to the custody of an illegitimate child, whether a parent or third party, the Court may order payment, to the person so entitled to the custody, by the father or mother or both of such sum in respect of aliment as, having regard to the means and position of the father and mother and the whole circumstances of the case, the Court may think reasonable.[1] Such orders for payment may be recalled or varied as in the case of an ordinary decree.[2] Where an illegitimate child dies under the age of sixteen the parents are (without prejudice to any liability on contract) liable for the funeral expenses jointly, or in such proportions as the Sheriff on summary application may determine, but nothing is recoverable in respect of such expenses from either parent beyond the amount fixed by the Sheriff unless the parent was a party to the incurring of the expenses.[3]

[1] 20 & 21 Geo. V c. 33, sec. 1 (3); as to amount of aliment, see p. 500, supra.
[2] Ibid., sec. 1 (4).   See p. 499, supra.
[3] Ibid., sec. 5.

Reference has already been made to the common practice in cases of affiliation and aliment of calling the defender as the first witness for the pursuer.[1] In many such cases the principle of corroboration by contradiction is applied and pursuer's evidence is held to be supported by the defender's false denials of circumstances which are otherwise proved against him.[2]

[1] See p. 218, supra.
[2] See Dawson v. M'Kenzie, 1908 S.C. 648; M'Whirter v. Lynch, 1909 S.C. 112; Lowdon v. M'Connachie, 1933 S.C. 574.

In a recent case the Court of Session decided that in awarding aliment the interlocutor should make an award at the rate of a specified sum payable weekly—or as the case may be—less tax.[1] By the Finance Act, 1944, it has since been provided that, in the case of a payment under an order of Court to or for the benefit of a woman for her maintenance, and to be made weekly at a rate not exceeding £2 a week, and in the case of such a payment to any person for the benefit of or the maintenance or education of a person under sixteen to be made weekly at a rate not exceeding £1 a week, the payments are to be made without deduction of tax and provision is made for the Court notifying the revenue authorities with a view to direct assessment of the recipient.[2] In cases outwith the Act the ruling laid down by the Court of Session would apparently require to be followed, although if the payment was one from which tax fell to be deducted in any case the addition of the words suggested seems to add nothing to what would be implied, and, if the payment was for some reason not in that category, it is difficult to see why the Court should seek to enforce a fiscal liability which the State has not itself imposed.

[1] Thomson v. Thomson, 1943 S.C. 154.
[2] 7 & 8 Geo. VI c. 23, sec. 25.

4. DIVISION OF COMMONTY.

The Sheriff has jurisdiction to deal with division of commonty as provided for under an old Statute of 1695.[1] Such an action may be competently raised in the Sheriff Court irrespective of value, but if the value of the subjects in dispute exceeds £50 by the year or £1000 in value either party is entitled, at the closing of the record or within six days thereafter, to require the cause to be remitted to the Court of Session.[2] The action, if raised in the Sheriff Court, must be brought in the Court of the district where the commonty is situated.[2] It may be at the instance of one or more of the joint proprietors, and any others should be called as defenders. Any person having an interest, although not a joint proprietor, as, for instance, the holder of a servitude right, should be called for his interest, but it is not necessary to call tenants. A common grazing is not necessarily a commonty.[3]

[1] 1695, c. 38 ; 7 Edw. VII c. 51, sec. 5 (3).
[2] 7 Edw. VII c. 51, sec. 5.
[3] Macandrew v. Crerar, 1929 S.C. 699.

The initial writ should describe the lands and set forth the pursuer's interest. It is convenient to produce and refer to a plan. The crave is for production of the titles instructing the various rights in the commonty, for declarator that the commonty should be divided amongst the proprietors according to their respective rights and interests, that each proprietor be allocated his portion, that the divisions be properly marked, and that the pursuer and defenders be ordained to grant or concur in granting the deeds necessary to complete a title to each portion of the lands.

If the necessity for division is disputed, or the respective interests of the proprietors are not agreed upon, it may be necessary to make up a record and take proof. When the necessity of division is not disputed, or after it has been established, a remit may be made to a land surveyor, or other man of skill, to prepare a scheme of division. If the scheme of division is approved by the Sheriff and decree of division is granted it has, by Statute, the effect of a conveyance to each party participating in the division who may complete his title by recording the extract decree in the Register of Sasines.[1]

[1] 37 & 38 Vict. c. 94, sec. 35.

5. DIVISION OR DIVISION AND SALE OF COMMON PROPERTY.

Any one of several joint proprietors may apply in the Sheriff Court to have a heritable property divided, or, if division is not possible or not practicable, to have it sold and the proceeds divided.[1] If the crave is for division only, and it appears during the proceedings that division is impracticable, an alternative crave for sale and division may be added. This action is subject to removal to the Court of Session if the property exceed the value of £1000 or £50 by the year in the same way as an action of division of commonty.[2] The crave is for declarator that the pursuer is entitled to insist in the action and for warrant to sell the subjects and divide the proceeds. If division of the subjects is a possible solution the crave may ask for a remit to a surveyor to report, and otherwise may be in similar terms to that in an action of division of commonty, including a crave that each joint proprietor be ordained to grant, or concur in granting, deeds necessary for the completion of titles. In the usual case a joint proprietor is entitled either to have the subjects divided or sold.[3]

[1] 7 Edw. VII c. 51, sec. 5 (3).
[2] Ibid., sec. 5. See p. 503, supra.
[3] See Thom v. Macbeth, 1875, 3 R. 161; Morrison v. Kirk, 1912 S.C. 44; Vincent v. Anderson, 1920, 36 Sh.Ct.Rep. 182.

The action must be raised in the Sheriff Court of the district where the property is situated,[1] and all the other joint proprietors are called as defenders. Any defences to the competency or relevancy of the action are first dealt with, and, if these are refuted or not propounded, a remit is usually made to a man of skill to report as to division or sale. There may be a debate on the report but the reporter's views on practical questions will not be readily disturbed. If there is to be a sale the reporter is asked, on the original or a subsequent remit, to suggest the upset price and any special conditions of sale. If this report is approved the Court orders the property to be sold at the sight of the Clerk of Court, or other suitable person, under articles of roup drawn by the reporter and approved by the Court (or adjusted at the sight of the Clerk of Court), and upon such advertisement or otherwise as the Court may order. The articles of roup may contain a clause authorizing any of the parties to bid.[2] When realized, the price is consigned in Court and divided amongst the parties, according to their respective rights and interests. The account of the pursuer's solicitor in carrying out the sale will generally be taxed as between solicitor and client.[3]

[1] 7 Edw. VII c. 51, sec. 5.
[2] See Thom v. Macbeth, 1875, 3 R. 161; Vincent v. Anderson, 1920. 36 Sh.Ct.Rep. 182.
[3] Reidford v. Liston, (O.H.) 1931 S.L.T. 418.

The disposition to the purchaser is usually adjusted at the sight of the Clerk of Court. If any of the parties refuses to sign it seems doubtful whether in the Sheriff Court it is competent to adjudge the subjects to the purchaser or to authorize the Clerk of Court to sign.[1] In the case of a division the extract decree can be recorded.[2]

[1] Cf. Whyte v. Whyte, (O.H.) 1913, 2 S.L.T. 85. See p. 498, supra.
[2] 37 & 38 Vict. c. 94, sec. 35.

6. Exhibition.

The object of this action is to obtain exhibition of writs in which the pursuer has an interest. This process is competent in the Sheriff Court, even if the writs sought relate to heritage and raise a question of heritable right or title.[1] It was formerly chiefly used at the instance of an heir, who desired to inform himself of the state of a title, before deciding to take up the succession to heritage, but its use is not confined to such circumstances.[2] It is an action *ad factum præstandum* directed against the holder of the writs, the crave of the initial writ being for production in the hands of the Sheriff-clerk. In a rarely used form of the action it may contain also a crave that copies of the writs be made and certified by the Court, in which event the process is known as an action of transumpt.[3] An action of exhibition is a competent process for recovery of any description of writing, to see which a pursuer can allege an interest.[2] If the recovery was merely for production as evidence in another pending process the action of exhibition was an accessory action,[4] and that form of it is now superseded by the modern system of recovery of documents by commission and diligence. If the action is for exhibition and delivery of writs to which pursuer has the sole right of property or custody, the process is one for delivery as already discussed.[5]

[1] 7 Edw. VII c. 51, sec. 5 (4).
[2] See Whyte v. Kilmarnock District Committee, 1912, 2 S.L.T. 15.
[3] Selkirk v. Service, 1880, 8 R. 29.
[4] Gilmour v. M'Clure, 1895, 12 Sh.Ct.Rep. 66.
[5] See p. 497, supra.

7. Interdict.

Suspension is competent in the Sheriff Court only in respect of certain Sheriff Court decrees and decrees of registration.[1] An action of interdict will not be competent in the Sheriff Court if it is in effect a suspension of a kind which the Sheriff cannot competently entertain.[2] The Sheriff may interdict a sale of poinded goods under a warrant granted by himself.[3] It is sufficient to found jurisdiction that the defender is responsible for an alleged wrong being committed, or threatened to be committed, within the jurisdiction and his residence within the jurisdiction is not necessary.[4]

[1] See p. 29, supra.
[2] Thom v. North British Bank, 1848, 10 D. 1254; Beattie & Son v. Pratt, 1880, 7 R. 1171; cf. M'Callum v. Cohen, &c., 1915, 32 Sh.Ct.Rep. 39.
[3] Jack v. Waddell's Trustees, 1918 S.C. 73.
[4] 7 Edw. VII c. 51, sec. 6 (e). See Gill v. Cutler, 1895, 23 R. 371; Toni Tyres v. Palmer Tyre, 1905, 7 F. 477.

An application for interdict is an ordinary action, and it follows the usual course of an Ordinary Court process. The crave for interdict may be combined with one for declarator, or for damages. If interim interdict is sought, it must be specially craved and averments should be made to justify it being granted. In such a case interim interdict may be granted *de plano* along with the warrant for service, or an early diet may be fixed for hearing parties on the crave for interim interdict. If granted in the defender's absence, he is not interpelled till the interdict order has been intimated to him; but it is sufficient that it has been brought to his notice informally.[1] If interim interdict is refused the motion for it may be renewed at any stage. The interlocutor of the Sheriff-Substitute granting or refusing interim interdict is appealable to the Sheriff although the case may not yet have been tabled, and although defences have not yet been put in.[2] But an interlocutor which merely reserves the question of interim interdict till defences are put in is not, for purposes of appeal, a refusal of interim interdict.[3] If interim interdict is refused appeal is competent within fourteen days of the interlocutor, if it is granted appeal may be taken within fourteen days from the date of intimation thereof.[4] Such interlocutors are not appealable to the Court of Session save with leave, but a defender may by motion at any stage of the cause ask that interim interdict be recalled. If recall is to be asked after an appeal has been taken the motion must be made before the Sheriff-Substitute and not in the appeal tribunal.[5] A pursuer may be liable in damages if he unreasonably take interim interdict which is granted *periculo petentis*.[6] The crave for interdict must in all cases be specific and precise.[7]

[1] Henderson v. Maclellan, 1874, 1 R. 920; Neville v. Neville, 1921, 40 Sh.Ct.Rep. 151. See also Matheson v. Fraser, (O.H.) 1911, 2 S.L.T. 493.
[2] 7 Edw. VII c. 51, sec. 27 (a).
[3] Gauldie v. Magistrates of Arbroath, 1936 S.C. 861.
[4] Ibid., Schedule I, Rule 86; 2 & 3 Geo. V c. 28, Schedule II.
[5] Ibid., Schedule I, Rule 91; Trainer v. Renfrewshire Upper District Committee, 1907 S.C. 1117. See p. 297, supra.
[6] Glasgow City and District Railway Co. v. Glasgow Coal Exchange, 1885, 12 R. 1287; Fife v. Orr, 1895, 23 R. 8.
[7] Kelso School Board v. Hunter, 1874, 2 R. 228; Cairns v. Lee, 1892, 20 R. 16; cf. Duncan v. Ballantyne, 1938, 55 Sh.Ct.Rep. 122.

A third party may intervene in an interdict process if the granting of the interdict would be prejudicial to his interests.[1]

Such person should put in a minute craving to be sisted as a party in the process.

¹ Glasgow Shipowners' Association, &c. v. Clyde Navigation Trustees, 1885, 12 R. 695; Gill v. Cutler, 1895, 23 R. 371; Gas Power, &c., Co. v. Power Gas Corporation, 1911 S.C. 27.

As a condition of obtaining interim interdict, the pursuer may be required to find caution for the damage the defender may sustain, if it ultimately appears that interim interdict ought not to have been asked.¹ The damage for which the cautioner may be liable may include legal expenses, judicial and extrajudicial, to which defender has been put,² as well as such elements as, for instance, deterioration in the value of a subject the sale of which had been interdicted, or loss of market, or the like. In certain cases caution from the defender has been asked as a condition of refusing interim interdict.³ Interdict granted on caution is not operative till caution is found.⁴

¹ See Dunnachie v. Young & Sons, 1883, 10 R. 874, p. 876; Stewart v. Forbes, 1897, 24 R. 1112.
² Henderson v. A B, 1907, 24 Sh.Ct.Rep. 40.
³ Johnston v. Dumfries Road Trustees, 1867, 5 M. 1127; Fergusson-Buchanan v. Dunbartonshire County Council, 1924 S.C. 42.
⁴ Wilson v. Gilchrist, 1900, 2 F. 391.

If a caveat has been lodged against the granting of interim interdict, it will not be granted till the defender has been afforded an opportunity of being heard. Such a caveat apparently holds good for a month.¹ In such circumstances, if the defender has a good objection to the competency of the action, or challenges the necessity for interim interdict, or means to offer caution to avoid interim interdict being granted, he must be prepared to substantiate his pleas at once. An interim interdict, although appealed against, is binding till it is recalled, for an appeal does not prevent the interdict being operative, pending that appeal being disposed of.² Apart from appeal, interim interdict continues effective though defences are lodged, and it remains in operation until final decree unless it has meantime been recalled.³ The fact that the action has fallen asleep does not terminate interim interdict which has been granted,⁴ but if interim interdict is granted with the warrant of service, or before the expiry of the induciæ, and nothing is done to bring the action into Court the whole process, and also the interdict, apparently falls in a year and day after the induciæ expires.⁵

¹ See Act of Sederunt, 16th July, 1929, Table of Fees, Part II, 26.
² 7 Edw. VII c. 51, sec. 29. See Home Drummond v. M'Lachlan, 1908 S.C. 12.

3 Clippens Oil Co. v. Edinburgh Water Trust, 1906, 8 F. 731; Home-Drummond v. M'Lachlan, supra. See also Reid v. Mitchell, 1899, 16 Sh.Ct.Rep. 61.
4 Hamilton v. Allan, 1861, 23 D. 589; Home-Drummond v. M'Lachlan, supra.
5 Home-Drummond v. Norman, 1902, 19 Sh.Ct.Rep. 16.

A defender who disobeys an interdict, interim or final, is liable to punishment by fine or imprisonment on prosecution for breach of interdict. This is in form a civil action, commenced by initial writ, and the crave is that the defender be ordained to appear personally to answer to that complaint, and that he be punished if the charge is admitted or proved. A crave for caution not to repeat the offence is competent, but any question of damages should be the subject of a separate action. The concurrence of the procurator-fiscal is required.[1] This is shown in the instance and the fiscal also endorses his concurrence upon the initial writ. The onus of proving the breach of interdict rests with the pursuer, and if necessary a record is made up and proof taken as in an ordinary civil process, the defender being a competent witness. Amendment is competent in the usual way.[2] The penalty for breach of interdict is in the Sheriff's discretion. It is usually a fine with an alternative of imprisonment, but occasionally imprisonment without the option of a fine may be appropriate.[3] If the case is defended, and the granting of interdict is not admitted, it must be proved by competent evidence in the usual way.[4]

1 Duke of Northumberland v. Harris, 1832, 10 S. 366; Beattie v. Rodger, 1835, 14 S. 6.
2 See Dunlop Pneumatic Tyre Co. v. Rose, 1901, 3 F. 635.
3 Boswell's Trustees v. Pearson, 1886, 24 S.L.R. 32; Mackenzie v. Coulthart, 1889, 16 R. 1127.
4 Home-Drummond v. Douglas, 1904, 20 Sh.Ct.Rep. 87.

If the defender fails to appear to answer to the complaint of breach of interdict, warrant may be granted for his apprehension, or the proceedings may go on in his absence, and though he is not personally present it is competent to impose a monetary penalty.[1] In serious cases it is preferable that the defender should be present, and if it is a case in which the penalty may be imprisonment the diet should be adjourned and a warrant granted to apprehend and bring him to the adjourned diet.[2]

1 Walker v. Junor, 1903, 5 F. 1035; Stark's Trustees v. Duncan, 1906, 8 F. 429.
2 Welsbach Incandescent Gas Co. v. M'Mann, 1901, 4 F. 395.

An interlocutor in a breach of interdict process is subject to review in the same manner as an interlocutor in any other Ordinary Court process.[1] Where imprisonment is ordered the marking of an appeal postpones the sentence being put into effect, and where the appellants had in the meantime been imprisoned the Court of Session ordered their interim liberation.[2] Applications for mitigation of sentence should be made to the Court which pronounced the sentence.[3]

[1] Stark's Trustees v. Duncan, 1906, 8 F. 429; Maclachlan v. Bruce, &c., 1912 S.C. 440; Macleay v. Macdonald, 1928 S.C. 776.
[2] Macleay v. Macdonald, supra.
[3] Johnson v. Grant, 1923 S.C. 789.

8. LAWBURROWS.

When a person dreads bodily harm or molestation by another person, of himself or his family, he may, in the Sheriff Court, present an application for lawburrows. This is a summary application,[1] commenced by initial writ, setting forth the grounds of the application, and craving that defender find caution that the pursuer and his family and dependants be kept scaithless, under a penalty to be fixed by the Sheriff, and craving also warrant, failing caution being found, for the defender's arrest and imprisonment till he find caution as ordered. The application is disposed of without written pleadings or record of evidence,[1] and the period of possible imprisonment is limited to six months.[2] The first deliverance usually includes a warrant to cite the defender and witnesses to a fixed diet when proof is led.[3] The evidence of one credible witness is sufficient and such witness may be a party.[4] Caution may be dispensed with, and the offender ordered to grant his own bond for duly implementing the terms of the Sheriff's order, under pain of imprisonment.[5] Expenses may be awarded on either side, and decree for these is granted in the usual way.[6] The pursuer does not require to aliment the defender if he is imprisoned.[7]

[1] 45 & 46 Vict. c. 42, sec. 6 (3); 7 Edw. VII c. 51, sec. 50.
[2] 45 & 46 Vict. c. 42, sec. 6 (6).
[3] Ibid., sec. 6 (2).
[4] Ibid., sec. 6 (4).
[5] Ibid., sec. 6 (7).
[6] Ibid., sec. 6 (3).
[7] Ibid., sec. 6 (8).

Under the older procedure a decree of lawburrows could be reviewed by suspension, but that remedy is no longer competent and review is now by way of stated case under the Summary

Jurisdiction Act.[1] Appeal by stated case would appear to be thus competent after final judgment whether decree of lawburrows is granted or refused.[2]

[1] Mackenzie v. Maclennan, 1916 S.C. 617.
[2] 8 Edw. VII c. 65, secs. 2, 60.

If the defender, despite the Sheriff's order, molests the pursuer or his family, he may be sued in an action of contravention of lawburrows. The cautioner is also called, if there is one. The concurrence of the procurator-fiscal is required, but the action is in form a civil application, craving forfeiture of the penalty.

9. MAILLS AND DUTIES.

An action of maills and duties is brought by a creditor heritably secured on certain subjects for the purpose of recovering the rents of the property, to the exclusion of the landlord's personal creditors. The heritable creditor, in the initial writ, must set forth his title. The proprietor of the property is called as defender, and under the former practice it was also necessary to call the tenants. The modern practice under which the tenants are not called as defenders is dealt with below.[1] If a question relating to heritable title arises it may now competently be settled in the Sheriff Court, irrespective of the value of the property.[2] When the creditor has obtained decree of maills and duties he has the same remedies as the proprietor for the recovery of rents, and may pursue an action of sequestration for rent, not only against tenants called in the maills and duties action, but also against tenants who have subsequently entered.[3] A creditor in possession under a decree of maills and duties may also, by poinding of the ground, attach moveables on the ground belonging to the proprietor, and also those belonging to the tenants, but only to the extent of their respective rents.[4]

[1] See next page.
[2] 7 Edw. VII c. 51, sec. 5 (4).
[3] Robertson's Trustees v. Gardner, 1889, 16 R. 705.
[4] Henderson v. Wallace, 1875, 2 R. 272.

The action of maills and duties is available to a heritable creditor, including the holder of a bond and disposition in security and the proprietor of a ground annual where the lands have been disponed in security.[1] It is not open to a superior,[2] nor the holder of an *ex facie* absolute conveyance,[3] but it is now available to the holder of a security over a superiority or ground annual.[4] A heritable creditor on a *pro indiviso* part of subjects may use the action to the extent of his debtor's share of the rents.[5] Maills and duties is competent only when the debtor is in default of principal or interest,[6] or when the owner of the security subject is notour bankrupt, or has granted a trust deed for creditors.[7] It is not a competent action against a proprietor who is in personal occupation,[8] but such a proprietor, if in default, may now be ejected.[9] An action of maills and duties is not open to the holder of a security over a registered lease,[10] but such a security holder may apply to the Sheriff for a warrant to enter on possession of the subjects leased.[11] This application may be made when payment of principal or interest is in default for six months, and intimation is made to the lessee for the time being and to the landlord.[11]

[1] Somerville v. Johnston, 1899, 1 F. 726. See 14 & 15 Geo. V c. 27, sec. 23 (4).
[2] Prudential Assurance Co. v. Cheyne, &c., 1884, 11 R. 871.
[3] Scottish Heritable Security Co. v. Allan, Campbell & Co., 1876, 3 R. 333, Lord President Inglis, p. 340; cf. Crichton's Trustees v. Clarke, (O.H.) 1909, 1 S.L.T. 467.
[4] 14 & 15 Geo. V c. 27, sec. 26.
[5] Schaw v. Black, 1889, 16 R. 336.
[6] 37 & 38 Vict. c. 94, sec. 119; 14 & 15 Geo. V c. 27, sec. 25 (1) (a); M'Ara v. Anderson, 1913 S.C. 931; Gibson v. Blair, 1918 S.C. 353. Tender of interest in arrear is no defence to the action when brought, M'Naughton, &c. v. Scott, 1912, 29 Sh.Ct.Rep. 83.
[7] 14 & 15 Geo. V c. 27, sec. 25 (1) (a). See Ritchie v. Kain, 1932, 48 Sh.Ct.Rep. 233.
[8] Smith's Trustees v. D. & J. Chalmers, 1890, 17 R. 1088; cf. Hutchison v. Alexander, 1904, 6 F. 532.
[9] 57 & 58 Vict. c. 44, sec. 5.
[10] Dunbar v. Gill, 1908 S.C. 1054.
[11] 20 & 21 Vict. c. 26, sec. 6. See Fleming v. Burgess, &c., 1867, 5 M. 856.

While the older writ of maills and duties, calling the tenants, is still competent the Heritable Securities Act of 1894 introduced an alternative and briefer process, in which the proprietor only need be called, the crave in the initial writ being for a general declarator that the creditor has right to the rents, or so much thereof as will satisfy principal, interest, and penalties.[1] A statutory style of writ is provided which is modified to conform to an initial writ in ordinary form. Notice of the raising of the action is given in statutory form by registered letter to the tenants, the effect of which notice when received by the tenants is to interpel them from paying to the proprietor, and to render them, if they do pay, liable to pay again to the creditor if he obtains decree, but without prejudice to the tenant's right upon any competent legal ground to withhold payment of rent.[2] Upon decree being obtained, notice thereof is again given in statutory form to the tenants by registered letter, the effect of which is to make the tenants direct debtors to the creditor, and to exonerate the tenants upon making payment to him.[3] The notices to the tenants are in each case signed by the pursuer, his solicitor or a messenger-at-arms or Sheriff-officer.[4] The pursuer is entitled to a decree of maills and duties despite the defender's offer to pay off the arrears of interest.[5]

[1] 57 & 58 Vict. c. 44, sec. 3, Schedule A.
[2] Ibid., Schedule B. See Marshall's Trustees v. Banks, 1934 S.C. 405.
[3] Ibid., Schedule C.
[4] Ibid., Schedules B, C.
[5] M'Naughton, &c. v. Scott, &c., 1912, 29 Sh.Ct.Rep. 83.

10. March Fences.

Notwithstanding the former limitation of Sheriff Court jurisdiction as regards questions relating to heritable property, the local Sheriff Court had always power to regulate questions relating to the erection or repair of march fences, and the straightening of marches. Actions for straightening marches[1] and the division of runrig lands[2] were and are competent only in the Sheriff Court, while those for erection of march fences can be brought either in the Sheriff Court or the Court of Session.[3] Even if there is a dispute as to the situation of the existing line of division, the whole questions relating to the regulation of march fences can now be settled in the Sheriff Court.[4] In a process for straightening marches, the Sheriff is required to visit the ground, and this duty he cannot delegate, although he may take the assistance of skilled persons in performing it.[5] An application of this sort is an ordinary action; the process is conducted in the usual manner, and the judgment is subject to review in common form. But, as a rule, the Supreme Court will not interfere unless there has been some grave error in procedure.[6]

[1] 1661, c. 41; 1669, c. 17. See Strang v. Steuart, 1864, 2 M. 1015; 4 M. (H.L.) 5.
[2] 1695, c. 23.
[3] Pollock v. Ewing, 1869, 7 M. 815.
[4] 7 Edw. VII c. 51, sec. 5 (4).
[5] Lord Advocate v. Sinclair, 1872, 11 M. 137.
[6] Kintore v. Kintore's Trustees, 1886, 13 R. 997.

It is usual in such cases for the Sheriff to remit to a man of skill for a report. It has been held that such a remit does not prevent a subsequent allowance of proof, although a second remit would be more appropriate.[1] The Sheriff's jurisdiction extends to ordering the reconstruction of a ruinous fence in a different style.[2] In general where the erection of a march fence is demanded it must not involve such a lack of common benefit, or such a grave disproportion of benefit, as to be unjust or oppressive to the defender.[3] The action must be raised before commencing the erection or repair of the fence, otherwise the defender will not be bound to contribute.[4]

[1] Steel v. Steel, 1898, 25 R. 715.
[2] Paterson v. MacDonald, 1880, 7 R. 958.
[3] Secker v. Cameron, 1914 S.C. 354.
[4] Duncan v. Ramsay, 1906, 23 Sh.Ct.Rep. 181.

11. MULTIPLEPOINDING.

The purpose of an action of multiplepoinding is to determine the rights in a fund, or in subjects, to which there are two or more competing claims. Apart from competing claims the process is also available to trustees for the purpose of obtaining exoneration when they cannot otherwise procure their discharge.[1] Where an action is raised any one or more of these matters may be found to be in dispute:—the competency of the action, the amount or extent of the fund *in medio*, or the parties entitled thereto. The fund *in medio* may be money, moveables, or moveable rights, or heritage or heritable rights.[2]

[1] Mackenzie's Trustees v. Sutherland, 1895, 22 R. 233; Davidson v. Ewen, (O.H.) 1895, 3 S.L.T. 162. See also Connell's Trustees v. Chalk, &c., 1878, 5 R. 735.
[2] As to heritage see Logan v. Byres, (O.H.) 1895, 2 S.L.T. 455; Edinburgh Merchant Maiden Hospital v. Greig's Executors, (O.H.) 1902, 10 S.L.T. 317; Boyd's Trustees v. Boyd, (O.H.) 1906, 13 S.L.T. 878.

Numerous cases have been decided as to the competency of an action of multiplepoinding, some of which are difficult to reconcile. It is impossible here to do more than indicate the general principles involved. Apart from an action brought by trustees for their exoneration the normal requisite is that there should be a fund held by one party and competing claims thereon by two or more other parties, and in general a demand by one or more of the claimants for payment. It is not enough that the ultimate division of the fund is in dispute if there are no competing claims made against the holder[1]; nor is it generally sufficient to justify a multiplepoinding in connexion with the division of an estate that certain claims of creditors are disputed by beneficiaries.[2] A multiplepoinding has been held to be competent at the instance of the holder of the fund when it was claimed both by a beneficiary and by assignees of the beneficiary,[3] and also where a sum due under a policy was claimed by the policy holder and also by an arrester.[4] Where an arrestment has been used on a fund in the hands of a third party, and claims are made both by the arrester and another party, the competency of a multiplepoinding will generally be

sustained.[5] If there are competing claims as to a certain part of
an estate that will justify a multiplepoinding in respect of that
portion, but not in respect of the whole estate.[6] A non-acceding
creditor under a trust deed who has arrested in the hands of the
trustee cannot bring a multiplepoinding in order to dispute the
trustee's administration.[7]

[1] Bank of Scotland v. Comrie, 1871, 8 S.L.R. 419; Clark v. Campbell,
1873, 1 R. 281; Royal Bank of Scotland v. Ellis, (O.H.) 1902, 10
S.L.T. 167; Commercial Union Assurance Co. v. Globe Co., (O.H.)
1916, 1 S.L.T. 343; cf. Commercial Bank of Scotland v. Muir, 1897,
25 R. 219.

[2] Robb's Trustees v. Robb, &c., 1880, 7 R. 1049; Gordon v. Gordon,
1894, 32 S.L.R. 355; Mackenzie's Trustees v. Sutherland, 1895,
22 R. 233. See also Glen's Trustees v. Miller, 1911 S.C. 1178.

[3] Fraser's Executrix v. Wallace's Trustees, 1893, 20 R. 374; cf. Connell's
Trustee v. Chalk, 1878, 5 R. 735.

[4] Colonial Mutual Life Assurance Society v. Brown, 1911, 1 S.L.T. 158.

[5] Park v. Watson, 1874, 2 R. 118; Pollard v. Galloway & Nivison, 1881,
9 R. 21; North British Railway Co. v. White, 1881, 9 R. 97; Dill
Wilson & Muirhead v. Ricardo's Trustee, 1885, 12 R. 404; Ross
v. Plano Co., (O.H.) 1902, 10 S.L.T. 314; cf. Mitchell v. Strachan,
1869, 8 M. 154.

[6] Macnab v. Waddell, 1894, 21 R. 827; MacGillivray's Trustees v. Dallas,
1905, 7 F. 733.

[7] Kyd v. Waterson, &c., 1880, 7 R. 884.

An action of multiplepoinding may be raised either in the
jurisdiction within which the fund or subject *in medio* is situated,
or in the Court to the jurisdiction of which the holder of the fund
is subject.[1] In the case of arrestments it is immaterial whether
or not the common debtor resides within either Sheriffdom[1]; and
jurisdiction does not require to be founded against him.[2] In view
of the statutory provisions above narrated it seems competent to
bring the action in any Sheriff Court to whose jurisdiction the
holder of the fund is subject, either by having his residence within
it, or by carrying on business within it and being cited personally
or at such place of business.[3] It seems more doubtful whether
jurisdiction by arrestment *ad fundandam jurisdictionem*, or that
arising from ownership of heritable property (when the dispute
does not relate to the property) or from contract could, on the
terms on which these classes of jurisdiction are conferred, be used
as founding an action of multiplepoinding.[4] In any event the
choice of jurisdiction is subject to the Sheriff's discretionary power
of transfer to a more convenient forum.[5]

[1] 7 Edw. VII c. 51, sec. 6 (g), Schedule I, Rule 128.
[2] Leggat Bros. v. Gray, 1912 S.C. 230.
[3] 7 Edw. VII c. 51, sec. 5 (a) (b); 2 & 3 Geo. V c. 28, Schedule I.
[4] Ibid., sec. 5 (c) (d) (f).
[5] Ibid., Schedule I, Rules 19, 20.

When a multiplepoinding is competent any claimant is entitled to raise the action as well as the holder of the fund or subject *in medio*. If raised by a claimant it is brought in name of the holder of the fund, who is called the pursuer and nominal raiser, and the party raising the action designs himself as real raiser.[1] If the real raiser is not the holder of the fund, the action must be served on such holder as if he were a defender.

[1] 7 Edw. VII c. 51, Schedule I, Rule 129.

All the known claimants having an interest in the fund or subject *in medio* should be called as defenders, whether they are domiciled in Scotland or not. It is unnecessary to found jurisdiction against them. Any who are resident furth of Scotland are cited edictally. Failure to call him does not preclude any person having an interest from lodging a claim (when claims have been ordered), and, subject to conditions as to expenses, the Court may allow a claimant to appear at a late stage of the process. Late claims have been received when the case was on appeal from a decree of ranking and preference,[1] but they cannot be accepted after final judgment.[2] Liability for expenses will generally depend on whether the claimant's appearance occasions any additional expense.[3] Not only are direct claimants upon the fund entitled to appear, but a claimant's creditor, in a liquid debt, is entitled to lodge a riding claim upon that of a claimant in order to obtain payment of his debt out of such portion of the fund as the claimant may be found entitled to.[4] A riding claim will be received after decree of ranking and preference has been pronounced but not after a decree for payment to the original claimant.[5]

[1] Binnie's Trustees v. Henry's Trustees, &c., 1883, 10 R. 1075; National Bank of Scotland v. Campbell, 1901, 4 F. 17.

[2] Landale v. Wilson, 1900, 2 F. 1047; Ramsay's Judicial Factor v. British Linen Bank, 1911 S.C. 832; cf. Dymond v. Scott, &c., 1877, 5 R. 196.

[3] See Dymond v. Scott, &c., supra; Binnie's Trustees v. Henry's Trustees, &c., supra; Sawers' Factor v. Sawers, 1889, 17 R. 1; National Bank of Scotland v. Campbell, supra. See also Cowan's Trustees v. Cowan, 1888, 16 R. 7; M'Farlane, &c. v. M'Gregor, &c., 1915, 31 Sh.Ct.Rep. 264.

[4] Royal Bank of Scotland v. Stevenson, &c., 1849, 12 D. 250; Gill's Trustees v. Patrick, 1889, 16 R. 403.

[5] Anglo-Foreign Banking Co., (O.H.) 1879, 16 S.L.R. 731; Scottish Life Assurance Co. v. Donald, (O.H.) 1902, 9 S.L.T. 348; Ramsay's Judicial Factor v. British Linen Bank, supra.

In an action of multiplepoinding, notice of appearance need not necessarily be lodged unless by one of the parties called as defender who desires to challenge the competency of the action, or where the action is brought by a claimant and the nominal raiser denies the existence of the fund *in medio*. If defences on these lines are put in a record will be made up and the competency of the action will be determined in the first instance. The claimants, whether called in the action or not, are not, properly speaking, defenders, and they are not liable in expenses merely because they have been called. The expenses of raising the action are a first charge upon the fund or subject *in medio*. The nominal raiser will be allowed out of the fund his expenses in connexion with the condescendence of the fund and the Sheriff may, and if the action was necessary, generally will, allow the real raiser his expenses, preferably, out of the fund *in medio*.[1]

[1] 7 Edw. VII c. 51, Schedule I, Rule 129; Hepburn's Trustee v. Rex, 1894, 21 R. 1024.

If there are no objections to the competency or relevancy of the action, or if these have been disposed of, the next step in the process is usually to settle the fund, which may be money or property, although this may competently be done at any time before decree for payment. If the initial writ contains a full statement of the fund *in medio* this may be held to be a condescendence of the fund; otherwise the holder will be ordered to lodge such a condescendence; claimants will be allowed to lodge objections and the holder may be allowed to answer these. If a dispute as to the amount of the fund arises in this way a record will be made up, and this issue disposed of before claims are entertained. When the amount of the fund has been determined, or where all parties interested agree upon the fund, an interlocutor is pronounced approving of the condescendence of the fund and this fixes the amount for which the holder is liable. Either at this, or at some other stage, the holder is found liable in once and single payment of the fund. The fund, if money, may then be consigned, or if it is a subject it may be realized and the proceeds consigned, or the subject itself deposited. On consignation or deposit, the holder may be exonerated and discharged, and found entitled to expenses. He then ceases to appear as a party, and the process becomes one of competition amongst the claimants. Consignation may be ordered under reservation of any claim the holder may have on the fund.[1] An interlocutor making no decerniture but merely exonerating the holder of the fund and ordering claims, has been held not appealable without leave.[2] As the holder's expenses are generally a preferable claim upon the fund *in medio*, the order upon him may be to consign under deduction of his expenses, modified at a named figure, or as taxed, or he may be ordered to consign, and found entitled to his expenses, as taxed, out of the fund.

1 Lang v. Downie, 1872, 9 S.L.R. 308.
2 Macduff v. Macduff, 1893, 9 Sh.Ct.Rep 243.

When the fund has been determined, the Sheriff orders claims to be lodged within a specified period.[1] A second order for claims is frequently made, and where it is doubtful whether all possible claimants have been cited an order for advertisement is usual. Claims consist of a condescendence of facts, a formal claim to a stated share of the fund, and pleas in law. If necessary answers to claims may be ordered, but in the normal case a record is made up upon the claims and is adjusted in the usual way. If necessary proof is allowed, and the question who has best right to the fund is disposed of in the same manner as any other issue in an ordinary defended action.[2] Only a party who has stated a claim can be preferred to any portion of the fund.[3] The facts upon which several claimants base their claims may be stated in one paper, but the formal claim, and pleas in law, may require to be separately stated.[4] A claimant may adopt all or part of the condescendence in another claim or in the initial writ. The position in regard to late claims and riding claims has been already discussed.[5] Holders who are trustees may lodge a claim to the whole fund for purposes of administration.[6] The claimant in a multiplepoinding is not usually required to sist a mandatory.[7] In a multiplepoinding the Court usually disposes of all such questions as may be necessary to decide as to competition between the parties. It seems that in the Sheriff Court there would not be power to set aside *ope exceptionis* a decree of Court, at any rate if granted *in foro*[8]; but it would be competent to set aside documents,[9] and to decide incidentally as to questions of marriage or legitimacy.[10] Where there is no competition claimants may be ranked without a record being made up, but if there is a possibility of other claimants being in existence the ranking may only be given " for aught yet seen," which is held to preserve the rights of claimants who have not been called.[11]

1 7 Edw. VII c. 51, Schedule I, Rule 130.
2 Ibid., Schedule I, Rule 132.
3 Connell v. Ferguson, 1861, 23 D. 683.
4 7 Edw. VII c. 51, Schedule I, Rule 131.
5 See p. 516, supra.
6 Hall's Trustees v. Macdonald, 1892, 19 R. 567.
7 See p. 92, supra.

8 Leggat Bros. v. Gray, 1912 S.C. 230; Jarvie's Trustees v. Bannatyne, 1927 S.C. 34.
9 7 Edw. VII c. 51, Schedule I, Rule 50.
10 See M'Donald v. Mackenzie, 1891, 18 R. 502.
11 See Kerr's Trustee, (O.H.) 1894, 2 S.L.T. 10; Gauden's Trustees v. Jamieson, (O.H.) 1902, 10 S.L.T. 326.

The mere raising of an action of multiplepoinding does not prevent diligence by creditors, but a creditor is not entitled to claim in a multiplepoinding, and at the same time to proceed with personal diligence.[1] If a person not in the multiplepoinding process proceed with diligence against the holder of the fund, the holder may bring a suspension and plead the pending multiplepoinding process as a ground of suspension.

1 Hendry v. Brown, 1851, 13 D. 1046; Ferguson v. Bothwell, 1882, 9 R. 687.

In a process of multiplepoinding, where the claims are numerous, it may be convenient for the Sheriff to determine the principle upon which the division of the fund is to proceed, and then to remit to a reporter to classify the claims, prepare a scheme of division, and report. The expense of such a remit may be made a charge upon the fund, to be deducted before division.

Decree preferring a claimant in a process of multiplepoinding is equivalent to a decerniture against all the other claimants, and if expenses are disposed of, it is a final judgment in the case of the claimants concerned, subject to review in the ordinary way.[1] But an interlocutor finding a claimant entitled to be ranked and containing no operative decree is not a final interlocutor.[2] If none of the interested parties appeals against an interlocutor ranking claimants to the whole fund that interlocutor becomes final and cannot thereafter be brought under review.[3] The holder of a fund, who allowed decree to go out in favour of a claimant after the condescendence of the fund had been lodged was held to be not entitled to suspend the decree, upon the ground that he had a claim of compensation against the common debtor,[4] but such a claim of compensation may be stated in giving in the condescendence of the fund though a decree of ranking has been already pronounced.[5]

1 See Glasgow Corporation v. General Accident, Fire and Life Assurance Corporation, 1914 S.C. 835.
2 Strichen Endowments v. Diverall, 1891, 19 R. 79.
3 Duncan's Factor v. Duncan, 1874, 1 R. 964; Terrell v. Ker, 1900, 2 F. 1055.
4 Downie v. Rae, 1832, 11 S. 51.
5 Ramsay's Judicial Factor v. British Linen Bank, 1912 S.C. 206.

The holder of the fund may obtain exoneration and discharge at any time after the condescendence of the fund has been approved, either on consignation or deposit as already explained,[1] or, if the competition has been determined, on paying over or delivering the funds or subjects *in medio* to the party found entitled thereto.

[1] See p. 517, supra.

In actions of multiplepoinding there are certain specialties in regard to expenses. If the action is competently brought the real raiser will get his expenses of raising the action and obtaining discharge out of the fund,[1] and such expenses will generally be taxed as between solicitor and client. But if the action is not justified the real raiser may be held liable in expenses, and in such circumstances trustees have been saddled with personal responsibility.[2] The nominal raiser will be found entitled to expenses relating to the condescendence of the fund, while litigation as to the amount of the fund is generally dealt with according to the ordinary rules.[3] Where the competition arises from the construction of a testamentary writing or a marriage contract all claimants, whether successful or not, will generally be allowed their expenses out of the fund.[4] Where the competition is not of this nature the matter is dealt with under the ordinary rules,[5] but where a claimant has made a justifiable, though not a successful, appearance these may not be so strictly applied as in an ordinary action.

[1] Hepburn's Trustee v. Rex, 1894, 21 R. 1024.
[2] Mackenzie's Trustees v. Sutherland, 1895, 22 R. 233; Cruickshank's Executor v. Cruickshank's Trustees, (O.H.) 1907, 14 S.L.T. 761.
[3] Walker's Trustee v. Walker, 1878, 5 R. 678; Pollard v. Galloway & Nivison, 1881, 9 R. 21, Lord Rutherfurd Clark, p. 26.
[4] See p. 315, supra.
[5] Bannerman's Trustees v. Bannerman, 1915 S.C. 398. See Agnew v. White, (O.H.) 1900, 8 S.L.T. 43 (abandonment of claim).

An interlocutor sustaining the competency of an action of multiplepoinding can only be appealed against with leave,[1] but an interlocutor dismissing the action as incompetent and disposing of the question of expenses is a final interlocutor which can be appealed without leave. An interlocutor which repels objections to the fund, approves the condescendence thereof and disposes of expenses is a final interlocutor which can be appealed without leave.[2] An interlocutor may be issued containing findings in fact and in law determining the principles on which the division of the fund is to proceed. This is usually done previous to the operative decree which may require adjustment in detail either

as a result of further discussion or of a remit. Such an interlocutor containing findings may conveniently grant leave to appeal
so that the principles of the decision can be disposed of before
the matter is worked out in detail.[3] Appeal in the case of decrees
of ranking and preference has been already noticed.[4] A decree for
payment is *res judicata* against other claimants in the multiplepoinding but not in a subsequent question—as in a reduction—
with parties who had not been claimants.[5]

[1] Gordon v. Graham, 1874, 1 R. 1081; Stewart v. Guthrie, 1889, 26
S.L.R. 656.
[2] Walker's Trustees v. Walker, 1878, 5 R. 678; School Board of Harris
v. Davidson, 1881, 9 R. 371.
[3] See Kennedy v. Taylor, 1873, 11 M. 603; Gowans' Trustees v. Gowans,
1889, 27 S.L.R. 210.
[4] See p. 519, supra.
[5] M'Caig v. Maitland, 1887, 14 R. 295; Elder's Trustees v. Elder, 1895,
22 R. 505.

In the case of a deceased's estate the need for an Inland
Revenue certificate as to death duties must be kept in view.[1]

[1] See p. 252, supra.

12. POINDING OF THE GROUND.

The object of the process of poinding of the ground is to
enable a creditor, whose debt constitutes a real burden on land,
to secure moveable effects upon the lands in satisfaction of his
debt, principal and interest. If he is in possession as owner he
cannot competently use this diligence. Thus, a creditor who holds
an absolute disposition qualified by a back letter cannot use
this process,[1] nor can a liferenter,[2] because in either case the
ex facie title for the time being is that of proprietor. But it is
available to a creditor in possession under a decree of maills
and duties.[3] It is competent to a bondholder, or to a superior,
or the holder of a ground annual,[4] but not to an assignee in
security of a long lease.[5] A postponed bondholder may raise a
poinding of the ground, but prior bondholders have a preference
on any proceeds of sale and they should be called as defenders.[6]
In the general case separate bondholders should not combine in
one process.[7] The initial writ is in ordinary form and sets forth
the pursuer's title, and the defenders called are the proprietor
and the tenants. The goods of third parties cannot in general
be attached.[8] The crave is for warrant to search for, poind, and
distrain the moveable effects upon the ground, for payment of the
heritable debt (the goods of tenants not being taken beyond the
value of rent due by them), and, meantime, for warrant to

inventory and secure.   Service of the writ creates a nexus upon
the effects which, at the date of service, are actually on the ground.[9]
Service by post does not appear to be incompetent but as the
process is of the nature of diligence it may be thought better
to serve by officer.   The warrant to inventory is included in the
first deliverance which is signed by the Sheriff,[10] and the warrant
is executed by officer as in a poinding but the effects are not
valued.[11]   No personal decree is craved, except for expenses (which
are asked against the proprietor and against the tenants only if
they oppose), and when decree has been granted a charge is not
necessary.   The debt or right founded upon must be duly constituted in the sense of infeftment, and the pursuer must not have
disposed of his interest[12]; but a person in right of the debt may
pursue the process, although his title is not yet heritably completed
as, for instance, an executor or assignee.[13]   It is immaterial that
the owner of the subjects affected is not feudally infeft.[14]   Poinding
in security of current interest is competent but payment cannot
be demanded till the interest is due.[15]   While other parties who
may have an interest in conflict with the pursuer (e.g., other
bondholders) should be called as defenders it is thought that any
such, though not called, may intervene to protect their interests.
Where a defender denied that he was owner of the goods poinded
but declined to specify the owner he was refused a proof on that
topic.[16]

[1] Scottish Heritable Security Co. v. Allan Campbell & Co., 1876, 3 R.
      333.
[2] Erskine IV, 1, 11.
[3] Henderson v. Wallace, 1875, 2 R. 272.
[4] Bell's Trustees v. Copeland & Co., 1896, 23 R. 650.
[5] Luke v. Wallace, 1896, 23 R. 634.
[6] Young's Trustees v. Hill's Trustee, (O.H.) 1893, 1 S.L.T. 357.
[7] Douglas v. Tait, 1884, 12 R. 10.
[8] Thomson v. Scoular, 1882, 9 R. 430.   See Kelly's Trustee v. Moncrieff's
      Trustee, 1920 S.C. 461 (partnership).
[9] Lyons v. Anderson, &c., 1880, 8 R. 24.
[10] 7 Edw. VII c. 51, Schedule I, Rule 7.
[11] See p. 276, supra.
[12] Scottish Heritages Co. v. North British Property Investment Co.,
      1885, 12 R. 550.   See Hardie, &c. v. Horn, &c., 1888, 4 Sh.Ct.Rep.
      409.
[13] Tweedie v. Beattie, 1836, 14 S. 337; Marquess of Ailsa v. Jeffray, 1859,
      21 D. 492.
[14] Mackenzie's Trustees v. Smith, 1883, 20 S.L.R. 351.
[15] Stewart v. Gibson's Trustee, 1880, 8 R. 270; cf. Martin's Trustees v.
      Hamilton, &c., 1908, 24 Sh.Ct.Rep. 351.
[16] Middleton v. Fleming, 1934, 51 Sh.Ct.Rep. 51.

The decree is in form a warrant to poind, and, after poinding,
a warrant of sale is obtained which is carried out under sec. 26

of the Debtors (Scotland) Act, 1838, as in the case of an ordinary poinding.[1] The pursuer has no claim to moveables removed from the subjects before the poinding is executed.[2]

[1] 1 & 2 Vict. c. 114, sec. 26. See p. 279, supra.
[2] Urquhart v. Macleod's Trustee, 1883, 10 R. 991; Traill's Trustees v. Free Church of Scotland, 1915 S.C. 655.

As all questions concerning heritable right or title are now competent in the Sheriff Court, the pursuer's title may be challenged, irrespective of the value of the lands, and all questions arising may be disposed of by the Sheriff.[1] This is subject to the right of either party in such circumstances at the closing of the record, or within six days thereafter, to require the cause to be remitted to the Court of Session where the value of the subjects in dispute exceeds £50 by the year or £1000 in value.[1]

[1] 7 Edw. VII c. 51, sec. 5 (4).

13. RELIEF.

An action of relief is the process by which a party, who is ex facie liable in implement of an obligation, but who is not the person ultimately liable, seeks to have the real obligant ordained to implement the obligation, and so to relieve the pursuer of a possible action against him at the instance of the creditor in the obligation. Thus, an ex facie joint obligant upon a bill, who is being held liable by the holder, may sue his joint obligant in relief if he is the real obligant. If he has been already forced to pay, the action will take the form of a claim for repayment; but an action of relief may be brought although the party ostensibly liable has not yet paid, in which case the crave is that defender be ordained to free and relieve the pursuer by meeting his obligation and producing a discharge in process. Any claim or action against a party who is entitled to relief by another should be intimated to that other at once.[1] Provision has been made by Statute in regard to relief as between joint wrongdoers.[2]

[1] See generally Gardiner v. Main, 1894, 22 R. 100; Clarke v. Scott, 1896, 23 R. 442; Duncan's Trustees v. Steven, 1897, 24 R. 880; Leith Harbour, &c., Commissioners v. North British Railway Co., (O.H.) 1904, 2 S.L.T. 192.
[2] 3 & 4 Geo. VI c. 42, sec. 3.

14. SEPARATION AND ALIMENT AND ADHERENCE AND ALIMENT.

Certain consistorial actions are now competent in the Sheriff Court which were formerly competent only in the Court of Session.[1] The peculiarities of procedure, which obtain in Court of Session practice in such actions, should be followed in the Sheriff Court, so far as these are not inconsistent with the general rules of procedure in Sheriff Court actions.[2] One of the peculiarities is that, although the action may be undefended, a decree in absence is not granted without inquiry.[3] The pursuer must first substantiate the grounds of action, and must submit to the Court the necessary evidence warranting the crave. By the rules it is provided that decree in absence, on failure to lodge a notice of appearance or to answer, is not available in actions of separation and aliment, adherence and aliment, interim aliment or actions regulating the custody of children.[4] Where an action of adherence and aliment was defended, and was settled on the basis of dropping the crave for adherence and granting a sum for aliment, it was held by the Supreme Court that such a decree was within the power of the Sheriff.[5] It is to be noted that this was not a decree in absence and therefore is not struck at by Rule 23, nor was it a type of decree that, under the practice of the Supreme Court, required to be substantiated by proof.[6] In this case the award was one of interim aliment only, otherwise it would have been outwith the jurisdiction of the Sheriff to grant it. The grounds of action in such cases should be clearly set forth in the condescendence annexed to the initial writ, but it is not the practice in the Sheriff Court as in the Court of Session to hold the libel relevant in the interlocutor allowing a proof when the action is undefended. In a proof in a consistorial action the pursuer should always lead.[7]

1 See p. 18, et seq., supra.
2 Grant v. Grant, 1908, 24 Sh.Ct.Rep. 114.
3 Muirhead v. Muirhead, 1846, 8 D. 786; M'Farlane v. M'Farlane, 1847, 9 D. 500.
4 7 Edw. VII c. 51, Schedule I, Rule 23; 2 & 3 Geo. V c. 28, Schedule II.
5 Christie v. Christie, 1919 S.C. 576.
6 Wood v. Wood, (O.H.) 1882, 19 S.L.R. 631; Wright v. Wright, (O.H.) 1894, 2 S.L.T. 29.
7 Paterson v. Paterson, 1938 S.C. 251.

The decree granted after proof in an undefended action of this kind is not a decree *in foro*, nor is it a decree by default. It is a decree in absence and while the legislature may not have intended that the ordinary rules in regard to reponing should apply to such a decree it has been held that they do, and that a defender may be reponed against a decree granted after proof.[1] Alternatively the defender may appeal.[2]

1 Christie v. Christie, 1917, 34 Sh.Ct.Rep. 123.
2 See next page.

When the Sheriff was empowered to deal with actions of separation and aliment and adherence and aliment no provision was made as to the nature of the jurisdiction which would enable such actions to be brought in any particular Sheriff Court. The ground of jurisdiction in such cases is not too clear,[1] and in the Sheriff Court it is thought that the general grounds of jurisdiction specified in sec. 6 of the Act of 1907[2] are, as a whole, inapplicable.[3] Such actions would appear to be competent in the Sheriffdom where the defender resides, and grounds of jurisdiction that might be available in the Court of Session do not necessarily apply.[4]

[1] Maclaren Court of Session Practice, 59; Thomson and Middleton Court of Session Procedure, 197.
[2] 7 Edw. VII c. 51, sec. 6; 2 & 3 Geo. V c. 28, Schedule I.
[3] Holt v. Holt, 1908, 25 Sh.Ct.Rep. 112; cf. Lindsay v. Lindsay, 1939, 56 Sh.Ct.Rep. 88.
[4] See M'Cord v. M'Cord, 1946 S.C. 198; see also Duncan and Dykes, Principles of Civil Jurisdiction, pp. 178-182; Wingrave v. Wingrave, 1918, 35 Sh.Ct.Rep. 97; Ramsay v. Ramsay, 1925 S.C. 216; cf. Jelfs v. Jelfs, (O.H.) 1939 S.L.T. 286.

The position in regard to service of consistorial actions has been already discussed.[1] It is a general rule in such cases that a defender may appear and defend the action although he has failed timeously to lodge a notice of appearance or to put in defences.[2] If decree has already been granted the defender may appeal, in which case he will generally be reponed on such terms as may seem appropriate in the circumstances.[3] It has been held that he may also lodge a reponing note in the usual way.[4]

[1] See p. 125, supra.
[2] Paul v. Paul, (O.H.) 1896, 4 S.L.T. 124; Ross v. Ross, 1897, 24 R. 1029; Cathcart v. Cathcart, 1899, 1 F. 781.
[3] Whyte v. Whyte, 1891, 18 R. 469; A B v. C D, 1912, 2 S.L.T. 255.
[4] Christie v. Christie, 1917, 34 Sh.Ct.Rep. 123.

As a general rule, arrestment on the dependence is not competent to secure future aliment. But it is not incompetent, in an action of separation and aliment or adherence and aliment, to crave a warrant to arrest on the dependence. The usual grounds on which arrestment on the dependence in such actions is justified is where the defender is *vergens ad inopiam*, or *in meditatione fugæ*, or is presently possessed of specified available funds, which are in danger of disappearing.[1] Arrestment would probably also be justified where the parties had been living apart by arrangement, and the defender was in arrear with the stipulated alimentary allowance. Each case must be judged of in the light of its own circumstances, and, if a warrant to arrest is craved, the grounds for craving it should be distinctly set forth in the condescendence

of the initial writ. Arrestment in execution on a decree in order
to secure future aliment has also to be justified by similar circumstances.[2]

[1] Burns v. Burns, 1879, 7 R. 355; Millar v. Millar, (O.H.) 1907, 15
S.L.T. 205; Noble v. Noble, (O.H.) 1921, 1 S.L.T. 57; Smith v.
Smith, 1932 S.L.T. 45; Johnson v. Johnson, 1910, 26 Sh.Ct.Rep. 134.
[2] See James v. James, 1886, 13 R. 1153.

The pursuer in an action of separation and aliment, or adherence and aliment, is entitled to an interim award of aliment,
sufficient to maintain her whilst the litigation is pending. This
may be granted at any time after the case has been tabled, but it
is generally undesirable to make an award till defences have been
lodged.[1] Both the making of an interim award, and the amount
of it, are matters within the discretion of the Court, and until
the pleadings on each side are available the circumstances cannot
be properly considered. Such an award will not as a rule be
granted when judgment against the wife has been appealed at her
instance.[2] An indigent husband may now be entitled to an award
of interim aliment against his wife.[3] It has been held that when
interim aliment is asked pending an appeal to the Sheriff, the
application is to be made to the Sheriff-Substitute under Rule 91.[4]

[1] Pirrie v. Pirrie, (O.H.) 1903, 10 S.L.T. 598; M'Donald v. M'Donald,
(O.H.) 1929 S.L.T. 512.
[2] Bonnar v. Bonnar, 1911 S.C. 854; Douglas v. Douglas, 1932 S.C. 680.
[3] Adair v. Adair, 1924 S.C. 798.
[4] A B v. C B, 1939 S.L.T. (Sh.Ct.) 11.

If evidence has been led to justify a separation the Court must
grant decree and is not entitled *ex proprio motu* to continue the
case in an endeavour to reach a reconciliation or resumption of
cohabitation.[1] Decree of separation when granted is final, and is
not subject to recall in respect that the grounds upon which it
was pronounced no longer exist.[2] Reference has already been
made to the Sheriff's power to remit to the Court of Session in
actions of adherence and aliment and separation and aliment,[3]
and to certain peculiarities in relation to actions of aliment in
general.[4] Where the pursuer in a separation action has failed
to establish his or her averments the appropriate decree is one of
absolvitor and not dismissal.[5]

[1] Dawson v. Dawson, 1925 S.C. 221.
[2] Strain v. Strain, 1890, 17 R. 297.
[3] See p. 499, supra.
[4] See p. 498, et seq., supra.
[5] Hutchison v. Hutchison, 1945 S.C. 427.

In actions of adherence and aliment, where an offer to adhere
is made and its genuineness is not admitted, the Court has sometimes, in place of allowing a proof, continued the case to enable
the offer to be tested by practical experience.[1] Whether this course
should be followed will depend on the circumstances of the case.[1]
Although there has been some doubt on the point, it seems competent
in the Sheriff Court to include a crave for custody of children in an
action of adherence and aliment.[2]

[1] Paterson v. Paterson, 1861, 24 D. 215; Samson v. Samson, 1924, 41
Sh.Ct.Rep. 251; Fletcher v. Young, (O.H.) 1936 S.L.T. 572; cf.
M'Cartan v. M'Cartan, 1943, 59 Sh.Ct.Rep. 49.
[2] Dunsmuir v. Dunsmuir, 1937, 53 Sh.Ct.Rep. 166; cf. Ramsay v.
Ramsay, (O.H.) 1945 S.L.T. 30.

Interim awards of expenses may be made, during the progress of
an action of separation and aliment or adherence and aliment,
either to a wife[1] with no separate estate,[2] or to an impecunious
husband where the wife has separate estate.[3] To justify such an
award a *prima facie* case must be disclosed,[4] and the award should
not be applied for until defences have been lodged.[5] The amount of
the award is generally measured by the necessary outlay which is
in prospect.[6] It is only in exceptional circumstances that an
unsuccessful party will get an interim award of expenses to
prosecute an appeal.[7]

[1] Symington v. Symington, 1874, 1 R. 1006; Linder v. Linder, 1902, 4 F.
465; Jaffray v. Jaffray, 1909 S.C. 577.
[2] See M'Ewan v. M'Ewan, (O.H.) 1903, 11 S.L.T. 169.
[3] Adair v. Adair, 1924 S.C. 798.
[4] Gunn v. Gunn, (O.H.) 1897, 5 S.L.T. 56; Stuart Brown v. Stuart
Brown, 1911, 2 S.L.T. 35.
[5] Pirrie v. Pirrie, (O.H.) 1903, 10 S.L.T. 598; Johnston v. Johnston,
1916, 2 S.L.T. 191.
[6] Mitchell v. Mitchell, (O.H.) 1893, 1 S.L.T. 141; Baird v. Clark, 1922
S.C. 290; Anderson v. Anderson, 1927 S.C. 561; 1927 S.L.T. 658.
[7] Bonnar v. Bonnar, 1911 S.C. 854; Cox v. Cox, 1942 S.C. 352.

An action of separation and aliment or of adherence and
aliment differs from actions in general as regards expenses. The
wife is usually awarded expenses irrespective of success or failure,
provided that her case was based on reasonable grounds.[1] On an
appeal taken by the wife, she must show that the case was a fair
one to try.[2] But if the wife is possessed of separate estate this
rule does not apply, and she may have to bear her own expense if
unsuccessful,[3] and possibly be held liable in expenses to her
husband.[4] When the wife is found entitled to expenses these are
usually taxed on the matrimonial scale, that is, as between solicitor
and client payable by a third party.[5] This rule is also applied to

an award to an impecunious husband where the wife has separate estate[4] but not where the husband, though found entitled to expenses, is not impecunious.[6] The principle underlying these rules is that a husband is liable for debts contracted by his wife for necessaries, and the cost of pursuing a necessary action at law is regarded as such a debt. A wife was refused expenses when her action was dismissed for want of jurisdiction and the husband had not appeared,[7] and a successful husband was refused expenses against a wife with separate estate who was furth of Scotland and who had not appeared.[8] Where a consistorial action is settled by the parties before inquiry into the facts the wife's solicitor may require to raise a separate action to recover his expenses.[9]

[1] Murray v. Murray, (O.H.) 1893, 1 S.L.T. 260; Liddell v. Liddell, (O.H.) 1903, 11 S.L.T. 488; Smith v. Smith, (O.H.) 1932 S.L.T. 199
[2] Thomson v. Thomson, 1908 S.C. 179.
[3] Henderson v. Henderson, 1888, 16 R. 84; Robertson v. Robertson, (O.H.) 1908, 16 S.L.T. 641; mere earnings are not necessarily separate estate, Milne v. Milne, 1885, 13 R. 304.
[4] A B v. C B, 1918 S.C. 19; Adair v. Adair, (O.H.) 1925 S.L.T. 286.
[5] Grant v. Grant, 1905, 43 S.L.R. 109; Wright v. Wright, 1910, 26 Sh.Ct.Rep. 111; Thomson v. Thomson, 1929, 45 Sh.Ct.Rep. 240; P v P, 1940 S.C. 389.
[6] A B v. C B, supra.
[7] Kelly v. Kelly, 1928 S.C. 43.
[8] Thomson v. Thomson, (O.H.) 1935 S.L.T. 24.
[9] Clark v. Henderson, 1875, 2 R. 428; Finnie v. Finnie, 1920, 37 Sh.Ct.Rep. 84.

The principle of taxation on the matrimonial scale, however, does not apply in other than consistorial causes proper, so it does not apply in actions relating to the custody of children, for these are not properly speaking consistorial actions.[1]

[1] Mackellar v. Mackellar, 1898, 25 R. 883; A B v. C B, 1906, 8 F. 973.

The position in regard to the deduction of income tax from alimentary payments has been already noticed.[1]

[1] See p. 503, supra.

15. SETT AND SALE.

This is not a very common form of action, for ships are not now extensively held on the sixty-fourth principle. The owner of one or more sixty-fourths, who desires to free himself from the joint ownership, but cannot arrange that with his co-owners, may offer to sell his interest to his co-owners, or to buy theirs at a named price. If his offer is not accepted, he may bring an action of sett and sale in the Sheriff Court, calling the other co-owners as

defenders. If each of the other co-owners is subject to the jurisdiction of a Sheriff Court, the action may be brought in the Sheriff
Court within whose jurisdiction any one of the defenders resides.[1]
If that is not the position, it would seem competent to bring the
action in the Court within whose jurisdiction the managing
owners have their office, for there all the co-owners (wherever
resident), through their managing owners, carry on the joint
adventure business of owning and employing the ship.[2] In that
case the defenders would be cited personally or at the place of
business.[2] It may possibly also be competent to bring the action
in the district of the ship's port of registry, if that port is in
Scotland.

[1] 7 Edw. VII c. 51, sec. 6 (a); 2 & 3 Geo. V c. 28, Schedule I.
[2] Ibid., sec. 6 (b); 2 & 3 Geo. V c. 28, Schedule I.

This is in form an ordinary action, and it follows the ordinary
course of procedure, including appeal. The initial writ should
narrate the offer made, and the refusal of the co-owners either to
buy or to sell. The crave is that the defenders be ordained to pay
to pursuer his fixed price, in exchange for a bill of sale for his
shares; or otherwise to grant bills of sale to pursuer in exchange
for the like price; and failing the defenders doing either, to appoint
the ship to be sold under direction of the Court, and the free
proceeds apportioned amongst the co-owners. Defences to the competency may be lodged, and, failing these, the defenders should by
minute declare their election, and decree is pronounced accordingly. If the defenders elect neither to buy nor to sell, the ship
is sold in the same way as an arrested vessel.[1]

[1] See p. 275, supra.

16. SUSPENSION.

The nature and extent of the Sheriff's jurisdiction in suspensions has been already considered.[1] Questions of procedure, like
those of jurisdiction, have been left by the Act in some confusion.
The application for suspension is made by initial writ in ordinary
form, and the rules provide that, on sufficient caution being found
in the hands of the Sheriff-clerk for the sum charged for, interest
and expenses, and a sum to be fixed by the Sheriff in respect
of expenses to be incurred in the suspension process, the Sheriff
may sist diligence, order intimation and answers, and proceed
to dispose of the cause in a summary manner.[2] This provision
applies only to a suspension of a charge, not of a threatened
charge, and on a strict reading of the rule the Sheriff would appear
to have no discretion as to the amount of caution save in connexion

with the prospective expenses in the suspension. It has been held, however, that despite the wording of the rule the Sheriff has a discretion as to the amount of caution to be found.[3] In the suspension of a threatened charge the Sheriff's authority is not fettered and he has seemingly full discretion as to the amount of caution to be found.[4] It is thought to be clear that the Sheriff has a discretion to allow or refuse a sist of diligence even if caution is offered, but that if he grants a sist he must order intimation and allow the defender to appear and be heard.

[1] See p. 28, supra.
[2] 7 Edw. VII c. 51, Schedule I, Rule 124.
[3] Maclachlan v. Glasgow, 1925 S.L.T. (Sh.Ct.) 77.
[4] See also 7 Edw. VII c. 51, Rule 123.

The first deliverance in a suspension usually grants warrant to cite the defender and appoints him to answer at a fixed diet, execution being meantime sisted till further orders of Court. An interim sist of execution when intimated prohibits poinding[1] or imprisonment,[2] but not arrestment or inhibition.[3] If a suspension is anticipated a caveat may be lodged and in that case the first order will be to appoint a hearing, the diet being intimated forthwith to the party who has lodged the caveat. As the Sheriff is apparently expected to dispose of the cause in a summary manner[4] the course of the procedure is largely in his hands. It will often be unnecessary to adjust pleadings or make up a record,[5] and if proof is required the evidence will not be recorded unless the Sheriff so orders.[6] The Sheriff's judgment must be in writing.[6]

[1] Stewart v. Stewart, 1751, M. 10535; Keltie v. Wilson, 1828, 7 S. 208.
[2] Keltie v. Wilson, supra; Graham Stewart, Diligence, 755.
[3] Graham Stewart, Diligence, 755, and cases cited.
[4] 7 Edw. VII c. 51, Schedule I, Rule 124.
[5] See Summerlee Iron Co. v. Duff, 1920 S.C. 291.
[6] 7 Edw. VII c. 51, secs. 3 (p), 50.

Rule 125 provides that, if objections are taken to the competency or regularity of suspension proceedings, the judgment of the Sheriff-Substitute on such objections may be appealed to the Sheriff but his judgment thereon shall be final.[1] Competency in this rule means an objection to suspension as a form of process and this provision does not cut off the right of appeal to the Court of Session where the point at issue arises on the merits of the suspension.[2] The general provisions of the Act, however, preclude appeal to the Court of Session where the cause does not exceed £50 in value, exclusive of interest and expenses, or is being tried as a summary cause, unless the Sheriff, after final judgment by him on an appeal, on the motion of either party made within seven days of the date of the final interlocutor, certifies the cause as suitable for appeal to the Court of Session.[3] As suspensions in the Sheriff Court are only competent where the debt, exclusive of interest and expenses, does not exceed £50.[4] and as suspensions are in any case usually disposed of in a summary manner,[5] right of appeal to the Court of Session, even on the merits, only seems to be competent after a final judgment by the Sheriff Principal on appeal and with a certificate by him obtained as above indicated.

[1] 7 Edw. VII c. 51, Schedule I, Rule 125.
[2] Wilsons & Clyde Coal Co. v. Cairnduff, 1911 S.C. 647.
[3] 7 Edw. VII c. 51, sec. 28 (1) (d); 2 & 3 Geo. V c. 28, sec. 2.
[4] Ibid., sec. 5 (5).
[5] Ibid., Schedule I, Rule 124.
[6] See Summerlee Iron Co. v. Duff, 1920 S.C. 291. (In this case it would seem to have been overlooked that appeal to the Court of Session is not competent from the judgment of the Sheriff-Substitute.)

CHAPTER XXV.

STATUTORY POWERS AND DUTIES.

I. GENERAL.

Over a long period legislation affecting Scotland has been made operative in the local Sheriff Courts. As a result a great number of Statutes dealing with many varied subjects impose duties on the Sheriff or his Substitutes. Thus there may be a right of appeal from the actings or decisions of a local authority or of some licensing body, or any dispute or question arising under an Act may be directed to be decided by the Sheriff, or the Sheriff Court may be the tribunal in which the procedure required to give effect to the statutory provisions is to be carried out. Some of these statutory provisions—such as those dealing with the adoption of children, the correction of entries of births, &c., and judicial factories—relate to applications which are comparatively common. Others provide for appeals or other applications which are almost unknown in practice. It would be impracticable and would be beyond the scope of this book to comment on every statutory provision under which the Sheriff Court is directed to function. All that can be done here is to provide some general observations on the nature of this statutory jurisdiction and the procedure thereunder, and to comment thereafter on such of the statutory powers conferred on the Sheriff as appear to justify more detailed treatment.

In some cases the Act conferring the jurisdiction on the Sheriff Court provides that the matter is to be dealt with summarily when the procedure will be by summary application as provided by the Sheriff Courts Act,[1] or procedure by summary application may be directed by Act of Sederunt.[2] But in the case of many Statutes no indication is given as to the form of procedure in the Sheriff Court. There is, however, a practice in many Courts to treat the bulk of applications under Statute as summary applications, and that remark may be taken as applying to all cases dealt with in detail later unless the contrary is stated.[3] In a few instances the statutory power or duty is conferred only upon the Sheriff, but in the vast majority of cases the jurisdiction can be exercised by either the Sheriff or the Sheriff-Substitute,[4] though—subject to any contrary practice in the particular Court— the application will normally come before the latter for disposal.

In all cases, unless otherwise stated, the application will be by
initial writ in the usual form, and this applies even where the
procedure in the Sheriff Court is described as an appeal against
the act or decision of some body or authority. In such cases
the writ is sometimes entitled a note of appeal, and this seems
justified by the terms of the Sheriff Courts Act,[5] but it is not
essential.

[1] 7 Edw. VII c. 51, sec. 50.
[2] E.g., Act of Sederunt, 14th December, 1923 (Rent Restrictions Acts).
[3] See Kirkpatrick v. Maxwelltown Town Council, 1912 S.C. 288.
[4] See Fleming v. Dickson, 1862, 1 M. 188; 52 & 53 Vict. c. 63, sec. 28.
[5] 7 Edw. VII c. 51, sec. 3 (k).

1. APPEALS IN GENERAL.

The most difficult questions which arise in relation to statutory
applications are whether there is a right of appeal from the
Sheriff-Substitute to the Sheriff, and whether appeal is competent
to the Court of Session. These difficulties are accentuated by
the variety of ways in which the question of appeal is dealt
with in the different Acts. In some cases nothing is said as to
appeal; in others the matter is dealt with in detail or is regulated
to some extent. In certain Acts a provision excluding review
may apply to the decision of first instance whether that of the
Sheriff or the Sheriff-Substitute; in others it may apply to the
Sheriff Court generally and while precluding appeal to the Court
of Session may leave open an appeal from the Sheriff-Substitute
to the Sheriff. By some Acts a peculiar right of appeal is conferred, and it may be uncertain whether this is intended to exclude
other rights of appeal that would be open according to the ordinary
practice of the Sheriff Court. In certain cases special provision
as to appeal may relate only to some of the applications falling
under the Act, and the position is left indefinite in regard to
the others. Sometimes a right of appeal may be specifically provided, but doubt exists as to whether it relates only to a final
decision and whether appeal against an interlocutory judgment
is competent.[1] In cases where appeal is limited to a stated case
there are other complications. Before passing to a detailed consideration of the various statutory applications to be dealt with
an attempt will be made to classify under separate heads certain
principles in regard to rights of appeal in statutory applications
in general.

[1] See Dumfries County Council v. Langholm Magistrates, 1913 S.C. 307,
Lord Dundas, p. 310.

The Sheriff Courts Act provides that nothing in the sections dealing with appeals to the Sheriff or the Court of Session is to affect any right of appeal, or exclusion of such right, provided by any Act of Parliament in force for the time being.[1] In regard to such statutory cases it has been pointed out that where a new and special jurisdiction is given to any Court the exercise of it must be regulated entirely by the conditions of the Statute under which it is conferred, and in the general case remedies which might have been competent in an ordinary civil process are not to be presumed or inferred to be given by the particular Statute.[2] On the other hand, where a well-known and recognized jurisdiction is invoked by the legislature for the purpose of carrying out a series of provisions without any specific form of process being prescribed, the presumption is that the ordinary forms of that Court are to be observed in carrying out the provisions.[2]

[1] 7 Edw. VII c. 51, secs. 27, 28; 2 & 3 Geo. V c. 28, sec. 2. See also 7 Edw. VII c. 51, sec. 7; 2 & 3 Geo. V c. 28, Schedule I.
[2] Magistrates of Portobello v. Magistrates of Edinburgh, 1882, 10 R. 130, Lord Justice-Clerk Moncreiff, p. 137. See also Marr & Sons v. Lindsay, 1881, 8 R. 784, Lord President Inglis, p. 785.

At the outset it should be pointed out that all provisions excluding review are subject to the general power in the Court of Session to intervene in order to set aside illegal or incompetent proceedings in Inferior Courts.[1] Often this may be done by reduction or suspension, but an appeal otherwise precluded has been held competent in respect of irregularities in the Sheriff Court,[2] and the Court of Session—like the Sheriff-Principal[3]—would be entitled to entertain any appeal where the Sheriff-Substitute had not exercised, or had exceeded, his jurisdiction.[4] When special or restricted rights of appeal are given by Statute these apply only to cases founded on and falling within the precise terms of the Statute, and not to cases which may arise as a result of the statutory provision but have not been definitely specified as falling under the statutory code of procedure.[5] The form in which the matter is brought before the Court may,[6] or may not,[7] be regarded as having some bearing on the question whether or not the application was a purely statutory one. Further, an action may be one of a class in regard to which, in the normal course of procedure, appeal is precluded or restricted, and yet by force of a special enactment appeal may be competent in a particular case. Thus an appeal under the Small Debt Acts is limited to review upon certain grounds by the Court of Justiciary,[8] but a dispute between a friendly society and a member might take the form of a small debt action, and either party might be entitled under the Friendly

Societies Acts[9] to ask the Court, prior to final judgment, to state
a case for the opinion of the Court of Session.[10] On the other
hand an appeal which would otherwise be competent may be precluded by want of material upon which it can be argued such as a
record of the evidence. In ordinary Sheriff Court procedure this
reduces the appeal to the Sheriff in a summary cause from a full
appeal on fact and law to one on law only.[11] In many cases of
statutory proceedings it may not be essential to keep a record of
the evidence,[12] but if the evidence has not been recorded the
Sheriff's judgment is not subject to review on the facts.[13]

[1] Moss' Empires v. Assessor for Glasgow, 1917 S.C. (H.L.) 1, Lord
    Kinnear, p. 6.
[2] See Dalgleish v. Leitch, 1889, 2 White 302; Allen & Sons v. Corpora-
    tion of Edinburgh, 1909 S.C. 70.
[3] See next paragraph.
[4] See Penny v. Scott, 1894, 22 R. 5; Heddle v. Magistrates of Leith,
    1898, 25 R. 801; Allen & Sons v. Corporation of Edinburgh, supra.
    Also see next paragraph.
[5] See Guthrie, Craig, Peter & Co. v. Magistrates of Brechin, 1885, 12 R.
    469; Galashiels Provident Building Society v. Newlands, 1893,
    20 R. 821; Mackenzie v. Cameron, 1894, 21 R. 427; Roxburgh, &c.,
    District Lunacy Board v. Selkirk Parish Council, 1902, 4 F. 468;
    Stirling Parish Council v. Dunblane Parish Council, 1912 S.C. 316.
[6] See Ross v. Ross, 1920 S.C. 530.
[7] Magistrates of Glasgow v. Glasgow District Subway Co., 1893, 21 R. 52.
[8] 7 Will. IV & 1 Vict. c. 41, sec. 31.
[9] See 59 & 60 Vict. c. 25, sec. 68 (7).
[10] Linton v. City of Glasgow Friendly Society, 1895, 23 R. 51; Smith v.
    Scottish Legal Life Assurance Society, 1912 S.C. 611.
[11] 7 Edw. VII c. 51, sec. 8; 2 & 3 Geo. V c. 28, Schedule I.
[12] Ibid., sec. 50.
[13] Sinclair v. Spence, 1883, 10 R. 1077.

Where a right of appeal to the Sheriff is given from the act or
decision of some outside body—such as a local authority, a licensing
body or the like—and nothing is said as to review of the decision
of the Sheriff, the presumption is that while such an appeal can
be dealt with by either the Sheriff-Substitute or the Sheriff, the
decision of either is intended to be final.[1] The result is the same
where the Statute provides that the Sheriff's decision is final, and
in that case also the matter can usually be dealt with by either
Sheriff-Substitute or Sheriff and the decision of either is not subject
to review.[2] But where there is irregularity of procedure before
the Sheriff-Substitute—as where instead of adopting summary
procedure as directed by the Act he made up a record and allowed
a proof—or where he has dismissed the application on some preliminary ground, an appeal to the Sheriff was held by the Court
of Session to have been competent, and the Sheriff's decision on
appeal was held to be the final determination of the matter and

not subject to review.[2] Apart from irregularities of the kind
indicated, if the Sheriff-Substitute exceeds his jurisdiction or
declines to exercise it, there would be a right of appeal to the
Sheriff in order to have the matter put right,[3] and the Court of
Session would be entitled to entertain an appeal in such circumstances as already explained.[4]

[1] Allen & Sons v. Edinburgh Corporation, 1909 S.C. 70.
[2] Bone v. School Board of Sorn, 1886, 13 R. 768; Roxburgh County
    Council v. Dalrymple's Trustees, 1894, 21 R. 1063; Strichen Parish
    Council v. Goodwillie, 1908 S.C. 835; cf. Leitch v. Scottish Legal
    Burial Society, 1870, 9 M. 40.
[3] Leitch v. Scottish Legal Burial Society, supra; Roxburgh County
    Council v. Dalrymple's Trustees, supra; Leggat v. Burgh of
    Barrhead, 1902, 19 Sh.Ct.Rep. 7, p. 11.
[4] See p. 299, supra.

The class of case falling within the principles last stated in
which applications may be dealt with by either Sheriff-Substitute
or Sheriff—the decisions of either being final—includes applications under the following statutory provisions.*

Midwives and Maternity Homes (Scotland) Act, 1927 (17 & 18
Geo. V c. 17, sec. 11 (4)).

Slaughter of Animals (Scotland) Act, 1928 (18 & 19 Geo. V c.
29, sec. 2 (4)).

Agricultural Marketing Act, 1931 (21 & 22 Geo. V c. 42, secs. 8,
19 (2)). The decision of the Sheriff Court judge would apparently
be final, but there is a right to remit to the Court of Session and
that Court may also of consent hear the appeal in the first instance.

Town and Country Planning (Scotland) Act, 1932 (22 & 23 Geo.
V c. 49, secs. 12 (1), 13 (4) (5), 46. See also 6 & 7 Geo. VI c. 43,
sec. 5 (2), Schedule I).

Pharmacy and Poisons Act, 1933 (23 & 24 Geo. V c. 25, secs.
21 (2), 30 (i); Act of Sederunt, 19th December, 1935).

Shops Act, 1934 (24 & 25 Geo. V c. 42, secs. 10 (6), 17 (a). See
p. 538 *infra*, for sec. 11). The appeal in this case is to the **Sheriff
Court**—not the Sheriff—and it might be suggested that this implies
a right of appeal to the Sheriff-Principal. It is thought, however,
that this is not the case.

Road Traffic Act, 1934 (24 & 25 Geo. V c. 50, secs. 31 (8), 41
(9). See also p. 538, *infra*, for sec. 6 (6).

Betting and Lotteries Act, 1934 (24 & 25 Geo. V c. 58, secs. 16
(2), 20 (1), (2), 31 (5), (6); Act of Sederunt, 19th December, 1935).

Restriction of Ribbon Development Act, 1935 (25 & 26 Geo. V
c. 47, secs. 17 (1), (4), 25 (5); Inverness County Council v. Palace
Hotel, (O.H.) 1938 S.N. 93). Right of further appeal is not
applicable to Scotland (sec. 25 (5)).

* Any Statutes dealt with in detail later are not included here.

Harbours, Piers and Ferries (Scotland) Act, 1937 (1 Edw. VIII & 1 Geo. VI c. 28, sec. 15 (1), (2)).

Methylated Spirits (Sale by Retail) Act, 1937 (1 Edw. VIII & 1 Geo. VI c. 48, sec. 2 (3); Act of Sederunt, 5th November, 1937; Rutherford v. Kirkcaldy Town Council, 1938, 54 Sh.Ct.Rep. 124; Renny v. Provost, &c., of Kirkcaldy, 1938 S.L.T. (Sh.Ct.) 41).

Nursing Homes Registration (Scotland) Act, 1938 (1 & 2 Geo. VI c. 73, sec. 3 (3)).

Cotton Industry (Reorganization) Act, 1939 (2 & 3 Geo. VI c. 54, Schedule IV, Part II, 2, 3, 4, sec. 40 (b). The position as to appeal is similar to that under the Shops Act, *supra.*

Nurses (Scotland) Act, 1943 (6 & 7 Geo. VI c. 33, sec. 8 (4)).

Another class of case into which a large number of these statutory applications falls differs from those last discussed because there is no provision as to finality, and the matter is not an appeal from an outside body. In the cases now to be considered some question or dispute or difference, arising from some statutory provision, is directed to be decided or determined or settled by the Sheriff, or in certain Statutes the function of the Sheriff is merely to appoint a valuer or grant a certificate. In these cases it can probably be stated as a general proposition that the applications fall to be regarded as forming a special statutory jurisdiction given to the Sheriff, to which the ordinary rules of procedure do not apply,[1] that such applications may be dealt with either by the Sheriff or Sheriff-Substitute and that, unless given by Statute, there is intended to be no right of appeal within the Sheriff Court— should the matter be dealt with by the Sheriff-Substitute—and no right of review by the Court of Session.[2] Appeal will be competent in respect of irregularities as already explained.[3] If the Statute in question directs that the matter is to be determined by the Sheriff summarily that may be regarded as emphasizing that there is no right of review,[4] but as a matter of practice all such applications are usually dealt with as summary applications.

[1] See Magistrates of Portobello v. Magistrates of Edinburgh, 1882, 10 R. 130, Lord Justice-Clerk Moncreiff, p. 137; Marr & Sons v. Lindsay, 1881, 8 R. 784, Lord President Inglis, p. 785.

[2] Dubs v. Crosshill Police Commissioners, 1876, 3 R. 758; Main v. Lanarkshire, &c., Railway Co., 1893, 21 R. 323; Cathcart v. Board of Agriculture, 1915 S.C. 166; Ross-shire County Council v. Macrae-Gilstrap, 1930 S.C. 808. See also Dove Wilson, Sheriff Court Practice, 4th edn., 367.

[3] See pp. 535, 536, supra.

[4] See Edgar v. Pollok, 1890, 6 Sh.Ct.Rep. 220; Leggat v. Burgh of Barrhead, 1902, 19 Sh.Ct.Rep. 7, p. 11.

Many applications falling within the class last referred to are dealt with in detail later. Those not so dealt with include applications arising under the following Statutes on which it is thought that the decision of the Sheriff or of the Sheriff-Substitute is intended to be final.

Boundaries of Burghs Extension Act, 1857 (20 & 21 Vict. c. 70). Certain rights of appeal to Court of Session will now be regulated by Rules of Court (1936, V 7-12); but there is no appeal to that Court save as provided by the Act (Dubs, &c. v. Police Commissioners of Crosshill, 1876, 3 R. 758).

Vaccination (Scotland) Act, 1863 (26 & 27 Vict., c. 108, secs. 29, 30).

Fish Teinds (Scotland) Act, 1864 (27 & 28 Vict. c. 33, secs. 2, 5, 6, 7, 15).

Roads and Bridges (Scotland) Act, 1878 (41 & 42 Vict. c. 51, secs. 3, 39 (3)). Other provisions under this Act are dealt with at p. 662, *infra.*

Dogs Act, 1906 (6 Edw. VII c. 32, sec. 5); Codifying Act of Sederunt, L. XII; Act of Sederunt, 31st January, 1917; Donaldson v. Chief Constable of Forfarshire, 1909, 25 Sh.Ct.Rep. 281; Ross v. Alexander, 1924 S.L.T. (Sh.Ct.) 69.

Protection of Animals (Scotland) Act, 1912 (2 & 3 Geo. V c. 14, sec. 5 (1)).

Celluloid and Cinematograph Film Act, 1922 (12 & 13 Geo. V c. 35, secs. 8, 10). No Act of Sederunt has apparently been issued but this might be held to be a case in which the ordinary rules of procedure and the normal rights of appeal applied.

Army and Air Force Act, 1925 (44 & 45 Vict. c. 58, secs. 113, 190 (37); 15 & 16 Geo. V c. 25, Schedule II; Dudgeon v. Lord Advocate, 1916, 32 Sh.Ct.Rep. 240; Ballantyne & Son v. Lord Advocate, 1917, 34 Sh.Ct.Rep. 103).

Roads Improvement Act, 1925 (15 & 16 Geo. V c. 68, secs. 9, 12 (c)). While the Sheriff Court seems intended to be final, it might be held that there was a right of appeal to the Sheriff-Principal.

Housing (Rural Workers) Act, 1926 (16 & 17 Geo. V c. 56, secs. 3 (5), 8 (a)). This might be held to be a case in which ordinary rules of procedure applied with the normal rights of appeal.

Shops Act, 1934 (24 & 25 Geo. V c. 42, sec. 11. See p. 536, *supra,* for sec. 10 (6)). In this case, while the Sheriff Court seems intended to be final, there might be held to be an appeal to the Sheriff-Principal.

Road Traffic Act, 1934 (24 & 25 Geo. V c. 50, secs. 6 (6), 41 (3). See also p. 536, *supra,* for sec. 31 (8)).

Livestock Industry Act, 1937 (1 Edw. VIII and 1 Geo. VI c. 50, secs. 19 (1), 57 (11). No Act of Sederunt has apparently been issued to regulate procedure. In the circumstances it is thought that the order of the judge of first instance is intended to be final.

Baking Industry (Hours of Work) Act, 1938 (1 & 2 Geo. VI c. 41, secs. 11, 14 (b)). The position here is similar to the preceding one.

Contrasted with the above classes is another in which there is an express provision as to finality, but this is applied, not to the determination of the Sheriff, but to the decision of the Sheriff Court, with the result that, while there is—save in respect of irregularities[1]—no appeal to the Court of Session, an appeal is competent from the Sheriff-Substitute to the Sheriff.

[1] See pp. 535, 536, supra.

Examples of this kind of provision are contained in the following Acts: *The Building Societies Act*, 1874. See p. 561, *infra*. *The Friendly Societies* and *Industrial and Provident Societies Acts*. See p. 592 *et seq.*, *infra*. *The Rent Restrictions Acts*. See p. 656 *et seq.*, *infra*. *Government Annuities Act*, 1929 (19 & 20 Geo. V c. 29, sec. 48).

In a few cases the ordinary procedure of the Sheriff Court and the ordinary rights of appeal apply. Thus where a dispute as to salvage has been determined summarily in the Sheriff Court appeal is declared to be competent in the same way as in the case of any other judgment,[1] and appeals under the Finance Act, 1894, are (subject to a specialty in regard to review by the Court of Session) regulated by the rules of ordinary procedure under the Rules of Court.[2] In the case of proceedings under the Rivers Pollution Prevention Act, 1876, ordinary procedure is partially applicable, for rules relating to proceedings in the Sheriff Courts are declared to apply, but a special right of appeal to the Court of Session is given by stated case.[3] Under the Town Councils Act an elector or ratepayer may within three months of the meeting of a town council approving of its annual accounts complain by petition against the accounts or any item, and the Sheriff is directed to hear and determine the matter of complaint, and his decision is subject to the same right of appeal as in ordinary actions in the Sheriff Court.[4] This latter provision suggests that the whole procedure is to be by ordinary action.[5] Under the Burgh Police Act[6] and the Town Councils Act[7] application may be made to the Sheriff Court or the Court of Session for an Order of Court to facilitate the execution of the Act or to determine any points of difficulty. The sections give certain directions as to procedure but *quoad ultra* the wording seems to suggest that the ordinary procedure of the Court is to be followed. Any Order pronounced either by the Sheriff or the Sheriff-Substitute is, however, expressly declared to be final.[6] The undernoted cases deal with applications under these provisions.[8] The apportionment of compensation consigned under the Coal Act appears to be a matter in which the ordinary jurisdiction of the Sheriff Court has been invoked by the legislature.[9]

[1] 57 & 58 Vict. c. 60, sec. 549 (1) (a). See p. 621, supra.
[2] See p. 589, infra.
[3] See p. 661, infra.
[4] 63 & 64 Vict. c. 49, sec. 96.
[5] See Eadie v. Glasgow Corporation, 1914, 30 Sh.Ct.Rep. 198; 1916 S.C. 163.
[6] 55 & 56 Vict. c. 55, sec. 17.
[7] 63 & 64 Vict. c. 49, sec. 113.
[8] Earlsferry Town Council, 1903, 20 Sh.Ct.Rep. 133; Mackay, 1904, 21 Sh.Ct.Rep. 46; Harrold v. Magistrates of Kirkwall, 1908, 24 Sh.Ct.Rep. 208; Thomson, 1935, 52 Sh.Ct.Rep. 233; Keith, 1936, 52 Sh.Ct.Rep. 350.
[9] 1 & 2 Geo. V c. 52, Schedule III, Part V, 23 (iv) (d). See also 23 (iii).

Statutes under which the right of appeal is regulated by express provision include the following :—

Burgh Police Act, 1892,* (55 & 56 Vict. c. 55, secs. 260, 292, 347, 373 (2) (b)).

Burghs Gas Supply (Scotland) Act, 1893 (56 & 57 Vict. c. 52, sec. 2); Helensburgh Commissioners v. M'Phee, 1899, 16 Sh.Ct.Rep. 98; Provost, &c., of Gourock, 1911, 2 S.L.T. 288; Lanark County Council, 1931, 49 Sh.Ct.Rep. 35.

Local Government (Scotland) Act, 1908 (8 Edw. VII c. 62, sec. 3).

House Letting and Rating (Scotland) Act, 1911 (1 & 2 Geo. V c. 53, sec. 7 (6); 10 & 11 Geo. V c. 17, secs. 16, 18 (1) (a); 19 & 20 Geo. V c. 25, sec. 20); Main, &c. v. Airdrie Water Trustees, 1912, 30 Sh.Ct.Rep. 105; Finlay, 1929, 46 Sh.Ct.Rep. 54; Kilmarnock Houseowners' Association v. Burgh of Irvine, 1932, 48 Sh.Ct.Rep. 138.

Water (Scotland) Act, 1946 (9 & 10 Geo. VI c. 42, secs. 31, 37, 38, 54 (3), 61 (2), 72, 82).

* For other applications under this Act see p. 630, et seq., infra.

2. Appeals by Stated Case.

In construing the various statutory provisions relating to stated cases the Court has drawn a distinction between two different kinds of stated case. In the first class of case there is a true right of appeal and the Court of Session can review, and if necessary reverse, the judgment of the Sheriff on any point of law which is put up to them in the case.[1] Stated cases falling within this category may be asked for after final judgment in the Sheriff Court, and that judgment may be reviewed on the question of law whether, on the facts as stated in the case, the Sheriff was entitled to reach the conclusion which he did.[1] In the other class of case there is no right of appeal in the proper sense, but the Court of Session may be asked to give an opinion on any question of law, and the Sheriff is bound to have regard to that opinion in dealing with the case.[1] Stated cases in this category must be applied for during the course of the proceedings in the Sheriff Court, and cannot be stated after judgment has been given.[1] Such cases are not excluded by findings made by the Sheriff if these are not in fact a final judgment.[2] The stating of the case by the Sheriff is not equivalent to his granting leave to appeal, and if the disposal of the case involves review of an interlocutor for which leave to appeal is required such leave may have to be obtained.[3] Where procedure by stated case is competent it will be available although the proceedings are in the Small Debt Court.[4]

[1] See Steele v. M'Intosh Brothers, 1879, 7 R. 192; Johnston's Trustees v. Glasgow Corporation, 1912 S.C. 300; Smith v. Scottish Legal Life Assurance Society, 1912 S.C. 611.
[2] Lanark County Council v. Magistrates of Motherwell, 1912 S.C. 1251.
[3] Dumfries County Council v. Langholm Magistrates, 1913 S.C. 307.
[4] Linton v. City of Glasgow Friendly Society, 1895, 23 R. 51; Smith v. Scottish Legal Life Assurance Society, supra.

The outstanding example of a statutory right of appeal—in the fuller sense above indicated—is that which was given under the Workmen's Compensation Act. But similar rights of appeal are provided by other Statutes including the following: *The Rivers Pollution Prevention Act*, 1876. The procedure under this is dealt with in detail later.[1]

[1] See p. 661, infra.

Burgh Police (Scotland) Act, 1892; *Burgh Police (Scotland) Act*, 1903.—Under these Acts resolutions or orders of a town council may be brought under appeal in the Sheriff Court, and it is expressly provided that the judgment of the Sheriff-Substitute is subject to review by the Sheriff.[1] Subject to this right of appeal to the Sheriff the Sheriff-Substitute's judgment is declared to be final,[1] but any party dissatisfied with the judgment of the Sheriff —which is defined to include Sheriff-Substitute—as erroneous in point of law may appeal to the Court of Session by applying for a stated case within six days.[2] The appeal may be taken either from the judgment of the Sheriff or of the Sheriff-Substitute.[3] The proceedings in the Court of Session are as laid down by the Rules of Court.[4]

[1] 55 & 56 Vict. c. 55, sec. 339; as to proceedings in the Sheriff Court, see p. 640, infra.
[2] 3 Edw. VII c. 33, sec. 104 (2) (s); 38 & 39 Vict. c. 62, sec. 3. See Magistrates of Cumnock v. Murdoch, 1910 S.C. 571.
[3] Magistrates of Buckhaven & Methil v. Wemyss Coal Co., 1928 S.C. 66. See also Little's Executors v. Magistrates of Troon, 1937 S.C. 657.
[4] Rules of Court, 1936, V, 22-24.

Local Government (Scotland) Act, 1908.—Any person who thinks himself aggrieved by any resolution or act of a county council under the powers conferred by secs. 10 and 11 of the Act has the same right of appeal and subject to the like incidents as are indicated above in regard to appeals from resolutions of a town council.[1]

[1] 8 Edw. VII c. 62, sec. 11 (6). See Kessock Ferry Joint Committee, 1916, 33 Sh.Ct.Rep. 178; Ross-shire County Council v. Macrae-Gilstrap, 1930 S.C. 808.

Police Pensions Act, 1921.—A person who has been refused a pension under this Act may apply to the Sheriff having jurisdiction in the place where the person concerned last served in the force, and appeal is competent on a point of law from any decision of the Sheriff to the Court of Session.[1] The procedure in appeals is intended to be regulated by Rules of Court, but no form of appeal has been prescribed. The most appropriate form of appeal would be by stated case, but in a recent case the application to the Sheriff was in the form of an ordinary action and the appeal to the Court of Session was taken as an ordinary appeal.[2]

[1] 11 & 12 Geo. V c. 31, secs. 17, 34. See also 9 & 10 Geo. VI c. 71, Schedule I, 7.
[2] Drummond v. Peebles County Council, 1937 S.C. 36.

Fire Brigade Pensions Act, 1925 (15 & 16 Geo. V c. 47, secs. 15, 25).—Provisions similar to those just mentioned are made for appeals under this Act.

Stated cases which do not provide a proper right of appeal, and which must be applied for before judgment for the purpose of obtaining the opinion of the Court of Session on a question of law are illustrated by the provisions of the *Elections (Scotland) (Corrupt and Illegal Practices) Act*, 1890[1]; the *Industrial and*

Provident Societies Act, 1893[2]; the *Friendly Societies Act,* 1896[3]; and the *Housing (Scotland) Act,* 1925.[4]

[1] See p. 634, infra.
[2] See p. 592, infra.
[3] See p. 593, infra.
[4] See p. 601, infra.

A similar provision is made in the Burgh Police (Scotland) Act, 1903. Under this Act the Sheriff Principal as a single arbiter may adjust the financial relations between a county and a burgh on the extension of the burgh, and may state a special case for the opinion of the Court of Session on any question of law.[1] No special procedure is prescribed but a stated case in customary form is appropriate.[2]

[1] 3 Edw. VII c. 33, sec. 96; 52 & 53 Vict. c. 50, sec. 50. See Midlothian County Council v. Magistrates of Musselburgh, 1911 S.C. 463; Lanark County Council v. Magistrates of Motherwell, 1912 S.C. 1251.
[2] Lanark County Council v. Magistrates of Motherwell, supra.

II. PARTICULAR STATUTES.

1. ADOPTION OF CHILDREN.*

Proceedings may be taken in the Sheriff Court for the adoption of a child under twenty-one who has never been married.[1] And where a child under twenty-one at the commencement of the Act on 1st October, 1930, was at that date, and had been for two years previously, in the custody of and under *de facto* adoption by the applicant it is immaterial that the child is over twenty-one when the application is made.[2] The petition for adoption may be by two spouses but otherwise one person only can adopt.[3] The applicant or both joint applicants must be not under the age of twenty-five[4] unless the applicant or one of the joint applicants is the mother of the child[5]; and the applicant or both joint applicants must be not less than twenty-one years older than the child[4] unless the applicants or one of them and the child are within the prohibited degrees of consanguinity or, in a joint application, the wife is the mother or the husband is the father of the child.[5] An adoption order may not be made where the sole applicant is a male and the child is a female unless (1) the Court is satisfied that there are special circumstances which justify the making of the order as an exceptional measure,[6] or (2) the child was on 1st October, 1930, under twenty-one and was at that date and had been for two years previously in the custody of and under

* See general observations, p. 532, et seq., supra.

544 SHERIFF COURT PRACTICE.

de facto adoption by the applicant and the Court is satisfied that
it is just and equitable and for the child's welfare to make the
adoption order.[7] Nor may an adoption order be granted upon
the application of one of two spouses without the consent of the
other, but such consent may be dispensed with if the Court is
satisfied that the other spouse cannot be found, or is incapable of
consenting, or that the spouses are living apart and that their
separation is likely to be permanent.[8] An illegitimate child may
be adopted by its father or its mother,[9] and spouses may adopt
the illegitimate child of either.[10] An adoption order may not be
made unless the applicant or applicants are resident in Scotland
and domiciled either there or in England and Wales, and unless
the child is a British subject resident in Scotland.[11]

[1] 20 & 21 Geo. V c. 37, sec. 1 (1). On the question of marriage, see
   N, 1946, 62 Sh.Ct.Rep. 76.
[2] Ibid., sec. 10; G, 1939 S.C. 782; cf. N, supra.
[3] Ibid., sec. 1 (3). As to proof of marriage see T, 1945, 61 Sh.Ct.Rep.
   172.
[4] Ibid., sec. 2 (1).
[5] 2 & 3 Geo. VI c. 27, sec. 15 (d); 3 & 4 Geo. VI c. 2, sec. 1, Schedule.
[6] 20 & 21 Geo. V c. 37, sec. 2 (2).
[7] Ibid., sec. 10.
[8] Ibid., sec. 2 (4).
[9] D, 1938 S.L.T. 26.
[10] A and B, 1932 S.L.T. (Sh.Ct.) 37. See also C, 1944, 60 Sh.Ct.Rep.
   61.
[11] 3 & 4 Geo. VI c. 2, sec. 2 (2), Schedule (infant is used in the section
   in place of child).

An adoption order may not be made save with the consent
of every person or body who is a parent or guardian of the child
or has the actual custody of the child, or is liable to contribute
to the child's support, and save with the consent of the child
itself if a minor.[1] Presumably the child should also consent if
major at the time of the application as it may be in the circumstances explained above.[2] Where an illegitimate child of nineteen
had consented to the adoption but was ignorant of his real status
the Court directed that he be informed of the circumstances of
his birth.[3] As to the mother's consent where the identity of the
adopters was unknown to her, see the cases undernoted.[4] The
foregoing consents may be dispensed with by the Court if satisfied
that the person in question has neglected or ill-treated the child,
or abandoned or deserted it, or cannot be found, or is incapable
of consenting, or, being liable to contribute to the child's support,
either has persistently neglected or refused to contribute, or is
a person whose consent should in the opinion of the Court in
all the circumstances of the case be dispensed with.[1] From the

wording of the sub-section it appears that the power of the Court to dispense with consents in respect of the general circumstances of the case applies only where the person is liable to contribute to the child's support—though that would generally include a parent.[5] The consent of a parent or guardian—but not apparently of any other person whose consent is needed—may be dispensed with where, at the commencement of the Act on 1st October, 1930, the child was and had been for two years in the custody of and *de facto* adopted by the applicant, and the Court is satisfied that it is just and equitable and for the child's welfare to dispense with the consent and make the adoption order.[6] A mother who had consented to the adoption was held entitled to an opportunity of seeing the child before the adoption order was made.[7]

[1] 20 & 21 Geo. V c 37, sec. 2 (3); D & D, 1945, 61 Sh.Ct.Rep. 65.
[2] See preceding paragraph.
[3] A, 1936 S.C. 255.
[4] C and C, 1936 S.C. 257; H and H, 1944 S.C. 347.
[5] This point does not appear to have been taken in Winchester v. Cuthbert, 1939, 55 Sh.Ct.Rep. 261.
[6] 20 & 21 Geo. V c. 37, sec. 10.
[7] B and B, 1946 S.L.T. (Sh.Ct.) 36.

Before making an adoption order the Court must be satisfied (a) that any person whose consent is required and has not been dispensed with has consented to, and understands, the nature and effect of the adoption order asked, and, if a parent, understands that the order will permanently deprive him or her of his or her parental rights; (b) that the order if made will be for the welfare of the child—consideration being given to the child's wishes, having regard to its age and understanding; and (c) that the applicant has not received or agreed to receive, and that no one has made or given or agreed to make or give the applicant, any payment or reward except such as the Court may sanction.[1] The Court may in the order impose conditions and may require the applicant by bond or otherwise to make provision for the child.[2] The Court may postpone determination of an application, and may make an interim order for custody in favour of the applicant for a probationary period not exceeding two years.[3] This is not an adoption order but it requires the same consents.[3] An adoption order or an interim order may be made in respect of a child already the subject of an adoption order, the first adopter being deemed to be the parent or guardian.[4] No adopter or parent or guardian may, save with sanction of the Court, receive any payment or reward in consideration of an adoption, and no person may give or agree to give any such payment or reward.[5] The effect of an adoption order is specified in the Act.[6]

[1] 20 & 21 Geo. V c. 37, sec. 3.
[2] Ibid., sec. 4.
[3] Ibid., sec. 6; S, 1945, 61 Sh.Ct.Rep. 131.
[4] Ibid., sec. 7. As to procedure where previous adoption in England, see E and E, 1939 S.C. 165; F, 1939 S.C. 166.
[5] Ibid., sec. 9.
[6] Ibid., sec. 5.

The Sheriff Court having jurisdiction under the Act is that within whose jurisdiction either the applicant or the child resides at the date of the application.[1] The application is made, not by initial writ, but by a special form of petition prescribed by Act of Sederunt.[2] All consents required by the Act must be in writing, signed and tested, and in the form prescribed.[2] Such consents and all other documents founded on to vouch the statements in the petition, including an extract birth certificate of the child, must be lodged with the petition.[2] The first deliverance is an order for service and it usually includes the appointment of a curator for the purpose aftermentioned. If consents have to be dispensed with that may be done at this stage or later. No express provision is made for intimation but the form of petition shows that it is to be served on the child—which is not usually done if the child is a pupil—its parents, its tutors and curators (if any), the persons having the actual custody, those liable to contribute to its support, and on such others as the Sheriff may think proper,[3] and that answers may be lodged. On presentation of the petition, or as soon as may be thereafter, the Court is directed to appoint a curator *ad litem* to the child whose duty it is to investigate and report on the circumstances of the child and the applicant and on other relevant matters.[4] The remit to the curator to report may be contained in the interlocutor appointing him or may be made after he has appeared and taken the oath *de fideli*. The curator must report in particular (a) whether the statements in the petition are true, and what steps he was able to take to verify that any parent giving consent understood the effect of the order; (b) whether there was any payment or reward in respect of the adoption, and whether the adoption is consistent with the child's welfare; (c) whether the means and status of the petitioner will enable him to maintain the child and what right or interest the child has in any property; (d) what insurance, if any, has been effected on the child's life; and (e) whether an interim order or the imposition of any terms and conditions is desirable.[4] In some Courts an official of the local authority—such as the public assistance officer—is appointed curator in all cases and performs his duties without further remuneration, but the practice is understood to vary and solicitors or other parties may be appointed and may receive fees in the usual way.

[1] 20 & 21 Geo. V c. 37, sec. 8 (1).
[2] Act of Sederunt, 30th October, 1930, sec. 1.
[3] In practice service is not made on the husband of a woman whose child—averred to be illegitimate—is in question if it is reasonably clear that the husband was not the father; E, 1944, 60 Sh.Ct.Rep. 127.
[4] Act of Sederunt, 30th October, 1930, sec. 2.

If the Court is not satisfied with the verification of the statements in the petition, as provided by the documents lodged or the curator's report, or if for any reason the Court thinks it right and proper, it may refuse to pronounce an order without further productions, or without oral evidence, and may order such productions to be lodged, or such evidence led.[1] The Court may also refuse to pronounce an order unless all or some of the parties and (if required) the child are in personal attendance, and may direct any of the parties or the child to attend apart from the others, or for a private interview by the Court.[2] In some Courts it is the practice to see the petitioner, in others it is not, but if the Sheriff is disposed to refuse the petition it is thought that before he does so he should give the petitioner or his solicitor an opportunity of being heard. If the documents and the curator's report are satisfactory, the Sheriff—with or without seeing the petitioner as the practice may be—grants decree in terms of the crave in the prescribed form of petition.[3] Unless the Court otherwise directs, all proceedings before it in an adoption petition are heard and determined in camera and all documents lodged in process, including the curator's report, are open only to the Court, the curator, and the parties, and are to be treated as confidential.[4] If the petitioner has lodged a previous petition, which has been refused, no order may be made except on a substantial change of circumstances.[5]

[1] Act of Sederunt, 30th October, 1930, sec. 3.
[2] Ibid., sec. 4.
[3] Ibid., Appendix, No. 1.
[4] Ibid., sec. 5.
[5] Ibid., sec. 8.

Every adoption order contains certain directions to the Registrar-General in relation to registration, and is communicated to him by the Sheriff-clerk to have such directions complied with.[1] Such communication is made by sending or delivering a certified copy of the order in a sealed envelope marked " Confidential."[2]

No extract of the order may be issued except by authority of the Sheriff on application to him setting forth the reasons for which the extract is required.[3] Immediately on the ˙communication to the Registrar-General (or on the issue of an extract as above) the process is enclosed by the Sheriff-clerk in a sealed envelope which may not be opened within twenty years of the order except (1) for the adopted child to whom the order refers and who has attained seventeen, or (2) by authority of the Sheriff on application to him setting forth the reasons for which the process is required.[4]

[1] 20 & 21 Geo. V c. 37, sec. 11 (5).
[2] Act of Sederunt, 30th October, 1930, sec. 9.
[3] Ibid., sec. 11.
[4] Ibid., sec. 12 (b).

The Court may make such order as to expenses (including the expenses of the curator) as it thinks fit and may modify such expenses or direct them to be taxed on such scale as it may determine.[1] In the ordinary unopposed petition no order for expenses is usually necessary. No provision is made as to appeal, but an appeal to the Sheriff on a question as to the competency of a petition has been entertained.[2] There is no provision nega- tiving an appeal to the Court of Session, and as jurisdiction in regard to adoption applications is not confined to the Sheriff Court, an appeal to the Court of Session is presumably competent.

[1] Act of Sederunt, 30th October, 1930, sec. 13.
[2] A and B, 1932 S.L.T. (Sh.Ct.) 37.

Under the Adoption of Children (Regulation) Act of 1939 adoption societies require to be registered by the local authority and there is a right of appeal against either a refusal of registra- tion or a cancellation of the registration.[1] The appeal must be lodged within twenty-one days after written notice of the decision has been given to the society, and it is made to the Sheriff within whose jurisdiction the administrative centre of the society is situated.[1] The initial writ will crave that the decision of the local authority should be recalled and in the case of refusal that they be ordained to register the society. Under sec. 11 of the Act a licence is required to permit a child to be transferred to a British subject resident abroad,[2] and such licence may be granted by the Sheriff within whose jurisdiction the child is resident.[3] The procedure is to be the same *mutatis mutandis* as in an action for regulating the custody of children.[4] Before granting a licence the Sheriff has to be satisfied on certain points[5] and the licence is granted in a prescribed form.[6] No appeal to the Court of Session appears to be competent in respect of either of the above proceedings. In the case of an appeal in regard to registration the application appears to fall into a class in which the decision of the Sheriff Court judge who deals with the matter is intended to be final,[7] and in the case of the licence this seems to be an application in which no right to review the decision of the judge of first instance is provided.[8]

[1] 2 & 3 Geo. VI c. 27, secs. 3 (3), 15 (a).
[2] Ibid., sec. 11 (2).
[3] Ibid., sec. 15 (e).
[4] Act of Sederunt, 5th November, 1943.
[5] 2 & 3 Geo. VI c. 27, sec. 11 (3).
[6] S.R. & O., 1943, No. 1455, S/45.
[7] See p. 535, supra.
[8] See p. 537, supra.

2. AGRICULTURAL HOLDINGS.*

(1) *Crofters, &c.*

The Crofters Holdings Acts have practically been superseded by the Small Landholders Act of 1911,[1] and the Sheriff's duties under the Crofters Acts have been mainly transferred to the Land Court. One matter which remains with the Sheriff is the hearing of complaints for contravention of the regulations for common grazings.[2] If the complaint is in respect of excessive stock the crave of the writ should be for an order to remove and failing that for warrant to sell. This statutory procedure appears to exclude other remedies.[3] The Sheriff is also directed by the Act of 1911 to grant decree conform to orders of the Land Court so that execution and diligence may proceed thereon.[4] The Sheriff's function in this connexion is purely ministerial,[5] but the procedure to obtain the decree varies. In some Courts the Land Court application and order are simply handed to the Sheriff, who grants decree if satisfied that the order has been recorded. In others a minute is endorsed asking the Sheriff to interpone authority to the order and ordain the appropriate party to conform thereto. There is no intimation and no process is made up.[5]

* See general observations, p. 532, et seq., supra.

[1] 1 & 2 Geo. V c. 49.
[2] 54 & 55 Vict. c. 41, sec. 5; 8 Edw. VII c. 50, sec. 2.
[3] M'Millan v. MacPhee, 1914, 30 Sh.Ct.Rep. 342.
[4] 1 & 2 Geo. V c. 49, sec. 25 (6).
[5] Duke of Argyll v. Cameron, 1888, 16 R. 139.

(2) *Arbitration.*

Under the Agricultural Holdings Acts[1] the Sheriff's duties are—
(a) To remove an arbiter who has misconducted himself[2]; (b) to

direct the arbiter upon questions of law arising in the arbitration[3]; (c) to set aside the arbiter's award if it has been improperly procured or if the arbiter has misconducted himself[4]; (d) to hear and decide objections to the report of the Sheriff Court Auditor upon any account of expenses awarded by the arbiter[5]; and (e) to deal with certain applications relating to compensation claims by cottagers for disturbance—such applications being directed to be made to the Court for the district where the house is situated.[6]

[1] 13 & 14 Geo. V c. 10; 21 & 22 Geo. V c. 44.
[2] 13 & 14 Geo. V c. 10, Schedule II (6).
[3] Ibid., Schedule II, 9.
[4] Ibid., Schedule II, 13.
[5] Ibid., Schedule II, 14.
[6] Ibid., sec. 14.

The Act of 1923 provides that, where an arbiter has misconducted himself, the Sheriff may remove him.[1]   There is no process direction and no definition of misconduct, but any behaviour in the conduct of the arbitration which though innocent may prevent justice being done would be sufficient to justify removal.[2]   One instance would be refusal by the arbiter to accept or act upon the opinion of the Sheriff upon a point of law submitted to him.[3]   The application may be at the instance of the landlord, or the tenant, or both, and if at the instance of one party the other as well as the arbiter will be called as defender.   The condescendence should narrate specific misconduct.[4]

[1] 13 & 14 Geo. V c. 10, Schedule II, 6.
[2] Adams v. Great North of Scotland Railway Co., 1890, 18 R. (H.L.) 1, Lord Watson, p. 8; Mitchell-Gill v. Buchan, 1921 S.C. 390, Lord President Clyde, p. 395; cf. Arbuthnott v. Williamson, &c., 1909, 25 Sh.Ct.Rep. 255.
[3] Mitchell-Gill v. Buchan, supra.
[4] For style see Encyclopædia of Scottish Legal Styles, I, 170.

In arbitrations under the Acts the arbiter himself may state questions of law for the opinion of the Sheriff, or either party may ask the Sheriff to direct the arbiter to do so.[1]   In either case if questions are submitted these are contained in the form of a special case for the opinion of the Sheriff.[1]   When the case is stated by the arbiter himself he, or his clerk, transmits the case to the Sheriff.   After hearing parties, the Sheriff answers the questions of law; and (unless appeal is taken) the Sheriff-clerk retransmits the process to the arbiter or his clerk.

[1] 13 & 14 Geo. V c. 10, Schedule II, 9.

Where one of the parties asks the Court to direct the arbiter to state a case, the writ narrates the arbitration, states the questions of law which have arisen, and craves the Court to direct the arbiter to embody them in a special case and meantime to interdict him from issuing any award.[1] If the application is dealt with by the Sheriff-Substitute there is no appeal to the Sheriff[2] and it is thought that there is no appeal from either to the Court of Session. If directed to state a case the arbiter does not seem to have any discretion; and must apparently state the questions of law, as they are contained in the direction by the Sheriff.[3] The application for such a direction should be served upon the other party, as well as upon the arbiter, and these parties are called as defenders.

[1] For style see Encyclopædia of Scottish Legal Styles, I, 168.
[2] 13 & 14 Geo. V c. 10, sec. 43.
[3] See 13 & 14 Geo. V c. 10, Schedule II, 9; Williamson v. Stewart, 1910, 27 Sh.Ct.Rep. 240.

As a matter of Court arrangement the stated case is frequently dealt with by the Sheriff and not by the Sheriff-Substitute. The interlocutor disposing of the matter contains categorical answers to the questions of law and a note explaining the reason for the answers is usually, if not invariably, appended. The interlocutor usually also disposes of the expenses of the stated case. Where expenses were not asked and were not dealt with in the interlocutor disposing of the questions in the stated case it was held that the Sheriff could not deal with expenses at a later date when his interlocutor had become final.[1] A second stated case has been refused on a matter acquiesced in when the first case was stated.[2]

[1] Jack v. King, 1932, 48 Sh.Ct.Rep. 242.
[2] Earl of Galloway v. M'Clelland, &c., 1917, 33 Sh.Ct.Rep. 351.

If the stated case is dealt with by the Sheriff-Substitute there is no appeal to the Sheriff[1] and the decision of the Sheriff-Substitute or the Sheriff is final unless an appeal is taken within twenty-one days after the date on which the decision was communicated to the appellant.[2] The appeal is taken by a written appeal to the Court of Session specifying certain prescribed particulars, lodged in the General Department of the Court of Session.[3]

[1] 13 & 14 Geo. V c. 10, sec. 43.
[2] Ibid., sec. 16 (2); Rules of Court, 1936, V, 16 (a).
[3] Rules of Court, 1936, V, 16 (a); for style see Encyclopædia of Scottish Legal Styles, I, 169.

The Schedule to the Act of 1923 provides that when an arbiter has misconducted himself, or an arbitration or award has been improperly procured, the Sheriff may set the award aside.[1] Misconduct is not defined and reference is made to what has been already' written on this point.[2] An application for removal may be combined with one for setting aside the award.[3] The statutory remedy is that of setting aside the award and not that of reduction.[4]

[1] 13 & 14 Geo. V c. 10, Schedule II, 13.
[2] See p. 550, supra.
[3] See Sim v. M'Connell, &c., 1936, 52 Sh.Ct.Rep. 324; Dundas v. Hogg, &c., 1936, 52 Sh.Ct.Rep. 329.
[4] See Paynter v. Rutherford, &c., 1939, 55 Sh.Ct.Rep. 305.

The Sheriff may sanction the appointment of a clerk in the arbitration where the parties do not consent to such an appointment.[1] The application is at the instance of the arbiter. The parties to the arbitration will be heard in reply but the matter will normally be disposed of in a summary manner and written answers to the application will not generally be required.[2] The existence of legal questions may be a ground for having a clerk appointed.

[1] 21 & 22 Geo. V c. 44, sec. 39 (2); for style see Encyclopædia of Scottish Legal Styles, I, 166.
[2] Henderson, 1933, 50 Sh.Ct.Rep. 17.

Under the Sheep Stocks Valuation (Scotland) Act, 1937, the arbiter is required to give certain details in his award and if he fails to comply with these requirements his award may be set aside by the Sheriff.[1] Provision is also made for a stated case on any question of law.[2] So far as procedure is concerned these applications will be dealt with in the same way as the corresponding applications under the Agricultural Holdings Acts.

[1] 1 Edw. VIII & 1 Geo. VI c. 34, sec. 1. See Paynter v. Rutherford, &c., 1939, 55 Sh.Ct.Rep. 305; Duke of Argyll v. MacArthur, 1941, 59 Sh.Ct.Rep. 91; and see also 9 & 10 Geo. VI c. 73, sec. 28 (2).
[2] Ibid., sec. 2.

(3) Bequest of Lease.

Under the Acts the Sheriff Court is the final Court of appeal in the matter of a bequest of a lease. The legatee of a lease must, within twenty-one days (unless prevented by some unavoidable cause), notify the landlord of the bequest.[1] Within one month after intimation, the landlord may notify his objection and the legatee may then apply in the Sheriff Court for declarator that he is the tenant.[1] The landlord is called as defender and intimation is made to him in common form. The Statute provides that the landlord may enter appearance and state his grounds of objection.[1]

The use of the term " enter appearance " does not, it is thought, imply that the procedure must be by way of ordinary action, and the matter will generally be disposed of in a summary manner so far as appropriate, the form of procedure being in the hands of the Sheriff. If the landlord's objection is to the validity of the bequest rather than to the person of the legatee there may be a right of appeal to the Court of Session.[2] Otherwise the decision of the Sheriff is final.[3]

[1] 13 & 14 Geo. V c. 10, sec. 28. See Sloss v. Agnew, 1923 S.L.T. (Sh.Ct.) 33; for style see Encyclopædia of Scottish Legal Styles, I, 172.
[2] See Mackenzie v. Cameron, 1894, 21 R. 427.
[3] 13 & 14 Geo. V c. 10, sec. 28 (f).

(4) Jurisdiction and Appeal.

In the absence of any statutory direction as to jurisdiction it is thought that applications under the Acts fall to be made to the Court having jurisdiction where the holding is situated, and this appears to be the practice.[1] If the matter is dealt with by the Sheriff-Substitute there is no appeal to the Sheriff.[2] Appeal to the Court of Session on a stated case has been already considered. Apart from this there is no provision as to appeals to that Court, and while these are not expressly excluded it is doubtful whether there is any right of review by the Court of Session apart from that conferred in relation to a stated case.[3]

[1] See Shanks v. Nisbet, 1900, 16 Sh.Ct.Rep. 316.
[2] 13 & 14 Geo. V c. 10, sec. 43.
[3] See Cathcart v. Board of Agriculture, 1915 S.C. 166.

3. ARBITRATION.*

(1) Purpose.

Under the Arbitration (Scotland) Act, 1894, the Sheriff Court has a concurrent jurisdiction with the Court of Session in relation to the appointment of an arbiter or oversman.[1] The Statute empowers the Court to appoint an arbiter or oversman in certain specified circumstances and when these are not present the aid of the Court cannot be invoked in the first instance to make an appointment.[2] The undernoted cases deal with the circumstances in which the jurisdiction of the Court is available.[3] Apart from the Act of 1894 provision may be made by other Statutes for the appointment of an arbiter by the Sheriff.[4]

* See general observations, p. 532, et seq., supra.

[1] 57 & 58 Vict. c. 13, sec. 6.
[2] See M'Millan & Son v. Rowan & Co., 1903, 5 F., 317.

³ Bryson & Manson v. Picken, 1895, 12 Sh.Ct.Rep. 26; Twibill v. Niven
   & Co., 1897, 13 Sh.Ct.Rep. 313; Cowie v. Kiddie, 1897, 14 Sh.Ct.Rep.
   26; British Westinghouse, &c., Co. v. Provost of Aberdeen, (O.H.)
   1906, 14 S.L.T. 391; Glasgow Parish Council v. United Collieries,
   (O.H.) 1907, 15 S.L.T. 232; M'Kechnie's Trustees v. Meiklam's
   Trustees, 1909, 2 S.L.T. 266, 340; Highgate & Co. v. British Oil
   and Guano Co., (O.H.) 1914, 2 S.L.T. 241.
⁴ E.g., 9 & 10 Geo. VI c. 30, sec. 14 (8).

(2) Procedure.

The Act of 1894 contains no process directions but normally the
proceedings will be treated as a summary application though in
difficult cases the procedure in an ordinary action may be followed.¹
The application may be made by any of the parties to the agreement to refer.² When the crave is to nominate an arbiter, only
the other referring party need be called as defender; but when
the crave is to nominate an oversman, not only the other party,
but the arbiters, should be called, for they are also interested
parties.³ The process is dealt with as judicial business. Expenses
are normally awarded in contested cases and there are the rights of
appeal appropriate to the form of process employed.⁴

¹ United Creameries Co. v. Boyd & Co., 1912 S.C. 617.
² 57 & 58 Vict. c. 13, secs. 2, 3.
³ For style see Encyclopædia of Scottish Legal Styles, I, 296, 297.
⁴ See United Creameries Co. v. Boyd & Co., supra; Ross v. Ross, 1920
   S.C. 530; Alison v. Blenkhorn, 1907, 23 Sh.Ct.Rep. 208; Thom &
   Sons v. Burrell, &c., 1929, 45 Sh.Ct.Rep. 187.

(3) Forum.

Any Sheriff having jurisdiction¹ is under the Act entitled to
entertain such an application, and this apparently means a Sheriff
to whose jurisdiction the defender is subject, upon one or other
of the appropriate grounds of jurisdiction set forth in the Sheriff
Courts Acts. The application is thus competent in the Sheriff
Court within whose jurisdiction the other party resides²; or
where he carries on business and has a place of business if the
defender is cited personally or at such place of business.³ It
may be competent (if the defender can be personally cited there)
to bring the action in the Sheriff Court of the district where the
arbitration is contracted to proceed, if the agreement to refer
has named a place because that is "the place of execution or
performance" of the contract to refer.⁴ Jurisdiction could not
it is thought be founded for such an application by arrestment.⁵
Specialties both in regard to procedure and jurisdiction may

arise where the application is not truly one under the Act but under a special clause in the contract.[6]

[1] 57 & 58 Vict. c. 13, sec. 6.
[2] 7 Edw. VII c. 51, sec. 6 (a).
[3] Ibid., sec. 6 (b).
[4] Ibid., sec. 6 (f).
[5] Union Electric Co. v. Holman & Co., 1913 S.C. 954, Lord President Dunedin, p. 957.
[6] See Magistrates of Glasgow v. Glasgow District Subway Co., 1893, 21 R. 52; Ross v. Ross, 1920 S.C. 530; Thom & Sons v. Burrell, &c., 1929, 45 Sh.Ct.Rep. 187.

(4) *Miscellaneous.*

Legal proceedings to compel an arbiter or oversman to execute his office are competent only in the Court of Session.[1] Apart from the Arbitration Act application may be made to the Sheriff for warrant to cite witnesses and havers in an arbitration following on an allowance of proof. It is not necessary to call any one as defender in such an application which is normally granted *de plano* by the Sheriff within whose jurisdiction the arbitration is proceeding. When an arbitration award has been made proceedings may be brought in the Sheriff Court for payment in implement of the award. Reduction of an arbiter's award is not competent in the Sheriff Court,[2] but in an action for implement objections may be taken *ope exceptionis.*[3] In certain statutory cases an award may be set aside by the Sheriff.[4]

[1] Forbes, &c. v. Underwood, 1886, 13 R. 465.
[2] See statutory authority to "set aside" awards in arbitrations under the Agricultural Holdings Acts, pp. 551, 552, supra.
[3] Kilmaurs Dairy Association v. Brisbane & Beattie's Dairies, 1927, 43 Sh.Ct.Rep. 210; Blythe Building Co. v. Mason's Executor, 1937, 53 Sh.Ct.Rep. 180; cf. Waugh v. Baxter & Sons, 1922, 38 Sh.Ct.Rep. 162.
[4] See pp. 551, 552, supra.

4. BIRTHS, &c., REGISTRATION.*

(1) *General.*

(a) *Officials.*—When a vacancy occurs in the office of a registrar the Sheriff may appoint an interim registrar[1] on the application of the local authority—the town council in large burghs, but otherwise the county council.[2] For the election of a new registrar application may be made by the town-clerk or the county-clerk either to the local authority or the Sheriff to call a meeting of the local authority to elect a successor.[3] Any difference as to the voting at that meeting is to be settled summarily by the Sheriff on hearing verbally the parties or their solicitors.[4] The local

* See general observations, p. 532, et seq., supra.

authority or the Sheriff must, within ten days, intimate to the Registrar-General the election of any registrar, or the nomination of any interim registrar.[4] The Sheriff also has power, on the application of the local authority or of the Registrar-General, to remove a registrar from office for incompetency or neglect of duty, after hearing parties and taking such proceedings as in his discretion he thinks necessary,[5] and under the Church of Scotland Act the Sheriff may determine questions as to the right to elect a registrar and as to assessments to be levied for registration purposes.[6]

[1] 17 & 18 Vict. c. 80, sec. 12. See Tait, 1903, 19 Sh.Ct.Rep. 345; for style see Encyclopædia of Scottish Legal Styles, VII, 402.
[2] 19 & 20 Geo. V c. 25, secs. 1 (1), 77 (1) (6).
[3] 17 & 18 Vict. c. 80, sec. 9.
[4] Ibid., sec. 12.
[5] Ibid., sec. 15; 18 Vict. c. 29, sec. 2.
[6] 15 & 16 Geo. V c. 33, sec. 43.

(b) *Custody of Books.*—Where a registrar who is superseded, or the representatives of a registrar who has died, are withholding delivery of the statutory books the local authority may apply to the Sheriff for warrant to arrest the person withholding delivery, and bring him before the Court.[1] If the Sheriff, after summary inquiry, is of opinion that delivery is being wilfully refused, he may commit such person to prison till delivery is made.[1]

[1] 17 & 18 Vict. c. 80, sec. 24.

(c) *Districts.*—The Sheriff is authorized to alter the areas and boundaries of registration districts.[1] He may divide or unite parishes or districts, or annex a portion of a parish to an adjoining parish, or a landward portion of a parish to a burgh, or *vice versa.*[1] Public intimation and an opportunity to hear objections are usually given in such applications, and the Sheriff should be satisfied that good reasons for the rearrangement exist.[2]

[1] 17 & 18 Vict. c. 80, secs. 10, 11; 23 & 24 Vict. c. 85, sec. 5.
[2] For style of application see Encyclopædia of Scottish Legal Styles, VII, 403.

(d) *Form of Action.*—The above proceedings are usually dealt with as summary applications.[1] In the case of removal of a registrar[2] and the union of landward and burghal parts of parishes,[3] and in relation to the right to elect a registrar, and questions as to assessments under the Church of Scotland Act,[4] it is expressly provided that the Sheriff's decision is final. No such provision is made in the case of other unions or divisions and annexations, and the position in regard to the right of appeal in such applications is left in doubt. A right of appeal within the Sheriff Court has been entertained in such an application,[5] but the competency of this may be doubted.[6] The remaining applications relate to comparatively trivial matters in regard to which appeals would not, it is thought, be entertained.[7]

[1] Forms for some of the applications are given in Lees, Sheriff Court Styles, 4th edn., pp. 322-3; Wallace, Sheriff Court Style Book, p. 521.
[2] 17 & 18 Vict. c. 80, sec. 15.
[3] 23 & 24 Vict. c. 85, sec. 5.
[4] 15 & 16 Geo. V c. 33, sec. 43.
[5] Neilson, &c., 1890, 7 Sh.Ct.Rep. 20.
[6] See p. 537, supra.
[7] See Milne v. Archibald, 1866, 1 Guthrie's Select Cases, 407.

(e) *Forum.*—Proceedings are apparently intended to be taken in the Sheriff Court within whose jurisdiction the parish is situated.[1] When a parish is situated in more than one Sheriffdom proceedings are to be taken in the Sheriff Court of the district within which the parish church is situated.[2]

[1] 17 & 18 Vict. c. 80, secs. 21, 76.
[2] Ibid. In present circumstances it is thought that this should be regarded as meaning where the parish church was situated before the Union.

(2) *Informant.*

If any person whose duty it is to give information to the registrar fails to do so after special intimation by the registrar, the latter may apply to the Sheriff for warrant to bring him to the registrar's office in custody.[1] Such a warrant is granted *de plano*, upon production of evidence that the intimations by the registrar have been made.[1] The warrant may be executed by any Sheriff-officer.[1]

[1] 17 & 18 Vict. c. 80, sec. 45.

(3) *Correction of Entries.*

Any person who discovers a mistake in the registration of a birth, marriage, or death is under a statutory duty to give information thereof to the Sheriff forthwith, whereupon the Sheriff may appoint a diet for inquiry, and require the attendance of all interested parties.[1] But in practice the registrar usually attends before the Sheriff, along with the necessary witnesses. The parties who may be required to attend are the person who made, and any person concerned in the making, of the erroneous entry, or having

knowledge of it, and also any person interested in the effect of
the entry.[1] Usually no written application is needed.[2] The
witnesses are examined on oath, and, if satisfied, the Sheriff
authorizes the correction. If the witnesses are not likely to attend
voluntarily formal warrant to cite may be granted, and a witness
who cannot attend may be examined on commission.[3] The Sheriff's
warrant directs that a fresh entry with the true particulars be
made in " The Register of Corrected Entries,"[1] and a reference
is made opposite the entry in the original register.[1] Correction
may take the form of cancellation of an entry made in the wrong
district or by an improper informant.[4]

[1] 17 & 18 Vict. c. 80, sec. 63.
[2] For written form of application see Encyclopædia of Scottish Legal
    Styles, VII, 406, 408-411.
[3] See Sellar's Forms, 319.
[4] See ibid., 322-3.

Within six months of the original registration of a birth the
registrar may himself correct the register by substituting for the
registered name that which a baptismal certificate, or (if there
is no baptism) a declaration of the parents shows to be the true
name of the child.[1] If more than six months have elapsed the
authority of the Sheriff is required to correct the register.[1] A
summary application by the parent or guardian may be presented
but the common practice is for a parent or guardian to attend
personally before the Sheriff, along with the registrar, and make
on oath the necessary explanation, whereupon the Sheriff, if
satisfied that an alteration is requisite, endorses upon the certificate
of baptism a warrant authorizing the registrar to enter the true
name in the Register of Corrected Entries.[1]

[1] 17 & 18 Vict. c. 80, secs. 32, 33; 23 & 24 Vict. c. 85, secs. 12, 13.

(4) Neglected Entries.

Where a birth, marriage, or death, which occurred in Scotland
between 31st December, 1800, and 1st January, 1885, has not been
registered the Sheriff may grant a warrant to enter it in the
Register of Neglected Entries.[1] Any person having interest may
present a summary application for the purpose[2] in the county in
which such birth, marriage or death occurred.[1] The first deliverance usually fixes a diet of proof and appoints intimation by
advertisement or otherwise, all parties desiring to oppose being
invited to appear at the diet. The evidence must be recorded,
as, if the warrant is granted, the notes of evidence, and any pro-

ductions made are transmitted to the Registrar-General and are
retained by him among the records of his office.[1]

[1] 23 & 24 Vict. c. 85, sec. 2.
[2] Forms in Lees, Sheriff Court Styles, 4th edn., p. 325; Wallace, Sheriff
Court Style Book, 518.

Where a birth is not registered within three months either of
the parents, or the guardians, of the child may make a declaration
before the Sheriff, who may authorize the registration.[1] The
declaration is written on the back of the Schedule of Particulars and
is signed by the declarant and the Sheriff, warrant to register being
appended.[2]

[1] 17 & 18 Vict. c. 80, sec. 31.
[2] Sellar's Forms 315; see also Encyclopædia of Scottish Legal Styles,
VII, 407.

(5) *Old Registers.*

If an error is discovered in a register kept prior to 1855
relative to a birth, marriage or death in Scotland after 31st
December, 1800, any person interested may apply in the Sheriff
Court within whose jurisdiction the register is kept, craving the
Court to authorize the Registrar-General, or the registrar in whose
custody the book is, to make the necessary correction.[1] If proof
is taken, the evidence must be recorded, and the notes of evidence
and the productions are transmitted to the Registrar-General.[1]

[1] 23 & 24 Vict. c. 85, sec. 3.

(6) *Legitimation of Child.*

The register discloses only the name of the mother of an illegitimate child, not that of the father, unless he signs the register with
the mother as an informant, or unless a decree finding paternity is
subsequently transmitted to the Registrar.[1] No entry may be
made in the Register of Corrected Entries respecting the legitimation *per subsequens matrimonium* of any child registered as
illegitimate except where legitimation is found by decree of a
competent Court.[2] If paternity has been registered, and if the
father afterwards marries the mother of the child, the Registrar-
General may authorize re-registration of the birth.[3] But, if
paternity has not been registered, re-registration is only competent
with the sanction of the Sheriff.[3] To obtain this application is
made on an official printed form by both parents or, if one is dead,
by the survivor.[3] The application narrates the birth, parentage,
and registration, and the parents' subsequent marriage, and the
crave is to sanction re-registration of the birth. The first deliver-

ance remits to the Registrar-General, and, on his report being obtained, the parties make a deposition before the Sheriff which is recorded on the application form. If sanction is granted the writ with productions and deliverance are forwarded to the Registrar-General. If necessary the deponents' evidence may be taken on commission and, if the father is not domiciled in Scotland, the Sheriff will normally require *prima facie* evidence that legitimation has resulted from the marriage. The Act provides for intimation of the application and for the hearing of any parties who may appear to oppose it,[3] but in practice no intimation is usually made.

[1] 17 & 18 Vict. c. 80, sec. 35. See next paragraph.
[2] 24 & 25 Geo. V c. 19, sec. 1.
[3] Ibid., sec. 2.

(7) *Decree of Paternity.*

When the paternity of a child has been established in a competent process provision is made for notice by the Clerk of Court to the registrar of the district of the father's domicile, or in which the child's birth is registered. On such notice being received the registrar enters the particulars in the register of corrected entries and makes a reference thereto in the margin of the original entry.[1] So also, if a Court decree has declared a child legitimate, which had been registered as illegitimate, the same procedure is followed and the corresponding marking is made in the register.[1]

[1] 17 & 18 Vict. c. 80, sec. 35, Form F; 23 & 24 Vict. c. 85, sec. 13.

(8) *Marriage.*

Where an irregular marriage by exchange of consent had been contracted application could formerly be made to the Sheriff to grant warrant for its registration. But by the Marriage (Scotland) Act of 1939 no irregular marriage by declaration *de praesenti*, or by promise *subsequente copula*, contracted after the commencement of the Act is valid.[1] The Sheriff's function in regard to marriage is now that of issuing a licence to take the place of a notice under the Marriage Notice (Scotland) Act, 1878, when such notice cannot be timeously obtained.[2] To obtain such a licence application is made by the parties to the intending marriage to the Sheriff within whose jurisdiction the marriage is to be contracted, and the Sheriff has to be satisfied that one of the parties has his usual residence in Scotland, or has lived in Scotland for fifteen days immediately preceding the presentation of the application; that there is no legal impediment to the marriage; that proclamation of banns or publication of the statutory notice could

not be made till after the day on which the marriage was intended
to take place and that there is reasonable excuse for the parties'
failure to secure proclamation or publication in time.[2] The
application is made in a prescribed form and the truth of the facts
stated is deponed to by two witnesses, at least one of whom ought
to be an applicant.[3] If the Sheriff is satisfied he grants the necessary licence and signs a separate licence which is delivered to the
parties and which becomes void if the marriage does not take place
within ten days of its date.[4]

[1] 2 & 3 Geo. VI c. 34, sec. 5.
[2] Ibid., sec. 2 (1).
[3] Act of Sederunt, 28th May, 1940.
[4] 2 & 3 Geo. VI c. 34, sec. 2 (2).

5. BUILDING SOCIETIES.*

(1) *General.*

In general disputes in connexion with building societies fall to
be settled by arbitration, but the aid of the Court may be invoked
(1) when the society's rules direct disputes to be referred to the
Court[1]; and (2) when the rules provide for arbitration, but (a) a
party has been called upon to arbitrate, but for forty days has
not complied[2]; (b) the arbiters nominated have refused to act[2]; or
(c) the arbiters have for twenty-one days failed to make an award.[2]
In such circumstances a writ[3] may be presented in the Sheriff Court
of the county within which the chief office or place of
meeting of the society is situated[4] craving the Court to
determine the dispute. Such decision is final, but, at the
request of either party, the Court may state a case for
the opinion of the Court of Session upon a question of law.[5]
Such a case must be stated prior to judgment in the Sheriff Court.[6]
As the finality provision applies to the Court—not the Sheriff—
an appeal from Sheriff-Substitute to Sheriff seems to be competent.[7]
Compliance with an arbitration award may be enforced by the
Court[8] but an action for this purpose is not subject to the finality
provision above referred to.[5] Where a society's rules provided
for arbitration, but no arbiter had been appointed, and an action
was brought in the Sheriff Court it was held that the Sheriff was
acting under his common law jurisdiction and that the usual rights
of appeal were available.[9]

* See general observations, p. 532, et seq., supra.

[1] 37 & 38 Vict. c. 42, secs. 16 (9), 35 (2). See also 47 & 48 Vict. c. 41,
sec. 2.
[2] Ibid., sec. 35 (1).

3 Forms in Lees, Sheriff Court Styles, 4th edn., 115; Wallace, Sheriff Court Style Book, 113.
4 37 & 38 Vict. c. 42, sec. 4. This is held to apply even when society is in liquidation; Glasgow Working Men's Building Society v. Kirkwood, 1888, 4 Sh.Ct.Rep. 165.
5 Ibid., sec. 36.
6 Johnston's Trustees v. Glasgow Corporation, 1912 S.C. 300; Smith v. Scottish Legal Life Assurance Society, 1912 S.C. 611.
7 See First Edinburgh Starr-Bowkett Building Society v. Munro, 1883, 11 R. 5; Glasgow Corporation v. Mickel, 1922 S.C. 228; cf. Greig v. City of Glasgow Friendly Society, 1939 S.L.T. (Sh.Ct.) 31.
8 37 & 38 Vict. c. 42, sec. 34.
9 Galashiels Provident Building Society v. Newlands, 1893, 20 R. 821.

Under the Building Societies Act, 1939, concurrent jurisdiction is conferred on the Sheriff Court and the Court of Session to deal with certain questions which may arise in relation to advances to a member where security is taken from a third party.[1] Such questions may be disposed of in an application by the society for leave to enforce its rights or on an application by the member.[1] It seems clear that such questions are not " disputes "[2] which fall within the finality provisions of the Act of 1874 above referred to,[3] and, although the point seems left in some doubt, it is thought that the particular jurisdiction conferred by the Act of 1874 on the Sheriff Court of the county where the chief office or the meeting place of the society is situated[4] is not applicable to the provision now under consideration, and that the ordinary rules in regard to jurisdiction apply.[5]

1 2 & 3 Geo. VI c. 55, secs. 7, 16 (7) (b).
2 See 47 & 48 Vict. c. 41, sec. 2.
3 37 & 38 Vict. c. 42, sec. 36.
4 Ibid., sec. 4.
5 The Acts are to be construed together. See 2 & 3 Geo. VI c. 55, sec. 18 (2), but secs. 7 and 16 (7) of the 1939 Act contain a separate definition of " Court."

(2) Officials.

If an official fail to pay over money in his hands, and to deliver securities, books, papers, and others in his possession the society may sue upon his bond of caution, or may apply to the Court under the Act, craving an accounting and delivery or as may be appropriate.[1] The Court is directed to proceed in a summary way, and make such order as may seem just.[1] As any such order is declared to be final and conclusive[1] there is no right of appeal to the Court of Session.[2] An appeal from the Sheriff-Substitute to the Sheriff would seem to be competent.[2]

1 37 & 38 Vict. c. 42, sec. 24.
2 First Edinburgh Starr-Bowkett Building Society v. Munro, 1883, 11 R. 5.

(3) *Liquidation.*

An application to the Court to wind up may be made (a) by a member authorized by three-fourths of the members present at a general meeting of the society specially called for the purpose; or (b) by a judgment creditor for not less than £50.[1] The condescendence of the writ[2] should set forth the circumstances justifying the order craved. The writ must be printed and members and creditors are entitled to demand copies.[3] It may crave winding up by the Court, in which case the Court nominates the liquidator, or it may crave that the winding up be under the supervision of the Court and that the nomination of liquidators by the society be confirmed.[4] The application, which will normally be served on the society, must be notified in the *Edinburgh Gazette,* and by such advertisement as the Court may order.[2]

[1] 37 & 38 Vict. c. 42, sec. 32.
[2] See Codifying Act of Sederunt, L, VII, 1.
[3] Ibid., L, VII, 2.
[4] Forms in Lees, Sheriff Court Styles, 4th edn., 268-9.

The Act of Sederunt contemplates that in the first deliverance a day is fixed for hearing parties and that proof for the applicant is to be led at the same diet.[1] If the application is by a creditor, or if the crave is for a supervision order, the actual proof required will usually be formal. Parties opposing the application may be heard at the same time, but answers may also be ordered, and the hearing may be adjourned.[1] In all matters connected with the winding up, the Court is to have regard to the wishes of the members and the creditors; and for ascertaining their views may order meetings to be held.[2] After parties have been heard the Court may dismiss the application, grant the order craved, or make such other order as may be just.[1]

[1] Codifying Act of Sederunt, L. VII, 1, 3.
[2] Ibid., L, VII, 4.

In a winding up under supervision, if a liquidator has not been appointed by the society, or if their nominee is not confirmed by the Court, the Court must appoint a liquidator, provisionally or otherwise.[1] The Court also determines the security to be found by the liquidator[1] and the remuneration to be paid to him.[2] The Court may remove a liquidator on cause shown, and make the necessary appointment to fill any vacancy.[2] Special powers may be granted by the Court on a note presented by the liquidator who may also apply to the Court for directions and instructions and for sanction to appoint a factor.[3] The Court appoints an auditor of the liquidator's accounts and deals with any question arising on his report.[4]

[1] Codifying Act of Sederunt, L, VII, 5.
[2] Ibid., L, VII, 6.
[3] Ibid., L, VII, 7, 8.
[4] Ibid., L, VII, 11.

The Court may approve or disapprove of the liquidator's state of liabilities and assets, and, if approved, may authorize distribution of the funds in terms thereof.[1] When all funds have been paid over or consigned the Court declares the winding up at an end and the society dissolved, discharges the liquidator and appoints his bond of caution to be delivered up.[1] Other subsidiary points in procedure can be found in the Act of Sederunt itself. See the case undernoted as to actions against a society in liquidation.[2]

[1] Codifying Act of Sederunt, L, VII, 10.
[2] Don v. Mein, 1898, 15 Sh.Ct.Rep. 270.

6. BURIAL GROUNDS.*

The county council, ten ratepayers, or certain other parties may apply in the Sheriff Court of the district where a burial ground, or land proposed to be so used, is situated for a finding that the same is or would be dangerous to health or offensive or contrary to decency.[1] The first order is for intimation, by *Gazette* notice and advertisement in the local press, fixing a diet not less than ten or more than twenty days after the date of presenting the application for hearing all parties interested.[2] Although not expressly provided by the Act the Sheriff may order inquiry, or visit the ground, or otherwise inform himself of the situation.[3] If he is satisfied that the objections are not well founded, he will dismiss the application. If he is of opinion that the pursuer's allegations are true, his duty is to pronounce an interlocutor to that effect.[2] If the application is dismissed no similar application can be presented till after the expiry of five years, except with the concurrence of the procurator-fiscal.[2] While the Act of 1855 does not define Sheriff as including Sheriff-Substitute, there seems little doubt that the application under that Statute can be dealt with by either.[4] The judgment of the Sheriff or Sheriff-Substitute is not subject to review.[5] An overcrowded or offensive

* See general observations, p. 532, et seq., supra.

cemetery may also be dealt with as a nuisance under the Public
Health Act.[6]

[1] 18 & 19 Vict. c. 68, sec. 4; 60 & 61 Vict. c. 38, sec. 146 (2).
[2] 18 & 19 Vict. c. 68, sec. 4; for forms of application see Encyclopædia
of Scottish Legal Styles, II, 256.
[3] See Ayr Town Council, 1891, 7 Sh.Ct.Rep. 196; Dunblane, &c., Parish
Council, 1923, 40 Sh.Ct.Rep. 3.
[4] See Fleming v. Dickson, 1862, 1 M. 188; Strichen Parish Council v.
Goodwillie, 1908 S.C. 835.
[5] Ibid., sec. 32; Strichen Parish Council v. Goodwillie, supra.
[6] See p. 648, infra.

The Sheriff's interlocutor is not in itself an operative judgment.
It is transmitted to the Secretary of State for Scotland, and it
may be provided by Order in Council that no new burial ground
shall be opened within specified limits, unless with the approval
of the Secretary of State, or that burials are to be discontinued
wholly or partly.[1] Notice of the representation to the Privy
Council by the Secretary of State, and of the time and place at
which the representation is to be taken into consideration by the
Council is given in manner prescribed by the Act.[1]

[1] 18 & 19 Vict. c. 68, sec. 5.

When a burial ground has been closed as above and another
is not provided within six months of the closing order, the same
parties may crave the Court to designate and set aside land
suitable for the purpose.[1] The procedure in this application is
more formal, and the first deliverance will order service on the
owners of the lands sought to be acquired, and probably also on
any occupiers, as well as intimation in the local press, and will
fix a diet at which parties will be heard and evidence taken.[2] Ten
days' notice of the hearing must be given to the landowners.[1]
The Sheriff is directed by the Act to examine such witnesses and
make such inquiry as he thinks proper, and, if proof is taken,
the evidence must be recorded.[1] An interlocutor designating the
land entitles the local authority to take the same by compulsory
purchase under the Lands Clauses Act.[3] The Sheriff's judgment
is subject to appeal within fourteen days of its date to the Court
of Session whose decision is final.[4] There is no appeal to the
Sheriff Principal.[5] Expenses are not awarded in such applications
as the Sheriff is regarded as acting in an administrative capacity.[6]

[1] 18 & 19 Vict. c. 68, sec. 10. See Dornoch Parish Council, 1929, 46
Sh.Ct.Rep. 33; Aberdeen County Council v. Roger, 1936, 53
Sh.Ct.Rep. 171.
[2] Sellar's Forms, 78; for form of application see Encyclopædia of Scottish
Legal Styles, II, 253.

3 18 & 19 Vict. c. 68, secs. 12, 13.
4 Ibid., sec. 10; Rules of Court, 1936, V, 7-12; the appeal being now in ordinary form by Note of Appeal which is dealt with in the Inner House.
5 Ibid., sec. 32; Strichen Parish Council v. Goodwillie, 1908 S.C. 835.
6 Liddall v. Ballingry Parish Council, 1908 S.C. 1082.

A writ for warrant to disinter a body falls under the common law jurisdiction of the Sheriff Court. The application is usually presented by relatives[1] and the approval of such as are not applicants may be evidenced by letters; otherwise they may be called as defenders. A certificate from the cemetery authority as to the feasibility of the disinterment should be provided. The Sheriff-Substitute's function in such cases has been held to be ministerial with no right of appeal to the Sheriff,[2] but in certain circumstances expenses have been awarded.[3] In a simple case, if the necessary consents and cemetery certificate are provided, the application is granted as a matter of course.

1 See M'Gruer, 1898, 15 Sh.Ct.Rep. 38; for form of application see Encyclopædia of Scottish Legal Styles, II, 260-263, 267.
2 Black v. M'Callum, &c., 1923, 40 Sh.Ct.Rep. 108; cf. M'Gruer, supra.
3 Black v. M'Callum, &c., supra; M'Gruer, supra; cf. Liddall v. Ballingry Parish Council, 1908 S.C. 1082.

The Sheriff may also be asked to sanction (a) the sale by the local authority of exclusive rights of burial and right to erect monuments, &c.,[1] and (b) the amount of the payments for interments.[2] Application is made by the local authority, intimation is made by advertisement or otherwise, and a diet is fixed for hearing parties and taking evidence if necessary, after which the Sheriff disposes of the matter, his decision being final.[3]

1 18 & 19 Vict. c. 68, sec. 18.
2 Ibid., sec. 24; County Council of Perth, 1941, 57 Sh.Ct.Rep. 98; Corporation of Troon, 1943, 60 Sh.Ct.Rep. 82.
3 18 & 19 Vict. c. 68, sec. 32.

7. CHILDREN AND YOUNG PERSONS ACT.

Under the Act of 1937 the education authority named in an approved school order—a copy of which has to be served on such authority—may contend that the person to whom the order relates was resident in the area of some other authority, or was resident outside Scotland.[1] In such circumstances the named authority may, by notice in writing given at any time within three months after service of the order on them, appeal to the Sheriff having jurisdiction in the place where the Court which made the order sat.[1] Notice of such appeal has also to be given to the other authority concerned (if any) and to the Sheriff-clerk.[1] It is suggested that, despite the reference to a notice in writing, the appeal should be taken in the form of an initial writ craving the Court to vary the order as desired. The matter will be dealt with by either the Sheriff or the Sheriff-Substitute, and the practice on this point appears to vary in the different Sheriffdoms. The Sheriff-clerk is required by the Act to give the parties to the appeal fourteen days' notice of the date fixed for the hearing, and the Sheriff is empowered, if satisfied as to the contention made, to vary the order by substituting therein the name of the other authority, or a statement that the person named in the order was resident outside Scotland.[1] Inquiry into the facts may be necessary in such cases, though an agreed statement of facts has usually been adjusted.[2] Although it is probably not incompetent to award expenses in such appeals this does not appear to have been done in any of the reported cases.[3] It seems probable that the decision of either the Sheriff or the Sheriff-Substitute is intended to be final.[4]

[1] 1 Edw. VIII & 1 Geo. VI c. 37, sec. 94 (2).
[2] Edinburgh Education Authority v. Perth, &c., Education Authority, 1934, 51 Sh.Ct.Rep. 23; Dundee Corporation v. Stirling County Council, 1940, 56 Sh.Ct.Rep. 189; Edinburgh Education Authority v. Perth, &c., Education Authority, 1941, 58 Sh.Ct.Rep. 27.
[3] See Fife Education Authority v. City of Edinburgh, 1934, 50 Sh.Ct.Rep. 245; Edinburgh Education Authority v. Perth, &c., Education Authority (1934), supra; Dundee Corporation v. Stirling County Council, supra; Edinburgh Education Authority v. Perth, &c., Education Authority (1941), supra.
[4] See p. 535, supra, and also County Council of Haddington v. Corporation of Edinburgh, 1915, 1 S.L.T. 200.

8. Church of Scotland Act.*

Under the Church of Scotland (Property and Endowments) Act various statutory duties are imposed on the Sheriff. Where all or part of a victual stipend is localled in victual not mentioned in the Schedule to the Act the minister, or the presbytery clerk (if the benefice is vacant), or any heritor may apply to the Sheriff to fix the average value of the victual, and the Sheriff is directed to fix such value after intimation to such parties as he may appoint and after such inquiry as he thinks fit.[1] The value so fixed is intimated by the Sheriff to the Clerk of Teinds.[1] Application may also be made to the Sheriff in connexion with any special method of calculating stipend customary in any particular parish.[2] Such application may be made by the minister, the presbytery, or a heritor and it craves the Sheriff to give such instructions to the Clerk of Teinds as he may deem necessary or proper for the purpose

* See general observations, p. 532, et seq., supra.

of such calculation.[2]   The application must be made before the
expiry of six months after the date of the standardization of the
stipend, and it is intimated to such persons as the Sheriff may
appoint.[2]   Although nothing is said as to inquiry this will presumably be necessary in some form in most cases.   The decision
of the Sheriff is in this case declared to be final unless an appeal
is taken to the Court of Session.[2]   Such an appeal will now fall to
be taken under the Rules of Court within twenty-one days of the
decision[3] and the ordinary rules in such appeals will apply.[4]   In
connexion with the valuation of teinds any heritor whose teinds are
wholly or partly unvalued, or the titular of any such teinds, or any
minister whose stipend comes wholly or partly from such teinds
or—if the benefice is vacant—the general trustees may, not later
than twelve months after the issue of the teind roll for the parish,
apply to the Sheriff to appoint a valuer to fix the annual agricultural value of the lands the teinds of which are unvalued.[5]   The
Sheriff is directed to make the appointment at his own hand,[5] and
provision is made for intimating the appointment to other parties
interested.[6]   The provisions as to removal of an arbiter and the
statement of a case under the Agricultural Holdings Acts[7] apply
in such valuations.[8]   The Sheriff may also be asked to appoint
an arbiter in connexion with the sale, feu, or disposal of a burgh
church[9] or a glebe.[10]

[1] 15 & 16 Geo. V c. 33, sec. 2 (1) (b), Schedule II B.
[2] Ibid., sec. 2 (2).
[3] Rules of Court, 1936, V, 7-12, which supersede 31 & 32 Vict. c. 96,
　 secs. 16-20.
[4] See p. 298, supra.
[5] 15 & 16 Geo. V c. 33, sec. 16, Schedule VI, 1.
[6] Ibid., Schedule VI, 2 (a).
[7] See p. 550, supra.
[8] 15 & 16 Geo. V c. 33, Schedule VI, 4.
[9] Ibid., sec. 22 (2) (h).
[10] Ibid., sec. 37.

In connexion with the transfer of rights in churches and
manses application to the Sheriff at the instance of the general
trustees to have repairs carried out by the heritors was competent
only within three years of the passing of the Act,[1] but any heritor
or the general trustees may apply to the Sheriff for a certificate
that all obligations on the heritors with respect to the church or
manse have been fulfilled.[2]   A statutory form of certificate is provided,[3] and this will be granted if the general trustees state or
admit that all the obligations on the heritors have been fulfilled,
or if the Sheriff is satisfied that any order or agreement as to
repairs has been implemented, or that no application for an order

was made within the three years above mentioned or that any
application for such an order was refused.[2] In cases where town
councils, or other bodies or persons, are liable along with or in
place of the heritors in obligations relating to a church or manse
the presbytery or the general trustees or any other person concerned may apply to the Sheriff to find and declare that the case
should be dealt with by the Scottish Ecclesiastical Commissioners.[4]
In any application under sec. 28 of the Act if a question arises as
to whether the church or manse to which the application relates is
the church or manse of a parish that question is to be determined by
the Sheriff in a summary manner and his determination is final.[5]

[1] 15 & 16 Geo. V c. 33, sec. 28 (1).
[2] Ibid., sec. 28 (2); Seafield Trustees v. General Trustees of Church of
   Scotland, 1928, 44 Sh.Ct.Rep. 189.
[3] Ibid., Schedule XI.
[4] Ibid., sec. 28 (4).
[5] Ibid., sec. 28 (5).

Where any annual sum is heritably secured in favour of a *quoad
sacra* parish and part of the subjects has been sold by the debtor,
he may, failing agreement between him and the creditor, apply to
the Sheriff of the county in which the subjects are situated to fix
the proportion of the annual sum which the debtor may allocate
on the subjects sold.[1] The powers of the Sheriff under a section
dealing with registration districts have been already noticed.[2]

[1] 15 & 16 Geo. V c. 33, sec. 35 (1).
[2] Ibid., sec. 43. See p. 556, supra.

All the above mentioned proceedings will normally be disposed
of by the Sheriff-Substitute. Although it is only so stated in one
instance,[1] it seems clear that the applications are intended to be
made to the Court within whose jurisdiction the subject matter of
the proceedings is situated. In applications relating to a special
method of calculating stipend appeal to the Court of Session only
is competent,[2] and in the incidental determination under sec. 28 of
whether a church or manse is the church or manse of a parish the
Sheriff's determination is final,[3] but in the other sections nothing is
laid down as to appeal. Applications which merely ask for the
appointment of a valuer or an arbiter[4] will generally be unopposed,
but even if contested it is thought that any appointment would not
be subject to review. The position as to appeal in the case of some
of the other applications is not too clear but it is thought that apart

from express provision in the Act the intention is that the judge
of first instance in the Sheriff Court should be final.[5]

1 15 & 16 Geo. V c. 33, sec. 35 (1).
2 Ibid., sec. 2 (2).
3 Ibid., sec. 28 (5).
4 Ibid., secs. 22 (2), 37, Schedule VI.
5 See p. 537, supra.

9. CLUBS.*

Under the Licensing (Scotland) Act of 1903, the Sheriff Court
became the registration authority for clubs. The Sheriff-clerk is
the statutory registrar,[1] and the Sheriff's powers include the granting,[2] renewing,[2] and cancelling[3] of club certificates. There is no
provision for endorsing an existing certificate to apply to new
premises.[4] The register of clubs is kept by the Sheriff-clerk of
each county and in practice applications in relation to certificates
are dealt with in the chief Court of the county even though the
club premises are situated within the jurisdiction of a district
Court. The proceedings may be taken before the Sheriff or the
Sheriff-Substitute and the jurisdiction of either is not excluded by
his being a member of the club. The decision of either is final.[5]

* See general observations, p. 532, et seq., supra.

1 3 Edw. VII c. 25, sec. 77.
2 Ibid., sec. 79.
3 Ibid., sec. 85.
4 Greenock Ex-Service Men's Club v. Town Council of Greenock, 1941,
   57 Sh.Ct.Rep. 123.
5 3 Edw. VII c. 25, sec. 88. See also sec. 103.

The procedure commences with the lodging with the Sheriff-
clerk of an application for registration or for renewal.[1] An
application for renewal must be made at least twenty-one days
before the expiry of the existing certificate.[1] Notice is given by the
Sheriff-clerk to (a) the chief officer of police; (b) the town council,
if the club premises are within a burgh; or (c) if not to the county
council.[2] These parties, or the procurator-fiscal or any person
owning or occupying property in the neighbourhood of the club,
are entitled to object to the granting or renewal of a certificate.[2]
There is no provision for intimation being made to the procurator-
fiscal or to neighbouring owners or occupiers but they have the
same right of objection as those parties who receive notice.[3]
Although no objection may be made, the Sheriff, before granting a
certificate, must be satisfied that the statutory formalities have
been observed, and that the club rules are in conformity with the

Statute.[2]   It has been held that the club must have existing premises.[4]

[1] 3 Edw. VII c. 25, sec. 78; 3 & 4 Geo. V c. 33, sec. 8; for form see Encyclopædia of Scottish Legal Styles, III, 13.
[2] Ibid., sec. 79; 3 & 4 Geo. V c. 33, sec. 8; 19 & 20 Geo. V c. 25, sec. 1 (1) (2) (d). As to challenge of certificate lodged with application, see Wellington Athletic Club v. Magistrates of Leith, 1904, 12 S.L.T. 570.
[3] Peeblesshire Social Club, 1922 S.L.T. (Sh.Ct.) 75; Edinburgh and District Motor Club, 1934, 50 Sh.Ct.Rep. 165.
[4] British Legion Club v. Burgh of Invergordon, 1936, 52 Sh.Ct.Rep. 295.

If objections are made, the objector must lodge his objections within twenty-one days of receiving notice from the Sheriff-clerk of an application having been made.[1]   He must at the same time send a copy of the objection to the secretary of the club.[1]   The procedure thereafter is in the discretion of the Sheriff.   He is required to hear parties, and he is entitled to order such inquiry as he thinks fit.[2]   Objection is competent only upon certain statutory grounds. These are both varied and numerous and they include the following : (a) that the club rules do not conform to the Statute; (b) that the club is not being conducted in good faith; (c) that the rules are not being observed; and (d) that the premises or situation are unsuitable.[3]

[1] 3 Edw. VII c. 25, sec. 79 (2); 3 & 4 Geo. V c. 33, sec. 8 (2); for form see Encyclopædia of Scottish Legal Styles, III, 15.
[2] Ibid., sec. 79 (3).
[3] Ibid., sec. 81; 3 & 4 Geo. V c. 33, sec. 8 (4).

The Sheriff has power to refuse to grant or to renew a certificate if objections are taken by a qualified person on one or other of the statutory grounds.[1]   The Sheriff may also cancel a certificate following upon a summary complaint made by a qualified objector or following upon a conviction as aftermentioned.   Such a complaint may be made to the Sheriff or a burgh magistrate for a finding that the club is being so conducted as to raise a ground of objection to renewal of the certificate.[2]   If such a finding is made or there is a conviction under sec. 84 of the Act— regarding supplying of liquor for outside consumption—a certified copy of the complaint and finding or conviction is transmitted to the Sheriff-clerk and laid before the Sheriff who may after such further inquiry as he thinks fit cancel the certificate subject to the club's right to apply for renewal at the time the certificate would have expired if there had been no cancellation.[2]   Expenses may be awarded by the Sheriff in contested applications for grant or renewal of a certificate[3] and in summary complaints[4], but not, it is thought, in proceedings for cancellation of a certificate.   When renewal is refused, or the certificate is cancelled, the Sheriff may make an order debarring the use of the premises as a club for a specified period.[5] Upon cause shown, the Sheriff may subsequently cancel or vary this closing order.[5]

[1] 3 Edw. VII c. 25, sec. 79; 3 & 4 Geo. V c. 33, sec. 8.
[2] Ibid., sec. 85.
[3] Ibid., sec. 79 (4).
[4] 3 & 4 Geo. V c. 33, sec. 8 (3).
[5] 3 Edw. VII c. 25, sec. 85 (3).

It is thought that the foregoing proceedings should be instituted by initial writ.[1] It has been held that the summary complaint referred to in the preceding paragraph may be in this form and that it may incorporate not merely a crave for a finding but also for an order cancelling the club's certificate, and also an order prohibiting the further use of the premises as a club.[1]

[1] Glasgow Corporation, &c. v. Railwaymen's Club, &c., 1915, 31 Sh.Ct.Rep. 220; for form of complaint see Encyclopædia of Scottish Legal Styles, III, 17.

10. COMPANIES.*

(1) *Liquidations.*

Where the amount of a company's share capital, paid up or credited as paid up, does not exceed £10,000 the Sheriff Court of the Sheriffdom in which the company's registered office is situated has concurrent jurisdiction with the Court of Session to wind up the company.[1] Registered office in this sense means the place which has longest been the registered office during the six months immediately preceding the presentation of the application for winding up.[2] When a company has passed a resolution for voluntary winding up, the Sheriff Court having jurisdiction as above may make an order to continue the voluntary winding up subject to the supervision of the Court.[3] The initial writ must contain certain prescribed particulars,[4] and may be presented by the company, a creditor or a contributory.[5] Unless it is summarily dismissed the application is intimated and served as directed by the Court, and it must be advertised once in the *Edinburgh Gazette*, and in one or two newspapers circulating in the district where the registered office is situated.[6] The advertisement must contain certain prescribed particulars and the Court may direct further advertisements than those above stated.[6] A provisional liquidator may be appointed on presentation of the application.[7] If a supervision order is granted the Court may appoint an additional liquidator,[8] and may also remove the

* See general observations, p. 532, et seq., supra.

liquidator and fill any vacancy.[8] There is no provision for a
caveat being lodged in a Sheriff Court application as there is
in the Court of Session,[9] but there seems no reason why a caveat
should not be competent in the Sheriff Court and it is understood
that in practice caveats are received.

[1] 19 & 20 Geo. V c. 23, sec. 166 (3).
[2] Ibid., sec. 166 (4).
[3] Ibid., secs. 256, 380 (1).
[4] Act of Sederunt, 20th March, 1930, secs. 2, 3; for form see Encyclo-
    pædia of Scottish Legal Styles, VI, 381.
[5] 19 & 20 Geo. V c. 23, sec. 170. See Miller v. Baxter & Co., 1931,
    48 Sh.Ct.Rep. 6; Coss & Morris v. Williams & Sons, 1931, 48
    Sh.Ct.Rep. 12; Wilson Harvey, 1934, 51 Sh.Ct.Rep. 15; Green &
    Sons v. Frasers, 1938, 55 Sh.Ct.Rep. 133.
[6] Act of Sederunt, 20th March, 1930, sec. 5.
[7] Ibid., sec. 6; 19 & 20 Geo. V c. 23, sec. 184 (3).
[8] 19 & 20 Geo. V c. 23, sec. 259.
[9] Rules of Court, 1936, IV, 15 (c).

If the original applicant withdraws, or does not proceed with
his application, another creditor or contributory may be sisted
in his place.[1] Answers to the application may be lodged by the
company or other interested parties such as creditors or the liquidator in a voluntary liquidation, and their opposition may be
confined to the appointment of any liquidator suggested in the
application.[2] At the hearing on the application and any answers
thereto the Court may dismiss the application, or adjourn it, or
make such other order as it thinks fit.[3] If a winding-up order
is made an official liquidator will usually be appointed at the
same time. Such an appointment is in the discretion of the Sheriff
and appeals against his interlocutor will be entertained only in
exceptional circumstances.[2] All orders for winding up by the
Court, or under supervision, or appointing a liquidator, must
be intimated to the Registrar of Companies and advertised in the
Edinburgh Gazette within a specified time and evidence of such
advertisement and intimation is lodged in process.[4] In appointing a liquidator in a winding up by the Court the Court fixes
the amount of caution to be found by the liquidator and provision
is made for such amount being limited to a specified sum either
at the time of appointment or on a separate note by the liquidator.[5]
Unless otherwise stated caution must be found within fourteen
days of the Court's interlocutor.[5]

[1] Rules of Court, 1936, IV, 18.
[2] Steel Scaffolding Co. v. Buckleys, 1935 S.C. 617. See also Jenkins v.
    Addie, 1932, 48 Sh.Ct.Rep. 129.
[3] 19 & 20 Geo. V c. 23, sec. 171.
[4] Rules of Court, 1936, IV, 19; 19 & 20 Geo. V c. 23, sec. 176.
[5] Rules of Court, 1936, IV, 20; 19 & 20 Geo. V c. 23, sec. 187 (1).

The Court of Session may in respect of the amount of the assets of any company remit to any Sheriff Court a petition for winding up presented to the Court of Session, or may require a Sheriff Court petition to be remitted to the Court of Session, and may also require any Sheriff Court petition to be remitted to another Sheriff Court.[1] A remit from the Court of Session to the Sheriff Court is competent only in cases where the capital of the company is such that the Sheriff Court could have dealt with a winding-up petition.[2] For the purpose of a remit from the Sheriff Court to the Court of Session, or from one Sheriff Court to another, a note is lodged in the Sheriff Court process by the liquidator, or by any creditor or contributory, asking transmission of the process to the Court of Session with a view to such remit, and this note may be lodged at any time after intimation, service and advertisement and the expiry of the induciæ.[3] Such note must contain a statement of the grounds on which a remit is applied for and, if a remit is asked to the Court of Session, it must include a statement of the company's assets.[4] On presentation of such a note the Sheriff-clerk forthwith transmits the process to the Petition Department of the Court of Session with the note and any report thereon which the Sheriff may think it expedient to make.[3] Apart from making any such report the Sheriff appears to take no part in these proceedings and the note is disposed of by the Court of Session, but the Sheriff may at his own hand order transmission of a winding up process if, after such hearing as he thinks proper, he considers that the process should be transmitted to the Court of Session or to another Sheriff Court.[5] The above provisions as to remits apply also to applications for winding up subject to the supervision of the Court.[6]

1 19 & 20 Geo. V c. 23, sec. 166 (3).
2 Chaney & Bull, 1930 S.C. 759.
3 Rules of Court, 1936, IV, 16 (b).
4 Ibid., IV, 16 (c).
5 Ibid., IV, 16 (d).
6 19 & 20 Geo. V c. 23, sec. 260; Rules of Court, 1936, IV, 16.

After a winding up application is presented, and before a winding up order is made, the company or any creditor or contributory may apply to the Court to restrain further proceedings in any action against the company,[1] and when a winding up order has been made, or a provisional liquidator has been appointed, no action may be commenced or proceeded with against the company except by leave of the Court and on such terms as the Court may impose.[2] These provisions apply also to any application for a supervision order,[3] and in a voluntary liquidation the liquidator may similarly apply to the Court to stay proceedings against the company.[4] Where the company is such that it may be wound up in the Sheriff Court that Court has concurrent jurisdiction with the Court of Session in connexion with the above applications,[5] but where proceedings are already depending—that is in cases other than a voluntary liquidation—the application will naturally be made in such proceedings.[6]

[1] 19 & 20 Geo. V c. 23, sec. 172.
[2] Ibid., sec. 177; as to expenses, see sec. 292.
[3] Ibid., secs. 257, 260.
[4] Ibid., sec. 253.
[5] Ibid., sec. 380 (1) (definition of " Court ").
[6] Rules of Court, 1936, IV, 29 (a).

In the course of proceedings for winding up, or for a super-vision order, the Sheriff may submit a stated case for the opinion of the Court of Session on any question of law.[1] This may be done either *ex proprio motu*, after such intimation and hearing as the Sheriff thinks necessary, or on application by any of the parties, and in either case before the Sheriff has decided the matter to which the question of law relates.[2] In the former case the Sheriff prepares the case and submits it to the parties to the dispute, who have to return the case within twenty-one days of its receipt with any additions, alterations or amendments.[2] Thereafter the Sheriff adjusts the case and the Sheriff-clerk transmits it to the General Department of the Court of Session.[2] If one of the parties desires a stated case he lodges a minute, prior to the decision of the Sheriff on the matter which is in question, stating the questions of law proposed to be put.[3] If the Sheriff considers that the questions do not arise on the facts admitted or proved, or that the application is frivolous, he may refuse to state a case, in which event he does not give any certificate of refusal.[3] The Sheriff-clerk forthwith intimates the application for a stated case to the other party or parties who may, within seven days of receipt of such intimation, lodge a minute with additional questions of law.[4] Within fourteen days of the Sheriff-clerk's intimation the Sheriff prepares the case and submits the draft to the parties, and within twenty-one days of its receipt the parties are required to return the draft to the Sheriff-clerk with any additions or alterations.[5] In preparing the case the Sheriff may include ques-tions proposed by both parties, and may add any questions he thinks necessary, and if parties do not agree as to the terms of the case the Sheriff adjusts these.[6] The case is in prescribed form and is signed by the Sheriff and delivered to the applicant or first applicant.[7] The Sheriff need not, unless he thinks it expedient to do so, append any note to the case.[8] The party receiving the case, within seven days of its receipt, gives written notice of his intention to proceed with it and sends a copy of the case to each of the other parties, and transmits the case to the General Department of the Court of Session with a certificate of intimation.[9] If the case is not transmitted the other party may apply to the Sheriff to dispose of the question at issue and to award him £2 2s. of expenses.[9] If in such circumstances both parties have applied for a case the other party may proceed with it.[9] In addition to this form of review by stated case there is a general right of appeal.[10]

[1] 19 & 20 Geo. V c. 23, secs. 166 (3) (c), 260 (2).
[2] Rules of Court, 1936, IV, 17.
[3] Ibid., IV, 17 (b); V, 28 (a).
[4] Ibid., V, 28 (b).
[5] Ibid., V, 28 (c).
[6] Ibid., V, 28 (c) (d).
[7] Ibid., V, 22 (b), 28 (e).
[8] Ibid., IV, 17 (b).
[9] Ibid., V, 28 (f).
[10] See below.

Where a winding up by the Court, or under the supervision of the Court, is proceeding in any Sheriff Court appeals against the liquidator's deliverances must be made to that Court by written note of appeal containing certain prescribed particulars which (unless by leave of the Court) must be lodged before the expiry of seven days after the deliverance.[1] An application to reverse or vary a liquidator's deliverance in a voluntary liquidation may be made by note of appeal lodged within the same time either to the Court of Session or to the Sheriff Court which would have jurisdiction to wind up the company.[1]

[1] Rules of Court, 1936, IV, 28. See Central Private Clinic, 1931, 48 Sh.Ct.Rep. 151.

In addition to review by stated case, already dealt with,[1] every order or decision of the Sheriff-Substitute in proceedings for winding up by the Court or under the supervision of the Court, and in applications to reverse or vary a liquidator's deliverance in a voluntary liquidation is open to appeal within fourteen days to the Sheriff or the Court of Session, and, in the former case, there is a further right of appeal from the Sheriff to the Court of Session also within fourteen days.[2] The appeals are made in the usual

form for appeals under the ordinary jurisdiction of the Court and
are subject to the same conditions.[3]

1 See p. 575, supra.
2 Rules of Court, 1936, IV, 31.
3 19 & 20 Geo. V c. 23, sec. 224 (1).

Provision is made for the removal of a liquidator on failure
to find caution, or to pay the annual premium on his bond, and
for other reasons, on application by note lodged in the process.[1]
Provision is also made for convening meetings of creditors and contributories[2] and for the appointment by the Court of a committee
of inspection to act with the liquidator.[3] In winding up by the
Court where a list of contributories has to be settled, the liquidator
applies by note on which intimation is ordered to each person on
the list[4]; and where calls are to be made he applies by note for
leave to do so.[5] In a winding up by the Court certain powers
may be exercised by the liquidator only with the sanction of the
Court, or of the committee of inspection, and any creditor or contributory may apply to the Court with respect to the exercise or
proposed exercise of such powers.[6] In a winding up by or subject
to the supervision of the Court the liquidator, on production of a
certified list of contributories, may obtain a decree against these
parties which can be extracted at once and is not subject to suspension except on caution or consignation save with special leave of
the Court.[7] Applications to the Court not otherwise provided for
are made by motion or by written note in the liquidation process
or, in a voluntary liquidation, by application similar to that for
winding up a company.[8]

1 Rules of Court, 1936, IV, 20 (e) (f), 21.
2 Ibid., IV, 22-24; 19 & 20 Geo. V c. 23, sec. 288.
3 19 & 20 Geo. V c. 23, sec. 198; for form see Encyclopædia of Scottish
  Legal Styles, VI, 382.
4 Rules of Court, 1936, IV, 25; 19 & 20 Geo. V c. 23, sec. 203.   See
  Glasgow Seating, 1934, 50 Sh.Ct.Rep. 295.
5 Rules of Court, 1936, IV, 26; 19 & 20 Geo. V c. 23, sec. 206; as to
  the position in the case of a supervision order, see sec. 260 (1).
6 19 & 20 Geo. V c. 23, sec. 191 (1) (3) (4) (5).
7 Ibid., sec. 222.   There is no right of appeal, see sec. 224 (4).
8 Rules of Court, IV, 29.   See British Legion Club, 1932, 48 Sh.Ct.Rep.
  188; Leon's Fabrics, 1932, 48 Sh.Ct.Rep. 190; Encyclopædia of
  Scottish Legal Styles, VI, 383.

When the affairs of a company have been completely wound up
the Court makes an order dissolving the company which order is,
within fourteen days, reported by the liquidator to the Registrar
of Companies.[1] The Court also directs as to the disposal of books
and papers.[2] Within two years of the dissolution the liquidator
or any interested party may apply to the Court—which is presum-

ably the Court that made the dissolution order—to declare the dissolution void.[3] If such an order is made an office copy must be sent to the Registrar of Companies by the applicant within seven days of the order or such other time as the Court may fix.[3]

[1] 19 & 20 Geo. V c. 23, sec. 221; for form see Encyclopædia of Scottish Legal Styles, VI, 384.
[2] Ibid., sec. 283.
[3] Ibid., sec. 294.

Certain powers for receiving evidence and conducting the examinations of witnesses and havers in connexion with the winding up of companies are conferred on Sheriffs by the Act.[1]

[1] 19 & 20 Geo. V c. 23, secs. 290, 291.

(2) *General.*

Apart from liquidation the Sheriff Court has now concurrent jurisdiction with the Court of Session in connexion with other applications under the Companies Act where the company is such that it could be wound up in the Sheriff Court.[1] Such applications are varied in their purpose, but the chief of them are : Alterations of a company's objects[2]; sanctioning the issuing of shares at a discount[3]; reduction of share capital[4]; variation of shareholders' rights[5]; rectification of share register[6]; reconstruction of the company by compromise with creditors or members[7]; various incidental applications following on a voluntary liquidation[8]; regulating the realization of heritage affected by heritable securities[9]; assessing damages against delinquent directors and others[10]; restoring to the register a company struck off as defunct.[11] In the Sheriff Court such applications will normally be instituted by initial writ in ordinary form.

[1] 19 & 20 Geo. V c. 23, sec. 166 (3), 380 (1).
[2] Ibid., sec. 5.
[3] Ibid., sec. 47; Rules of Court, 1936, IV, 32.
[4] Ibid., secs. 55-58; for form see Encyclopædia of Scottish Legal Styles, III, 378.
[5] Ibid., sec. 61.
[6] Ibid., sec. 100.
[7] Ibid., secs. 153-5.
[8] Ibid., secs. 236 (4), 239, 240, 243, 245 (4), 248 (1) (a), 249, 251 (2), 252.
[9] Ibid., sec. 270 (1) (c); 3 & 4 Geo. V c. 20, secs. 108-113.
[10] Ibid., sec. 276.
[11] Ibid., sec. 295 (6).

11. CONVEYANCING ACTS.*

Under sec. 39 of the Conveyancing Act of 1874 where a deed, instrument or writing has been signed by the granter and bears

to be attested by two subscribing witnesses, but contains some
informality of execution, proof to set up the deed may be led in
any action in which it is founded on, or objected to,[1] or in a special
application to the Court of Session, or to the Sheriff within whose
jurisdiction the defender in any such application resides, to have
it declared that the deed was subscribed by the granter and
witnesses.[2] Anyone interested in maintaining the invalidity of
the deed should be called as defender. Proof will be required even
though the application is not contested.[3]

* See general observations, p. 532, et seq., supra.

[1] See Farquharson v. Neish, 1909, 26 Sh.Ct.Rep. 139, as to using provision in commissary proceedings.
[2] 37 & 38 Vict. c. 94, sec. 39.
[3] See Richardson's Trustees, 1891, 18 R. 1131.

By sec. 23 (5) of the Conveyancing Act of 1924 a creditor infeft
in a ground annual, which is in arrear for two years together,
may raise an action of adjudication against the proprietor of the
subjects from which the ground annual is payable, and any other
persons interested therein whose rights are postponed to the pursuer's.[1] The crave is for adjudication of the subjects to the pursuer in the terms set forth in the sub-section.[1] Service is made
on the defenders, and the Court may order further intimation.[1]
If the application is unopposed decree may be granted in absence,
but in some Courts a remit is made to a solicitor to examine the
titles and report. The form of decree is provided by the Act,[2] and
an extract is recorded in the Register of Sasines with certain
statutory effects.[1] If the amount of the ground annual is less than
£2 10s. per annum the application must be made in the Sheriff
Court, and it has to be brought in the Court of the county in
which the land out of which it is payable, or any part of it, is
situated.[3]

[1] 14 & 15 Geo. V c. 27, sec. 23 (5).
[2] Ibid., Schedule K, Form No. 8.
[3] Ibid., sec. 23 (6).

By sec. 21 of the 1924 Act actions of serving to terce and of
kenning to terce are abolished, and new forms of procedure are
provided for declarator of a right of terce, declarator of the amount
of terce, and redemption of terce.[1] Such proceedings may be
raised in the Court of Session, or alternatively (if the lands in
question are wholly in one county or in two or more contiguous
counties) in the Sheriff Court where the lands or the greater part
of them lie.[2] Although the jurisdiction of the Sheriff is conditioned
by the situation of "land"[3] it seems too narrow a reading to

exclude that Court in applications under sec. 21 (2), with regard to terce out of heritable securities only, for the action can still be said to relate to the land on which these are secured. To establish her right to terce a widow may raise an action for declarator that she has a right of terce out of the items of her husband's estate from which she claims it.[4] Such items are specified, and the husband's heir-at-law and any other persons interested in the estate, whose rights may be affected by the claim, are called as defenders.[4] Decree of declarator in such an action gives the widow the same rights as if she had served to her terce.[4] If the action is not defended decree in absence may apparently be granted. Special provision is made for the case where the property subject to terce is in the personal occupation of the owner.[4] To the above declarator could be added a crave for payment of one third of the net revenue[5] but this would seem to have little practical effect, and the amount of the terce would fluctuate with any changes in income or deductions.

[1] 14 & 15 Geo. V c. 27, sec. 21.
[2] Ibid., sec. 21 (8).
[3] Ibid., sec. 2 (1) (a), 21 (8).
[4] Ibid., sec. 21 (2).
[5] See Encyclopædia of Scottish Legal Styles, VI, 247.

Under the next sub-section either the widow, or the proprietor, or any security holder,[1] postponed to the terce, may bring an action to declare the annual amount of the terce, and where this is so fixed it is not affected by any fluctuations of income or deductions.[2] The other parties interested in the subjects will be called as defenders and the Court is directed to inquire into the average free rental and deductions[3] for such period as it thinks fit and it may take into account prospective income and deductions for the presumptive period of the widow's life.[2] The sum to be determined is that which, one year with another, may be taken as the annual amount of the terce and the determination takes effect from the date of the decree, or from any succeeding term of Whitsunday or Martinmas to be named by the Court.[2] It seems clear that the latter part of sub-sec. (2) does not prevent the Court under this sub-section from inquiring into prospective future revenue where the owner is in personal occupation.[4]

[1] For definition see 14 & 15 Geo. V c. 27, sec. 21 (3) (f).
[2] Ibid., sec. 21 (3) (a).
[3] For definition see ibid., sec. 21 (6). See Brown's Trustees v. Brown, 1925 S.L.T. (Sh.Ct.) 146; Serra Largo v. Serra Largo's Trustees, (O.H.) 1933 S.L.T. 391; Thomson's Trustees v. Thomson, (O.H.) 1942 S.L.T. 22.
[4] As to incidental profits in such cases see M'Innes v. M'Innes, 1939, 56 Sh.Ct.Rep. 83.

Where the amount of terce is fixed as above the proprietor of the subjects or any security holder[1] postponed to the terce—but not the widow—may redeem the terce and may, either in the action above described or in a subsequent action, crave the Court to declare the capital sum to be paid in redemption, the method of fixing which is laid down in the Act.[2] If the subjects have been sold at what the Court is satisfied is a fair price the redemption price may not exceed one third of such sale price,[2] but this is a limit in favour of the owner and not an option to the widow. Sub-secs. 3 (a) and (b) (which provide for actions to fix the annual amount of terce and to determine the redemption price) refer expressly to " land " and do not appear to apply to terce due out of heritable securities.[3] Provisions generally corresponding to those above dealt with are made in connexion with lesser terce and a surviving husband's right to courtesy,[4] but in the case of courtesy proceedings are only competent in relation to redemption, and the redemption price is not limited by the amount of any price received on a sale of the subjects. The inquiries in connexion with fixing the amount of terce are to be made by proof even where the matter is not contested.[5] The Court may declare that there are no free rents and that the subjects are free and disburdened of terce or courtesy.[6] Where terce or courtesy is due from more than one property the defender may require the Court to fix the amount payable from each[7]; where the proprietor of the subjects is pursuer he already has this right in framing the crave of the writ.[8]

[1] Defined 14 & 15 Geo. V c. 27, sec. 21 (3) (f).
[2] Ibid., sec. 21 (3) (b).
[3] See ibid., sec. 2 (1) (a); 37 & 38 Vict. c. 94, sec. 3, and contrast with 14 & 15 Geo. V c. 27, sec. 21 (2) and (4) (a) and (b).
[4] Ibid., sec. 21 (3) (a) (b) (c) and (d).
[5] Dickson v. Dickson, (O.H.) 1931 S.L.T. 75.
[6] 14 & 15 Geo. V c. 27, sec. 21 (3) (g). See M'Innes v. M'Innes, 1939, 56 Sh.Ct.Rep. 83.
[7] Ibid., sec. 21 (7).
[8] See Thomson's Trustees v. Thomson, (O.H.) 1942 S.L.T. 22.

On consignation in the hands of the Clerk of Court, on or before a date to be fixed by the Court, of the redemption price of terce or courtesy as ascertained by the Court, the Court may declare the subjects to be free and disburdened of the terce or courtesy[1] and an extract of the decree may be recorded in the Register of Sasines.[2] As to expenses, see the case noted.[3]

[1] 14 & 15 Geo. V c. 27, sec. 21 (3) (e).
[2] Ibid., sec. 21 (9).
[3] Serra Largo v. Serra Largo's Trustees, (O.H.) 1933 S.L.T. 391.

The Sheriff's jurisdiction in relation to the commutation of carriages and services due to a superior[1] has fallen with the extinction of these exactions.[2]

[1] 37 & 38 Vict. c. 94, sec. 20.
[2] 14 & 15 Geo. V c. 27, sec. 12 (7).

In proceedings under the Conveyancing Acts the ordinary rules as to appeal[1] appear to apply.

[1] See p. 298, supra.

12. CUSTODY OF CHILDREN.

(1) *Custody Orders.*

At common law the Sheriff Court had jurisdiction only in regard to interim orders for custody. Now the jurisdiction is extended to cover actions for regulating the custody of children,[1] which is held to include actions for permanent as distinguished from temporary custody.[2] But in such actions the Sheriff may remit the cause to the Court of Session at any stage and that either *ex proprio motu* or on cause shown.[3] It has been indicated that in cases of delicacy the Sheriff should exercise his power to remit, and that a remit should be made in all cases where it becomes clear that a question arises under the Custody of Children Act of 1891.[4] That Act qualified a parent's abstract right to custody and entrusted the Court of Session with a discretion (a) to refuse custody if the parent's conduct made him an unsuitable guardian; (b) to make it a condition of granting the custody of a child to its parent that the costs of the upbringing of the child should be paid; (c) to refuse a parent custody where a child has been abandoned or deserted, or has been brought up by another person, or by the parochial authorities; (d) to order, when refusing custody, that a child should be educated in the parent's religion.[5] For the purposes of this Statute, " parent " includes any person or institution liable at law to maintain a child, or entitled to the custody.[6] Orders as to custody, maintenance and access may now be made in relation to a child up to the age of sixteen.[7] In such a case service should be made on the child who has attained minority.[8] If an order for custody does not fall within the common law jurisdiction of the Sheriff the proceedings must apparently be brought in the Sheriff Court, within whose territory the defender resides.[9]

[1] 7 Edw. VII c. 51, sec. 5 (2).
[2] Murray v. Forsyth, 1917 S.C. 721.
[3] 7 Edw. VII c. 51, sec. 5.

4 Murray v. Forsyth, supra, Lord Skerrington, p. 725; Kitson v. Kitson, 1945 S.C. 434. See Shannon v. Gowans, &c., 1921, 37 Sh.Ct.Rep. 235; Dawkins v. Muir, 1922, 39 Sh.Ct.Rep. 45; Raeburn v. Dunleavy, 1934, 50 Sh.Ct.Rep. 107.
5 54 & 55 Vict. c. 3, secs. 1-4.
6 Ibid., sec. 5.
7 2 & 3 Geo. VI c. 4, sec. 1.
8 Morrison, 1943 S.C. 481.
9 Kitson v. Kitson, supra.

(2) *Guardianship.*

The Sheriff Court is, under the Guardianship of Infants Acts of 1886 and 1925, entrusted with certain powers for regulating the care and upbringing of children. The Sheriff Court, which has jurisdiction under this Statute, is the Court within whose jurisdiction the defender, or any one of several defenders, resides,[1] and other grounds of jurisdiction under the Sheriff Courts Act are not available.[2] The Sheriff's powers include (a) nominating guardians[3]; (b) settling differences amongst guardians[4]; (c) regulating the custody of and access to children where a guardian is appointed.[5] Although he has power to appoint, the Sheriff has not power to remove, guardians.[6]

1 49 & 50 Vict. c. 27, sec. 9.
2 Kitson v. Kitson, 1945 S.C. 434.
3 15 & 16 Geo. V c. 45, sec. 4.
4 Ibid., sec. 6.
5 49 & 50 Vict. c. 27, sec. 5; 15 & 16 Geo. V c. 45, secs. 3, 5; 18 & 19 Geo. V c. 26, sec. 16.
6 49 & 50 Vict. c. 27, sec. 6.

(3) *Form of Action.*

There is no statutory direction that procedure under these various Statutes is to be summary, and applications under them will take the form, and follow the course of, ordinary actions.[1] Reference has already been made to the Sheriff's power to remit to the Court of Session in custody applications.[2] In applications under the Guardianship of Infants Acts any party may require the proceedings to be removed to the Court of Session at the closing of the record or within six days thereafter,[3] and any orders made in the Sheriff Court may be appealed to the Court of Session.[4] This last provision does not, it is thought, preclude an appeal from the Sheriff-Substitute to the Sheriff[5]—when it would be otherwise competent—and the time limit and form of appeal in either case will be as in an ordinary action. In the case of custody applications the ordinary rules in regard to appeals will apply.

1 For forms see Encyclopædia of Scottish Legal Styles, II, 408-9.
3 See p. 582, supra.
3 49 & 50 Vict. c. 27, sec. 10; 7 Edw. VII c. 51, sec. 5.
4 Ibid., sec. 10.
5 See Kitson v. Kitson, 1945 S.C. 434.

13. EDUCATION ACT.*

Any parent—which includes a guardian, and any person liable to maintain, or having the actual custody of, a child—aggrieved by the making or amending of an attendance order by the education authority may, within fourteen days after a copy of the order was served on him, appeal to the Sheriff, who may confirm, vary or annul the order.[1] The writ should crave the annulment or variation of the order, and call the education authority as defenders. Defences may be ordered, and the case disposed of after a hearing or proof if such procedure seems necessary. The matter could be dealt with by either the Sheriff or the Sheriff-Substitute, and the decision of either is final.[2] A similar right of appeal is given to a parent aggrieved by the refusal of, or the failure to deal with, an application for the modification or revocation of an attendance order in respect the child should be educated elsewhere than in the school named in the order. It is not clear that the time limit of fourteen days applies in such an appeal.[3]

* See general observations, p. 532, et seq., supra.

1 9 & 10 Geo. VI c. 72, sec. 36 (4) (5). See also Farquhar v. Aberdeen School Board, 1918, 34 Sh.Ct.Rep. 217; Frater v. Linlithgow Education Authority, &c., 1923, 39 Sh.Ct.Rep. 262; Weir v. Kirkcaldy 'School Management Committee, 1935, 51 Sh.Ct.Rep. 273; Birnie v. Aberdeen Education Committee, 1937, 53 Sh.Ct.Rep. 221; and see similar right of appeal under sec. 55 (4) of the Act.
2 Ibid., Bannon v. Dunbarton County Council, 1934, 50 Sh.Ct.Rep. 301.
3 Ibid., sec. 36 (6).

14. EMPLOYERS' LIABILITY.

(1) Action.

The Employers' Liability Act, 1880, introduced a statutory kind of action, which can competently be raised only in the Sheriff Court.[1] In many cases the action is raised with an alternative crave at common law, but even in this alternative form the action must be brought in the Sheriff Court. Originally it was competent for either party to require cases under the Act to be removed to the Court of Session[1] but this privilege was abolished by the Workmen's Compensation Act of 1906.[2] The latter provision is itself

repealed[3] and the position is now regulated by the Sheriff Courts
Act.   In actions under the Employers' Liability Act, or at common
law, or alternatively under the Act and at common law, if the
claim exceeds £50 either party may apply for a jury trial in the
Sheriff Court[4] and such actions are excluded from those which
may be removed to the Court of Session for jury trial.[5] Where a
proof and not a jury trial is allowed in the Sheriff Court the
ordinary rules as to appeals apply.   An action laid under the
Employers' Liability Act may be conjoined with another action or
actions arising out of the same occurrence, or cause of action,
although such actions may be at the instance of different parties
and in respect of different injuries.[1]

[1] 43 & 44 Vict. c. 42, sec. 6.
[2] 6 Edw. VII c. 58, sec. 14.
[3] 13 & 14 Geo. V c. 42, sec. 24 (10).
[4] 7 Edw. VII c. 51, sec. 31.   See p. 339, et seq., supra.
[5] Ibid., sec. 30.   See p. 305, supra.

(2) *Notice.*

An action laid under this Statute is not competent unless notice
has been given within six weeks, to the employer, that the workman
(whose name and address must be stated) has sustained injury, the
date and cause of which must be set forth.[1]   Such notice may be
delivered to the employer or at his residence or place of business,
or it may be sent by post in a registered letter addressed to the
employer at his last known place of residence or place of business.[2]
Postal service is deemed to take place when the letter would be
delivered in the ordinary course of post, and proof of the addressing and registering of the notice is sufficient.[2]   If the employer is
a body of persons, corporate or unincorporate, the notice may be
given at any office of the body.[2]   A defect or inaccuracy in the
notice is not fatal, unless the Sheriff is of opinion that the employer
has been prejudiced in his defence and that the defect or inaccuracy
was for the purpose of misleading.[2]   In case of death, failure to
give notice does not bar the action, if the Sheriff is of opinion
that there was reasonable excuse for the omission.[3]

[1] 43 & 44 Vict. c. 42, secs. 4, 7.
[2] Ibid., sec. 7.
[3] Ibid., sec. 4.

The notice must be written and not merely oral[1] and the
statutory requirement of timeous notice and of reasonable excuse for
its omission in fatal cases has usually been strictly enforced,[2]
although more latitude has been allowed in regard to the form and
contents of the notice.[3]   The question of prejudice through defect

in the notice ought to be dealt with as a preliminary point and this is not a matter which can be put to the jury at the trial.[4] A wrongly addressed notice may be held good on proof or admission of its receipt[5] and when notice was delivered to a head official at one of a limited company's offices it was held that this was sufficient.[6]

[1] Moyle v. Jenkins, [1881] 8 Q.B.D. 116.
[2] Keen v. Millwall Dock Co., [1882] 8 Q.B.D. 482; M'Donagh v. P. & W. MacLellan, 1886, 13 R. 1000; Connolly v. Young's Paraffin Oil Co., 1894, 22 R. 80; MacFadyen v. Dalmellington Iron Co., 1897, 24 R. 327.
[3] Stone v. Hyde, [1882] 9 Q.B.D. 76; Carter v. Drysdale, [1883] 12 Q.B.D. 91; Thomson v. Robertson & Co., 1884, 12 R. 121; cf. Thomson v. Baird & Co., 1903, 6 F. 142.
[4] Duncan v. Fife Coal Co., 1905, 7 F. 958; cf. Trail v. Kelman & Co., 1887, 15 R. 4.
[5] M'Govan v. Tancred Arrol & Co., 1886, 13 R. 1033.
[6] Duncan v. Fife Coal Co., supra.

An action is not timeously brought under this Statute unless it is commenced within six months after the occurrence of the accident which caused the injury, or in the case of death within twelve months from the time of death.[1] This is not a condition which the parties, or the Sheriff, can waive.[2]

[1] 43 & 44 Vict. c. 42, sec. 4.
[2] Johnston v. Shaw. (O.H.) 1883, 21 S.L.R. 246; Clark v. Adams, 1885, 12 R. 1092.

(3) Assessor.

In actions under this Statute it is competent to call in one or more assessors, where the case is tried before the Sheriff without a jury.[1] A medical assessor is what is contemplated by the Act as he is appointed for the purpose of ascertaining the amount of compensation.[1] The power to call in an assessor skilled in machinery, to help in ascertaining whether there was a defect in an employer's plant, or negligence on the part of his servants is not provided for. In practice assessors are seldom called in.

[1] 43 & 44 Vict. c. 42, sec. 6 (2).

15. ENTAILS.*

(1) Jurisdiction.

Under various entail Statutes the Sheriff Court has in some matters a concurrent jurisdiction with the Court of Session, and under the 1914 Act it alone can authorize the granting of a feu

* See general observations, p. 532, et seq., supra.

where the next heir's consent is refused or not available.[1] Applications are brought in the Sheriff Court of the district where the lands proposed to be affected are situated.[2] The Sheriff has power to grant authority (a) to grant feus or leases[3] ; (b) to excamb[4] ; (c) to charge the entailed estate with improvement expenditure.[5]

[1] 4 & 5 Geo. V c. 43, sec. 4 (a).
[2] 10 Geo. III c. 51, secs. 11, 26; 31 & 32 Vict. c. 84, sec. 4; 45 & 46 Vict. c. 53, sec. 5; 4 & 5 Geo. V c. 43, sec. 4 (a).
[3] 3 & 4 Vict. c. 48, sec. 1; 31 & 32 Vict. c. 84, sec. 4; 45 & 46 Vict. c. 53, secs. 5, 6; 4 & 5 Geo. V c. 43, sec. 4 (a).
[4] 10 Geo. III c. 51, sec. 33.
[5] 45 & 46 Vict. c. 53, sec. 5.

(2) *Procedure.*

An application under the Entail Acts is brought at the instance of the heir of entail in possession. If the application has to be made by a tutor, curator, or legal guardian the proceedings appear to be competent only in the Court of Session.[1] The application must be intimated to the next heir of entail in such manner as the Sheriff may direct.[2] In practice the next heir will be called as defender and service will be made on him in the usual way. If he is under age or *incapax* a curator *ad litem* will be appointed.[2] Advertisement in the *Edinburgh Gazette*, or in the public press, may in some cases be appropriate. Inquiry must be made, whether the application is opposed or not, and in practice a remit is made to a man of skill to report.[2] If an application is to be opposed defences can be lodged in the ordinary way.[3]

[1] See 38 & 39 Vict. c. 61, sec. 12; 45 & 46 Vict. c. 53, sec. 11.
[2] 31 & 32 Vict. c. 84, sec. 4; 45 & 46 Vict. c. 53, sec. 5.
[3] Pringle, 1889, 5 Sh.Ct.Rep. 408.

The procedure above outlined applies to entail applications in general, and those for authority to grant feus or leases and to borrow and charge for improvement expenditure under the Entail Amendment Acts of 1875 and 1878, are all assimilated in relation to procedure in the Sheriff Court.[1] The cost of improvement expenditure may be constituted in the Sheriff Court under the Montgomery Act of 1770[2] though this course is not often resorted to, and that Act also regulates the procedure by which authority to excamb may be obtained in the Sheriff Court.[3] In the latter case the Sheriff is directed to appoint two or more men of skill to inspect and adjust the value of the lands to be excambed, and on their settling the marches and reporting on oath that the exchange is just and equal, the Sheriff authorises the excambion.[3] In the Act of 1914 the only procedural direction in regard to the application for power to feu is that it is to be intimated to the nearest heir who is entitled to appear and object.[4]

[1] 45 & 46 Vict. c. 53, sec. 5.
[2] 10 Geo. III c. 51, sec. 26.
[3] Ibid., sec. 33—applications under later Acts are competent only in the Court of Session.
[4] 4 & 5 Geo. V c. 43, sec. 4 (a).

(3) *Appeal.*

In the case of applications for authority to borrow and charge under the Entail Amendment Acts of 1875 and 1878, applications for authority to grant leases, and applications for authority to feu under the Entail Amendment Act of 1868 appeals from the Sheriff-Substitute to the Sheriff are excluded[1] and this exclusion is not affected by the Sheriff Courts Act.[2] Appeal to the Court of Session from the judgment of the Sheriff-Substitute in such applications is competent within six months of the date of the decree[1] and is taken by note of appeal in ordinary form.[3] In the case of applications for authority to excamb under the Montgomery Act of 1770[4] and in applications for power to feu under the Act of 1914[5] no special provisions as to appeal are made and in such applications the ordinary rights of appeal would appear to apply.

[1] 31 & 32 Vict. c. 84, sec. 4; 45 & 46 Vict. c. 53, sec. 5.
[2] 7 Edw. VII c. 51, sec. 28 (2).
[3] Rules of Court, 1936, V, 7, 8. See p. 301, supra.
[4] 10 Geo. III c. 51, sec. 33.
[5] 4 & 5 Geo. V c. 43, sec. 4 (a).

16. FINANCE ACT, 1916.*

Under sec. 66 of this Act any order or decree of any Court in the United Kingdom, whereby the right to transfer, or call for a transfer of, any Government Stock, or to receive any dividends thereon, is expressed to be vested in any person, is declared to be sufficient authority to the appropriate bank or other authority to allow the transfer, or pay the dividends, as stated in the order or decree.[1] It is understood that this section can be used in cases where a transfer by (say) a certain number of trustees would be accepted in Scotland but will not be taken by the Bank of England, and an application is made to the Sheriff to grant warrant to the trustees in question to transfer the stock. Such an application will normally be granted *de plano* when the right to transfer is clear.

* See general observations, p. 532, et seq., supra.
[1] 6 & 7 Geo. V c. 24, sec. 66.

17. FINANCE APPEALS.*

(1) *Estate Duty.*

Under the Finance Act of 1894 any person aggrieved by the decision of the commissioners of Inland Revenue with respect to repayment of excess estate duty, or the amount of such duty claimed by the commissioners, has a right of appeal to the Court of Session.[1] But, when the value of the property as alleged by the commissioners in respect of which a dispute arises does not exceed £10,000, the Sheriff Court has a concurrent appellate jurisdiction.[1] The appeal, if taken in the Sheriff Court, is brought in the Court of the district (a) where the appellant resides; or (b) where the property is situated.[1]

* See general observations, p. 532, et seq., supra.

[1] 57 & 58 Vict. c. 30, secs. 10, 23.

Within a month from the date of notification by the commissioners of a decision or claim, an appellant may deliver to the commissioners a written appeal containing a statement of the grounds of appeal, incorporating certain prescribed particulars.[1] Within a month of the receipt of such appeal, the commissioners must notify the appellant or his solicitor whether they withdraw their decision or claim, or are to maintain it in whole or in part.[2] Within a month of the date of this notification, the appellant may present in the Sheriff Court an application, narrating the claim or decision of the commissioners which is complained against, and crave the Court to make the necessary order to give effect to his contentions.[3] Service is made upon the commissioners, or upon the solicitor of Inland Revenue on their behalf, and the Sheriff may appoint answers to be lodged.[3] The Sheriff hears parties, with or without answers, and thereafter he may give decree granting or refusing the crave, or he may take such other course in regard thereto as to him may seem proper.[3] While the Rules of Court refer to a petition and answers the application should be in the form of an initial writ and the commissioners will be called as defenders.[4] The application may not contain any ground of appeal not included in the original statement, but the Court may allow amendment on such terms as it may think right.[5] The proceedings are summary and the ordinary rules of procedure in the Sheriff Court apply.[6] There is an appeal from the Sheriff-Substitute to the Sheriff[7] and from either to the Court of Session.[8] In either case the ordinary procedure in regard to appeals applies,[6] but in the case of an appeal from the Sheriff-Substitute or the Sheriff to the Court of Session leave must apparently be got in the Sheriff Court.[9]

[1] Rules of Court, 1936, V, 20 (a).
[2] Ibid., V, 20 (b).
[3] Ibid., V, 20 (c).
[4] See form in Encyclopædia of Scottish Legal Styles, I, 222.
[5] Rules of Court, 1936, V, 20 (d).
[6] Ibid., V, 20 (g).
[7] Wylie v. Commissioners of Inland Revenue, 1918, 34 Sh.Ct.Rep. 178.
[8] 57 & 58 Vict. c. 30, sec. 10 (5); 59 & 60 Vict. c. 28, sec. 22.
[9] 57 & 58 Vict. c. 30, sec. 10 (2) (5). See Wylie v. Commissioners of Inland Revenue, supra.

In general, the duties, as assessed by the commissioners, must be paid, notwithstanding an appeal, but the Court has power to allow an appeal without payment, or on part payment only, of the duty, if an application is made within fourteen days of the date of notification by the commissioners that they maintain their claim or decision.[1] The rules direct that the application is to be by note to the Sheriff specifying the grounds of the application[2] but it is probably not incompetent to include a crave to dispense with present payment of the duty in the principal appeal application. The Sheriff is bound to afford the commissioners an opportunity of being heard, but the proceedings are summary.[2] If the application for leave is by separate note the appeal application must be made within ten days of the interlocutor disposing of the preliminary application.[3]

[1] 57 & 58 Vict. c. 30, sec. 10 (4) (5); Rules of Court, 1936, V, 20 (e).
[2] Rules of Court, V, 20 (e).
[3] Ibid., V, 20 (c).

(2) Other Duties.

The Finance Act, 1910,[1] created certain duties on land, viz. : increment value duty, reversion duty, undeveloped land duty and mineral rights duty. These have all been repealed with the exception of mineral rights duty.[2] Certain rights of appeal to the Court of Session are provided and also a right of appeal to the Sheriff Court, but as the latter right of appeal is concerned only with the duties now repealed the Sheriff Court does not now appear to have any function under the Act.[3]

[1] 10 Edw. VII c. 8, Part I.
[2] 10 & 11 Geo. V c. 18, sec. 57.
[3] 10 Edw. VII c. 8, sec. 33

18. Firearms Act, 1937.*

Under this Act any person aggrieved by the refusal to grant, vary or renew a firearms certificate, or by the revocation of such a certificate, may appeal to the Sheriff within whose jurisdiction he resides,[1] and any person aggrieved by the refusal to register him as a firearms dealer, or by the removal of his name from the register,[2] or the refusal to register a place of business, or its removal from the register,[3] may appeal to the Sheriff within whose jurisdiction his place of business is situated. Such appeals are directed to be made by initial writ under the Sheriff Courts Acts and the proceedings are to be as laid down in these Acts.[4] No time for appeal is apparently prescribed. The writ should ask the Court to reverse the decision complained of, and to find the applicant entitled to a certificate or to direct the chief constable to grant the certificate, or as the case may be. The chief officer of police will be called as defender and defences may be ordered and the appeal disposed of after debate or proof as may be necessary—the procedure being that of a summary application.[5] Certain persons convicted of crime are not entitled to possess a firearm, but they may apply to the Sheriff within whose jurisdiction they reside for the removal of the statutory prohibition.[6] Not less than twenty-one days' notice of the appeal must be given to the chief officer of police for the area in which the applicant resides.[6] This presumably means notice given before the application is presented. Otherwise the procedure suggested is as above. The rules of procedure for England provide for expenses being awarded against the applicant but not against the police and this provision has been taken into account in Scotland,[5] though it is not operative here. It might be thought that the decision of the Sheriff is intended to be final, although the reference to proceedings being as laid down in the Sheriff Court Acts may suggest that the ordinary rules as to appeal should apply.

* See general observations, p. 532, et seq., supra.
[1] 1 Edw. VIII & 1 Geo. VI c. 12, sec. 2 (8).
[2] Ibid., sec. 8 (5).
[3] Ibid., sec. 10 (4).
[4] Act of Sederunt, 11th June, 1937.
[5] See Todd v. Neilans, 1940 S.L.T. (Sh.Ct.) 12; Anderson v. Neilans, 1940 S.L.T. (Sh.Ct.) 13.
[6] 1 Edw. VIII & 1 Geo. VI c. 12, sec. 21 (3).

19. Friendly Societies.*

(1) General.

A leading principle in legislation affecting friendly societies is that disputes, failing adjustment by the parties interested, are to

* See general observations, p. 532, et seq., supra.

be settled by arbitration. The rules of such societies generally prescribe the manner in which disputes are to be settled, but in some circumstances resort may be had to a Court of law.

(2) *Industrial Societies.*

Under the Industrial and Provident Societies Act of 1893 disputes between the society, or an officer thereof, and a member or past member or person claiming through such parties, or claiming under the society's rules, are decided as provided by the rules, and application may be made to the Sheriff Court to enforce the decision.[1] A determination of the assistant registrar may be enforced in the same way.[2] Where under the rules a dispute is cognizable by a Court of summary jurisdiction the parties may refer the dispute to the Sheriff Court, and, where the rules contain no direction as to disputes or where no decision is made on a dispute within forty days after application to the society for a reference under its rules, the member or person aggrieved may apply to the Sheriff Court to hear and determine the dispute.[3] It appears to be the result of the statutory provisions that there is a right of appeal from the Sheriff-Substitute to the Sheriff[4] but that there is no appeal in the ordinary way to the Court of Session. Either party, however, may request a case on any question of law for the opinion of the Court of Session.[5] The Court is not compelled to state such a case,[5] and if it is to do so the case must be stated prior to judgment in the Sheriff Court.[6] This restricted right of appeal appears to apply where the dispute is determined by the Court, and an application to enforce an award by the assistant registrar or other referee is subject to the ordinary right of appeal.[7] The Court has refused legal effect to an order to reinstate a member on the ground that a decree conform in such a case would not be enforceable.[8] Where a dispute is dealt with in the Small Debt Court there is an appeal by stated case as above and not under the Small Debt Acts.[9] The Sheriff may have jurisdiction at common law where a dispute is not within the terms of the Statute,[10] and where an English society had not registered its rules in Scotland it was held that it could not insist upon arbitration in terms of the rules.[11]

1 56 & 57 Vict. c. 39, secs. 49 (1), 79.

2 Ibid., sec. 49 (2).

3 Ibid., secs. 49 (4) (5), 79. For style see Encyclopædia of Scottish Legal Styles, IX, 41.

4 See First Edinburgh Starr-Bowkett Building Society v. Munro, 1883, 11 R. 5; Glasgow Corporation v. Mickel, 1922 S.C. 228; cf. Greig v. City of Glasgow Friendly Society, 1939 S.L.T. (Sh.Ct.) 31.

[5] 56 & 57 Vict. c. 39, sec. 49 (6); Rules of Court, 1936, V, 22-24.
[6] Smith v. Scottish Legal Life Assurance Society, 1912 S.C. 611.
[7] See Glasgow District of Order of Foresters v. Stevenson, 1899, 2 F.
      14; Collins v. Barrowfield United Oddfellows, 1915 S.C. 190.
[8] Gall v. Loyal Glenbogie Lodge of Oddfellows Friendly Society, 1900,
      2 F. 1187; cf. Collins v. Barrowfield United Oddfellows, supra.
[9] Linton v. City of Glasgow Friendly Society, 1895, 23 R. 51.
[10] Galashiels Provident Building Society v. Newlands, 1893, 20 R. 821;
      M'Gowan v. City of Glasgow Friendly Society, 1913 S.C. 991;
      Gow v. Portobello Co-operative Society, 1926, 43 Sh.Ct.Rep. 127.
[11] Conway v. Ideal Benefit Society, 1918, 35 Sh.Ct.Rep. 29.

A society may sue a member for a debt either in the Sheriff Court of the district where the registered office of the society is situated, or in that of the district where such member resides.[1] Privileges are granted to certain forms of documentary evidence as in the case of friendly societies.[2]

[1] 56 & 57 Vict. c. 39, sec. 23.   This privilege extends to an action by
      the liquidator of a society; Glasgow Working Men's Building
      Society v. Kirkwood, 1888, 4 Sh.Ct.Rep. 165.
[2] Ibid., sec. 75.   See next page.

The Sheriff Court alone has jurisdiction in all proceedings for winding up an industrial society in Scotland.[1] The provisions of the Companies Act are applied to such a winding up[2] and the forms and procedure in company liquidations should be followed.[3]

[1] 58 & 59 Vict. c. 30, sec. 2.
[2] 56 & 57 Vict. c. 39, sec. 58 (a).
[3] See p. 572, et seq., supra.

(3) *Friendly Societies.*

Under the Friendly Societies Acts, 1896 and 1908, disputes may be settled in the same way as those under the Industrial and Provident Societies Act.[1] The disputes are those arising between the parties specified in that Act and also between a society and any branch, an officer of a branch and the society or branch and any two or more branches or any officers thereof.[1] Reference is made to what has been written above in regard to the settlement of disputes in industrial societies and on the rights of appeal.[2]

[1] 59 & 60 Vict. c. 25, sec. 68; 8 Edw. VII c. 32, sec. 6.
[2] See previous page.

Application may be made to the Sheriff Court on failure by an officer of a society to account for money or to deliver property.[1] An order of the Sheriff Court is final, which seems to imply that an appeal from Sheriff-Substitute to Sheriff is not excluded.[2] Proceedings may also be taken against such an officer in the form of a criminal complaint for withholding or misapplying property, and a fine may be imposed, and the officer ordered to deliver property or repay money and in default of such delivery or repayment, or payment of the fine, imprisonment may be imposed.[3] It was later provided, however, that if it is not proved that the respondent acted with fraudulent intent a conviction is not to follow; but he may be ordered to deliver property or pay money and be found liable in expenses, and such order is enforceable as an order for payment of a civil debt recoverable before a Court of summary jurisdiction.[4] Such an order made in connexion with a criminal complaint is apparently open to review by stated case on a question of law.[5]

[1] 59 & 60 Vict. c. 25, secs. 55, 102.
[2] See First Edinburgh Starr-Bowkett Building Society v. Munro, 1883, 11 R. 5.
[3] 59 & 60 Vict. c. 25, sec. 87 (3).
[4] 8 Edw. VII c. 32, sec. 9.
[5] 59 & 60 Vict. c. 25, sec. 93; cf. sec. 55 (2).

A member of a registered friendly society, or a person claiming through him, may sue either the society or its trustees or any officer or person who receives contributions or issues policies on behalf of the society or branch within the jurisdiction of the Court in which the action is brought with the addition of the words " on behalf of the society or branch " (naming the same).[1] A society with officers in all parts of Scotland accordingly appears liable to be sued by a member in any Sheriff Court within whose jurisdiction any of its collecting agents has a place of business. Such an action has also this service privilege—it may be served (a) personally on the above mentioned officer or person; (b) by leaving a copy of the writ at the registered office of the society or branch, or at any place of business of the society or branch within the jurisdiction of the Court in which the action is brought; or (c) if such office or place of business is closed, by fixing the service copy of the writ upon the outer door.[2] If the writ is not served personally, or by leaving a copy at the registered office, a copy writ must also be sent, by registered letter, to the committee at the registered office of the society or branch, posted at least six days before any further step in the process is taken.[2]

[1] 59 & 60 Vict. c. 25, sec. 94 (1) (2).
[2] Ibid., sec. 94 (4) (5).

In friendly society actions, certain statutory privileges are accorded to some documentary evidence. A document bearing the seal or stamp of the central office (that is the office of the chief registrar and assistant registrar for England)[1] is received in evidence without further proof[2]; and a document bearing to be signed by the chief or any assistant registrar or any inspector or public auditor or valuer under the Act is received in evidence without proof of the signature, unless there is evidence to the contrary.[2]

[1] 59 & 60 Vict. c. 25, sec. 1.
[2] Ibid., sec. 100.

20. HERITABLE SECURITIES.

(1) *Jurisdiction.*

The Heritable Securities (Scotland) Act of 1894 materially extended the powers of a heritable creditor in dealing with the security subjects. Proceedings under the Act are competent in the Sheriff Court of the county where the security subjects are situated, or, if they lie in different counties, then in the Court of either county.[1] The Sheriff has jurisdiction irrespective of the value of the lands.[2] The alterations made by the Act on the procedure in an action of maills and duties have been already considered.[3]

[1] 57 & 58 Vict. c. 44, sec. 15.
[2] Ibid. As to appeal, see p. 598, infra.
[3] See p. 512, supra.

(2) *Interdict against Heritable Creditor.*

The Act provides that any person interested may take proceedings to interpel the creditor from entering into possession of the security subjects or collecting the rents thereof.[1] This provision appears to contemplate an action of interdict, which would follow the usual course of an ordinary action. The jurisdiction laid down by the Act would apply,[2] but the limited right of review is not applicable to an action of this kind[3] and the ordinary rules will obtain.

[1] 57 & 58 Vict. c. 44, sec. 4.
[2] Ibid., sec. 15.
[3] Ibid., sec. 12.

(3) *Ejection of Proprietor.*

When a proprietor is in personal occupancy of the security subjects or any part of them and has failed to make punctual payment of interest, or after formal requisition has failed to pay the principal sum, he is deemed to be an occupant without a title, and the heritable creditor may take proceedings to eject him in all respects as if he were such occupant.[1] The proceedings take the form of an ordinary action and while the jurisdiction laid down

by the Act applies[2] the ordinary rules as to appeal are available
and not ,the limited right of review under the Act.[3] A proprietor
in occupancy, who defends such an action, is not required to find
caution for violent profits.[4]

[1] 57 & 58 Vict. c. 44, sec. 5.
[2] Ibid., sec. 15.
[3] Ibid., sec. 12. See as to appeal, p. 298, et seq., supra.
[4] Inglis' Trustees v. Macpherson, 1910 S.C. 46. See also Douglas v.
Frew, &c., 1910, 26 Sh.Ct.Rep. 355.

(4) *Leasing Security Subjects.*

The Act authorizes a heritable creditor in possession to lease
the security subject for a period not exceeding seven years at his
own hand[1] and he may apply to the Sheriff for warrant to lease all
or part of the subjects for a period not exceeding twenty-one years,
in the case of heritable property in general, or thirty-one years in
the case of minerals.[2] The writ must state the name of the proposed
tenant and the duration and conditions of the proposed lease,[2] and
the crave is for authority to lease on these terms.[3] Service is
directed to be made upon the proprietor and any other heritable
creditors,[2] and these parties will be called as defenders. There
is the qualified right of appeal laid down in the Act.[4] The Sheriff
may order further intimation if he thinks proper.[2] Whether
appearance is made or not, the Sheriff should institute inquiry and
he may do so by making a remit to a reporter. He is not to approve
of the proposed lease unless he is satisfied that the let is expedient
for the beneficial occupation of the lands, and he may approve of
the terms proposed or such other terms and conditions as appear to
him expedient.[2]

[1] 57 & 58 Vict. c. 44, sec. 6.
[2] Ibid., sec. 7.
[3] For style see Lees, Sheriff Court Styles, 4th edn., 210.
[4] 57 & 58 Vict. c. 44, sec. 12. See further, p. 598, infra.

(5) *Realizing Security Subjects.*

Under the Act a special form of declarator may be brought to
convert the bondholder into an absolute proprietor. The writ
describes the security and security subjects, and narrates the
exposure for sale, and the failure to sell. The crave is for
declarator of forfeiture of the right of redemption, and that the
heritable creditor is vested in the subjects as absolute proprietor,
at the price at which the lands were exposed and failed to find a
purchaser ; and for warrant to record the decree of Court in the
Register of Sasines.[1] Service is made on the proprietor and any

other heritable creditors and the Sheriff may order further intimation.[2]

[1] 57 & 58 Vict. c. 44, sec. 8, Schedule D; 14 & 15 Geo. V c. 27, sec. 9 (1).   See styles in Encyclopædia of Scottish Legal Styles, II, 124; Lees, Sheriff Court Styles, 4th edn., 208.
[2] Ibid., sec. 8.

If appearance is entered, it may be necessary to make up a formal record and take proof, but the action is generally undefended.   In that case the usual course is to remit to a conveyancer, and if the proceedings are reported to have been regular, decree is granted.   The extract when recorded in the Register of Sasines, disencumbers the lands of all securities and diligences posterior to that of the pursuer.[1]   The decree attracts *ad valorem* stamp duty.[2]   These proceedings are competent only in respect of the whole—and not a part—of the security subjects contained in the bond or bonds held by the pursuer.[3]

[1] 57 & 58 Vict. c. 44, sec. 8.
[2] Inland Revenue v. Tod, 1898, 25 R. (H.L.) 29.
[3] Webb's Executors v. Reid, 1906, 14 S.L.T. 323.

The Sheriff is not bound to grant decree and he may appoint the subjects to be exposed at a price fixed by him in which event the pursuer may bid at the sale.[1]   If he purchases, the decree is expressed in the same terms, except that the pursuer is declared to have become proprietor at the price at which he purchased at the judicial sale.   As an alternative to such decree the pursuer may dispone in his own favour.[1]   If a surplus arises upon the sale, it is consigned in bank.[2]   If there is no surplus a notarial certificate to that effect is obtained, and recorded.[3]   Consignation of a surplus, or recording a certificate of no surplus, has the effect of disencumbering the lands of other securities and diligences as provided by the Conveyancing Acts, but the debtor's personal obligation remains so far as not extinguished by the price at which the lands have been acquired.[4]   Questions as to appeal and expenses are dealt with below.[5]

[1] 57 & 58 Vict. c. 44, sec. 8.   See Lusk, &c. v. Tait, 1899, 15 Sh.Ct.Rep 249.
[2] 57 & 58 Vict. c. 44, sec. 9; 31 & 32 Vict. c. 101, sec. 122.
[3] 57 & 58 Vict. c. 44, sec. 9; 37 & 38 Vict. c. 94, sec. 48.
[4] 57 & 58 Vict. c. 44, sec. 9.
[5] See next page.

(6) *Pari Passu Security*.

A heritable creditor, who ranks *pari passu* with another and who cannot get the consent of his fellow bondholder to bring the

subjects to sale, may apply to the Court for authority to sell.[1] The
initial writ should describe the lands, and the *pari passu* securities,
and should crave warrant to expose the subjects for sale at an
upset price to be fixed by the Court. The other bondholder must
be called as defender.[1] If appearance is entered, the normal procedure follows, but even if no appearance is made the Act contemplates inquiry[1] and the practice is to remit to a reporter. If
the Sheriff is satisfied that a sale should take place he fixes an upset
price, and nominates one of the bondholders or another person to
carry through the sale, and to grant the necessary deeds to give the
purchaser a title.[1] The expenses of the sale are payable preferably
out of the price, and the balance is paid to the creditors according to their rights.[1] Questions as to appeal are dealt with below.[2]

[1] 57 & 58 Vict. c. 44, sec. 11; for styles see Encyclopædia of Scottish
Legal Styles, II, 121; Lees, Sheriff Court Styles, 4th edn., 209.
[2] See foot of this page.

(7) *Notice.*

The formal demand for payment of a heritable debt may in
certain circumstances be made edictally[1] and the heritable creditor
may make an *ex parte* application to the Sheriff Court of the
district where any part of the security subjects is situated, for
warrant to make premonition edictally.[2] The writ should narrate
the circumstances sufficiently to enable the Court to judge whether
a warrant should be granted. No one need apparently be called
as defender except where some other party entitled also to receive
notice is known and should be made a defender. The Sheriff may
make such inquiry as he thinks fit, and before granting the warrant
he may order intimation by advertisement or otherwise. The interlocutor granting the warrant should state the particular persons,
or their representatives, to whom the edictal intimation is to be
made. These provisions of the 1894 Act are to some extent superseded by the Conveyancing Act of 1924.[3]

[1] 31 & 32 Vict. c. 101, sec. 119; 57 & 58 Vict. c. 44, sec. 16.
[2] 57 & 58 Vict. c. 44, sec. 16.
[3] 14 & 15 Geo. V c. 27, secs. 33, 34.

(8) *Appeal and Expenses.*

No special provisions as to appeal are made in relation to
applications for interdict against a heritable creditor, ejection of a
proprietor, and for warrant to serve notice edictally. In the last
case no appeal would appear to be possible or competent. The
others would appear to be cases in which the ordinary rules of procedure and of appeal would apply.[1] As regards applications for

authority to lease, or for decree of declarator that the right of
redemption is forfeited, or for sale by a *pari passu* bondholder, the
Statute provides that the interlocutor of the Sheriff who pronounces
any order or decree is final, and not subject to review, except (1)
as to questions of title; and (2) where the principal sum due
under the heritable security exceeds £1000.[2] This provision is
held to exclude appeal to the Sheriff-Principal[3] but such appeal has
been allowed where the order made was challenged as incompetent,[4]
and where questions of title were involved, not in the interlocutor
appealed against but in earlier interlocutors, which would be open
to review.[4] In the case of the three forms of application last
referred to, the Sheriff may award expenses or may direct that
these be treated as expenses of sale.[2] The latter alternative seems
inappropriate in any application for power to lease.

[1] See p. 298, supra.
[2] 57 & 58 Vict. c. 44, sec 12.
[3] Thomson, &c. v. Smith, 1921, 37 Sh.Ct.Rep. 251; Nicholson v. Murray,
    1927, 43 Sh.Ct.Rep. 108; cf. Webb's Executors v. Reid, 1906, 14
    S.L.T. 325.
[4] Thomson, &c. v. Smith, supra.

21. HOUSING AND TOWN PLANNING.*

Under the Acts relating to housing the Sheriff may be ordered
to determine questions arising in relation to water supply[1] or
sanitary conveniences[2] for houses outside a burgh. The decision
of either the Sheriff or Sheriff-Substitute is final.[1] In certain
circumstances a superior may make application to the Sheriff for
an order empowering him to enter on subjects and carry out operations.[3] The local authority and the owner of the subjects will be
called as defenders. The Sheriff may also be asked to determine
a lease in certain cases.[4] There is no express exclusion of review
but the sections seem to contemplate a jurisdiction exercisable by
either Sheriff or Sheriff-Substitute but with no right of appeal.[5]
The Court is presumably that having jurisdiction where the property is situated.

* See general observations, p. 532, et seq., supra.
[1] 9 & 10 Geo. V c. 60, sec. 40; Sinclair v. Berwick County Council,
    1933, 49 Sh.Ct.Rep. 116.
[2] 15 Geo. V c. 15, sec. 20; Sinclair v. Berwick County Council, supra;
    for style see Encyclopædia of Scottish Legal Styles, V, 341.
[3] 15 Geo. V c. 15, sec. 23; 20 & 21 Geo. V c. 40, sec. 50. See also
    25 & 26 Geo. VI c. 41, sec. 55 (a).
[4] 20 & 21 Geo. V c. 40, sec. 29. See also 25 & 26 Geo. VI c. 41, sec.
    55 (f).
[5] See p. 537, supra.

Where owing to changes in the character of a neighbourhood a house cannot readily be let as a single dwelling, but could be so let if converted into two or more dwellings, and such conversion is not permissible owing to the terms of the feu or lease, the local authority or the feuar or lessee may apply to the Sheriff to vary such terms so as to permit the conversion.[1] Any persons interested in the house or entitled to enforce the terms should be called as defenders, but advertisement may also be ordered.[1] The facts above mentioned must be proved to the satisfaction of the Sheriff[1] so that inquiry seems necessary even if the application is not contested. The application can only be dealt with by the Sheriff and not the Sheriff-Substitute, and his decision is final. The conditions may be varied on such terms as the Sheriff thinks fit.[1] In the only reported cases no expenses were awarded.[2]

[1] 15 Geo. V c. 15, sec. 85; for style see Encyclopædia of Scottish Legal Styles, V, 215.
[2] Henry v. George Heriot's Trust, 1934, 50 Sh.Ct.Rep. 111; Hutton v. Hatrick, &c., 1937, 54 Sh.Ct.Rep. 16.

Appeals are competent in the Sheriff Court against the following : (1) notice requiring the execution of works[1]; (2) demand for recovery of expenses of a local authority in executing works[2]; (3) order by local authority with respect to such expenses[2]; (4) demolition order[3]; (5) closing order or refusal to determine a closing order[3]; and (6) charging order for cost of works.[4] The Acts provide that notice of appeal is to be given within twenty-one days after the service of the notice, demand or order, or after the refusal, in the case of (1) to (5) above[5] and within one month after service of the charging order in the case of (6) above,[4] but by Act of Sederunt appeals are to be made by initial writ in ordinary form presented within the time above specified.[6] When the appeal is against an order the crave is for recall of the order. Before considering any appeal the Sheriff may, on a motion by the respondent, order the appellant to deposit within a stated time a sum not exceeding £10 to cover the costs of the appeal.[7] In such appeals expenses are usually awarded.[8] Primarily such appeals are concerned with the merits of the question in dispute,[9] but fundamental irregularities, as in the service of the notice, may be grounds for recalling the order.[10]

[1] 20 & 21 Geo. V c. 40, secs. 14, 15, 20; 25 & 26 Geo. V c. 41, sec. 74.
[2] Ibid., secs. 15, 20; 25 & 26 Geo. V c. 41, sec. 74.
[3] Ibid., secs. 16, 20; 25 & 26 Geo. V c. 41, sec. 74; Kirkpatrick v. Town Council of Maxwelltown, 1912 S.C. 288; for styles see Encyclopædia of Scottish Legal Styles, V, 343, 344. As to undertaking by owner in relation to determination of closing order, see Peters v. Coupar Angus Town Council, 1938, 55 Sh.Ct.Rep. 84.

[4] 15 Geo. V c. 15, sec. 21.

[5] 20 & 21 Geo. V c. 40, sec. 20; 25 & 26 Geo. V c. 41, sec. 74.

[6] Act of Sederunt, 10th July, 1931, secs. 1, 2.

[7] Ibid., sec. 3.

[8] Bell v. Gourock Corporation, 1923, 40 Sh.Ct.Rep. 296; Steele v. Lanark Middle Ward, 1928, 44 Sh.Ct.Rep. 249; Gilchrist v. Glasgow Corporation, 1934, 50 Sh.Ct.Rep. 171; Grieve v. West Lothian County Council, 1935, 51 Sh.Ct.Rep. 248; Burgh Property Investment Co. v. Stirling County Council, 1938, 55 Sh.Ct.Rep. 87; Lawson v. Coupar Angus Town Council, 1938, 55 Sh.Ct.Rep. 137; cf. Sinclair v. Berwick County Council, 1933, 49 Sh.Ct.Rep. 116; Flynn v. Glasgow Corporation, 1937, 54 Sh.Ct.Rep. 63.

[9] Thom, &c. v. Glasgow Corporation, 1941, 58 Sh.Ct.Rep. 94.   See also Gilchrist v. Glasgow Corporation, supra; and cf. Lawson v. Coupar Angus Town Council, supra.

[10] Grieve v. West Lothian County Council, supra.

There is no right of appeal to the Sheriff,[1] but the Sheriff-Substitute may, at any stage of the proceedings before him, and shall if so directed by the Court of Session, state in the form of a stated case any question of law arising on the appeal to him.[2] The case is applied for by any party to an appeal at any time prior to the issue of the Sheriff's decision.[3] The application is made by minute lodged in the process setting forth the question of law.[3] If made before the facts in the appeal are fully ascertained by the Sheriff he may postpone consideration of the application till the facts are ascertained.[4] If the Sheriff considers that the proposed question of law does not arise, or that a decision on it is unnecessary for the purposes of the appeal or that it is frivolous he may refuse to state a case.[5] In the latter event he grants a certificate specifying the cause of refusal, and bearing the date of refusal, and also a note which, if the facts have been ascertained, contains the proposed findings and the facts on which the Sheriff is to base his decision, or otherwise sets forth or refers to the parties' averments or admissions on which the refusal is based.[5] Where an appeal has been disposed of on preliminary pleas without any proof being led it is too late thereafter to ask for a stated case.[6]

[1] See M'Mikin's Curator v. Carrick District of Ayr County Council, 1922, 38 Sh.Ct.Rep. 194.

[2] 15 Geo. V c. 15, sec. 103; 20 & 21 Geo. V c. 40, Schedule 4.

[3] Rules of Court, 1936, V, 29 (a).

[4] Ibid., V, 29 (b).

[5] Ibid., V, 29 (c).

[6] Burgh Property Investment Co. v. Stirling County Council, 1938, 55 Sh.Ct.Rep. 87.

The person applying for a stated case must intimate the application and the proposed question of law to the other parties, any of whom may within seven days of receiving such intimation apply in writing for a case on any additional question of law.[1] If the

Sheriff decides to state a case his decision is intimated to the parties and the draft case is submitted to them within fourteen days thereafter.[2] Within twenty-one days of receipt of the case each party is to return it with any additions, alterations or amendments,[2] and if the parties fail to agree as to the terms of the case or any of them fail to return the draft the Sheriff is to adjust the case[3] and he may add any further proposed findings in fact or questions of law that he considers necessary.[3] The case is signed by the Sheriff and is transmitted to the Court of Session and intimation is made that this has been done.[4] If the case is refused the applicant may within seven days of the refusal apply in the Court of Session for an order on the other parties to show cause why a case should not be stated.[5]

[1] Rules of Court, 1936, V, 29 (d), 31 (d); the reason for also incorporating the provisions of Rule 26 is not clear. See V, 29 (d).
[2] Ibid., V, 29 (d), 31 (e).
[3] Ibid., V, 29 (d), 31 (f).
[4] Ibid., V, 29 (d), 26 (c), 31 (g).
[5] Ibid., V, 29 (d), 31 (i); Encyclopædia of Scottish Legal Styles, V, 347; Kirkpatrick v. Town Council of Maxwelltown, 1912 S.C. 288.

Under sec. 56 of the Town and Country Planning (Scotland) Act, 1945, the Sheriff has jurisdiction to determine any question arising on a claim thereunder, whether the claimant is a person who is to be deemed, for the purposes of the Act, to be an owner-occupier.[1] By the same section it is provided that an arbiter under the Act may, at any stage of the proceedings before him, and shall, if so directed by the Sheriff, state in the form of a special case for the opinion of the Sheriff any question of law arising in the course of the proceedings, and may state his award, as to the whole or part thereof, in the form of a special case for the opinion of the Sheriff.[2] The opinion of the Sheriff on any question brought before him under the above provision is declared to be final, unless either party appeals to the Court of Session from whose decision no appeal lies.[1] In the absence of any special provision such appeals would apparently be made by note of appeal written within twenty-one days of the Sheriff's decision.[3]

[1] 8 & 9 Geo. VI c. 33, sec. 56.
[2] Ibid. See the similar provision under the Agricultural Holdings Act, p. 550, supra.
[3] Rules of Court, 1936, V, 7-13.

22. HUSBAND AND WIFE.

(1) *Protection Order.*

A deserted wife may apply for an order protecting property acquired after desertion against her husband and his creditors, and

the husband or his creditors may ask the recall of any such order.[1]
An application for recall is competent only in the Court to whose
jurisdiction the wife is for the time being subject.[1] Such an
application is to be treated as an ordinary action. Service upon
the husband as defender is made in the usual manner, and if his
address is unknown or if he is furth of Scotland it may be edictal.[1]
In view of subsequent legislation, including the Married Women's
Property (Scotland) Act, 1920,[2] applications for a protection order
are now practically unknown.

[1] 37 & 38 Vict. c. 31, sec. 2.
[2] 10 & 11 Geo. V c. 64, sec. 1.

(2) Husband's Consent to Deeds.

Where a wife has been deserted, or is living separate with her
husband's consent, the Sheriff may dispense with the husband's
consent to any deed relating to the wife's estate.[1] This is an *ex
parte* summary application at the instance of the wife. If the
husband's address in Scotland is known it should be brought in the
Court to whose jurisdiction he is subject. Otherwise it can probably be brought in the Court within whose jurisdiction the wife
resides. As the husband's right of administration is now wholly
abolished, and he is his wife's curator only during her minority,
such an application is now of little importance.[2]

[1] 44 & 45 Vict. c. 21, sec. 5.
[2] 10 & 11 Geo. V c. 64, secs. 1, 2, 3.

23. INCOME TAX.

Under the Income Tax Act, 1918, the Sheriff or Sheriff-Substitute, on certificate by a collector of taxes that any tax is due and
unpaid, is directed to issue a warrant for recovery by poinding
which is executed by Sheriff officer.[1] Provision is made for the
manner of executing the diligence and if no purchaser appears at
the sale the effects poinded are to be left with the Sheriff to be sold
and disposed of as he shall appoint.[2] If goods sufficient to pay
the tax are not found to be poinded and the person liable does not
pay it the Sheriff may commit him to prison.[3] The original
application for the summary warrant is made by printed form,
which is usually granted by the Sheriff *de plano*, no notice to the
debtor being necessary. If any further steps have to be taken a
minute on the original application seems to be appropriate. If a
summary warrant is wrongly granted the debtor's remedy appears

to be by way of suspension.[4] Provisions similar to the above in the Taxes Management Act of 1880 are applicable to the recovery of land tax.[5]

[1] 8 & 9 Geo. V c. 40, sec. 166 (1) (2).
[2] Ibid., sec. 166 (3) (10).
[3] Ibid., sec. 166 (8).
[4] Rutherford v. Lord Advocate, (O.H.) 1931 S.L.T. 405.
[5] 43 & 44 Vict. c. 19, sec. 97; 8 & 9 Geo. V c. 40, sec. 238, Schedule VII.

24. JUDICIAL FACTORS.

By the Judicial Factors (Scotland) Act of 1880 the Sheriff Court was empowered to appoint judicial factors if the factor desired was either a factor *loco tutoris* or a *curator bonis*.[1] The jurisdiction is further restricted to cases where the yearly value of the heritable and moveable estate together does not exceed £100. A judicial factor under the Bankruptcy Act may also be appointed by the Sheriff in circumstances already explained.[2]

[1] 43 & 44 Vict. c. 4, secs. 3, 4.
[2] See p. 393, supra.

(a) *Procedure.*—Within the above limits of jurisdiction, the Sheriff may (a) appoint a factor; (b) recall an appointment; (c) fix caution to be found by the factor; (d) grant the factor special powers; and (e) discharge the factor. There is an appeal from the Sheriff-Substitute to the Sheriff in all cases where in the Court of Session the determination of a Lord Ordinary could be reviewed by the Inner House.[1] This limits appeals to interlocutors finally disposing of the merits of the application.[2] The time for appealing is thought to be that under the Sheriff Courts Act and not that under the Act of 1857.[3] The decision of the Sheriff is final,[4] but this does not preclude an appeal to the Court of Session where the Sheriff for any reason has declined to exercise his jurisdiction.[5]

[1] 43 & 44 Vict. c. 4, sec. 4 (5).
[2] 20 & 21 Vict. c. 56, sec. 6.
[3] See Paul, &c. v. Logan, 1902, 18 Sh.Ct.Rep. 223.
[4] 43 & 44 Vict. c. 4, sec. 4 (10).
[5] Penny v. Scott, 1894, 22 R. 5.

An application to the Sheriff Court for the appointment of a judicial factor is a summary application[1] made by initial writ,[2] and the procedure is to be as nearly as may be that followed in the Court of Session.[2] When an appointment has been made, the process subsists till the factor has been discharged, and later applications such as for special powers, or for discharge, are made by a note lodged in the original process.[3] The note may conveniently be framed in the form of an initial writ. Where a new factor has to be appointed the application must be made in the Court which made the original appointment irrespective of the then place of residence of the ward.[4] The process does not fall asleep by the lapse of year and day.[5] Decrees in absence in such applications may not be opened up after the lapse of twelve months.[6]

[1] Codifying Act of Sederunt, L, VIII, 1.
[2] 43 & 44 Vict. c. 4, sec. 4 (1).
[3] Codifying Act of Sederunt, L, VIII, 3.
[4] Accountant of Court, 1893, 20 R. 573.
[5] Codifying Act of Sederunt, L, VIII, 2.
[6] 43 & 44 Vict. c. 4, sec. 4 (8).

The application for appointment is competent only in the Sheriff Court of the district where the pupil or insane person resides[1]— that is where he has his house, not where he is detained as an *incapax*.[2] It is made at the instance of a relative or creditor or someone with an interest in the ward or the estate. The writ should state the interest of the applicant, the circumstances in which the appointment is necessary, and that the estate does not exceed £100 in yearly value, and should crave the Court to nominate a factor. The application is intimated on the Court walls, to the Accountant of Court, and to any other interested parties.[3] It should also be served personally on the *incapax*, although in special circumstances this may be dispensed with.[4] The Sheriff may also order public intimation by newspaper advertisement in prescribed form.[5] The matter is usually disposed of upon a hearing, but, if the circumstances require it, proof may be taken. The Sheriff must be satisfied by reasonable evidence that the estate does not exceed £100 in yearly value, and the interlocutor making the appointment must contain a finding to that effect which is final.[5] The yearly value of heritage is taken from the valuation roll and in the case of moveables is taken at 4 per cent. on the estimated value.[6] If yearly value cannot be ascertained in this way it is ascertained in such way as the Sheriff may think fit.[6] In the case of an *incapax* two medical certificates on soul and conscience must be produced with the application and one at least should be by a doctor not connected with any asylum in which the *incapax* may be detained.[7] The medical reports should be of recent date and a report is in practice not usually accepted if it is not dated within a month of the application being presented. If a medical examination cannot

be obtained the application may be made without certificates and
a remit made by the Court.[8]   The incapacity need not be mental.[9]

[1] 43 & 44 Vict. c. 4, sec. 4 (1).
[2] Henry, 1896, 12 Sh.Ct.Rep. 121; M'Cormick, 1896, 13 Sh.Ct.Rep.
    184.
[3] Codifying Act of Sederunt, L, VIII, 4, Schedule A.
[4] Buyers, (O.H.) 1910, 2 S.L.T. 201.
[5] 43 & 44 Vict. c. 4, sec. 4 (3).
[6] Ibid., sec. 4 (2).
[7] Kennedy, (O.H.) 1901, 8 S.L.T. 415.
[8] Davies, (O.H.) 1928 S.L.T. 142
[9] Duncan, (O.H.) 1915, 2 S.L.T. 50; cf. Key, &c. v. Swan, &c., 1913,
    30 Sh.Ct.Rep. 77.

The appointment of a curator on an application by the *incapax*
himself has been held to be competent.[1]   If there has been a previous application relating to the same ward or estate the accountant
of Court reports this to the Sheriff-clerk when intimation is made
to him.[2]   A married woman may be appointed as factor.[3]   A
factor cannot be appointed by the Court to act jointly with another
person.[4]

[1] A B, (O.H.) 1908, 16 S.L.T. 557; Fraser, 1946, 62 Sh.Ct.Rep. 132.
[2] Codifying Act of Sederunt, L, VIII, 5.
[3] Crombie, &c. v. Crombie, &c., 1920, 36 Sh.Ct.Rep. 109.   See also
    Smith Sligo, (O.H.) 1914, 1 S.L.T. 287.
[4] Speirs, (O.H.) 1946 S.L.T. 203.

Appointment of a factor is made subject to his finding caution
within three weeks, unless some other time limit is stated.[1]   The
time may be extended on motion made before its expiry, but otherwise the appointment falls if caution is not timeously found.[1]   The
cautioner may be a private person who signs a bond in prescribed
form with certificate of sufficiency appended.[2]   But caution is
usually found through a guarantee company and the premium and
expenses of obtaining caution are allowed out of the estate.[3]   The
Sheriff-clerk transmits the bond to the accountant and he may then
issue extract of the appointment.[4]   The factor cannot act until he
has obtained extract[2] but this has been held not to invalidate acts
done in an emergency.[5]

[1] Codifying Act of Sederunt, L, VIII, 6.
[2] Ibid., VIII, 7.
[3] Ibid., VIII, 8.
[4] Ibid., VIII, 9.
[5] Calver v. Howard Baker & Co., 1894, 22 R. 1.

(b) *Special Powers.*—An application for special powers is made,
in the first instance, to the Accountant of Court, and his report
is presented to the Court, along with a note by the factor, setting

forth the special powers craved, and the circumstances in which they are necessary.[1] The procedure is summary, and in the discretion of the Sheriff-Substitute, who after intimation and service disposes of the application.[1] As such a judgment is one which is open to review in a Court of Session application[2] there is a right of appeal to the Sheriff,[3] whose decision is final.[4] Special powers are not granted till the factor has extracted the decree appointing him.[5]

[1] Codifying Act of Sederunt, L, VIII, 11.
[2] See Macqueen v. Tod, 1899, 1 F. 1069.
[3] 43 & 44 Vict. c. 4, sec. 4 (5).
[4] Ibid., sec. 4 (10).
[5] Codifying Act of Sederunt, L, VIII, 11.

(c) *Recall of Appointment.*—Any person interested may apply in the Sheriff Court or the Court of Session for the recall of the appointment of a factor.[1] If made in the Sheriff Court, it is a step in the original process, and is made by note[2] setting forth the interest of the applicant, and the circumstances in which recall is craved. There would appear to be a right of appeal to the Sheriff,[3] whose decision is final.[4]

[1] 43 & 44 Vict. c. 4, sec. 4 (9).
[2] Codifying Act of Sederunt, L, VIII, 3.
[3] See preceding paragraph.
[4] 43 & 44 Vict. c. 4, sec. 4 (10).

(d) *Discharge of Factor.*—The factor's application for discharge is made by note lodged in the original process.[1] Intimation and service is made in the same manner as in an application for the appointment of a factor, and a remit is made to the Accountant of Court, who makes a report to the Court.[1] If the report is satisfactory, the Sheriff will discharge the factor.

[1] Codifying Act of Sederunt, L, VIII, 3, 12.

25. LANDS CLAUSES ACT.

(1) *Capital Certificate.*

Under the Lands Clauses Act of 1845, or other Statutes into which it is incorporated, the fact that the prescribed sum of capital of an undertaking has been subscribed is certified by the Sheriff.[1] The appropriate Court is presumably that of the district where the promoters carry on business, and where the share register is kept. No formal application is necessary,[2] and the Sheriff is directed to grant the certificate upon such evidence as he thinks proper and sufficient.[1]

[1] 8 & 9 Vict. c. 19, secs. 15, 16.
[2] For style of a written application, see Lees, Sheriff Court Styles, 4th edn., 255.

(2) *Assessment of Compensation.*

When lands are taken compulsorily under the Act compensation is normally assessed by arbitration. But if the claim is less than £50 the matter must be determined by the Sheriff unless both parties agree to arbitration.[1] Application may be made by either party[2] in the Sheriff Court of the district where the lands are situated. The decision of either Sheriff or Sheriff-Substitute is final.[2] The first deliverance orders service and fixes a diet. At that diet the Sheriff may proceed in the absence of either party provided proof of service is given,[2] but it may be more convenient to adjourn the inquiry to a later date. The proceedings are summary and no written pleadings, or record of evidence, is necessary.[2] The Sheriff must give his decision in writing and expenses are in his discretion.[2]

[1] 8 & 9 Vict. c. 19, sec. 21.
[2] Ibid., sec. 22; for style see Lees, Sheriff Court Styles, 4th edn., 255. See also Sutherland v. Caledonian Railway Co., 1892, 10 Sh.Ct.Rep. 90.

If the claim exceeds £50, the claimant may require it to be assessed by a jury.[1] This mode also falls to be adopted if a claimant does not ask for arbitration; or if an arbitration has been entered upon and the arbiter or oversman fails for three months to make an award.[2] In all such cases the promoters present a summary application craving the Sheriff to summon a jury to determine the amount of compensation.[1] The jury consists of thirteen persons, drawn from a panel of twenty-five summoned by the Sheriff,[3] or upon the request of either party the Sheriff may nominate a special jury.[4] The promoters must give the claimant ten days' notice of presenting their application,[5] and the claimant may require a special jury to be called by so intimating to the promoters before their application is presented.[4] Where there is to be a special jury the first deliverance grants warrant to the Sheriff-clerk to return a list of thirty-six special persons at the first diet of appearance. At such diet (of which four days' notice must be given to the parties)[4] these persons are nominated as a special jury and another diet is fixed for having their number reduced to twenty by the parties' alternate suggestions.[4] When the numbers have been so reduced warrant is granted for citing the twenty persons on the day of trial and for citing witnesses and havers. The jury chosen consists of thirteen.[6] Not less than ten days' notice of the time and place of inquiry must be given by the promoters to the claimant or his solicitor in writing.[7]

[1] 8 & 9 Vict. c. 19, sec. 36; for style see Lees, Sheriff Court Styles, 4th edn., 256.
[2] Ibid., sec. 35.
[3] Ibid., secs. 38, 39, 41.
[4] Ibid., sec. 53.
[5] Ibid., sec. 37. This applies to special as well as common juries; Lang v. Glasgow Court House Commissioners, 1871, 9 M. 768. See also Houston Local Authority v. M'Phedran, 1890, 6 Sh.Ct.Rep. 267.
[6] Ibid., sec. 54.
[7] Ibid., sec. 40.

The proceedings at the inquiry are conducted in the manner of a criminal jury trial.[1] The Sheriff presides, and, if either party so request, the Sheriff may order the jury or any seven or more of them to inspect the *locus*.[1] The amount assessed by the jury is decerned for by the Sheriff, and his decision is not subject to review though it may be set aside by reduction.[2] The costs of the inquiry are borne by the promoters unless (a) the claimant fails to appear ; or (b) the jury award the same or a less sum than the promoters had offered, in either of which cases one half of the promoters' expenses has to be met by the claimant.[3] Where a claimant fails to appear the inquiry cannot proceed and compensation is fixed by a valuer appointed by the Sheriff.[4]

[1] 8 & 9 Vict. c. 19, sec. 42.
[2] See City of Glasgow Union Railway Co. v. Hunter, 1870, 8 M. (H.L.) 156.
[3] 8 & 9 Vict. c. 19, sec. 50.
[4] Ibid., sec. 46. See next paragraph.

(3) *Absent Owner*.

When an owner of lands compulsorily taken is outwith the United Kingdom, or cannot be found, or where he has failed to appear at the inquiry, the promoters may present a summary application to the Sheriff to nominate a valuator to determine the amount of compensation.[1] Before granting the application the Sheriff must be satisfied that the party is absent or cannot be found, and the first deliverance may fix a diet at which proof on this point is to be led.[2] The valuator, when nominated, appears before the Sheriff, and makes oath that he will faithfully execute the office.[3] The promoters are bound to preserve the nomination and valuation, and to produce them to the owner, and all other parties, if after-

wards called upon.[3] The expenses of and incident to the valuation
are in this case borne wholly by the promoters.[4]

[1] 8 & 9 Vict. c. 19, sec. 56; for style see Lees, Sheriff Court Styles,
    4th edn., 259.
[2] Ibid., sec. 57.
[3] Ibid., secs. 58, 59.
[4] Ibid., sec. 60.

(4) *Miscellaneous.*

Other proceedings under the Act include applications to
nominate an arbiter where a claimant is under disability,[1] or for
the purpose of getting entry to the lands before purchase,[2] or in the
case of common property,[3] to recover a penalty for unlawful entry,[4]
to obtain entry for the promoters[5] or to determine the compensation
to be paid to a yearly tenant.[6] Save in the case of recovery of
penalties the applications are made by initial writ.[7] In such
cases there is a right of appeal from the Sheriff-Substitute to the
Sheriff if written pleadings have been allowed, a record has been
made up and any evidence led has been recorded.[8] The appeal is
competent against a final judgment within seven days of its date.[8]
Otherwise there is no right of appeal.[8] A penalty has been held to
be not recoverable by civil action but only under the Summary
Jurisdiction Act.[9]

[1] 8 & 9 Vict. c. 19, sec. 9.
[2] Ibid., sec. 84.
[3] Ibid., sec. 97.
[4] Ibid., sec. 87.
[5] Ibid., sec. 89.
[6] Ibid., sec. 114; Glasgow District Subway Co. v. Albin & Son, 1895,
    23 R. 81.
[7] See Lees, Sheriff Court Styles, 4th edn., pp. 260-5. See also Sellar's
    Forms, p. 194, et seq.
[8] 8 & 9 Vict. c. 19, sec. 139; Bridge of Allan Water Co. v. Alexander,
    1868, 6 M. 321.
[9] Dennison v. Paisley, &c., Railway Co., 1899, 16 Sh.Ct.Rep. 17.

26. LAND DRAINAGE.*

Under the Land Drainage (Scotland) Act, 1930, an owner or
occupier of agricultural land may serve a notice on another owner
or occupier to have certain operations carried out to save injury
to the former's land.[1] If the notice is not complied with within
two months after service the server of the notice may apply to the
Sheriff—presumably within whose jurisdiction the lands in which
the operations are to be carried out lie—for a warrant authorizing
the applicant to cause the required operations to be carried out,
or to join with others in so doing.[2] The other party will be called

* See general observations, p. 532, et seq., supra.

as defender, and the Sheriff may appoint a skilled assessor, or remit to a man of skill to report.[3] The Sheriff may ordain the defender to carry out the operations within a specified time and on failure may authorize another person to carry them out and to enter on the lands to do so.[4] If either party so require the Sheriff must direct the operations to proceed under the supervision of a man of skill.[4] Before the Sheriff can grant the application he must be satisfied that the applicant's land is in danger of injury, that the defender is unreasonably refusing or delaying operations and that the cost of these is such as may reasonably be borne by the parties.[4]

[1] 20 Geo. V c. 20, sec. 1 (1).
[2] Ibid., sec. 1 (2).
[3] Ibid., sec. 1 (3).
[4] Ibid., sec. 1 (4).

If the Sheriff considers it unreasonable to make the order he may direct intimation to the Department of Agriculture for Scotland,[1] who are empowered to prepare schemes and carry out works.[2] If the Sheriff grants the application he may direct that the cost of the works, including the remuneration of the skilled person under whose supervision they were carried out, shall be borne by the parties in such proportions as he may think fit.[3]

[1] 20 Geo. V c. 20, sec. 1 (5).
[2] Ibid., sec. 3.
[3] Ibid., sec. 1 (6) (7).

An owner or occupier of agricultural land may also apply to the Sheriff for warrant to make underground main drains through other land,[1] and the Sheriff may grant such application if satisfied that the applicant's land is injured or endangered by the owner of the other land refusing to allow such drains to be made and that his refusal is unreasonable.[2] The Sheriff may make inquiry by remit, report, or otherwise, and the person authorized in the warrant is empowered to enter on the other land and carry out the work.[2] If the defender so requires, the Sheriff must direct that the work be carried out under the supervision of a man of skill.[2] The Sheriff's warrant must provide for payment of compensation for any loss or damage caused by the operations (the amount of which failing agreement is fixed by the Sheriff after inquiry) and for the maintenance or renewal of the drains at the expense of the owner of the agricultural land.[3]

[1] 20 Geo. V c. 20, sec. 2 (1).
[2] Ibid., sec. 2 (2).
[3] Ibid., sec. 2 (3).

In applications under the Act the Sheriff may award expenses to or against any party.[1] There is no provision as to review but the intention seems to be that the decision of the Sheriff is not subject to appeal.[2]

[1] 20 Geo. V c. 20, sec. 2 (4).
[2] See p. 537, supra.

27. LUNACY AND MENTAL DEFICIENCY.

I. LUNACY.

(1) *Committal of Lunatic.*

For detention of a lunatic beyond a period of three days a summary application is made in the Sheriff Court of the District where the lunatic is resident or is found; or where the place of proposed detention is situated.[1] Any person who has the custody of the insane person may apply. In general, the applicant is a relative, but in the case of paupers, the inspector of poor makes the application. The crave is to authorize the superintendent of the asylum to receive the patient.[2]

[1] 25 & 26 Vict. c. 54, sec. 14; 20 & 21 Vict. c. 71, Schedule C.
[2] For style see Encyclopædia of Scottish Legal Styles, V, 398.

Before a warrant is granted there must be produced to the Sheriff two medical certificates in statutory form, dated within fourteen days prior to the date of the application.[1] A doctor signing such a certificate must have no immediate or pecuniary interest in the asylum in which the lunatic is to be detained, and a doctor engaged at the asylum may not sign save in the case of a pauper lunatic.[2] The medical certificates state the facts upon which the opinion is based that the person certified is insane, and this is done under two heads: (a) facts observed by the doctor himself; and (b) facts (if any) communicated to him by others. The Sheriff himself does not make any finding of insanity, and his interlocutor merely records the fact that this has been certified, and, because of that, warrant is granted authorizing the transmission of the lunatic to a named asylum.[3] Provision is made for applications to the Sheriff for removal of a lunatic from one asylum to another.[4]

[1] 25 & 26 Vict. c. 54, sec. 14; 20 & 21 Vict. c. 71, Schedule D.
[2] 25 & 26 Vict. c. 54, sec. 14; 29 & 30 Vict. c. 51, sec. 4.
[3] 20 & 21 Vict. c. 71, Schedule E.
[4] 20 & 21 Vict. c. 71, sec. 91; Lees, Sheriff Court Styles, 4th edn., 462.

(2) *Dangerous Lunatic.*

When a lunatic (a) has been apprehended charged with an offence dangerous to the lieges; or (b) is found in a state threatening danger to the lieges, or to public decency, the Sheriff of the district where the lunatic is apprehended or found, on the application of the procurator-fiscal, or the inspector of poor, or other person, and on production of a medical certificate bearing that the lunatic is in a state threatening danger, or offensive to public decency, may in the first place commit the lunatic to a place of safe custody.[1] Thereupon the Sheriff directs notice, by newspaper advertisement, to be given that, at a named time and place, inquiry will be made into the condition of the lunatic.[1] Notice of the application is given to the inspector of poor of the locality where the lunatic was apprehended or found (unless he presented the application) and any further notice may be given as the Sheriff thinks fit.[1] Within twenty-four hours the inspector may make arrangements for the custody of the lunatic,[1] and thereafter the Sheriff, if necessary, proceeds to take evidence as to the lunatic's condition.[1] The proceedings are summary, and the evidence need not be recorded. The Sheriff, upon being satisfied that the person is a lunatic, and in a state threatening danger to the lieges or offensive to public decency, commits him to an asylum, to be detained until cured, or until caution is found for his safe custody.[1] It has been held that the Sheriff need not accept or act upon any arrangements made by the inspector; that the diet of inquiry should in general be held; and that if the procurator-fiscal desires the inquiry to proceed, notwithstanding any undertaking by the inspector, this request should receive special consideration.[2] Before authorizing the release of the lunatic on caution the Sheriff must be satisfied, not only as to the caution, but also of the safety and propriety of the custody proposed.[1] The Sheriff may also authorize the discharge of a dangerous lunatic on certificates from two medical men, approved by the procurator-fiscal, to the effect that the lunatic may be discharged without risk of injury to himself or to the public.[3] The provisions above narrated are not limited to pauper lunatics.[4]

---

[1] 25 & 26 Vict. c. 54, sec. 15; for style see Encyclopædia of Scottish Legal Styles, V, 402; Lees, Sheriff Court Styles, 4th edn., 458. See also Sellar's Forms, p. 220, et seq.

[2] M'Knight v. Ramsay, 1935 J.C. 94.

[3] 29 & 30 Vict. c. 51, sec. 19.

[4] 34 & 35 Vict. c. 55, sec. 8.

(3) *Expenses.*

In ordinary circumstances no order for expenses is made in lunacy applications, but, where the condition of a dangerous lunatic is inquired into by the Sheriff he is directed to grant a decree for expenses in favour of the procurator-fiscal, or other applicant against the local authority within whose area the lunatic is apprehended or found at large.[1] If the Sheriff commits the person he is also directed to grant decree against the authority in favour of the superintendent of the asylum, for a sum sufficient to maintain the lunatic.[1] Such decrees are final, but the local authority has a right of relief against the authority of the lunatic's settlement or against his estate, or against relatives who may be legally liable for his maintenance.[1] If in such a case a pauper lunatic has a known settlement in another county the Sheriff may transmit the application to the other county.[2]

[1] 25 & 26 Vict. c. 54, sec. 15; 34 & 35 Vict. c. 55, sec. 8. See also 20 & 21 Vict. c. 71, sec. 78; Roxburgh, &c., District Board of Lunacy v. Selkirk Parish Council, 1902, 4 F. 468.
[2] 20 & 21 Vict. c. 71, sec. 86.

(4) *Criminal Lunatic.*

Where a person confined in prison becomes insane the Sheriff of the county where he is detained may, with two doctors, inquire as to the insanity, and if these parties certify that the prisoner is insane a Secretary for State may direct him to be removed to an asylum.[1] When any person confined in a local prison becomes insane summary application for his removal may be made by the **prison** authorities,[2] in the Sheriff Court within whose jurisdiction the prison is situated.[3] The application must be accompanied by two medical certificates on soul and conscience.[2] If satisfied that the certificates are in order, the Sheriff grants warrant for removal to any asylum.[2] The same Sheriff may grant warrant for the prisoner's reconveyance to prison, if he recover his reason before his term of sentence has expired.[3] Warrants granted under this Statute may be put in force anywhere within Scotland.[3] Under the Criminal Lunatics (Scotland) Act, 1935, the Prisons Department for Scotland may itself act on the medical certificates relating to an insane prisoner.[4]

[1] 20 & 21 Vict. c. 71, sec. 89.
[2] 34 & 35 Vict. c. 55, sec. 6.
[3] Ibid., sec. 7.
[4] 25 & 26 Geo. V c. 32, sec. 4.

(5) *Discharge of Lunatic.*

The Sheriff may order the liberation of a lunatic on application by any person, accompanied by two medical certificates that the lunatic has recovered or that he may be liberated without risk of injury to himself or the public.[1] The authority of the Court is also required for liberation of a lunatic detained under sentence of the Court[2] and dangerous lunatics may be liberated on the authority of the Sheriff on caution being found.[3] But in the majority of cases no judicial procedure is necessary for discharge of a lunatic.[4]

[1] 20 & 21 Vict. c. 71, sec. 92.   See Encyclopædia of Scottish Legal Styles, V, 400; Lees, Sheriff Court Styles, 4th edn., 460.
[2] Ibid., sec. 93.
[3] See p. 613, supra.
[4] See 25 & 26 Vict. c. 54, sec. 17; 20 & 21 Vict. c. 71, sec. 92; 3 & 4 Geo. V c. 38, sec. 55 (5).

(6) *Escaped Lunatic.*

The Sheriff may grant warrant for the restoration to England or Ireland of an escaped lunatic found in Scotland.[1] Warrant by an English or Irish justice for his return is *prima facie* evidence that the person named is an escaped lunatic, and is authority to the Sheriff within whose jurisdiction the lunatic is found to countersign it.[1] No application other than the production of the warrant seems to be necessary. Upon this warrant the lunatic may be taken back to the custody from which he has escaped.[1] In like manner a lunatic who has escaped from Scotland into England or Ireland may be brought back upon the warrant of the Sheriff having jurisdiction in the place whence he escaped, countersigned by a justice in England or Ireland, having jurisdiction in the place where the lunatic is found.[1] A summary application will be made to the Sheriff for such a warrant.

[1] 53 Vict. c. 5, secs. 85-89; 3 & 4 Geo. V c. 38, sec. 19 (5).

II. MENTAL DEFICIENCY.

Under the Mental Deficiency and Lunacy (Scotland) Act, 1913, a defective as therein defined who is not otherwise dealt with may be subject to an order by the Sheriff.[1] To obtain such an order a petition—which may be made on an official printed form—is presented by a relative or certain other parties, and is accompanied by two medical certificates signed not more than one month prior to such presentation.[2] One certificate must be by a doctor approved for the purpose by the Board of Control and the other must, where practicable, be by the defective's usual medical attendant.[2] With the application there must also be a statutory declaration, signed by

or on behalf of the applicant and by one other person who may
be one of the certifying doctors, testifying to the facts in the
petition.[2] The official form contains the petition, certificates and
declaration. Where the application is not by a relative or a local
authority there must be averments explaining the applicant's
connexion with the defective and the circumstances under which
he is making the application.[3]

[1] 3 & 4 Geo. V c. 38, sec. 5.
[2] Ibid., sec. 6 (1) (2) (4).
[3] Ibid., sec. 6 (3).

Unless cause is shown to the contrary—as where he is unfit to
travel or it is not advisable for him to do so—the defective is cited
to appear personally.[1] The local authority liable to contribute
towards maintenance and the parent or guardian (when not the
petitioner) are usually cited to the first diet. The Sheriff may
adjourn the case for further information or evidence, and may
remit to some person to make inquiries or an examination of the
defective, or to take evidence on commission, or the Sheriff may
himself visit the defective.[2] It is thought that such inquiries would
only be necessary if the application was opposed or if the medical
certificates did not satisfy the Sheriff. The proceedings may,
and must if the defective so requires, be held in camera,[3] and the
Sheriff may examine witnesses on oath, and may award expenses
as if acting in his ordinary jurisdiction.[4]

[1] 3 & 4 Geo. V c. 38, sec. 7 (1).
[2] Ibid., sec. 7 (2).
[3] Ibid., sec. 7 (3).
[4] Ibid., sec. 7 (5).

If the Sheriff is satisfied that the person is a defective, and is
liable to be dealt with under the Act, he may order him to be
sent to an institution or he may appoint a guardian.[1] The order
must state the class of defective to which he belongs, and the circumstances rendering him liable to be dealt with under the Act.[1]
If the applicant is not a parent or guardian[2] an order is not to be
made without the consent of the parent or guardian unless the
Sheriff is satisfied that he cannot be found, or that consent is
unreasonably withheld, or that such withholding prejudices the
defective's interests.[1] An order may be made though the defective
is found not to belong to the class of defectives described in the
petition.[1] The Sheriff's order may be varied by the Board of
Control,[3] but it is thought it is not otherwise subject to review.

[1] 3 & 4 Geo. V c. 38, sec. 7 (4); as to religious persuasion, see sec. 17.
[2] See ibid., sec. 76 (1).
[3] Ibid., sec. 8.

An order that a defective be sent to an institution authorizes his conveyance and reception within fourteen days of its date,[1] and such an order and the appointment of a guardian expire after certain periods unless continued by the Board of Control.[2] Such continuation by the board may be appealed by the defective or certain other parties to the Sheriff.[3] The appeal will be made by initial writ and the Sheriff is directed to hold an inquiry and dispose of the appeal.[3] A similar right of appeal is open in cases of continuance of guardianship where a guardian has been appointed of consent.[4] The decision of the Sheriff is thought to be not subject to review.[5]

[1] 3 & 4 Geo. V c. 38, sec. 11 (1).
[2] Ibid., sec. 12 (1) (2); 3 & 4 Geo. VI c. 8, secs. 1, 4.
[3] Ibid., sec. 12 (3); 3 & 4 Geo. VI c. 8, secs. 1, 4; the Sheriff's power to order the discharge of criminal defectives is restricted by sec. 25 (2).
[4] Ibid., sec. 13 (2); 3 & 4 Geo. VI c. 8, secs. 2, 4.
[5] See p. 535, supra.

Where an order under the Act is made by a Sheriff or otherwise, either for detention in an institution or for appointment of a guardian, the defective or anyone liable to maintain him may be ordered to contribute to his maintenance.[1] The application for this may be made by the local authority concerned, the manager of the institution, the guardian, or the original applicant, and it is made to any Sheriff having jurisdiction, which presumably means over the defender.[1] Any order pronounced may be enforced as if it were a decree in the Small Debt Court, and it may be varied or revoked by any Sheriff having jurisdiction.[2] It is thought that an application to vary or revoke might be made by minute in the original process.[3] Provision is made for the Sheriff granting an interim warrant for removal to a place of safety in the case of a defective who is abandoned, neglected or cruelly treated within his jurisdiction if information on oath is laid before him by an officer of, or some person authorized by, the local authority.[4] Application by initial writ seems appropriate.

[1] 3 & 4 Geo. V c. 38, sec. 14 (1).
[2] Ibid., sec. 14 (2) (3).
[3] See 7 Edw. VII c. 51, Schedule I, Rule 171; Act of Sederunt, 16th July, 1936.
[4] 3 & 4 Geo. V c. 38, sec. 15 (2).

28. MARITIME.

(1) *General.*

It is provided by the Sheriff Court Act that the jurisdiction formerly competent to the High Court of Admiralty in Scotland in all maritime cases and proceedings including such as may apply to persons furth of Scotland, is competent in the Sheriff Court provided the defender is upon any legal ground of jurisdiction amenable to the Court in question.[1] By the Rules of the Court of Session special forms of procedure are provided in that Court for maritime causes as therein defined.[2] In the Sheriff Court maritime causes have no procedural peculiarities, and, save in special instances as noted hereafter, they proceed according to the ordinary rules and are subject to the usual principles in relation to jurisdiction.[3] Incidental applications will usually be disposed of summarily.

[1] 7 Edw. VII c. 51, sec. 4. As to jurisdiction by arrestment, see Sheaf Steamship Co. v. Compania Transmediterranea, 1930 S.C. 660.
[2] Rules of Court, 1936, III, 1-13.
[3] See Sheaf Steamship Co. v. Compania Transmediterranea, supra.

(2) Seamen's Wages.

Wages of a seaman may be sued for in common form by small debt action or otherwise. But special provisions are available to a seaman or apprentice for recovery of wages not exceeding £50.[1] Such an action may be brought in a Court of summary jurisdiction in or near the place where pursuer's service has terminated, or where he has been discharged, or where any person on whom the claim is made is or resides.[1] The decision of the Court is declared to be final.[1] It has been held that such an action may be brought as a summary cause in the Sheriff Court and that the right of appeal to the Sheriff is not excluded.[2] It might also if appropriate be brought in the Small Debt Court.

[1] 57 & 58 Vict. c. 60, sec. 164. See also sec. 693.
[2] Bain v. Ormiston, 1928 S.C. 764.

The above remedy is open to a shipmaster for his wages and to a master, or a person acting as master in consequence of the decease or incapacity of the master, for recovery of disbursements, or liabilities made or incurred on account of the ship.[1] In such an action questions of accounting between the master and owners may be entertained, and decree may be granted for any balance found due.[1] A master may also recover damages in addition to wages, if payment has been unreasonably delayed.[2]

[1] 57 & 58 Vict. c. 60, sec. 167.
[2] 6 Edw. VII c. 48, sec. 57.

Various other claims may be recovered in the same way as seamen's wages. These include (1) maintenance or passage money to a seaman discharged abroad[1]; (2) expenses of relief of distressed seamen[2]; (3) allowances for short or bad provisions[3]; (4) expenses for failure to provide medicine, &c.[4]; (5) expenses attendant on illness, &c.[5] An inspector of poor may obtain reimbursement for relief to a seaman's family on application to a Court of summary jurisdiction in the area where the relief was given.[6] Proceedings in these cases will be taken in the Small Debt Court or in the Ordinary Sheriff Court.

[1] 57 & 58 Vict. c. 60, sec. 186 (4).
[2] Ibid., sec. 193 (2).
[3] Ibid., sec. 199.
[4] Ibid., sec. 207 (4).
[5] Ibid., sec. 208 (2).
[6] Ibid., sec. 183.

(3) *Contracts.*

The Court has power in any action relating to a dispute between an owner or master, and a seaman, or apprentice, arising out of their relationship, to rescind any contract of service upon such terms as the Court thinks fit.[1]

[1] 57 & 58 Vict. c. 60, sec. 168.

(4) *Passage Brokers and Emigrant Runners.*

In Scotland the Sheriff is the authority for granting licences to passage brokers,[1] and emigrant runners.[2]

[1] 57 & 58 Vict. c. 60, sec. 343.
[2] Ibid., sec. 348.

(5) *Salvage.*

The Merchant Shipping Act restricts the jurisdiction of the Sheriff Court in disputes as to the amount of salvage to cases where (a) irrespective of value, parties consent to try the case in the Sheriff Court; or (b) the value of the property saved does not exceed £1000; or (c) the amount claimed does not exceed £300.[1] In such cases the action must be brought in the Sheriff Court.[1] In all other cases the action is brought in the Court of Session, but if the claimant does not there get decree for more than £300, he does not get expenses unless the Court of Session certifies that the case was a fit one to be tried otherwise than summarily in the Sheriff Court.[1] The position as to actions relating to salvage which do not fall under the Statute is discussed in the next paragraph. When a salvage claim falls under one of the three heads specified at the beginning of this paragraph the Act provides that such claim is to be determined summarily in manner provided by the Act which in Scotland means that it is to be determined by the Sheriff Court.[2] That direction has been interpreted—and it is thought rightly interpreted—as meaning that the action in the Sheriff Court is not a summary application, but an ordinary action or, if the claim does not exceed £50, a summary cause.[3] Certain later provisions in the Act relating to legal proceedings do not, it is thought, apply to claims for salvage.[4] If the claim does not exceed £20 it will be sued for in the Small Debt Court; if it is over that amount but does not exceed £50 it will be sued for as a summary cause in the Sheriff Court; if it exceeds £50 but is appropriated to the Sheriff Court in one of the ways above specified it will be sued for as an ordinary action in the Sheriff Court. The Court is entitled under the Act to call in a nautical assessor.[5] Unless the Court extends the period all actions must be brought within two years of the date when the salvage services were rendered.[6]

---

[1] 57 & 58 Vict. c. 60, sec. 547; Swanson v. Craig, (O.H.) 1939 S.L.T. 297. It seems clear that the jurisdiction of the Sheriff Court is still subject to this limitation, Bain, Morrison & Co. v. Stangeland, 1920, 36 Sh.Ct.Rep. 250; cf. Waterford, &c., Steamboat Co. v. Ford Shipping Co., 1915, 2 S.L.T. 192. See also next paragraph.
[2] Ibid., sec. 547 (1) (4) (b).
[3] Thirtle v. Copin, 1912, 29 Sh.Ct.Rep. 13.
[4] 57 & 58 Vict. c. 60, secs. 702, et seq. See Sinclair v. Spence, 1883, 10 R. 1077; Bain v. Ormiston, 1928 S.C. 764.
[5] Ibid., sec. 548 (2). See p. 135, supra.
[6] 1 & 2 Geo. V c. 57, sec. 8. This provision is not limited to actions brought under the Act of 1894.

A salvage action in the Sheriff Court must under the Act be brought in a Sheriff Court which has jurisdiction (a) at or near the place where the salved vessel is lying, or where a wreck is found; or (b) at or near the port into which the vessel is first brought after the occurrence out of which the salvage claim arises.[1] It has been held that the place where a vessel is lying under the first of these alternatives means the place where it is lying immediately after the act of salvage and not any place where it may be lying at a later stage when the dispute as to salvage arises.[2] The statutory provisions as to procedure apply to disputes as to the amount of salvage,[3] and where parties are in dispute as to whether or not salvage services have been rendered an action at common law would appear to be competent.[4] An action at common law may also be competent where the defender is subject to the jurisdiction of a Sheriff Court by residence, arrestment or otherwise, but is not amenable under this section because the vessel has not been brought into a port in this country.[5] In such a case the ordinary rules as to procedure and jurisdiction would apparently apply. If the salvage claim is within the ambit of the statutory provisions and if the statutory jurisdiction can be invoked it is thought that an action at common law would not be competent.[6]

[1] 57 & 58 Vict. c. 60, sec. 548.
[2] Summers v. Buchan, 1891, 18 R. 879; cf. Reid v. Couper, 1907, 23 Sh.Ct.Rep. 234.
[3] 57 & 58 Vict. c. 60, sec. 547 (1).
[4] See Thirtle, &c. v. Copin, 1912, 29 Sh.Ct.Rep. 13; Waterford, &c., Steamboat Co. v. Ford Shipping Co., 1915, 2 S.L.T. 192; but cf. Swanson v. Craig, (O.H.) 1939 S.L.T. 297.
[5] Thirtle, &c. v. Copin, supra, p. 18. See also Summers v. Buchan, supra, p. 883.
[6] Duncan and Dykes, Civil Jurisdiction, 356; cf. Thirtle, &c. v. Copin, supra, p. 19.

Whether the action is one under the Statute or at common law the ordinary rules in regard to appeal apply.[1]

[1] 57 & 58 Vict. c. 60, sec. 549; cf. Sinclair, &c. v. Spence, 1883, 10 R. 1077.

Where a dispute as to unclaimed wreck arises it may be determined in the Sheriff Court in the same way as the amount of salvage may be determined there,[1] but any party may object to such determination, and in that case, or if he is dissatisfied with the decision in the Sheriff Court, he may take proceedings in any Court having jurisdiction for establishing his title.[2] The effect of this provision would appear to be that, if parties do not agree to accept the decision of the Sheriff Court, then, except in cases where by reason of the amount involved that Court has privative jurisdiction, any party to such a dispute may raise proceedings to establish his title by declarator or otherwise in the Court of Session, either in the course of the proceedings in the Sheriff Court, or after they have been terminated by final judgment, and such proceedings in the Supreme Court will supersede those in the Lower Court.

[1] See p. 619, supra.
[2] 57 & 58 Vict. c. 60, sec. 526.

(6) Apportionment of Salvage.

Where an ascertained or agreed upon amount of salvage requires to be apportioned amongst the parties entitled thereto, the Sheriff Court, as a Court of Admiralty jurisdiction in Scotland, has jurisdiction to apportion salvage for services rendered in Great Britain if the amount exceeds £200, and for services rendered elsewhere whatever the amount.[1] If the salvage for services rendered in Great Britain does not exceed £200, the apportionment is made by

the Receiver of Wrecks.[2] The value qualification of the Act relating
to disputes as to the amount of salvage does not apply to apportionment.[3] The writ may crave the Court to apportion the amount,
or to appoint a person to do so; or the holder of the fund, or any
claimant, may raise a multiplepoinding[4] in the Sheriff Court within
whose jurisdiction the fund lies, or to which the holder of the fund
(e.g., the managing owner of the salved vessel) is subject. In either
case the ordinary rule as to procedure will apply. If all those
entitled to share are parties to an action for payment of salvage
a crave for apportionment could be included in the action.[5]

[1] 57 & 58 Vict. c. 60, sec. 556.   See Shaw v. s.s. Falls of Inversnaid Co.,
      1891, 8 Sh.Ct.Rep. 18.
[2] Ibid., sec. 555.
[3] Ibid., sec. 547.
[4] See Robinson, &c. v. Thoms, &c., 1857, 13 D. 592.
[5] For form see Lees, Sheriff Court Styles, 4th edn., 362.

(7) *Detention of Foreign Ship.*

When, in any part of the world, injury has been caused to a
ship, or any other kind of property, belonging to a British subject,
by any foreign ship,[1] or where such a ship has caused damage by
loss of life or personal injury,[2] and subsequently that ship is found
in any port or river within his jurisdiction, the Sheriff is
empowered to detain the ship, till caution be found for damages and
expenses in an action for reparation.[1] This is an *ex parte* summary application by the person entitled to claim damages. The
writ should set forth the nature of the injury done and that it was
the result of misconduct or want of skill on the part of the master
or mariners of the foreign ship.[1] The crave will be for warrant to
arrest (and, if necessary, to dismantle) the ship, to remain till the
owner or master finds security to the satisfaction of the Court.[1] The
cautioner then becomes the defender in the ensuing action for
reparation,[1] which follows the usual course of a small debt action,
summary cause, or ordinary action, according to its value.

[1] 57 & 58 Vict. c. 60, sec. 688; Lees, Sheriff Court Styles, 4th edn., 391.
[2] 1 & 2 Geo. V c. 57, sec. 5.

(8) *Sale of Goods.*

To avoid detention of ships, goods may be landed from a ship,
and placed in the custody of a warehouseman or wharfinger, and
yet remain subject to the shipowner's lien for freight and charges.[1]
But a shipowner is not bound to wait longer than ninety days for
payment of his freight, and at the end of that time he may
require the warehouseman to realize the goods, or so much thereof

as may be necessary to pay the freight and charges after notice given in two local newspapers, and notice sent by post to the owner of the goods, if known.[2] Under the Statute, the warehouseman has authority, after giving notice, to realize the goods at his own hand.[2] But it is the practice in Scotland to obtain judicial authority so to sell, by an *ex parte* summary application in the Sheriff Court of the district where the goods lie.

[1] 57 & 58 Vict. c. 60, secs. 494-496.
[2] Ibid., sec. 497.

(9) *Miscellaneous Claims.*

Under the Act various claims may be sued for summarily, or in a Court of summary jurisdiction, and in Scotland these will be brought in the Small Debt Court, or as summary causes in the Ordinary Court as may be appropriate.[1] These include (1) claims for breach of contract by a cabin or steerage passenger (the award in this case is not to exceed the amount of passage money and £20 in addition[2]); (2) similar claims where passage is not provided for a steerage passenger (the award here is not to exceed the amount of passage money and £10 in addition)[3]; and (3) claims for passage money, subsistence money, damages, compensation, or costs falling under Part III of the Act which deals with passenger and emigrant ships.[4]

[1] Bain v. Ormiston, 1928 S.C. 764.
[2] 57 & 58 Vict. c. 60, sec. 321.
[3] Ibid., sec. 328.
[4] Ibid., sec. 357.

(10) *Appeals.*

Certain rights of appeal in different kinds of maritime causes have been already dealt with. Part XIII of the Act deals with legal proceedings under various subheads, one of which, covering secs. 702 to 710, relates to procedure in Scotland. There is some doubt as to whether these sections are intended to deal with other than criminal or quasi-criminal proceedings.[1] The section of importance is 709, which provides that the Sheriff's decision is final save in cases of corruption or malice. This section has been held inapplicable to salvage cases where a right of appeal is specially referred to in the part of the Act relating to salvage.[2] It has been applied to summary proceedings in the Justices of the Peace Court for recovery of seamen's wages,[3] but not to a claim for wages made as a summary cause in the Sheriff Court.[4] Despite what was said in the later of these two cases, it is difficult to reconcile it with the earlier decision.

1 Sinclair, &c. v. Spence, 1883, 10 R. 1077; Alexander v. Little & Co., 1906, 8 F. 841 ; Bain v. Ormiston, 1928 S.C. 764.
2 Sinclair v. Spence, supra.
3 Alexander v. Little & Co., supra.
4 Bain v. Ormiston, supra.

(11) *Evidence.*

There are certain relaxations of the rules of evidence in maritime cases. A document required under the Act to be attested by witnesses may be proved by the evidence of any person who can speak to the fact although not one of the witnesses to the document.[1] Where the Act declares a document to be admissible in evidence then, subject to any exceptions that may be taken against it, it is evidence of matters stated in it in pursuance of the Act or by any officer in pursuance of his duties.[2] A copy or certified copy of a document is admissible in evidence in certain circumstances.[2] In the case of a necessary witness who cannot be found, a deposition on oath before a British magistrate, or consular officer, may be used as evidence in the cause.[3] But this latter section is one of three which deal with offences abroad and it is thought to be inapplicable to civil proceedings in this country.[4] The provisions in relation to nautical assessors have been already discussed.[5]

1 57 & 58 Vict. c. 60, sec. 694.
2 Ibid., sec. 695.
3 Ibid., sec. 691.
4 See Bain v. Ormiston, 1928 S.C. 764, p. 772.
5 See p. 185, supra.

(12) *Citation.*

The ordinary rules as to citation are qualified by the Statute. When citation is necessary in proceedings under the Merchant Shipping Act, it may be made personally, or at the last place of abode of the person to be cited.[1] If service is to be made on the master, or on some person belonging to a ship, it may be made by leaving the writ for him on board the ship with the person appearing to be in command. If service is to be made on the master, and there is no master, and the ship is in Great Britain, it may be made upon the managing owner, or if there is no managing owner on some agent of the owner residing in Great Britain, or if no such agent can be found by affixing a copy to the mast of the ship.[1]

1 57 & 58 Vict. c. 60, sec. 696.

(13) *Damage to Harbour.*

The owners of a vessel[1] which does damage to harbour works
may be liable at common law to the harbour authorities in reparation, but if the damage does not exceed £50, the authorities, if
they can invoke the Harbours, Docks, and Piers Clauses Act of
1847, have a summary remedy under that Act.[2] They may detain
the vessel till security is found for their claim, and they may sue
the masters or owners in the Sheriff Court of the district where the
harbour is situated,[3] craving the Court to find that the harbour
works have been damaged through the negligence of the master or
others in charge of the vessel; to assess the damage, and to decern
for payment thereof; to distrain and keep the vessel till payment
is made, and if payment is not made within seven days, to grant
warrant for the sale of the vessel; to authorize the authorities, out
of the proceeds, to retain the amount assessed and expenses; and
to appoint them to consign in Court any balance which may
remain.[3]

[1] Vessel is defined in 10 & 11 Vict. c. 27, secs. 3, 28; 1 Edw. VIII &
    1 Geo. VI c. 28, sec. 10 (2).
[2] As now extended by 1 Edw. VIII and 1 Geo. VI c. 28, sec. 10 (1).
[3] 10 & 11 Vict. c. 27, secs. 74, 75.

(14) *Pilotage Appeal.*

The Pilotage Act, 1913, gives a right of appeal in the Sheriff
Court, to a pilot (a) if the pilotage authority suspend or revoke
his licence; (b) if they refuse or fail to renew it; (c) if they have
obtained possession of the licence, and refuse or fail to return it;
and (d) if they have fined the pilot a sum exceeding £2.[1] The pilot
may present a summary application in the Sheriff Court having
jurisdiction at the port where the decision of the pilotage authority
is given (which in the case of (b) and (c) must presumably be read
as meaning where the office of the authority is situated)[1] craving
review of the decision of the pilotage authority, and the Court
may confirm or reverse the suspension or revocation of the licence or
make such order in the case as may seem just.[2] The appeal is
made by initial writ presented within twenty-one days from the
date of the decision appealed against.[3] With it there are produced
two copies of the decision, one being certified by the clerk or secretary of the pilotage authority.[3] (These latter provisions may not
apply in terms to a failure or refusal by the authority.) Warrant
is granted to cite the authority and citation is made by serving a
copy of the writ and warrant on the clerk or secretary of the

authority.[3] The rules as to expenses in civil causes apply.[3] The Sheriff may, but apparently need not, sit with an assessor,[4] to whom objection may be taken by either side either personally or in respect of his qualifications.[5] The general provisions as to nautical assessors apply.[6] The Sheriff Court judgment is final, unless leave is given to appeal to the Court of Session on a question of law or a question of mixed law and fact.[2] The appeal to the Court of Session is taken in the ordinary way by note of appeal on the interlocutor sheet and is not by stated case.[7]

[1] 2 & 3 Geo. V c. 31, sec. 28 (1) (7).
[2] Ibid., sec. 28 (4). See Manson v. Forth Pilotage Authority, 1933, 49 Sh.Ct.Rep. 243; Moore v. Clyde Pilotage Authority, 1943 S.C. 457.
[3] C.A.S. L, XI; Act of Sederunt, 29th October, 1919.
[4] 2 & 3 Geo. V c. 31, sec. 28 (7); cf. sec. 28 (2).
[5] Ibid., sec. 28 (3).
[6] C.A.S. L, XI, 5; Act of Sederunt, 29th October, 1919. See p. 185, supra.
[7] Moore v. Clyde Pilotage Authority, 1943 S.C. 30.

29. MILK AND DAIRIES ACTS.*

If the local authority grant a certificate to a dairyman, or refuse a certificate, or grant one provisionally, or revoke a certificate, any person aggrieved may appeal in a summary manner to the Sheriff who may order the local authority to grant, restore or revoke the certificate.[1] The application can be dealt with either by the Sheriff or the Sheriff-Substitute.[1] The decision of the former is final, but that of the Sheriff-Substitute is open to appeal to the Sheriff.[1] Expenses may be awarded to either party.[1] Under the later Act of 1922 a local authority may, after certain procedure, refuse to register a purveyor of milk, or may remove him from the register, and any person aggrieved may within twenty-one days give notice of appeal to the Sheriff who may require the local authority to register the purveyor, or not to remove him from the register.[2] The appeal may be disposed of either by the Sheriff or the Sheriff-Substitute and if by the latter there is a further right of appeal to the Sheriff if notice of appeal is given within seven days of the Sheriff-Substitute's decision.[2] It seems to be implied that there is no further right of appeal. The crave of the writ will be to recall or annul the decision of the local authority—who will be called as defenders—and to direct them to register the applicant or as the case may be. Answers or defences will usually be ordered and the matter disposed of after a hearing or proof. Where appeal from the Sheriff-Substitute to

* See general observations, p. 532, et seq., supra.

the Sheriff is competent it should be marked in the usual way, and under the Act of 1914—where no time is specified—it is presumably competent within the normal time for appeal.

1 4 & 5 Geo. V c. 46, sec. 7 (7).
2 12 & 13 Geo. V c. 54, secs. 2 (1) 14 (c).

If the local authority fail to perform any duty under the Act of 1914 the Department of Health may present a summary application to the Sheriff to order the performance of the duty.[1] This will be done by initial writ calling the authority as defenders and expenses may be awarded.[1] The ordinary rules in regard to appeal will apparently apply. In the interests of public health a local authority may order the stoppage of supplies from any dairy and may later withdraw any such order.[2] Any local authority or dairyman, aggrieved by an order or withdrawal or a failure to make an order, may appeal by summary application to the Sheriff having jurisdiction in the district where the dairy is situated, and the Sheriff may either make an order requiring the dairyman to cease supplies or may vary or rescind or withdraw any order made.[3] As a further limited right of appeal is expressly provided in relation to registration under the Act it was presumably intended that the decision in this case should not be subject to review. Otherwise the procedure will be as indicated in the previous paragraph. If an order under sec. 18 of the 1914 Act causes damage to a dairyman, and such damage has not arisen by his default, the local authority are liable to him in full compensation.[4] If the compensation claimed does not exceed £50 it is ascertained in a summary application by either party to the Sheriff, whose decision is final and not subject to review unless it is pronounced by the Sheriff-Substitute when it may be appealed to the Sheriff.[4] The appeal will be taken in the usual way and within the usual time.

1 4 & 5 Geo. V c. 46, sec. 10.
2 Ibid., sec. 18.
3 Ibid., sec. 18 (7).
4 Ibid., sec. 18 (10) ; 60 & 61 Vict. c. 38, sec. 164.

30. MONEYLENDERS' CLAIMS.

Under the Moneylenders Act of 1900 where proceedings are taken by a moneylender in any Court for recovery of money lent or the enforcement of an agreement or security, and there is evidence which satisfies the Court that the interest charged, or the amounts charged for expenses or other similar charges, are excessive, and that, in either case, the transaction is harsh and unconscionable the Court may reopen the transaction and relieve the debtor, or if necessary may order repayment, and may set aside or alter the security or agreement.[1] The above is largely superseded by the more drastic provisions in the Act of 1927, referred to below, but it is still available where the transaction does not fall within the later Act. The 1900 Act (as now amended) also provides that the borrower, his cautioner or other person liable, or the borrower's trustee in bankruptcy[2] may bring proceedings to have the above provisions of the Act exercised though the time for repayment of the loan or any instalment has not arrived.[3] The appropriate action by the borrower or other person would seem to be a declarator.

[1] 63 & 64 Vict. c. 51, sec. 1 (1).
[2] 17 & 18 Geo. V c. 21, sec. 10 (4).
[3] 63 & 64 Vict. c. 51, sec. 1 (2).

By the Act of 1927 where, in any proceedings in respect of any money lent by a moneylender, or of any agreement or security in respect of money lent, the interest charged exceeds 48 per cent., the Court must, unless the contrary is proved, presume for the purposes of sec. 1 of the 1900 Act that the interest charged is excessive and that the transaction is harsh and unconscionable.[1] By Act of Sederunt it is provided that in such a case the Sheriff may not grant decree in absence or otherwise unless he is satisfied by sworn evidence led in a proof before him in the ordinary manner that, in the circumstances of the case, the rate sued for is not excessive and the transaction is not harsh and unconscionable.[2] As the operative provision in this connexion is sec. 1 of the 1900 Act and as it authorizes the reopening of transactions only if the rate of interest is excessive and the transaction is harsh and unconscionable it seems clear that the moneylender avoids interference with the transaction if he disproves either of these factors which are now assumed against him.[3] So far as it requires proof of both the Act of Sederunt would seem to go beyond the Statutes, and it is thought that to that extent it must be regarded as inoperative. In many Courts the evidence of one witness is regarded as sufficient to meet the requirements of the Act of Sederunt. The evidence is usually not recorded.[4] Interest runs from the date of decree at 5 per cent. and not at the rate in the transaction.[5]

[1] 17 & 18 Geo. V c. 21, sec. 10 (1).
[2] Act of Sederunt, 24th February, 1933, sec. 5.
[3] 63 & 64 Vict. c. 51, sec. 1.
[4] Cf. M'Coll v. Leitch, 1933, 49 Sh.Ct.Rep. 189.
[5] Jackson v. Morris, 1931, 47 Sh.Ct.Rep. 307.

The Act of Sederunt makes various provisions in regard to procedure in the Sheriff and Small Debt Courts. Every writ at the instance of a moneylender for recovery of money lent by him must be headed and backed " Moneylenders Action."[1] In small debt causes the claim or account must be headed and backed in the same way.[1] Strictly read, the Act of Sederunt does not appear to apply to actions, not for recovery of money, but for enforcement of a security or agreement and actions at the instance of an assignee. The condescendence, or the account or claim in a small debt case, must set forth (a) the amount and date of actual receipt of principal sums received by the defender; (b) the percentage rate of interest; (c) any sums paid to account with dates and allocation; (d) the balance outstanding, distinguishing principal and interest; (e) the date when the cause of action accrued; and (f) a statement of any securities and whether still held or liquidated.[2] If the interest exceeds 48 per cent. there must also be stated the circumstances to justify the higher rate charged.[3] If these provisions are not complied with the defender may be assoilzied or the action dismissed.[4] When the writ is lodged, or the summons applied for, the pursuer must lodge the note or memorandum of the contract required by the Act of 1927, and any other document signed by the defender in relation to the loan.[5] Where the interest exceeds 48 per cent. the interlocutor or decree must find whether or not the rate charged is in the circumstances excessive, and whether or not the transaction is harsh and unconscionable, and in the Small Debt Court the same finding must be entered in the Cause Book.[6] Without such finding extract cannot be issued.[5] Where the interest claimed exceeds 48 per cent., and the pursuer fails to satisfy the Sheriff that he is entitled to the rate charged, he is not to be awarded the expenses of the proof.[7] Presumably the proof in question is that led in an undefended action, or in a defended action any proof led to justify the rate of interest charged. On a strict reading the pursuer would seem to lose such expenses whenever he failed to recover the full interest charged, even though only a slight modification in the rate was made. If the rate of interest is sustained the pursuer is entitled to the expenses of the proof.[8] In granting decree to a moneylender the Court may order payment by instalments and may make a similar order after decree but before payment.[9] If a transaction is reopened by the Court the moneylender's certificate may be endorsed.[10]

[1] Act of Sederunt, 24th February, 1933, sec. 1.
[2] Ibid., sec. 2.
[3] Ibid., sec. 3.
[4] Campbell v. Christie, 1934, 51 Sh.Ct.Rep. 75.
[5] Act of Sederunt, 24th February, 1933, sec. 4.

6 Ibid., sec. 6.
7 Ibid., sec. 7.
8 M'Coll v. M'Caig, &c., 1940, 57 Sh.Ct.Rep. 35.
9 17 & 18 Geo. V c. 21, sec. 18 (f).
10 Ibid., sec. 10 (2).

The Act of 1927 contains various other provisions which affect the right of a moneylender to recover from his debtor. In certain circumstances and for different reasons the transaction may be illegal[1] or the contract unenforceable[2] either in whole or in part[3] or while the moneylender is in default under some provision of the Act.[4] With certain exceptions proceedings for recovery of money lent, or interest thereon, or for enforcing any agreement or security, must be brought within twelve months from the date on which the cause of action accrued.[5] Certain relaxations of the provisions of the Act are allowed in the case of assignees of a moneylender.[6]

1 17 & 18 Geo. V c. 21, secs. 5 (6), 12.
2 Ibid., sec. 6. See M'Coll v. Letham, &c., 1937, 53 Sh.Ct.Rep. 101;
   Shaw v. Clark, 1940, 60 Sh.Ct.Rep. 3; Shaw v. Duffy, 1943 S.C.
   350; Smith v. Connor, 1943, 60 Sh.Ct.Rep. 5; Shaw v. Holmes,
   1946, 62 Sh.Ct.Rep. 120. Even the money lent is not recoverable,
   Miller & Sons v. A. S., &c., 1933, 50 Sh.Ct.Rep. 127.
3 Ibid., sec. 7; Malcolm Muir v. Jamieson, 1947 S.N. 59.
4 Ibid., sec. 8 (3).
5 Ibid., sec. 13; Duncan v. Kennaway, 1936, 52 Sh.Ct.Rep. 306; Smith
   v. Craig, 1938 S.C. 620.
6 Ibid., sec. 17.

31. MUNICIPAL.†

(1) *Creation of Burgh.*

An application to erect a populous place into a burgh may be made by any seven or more householders to the Sheriff or Sheriffs of the county or counties within which the place is situated.[1] Such applications cannot be dealt with by a Sheriff-Substitute.[2] The writ will crave the Sheriff to find that the area proposed is suitable for being formed into a police burgh, and to define the boundaries thereof. If the population is 5000 or over the place may be divided into wards.[1] Notice is given by advertisement and all parties interested are entitled to be heard, and may be appointed to lodge a notice of appearance. The population is ascertained by remit to a reporter.[1] The boundaries having been defined, a meeting of householders is convened by the Sheriff, on a requisition of seven or more householders, and is advertised in

† Certain of the matters under this sub-head may be affected by the
   provisions of the new Local Government (Scotland) Bill when that
   comes into effect.

prescribed fashion.[1] The Sheriff—or one of the Sheriffs—presides, and, if necessary, a poll is taken.[1] If the resolution to adopt the Act is carried, the Sheriff finds and declares that the populous place is a burgh.[1] His finding is recorded in the Court books and reported to the Secretary of State for Scotland.[1] There is no appeal in the proper sense though the Sheriff has power to rectify any accidental error,[3] but certain parties are given a right to apply in the Court of Session to have the Sheriff's order recalled.[4] If two or more Sheriffs are concerned and they are not unanimous they must state a case for the Court of Session.[4] Provisions similar to the above are laid down in regard to fixing of boundaries in the case of certain other burghs.[5]

1 55 & 56 Vict. c. 55, sec. 9; 56 & 57 Vict. c. 25, sec. 2.   See Lees, Sheriff Court Styles, 4th edn., 116-7.
2 Ibid., sec. 4 (30).
3 Ibid., sec. 10.
4 Ibid., sec. 13; Glengarnock Iron, &c., Co. v. M'Gregor, 1904, 6 F. 955.
5 Ibid., sec. 8.

(2) Revision of Boundaries.

Upon the application of a town council, after notice by public advertisement, and after hearing all parties interested and making such inquiry as he may deem necessary, the Sheriff may alter the burgh boundaries.[1] The Court is that of the county where the burgh is situated, but where the burgh and the lands proposed to be included lie in more than one county the Sheriffs of all the counties concerned form the tribunal.[1] The Sheriff may not sanction an alteration of boundaries merely because the application is not opposed.[2] If more than one Sheriff sits, and they are not unanimous, the application is not granted and the Sheriffs must state a case for the Court of Session.[3] There is a right to apply, by separate petition, to the Court of Session to have the Sheriff's order recalled, and a right in the Sheriff to correct errors all as above stated.[4] The Sheriff alone, not the Sheriff-Substitute, may act in such applications.[5] It is not usual, though it appears competent, to award expenses.[6]

1 55 & 56 Vict. c. 55, sec. 11; 63 & 64 Vict. c. 49, sec. 3.   See Lees, Sheriff Court Styles, 4th edn., 117.
2 Lindsay v. Magistrates of Leith, 1897, 24 R. 867.
3 55 & 56 Vict. c. 55, secs. 11, 13.
4 See preceding paragraph.   See also Magistrates of Kilsyth v. Stirling County Council, 1936 S.C. 149.
5 55 & 56 Vict. c. 55, sec. 4 (30).
6 Dunbarton County Council v. Clydebank Commissioners, 1901, 4 F. 111; Burgh of Motherwell v. Lanarkshire County Council, 1902, 18 Sh.Ct.Rep. 317; Lanarkshire County Council v. Motherwell Corporation, 1904, 6 F. 962; Rothes Town Council v. Elgin County Council, 1907, 23 Sh.Ct.Rep. 147.

(3) *Wards.*

As regards certain burghs the Sheriff or the Sheriff-Substitute, upon the application of a town council, may divide or redivide the burgh into wards, apportion councillors to the wards, and determine incidental questions.[1] Advertisement and inquiry are in the discretion of the Sheriff, but he must hear interested parties,[1] and cannot grant the application merely because there is no opposition.[2] If the applicaton is dealt with by the Sheriff-Substitute, there is appeal to the Sheriff whose decision is final,[3] but where a burgh is situate in more than one county the application is made to the Sheriffs—which presumably excludes Sheriffs-Substitute —of such counties, to be dealt with as in cases under the Burgh Police Act.[4]

[1] 63 & 64 Vict. c. 49, sec. 19; Encyclopædia of Scottish Legal Styles, II, 235.
[2] Lindsay v. Magistrates of Leith, 1897, 24 R. 867. See also Kintore Town Council, 1938, 54 Sh.Ct.Rep. 241.
[3] 63 & 64 Vict. c. 49, sec. 114.
[4] Ibid. See previous page.

(4) *Acquisition of Land.*

As a necessary preliminary to acquiring land compulsorily a town council may present a summary application craving authority to put in force the powers of the Lands Clauses Act.[1] The proceedings are not competent before the Sheriff-Substitute, but only before the Sheriff.[2] There must be produced with the initial writ a plan and a book of reference showing owners and occupiers.[1] A time and place for inquiry is fixed and intimated to the owners and occupiers on fourteen days' notice, and such other intimation is made as the Sheriff may order.[1] After inquiry and hearing parties the Sheriff may (a) grant the crave; (b) grant it in a modified form; or (c) refuse it.[1] There is no appeal to the Court of Session, but there is what is called an appeal (but seems rather to be a power to represent) to the Secretary of State for Scotland, who may order further inquiry.[1]

[1] 55 & 56 Vict. c. 55, secs. 60, 154.
[2] Ibid., sec. 4 (30).

(5) *Councillors.*

Where the number of magistrates or councillors differs or comes to differ from the statutory scale the town council may apply to the Sheriff to have the matter remedied.[1] After such advertisement and inquiry as he may deem proper the Sheriff is required to ascertain and declare the population and declare that the number of magistrates and councillors shall be increased or diminished, and also to determine certain incidental matters.[1] Where the application is dealt with by the Sheriff-Substitute there is an appeal to the Sheriff, and the decision of the Sheriff, either on appeal or in the first instance, is final.[2] If the numbers are disproportionate the Sheriff has apparently no option but to carry out the statutory direction.[3]

[1] 63 & 64 Vict. c. 49, sec. 11; Kintore Town Council, 1938, 54 Sh.Ct.Rep. 241; Encyclopædia of Scottish Legal Styles, II, 236.
[2] Ibid., sec. 114.
[3] Magistrates of Cupar, 1904, 21 Sh.Ct.Rep. 9.

(6) Election Petition.

The disqualification of a town councillor may be declared by the Sheriff Court of the county within which the election took place or to which the larger part of the electoral area belongs.[1] The proceedings may be taken at the instance of (a) the town council; (b) any four or more electors; or (c) an opposing candidate if the disqualification existed at the time of nomination or election.[2] The crave is for declarator that the defender is disqualified for election as a town councillor, and if pursuer is the opposing candidate a further crave may be made for declarator that the pursuer was duly elected.[3] The condescendence of the writ should narrate the specific disqualification founded on.

[1] 53 & 54 Vict. c. 55, sec. 31.
[2] 63 & 64 Vict. c. 49, sec. 14 (2).
[3] As to facts entitling pursuer to have this crave granted, see Templeton v. M'Leod, 1939, 56 Sh.Ct.Rep. 44. See also Moore, &c. v. Houston, 1905, 22 Sh.Ct.Rep. 55.

The procedure in election petitions is regulated by the Elections (Scotland) (Corrupt and Illegal Practices) Act, 1890,[1] and relative Act of Sederunt[2] which should be consulted for details. Application is made by initial writ in the usual form,[3] which must be presented within a specified time[4] and must be signed by the petitioner personally.[5] With certain exceptions in relation to incidental matters referred to below,[6] applications under the Act are dealt with by the Sheriff and not the Sheriff-Substitute.[7] The first deliverance fixes the amount of security to be given by the petitioner and may appoint answers to be lodged.[3] The method of service on the respondents is prescribed,[3] and, within five days of presentation, formal notice of presentation has to be given to the respondent.[8] The respondent may object in writing to any bond of caution,[9] and such objection is disposed of by the Sheriff-clerk.[10] Special provision is made as to amendment and for notice of the date and place of trial.[11] Any party may apply by minute[12] in the process to have the point raised in the petition stated as a case to be heard by the Court of Session,[13] and at the trial the Sheriff may himself reserve any question of law for consideration of the Court of Session.[13] It seems clear that any such case is competent only before judgment is given by the Sheriff. In either event such case is in form prescribed by, and is dealt with under the procedure laid down in, the Rules of Court.[14] The evidence at the trial is taken down in shorthand,[15] and the shorthand writer's charges as fixed by the Sheriff are met in the first instance by the petitioner.[16] The Lord Advocate is represented at the trial.[17] Provision is made for compelling the attendance of witnesses and for their examination and expenses.[18] The Court does not appear to have the power to grant a specification for recovery of documents prior to the trial.[19]

[1] 53 & 54 Vict. c. 55, secs. 30-46.
[2] C.A.S., L, X.
[3] C.A.S., L, X, 1; Lees, Sheriff Court Styles, 4th edn., 176-8.
[4] 53 & 54 Vict. c. 55, sec. 32.
[5] Baxter v. Stevenson, 1913, 30 Sh.Ct.Rep. 159; Waddelow v. Johnston, 1945, 62 Sh.Ct.Rep. 55.
[6] See next page.
[7] 53 & 54 Vict. c. 55, sec. 35.
[8] Ibid., sec. 33 (3); Hunter v. Kennedy, 1896, 12 Sh.Ct.Rep. 95; Baxter v. Stevenson, supra; Fairley v. Young, 1933, 49 Sh.Ct.Rep. 108.
[9] Ibid., sec. 33 (4).
[10] C.A.S., L, X, 2.
[11] Ibid., 3, 4; as to amendment see Waddelow v. Johnston, supra.
[12] Ibid., 7. See Rules of Court, 1936, V, 22-24.
[13] 53 & 54 Vict. c. 55, sec. 36 (7) (8).
[14] Rules of Court, 1936, V, 22-24.
[15] 53 & 54 Vict. c. 55, sec. 36 (12).
[16] C.A.S., L, X, 6.
[17] 53 & 54 Vict. c. 55, sec. 41.
[18] Ibid., sec. 37; C.A.S., L, X, 10.
[19] Ibid., sec. 35 (2); Hood v. Gordon, 1895, 23 R. 171.

An election petition can only be withdrawn after certain formalities have been complied with.[1] A minute in prescribed form is lodged, and intimated to the respondent and certain officials, a time is fixed for a hearing on the minute, and notice is given by advertisement.[2] Affidavits by the petitioner and his solicitor are produced and copies delivered to the Lord Advocate who may appear or be represented.[1] At the hearing any other person who is eligible may be substituted as petitioner.[1] If leave to withdraw is granted the petitioner must pay the respondent's expenses.[1] If the petitioner dies the petition is abated,[3] but notice is given by newspaper advertisement and another eligible person may apply to be substituted.[4] If the petition is not to be opposed the

respondent must give written intimation to that effect at the
Sheriff-clerk's office at least six days (exclusive of the day of giving
the notice) before the trial.[5]   Where such notice is given, or the
respondent dies or otherwise ceases to hold the office in question,
any other eligible person may apply to appear as respondent.[6]
Where necessary public notice is given by the Sheriff-clerk that
a trial is not to proceed by reason of withdrawal or otherwise.[7]
Expenses are in the hands of the Court and special provision may
be made in respect of expenses caused by vexatious or unfounded
allegations.[8]   Expenses are taxed as between solicitor and client
on the higher scale.[9]

[1] 53 & 54 Vict. c. 55, sec. 38.
[2] C.A.S., L, X. 11.
[3] 53 & 54 Vict. c. 55, sec. 39.
[4] C.A.S., L, X, 12.
[5] Ibid., 13.
[6] 53 & 54 Vict. c. 55, sec. 40; C.A.S., L, X, 14.
[7] C.A.S., L, X, 15.
[8] 53 & 54 Vict. c. 55, sec. 42.
[9] Ibid., sec. 42 (7); C.A.S., L, X, 18.

The Sheriff-Substitute may deal with applications to allow late
claims to be submitted and settled and for an authorized excuse in
respect of failure or error in the return or declaration,[1] incidental
applications in relation to the time of presenting a petition or
the amending thereof,[2] the arrangements for security for expenses,[3]
the abatement of a petition on the death of the petitioner,[4] and
the withdrawal and substitution of respondents.[5]

[1] 53 & 54 Vict. c. 55, secs. 25, 35 (3); Caddell, 1935, 52 Sh.Ct.Rep. 203.
[2] Ibid., secs. 32, 35 (3).
[3] Ibid., secs. 33, 35 (3).
[4] Ibid., secs. 35 (3), 39.
[5] Ibid., secs. 35 (3), 40.

An alternative mode of challenging the election of a councillor
is for the town council to pass a resolution declaring his office
vacant.[1]   In that event the councillor may appeal against the
resolution in the manner allowed by the Burgh Police Act, 1892.[2]
Difficulties arising in connexion with elections and otherwise in
relation to municipal administration may be dealt with by a special
application for an order to facilitate the execution of the statutory
provisions.[3]

[1] 63 & 64 Vict. c. 49, sec. 14 (3).
[2] 55 & 56 Vict. c. 55, sec. 339.   See p. 640, infra.
[3] Ibid., sec. 17; 63 & 64 Vict. c. 49, sec. 11.   See further at p. 539, supra.

(7) Bye-Laws.

Bye-laws made by a town council for carrying out the provisions of the Burgh Police Acts are not operative until they have been confirmed by the Sheriff who is directed to inquire into the bye-laws, and to allow or disallow them as he thinks fit.[1] The Burgh Police Act of 1892 provides that the bye-laws must be not contrary to Scots law or to anything contained in that Act.[2] Bye-laws must also be confirmed by the Secretary of State for Scotland.[1]

[1] 55 & 56 Vict. c. 55, sec. 318. See also secs. 55 (6), 316; 3 Edw. VII c. 33, secs. 80, 82 (2), 93.
[2] Ibid., sec. 55 (6).

The application for approval of bye-laws is an *ex parte* summary application at the instance of the town council. But before the application is presented the town council must make certain publication and advertisement.[1] Any person desiring to object must give the council notice of the nature of his objection ten days before the hearing of the application, and he may then be heard personally or by counsel or solicitor, only one objector being heard on the same point without leave of the Sheriff.[1] The initial writ should refer to any objection stated, and it should be produced with the writ. Objectors will usually be allowed to lodge written objections in reply to the averments in the writ, and inquiry by proof in such a case will usually be necessary. The matter may be disposed of either by the Sheriff-Substitute or the Sheriff,[2] and there is no right of appeal in either case.[3] It seems doubtful whether the bye-laws can be varied by the Sheriff or must be simply allowed or disallowed,[4] but the town council can be given the opportunity of amending.[5] The jurisdiction of the Sheriff is not confined to the question whether the bye-laws are legally unchallengeable, and his function is to consider also questions of reasonableness and expediency.[6] It is not the practice, and is inappropriate if not incompetent, to award expenses.[7]

[1] 55 & 56 Vict. c. 55, secs. 319, 320; Encyclopædia of Scottish Legal Styles, II, 249.
[2] Ibid., sec. 4 (30). See also sec. 49.
[3] Glasgow Corporation v. Glasgow Churches' Council, 1944 S.C. 97, Lord Jamieson, p. 118.
[4] See White v. Magistrates of Rutherglen, 1897, 24 R. 446; Biggar Town Council, 1912, 28 Sh.Ct.Rep. 348; cf. Provost, &c., of Dundee, 1912, 29 Sh.Ct.Rep. 49.
[5] Rothesay Town Council, 1898, 14 Sh.Ct.Rep. 189; Provost, &c., of Dundee, supra.
[6] Glasgow Corporation v. Glasgow Churches' Council, supra. See also other cases, supra, and Glasgow Corporation, 1932, 48 Sh.Ct.Rep. 222; Burgh of Turriff, 1933, 50 Sh.Ct.Rep. 33; Oban Town Council v. Oban Sabbath Observance Society, 1935, 52 Sh.Ct.Rep. 27.
[7] See White v. Magistrates of Rutherglen, supra; Tobermory Town Council v. Capaldi, 1938, 54 Sh.Ct.Rep. 175.

(8) *Recovery of Rates.*

In addition to procedure in the ordinary way,[1] a special summary process is competent and is generally adopted for the recovery of municipal rates. The collector is required to issue an assessment notice, setting forth the rates claimed, and fixing a time within which payment must be made.[2] If payment is not made within that time the collector may apply to the Sheriff for a summary warrant for recovery of the assessments in arrear with 10 per cent. added.[2] Any number of persons in arrear may be included in the same application, and no service or intimation is required. The Sheriff must be satisfied by certificate by the collector that statutory notice has been given to each person, and upon production of this certificate warrant must be granted.[2] The warrant authorizes arrestment in common form, and also authorizes the collector, or any officer of Court, to enter into premises and to poind, seize, remove, or secure effects.[2] The statutory form does not contain warrant to open shut and lockfast places, but the collector or officer can apply to the Court for a supplementary warrant to that effect.[3] If proceedings for recovery of rates are taken by ordinary action the Sheriff may entertain defences challenging the legality of the assessments.[4] It has been held that a summary warrant may be abandoned and an ordinary action thereafter brought for recovery.[5]

[1] See Govan Commissioners v. Clark, 1889, 5 Sh.Ct.Rep. 156; Magistrates of Kilmarnock v. Sloan, 1914, 30 Sh.Ct.Rep. 238; Lanark County Council v. Burns, 1915, 31 Sh.Ct.Rep. 301.
[2] 55 & 56 Vict. c. 55, secs. 352, 353, Schedule VIII.
[3] Scott v. Letham, 1846, 5 Bell's App. 126.
[4] M'Tavish v. Caledonian Canal Commissioners, 1896, 3 R. 412.
[5] Wright v. Craig, 1919, 35 Sh.Ct.Rep. 22; Lanark County Council v. Burns, supra; Muir v. Sands, 1927, 44 Sh.Ct.Rep. 79; Staig v. M'Meekin, 1943, 59 Sh.Ct.Rep. 126.

The proprietor of goods poinded or sold, who feels aggrieved by any proceedings taken under the summary warrant, may apply to the Sheriff who granted the warrant.[1] The Sheriff is then directed to call summarily before him the party complained of, and the applicant, and without written pleadings, to inquire into and decide any dispute, question or claim of damage raised by the application.[1] The Sheriff may award expenses to either party and his decision is final.[1] Apart from this limited right of review the propriety of the assessment would be open to challenge by suspension.[2]

[1] 55 & 56 Vict. c. 55, sec. 354.
[2] See Winter v. Magistrates of Edinburgh, 1837, 16 S. 276; Watson v. Adams, 1849, 11 D. 1263; Sharp v. Latheron Parochial Board, 1883, 10 R. 1163.

If any persons included in the summary warrant leave the
jurisdiction, it is necessary, before the warrant can be executed
in another Sheriffdom, to have it endorsed by the Sheriff of the
jurisdiction where it is to be enforced.[1] A summary warrant may
be executed by the collector, or a Sheriff-officer,[2] and in the case
of a warrant executed out of the original jurisdiction it is provided that any police constable may also put the warrant in force.[1]

[1] 55 & 56 Vict. c. 55, sec. 357.
[2] Ibid., sec. 353.

(9) *Dangerous Buildings.*

If the owner of a building or wall fail to carry out operations
to render it safe the burgh surveyor may apply to the Sheriff for
an order upon the owner, within a specified time, to execute the
required work.[1] The Sheriff's order is to be made after inquiry.[1]
The Statute authorizes the municipal authority, in the event of
the owner not complying with the Sheriff's order within the set
time, to do the work themselves,[1] and there should be an alternative
crave for decree for the cost of executing the work if the owner
fails to do this.[2] These sections seem to confer a special jurisdiction on the Sheriff which would not be subject to any right of
review.[3]

[1] 55 & 56 Vict. c. 55, sec. 191; Lees, Sheriff Court Styles, 4th edn., 119.
[2] Ibid., sec. 192.
[3] See p. 537, supra; but cf. Somerville v. Macdonald's Trustees, 1901,
    3 F. 390.

(10) *Ruinous Property.*

When property in a burgh, held by two or more joint owners,
has become ruinous, owing to the proprietors being unable to agree
what should be done with it, the burgh surveyor, or sanitary
inspector, or any of the joint proprietors may apply to the Sheriff,
who may call all parties interested before him " in the usual
manner and form followed in the Court."[1] The appropriate form
of process seems to be an ordinary action calling as defenders all
parties interested, and in respect of which the ordinary right of
appeal will apparently apply. The first stage of procedure is a
remit to three men of skill to value the property and apportion
the valuation amongst the joint proprietors according to their
respective rights and interests.[1] The Sheriff must then fix a time,
not exceeding six weeks, within which the parties may buy or sell
to each other,[1] and failing the owners so agreeing the Sheriff may
authorize the exposure of the subjects for sale at an upset price
not less than the appraised value, and, if necessary, may reduce

the upset price from time to time.[2]   Provision is made for advertisement, consignation of the price,[2] and for warrant to complete the title of the purchaser.[3]   On failure of the original purchase a resale may be ordered.[4]   When the sale is completed the Sheriff is directed to ascertain who are entitled to share in the price and to order payment accordingly.[5]

[1] 55 & 56 Vict. c. 55, sec. 195.
[2] Ibid., sec. 196.
[3] Ibid., sec. 197.   See Young's Trustees v. Grainger, 1904, 7 F. 232.
[4] Ibid., sec. 198.
[5] Ibid., sec. 199.   See Young's Trustees v. Grainger, supra.

If the ruinous subject is held by a single proprietor the owner is notified to put the place into repair within three months, and, if he fails to carry out the operations required, application may be made to the Sheriff for warrant of sale.[1]   The procedure as regards valuation, exposure, and completion of the purchaser's title is, *mutatis mutandis*, the same as in the case of joint proprietors.[2]   The ordinary right of appeal will apparently apply.[3]

[1] 55 & 56 Vict. c. 55, sec. 200; 3 Edw. VII c. 33, sec. 104 (1), Schedule.
[2] See preceding paragraph.
[3] See preceding paragraph; also Provost, &c., of Airdrie v. Andrew, &c., 1905, 21 Sh.Ct.Rep. 255.

(11) *Street Register.*

Any person aggrieved by an entry in the register of streets made in a burgh, or a marking on the plan relative thereto, may, within three months from publication of notice thereof, appeal to the Sheriff or the Court of Session,[1] and any deliverance of a town council making alterations or additions to such register or plan is subject to appeal in the same way.[2]   The Sheriff is directed[1] to deal with the appeal in the manner provided by sec. 339 of the 1892 Act which deals with the general right of appeal.[3]   Where such an appeal is taken to the Sheriff—which includes the Sheriff-Substitute[4]—either party may, within fourteen days from the date of his decision, appeal thereagainst to the Court of Session whose decision is final.[1]   The above reference to sec. 339 relates only to procedure before the Sheriff, and the appeal to the Court of Session under this section would appear to be an ordinary appeal and not one by stated case as under sec. 339.   It is thought that there is no right of appeal from the Sheriff-Substitute to the Sheriff and that the appeal from either to the Court of Session is from a final determination only.

[1] 3 Edw. VII c. 33, sec. 7.
[2] Ibid., sec. 9.
[3] See next page.
[4] 3 Edw. VII c. 33, sec. 103; 55 & 56 Vict. c. 55, sec. 4 (30).

The existence of the above statutory machinery for determining the width of streets does not preclude private parties from asking the Court to determine their rights.[1] Where a town council has failed to perform its statutory duty by preparing a register an action of declarator may be brought to settle the limits of a street. This is an ordinary action subject to review in common form.

[1] Campbell v. Craig, 1911 S.C. 516.

(12) *General Appeal.*

In addition to special procedure in matters otherwise provided for, the Burgh Police Acts give to aggrieved persons a general right of appeal in wide terms to the Sheriff or the Court of Session against orders or resolutions of a town council.[1] The orders of municipal authorities against which appeal is thus competent are very varied, and the appellants may include persons liable to pay or contribute towards the expense of works ordered or required by the town council, or persons whose property may be affected, or who think themselves aggrieved by any order, resolution, deliverance or act of the council.[1] An appeal under this section is not an appropriate way for a ratepayer to raise a general question of public expenditure.[2] Further, such appeals are not likely to be successful if they are in effect a challenge of the general policy of a town council in discharging their statutory duties, for the Court is usually unwilling to set aside an order relating to some practical matter of administration which the Statutes have entrusted to the local authority.[3] It has been held that appeal under this section is competent only to persons within, or having property within, the burgh,[4] and it has been suggested that the word " act " as used in this section is not a mere physical act but rather something of the nature of an order or deliverance.[5] A notice by a sanitary inspector requiring premises to be whitewashed is appealable under the section.[6] Various rights of appeal given earlier in the Act are apparently intended (so far as an appeal to the Sheriff is concerned[7]) to apply to the procedure under this section.[8] But where a special right of appeal is given by another section an appeal under sec. 339 is not available.[9] Orders, resolutions, deliverances or acts of a Town Council made or done under the Burgh Police Act of 1903 are appealable under sec. 339 of the earlier Act,[10] and the section seems to justify an appeal against the council's decision in places where no Dean of Guild Court is in existence.[11]

[1] 55 & 56 Vict. c. 55, sec. 339; 3 Edw. VII c. 33, sec. 104 (2) (s).
[2] Freebairn v. Kilsyth Commissioners, 1895, 11 Sh.Ct.Rep. 257; Heddle v. Magistrates of Leith, 1897, 24 R. 662; cf. Ferrier v. Provost, &c., of Melrose, 1907, 24 Sh.Ct.Rep. 178.

3 Small v. Dundee Commissioners, 1884, 12 R. 123. See also Glen v. Commissioners of Dumbarton, 1897, 13 Sh.Ct.Rep. 244; Hayes-Watson v. Carnoustie Town Council, 1901, 17 Sh.Ct.Rep. 325; Gray v. Coupar Angus Town Council, 1904, 21 Sh.Ct.Rep. 214; Shaw's Trustees v. Provost, &c., of Inverness, 1907, 24 Sh.Ct.Rep. 89; Port Glasgow Property Investment Co. v. Provost, &c., of Port Glasgow, 1909, 25 Sh.Ct.Rep. 86; Aberdeen Cemetery Co. v. Clapperton, 1918, 35 Sh.Ct.Rep. 102.

4 Christie v. Magistrates of Leven, 1912 S.C. 678.

5 Magistrates of Crieff v. Young, 1906, 8 F. (J.) 48, Lord Justice-Clerk Macdonald, p. 51.

6 Magistrates of Leith v. Irons, 1907 S.C. 384.

7 Cf. Laurenson v. Lerwick Commissioners, 1896, 24 R. 135.

8 55 & 56 Vict. c. 55, secs. 132, 143, 165, 182, 233, 237, 245, 267. As to some of these it may be difficult to say from what date the fourteen days for appealing should run, on which point see the next paragraph. Appeals under sec. 251 (where the Sheriff's judgment is declared to be final) have usually been regarded as falling under sec. 339 and not as being a separate right of appeal. (Campbeltown Building Co. v. Magistrates of Campbeltown, 1893, 10 Sh.Ct.Rep. 16; Hill v. Kilwinning Town Council, 1928, 44 Sh.Ct.Rep. 359.)

9 Brown v. Magistrates of Leith, 1896, 23 R. 654, Lord President Robertson, p. 658; Lambie v. Provost, &c., of Port Glasgow, 1906, 22 Sh.Ct.Rep. 150.

10 3 Edw. VII c. 33, sec. 104 (2) (s).

11 Walker v. Saltcoats Commissioners, 1898, 14 Sh.Ct.Rep. 361.

An appeal to the Sheriff is taken by initial writ (which the section describes as a note of appeal), and the proceedings will normally be treated as a summary application. Under the Act the appeal is directed to be taken within fourteen days of the date of the intimation of the order or deliverance, or within fourteen days after the commission of the act complained of.[1] Whilst the fourteen days' limit might be rigidly enforced in cases relating to works the effect of which is immediately evident, or to orders or deliverances duly notified to the appellant, in other cases an appeal might be regarded as competent if taken within fourteen days of the matter complained of becoming evident.[2] But appellants who did not appeal following on intimation made to them were not allowed to appeal at a later stage against an act following on the order intimated to them.[3]

1 55 & 56 Vict. c. 55, sec. 339.

2 See Adam v. Alloa Commissioners, 1875, 2 R. 143; Phillips v. Dunoon Commissioners, 1885, 12 R. 159; Muirhead, Municipal and Police Government, 3rd edn., ii, 719. See also Dougan v. Armadale Town Council, 1923, 40 Sh.Ct.Rep. 70, p. 72.

3 Mackay v. Provost, &c., of Helensburgh, 1903, 20 Sh.Ct.Rep. 61.

Appeals are taken in the Sheriff Court of the county or district where the burgh is situated.[1] The writ should crave the Court to recall the order or resolution complained of and the Act provides that the Sheriff's deliverance may confirm, quash, vary or redress the order in question.[1] The Sheriff is directed to order a copy of the writ to be served on the clerk to the local authority and to appoint answers to be lodged within six days after service, and it is specially provided that expenses may be awarded to either party.[1] This has been held to be competent whether they have been craved or not.[2] Persons not called, but who have an interest, have been allowed to be sisted as parties.[3]

[1] 55 & 56 Vict. c. 55, sec. 339.
[2] Jack v. Lanark Commissioners, 1895, 12 Sh.Ct.Rep. 7.
[3] Hamilton's Trustees v. Perth Commissioners, 1897, 14 Sh.Ct.Rep. 325.

The position in regard to appeals within the Sheriff Court and from that Court to the Court of Session has been already dealt with.[1]

[1] See p. 541, supra.

The statutory appeal rights do not necessarily exclude a common law remedy against a corporation whose proceedings are *ultra vires* of their powers or are irregular.[1] And where it is, for some reason, not competent to appeal against a particular order, it may be competent to raise a civil process, such as an interdict, suspension or declarator.[2] But in general when a statutory remedy has been provided, the Court will not entertain an action at common law when the appropriate right of appeal has not been exercised.[3]

[1] See Adam v. Alloa Commissioners, 1874, 2 R. 143; Phillips v. Dunoon Commissioners, 1884, 12 R. 159. See also Caledonian Railway Co. v. Glasgow Corporation, 1905, 7 F. 1020; 1907 S.C. (H.L.) 7; Magistrates of Crieff v. Young, 1906, 8 F. (J.) 48; cf. Brand v. Arbroath Commissioners, 1890, 17 R. 790.
[2] See Campbell v. Craig, 1911 S.C. 516; Christie v. Magistrates of Leven, 1912 S.C. 678.
[3] John Darney & Son v. Calder District Committee, 1904, 7 F. 239, Lord Adam, p. 244; Minty v. Provost, &c., of Macduff, 1908, 25 Sh.Ct.Rep. 194. See also Govan Commissioners v. Caledonian Railway Co., 1890, 6 Sh.Ct.Rep. 365.

32. PARTNERSHIP.

Under the Partnership Act of 1890 the Court may, on application by a partner, decree a dissolution of the partnership in certain specified cases.[1] The Court is defined as including every Court and judge having jurisdiction in the case.[2] As a matter of jurisdiction a bare declarator that a partnership is at an end would now be competent in the Sheriff Court.[3] The Act, however, does not contemplate an action of this kind but one craving the dissolution of the firm.[1] This does not seem to be a form of action competent in the Sheriff Court,[4] apart from the limited jurisdiction now expressly conferred in relation to the winding up of companies.[5] Nor has the Sheriff power to appoint a judicial factor on a partnership estate.[6] For these reasons it is difficult to see how an action for dissolution of a partnership can be competent in the Sheriff Court, but in a recent case such an action was brought and discussed without any question as to competency being raised.[7] An action of declarator of partnership is competent as are also actions of accounting and other causes relating to partnership which are within the ordinary jurisdiction of the Sheriff.

[1] 53 & 54 Vict. c. 39, sec. 35.
[2] Ibid., sec. 45.
[3] 7 Edw. VII c. 51, sec. 5 (1).
[4] See Weir v. Weir, 1907, 23 Sh.Ct.Rep. 233.
[5] See p. 572, supra.
[6] 43 & 44 Vict. c. 4, secs. 3, 4.
[7] Duthie v. Milne, 1946, 63 Sh.Ct.Rep. 9.

33. Poor Law.

(1) *Relief Order.*

A person who is refused poor law relief has a right of appeal in the Sheriff Court of the district where refusal is made.[1] The inspector must deliver to the applicant for relief a certificate stating the grounds of refusal.[2] If the refusal proceeds upon a medical report, as to the applicant's state of health, and a copy of that report has been furnished to the applicant, it should also be produced to the Sheriff. No written complaint or appeal is necessary. Production of the certificate of refusal is sufficient warrant to the Sheriff to deal with the appeal. The Sheriff cannot entertain an appeal upon the amount of relief afforded, and if the pauper is dissatisfied with that his remedy is to complain to the Department of Health for Scotland.[3] The proceedings before the Sheriff proceed *viva voce*, and if the Sheriff considers that relief is not due he refuses the application. If he considers that, on the facts stated to him, the applicant is entitled to relief he orders the inspector to lodge a written statement showing his reasons for refusal and orders interim relief to be given till the statement is lodged.[1] This order may be intimated to the inspector by post,[4] but in practice the order is directed to be intimated by the pauper, who is furnished with a certified copy for delivery to the inspector. The inspector must then grant interim relief; but he may lodge a written statement with his reasons for not granting relief. The Sheriff may allow answers and hear parties, and, if necessary, make up a record and take proof.[5] He may also nominate a solicitor to appear for the poor person and continue the interim relief till judgment on the merits.[5] The interlocutor should contain the usual findings in fact and law.[6] The only competent decision of the Sheriff is that the applicant is, or is not, entitled to relief. If he is not the interim order for relief falls; if he is there is a finding to that effect, the amount being fixed by the poor law authorities. An appeal to the Sheriff, or to the Court of Session, appears to be competent.[7]

[1] 8 & 9 Vict. c. 83, sec. 73. See Duncan v. Aberdeen County Council, 1936 S.C. (H.L.) 47.
[2] Graham, Poor Law, 284.
[3] 8 & 9 Vict. c. 83, sec. 74.
[4] Act of Sederunt, 12th February, 1846, sec. 4.
[5] Ibid., secs. 6, 7; 8 & 9 Vict. c. 83 sec. 73.
[6] Carnwath v. West Calder Parish Council, 1928, 45 Sh.Ct.Rep. 124.
[7] Harper v. Inspector of Rutherglen, 1903, 6 F. 23; Carnwath v. West Calder Parish Council, supra; Goldie v. Glasgow Corporation, 1932, 48 Sh.Ct.Rep. 198.

(2) *Removal of Paupers.*

Paupers who are being relieved in Scotland, but who have not acquired a settlement in Scotland, may be removed to the place of their birth in England, Ireland, or the Isle of Man.[1] The Sheriff Court has privative jurisdiction in this matter.[2] The application is made in the Sheriff Court of the district within which the pauper has become chargeable.[1] It is an *ex parte* summary application, at the instance of the inspector of poor of the area to which the pauper has become chargeable, setting forth the nativity and reputed age of the pauper, and the fact that he has not acquired a settlement in Scotland, and that he is presently being relieved by the applicant.[1] The crave is for an order authorizing the removal of the pauper with his wife and children (if any) to the workhouse of the place where he was born, or where he last resided.[1] The Sheriff, before granting such an order, must see the person proposed to be removed, and must be satisfied that he is in a fit state of health to be removed.[1] In the case of a pauper lunatic the Sheriff may dispense with seeing the pauper if satisfied that he is detained as a lunatic and that his presence in Court is not desirable.[3] Depositions of witnesses must apparently be taken in writing.[4] The decision of the Sheriff or Sheriff-Substitute who grants the order is final, as regards the judicial proceedings, but, upon an order of removal being granted, intimation is made by the inspector who has obtained the order, to the pauper, and also to the board of the union or parish to which it is proposed to remove the pauper (who must also receive notice of their right of appeal and a copy

of the depositions taken before the Sheriff), and within fourteen
days the pauper (in certain circumstances), or the English or Irish
authorities may appeal to the Department of Health for Scotland.[5]

[1] 8 & 9 Vict. c. 83, sec. 77; 25 & 26 Vict. c. 113, secs, 1, 4; 55 & 56
   Vict. c. 19, Schedule; 61 & 62 Vict. c. 21, sec. 5.   See Edinburgh
   Parish Council v. Local Government Board, 1914 S.C. 241; 1915
   S.C. (H.L.) 44.
[2] 61 & 62 Vict. c. 21, sec. 6.
[3] 3 & 4 Geo. V c. 38, sec. 63.
[4] See 61 & 62 Vict. c. 21, sec. 5 (2).
[5] Ibid., sec. 5: 57 & 58 Vict. c. 58, sec. 3; 9 & 10 Geo. V c. 20, sec. 4;
   18 & 19 Geo. V c. 34, sec. 1.

34. PUBLIC HEALTH.†

(1) *Statutory Procedural Directions.*

The Public Health Act contains certain directions in regard to
procedure in actions necessary to carry into effect the provisions
of the Statute.   These are to be brought by way of summary
application and will be commenced by initial writ which may refer
to the sections of the Act without narrating them.[1] Special provisions are made for service of notices, intimations and orders,
and also of applications under the Act by any person authorized
in certain specified ways,[2] but in practice service of the writ is
usually effected in the customary fashion.   The Sheriff may appoint
answers to be lodged within three days after service, or may ordain
parties to appear, and he may grant decree after a hearing or
in default of appearance.[1] The Sheriff may also remit for a report
on any premises and may act on such report or he may order
proof (which is directed to be taken within five days), and he is
directed to give decree within three days thereafter.[1] Copies of
orders, resolutions and regulations (other than bye-laws) of a local
authority and their committee, purporting to be signed by their
clerk, must, unless the contrary is shown, be received in evidence
without proof of the meeting or of the official character or signature
of the clerk.[3] Apart from the writ and answers no further pleadings are to be allowed.   Diligence against witnesses and havers
may be granted in common form.[4] It will generally be thought
unnecessary, though it would appear to be quite competent, to
have the evidence recorded, but in certain cases where appeal is
allowed[5] it is provided that the Sheriff shall take the evidence in
like manner as in civil proofs.[4] In such cases the evidence should
be recorded.   Apart from these cases there is no right of appeal

† Certain of the matters under this sub-head may be affected by the
  provisions of the new Local Government (Scotland) Bill when that
  comes into effect.

and the Sheriff's decree is not subject to review.[6] Applications
under the Act may be dealt with either by the Sheriff or the Sheriff-
Substitute,[7] and membership of the local authority concerned in
the matter is not a disqualification.[8] Apart from the special
cases where appeal is allowed[5] there is no appeal from the Sheriff-
Substitute to the Sheriff.[9] Expenses may be awarded and may
be modified.[1] A local authority may be represented in such applications by an authorized official or member in place of a solicitor.[10]
Actions in respect of wrongs done in operations under the Act are
subject to a time limit of two months from the time the cause
of action arose.[11]

[1] 60 & 61 Vict. c. 38, sec. 154.
[2] Ibid., sec. 159; M'Dougall v. Duke of Argyll, 1864, 3 M. 248. See
Waddell v. Stirling County Council, 1942, 59 Sh.Ct.Rep. 78.
[3] Ibid., sec. 160; as to bye-laws, see sec. 187.
[4] Ibid., sec. 155.
[5] Ibid., secs. 16 (9) (10) (11), 156. See p. 649, infra.
[6] Ibid., sec. 157. See also Wright v. Kennedy, 1946 J.C. 142, and cf.
Guthrie, Craig, Peter & Co. v. Magistrates of Brechin, 1885, 12 R.
469 (where the matter was held to be not wholly under the Act).
[7] 52 & 53 Vict. c. 63, sec. 28.
[8] 60 & 61 Vict. c. 38, sec. 158.
[9] Leggat, &c. v. Burgh of Barrhead, 1902, 19 Sh.Ct.Rep. 7; cf. Veitch
v. Crieff Local Authority, 1912, 28 Sh.Ct.Rep. 264.
[10] Ibid., sec. 152.
[11] Ibid., sec. 166; Ramsay v. Midlothian County Council, 1928, 45
Sh.Ct.Rep. 132; cf. Mitchell v. Magistrates of Aberdeen, 1893,
20 R. 253; Oatman v. Leslie, 1913, 29 Sh.Ct.Rep. 317.

Save in so far as otherwise stated the above provisions as to
procedure may be taken as applying to all applications under
the Act to which reference is made hereafter. Penalties due
under the Act will be recoverable under the Summary Jurisdiction
Act and not by civil procedure.[1]

[1] See Rae v. Hamilton, 1904, 6 F. (J.) 42; Glasgow Goldsmiths' Co. v.
Mackenzie & Co., 1911, 28 Sh.Ct.Rep. 27.

(2) *Nuisances.*

The aid of the Sheriff Court may be invoked under the Public
Health Act for the suppression of nuisances.[1] To obtain access
to premises a summary application[2] may be made in the Sheriff
Court of the district where the nuisance exists,[3] narrating the
nature of the nuisance, and that entry has been refused. The
application is made by the authority, or their medical officer or
sanitary inspector,[3] and the occupier or person who has refused
admission should be called as defender. The crave is to ordain
the defender to admit the pursuer and, if he refuses, to find him

liable in a penalty and to grant warrant to the pursuer to obtain forcible entry.[3] The writ will be served on the defender and the Act contemplates that evidence on oath will be given by or for the pursuer of his belief in the existence of the nuisance.[3] Any order for entry remains in force till the nuisance is removed or the necessary work has been done.[3]

[1] 60 & 61 Vict. c. 38, secs. 16-31; 2 & 3 Geo. VI c. 23.
[2] Ibid., sec. 154. See p. 645, supra; Encyclopædia of Scottish Legal Styles, VII, 360.
[3] Ibid., sec. 18.

Before any application to the Court is competent for removal of a nuisance notice must be served by the local authority on the author of the nuisance,[1] that is, the person through whose act or default the nuisance is caused or exists or is continued.[2] If the author cannot be found the notice is served on the owner or occupier of the premises where the nuisance is alleged to exist.[1] If the nuisance arises from structural defect notice must be served on the owner.[1] It may be served, as directed in the Act, by any person authorized to do so,[3] but service on an owner per his solicitor is not enough.[4]

[1] 60 & 61 Vict. c. 38, sec. 20.
[2] Ibid., sec. 3.
[3] Ibid., sec. 159.
[4] Waddell v. Stirling County Council, 1942, 59 Sh.Ct.Rep. 78.

Proceedings for removal of a nuisance, following non-compliance with the notice above referred to, are directed against the author of the nuisance, and, if he is not the owner or the occupier of the premises, such owner or occupier should also be called as defender. The crave is to find that the nuisance exists and to ordain the defender, within a set time, to remove it. If the Sheriff is satisfied that a nuisance exists he may order its removal.[1] No formal record of evidence is in most cases essential, but where appeal is competent[2] the evidence is to be taken as in civil proofs[3] and should be recorded. Proceedings may be taken although the nuisance has been removed if the local authority think it may recur.[4]

[1] 60 & 61 Vict. c. 38, sec. 22; for forms see Encyclopædia of Scottish Legal Styles, VII, 361, et seq.
[2] Ibid., secs. 16 (9) (10) (11), 156. See p. 649, infra.
[3] Ibid., sec. 155.
[4] Ibid., secs. 21, 22.

Under the Act various different things are defined as nuisances.[1] In the case of offensive trades, or want of cleanliness, or ventilation, or of overcrowding in a schoolhouse application to the Sheriff is only competent following on a medical certificate, a representation by a local authority, or a written requisition by ten ratepayers.[2] In the case of an overcrowded or offensive cemetery or churchyard no one need be cited as the author of the nuisance, but the Sheriff may order intimation to the collector of churchyard dues or other persons interested, and such persons may appear and be heard.[2] In the case of certain nuisances penalties may be imposed for non-compliance with or infringement of a decree, and in the case of a nuisance from industrial smoke final determination may be suspended to enable the defender to adopt some better means of mitigating the nuisance.[3]

[1] 60 & 61 Vict. c. 38, sec. 16.
[2] Ibid., sec. 22; as to reservations in such an order, see Provost, &c., of Paisley, 1901, 18 Sh.Ct.Rep. 273.
[3] Ibid., sec. 24.

The order of the Sheriff is not restricted to the particular remedy craved and he may ordain the defender to execute certain specified work within a specified time, or to cease from doing certain specified acts.[1] If the nuisance is one likely to recur, the Sheriff may grant interdict; and if it is such as to render premises unfit for habitation or use, he may temporarily prohibit their occupancy or use, and after the remedial work has been executed he may authorize them again to be inhabited or used.[1] If the nuisance arose from the wilful fault or culpable neglect of the owner or occupier, who had previously been served with a notice in respect thereof, the Sheriff may impose a fine in addition to granting decree.[2]

[1] 60 & 61 Vict. c. 38, sec. 23.
[2] Ibid., sec. 22.

When structural works are necessary the Sheriff may appoint these to be carried out under the superintendence of a person appointed by him, and before making such order he may require the local authority to furnish an estimate of the cost.[1] Where any decree of the Sheriff is not complied with or is infringed he may authorize some person to do what is necessary to execute the decree, and where, in the original application, the author of the nuisance cannot be ascertained the local authority may be ordained to execute the works thereby directed.[2] When anything creating a nuisance is ordered to be removed, the Sheriff may order its destruction, or authorize it to be sold, and the price applied *primo loco* towards the expense incurred by the local authority with reference to the nuisance, the surplus, if any, being payable on demand to the owner of the thing sold.[3] Foul ditches and the like may be replaced by sewers constructed by the local authority who may enter and use premises to do so.[4] Damages for such use may be fixed by the Sheriff.[4]

[1] 60 & 61 Vict. c. 38, sec. 25.
[2] Ibid., sec. 26. See United Kingdom Temperance, &c., Institution v. Cadder Parochial Board, 1877, 4 R. (J.) 39; Cadder Local Authority v. Lang, 1879, 6 R. 1242.
[3] Ibid., sec. 27.
[4] Ibid., sec. 28.

Special rights of appeal are provided when the nuisance complained of is (a) that a factory furnace does not consume its own smoke[1]; (b) that a chimney other than that of a private dwelling-house emits smoke in such quantities as to be injurious to health; or (c) that a cemetery is by its situation, or by overcrowding, or otherwise, dangerous or injurious to health.[2] In these cases if the Sheriff-Substitute certifies in the decree that (a) the value of the subject alleged to be a nuisance; (b) the cost of operations for its amendment or removal; or (c) the value of the trade or business which would be interfered with, exceeds £25, and does not exceed £50, an appeal to the Sheriff is competent by note of appeal lodged with the Sheriff-clerk within three days of the decree and served upon the respondent or his solicitor.[3] The Sheriff's decision is final.[3]

[1] See Dumfries Local Authority v. Murphy, 1884, 11 R. 694.
[2] 60 & 61 Vict. c. 38, secs. 16 (9) (10) (11), 156.
[3] Ibid., sec. 156.

If the value is certified to exceed £50 there is an appeal from the Sheriff-Substitute or the Sheriff, whether the latter's is an original judgment or one on appeal.[1] This is made by note of appeal written on the interlocutor sheet signed by the appellant or his solicitor and dated.[2] The note must be lodged and a copy be served upon the respondent or his solicitor within eight days of the interlocutor appealed against.[1] Along with the note of appeal the appellant must lodge a bond of caution for £50 for implement of the judgment which may be pronounced.[1]

[1] 60 & 61 Vict. c. 38, sec. 156.
[2] Rules of Court V, 7, 8.

(3) Offensive Trades.

Bye-laws of local authorities may empower the Sheriff by summary order to deprive any person of the right to carry on an offensive trade as a punishment for breaking the bye-law.[1]

Such an order is not subject to appeal from the Sheriff-Substitute to the Sheriff, but there is an appeal to the Court of Session in the same way as in applications regarding nuisances.[2] There is no other form of review.[3] In view of the method of appeal provided, this is apparently intended to be a civil proceeding.

[1] 60 & 61 Vict. c. 38, sec. 32.
[2] Ibid., secs. 32 (4), 156. See previous page.
[3] Ibid., sec. 157.

(4) Drainage, &c., Districts.

The Sheriff Court is a Court of Appeal against resolutions or orders of the local authority in regard to the formation, or combination of scavenging, drainage, and water districts.[1] Such appeals may be heard either by the Sheriff or (subject to what is stated in the next paragraph) by the Sheriff-Substitute.[2] The same right of appeal is held to be available in the case of enlarging an existing district.[3] Any person interested may appeal to the Sheriff within twenty-one days of the date of the first publication of the resolution or the date of the order.[1] The writ will crave the Court to disapprove of the resolution or order,[4] but the Court has extensive powers of amending or modifying, as well as rejecting, the resolution.[1] The Sheriff may order answers and may dispose of the appeal at a hearing or take proof. If the application is entertained by the Sheriff no record of evidence appears to be necessary, for the Sheriff's decision is final; but if the process is before a Sheriff-Substitute the recording of the evidence seems desirable as there is an appeal from the Sheriff-Substitute to the Sheriff.[1] Any party to an appeal may be found liable in expenses.[5] The order of the Sheriff is to determine any question as to debt affecting a district, and questions of assessment, and it is to fix the date when the determination takes effect.[6] A copy of the order is to be published by newspaper advertisement or by handbills,[6] and the order itself should provide how and by whom this is to be done.

[1] See 57 & 58 Vict. c. 58, sec. 44; 60 & 61 Vict. c. 38, secs. 38, 39, 122, 131. See generally as to principles applied in such appeals, Montrose Lunatic Asylum v. Brechin District Committee, 1900, 16 Sh.Ct.Rep. 336; Reid Gear Co. v. Renfrewshire District Committee, 1923, 39 Sh.Ct.Rep. 194; Spence v. Linlithgow District Committee, 1926, 43 Sh.Ct.Rep. 62; L.M.S. and L.N.E. Railway Companies v. Dunbarton County Council, 1936, 53 Sh.Ct.Rep. 61, 64.
[2] 52 & 53 Vict. c. 63, sec. 28.
[3] Glasgow and South Western Railway Co., &c. v. Renfrew District Committee, 1906, 23 Sh.Ct.Rep. 44.
[4] See Carnbroe Chemical Co. v. Lanark Middle Ward, 1926, 43 Sh.Ct.Rep. 163.

5 8 Edw. VII c. 62, sec. 14 (4); cf. Lornie, &c. v. Highland District Committee of Perthshire, 1908, 25 Sh.Ct.Rep. 124, which was brought before this Act was in force.
6 60 & 61 Vict. c. 38, secs. 122 (2), 131 (2).

The Sheriff-Substitute may not act in such appeals if he is resident within the district,[1] and "district" is defined as the district of any local authority under the Act,[2] so that the Sheriff-Substitute is disqualified if he resides within the district of the local authority although not within the proposed special district.[3] This disqualification does not apply to the Sheriff.[1] Orders to level or make good streets or footways in a special scavenging district are subject to appeal in the way above described.[4]

1 60 & 61 Vict. c. 38, secs. 3, 122 (1), 131 (1).
2 Ibid., sec. 3.
3 See Kenneth & Sons v. Ayrshire County Council, 1900, 2 F. 511.
4 60 & 61 Vict. c. 38, sec. 39; Waddell v. Stirling County Council, 1942, 59 Sh.Ct.Rep. 78.

Under the Local Government Act of 1908 a town council has, in certain circumstances, a title to appeal against the resolution for formation of a special district.[1] When burgh boundaries are extended to encroach on a special district the town council supersedes the county council on matters of administration on such terms as, failing agreement, may be fixed by the Sheriff whose decision is final.[2]

1 8 Edw. VII c. 62. sec. 14 (3).
2 60 & 61 Vict. c. 38, sec. 38.

(5) Sewer Construction.

A local authority may enter upon lands for the construction or maintenance of sewers.[1] If an owner or occupier refuse access a summary application may be presented in the Sheriff Court craving warrant to enter upon the lands.[1] The Sheriff's decision may be given after a hearing, or on a proof being taken, or a remit to a man of skill.[2] The Sheriff may also determine summarily any dispute as to the terms on which a sewer may be used by a person outwith the district to which it belongs,[3] or as to the allocation of the cost of a new sewer among the owners of houses which drain into it.[4]

1 60 & 61 Vict. c. 38, sec. 109; for style see Encyclopædia of Scottish Legal Styles, VII, 366.
2 Brown v. Magistrates of Kirkcudbright, 1905, 8 F. 77. See also Montgomerie & Co. v. Haddington Corporation, 1908 S.C. 127; 1908 S.C. (H.L.) 6; Johnstone Corporation v. Smith & M'Laurin, 1937, 53 Sh.Ct.Rep. 317.

3 60 & 61 Vict. c. 38, sec. 111. See Leggat v. Burgh of Barrhead, 1902,
19 Sh.Ct.Rep. 7; Telford, &c. v. Perth District Committee, &c.,
1907, 24 Sh.Ct.Rep. 241.
1 Ibid., sec. 120.

(6) *Boundary Ditches.*

If a water course, or open ditch, lying near to, or forming
the boundary between, the districts of two local authorities is
offensive, either local authority may present a summary application in the Sheriff Court of the other district craving the Court
to make an order for cleansing the ditch, or for executing such
works as may be necessary.[1] The other local authority will be
called as defenders. The Sheriff may inform himself of the circumstances by proof, remit, or inspection.[2] He may make such order
as seems to him reasonable in regard to the execution of works;
the persons by whom the work is to be done; and the allocation
of the cost.[1]

1 60 & 61 Vict. c. 38, sec. 41.
2 See Brown v. Magistrates of Kirkcudbright, 1905, 8 F. 77.

(7) *Unsound Food.*

Certain officers of a local authority may seize and remove any
article intended for human food, if in their opinion the food is
unsound,[1] but the officer requires the authority of the Court to
destroy it. An order for destruction may be made in a judgment
imposing a penalty, but the right to obtain a warrant to destroy
is not affected by whether there is liability to a penalty or not.[2]
A summary application craving warrant to destroy may be presented in the Sheriff Court of the district where the food was seized,
and the Sheriff may order intimation and may hear any interested
persons.[3] The only matter upon which the Sheriff has to be satisfied
in this process is the condition of the food, and he is apparently
entitled to dispose of the application without hearing the owner of
the article seized.[4] There is no appeal against the warrant to
destroy.[5]

1 60 & 61 Vict. c. 38, sec. 43 (1).
2 Couper v. Lang, 1889, 17 R. (J.) 15.
3 60 & 61 Vict. c. 38, secs. 43 (2), 154.
4 Henderson v. Riddoch, (O.H.) 1912, 2 S.L.T. 375.
5 60 & 61 Vict. c. 38, sec. 157; Couper v. Lang, supra.

(8) *Miscellaneous.*

Under the Act the Sheriff may grant warrant to remove or
detain persons in hospital in respect of infectious diseases[1]; order

a dead body to be removed and buried[2]; grant warrant to remove
a lodging-house from the register or order it to be restored[3]; and
authorize necessary works to be executed where an occupier is
preventing the owner from doing so.[4]

[1] 60 & 61 Vict. c. 38, secs. 47 (4), 54, 55.   See Local Authority of
   Aberdeen, 1893, 1 S.L.T. 210.
[2] Ibid., sec. 69.
[3] Ibid., secs. 89, 90, 94, 154.
[4] Ibid., sec. 162.

(9) *Proceedings against Local Authority.*

If a local authority permits a nuisance to exist on their own
premises, or if they fail to perform any of their duties under the
Act, the Secretary of State for Scotland (as coming in place of
the Department of Health for Scotland),[1] or ten ratepayers in the
district, or the procurator-fiscal may present a summary petition
to the Sheriff, who is directed to inquire into the matter and grant
a decree to enforce the removal of the nuisance, or compel execution
of the statutory duty.[2]   The Department also has power to instruct
proceedings in the Sheriff Court against a local authority to compel
them to carry out their duties.[3]   On the sanction of the Lord
Advocate being obtained the proceedings are taken at the instance
of the local procurator-fiscal.[3]   These actions are commenced by
initial writ, and follow the procedure prescribed for summary
applications.[4]   Proceedings of this kind are more usually brought
in the Court of Session under another section of the Act.[5]

[1] 2 & 3 Geo. VI c. 20, sec. 1.
[2] 60 & 61 Vict. c. 38, sec. 146.
[3] Ibid., sec. 148.
[4] Ibid., sec. 154.
[5] Ibid., sec. 147; e.g., Board of Supervision v. Local Authority of
   Pittenweem, 1874, 1 R. 1124.

(10) *Compensation.*

Full compensation is payable to all persons suffering damage
by the exercise of any of the powers of the Act except when otherwise specially provided.[1]   If the amount in dispute does not exceed
£50 it may be ascertained on a summary application by either
party to the Sheriff.[1]   If the matter is dealt with by the Sheriff
his decision is final, but if disposed of by the Sheriff-Substitute,
his judgment may be reviewed by the Sheriff on appeal.[1]   No
provision is made for a record of the evidence, so that matter is
apparently in the discretion of the Sheriff-Substitute.[2]   If the
evidence is not recorded any appeal would be limited to a question
of law.[3]   Questions may arise as to whether a claim is for com-

pensation to be ascertained as above, and to which the time limit in sec. 166 of the Act does not apply, or for damages to which that time limit does apply.[4]

1 60 & 61 Vict. c. 38, sec. 164.
2 7 Edw. VII c. 51, sec. 50.
3 See Sinclair v. Spence, 1883, 10 R. 1077.
4 Thomson v. Broughty Ferry Commissioners, 1898, 14 Sh.Ct.Rep. 365; Cessford v. Commissioners of Millport, 1899, 15 Sh.Ct.Rep. 362; Barbour v. Renfrew District Committee, 1906, 8 F. 448; Craig v. Lorn District Committee, 1911, 28 Sh.Ct.Rep. 14; Oatman v. Provost, &c., of Buckhaven, &c., 1914, 30 Sh.Ct.Rep. 258.

35. RAILWAYS.

The Railways Clauses Consolidation (Scotland) Act of 1845 is a Statute similar to the Lands Clauses Act, and may be incorporated by reference in other Acts, public or private. When lands are taken or used for railway purposes the compensation is ascertained in the manner prescribed in the Lands Clauses Act.[1]

1 8 & 9 Vict. c. 33, sec. 37. See p. 607, supra.

(1) *Level Crossings.*

If a railway is to be carried across a road, on the level, the consent of the Sheriff (or two justices) is required.[1] Notice of intention to apply for such consent is given as prescribed.[2] The process is a summary application[3] and will normally be begun by initial writ. It seems unnecessary to call any defenders and the Sheriff may hear parties, with or without written proceedings or a record, and may hear evidence without having it recorded.[3] The question at issue is whether the level crossing is consistent with public safety and convenience.[2] The matter may be dealt with by the Sheriff or the Sheriff-Substitute,[4] and, if there are written pleadings and a record, and the evidence has been recorded, there is an appeal to the Sheriff from the final judgment of the Sheriff-Substitute[5]; but otherwise there is no right of appeal.[5]

1 8 & 9 Vict. c. 33, sec. 39.
2 Ibid., sec. 53.
3 Ibid., sec. 147.
4 Ibid., sec. 3.
5 Ibid., sec. 150. See Main v. Lanarkshire and Dunbartonshire Railway Co., 1893, 21 R. 323; Paisley and Barrhead District Railway Co. v. Coats, 1902, 19 Sh.Ct.Rep. 12.

(2) *Accommodation Works.*

A railway company is bound to provide certain accommodation works,[1] and differences arising in regard to the construction or maintenance of these may be settled by the Sheriff.[2] The aggrieved party, or the company, may present a summary application in the Sheriff Court of the district where the works are required. The writ should crave the Court to order the company to execute the works, within a time to be fixed by the Court, and (failing that) to authorize the pursuer himself to execute them, and to grant decree for the cost. The first deliverance will fix a diet for hearing the application.[3] By remit, inspection, proof, or otherwise, the Sheriff may satisfy himself as to the matters at issue.[3] The procedure before the Sheriff (or Sheriff-Substitute) and right of appeal are as stated in the preceding paragraph. The Sheriff may also authorize additional works, and under similar procedure may order the railway company to repair roads,[4] bridges, fences and others,[5] and to make approaches and other works at certain level crossings.[6] In connexion with the construction of railways the Sheriff may certify the correction of errors in the plans or books of reference[7] and authorize deviations from original levels.[8]

[1] 8 & 9 Vict. c. 33, sec. 60.
[2] Ibid., sec. 61.
[3] Ibid., sec. 147.
[4] Ibid., sec. 51.
[5] Ibid., sec. 57.
[6] Ibid., sec. 54.
[7] Ibid., sec. 7.   See Glasgow District Subway Co. v. M'Callum, 1896, 12 Sh.Ct.Rep. 148; Paisley and Barrhead District Railway Co. v. Coats, 1902, 19 Sh.Ct.Rep. 12.
[8] Ibid., sec. 11.

(3) Sheriff-clerk's Duties.

The Statute requires the principal Sheriff-clerk in the county in which the lands affected are situated to receive the deposited plans and books of reference of railway undertakings; to arrange for the public inspecting them; and to furnish parties with certified copies or excerpts.[1] The Sheriff-clerk's certificate makes these receivable as evidence in any Court of law.[2]

[1] 8 & 9 Vict. c. 33, secs. 7, 9.
[2] Ibid., sec. 10.

36. RENT RESTRICTIONS ACTS.

Apart from their effect on actions brought to remove tenants—which has been already dealt with[1]—these Acts provide for certain applications being presented in the Sheriff Court.[2] By Act of Sederunt it is provided that applications under the Acts of 1920 and 1923—which comprise nearly all of such applications—may be made by initial writ or by minute in any pending process, and

that, if made by writ, they are to be summary applications.[3] But
any questions arising under or in connexion with the Acts referred
to (other than Parts II and III of the later Act of 1923), including
any question as to amendment of notices to increase rent, may
be decided by the Sheriff without additional procedure if it arises
in any cause pending before him.[4] Whether any particular question
should be disposed of incidentally in this way in a pending process,[5]
or should be raised by minute, will depend on the circumstances
of each case.

1 See p. 419, supra.
2 See 10 & 11 Geo. V c. 17, sec. 18 (1).
3 Act of Sederunt, 14th December, 1923, sec. 2.
4 Ibid., sec. 3.
5 E.g., Langdon v. Elliott, 1924 S.L.T. (Sh.Ct.) 9.

Under the Acts applications may be made to the Court to
suspend or reduce an increase of rent in certain circumstances,[1]
or to determine the amount of increase in respect of repairs where
the landlord is not wholly responsible for these.[2] In the last case
the application may be by landlord or tenant[2]; in the case of a
suspension or reduction in respect that expenditure on improve-
ments was unnecessary the application is by the tenant alone[3];
and in the case of a suspension on the ground that the house is
not fit for habitation the application may be by the tenant or
the sanitary authority.[4] Such questions are by a later sub-section
to be determined on the application of the landlord or tenant and
the decision of the Sheriff Court is declared to be final and conclusive.[5] It is held that this finality applies even where the application is by the sanitary authority.[6] Such applications are competent before either the Sheriff-Substitute or the Sheriff in the
usual way, and if dealt with by the former an appeal to the Sheriff
appears to be competent.[6] If questions under these sub-sections
are raised incidentally in another action, such as one for payment
of rent, the statutory finality provision would not apparently
apply and the ordinary rights of appeal would seem to be available.[7]

1 10 & 11 Geo. V c. 17, sec. 2 (1) (a) (2). See also 13 & 14 Geo. V c.
    13, sec. 3; 23 & 24 Geo. V c. 32, sec. 7.
2 10 & 11 Geo. V c. 17, sec. 2 (1) (d).
3 Ibid., sec. 2 (1) (a).
4 Ibid., sec. 2 (2). As to such applications see Wilson v. Brown, 1921,
    37 Sh.Ct.Rep. 212; Britton v. Anderson, 1921, 38 Sh.Ct.Rep. 142;
    Harcus v. Balfour Hospital Trustees, 1921, 39 Sh.Ct.Rep. 62.
5 Ibid., sec. 2 (6).
6 Glasgow Corporation v. Mickel, 1922 S.C. 228.
7 Strickland v. Palmer, [1924] 2 K.B. 572.

The holder of a bond over leasehold subjects may, in certain circumstances, apply to the Sheriff Court for an order authorizing him to call up his bond and this may be granted, despite the Acts, on the Court being satisfied that the security is in jeopardy.[1] The terms of the section seem to imply that, though the application is undefended, *prima facie* evidence of the risk to the security should be adduced. The tenant of a furnished house may also apply to the Sheriff Court for an order that the rent above a certain amount is irrecoverable and for repayment of the excess if necessary.[2] Such order is to be given on proof to the satisfaction of the Court that a certain percentage of profit is exceeded,[2] which seems to imply proof even though no appearance is made for the defender. These sections make no provision as to appeal but their terms suggest a jurisdiction conferred on the Sheriff Court alone, and this view has been judicially expressed.[3] The position is, however, by no means clear and appeal to the High Court appears to be competent in England.[4] There will be a right of appeal in any case from the Sheriff-Substitute to the Sheriff.[5] Questions under sec. 9 might arise incidentally in an ordinary action for payment of rent, and in such a case the ordinary rules as to appeal would apparently apply.[6]

[1] 10 & 11 Geo. V c. 17, sec. 7 (ii).
[2] Ibid., sec. 9. See 2 & 3 Geo. VI c. 71, Schedule I. (This section is now to some extent superseded by the Rent of Furnished Houses Control (Scotland) Act, 1943. See also Langdon v. Elliott, 1924 S.L.T. (Sh.Ct.) 9.
[3] Glasgow Corporation v. Mickel, 1922 S.C. 228, Lord Ormidale, p. 233.
[4] See Truss v. Olivier, 1924, 40 T.L.R. 588.
[5] Glasgow Corporation v. Mickel, supra.
[6] Strickland v. Palmer, [1924] 2 K.B. 572.

On application by either landlord or tenant the Sheriff Court may apportion rent in order to enable standard rent to be fixed, and in such an application the decision of the Sheriff Court as to the amount to be apportioned is declared to be final and conclusive.[1] The finality in this case applies only to the fixing of the amount, not, for example, to a question as to the competency of the apportionment.[2] Under the Rent Restrictions (Notices of Increase) Act, 1923, any question as to the amount of arrears due from a tenant or the amount of any instalment is to be determined on the application of landlord or tenant to the Sheriff Court, and the decision of that Court is declared to be final and conclusive.[3] In both these cases appeal to the Sheriff Principal is available[4] and the usual right of appeal will apparently be open if the point under the Act is merely raised incidentally in other proceedings.[5] In certain circumstances the Court may discharge or rescind an order for recovery of possession which has been already made but not executed.[6] The procedure in regard to such applications has been already considered in relation to removings.[7]

[1] 10 & 11 Geo. V c. 17, sec. 12 (3). See also 2 & 3 Geo. VI c. 71, sec. 7 (2).
[2] See Balderston & Co. v. Hutchison, 1921, 37 Sh.Ct.Rep. 166.
[3] 13 & 14 Geo. V c. 13, sec. 2 (4).
[4] See Glasgow Corporation v. Mickel, 1922 S.C. 228.
[5] Strickland v. Palmer, [1924] 2 K.B. 572.
[6] 10 & 11 Geo. V c. 17, sec. 5 (2) (3); 13 & 14 Geo. V c. 32, sec. 4; 2 & 3 Geo. VI c. 71, sec. 4.
[7] See p. 420, supra.

If satisfied that any error or omission in a notice to increase rent is due to *bona fide* mistake on the part of the landlord the Sheriff Court may amend the notice on such terms as appear to the Court to be just.[1] It is expressly provided by Act of Sederunt that this power may be exercised without additional procedure if the question arises in any cause pending in the Sheriff Court.[2] Such power of amendment is conferred on the Sheriff Court only, which means that it could be exercised either by the Sheriff-Substitute or the Sheriff, but not by the Court of Session in the event of the ·question being raised in an action which was on appeal to that Court.

[1] 13 & 14 Geo. V c. 32, sec. 6.
[2] Act of Sederunt, 14th December, 1923, sec. 3.

The Sheriff Court has power, on the application of either landlord or tenant, to determine summarily any question as to the amount of the rent, standard rent or net rent of any dwelling-house to which the Acts apply, or as to any increase of rent permitted by the Acts.[1] Such questions may arise as mere incidents in a pending action and will then be dealt with without additional procedure.[2] If raised in a substantive application the terms of the section seem to imply a determination of the question within the Sheriff Court, thus presumably permitting an appeal to the Sheriff but not to the Court of Session.[3] Where the recoverable rent of a house to which the Acts apply is determined by any Court, that Court may, on the application of the tenant in those or in any subsequent proceedings, call for production of the rent book and make any necessary corrections.[4] Such an application does not fall within the scope of the Act of Sederunt of 1923, but if made in a separate proceeding in the Sheriff Court it will normally be treated as a summary application.

[1] 13 & 14 Geo. V c. 32, sec. 11. See also 23 & 24 Geo. V c. 32, sec. 6.
[2] Act of Sederunt, 14th December, 1923, sec. 3.

³ In England where different considerations may apply there is apparently
    a right of appeal to the Court of Appeal. See Chamberlain v.
    Farr, 1942, 2 All E.R. 567.
⁴ 23 & 24 Geo. V c. 32, sec. 8.

Of consent of parties any questions arising under or in connexion with the Act of 1920 or Part I of the Act of 1923 may be
referred for final determination by the Sheriff or Sheriff-Substitute
sitting as arbitrator, or by an arbitrator appointed by the Sheriff
or Sheriff-Substitute.¹ The procedure is to be by summary application begun by initial writ or by minute in a pending process.²
Under sec. 16 (2) of the Act of 1920 a tenant protected by the Acts
is required to afford to the landlord access to the house and all
reasonable facilities to execute repairs.³ If such facilities are
not afforded a summary application may be made to the Sheriff
to order the defender to allow access.⁴

¹ 13 & 14 Geo. V c. 32, sec. 11 (2).
² Act of Sederunt, 14th December, 1923, secs. 2, 4.
³ 10 & 11 Geo. V c. 17, sec. 16 (2).
⁴ Russell v. Keary, 1933, 49 Sh.Ct.Rep. 298.

37. Representation of the People Acts.

Under the Act of 1918 there is an appeal to the Sheriff Court
from any decision of the registration officer on any claim or
objection, or the placing or refusal to place a mark against any
name on the register, provided the appellant has availed himself
of his opportunity of being heard by the registration officer on the
matter at issue.¹ Similar rights of appeal are given under the
Act of 1945.² If an appeal is to be taken, notice of appeal in a
prescribed form, specifying the grounds of appeal, must be given
to the registration officer and to the opposite party, if any, either
when the decision is given or within five days thereafter.³ Within
ten days of receipt of such notice the registration officer must
forward same to the Sheriff-clerk of the county within which the
qualifying premises are situate, along with a statement of the
material facts which, in his opinion, have been established, and
of his decision on the case, and on any point specified as a ground
of appeal.⁴ He must also furnish the Court with further information if required,³ and if he considers that any appeals are based
on similar grounds he must so inform the Court to enable the
Court, if it thinks fit, to consolidate the appeals or select a test
case.⁵ No procedural directions are given, but the proceedings
will normally be treated as a summary application and should be
begun by initial writ. The registration officer is deemed to be
a party to any appeal, and should be called as a defender.⁶ The

appeal may be disposed of either by the Sheriff or the Sheriff-Substitute, and the practice on this point appears to vary in different Sheriffdoms. No provision is made for an allowance of proof if either party refuses to accept the facts as stated by the registration officer, but, as the appeal is not limited to a question of law, some inquiry into the facts may be necessary if these are in dispute. The appeal is to be disposed of with all convenient speed, and within seven days of the judgment the Sheriff-clerk must send notice to the registration officer of the decision, unless an appeal against the decision has been intimated.[7] In view of the possibility of such further appeal the Sheriff-clerk will presumably intimate the decision to all parties to the appeal.

[1] 7 & 8 Geo. V c. 64, secs. 14, 43 (1) (h).
[2] 8 & 9 Geo. VI c. 5, sec. 21.
[3] 7 & 8 Geo. V c. 64, Schedule I, 29; the time limit for giving notice is held to be peremptory; Fletcher v. Wheeler, 1922, 38 Sh.Ct.Rep. 165.
[4] Ibid., Act of Sederunt, 19th July, 1918, I (1).
[5] Ibid., Schedule I, 30. See also Crawford v. M'Blain, 1922, 39 Sh.Ct.Rep. 46, p. 49.
[6] Ibid., sec. 14 (5).
[7] Act of Sederunt, 19th July, 1918, I (2).

A further appeal is competent on any point of law from any decision in the Sheriff Court to the Registration Court of Appeal,[1] and any person entitled to appeal, which includes the registration officer, may by minute lodged with the Sheriff-clerk within seven days of intimation of the decision require the Sheriff to state a case.[2] The minute is to state the circumstances of the case and the Sheriff's decision and to specify the question or questions of law for submission to the Court.[2] It is to be intimated by the appellant to the opposite party by delivery of a copy thereof.[2] No provision is made for the adjustment of the case, and the Sheriff is merely directed to prepare forthwith and deliver to the appellant a special case stating articulately in numbered paragraphs (i) the facts found proved or admitted, (ii) the questions of law submitted to the Sheriff and his decision thereon, and (iii) the questions of law submitted for the Registration Court of Appeal.[3] Within fourteen days after delivery to him of the case the appellant must lodge same with the General Department of the Court of Session, and, at the same time, must intimate the lodging by sending copies of the case to the respondent and the registration officer.[4] The lodging of the case may be done by transmitting it to the Deputy Principal-clerk of the General Department of the Court of Session.[4] At any time before final disposal of the case the Court may remit it to the Sheriff for restatement or further statement in whole or in part,[5] but it seems that the Appeal Court will not deal with any point which has not been raised before the Sheriff.[6]

[1] 7 & 8 Geo. V c. 64, sec. 14 (2).
[2] Rules of Court, 1936, V, 26 (a).
[3] Ibid., V, 26 (b).
[4] Ibid., V, 26 (c).
[5] Ibid., V, 26 (g).
[6] M'Kergow v. White, 1910 S.C. 215.

When it appears to the Sheriff that any two or more minutes requiring a case raise the same questions of law he may consolidate the appeals in one case, and in that event he states in the case the circumstances in which he has consolidated the appeals and names one of the appellants as the appellant for the purpose of transmitting the case to the Appeal Court.[1] Such appellant must supply copies of the case as lodged to any other appellants on their request, and at their charges.[1]

[1] Rules of Court, 1936, V, 26 (d).

In all appeals under the Act the Court may award and decern for expenses.[1]

[1] Act of Sederunt, 19th July, 1918, III.

38. Rivers' Pollution Prevention Act.

Subject to the giving of notice before proceedings are brought,[1] the Sheriff-Substitute or Sheriff having jurisdiction in the place where any offence against the above Act is committed may, by summary order, require any person to abstain from committing the offence, or to perform any duty of which he is in default.[2] Such an order may be suspended or rescinded on an undertaking being given, and directions may be given by the Court for carrying the order into effect.[2] Subject to what is stated later as to appeal, the usual rules in the Sheriff Court are expressly provided to apply to such proceedings,[3] which are ordinary civil actions begun by initial writ asking that the defender be prohibited or interdicted from doing the act complained of.[4] It is specially provided that the Court may remit to a man of skill to report,[5] and it seems to be intended that the evidence in any proof should be recorded.[6] If default is made in complying with an order made by the Court, action may be taken for payment of a penalty—this being a civil action brought by initial writ[4]—and, in the case of persistent disobedience, the Court may, in addition to any penalty, appoint some person to carry out the work at the expense of the defaulter.[5]

In proceedings under the Act there is a special right of removal of the case to the Court of Session.[7]

[1] See 39 & 40 Vict. c. 75, secs. 6, 13.   See also Midlothian County Council v. Oakbank Oil Co., &c., 1903, 5 F. 700.
[2] Ibid., secs. 10, 21 (5).
[3] Ibid., secs. 11, 21 (5); Magistrates of Portobello v. Magistrates of Edinburgh, 1882, 10 R. 130, Lord Justice-Clerk Moncreiff, p. 138.
[4] For style see Lees, Sheriff Court Styles, 4th edn., 300.
[5] 39 & 40 Vict. c. 75, sec. 10.
[6] Magistrates of Portobello v. Magistrates of Edinburgh, supra, p. 138.
[7] 39 & 40 Vict. c. 75, sec. 11.   See Midlothian County Council v. Pumpherston Oil Co., 1902, 4 F. 996; Lanark County Council v. Magistrates of Airdrie, &c., 1906, 8 F. 802.

Right of appeal from the Sheriff-Substitute to the Sheriff is regulated by the ordinary rules of the Sheriff Court,[1] but appeal to the Court of Session is regulated by the Act itself which provides for an appeal against the decision of the Court in point of law, or on the merits, or in respect of the admission or rejection of evidence.[2]   Such appeal is to be by special case agreed on by both parties or settled by the Sheriff.[2]   An appeal which is not in the form of such a case is incompetent.[3]   There appears to be some doubt as to whether there is a right of appeal against an interlocutory judgment in the Sheriff Court, but such an appeal, if competent, must be taken in the form of a stated case, and with leave, if such leave would have been required for an appeal in an ordinary action under the Sheriff Court Rules.[4] The form of the case and the procedure in the Court of Session are as laid down in the Rules of Court.[5]   There would appear to be a right of appeal by stated case from the Sheriff-Substitute direct to the Court of Session where appeal would otherwise be competent.

[1] 39 & 40 Vict. c. 75, sec. 11; Magistrates of Portobello v. Magistrates of Edinburgh, 1882, 10 R. 130.
[2] Ibid., sec. 11.
[3] Lanark County Council v. Magistrates of Airdrie, 1906, 8 F. 802.
[4] Dumfries County Council v. Langholm Magistrates, 1913 S.C. 307.
[5] Rules of Court, 1936, V, 22-24.

39. Roads and Bridges.

(1) Extraordinary Traffic.

A person or body, responsible for causing excessive weight or extraordinary traffic on a road, resulting in extraordinary cost of repair, is liable for the excess cost of upkeep beyond the average expense of road repair.[1]   Any sum recoverable under the above provision is to be recovered, if not over £50, before the Sheriff whose decision is final, and if over that amount either before the Sheriff, subject to an appeal to the Court of Session, or in the Court of Session.[2] The action is preceded by a certificate by the road surveyor,[1] which will be produced with the writ. It must be proved that the extra cost of maintenance has been incurred, and that it has been necessitated by the extra traffic condescended on. The action is brought against the person by or in consequence of whose order the traffic was conducted.[3] If the claim is for not more than £50 the matter could be dealt with either by the Sheriff or the Sheriff-Substitute, but the decision of either is final.[4] If over that amount the right of appeal from the Sheriff-Substitute to the Sheriff may not be excluded.[5] If the amount claimed is within the limits of the Small Debt Court the action may be brought there.[6] Proceedings must be brought within twelve months of the damage being done, or if the operations are continuous within six months of completion.[7]

[1] 20 & 21 Geo. V c. 43, sec. 54 (1).
[2] Ibid., sec. 60 (c).
[3] Ibid., sec. 54 (1). See Partick Town Council v. Muir & Sons, 1905, 21 Sh.Ct.Rep. 196.
[4] See Bone v. School Board of Sorn, 1886, 13 R. 768.
[5] Thornhill District Committee v. M'Gregor & Son, 1922 S.C. 512. This decision was given of consent on a similar but not identical provision.
[6] Annan District Committee v. Pattie, 1908, 25 Sh.Ct.Rep. 157.
[7] 20 & 21 Geo. V c. 43, sec. 54 (2); Deer District Committee v. Shanks & M'Ewan, 1911, 1 S.L.T. 314; Arbroath District Committee v. Provost, &c., of Carnoustie, 1911, 28 Sh.Ct.Rep. 101.

(2) *Barbed Wire Fences.*

If a notice for removal of a barbed wire fence is not complied with the local authority may apply in the Sheriff Court[1] to have the defender ordained to abate the nuisance, and, failing his doing so, to authorize the pursuers to execute the necessary work, and to find the defender liable for the cost. Either the Sheriff or the Sheriff-Substitute may deal with the matter,[2] and the intention appears to be that the order of either should be final. When a local authority occupy the lands upon which the fence exists the like proceedings may be instituted by a ratepayer, the preliminary notice being served upon the clerk to the local authority.[3]

[1] 56 & 57 Vict. c. 32, secs. 2, 3 (1) (2).
[2] Ibid., sec. 2.
[3] Ibid., sec. 4.

(3) *Bye-laws.*

Bye-laws by the local authority in charge of highways and bridges are not binding until approved by the Sheriff.[1] On the local authority making application for approval the Sheriff, or Sheriff-Substitute,[2] will order publication, in a newspaper circulating in the district, of the text of the proposed bye-laws, and of the date upon which they will be considered, which must be at least ten days from the date of the advertisement.[1] At such diet any interested party may appear and be heard.

[1] 41 & 42 Vict. c. 51, sec. 104.
[2] Ibid., sec. 3.

(4) *Miscellaneous.*

A declaration by the local authority that a highway has ceased to be a highway, or that a road or bridge is to be a highway, may be appealed to the Sheriff by any three ratepayers within fourteen days, and a resolution to shut up a disused highway may be similarly appealed by any three inhabitants within six months.[1] The appeal is initiated by initial writ calling the authority as defenders, and it may be dealt with by the Sheriff or the Sheriff-Substitute.[2] It is to be dealt with summarily and the decision of either Sheriff or Sheriff-Substitute is final.[1] Expenses may be awarded.[1] The Sheriff or Sheriff-Substitute may also be asked to name a valuator in connexion with the sale of a toll-house.[3] This will also be a summary application and will not, it is thought, be open to review. The Sheriff may also authorize or prohibit the taking of materials from enclosed ground,[4] determine the damages payable on such being done,[4] or in respect of ground used as a temporary road,[5] and order the pulling down and removal of any unauthorized building on the side of a road.[6] These would appear to be summary applications to the Sheriff or Sheriff-Substitute,[2] and although in one case the ordinary rules as to appeal have been assumed to apply,[7] it is thought that the determination of the Sheriff (or Sheriff-Substitute) is intended to be final.[8] Expenses may be awarded at any rate in the applications dealing with damages.[9]

[1] 41 & 42 Vict. c. 51, secs. 42, 43; Maclean, &c. v. Inverness Road Trustees, &c., 1891, 7 Sh.Ct.Rep. 246. See also 55 & 56 Vict. c. 43, secs. 13 (1), 25 (7); cf. Roxburgh County Council v. Dalrymple's Trustees, 1894, 21 R. 1063, as to disposal by Sheriff on appeal after irregularities before Sheriff-Substitute.
[2] Ibid., sec. 3.
[3] Ibid., sec. 44.
[4] Ibid., Schedule (C) 80.
[5] Ibid., Schedule (C) 83.

6 Ibid., Schedule (C) 91.
7 See Argyllshire County Council v. Urquhart, 1892, 9 Sh.Ct.Rep. 56.
8 Whitson v. Blairgowrie District Committee, 1897, 24 R. 519, pp. 522, 523; cf. Ovenstone v. Dundee District Committee, (O.H.) 1919, 2 S.L.T. 35.
9 41 & 42 Vict. c. 51, Schedule (C) 80, 83. See Argyllshire County Council v. Urquhart, supra.

(5) *Interest of Judge.*

A Sheriff may act in the execution of the Roads and Bridges Act although he is a road trustee[1]—now a county councillor.[2] Thus a county councillor who is also an honorary Sheriff-Substitute could preside in the Sheriff Court in proceedings under the Act.

1 41 & 42 Vict. c. 51, sec. 113.
2 52 & 53 Vict. c. 50, sec. 11 (2).

40. SEA FISHERIES (SCOTLAND) AMENDMENT ACT.

Under this Act provision is made for a report by a fishery officer in regard to injury to boats, nets, lines and gear as the result of an offence under the Sea Fisheries Acts and in any legal proceedings for recovery of damages the report may be transmitted to the Clerk of Court when it will be received in evidence without the attendance of the fishery officer, and no other evidence as to damage is competent unless the Court consider such other evidence necessary.[1] This provision appears to relate to a question of evidence only and the proceedings are presumably such action as is competent in the circumstances. The section concludes by providing that if the damages awarded exceed £12—the then limit of the Small Debt Court—appeal is to be competent as in ordinary causes before the Sheriff Court.[1] This appears to mean that the ordinary rights of appeal are available according to the value of the cause, and it does not seem to enlarge the restricted right of appeal in summary causes.[2] Sec. 8 of the Act provides that if such an offence is committed the party claiming damages may notify the other party, and also the Sheriff-clerk of the Court where the offence is to be tried, that at the trial the Sheriff will be asked to dispose of the question of damages, and in that case the evidence at the trial is to be evidence on the question of damages, and at the close of the trial the Sheriff is directed to consider and dispose of the question of damages, and if a fishery officer's report is produced no additional evidence is to be heard—presumably on the question of damages—unless the Sheriff considers that necessary.[3] If additional evidence is taken the accused is a competent witness on this point.[3] After hearing parties the Sheriff is directed to give decree as in an ordinary action.[3] From the nature of this provision it would seem that no appeal in the normal sense is competent, as the evidence will not be recorded. The accused's liability for damages rests upon his conviction and it seems as if he could only avoid that liability by having the conviction upset. Procedure under sec. 8 is alternative and does not seem to exclude actions taken in the ordinary way.[4]

[1] 48 & 49 Vict. c. 70, sec. 7.
[2] 7 Edw. VII c. 51, sec. 8.
[3] 48 & 49 Vict. c. 70, sec. 8.
[4] Macleod, &c. v. Dobson, 1899, 16 Sh.Ct.Rep. 33; Ferrier, &c. v. Coull, &c., 1906, 22 Sh.Ct.Rep. 263.

41. SUMMARY JURISDICTION (PROCESS) ACT.

This Act provides that any process—which includes summons, warrant of citation as a party or as a witness, warrant for diligence, or order or minute[1]—issued by a Court of summary jurisdiction in England (with the exception noted below), if endorsed by a Court of summary jurisdiction in Scotland, may be served and executed within the jurisdiction of the endorsing Court and by an officer of that Court.[2] There is a general exception of English process for recovery of money which is a civil debt.[3] In Scotland a Court of summary jurisdiction includes the Sheriff or Sheriff-Substitute,[1] who may endorse such process in form prescribed by the Act,[4] or in a like form, on proof of the handwriting of the person who issued the process, which may be given on oath or by declaration.[4] An English warrant of distress when so endorsed is to be executed in Scotland as if it were for poinding and sale,[5] and an English bastardy order may be registered in the books of a Sheriff Court in Scotland, and thereupon a warrant for arrestment may be issued.[6] No special form of procedure is indicated by the Act, and it is presumably intended that the English process should merely be produced, with the necessary evidence as to handwriting, and the form of endorsement be written thereon and signed. The functions of the endorsing Court are purely ministerial.[7] Corresponding provision is made for the endorsement in England of any process—in the sense above indicated—issued by a Sheriff Court in Scotland.[4]

[1] 44 & 45 Vict. c. 24, sec. 8.
[2] Ibid., sec. 4. See also M'Queen v. M'Queen, (O.H.) 1920, 2 S.L.T. 405; Forsyth v. Forsyth, [1947] All E.R. 406.
[3] Ibid., sec. 4 (4).
[4] Ibid., sec. 4 (1), Schedule.
[5] Ibid., sec. 5.
[6] Ibid., sec. 6.
[7] Murphy v. Brooks, 1935 J.C. 11.

42. TELEGRAPHS.

By the Telegraphs Act, 1863,[1] claims for damages and compensation are to be determined under the provisions of the Lands Clauses and Railway Clauses Acts.[2] By the Telegraph Act, 1878, differences arising between the Postmaster-General and any body or person having control over public roads fall to be determined by the Sheriff.[3] The Telegraph Act, 1908, broadened this provision to include differences arising with certain private owners or occupiers.[4] Any person interested may bring a summary application in the Sheriff Court of the district where the subject-matter of the dispute arises,[5] narrating the circumstances and formulating the point upon which the decision of the Sheriff is desired. The crave is to determine the difference in dispute and the procedure is that appropriate in a railway arbitration.[3] The award of the Sheriff is not subject to review unless either party gives written notice within twenty-one days to the other party requiring the difference to be referred to the Railway and Canal Commission.[3] The Telegraph Arbitration Act of 1909 made it competent for parties, by agreement, to dispense with the Sheriff Court proceedings, and refer a dispute direct to the Railway and Canal Commission.[6]

[1] 26 & 27 Vict. c. 112, secs. 4, 7.
[2] See pp. 607, 654, supra.
[3] 41 & 42 Vict. c. 76, sec. 4. See Postmaster General v. Grimmond, 1922, 38 Sh.Ct.Rep. 204.
[4] 8 Edw. VII c. 33, sec. 1.
[5] 26 & 27 Vict. c. 112, sec. 3; 41 & 42 Vict. c. 76, secs. 2, 4.
[6] 9 Edw. VII c. 20, sec. 1.

43. TRUSTS.

The powers of the Trust Act are in general exercised by the Court of Session. But where a trustee in a *mortis causa* or marriage trust has become insane or incapable of acting by reason of physical or mental disability, or has been continuously absent from the United Kingdom for at least six months, or has disappeared for a like period, the Sheriff Court may entertain an application for his removal from office.[1]

[1] 11 & 12 Geo. V c. 58, sec. 23.

The aid of the Court may be invoked at the instance of any co-trustee, or of any beneficiary or other person interested in the trust estate.[1] The application is made in the Court whence issued the original confirmation of the trustees; and in the case of a marriage contract trust in the Court of the district within

which the spouses are, or the survivor is, domiciled.[1] The trustee
to be removed is called as defender, and the crave of the writ is
for declarator that the trustee is incapable of acting in respect of
one or more of the statutory reasons and for his removal from
office. If the defending trustee is insane personal service on him
is usually ordered. There are no statutory process directions save
that the removal is to be made on such evidence as satisfies the
Court of the grounds for removal.[1] In cases of insanity similar
medical certificates to those required for the appointment of a
curator will generally suffice,[2] but in the case of absence or disappearance a proof will be required though in one case in the
Court of Session affidavits were accepted.[3] Where the incapacity
is disputed a remit may be appropriate.[4]

[1] 11 & 12 Geo. V c. 58, sec. 23.
[2] Lees, (O.H.) 1893, 1 S.L.T. 42.
[3] Dickson's Trustees, (O.H.) 1894, 2 S.L.T. 61.
[4] A, (O.H.) 1898, 6 S.L.T. 149.

In the Sheriff Court proceedings are competent only for the
removal of a trustee. The Sheriff cannot replace a trustee so
removed, for the Court of Session alone has power to appoint
new trustees.[1] The trustee to be removed in the Sheriff Court
includes one judicially appointed or acting *ex officio* in a *mortis
causa* or marriage contract trust, and the expression trustee
includes an executor nominate.[2]

[1] 11 & 12 Geo. V c. 58, sec. 22.
[2] Ibid., secs. 2, 23.

APPENDIX.

THE SHERIFF COURTS (SCOTLAND) ACT, 1907 (7 Edw. VII c. 51), as amended by THE SHERIFF COURTS (SCOTLAND) AMENDMENT ACT, 1913 (2 & 3 Geo. V c. 28), and by LATER STATUTES AND ACTS OF SEDERUNT.

An Act to regulate and amend the Laws and practice relating to the civil procedure in Sheriff Courts in Scotland, and for other purposes. [28th August, 1907.]

B E it enacted by the King's most Excellent Majesty, by and with the advice and consent of the Lords Spiritual and Temporal, and Commons, in this present Parliament assembled, and by the authority of the same, as follows :—

Preliminary.

1. This Act may be cited for all purposes as the Sheriff Courts Short title. (Scotland) Act, 1907.

* 2. Unless otherwise specially enacted this Act shall come into Commence- operation on the first day of January one thousand nine hundred ment. and eight.

3. In construing this Act (unless where the context is repugnant Interpreta- to such construction)— tion.

(*a*) " Sheriff " includes Sheriff-substitute ;

(*b*) " Tenant includes sub-tenant ;

(*c*) " Lease " includes sub-lease ;

† (*d*) " Action [or cause "] includes every civil proceeding com- petent in the ordinary Sheriff Court ;

(*e*) " Person " includes company, corporation, or association and firm of any description nominate or descriptive, or any Board corporate or unincorporate ;

* This section is now repealed by the Statute Law Revision Act, 1927 (17 & 18 Geo. V c. 42, sec. 1, Schedule).

† As amended by the 1913 Act, Schedule I.

(f) " Sheriff-clerk " includes Sheriff-clerk depute ;

(g) " Agent " means a law-agent enrolled in terms of the **Law** Agents (Scotland) Act, 1873 ;

(h) " Final judgment " means an interlocutor which, **by** itself, or taken along with previous interlocutors, disposes of the subject-matter of the cause, notwithstanding that judgment may not have been pronounced **on** every question raised, and that expenses found due **may** not have been modified, taxed, or decerned for ;

† (i) " Summary cause " includes [actions (other than actions brought and conducted in the Small Debt Court **and** claims under the Workmen's Compensation Act) **for** payment of money not exceeding fifty pounds in amount, exclusive of interest and expenses, and **all** actions in which either the parties admit that the value of the action, exclusive of interest and expenses, **does** not exceed fifty pounds, or which they consent at **any** stage shall be tried summarily] ;

(j) " Small Debt Acts " means and includes the Small **Debt** (Scotland) Acts, 1837 to 1889, and Acts explaining **or** amending the same ;

(k) " Initial writ " means the statement of claim, petition, note of appeal, or other document by which the action is initiated ;

(l) " Procurator fiscal " means procurator fiscal in **the** Sheriff Court ;

(m) " Workmen's Compensation Act " means the Workmen's Compensation Act, 1906, and any Acts explaining **or** amending the same ;

(n) " Pursuer " means and includes any person making **a** claim or demand, or seeking any warrant or **order** competent in the Sheriff Court ;

(o) " Defender " means and includes any person **who is** required to be called in any action ;

(p) " Summary application " means and includes all applications of a summary nature brought under the common law jurisdiction of the Sheriff, and all applications, whether by appeal or otherwise, brought under **any** Act of Parliament which provides, or, according to **any**

† As amended by the 1913 Act, Schedule I.

practice in the Sheriff Court, which allows that the **Sec. 3.**
same shall be disposed of in a summary manner, but
which does not more particularly define in what form
the same shall be heard, tried, and determined.

*[(*q*) " Employee " includes the legal personal representative of
an employee, and any person who by the law of Scotland
may be entitled to solatium in respect of the death of
an employee.]

* Added by the 1913 Act, Schedule I.

JURISDICTION.

4. The jurisdiction of the Sheriffs, within their respective **Jurisdiction.**
Sheriffdoms shall extend to and include all navigable rivers, ports,
harbours, creeks, shores, and anchoring grounds in or adjoining
such Sheriffdoms. And the powers and jurisdictions formerly
competent to the High Court of Admiralty in Scotland in all
maritime causes and proceedings, civil and criminal, including
such as may apply to persons furth of Scotland, shall be competent
to the Sheriffs, provided the defender shall upon any legal ground
of jurisdiction be amenable to the jurisdiction of the Sheriff before
whom such cause or proceeding may be raised, and provided also
that it shall not be competent to the Sheriff to try any crime
committed on the seas which it would not be competent for him
to try if the crime had been committed on land : Provided always
that where Sheriffdoms are separated by a river, firth, or estuary,
the Sheriffs on either side shall have concurrent jurisdictions over
the intervening space occupied by water.

5. Nothing herein contained shall derogate from any jurisdic- **Extension of**
tion, powers, or authority presently possessed or in use to be **jurisdiction.**
exercised by the Sheriffs of Scotland, and such jurisdiction shall
extend to and include—

(1) Actions of declarator (except declarators of marriage or
nullity of marriage, and actions the direct or main
object of which is to determine the personal status of
individuals) :

* (2) [Actions of aliment, provided that as between husband and
wife they are actions of separation and aliment,
adherence and aliment, or interim aliment, and actions
for regulating the custody of children :]

* As amended by the 1913 Act, Schedule I.

(3) Actions of division of commonty and of division or division and sale of common property, in which cases the Act of 1695 concerning the division of commonties shall be read and construed as if it conferred jurisdiction upon the Sheriff Court in the same manner as upon the Court of Session :

(4) Actions relating to questions of heritable right or title (except actions of adjudication save in so far as now competent and actions of reduction) including all actions of declarator of irritancy and removing, whether at the instance of a superior against a vassal or of a landlord against a tenant :

(5) Suspension of charges or threatened charges upon the decrees of Court granted by the Sheriff or upon decrees of registration proceeding upon bonds, bills, contracts or other obligations registered in the books of the Sheriff Court, the books of council and session, or any others competent where the debt exclusive of interest and expenses does not exceed fifty pounds :

Provided that actions relating to questions of heritable right or title, including irritancy and removing or to division of commonties or division or divisions and sale, of common property shall, if raised in the Sheriff Court, be raised in the Sheriff Court of the jurisdiction and district where the property forming the subject in dispute is situated, and all parties against whom any such action may be brought shall in such action be subject to that jurisdiction : Provided also that it shall be competent for either party at the closing of the record or within six days thereafter to require the cause to be remitted to the Court of Session in the case of actions—

(a) Relating to questions of heritable right and title where the value of the subject in dispute exceeds fifty pounds by the year or one thousand pounds in value :

(b) Relating to the right of succession to moveables where the value of the subject in dispute exceeds one thousand pounds :

(c) Relating to division of commonty or division or division and sale of common property where the value of the subject in dispute exceeds fifty pounds by the year or one thousand pounds value :

* Provided also, that on cause shown or *ex proprio motu* the Sheriff may at any stage remit to the Court of Session any action [mentioned in the second sub-section of this section.]

6. Any action competent in the Sheriff Court may be brought within the jurisdiction of the Sheriff—

* * (*a*) Where the defender (or when there are several defenders, [over each of whom a Sheriff Court has jurisdiction in terms of this Act,] where one of them) resides within the jurisdiction, or having resided there for at least forty days has ceased to reside there for less than forty days [and has no known residence in Scotland.]
* * (*b*) Where the defender carries on business, and has a place of business within the [jurisdiction,] and is cited either personally or at such place of business :
* (*c*) Where the defender is a person not otherwise subject to the jurisdiction of the Courts of Scotland, and a ship or vessel of which he is owner or part owner or master, or goods, debts, money, or other moveable property belonging to him, have been arrested within the jurisdiction :
* (*d*) Where the defender is the owner or part owner or tenant or joint tenant, whether individually or as a trustee, of heritable property within the jurisdiction, and the action relates to such property or to his interest therein :
* (*e*) Where the action is for interdict against an alleged wrong being committed or threatened to be committed within the jurisdiction :
* (*f*) Where the action relates to a contract the place of execution or performance of which is within the jurisdiction, and the defender is personally cited there :
* (*g*) Where in an action of furthcoming or multiplepoinding the fund or subject in medio is situated within the jurisdiction; or the arrestee or holder of the fund is subject to the jurisdiction of the Court :
* (*h*) Where the party sued is the pursuer in any action pending within the jurisdiction against the party suing :
* (*i*) Where the action arises out of the delict of the defender within the jurisdiction, and he is personally cited there :
* (*j*) Where the defender prorogates the jurisdiction of the Court.

* As amended by the 1913 Act, Schedule I.

1x

Sec. 7.
Privative
jurisdiction
in causes
under fifty
pounds
value.

† **7.** Subject to the provisions of this Act and of the Small Debt Acts, all causes not exceeding fifty pounds in value exclusive of interest and expenses competent in the Sheriff Court shall be brought and followed forth in the Sheriff Court only, and shall not be subject to review by the Court of Session : Provided that nothing herein contained shall affect any right of appeal competent under any Act of Parliament in force for the time being.

Summary
cause pro-
cedure and
appeal.

* **8.** In a summary cause the Sheriff shall order such procedure as he thinks requisite, and (without a record of the evidence, unless on the motion of either party [made before the examination of witnesses is begun] the Sheriff shall order that the evidence be recorded) shall dispose of the cause without delay by interlocutor containing findings in fact and in law. Where the evidence has been recorded the judgment of the Sheriff-Substitute upon fact and law may in ordinary form be brought under review of the Sheriff, but where the evidence has not been recorded, the findings in law only shall be subject to review.

Value of
cause. How
determined.

9. [Repealed by Act of 1913, sec. 1.]

Privilege not
to exempt
from juris-
diction.

10. No person shall be exempt from the jurisdiction of the Sheriff Court on account of privilege by reason of being a member of the College of Justice.

SHERIFFS.

Appointment
of Sheriffs
and salaried
Sheriffs-
Substitute.

11. The right of appointing to the salaried offices of Sheriff and salaried Sheriff-Substitute shall be vested in His Majesty, and shall be exercised on the recommendation of the Secretary for Scotland.

Qualification
for Sheriff
and salaried
Sheriff-
Substitute.

36 & 37 Vict.
c. 63.

12. Every person appointed to the office of Sheriff shall be an advocate of five years' standing at least or, if not an advocate, a Sheriff-Substitute of five years' standing at least; and every person appointed to the office of salaried Sheriff-Substitute shall be an advocate, or a law agent within the meaning of the Law Agents (Scotland) Act, 1873 : Provided always that such advocate or law agent shall be of not less than five years' standing in his profession.

† As amended by the Act of 1913, Schedule I. It is also affected by the Administration of Justice (Scotland) Act, 1933 (23 & 24 Geo. V c. 41, sec. 10) in terms of which a dispute which could be the subject of a cause in the Outer House of the Court of Session or which might competently have been the subject of such a cause but for this section of the Sheriff Courts Act may be disposed of by summary trial in the Court of Session.

* As amended by the Act of 1913, Schedule I.

APPENDIX. 675

13. It shall be lawful for the Secretary for Scotland, upon a report prepared at his instance by the Lord President of the Court of Session and the Lord Justice-Clerk for the time being, declaring that a Sheriff in Scotland is by reason of inability, neglect of duty, or misbehaviour unfit for his office, to issue an order for his removal from office : Provided always that such order shall lie before both Houses of Parliament for a period of four consecutive weeks while Parliament is sitting, and, if either House of Parliament within that period resolve that such order ought not to take effect, the same shall be of no effect, but otherwise shall come into operation at the expiration of the said period. In this paragraph " Sheriff " does not include " Sheriff-Substitute."

A salaried Sheriff-Substitute shall be removeable from his office by the Secretary for Scotland for inability or misbehaviour upon the report of the Lord President of the Court of Session and the Lord Justice-Clerk for the time being.

Sec. 13.
Removal from office of Sheriff and salaried Sheriff-Substitute.

14. It shall be lawful to grant to any Sheriff or Sheriff-Substitute such salary as to the Treasury may seem meet, and every such salary shall be paid by four equal quarterly instalments, and shall be charged upon and be payable out of the Consolidated Fund.

Salaries of Sheriffs and Sheriffs-Substitute.

* 15. It shall be lawful for the Secretary for Scotland, on an application made by or on behalf of any Sheriff for leave of absence on account of temporary illness or other reasonable cause, to grant such leave of absence for such period as he shall deem proper, and to appoint some other person who shall be a Sheriff of some other Sheriffdom, or an advocate of not less than five years' standing, to act as interim Sheriff in the place and during the absence of such Sheriff, and on such interim appointment being made to fix what proportion of the salary of the Sheriff shall be paid to the interim Sheriff, and to certify the same in writing, and such certificate when presented in Exchequer to the King's and Lord Treasurer's

Leave of absence to Sheriff.

* Sec. 32 of the Administration of Justice (Scotland) Act, 1933 (23 & 24 Geo. V c. 41) provides : Where the Secretary of State in pursuance of sec. 15 of the Sheriff Courts (Scotland) Act, 1907, appoints an interim Sheriff to act in the place and during the absence on leave, granted on account of temporary illness, of a Sheriff who is restricted by the terms of his appointment from engaging in private practice, the provisions of the said section with regard to payment to the interim Sheriff shall not apply and it shall be lawful for the Treasury to allow any interim Sheriff so appointed such remuneration as they think fit out of moneys to be provided by Parliament, and in the event of a vacancy in the office of such Sheriff prior to the expiry of the period of leave of absence so granted to him, the appointment of the interim Sheriff shall have effect as an appointment to act as Sheriff until such vacancy shall be filled.

Sec. 15. Remembrancer shall be sufficient warrant for him for payment to such interim Sheriff of the proportion of the Sheriff's salary therein mentioned. A Sheriff appointed to be interim Sheriff under this section shall not by accepting such interim appointment vacate his office as Sheriff. An interim Sheriff appointed under this section shall have and exercise all the powers and privileges and perform all the duties of the Sheriff, and his acts, orders, and judgments shall have the same force and effect as if done, made, or pronounced by the Sheriff. In this section " Sheriff " does not include Sheriff-Substitute.

Leave of absence to salaried Sheriff-Substitute.

* 16. In the event of any salaried Sheriff-Substitute, by reason of ill-health [or other reasonable cause], being temporarily unable to discharge the duties of his office, it shall be lawful for the Secretary for Scotland on application being made to him by or on behalf of such Sheriff-Substitute to appoint a person qualified to fill the office of Sheriff-Substitute to act *ad interim* in the place and during the absence of such Sheriff-Substitute, and on such interim appointment being made the Treasury may, on the recommendation of the Secretary for Scotland, allow such interim Sheriff-Substitute such remuneration as they think fit out of monies to be provided by Parliament.

Honorary Sheriff-Substitute.

17. The Sheriff may by writing under his hand appoint such persons as he thinks proper to hold the office of honorary Sheriff-Substitute within his Sheriffdom during his pleasure, and for whom he shall be answerable. An honorary Sheriff-Substitute, during the subsistence of his commission, shall be entitled to exercise the powers and duties appertaining to the office of Sheriff-Substitute. An honorary Sheriff-Substitute shall hold office, notwithstanding the death, resignation, or removal of the Sheriff, until his commission shall be recalled by a succeeding Sheriff. In this section " Sheriff " does not include Sheriff-Substitute.

---

* As amended by the Sheriff Courts (Scotland) Act, 1939 (2 & 3 Geo. VI c. 98). It is also provided by the Sheriff Courts and Legal Officers (Scotland) Act, 1927 (17 & 18 Geo. V c. 35, sec. 14) that an appointment in pursuance of sec. 16 of the Sheriff Courts (Scotland) Act, 1907, of a person to act ad interim, in the place of a Sheriff-Substitute to whom leave of absence has been granted, shall, in the event of a vacancy occurring in the office of such Sheriff-Substitute prior to the expiry of the period of leave of absence, have effect as an appointment to act as Sheriff-Substitute until the vacancy shall be filled.

18. Every Sheriff shall, unless prevented by indisposition or *Sec. 18.*
other unavoidable cause, hold annually in his Sheriffdom Courts
for the discharge of the judicial business of the Sheriffdom; and *Courts to be*
such Courts shall continue until the causes ready for trial or hear- *held by*
Sheriffs in
ing when such Courts commence shall be disposed of; and each *their Sheriff-*
Sheriff shall give due notice of the times and places of such Courts; *doms.*
and, unless otherwise prescribed, each Sheriff shall, once in the
year, go on the small debt circuit, in use to be held by the Sheriff-
Substitute, and shall on such occasions, in addition to holding the
Small Debt Court, despatch as much of the ordinary business as
may be ready for adjudication, or as time may permit; and each
Sheriff shall annually, within ten days after the twelfth day of
November, make a return to the Secretary for Scotland of the
number of Courts and sittings held by him, and of the periods
of holding each such Court, in the immediately preceding year,
stating the cause of absence in case the Courts hereinbefore directed
shall not have been held by him in terms of this Act, provided
that the above provisions shall not extend to the Sheriffs of the
Lothians and Peebles and of Lanarkshire: Provided always that it
shall be lawful for the Secretary for Scotland to prescribe from
time to time the number of Courts to be held by the several Sheriffs
and the times and places for holding such Courts, and also from
time to time to prescribe the duties of the office of Sheriff which
such Sheriffs respectively are required to perform personally. In
this section " Sheriff " does not include Sheriff-Substitute.

19. It shall be lawful for the Secretary for Scotland from time *Secretary for*
to time to prescribe the number of salaried Sheriffs-Substitute of *Scotland to*
regulate
the several Sheriffdoms, and the places at which such salaried *number,*
Sheriffs-Substitute respectively are required generally to reside and *duties, and*
to attend for the performance of their duties, the number of Courts *residence of*
salaried
to be held by such Sheriffs-Substitute, the times and places of *Sheriffs-*
holding such Courts, and the duties to be performed by such *Substitute.*
Sheriffs-Substitute; and it shall also be lawful for the Secretary
for Scotland, if he shall think fit, to direct that the Sheriff-
Substitute of one county shall perform the duties of Sheriff-Substitute in an adjacent county; and any such direction shall be equivalent in all respects to a commission to act in such adjacent county
in favour of the Sheriff-Substitute so directed; and no salaried
Sheriff-Substitute shall be absent from the Sheriffdom for more
than six weeks in any year nor for more than two weeks at any
one time nor so as to interfere with the regular sittings of his
Court, without the special consent in writing of the Sheriff, who
shall be bound, in the event of his giving such consent, either to

Sec. 19.

attend personally during the absence of such substitute, or to appoint another person qualified as in section twelve hereof to act as substitute in his stead.

Annuities to
Sheriffs and
salaried
Sheriffs-
Substitute.

* **20.** It shall be lawful for the Treasury, upon the recommendation of the Secretary for Scotland, to grant an annuity payable in like manner as the salaries to any person who has held, now holds, or may hereafter hold the office of Sheriff or salaried Sheriff-Substitute whose period of service (notwithstanding that such service may not have been continuous and may have been in different Sheriffdoms and may have been partly as Sheriff-Substitute and partly as Sheriff) has been not less than ten years. Provided always that such annuity shall not exceed one-third of the salary payable to such person in case the period of his service shall have been not less than ten years, and shall not exceed two-thirds of such salary in case the period of service shall have been not less than fifteen years, and shall not exceed three-fourths of such salary in case the period of service shall have been not less than twenty years or upwards : Provided also that (except as hereinafter provided) no such annuity shall be granted to any Sheriff or Sheriff-Substitute unless the periods of his actual service shall, when taken together, extend to one or other of the periods of service before mentioned, and that in computing the amount of said annuity the emoluments drawn by him on an average of the five preceding years shall be held to constitute his salary : Provided also that no such annuity shall be granted unless such Sheriff or Sheriff-Substitute shall have duly fulfilled the duties of his office during one of the periods before mentioned, and is from age or permanent infirmity disabled from the due exercise of his office, which facts shall be certified by the Lord President, the Lord Justice-Clerk, and the Lord Advocate for the time being as having been established to their satisfaction : Provided also that if a Sheriff is removed under section thirteen hereof before he has completed ten years' service on the ground that he is by reason of inability unfit for his office, it shall be lawful for the Treasury to grant him an annuity of such amount and for such period as they shall consider just in all the circumstances, but in no case exceeding three-tenths of the salary payable to such Sheriff, and any such annuity shall be

* Amended by the Administration of Justice (Scotland) Act, 1933 (23 & 24 Geo. V c. 41), which provides by sec. 33 :—(1) Sec. 20 of the Sheriff Courts (Scotland) Act, 1907 (which relates to annuities to Sheriffs and salaried Sheriffs-Substitute) shall not apply to any Sheriff (other than a Sheriff holding office at the passing of this Act) unless he is restricted by the terms of his appointment from engaging in private practice ; (2) in this section " Sheriff " shall not include a Sheriff-Substitute.

charged upon and payable out of the same fund and in the same
manner as annuities to Sheriffs are paid and charged under the
first section of the Public Revenue and Consolidated Fund Charges
Act, 1854. In the last proviso of this section " Sheriff " shall not
include Sheriff-Substitute.

  * **21.** It shall not be lawful for a Sheriff to advise, plead, or
otherwise act as an advocate before any of the King's Courts at
Edinburgh, or at the Circuit Court, in any cause civil or criminal
arising within or coming from his Sheriffdom ; and no Sheriff or
salaried Sheriff-Substitute shall be steward, chamberlain, factor,
agent, or commissioner to any subject whatsoever, or shall exercise,
or act in the employment, service, or office of such steward,
chamberlain, factor, agent, or commissioner ; and no Sheriff or
salaried Sheriff-Substitute shall be capable of being elected or of
sitting or voting as a member of the House of Commons, nor shall
he be entitled to vote at any election for any member of Parliament
held within his Sheriffdom ; nor shall he act directly or indirectly
as an agent for any candidate in any matter connected with, or
preparatory to, any election [occurring within his jurisdiction] ;
and it shall not be lawful for a salaried Sheriff-Substitute to engage
in legal, banking, or other private practice or business, or to act
directly or indirectly as a procurator before any Court, or to be
in partnership with any person so engaged or acting, nor shall
such Sheriff-Substitute be appointed to any office, except such office
as shall be by Statute attached to the office of Sheriff-Substitute.
  Any Sheriff or salaried Sheriff-Substitute acting contrary to the
provisions of this section shall be guilty of misbehaviour within the
meaning of section thirteen of this Act.

PROCURATORS-FISCAL.

22-24. (These sections are repealed by the Sheriff Courts and
Legal Officers (Scotland) Act, 1927 (17 & 18 Geo. V c. 35, sec. 23.)

SESSIONS.

25. In each Sheriff Court there shall be held two sessions in the
year, a winter and a summer session. The winter session shall
extend from the first Ordinary Court day in October to the last
Ordinary Court day in March. The sittings of the Court may, at
Christmas time, be suspended for a period not exceeding fifteen
days. The summer session shall extend from the first Ordinary
Court day in May to the last Ordinary Court day in July.

  * As amended by the 1913 Act, Schedule I.

Sec. 26.
Vacation
Courts.

26. The Sheriff shall, before the termination of each winter session, appoint at least one Court day during the spring vacation for the despatch of civil business, and before the termination of each summer session he shall in like manner appoint at least two Court days during the autumn vacation for the same purpose. Any cause may proceed during vacation as during session, and in all causes interlocutors may competently be pronounced during vacation.

APPEALS.

Appeal to
Sheriff.

27. Subject to the provisions of this Act an appeal to the Sheriff shall be competent against all final judgments of the Sheriff-Substitute and also against interlocutors—

(A) Granting or refusing interdict, interim or final;

(B) Granting interim decree for payment of money other than a decree for expenses, or making an order *ad factum præstandum;*

(c) Sisting an action;

(D) Allowing or refusing or limiting the mode of proof not being an interlocutor fixing a diet for jury trial;

(E) [Refusing a reponing note; or

(F)] Against which the Sheriff-Substitute either *ex proprio motu* or on the motion of any party grants leave to appeal;

Provided always that notwithstanding the death, resignation, or removal of a Sheriff, appeals may be taken from the judgment of the Sheriff-Substitute, which appeals shall be heard by the succeeding Sheriff when he shall enter upon office. [It shall be competent for the Sheriff when the action is before him on appeal on any point, to open the record *ex proprio motu,* if the record shall appear to him not to have been properly made up, or to allow further proof.]

Appeal to
Court of
Session.

† **28.**—[(1) Subject to the provisions of this Act, it shall be competent to appeal to the Court of Session against a judgment either of a Sheriff or of a Sheriff-Substitute if the interlocutor appealed against is a final judgment or is an interlocutor—

(A) Granting interim decree for payment of money other than a decree for expenses; or

* As amended by the Act of 1913, Schedule I.

† Substituted for the original section by the Act of 1913, sec. 2.

(B) Sisting the action; or

(C) Refusing a reponing note; or

(D) Against which the Sheriff or Sheriff-Substitute, either *ex proprio motu* or on the motion of any party, grants leave to appeal:

Provided that no appeal shall be competent where the cause does not exceed fifty pounds in value exclusive of interest and expenses or is being tried as a summary cause unless the Sheriff, after final judgment by him on an appeal on the motion of either party made within seven days of the date of the final interlocutor certifies the cause as suitable for appeal to the Court of Session.

(2) Nothing in this section nor in section twenty-seven of this Act contained shall affect any right of appeal or exclusion of such right provided by any Act of Parliament in force for the time being.]

29. An appeal shall be effectual to submit to review the whole of the interlocutors pronounced in the cause, and shall be available to and may be insisted in by all other parties in the cause notwithstanding they may not have noted separate appeals. An appeal shall not prevent immediate execution of a warrant of sequestration for rent, or of warrants to take inventories, or place effects in custody *ad interim*, or warrants for interim preservation, and an interim interdict, although appealed against, shall be binding till recalled.

Effect of appeal.

REMOVAL OF CAUSE TO COURT OF SESSION FOR JURY TRIAL.

* **30.** In cases originating in the Sheriff Court (other than claims by employees against employers in respect of injury caused by accident arising out of and in the course of their employment and concluding for damages under the Employers Liability Act, 1880, [or at common law], or alternatively at common law or under the Employers Liability Act, 1880), where the claim is in amount or value above fifty pounds, and an order has been pronounced allowing proof (other than an order for proof to lie *in retentis* or for recovery of documents) it shall, within six days thereafter, be competent to either of the parties, who may conceive that the cause ought to be tried by jury, to require the cause to be remitted to the Court of Session for that purpose where it shall be so tried:

Removal of cause for jury trial.

43 & 44 Vict. c. 42.

---

* As amended by the Act of 1913, Schedule I. Reference should also be made to the Rules of Court, 1936, **V**, 14, 15.

Sec. 30. Provided, however, that the Court of Session shall, if it thinks the case unsuitable for jury trial, have power to remit the case back to the Sheriff, or to remit it to a Lord Ordinary, or to send it for proof before a Judge of the Division before whom the cause depends

JURY TRIAL IN SHERIFF COURT.

Jury trial in Sheriff Court.

* **31.** In any action raised in the Sheriff Court by an employee against his employer concluding for damages under the Employers Liability Act, 1880, [or at common law], or alternatively under that Act or at common law in respect of injury caused by accident arising out of and in the course of his employment, where the claim exceeds fifty pounds, either party may so soon as proof has been allowed, or within six days thereafter, require that the cause shall be tried before a jury, in which case the Sheriff shall appoint the action to be tried before a jury of seven persons. The verdict of the jury shall be applied in an interlocutor by the Sheriff, which shall be the final judgment in the cause, and may, subject to the provisions of this Act, be appealed to either division of the Court of Session but that only upon one or more of the following grounds—

(1) That the verdict has been erroneously applied by the Sheriff;

(2) That the verdict is contrary to the evidence;

(3) That the Sheriff had in the course of the trial unduly refused or admitted evidence or misdirected the jury

(4) That an award of damages is inadequate or is excessive

Upon such appeal the Court may refuse the appeal or may find that the verdict was erroneously applied, and give judgment accordingly, or may set aside the verdict and order a new trial provided that if the judges are equally divided in opinion the verdict shall stand.

Procedure at jury trials.

† **32.** [Where a jury trial has been ordered, the Sheriff shall issue an interlocutor fixing a time and place for the trial, being not sooner than fourteen days from the date of his interlocutor and at the trial he may, or if required by either party, shall, after the conclusion of the evidence, propone to the jury question or questions of fact to be answered by them, and the jury shall, in their verdict, give specific answers to such question or questions.

* As amended by the Act of 1913, Schedule I; so far as disposal of an appeal is concerned the section is also affected by the Jury Trial Amendment (Scotland) Act, 1910 (10 Edw. VII & 1 Geo. V c. 31 sec. 2) and the Rules of Court, 1936, V, 7-13.

† This section, which is sec. 6 of the Act of 1913, supersedes the original sec. 32.

33. Where jury trial has been ordered the party moving for it shall, on each day the trial proceeds, before the proceedings commence, deposit with the Sheriff-clerk the sum of three pounds ten shillings, which deposit shall form part of the expenses of the cause; failing any such deposit being made, the Sheriff may dismiss the cause. Out of said fund the Sheriff-clerk shall pay to each juror a fee of ten shillings for each day on which he is empanelled. When a jury trial is not proceeded with, said deposit shall be returned to the depositor.

Sec. 33.

Remunera-
tion of jurors.

REMOVINGS.

34. Where lands exceeding two acres in extent are held under a probative lease specifying a term of endurance, and whether such lease contains an obligation upon the tenant to remove without warning or not, such lease, or an extract thereof from the books of any Court of record, shall have the same force and effect as an extract decree of removing obtained in an ordinary action at the instance of the lessor, or any one in his right, against the lessee or any party in possession, and such lease or extract shall along with authority in writing signed by the lessor or any one in his right or by his factor or law agent, be sufficient warrant to any Sheriff-officer or messenger-at-arms of the Sheriffdom within which such lands or heritages are situated to eject such party in possession, his family, sub-tenants, cottars, and dependants, with their goods, gear and effects, at the expiry of the term or terms of endurance of the lease: Provided that previous notice in writing to remove shall have been given—

Removings.

(A) When the lease is for three years and upwards not less than one year and not more than two years before the termination of the lease; and

(B) In the case of leases from year to year (including lands occupied by tacit relocation) or for any other period less than three years, not less than six months before the termination of the lease (or where there is a separate ish as regards land and houses or otherwise before that ish which is first in date):

Provided that if such written notice as aforesaid shall not be given the lease shall be held to be renewed by tacit relocation for another year, and thereafter from year to year: Provided further that nothing contained in this section shall affect the right of the landlord to remove a tenant who has been sequestrated under the Bankruptcy (Scotland) Act, 1856, or against whom a decree of

19 & 20 Vict.
c. 79.

Sec. 34.
43 & 44 Vict.
c. 34.

cessio has been pronounced under the Debtors (Scotland) Act, 1880, or who by failure to pay rent has incurred any irritancy of his lease or other liability to removal : Provided further that removal or ejectment in virtue of this section shall not be competent after six weeks from the date of the ish last in date : Provided further that nothing herein contained shall be construed to prevent proceedings under any lease in common form ; and that the foregoing provisions as to notice shall not apply to any stipulations in a lease entitling the landlord to resume land for building, planting, feuing, or other purposes or to subjects let for any period less than a year.

Letter of removal.

35. Where any tenant in possession of any lands exceeding two acres in extent (whether with or without a written lease) shall, either at the date of entering upon the lease or at any other time, have granted a letter of removal, either holograph or attested by one witness, such letter of removal shall have the same force and effect as an extract decree of removing, and shall be a sufficient warrant for ejection to the like effect as is provided in regard to a lease or extract thereof, and shall be operative against the granter of such letter of removal or any party in his right within the same time and in the same manner after the like previous notice to remove : Provided always that where such letter is dated and signed within twelve months before the date of removal or before the first ish, if there be more than one ish, it shall not be necessary that any notice of any kind shall be given by either party to the other.

Notice to remove.

36. Where lands exceeding two acres in extent are occupied by a tenant without any written lease, and the tenant has given to the proprietor or his agent no letter of removal, the lease shall terminate on written notice being given to the tenant by or on behalf of the proprietor, or to the proprietor by or on behalf of the tenant not less than six months before the determination of the tenancy, and such notice shall entitle the proprietor, in the event of the tenant failing to remove, to apply for and obtain a summary warrant of ejection against the tenant and every one deriving right from him.

Notice of termination of tenancy.

37. In all cases where houses, with or without land attached, not exceeding two acres in extent, lands not exceeding two acres in extent let without houses, mills, fishings, shootings, and all other heritable subjects (excepting land exceeding two acres in extent) are let for a year or more, notice of termination of tenancy shall be given in writing to the tenant by or on behalf of the

proprietor or to the proprietor by or on behalf of the tenant: **Sec. 37.**
Provided always that notice under this section shall not warrant
summary ejection from the subjects let to a tenant, but such notice,
whether given to or by or on behalf of the tenant, shall entitle the
proprietor to apply to the Sheriff for a warrant for summary
ejection in common form against the tenant and every one deriving
right from him : Provided further that the notice provided for by
this section shall be given at least forty days before the fifteenth
day of May when the termination of the tenancy is the term of
Whitsunday, and at least forty days before the eleventh day of
November when the termination of the tenancy is the term of
Martinmas.

SUMMARY REMOVINGS.

38. Where houses or other heritable subjects are let for a **Summary**
shorter period than a year, any person by law authorized may **removing.**
present to the Sheriff a summary application for removing, and a
decree pronounced in such summary cause shall have the full force
and effect of a decree of removing and warrant of ejection. Where
such a let is for a period not exceeding four months, notice of
removal therefrom shall, in the absence of express stipulation, be
given as many days before the ish as shall be equivalent to at
least one-third of the full period of the duration of the let ; and
where the let exceeds four months, notice of removal shall, in the
absence of express stipulation, be given at least forty days before
the expiry of the said period.

PROCEDURE RULES.

39. Subject to the provisions of any Act of Parliament in **Procedure**
force after the passing of this Act, the procedure in all civil causes **rules.**
shall be conform to the rules of procedure set forth in the First
Schedule hereto annexed. Such rules shall be construed and have
effect as part of this Act.

* **40.** The Court of Session may from time to time, by Act of **Court of**
Sederunt, make such regulations for regulating the fees of agents, **Session to**
officers, shorthand writers, and others, and, with the concurrence **regulate**
of the Treasury, for regulating the fees of Court : Provided that **fees, &c.**
every such Act of Sederunt shall, within one week from the date
thereof, be transmitted by the Lord President of the Court of
Session to the Secretary for Scotland, in order that it may be laid

---

* As amended by (a) the Act of 1913, Schedule I, and (b) the Administration of Justice (Scotland) Act, 1933 (23 & 24 Geo. V c. 41,
sec. 34 (2)).

Sec. 40.

before the Houses of Parliament; and, if either of the Houses of Parliament shall within thirty-six days after it has been laid before them resolve that the whole or any part of such Act of Sederunt ought not to continue in force, the whole or such part thereof as shall be included in such resolution shall from and after the date of the passing of such resolution cease to be binding.

Meetings of Sheriffs.

41. (Repealed by the Administration of Justice (Scotland) Act, 1933 (23 & 24 Geo. V c. 41, sec. 39).)

SMALL DEBT ACTS.

Extension of small debt jurisdiction to £20.

42. The provisions of the Small Debt Acts shall extend and apply to all causes competent thereunder where the value of the cause does not exceed twenty pounds, and wherever the words " eight pounds six shillings and eightpence " or the words " twelve pounds " occur in these Acts they shall be read and construed as if for these words there were substituted the words " twenty pounds."

Small debt sequestration for rent.

43. The provisions of the Small Debt Acts for sequestration for rent shall extend to all sequestrations applied for *currente termino* or in security.

Parties may appear by agents in Small Debt Court.

52 & 53 Vict. c. 26.

* **44.** [Section eight of the Small Debt Amendment (Scotland) Act, 1889, is hereby repealed, and in lieu thereof it is enacted that] in any cause brought under the Small Debt Acts any party may appear by or along with an agent, and the Sheriff may allow and include in the expenses of the cause a fee to such agent.

* Portion within brackets is repealed by the Statute Law Revision Act, 1927 (17 & 18 Geo. V c. 42, sec. 1, Schedule).

Procedure rules applicable to small debt causes.

* **45.** The provisions of section three (except sub-sections (*d*), (*h*), (*i*), (*k*), (*l*), (*m*), and (*p*)), section four, sub-section (2) of section five, so far as relating to claims for aliment, section six (except sub-section (*e*)), section forty-nine and section fifty-one hereof, and the rules ten, eleven, twelve, thirteen, fourteen, fifteen, seventeen, nineteen, twenty-one, twenty-six, fifty, fifty-five, sixty, sixty-three, sixty-eight (*b*), seventy, seventy-nine, eighty, one hundred and twenty-six, one hundred and twenty-seven, one hundred and twenty-eight, one hundred and twenty-nine, one hundred and fifty-one, in the First Schedule hereto shall, so far as appropriate, apply to causes under the Small Debt Acts.

* As amended by Act of Sederunt, 16th July, 1936, which added the reference to Rule 68 (b).

† **46.** The provisions of sections ten and eleven of the Debtors (Scotland) Act, 1838, shall not apply to decrees of delivery under the Small Debt Amendment (Scotland) Act, 1889, but such decrees shall be enforceable by imprisonment under the warrant for execution contained in Schedule B of the Small Debt Amendment (Scotland) Act, 1889.

Sections 10 and 11 of the Debtors (Scotland) Act, 1838, not to apply to small debt causes. 1 & 2 Vict. c. 114.

47. It shall be lawful to issue a second or further extract of any decree under the Small Debts Acts, in the form as nearly as may be of Schedule B or C of the Small Debt Amendment (Scotland) Act, 1889, which extract may be written upon a separate paper, and shall have the same force and effect in all respects as the first extract.

Second extract of small debt decree competent.

48. If the Sheriff is of opinion that the importance of the questions raised in any cause brought under the Small Debt Acts warrants that course, he may at any stage remit the cause to his Ordinary Court roll either on cause shown or *ex proprio motu*, in which case the cause shall proceed in all respects (including appeal) as if it had been originally raised in the Ordinary Court.

Small debt cause may be remitted to Ordinary Court roll.

POSTAL CHARGE.

49. (Repealed by the Execution of Diligence (Scotland) Act, 1926 (16 & 17 Geo. V c. 16, sec. 7) which, by sec. 2, makes other provisions for a postal charge.)

Postal charge.

SUMMARY APPLICATIONS.

50. In summary applications (where a hearing is necessary) the Sheriff shall appoint the application to be heard at a diet to be fixed by him, and at that or any subsequent diet (without record of evidence unless the Sheriff shall order a record) shall summarily dispose of the matter and give his judgment in writing : Provided that wherever in any Act of Parliament an application is directed to be heard, tried, and determined summarily or in the manner provided by section fifty-two of the Sheriff Courts (Scotland) Act, 1876, such direction shall be read and construed as if it referred to this section of this Act : Provided also that nothing contained in this Act shall affect any right of appeal provided by any Act of Parliament under which a summary application is brought.

Summary applications. 39 & 40 Vict. c. 70.

† This section is affected and largely annulled by the Hire Purchase and Small Debt (Scotland) Act, 1932 (22 & 23 Geo. V c. 38, secs. 6, 7) in regard to which see p. 478, supra.

THE POOR'S ROLL.

51. Where parties are unable from poverty to pursue or defen
an action, it shall be lawful for the Sheriff to admit such parties t
the benefit of the poor's roll if, upon the report of the procurator
for the poor, he is satisfied that such person is entitled thereto.

REPEAL.

* **52.** The enactments mentioned in the Second Schedule heret
annexed are hereby repealed to the extent mentioned in the thir
column of that Schedule, and all laws, Statutes, Acts of Sederunt
orders and usages now in force so far as the same are inconsisten
with the provisions of this Act, are also hereby repealed.   Bu
provided that all actions pending at the date of the commencemen
of this Act shall nevertheless proceed to final determination in a
respects as if this Act had not been passed.

* This section is now repealed by the Statute Law Revision Act, 192
    (17 & 18 Geo. V c. 42, sec. 1, Schedule).

SCHEDULES.

FIRST SCHEDULE.

RULES FOR REGULATING PROCEDURE IN THE ORDINARY COURT.

FORMS OF PROCESS.

1. Subject to the provisions of the Titles to Land Consolidatio
(Scotland) Act, 1868, and the Conveyancing and Land Transfe
(Scotland) Act, 1874, as regards service of heirs and completion o
title, all actions shall be commenced by writ as nearly as may b
in the Form A hereto annexed.

* 2. [There shall be annexed to the initial writ a statement (i
the form of an articulate condescendence) of the facts which form
the ground of action, and a note of the pursuer's pleas in law
which condescendence and note of pleas in law shall be held t
constitute part of the initial writ.]

* This rule, introduced by the Act of 1913, Schedule II, supersedes th
    original Rule 2.

3. The writ shall be signed by the pursuer or complainer or by his agent, and the name and address of pursuer's agent (if any) shall be upon the back of every service copy. **Sched. I.** Writ to be signed.

4. The warrant of citation shall be as nearly as may be—

(a) In summary causes and summary removings, and also in summary applications when citation is necessary and in cases under the Workmen's Compensation Act, in the Form B hereto annexed : Form of first warrant.

(b) In all other causes, in the Form C hereto annexed.

Induciæ.

5. Actions shall proceed upon seven days' warning or *induciæ* when the defender is within Scotland, or fourteen days when he is in Orkney or Shetland or in any other island within Scotland or is furth of Scotland. Induciæ of citation.

6. The Sheriff may shorten or may extend the *induciæ*, but not so as to be in any case less than forty-eight hours. Special induciæ.

Citation.

7. Warrants may be signed by the Sheriff-clerk, but any warrant may be signed by the Sheriff or Sheriff-Substitute, and must be so signed if it contains an order for shortening or extending the *induciæ* or for interim interdict, sequestration, or other order not being an order for citation or warrant to arrest. In actions against persons furth of Scotland the warrant may authorize service edictally. Signature of warrants.

8. Citation may be in the Form D hereto annexed, and the form of execution of citation, which shall be appended to or endorsed upon the initial writ, may be in the Form E hereto annexed. Mode of citation.

9. If a warrant is executed by an officer, one witness shall be sufficient for the execution of citation and the execution shall be signed by the officer and the witness, and shall specify whether the citation was personal, or, if otherwise, the mode of citation. Attestation of officer's execution of citation.

10. Any warrant of citation or any warrant or precept of arrestment proceeding upon a depending action or liquid document of debt may in any competent manner be lawfully executed within the jurisdiction of any Sheriff without indorsation by the Sheriff-clerk of that jurisdiction, and, if executed by an officer, may be so Endorsation of warrant by Sheriff-clerk of defender's residence not necessary

Sched. I. executed by an officer of the Court which granted the warrant or precept, or by an officer of the jurisdiction within which it is to be executed.

* [11. Any individual or individuals, or any corporation or association, carrying on business under a firm or trading or descriptive name may sue or be sued in such name without the addition of the name or names of such individual or individuals or any of them, or of any member or official of such corporation or association, and any extract of a decree pronounced in the Sheriff Court, or of a decree proceeding upon any deed, decree arbitral, bond, protest of a bill, promissory note or banker's note, or upon any other obligation or document on which execution may competently proceed, recorded in the Sheriff Court books against such individual or individuals, or against such corporation or association, under such firm, trading, or descriptive name, shall be a valid warrant for diligence against such corporation, association, or firm, and such individual or individuals. Citation in any action may be made at the principal place where such business is carried on (including the place of business or office of the clerk or secretary of any corporation or association) when such place is within the jurisdiction of the Sheriff Court in which such action is brought, or otherwise at any place of business or office at which such business is carried on within the jurisdiction of such Sheriff Court.]

Service of new.
12. If it appear to the Sheriff that there has been any irregularity in service upon a defender who has not appeared, the Sheriff may authorize the pursuer or complainer to make service of new upon such conditions as to the Sheriff shall seem just.

Defender appearing barred objecting to citation.
13. A party who appears may not state any objection to the regularity of the service upon himself, and his appearance shall be deemed to remedy any defect in the service, unless where jurisdiction has been constituted by citation or by arrestment *ad fundandam jurisdictionem.*

Citation of a minor.
14. Service in ordinary form on a minor and on his father, as curator-at-law, or upon a minor and his tutors and curators if known to pursuer, or, if they are not known, upon the minor himself in ordinary form, and his tutors and curators edictally, shall be good and sufficient service on the minor for every purpose of law.

* This rule, introduced by the Act of 1913, Schedule II, supersedes the original Rule 11.

* 15. It shall be competent to execute edictally any warrant of **Sched. I.** citation granted or charge on an extracted decree pronounced by a Edictal Sheriff against any person furth of Scotland, by delivery of a copy citation. thereof at the office of the keeper of edictal citations at Edinburgh according to the mode established in regard to the execution edictally of citations and charges on warrants of the Court of Session; or by sending to such keeper in a registered post-letter a certified copy of such warrant or charge, of which copy the keeper shall acknowledge receipt. Every citation or charge so executed edictally shall be recorded in the record of edictal citations in Edinburgh in a separate record of edictal citations or charges against persons furth of Scotland cited or charged upon warrants proceeding from any Sheriff Court. Where the party cited or charged has a known residence or place of business in England or Ireland a copy of the writ and citation or of the decree and charge on fourteen days' *induciæ* shall be posted in a registered letter to the party at such address, and the execution shall express that this has been done. The Sheriff-clerk shall in all warrants to cite persons furth of Scotland insert a warrant to cite edictally, and along with the execution of edictal citation pursuer's agent shall lodge a certificate of such postal intimation and the post office registered letter receipt.

CUSTODY OF PROCESS.

† 16. Every initial writ shall after tabling remain in the custody Custody of of the Sheriff-clerk, unless the Sheriff shall grant a special order to process. the contrary. A process may be borrowed only by an agent entitled to practice in the jurisdiction, or by his duly authorized clerk, for whom he shall be responsible. [All remedies (including caption) competent to enforce the return of a borrowed process may proceed on the warrant of the Court from whose custody the process was obtained, and that whether the borrower is or is not resident within its jurisdiction.]

17. When any number of process is lost or destroyed, a copy Lost docu- thereof, authenticated in such manner as the Sheriff may require, ments may be may be substituted, and shall, for the purposes of the action, be replaced by equivalent to the original. copies.

---

* Edictal citation is now made at the office of the Extractor of the Court of Session. See p. 121, supra.

† As amended by the Act of 1913, Schedule II. See also Solicitors (Scotland) Act, 1933 (23 & 24 Geo. V c. 21, sec. 46).

Sched. I.
Interlocutor sheets, &c., to be lodged by pursuer.

18. In a defended action the pursuer shall lodge with the Sheriff-clerk principal and duplicate interlocutor sheets and a principal and borrowing inventory of process; and the Sheriff-clerk shall endorse upon all pleadings the date when the same are lodged. The principal interlocutor sheets and the borrowing inventory shall remain in the custody of the Sheriff-clerk.

Transfer of Causes.

Transfer of cause to more convenient Sheriffdom where several defenders in different Sheriffdoms.

19. Where an action in which there are two or more defenders has been brought in the Court of the domicile of one of them, the Sheriff may transfer the cause to any other Court which has jurisdiction over any of the defenders, if in his opinion it is expedient that this should be done, and an action so transferred shall proceed in all respects as if it had been originally brought in that Court.

Sheriff on cause shown may remit to another Sheriffdom.

20. The Sheriff may upon sufficient cause, by interlocutor stating his reasons, remit any cause to another Sheriffdom, and such interlocutor, when issued by a Sheriff-Substitute, shall by leave of the Sheriff-Substitute, and within seven days only, be subject to review by the Sheriff, but shall not be further subject to review.

Where plea of no jurisdiction stated cause may be remitted to proper Sheriffdom.

21. Where a plea of no jurisdiction is sustained, the Sheriff may, if he think proper, and upon such conditions as to costs as he may think fit, remit the cause to the Sheriff before whom it appears to him it ought to have been brought, and it shall thereafter proceed in all respects as if it had been originally there brought. When such remit is made by the Sheriff-Substitute, the interlocutor remitting shall by leave of the Sheriff-Substitute and within seven days only be subject to review by the Sheriff but shall not be further subject to review.

Appearance.

Notice of appearance.

* 22. If a defender intend to state a defence he shall (except in a summary cause), before the expiry of the *induciæ* [exhibit to the Sheriff-clerk the service copy of the writ and lodge with him], a notice of appearance in the following terms:—

[Place and date]—C. D., [design him] defender, intends to defend the action against him [and others] at the instance of A. B. [design him].

C. D., *Defender*,
or X. Y. [add address],
Defender's Agent.

* As amended by the Act of 1913, Schedule II.

UNDEFENDED CAUSES.

* [23. If the defender does not lodge a notice of appearance, or **Sched. I.** does not answer, the Sheriff may, at any time after the expiry of the *induciæ*, upon a written craving being endorsed on the initial writ by the pursuer or his agent, decern in terms of the crave of the initial writ, and at the same time or thereafter, for expenses as the same may be certified by a note endorsed upon the initial writ by the auditor of Court subject to any restriction so endorsed or set forth in a minute by the pursuer or his agent : Provided that this rule shall not apply to actions of separation and aliment, adherence and aliment, or interim aliment, or to actions regulating the custody of children.]

In undefended cause decree may be granted at any time after expiry of induciæ.

24. The Sheriff-clerk may issue an extract of such decree after the expiry of seven days from the date of the Sheriff's judgment.

Extract of decree in absence in seven days.

25. A decree pronounced in absence, and which has not been recalled or brought under review by suspension, where suspension is competent, or by reduction, shall become final, and be entitled to all the privileges of a decree *in foro*—

Finality of decree in absence.

    (*a*) In six months from its date, or from the date of charge under it, where the service of the writ or of the charge has been personal ;

    (*b*) In any event after the lapse of twenty years from its date.

26. In an undefended action the Sheriff may allow the pursuer or his agent to amend any error or defect in the initial writ, and may, if he see fit, order the amended writ to be served upon the defender, and may allow him to appear within such time as he may think proper. But the expense occasioned by such amendment shall not be chargeable against the defender, and such amendment shall not have the effect of validating diligence used on the dependence of the action so as to prejudice creditors of the defender, but such amendment shall be operative to the effect of obviating objections to such diligence when stated by the defender himself, or by any persons representing him by a title, or in right of a debt contracted by him subsequent to the using of such diligence, and any diligence which was competent upon the original writ shall be competent upon the amended writ.

Amendment of writ in undefended action.

* This rule, introduced by the Act of 1913, Schedule II, supersedes the original Rule 23.

Reponing.

Sched. I.
Defender may be reponed against decree in absence.
27. At any time before implement of a decree in absence, the defender may apply to be reponed by lodging with the Sheriff-clerk and serving upon pursuer a note setting forth his proposed defence, and his explanation of his failure to appear.

Upon consignation.
28. Along with this reponing note the defender shall consign the sum of two pounds in the hands of the Sheriff-clerk.

Sheriff may recall the decree in absence.
29. Upon such consignation the Sheriff, if satisfied with the defender's explanation, may recall the decree so far as not implemented, whereupon the action shall proceed in all respects as if the defender had appeared.

Or refuse to recall.
30. If the Sheriff is not satisfied with the defender's explanations he may refuse the reponing note.

Pursuer entitled to consigned money.
31. In either case the pursuer shall be entitled to uplift the consigned money.

Reponing note to operate as sist of diligence.
32. A reponing note, when duly lodged and intimated to the pursuer or his agent, shall operate as a sist of diligence.

Judgment upon a reponing note final.
* 33. Any interlocutor or order recalling, or incidental to the recall of a decree in absence, shall be final and not subject to review.

Defended Causes.

Defended cause to be tabled.
34. Where appearance has been entered the Sheriff-clerk shall enrol the cause for tabling on the first Court day occurring after the expiry of the *induciæ*.

If not tabled to drop from roll.
35. An action which has not been tabled, and in which protestation has not been craved, shall drop from the roll, but within three months the Sheriff may direct it to be again enrolled for tabling under such conditions as to notice, or re-service, or expenses, or otherwise as he shall think fit.

If case not tabled defender may crave protestation.
36. If the pursuer do not then table the cause, the defender or his agent, upon producing the service copy of the writ, may crave protestation for not insisting, which the Sheriff may grant, and may modify the amount of protestation money payable to defender.

* As amended by the Act of 1913, Schedule II.

37. Protestation shall not be extracted till the expiry of seven **Sched. I.** free days from the date of its granting, except where arrestments Extract of have been used, in which case extract may be given out after the protestation. lapse of forty-eight hours.

38. Upon protestation being extracted, the instance shall fall. Effect of protestation.

39. Before extract protestation may be recalled, and the pursuer Recall of may be allowed to proceed with his action upon making payment protestation. to the defender of the amount of the protestation money, and upon such other conditions as to the Sheriff shall seem just.

40. When any defended action (other than a claim under the Sheriff may Workmen's Compensation Act) has been tabled, the Sheriff of direct any consent of parties, notwithstanding that its value exceeds fifty cause to be tried as a pounds, may, at any stage, direct that it be tried as a summary summary cause, and his decision as to this shall be final. cause.

† 41. In a summary cause the Sheriff may order defences if he Procedure in thinks fit or may make or certify a note upon the writ or separately a summary of the defender's pleas, and may appoint a diet for the trial of the cause. cause, or may order such other procedure as the circumstances seem to him to require.

* [42. In all other defended actions the defender shall, at the tabling of the action, or within six days thereafter, lodge defences.]

* [43. Defences shall be in the form of articulate answers to the Form of condescendence and shall have appended a note of the defender's defences. pleas in law and, where necessary, or where a counter-claim is made, a separate statement of facts founded on by the defender which shall be set forth succinctly.]

* [44. Every statement of fact made by one party shall be answered by the other party, and, if a statement made by one party of a fact within the knowledge of the other party is not denied by that other party, the latter shall be held as admitting the fact so stated.]

* [45. Upon defences being lodged, the Sheriff-clerk shall enrol Enrolment the action for adjustment at an Ordinary Court held on a day for adjust-occurring not less than four days thereafter. Such adjustment shall ment. not be adjourned more than once except on special cause shown.]

† As amended by the Act of 1913, Schedule II.

* These rules, introduced by the Act of 1913, Schedule II, supersede the original Rules 42-46.

Sched. I.
Certified copy
writ warrant
for arrest-
ment,

* [46. In every defended action the pursuer shall, after defences have been lodged, and before the diet for adjustment, lodge in process a copy of the initial writ and warrant thereon, certified by him or his agent, which may thereafter be borrowed by the agent of any party to the process, and such certified copy shall be sufficient warrant where competent to arrest on the dependence. Separate precepts of arrestment may be issued by the Sheriff-clerk upon production to him of a writ containing pecuniary conclusions upon which a warrant of citation has been granted, or of a liquid document of debt.]

Documents
founded on to
be produced
before record
closed.

47. Each party shall, along with his pleadings, or at least before the closing of the record, if required by any other party in the action or by the Sheriff, lodge any documents founded upon in the pleadings, so far as the same are within his custody or power.

Diligence for
recovery of
such
documents.

48. Where such documents are not produced by either party, or where they are in the hands of third parties, the Sheriff may, on the motion of either party, grant commission and diligence for their recovery, and may on that account delay closing the record.

Revisal may
be ordered.

49. The Sheriff may upon cause shown, or *ex proprio motu*, order a revisal of the pleadings, or may order pursuer to answer defender's separate statement of facts.

Documents
may be chal-
lenged *ope
exceptione.*

50. When a deed or writing is founded on by any party in a cause, all objections thereto may be stated and maintained by way of exception, without the necessity of bringing a reduction thereof.

Caution may
be ordered
when action
of reduction
competent.

51. The Sheriff may, where an objection is so stated and where an action of reduction would be competent, order the objector to find caution, or to make consignation as he shall direct.

Closing
record.

† [52. When the pleadings have been adjusted the Sheriff shall close the record; and not later than six days thereafter the pursuer shall lodge in process a certified copy of the closed record.]

Alterations to
be initialed
by Sheriff.

53. All alterations or additions made on the record shall be authenticated by the Sheriff's initials.

* These rules, introduced by the Act of 1913, Schedule II, supersede the original Rules 42-46.

† This rule, introduced by the Act of 1913, Schedule II, supersedes the original Rule 52.

54. If preliminary pleas have been stated the Sheriff shall first dispose of them, unless he thinks that from their being connected with the merits, or on any other ground, they should be reserved till a future stage of the cause.

Sched. I.
Preliminary pleas to be first disposed of.

55. Where a defender pleads a counter claim it shall suffice that he state the same in his defences, and the Sheriff may thereafter deal with it as if it had been stated in a substantive action, and may grant decree for it in whole or in part, or for the difference between it and the claim sued on.

Counter claim may be stated in defences.

56. In a defended action (including a jury cause) when any production or pleading has not been lodged or order implemented within the time required by Statute or ordered by the Sheriff or where in a defended action either party fails to appear by himself or his agent at any diet, or fails to make payment of any Court dues or deposit, the Sheriff may grant decree as craved, or of absolvitor, or may dismiss the action, with expenses, but the Sheriff may upon cause shown prorogate the time for lodging any production or pleading or implementing any order. If all parties fail to appear the Sheriff shall, unless sufficient reason appear to the contrary, dismiss the action.

Failure of either party to appear or to implement orders of court entitles other party to decree.

57. When an agent has borrowed a process, or any part thereof, and fails to return it for any diet at which it is required, the Sheriff may impose upon such agent a fine not exceeding one pound, which shall be payable to the Clerk of Court for behoof of His Majesty's Exchequer, but an order so imposing a fine may, on cause shown, be recalled by the Sheriff who granted it. Orders made under this section shall not be subject to review. For the purposes of this section every agent practising before his Court shall be subject to the jurisdiction of the Sheriff.

Agent failing to return process may be fined.

58. If at the time of closing the record the parties renounce probation, they shall sign a minute to that effect on the inter-locutor sheet, and the Sheriff may order the case to be debated then or at a subsequent diet.

If probation renounced parties to sign minute

59. If proof is necessary, the Sheriff shall (unless the cause has been ordered for jury trial), with the least possible delay, fix a date for taking the proof, and may limit the mode of proof.

Proof may be ordered.

60. The Sheriff may remit to any person of skill, or other person, to report on any matter of fact; and, when such remit is

Remit to person of skill.

Sched. I. made of consent of both parties, the report of such person shall be final and conclusive with respect to the matter of the remit. When such a remit is made, upon the motion of either party, the expense attending its execution shall in the first instance be paid by the party moving for it. When the remit is on joint motion, or by the Sheriff *ex proprio motu*, the expense shall in the first instance be paid by the parties equally, unless the Sheriff shall otherwise order.

Parties may by minute agree to cause being tried as small debt cause.

61. The parties to any action may lodge in process a minute signed by themselves or their agents, agreeing to the cause being disposed of in the manner provided under the Small Debt Acts, whereupon the Sheriff shall remit the action to his Small Debt Court roll, and the whole powers and provisions of the Small Debt Acts shall become applicable to the cause.

Diligence for recovery of documents.

62. At any time after a proof has been allowed, or an order made for jury trial, the Sheriff, upon the motion of either party, may grant commission and diligence for the recovery of such documents as the Sheriff shall deem relevant to the cause.

Evidence to lie in retentis.

63. Evidence in danger of being lost may be taken to lie *in retentis*, and, if satisfied that it is desirable so to do, the Sheriff may, upon the motion of either party at any time, either take himself, or grant authority to a commissioner to take, such evidence.

Reference to oath.

64. When any person desires to refer to the oath of his adversary, he shall lodge a minute to that effect, signed by himself or his agent. If the party to whose oath reference has been made fail to appear at the diet for taking his deposition, the Sheriff may hold him as confessed, and decern accordingly.

Recording of evidence.

65. Evidence in a cause or a deposition, whether before the Sheriff or a commissioner, may be taken down by the Sheriff or commissioner, or by a clerk or shorthand writer nominated by the Sheriff or commissioner, to whom the oath *de fideli administratione* shall be administered and evidence may be recorded in narrative form or by question and answer as the Sheriff or commissioner shall direct, and the extended notes of evidence certified by such clerk or shorthand writer shall be the notes of the oral evidence in the cause. The Sheriff or commissioner may, if he think fit, dictate to the clerk or shorthand writer what he is to record.

Sheriff may amend record of evidence.

66. If the correctness of the notes of evidence or of a deposition be questioned, the Sheriff may satisfy himself in regard thereto by the examination of witnesses or otherwise, and may amend the record of evidence or a deposition.

67. When a shorthand writer is so employed to record evidence, he shall in the first instance be paid, as regards commissions by the party moving for the commission, and as regards proofs or jury trials by the parties equally. The agents of parties shall be personally liable for the shorthand writer's fees. And it shall be competent for the Sheriff to make an order directing payment to be made.

Sched: I.
Shorthand
writer's fees.

* 68. In all causes in which a proof shall be allowed, all documents, plans, maps, models and other productions which are intended to be used or put in evidence at the proof, shall be lodged according to inventory in the office of the Sheriff-clerk on or before the fourth day prior to the day appointed for the proof, and notice of the lodging thereof shall at the same time be sent to the solicitor of the opposite party : and no other production shall be used or put in evidence at the proof unless by consent of parties or by permission of the judge presiding thereat, on cause shown to his satisfaction, and on such terms, as to expenses or otherwise, as to him shall seem proper. All steps of process and productions borrowed shall be returned to process before noon on the day preceding the date of the proof.

Lodging and
returning
productions
for proofs.

† 68(a) The Sheriff may order production of documents at any stage of the cause, and the Sheriff may allow a party, at any time before judgment, to produce any document which he has failed to produce timeously, upon such conditions as to payment of expenses and allowing further proof as to the Sheriff shall seem just.

Production of
documents
may be
ordered.

‡ 68(b). (a) Where any party to a cause desires to obtain from the Keeper of the Registers and Records of Scotland production of the original of any register or deed under his custody, he shall apply by motion to the Sheriff or Sheriff-Substitute before whom the cause depends, after seven days' notice of such application given in writing to the Keeper in charge of the original.

Warrant for
production of
original docu-
ments from
public
Records.

(b) Upon such application the Sheriff or Sheriff-Substitute may, by interlocutor, certify that it is necessary for the ends of justice that the application should be granted, and the party may make application by letter (enclosing a copy of the interlocuor duly certified by the Sheriff-clerk or one of his deputes) addressed to the Principal Clerk of Session, for an order from the Lords of Council and Session authorizing the Keeper to exhibit the original of any

* New rule added by Act of Sederunt, 16th July, 1936.
† Formerly Rule 68, but renumbered 68 (a) by Act of Sederunt, 16th July, 1936.
‡ New rule added by Act of Sederunt, 16th July, 1936.

Sched. I. register or deed to the Sheriff or Sheriff-Substitute, and that in the hands of an officer to be selected by the said Keeper.

(*c*) The Principal Clerk of Session shall submit the same to a Lord Ordinary in Chambers, who, if satisfied, shall grant a warrant on behalf of the Lords of Council and Session. A certified copy of said warrant shall be served upon the Keeper of the Registers and Records of Scotland.

(*d*) The expense attending the transmission and exhibition of such original register or deed shall be defrayed in the first instance by the party or parties on whose application they are exhibited.

Proof to be taken continuously. 69. The proof shall be taken so far as possible continuously, but the Sheriff may adjourn the diet from time to time.

Evidence may be taken on commission. 70. The evidence of any witness or haver resident beyond the jurisdiction of the Court, or who although resident within the jurisdiction resides at some place remote from the seat of the Court, or who is by reason of illness, age, or infirmity unable to attend the diet of proof, or a jury trial, may be taken by commission in like manner as evidence to lie *in retentis*.

Citation of witnesses. 71. A copy of an interlocutor certified by the Sheriff-clerk allowing a proof or fixing a diet for the trial of any action or for the examination of witnesses or havers, or fixing a date for a jury trial, shall be sufficient warrant for citation of witnesses or havers. If any witness or haver duly cited on an *induciæ* of at least forty-eight hours, and after having been tendered his travelling expenses, if the same shall have been demanded, fail to attend a diet, either before the Sheriff or before his commissioner, such witness or haver may be ordained by the Sheriff to forfeit and pay a penalty not exceeding forty shillings, unless a reasonable excuse be offered and sustained, and the Sheriff may grant decree for said penalty in favour of the party on whose behalf said witness or haver was cited.

Form of citation. 72. Witnesses and havers may be cited as nearly as may be in Form F hereto annexed, and the execution of citation shall be as nearly as may be in the Form G, and an agent who cites a witness shall be personally liable for the fees of the witness.

Second diligence against witness failing to attend. 73. It shall further be competent to the Sheriff to grant second diligence (which shall be effectual in any Sheriffdom within Scotland without endorsation) for compelling the attendance of said witness or haver under pain of arrest and imprisonment, until caution be found as the Sheriff may require for his due attendances, the **Sched. I.** expense whereof may in like manner be decerned for against the witness or haver.

74. When the Sheriff or a commissioner repels or sustains an *Objections.* objection taken in the course of a proof, the objection stated, and *taken in* any answer made to it, shall, if desired by the objector, be shortly *course of* noted on the notes of evidence to the Sheriff's or commissioner's *proof to be noted.* dictation, but the examination of the witness shall nevertheless proceed. The Sheriff or commissioner may, if he consider the objections of sufficient importance, direct the evidence objected to to be taken on a separate paper; but it shall not be competent during the course of a proof to submit to review any judgment pronounced upon the competency of the evidence.

75. On the proof being declared closed, or within seven days *Appeal on* thereafter, if the Sheriff-Substitute has not in the interval pro- *questions of* nounced judgment, it shall be competent by leave of the Sheriff- *admissibility* Substitute to appeal to the Sheriff upon objections to the admissi- *of evidence.* bility of evidence taken during the course of the proof, and the Sheriff shall, with or without a hearing, dispose of such appeal with the least possible delay, and, if he think that evidence accepted should not have been allowed, he may delete the same from the notes of evidence, and, if he think that evidence has been improperly rejected, he may appoint the same to be taken before the case is advised on its merits.

* 76. If any person, whether a party to the cause or other person, *Appeal on* plead before the Sheriff-Substitute confidentiality with reference to *ground of con-* documentary or oral evidence, or, on pleas of alleged hypothec or *fidentiality.* otherwise, shall object to produce documents, the Sheriff-Substitute shall, on the notes of evidence, minute his decision on such pleas, and any party in the cause or the party pleading [confidentiality] by leave of the Sheriff-Substitute may, in open Court, take an appeal to the Sheriff, who shall, with or without a hearing and with the least possible delay, dispose of such appeal.

77. Such incidental appeal shall not remove the cause from the *Proof to pro-* Sheriff-Substitute, who may proceed with the cause as regards points *ceed not with-* not necessarily dependent upon the ruling so appealed against. *standing such appeal.*

78. At the close of the proof, or at an adjourned diet, if for any *Parties to be* reason the Sheriff shall see fit to postpone the hearing, the Sheriff *heard at close of proof.*

* As amended by the Act of 1913, Schedule II.

Sched. I. shall hear the parties or their agents, and thereafter shall pronounce judgment with the least possible delay.

AMENDMENT OF PLEADINGS.

Record may be amended by Sheriff. 79. Upon the motion of either party the Sheriff may, at any stage of the cause, and upon such conditions as to expenses, reservice, or otherwise as he shall deem proper, allow a record to be altered or amended to the effect of determining the real question in controversy (including amendment of the instance and the initial writ and the adding of parties) notwithstanding that the conclusions of the action may thereby be enlarged or altered.

Effect of amendment. 80. No such amendment shall have the effect of validating diligence used prior thereto on the dependence of the action so as to prejudice the rights of creditors of the defender interested in defeating such diligence, but such amendment shall be operative to the effect of obviating objections to such diligence when stated by the defender himself, or by any person representing him by a title, or in right of a debt contracted by him subsequent to the execution of such diligence.

ABANDONMENT.

Abandonment of action. 81. A pursuer may at any stage of an action before an interlocutor granting absolvitor or dismissing the action has been pronounced offer to abandon his action by lodging a minute to that effect, signed by himself or his agent, in which case, upon payment to defender of his expenses, the Sheriff may dismiss the action, and pursuer may bring a new action if otherwise competent. If the pursuer fails, within fourteen days of the date of taxation, to pay the defender's expenses, the defender shall be entitled to decree of absolvitor, with expenses.

JUDGMENT.

Sheriff to state reasons for judgment. 82. To all interlocutors, except those of a formal nature, the Sheriff shall append a note setting forth the grounds upon which he has proceeded, and in his final judgment on the merits he shall set forth his findings in fact and in law separately.

Date of judgment to be date of entry in court books. 83. The Sheriff may pronounce or sign any judgment or interlocutor when furth of his Sheriffdom, but the date of every interlocutor shall be deemed to be the date upon which it is entered in the books of the Court.

84. At any time before extract, or before the transmission of a **Sched. I.**
process in which an appeal has been taken the Sheriff may correct Clerical error
any clerical or incidental error in his judgment. in judgment
may be
corrected.

EXTRACT.

* 85. Extract of any decree, interlocutor, or order of the Sheriff Time of
(other than a decree in absence or a decree for expenses) [unless extract.
either an appeal has been taken or leave to appeal has been applied
for] may be issued in a summary cause after the lapse of seven
days; and in any other cause, after the lapse of fourteen days
from its date, or at such earlier date as the Sheriff shall allow
extract [provided that an application for leave to appeal shall not
preclude the issuing of extract unless leave is granted and an appeal
is taken within seven days after leave is granted].

* As amended by the Sheriff Courts and Legal Officers (Scotland) Act,
1927 (17 & 18 Geo. V c. 35, sec. 21).

APPEAL.

† 86. A final judgment of the Sheriff-Substitute may if appeal Appeal from
be competent and unless otherwise provided be appealed to the the Sheriff-
Sheriff or to the Court of Session at any time within three months Substitute.
of its date (but not later), if the same shall not sooner have
been extracted or implemented. Any other appealable interlocutor
of the Sheriff-Substitute may be appealed within fourteen days (but
not later), if not sooner extracted [provided that an interlocutor
granting interim interdict may be appealed within fourteen days
from the date of intimation thereof].

* 87. An appeal shall be taken by the appellant or his agent Form of
dating and signing a note on the interlocutor sheet in the follow- appeal.
ing terms :—

> The pursuer [or defender or other party] appeals [to the
> Sheriff] or [to the Division of the Court of
> Session].
> Or if the interlocutor sheet is not in the hands of the Sheriff-
> clerk (which fact shall be certified by him), the note of
> appeal may be written upon a separate paper, and
> lodged along with the Sheriff-clerk's said certificate.

† As amended by the Act of 1913, Schedule II.
* This rule is affected by the Rules of Court, 1936, V, 8 (a), which
provide inter alia that so far as appeal to the Court of Session
is concerned the form of note of appeal is now " The (pursuer,
applicant, claimant, defender, respondent, or other party) appeals
to the Court of Session."

On appeal
process to go
to Sheriff or
clerk of
Session.

† 88. On an appeal being taken, the Sheriff-clerk shall within two days transmit the process to the Sheriff or to the Principal Clerk of Session as the case may be, and also send written notice of the appeal to the other parties or their agents, but failure to give such notice shall not invalidate the appeal.

> † So far as appeal to the Court of Session is concerned this rule is now superseded by the Rules of Court, 1936, V, 8 (b) (c), which provide for the process being transmitted to the deputy principal clerk of the General Department within four days after an appeal has been taken, and for notice being sent to the other party within the same period.

Reclaiming
petition or
oral hearing
may be
ordered.

‡ 89. The Sheriff may order a [reclaiming petition] and answers, or may hear parties orally.

But may be
dispensed
with.

‡ 90. The Sheriff may, on the motion of both parties and if he see fit, dispose of the appeal without ordering either a [reclaiming petition] and answers or an oral hearing.

> ‡ As amended by the Act of 1913, Schedule II.

Sheriff to
regulate
interim
possession,
&c., pending
appeal.

91. Notwithstanding an appeal, the Sheriff shall have power to regulate all matters relating to interim possession, to make any order for the preservation of any property to which the action relates or for its sale if perishable, or for the preservation of evidence, or to make in his discretion any interim order which a due regard to the interests of the parties may require. Such orders shall not be subject to review except by the Appellate Court at the hearing of the appeal.

Appeal to
Court of
Session.

92. Within three months from its date (but not later) a final judgment of the Sheriff, if not sooner extracted or implemented, may, if appeal be competent, be appealed to the Court of Session. Any other appealable judgment of the Sheriff may, if not sooner extracted or implemented, be appealed within fourteen days (but not later).

Form of
appeal.

‡ 93. The party desiring so to appeal, or his agent, shall do so by writing on the interlocutor sheet (or on a separate paper, in like manner as in the case of an appeal from the Sheriff-Substitute) a note in the following terms:—

> The pursuer [or defender or other party] appeals to the Division of the Court of Session.

> ‡ This rule is affected by the Rules of Court, 1936, V 8 (a) which provide inter alia that so far as appeal to the Court of Session is concerned the form of note of appeal is now " The (pursuer, applicant, claimant, defender, respondent or other party) appeals to the Court of Session."

* 94. On receiving such note of appeal the Sheriff-clerk shall within two days transmit the process to the Principal Clerk of Session at Edinburgh, and shall also send written notice of the appeal to the other parties or their agents, but failure to give such notice shall not invalidate the appeal.

Sched. I. Sheriff-clerk to transmit process to Edinburgh.

† 95. If any action is desired to be removed to the Court of Session in terms of sections five and thirty of this Act, the party so desiring its removal shall write a minute to that effect upon the interlocutor sheet, whereupon the Sheriff-clerk shall give intimation to the other parties or their agents and shall transmit the process to the keeper of the roll of the Court of Session, who shall, under the direction of the Lord President, allocate the cause to a Division and a Lord Ordinary, and thereafter the cause shall proceed in all respects as if it had originally been raised in the Court of Session.

Form of appeal to Court of Session in actions cated un this Act.

‡ 96. After an appeal has been noted, the appellant shall not be entitled to abandon it unless of consent of all parties, or by leave of the Appellate Court.

Abandonment of appeal.

97. In sections 86, 87, 88, 89, 90, and 92 " Sheriff " does not include Sheriff-Substitute.

Expenses.

98. Every decree for expenses shall be deemed to include a decree for the expense of extracting the same, and extract of such decree for expenses may be issued after the lapse of seven days unless otherwise directed by the Sheriff.

Decree for expenses to include dues of extract.

99. Expenses allowed in any action, whether in absence or *in foro*, shall, unless modified at a fixed amount, be taxed before

Decree for expenses may be extracted in agent's name.

* So far as appeal to the Court of Session is concerned this rule is now superseded by the Rules of Court, 1936, V, 8 (b) (c), which provide for the process being transmitted to the deputy principal clerk of the General Department within four days after an appeal has been taken, and for notice being sent to the other party within the same period.

† This rule is now superseded by the Rules of Court, 1936, V, 14, 15, which provide inter alia that the note to be written on the interlocutor sheet is to be in these terms : " The pursuer (or defender or other party) requires the cause to be remitted to the Court of Session," and that within four days after such application the Sheriff-clerk shall give notice to the opposite party and within the same period shall transmit the process to the deputy principal clerk of the General Department. The procedure in the Court of Session is as laid down in the Rules of Court.

‡ See also Rules of Court, 1936, V, 9 (b), 12.

Sched. I.

decree is granted for them, and the Sheriff may allow a decree for expenses to go out and be extracted in name of the agent who conducted the cause.

Objection to auditor's report.

100. Within two days after the lodging of the auditor's report on taxation it shall be competent to lodge a note of objections to an auditor's report, and the Sheriff shall dispose of such objections in a summary manner, with or without answers.

WAKENING.

Wakening action.

101. If no interlocutor shall have been pronounced in a cause for a year and a day it shall be held to have fallen asleep.

To be by minute.

102. Where the whole of the parties or their agents subscribe a minute on the interlocutor sheet consenting to the cause being wakened the Sheriff may pronounce an interlocutor wakening the cause, and thereafter proceed with it.

Publication of application for wakening.

103. Where all parties do not so consent, the party desiring to have the cause wakened may lodge a minute to that effect, which the Sheriff may order to be intimated to the other parties or their agents, and to be published in such manner as the Sheriff shall direct, and the agent for the party applying for wakening shall lodge a certificate that the intimation and publication ordered have been made. If satisfied, the Sheriff may thereafter pronounce an interlocutor wakening the cause, and proceed with it.

SEQUESTRATION FOR RENT.

In sequestration for rent.

104. In actions for sequestration, and sale, for recovery, or in security of rent, whether brought after the term of payment or *currente termino*, payment of rent may be concluded for, and decree for payment of such rent or part thereof, when the same has become due and payable, may be pronounced and be extracted in common form.

Warrant may be granted to inventory and secure.

105. In the first deliverance upon a writ for sequestration for rent the Sheriff may sequestrate the effects of a tenant, and grant warrant to inventory and secure the same, and all warrants to sequestrate, inventory, sell, eject, or relet shall be deemed to include authority, if need be, to open shut and lockfast places for the purpose of carrying such warrants into execution.

Sequestrated effects may be sold.

106. The Sheriff may order the sequestrated effects to be sold at the sight of an officer of Court or other person named.

107. When a sale follows, it shall be reported within fourteen days, and pursuer shall lodge the roup rolls or certified copies thereof and a state of debt.

108. In the interlocutor approving the report of sale, or by separate interlocutor, the Sheriff may give decree against the defender for any balance remaining due.

109. The Sheriff may at any stage appoint a fit person to take charge of the sequestrated effects, or may require the tenant to find caution that they shall be made forthcoming.

REMOVINGS.

110. An action of removing may be raised at any time, provided the tenant has bound himself to remove by writing, dated and signed within twelve months of the term of removal, or, where there is more than one ish, of the ish first in date to remove. When the tenant has not so bound himself, an action of removing may be raised at any time provided that—

(a) In the case of a lease of lands exceeding two acres in extent for three years and upwards, an interval of not less than one year nor more than two years shall elapse between the date of notice of removal and the term of removal first in date;

(b) In the case of leases of lands exceeding two acres in extent, whether such leases be written or verbal, held from year to year or under tacit relocation, or for any other period less than three years, an interval of not less than six months shall elapse between the date of notice of removal and the term of removal first in date; and

(c) In the case of houses let with or without land attached not exceeding two acres in extent, as also of land not exceeding two acres in extent without houses, as also of mills, fishings, shootings, and all other heritable subjects excepting land exceeding two acres in extent, and let for a year or more, forty days at least shall elapse between the date of notice of removal and the term of removal first in date.

Provided that nothing herein contained shall affect section 27 of the Agricultural Holdings Act, 1883: Provided also that in any defended action of removing, the Sheriff may order the defender to find caution for violent profits: Provided also that, in actions of

Sched. I. declarator of irritancy and removing by a superior against a vassal, the pursuer shall call as parties the last entered vassal and such heritable creditors and holders of postponed ground burdens as are disclosed by a search for twenty years prior to the raising of the action, and the expense of the search shall form part of pursuer's expenses of process.

Form of notice of removal. 111. Notices under sections 34, 35, and 36 of this Act shall be as nearly as may be in the Form H annexed hereto, and a letter of removal may be in the terms of Form I.

Form of notice under section 37. 112. Notices under section 37 of this Act shall be as nearly as may be in the Form J hereto annexed, and such form may be used, *mutatis mutandis*, also for notices to the proprietor by or on behalf of the tenant.

Removal notices. 113. Removal notices under sections 34, 35, 36, 37, and 38 of the Act may be given by a messenger-at-arms or Sheriff-officer, or by registered letter signed by the person entitled to give such notice, or by the law agent or factor of such person, posted at any post office within the United Kingdom in time to admit of its being delivered at the address thereon on or prior to the last date upon which by law such notice must be given, addressed to the person entitled to receive such notice, and bearing the particular address of such person at the time if the same be known, or, if the same be not known, then to the last known address of such person.

Evidence of notice to remove. 114. A certificate of notice under Rule 111, dated and endorsed upon the lease or extract, or upon the letter of removal, and signed by the Sheriff-officer, messenger-at-arms, or by the person giving the notice, or his law agent, or factor, or an acknowledgment of notice endorsed on the lease or extract or letter of removal by the party in possession or his agent shall be sufficient evidence that notice has been given. Where there is no lease, a certificate endorsed upon a copy of the notice or letter, certified to be correct, by the person, Sheriff-officer, messenger-at-arms, law agent, or factor sending the same, which certificate shall be signed by such party sending the notice or letter, shall also be sufficient evidence that notice has been given. A certificate of notice under Rule 112, dated and endorsed upon a copy of the notice or letter signed by the party sending the notice, shall be sufficient evidence that such notice has been given.

Summary Removings.

115. The action for summary removing as authorized by section 38 of this Act may be at the instance of a proprietor or his factor, or any other person by law authorized to pursue a process of removing, and be in the Form K hereto annexed. **Sched. I.** Form of action for summary removing.

116. The warrant to be granted thereon may be in the Form B hereto annexed upon two days *induciæ* and may be signed by the Sheriff-clerk. Form of warrant.

117. If the defender fail to appear, the Sheriff may dispose of the cause in his absence, but, if within three days the defender shall satisfy the Sheriff that there was reasonable excuse for his non-appearance, the Sheriff may rehear the cause, and, if decree has been granted and not implemented, may recall the decree upon such conditions as to expenses and otherwise as the Sheriff shall deem reasonable. Where decree is pronounced in absence, the Sheriff may give such directions as he may deem proper for the preservation of the defender's goods and effects. Decree in absence may be recalled within three days.

118. The warrant upon the petition or complaint or the defender's service copy thereof shall be sufficient warrant for the citation of witnesses. Service copy warrant sufficient to cite witnesses.

* [119. Except as hereinafter provided, such action for summary removing shall be conducted and disposed of in the summary manner in which proceedings are conducted under the Small Debt Acts and shall not be subject to review.] Small debts procedure applies to summary removing.

† 120. When decree and warrant of ejection is granted it shall be in the Form L hereto annexed. Form of decree.

* [121. In all such actions for summary removing, where the defender has found caution for violent profits, or where such caution has been dispensed with, he shall be entitled to give in written answers.]

122. Where a defender has given in answers, and caution for violent profits has been found or has been dispensed with, such When caution found procedure as ordinary action.

* This rule, introduced by the Act of 1913, Schedule II, supersedes the original rule.

† This rule is affected by Act of Sederunt of 3rd February, 1933, sec. 7, which also provides new forms of extracts of decrees (see p. 722, infra).

Sched. I.   causes shall, as nearly as may be thereafter, be conducted according to the procedure in ordinary actions of removing, and shall be subject to review in common form.

SUMMARY SUSPENSION.

Summary
application
for suspension
of charge may
be brought
in court of
defender's
domicile.

123. Where a charge has been given on a decree of Court granted by the Sheriff or a decree of registration proceeding upon a bond, bill, contract, or other form of obligation registered in any Sheriff Court books, or in the books of council and session, or any others competent, or on letters of horning following on such decree, for payment of any sum of money not exceeding fifty pounds, exclusive of interest and expenses, the person so charged may apply in the Sheriff Court of his domicile for suspension on caution of such charge and diligence.

Diligence
may be sisted
on caution.

124. On sufficient caution being found in the hands of the Sheriff-clerk for the sum charged for interest and expenses, and a sum to be fixed by the Sheriff in respect of expenses to be incurred in the suspension process, the Sheriff may sist diligence, order intimation and answers, and proceed to dispose of the cause in a summary manner.

Judgment of
Sheriff final on
competency.

125. If objections be taken to the competency or regularity of suspension proceedings, the judgment of the Sheriff-Substitute on such objections may be appealed to the Sheriff, but his judgment thereon shall be final.

ARRESTMENT.

When arrest-
ment schedule
not served
personally
copy to be
sent by post.

‡ 126. If a schedule of arrestment has not been personally served upon an arrestee, it shall be necessary to make the arrestment effectual, that a copy of the schedule be also sent by postal registered letter to the last known place of abode of the arrestee, or, if such place of abode is unknown, or, if the arrestee is a firm or corporation, to the arrestee's principal place of business if known, or if not known, to any known place of business of the arrestee, and the officer shall in his execution certify that this has been done, and specify the said address.

Arrestment
to be
reported.

* [127. An arrestment on the dependence of an action used prior to service shall fall unless the action shall have been served within

‡ This rule is affected by the Execution of Diligence (Scotland) Act, 1926 (16 & 17 Geo. V c. 16, sec. 2 (2)).

* This rule, introduced by the Act of 1913, Schedule II, supersedes the original Rule 127.

twenty days from the date of execution of arrestment; and in the case of defended actions tabled within twenty days of the first Ordinary Court day, occurring subsequent to the expiry of the *induciæ*, and in the case of undefended actions decree in absence be taken within twenty days of the expiry of the *induciæ*, and, when such an arrestment has been executed, the party using it or his agent shall forthwith report the execution to the Sheriff-clerk.] *Sched. I.*

Forthcoming and Multiplepoinding.

128. An action of forthcoming or multiplepoinding may be raised in the Sheriffdom where the fund or subject *in medio* is situated, or in that to whose jurisdiction the arrestee or the holder of the fund is subject, although the common debtor may not reside within either Sheriffdom. *Forum of action of multiplepoinding*

129. The party raising an action of multiplepoinding shall set forth in the initial writ who is the real raiser. The Sheriff may, in an action of multiplepoinding, allow the real raiser his expenses preferably out of the fund *in medio;* and, in an action of forthcoming, the expenses of bringing the action shall be deemed to be part of the arrestor's claim, which may be made good out of the arrested fund or subject. *Real raiser to be set forth.*

130. Where, in an action of multiplepoinding, no defences are stated, and where defences are stated and repelled, the Sheriff shall order claims and, if necessary, answers within a short space. *Claims to be ordered.*

131. Several claimants may state the facts on which they base their claims on the same paper, but, where necessary, they shall append separate claims and separate pleas in law. *Several claimants may state one paper.*

132. Where there are defences in an action of forthcoming or competing claims in a multiplepoinding process the procedure shall be as near as may be that in ordinary actions where defences have been lodged. *When competing claims procedure as in ordinary action.*

Jury Trial.

133. The jury shall consist of two special, and five common jurors, who shall be chosen from a panel of five special and ten common jurors to be cited for the diet. *Jury.*

134. The jury shall be cited by the Sheriff-clerk from the Sheriff Court jury book in the manner prescribed by law or in use to be. *Citation of jury.*

Sched. I. followed for the citation of jurors in Scotland; and all statutory or other regulations and customs relative to the citation, non-attendance, selection, and swearing of jurors shall (subject to Rule 135) apply to jury trial in the Sheriff Court.

Challenge of jurors. 135. Each party in the cause shall have right to challenge one special and one common juror, but not more; and in this matter, where there are more pursuers or defenders than one, they shall act collectively and not individually.

Jury to have copy issue. 136. (Repealed by the 1913 Act, Schedule II.)

Practice in proofs to apply. 137. The law and practice relating to the taking of evidence in proofs before the Sheriffs shall apply to jury trials. Unless all the parties appearing put in a minute (which may be signed by their agents) dispensing with a record of the proceedings, the same shall be taken by an official shorthand writer of the Court, but the notes need not be extended unless, in the case of an appeal, their production shall be ordered by the Appellate Court, in which event it shall be the duty of the appellant to procure the extended notes, certified by the shorthand writer, and to lodge the same with the Principal Clerk of Session.

Evidence on commission. 138. When evidence has been taken to lie *in retentis*, if the Sheriff is satisfied that the deponing witness is dead, or that he cannot attend at the trial owing to absence or infirmity or other sufficient cause, it shall be competent for the Sheriff, on the motion of any party in the cause (irrespective of which party moved for the commission to take such evidence) to direct that the report of the commission be read to the jury, and when so read such report shall form part of the evidence in the cause; but depositions shall not be read or referred to if the deponing witness attends at the trial.

Exceptions. 139. Exceptions taken in the course of the trial to rulings of the Sheriff in regard to admission or rejection of evidence, or in regard to points of law laid down in the course of the trial or in the Sheriff's charge to the jury, shall, if required by the party taking the exception, be recorded to the Sheriff's dictation upon the official shorthand notes before the jury proceed to consider their verdict.

Addressing jury. 140. (Repealed by the 1913 Act, Schedule II.)

Charge to jnry. 141. If the Sheriff deem it necessary to charge the jury, he shall do so immediately after, or as soon as practicable after, the con-

clusion of the speeches, or, if none be made, after the conclusion Sched. I.
of the evidence.

142. Documents or productions intended to be put in evidence Productions.
or referred to at the trial shall be lodged with the Clerk of Court
four days before the date fixed for the trial, but the Sheriff may
allow productions to be exhibited and produced at the trial if he is
satisfied that they could not reasonably have been lodged earlier
and that reasonable notice had been given to the other parties of
intention to produce at the trial.

143. The jury may return a verdict by a majority of its number Verdict by
at any time not less than one hour after the jury has been enclosed. majority.

144. (Repealed by the 1913 Act, Schedule II.)

145. The verdict returned by the jury shall be recorded upon Verdict to be
the interlocutor sheets and signed by the Clerk of the Court, and recorded.
this having been done the jury shall be discharged.

146. Any party in the cause may, so soon as the verdict has been And followed
so recorded or within fourteen days thereafter, move the Sheriff to by inter-
apply the verdict, and upon this motion the Sheriff may hear locutor.
parties and may make avizandum. As soon as practicable the
Sheriff shall issue an interlocutor applying the verdict and grant
decree accordingly. In this interlocutor the Sheriff shall also dispose of the question of expenses.

147. Where no shorthand notes of the proceedings have been Interlocutor
taken, the interlocutor applying the verdict shall not be subject to final if no
review. shorthand
notes.

* 148. If shorthand notes have been taken, it shall be competent Grounds of
for any party in the cause within fourteen days after the date of appeal to
the final interlocutor of the Sheriff applying the verdict (but not Session.
later) to appeal to a division of the Court of Session by lodging
with the Sheriff-clerk a note of appeal in the Form M annexed
hereto.

* 149. The Sheriff-clerk shall, within three days of his receiving Transmission
the note of appeal, notify the other parties in the cause, and of process.
transmit the process to the Principal Clerk of Session at Edinburgh.

* 150. If the Court shall order a new trial, the Principal Clerk New trial.
of Session shall retransmit the process to the Sheriff-clerk, and the

* These rules are affected by the Rules of Court, 1936, V, 7-13.

Sched. I.

Sheriff shall as soon as practicable fix a date of new trial, which shall proceed as herein directed as regards the original trial.

CHARGE.

Charge against a corporation.

† [151. It shall be competent to charge any corporation or association or any individual or individuals carrying on business under a firm or trading or descriptive name under such name at the principal place where such business is carried on (including in the case of a corporation or association the place of business or office of their clerk or secretary) or where such principal place of business is furth of Scotland, at any place of business in Scotland at which such business is carried on.]

THE POOR'S ROLL.

Agents to meet to nominate agents for poor.

* 152. The Sheriff shall annually make an order appointing the agents enrolled in his Court (or, where the [county] is divided into districts having separate local Courts, the agents enrolled in the district Courts) to meet to nominate a specified number of agents for the poor.

Notice of meeting on court-house walls.

* 153. Notice of such order shall be given by a copy thereof being affixed on the walls of the Court houses and the Sheriff-clerk's offices in the [county or district].

Nomination to be reported to Sheriff.

154. At said meeting the agents present shall, by a majority of votes, nominate the required number of agents, and cause the nominations to be reported to the Sheriff.

Sheriff may confirm or refuse.

155. The Sheriff shall have power to confirm the nominations, in whole or in part, or to decline to do so.

Notice to agents.

156. Six days before the list is submitted to the Sheriff, the Sheriff-clerk shall notify each agent who has been nominated, and such agent may, before the nominations are confirmed, represent to the Sheriff any reason why his nomination should not be confirmed.

If agents fail to do so Sheriffs may nominate.

157. In the event of the agents failing to nominate as above provided for, or the Sheriff not confirming the nomination, the Sheriff may himself make the requisite nomination, or may appoint another meeting to be held.

† This rule, introduced by the Act of 1913, Schedule II, supersedes the original Rule 151.

* As amended by the Act of 1913, Schedule II.

* 158. The agents nominated shall act as agents for the poor in the [county] or the district in which they are appointed, for one year, but they shall be eligible for renomination.

Sched. I.
Agents to act for one year.

159. The agents so nominated shall as they themselves arrange, or as the Sheriff shall direct, act as procurators for the poor in all causes, civil and criminal, including attendance at the Circuit Court.

Agents to act as directed by Sheriff.

160. The agents for the poor, in their respective districts, shall assist each other by taking precognitions, or proofs on commission, or otherwise as may be requisite and reasonable.

Agents to assist each other.

161. In sections 152 to 157 " Sheriff " does not include Sheriff-Substitute.

162. Along with his application for the benefit of the poor's roll, the applicant shall produce a certificate signed by the inspector or an assistant inspector of poor of the parish or district where the applicant resides, bearing that the applicant is unable, through poverty, to pay for the conduct of legal proceedings.

Applicant to produce certificate of poverty.

163. The Sheriff shall remit the application to the procurators for the poor who shall notify the parties, and after inquiry shall make a report to the Sheriff.

Application to be remitted to procurators for poor.

164. If they report that the applicant has a probable cause of action and is entitled to the benefit of the poor's roll, the Sheriff shall appoint one of the agents to take charge of the applicant's case.

If they report applicant entitled, Sheriff to appoint an agent to conduct cause.

165. Such agent shall conduct the cause to its final issue, notwithstanding that during its progress he may have ceased to be an agent for the poor.

Agent to conclude cause.

166. Unless expenses shall be awarded against and recovered from the opposite party, the agent shall have no claim for fees; but the litigant shall be liable to him for actual outlays incurred with the litigant's sanction.

Agent to have no claim for fees unless recovered from other party.

167. The agent shall not be liable for witnesses' fees, shorthand writers' fees, or Court dues unless they are recovered by the agent personally.

Agent not liable for fees.

* As amended by the Act of 1913, Schedule II.

Agent not liable for court dues.

168. Neither the agent nor the litigant shall be liable for dues of Court or officers' fees, unless these are awarded against and recovered from the opposite party, in which case the litigant (or the agent, if he personally recovers the same) shall be liable.

Sheriff may remove litigant from poor's roll.

169. It shall be in the power of the Sheriff at any time to deprive any litigant of the benefit of the poor's roll.

Judicial Factors under the Bankruptcy (Scotland) Act, 1913.

* [170. The procedure applicable to the appointment of judicial factors appointed under section 4 of the Judicial Factors (Scotland) Act, 1880 (43 & 44 Vict. c. 4), shall apply to the appointment of judicial factors by the Sheriff under sections 163 and 164 of the Bankruptcy (Scotland) Act, 1913 (3 & 4 Geo. V c. 20).]

Recall or variation of decrees for aliment and of decrees regarding the custody of and access to children.

* [171. Applications for the recall or variation of any decree for payment of aliment, whether pronounced in favour of a spouse, a parent, or any other person, or pronounced in respect of a child legitimate or illegitimate, and applications for the recall or variation of any decree regulating the custody of or access to children legitimate or illegitimate, shall be made by minute lodged in the original process in which decree was pronounced. The Court shall order the minute to be served on the opposite party or parties and appoint answers to be lodged within a specified time, and shall thereafter, without closing a record, and after such proof or other procedure as to the Court seems necessary, dispose of the application.]

Disposal of money payable to persons under legal disability.

† [172. (a) Where in an action of damages by or for behoof of a person under legal disability, arising either out of injury sustained by such person, or out of the death of some other person in respect of whose death the person under legal disability is entitled to damages, a sum of money becomes payable to such person, such sum shall, unless otherwise ordered, be paid into Court, and shall be invested, applied or otherwise dealt with and administered by the Court in such manner as the Court in its discretion thinks fit for the benefit of the person entitled thereto, and the receipt of the Sheriff Clerk shall be a sufficient discharge in respect of the amount paid in.

(b) The Sheriff-clerk of any Sheriff Court is also authorized at the request of any competent Court within the British Dominions to accept custody of any sum of money paid into such Court in any

* New rule added by Act of Sederunt, 16th July, 1936.

† New Rule 172 (a) (b) (c) (d) added by Act of Sederunt, 16th July, 1936; (e) and (f) added by Act of Sederunt, 9th February, 1939.

action of damages by or for behoof of a person under legal disability, provided always that such person is then resident within the jurisdiction of such Sheriff Court and such sum shall be invested or otherwise dealt with as in this section.

(c) Where any money is paid into Court under this section, it shall thereafter be paid out by the Sheriff-clerk, or otherwise applied for the benefit of the person entitled thereto, after such intimation and service and such inquiry as the Sheriff may direct.

(d) All applications under the immediately preceding sub-sections shall be by minute by or on behalf of the person entitled to such payment.

(e) On payment into Court under this rule of money which has become payable to a person under legal disability, the Sheriff-clerk shall (1) issue to the person making the payment a receipt in or as nearly as may be in the terms of Form No. 1 of Schedule A hereto annexed, to which receipt there shall be attached a form in the terms of Form No. 2 of said Schedule A; (2) transmit forthwith to the King's and Lord Treasurer's Remembrancer a copy of the said receipt, having appended thereto the additional particulars specified in Schedule B hereto annexed; and the person making the payment shall forthwith complete and transmit to the King's and Lord Treasurer's Remembrancer Form No. 2 of Schedule A hereto annexed, intimating the payment into Court.

(f) Any sum which in terms of this rule is ordered to be invested, applied or otherwise dealt with by the Court in such manner as the Court in its discretion thinks fit, may be either :—

(1) Deposited in the Post Office Savings Bank; or

(2) Deposited in the ordinary department of any Trustee Savings Bank in Scotland " certified under the Act of 1863 "; or

(3) Invested in the purchase of an annuity in accordance with paragraphs 4 and 5 of the Second Schedule to the Workmen's Compensation Act, 1925; or

(4) Invested through the Post Office Savings Bank or a Trustee Savings Bank in Scotland certified as aforesaid in such British Government security as the Court may direct:

And no such sum shall be invested otherwise than in accordance with this Act.]

Sched. I.

* [FORM A.

SHERIFFDOM OF　　　　　　　　　　AT

A. B. [*design him; if he sues in any special character set that forth; as also, where necessary, set forth relationship to defender, e.g., wife, creditor, &c.*],
Pursuer.

Against

C. D. [*design him; if sued in any special character set that forth, e.g., as trustee, vitious intromitter, &c.*],
Defender.

The pursuer craves the Court [*here set forth the specific decree, warrant, or order asked*].

(*To be signed*)　　　*A. B.*, Pursuer;
　　　　　　　　　　　　or
　　　　　　　X. Y. [*add designation and business address*]
　　　　　　　　　　　　　　　　Pursuer's Agent.

CONDESCENDENCE.

[*State articulately the facts which form the ground of action.*]

PLEAS IN LAW.
[*State them articulately.*]]

* This form, introduced by the Act of 1913, Schedule II, supersedes the original Form A.

FORM B.

[*Place and date.*]　Grants warrant to cite the defender [*or respondent*] by serving a copy of the writ and warrant upon an *induciæ* of　　　　　　　, and appoints him to answer within the Sheriff Court house at　　　　, [*in Room No.　, or in Chambers, or as the case may be*], on the　　　day of　　　at　　　o'clock　　　noon, under certification of being held as confessed. [When necessary add (meantime sequestrates and grants warrant to inventory and secure); or (grants warrant to arrest on the dependence) or (otherwise as the case may be).]

Form C.

[*Place and date.*] Grants warrant to cite the defender by serving a copy of the writ and warrant upon an *induciæ* of days, and appoints him, if he intend to defend, to lodge a notice of appearance with the Sheriff-clerk at   within the *induciæ*, under certification of being held as confessed. [*Meantime grants interim interdict, or warrant to arrest on the dependence, or sequestrates and grants warrant to inventory, or otherwise, as the case may be.*]

Form D.

[*Place and date, and, if necessary, hour.*] C. D., defender. You are hereby served with the foregoing [*or within-written*] writ and warrant, and required to answer thereto, conform to the said warrant. [*If posted and if necessary add (the* induciæ *is reckoned from twenty-four hours after date of posting).*]

(*To be signed*) P. Q., Sheriff-officer,

or

X. P. [*add designation and business address*].

Pursuer's Agent.

Form E.

[*Place and date.*] I,   , do hereby certify that upon the   day of   [*if necessary add between the hours of*   *and*   ] I duly cited C. D., the defender [*or respondent*], to answer to the foregoing [*or within-written*] writ. This I did by [*set forth mode of service, if by officer and not by post, add in presence of L. M. (design him),* witness, hereto with me subscribing*].

(*To be signed*) P. Q., Sheriff-officer ;

L. M., Witness ;

or

X. Y. [*add designation and business address*].

Pursuer's Agent.

Form F.

K. L. [*design him*], you are hereby required to attend at the Sheriff Court house at [*street address*] [*if necessary, add within*

Sched. I. *Court Room, No.   , or in Chambers*], on   , the
day of   , at   o'clock   noon, to give
evidence for pursuer [*or appellant or complainer*] [*or defender or
respondent*] in the action *A. B.* [*design him*], pursuer, against
C. D. [*design him*], and [*if necessary*] you are required to bring
with you [*specify documents*] under penalty of forty shillings if
you fail to attend.

> Dated this   day of   [*if necessary
> add between the hours of   and   noon*].
>
> [*Signed*]   *P. Q.*, Sheriff-officer ;
>
> or
>
> *X. Y.* [*add designation and business address*].
> Pursuer's [*or defender's or appellant's or
> respondent's*] Agent.

Form G.

[*Place and date*] I,
do hereby certify that upon the   day of   [*if necessary,
add between the hours of   and   noon*], I duly cited *K. L.*,
[*design him*], to attend at   o'clock   noon, within
        to give evidence for the   in the
action *A. B.* [*design him*], against *C. D.* [*design him*], and I also
required him to bring with him [*specify documents*]. This I did by
[*set forth mode of citation*].

> [*Signed*]   *P. Q.*, Sheriff-officer ;
>
> or
>
> *X. Y.* [*add designation and business address*].
> Pursuer's [*or defender's or appellant's or
> respondent's*] Agent.

Form H.

To [*name, designation, and address of party in possession*].
    You are required to remove from [*describe subjects*] at the
term of   [*or if different terms, state them and the subjects
to which they apply*], in terms of lease [*describe it*] or [*in terms of
your letter of removal of date   ] or [*otherwise as
the case may be*].

Form I.

To [*name and designation of addressee*].

[*Place and date.*] I am to remove from [*state subjects by usual name or short description sufficient for identification*] at the term of

K. L. [*add designation and address*].

If not holograph to be attested thus—

M. N. [*add designation and address*], witness.

Form J.

[*Place and date.*]

You are required to remove from [ ] that portion of ground [*describe it*]; *or* the mill of [*describe it*]; *or* the shootings of the lands and estate of [*describe them*]; *or* [*other subjects to which this notice is applicable*], at the term of Whitsunday [*insert year*] [*or Martinmas, as the case may be, inserting after the year the words, being the 15th day of May*, or *the 11th day of November*, or *the 28th day of May*, or *the 28th day of November, as the case may be*].

To K. L. [*designation and address*].

Form K.

In the Sheriff Court of
at

A. B. [*design him*], pursuer, complains that he [*or his author, as the case may be*], let to C. D. [*design him*], defender [*or his author, as the case may be*], a dwelling-house, garden, and pertinents [*or other subjects, as the case may be*], situated at ,
for the period from to ,
and that the defender refuses or delays to remove therefrom, although his term of occupancy has expired, and it is necessary to obtain warrant for his ejection; therefore decree ought to be granted for removing and ejecting the defender, his family, sub-tenants, cottars, and dependants, with their goods and gear, furth and from the said subjects [*here insert date at which removal or ejection is sought*], that the pursuer or others in his right may then enter to and possess the same. [*If expenses are sought add, " and the defender ought to be found liable in the expenses of process and dues of extract."*]

[*Signature of pursuer or his agent.*]

* Form L.

[Forms of Extracts of Decrees in Summary Removing Petition
or Complaint.

(1) EXTRACT OF DECREE AND WARRANT OF EJECTION.

At the day of 19 , the
Sheriff of Decerned and hereby Decerns, Granted
and hereby Grants Warrant for Ejecting the said
Defender, and others mentioned in the Complaint, from the subjects
therein specified, such Ejection not being sooner than
19 , at Twelve o'clock noon, Found and hereby Finds the said
Defender liable to the Pursuer in the sum of
of Expenses, and Decerns and Ordains instant Execution by Arrestment, and also Execution to pass hereon by Poinding and Sale for
said Expenses, after a of Ten free days.

Sheriff-clerk.

(2) EXTRACT OF DECREE OF ABSOLVITOR.

At the day of 19 , the
Sheriff of Assoilzied and hereby Assoilzies the
within designed Defender from the foregoing
Complaint, and Found and hereby Finds the within designed
Pursuer, liable to the
Defender in the sum of
of Expenses, and Decerns and Ordains instant execution by Arrestment, and also execution to pass hereon by Poinding and Sale,
after a of Ten free days.

Sheriff-clerk.

(3) EXTRACT OF DECREE OF DISMISSAL.

At the day of 19 , the
Sheriff of Dismissed and hereby Dismisses the
foregoing Complaint, Found and hereby Finds the within designed
Pursuer , liable to the Defender in the
sum of of Expenses; and

* This form, introduced by the Act of Sederunt of 3rd February, 1933,
supersedes the original Form L. The Act of Sederunt provides
that the forms shall be signed by the Sheriff-clerk, shall have the
force and effect of extracts, and may be written on the principal
complaint, on the copy thereof, or, with necessary modifications,
separately.

Decerns and Ordains instant execution by Arrestment, and also **Sched. I.**
execution to pass hereon by Poinding and Sale after a
of Ten free days.

Sheriff-clerk.]

---

† FORM M.

[At the jury trial in the action at the instance of *A. B.* [*design him*], pursuer, against *C. D.* [*design him*], defender, held at , on the day of , before Sheriff of

The verdict of the jury was [*here quote the recorded verdict setting forth, where the Sheriff has proponed to the jury a question or questions of fact, such question or questions, and the answer or answers thereto returned by the jury*].

The interlocutor of the Sheriff applying the verdict was pronounced on , and was in these terms :— [*here quote the interlocutor*].

The [*state party appealing*] appeals to the [‡ Division of the] Court of Session upon the ground [*here state the grounds conform to section* 31 *of the Act*].

(*a*) That in the interlocutor complained of the verdict was erroneously applied.

(*b*) That the verdict of the jury was contrary to evidence in respect [*here set forth clearly and succinctly the particulars in which it is alleged the evidence led and the verdict returned are inconsistent*].

(*c*) That evidence was unduly admitted [*or rejected*] in regard to [*here set forth shortly the fact in regard to which the evidence was admitted or rejected*].

(*d*) That the Sheriff misdirected the jury in regard to [*here state shortly the point of law alleged to be misdirection*].

(*e*) That the damages awarded by the jury were excessive.

M. P., pursuer [or other party],

or

X. Y. [<i>signature and business address</i>],
Agent for the .]

† This form, introduced by the Act of 1913, Schedule II, supersedes the original Form M.

‡ As the right of a party to appeal to a specified Division of the Court of Session is now abolished (23 & 24 Geo. V c. 41, sec. 5) these words will now be omitted (see also Rules of Court, 1936, V, 8 (a)).

* [SCHEDULE A.

Form No. 1.

In the Sheriff Court of   *at*
       Receipt for a Payment into Court.

In the cause, matter or proceeding (*state names of parties or other appropriate description*).

(*Place and date*)
(*A. B. design*)

has this day paid into Court the sum of £   , being a payment into Court in terms of Rule 172 of the Sheriff Courts (Scotland) Act, 1907, as amended by the Act of Sederunt of 16th July, 1936, of money which in an action of damages, has become payable to a person under legal disability. (*Note*) If the payment is made under Rule 172(*b*) add " the custody of which money has been accepted at the request of " (*name of Court making request*).

....
Sheriff-clerk.

N.B.—The person paying the money into Court is required by the Act of Sederunt of 9*th February*, 193?, to complete and transmit the subjoined Form No. 2 to the King's and Lord Treasurer's Remembrancer, *forthwith*.

TO BE PERFORATED
————

Form No. 2.

(*Address*).......................................
....
(*Date*)...................................19.......
To
     The King's and Lord Treasurer's Remembrancer,
         Exchequer Chambers, Edinburgh, 1.
Sir,
     I/We paid into the Sheriff Court at...............on..................
19   , the sum of..
in the (*state name of cause, matter or proceeding*).
         Yours faithfully,
           (*Signature*)..................................

SCHEDULE B.

Additional particulars to be noted by the Sheriff-clerk on the copy receipt to be sent by him to the King's and Lord Treasurer's Remembrancer:—

The above-mentioned payment into Court was :—

   (*a*) Lodged on Deposit Receipt No.......... with the (*state name of Bank*)...

      pending the Orders of the Court.

   (*b*) Deposited in the Post Office Savings Bank, Account No.......

   (*c*) (otherwise as the case may be, stating similar particulars).

Name and address of Solicitor (or Insurance Company) representing the person who made the payment into Court :—

....

                Date...................................19   .

           ....

                Sheriff-clerk.]

* These Schedules A and B were added by the Act of Sederunt of 9th February, 1939.

Sched. II.   * SECOND SCHEDULE.

Session and Chapter.	Short Title.	Extent of Repeal.
20 Geo. 2 c. 43.	The Heritable Jurisdictions (Scotland) Act, 1746.	Section 29.
21 Geo. 2 c. 19.	The Sheriffs (Scotland) Act, 1747.	Sections 10 and 11.
28 Geo. 2 c. 7.	The Sheriffs (Scotland) Act, 1755.	The whole Act.
50 Geo 3 c. 112.	The Court of Session Act, 1810.	Sections 36, 37, 38, and 40, so far as these sections relate to Sheriff Court.
5 Geo. 4 c. 23.	The Sheriff Courts (Scotland) Act, 1825.	Sections 1, 3, 4, 5, and 8, so far as these sections relate to civil causes in the Sheriff Court, and section 10.
6 Geo. 4 c. 120.	The Court of Session Act, 1825.	Section 40, so far as relating to appeal for jury trial from Sheriff Court to Court of Session.
9 Geo. 4 c. 29.	The Circuit Courts (Scotland) Act, 1828.	Section 22.
11 Geo. 4 and 1 W. 4 c. 69.	The Court of Session Act, 1830.	Sections 22, 23, 24, and 32, as also in section 33 the words " and all actions of separation a mensa et thoro."
2 & 3 W. 4 c. 65.	The Representation of the People (Scotland) Act, 1832.	Section 36, so far as relating to Sheriff and Sheriff-Substitute.
1 & 2 Vict. c. 114.	The Debtors (Scotland) Act, 1838.	Section 19.
1 & 2 Vict. c. 119.	The Sheriff Courts (Scotland) Act, 1838.	The whole Act, except sections 25, 27, and 28, and section 31, so far as that section relates to courts other than Sheriff Courts.
16 & 17 Vict. c. 80.	The Sheriff Courts (Scotland) Act, 1853.	The whole Act, except section 34.
27 & 28 Vict. c. 106.	The Sheriffs-Substitute Act, 1864.	The whole Act.

Sched. II.

Session and chapter.	Short Title.	Extent of Repeal.
30 & 31 Vict. c. 96.	Tht Debts Recovery (Scotland) Act, 1867.	The whole Act.
31 & 32 Vict. c. 100	The Court of Session Act, 1868.	Sections 65, 66, 67, 68, 69, 70, 73, and 79, so far as those sections relate to appeals from Sheriff Court.
33 & 34 Vict. c. 86.	The Sheriff Courts (Scotland) Act, 1870.	Sections 13 and 14.
38 & 39 Vict. c. 81.	The Sheriffs-Substitute (Scotland) Act, 1875.	Sections 1 and 2.
39 & 40 Vict. c. 70.	The Sheriff Courts (Scotland) Act, 1876.	Sections 4 to 25, both inclusive. Sections 27 to 34, both inclusive. Sections 46 to 52, both inclusive. Section 54, except in so far as it relates to commissary regulations. All the schedules.
40 & 41 Vict. c. 50.	The Sheriff Courts (Scotland) Act, 1877.	The whole Act.
52 & 53 Vict. c. 26.	The Small Debt Amendment (Scotland) Act, 1889.	Section 8.
61 & 62 Vict. c. 8.	The Sheriffs Tenure of Office (Scotland) Act, 1898.	The whole Act.

* This Schedule is now repealed by the Statute Law Revision Act, 1927 (17 & 18 Geo. V c. 42, sec. 1, Schedule).

INDEX.

INDEX.

ABANDONMENT, 243-246.
    against one of several defenders, 234, 243.
    by letter, whether competent, 243.
    by one of several pursuers, 235, 245, 318.
    common law abandonment still competent, 243.
    defender does not abandon, 245.
    effect on counter claim, 153, 245.
    expenses, 243, 244, 245.
    mandate to solicitor, 244.
    partial abandonment or restriction, 245.
    procedure, 243.
    withdrawal of minute, 244.

ABSENCE, DECREE IN. *See* DECREE IN ABSENCE.

ABSOLVITOR—
    or dismissal, 168, 169, 249, 526.

ACTION—
    definition of, 95.

ACCOUNTING—
    action of, 495-496.
    arrestment on dependence competent, 262, 495.
    consignation, 496.
    continuing account to date of decree, 495.
    decree not limited to amount craved, 495.
    not competent in Small Debt Court, 467.
    procedure, 495.
    when competent, 495.
    value of cause, 51.

ADDRESS—
    party ordered to disclose, 111.

AD FACTUM PRÆSTANDUM—
    action, 496-498.
    alternative crave, 496.
    appeal against order, 290.
    discretion in Court to grant decree, 496, 497.
    imprisonment on decree, 35, 36, 281, 284, 496, 497. *See also* IMPRISON-
        MENT.
    remedy asked must be possible, 496.
    signature to document, 498.
    two defenders, 497.
    value of cause, 48.
    warrant to search, 497.
    when action competent, 496. *See also* DELIVERY, ACTION OF; SMALL DEBT
        COURT—delivery.

731

ADHERENCE AND ALIMENT—
 appeal against decree in absence after proof, 524, 525.
 arrestment on the dependence and in execution, 525.
 citation of defender, 125.
 crave for custody of children, 527.
 decree after proof still in absence if case undefended, 130, 524.
 decree in absence incompetent without proof, 19, 130, 498, 524.
 decree of consent, 499, 524.
 defender may appear at any stage, 130, 525.
 expenses, 527.
 income tax on aliment, 503.
 interim aliment, 298, 526.
 interim award of expenses, 527.
 jurisdiction, 18, 498, 525.
 offer to adhere, genuineness of, 527.
 pursuer must lead at proof, 524.
 remit to Court of Session, 19, 170, 499.
 reponing against decree after proof, 136, 524, 525.
 review of aliment, 498.
 solicitor for wife cannot get decree for expenses against husband if
   case settled before proof, 528.

ADJUDICATION—
 as diligence following on inhibition, 285.
 jurisdiction in Sheriff Court, 26, 285.
 statutory process for ground annual creditor, 579.

ADJUSTMENT OF PLEADINGS—
 adjournment of diet, 156, 157.
 alternative averments, 158, 167.
 alternative legal grounds, 157.
 answers to statement of facts, 156.
 authentication of alterations, 158.
 deletion of irrelevant or improper matter, 157.
 fair notice of evidence to be led, 157.
 lodging certified copy record, 156, 162.
 summary cause, 99.
       See also CLOSING RECORD.

ADMINISTRATIVE JURISDICTION, 34-36.

ADMIRALTY—
 jurisdiction of Sheriff Court, 31, 32, 617.
 law applied in Admiralty cause, 31.
       See also SHIPPING.

ADMISSION—
 failure to deny may imply, 147, 157.
 qualified, effect of, 147.

ADOPTION OF CHILDREN, 543-549.
 adoption societies, appeals by, 548.
 appeal, 548.
 applicants, who may be, 543.
 children who may be adopted, 543.
 confidentiality of documents, 547.
 consents required, 544, 546.

ADOPTION OF CHILDREN—*continued.*
curator ad litem, 546.
expenses, 548.
interim order, 545.
jurisdiction, 544, 546.
licence to send child abroad, 548.
matters on which Court to be satisfied, 545, 547.
procedure, 546, 547.
registration, 547.

AFFIDAVIT—
in lieu of parole evidence, 213.

AFFILIATION AND ALIMENT, 500-503.
action before birth of child, 501.
    arrestment, 262, 502.
    expenses, 502.
action by person having custody, 502.
action not based on delict, 70.
corroboration by contradiction, 503.
custody and access, order for, 21, 501.
declarator of paternity unnecessary, 500.
decree in absence must be for amount craved, 500.
decree may be to inspector of poor, &c., 502.
defender as pursuer's first witness, 218.
duration of award, 501.
failure by defender to give evidence, 218.
funeral expenses, 502.
income tax on aliment, 503.
in Small Debt Court, 466.
offer by father of custody, 501.
rate of aliment, 500.
review of amount awarded, 500, 501.
Summary Jurisdiction (Process) Act, jurisdiction under, 70.
value of cause, 49.

AGENT DISBURSER. *See* EXPENSES (3).

AGRICULTURAL HOLDINGS ACTS, 549-553.
appeal in applications under Acts, 553.
arbiter—
    appeal to Court of Session, 551.
    appointment of clerk, 552.
    direction to, on question of law, 550.
    expenses awarded by, objections to auditor's report, 550.
    expenses in connexion with stated case, 551.
    procedure to obtain stated case from arbiter, 550, 551.
    removal of, 550, 552.
    setting aside award, 551.
bequest of lease, declarator in Sheriff Court, 552.
common grazings, complaints for contravention of regulations, 549.
compensation claims by cottagers for disturbance, 550.
crofters, applications relating to, 549.
jurisdiction in applications under Acts, 553.
Land Court, decree conform to order of, 549.
removings from holdings. *See* REMOVINGS.

AGRICULTURAL MARKETING ACT—
applications under, 536.

AIRCRAFT—
jurisdiction in relation to, 32.

ALIMENT—
action of, 498-503.
as between spouses, decree in absence only after proof, 19, 130, 499.
decree of consent, 499, 524.
jurisdiction, 18, 20, 498.
remit to Court of Session, 19, 170, 499.
review of aliment under decree or contract, 498.

ALIMENT, INTERIM—
action for, decree in absence only after proof, 130, 498, 524.
jurisdiction, 18, 20, 498.
    See also ADHERENCE AND ALIMENT; SEPARATION AND ALIMENT.

AMENDMENT, 234-242.
adding a party, 111, 236.
adding alternative crave, 496.
after time limit for action has expired, 43, 239.
amending amendment, 239.
appeal, amendment by sheriff *ex proprio motu*, 241, 297.
asked before avizandum if made to meet attack on relevancy, 167.
at what stage competent, 235, 239.
breach of interdict process, 509.
competent to increase sum craved though defender has consented to decree, 240.
defender to be added must be subject to jurisdiction, 236.
deleting one defender done by abandonment, 234, 243.
deleting one pursuer may be abandonment or amendment, 235, 245.
diligence, effect of amendment on, 238, 241.
discretion of sheriff to allow, 235, 240.
effect on jurisdiction by arrestment, 64.
expenses of, 237, 240.
    payment of as condition, 238.
extent to which competent, 235-237.
how made, 239.
instance, 111, 235.
irrelevant amendment, 237.
judicial reference, not usually competent after, 171, 239.
jury trial, 345.
may be refused if inconsistent with prior interlocutors, 239.
necessary if new ground of action proved and relied on, 240.
other party must have opportunity of meeting, 240.
radical defect may not be curable by, 235, 237, 240, 241.
reopening of proof on, 225.
service on new defender, 236.
sist of new party, 236.
Small Debt Court, 472
substituting new for original defender, 111, 235.
summary cause, 240.
undefended action, 111, 241.

ARBITRATION—

action for payment in implement of award, 555.
arbitration clause as bar to action, 43.
position when appointment of arbiter not under Act, 554.
proceedings to compel arbiter to act not competent, 17, 555.
setting aside award, 555.
witnesses and havers, application for warrant to cite, 555.
 See also AGRICULTURAL HOLDINGS ACT; ARBITRATION ACT.

ARBITRATION ACT, 553-555.

appointment of arbiter under, 553.
jurisdiction, 554.
procedure, 554.
 See also ARBITRATION.

ARMY—

exclusion of jurisdiction of Civil Courts, 44, 55.

ARMY AND AIR FORCE ACT—

applications under, 538.

ARRESTMENT (diligence), 260-273.

against firm with descriptive name, 263, 270.
breach of, action for, 273.
competent only within Scotland, 261.
creditor of poinder using, 279.
does not transfer fund, 272.
errors in schedule or execution, 273.
execution of, 263-264.
 specialties when funds in hands of trustees and various other
  parties, 270-271.
expenses of, 266.
expenses secured by, 271.
in execution—
 against firm or corporation, 263, 264.
 decree for future debt, 526.
 endorsement of warrant, 261.
 not prevented by interim sist on suspension, 530
 warrant must be in officer's hands, 264.
on dependence—
 actions in which competent, 105, 262.
  accounting, 262.
  adherence and aliment, and separation and aliment, 105, 262, 525.
  affiliation and aliment raised before birth, 262, 502.
 against firm and corporation, 263, 264, 270.
 available till extract decree got, 265.
 can be used before service, 260.
 defender cannot arrest on counter claim, 262.
 effect of transfer to another Court, 265.
 endorsement of warrant, 261.
 future and contingent debts, 105, 262.
 grant of warrant though not craved, 105, 261.
 must be pecuniary crave, 105, 262.
 precept issued by Sheriff-clerk, 261.
 report to Sheriff-clerk, 265.
 time limit for service and tabling or decree in absence, 115, 129,
  140, 260.

BANKRUPTCY. *See* Sequestration in Bankruptcy.

BARBED WIRE FENCES—
applications relating to, 663.

BASTARDY ORDER—
English, registration in Sheriff Court, 666.

BETTING AND LOTTERIES ACT—
applications under, 536.

BIRTHS, &c., REGISTRATION, 555-561.
appeal in applications under Acts, 556.
baptism, change of name on, 558.
books, application for delivery, 556.
correction of entries, 557.
correction of old registers, 559.
informant, application to apprehend, 557.
jurisdiction in applications, 557.
legitimation, re-registration on, 559.
marriage, application for licence, 560.
neglected entries, 558.
paternity, decree of, entry of particulars, 560.
procedure in applications, 556, 558, 559, 560.
registrar, application to call meeting to elect, 555.
    interim appointment, 555.
    removal, 556.
registration districts, alteration of, 556.

BOARD OF TRADE INQUIRIES. *See* Shipping.

BOND AND DISPOSITION IN SECURITY. *See* Heritable Securities Act; Rent Restrictions Acts.

BORROWING PROCESS. *See* Process.

BOUNDARIES OF BURGHS EXTENSION ACT—
applications under, 538.

BREACH OF INTERDICT. *See* Interdict.

BUILDING SOCIETIES, 561-564.
action against society in liquidation, 564.
advances to members, jurisdiction in Sheriff Court, **562.**
appeal in applications under Acts, 561, 562.
common law applications, 561.
disputes, when cognizable by Court, 561.
jurisdiction in applications, 561, 562.
officials, applications for accounting, &c., against, **562.**
winding up, 563.

BURGH. *See* Municipal.

BURGH COURTS—
jurisdiction of Sheriff Court may be concurrent, **28.**

BURGH POLICE ACTS. *See under* Municipal.

BURGHS GAS SUPPLY ACT—
applications under, 540.

BURIAL GROUNDS, 564-566.
closing order, 564, 648.
designation of land for, 565.
disinterring body, 566.
dispute as to right to lair, 75.
preventing ground being used as, 564.
sanctioning sale of lairs, &c., 566.

BUSINESS, CARRYING ON—
jurisdiction from, 59-61.

BUSINESS NAMES ACT—
effect of default in registration on title to sue, 86.

BYE-LAWS. *See* MUNICIPAL ; ROADS AND BRIDGES.

CAPTION. *See* PROCESS.

CAUSE—
definition of, 95.

CAUTIONER—
action for relief, 85.
as litigant, 84.

CAVEAT. *See under heading of particular action.*

CELLULOID AND CINEMATOGRAPH FILM ACT—
applications, under, 538.

CEMETERY. *See* BURIAL GROUNDS.

CHANCERY, SHERIFF OF, 2.

CHARGE, 256-260.
endorsement of decree, when necessary, 257.
execution of, 256-259.
by registered letter, when competent, 256.
challenge of, 258.
contents of charge, 259.
edictal, 257, 259.
errors in, 257.
personally or at dwelling-place, 257.
service on corporations, &c., 258.
where no officer or messenger available, 257.
induciæ, 259.
on certificate under Judgments Extension Act, 287.
mandatory not necessary for person charging, 256.
not necessary on decree for summary ejection, 418.
party in right of decree, 256.
registration in Register of Hornings, 260.
Small Debt decree. *See* SMALL DEBT COURT.

COMMISSION TO TAKE EVIDENCE—
  (1) EVIDENCE TO LIE IN RETENTIS, 205-208.
  citation of witness, 197, 206.
  commissioner, qualification of, 207.
  interrogatories, 207.
  jury trial, 344.
  liability for expenses of, 207.
  objections to evidence, 207.
  procedure to obtain, 206.
  record of evidence, 207.
  report by commissioner, 208.
    when usable as evidence, 208.
  when granted, 205.
  (2) WITNESS UNABLE TO ATTEND PROOF—
  commissioner, qualification of, 207, 209.
  doubts as to sanity of witness, 209.
  evidence of party, 209, 211.
  incriminating questions, 210.
  interrogatories, 211.
  liability for expense of, 210, 211.
  reference to oath, how far competent, 231.
  report as evidence, 210.
  when granted, 209.
  witness in British Dominions, 210.
    England or Northern Ireland, 209.
    foreign country, 210.

COMMISSION TO RECOVER DOCUMENTS. *See* DILIGENCE.

COMMON GRAZINGS—
  complaints for contravention of regulations, 549.

COMPANY, JOINT STOCK—
  caution for expenses, 313.
  citation of, 127.
  incidental applications under Act, 578.
  jurisdiction against, where registered office situated, 60.
  liquidation—
    appeals against liquidator's deliverance, 576.
    applications for incidental purposes, 577.
    applications for winding up or supervision order, 572-578.
      appeals, 575, 576.
      caveat, 573.
      dissolution order, 577.
        expenses in, 321.
      remit to and from Court of Session, 574.
      restraining of proceedings, 574.
      sisting of mandatory by claimant, 92.
      sisting new applicant, 573.
      stated case, 575.
      transmission of process, 574.
    applications to remove liquidator, 577.
    applications to stay proceedings in voluntary liquidation, 575.
    jurisdiction in Sheriff Court, 572.
    witnesses and havers, examination of by Sheriff, 578.

COMPENSATION, ASSESSMENT OF, under Lands Clauses Act.
    See LANDS CLAUSES ACT.

CORPORATION—
  as litigant, 87.
  citation of, 89, 90, 127, 128.
  execution of charge, 258.

COTTON INDUSTRY (RE-ORGANIZATION) ACT—
  applications under, 537.

COUNSEL—
  appearance for party, 12.
  expenses of, 327, 334, 335.

COUNT, RECKONING AND PAYMENT. *See* ACCOUNTING.

COUNTER-CLAIM—
  abandonment of principal action, effect of, 153, 245.
  arrestment on dependence incompetent on counter claim, 262.
  dismissal of, when defender may raise separate action, 153.
  effect of, in summary cause, 153.
    on value of cause, 50.
  may be for over £50 in summary cause, 50, 98, 153.
  nature of claim to be set off, 151, 152.
  proof may be allowed though decree on principal claim, 152.
  Public Authorities Protection Act may not exclude, 152.
  separate statement of facts essential, 147, 151.
  Small Debt practice. *See* SMALL DEBT COURT.
  when unnecessary, 151.

COURTESY—
  redemption of, 581.

CROFTERS—
  applications relating to, 549.

CROWN—
  as litigant, 88.
  citation of Lord Advocate for, 89, 128.
  jurisdiction over, 39.

CURATOR AD LITEM—
  appointment, 81, 82, 83, 128.
  expenses of and against, 81.
  power to compromise, 81.

CURATOR BONIS—
  action by, 83.
        See also JUDICIAL FACTOR.

CUSTODY OF CHILDREN—
  affiliation and aliment, application in process of, 501.
  appeal, 583.
  crave for, in adherence and aliment action, 527.
  decree in absence incompetent without proof, 19, 21, 130.
  expenses, 321, 528.
  jurisdiction in custody applications, 18, 21, 498, 582.
        guardianship applications, 583.

CUSTODY OF CHILDREN—*continued.*

  procedure generally, 583.
  remit to Court of Session, 21, 170, 582.
  removal to Court of Session, 21, 583.
  warrant to search, 21.

DAIRY. *See* MILK AND DAIRIES ACT.

DAMAGES.

  custody of sum from Dominions, 82.
  payment into Court where person under disability, 82.
  right of executor to sue for, 84, 113.
  scale of expenses in action of, 321.
  value of cause, 51.

DANGEROUS BUILDING. *See* MUNICIPAL.

DATE—

  of commencement of action, 116.
  of interlocutor, 132, 248, 295, 301.

DEAF AND DUMB PERSON—

  as litigant, 83.

DEAN OF GUILD COURTS, jurisdiction of, 28.

DEATH—

  common law declarator held incompetent in Sheriff Court, 33.
  fixing presumed date of. *See* PRESUMPTION OF LIFE ACT.
  registration of. *See* BIRTHS, &c., REGISTRATION.

DEBATE ROLL, 180.

DECLARATOR—

  common law declarator of death held incompetent, 33, 445.
  incompetent if really reduction, 33.
  interest necessary to render competent, 34.
  jurisdiction, 18, 19, 25, 33, 34, 65.
  of irritancy and removing competent, 25.
  of negative competent, 34.
  that will holograph, 130, 451.
  that deed duly executed, 578.
  value of cause, 48.

DECLINATURE—

  of jurisdiction. *See* JURISDICTION (1).

DECREE BY DEFAULT, 249-252.

  appeal competent, 250.
    grounds for reponing, 250.
  cause must have been defended, 132, 249, 250, 251.
  discretion of Court when default occurs, 251.
  failure to appear, lodge paper or implement order, 249.
  for non-appearance at proof, 183, 249.
  failure to lodge defences, 250.

DEFENCES—*continued.*

failure to deny fact may imply admission, 147, 157.
failure to lodge justifies decree by default, 250.
lodging, prorogation competent though time expired, 147.
    vacation does not extend time, 147.
preliminary plea does not justify reservation of defence on merits, **147.**
qualified admission, 147.
several defenders, 148.
statement of facts, essential when counter-claim, 147, 151.
    when otherwise appropriate, 147.
tender in, 149.
unauthorized defences, 149.
when due, 146.
whole defence stated at once, 147.
withdrawal of, and consent to decree, 149. 245.

DEFENDERS—

abandonment against one of several, 234, 243.
action against several, 108.
apportionment of damages and expenses between several, 110, 247.
deletion of one of several, 234.
joint, jurisdiction against, 52, 53, 58-59.
plurality of, action may proceed against one only, 109, 235.
    See also INSTANCE; TITLE TO SUE.

DELETION—

of irrelevant or scandalous averments, 157, 242.

DELICT—

jurisdiction arising from, 69, 71.

DELIVERY, ACTION OF, 497.

joint and several crave competent, 109, 497.
value of cause, 48.
warrant to search on decree, 497.
    See also AD FACTUM PRÆSTANDUM; SMALL DEBT COURT.

DEMOLITION ORDER—

under Housing, &c., Acts, appeal against, 600.

DESCRIPTIVE FIRM—

as litigant, 86.
arrestment against, 263, 270.

DESCRIPTIVE NAME—

association having, as litigant, 87.

DILIGENCE—

effect of amendment on, 238, 241.
effect of multiplepoinding on, 519.
    See also ARRESTMENT; CHARGE; IMPRISONMENT; POINDING;
    SMALL DEBT COURT.

DILIGENCE FOR RECOVERY OF DOCUMENTS—

accountant's assistance for books, 197.
after proof allowed, 193.

ELECTOR.   *See* REPRESENTATION OF THE PEOPLE ACTS.

ELECTORAL DUTIES OF SHERIFF, 2.

EMPLOYERS' LIABILITY ACT—
    action under, 584-586.
    assessor, 586.
    conjunction of actions, 585.
    form of action, 584.
    jury trial, 585.
    not removeable for jury trial, 585.
    notice as statutory preliminary, 585
    time limit for proceedings, 586.

EMPLOYERS AND WORKMEN ACT.   *See* SMALL DEBT COURT.

ENDORSATION—
    of English warrant.   *See* SUMMARY JURISDICTION (PROCESS) ACT.

ENGLISH DECREE—
    registration of.   *See* JUDGMENTS EXTENSION ACT; SUMMARY JURISDICTION
      (PROCESS) ACT.

ENTAILS—
    applications relating to, 586-588.

ERRORS—
    correction in decree, 248.

ESTATE DUTY APPEALS, 589, 590.

EVIDENCE—
    recording of, effect on appeal when no record, 224.
    to lie *in retentis*.   *See* COMMISSION TO TAKE EVIDENCE.
        See also PROOF; WITNESSES (1).

EXCEPTION—
    plea by way of.   *See* REDUCTION.

EXCHEQUER—
    functions of Sheriff Court in relation to, 24

EXCLUSION OF JURISDICTION, 38-44.

EXECUTION—
    of warrant, &c., outside sheriffdom, 10, 126, 257, 261.

EXECUTOR—
    cannot raise damages action for injury to deceased, 84, 113.
    foreign, specialties of jurisdiction, 61.
    jurisdiction against, 58, 61.
    may sue before obtaining confirmation, 113, 438.
    sist of, 84, 236.
        See also COMMISSARY PRACTICE.

EXHIBITION—
 action of, 506.

EXPENSES—
 (1) AWARDING OF—
 abandonment, 243, 244, 245, 318.
 adherence and aliment and separation and aliment, 527.
 administrative processes, 310, 565.
 affiliation and aliment when no denial, 316.
  raised before birth, 502.
 amendment, 236, 240.
  payment as condition precedent, 238.
 arrestment, laying on and recalling, 266.
  expenses secured by, 271.
 combination of parties on same side, 107, 316, 317, 318, 319.
 commission to take evidence, 208.
 consenter, 110, 316.
 consistorial cause, 527.
 constituting claim, 316.
 construction of wills, &c., 315.
 counter claim, 316.
 decree in absence, 131.
 determination of scale, when competent, 326, 327.
 disclaimer, 246.
 discretion must be exercised judicially, 315.
 divided success, 315.
 divided success where several parties, 317, 319.
 dominus litis, 112, 317.
  separate action against, 112, 317.
 " expenses in the cause," 309, 324.
 failure to ask when merits disposed of, 248, 311.
 furthcoming, 275.
 general principles, 309, 314.
 husband, 110, 316, 317.
 instalment award probably incompetent, 322.
 interim award, 311.
  consistorial cause, 527.
  effect on later finding, 311.
  payment as condition of proceeding, 238, 337.
 joint and several liability, 319.
 judicial reference, 172.
 jury trial, when refused in Court of Session, 307.
 mandatory, 93.
 minute for warrant to imprison, 282.
 multiplepoinding, 311, 516, 517, 520.
 no demand for payment before writ served, 310.
 no expenses if settled before service, 309.
 party sisted, 236.
 record of evidence in summary causes, 228.
 remit to man of skill, 176.
 reponing note, effect of sum consigned, 138.
 reserved expenses, 309.
 separate actions when same subject matter, 107, 318.
 separate defences, 148.
 sequestration in bankruptcy—
  application by bankrupt for discharge, 312, 387.
  trustee's liability for expenses, 80.
   See also SEQUESTRATION.

EXPENSES—*continued.*

on expenses only, 290, 337.
utilizing opponent's appeal to raise question, 338.
apportionment of, between several defenders, 110, 319.
charging order, 331-332.
consignation before service of writ, 310.
continuation of action by representative for expenses only, 84.
crave for expenses, how far necessary, 104, 310.
deduction of items unincurred, 255, 328.
cost of extract, when recoverable, 255, 328.
dominus litis, action against for expenses, 112, 317.
extract of decree for expenses, 254, 296, 328.
inclusive fee in undefended causes, 131, 325.
interest on expenses decree, 329.
payment of expenses as condition of proceeding, 238, 337.
not implied from mere award, 337.
prior action, expenses of, 337.
remit to Court of Session, Sheriff Court expenses should be taxed and decerned for, 109.
separate action for expenses usually incompetent, 315.
tenders and offers, 335, 336.
extrajudicial offer repeated on record, 150.
not repeated, 150.
non-timeous acceptance, 336.
tender must include expenses, 149. *See also* TENDER.

EXTRACT—

absolvitor, pursuer paying expenses not entitled to delivery, 329.
decree in absence—
reponing note does not prevent issue, 133.
time for applying for, 132, 254.
expenses decree extractable after decree on merits, 254.
expenses of extract, how far recoverable, 255, 328.
form of, 133, 253.
interest on sum decerned for, 133, 255, 329.
no step competent after final judgment extracted, 253.
protestation, 143.
registration decree, 255.
removings, 418.
statutory form may supplement interlocutor, 134.
stay of execution incompetent after final extract, 254.
time for extract, 132, 251, 254.
alteration by Sheriff, 132, 254, 255.
application for leave to appeal, 254.
use of " decerns " not necessary for extract, 133.
when necessary, 134.

EXTRAORDINARY TRAFFIC—
action for cost of repairs, 662.

FACTOR, JUDICIAL. *See* JUDICIAL FACTOR.

FATAL ACCIDENT INQUIRIES, 452-454.

FIARS PRICES—
striking of, 34.

HEARING ON EVIDENCE, 228.

HERITABLE SECURITIES ACT, 595-599.
    ejection of proprietor in default, 595.
    expenses, 599.
    interdict against heritable creditor, 595.
    jurisdiction, 595.
    leasing security subjects, application for warrant, 596.
    notice to debtor, warrant to make edictally, 598.
    pari passu security, warrant to sell, 597.
    realizing subjects, foreclosure, 596, 597.
    rights of appeal, 598.

HERITAGE—
    actions relating to, jurisdiction in, 25-28, 47, 52, 71-74, 106.
    remit to Court of Session, 27, 162, 169.

HERRING FISHERY ACT, 1908—
    jurisdiction under, 32.

HIGHWAY. *See* ROADS AND BRIDGES.

HIRE PURCHASE AGREEMENT. *See* JURISDICTION (2) (*f*); SMALL
        DEBT COURT.

HONORARY SHERIFF-SUBSTITUTE, 4.

HOUSE LETTING AND RATING ACT—
    applications under, 540.

HOUSING AND TOWN PLANNING—
    applications under Acts and rights of appeal, 599-602.

HOUSING (RURAL WORKERS) ACT—
    applications under, 538.

HUSBAND AND WIFE—
    dispensing with consent to deeds, 603.
    protection order, 602.
        See also ADHERENCE AND ALIMENT; ALIMENT; CUSTODY OF
            CHILDREN; SEPARATION AND ALIMENT.

HYPOTHEC—
    appeal to Sheriff on question of, 224.

IMPRISONMENT FOR CIVIL DEBT, 281-284.
    ad factum præstandum decree, 35, 36, 281, 284, 496, 497.
        procedure to obtain warrant, 284.
    aliment of debtor in prison, 283.
    alimentary debts, 35, 281.
        minute for warrant to imprison, 282.
        on what debts competent, 283.
        review, 282.
    Crown taxes, 35, 281.
    fugæ warrant, 35, 281.
    induciæ of charge, 284.

INSANE PERSON—
    appointment of curator *ad litem* if no appearance, 83.
    as litigant, 83.
    as witness, 189, 209.
    damages recovered for, 82.
    doubts of condition when evidence taken on commission, 209.
    proof of supervening insanity in pending process, 83, 185.
    pursuer, request for medical examination, 185.
        See also LUNACY; JUDICIAL FACTOR.

INSPECTION—
    by Court, 184.
    by parties, order for by Court, 184.
        production of portable article, 184.

INSTANCE, 106-114.
    assignee, 84, 113.
    combination of defenders, 108.
        pursuers, 107.
    consenter, 110.
    dominus litis, 112.
    executor unconfirmed, 113.
    identification of party, 111.
    interest, calling party for, 110.
    joint and several liability, 108.
    joint delinquents, 108.
    new defender cannot always be substituted, 111.
    party ordained to disclose true address, 111.
    title to defend though not called, 148.
    trustees, must give personal names, 113.
        sued as individuals, 114.
        See also TITLE TO SUE.

INTERDICT, 506-510.
    against sale, in sequestration for rent, 428.
        under poinding, 280, 506.
    appeal, 290, 298, 507.
        interim interdict, 290, 298, 301, 304, 507.
    breach of interdict, 8, 509, 510.
        amendment, 509.
        appeal, 510.
        failure to appear, 509.
        penalty, 509.
    caveat, 508.
    expenses : scale, 322.
    heritable creditor, interdict under Act of 1894, 595.
    incompetent, if really suspension, 506.
    interim interdict, 507, 508.
        appeal, 290, 298, 301, 304, 507.
        binding till recalled despite appeal, 290, 298, 508.
        caution, 508.
        falls if process falls, 508.
        not ended by cause falling asleep, 508.
        recall, 507.
    jurisdiction, 25, 506.
    sist of third party, 507.
    value of cause, 49.

JOINT DELINQUENTS—
action against, 108, 109.
apportionment of damages and expenses, 110.
jurisdiction against, 70.
one delinquent cannot appeal against absolvitor to other, 109.
relief between, 523.
subsequent action against one not sued originally, 109.
unsatisfied decree against one, 109.
See also DEFENDERS.

JOINT AND SEVERAL LIABILITY—
of defenders, 108, 109.
apportionment of damages and expenses, 110.

JOINT STOCK COMPANY. See COMPANY.

JUDGMENT, FINAL—
apportionment of damages where contributory negligence, 247.
of liability between joint defenders, 247.
definition of, 291-293.
findings in fact and law, 247.
no further step competent after extract of, 253.
summary application, 102.
See also DECREE; EXTRACT; INTERLOCUTOR.

JUDGMENTS EXTENSION ACT, 286, 288.
control of Court issuing certificate, 288.
decree conform not competent, 287.
induciæ of charge on certificate, 287.
registration, of English or Northern Irish judgment, 286.
of Sheriff Court decree in England, &c., 286.
time limit for registration, 287.
See also SUMMARY JURISDICTION (PROCESS) ACT.

JUDICIAL FACTOR AND CURATOR BONIS, 604-607.
absent person, interim appointment, 39.
action relating to duties may be incompetent, 18.
appointment in Sheriff Court, 604.
commissary factor, 39, 441, 442.
discharge of factor, 607.
interim factor, 39.
judicial manager on farm, 26, 39.
jurisdiction, 39, 55, 604, 605.
partnership, appointment on, incompetent, 643.
procedure, 604-606.
    appeal, 604, 607.
    caution, 606.
    medical certificates, 605.
    special powers, 606.
recall of appointment, 607.
sequestration : appointment for interim preservation, 39, 367.
    on deceased's estate, 39, 393.
    competition between factory and sequestration, 394.

JUDICIAL REFERENCE, 171-173.
action may fall asleep, 172.
amendment not usually competent after, 171, 239.

JURISDICTION—*continued.*

    forum non conveniens, 44.
    fugæ warrant, detention on, 35.
    geographical limits of jurisdiction, 31, 32.
    Herring Fishery Act, action under, 32.
    leases, actions relating to, 26.
    must be exercised if action competent, 37.
    nobile officium, if involved action incompetent, 17.
    proving of tenor incompetent, 18, 33.
    privative in Sheriff Court, 47-51, 289.
        encroachment by Administration of Justice Act, 47.
    Sea Fisheries Act, damages under, 32.
    sequestration, 355, 356.
    statutory grounds not exhaustive, 52.
    Summary Jurisdiction (Process) Act, 70.
    transfer of causes, 44-47, 106.
    trustees and executors, 58, 61.
        See also SMALL DEBT COURT *and under separate actions.*

  (2) GROUNDS OF JURISDICTION—

  (*a*) *Arrestment to found jurisdiction,* 61-67.
    amendment, effect of, 64.
    death of defender terminates, 64.
    defender must not be otherwise subject to Scottish Courts, 48, 61.
    foreign executors, specialties in relation to, 61.
    foreign pursuer may use, 66.
    ineffective if defender owns Scottish heritage, 48, 61.
    limited to action in which used, 64.
    nexus not created by, 62.
    ownership of subject by defender essential, 63.
    plea of invalidity of arrestment, 65.
    police, money in hands of, 64.
    possession by third party essential, 64.
    procedure—
        application for letters, 67.
            Court of Session application, 67.
        expenses, 67.
        time limit for action after arrestment, 66.
    ship arrested may found jurisdiction against master, 63, 64.
    subjects arrestable, 62, 63, 267-270.
    whether competent for all actions, 65, 103.

  (*b*) *Carrying on business,* 59-61.
    common law rule, 59.
    limited company's registered office, 60.
    nature of business, 60.

  (*c*) *Contract,* 75-76.
    nature of action which is competent, 76.
    personal citation essential, 75, 76.

  (*d*) *Delict,* 69-71.
    affiliation and aliment not founded on, 70.
    common law rule, 71.
    interdict does not need personal service, 71, 506.
    joint delinquents, 70.
    personal citation necessary, 69, 70, 71.
    servant's negligence probably enough, 71.

  (*e*) *Joint defenders,* 52, 53, 58-59.
    trustees and executors, 58.

LAW OF OTHER COUNTRIES—
proof of, 212-213.

LAWBURROWS, ACTION OF—
procedure and review, 510, 511.

LEASE—
action to appoint judicial manager, 26, 39.
to compel tenant to take possession, 26.
to ordain stocking or plenishing, 26.
to order inspection and repair, 26.
jurisdiction in actions relating to leases, 26.

LEGITIMATION. *See* Births, &c., Registration.

LICENSING AUTHORITY—
appeal against. *See* Statutory Powers and Duties, Appeals.

LICENSING (SCOTLAND) ACT. *See* Club.

LIFE, PRESUMPTION OF. *See* Presumption of Life.

LIMITATION OF TIME—
for bringing action, 41, 42, 43, 586.
amendment after time limit expired, 43

LIMITED COMPANY. *See* Company.

LIQUIDATION—
sisting of mandatory by claimant, 92.
See also Building Society ; Company ; Industrial Societies.

LIVESTOCK INDUSTRY ACT—
applications under, 539.

LOCAL AUTHORITY—
as litigant, 90.
citation of, 128.
proceedings against under Public Health Act, 653.
review of Sheriff Court decision where appeal to Sheriff from decision of, 535.

LOCAL GOVERNMENT ACT—
applications under, 540.
appeal by stated case from Sheriff Court decision, 542.

LORD ADVOCATE—
service of writ on, 128.
specification of documents, intimation of, 195, 202.

LOST NUMBER OF PROCESS, 141, 143, 228.

LUNACY, 612-615.
committal of lunatic, 612.
criminal lunatic, committal of, 614.
dangerous lunatic, committal of, 613.

MESSENGER-AT-ARMS—
  power to act as officer of Court, 11, 117, 263.

METHYLATED SPIRITS ACT—
  applications under, 537.

MIDWIVES AND MATERNITY HOMES ACT—
  applications under, 536.

MILITARY AFFAIRS—
  exclusion of Civil Courts, 44.

MILK AND DAIRIES ACT, 626, 627.
  appeal as to certificate, 626.
    registration, 626.
    stoppage of supplies, 627.
  application to order local authority to perform duty, 627.
  compensation, action by dairyman for, 627.

MINISTERIAL JURISDICTION, 34-36.

MINOR—
  as litigant, 81.
  damages paid into Court, 82.
  service on, 55, 82, 128, 582.
    See also CURATOR AD LITEM.

MINUTE—
  defender cannot usually appear by, 149.

MONEYLENDERS' CLAIMS, 627-630.
  presumptions under Act of 1927, 628.
    evidence to overcome, 628.
  procedural specialties under Act of 1927, 629.
  rate of interest on decree, 628.
  reopening transaction under Act of 1900, 627.
  time limit for proceedings, 630.

MOTIONS IN CAUSE, 234.

MOVEABLE PROPERTY—
  jurisdiction from situation of, 52, 74.

MOVEABLE SUCCESSION—
  remit of case to Court of Session, 162, 170.

MULTIPLEPOINDING, 514-521.
  appeals, 517, 519, 520, 521.
  appearance not necessary in all cases, 516.
  claimant may raise action, 516.
  competency of action, 514.
    dispute as to, 516.
    record in, 517.
  competition for fund, 518.
    decision on principle of division, 519, 520.
    late claims, 516.

MULTIPLEPOINDING—*continued.*

    record in, 518.
  condescendence and claim, 518.
  decree to claimant precludes set-off by holder, 519.
    ranking itself does not, 519.
  defenders to be called, 516.
  diligence, effect of multiplepoinding on, 519.
  exception, plea by in, 22, 518.
  expenses, 311, 516, 517, 520.
  final judgment, what decrees are, 292-293, 519, 520.
  fund *in medio*, 514, 517.
    condescendence of, 517.
    discharge of holder, 517, 520.
    settlement of, 517.
  furthcoming as alternative process, 276.
  inland revenue certificate before decree, 521.
  jurisdiction, 74, 515.
  nominal raiser, 516.
  order for claims, 518.
  real raiser, 516.
  res judicata, how far decree is, 521.
  riding claims, 516.
  sisting of mandatory by claimant, 92, 518.
  trustees' claim to whole fund for administration, 518.
  trustees may bring, for exoneration, 514.

MUNICIPAL, 630-642.

  acquisition of land by town council, 632.
  appeal, general rights of, under Burgh Police Acts, 540, 541, 640-642.
    common law remedy, how far excluded, 642.
    expenses in, 642.
    local administration, how far challengeable, 640.
    procedure in, 641.
  review of judgment by Sheriff, 541.
    special right of appeal may supersede, 640.
  stated case to Court of Session, 541, 543.
    See also under other subheads below.
  arbitration before Sheriff under Burgh Police Act, 543.
  burgh, creation of, application for, 630.
    revision of boundaries, application for, 631.
    wards, division into, &c., 632.
  Burgh Police Act, appeal from Sheriff Court, express provision as to, 540, 541.
  bye-laws, application for confirmation, 636.
  councillor, appeal against resolution declaring office vacant, 635.
    declarator of disqualification of, 633.
  councillors, application to have numbers altered, &c., 632.
  dangerous buildings, application to order repairs, 638.
  election petition, 633-635.
    certain applications before Sheriff-Substitute, 635.
    expenses, 634, 635.
    petition to disqualify councillor, 633.
    procedure in petition, 633-635.
    stated case to Court of Session, 634.
    substitution of petitioner, 634, 635.
    unopposed petition, 634.
    withdrawal of petition, 634.

PROCESS—
  borrowing of—
    caption, 142.
    numbers not borrowable, 141.
    penalty for failure to return, 141.
    returning before proof or trial, 201.
    who may borrow, 12, 106, 141.
  date of lodging numbers noted, 141.
  lodging certified copy record, 156, 162.
  lost numbers, substitution of copies, 141, 143, 228.
  making up, 141.
  returning for proof or trial, 201.
  transmission of, to Court of Session, 161.

PROCURATOR-FISCAL, 8.

PRODUCTIONS—
  banker's books, 194, 203.
  business books, 198, 199.
  chemical test of document in public register, 202.
  documents founded on in pleadings, 154, 155, 193.
  documents, diligence for recovery, 154, 155, 193.
    illegally obtained, 203.
    recovered by diligence must be formally produced, 198.
    required to adjust pleadings, 155.
  failure to produce may entail decree by default, 154.
  lodging before proof or trial, 201.
  may be lodged at any time before judgment, 154, 193.
  notes to refresh memory not necessarily produced, 217.
  official documents when probative, 205.
  order to produce at any stage, 193.
  public records : procedure to get originals, 201.
  re-opening proof after document produced, 154.
  required from another process, 202.
  returning before proof or trial, 201.
  stamping, liability for duty, 204.
    not matter for commissioner at diligence, 198.
    procedure to get rectified, 203.
      See also DILIGENCE FOR RECOVERY OF DOCUMENTS.

PROOF—
  affidavits in lieu of, 213.
  allowance of, 181, 233.
  amendment necessary when facts proved not averred, 240.
  appeal against allowance, refusal or limitation, 181, 183, 290.
    to Sheriff on admission, &c., of evidence, 222-224.
      failure to appeal may bar review later, 223.
  averments provable by writ or oath only, 182.
  before answer, 168, 181, 182.
  closing of proof, 224.
  confidentiality, appeal on plea of, 223.
  death of Sheriff-Substitute, 225.
  exclusion of improper or irrelevant matter, 158, 182, 242.
  form of order for proof, 181.
  hearing on evidence, 228.
  incriminating questions, instructions to commissioner, 210.
  law of Dominions or other countries, 212-213.
  leading in proof, 182, 224, 524.

PROOF—*continued.*

non-appearance of party or solicitor, 183.
persons entitled to be in Court during, 214.
preliminary, to ascertain *dominus litis*, 112.
  to dispose of preliminary pleas, 169.
  to inquire into pursuer's sanity, 83.
proof, *habili modo*, 182.
  in chief and conjunct probation led together, 220.
  in replication, 222.
record of evidence, 227-228.
  correction of notes, 228.
  in summary causes either party may require, 99, 145, 227.
    expenses of, 228.
  use of notes when Sheriff-Substitute has died, 225.
reference to oath. *See* REFERENCE TO OATH.
refusal of proof of irrelevant averments, 182.
re-opening proof by Sheriff on appeal, 225, 226, 227, 297.
  on amendment, or production of document, 154, 225, 226.
  on appeal to Court of Session, 226, 227.
  otherwise not generally competent, 225, 226.
restricting proof to writ or oath, 182.
taking whole proof of new, 225, 228.
    See also WITNESSES.

PROROGATION OF JURISDICTION, 76-77.

PROROGATION OF TIME—

for appearance, implementing order, &c., 139, 249, 251.
for lodging defences, 147.

PROTECTION OF ANIMALS ACT—
applications under, 538.

PROTESTATION, 142-143.

defender may re-enrol to crave protestation, 143.
extract, 143.
how obtained, 142.
recall competent but not appeal, 143.
several defenders, 143.
where pursuer fails to appear at first diet in summary cause, 143, 251.

PROVING OF TENOR—

action incompetent in Sheriff Court, 18, 33.
incidental proof of terms of writ may be competent, 33.

PROVISIONAL ORDER INQUIRY, 461.

PUBLIC AUTHORITIES PROTECTION ACT—
amendment after time limit expired, 43.
effect on counter claim, 152.
expenses under, 319.
time bar on action, 41, 42.

PUBLIC DEPARTMENT—
as litigant, 88.
citation of, 88, 128.

RIVERS' POLLUTION PREVENTION ACT—
applications under, 661.
removal to Court of Session, 662.
rights of appeal, 662.

ROAD TRAFFIC ACT—
applications under, 536, 538.

ROADS AND BRIDGES, 662-665.
barbed wire fences, application relating to, 663.
bye-laws, approval of by Sheriff, 664.
extraordinary traffic, action for reparation, 662.
miscellaneous applications under Act, 538, 664.
Sheriff may act through county councillor, 665.

ROADS IMPROVEMENT ACT—
applications under, 538.

RUINOUS PROPERTY. *See* MUNICIPAL.

SALVAGE. *See* SHIPPING.

SCANDALOUS AVERMENTS—
deletion of, 157, 242.

SEA FISHERIES ACT—
assessment of damages under, 665.
fishery officer's report as evidence, 665.
jurisdiction under, 32.

SEAMEN. *See* SHIPPING.

SEPARATION AND ALIMENT—
appeal against decree in absence after proof, 524, 525.
arrestment on dependence and in execution, 105, 262, 525.
citation of defender, 125.
decree after proof still in absence if undefended, 130, 524.
decree in absence incompetent without proof, 19, 130, 499, 524.
decree must be granted if justified, 526.
decree not subject to recall, on change of circumstances, 526.
decree of consent, competency of, 499.
defender may appear at any stage, 130, 525.
expenses, 527.
income tax on aliment, 503.
interim aliment, 298, 526.
interim award of expenses, 527.
jurisdiction, 18, 498, 525.
pursuer must lead at proof, 524.
remit to Court of Session, 19, 170.
reponing against decree after proof, 136, 524, 525.
review of amount of aliment, 498.
wife's solicitor cannot get decree for expenses against husband if case
settled before proof, 528.

SEQUESTRATION FOR FEU DUTY, 428.

SHIPPING—*continued.*

 passage broker's and emigrant runner's licences, 619.
 pilotage appeal, 625.
 procedure generally in shipping cases, 618.
 sale of goods from ship, 622.
 salvage, apportionment of, 621.
  jurisdiction under Act and at common law, 619, 620
  rights of appeal, 621.
  time limit for actions, 620.
 seamen's claims, various, how recoverable, 618.
  wages, actions for recovery, 618.
 sett and sale, action of, 528, 529.
 ship, arrestment and dismantling, 272.
  arrestment to found jurisdiction, 63, 64.
  not poindable, 277.
  warrant to sell, 275.
 ship's officer's conduct, inquiry into, 460.
 shipmaster's disbursements, actions for recovery, 618.
 survey inquiry, 459.
 wreck, unclaimed, determination of dispute, 621.
    See also NAUTICAL ASSESSORS; SEA FISHERIES ACT.

SHOPS ACT—

 applications under, 536, 538.

SIST OF PARTY—

 assignee, 84, 236.
 competent after judgment, 84, 236.
 executor or trustee, 84, 236.
 interdict, intervention of third party, 506.
 liability for expenses, 236.
 not competent against party's wishes, 236.
  nor when sole or all pursuers disclaim, 246.
 party with legitimate interest, 236.
 sequestration in bankruptcy, sist of new creditor, 360.
 solicitor, to obtain expenses award, 329.

SIST OF PROCESS, 176-178.

 appeal against, 178, 290, 299.
 does not prevent cause falling asleep, 178, 243.
 recall of, 178.
 when appropriate, 176, 177.

SLAUGHTER OF ANIMALS ACT—

 applications under, 536.

SMALL DEBT COURT—

 appeal, 487-490.
  caution, 489.
  exclusion of reduction, &c., 489.
  grounds of appeal, 487, 488.
  procedure, 489.
  stated case under Friendly Societies Acts, 490, 534, 541.
  statutory rights of appeal still open, 490.
  suspension, 487.
  where process treated as summary application, 487.
 damages for irregularities, &c., 490.

SOLICITOR—*continued.*

    striking off roll, 13.
    unqualified person may not act as, 13, 96.
        when allowed to represent litigant, 12, 96, 471.
    woman may enrol as, 13.
        See also under CITATION.

SPECIFICATION OF DOCUMENTS. *See* DILIGENCE.

STAMPING OF DOCUMENT. *See* PRODUCTION.

STATED CASE—

    appeal by, in statutory applications, 540-543.
    to ascertain law of British Dominion, 212, 213.

STATUS—

    action relating to, jurisdiction by arrestment, 65.
    declarator, limitation of jurisdiction in, 18, 19.
    question merely ancillary may be declared in another process, 20.

STATUTORY POWERS AND DUTIES OF SHERIFF—

    appeals—
        by stated case, when full right of review, 540, 541, 542.
            when leave to appeal required, 541.
            when opinion only obtainable, 541.
        effect of evidence not being recorded, 535.
            finality provision, 535, 539.
            irregularities in Sheriff Court, 534, 535.
            provision that matter be determined summarily, 532, 537.
        existing rights of appeal reserved by Act, 534.
        express provision as to, 539, 540.
        general provisions as to, 533-540.
        review of Sheriff Court decision, when Sheriff directed to determine
            differences, &c., 537.
            when Sheriff deals with appeal from decision of local or
            licensing authority, 535.
    applications usually by initial writ, 533.
    general, 532, 533.
    ordinary procedure, how far applicable, 534, 539.
    when applications treated as summary applications, 532.
    whether exercisable by Sheriff or Sheriff-Substitute, 532, 535, 537.
        See also under names of various Statutes.

STIPEND. *See* CHURCH OF SCOTLAND ACT.

STREET REGISTER. *See* MUNICIPAL.

SUMMARY APPLICATIONS—

    appeals in, 102, 305.
    applications under Statute, when treated as, 101.
    common law applications, 101.
    definition, 101.
    findings in judgment not always necessary, 102, 247.
    form of final judgment, 102, 247.
    jurisdiction in, 103.
    ordinary procedure does not involve incompetency, 102.
    procedure generally, 101-103.

SUMMARY APPLICATIONS—*continued.*

recovery of penalties by, 103.
service of, 102.
Small Debt action may be held to be, 103, 487.
Statute may prescribe procedure, 103.
warrant for service, 102, 115.
    effect of use of wrong form, 102, 115.

SUMMARY CAUSE—

adjustment of pleadings, 99
allowance of proof generally forecloses relevancy, 168.
amendment, 240.
appeal, right of, may depend on how case dealt with, 98.
    See also under APPEAL.
ascertainment of value, 96.
competency of incidental appeal on evidence, 224.
conjunction with ordinary action, 98.
consent of parties to action becoming, 98, 146.
counter claim, effect of, 98, 153.
    of over £50 competent, 98, 153.
definition of, 96.
diet of appearance, whether competent in chambers, 100, 129.
evidence must be recorded if either party require, 99, 145, 227.
    expenses of so recording, 228.
extract, time for, whether Sheriff may shorten, 255.
failure of pursuer to appear at first diet, 251.
if no appearance for defender continuation does not bar decree in absence, 130.
instalment decree probably incompetent, 145.
non-professional pleaders in, 96.
not tabled but diet for appearance is equivalent, 140, 143.
procedure in, 99, 141, 145.
record need not be closed, 99, 145, 162.
reference to oath, 233.
Sheriff may decide whether summary cause or not, 97.
warrant for service, 97, 99, 115.
    effect of use of wrong form, 98, 115.

SUMMARY JURISDICTION (PROCESS) ACT, 666.

endorsement of English warrant, &c., 666.
endorsement of Scottish warrant in England, 666.
jurisdiction under, 70.
registration of English bastardy, &c., order, 666.

SUMMARY REMOVING. *See* REMOVING.

SUPERIOR—

action for removing against vassal, 25, 420.
sequestration for feu duty, 428.

SURVEY. *See* SHIPPING.

SUSPENSIONS, 529-531.

appeal, 530.
caution, 529, 530.
caveat, 530.
interdict may be incompetent if really suspension, 506.

SUSPENSIONS—*continued.*
> interim sist, effect on diligence, 530.
> jurisdiction in, 28-31.
> recording of evidence not necessary, 530.
> Small Debt decree, 487, 489.
> summary procedure, 529, 530.
> summary warrant to recover rates, 31, 637.
> value of cause, 29.
> when competent remedy, 29-31.

SYNOD—
> citation of, 128.

TABLING OF CAUSE—
> arrestment on dependence falls if not timeously tabled, 140.
> case drops if not tabled, 140.
> date of tabling if several defenders, 140.
> failure to table does not justify absolvitor, 143.
> irregularities in, 140.
> method of, 140.
> protestation, 142-143.
> re-enrolment for, 140.
>> action falls if not re-enrolled, 140.
>> defender may re-enrol to crave protestation, 143.
> summary cause, position in, 140, 143.
> undefended cause not tabled, 129.

TELEGRAPHS—
> applications relating to, 667.

TENDER—
> acceptance of, 150.
> allocation between several pursuers, 108, 149, 336.
> apology in slander action, 149.
> by one of several defenders, 149.
> does not imply waiver of jurisdiction plea, 150.
> effect on expenses, 149, 335.
>> *See also under* EXPENSES.
> expenses must be offered, 149.
>> unless no claim till writ served, 149.
> method of making, 149.
> must meet crave, or one of several craves, 149.
> non-timeous acceptance, 336.
> repetition of offer made before action raised, 150.
> usually sealed up on lodging, 150.
> withdrawal of, 150.

TERCE—
> appeal in applications relating to, 582.
> declarator of amount, 580.
> declarator of right to, 579.
> inquiry by proof, 174, 581.
> expenses in applications, 581.
> redemption of, 581.

TIME-BAR—
> to action, 41-43, 586.

TRUST—*continued.*
>   application to remove trustee, 667, 668.
>   dissenting trustees may disclaim action, 246.
>   jurisdiction against trustees, 58.
>   sist of trustees, 84, 236.
>   trustee's personal liability for expenses, 80, 114, 309, 316.

TUTOR—
>   citation of when known, 81, 128.
>   *See also* PUPIL.

TUTOR AD LITEM—
>   appointment, 80.
>   expenses of and against, 81.
>   power to compromise, 81.

TYPEWRITER—
>   not recoverable by diligence, 195.

UNDEFENDED CAUSE.   *See* DECREE IN ABSENCE.

VACCINATION (SCOTLAND) ACT—
>   applications under, 538.

VALUE OF CAUSE—
>   factors determining, 29, 48-51, 170.

VEXATIOUS LITIGANT, 90

VOLUNTARY ASSOCIATION OR SOCIETY—
>   as litigant, 87.
>   citation of, 89, 90, 127.
>   effect of decree *quoad* members, 88.

WAKENING, 242-3.
>   action not tabled cannot be wakened, 140.
>   if no procedure for year and day after last date for appearance instance
>   falls, 126, 243.
>   procedure to waken, 242.
>   when necessary, 242.

WARRANT OF CITATION.   *See* CITATION.

WATER, &c., DISTRICTS.   *See* PUBLIC HEALTH.

WATER (SCOTLAND) ACT—
>   applications under, 540.

WILL—
>   declarator that holograph, 451.
>   setting up incidentally in another process, 451.

WINDING-UP.   *See* BUILDING SOCIETY; COMPANY; INDUSTRIAL SOCIETIES.

WITNESSES—*continued.*

    interest or relationship no disability, 188, 189.

    list of, how far recoverable by diligence, 189.

    opinion witness not generally compellable, 192.

    outwith Scotland cannot be compelled to attend, 191, 209.

    penalty for failure to attend, 191.

    right to tender of travelling, &c., expenses, 191.

    unable to attend Court. *See* COMMISSION TO TAKE EVIDENCE.

        See also CITATION; OATH; PRECOGNITION.

WRITING—

    parole evidence to prove or qualify terms, 216.